THE
BOOK
OF THE
STATES

1994-95 EDITION
VOLUME 30

The Council of State Governments
Lexington, Kentucky

Copyright 1994
The Council of State Governments
3560 Iron Works Pike
P.O. Box 11910
Lexington, Kentucky 40578-1910

Manufactured in the United States

C-074-94
ISBN 0-87292-986-8
Price $79.00

Contents

CONTENTS

Chapter Three
STATE LEGISLATIVE BRANCH 97
*An overview of state legislatures and legislative processes in the states, with special
emphasis on activities during 1992-93. Includes basic information on the legislatures
— such as legal provisions for legislative sessions and a variety of information on legislative procedures — along with legislative compensation, statistics on 1992 and 1993
bill introductions and enactments, committee appointments and procedures, and review of administrative regulations.*

ESSAY
State Legislatures

TABLES
Legislatures

Chapter Four
*An exploration of the current status of state judicial systems, with a focus on efforts
to make the judiciary more accessible to the public and on long-term planning goals
for state courts. Includes information on the state courts of last resort, intermediate
appellate courts and general trial courts, as well as the selection and compensation
of judges and judicial administrators.*

CONTENTS

Chapter Five
STATE ELECTIONS, CAMPAIGN FINANCE & INITIATIVES 203
A review of election legislation and developments in campaign financing and initiatives across the states in recent years. Includes information on which state offices will be up for election in the years 1994-2003, formulas for election dates, voting statistics, campaign finance laws, and procedures for initiatives, referenda and recalls.

Chapter Six
STATE FINANCES 309

A focus on the states' financial situation, with an update on recent trends in taxation and tax collections, and federal spending in the states. Includes information on state budgetary procedures and funds management activities, their revenue sources, expenditures and debt for 1991 and 1992, and tax rates for 1994.

ESSAYS

CONTENTS

Chapter Seven
STATE MANAGEMENT, REGULATION & PERSONNEL 405

An overview of several components of state administration and regulation, including recent reforms in state management, personnel, and lobby laws. Includes information on state personnel systems, information resource management, and regulatory activities. Statistics on state government employment and payrolls, as well as public employee retirement systems, are presented for 1991 and 1992.

TABLES

State Management

Personnel

Information/Records Management

State Purchasing

Public Employment

Chapter Eight
A review of several state program and issue areas — including education, corrections and criminal justice, environmental management, labor, health care, and highways — with current information and statistics. Includes a special feature on innovators in state government.

TABLES

Chapter Nine
INTERGOVERNMENTAL AFFAIRS 575

A recap of recent developments in the relations between the federal government and the states, the states and local governments, and the impact of free trade agreements on the states. Includes statistics on federal aid and state intergovernmental revenues and expenditures for 1991 and 1992.

ESSAYS

A variety of statistics and information about the states — including capitals, population, land areas, historical data, elected executive branch officials, legislative leaders, and judges of the state high courts. State mottos, flowers, songs, birds and other items unique to the states and other U.S. jurisdictions also are presented.

Foreword

The 1994-95 edition of *The Book of the States* represents the 30th volume of this premier reference work on state government. As noted in the Foreword to the first volume produced in 1935, "your interest in this book will vary with your interest in state government." We can assure you that if you have *any* interest in state government, you will have a keen interest in the essays and tables included here.

The Council of State Governments has served state governments across the country for over 60 years, and we are proud that *The Book of the States* has been our flagship publication since the beginning. We trust that this volume reflects the challenges and opportunities facing states today. As states confront a greater diversity and complexity of issues presented by new global linkages and rapidly changing technologies, CSG's mission is more important than ever. We pledge that through all of our products and services, CSG will be a partner to state governments and state leaders, a champion of excellence in their institutions, and an active participant in putting the best and newest ideas and solutions into practice.

May 1994

Daniel M. Sprague
Executive Director
The Council of State Governments

The Book of the States 1994-95 Project Staff

Project Coordinator:
Joan F. Minton

Editor-in-Chief:
Robert A. Silvanik

Senior Advisor:
Deborah A. Gona

Chapter Editors:
Joyce Bullock (ch. 5)
Benjamin J. Jones (ch. 4)
Joan F. Minton (chs. 1, 2)
Douglas J. Olberding (ch. 6)
Julie Cencula Olberding (ch. 7)
Nancy L. Olson (ch. 3)
Sari Siegel (ch. 9)
Robert A. Silvanik (ch. 8)

Production Assistance:
Debbie Jones
Pam Walters

Editing Assistance:
Carla Nielsen
Christopher Schwarz

Typographers:
Connie P. LaVake
A. Turner Williams

Acknowledgments

The project staff wish to thank the hundreds of individuals in the states who provided data and information, the authors who graciously shared their expertise, and the thousands of state officials who, through their daily work, contributed to the story of state government presented in this volume.

Chapter One

STATE CONSTITUTIONS

A review of constitutional revision and actions on proposals in the states during 1992-93, including general information on state constitutions, amendment procedures, and constitutional commissions. Includes a special essay on the term limits movement in the states.

State Constitutions and Constitutional Revision, 1992-93

States can modify their constitutions several ways, and the processes have become more popular recently.

by Janice C. May

State constitutional activity in 1992-93 was generally similar to that of the past biennium and the 1980s, but there were some significant changes. Compared with the last two years, proposals and adoptions of constitutional amendments were more numerous. No new constitution or general revision was on the ballot, but the Louisiana Legislature convened briefly as a constitutional convention, and constitutional revision commissions were authorized in New York and California. In addition, history was made when the Florida Commission won approval for two amendments it submitted directly to the voters. As a method of constitutional change, the constitutional initiative was more popular than ever with adoptions reaching new heights. Interest in state constitutional law by the legal profession and others continued to add to the literature on state constitutions.

Use of Authorized Methods

As Table A shows, constitutional changes by all methods were higher in 1992-93 than in 1990-91. There were 239 proposals and 160 adoptions, including two approved by Delaware through legislative action only. The number of states with some activity also increased. Although more than in 1990-91, the new figures are far below those of 10 years ago (345 proposals and 258 adoptions) and the averages per biennium in the 1970s (418.8 proposals and 261 adoptions). The approval rate in the current biennium of 66.6 percent was somewhat more than in 1990-91, but lower than the other biennium on the table.

The constitutional initiative generated 34 proposals compared with 29 during the last biennium, a record high as measured by biennium averages during the past 60 years. The approval of 21 of the 34 propositions in 1992-93 was significant, as the 62 percent rate is almost double the average rate of 33 percent.

Table A also includes the first constitutional convention since the Rhode Island limited convention of 1986. However, the authenticity of the convention might be questioned since it was the Louisiana Legislature convening as a convention. Its proposed "revision" failed at

Janice C. May is an associate professor of government at the University of Texas at Austin.

Table A
STATE CONSTITUTIONAL CHANGES BY METHOD OF INITIATION
1986-87, 1988-89, 1990-91 AND 1992-93

Method of installation	Number of states involved				Total proposals				Total adopted				Percentage adopted			
	1986-87	1988-89	1990-91	1992-93	1986-87	1988-89	1990-91	1992-93	1986-87	1988-89	1990-91	1992-93	1986-87	1988-89	1990-91	1992-93
All methods	47	45	41	43	275	267	226	239	204	199	145	160	74.3*	74.0*	63.3*	66.1*
Legislative proposal	46	45	41	42	243	246	197	201	191	188	134	137	77.7*	75.6*	67.0*	67.1*
Constitutional initiative	9	11	10	13	18	21	29	34	5	11†	11	21	77.7†	55.0†	37.9	61.7
Constitutional convention	1	...	...	1	14	...	...	1	8	...	...	0	57.1	...	...	0.0
Constitutional commission	...	...	...	1	...	...	...	3	...	...	...	2	...	...	...	66.6

Key:
* — In calculating these percentages, the amendments adopted in Delaware (where proposals are not submitted to the voters) are excluded.
† — Excludes one Nevada constitutional initiative whose final adoption requires a second favorable vote.
.... — Not applicable

the polls, however. Of considerable significance was the addition of a Florida constitutional commission for the first time since 1978.
Two of the three proposals on the ballot were
adopted, the first ever for a commission that
has the authority to submit them directly to
the voters.

Tables 1.2, 1.3, and 1.4 summarize the procedures associated with the three major methods used to initiate amendments and revisions
to state constitutions: proposal by the state legislature, which is permitted in all states; constitutional initiative, authorized in 18 states during
the biennium but available in only 17; and the
constitutional convention, accepted as legal
in all states although not expressly authorized
in nine state charters. A fourth method used
to initiate and refer proposed constitutional
amendments to the voters, the constitutional
commission, is authorized only in Florida.

Legislative Proposal

Legislative proposal, the most commonly
employed method for initiating constitutional
amendments, accounted for 201 of the 239
amendments submitted to the voters during
the biennium. Of the 201, 137 were adopted
(including two Delaware propositions that were
not submitted to voters), and 135 were approved
by the electorate (excluding the Delaware measures) for a 67.6 percent voter approval rate.
Legislative proposals represented 84 percent of
all proposals, somewhat less than in the preceding biennium because of the larger number of
constitutional initiatives and proposals of the
constitutional convention and the commission.

Constitutional Initiative

The constitutional initiative, which empowers
citizens by petition to propose amendments
directly to the electorate (except in Massachusetts and Mississippi where the indirect form
is used) is available in one-third of the states.
Appropriate only for making limited constitutional change, the method accounted for
14.2 percent of the total number of proposals
and 13.1 percent of adoptions, which is un-
usually high compared with other years.

The number of initiative proposals and adoptions by state during the 1992-93 biennium
were as follows: Arizona (3-2), Arkansas (1-1),

California (4-2), Colorado (9-3), Florida (2-2),
Michigan (2-1), Missouri (2-2), Montana (2-1),
Nebraska (1-1), Ohio (4-2), Oklahoma (1-1),
Oregon (3-1), and South Dakota (1-1). As the
figures indicate, Colorado led the states in
usage.

During the biennium, Mississippi became
the 18th state to adopt the constitutional initiative. Mississippi voters had approved the
initiative and referendum in 1914, but the Mississippi Supreme Court had struck the amendment from the constitution in 1922. An indirect
initiative, the new Mississippi version is ex-
ceedingly complicated and restrictive, both as
to procedures for putting measures on the ballot and their content.

The initiative is indirect because the measure
must be submitted to the Legislature before it
is placed on the ballot. The Legislature, which
receives initiatives on the first day of the regular
session, may adopt, amend or reject a proposal,
or take no action. But whatever the Legislature does or does not do, a proposal, if it
meets all the requirements outlined, will be
placed on the ballot. However, ballot forms
and choices depend on what course of action
the Legislature takes. If no legislative action
occurs in four months, or if the Legislature
adopts the proposal without any changes, the
measure goes on the ballot in its original form
as received by the Legislature. If the Legislature amends the proposal, the original constitutional initiative and the amended version
are both placed on the ballot. If the Legislature rejects the proposal and submits an alternative, both the original and the alternative
will be on the ballot. A constitutional initiative
is adopted only if it receives a majority of the
votes on the proposition and at least 40 percent of the total vote cast in the election.

In addition, a fiscal analysis must be attached to ballot measures; no more than five initiative proposals can be placed on a single
ballot, and a defeated proposition cannot be
considered again for two years.

During the last biennium, two state supreme
courts denied a place on the ballot to a constitutional initiative on the grounds that the
content violated the U.S. Constitution. It is
unusual for courts to strike from the ballot

propositions for substantive rather than procedural reasons. In *Strumpf v. Lau, 839 P.2d 120 (Nev. 1992)*, the Nevada Supreme Court ruled invalid a measure to impose term limits on members of Congress. In *Re Initiative Petition No. 349*, 838 P.2d 1 (Okla. 1992), the Oklahoma Supreme Court refused to allow an anti-abortion proposal on the ballot.

In addition, two state supreme courts held unconstitutional two initiatives adopted by the voters. In Colorado, a state district court held invalid the initiative to restrict the legal status of gays, lesbians, and bisexuals; and the Arkansas Supreme Court found unconstitutional the proposition imposing term limits on members of Congress. (For a full discussion of term limits, see the essay "Term Limits in the States," by Thad Beyle and Rich Jones, pp. 28-33 of this volume.)

Constitutional Convention

The constitutional convention is the oldest, best known and most traditional method for extensively revising an old constitution or writing a new one. As of January 1, 1992, 233 conventions, including the 1982 convention in the District of Columbia, had been held in the United States. No convention had been held since 1986 until the Louisiana Legislature called itself into session as a convention in 1992.

Governor Edwin Edwards, a Democrat who had won the governorship for the fourth time in 1991, proposed a constitutional convention as a means of resolving fiscal problems early in the 1992 Louisiana legislative session. His initial proposal called for a convention of 85 delegates, 50 of whom would be elected by districts and the remainder appointed by the governor or would serve ex officio. When the Legislature remained unpersuaded, the governor suggested a one-house convention composed solely of legislators. Upon its rejection, Edwards proposed a bicameral convention composed of the legislators. The Legislature passed a statute containing the necessary provisions for a convention, retaining legislative compensation, rules, leadership and organization. The convention was limited to "state and local revenues" and related matters; the Transportation Trust Fund was expressly excluded.

The convention/Legislature met as scheduled on August 23, 1992, and adjourned as required after one month, on September 22. The governor was unsuccessful in adoption of his plan to expand the tax base but the convention agreed to other proposals in its "revision" package. The most controversial proposal would have given the Legislature more control over dedicated funds. In the event of a pending deficit, the Legislature by majority rather than a two-thirds vote could shift up to 10 percent of dedicated funds to the general fund. Supporters of the public schools were particularly concerned because the Minimum Foundation Fund is a major dedicated fund.

The voters defeated the "revision" in the November 1992 general election by a large margin, 38 percent for, 62 percent against. Legislators had turned against it, and after the election, Governor Edwards apologized to teachers for supporting it.[1]

Fourteen state constitutions require a regular periodic vote on the question of calling a convention (See Table 1.4). Eight states mandate one every 20 years; one state, every 16 years; four, every 10 years; and one, every nine years. During 1992-93 a referendum for a convention call required by their state constitutions were on the ballots of three states — Alaska and New Hampshire, where a vote is taken every 10 years, and Ohio, where it occurs every 20 years. The voters rejected the referendum in all three states. The votes were: Alaska, 84,929 - 142,735; New Hampshire, 210,346 - 217,575; and Ohio, 1,672,320 - 2,660,222.

In 1994 the state of Michigan will face the prospect of a constitutional convention because the 16-year mandatory referendum on a convention call will be on the ballot in November. The Research Council of Michigan has undertaken a voter education campaign to identify and analyze major constitutional issues. The Council took an active role in providing citizen information and services at the time of the Michigan Constitutional Convention of 1962 and when mandatory calls were on the ballot.

Although no convention call was approved in the states during the biennium, the voters in the Northern Marianas Commonwealth, on November 6, 1993, approved a constitutional convention to propose amendments to their constitution.

Constitutional Commissions

Constitutional commissions generally serve two major purposes: to study the constitution and propose changes; and to prepare for a constitutional convention. In 1992-93 four commissions were operative (Florida, Utah, Alaska and New York) and a fifth was authorized by statute (California).

The unique Florida Taxation and Budget Reform Commission completed its work during the biennium and was officially dissolved on June 20, 1993. Originally authorized by a constitutional amendment adopted in 1988, the body was established in 1990 for a three-year period. Commissions will be organized every decade in the future.

After numerous meetings, the commission approved four proposed constitutional amendments for approval or rejection by the voters at the November 1992 general election. The Florida Supreme Court removed from the ballot one amendment because it violated statutory requirements on clarity of ballot language. The voters approved two of the three remaining measures. Adopted were a comprehensive change in budgeting and planning and a directive to the Legislature to prepare and adopt a "Taxpayers' Bill of Rights." The rejected measure would have allowed city and county governments, upon voter approval, to levy a sales tax.

The fact that the commission's proposals were approved at the polls was historic. The Florida Constitution Revision Commission of 1978 proposed eight amendments, all of which failed. Thus, 1992 marked the first success at the polls for amendments proposed directly to the voters by a commission.

Utah's Constitutional Revision Commission, a permanent body since 1977, is required by statute to submit recommendations for constitutional changes to the Legislature at least 60 days before each regular session. The commission had resubmitted six proposals to the 1992 Legislature: major revisions of the labor, corporations, legislative and executive articles; and two lesser changes, legislative eligibility and separation of powers and elimination of the dedication of the income tax for public schools. Three of the revisions (legislative, executive and corporations), after referral to the voters by the Legislature, were adopted at the general election in 1992.

In 1993, the commission, at the instigation of the Utah Governor's Council of Victims Rights, reviewed and endorsed (with a reservation about wording) a "Proposed Declaration of the Rights of Crime Victims." The commission also studied briefly the constitutional issue of church and state raised by the offering of a prayer before Salt Lake City Council meetings. The issue was resolved by the Utah Supreme Court, which found no violation of the separation of church and state in the case of *Society of Separationists v. Whitehead, 227 Utah Adv. Rep. 67 (Dec. 1993)*. The commission's most ambitious project of the biennium was the completion of a comprehensive study, begun in 1990, of the revenue and taxation article. Recommendations for revision were incorporated in its 1994 report to the Legislature. The commission underwent sunset review in 1992 by the State and Local Affairs Interim Committee, which approved its re-authorization.

Following the defeat of the call for a constitutional convention in Alaska in 1992, the House of Representatives of the Alaska Legislature created the House Constitutional Revision Task Force by resolution (HR 5) during the regular session in 1993. The purpose of the Task Force was to study and make recommendations concerning methods of constitutional revision in addition to the two provided for in the state charter — amendments by the Legislature subject to voter approval and the constitutional convention. The resolution stated that neither method "lends itself to adequate citizen involvement" in constitutional change, an issue that was raised during the consideration of the referendum on the convention call. In accordance with the resolution, a five-member group was appointed by the Speaker — who also designated the chair.

Teleconferences were used extensively to obtain information on methods of constitutional revision and how they had worked. In April 1994, the Task Force released its final report. It recommended a permanent statutory citizens advisory commission called "The Alaska Commission on the Constitution" to be composed of seven members. The bipartisan commission was to be chosen by a five-member selection committee, four of whom were state officers (the governor, the chief justice, the Senate president and the House speaker), who jointly would appoint a fifth member. The commission would offer opportunities for citizens to participate in discussions and proposals concerning the Alaska Constitution and have power to propose amendments to the Legislature. The Task Force also recommended that a new standing committee, the Joint Committee on the Constitution, be created to handle constitutional amendments. It remains to be seen whether the Alaska Legislature will adopt any or all of the innovative suggestions.

New York Governor Mario Cuomo supported constitutional revision by convention in his 1992 state of the state address. On May 26, 1993, the governor, by executive order, created the Temporary State Commission on Constitutional Revision. The 18-member nonpartisan body was appointed by the governor and included members of diverse backgrounds, interests and areas of New York.

The general mission of the new commission is to prepare New Yorkers for the mandatory vote on a convention call in 1997 or on an earlier call. More specifically, the group is to look at the processes for holding a convention and to make recommendations to improve them and to develop "a broad-based agenda of interests and concerns which might be considered by a convention." Their first interim report, "Delegate Selection Process," was released on March 17, 1994, and a 251-page compilation of articles, "The New York State Constitution Briefing Book," became available in April. Public hearings were scheduled for later in the year.

The California Constitutional Revision Commission is the most recent commission to be authorized. The Legislature passed and the governor signed the statute creating the commission in October 1993, after two attempts to do so in 1991 and 1992 had been vetoed by the governor. The commission is composed of 23 members, 20 appointed and three serving ex-officio. The commission members were appointed in April 1994. The Legislature appropriated $200,000 to support the commission in 1993-94. The commission will be "sunset" on July 1, 1996.

The mission of the commission is to study and make recommendations regarding the budget process, state governmental structure and proposed modifications, state and local governmental duties and relationships, and community resources and service delivery systems. The statute emphasizes the need to improve the budget process, which "has become crippled" and hampered by "gridlock." It is the hope of the sponsors that an independent citizens commission can provide the Legislature with recommendations for making needed changes. A final report is due no later than August 1, 1995.

Substantive Changes

In 1992-93 no new constitution or other general revision was on the ballot. There were, however, three budget proposals of some breadth: the "revision" drafted by the Louisiana Constitutional Convention, which was defeated at the polls, the budgeting and planning amendment of the Florida Taxation and Budget Reform Commission, which passed, and a budget proposal supported by Governor Pete Wilson in California, which failed. Also, the so-called "Taxpayers Bill of Rights" (TABOR), the constitutional initiative adopted in Colorado, while limited to the revenue article, made major changes.

The corporations article of the Utah Constitution underwent major revision. Several specific reforms also were important. The amendments to limit legislative terms may well be the most distinctive development historically. Among other changes were the extension of the recall to two states, authorization of county home rule in Arizona, executive reforms in Kentucky and Rhode Island, and judicial innovations in Arizona. School vouchers, which were on the ballot for the first time, were defeated. A limitation on the legal status of gays, lesbians and bisexuals was held unconstitutional in Colorado and defeated by the voters in Oregon.

One general trend that stands out during the biennium is the drive to increase direct citizen control of institutions and policymaking. The constitutional initiative was used more than ever, and direct democracy methods were added in Mississippi (the constitutional initiative), Rhode Island (the recall) and New Jersey (the recall). In Arizona, citizen committees were created to assist in the nomination of judges and the number of public members on nominating commissions was doubled. An Alaska task force recommended a citizens' commission to propose constitutional amendments to the legislature. Voter approval was required before certain fiscal policies could be adopted in Colorado (a special case), Arizona, Oklahoma (an alternative) and Texas. And the popularity of term limits can be explained at least partially by the desire to break the hold of incumbents so that more citizens can run for office.

Table B offers an overview of the general subject matter of state constitutional change in 1992-93 and the three preceding biennia. As indicated, finance and taxation drew the most propositions (54), and the legislative article was next (42), a familiar pattern in most biennia. Barely half of the fiscal amendments were adopted, the smallest percentage on the table, whereas close to three-fourths of the legislative proposals were approved. The most popular article was suffrage and elections; all measures were approved, including a Delaware proposal adopted by the Legislature. Least popular were the "State Functions" articles; only about one-third were approved, the lowest number on the table.

Bill of Rights, Suffrage and Elections

Compared with the last biennium, the number of constitutional proposals to change state bills of rights rose from 13 to 18. Fifteen were approved, or 83 percent and almost half of those concerned crime. Rights of crime victims were adopted in six states (Colorado, Illinois, Kansas, Missouri, New Mexico and Wisconsin). Two provisions restricted the rights of the accused. In Texas, voters approved another limit on the right to bail. Bail could be denied to a person accused of certain violent or sexual offenses committed while under supervision of a criminal justice agency for a prior felony. In New Jersey, the voters approved a measure declaring that the death penalty was not cruel or unusual punishment when imposed on a person who purposely or knowingly caused death or serious bodily injury resulting in death. The Arizona electorate approved of lethal injection as the sole method of execution. (Persons condemned before the effective date of the new provision could choose between lethal injection and lethal gas.) The only proposal on juries in criminal cases was defeated. The New Hampshire proposal would have retained 12-person juries in capital cases and in cases of imprisonment exceeding one year; six-person juries would be allowed in other cases.

Two proposals opposed to a protected legal status for persons of "homosexual, lesbian, or bisexual orientation" were on the ballot. The Oregon voters turned down the measure,

Table B
SUBSTANTIVE CHANGES IN STATE CONSTITUTIONS:
PROPOSED AND ADOPTED 1986-87, 1988-89, 1990-91 AND 1992-93

Subject matter	Total proposed				Total adopted				Percentage adopted			
	1986-87	1988-89	1990-91	1992-93	1986-87	1988-89	1990-91	1992-93	1986-87	1988-89	1990-91	1992-93
Proposals of statewide applicability	251*	228*	195*	211*	184†	164†	121†	139†	72.9*	71.6*	61.5*	64.9*
Bill of Rights	12*	21	13	18	10	19	8	15	81.8*	90.5	61.5	83.3
Suffrage & elections	11	12	3	8†	10	8	2	8	90.9	66.7	66.6	100.0
Legislative branch	49	44	45	42	35	33	28	31	71.4	75.0	62.2	73.8
Executive branch	23	22	9	15	19	14	8	13	82.6	63.6	88.8	86.6
Judicial branch	18	18	13	12†	15	14	7	9	83.3	77.8	53.8	75.0
Local government	17	14	7	10	11	10	3	6	64.7	71.4	42.8	60.0
Finance & taxation	45	54	58	54	29	33‡	36	29	64.4	62.9‡	62.0	53.7
State & local debt	12	6	4	4	8	5	3	2	66.6	83.3	75.0	50.0
State functions	29	22	29	25	22	17	18	9	75.8	77.3	62.0	36.0
Amendment & revision	0	5	0	2	0	2	0	1	0.0	40.0	0.0	50.0
General revision proposals	14	0	0	0	8	0	0	0	57.1	0.0	0.0	0.0
Miscellaneous proposals	22	12	15	23	17	9	9	16	77.2	75.0	60.0*	69.5
Local amendments	24	39	31	28	20	35	24	21	79.1	89.7	74.1*	75.7

Key:
* — Excludes Delaware where proposals are not submitted to voters
† — Includes Delaware
‡ — Excludes one Nevada constitutional initiative whose final adoption requires a second favorable vote.

but the voters in Colorado approved it. The Colorado Supreme Court upheld a preliminary injunction against its enforcement in 1993 and a state district court ruled the amendment invalid under the equal protection clause of the 14th Amendment to the U.S. Constitution.

In other significant actions, Iowa voters turned down an equal rights amendment, the Florida electorate approved an amendment to require the Legislature to draw up a taxpayers' bill of rights and Washington voters ratified an amendment allowing chaplains in public hospitals. In addition, Florida voters approved an amendment that required public access to public records and meetings in all three branches of government, Maryland voters approved an amendment that allowed six-member civil juries and raised the amount in dispute ($5,000) that would entitle a party to a jury trial in civil suits, and Arizona's "Pre-born Child Protection Act," which included a ban on public funding of abortions, was defeated.

Unlike the last biennium in which only three suffrage and election proposals were on the ballot, there were eight proposals this biennium. Very significant was the adoption of the recall for state officials in Rhode Island and in New Jersey. In two states, amendments were passed to make it easier to vote. In Connecticut, the Legislature may allow any qualified voter to vote absentee, while in Delaware absentee registration was extended to spouses and dependents of persons in the armed forces or merchant marine temporarily absent from the state or for certain other reasons. Obsolete voting or office-holding provisions were removed in Nevada and Iowa. A Mississippi amendment disqualified from public office persons convicted of a felony in other states or by the United States. A New Hampshire proposal to allow National Guardsmen and certain others to hold public office was defeated. In Florida, suspension of an election in an emergency was approved, as was a Kentucky executive reform amendment that changed elections for all but constitutional officers from odd-numbered years to even-numbered years.

Three Branches of Government

Proposals to change the legislative, executive and judicial articles accounted for about one-third of the statewide propositions in 1992-93, the same as two years ago. Legislative proposals continued to outnumber those regarding the other two branches, but the number of executive questions grew from two years ago. Proposed changes to the judiciary continued to decline, though slightly, while the approval rate was higher than two years ago.

The movement to limit legislative terms by constitutional initiative picked up speed in the biennium after its beginnings in Oklahoma, Colorado and California in 1990. (For a full discussion of term limits, see the essay "Term Limits in the States" by Thad Beyle and Rich Jones, pp. 26-31 of this volume.)

Three measures in Hawaii, all of which passed, addressed reapportionment, a perennial topic in the state. The major change was in the population base — from the total number of registered voters to the total number of permanent residents. Legislative compensation items were on the ballot in three states. The only one to pass was a Wisconsin amendment that requires an intervening election between a legislative-sponsored pay raise and its adoption. In New Mexico, the long quest to substitute a salary for per diem compensation failed when the voters turned down an amendment creating a citizens' salary commission to set legislative compensation.

In Louisiana, significant changes in sessions and procedures won approval at the polls in 1993. The regular session in the even-numbered years was reduced from 60 to 30 days and limited to taxes and other fiscal subjects. Sessions in odd-numbered years were limited to 60 days in an 85-day period and cannot address tax issues. Various deadlines have been inserted into the procedural rules. After a pre-filing deadline, legislators are limited to the introduction of five bills unless joint rules permit otherwise. Another Louisiana amendment and one in North Dakota were passed to change the date on which laws become effective. Finally, Utah clarified certain provisions of its legislative article, such as the beginning date for legislative terms, and added some new sections on deadlines: the regular sessions will begin one week later than before, the Senate will have more time to approve judicial appointments, and the legislature must call itself into session to override vetoes no later than 60 days after a session ends.

Two legislative oversight questions were also on the ballot. A New Jersey amendment allowing the legislature to review administrative rules and regulations and invalidate or prohibit them was adopted, but a similar amendment involving delegation of legislative authority and its control failed in New Hampshire.

In California, amendments to elevate the legislative analyst and the auditor general to constitutional status were rejected by the voters. Financing of the two offices would have been removed from legislative budget limits. Also in California, two amendments to change budgeting procedures were turned down. The more comprehensive of the two, which was supported by Governor Wilson, would have granted more power to the governor over the budget. The second amendment concerned implementation procedures, and would have been permitted the Legislature to disregard the single-subject rule for bills implementing the appropriations act.

All but two of the proposed changes to the executive articles were ratified. With respect to terms of office, nine of the constitutional initiatives on legislative term limits extended them to the executive office. In addition, the Mississippi charter was amended to restrict the lieutenant governor to two consecutive terms. There were counter-moves as well. The Rhode Island electorate approved a historic increase in the term of governor from two to four years. However, the governor would be able to serve only two consecutive terms. Also, in Kentucky, the voters repealed the present one four-year term provision and allowed the governor and other high executive officers to serve two consecutive four-year terms. In Arizona, the term of the office of mine inspector was increased from two to four years.

A major reform in Kentucky was the selection of the governor and lieutenant governor as a team — that is, on a single ticket. And an interesting amendment in Arizona repealed an amendment adopted in 1986 that required a majority vote to win the governorship, and a runoff if no majority were obtained. The 1986 change was a reaction to the election of Governor Evan Mecham by 39 percent of the vote. Mecham was impeached and removed from office during the first term. An argument for repeal was that in elections after 1986 the runoff did not change the outcome of the first election.

Several ballot questions concerned what happens when the governor is absent from the state or unable to serve, and succession to executive offices. The Kentucky amendment providing for the single-ticket and other reforms also allowed the governor, if unable to perform duties temporarily, to transfer them to the lieutenant governor; and if both the officers were unable to act, the attorney general and then the auditor would be in line to perform gubernatorial duties. In both Kentucky and Rhode Island, amendments repealed the prohibition against the governor serving in his or her capacity while absent from the state. In addition, the Kentucky charter was amended to repeal the requirement of an election to fill a vacancy in the governorship during the first two years of tenure. In Maine, the voters adopted a measure to provide for a method for interim occupancy of the offices of treasurer and secretary of state in the event of a vacancy. A deputy would be assigned until the Legislature appointed a replacement.

Compensation of executive officers was addressed in two ballot questions, both approved. Voters in Mississippi prohibited the lieutenant governor from receiving the lieutenants' and the governor's salary when acting as governor. In Arkansas, a measure that expressly excluded "public relations funds" from reimbursable expenses of executive and legislators was adopted.

The revision of the executive article in Utah, which was adopted at the polls, allowed the governor and the judiciary to appoint legal counsel and clarified the qualifications, terms and duties of several officers. One change was the establishment, for the first time, of a minimum age for the state auditor and state treasurer.

The proposed amendments to the judiciary articles included changes in judicial selection, discipline, jurisdiction, courts and costs. Arizona voters ratified comprehensive changes in the merit selection system used to appoint and retain state appellate judges and trial judges in the two largest counties, Maricopa (Phoenix) and Pima (Tucson). Other judicial selection proposals were less comprehensive. Nevada voters turned down a proposal to require the selection of the chief justice by a majority of the members of the court to serve one or more four-year terms. In Montana, the electorate opposed a change in the state's merit selection system to require timely elections of judges who are appointed to fill a vacancy; under the existing law a judge may serve up to three years without facing the voters. The Pennsylvania Legislature referred to the voters a new method for regulating judicial conduct, which was ratified.

Four measures, all but one of which passed, concerned jurisdiction. The rejected proposal would have allowed the Louisiana Legislature to authorize family courts to hear certain community property partition cases. A Delaware provision permitted the supreme court of that state to hear questions of law certified to it by the U.S. Supreme Court and other constitutional federal courts and the highest court of other states in addition to the Delaware courts and the federal district court in Delaware. In Nevada, the district courts were allowed to issue writs of prohibition and writs of habeas corpus before the sentence was completed. And in Washington, the district courts as well as superior courts can now hear cases in equity.

In Mississippi, the Legislature was allowed by the voters to change the number of circuit and chancery courts; but in Nevada, the electorate refused to approve the establishment of intermediate appellate courts. And in New Jersey, the voters approved an amendment to require the state to assume more of the costs of courts now supported by the county property tax.

Local Government

The proposed amendments to local government articles were few, but not insignificant. In Arizona, the voters approved a procedure for allowing county home rule in the two largest counties. An amendment was added to the New Mexico constitution requiring all elective county officials to serve four-year terms in-

stead of two, with a limit of two successive terms. Also, five-member boards of county commissioners are allowed upon the unanimous vote of the board but single-member districts would be mandatory. In Texas, the voters approved an amendment to permit the Legislature to prescribe qualifications for sheriffs and to enable county commissioners' courts to hold an election to abolish the county surveyor. Two rejected Alabama measures would have allowed county tax officials and mayors, sheriffs and other local elective offices to join a local or a state government retirement system.

Other local government proposals concerned fiscal matters. New Yorkers voted to allow more flexibility in the handling of local debt (extending to the year 2004 the exclusion of debt for sewage facilities from the local debt limits, and allowing a different calculation of debt) and Arizona voters approved an amendment to add general elections to four-year local elections in which to vote on expansion in the permanent tax base that determines spending limits. However, New Mexico voters voted against an amendment to allow county debt to repair buildings. Missourians also rejected a proposal to increase local bonded debt to retrofit buildings damaged in an earthquake.

Finally, there were three provisions scattered in different amendments and articles on state mandates, two of which passed. The rejected measure was a Texas school finance law that exempted a school district from complying with unfunded state educational mandates under certain conditions.

Provisions in Maine and Colorado were adopted. Now no state mandates to local governments are lawful in Maine unless the state provides 90 percent of the funding; the Legislature, by a two-thirds vote, can make an exception to the ban. The Colorado provision was part of the Taxpayers' Bill of Rights. It allowed local governments to end or reduce, over a three-year period, subsidies to a program delegated to them by the Legislature with certain exceptions.

Finance

There were 54 proposals to change finance and taxation articles and four more on local and state debt, during the biennium. In addition, fiscal measures were not infrequently located in other articles. It is clear that state constitutions are documents about raising and spending money.

Taxes were the target of most of the amendments in 1992-93, a common pattern, but the severity of tax restrictions in a few states was one highlight of the biennium. The most restrictive was the Colorado "Taxpayers' Bill of Rights" (TABOR), a constitutional initiative adopted in 1992 after defeat in 1988 and 1990. A distinctive feature of the Colorado proposal is the requirement for voter approval of state and local governmental changes that increase taxes and important decisions concerning spending and debt.

The amendment added new limits on spending and debt. Before TABOR, no limitations on spending applied generally to all local governments and no limits were imposed on local or state revenue bonds or multi-year lease agreements. Under the new law, existing spending limits have been changed to reflect the rate of inflation and certain other factors and new local limits have been imposed. Also, voter approval is probably required for revenue bonds and the multi-year financial arrangements.

New restrictive tax procedures were added to the constitutions of two other states. An Oklahoma constitutional initiative required a bill raising revenue either to receive three-fourths of the vote of each house of the Legislature or voter approval. A measure receiving the extraordinary majority would not go into effect for 90 days. The Arizona charter was changed so that a two-thirds majority of each house of the Legislature, rather than a simple majority, must be obtained to increase state revenue. If the governor vetoes the bill, it takes a three-fourths vote to override the veto. The new amendment would not apply if the revenue increases resulted purely from economic effects.

Most tax proposals in other states concerned the property tax. In addition to TABOR, 28 such proposals were on the ballot and 13 were adopted. Fifteen were designed to offer a "tax break" by exemption, postponement or other means. Only one of the exemption measures failed, and it was passed when it was on the

ballot the next year (Louisiana). In contrast, only two of eight other "breaks" were adopted.

Another group of property tax measures was designed to increase tax revenue either directly or indirectly by such means as lowering the vote for tax increases or allowing exceptions to limits. Only one of nine was approved, an Arkansas amendment to allow a tax for libraries. Most of the remaining property tax propositions concerned classification of property.

Only one amendment was devoted solely to the income tax. In Texas, where the constitution explicitly allows an income tax, the voters approved a requirement that voter approval is necessary before a personal income tax can be levied. Also, if the tax is adopted, a vote is also necessary to increase the tax when the result is to increase income tax liability. Proceeds from the tax are dedicated solely to education, and at least two-thirds must be used to reduce local school property taxes.

The remaining tax measures were directed at the sales and excise taxes. Three of the seven passed. In California, the voters approved the repeal of a sales tax on certain foods and the dedication of 1/2 cent of the current sales tax to law enforcement. Missouri voters approved the distribution of 5 percent of a new fuels tax to cities and counties.

Regarding spending, the voters in three states adopted state limits for the first time. In Connecticut, general budget expenditures must not exceed the estimated amount of revenue each fiscal year and, in addition, may not grow faster than the increase in personal income or inflation unless the governor declares an emergency. In Rhode Island, appropriations are limited to 98 percent of state revenue and a budget reserve account is created for the remaining 2 percent. In Virginia, a contribution to the Budget Stabilization Fund is mandated when taxes exceed an average tax growth rate.

Several amendments concerned expenditures for specific purposes. A Louisiana proposal to allow the state and local governments, by a two-thirds vote, to spend money for economic diversification was defeated. Also rejected was a North Carolina measure to enact laws without a referendum to promote private industrial economic development. Maine voters approved a proposition to ensure that a certain level of appropriations for the Department of Inland Fisheries and Wildlife, and North Dakota and West Virginia voters approved of payments to veterans of the Gulf War and military service in certain other areas.

Various proposals concerning trust and other funds were on the ballot. Six were trust fund amendments, of which two were adopted: the Alabama Forever Wild Land Trust and the Georgia Indigent Care Trust Fund. Rejected were: the Georgia Transportation Trust Fund, a North Dakota bicentennial trust fund for the year 2089, a proposal to divert the principal from the Montana Coal Trust Fund for infrastructure, and in Louisiana, a proposal to allow the Louisiana Education Trust Fund to be invested in stocks. Also, Wyoming voters rejected an amendment allowing the Legislature to invest state funds in stocks of major corporations. Public pension funds were the subject of three propositions, the most comprehensive of which was adopted in California by constitutional initiative. It was designed to ensure the independence of the boards in investment decisions.

Unlike proposals for tax and spending increases, amendments to authorize bonds were relatively popular at the polls. Of 11 authorizations of general obligation (GO) bonds, seven were adopted. Texas led the way with five GO bond issues, but only two passed, one for veterans housing and land purchases and the other for corrections and mental health and mental retardation facilities. Bonds for local and regional solid waste and other facilities (Georgia), public universities and certain other agencies (Oklahoma), funding of internal improvements for railways (Wisconsin), capital improvements for state parks and recreation (Ohio), and construction of higher education facilities (Florida) were accepted by voters.

Of the four remaining propositions, all of which passed, three were derived from the revision proposed by the Louisiana convention and included a new limit on net state supported debt. The fourth is a New York amendment that allows new methods for payment of state bonds.

Functions, Amendments and Revisions, and Miscellaneous

In 1992-93, the total number of proposed changes to the policy articles dropped slightly from the past biennium (from 29 to 25), but only nine were approved. The main reason for the low adoption rate is the appearance on the ballot of highly controversial education proposals, such as vouchers and various public school financing alternatives. Only three of the 14 education amendments were approved. Six of the 11 proposals to change other policy articles were approved, and they were mostly noncontroversial.

The placement in 1992-93 of school voucher proposals by constitutional initiative on the ballot in California and Colorado attracted national attention. Both were defeated. The California initiative would have required the state to offer to every resident school-age child an annual scholarship in the form of a voucher equal to at least 50 percent of the prior fiscal year's per pupil spending on public schools (K-12), an amount estimated to be $2,600 per child. The voucher could be used at any "scholarship redeeming school," which must have at least 25 pupils. The Colorado plan intended to apportion, in the form of vouchers, all state money for the general support of public school education (K-12) among students from age 5 through 21. The value of the voucher was to be at least 50 percent of the average per pupil expenditure in the district of the student's residence. The voucher could be used at any school — public, private or home.

Controversial issues on school funding also were on the ballot in Texas, Oregon and Michigan. The Texas Legislature, in an attempt to avoid another state Supreme Court decision holding the public school financing system unconstitutional, referred an amendment to the voters at a special election in May 1993 allowing the Legislature to redistribute among other school districts the property taxes levied and collected by a district (the "recapture principle") and to consolidate tax bases by means of county education districts. The voters rejected the amendment, often referred to as "Robin Hood." In Oregon an unsuccessful effort was made to amend a school property tax amendment adopted in 1990 whose purpose was to reduce the tax as a source of public school funding. The new proposal would have doubled the rate of the property tax limit and retained it at that level. Another measure, to levy a 5 cent sales tax for schools, was also defeated. Michigan proposed two measures, both of which were rejected. Property taxes would have been reduced, and the state sales and use tax rates increased to 6 percent. The new money would have been dedicated to the schools. A minimum state and local per pupil funding would have been guaranteed.

The voters in Illinois turned down a public school amendment devoted to basic principles: Education was a "fundamental right"; the state had the "paramount duty" to provide a thorough and efficient system of quality public education and equality of educational opportunity; and the state had the "preponderate financial responsibility" for financing public education.

Other rejected public school measures concerned education boards and school lands. Two were Louisiana amendments to change education boards to conform to new congressional districts, and one was a Montana measure to increase the number of regents on the board of education and to require that one seat be reserved for a native American; another Montana proposal would have transferred certain public school lands to local governments.

The three measures adopted were: requiring elective local school boards (Georgia), adding state Institutes of Technology to the guaranteed building fund for colleges and universities not eligible for the Permanent University Fund (Texas) and overruling a state supreme court decision on oil and gas leases affecting school revenues (Mississippi).

Proposed amendments to policy articles other than education included a measure to require businesses to provide labels with warning about toxic chemicals (rejected in Ohio) and the repeal of the requirement for a referendum before the construction of low-rent housing projects (defeated in California). Adopted was a revision of the corporations article in Utah; included was a general prohibition of all forms of restraint on trade or commerce.

In contrast to the past biennium when no amendments were proposed to the amending article, two were on the ballot in 1992-93. Only one passed, the indirect constitutional initiative in Mississippi. Defeated was a Louisiana proposal to allow the Legislature to refer to the voters as single amendment changes or additions to certain fiscal provisions, such as dedication of state revenues.

Most state charters contain a miscellaneous or general provisions article for propositions that apply to more than one article or that do not fit anywhere else. For convenience, a Colorado measure repealing obsolete provisions in four articles was included in Table B under "Miscellaneous." Counting Colorado, there were 23 proposals and 16 adoptions for a high approval rate of almost 70 percent. The number of proposals was the largest of any of the biennia in Table B.

Over half of the measures (13) dealt with lottery and gambling, and eight passed. Voters in Georgia, Nebraska and Mississippi approved a state lottery for the first time. (In Mississippi the prohibition against lotteries was simply lifted.) In Kentucky, the electorate permitted charitable groups to conduct lotteries under legislative authorization. Two of three amendments to dedicate lottery proceeds were adopted: for the Great Outdoors Project in Colorado and for education in Missouri, but not for the Louisiana Health Insurance Association Fund. In Colorado, three statewide (and two local) amendments concerned gaming. The only measure to pass required the approval of local voters for gaming to be allowed in local areas. Propositions were approved in Wisconsin and Idaho that clarified the meaning of "gambling" in current law: to prohibit further extension of gaming (Wisconsin) and to exclude expressly casino gambling (Idaho). The voters rejected simulcast horse racing in Missouri.

Remaining proposals not already reviewed elsewhere are: changes in the oath of office to exclude university faculty and certain other officials (Hawaii), a repeal of the prohibition against devising property to a charitable or education institution within a given time period (Mississippi), requiring a two-thirds vote of the legislature to reduce state park land

(Maine), and ending tolls on toll roads leased to private interests after 35 years or when the lease expires (California). The California proposal was rejected as was a Missouri proposal to allow construction of toll roads (located in the executive article). All the others were adopted.

Sources and Resources

As was true of the past biennium and the 1980s, publications on state constitutions and state constitutional law have continued to multiply. Ongoing series initiated in the late 1980s have been joined by new sources including state constitutional commissions.

The National Association of Attorneys General has continued to publish its *State Constitutional Law Bulletin*, a 10-issue monthly inaugurated in December 1987. The *Temple Law Review* (Temple University School of Law), by agreement with the Attorneys General, began publication in 1992 of an annual winter issue, "Emerging Issues in State Constitutional Law." To date, the 1992 and 1993 issues have been published. Emerging Issues was originally an annual law journal sponsored by the Attorneys General which also offered a state constitutional law student writing competition. The *Temple Law Review* has kept this feature of the journal, and in addition, has sponsored a state constitutional law symposium.

Annual reviews of state constitutional law first published by the *Rutgers Law Journal* (Rutgers University School of Law at Camden) in 1989 have entered the fifth year with the 1993 issue. In addition to articles, the reviews contain yearly summaries of state constitutional law cases.

The Edward McNall Burns Center for State Constitutional Studies at Rutgers University in New Brunswick has continued its *State Constitutional Commentaries and Notes*, which made its debut in 1989, and has added other materials under the editorship of Stanley Friedelbaum.

Robert F. Williams, one of the editors of the state constitutional law series in the *Rutgers Law Journal*, has revised his book on state constitutional law with a new publisher, the Michie Company of Charlottesville, Va. *State Constitutional Law Cases and Materials*, sec-

ond edition, came out in 1993. A legal treatise on state constitutional law was also made available during the biennium: Jennifer Friesen's *State Constitutional Law Litigating Individual Rights, Claims and Defenses*, Mathew Bender and Company of New York, publisher.

State constitutional commissions were sources of several publications directly or indirectly. The recommendations of the Oklahoma Revision Study Commission were incorporated in the first of two issues on the Oklahoma Constitution in the *Oklahoma City University Law Review* (Oklahoma City University School of law), fall 1991. A leading article in the second issue (summer 1992) by Robert H. Henry, chairman of the Oklahoma commission, was entitled, "The Oklahoma Constitutional Revision Commission: A Call to Arms or the Sounding of Retreat."

The New York Temporary State Commission on Constitutional Revision completed two reports in 1994: "Delegate Selection Process" and "The New York State Constitution Briefing Book." The latter is a 257-page volume of articles by experts on various constitutional subjects. More works can be expected during the Commission's tenure. In April 1994, the Alaska Constitutional Revisision Task Force completed its final report which contains recommendations for alternative methods of constitutional revision. A consultant to the commission, Gordon S. Harrison, who is director of the Alaska Legislative Research Agency, revisited the Alaska constitution in the third edition of his book, *Alaska's Constitution, A Citizen's Guide*. More comprehensive than and in a different format from the two earlier editions, the book came out in time for guidance to voting in the November 1992 election on the call for a constitutional convention.

A very substantial contribution to state constitutional literature occurred with the release of 15 more legal reference guides to state constitutions for the projected 52-volume series edited by G. Alan Tarr and published by the Greenwood Publishing Group. Five such guides were complete during the past biennium. A list of the 20 states for which guides have been published and their authors appears in the bibliography at the end of this essay.

Among other developments of interest, the Pennsylvania Constitution was highlighted in an issue of the *Widener Journal of Public Law* (the Widener University School of Law) in 1993. It contained papers from a symposium, "Securing Individual Rights Under the Pennsylvania Constitution." Cosponsored by the Roscoe Pound Foundation and the Yale Law School, a forum on "Protecting Individual Rights: The Role of State Constitutionalism" to which more than 100 state court judges were invited was held in 1992. Also, a history of three Western states that focused on the writing of their constitutions was also published during the biennium: David Alan Johnson, *Founding of the Far West: California, Oregon and Nevada 1840-1890*, the University of California Press, 1992.

The selected list of references at the end of this summary analysis includes several works of particular significance: *Sources and Documents of United States Constitution* (edited and annotated by William F. Swindler with Donald Musch) designed to integrate national and state constitutional documents into a reference collection on American constitutional developments; *Model State Constitution*, first published by the National Municipal League in 1923 and since revised six times; and the *Index Digest of State Constitutions* prepared by the Legislative Drafting Research Fund of Columbia University. The selected list necessarily excludes many specific items developed for constitutional reform of particular state constitutions, including official documents, special studies, and vast quantity of ephemeral material stored in state libraries and archives. Of particular value are the complete, annotated and comparative analyses of the Illinois and Texas constitutions, prepared for delegates to the constitutional conventions of those states. Also excluded from the list are numerous materials prepared by groups long identified with state constitutions, the League of Women Voters, the National Civic League, and The Council of State Governments. Excepting the holdings of the Library of Congress, probably the most extensive collection of fugitive and published materials are those of the National Civic League and The Council of State Governments.

Sources of periodic reviews and updates of state constitutional developments include the biennial summary of official activities in *The Book of the States*. The 1982-83 volume featured a 50-year review of state constitutional history and bibliography. From 1982-1986, Ronald K.L. Collins authored articles on state constitutional law that appeared periodically in *The National Law Journal*. From 1970 through 1985, Albert L. Sturm contributed an annual survey of state constitutional developments to the *National Civic Review*.

Footnotes

[1] Thomas H. Ferrell, "The Louisiana Constitutional Convention of 1992," State Constitutional Commentaries and Notes, 3, 4 (Summer 1992): 9-12.

Selected References

"Annual Issue on State Constitutional Law." *Rutgers Law Journal* 20, 4 (Summer 1989): 877-1113. Includes Bibliography, 1980-89. Subsequent annual issues (Summer) to present.

Bamberger, Phylis Skloot, ed. *Recent Developments in State Constitutional Law*, New York, N.Y.: Practicing Law Institute, 1985.

Brammer, Dana B. and John Winkle III, eds. *A Contemporary Analysis of Mississippi's Constitutional Government: Proceedings of a Forum May 2-3, 1986*. Oxford, Miss.: The Public Policy Research Center, University of Mississippi, October 1986.

Brown, Cynthia E., comp. *State Constitutional Conventions: From Independence to the Completion of the Present Union, A Bibliography*. Westport, Conn.: Greenwood Press, 1973.

Clem, Alan L., ed. *Contemporary Approaches to State Constitutional Revision*. Vermillion, S.D.: Governmental Research Bureau, University of South Dakota, 1970.

Collins, Ronald K.L., comp. and ed. "Bills and Declarations of Rights Digest." *The American Bench, Judges of the Nation*. 3rd ed. Minneapolis, Minn.: Reginald Bishop Forster and Associates, Inc., 1985, 2483-2655.

"The Constitution of the State of Oklahoma: Recommendations for Revision." *Oklahoma City University Law Review* 16,3 (Fall 1991) — entire issue. Untitled second issue on the Oklahoma Constitution. *Oklahoma City University Law Review* 17,1 (Summer 1992).

Constitutions of the United States: National and State, 2nd ed. 2 vols. Dobbs Ferry, N.Y. Oceana Publications, 1974. Loose leaf. Updated periodically.

Cornwell, Elmer, E. Jr., et al. *Constitutional Conventions: The Politics of Revision*. New York, N.Y.: National Municipal League, 1974. (In second series of the National Municipal League's State Constitution Studies.)

Dishman, Robert B., *State Constitutions: The Shape of the Document*. Rev. ed. New York, N.Y.: National Municipal League, 2968 (In first series of the National Municipal League's State Constitution Studies.)

Edwards, William A., ed. *Index Digest of State Constitutions* 2nd ed. Dobbs Ferry, N.Y.: Oceana Publications, 1959. Prepared by the Legislative Drafting Research Fund, Columbia University.

Elazar, Daniel J., ed. Series of articles on American state constitutions and the constitutions of selected foreign states. *Publius: The Journal of Federalism* 12, 2 (Winter 1982): entire issue.

Emerging Issues in State Constitutional Law. Annual Law Review. Washington, D.C.: National Association of Attorneys General 1988-1991.

"Emerging Issues in State Constitutional Law." *Temple Law Review* 65, 4 (Winter 1992): entire issue. Subsequent annual issues (Winter) to present.

Friedelbaum, Stanley, H. ed. *Human Rights in the States, New Directions in Constitutional Policy-making*. Westport, Conn.: Greenwood Press, 1988.

Friesen, Jennifer. *State Constitutional Law: Litigating Individual Rights, Claims and Defenses*. New York: Mathew Bender and Co., Inc., 1992.

Grad, Frank P., *The State Constitutions: Its Function and Form for Our Time*. New York, N.Y.: National Municipal League, 1968. Reprinted from *Virginia Law Review* 54, 5 (June 1968). (In first series of the National Municipal League's State Constitution Studies).

Graves, W. Brooke, "State Constitutional Law: A Twenty-five Year Summary." *William and May Law Review* 8,1 (Fall 1966): 1-48.

_____, ed. *Major Problems in State Constitutional Revision*. Chicago: Public Administration Service, 1960.

Harrington, James C. *The Texas Bill of Rights: A Commentary and Litigation Manual*, 2nd edition. Austin, Texas: Butterworth, 1993.

Harrison, Gordon S. *Alaska's Constitution: A Citizen's Guide*. 3rd ed. Juneau: Alaska Legislative Research Agency, 1992.

Kincaid, John, special ed. "State Constitutions in a Federal System." *The Annals of the American Academy of Political and Social Sciences* 496 (March 1988): entire issue.

Leach, Richard H., ed. *Compacts of Antiquity: State Constitutions*. Atlanta, Ga.: Southern Newspaper Publishers Association Foundation, 1969.

Leshy, John D. "The Making of the Arizona Constitution." *Arizona State law Journal* 20, 1 (Spring 1988): 1-113.

May, Janice C. "Constitutional Amendment and Revision Revisited." *Publius: The Journal of Federalism* 17, 1 (Winter 1987): 153-179.

_____. "The Constitutional Initiative: A Threat to Rights?" In *Human Rights in the States, New Directions in Constitutional Policy-making*, Stanley H. Freidelbaum, ed.: 163-184.

_____. "Texas Constitutional Revision: Lessons and Laments." *National Civic Review* 66, 2 (February 1977): 64-69.

_____. *The Texas Constitutional Revision Experience in the Seventies*. Austin, Tex.: Sterling Swift Publishing Company, 1975.

McGraw, Bradley D., ed. *Developments in State Constitutional Law*, The Williamsburg Conference, St. Paul, Minn. West Publishing Co., 1985.

Model State Constitution. 6th ed. New York, N.Y.: National Municipal League, 1963. Revised 1968.

Pisciotte, Joseph P., ed. *Studies In Illinois Constitutional Making*. 10 vols. Urbana, Ill.: University of Illinois Press, 1972-1980.

Report of the Special Commission on Constitutional Revision. Research Report No. 226. Frankfort, Ky.: Legislative Research Commission, September 1987.

Sachs, Barbara Faith, ed. *Index to Constitutions of the United States: National and State*. London, Rome and New York: Oceana Publications. 1980. Prepared by the Legislative

Drafting Research Fund. Columbia University. The first two in the series are: *Fundamental Liberties and Rights: A Fifty-State Index* (1980), and *Laws, Legislatures and Legislative Procedures: A Fifty-State Index* (1982).

Schrag, Philip G., *Behind the Scenes: The Politics of a Constitutional Convention.* Washington, D.C.: Georgetown University Press, 1985.

Southwick, Leslie H. "State Constitutional Revision: Mississippi and the South." *The Mississippi Lawyer* 32, 3 (November-December 1985): 21-25.

_____ and C. Victor Welsch, III. "Method of Constitutional Revision: Which Way Mississippi?" *Mississippi Law Journal* 56, 1 (April 1986): 17-71.

State Constitutional Commentaries and Notes, A Quarterly Review. New Brunswick, N.J.: Edward McNall Burns Center for State Constitutional Studies, Fall 1989 to present.

State Constitutional Conventions, Commissions, and Amendment, 1979-1988. Annotated Bibliography and Microfiche Collection, Part 5. Bethesda, Maryland: Congressional Information Service. 1989. Parts 1-4 (1776-1978) published irregularly. For annotated bibliography published separately for Part I (1776-1959) see Cynthia Brown entry.

State Constitutional Convention Studies. 11 vols. New York, N.Y.: National Municipal League, 1969-1978.

State Constitutional Studies. 10 vols. in two series. New York, N.Y.: National Municipal League, 1960-1965.

State Constitutional Law Bulletin. Monthly from July-August. Washington, D.C.: National Association of Attorneys General, Dec. 1987 to present.

Sturm, Albert L., *A Bibliography on State Constitutions and Constitutional Revision, 1945-1975.* Englewood, Colo.: The Citizens Conference on State Legislatures, August 1975.

_____. Annual summary analyses of state constitutional developments. Published in the January or February issues of the *National Civic Review* 1070-1985.

_____. "The Development of American State Constitutions." *Publius: The Journal of Federalism* 12.2 (Winter 1982): 57-98.

_____. *Thirty Years of State Constitution Making, 1938-1968.* New York, N.Y.: National Municipal League, 1970.

Swindler, William F., ed. *Sources of Documents of United States Constitutions.* 10 vols. Dobbs Ferry, N.Y.: Oceana Publications, Inc. 1973-1979.

_____, ed. (vol. 1), with Donald Musch (vols, 2-4). *Sources and Documents of United States Constitutions, Second Series 1492-1800.* 4 vols. Dobbs Ferry, N.Y.: Oceana Publications, Inc. 1982-1986.

"Symposium Articles." (Pennsylvania Constitution). *Widener Journal of Public Law* 3, 1 (1993): entire issue.

"A Symposium on State Constitutional Revision." *Oregon Law Review* 67, 1 (1988): 1-238.

"Symposium on the Arizona Constitution." *Arizona State Law Journal* 20, 1 (Spring 1988): 1-368.

"Symposium on Constitutional Revision in Mississippi." *Mississippi Law Journal*, 56, 1 (April 1986): 1-163.

"Law School Symposium of the 1972 Constitution." *Montana Law Review* 51, 2 (Summer 1990): 237-508.

"Symposium: The Emergence of State Constitutional Law." *Texas Law Review* 63, 6 and 7 (March/April 1985): 959-1375.

"Symposium on the Texas Constitution." *Texas Law Review* 68, 7 (June 1990): 1337-1671.

Tarr, G. Alan and Mary Cornelia Porter, eds. "New Developments in State Constitutional Law." *Publius: The Journal of Federalism* 17, 1 (Winter 1987): entire issue.

Tarr, G. Alan, ed. *Reference Guides to the State Constitutions of the United States* (Projected 52 Vols.) Westport, Conn.: Greenwood Publishing Group, 1990 to present. States and authors: Alabama — William H. Stewart, Arizona — John D. Leshy, Arkansas — Kay Collett Goss, California — Joseph R. Grodin, Calvin R. Massey and Richard B. Cunningham, Connecticut — Wesley W. Horton, Florida — Talbot D'Alemberte, Hawaii — Anne Feden Lee, Idaho — Donald Crowley and Florence Heffron, Kansas — Francis H. Heller, Louisiana — Lee Hargrave, Maine — Marshall J. Tinkel, Mississippi — John W. Winkle III, Nebraska — Robert D. Miewald and Peter J. Longo, Nevada — Michael W. Bowers, New Jersey — Robert F. Williams, New York — Peter Galie, North Carolina — John V. Orth, Tennessee — Lewis L. Laska, Vermont — William C. Hill, Wyoming — Robert S. Keiter and Tim Newcomb.

Wheeler, John P. Jr. *The Constitutional Convention: A Manual on Its Planning, Organization and Operation*. New York, N.Y.: National Municipal League, 1961.

_____. ed. *Salient Issues of Constitutional Revision*. New York, N.Y.: National Municipal League, 1961.

Williams, Robert F. *State Constitutional Law: Cases and Materials*. 2d ed. Charlottesville, Va.: The Michie Company, 1993.

Table 1.1
GENERAL INFORMATION ON STATE CONSTITUTIONS
(As of January 1, 1994)

State or other jurisdiction	Number of constitutions*	Dates of adoption	Effective date of present constitution	Estimated length (number of words)	Number of amendments Submitted to voters	Adopted
Alabama	6	1819, 1861, 1865, 1868, 1875, 1901	Nov. 28, 1901	174,000	783	556
Alaska	1	1956	Jan. 3, 1959	16,675 (a)	32	23
Arizona	1	1911	Feb. 14, 1912	28,876	215	119
Arkansas	5	1836, 1861, 1864, 1868, 1874	Oct. 30, 1874	40,720	171	81 (b)
California	2	1849, 1879	July 4, 1879	33,350	814	485
Colorado	1	1876	Aug. 1, 1876	45,679	254	124
Connecticut	4	1818 (c), 1965	Dec. 30, 1965	9,564	29	28
Delaware	4	1776, 1792, 1831, 1897	June 10, 1897	19,000	(d)	123
Florida	6	1839, 1861, 1865, 1868, 1886, 1968	Jan. 7, 1969	25,100	92	65
Georgia	10	1777, 1789, 1798, 1861, 1865, 1868, 1877, 1945, 1976, 1982	July 1, 1983	25,000	52 (e)	39
Hawaii	1 (f)	1950	Aug. 21, 1959	17,453	102	86
Idaho	1	1889	July 3, 1890	21,500	189	109
Illinois	4	1818, 1848, 1870, 1970	July 1, 1971	13,200	14	8
Indiana	2	1816, 1851	Nov. 1, 1851	9,377 (a)	70	38
Iowa	2	1846, 1857	Sept. 3, 1857	12,500	52	49 (g)
Kansas	1	1859	Jan. 29, 1861	11,865	118	90 (g)
Kentucky	4	1792, 1799, 1850, 1891	Sept. 28, 1891	23,500	65	32
Louisiana	11	1812, 1845, 1852, 1861, 1864, 1868, 1879, 1898, 1913, 1921, 1974	Jan. 1, 1975	51,448	92	54
Maine	1	1819	March 15, 1820	13,500	192	162 (h)
Maryland	4	1776, 1851, 1864, 1867	Oct. 5, 1867	41,349	238	205 (i)
Massachusetts	1	1780	Oct. 25, 1780	36,690 (j)	144	117
Michigan	4	1835, 1850, 1908, 1963	Jan. 1, 1964	20,000	51	17
Minnesota	1	1857	May 11, 1858	9,500	207	113
Mississippi	4	1817, 1832, 1869, 1890	Nov. 1, 1890	24,000	148	116
Missouri	4	1820, 1865, 1875, 1945	March 30, 1945	42,000	132	81
Montana	2	1889, 1972	July 1, 1973	11,866	32	18
Nebraska	2	1866, 1875	Oct. 12, 1875	20,048	293	197
Nevada	1	1864	Oct. 31, 1864	20,770	184	113 (g)
New Hampshire	2	1776, 1784	June 2, 1784	9,200	280 (k)	143 (k)
New Jersey	3	1776, 1844, 1947	Jan. 1, 1948	17,086	57	44
New Mexico	1	1911	Jan. 6, 1912	27,200	240	123
New York	4	1777, 1822, 1846, 1894	Jan. 1, 1895	80,000	280	213
North Carolina	3	1776, 1868, 1970	July 1, 1971	11,000	35	27
North Dakota	1	1889	Nov. 2, 1889	20,564	235 (l)	129 (l)
Ohio	2	1802, 1851	Sept. 1, 1851	36,900	253	151
Oklahoma	1	1907	Nov. 16, 1907	68,800	293 (m)	146 (m)
Oregon	1	1857	Feb. 14, 1859	26,090	383 (n)	(n)
Pennsylvania	5	1776, 1790, 1838, 1873, 1968 (n)	1968 (n)	21,675	26	56
Rhode Island	2	1842 (c)	May 2, 1843	19,026 (o)	102	36
South Carolina	7	1776, 1778, 1790, 1861, 1865, 1868, 1895	Jan. 1, 1896	22,500 (o)	648 (p)	463
South Dakota	1	1889	Nov. 2, 1889	23,300	191	99
Tennessee	3	1796, 1835, 1870	Feb. 23, 1870	15,300	55	32
Texas	5	1845, 1861, 1866, 1869, 1876	Feb. 15, 1876	76,000	518 (q)	353
Utah	1	1895	Jan. 4, 1896	11,000	131	82
Vermont	3	1777, 1786, 1793	July 9, 1793	6,600	208	50
Virginia	6	1776, 1830, 1851, 1869, 1902, 1970	July 1, 1971	18,500	28	23
Washington	1	1889	Nov. 11, 1889	29,400	158	88
West Virginia	2	1863, 1872	April 9, 1872	25,600	110	64
Wisconsin	1	1848	May 29, 1848	13,500	174	129 (g)
Wyoming	1	1889	July 10, 1890	31,800	102	61
American Samoa	2	1960, 1967	July 1, 1967	6,000	14	7
No. Mariana Islands	1	1977	Jan. 9, 1978	11,000	49 (r)	47 (r,s)
Puerto Rico	1	1952	July 25, 1952	9,281 (a)	6	6

See footnotes at end of table.

GENERAL INFORMATION ON STATE CONSTITUTIONS—Continued

Note: An authoritative revision of the number of words in each of the 50 state constitutions will be included in *The Book of the States, 1996-97.*

* The constitutions referred to in this table include those Civil War documents customarily listed by the individual states.

(a) Actual word count.

(b) Eight of the approved amendments have been superseded and are not printed in the current edition of the constitution. The total adopted does not include five amendments that were invalidated.

(c) Colonial charters with some alterations served as the first constitutions in Connecticut (1638, 1662) and in Rhode Island (1663).

(d) Proposed amendments are not submitted to the voters in Delaware.

(e) The new Georgia constitution eliminates the need for local amendments, which have been a long-term problem for state constitution makers.

(f) As a kingdom and a republic, Hawaii had five constitutions.

(g) The figure given includes amendments approved by the voters and later nullified by the state supreme court in Iowa (three), Kansas (one), Nevada (six) and Wisconsin (two).

(h) The figure does not include one amendment approved by the voters in 1967 that is inoperative until implemented by legislation.

(i) Two sets of identical amendments were on the ballot and adopted in the Maryland 1992 election. The four amendments are counted as two in the table.

(j) The printed constitution includes many provisions that have been annulled. The length of effective provisions is an estimated 24,122 words (12,400 annulled) in Massachusetts, and in Rhode Island before the "rewrite" of the constitution in 1986, it was 11,399 words (7,627 annulled).

(k) The constitution of 1784 was extensively revised in 1792. Figures show proposals and adoptions since the constitution was adopted in 1784.

(l) The figures do not include submission and approval of the constitution of 1889 itself and of Article XX; these are constitutional questions included in some counts of constitutional amendments and would add two to the figure in each column.

(m) The figures include five amendments submitted to and approved by the voters which were, by decisions of the Oklahoma or U.S. Supreme Courts, rendered inoperative or ruled invalid, unconstitutional, or illegally submitted.

(n) Certain sections of the constitution were revised by the limited constitutional convention of 1967-68. Amendments proposed and adopted are since 1968.

(o) Of the estimated length, approximately two-thirds is of general statewide effect; the remainder is local amendments.

(p) As of 1981, of the 626 proposed amendments submitted to the voters, 130 were of general statewide effect and 496 were local; the voters rejected 83 (12 statewide, 71 local). Of the remaining 543, the General Assembly refused to approve 100 (22 statewide, 78 local), and 443 (96 statewide, 347 local) were finally added to the constitution.

(q) The number of proposed amendments to the Texas Constitution exclude three proposed by the legislature but not placed on the ballot.

(r) The number of amendments is from 1984-1994.

(s) The total excludes one amendment ruled void by a federal district court.

Table 1.2
CONSTITUTIONAL AMENDMENT PROCEDURE: BY THE LEGISLATURE
Constitutional Provisions

State or other jurisdiction	Legislative vote required for proposal (a)	Consideration by two sessions required	Vote required for ratification	Limitation on the number of amendments submitted at one election
Alabama	3/5	No	Majority vote on amendment	None
Alaska	2/3	No	Majority vote on amendment	None
Arizona	Majority	No	Majority vote on amendment	None
Arkansas	Majority	No	Majority vote on amendment	3
California	2/3	No	Majority vote on amendment	None
Colorado	2/3	No	Majority vote on amendment	None (b)
Connecticut	(c)	(c)	Majority vote on amendment	None
Delaware	2/3	Yes	Not required	No referendum
Florida	3/5	No	Majority vote on amendment	None
Georgia	2/3	No	Majority vote on amendment	None
Hawaii	(d)	(d)	Majority vote on amendment (e)	None
Idaho	2/3	No	Majority vote on amendment	None
Illinois	3/5	No	(f)	3 articles
Indiana	Majority	Yes	Majority vote on amendment	None
Iowa	Majority	Yes	Majority vote on amendment	None
Kansas	2/3	No	Majority vote on amendment	5
Kentucky	3/5	No	Majority vote on amendment	4
Louisiana	2/3	No	Majority vote on amendment (g)	None
Maine	2/3 (h)	No	Majority vote on amendment	None
Maryland	3/5	No	Majority vote on amendment	None
Massachusetts	Majority (i)	Yes	Majority vote on amendment	None
Michigan	2/3	No	Majority vote on amendment	None
Minnesota	Majority	No	Majority vote in election	None
Mississippi	2/3 (j)	No	Majority vote on amendment	None
Missouri	Majority	No	Majority vote on amendment	None
Montana	2/3 (h)	No	Majority vote on amendment	None
Nebraska	3/5	No	Majority vote on amendment (e)	None
Nevada	Majority	Yes	Majority vote on amendment	None
New Hampshire	3/5	No	2/3 vote on amendment	None
New Jersey	(k)	(k)	Majority vote on amendment	None (l)
New Mexico	Majority (m)	No	Majority vote on amendment (m)	None
New York	Majority	Yes	Majority vote on amendment	None
North Carolina	3/5	No	Majority vote on amendment	None
North Dakota	Majority	No	Majority vote on amendment	None
Ohio	3/5	No	Majority vote on amendment	None
Oklahoma	Majority	No	Majority vote on amendment	None
Oregon	(n)	No	Majority vote on amendment	None
Pennsylvania	Majority (o)	Yes (o)	Majority vote on amendment	None
Rhode Island	Majority	No	Majority vote on amendment	None
South Carolina	2/3 (p)	Yes (p)	Majority vote on amendment	None
South Dakota	Majority	No	Majority vote on amendment	None
Tennessee	(q)	Yes (q)	Majority vote in election (r)	None
Texas	2/3	No	Majority vote on amendment	None
Utah	2/3	No	Majority vote on amendment	None
Vermont	(s)	Yes	Majority vote on amendment	None
Virginia	Majority	Yes	Majority vote on amendment	None
Washington	2/3	No	Majority vote on amendment	None
West Virginia	2/3	No	Majority vote on amendment	None
Wisconsin	Majority	Yes	Majority vote on amendment	None
Wyoming	2/3	No	Majority vote in election	None
American Samoa	2/3	No	Majority vote on amendment (t)	None
No. Mariana Islands	3/4	No	Majority vote on amendment	None
Puerto Rico	2/3 (u)	No	Majority vote on amendment	3

See footnotes at end of table.

CONSTITUTIONAL AMENDMENT PROCEDURE: BY THE LEGISLATURE—Continued

(a) In all states not otherwise noted, the figure shown in the column refers to the proportion of elected members in each house required for approval of proposed constitutional amendments.

(b) Legislature may not propose amendments to more than six articles of the constitution in the same legislative session.

(c) Three-fourths vote in each house at one session, or majority vote in each house in two sessions between which an election has intervened.

(d) Two-thirds vote in each house at one session, or majority vote in each house in two sessions.

(e) Majority vote on amendment must be at least 50 percent of the total votes cast at the election; or, at a special election, a majority of the votes tallied which must be at least 30 percent of the total number of registered voters.

(f) Majority voting in election or three-fifths voting on amendment.

(g) If five or fewer political subdivisions of the state are affected, majority in state as a whole and also in affected subdivision(s) is required.

(h) Two-thirds of both houses.

(i) Majority of members elected sitting in joint session.

(j) The two-thirds must include not less than a majority elected to each house.

(k) Three-fifths of all members of each house at one session, or majority of all members of each house for two successive sessions.

(l) If a proposed amendment is not approved at the election when submitted, neither the same amendment nor one which would make substantially the same change for the constitution may be again submitted to the people before the third general election thereafter.

(m) Amendments concerning certain elective franchise and education matters require three-fourths vote of members elected and approval by three-fourths of electors voting in state and two-thirds of those voting in each county.

(n) Majority vote to amend constitution, two-thirds to revise ("revise" includes all or a part of the constitution).

(o) Emergency amendments may be passed by two-thirds vote of each house, followed by ratification by majority vote of electors in election held at least one month after legislative approval.

(p) Two-thirds of members of each house, first passage; majority of members of each house after popular ratification.

(q) Majority of members elected to both houses, first passage; two-thirds of members elected to both houses, second passage.

(r) Majority of all citizens voting for governor.

(s) Two-thirds vote senate, majority vote house, first passage; majority both houses, second passage. As of 1974, amendments may be submitted only every four years.

(t) Within 30 days after voter approval, governor must submit amendment(s) to U.S. Secretary of the Interior for approval.

(u) If approved by two-thirds of members of each house, amendment(s) submitted to voters at special referendum; if approved by not less than three-fourths of total members of each house, referendum may be held at next general election.

Table 1.3
CONSTITUTIONAL AMENDMENT PROCEDURE: BY INITIATIVE
Constitutional Provisions

State or other jurisdiction	Number of signatures required on initiative petition	Distribution of signatures	Referendum vote
Arizona.............	15% of total votes cast for all candidates for governor at last election.	None specified.	Majority vote on amendment.
Arkansas	10% of voters for governor at last election.	Must include 5% of voters for governor in each of 15 counties.	Majority vote on amendment.
California..........	8% of total voters for all candidates for governor at last election.	None specified.	Majority vote on amendment.
Colorado	5% of total legal votes for all candidates for secretary of state at last general election.	None specified.	Majority vote on amendment.
Florida	8% of total votes cast in the state in the last election for presidential electors.	8% of total votes cast in each of 1/2 of the congressional districts.	Majority vote on amendment.
Illinois (a)	8% of total votes cast for candidates for governor at last election.	None specified.	Majority voting in election or 3/5 voting on amendment.
Massachusetts (b)	3% of total votes cast for governor at preceding biennial state election (not less than 25,000 qualified voters).	No more than 1/4 from any one county.	Majority vote on amendment which must be 30% of total ballots cast at election.
Michigan	10% of total voters for all candidates at last gubernatorial election.	None specified.	Majority vote on amendment.
Mississippi	12% of total votes for all candidates for governor in last election	No more than 20% from any one Congressional district	Majority vote on amendment and not less than 40% of total vote cast at election
Missouri	8% of legal voters for all candidates for governor at last election.	The 8% must be in each of 2/3 of the congressional districts in the state.	Majority vote on amendment.
Montana...........	10% of qualified electors, the number of qualified electors to be determined by number of votes cast for governor in preceding general election.	The 10% to include at least 10% of qualified electors in each of 2/5 of the legislative districts.	Majority vote on amendment.
Nebraska	10% of total votes for governor at last election.	The 10% must include 5% in each of 2/5 of the counties.	Majority vote on amendment which must be at least 35% of total vote at the election.
Nevada	10% of voters who voted in entire state in last general election.	10% of total voters who voted in each of 75% of the counties.	Majority vote on amendment. in two consecutive general elections.
North Dakota	4% of population of the state.	None specified.	Majority vote on amendment.
Ohio	10% of total number of electors who voted for governor in last election.	At least 5% of qualified electors in each of 1/2 of counties in the state.	Majority vote on amendment.
Oklahoma	15% of legal voters for state office receiving highest number of voters at last general state election.	None specified.	Majority vote on amendment.
Oregon	8% of total votes for all candidates for governor at last election at which governor was elected for four-year term.	None specified.	Majority vote on amendment.
South Dakota	10% of total votes for governor in last election.	None specified.	Majority vote on amendment.
No. Mariana Islands ...	50% of qualified voters of commonwealth.	In addition, 25% of qualified voters in each senatorial district.	Majority vote on amendment if legislature approved it by majority vote; if not, at least 2/3 vote in each of two senatorial districts in addition to a majority vote.

(a) Only Article IV, the Legislature, may be amended by initiative petition.
(b) Before being submitted to the electorate for ratification, initiative measures must be approved at two sessions of a successively elected legislature by not less than one-fourth of all members elected, sitting in joint session.

Table 1.4
PROCEDURES FOR CALLING CONSTITUTIONAL CONVENTIONS
Constitutional Provisions

State or other jurisdiction	Provision for convention	Legislative vote for submission of convention question (a)	Popular vote to authorize convention	Periodic submission of convention question required (b)	Popular vote required for ratification of convention proposals
Alabama.............	Yes	Majority	ME	No	Not specified
Alaska..............	Yes	No provision (c,d)	(c)	10 years (c)	Not specified (c)
Arizona.............	Yes	Majority	(e)	No	MP
Arkansas	No		No		
California...........	Yes	2/3	MP	No	MP
Colorado	Yes	2/3	MP	No	ME
Connecticut	Yes	2/3	MP	20 years (f)	MP
Delaware	Yes	2/3	MP	No	No provision
Florida	Yes	(g)	MP	No	Not specified
Georgia.............	Yes	(d)	No	No	MP
Hawaii	Yes	Not specified	MP	9 years	MP (h)
Idaho	Yes	2/3	MP	No	Not specified
Illinois.............	Yes	3/5	(i)	20 years; 1988	MP
Indiana.............	No		No		
Iowa	Yes	Majority	MP	10 years; 1970	MP
Kansas	Yes	2/3	MP	No	MP
Kentucky	Yes	Majority (j)	MP (k)	No	No provision
Louisiana	Yes	(d)	No	No	MP
Maine	Yes	(d)	No	No	No provision
Maryland	Yes	Majority	ME	20 years; 1970	MP
Massachusetts	No			No	Not specified
Michigan	Yes	Majority	MP	16 years; 1978	MP
Minnesota	Yes	2/3	ME	No	3/5 voting on proposal
Mississippi	No		No		
Missouri	Yes	Majority	MP	20 years; 1962	Not specified (l)
Montana.............	Yes (m)	2/3 (n)	MP	20 years	MP
Nebraska	Yes	3/5	MP (o)	No	MP
Nevada	Yes	2/3	ME	No	No provision
New Hampshire	Yes	Majority	MP	10 years	2/3 voting on proposal
New Jersey...........	No		No		
New Mexico..........	Yes	2/3	MP	No	Not specified
New York	Yes	Majority	MP	20 years; 1957	MP
North Carolina	Yes	2/3	MP	No	MP
North Dakota	No		No		
Ohio	Yes	2/3	MP	20 years; 1932	MP
Oklahoma	Yes	Majority	(e)	20 years	MP
Oregon	Yes	Majority	(e)	No	No provision
Pennsylvania	No		No		
Rhode Island	Yes	Majority	MP	10 years	MP
South Carolina	Yes	(d)	ME	No	No provision
South Dakota	Yes	(d)	(d)	No	(p)
Tennessee	Yes (q)	Majority	MP	No	MP
Texas................	No		No		
Utah	Yes	2/3	ME	No	MP
Vermont	No		No		
Virginia.............	Yes	(d)	No	No	MP
Washington	Yes	2/3	ME	No	Not specified
West Virginia	Yes	Majority	MP	No	Not specified
Wisconsin...........	Yes	Majority	MP	No	No provision
Wyoming	Yes	2/3	ME	No	Not specified
American Samoa	Yes	(r)	No	No	ME (s)
No. Mariana Islands	Yes	Majority (t)	2/3	No (u)	MP and at least 2/3 in each of 2 senatorial districts
Puerto Rico	Yes	2/3	MP	No	MP

PROCEDURES FOR CALLING CONSTITUTIONAL CONVENTIONS—Continued

Key:

MP — Majority voting on the proposal.

ME — Majority voting in the election.

(a) In all states not otherwise noted, the entries in this column refer to the proportion of members elected to each house required to submit to the electorate the question of calling a constitutional convention.

(b) The number listed is the interval between required submissions on the question of calling a constitutional convention; where given, the date is that of the first required submission of the convention question.

(c) Unless provided otherwise by law, convention calls are to conform as nearly as possible to the act calling the 1955 convention, which provided for a legislative vote of a majority of members elected to each house and ratification by a majority vote on the proposals. The legislature may call a constitutional convention at any time.

(d) In these states, the legislature may call a convention without submitting the question to the people. The legislative vote required is two-thirds of the members elected to each house in Georgia, Louisiana, South Carolina and Virginia; two-thirds concurrent vote of both branches in Maine; three-fourths of all members of each house in South Dakota; and not specified in Alaska, but bills require majority vote of membership of each house. In South Dakota, the question of calling a convention may be initiated by the people in the same manner as an amendment to the constitution (see Table 1.3) and requires a majority vote on the question for approval.

(e) The law calling a convention must be approved by the people.

(f) The legislature shall submit the question 20 years after the last convention, or 20 years after the last vote on the question of calling a convention, whichever date is last.

(g) The power to call a convention is reserved to the people by petition.

(h) The majority must be 50 percent of the total votes cast at a general election or at a special election, a majority of the votes tallied which must be at least 30 percent of the total number of registered voters.

(i) Majority voting in the election, or three-fifths voting on the question.

(j) Must be approved during two legislative sessions.

(k) Majority must equal one-fourth of qualified voters at last general election.

(l) Majority of those voting on the proposal is assumed.

(m) The question of calling a constitutional convention may be submitted either by the legislature or by initiative petition to the secretary of state in the same manner as provided for initiated amendments (see Table 1.3).

(n) Two-thirds of all members of the legislature.

(o) Majority must be 35 percent of total votes cast at the election.

(p) Convention proposals are submitted to the electorate at a special election in a manner to be determined by the convention. Ratification by a majority of votes cast.

(q) Conventions may not be held more often than once in six years.

(r) Five years after effective date of constitutions, governor shall call a constitutional convention to consider changes proposed by a constitutional committee appointed by the governor. Delegates to the convention are to be elected by their county councils. A convention was held in 1972.

(s) If proposed amendments are approved by the voters, they must be submitted to the U.S. Secretary of the Interior for approval.

(t) The initiative may also be used to place a referendum convention call on the ballot. The petition must be signed by 25 percent of the qualified voters or at least 75 percent in a senatorial district.

(u) The legislature was required to submit the referendum no later than seven years after the effective date of the constitution. The convention was held in 1985; 45 amendments were submitted to the voters.

Table 1.5
STATE CONSTITUTIONAL COMMISSIONS
(Operative during January 1, 1992 to January 1, 1994)

State	Name of commission	Method and date of creation and period of operation	Membership: number and type	Funding	Purpose of commission	Proposals and action
Alaska	Constitutional Revision Task Force	Legislative: House Resolution 5 (18th Leg. 1st Sess.), 1993-Jan. 1995.	5: speaker of the House appointed 3 representatives and 2 public members and named chair.	From regular appropriations for legislature.	To study alternatives to present methods of revising the constitution and present recommendations.	Five formal meetings: Sept. 9 - March 24. Teleconferences and other outreach methods to acquire information. Public testimony encouraged. Final report on April 1, 1994. Recommendation for a permanent seven-member statutory advisory commission on the Constitution to study and submit recommendations to the legislature; recommend legislative rule changes to create Joint Committee on the Constitution and to require a vote on advisory commission's recommendations for amendments.
California	California Constitutional Revision Commission	Statutory: Ch. 1243, *Laws of California*, 1993. April 1994 - July 1, 1996. Act expires Jan. 1997.	23: 3 ex officio, 20 appointed. 10 appointed by the governor; 5 by speaker of the House; 5 by the Senate Rules Committee; bipartisan appointments required. Ex officio - Chief Justice Legislative Analyst, Director of Finance. No lobbyist eligible. No more than one legislator appointed by each of the appointing authorities.	$200,000 appropriation, 1993-94.	To study and make recommendations on budget process, state government structure, state and local government duties and relationships, and community resources and delivery systems.	No action in 1993. Commission appointed in 1994.
Florida	Florida Taxation and Budget Reform Commission	Constitutional/statutory: Art. XI, sec. 6 of Florida Const.; *Laws* 1990, c.90-203 (West's F.S.A. sec. 286.036), 1990 - June 30, 1993.	29: 25 non-legislative voting members: by governor (11), by speaker of House (7), by president of Senate (7); 4 nonvoting legislative members: - by speaker (1 majority and one minority representative), by president of Senate (1 majority and one minority senator). Voting members elect chairman.	$1.5 million for 1990-1992; administrative support from Florida State University.	Citizen evaluation, recommendations for tax and budget reforms. Commission may submit statutory recommendations to legislature and constitutional amendments directly to electorate.	Numerous meetings and public hearings, two major reports; statutory recommendations to legislature in 1991 and 1992; budget reform bill adopted. April 1992 meetings to finalize proposed constitutional amendments for 1992 general election. Commission approval of amendments requires: 2/3 of voting members and majority of each of three subgroups of voting members. May 7, 1992 deadline to submit proposed amendments for November 1992 election. Four amendments on ballot; one removed by Florida Supreme Court; one defeated and two adopted by voters.
New York	Temporary State Commission on Constitutional Revision	Executive: Executive Order 172. May 26, 1993 - at least May 15, 1995 when final report due.	18: appointed by governor. Chair named by governor. Membership nonpartisan and diverse, representative of state's areas, interests, occupations.	Funding and staff through Rockefeller Institute of Government of the State of New York.	To prepare for referendum on convention call in 1997; to evaluate convention processes and make recommendations; to start state discussion of government structure, purposes.	Regular monthly meetings began Fall 1993; "Delegate Selection Process," first interim report Mar. 17, 1994; "The New York State Constitution Briefing Book" April 1994. Newsletters. Public hearings planned in 1994.

STATE CONSTITUTIONAL COMMISSIONS—Continued

State	Name of commission	Method and date of creation and period of operation	Membership: number and type	Funding	Purpose of commission	Proposals and action
Utah	Utah Constitutional Revision Commission	Statutory: Ch. 89, *Laws of Utah,* 1969; amended by Ch. 107, *Laws* 1975, *Laws* 1977, which made the commission permanent as of July 1, 1977. (Codified at Ch. 54, Title 63, *Utah Code Annotated,* 1953.)	16: 1 ex officio, 9 appointed—by the speaker of the House (3), president of Senate (3), and governor (3) no more than 2 of each group to be from same party); and 6 additional members appointed by the 9 previously appointed members.	Appropriation through 1993 totaled $913,000 (1993 appropriation was $55,000, same as in 1992).	Study constitution and recommend desirable changes, including proposed drafts.	Mandated to report recommendations at least 60 days before legislature convenes. Voter action on commission's recommendations through 1993 include: approval of revised articles on legislature, elections and rights of suffrage, revenue and taxation, executive, judicial, education, and corporations. In 1992, the legislature referred revised articles on the legislature, executive, and corporations to the voters who approved them; they are included in the list above. In 1993 the commission completed work on a revised Revenue and Taxation Article.

Table 1.6
STATE CONSTITUTIONAL CONVENTIONS
(Operative during January 1, 1992 - January 1, 1994)

State	Convention dates	Type of convention	Referendum on convention questions	Preparatory bodies	Appropriations	Convention delegates	Convention proposals	Referendum on convention proposals
Louisiana	Aug. 23, 1992 - Sept. 22, 1992	Limited	No referendum; legislature called itself into session as a convention by statute (La. Acts 1992, No. 1066, sections 1-10.)	None	Appropriations for expenses; delegates receive compensation as provided for legislators, including per diem and travel allowances; staffing provided by legislature and its agencies.	144 (all members of the legislature) meeting as a bicameral body.	One "revision" proposal on fiscal topics only. Amends Arts. VI, VII, and XII. Proposals include: limit amount of GO bonds sold in particular fiscal years; mandate debt management plan; limit nonrecurring money to capital outlay and extraordinary expenses; allow reduction in mandatory expenditures in event of revenue shortages; require a 2/3 vote of legislature to provide exemptions from local sales taxes; permit constitutional change of state funds by a single amendment; authorize local funds for aid to students attending college and vocational-technical schools.	November 3, 1992; Revision rejected—441,658 for, 729,511 against.

Term Limits in the States

Voter discontent fuels the term-limits movement in many states, but the courts may halt it.

by Thad Beyle and Rich Jones

One measure of the public's recent disdain for professional politicians is the movement throughout the states to limit the terms of state legislators, members of Congress and state executive branch officials.[1] Voters in California, Colorado and Oklahoma approved citizen initiatives in 1990 that limit the terms of state lawmakers.[2] The Colorado initiative also applies to members of the U.S. Congress.[3] The movement suffered a setback in 1991 when Washington state voters narrowly rejected a term-limits initiative.

In November 1992, while most eyes were on the presidential election, 14 states passed citizen initiatives that limit the terms of their elected officials. This includes California, which expanded its ban adopted in 1990 to include its congressional delegation, and Washington state voters who reversed their 1991 decision. Wyoming's new term limits also stated that "fractions of terms served after the resignation of an incumbent . . . are counted as a full term,"[4] joining several other states that have such a provision. However, the Nevada state Supreme Court recently refused a petition to invoke that state's restriction on the incumbent governor.[5]

In 1993, Maine voters adopted an initiative that limits the terms of state lawmakers and constitutional officers. The restrictions in the Maine law become effective with the 1996 elections and count years already served when applying the limit.

Currently, there are 18 states that recently have adopted term limits for elected officials. North Dakota limits the terms of federal officials only, Oklahoma and Maine laws apply only to state officials and the remainder apply to both state and federal officeholders.[6] (See Table A for more details on each state.) In 1994, Utah became the first state to impose limits on state and federal elected officials' terms through state legislation, effective January 1995.

In the Washington state case, voters defeated a 1991 proposal that would have limited the terms of both state and federal officeholders.[7] This proposal would have counted years already served when applying the term limit. A last minute campaign by the state's congressional incumbents raised the fear of losing the clout of long-tenured members of Congress such as U.S. House Speaker Thomas Foley and Rep. Al Swift and turned what had looked like a victory for term limit proponents into a 54 percent to 46 percent defeat of the measure. The term limit opponent's theme was "there is too much to lose," and the target of this fearful losing prospective was California and its large congressional delegation gaining power over the state.[8]

Washington voters approved a modified term limit measure in 1992 that did not count terms served prior to November 1992 when applying the limit and would limit federal officials only when nine other states limited ballot access or terms. There is still the possibility the Legislature can change the intent of the popular vote as "an initiative can be amended by a two-thirds legislative vote and after two years, changed by simple majorities."[9] But a partially successful lawsuit, discussed below, has made this possibility moot for the time being.

Thad L. Beyle is a professor of political science, The University of North Carolina at Chapel Hill and Rich Jones is the director of legislative programs at the National Conference of State Legislatures. Nancy Rhyme and Karl Kurtz of NCSL contributed to this article.

Table A
TERM LIMITS IN THE STATES: FEDERAL AND STATE LEGISLATORS

State	Year	Federal level: Senate	Federal level: House	State Level: Senate	State Level: House	Combined House/Senate service limit	Vote*	Date	Notes
Adopted									
Arizona	1992	12	6	8	8	. . .	74-26		a,b
California	1990	. . .	. . .	8	6	. . .	52-48	11/90	a
California	1992	12/17y	6/11y	8	6	. . .	63-37		a
Colorado	1990	12	12	8	8	. . .	71-29	1/91	a,b,c
Florida	1992	12	8	8	8	. . .	77-23		a,b
Maine	1993	. . .	. . .	8	8	. . .	67-33	1996	aa,d
Michigan	1992	12/24y	6/12y	8	6	. . .	59-41		a
Missouri	1992	12	8	8/sh	8/sh	16	74-26		a,e,f
Montana	1992	12/24y	6/12y	6/12y	8/16y	. . .	67-33		a
Nebraska	1992	12	8	8	8	. . .	68-32		a,b
North Dakota	1992	12	12	. . .	. . .	. . .	55-45		a,g,h
Ohio	1992	12	8	8	8	. . .	66-34		a,b,i
Oklahoma	1992	. . .	. . .	12	12	12	67-33	1/91	a
Oregon	1992	12	6	8	6	12	69-31		a,j
South Dakota	1992	12	12	8	8	. . .	63-37		a,b
Utah	1994	12	12	12	12	. . .	N.A.		b,k
Wyoming	1992	12/24y	6/12y	12/24y	6/12y	. . .	77-23		aa
Under Court Challenge									
Arkansas**	1992	12	6	8	6	. . .	60-40		a
Washington***	1992	12/18y	6/12y	8/14y	6/12y	. . .	52-48		a,l
Defeated									
Washington	1991	12	6	8	6	10	46-54	N.A.	a,m

Sources: <u>Overall</u>: Gerald Benjamin and Michael J. Malbin (eds), Limiting Legislative Terms (Washington, D.C.: CQ Press, 1992); "States with Term Limits," National Conference of State Legislatures (1994); and "Term Limits," Center for Policy Alternatives (1994), and Thomas Galvin, "Limits Score a Perfect 14-for-14, But Court Challenges Loom," CQ Weekly Report, November 7, 1992, 3596-94.

<u>Courts</u>: "Lawyers Argue Limits on Terms in Congress," CQ Weekly Report, January 15, 1994, 83; "Term Limits Opponents Win First Round," CQ Weekly Report, February 12, 1994, 342; "Term Limit Backers Seek Supreme Court Help," CQ Weekly Report, March 19, 1994, 689.

* Percentage of vote for and against measure.

** The Arkansas Supreme Court ruling on March 7, 1994 upheld the state provisions in the 1992 term limits initiative, but ruled the limits on federal offices were unconstitutional as only an amendment to the U.S. Constitution could change the three basic congressional qualifications of age, residency and citizenship. The decision is currently under appeal by term limit supporters to the U.S. Supreme Court as the first term limit test to reach that body.

*** A U.S. District Court judge in Washington State ruled on February 10, 1994, that the 1992 term limit initiative was unconstitutional. The decision is currently under appeal to the 9th U.S. Circuit Court of Appeals.

Key:

#/# — number of years in limit adopted/out of this number of years

. . . — Not applicable

sh — In the same house

y — Years

N.A. — Not available

(a) Direct constitutional or statutory initiative used.

(aa) Indirect statutory initiative used.

(b) Applies to consecutive years.

(c) Limitations will not effect currently elected members of Congress until 2002.

(d) Provisions apply to individuals currently holding office.

(e) No more than 16 total years in state legislature.

(f) Federal office term limits do not go into effect until one-half of the states adopt term limits.

(g) U.S. senators and representatives limited to no more than 12 years in any combination.

(h) After a two year break in service, can re-enter service.

(i) Terms are considered consecutive unless there is a break of four years.

(j) State representatives can have no more than 12 years of legislative experience.

(k) Federal office limits do not go into effect until 24 states adopt term limits.

(l) Federal office term limits do not go into effect until nine other states limit ballot access or terms.

(m) Provisions were retroactive.

Table B
THE TERM LIMITS MOVEMENT AND THE GOVERNORS

State	Year	Pre-1990 status (1)	Change	New Status (2)
Arizona	1992	no limit	Yes	two 4-year terms
Arkansas	1992	no limit	Yes	two 4-year terms
California	1990	no limit	Yes	two 4-year terms (a)
Colorado	1990	no limit	Yes	two 4-year terms
Florida	1992	two 4-year terms	No	
Maine	1993	two 4-year terms	No	
Michigan	1992	no limit	Yes	two 4-year terms
Missouri	1992	two 4-year terms (b)	No	
Montana	1992	no limit	Yes	8 years in 16 years
Nebraska	1992	two 4-year terms (c)	No	
North Dakota	1992	no limit	No	
Ohio	1992	two 4-year terms	No	
Oklahoma	1990	two 4-year terms	No	
Oregon	1992	two 4-year terms	No	
South Dakota	1992	two 4-year terms	No	
Utah	1994	no limit	Yes	three 4-year terms (d)
Washington	1992	no limit	Yes	8 years in 14 years
Wyoming	1992	no limit	Yes	8 years in 16 years

Notes:

(1) From *Directory of Governors of the American States, Commonwealths, & Territories* (Washington, D.C.: National Governors' Association, 1990).

(2) From the election reports in *The New York Times, USA-Today* and *CQ Weekly Report, The Book of the States, 1992-93, State Legislatures* (November 1992), 27 and (December 1992), 15, and National Conference of State Legislatures, "States with Term Limits" (January 1994).

(a) Legislature can waive the limitation.

(b) Absolute two-term limit, but not necessarily consecutive.

(c) After two consecutive terms, must wait four years before being eligible again.

(d) Consecutive 12 years, effective 1995. Does not affect current govenor.

Gubernatorial Term Limits

Limits on the terms of gubernatorial terms are nothing new. In fact, during the past few decades the direction of reform has been to remove or relax some of these term limits. For example, in 1955, 17 states limited their governors to one four-year term or banned immediate succession, while six other states limited their governors to two four-year terms. By 1981, only four states limited their governors to only one four-year term or banned immediate succession, while 24 limited their governors to two four-year terms.[10] As of 1994, only Virginia will limit its governor to a single four-year term while 28 others will limit their governors to two four-year terms either consecutively or absolutely. The direction in this reform clearly has been to trade the single term limit for a two-term limit.

As can be seen in Table B, "The Term Limits Movement and the Governors," the passing of a term-limit initiative in the states has had about a 50-50 chance of changing gubernatorial succession possibilities. In eight states, the governors' terms were already limited to two four-year terms.[11] In six states, formerly unlimited terms for governors were restricted to two four-year terms,[12] while Montana and Wyoming moved to a limit of eight years of service in a 16-year period, and Washington to eight years of service in a 14-year period. North Dakota's term limits applied only to the federal offices.

Term Limits Move Into the Courts

Court challenges to a state's authority to limit congressional terms are the next step in this battle.[13] Speaker Foley and other members of Congress challenged the initiative in the federal courts and on February 10, 1994, a U.S. District Court judge in Seattle overturned the term-limits initiative by ruling that the measure deprives voters of the right to elect qualified candidates. U.S. District Judge William Dwyer wrote "voters freedom to choose must not be abridged by laws that make qualified persons ineligible to serve."[14]

The judge cited the 1969 U.S. Supreme Court *Powell v. McCormick* 7-1 decision that "no one, not even Congress itself, could add to the age, citizenship, and residency requirements" established in the U.S. Constitution. In the 1969 decision, the justices argued that term limits violated the First Amendment by constraining a member's freedom of association and the 14th Amendment by imposing undue restrictions on ballot access for one "disfavored group of candidates."[15] Legal experts expect the case eventually will be appealed to the U.S. Supreme Court, but it must first be appealed to the 9th U.S. Circuit Court of Appeals.[16]

On a faster track to the U.S. Supreme Court is an appeal of a March 7, 1994 decision coming out of Arkansas in which the state's Supreme Court overturned that state's limits on federal officials' terms but let stand term limits for state lawmakers. The Arkansas court ruled that only an amendment to the U.S. Constitution could alter the three basic qualifications of age, residency and citizenship for membership in Congress. Term-limit supporters appealed this decision to the U.S. high court.[17]

Other court challenges to the states' authority to limit congressional terms are likely. In Wyoming, in a 1991 letter to the secretary of state, a senior assistant attorney general indicated it was "doubtful that the statutory imposition of term limits could withstand a [constitutional] challenge."[18]

Proponents of term limits in Arizona, California, Nebraska and North Dakota hope to avoid court challenges by wording their initiatives to deny ballot access to incumbents who have served a certain number of years. They reason that the U.S. Constitution, by giving the states the right to control suffrage in elections, allows states to regulate ballot access. However, the Congress can alter those regulations by law as in the Voting Rights Act of 1965 and its amendments.

Court challenges to ballot proposals to limit terms in Florida and Missouri were unsuccessful. In California, the Legislature challenged the term-limit initiative arguing that a lifetime ban on state legislative service would disqualify the most qualified candidates — incumbents — and deny the voters the right to choose their representatives. The California Supreme Court rejected these arguments and upheld the measure's constitutionality.[19]

Is Turnover the Problem?

Proponents of term limits argue that legislatures are dominated by entrenched members with long tenures who are out of touch with the needs of the citizens. Because incumbents have electoral advantages by virtue of their positions, term limits are necessary to force turnover and bring new people with new ideas into state legislatures.

Although turnover has been declining in state legislatures for the past 20 years, it is still significant. For example, nationwide, 72 percent of the House members and 75 percent of senators who served in 1979 had left their respective chambers by 1989. Turnover in the houses exceeded 80 percent in 23 states while 16 Senates had comparable rates.[20] There is a similar turnover among legislative leaders. During the past decade, 88 percent of Senate presidents and 94 percent of House speakers turned over.[21] Membership turnover in state legislatures continued at a similar pace in the 1990s. Nationwide, 19 percent of all house members were new following the 1990 election, and 29 percent were new following the 1992 election.[22]

Term limits will begin to force incumbent lawmakers from office in the mid-1990s. As they take effect, these limits are likely to significantly affect the selection of leaders, professionalization of legislatures and the distribution of power between the branches of government — all to the detriment of the legislative branch. Term limits also will significantly alter the leadership selection process in those states adopting limits. For example, in California, which currently has leaders with long tenures, the next speaker of the Assembly who will preside in 1997 will come from the freshmen class elected in 1992.

One analysis of the initial California vote on term limits indicates that minorities may see the term-limits movement as "an attack upon their power by abolishing the seniority that accrues to leaders elected from 'safe' ethnic districts." In effect, imposition of legislative term limits may do as much or more to undermine the ability of minorities to achieve representation and power than court decisions negating the newly created "safe" minority districts.[23]

A Break in the Action?

The term-limits movement has been driven by both national groups and local supporters. It has been heavily financed by certain individuals and groups at the national level mainly from the right side of the political spectrum and, most usually, Republicans. The ability to target different states has been facilitated by direct democracy provisions in some state constitutions.[24]

The initiative and referendum provisions in these state constitutions have opened the door to placing term-limit proposals before the voters for action. Of the 18 states that have adopted term limits in some form, all but Maine, Washington and Wyoming allow the direct citizen initiative to place constitutional amendments on the ballot. Washington and Wyoming allow the direct citizen initiative to place proposed statutory changes on the ballot, while Maine allows the indirect citizen initiative process, which means the Legislature must take the final step of placing the proposal on the ballot. (See Table A notes a and aa).

Now the field of states in which such direct citizen initiatives can be used is narrowing. Only Illinois, Nevada and Oklahoma remain as states in which the direct citizen initiative can place these controversial limits on the ballot whether they are constitutional amendments or statutory changes. In Illinois, only the legislative article (IV) of the constitution can be so amended — governors are immune to such action.

Indirect citizen initiatives to amend the constitution can be placed on the ballot in

Massachusetts and Mississippi, but in Massachusetts only after it is "approved by two sessions of a successively elected legislature by not less than one-fourth of all members sitting in joint session."[25] The direct citizen initiative can be used to place statutory changes on the ballot in Alaska and Utah.[26]

These citizen-based provisions for gaining access to the ballot in Maine and Oklahoma apply only to possible limitations on the federal offices, as state level limits already have been adopted there. For governors, the fear of possible term limitations is even less as only Massachusetts remains as a state with access provisions that allow its governor unlimited terms. All the other states with these initiative provisions already limit their governors to two four-year terms.

The message of this is that for most of the term-limit proponents easy access to the states' ballots to achieve a term-limit vote has been accomplished. With the few exceptions noted, from now on the term limit fight to gain access to the ballot has to be undertaken on the turf of those who would be most affected by any such change. This will also be true for changes in the federal offices if the U.S. Supreme Court upholds either or both of the Arkansas and Washington state court decisions — Congress would have to approve and send to the states an amendment to the U.S. Constitution. To date, only the Utah Legislature and governor have agreed to pass term limitations into statutory law.

Notes

[1] See Gerald Benjamin and Michael J. Malbin, eds, *Limiting Legislative Terms* (Washington, D.C.: CQ Press, 1992) for background, analysis and a series of case studies on the current term-limit movement.

[2] For a discussion of the 1990 campaigns in California and Oklahoma see Charles M. Price, "The Guillotine Comes to California: Term-Limit Politics in the Golden State," and Gary W. Copeland, "Term Limitations and Political Careers in Oklahoma: In, Out, Up, or Down," in Benjamin and Malbin, 117-158.

[3] John A. Straayer, "Possible Consequences of Legislative Term Limits," *Comparative State Politics* 13:3, June 1992, 1-15.

[4] James D. King, "Term Limits in Wyoming," *Comparative State Politics* 14:2 (April 1993), 9.

[5] "Nevada: Court Rules Miller Is Eligible to Dismay of Jones," *The Hotline* 7:41 (April 19, 1994), 18.

[6] Nancy Rhyme, "Throwing Out the Rascals (And Those who Aren't)," *State Legislatures*, November 1992, 26-27.

[7] For a discussion of the 1991 campaign see David J. Olson, "Term Limits Fail in Washington," in Benjamin and Malbin, 65-96.

[8] Olson, 79-82.

[9] Hugh Bone, "Aspects of the Washington State Elections," *Comparative State Elections* 14:4 (September 1993), 11.

[10] A Commission Report, *The Question of State Government Capability* (Washington, D.C.: Advisory Commission on Intergovernmental Relations, January 1985), 129.

[11] These states are Florida, Maine, Missouri, Nebraska, Ohio, Oklahoma, Oregon and South Dakota.

[12] These states are Arizona, Arkansas, California, Colorado, Michigan and Washington.

[13] For a discussion of the legal aspects of this controversy see Appendix 3, "Can the States Constitutionally Impose Term Limits on Members of Congress?: A Legal Debate," in Benjamin and Malbin, 251-261.

[14] *Thorsted v. Gregoire*, U.S. District Court of Washington, Opinion number C93-770WD, February 1994. (No citation available). See also "Term Limits: WA Battle Likely Headed for U.S. Supreme Court," *The Hotline* 7:77 (January 12, 1994), 9.

[15] "Term Limits Opponents Win First Round," *CQ Weekly Report*, February 12, 1994, 342.

[16] "Term Limit Backers Seek Supreme Court Help," *CQ Weekly Report*, March 19, 1994, 689.

[17] Ibid.

[18] King, 15.

[19] *Legislature of the State of California v. Eu*, 54 cal. 3D 492, 286 Cal. Rptr. 283, 816 P 2d 1309, 1991. See also Appendix A-4, Benjamin and Malbin, 263-274.

[20] National Conference of State Legislatures, *Turnover in State Legislatures, 1979-1989*, April 1991.

[21] Rhyme, 26.

[22] Karl T. Kurtz, "The Election in Perspective," *State Legislatures*, January 1993, 16-19.

[23] David L. Martin, "How Minority Voters Reacted to Term Limits in California," *Comparative State Politics* 13:3 (June 1992), 34-39.

[24] Amy E. Young, "The Money Behind the Movement," *Common Cause Magazine*, 19:2 (Summer 1993), 37-39. For a discussion and analysis of these provisions see Thomas E. Cronin, *Direct Democracy: The Politics of Initiative, Referendum, and Recall* (Cambridge: Harvard University Press, 1989).

[25] Table B-9, "State Provisions for Initiative," taken from Harold W. Stanley and Richard G. Niemi, *Vital Statistics on American Politics* (Washington, D.C.: CQ Press, 1992), 23-24 reprinted in Benjamin and Malbin, 302. See also Table 1.3, "Constitutional Amendment Procedure: By Initiative," *The Book of the States, 1992-93* (Lexington, Ky: The Council of State Governments, 1992), 24.

[26] Table 5.15, "Statewide Initiative and Referendum," *The Book of the States, 1992-93*, (Lexington, Ky: The Council of State Governments, 1992), 329.

Chapter Two

STATE EXECUTIVE BRANCH

An overview of the states' chief executives, other constitutional officers, and executive branch activities in 1992-93. Current information on the office of governor — including qualifications for office, compensation, powers, cabinet systems — and the duties, qualifications for office, annual salaries, methods of selection, and length of terms for selected executive branch officials. Includes information on lieutenant governors, secretaries of state, attorneys general, and state treasurers.

The Governors, 1992-93

*A roundup of the activities of the states' chief executives:
who won, who lost, who is popular and who was indicted.*

by Thad L. Beyle

Much has happened in the gubernatorial arena in the past two years, both positive and negative. Long-time Arkansas Gov. Bill Clinton (D, 1979-81, 1983-92) ran for and won the presidency in 1992. He became the third of the last four presidents who had served as governor just prior to seeking and winning the presidency.[1] In the 1988 election when George Bush, a non-governor, won the presidential election, he was challenged by a governor, Michael Dukakis (D-Massachusetts). Clearly, presidential politics in the last quarter of the 20th century finds governors as major actors.

Additionally, given the health, legal and personal problems, as well as the normal state demands, encountered by governors over the last two years, the governorship remains a "hot seat" in more ways than one.

Gubernatorial Elections[2]

Only 14 governorships were contested and decided by the elections of 1992 and 1993. In 10 of these states, incumbents were eligible to seek re-election, and of those, five incumbents (all Democrats) or 50 percent did run. Four were successful (80 percent). The winning incumbents, all in 1992, were Evan Bayh (Indiana), Bruce Sundlun (Rhode Island), Howard Dean (Vermont) and Gaston Caperton (West Virginia). Each won handily with an average winning margin of 31 points led by Dean's 52-point victory.

Jim Florio of New Jersey was the one incumbent governor who lost a bid for re-election when he was narrowly defeated by Christine Todd Whitman (R) in the 1993 general election. The aftershocks of this campaign became significant when Ed Rollins, the major campaign adviser for the winner, indicated their campaign had used "street money" paid to certain minority leaders to "depress" the voter turnout among minorities who historically vote heavily Democratic. He later recanted this allegation. After much media comment, Rollins' repeated recantations and two investigations — one federal and one state — no evidence of such activity was found and no charges filed. However, the newly-elected governor was wounded by the ferment over the issue as her "honeymoon period" ended the day after the election.[3]

As can be seen in Table A, in the 326 gubernatorial elections held between 1970 and 1993, incumbents were eligible to seek another term in 253 (or 78 percent) of the contests: 193 eligible incumbents sought re-election (76 percent) and 139 of them succeeded (72 percent). Those who were defeated for re-election were more likely to lose in the general election than in their own party primary by a three-to-one ratio. (See Table A) Democrats were more likely to win the governorship by a three-to-two ratio over the 24-year period.

But there was still considerable turnover in the governorships over the period as 187 of the 326 incumbents (57 percent) did not receive another term. The reasons were constitutional, as 73 of these non-returning governors were ineligible to seek re-election (39 percent); personal, as 60 decided not to seek another term (32 percent); and political, as 54 were defeated in their bids for another term (29 percent).

Comparing the 1992-93 elections with those conducted between 1970 and 1991, fewer incumbents were eligible to seek re-election (71 percent in two-year period versus 78 percent

*Thad L. Beyle is a professor of political science,
The University of North Carolina at Chapel Hill.*

Table A
GUBERNATORIAL ELECTIONS: 1970-1993

Year	Number of races	Democratic winner		Eligible to run		Did run		Won		Lost			
		Number	Percent	Number	Percent	Number	Percent	Number	Percent	Number	Percent	In primary	In general election
1970	35	22	63	29	83	24	83	16	64	8	36	1 (a)	7 (b)
1971	3	3	100	0	...	...	...	...	...	...	...	...	...
1972	18	11	61	15	83	11	73	7	64	4	36	2 (c)	2 (d)
1973	2	1	50	1	50	1	100	...	...	1	100	1 (e)	...
1974	35	28 (f)	80	29	83	22	76	17	77	5	24	1 (g)	4 (h)
1975	3	3	100	2	66	2	100	2	100	...	...	...	...
1976	14	9	64	12	86	8	67	5	63	3	33	1 (i)	2 (j)
1977	2	1	50	1	50	1	100	1	100	...	...	...	...
1978	36	21	58	29	81	22	76	16	73	6	27	1 (k)	5 (l)
1979	3	2	67	0	0	...	...	...	...	...	...	...	...
1980	13	6	46	12	92	12	100	7	58	5	42	2 (m)	3 (n)
1981	2	1	50	0	0	...	...	...	...	...	...	...	...
1982	36	27	75	33	92	25	76	19	76	6	24	1 (o)	5 (p)
1983	3	3	100	0	0	...	...	...	...	...	...	...	...
1984	13	5	38	9	69	6	67	4	67	2	33	...	2 (q)
1985	2	1	50	1	50	1	100	1	100	...	...	...	...
1986	36	19	53	24	67	18	75	15	83	3	18	1 (r)	2 (s)
1987	3	3	100	2	67	1	50	0	0	1	100	1 (t)	...
1988	12	5	42	9	75	9	100	8	89	1	11	...	1 (u)
1989	2	2	100	0	0	...	...	...	...	...	...	...	...
1990	36	19 (v)	53	33	92	23	70	17	74	6	26	...	6 (w)
1991	3	2	67	2	67	2	100	0	0	2	100	1 (x)	1 (y)
1992	12	8	67	9	75	4	44	4	100	0	0	...	...
1993	2	0	0	1	50	1	100	0	0	1	100	...	1 (z)
Totals:													
Number	326	202		253		193		139		54		13	41
Percent	100%	62%		78%		76%		72%		28%		24%	76%

Source: Thad L. Beyle, "Term Limits in the State Executive Branch," in Gerald Benjamin and Michael J. Malbin, eds., *Legislating Legislative Terms* (Washington: CQ Press, 1992), 169 (revised); and selected issues of *CQ Weekly Reports*, 1970-date.
(a) Albert Brewer, D-Alaska.
(b) Keith Miller, R-Alaska; Winthrop Rockefeller, R-Ark.; Claude Kirk, R-Fla.; Don Samuelson, R-Idaho; Norbert Tieman, R-Neb.; Dewey Bartlett, R-Okla.; Frank Farrar, R-S.D.
(c) Walter Peterson, R-N.H.; Preston Smith, D-Texas.
(d) Russell Peterson, R-Del.; Richard Ogilvie, R-Ill.
(e) William Cahill, R-N.J.
(f) One Independent candidate won: James Longley of Maine.
(g) David Hall, D-Okla.
(h) John Vanderhoof, R-Colo.; Francis Sargent, R-Mass.; Malcolm Wilson, R-N.Y.; John Gilligan, D-Ohio.
(i) Dan Walker, D-Ill.
(j) Sherman Tribbitt, D-Del.; Christopher "Kit" Bond, R-Mo.
(k) Michael S. Dukakis, D-Mass.
(l) Robert F. Bennett, R-Kan.; Rudolph G. Perpich, D-Minn.; Meldrim Thomson, R-N.H.; Robert Straub, D-Oreg.; M.J. Schreiber, D-Wis.
(m) Thomas L. Judge, D-Mont.; Dixy Lee Ray, D-Wash.
(n) Bill Clinton, D-Ark.; Joseph P. Teasdale, D-Mo.; Arthur H. Link, D-N.D.
(o) Edward J. King, D-Mass.
(p) Frank D. White, R-Ark.; Charles Thone, R-Neb.; Robert F. List, R-Nev.; Hugh J. Gallen, D-N.H.; William P. Clements, R-Texas.
(q) Allen I. Olson, R-N. D.; John D. Spellman, R-Wash.
(r) Bill Sheffield, D-Alaska.
(s) Mark White, D-Texas; Anthony S. Earl, D-Wis.
(t) Edwin Edwards, D-La.
(u) Arch A. Moore, R-W. Va.
(v) Two Independent candidates won: Walter Hickel (Alaska) and Lowell Weiker (Conn.). Both were former statewide Republican office holders.
(w) Bob Martinez, R-Fla.; Mike Hayden, R-Kan.; James Blanchard, D-Mich.; Rudy Perpich, DFL-Minn.; Kay Orr, R-Neb.; Edward DiPrete, R-R.I.
(x) Buddy Roemer, R-La.
(y) Ray Mabus, D-Miss.
(z) James Florio, D-N.J.

over the 22-year period), fewer eligible incumbents actually sought election (50 percent versus 77 percent), although those seeking re-election were slightly more likely to win (80 percent versus 72 percent).

Another factor in determining how many governors have served in the states is how many of the newly-elected governors are truly new to the office, and how many are returning after complying with constitutional term limits or holding other positions. Looking only at the number of actual new governors taking office

over a decade, we noted in the 1992-93 edition of *The Book of the States* that the average number of new governors in the states had dropped from 2.3 new governors in the 1950s to 1.9 in the 1970s and 1.1 in the 1980s.[4]

So far, in the 1990s there have been 26 actual new governors elected in the states, while five others elected are "comebackers." At this pace, only four election years into the decade, it would appear the average number of actual new governors in the 1990s might be greater than in most recent decades. Additionally, there will be a minimum of 10 turnover gubernatorial elections in 1994 due to term limits and incumbent's personal decisions.[5]

The 1990s "comebackers" re-elected after a period out of office were: Walter Hickel (I-Alaska), who had served as a Republican (1967-69) when he was appointed U.S. Secretary of the Interior by President Richard Nixon; Bruce King (D-New Mexico), who had served two previous terms (1971-75 and 1979-82); Richard Snelling (R-Vermont), who had served previous four terms (1977-85); Edwin Edwards (D-Louisiana), who had served three previous terms (1972-80 and 1984-1988); and Jim Hunt (D-North Carolina), who had served two previous terms (1977-1985). Hickel, King and Snelling were re-elected in 1990, Edwards in 1991 and Hunt in 1992.

The New Governors

The partisan division among the 10 new governors elected in 1992-93 tilted to the Republican side, six to four, with the Republicans sweeping the two 1993 elections in New Jersey and Virginia. Overall, the partisan division in the governorships entering 1994 was 29 Democrats, 19 Republicans and two independents.

The same three main routes to gaining the governor's office appear among these 10 new governors as in past years. First were the five new governors who had previously run and held statewide office (Lt. Governor Mel Carnahan of Missouri, Attorney General Mark Racicot of Montana, former Attorney General Steve Merrill of New Hampshire, former Governor Jim Hunt of North Carolina and Tom Carper of Delaware).

Three others had served in Congress as their most recent political experience (Carper of Delaware, George Allen Jr. of Virginia and Mike Lowery of Washington). In fact, Carper had run statewide as a congressman since 1982 (Delaware has only one seat in Congress); prior to that he had run and won the state treasurer's seat three times. Of special interest is the 1993 Delaware election where out-going Governor Michael Castle (R, 1985-93) ran and won Carper's congressional seat. The two just switched seats beginning in 1993.

Of the two other new governors, Christine Todd Whitman had served as an appointed head of the state board of utilities, resigning in 1990 to challenge U.S. Senator Bill Bradley in a very close race. Whitman, therefore, had some level of statewide political recognition. The last of the new governors, Mike Leavitt of Utah, was a newcomer to electoral politics and was starting at the top. However, he could not be called an "outsider" candidate, as he had been active in managing several statewide campaigns. The last of the new governors, Edward Schafer of North Dakota, was a bona-fide newcomer shifting from the business world to the governor's seat.

Looking at the most recent four-year cycle of gubernatorial elections (1990-92) and where the new governors came from continues to reveal a more constricted path to the office than in the past. Of the 32 new governors elected over the four-year period, 21 (or nearly two-thirds) came from previous statewide elected positions (15 or 47 percent) or federal elective positions (6 or 19 percent). Two others had held major state level appointive positions, another was mayor of the state's largest city. One other winning governor moved from a leadership position in the state legislature into the governorship. Six other winners were from the business sector winning their first elective office (19 percent), and the last had served as a federal attorney. The impact of media politics is clear. Those who already have name recognition from previous political campaigns, or positions they hold, have an advantage as do those who can afford to run expensive campaigns.

Who didn't win races for the governorship in 1992-93? Aside from the array of incumbents and former state legislators, this two-year period was not politically prosperous for state attorneys general and a few other statewide office holders. Of the eight sitting or former state attorneys general seeking the governorship, only two won.[6] One of the two lieutenant governors who ran won, while the only agricultural commissioner running lost.[7]

Looking at the 216 gubernatorial races between 1977 and 1993, there were 61 lieutenant governors (17 won), 53 attorneys general (14 won), and 26 speakers of the House (nine won) who were gubernatorial candidates. Looking at these numbers from a bettor's point of view,

Table B
COST OF GUBERNATORIAL CAMPAIGNS, MOST RECENT ELECTION
Total campaign expenditures (a)

State	Year	W	All candidates	Cost per vote (b)	Winner Spent	Winner Percent of all expenditures	Winner Vote percent
Alabama	1990	R★	14,848,688	$11.92	$ 4,144,640	28	53
Alaska	1990	I#	6,200,682	35.32	1,181,565	19	39
Arizona	1990	R#	6,416,195	6.82	3,539,641	55	52
Arkansas	1990	D★	6,020,788	8.65	2,556,344	42	57
California	1990	R#	53,165,881	6.90	25,192,202	47	49
Colorado	1990	D★	1,248,652	1.27	1,028,787	82	64
Connecticut	1990	I#	7,581,885	6.64	2,734,127	36	41
Delaware	1992	D#	2,709,940	9.78	1,393,784	51	65
Florida	1990	D★★★	25,086,370	7.14	7,755,190	31	57
Georgia	1990	D#	17,269,807	11.91	6,212,659	36	53
Hawaii	1990	D★	3,730,712	10.97	3,046,044	82	60
Idaho	1990	D★	1,351,152	4.23	1,062,792	79	68
Illinois	1990	R#	23,914,628	7.34	11,700,314	49	51
Indiana	1992	D★	6,700,884	3.04	4,223,141	63	62
Iowa	1990	R★	6,400,755	6.59	3,842,199	60	61
Kansas	1990	D★★★	5,386,320	6.88	715,762	13	49
Kentucky	1991	D#	19,595,885	23.50	7,334,670	37	65
Louisiana	1991	D★★	9,778,386	5.66	4,709,339	48	61
Maine	1990	R★	3,062,678	5.87	1,557,766	51	47
Maryland	1990	D★	2,679,446	2.41	2,516,072	94	60
Massachusetts	1990	R#	14,778,198	6.31	3,453,281	23	50
Michigan	1990	R★★★	6,939,601	2.71	3,368,504	49	50
Minnesota	1990	R★★★	8,209,957	4.62	1,557,368	19	51
Mississippi	1991	R★★★	5,234,205	7.45	901,823	17	51
Missouri	1992	D#	13,834,134	5.90	3,834,558	28	59
Montana	1992	R#	2,657,748	6.52	1,052,250	40	51
Nebraska	1990	D★★★	5,364,814	9.15	1,706,515	32	50
Nevada	1990	D★	1,994,430	6.38	1,322,478	66	66
New Hampshire	1992	R#	2,446,615	4.74	794,438	32	56
New Jersey	1993	R★★★	22,458,552	9.24	9,339,848	42	50
New Mexico	1990	D#	4,116,227	10.03	1,414,723	34	55
New York	1990	D#	6,936,791	1.69	5,419,031	78	54
North Carolina	1992	D#	13,353,473	5.15	6,978,623	52	53
North Dakota	1992	R#	762,322	2.54	376,626	49	58
Ohio	1990	R#	16,016,528	4.61	8,175,556	51	56
Oklahoma	1990	D#	9,225,182	10.21	2,651,478	29	57
Oregon	1990	D#	5,546,051	4.99	1,763,140	32	43
Pennsylvania	1990	D★	8,770,476	2.87	7,205,746	82	68
Rhode Island	1992	D★	2,569,652	6.05	1,482,849	58	62
South Carolina	1990	R★	2,218,997	2.92	1,868,131	84	69
South Dakota	1990	R★	1,271,841	4.95	925,451	73	59
Tennessee	1990	D★	1,788,592	2.26	1,587,804	89	61
Texas	1990	D	50,537,239	13.56	11,479,136	23	51
Utah	1992	R#	3,908,301	5.18	1,744,265	45	42
Vermont	1992	D#	389,112	1.12	257,706	66	75
Virginia	1993	R#	13,507,697	7.58	5,467,000	40	58
Washington	1992	D#	6,994,269	3.08	1,633,124	23	53
West Virginia	1992	D★	3,941,775	6.00	2,402,621	61	56
Wisconsin	1990	R★	5,769,541	4.28	4,577,650	79	58
Wyoming	1990	D★	1,026,567	6.41	310,031	30	65
Election totals, 53 state gubernatorial elections: (c)							
1990 election totals 19D/15R/2I			345,511,402		137,572,135	40	54
1991 election totals 2D/1R			34,612,476		12,945,832	37	59
1992 election totals 8D/4R			60,268,231		26,173,985	43	58
1993 election totals — 2R			35,966,249		14,806,848	41	54
Total 29D/22R/2I							56

Source: State campaign filing offices and others within the states.
Key:
D — Democrat
R — Republican
I — Independent
★ — Incumbent ran and won
★★ — Incumbent ran and lost in party primary
★★★ — Incumbent ran and lost in general election
— Open seat
(a) Includes primaries and general elections; all figures are actual dollars for the year involved.
(b) Determined by dividing total campaign expenditures by total general election votes for the office.
(c) There were 53 separate elections in the four-year period as New Hampshire, Rhode Island and Vermont governors only serve a two-year term, hence each of these states held two elections in the four-year period. The winner's percent of all expenditures by each election year in the summary differs from earlier tables as it is derived by dividing the total expenditure of all candidates in that election year.

the odds of a lieutenant governor winning were 3.6 to 1, an attorney general 3.8 to 1, and a speaker 2.9 to 1. Therefore, while fewer speakers do enter these contests, they have a greater potential of winning when they do.[8]

Timing of Gubernatorial Elections

The election cycle for governors continues to shift ever so slightly. Over the past few decades, many of the states have moved their elections to the off-presidential years in order to decouple the state and national level campaigns. In the last four-year cycle, there were 36 gubernatorial elections in 1990, including the three states with two-year terms,[9] three elections in 1991, 12 elections in 1992, and two elections in 1993. Table B indicates where states fit into this cycle.

With the 1994 election, the newly-elected governor of Rhode Island will serve a four-year term changing the number of elections in the cycle to 11 in presidential years and 36 in the even non-presidential years, while the number of elections in the two odd-year elections will remain the same. The Kentucky General Assembly considered moving its statewide elections from an odd year to the even, non-presidential year by developing a constitutional amendment that voters adopted in 1992. However, this specific provision was killed by legislative leaders "because they feared that it would somehow weaken the power of the legislators if members ran the same time the governor did."[10]

Cost of Gubernatorial Elections

Tables B and C present data on the costs of the most recent gubernatorial elections across the 50 states. Table B shows the cost of the most recent gubernatorial campaigns for each of the states in the actual dollars for the year involved. Table C presents the total cost of gubernatorial elections by year between 1977 and 1993, normalized to 1993 dollars.

Since 1981, we have been able to compare the costs of each year's elections with those held four years earlier in the same states.[11] In seven of these comparisons, the elections have cost more, ranging from an increase of 94 percent between the 1985 and 1989 elections in New Jersey and Virginia to only 6 percent between the 1986 and 1990 elections when there were contests in 36 states. In six of these comparisons, the elections have cost less, with three of them in the 1990s.

After a period in which it appeared that the cost of becoming governor was going to continue to escalate, both in terms of expenditures by individual candidates and the total expenditures by all candidates in a race, we now see a leveling off in the 1990s. While there are still expensive races and campaigns, in general the costs seem to have stabilized. Why?

One reason is that the new style of campaigning with the candidates developing their own personal political party by the use of outside consultants, opinion polls, media adds and buys, and extensive money-raising efforts to pay for all this has reached into most all of the states. Few states will be surprised by a high price, high-tech campaign suddenly exploding there; they are commonplace now. This suggests there may be some limits to just how much can be spent in gubernatorial campaigns — until the next costly innovations appear.

Another reason is tied to the effects of providing more governors with the possibility of running for re-election (succession). Looking just at the 53 gubernatorial elections held in the 1990s, the average cost of the 30 elections with an incumbent governor running was $6.4 million (in 1993 dollars); in those 23 states with an open seat and no incumbent governor on the ballot, the average cost was $13.7 million. So term limits, or the reduction of their impact, has an effect on the costs of these elections.

In the same 53 elections held in the 1990s, there have been fewer very expensive gubernatorial races than in previous years, but there have been several that have done much to heighten the averages we see at the bottom of Table B. For example, using 1993 dollars, the 1990 races in California ($57.9 million), Texas ($55.5 million), Florida ($27.3 million) and Illinois ($26.1 million) were mainly responsible for the 36 races costing 6 percent more than they had four years earlier in 1986. Only the Florida race was less expensive than in 1986. Each of these 1990 races was for an open seat; only Florida had an open seat in 1986.

Table C
TOTAL COST OF GUBERNATORIAL ELECTIONS: 1977-1993
(in thousands of dollars)

Year	Number of races	Total campaign costs		Average cost per state 1993 $ (a)	Percent change in similar elections (b)
		Actual $	1993 $ (a)		
1977	2	12,312	28,901	14,451	. . .
1978	36	99,981	215,013	5,973	. . . (c)
1979	3	32,744	62,251	20,750	. . .
1980	13	35,623	60,174	4,629	. . .
1981	2	24,648	37,920	18,960	+31%
1982	36	181,306	270,606	7,517	+26% (d)
1983	3	39,966	57,505	19,168	-8%
1984	13	47,156	65,223	5,017	+8%
1985	2	21,450	28,600	14,300	-25%
1986	36	270,383	356,706	9,908	+32%
1987	3	40,212	50,773	16,924	-12%
1988	12 (e)	52,161	63,073	5,256	+5%
1989	2	47,902	55,378	27,689	+94%
1990	36	345,511	376,374	10,455	+6%
1991	3	34,612	36,588	12,196	-28%
1992	12	60,268	61,877	5,156	-2%
1993	2	35,966	35,966	17,983	-25%
Totals	216		1,862,928	8,625	

(a) From Table 24: "Historical Consumer Price Index for All Urban Consumers, (CPI-U): U.S. city average, all items," Bureau of Labor Statistics, U.S. Department of labor, *CPI Detailed Report*, October 1993, 67.

(b) This represents the percent increase or decrease over the last bank of similar elections, i.e., 1977 v. 1981, 1978 v. 1982. 1979 v. 1983, etc.

(c) The year-by-year data in this table differ from the data presented in the 1992-93 edition of *The Book of the States*. The reasons for the changes are due to availability of additional data and/or revised data from some states and other sources, a very careful review of the cost of each election in each state over the period, and the correction of errors found in the earlier reported data. The data for 1978 are a particular problem as the two sources which compiled data on this year's elections did so in differing ways which excluded some candidates. Further, all research notes and material in both organizations have been discarded so there was no chance to mend the differences. The net of this is that the numbers for 1978 under-represent the actual costs of these elections by some unknown amount. The sources for the 1978 data are: Rhodes Cook and Stacy West, "1978 Advantage," *CQ Weekly Report*, 37 (1979): 1757-1758, and "The Great Louisiana Spendathon," (Baton Rouge: Public Affairs Research Council, March 1980).

(d) This particular comparison with 1978 is not what it would appear to be for the reasons noted in note (c). The amount spent in 1978 was more than indicated here so the increase is really not as great as it appears.

(e) As of the 1986 election, Arkansas switched to a four-year term for the governor, hence the drop from 13 to 12 races for this off year.

All three 1991 elections cost less than they did in 1987 (in 1993 dollars). In 1992, only the Delaware, New Hampshire and Washington state elections were more expensive than they were in 1988 but only by $6.4 million (in 1993 dollars) between them. In 1993, both the New Jersey and Virginia elections were less expensive than they were in 1989, but the New Jersey race still cost $22.5 million.

In these 53 1990s elections, there were 25 candidates who spent more than $5 million on their own campaign — eight of them spending more than $10 million (1993 dollars). Sixteen of these high-priced candidacies were in those 1990 expensive elections in California, Florida, Illinois and Texas; in fact, all eight of the most expensive candidacies of over $10 million occurred in these races.[12] Spending a great deal of money doesn't guarantee success, however, as only 13 of these 25 candidacies won. And despite common political wisdom suggesting that Republicans have the most money, 16 of the 25 candidates were Democrats. The most expensive race to date still is the 1990 race in California at $57.9 million (1993 dollars), which had three high-spending candidates.[13]

Gubernatorial Problems

Several governors faced serious personal problems over the two-year period. South Dakota Governor George Mickelson (R, 1987-93) died in an airplane crash April 19, 1993, and was replaced by Lt. Governor Walter Miller (R). Mickelson was the second sitting governor to die in the 1990s, following Richard Snelling of Vermont who died in 1991.

Another governor, Guy Hunt (R-Alabama, 1987-93), was indicted and then convicted of a felony, which automatically led to his removal from office on April 22, 1993. He was the eighth 20th century governor to be indicted in office.[14] His specific problem concerned an ethics violation in which he used $200,000 of the $800,000 tax exempt, nonprofit inauguration fund for his own personal use, including making mortgage payments, buying furniture for his son and buying fencing for his farm. Hunt was replaced by Democrat Lt. Governor

Jim Folsom Jr., the son of former Alabama Governor James "Big Jim" Folsom (D, 1947-51, 1955-59).[15]

Oklahoma Governor David Walters (D, 1991-Present) pleaded guilty to a misdemeanor in relation to a campaign finance violation tied to his 1990 gubernatorial campaign. In the plea bargain, two counts of conspiracy and six counts of perjury were dismissed; conviction on any of these felony counts would have forced Walters from office.[16] Governor Walters, the first sitting governor in the state's history to plead guilty to a crime, also announced he would not seek re-election to a second term in 1994. Some state legislators began a movement to impeach Walters, but the effort soon lost steam without much public or legislative support. The House voted 52-47 not to pursue an impeachment investigation.[17]

Rhode Island Governor Bruce Sundlun (D, 1991-present) was faced with a paternity lawsuit over a situation he thought had been settled previously. Within two weeks, Sundlun had settled with his now-acknowledged daughter; the lawsuit was dropped.[18] His predecessor, former Governor Edward DiPrete (R, 1985-91), was indicted on March 29, 1994, of 23 felony counts of bribery, extortion, perjury and racketeering while serving as governor.[19] Finally, as 1994 began, Arizona Governor Fife Symington (R, 1991-present) was under investigation by a federal grand jury over actions taken relating to a failed savings and loan bank prior to his run for governor.[20]

In another twist, a former governor's spouse was found guilty of political corruption and sentenced to five years in federal prison. Bill Collins, husband of former Kentucky Governor Martha Layne Collins (D, 1983-87), was charged with extortion of funds from state contractors and disguising kickbacks as political contributions to his wife while she was serving as governor.[21]

Rating Gubernatorial Performance

Recently, there have been several attempts to provide some comparative ratings on how well governors are performing their jobs. Those doing the rating include the governors themselves, citizens and voters in the states, and a conservative "think tank." The first two are in the eyes of the observers and are fleeting. The third is based on some specific indicators, but with a bias in what is included as indicators and what is good or not good.

The first source of such ratings are the governors themselves who are asked about their colleagues: "excluding yourself, which governors would you say are most effective in their positions?" The most recent such rating, based on interviews with 46 of the 50 state governors in May-June 1991, found Bill Clinton (D-Arkansas) rated most effective by 18 of his peers (39 percent), Roy Romer (D-Colorado) by 15 (33 percent), Booth Gardner (D-Washington) by 12 (26 percent), Carroll Campbell (R-South Carolina) by seven (15 percent), John Ashcroft (R-Missouri), Mike Sullivan (D-Wyoming) and Tommy Thompson by five (11 percent) each, Norman Bangerter (R-Utah) and Mario Cuomo (D-New York) by four (9 percent) each, and Terry Branstad (R-Iowa) by three (7 percent). All were in their second terms at least, and were split equally between Democrats and Republicans.[22]

Of interest here is what has happened to the governors who come out on top of the ratings by their peers. In 1986, a similar poll of 43 of the 50 governors found Michael Dukakis (D-Massachusetts) in the top spot. He became the Democratic candidate for president in 1988.[23] Top-ranked Bill Clinton in the 1991 poll became the Democratic candidate for president in 1992.[24]

The second source of ratings is the growing number of state public opinion polls being conducted with citizens and registered voters. Some of these ratings are conducted on a regular basis, others only when there is an upcoming political contest, and others on a very sporadic basis, if at all. The respondents are asked a variation of a question such as "generally speaking, do you think that Governor X is doing an (excellent, good, fair, poor) job?"

Looking at those ratings compiled in 1993, there appear to be at least three patterns. First are those governors who have rather steady and positive job performance ratings ranging from the mid 40s to the mid 70s or even higher percentages. Topping the list of the fourth quarter 1993 ratings was Tommy Thompson (R-Wisconsin), with a 73 percent positive job performance rating, followed by Carroll Campbell (R-South Carolina), with a 62 percent positive rating, and George Voinovich (R-Ohio) with a 60 percent positive rating.

At the other end of the scale are those governors who have sunk quite low in the public's esteem over their job performance. Again, looking at the fourth quarter 1993 ratings, we see Edwin Edwards (D-Louisiana) with only a 30 percent positive job performance rating, Pete Wilson (R-California) with a 31 percent positive rating, Mario Cuomo (D-New York) with a 35 percent positive rating, and Lawton Chiles with a 38 percent positive rating. Actually, Wilson and Chiles could be classified as "comebackers," a third category for these ratings, as they had sunk to as low as 15 percent and 22 percent positive ratings in their gubernatorial careers. Jim Florio (D-New Jersey) was another "comebacker" who had sunk to a low of 18 percent job approval rating, rising to a 43 percent rating one month before being unseated in the 1993 election.[25]

Analyzing the 1993 job performance ratings of 32 governors found there was "no obvious single key to popularity with the state electorates."[26] Theories such as governors are hurt by factors beyond their control, helped by a thriving economy, hurt in a "rough-and-tumble partisan political environment," helped by cutting taxes or by calling for more programs to help the state, helped by their effectiveness in achieving goal, or by their personal style or lack of it did not hold as there was conflicting evidence under each.[27] Like President George Bush, who had a 90 percent job effectiveness rating following the 1991 Gulf War, and Jim Florio, basing your probabilities of being re-elected on such job ratings is at best a gamble.

The third source of rating gubernatorial performance comes from the conservative CATO Institute, which has issued two such listings that were carried prominently on the editorial page of *The Wall Street Journal*.[28] The grades in the first report were in both numerical scores from 25 to 85 and school-like letter grades from A to F. The 1994 report only reported

the letter grades. The criteria for the scores are fiscal restraint "to determine which governors have raised spending the most and which the least." The bias in the analysis is that low spending is good and, by inference, increasing spending and/or taxes for whatever reason (including to meet needs) is bad.

Hal Hovey of *State Policy Reports*, in evaluating the first report, argued that the grades did not totally correspond "to governors' records in advocating higher taxes," nor did they "correspond to assessments of fiscal management inherent in (state) bond ratings." Importantly, the study evaluated people (the governors) but "the data deal only with the policy decisions and fiscal circumstances of state governments: This latter critique thus indicates some clear fallacies in the analysis: governors get credit for frugality forced on them by legislatures and voters . . . governors get credit or blame for the actions of their predecessors . . . and governors get credit or blame for their economic circumstances."[29] He also listed several of the many technical problems in the methodology, but agreed that the results are very "politically potent in some states."[30]

In each of these evaluation processes, beauty (or ugliness) is in the eyes of the beholder. Each measure has its own biases ranging from the gubernatorial eyes of positive performance to the CATO Institute's eyes of fiscal restraint. In the end, it is in the eyes of the voters as translated by their votes that counts as the basic measurement.

Gubernatorial Powers

Term Limits and Succession

The major action during the past two years in the area of gubernatorial powers is tied to the rapidly spreading term limits movement.[31] For a complete discussion of term limits, see the essay, "Term Limits in the States" on pages 28-33 of this volume.

One especially interesting and unique term limits court case involves the question of whether incumbent Governor Bob Miller (D-NV, 1998-date) was eligible to seek re-election to a second full term in 1994. Nevada has a two four-year term limit for governors. The problem was that as lieutenant governor, Miller

succeeded to the governorship when then incumbent Governor Richard Bryan (D, 1983-
1989) resigned to take his newly-won seat in
the U.S. Senate in January 1989. Miller ran
for and won a four-year term on his own in
1990 after serving nearly two years of Bryan's
second term. In Nevada, if Miller served as
governor or as acting governor when Bryan
was out of state for more than two years prior
to his win in 1990 he would be ineligible, according to the Legislative Counsel Bureau.[32]
The State of Nevada Employees Association
had petitioned the state's Supreme Court to
keep Miller's name off the 1994 ballot.[33] On
April 15, the Court ruled without comment
that Miller was eligible to seek re-election.[34]

In 1992, Kentucky joined 48 other states
that allow their governors to succeed themselves for a second term. While the current
governor, Brereton Jones (D, 1991-1995) is not
eligible to do so, the winner of the 1995 gubernatorial election will be allowed to seek a second term in 1999. This leaves Virginia as the
only state to retain the one-term limit on its
governor.[35] As noted earlier, beginning with
the 1994 election, the new governor of Rhode
Island will begin serving a four-year term. This
will leave only New Hampshire and Vermont
restricting their governors to two-year terms.

Finally, the Arkansas Supreme Court had
to sort out the status of the governorship in
that state when Governor Bill Clinton resigned
to assume the presidency with more than 12
months to serve as governor. The question was
whether the lieutenant governor became governor for the remainder of the elected term,
or only until a special election determined
who the governor would be. The Court ruled
the "the powers and duties of the Office of
Governor devolved upon the lieutenant governor for the remainder of the four-year term"
and that the Office of the Governor itself de-
volves upon the lieutenant governor.[36]

Gubernatorial Veto

Two recurring themes were heard during the
past two years in relationship to veto. First,
the 1993 North Carolina General Assembly
again killed a proposed amendment to the
state's constitution providing the governor with
the veto. It cannot be reconsidered until the

1995 legislative session. So North Carolina re-
tains its unique position as the only state without a gubernatorial veto caught in a separation
of powers fight between the two branches.[37]

Second, Wisconsin Governor Thompson (R,
1987-date) continues to bedevil his state legislature with his use of the partial and amen-
datory veto. He has taken the constitutional
power allowing him to veto appropriations bills
"in whole or in part" and vetoed words, including "shalt" and "not," punctuation such
as commas and periods, and "then cobbled
together the surviving words into whole new
sentences — and new law." As of mid-1993, he
had executed at least 1,300 vetoes. A legislative effort to change this power by amending
the state's constitution was blocked by the
results of the 1992 elections in which the Republicans gained control of the state Senate.[38]

There were several state court decisions on
the veto and its use. In Maryland, the state's
high court ruled that a judicial investigation
into a governor's motives for exercising a veto
was violation of the separation of powers doctrine in the state's constitution.[39] The Colorado Supreme Court ruled that a governor must
provide a statement of his or her objections
to a bill when exercising the veto. At issue were
six bills that were vetoed with the notation
"disapproved and vetoed" on each. The Court
indicated that the Legislature needs "to mean-
ingfully evaluate and consider the reasons"
for the veto. However, the Court also indicated
it would not inquire into the governor's jus-
tifications when stated.[40]

In two Minnesota cases, the definition of
what could be constitutionally vetoed was clarified. In a 1991 case, the state's high court ruled
against the governor in the use of an item veto
on an estimated or unspecified amount of
money. In a 1993 case, in which the governor
vetoed a law directing revenues from a specific
1990 tax increase to the state's higher education
program, the court sided with the governor as
the veto was used on an item of appropriated
funds. In this decision, the court provided the
rationale for the use of the item veto to coun-
teract legislative "pork-barreling" by the legislature without having to veto an entire appropriations bill.[41]

On a related matter, the New York Court of Appeals ruled the long-time bill recall procedure used by the state Legislature is not allowed under the state's constitution. Used since 1865, this procedure allowed the legislature to recall a passed bill from the governor prior to his taking action. Since it had been used for so long, the decision was prospective only.[42] The procedure, also used in Massachusetts, New Jersey and Virginia, has the effect of reducing the number of vetoes as the Legislature can recall "to amend bills to make them acceptable to the governor." The recall procedure has been used to give the governor more time to consider a bill by breaking the 10-day consideration period, to correct defects in the bill, or to even kill the bill without a veto involved.[43]

In Mississippi, Governor Kirk Fordice vetoed parts of two bills proposed to provide construction and renovation bond funds for state universities and community colleges. Legislators questioned the constitutionality of extending the use of the line-item veto to bond bills and threatened a lawsuit.[44]

Gubernatorial Appointment Power

In a long overdue 1993 reorganization of the executive branch of state government, the South Carolina governorship for the first time gained significant appointment powers for directors of many state agencies.[45] The governor traditionally has been seen as very weak in good part due to quite limited appointment powers.[46]

At the other end of the appointment power, the state of Illinois and especially the governor's office have been reacting to the 1990 U.S. Supreme Court decision in the *Rutan et al. v. Republican Party of Illinois* case. The Court ruled that using party affiliation in personnel decisions such as hiring, promoting or transferring personnel was violation of their First Amendment rights. In a study of the aftermath, it appears there is more interest in compliance with the decision than improving the system. They have replaced "a centralized patronage system with a centralized bureaucratic system . . . creating even greater rigidities and inefficiencies."[47]

Settling a legislative-executive battle, the New Jersey Supreme Court ruled legislation ordering the governor to lay off certain categories of individuals was an unconstitutional breach of the separation of powers doctrine.[48]

Gubernatorial Budgetary Power

The past two years saw governors and legislatures struggling to keep their state budgets balanced. The passing of a state budget is a joint legislative-executive effort, and with the exceptions of Indiana and North Carolina, governors have the veto power over budgets both in toto or specific lines. However, there are questions involved in what must happen when actual revenues fall short of the estimates on which the budget is based and the budget is out of balance during the budget year.

In most states, the governor clearly has the responsibility and power to act to rectify any shortfall. In 36 states the governor can take necessary action without legislative approval, while some states put limits on the governor's power to do so. For example, statutes may specify that any cuts must be across the board, or cannot exceed a certain level. No governor has the ability to increase taxes to cover a shortfall.[49] And while a governor may be able to adjust appropriations and expenditures downward to respond to a shortfall, there might not be gubernatorial power to adjust substantive legislation setting certain levels of expenditures such as welfare. This has been a recent problem in California, for example.[50]

However, in Maryland, the state's Court of Appeal upheld the governor's cuts in indigent benefits in order to keep the state's budget in balance. The court ruled that taking such action to balance the budget was "necessary and proper for the functioning of the process."[51]

The problems with state revenue estimates has led to concern over the process of fiscal planning. A study of the recent New York State fiscal situation concluded that "the lack of long-term fiscal planning and short-term discipline were the root causes" of that state's problems.[52] A review of the first two years of Connecticut Governor Lowell Weicker's tenure in office indicated that the goal of his first year was to restructure the revenue system; the second year was to reform the expenditure side.[53]

Governors' Priorities

Looking at the priorities set by the governors in their own 1993 "state of the state" addresses, the three top issues facing the states were education reform, health reform and economic development.[54] As has been true in recent years, the National Governors' Association has continued to further the governors' interests in education.[55] Under the leadership of chairmen Governor Roy Romer (D-Colorado) in 1992-93 and Governor Carroll Campbell (R-South Carolina) in 1993-94, NGA also took steps to further the states' interest in healthcare reform,[56] as well as welfare reform.[57] With one of their former peers in the White House, they are hoping for substantive results in working with the federal government on these concerns.

But NGA also has been helping governors in how they redesign their own state governmental structures. A major report was issued based on the findings of four strategy groups of governors.[58] And as usual, NGA conducted a "New Governors Seminar" for those new governors elected in 1992, and will do so again for those elected in 1994.

Concluding Note

One curiosity is that there are five states that continue to walk to a different drummer than other states: Nebraska with its unicameral legislature, North Carolina with its lack of a gubernatorial veto, Virginia as the only state to restrict its governor to one term, and New Hampshire and Vermont, the only states restricting their governors to two-year terms. These states will continue to be noted in textbooks, governmental reports and news stories for their persistence in hewing to a singular direction.

Footnotes

[1] The former governors winning the presidency were Ronald Reagan (R-CA, 1967-1975); Jimmy Carter (D-GA, 1971-75); and Clinton.

[2] For an interesting perspective on gubernatorial elections and the likelihood of a turnover in the governor's chair see Larry Sabato, "The Keys to the Governor's Mansion," *University of Virginia Newsletter* 69 (October 1993), 1-5. The 10 keys he used were: the economy, party unity, scandal, campaign organization and technology, campaign money, candidate personality and appeal, prior office experience of candidates, retrospective judgement on previous governor, presidential popularity, and special issues and dominant circumstances.

[3] For a discussion of what "street money" is and has been, see "Street Money" in *The Hotline* (Nov. 17, 1993), 16-17; (Nov. 18, 1993), 20-21; and (Nov. 19, 1993), 18-19.

[4] Beyle, "The Governors, 1990-92," *The Book of the States, 1992-93*, pp. 30-31. See also Beyle, "Term Limits for Governors," in Malbin (Washington, D.C.: CQ Press, 1992), 162-168.

[5] States in which there will be a new governor following the 1994 elections are: Connecticut, Hawaii, Idaho, Maryland, Pennsylvania, Oklahoma, Oregon, South Carolina, Tennessee and Wyoming. The governor of Nevada, Bob Miller, faces a constitutional challenge regarding his moving up from the lieutenant governor's chair when then-Governor Richard Bryan vacated the governorship in January 1989 to begin his service in the U.S. Senate earlier than other senators elected in 1988 for seniority purposes.

[6] The two winners were incumbent state Attorney General Marc Racicot (R-MT) and former state Attorney General Steve Merrill (R-NH) in 1992. The six losing attorneys general candidates were: Linley Pearson (R-IN), William Webster (R-MO), Lacy Thornburg (D-NC), Nicholas Spaeth (D-ND), Ken Eichenberry (R-WA), and Mary Sue Terry (D-VA). All except Terry (1993) ran in 1992.

[7] The lieutenant governor winner was Mel Carnahan (D-MO) who defeated the attorney general in the race while Lt. Governor Jim Gardner (R-NC) lost to former Governor Jim Hunt (D-NC, 1977-85). The losing agriculture commissioner was Cleve Benedict (R-WV). All were 1992 races.

[8] Thad Beyle, "The Speaker's Office as a Political Stepping Stone?," *North Carolina Insight* 15:1 (January 1994), 30-31.

[9] New Hampshire, Rhode Island, and Vermont.

[10] Malcolm Jewell, "Amendment Changes Elections," *Kentucky Journal* 6:1 (March 1993), 16.

[11] The year-by-year data in this Table differ from the data presented in the last edition of *The Book of the States*. The reasons for the changes are due to availability of additional data from some states and additional sources, a very careful review of the cost of each election in each state over the period, and the correction of errors found in the earlier reported data. As noted in the Table, 1978 data are a particular problem as the two sources which had compiled the data on these elections did so in differing ways that excluded some candidacies. Further, all research notes and material in both organizations have been discarded. The net of this is that the numbers for 1978 under-represent the actual costs of these elections by some unknown amount.

[12] These candidacies were: Pete Wilson (R-CA) $27.4 million; Diane Feinstein (D-CA) $26.5 million; Clayton Williams (R-TX) $21.1 million; Jim Edgar (R-IL) $12.7 million; incumbent Bob Martinez (R-FL) $12.6 million; Ann Richards (D-TX) $12.5 million; Neil Hartigan (D-IL) $12.2 million; and Jim Mattox (D-TX) $10.5 million (all in 1993 dollars).

[13] In addition to Wilson and Feinstein noted in the previous footnote, Attorney General John Van De Kamp, who lost in the Democratic primary to Feinstein, spent $7.6 million on his race.

[14] Associated Press, "Folsom to take over Ala. governor post," *The Herald Sun* (Durham), April 23,1993, A3; Tom Watson and Carl Weiser, "Alabama Gov. convicted, removed from office," *USA Today* (April 23, 1993); and "Alabama: Guilty Verdict Ushers in Time of Sorrow," *The Hotline* 6:144 (April 23,1993), 13.

[15] David L. Martin, "Alabama's Governor Removed on Ethics Conviction: Implications for Other States," *Comparative State Politics* 14:3 (June 1993), 1-4.

[16] "Oklahoma: Governor pleads guilty to campaign violation," *News and Observer* (Raleigh) October 22, 1993. See also "Oklahoma: Walters Pleads Guilty to Misdemeanor," *The Hotline* 7:27 (October 22, 1993). See also Richard R. Johnson, "Oklahoma Governor Pleads Guilty," *Comparative State Politics* 15:1 (February 1994), 4-5.

[17] "Oklahoma: House Votes to Delay Impeachment Proceedings," *The Hotline* 7:63 (December 15, 1993), 12-13; "Oklahoma: Poll Finds No Gung-Ho Impeachment Mood," *The Hotline* 7:69 (December 23, 1993), 23; "Oklahoma: Impeachment Moves Seem to Lose Steam," *The Hotline* 7:81 (January 19, 1994, 17; and "Oklahoma: Walters Survives Vote on Impeachment," *The Hotline* 7:97 (February 10, 1994), 18.

[18] Steve Marshall, "R.I. governor may face paternity lawsuit," *USA Today* (June 9, 1993), 3A; "Rhode Island: Sundlun Discloses Paternity Suit," *The Hotline* 6:176 (June 9, 1993), 18; "Rhode Island: 'Accept Me, Kara Asks Sundlun,'" *The Hotline* 6:177 (June 10, 1993), 17-18; and "Rhode Island: One Big Happy Family," *The Hotline* 6:183 (June 18, 1993), 17.

[19] "Rhode Island: Ex-Governor Indicted on 23 Felony Counts," *The Hotline* 7:130 (March 31, 1994), 19.

[20] "Arizona: Symington Roles in Savings & Loan is Probed by Grand Jury," *The Hotline* 7:88 (January 28, 1994), 11-12.

[21] "Political Corruption," *USA Today* (December 23, 1993).

[22] "Ranking the Governors," *Newsweek* (July 1, 1991), 27.

[23] "How the Governors See It: A *Newsweek* Poll," *Newsweek* (March 24, 1986), 32.

[24] "Ranking the Governors," 1991.

[25] Thad Beyle, "1993 Approval Ratings of Current Governors," *National Network of State Polls Newsletter* No. 18 (Winter 1994), 3-5.

[26] "Getting Re-elected," *State Policy Reports* 12:1 (January 1994), 20.

[27] Ibid., 20-22. Earlier analyses of these job ratings in *State Policy Reports* were: "Governors' Popularity and Tax Policy," 11:9 (May 1993), 19-20; "Governors' Popularity Ratings," 11:13 (July 1993), 20; and "Governor's Popularity," 11:16 (August 1993), 9-10.

[28] "The Good Governor Guide," *Wall Street Journal* (February 5, 1992, A14) and "Gover-

nors' Dilemma: Budgets Out of Control," (January 31, 1994), A12.

[29] "Good Governors," State Policy Reports 10:6 (March 1993), 15; and "Junk Data on Governors' Fiscal Policies," State Policy Reports 12:4 (February 1994), 21.

[30] "Evaluating Governors and State Policies," State Policy Reports 10:6 (March 1992), 23-24.

[31] "Term Limit Initiatives," State Legislatures 18:11 (October 1992), 27 and "Their Terms are Limited," State Legislatures 18:12 (December 1992), 15.

[32] "Nevada: Will Constitutional Glitch Rule Out a Miller Bid?," The Hotline 7:76 (Jan. 11, 1994), 12-13.

[33] "Nevada: Miller's Big Day to be Shrouded by Lawsuit," The Hotline 7:113 (March 8, 1994), 15-16.

[34] "Nevada: Court Rules Miller Is Eligible to Dismay of Jones," The Hotline 7:141 (April 18, 1994), 18.

[35] Michael Barone and Grant Ujifusa, The Almanac of American Politics, 1994 (Washington, D.C.: National Journal, Inc., 1993), 508, 1302.

[36] Bryant v. English, 311 Ark. 187 (1992) (12/4/92) as reported in the State Constitutional Law Bulletin 6:6 (March 1993), 5.

[37] Joel Thompson, "The 1993 North Carolina General Assembly: Back to the Future," Comparative State Politics 14:6 (December 1993), 1-5.

[38] Dennis Farney, "When Wisconsin Governor Wields Partial Veto, The Legislature Might as Well Go Play Scrabble," Wall Street Journal (July 1, 1993), A16. See also "Wisconsin voters may look at the funny veto law," State Legislatures 19:5 (May 1993), 11.

[39] O'Hara v. Kovens 1 MLR 3373 (5/26/93) as reported in the State Constitutional Law Bulletin 5:9 (June 1993), 2.

[40] Romer v. Colorado General Assembly, No. 92 SA 118 (11/23/92) Reported in the State Constitutional Law Bulletin 6:4 (January 1993), 3-4.

[41] The two cases were Inter Faculty Organization v. Carlson, 478 N.W. 2d 192 (Minn. 1991) and Johnson v. Carlson, 507 N.W. 2d 232 (1993). "Exercise by Minnesota's Gover-

nor of Line Item Veto Upheld," State Constitutional Law Bulletin 7:5 (February 1994), 19, 23.

[42] King v. Cuomo, No. 78 (5/6/93) as reported in the State Constitutional Law Bulletin 6:9 (June 1993), 2.

[43] Joseph F. Zimmerman, "The Recall of Bills from the Governor of New York," Comparative State Politics 15:1 (February 1994), 19, 23.

[44] "Mississippi governor uses line item veto on bond bill," State Legislatures 19:7 (July 1993), 17.

[45] "Initiatives to Redesign Government," Governors Bulletin 27:14 (July 19, 1993), 5. See also special section, "Restructuring: The players and politics," The (Columbia) State, a reprint of articles published between January 10 and July 1, 1993.

[46] Thad L. Beyle, "The Powers of the Governor in North Carolina," North Carolina Insight 12:2 (March 1990), 30, 41-45.

[47] David K. Hamilton, "The Staffing Function in Illinois State Government after Rutan," Public Administration Review 53:4 (July/August 1993), 385.

[48] "Florio wins pink-slip battle," State Government News 36:2 (February 1993), 33.

[49] "Assessing Balanced Budget Requirements," State Policy Reports 10:13 (July 1992), 7-8.

[50] Ibid.

[51] Judy v. Schaefer, 331 Md. 239, 627 A.2d 1039 (1993) as reported in the State Constitutional Law Bulletin 7:1 (October 1993), 1-2.

[52] Roy Bahl and William Duncombe, "Economic Change and Fiscal Planning: The Origins of the Fiscal Crisis in New York State," Public Administration Review 52:6 (November-December, 1992), 547.

[53] Robert Kravchuck, "The 'New Connecticut': Lowell Weicker and the Process of Administrative Reform," Public Administration Review 53:4 (July-August, 1993), 334-335.

[54] "Governors' Top Priorities," Governors' Bulletin 27:6 (March 15, 1993), 1.

[55] Transforming Education: Overcoming Barriers and a Guide to Building Public Support for Education Reform (Washington, D.C.: NGA, 1993). See also Carroll Campbell, "Governors Must Renew Focus on the Edu-

cational Goals," *Governors' Bulletin* 27:20 (Oct. 11, 1993), 2-3.

[56] On health reform, see *State Progress in Health Care Reform*, 1992 (Washington, D.C.: NGA, 1993) and an earlier report, *A Healthy America: The Challenge for States* (NGA, 1991).

[57] Shelley Borysiewica, "Governors using Innovative Approaches to Reform Welfare," *Governors' Bulletin* 27:20 (Oct. 11, 1993), 1, 405. See also *Putting Families First* (NGA, 1993).

[58] *An Action Agenda to Redesign State Government* (NGA, 1993).

Table 2.1
THE GOVERNORS, 1994

State or other jurisdiction	Name and Party	Length of regular term in years	Date of first service	Present term ends	Number of previous terms	Maximum consecutive terms allowed by constitution	Joint election of governor and lieutenant governor (a)	Official who succeeds governor	Birthdate	Birthplace
Alabama	Jim Folsom (D)	4	04/93 (b)	01/95	1 (c)	2 (d)	No	LG	05/14/49	Ala.
Alaska	Walter J. Hickel (I)	4	12/66	12/94	...	2 (d)	Yes	LG	08/18/19	Kan.
Arizona	Fife Symington (R)	4	03/91 (e)	01/95	...	2	(f)	SS	08/12/45	N.Y.
Arkansas	Jim Guy Tucker (D)	4	03/92 (g)	01/95	...	2	No	LG	06/13/43	Okla.
California	Pete Wilson (R)	4	01/91	01/95	...	2	No	LG	08/23/33	Ill.
Colorado	Roy Romer (D)	4	01/87	01/95	1	2	Yes	LG	10/31/28	Kan.
Connecticut	Lowell P. Weicker, Jr. (ACP)	4	01/91	01/95	...	2	Yes	LG	05/16/31	France
Delaware	Tom Carper (D)	4	01/93	01/97	...	2 (h)	No	LG	01/23/47	W.V.
Florida	Lawton Chiles (D)	4	01/91	01/95	...	2 (d)	Yes	LG	04/03/30	Fla.
Georgia	Zell Miller (D)	4	01/91	01/95	...	2 (d)	No	LG	02/24/32	Ga.
Hawaii	John D. Waihee III (D)	4	01/86	12/94	1	2	Yes	LG	05/19/46	Hawaii
Idaho	Cecil D. Andrus (D)	4	01/71	01/95	3 (i)	...	No	LG	08/25/31	Ore.
Illinois	Jim Edgar (R)	4	01/91	01/95	...	...	Yes	LG	07/22/46	Okla.
Indiana	Evan Bayh (D)	4	01/89	01/97	1	(j)	Yes	LG	12/26/55	Ind.
Iowa	Terry E. Branstad (R)	4	01/83	01/95	2	...	Yes	LG	11/17/46	Iowa
Kansas	Joan Finney (D)	4	01/91	01/95	...	2	Yes	LG	02/12/25	Kan.
Kentucky	Brereton C. Jones (D)	4	12/91	12/95	...	2	Yes (k)	LG	06/27/39	Ohio
Louisiana	Edwin W. Edwards (D)	4	05/72	01/96	3 (l)	2	No	LG	08/07/27	La.
Maine	John R. McKernan, Jr. (R)	4	01/87	01/95	1	2	(f)	PS	05/20/48	Maine
Maryland	William Donald Schaefer (D)	4	01/87	01/95	1	2 (d)	Yes	LG	11/02/21	Md.
Massachusetts	William F. Weld (R)	4	01/91	01/95	...	...	Yes	LG	07/31/45	N.Y.
Michigan	John Engler (R)	4	01/91	01/95	...	2	Yes	LG	10/12/48	Mich.
Minnesota	Arne H. Carlson (R)	4	01/91	01/95	...	...	Yes	LG	09/24/34	N.Y.
Mississippi	Kirk Fordice (R)	4	01/92	01/96	...	2	No	LG	02/10/34	Tenn.
Missouri	Mel Carnahan (D)	4	01/93	01/97	...	2 (h)	No	LG	02/11/34	Mo.
Montana	Marc Racicot (R)	4	01/93	01/97	...	(m)	Yes	LG	07/24/48	Mont.
Nebraska	E. Benjamin Nelson (D)	4	01/91	01/95	...	2 (d)	Yes	LG	05/17/41	Neb.
Nevada	Bob Miller (D)	4	01/89 (n)	01/95	(n)	2	No	LG	03/30/45	Ill.
New Hampshire	Stephen Merrill (R)	2	01/93	01/95	1	...	(f)	PS	06/21/46	Conn.
New Jersey	Christine T. Whitman (R)	4	01/94	01/98	...	2 (d)	(f)	PS	09/26/46	N.J.
New Mexico	Bruce King (D)	4	01/71	01/95	2 (o)	2 (d)	Yes	LG	04/06/24	N.M.
New York	Mario M. Cuomo (D)	4	01/83	01/95	2 (p)	...	Yes	LG	06/15/32	N.Y.
North Carolina	James B. Hunt, Jr. (D)	4	01/77	01/97	2	2	No	LG	05/16/37	N.C.
North Dakota	Edward T. Schafer (R)	4	01/93	01/97	...	...	Yes	LG	08/08/46	N.D.
Ohio	George V. Voinovich (R)	4	01/91	01/95	...	2 (h)	Yes	LG	07/15/36	Ohio
Oklahoma	David Walters (D)	4	01/91	01/95	...	2 (d)	No	LG	11/20/51	Okla.
Oregon	Barbara Roberts (D)	4	01/91	01/95	...	2 (q)	(f)	SS	12/21/36	Ore.
Pennsylvania	Robert P. Casey (D)	4	01/87	01/95	1	2	Yes	LG	01/09/32	N.Y.
Rhode Island	Bruce Sundlun (D)	2 (r)	01/91	01/95	1	...	No	LG	01/19/20	R.I.
South Carolina	Carroll A. Campbell, Jr. (R)	4	01/87	01/95	1	2	No	LG	07/24/40	S.C.
South Dakota	Walter D. Miller (R)	4	04/93 (b)	01/95	...	2	Yes	LG	10/05/25	S.D.
Tennessee	Ned Ray McWherter (D)	4	01/87	01/95	1	2	No	SpS (s)	10/15/30	Tenn.
Texas	Ann W. Richards (D)	4	01/91	01/95	...	...	No	LG	09/01/33	Texas
Utah	Mike Leavitt (R)	4	01/93	01/97	...	3	Yes	LG	02/11/51	Utah
Vermont	Howard Dean (D)	2	08/91 (t)	01/95	1	...	No	LG	11/17/48	N.Y.

THE GOVERNORS—Continued

State or other jurisdiction	Name and Party	Length of regular term in years	Date of first service	Present term ends	Number of previous terms	Maximum consecutive terms allowed by constitution	Joint election of governor and lieutenant governor (a)	Official who succeeds governor	Birthdate	Birthplace
Virginia	George Allen (R)	4	01/94	01/98	...	(u)	No	LG	03/08/52	Calif.
Washington	Mike Lowry (D)	4	01/93	01/97	...	(v)	No	LG	03/08/39	Wash.
West Virginia	Gaston Caperton (D)	4	01/89	01/97	1	2 (w)	(f)	PS	02/21/40	W.V.
Wisconsin	Tommy G. Thompson (R)	4	01/87	01/95	1	..	Yes	LG	11/19/41	Wisc.
Wyoming	Michael (Mike) J. Sullivan (D)	4	01/87	01/95	1	2 (m)	(f)	SS	09/22/39	Neb.
American Samoa	A.P. Lutali (D)	4	01/85	01/97	1	2 (x)	Yes	LG	12/24/19	A.S.
Guam	Joseph F. Ada (R)	4	01/87	01/95	..	2 (d)	Yes	LG	12/03/43	Guam
No. Mariana Islands	Froilan C. Tenorio (D)	4	01/94	01/98	..	2 (h)	Yes	SS	09/09/39	Saipan
Puerto Rico	Pedro Rossello (NPP)	4	01/93	01/97	..	..	(f)	SS	04/05/44	P.R.
U.S. Virgin Islands	Alexander A. Farrelly (D)	4	01/87	01/95	1	2 (d)	Yes	LG	12/29/23	V.I.

Sources: National Governors' Association and The Council of State Governments.

Key:
ACP — A Connecticut Party
D — Democrat
I — Independent
R — Republican
NPP — New Progressive Party
LG — Lieutenant Governor
SS — Secretary of State
PS — President of the Senate
SpS — Speaker of the Senate
... — Not applicable

(a) The following also choose candidates for governor and lieutenant governor through a joint nomination process: Florida, Kansas, Maryland, Minnesota, Montana, North Dakota, Ohio, Utah, American Samoa, Guam, No. Mariana Islands and U.S. Virgin Islands.
(b) Succeeded to governor's office April 1993 to serve remainder of unexpired term.
(c) Served 1966-69, when he resigned to become Secretary, U.S. Department of Interior.
(d) After two consecutive terms, must wait four years before being eligible again. In Nebraska, this provision begins in January 1995.
(e) Elected in runoff election February 1991 due to no one candidate receiving a majority of votes in November 1990 election.
(f) No lieutenant governor.

(g) Succeeded to governor's office March 1992 to serve remainder of unexpired term.
(h) Absolute two-term limit, but not necessarily consecutive.
(i) Served from 1971 to 1977 when he resigned to accept appointment as Secretary, U.S. Dept. of Interior; reelected in 1986 and 1990.
(j) Prohibited from serving more than eight years out of a 12-year period.
(k) Effective with the winner of the 1995 election.
(l) Served 1972-76, 1976-1980, 1984-88.
(m) Prohibited from serving more than eight years out of 16-year period.
(n) Succeeded to governor's office November 1988 to serve remainder of unexpired term.
(o) Served 1971-75 and 1979-83.
(p) Served 1977-1981 and 1981-1985.
(q) Prohibited from serving more than eight years out of a 12-year period.
(r) Effective January 1995, the term length increases to four years.
(s) Official bears the additional statutory title of "lieutenant governor."
(t) Succeeded to governor's office August 1991 to serve remainder of unexpired term.
(u) Successive terms forbidden.
(v) Prohibited from serving more than eight years out of 14-year period.
(w) A person who has been elected or who has served as governor during all or any part of two consecutive terms shall be ineligible for the office of governor during any part of the term immediately following the second of the two consecutive terms.
(x) Limit is statutory.

Table 2.2
THE GOVERNORS: QUALIFICATIONS FOR OFFICE

State or other jurisdiction	Minimum age	State citizen (years)	U.S. citizen (years)	State resident (years)	Qualified voter (years)
Alabama*	30	7	10	7	...
Alaska	30	...	7	7	★
Arizona	25	5	10	...	...
Arkansas	30	...	★	7	...
California	18	...	5	5	★
Colorado	30	...	★	2	...
Connecticut	30	...	...	...	★
Delaware	30	...	12	6	...
Florida	30	...	...	7	★
Georgia	30	...	15	6	...
Hawaii	30	...	...	5	★
Idaho*	30	...	★	2	...
Illinois	25	...	★	3	...
Indiana	30	...	5	5	...
Iowa	30	...	★	2	...
Kansas	...	...	...	...	...
Kentucky	30	6	★	6	...
Louisiana	25	5	5	...	★
Maine	30	...	15	5	...
Maryland	30	...	(a)	5	5
Massachusetts	...	...	...	7	...
Michigan	30	...	...	...	4
Minnesota	25	...	★	1	...
Mississippi*	30	...	20	5	...
Missouri	30	...	15	10	...
Montana* (b)	25	★	★	2	...
Nebraska (c)	30	5	5	5	...
Nevada	25	2	...	2	★
New Hampshire	30	...	...	7	...
New Jersey	30	...	20	7	...
New Mexico*	30	...	★	5	★
New York	30	...	★	5	...
North Carolina	30	...	5	2	...
North Dakota	30	...	★	5	★
Ohio	...	...	★	...	★
Oklahoma	31	...	★	...	10
Oregon	30	...	★	3	...
Pennsylvania	30	...	★	7	...
Rhode Island	...	...	...	...	★
South Carolina	30	5	★	5	...
South Dakota	...	...	2	2	...
Tennessee	30	7	★	...	...
Texas	30	...	★	5	...
Utah	30	5	...	5	★
Vermont	...	...	...	4	...
Virginia*	30	...	★	5	5
Washington	18	...	★	...	★
West Virginia	30	5	★	★	★
Wisconsin	18	...	★	...	★
Wyoming	30	...	★	5	★
American Samoa	35	...	★	5	...
Guam	30	...	5	5	★
No. Mariana Islands	35	...	...	10	★
Puerto Rico	35	5	5	5	...
U.S. Virgin Islands	30	...	5	5	★

Source: The Council of State Governments' survey, February 1994; except as noted by * where information is from *The Book of the States 1992-93.*

Note: The information in this table is based on a literal reading of the state constitutions and statutes.

Key:
★ — Formal provision; number of years not specified.
. . . — No formal provision.

(a) *Crosse* v. *Board of Supervisors of Elections* 243 Md. 555, 221A.2d431 (1966) — opinion rendered indicated that U.S. citizenship was, by necessity, a requirement for office.

(b) No person convicted of a felony is eligible to hold office until final discharge from state supervision.

(c) No person in default as a collector and custodian of public money or property shall be eligible to public office; no person convicted of a felony shall be eligible unless restored to civil rights.

Table 2.3
THE GOVERNORS: COMPENSATION

State or other jurisdiction	Salary	Governor's office staff (a)	Access to state transportation			Travel allowance	Official residence
			Automobile	Airplane	Helicopter		
Alabama*	$ 81,151	22	★	★	★	(b)	★
Alaska	81,648	66	★	★	★	(b)	★
Arizona	75,000	41	★	★	. . .	(b)	. . .
Arkansas	60,000	48	★	. . .	. . .	(c)	★
California	114,286 (d)	86	★	. . . ■	. . .	(c)	(e)
Colorado	60,000	39	★	★	. . .	(f)	★
Connecticut	78,000	38	★	. . .	. . .	(f)	★
Delaware	95,000	25	★	. . .	★	$13,000 (c)	★
Florida	97,850	264	★	★	. . .	(b)	★
Georgia	94,390	41	★	★	★	(f)	★
Hawaii	94,780	28 (g)	★	. . .	. . .	(f)	★
Idaho*	75,000	21	★	★	. . .	(f)	. . .
Illinois	103,097	140	★	★	★	(b)	★
Indiana	77,200 (h)	35	★	★	★	0	★
Iowa	76,700	10	★	★	. . .	(b)	★
Kansas	76,476	29	★	★	. . .	(f)	★
Kentucky	81,647	43	★	★	★	(b)	★
Louisiana	73,440	45	★	. . .	★	(b)	★
Maine	69,992	21	★	. . .	. . .	(f)	★
Maryland	120,000	98	★	★	★	(f)	★
Massachusetts	75,000	80	★	★	★	(f)	. . .
Michigan	112,025 (i)	66	★	★	★	(b)	★
Minnesota	109,053	36	★	★	★	(f)	★
Mississippi*	75,600	39 (j)	★	★	★	$24,017 (c,f)	★
Missouri	91,615	33.5	★	★	. . .	(c)	★
Montana*	55,850	24	★	★	★	(b)	★
Nebraska	65,000	18	★	★	★	(b)	★
Nevada	90,000	18	★	★	. . .	(c)	★
New Hampshire	82,325 (k)	23	★	★	. . .	(f)	★ (l)
New Jersey	85,000	125	★	. . .	★	$61,000	★
New Mexico*	90,000	54	★	★	★	$95,300 (c)	★
New York*	130,000 (m)	216	★	★	★	(b)	★
North Carolina	93,777	86	★	★	★	$11,500	★
North Dakota	68,280	19	★	★	. . .	(f)	★
Ohio	110,250	66	★	★	★	(f)	★
Oklahoma	70,000	34	★	★	. . .	(f)	★
Oregon	80,000	27	★	. . .	. . .	(f)	★
Pennsylvania	105,000	87	★	★	. . .	(b)	★
Rhode Island	69,900	33	★	★	★	(n)	. . .
South Carolina	103,998	22	★	★	★	(f)	★
South Dakota	72,475	18	★	★	. . .	(f)	★
Tennessee	85,000	30	★	★	★	(f)	★
Texas	99,122	190	★	★	★	(b)	★
Utah	77,250	16	★	★	. . .	$26,000	★
Vermont	80,724	17	★	. . .	. . .	(f)	. . .
Virginia*	110,000	36	★	★	★	(b)	★
Washington	121,000 (o)	37	★	★	. . .	$120,000 (c)	★
West Virginia	72,000	48	★	★	★	(p)	★
Wisconsin	92,283	38	★	★	. . .	(f)	★
Wyoming	70,000 (n)	7.5 (q)	★	★	. . .	(c)	★
American Samoa	50,000	23	★	. . .	. . .	$105,000 (c)	★
Guam	90,000	42	★	. . .	. . .	$218/day	★
No. Mariana Islands	70,000	16	★	. . .	. . .	(f,r)	★
Puerto Rico	70,000	22	★	★	★	(f)	★
U.S. Virgin Islands	80,000	(s)	★	. . .	. . .	(f)	★

See footnotes at end of table.

THE GOVERNORS: COMPENSATION—Continued

Source: The Council of State Governments' survey, February 1994; except as noted by * where information is from *The Book of the States 1992-93.*

Key:
★ — Yes
. . . — No
N.A. — Not available

(a) Definitions of "governor's office staff" vary across the states — from general office support to staffing for various operations within the executive office.

(b) Reimbursed for travel expenses. Alabama — reimbursed up to $40/day in state; actual expenses out of state. Alaska — receives per diem based on location or actual expenses if exceeds per diem. Arizona — $26/day per diem for food; actual expenses for lodging. Florida — reimbursed at same rate as other state officials: in state, choice between $50 per diem or actual expenses; out of state, actual expenses. Illinois — no set allowance. Iowa — limit set in annual office budget. Kentucky — mileage at same rate as other state employees. Louisiana — reimbursed for actual expenses. Michigan — $35-50/day for in state; no state tax dollars used for out of state. Montana — reimbursed for actual and necessary expenses in state up to $55/day, and actual lodging plus meal allowance up to $30/day out of state (no annual limit). Nebraska — reasonable and necessary expenses. New York — reimbursed for actual and necessary expenses. Pennsylvania — reimbursed for reasonable expenses. Texas — reimbursed for actual expenses.

(c) Amount includes travel allowance for entire staff. Arkansas, Missouri — amount not available. California — $145,000 in state; $36,000 out of state. Nevada — $21,995 in state; $10,640 out of state. New Mexico — $95,300 (in state $40,800, out of state $54,500). Wyoming — $42,375 in state; $36,000 out of state.

(d) Governor has taken a voluntary 5 percent cut in statutory salary.

(e) In California—provided by Governor's Residence Foundation, a non-profit organization which provides a residence for the governor of California. No rent is charged; maintenance and operational costs are provided by California Department of General Services.

(f) Travel allowance included in office budget.

(g) In Hawaii, does not include offices and commissions attached to governor's office.

(h) Accepts $66,000.

(i) Salary was increased to $110,700, but governor rejected the increase.

(j) Currently 18; budget request is for 39.

(k) Governor refused a pay raise and has given 10 percent of his salary back to the state. Actual salary is $71,587.

(l) Governor does not occupy residence.

(m) Accepts $100,000.

(n) Effective January 1995, salary will be $95,000.

(o) Governor has taken voluntary cut of $31,000 in statutory salary.

(p) Included in general expense account.

(q) Also has state planning coordinator.

(r) Governor has a "contingency account" that can be used for travel expenses and expenses in other departments or other projects.

(s) Governor's office staff includes office staff to various agencies of the U.S. Virgin Islands government.

Table 2.4
THE GOVERNORS: POWERS

State or other jurisdiction	Budget-making power		Veto power (a)					Authorization for reorganization through executive order (b)	Other statewide elected officials (c)	
	Full responsibility	Shares responsibility	No item veto	Item veto—2/3 legislators present to override	Item veto—majority legislators elected to override	Item veto—3/5 legislators elected to override	Item veto—at least 2/3 legislators elected to override		Number of officials	Number of agencies
Alabama*	★				★				9	7
Alaska	★						★★	C	1	0 (d)
Arizona	★				★				8	6
Arkansas	★				★		'	S	6	6
California	★						★★		7	7
Colorado		★							4	4
Connecticut	★ (f)						★★	C	5	5
Delaware		★		★					1	1
Florida		★	★					S	7	7
Georgia	★						★	S	12	8
Hawaii	★			★			★	(e)	1	1
Idaho*	★		★			★		C	6	6
Illinois	★								14	6
Indiana	★		★						6	6
Iowa	★						★	S	6	6
Kansas	★			★	★			C	5	5
Kentucky		★★		★	★			S	7	7
Louisiana		★		★			★ (g)		7	7
Maine	★								0	0
Maryland	★★			★		★	★	C	3	3
Massachusetts	★ (f)			★				C	5	7
Michigan	★						★★★★	C	35	7
Minnesota		★						S	5	5
Mississippi*	★							S	7	7
Missouri	★			★		★	★	C	5	5
Montana*	★			★		★		S	5	5
Nebraska	★								5	5
Nevada	★		★★ (h)						5	5
New Hampshire	★		S						0	0
New Jersey	★						★	S	0	0
New Mexico*	★		(h)	★			★ (g)	C	9	7
New York	★		S				★		3	3
North Carolina		★		★				C	13	11
North Dakota	★ (f)		S						5	5
Ohio	★ (f)			★		★		(e)	10	8
Oklahoma	★ (f)		★				★	S	5	5
Oregon	★ (f)			★			★		5	5
Pennsylvania	★	★							4	4
Rhode Island	★ (f)		★						4	4
South Carolina		★							8	10 (i)
South Dakota	★						★	C	9	7
Tennessee	★				★			S	3	1
Texas		★	★★						9	7
Utah	★★		★						4	4
Vermont	★	★						S	5	5

See footnotes at end of table.

THE GOVERNORS: POWERS—Continued

State or other jurisdiction	Budget-making power		Veto power (a)					Authorization for reorganization through executive order (b)	Other statewide elected officials (c)	
	Full responsibility	Shares responsibility	No item veto	Item veto—2/3 legislators present to override	Item veto—majority legislators elected to override	Item veto—3/5 legislators elected to override	Item veto—at least 2/3 legislators elected to override		Number of officials	Number of agencies
Virginia*	★	. . .	. . .	★	. . .	. . .	. . .	S (j)	2	2
Washington	★	. . .	. . .	★	. . .	. . .	. . .	S	8	8
West Virginia	. . .	★	. . .	★	. . .	. . .	. . .	S	5	7
Wisconsin	★	. . .	. . .	★ (k)	. . .	. . .	. . .	. . .	5	5
Wyoming	★	. . .	. . .	. . .	. . .	. . .	★	. . .	4	4
American Samoa	. . .	★	. . .	. . .	. . .	. . .	★	S	1	1
Guam	. . .	★	(l)	. . .	. . .	. . .	★	★	1	1
No. Mariana Islands	. . .	★	(l)	. . .	. . .	. . .	★	★	0	0
Puerto Rico	★	. . .	. . .	. . .	. . .	. . .	★	. . .	1	
U.S. Virgin Islands	. . .	. . .	. . .	. . .	. . .	. . .	. . .	. . .		1

Source: The Council of State Governments' survey, February 1994; except as noted by * where information is from The Book of the States 1992-93.

Key:
★—Yes; provision for.
. . .—No; not applicable.
C — Constitutional
S — Statutory

(a) In all states, except North Carolina, governor has the power to veto bills passed by the state legislature. The information presented here refers to the governor's power to item veto—veto items within a bill—and the votes needed in the state legislature to override the item veto. For additional information on vetoes and veto overrides, as well as the number of days the governor is allowed to consider bills, see Table 3.16, "Enacting Legislation: Veto, Veto Overrides and Effective Date."
(b) For additional information on executive orders, see Table 2.5, "Gubernatorial Executive Orders: Authorization, Provisions, Procedures."
(c) Includes only executive branch officials who are popularly elected either on a constitutional or statutory basis (elected members of state boards of education, public utilities commissions, university regents, or other state boards or commissions are also included); the number of agencies involving these officials is also listed.
(d) Lieutenant governor's office is part of governor's office.
(e) Implied through a broad interpretation of gubernatorial authority; no formal provision.
(f) Full responsibility to propose; legislature adopts or revises and governor signs or vetoes.
(g) In New York, governor has item veto over appropriations. In Louisiana, governor has item veto over appropriation bill only.
(h) Governor has no veto power.
(i) Divisions within governor's office.
(j) For shifting agencies between secretarial offices; all other reorganizations require legislative approval.
(k) In Wisconsin, governor has "partial" veto over appropriation bills. The partial veto is broader than item veto.
(l) The governor has an item veto over appropriations only.

Table 2.5
GUBERNATORIAL EXECUTIVE ORDERS: AUTHORIZATION, PROVISIONS, PROCEDURES

State or other jurisdiction	Authorization for executive orders	Civil defense disasters, public emergencies	Energy emergencies and conservation	Other emergencies	Executive branch reorganization plans and agency creation	Create advisory, coordinating, study or investigative committees/commissions	Respond to federal programs and requirements	State personnel administration	Other administration	Filing and publication procedures	Subject to administrative procedure act	Subject to legislative review
		Provisions								Procedures		
Alabama*	S,I (a)			★ (b)						★ (c,d)		
Alaska	C	★	★ (a)	★ (a)	★	★	★	★		★ (c)		★
Arizona	I	★	★ (a)	★	★	★	★	★	★★	★★		
Arkansas	S,I (e)	★	★	★	★	★	★	★		★		
California	S	★★		★★	★★	★★	★★	★★		★		
Colorado	S	★	★	★ (f)		★	★			★		
Connecticut	S	★	★	★		★	★			★		
Delaware	C	★	★	★	★	★	★	★	(g,h)	★ (c)		★ (k)
Florida	C,S	★	★	★ (i)	★	★	★	★	(g,h)	★		
Georgia	S,I (e)	★	★		★	★	★	★		★★		
Hawaii		(a)							(j)	★ (c)		
Idaho*	S		I	I		I	I	I		★ (c)		
Illinois	C	S										
Indiana	I		★		★	★					★	★
Iowa	S		★		★	★	★	★		★	★	
Kansas	S	★★	★★		★★★	★	★	★★	(l)	★★ (c,d,m)		★★ (t,u)
Kentucky	S	S	S	★ (n)	★★	★★	★★	★★	(k,o,p,q)	★★ (c)	★	★★
Louisiana	S (r)	S	S	★ (v,w)	★	C,S	★	★	(s,t,u)	★ (m)	★	
Maine	C,S	★★			★	★★	★★	★	(x)	★★ (d)	★	★ (y)
Massachusetts	C,I	★	★	★ (f,v)	★	★	★	★	(q)	★ (m)		
Michigan	C,S	★	★ (aa)	★★	★	★	★★	★	(bb)	★★ (c,m)		★★ (z)
Minnesota	S	★	★	★	★★	★	★	★	(cc,dd)	★ (c)		★★
Mississippi*	C	★	★	★	★	★	★	★	(y)	★★ (y)		★ (y)
Missouri	S,I	★	★★	★	★	★	★	★★	(q)	★ (c)		
Montana*	S	★				★	★★			★★★		
Nebraska	S,I	★				★	★			★		
Nevada	S	★				★	★			★		
New Hampshire	S	★	★ (a)	★★ (ff)	(gg)	I	★	★★	(q)	★		★ (t,u)
New Jersey	S			★		I			(dd)	★	★	★★
New Mexico*	S	★		★		★	★			★		★
New York*	I	S	S	S	S,C	I	S	S	S,C	S		
North Carolina	S,I		S	S		I	I	S		★		
North Dakota	S,I	★	★		I				(h,q,s,t,bb,dd)			★ (y,ee)
Ohio	C,S,I	★	★★	★	★	★	★	★		★ (c)	★	★ (y)
Oklahoma	S,I	★★	★★	★ (v)	★	★	★	★★	(hh)	★★ (c)		
Oregon	S	★★	★	★ (n,v,x,ii)		★			(jj)	★★ (c,m)		★★ (y)
Pennsylvania	C,S	★★	★			(a)	S		(l)	★ (c,m)	★	★
Rhode Island	S (a)						I					
South Carolina	I (e)	★ (dd)	★	★ (h,hh)	★	★	★	★		★ (c,d,kk)	★	★ (y)

See footnotes at end of table.

GUBERNATORIAL EXECUTIVE ORDERS—Continued

State or other jurisdiction	Authorization for executive orders	Provisions								Procedures		
		Civil defense disasters, public emergencies	Energy emergencies and conservation	Other emergencies	Executive branch reorganization plans and agency creation	Create advisory, coordinating, study or investigative committees/commissions	Respond to federal programs and requirements	State personnel administration	Other administration	Filing and publication procedures	Subject to administrative procedure act	Subject to legislative review
South Dakota	C	★	★	★	★	★			★ (t)	★ (t)		★
Tennessee	S,I	★	★	★		★	★	★	★	★ (c)	★	★
Texas	S	★	★			★	★			★ (c)		
Utah	S	★	★		(ll)	★						
Vermont	S,I	★	★ (r)		★	★	★	★	★ (h,ii,pp)	★ (mm)	★ (mm)	★ (mm)
Virginia*	S,I	★		★	(oo)	★		★	★ (h,ii,pp)	★ (c)		
Washington	S	★	★	★	★	★	★	★	★ (qq)	★ (c)	★	★
West Virginia	S,I (e)	★		★		★	★	★	★ (p,dd.gg)	★ (c.m)	★	
Wisconsin	S	★		★		I		★		★ (c)		
Wyoming	I	I										★
American Samoa	C,S	★	★	★	★	★	★	★	★	★ (rr)	★ (rr)	
Guam	C	★	★		★	★	S	★	★	S		
No. Mariana Islands	C	★	I	★	C	S,I	S	★	★	S	I	
Puerto Rico	I	★		★		★						
U.S. Virgin Islands	C	★	★	★	★				★	★	★	★

Source: The Council of State Governments' survey, February 1994; except as noted by ★ where information is from *The Book of the States 1992-93.*

Key:
C — Constitutional
S — Statutory
I — Implied
★ — Formal provision
... — No formal provision
(a) Broad interpretation of gubernatorial authority.
(b) To activate or veto environmental improvement authorities.
(c) Executive orders must be filed with secretary of state or other designated officer. In Idaho, must also be published in state general circulation newspaper.
(d) Governor required to keep record in office. In Maine, also sends copy to Legislative Counsel, State Law Library, and all county law libraries in state.
(e) Some or all provisions implied from constitution.
(f) To regulate distribution of necessities during shortages.
(g) To reassign state attorneys and public defenders.
(h) To suspend certain officials and/or other civil actions.
(i) Local financial emergency, shore erosion, polluted discharge and energy shortage.
(j) Delegation of authority over real property (e.g., to counties for park purposes).
(k) Only if involves a change in statute.
(l) To transfer allocated funds.
(m) Included in state register or code.
(n) To give immediate effect to state regulations in emergencies.
(o) To control administration of state contracts and procedures.
(p) To impound or freeze certain state matching funds.
(q) To reduce state expenditures in revenue shortfall.
(r) Broad grant of authority.
(s) To designate game and wildlife areas or other public areas.
(t) Appointive powers.
(u) To suspend rules and regulations of the bureaucracy.
(v) For fire emergencies.
(w) For financial institution emergencies.
(x) To control procedures for dealing with public.
(y) Reorganization plans and agency creation.
(z) Legislative appropriations committees must approve orders issued to handle a revenue shortfall.
(aa) If an energy emergency is declared by the state's Executive Council or Legislature.
(bb) To assign duties to lieutenant governor, issue writ of special election.
(cc) To control prison and pardon administration.
(dd) To administer and govern the armed forces of the state.
(ee) For meeting federal program requirements.
(ff) To declare air pollution emergencies.
(gg) Relating to local governments.
(hh) To declare water, crop and refugee emergencies.
(ii) To transfer funds in an emergency.
(jj) Must be published in register if they have general applicability and legal effect.
(kk) Can reorganize, but not create.
(ll) Filed with legislature.
(mm) Only executive branch reorganization.
(nn) To shift agencies between secretarial offices; all other reorganizations require legislative approval.
(oo) To control state-owned motor vehicles and to delegate powers to secretaries and other executive branch officials.
(pp) Regarding annual reports of state agencies.
(qq) To transfer functions between agencies.
(rr) If executive order fits definition of rule.

Table 2.6
STATE CABINET SYSTEMS

State or other jurisdiction	Authorization for cabinet system				Criteria for membership			Number of members in cabinet (including governor)	Frequency of cabinet meetings	Open cabinet meetings
	State statute	State constitution	Governor created	Tradition in state	Appointed to specified office (a)	Elected to specified office (a)	Gubernatorial appointment regardless of office			
Alabama*	...	...	...	★	...	...	★	28	Gov.'s discretion (a)	...
Alaska	...	...	★	...	★	...	...	19	Regularly	★ (b)
Arizona	...	...	★	...	★	...	...	25	Gov.'s discretion	...
Arkansas	★	...	...	...	★	...	...	18	Regularly	...
California	★	...	★	...	★	...	★	12	Every two weeks	...
Colorado	...	★	...	...	★	...	...	21	Twice monthly	★
Connecticut	★	...	...	...	★	...	...	24	Gov.'s discretion	...
Delaware	★	...	...	...	★	...	★ (c)	17	Gov.'s discretion	...
Florida	...	★	...	...	...	★	...	7	Every two weeks	★
Georgia	------- (d) -------									
Hawaii	...	...	...	★	★	★	★	24	Gov.'s discretion	...
Idaho*	------- (d) -------									
Illinois	★	...	...	...	★ (e)	...	...	30	Gov.'s discretion (e)	★
Indiana	------- (d) -------									
Iowa	------- (e) -------									
Kansas	...	...	★	...	...	...	★	16	Monthly or as needed	...
Kentucky	★	...	...	...	★	...	...	20	Gov.'s discretion	...
Louisiana	★	★	...	...	★	★	...	13	Monthly	...
Maine	...	...	...	★	...	...	★ (c)	17	Weekly	...
Maryland	★	...	...	...	★ (c)	...	...	20	Weekly	...
Massachusetts	★	...	...	...	★	...	...	12	Twice monthly	...
Michigan	...	...	★	...	★	★	★	18	Gov.'s discretion	...
Minnesota	...	...	★	...	★	...	...	26	Regularly	...
Mississippi*	------- (d) -------									
Missouri	...	★	...	★	★	...	...	17	Gov.'s discretion	...
Montana*	...	...	★	...	★	...	...	24	Monthly	★
Nebraska	...	...	★	...	★	...	...	27	Monthly	...
Nevada	------- (d) -------									
New Hampshire	------- (d) -------									
New Jersey	★	★	...	...	★	...	...	20	Monthly	...
New Mexico*	★	...	...	...	★	...	...	17	Monthly	...
New York	...	...	...	★	★	...	...	7	Gov.'s discretion	...
North Carolina (f)	...	...	★	...	...	...	★	10	Monthly	...
North Dakota	------- (d) -------									
Ohio	★	...	...	...	★	...	★	30	Weekly	...
Oklahoma	★	...	★	...	...	...	★	16 (g)	Gov.'s discretion	...
Oregon	------- (d) -------									
Pennsylvania	★	...	...	...	★ (c)	...	...	19	Weekly	★
Rhode Island	------- (h) -------									
South Carolina	★	...	...	...	...	...	...	13 (i)	Gov.'s discretion	...
South Dakota	...	...	...	...	★	...	★	22	Gov.'s discretion	...
Tennessee	★	...	...	★	★	...	...	29	Gov.'s discretion	★
Texas	------- (d) -------									
Utah	...	...	★	(h)	★	...	...	23	Monthly	★
Vermont	★	...	...	...	★	...	...	6	Gov.'s discretion	...
Virginia*	★	...	...	...	★	...	...	9	Gov.'s discretion	...
Washington	...	...	★	...	★	...	...	26	Twice monthly	...
West Virginia	★	...	...	...	★	...	...	8	Weekly	...
Wisconsin	★	...	...	...	★	...	...	9	Monthly	★
Wyoming (j)	★	...	...	...	★	...	...	14	Gov.'s discretion	★
American Samoa	★	...	...	...	★	...	...	16	Gov.'s discretion	★
Guam	...	...	★	...	★	...	...	79	Monthly	...
No. Mariana Islands	...	★	...	...	★	...	...	16	Gov.'s discretion	★
Puerto Rico	★	★	...	...	★	...	...	17	Weekly	...
U.S. Virgin Islands	...	...	...	...	...	...	★	16	Gov.'s discretion	...

See footnotes at end of table.

STATE CABINET SYSTEMS—Continued

Source: The Council of State Governments' survey, February 1994; except as noted by * where information is from *The Book of the States 1992-93.*

Key:

★ — Yes

. . . — No

(a) Individual is a member by virtue of election or appointment to a cabinet-level position.

(b) Except when in executive session.

(c) With the consent of the Senate.

(d) No formal cabinet system. In Idaho, however, sub-cabinets have been formed, by executive order; the chairmen report to the governor when requested.

(e) Sub-cabinets meet quarterly.

(f) Constitution provides for a Council of State made up of elective state administrative officials, which makes policy decisions for the state while the cabinet acts more in an advisory capacity.

(g) Includes secretary of state; most other cabinet members are heads of state agencies.

(h) In Rhode Island, department heads require advice and consent of the Senate. In Utah, department heads serve as cabinet; meets at discretion of governor.

(i) Five additional members to be phased in through July 1995.

(j) A four-year, phased-in executive reorganization currently being implemented. The first three cabinet-level agencies went on-line in July 1990; seven in 1991; two in 1992.

Table 2.7
THE GOVERNORS: PROVISIONS AND PROCEDURES FOR TRANSITION

State or other jurisdiction	Legislation pertaining to gubernatorial transition	Appropriations available to gov-elect	Gov-elect's participation in state budget for coming fiscal year	Gov-elect to hire staff to assist during transition	State personnel to be made available to assist gov-elect	Office space in buildings to be made available to gov-elect	Acquainting gov-elect staff with office procedures and routine office functions	Transfer of information (files, records, etc.)
Alabama*	. . .	. . .	•	(a)	•	•	•	. . .
Alaska	. . .	★	. . .	. . .	★	•	★	•
Arizona	. . .	. . .	★	. . .	•	•	•	•
Arkansas	★	$ 60,000 (b)	★	★	•	•	. . .	. . .
California	★	450,000	★	★	★	★	•	•
Colorado	★	10,000	. . .	★	★	★	★	★
Connecticut	★	25,000	•	★	•	★	. . .	•
Delaware	★	(c)	(d)	(e)	•	★	•	•
Florida	. . .	250,000	★	•	•	•	•	•
Georgia	★	★	•	•	★	★	•	★
Hawaii	★	100,000	★	★	★	★	★	★
Idaho*	★	15,000	★	★	★	★	★	★
Illinois	★	. . .	★	★ (f)	★	★	★	★
Indiana	★	40,000	★	★	★	★	★	★
Iowa	★ (g)	10,000	★	★	• (h)	•	•	★ (i)
Kansas	★	100,000	★	★	★	★	★	★
Kentucky	★	Unspecified	★	★	★	★	★	★
Louisiana	★	10,000	★	★	★	★	★	•
Maine	★	5,000	★	★	★ (j)	•	★	★
Maryland	★	50,000	★	★	★	★	•	★
Massachusetts	. . .	★	★	•	•	•	•	★
Michigan	★	1,000,000 (k)	•	★	★	•	★	★
Minnesota	★	35,000	★	★	★	★	•	★
Mississippi*	★	30,000	★	★	★	★	★	•
Missouri	★	100,000	★	★	•	★	•	• (l)
Montana*	★	5,000	★	★	★	•	★	★
Nebraska	. . .	50,000	★	★	•	★	★	★
Nevada	★	. . .	★	. . .	•	•	•	• (g)
New Hampshire	★	5,000	★	★	★	★	★	. . .
New Jersey	★	200,000	★	★	★	★	•	★
New Mexico*	★	(m)	★	★	•	★	•	•
New York	. . .	. . .	•	•	•	•	•	•
North Carolina	★	50,000 (n)	• (o)	★	★	★	•	•
North Dakota	. . .	(p)	. . .	. . .	. . .	. . .	. . .	★
Ohio	★	(m)	. . .	★	★	★	. . .	. . .
Oklahoma	★	40,000	★	★	. . .	•	. . .	. . .
Oregon	★	20,000	★	★	★	★	★	★
Pennsylvania	★	100,000	. . .	★	•	. . .	. . .	. . .
Rhode Island	. . .	•	★	• (a)	•	•	•	•
South Carolina	★	50,000 (q)	. . .	★	★	★	★	★
South Dakota	•	10,000 (r)	•	•	•	•	•	•
Tennessee	★	★	•	. . .	. . .	. . .	. . .	•
Texas	. . .	. . .	★	★	•	. . .	. . .	. . .
Utah	. . .	Unspecified	. . .	. . .	. . .	. . .	. . .	. . .
Vermont	. . .	(c)	★ (s)	•	•	•	. . .	(t)
Virginia*	. . .	(c)	. . .	★ (l)	★ (l)	★ (l)	★ (l)	★ (l)
Washington	★	Unspecified	•	•	•	•	•	•
West Virginia	. . .	. . .	. . .	. . .	. . .	. . .	. . .	. . .
Wisconsin	★	Unspecified	★	★	★	★	★	★
Wyoming	. . .	(m)	★	★	•	•	•	•
American Samoa	. . .	Unspecified	★ (u)	•	•	•	•	•
Guam	. . .	(v)	. . .	. . .	. . .	. . .	. . .	. . .
No. Mariana Islands	★	Unspecified	. . .	★	★	★	★	★
Puerto Rico	. . .	250,000 (n)	. . .	•	•	•	•	•
U.S. Virgin Islands	. . .	. . .	. . .	. . .	. . .	. . .	. . .	. . .

See footnotes at end of table.

THE GOVERNORS: PROVISIONS AND PROCEDURES FOR TRANSITION

Source: The Council of State Governments' survey, February 1994; except as noted by * where information is from *The Book of the States 1992-93.*

Key:

. . . — No provisions or procedures

★ — Formal provisions or procedures

• — No formal provisions, occurs informally

(a) Governor usually hires several incoming key staff during transition.

(b) Made available in 1983.

(c) Determined prior to each election by legislature.

(d) Can participate in budget office hearings before taking office.

(e) Subject to appropriations.

(f) On a contractual basis.

(g) Pertains only to funds.

(h) Provided on irregular basis.

(i) Arrangement for transfer of criminal files.

(j) Budget personnel.

(k) Made available in 1990.

(l) Activity is traditional and routine, although there is no specific statutory provision.

(m) Legislature required to make appropriation; no dollar amount stated in legislation. In New Mexico, $50,000 was made available in 1990. In Wyoming, $12,500 for transition following 1994 election.

(n) Inaugural expenses are paid from this amount.

(o) New governor can submit supplemental budget.

(p) If necessary, submit request to State Emergency Commission.

(q) Governor's executive budget recommendation for FY94-95 is to increase this appropriation to $150,000 for transition purposes. This will require legislative approval in the 94-95 Appropriations Bill.

(r) Made available for 1987.

(s) Responsible for the preparation of the budget; staff made available.

(t) Not transferred, but use may be authorized.

(u) Can submit reprogramming or supplemental appropriation measure for current fiscal year.

(v) Appropriations given upon the request of governor-elect.

Table 2.8
IMPEACHMENT PROVISIONS IN THE STATES

State or other jurisdiction	Governor and other state executive and judicial officers subject to impeachment	Legislative body which holds power of impeachment	Vote required for impeachment	Legislative body which conducts impeachment trial	Chief justice presides at impeachment trial (a)	Vote required for conviction	Official who serves as acting governor if governor impeached (b)	Legislature may call special session for impeachment
Alabama	★ (c)	H	...	S	★	...	LG	★
Alaska	★	S	2/3 mbrs.	H	(d)	2/3 mbrs.	SS	★
Arizona	★ (e)	H	maj. mbrs.	S	★	2/3 mbrs.	LG	★
Arkansas	★	H	...	S	★	2/3 mbrs.	LG	...
California	★	H	...	S	...	2/3 mbrs.	LG	★
Colorado	★ (e)	H	maj. mbrs.	S	★	2/3 mbrs.	LG	★
Connecticut	★	H	...	S	★	2/3 mbrs. present	LG	...
Delaware	★	H	2/3 mbrs.	S	★	2/3 mbrs.	LG	...
Florida	★	H	2/3 mbrs.	S	★	2/3 mbrs. present	LG	★
Georgia	★	H	...	S	...	2/3 mbrs. present	...	★
Hawaii	★ (f)	H	...	S	★	2/3 mbrs.	LG	★
Idaho	★	H	...	S	★	2/3 mbrs.	LG	...
Illinois	★	H	maj. mbrs.	S	★	2/3 mbrs.	LG	★
Indiana	★	H	...	S	...	2/3 mbrs.	...	...
Iowa	★	H	...	S	...	2/3 mbrs. present	LG	...
Kansas	★	H	...	S	...	2/3 mbrs.	...	...
Kentucky	★	H	...	S	...	2/3 mbrs. present	...	...
Louisiana	★	H	...	S	...	2/3 mbrs.	...	★
Maine	★	H	...	S	...	2/3 mbrs. present	...	★
Maryland	★	H	maj. mbrs.	S	...	2/3 mbrs.	...	...
Massachusetts	★	H	...	S (g)	...	...	...	★
Michigan	★	H	maj. mbrs.	S	★	2/3 mbrs.	LG	...
Minnesota	★	H	maj. mbrs.	S	...	2/3 mbrs. present	...	...
Mississippi	★	H	2/3 mbrs. present	S	★	2/3 mbrs. present	...	★
Missouri	★	H	...	(h)	(h)	(h)	LG	...
Montana	★	H	2/3 mbrs.	S	...	2/3 mbrs.	...	★
Nebraska	★ (e)	S (i)	maj. mbrs.	(j)	(j)	(j)	...	★
Nevada	★ (e)	H	maj. mbrs.	S	★	2/3 mbrs.	LG	...
New Hampshire	★ (k)	H	...	S	★	...	...	...
New Jersey	★	H	maj. mbrs.	S	★	2/3 mbrs.	...	★
New Mexico	★	H	maj. mbrs.	S	★	2/3 mbrs.	LG	★
New York	★	H	maj. mbrs.	(l)	...	2/3 mbrs. present	LG	★
North Carolina	★ (e)	H	...	S	★	2/3 mbrs. present	LG	★
North Dakota	★	H	maj. mbrs.	S	★	2/3 mbrs.	LG	...
Ohio	★ (c)	H	maj. mbrs.	S	...	2/3 mbrs.	...	★
Oklahoma	★ (c)	H	...	S	★	2/3 mbrs. present	LG	★
Oregon	...	—(m)—		(m)	(m)	...	...	...
Pennsylvania	★	H	(n)	S	...	2/3 mbrs. present	LG	...
Rhode Island	★	H	2/3 mbrs.	S	★	2/3 mbrs.	LG	...
South Carolina	★	H	...	S	★	2/3 mbrs.	...	...
South Dakota	★ (e)	H	maj. mbrs.	S	★	2/3 mbrs.	LG	...
Tennessee	★	H	...	S	★	2/3 mbrs. (o)	...	★
Texas	★ (e)	H	2/3 mbrs.	S	...	2/3 mbrs. present	LG	...
Utah	★	H	2/3 mbrs.	S	★	2/3 mbrs.	LG	...
Vermont	★	H	2/3 mbrs.	S	...	2/3 mbrs. present	...	...

See footnotes at end of table.

IMPEACHMENT PROVISIONS IN THE STATES—Continued

State or other jurisdiction	Governor and other state executive and judicial officers subject to impeachment	Legislative body which holds power of impeachment	Vote required for impeachment	Legislative body which conducts impeachment trial (a)	Chief justice presides at impeachment trial (a)	Vote required for conviction	Official who serves as acting governor if governor impeached (b)	Legislature may call special session for impeachment
Virginia	★	H	...	S	...	2/3 mbrs. present	...	★
Washington	★ (e)	H	maj. mbrs.	S	★	2/3 mbrs.	...	★
West Virginia	★	H	...	S	★	2/3 mbrs.	LG	★
Wisconsin	★	H	maj. mbrs.	S	...	2/3 mbrs. present	LG	...
Wyoming	★ (e)	H	maj. mbrs.	S	★	2/3 mbrs.	SS	...
Dist. of Columbia	———(p)———							
American Samoa	(q)	H	2/3 mbrs.	S	★	2/3 mbrs.	...	...
Guam	———(p)———							
No. Mariana Islands	★	H	2/3 mbrs.	S	...	2/3 mbrs.	...	...
Puerto Rico	(r)	H	2/3 mbrs.	S	★	3/4 mbrs.	...	★
U.S. Virgin Islands	———(p)———							

Source: State constitutions and statutes.

Note: The information in this table is based on a literal reading of the state constitutions and statutes. For information on other methods for removing state officials, see Table 4.5, "Methods for Removal of Judges and Filling of Vacancies," and Table 5.24, "State Recall Provisions: Applicability to State Officials and Petition Circulation."

Key:
★ — Yes; provision for
... — Not specified, or no provision for
H — House or Assembly (lower chamber)
S — Senate
LG — Lieutenant governor
PS — President or speaker of the Senate
SS — Secretary of state

(a) Presiding justice of state court of last resort. In many states, provision indicates that chief justice presides only on occasion of impeachment of governor.
(b) For provisions on official next in line on succession if governor is convicted and removed from office, refer to Table 2.1, "The Governors."
(c) Includes justices of Supreme Court. Other judicial officers not subject to impeachment.
(d) A. Supreme Court justice designated by the court.
(e) With exception of certain judicial officers. In Arizona, Washington, and Wyoming—justices of courts not of record. In Colorado—county judges and justices of the peace. In Nevada and Utah— justices of the peace. In North Dakota and South Dakota—county judges, justices of the peace, and police magistrates.
(f) Governor, lieutenant governor, and any appointive officer for whose removal the consent of the Senate is required.
(g) House elects three members to prosecute impeachment.
(h) All impeachments are tried before the state Supreme Court, except that the governor or a member of the Supreme Court is tried by a special commission of seven eminent jurists to be elected by the Senate. A vote of 5/7 of the court of special commission is necessary to convict.
(i) Unicameral legislature; members use the title "senator."
(j) Court of impeachment is composed of chief justice and all district court judges in the state. A vote of 2/3 of the court is necessary to convict.
(k) All state officers while in office and for two years thereafter.
(l) Court for trial of impeachment composed of president of the Senate, senators (or major part of them), and judges of Court of Appeals (or major part of them).
(m) No provision for impeachment. Public officers may be tried for incompetency, corruption, malfeasance, or delinquency in office in same manner as criminal offenses.
(n) Vote of 2/3 members required for an impeachment of the governor.
(o) Vote of 2/3 of members sworn to try the officer impeached.
(p) Removal of elected officials by recall procedure only.
(q) Governor, lieutenant governor.
(r) Governor and Supreme Court justices.

The Executive Branch: Organization and Issues, 1992-93

The number of multiple executives remains high as state elected officials garner enough support to keep their offices intact.

by Thad L. Beyle

Separately Elected Officials

The states continue to hold to the concept of the multiple executive in terms of how many statewide elected officials there are. In 1992, there were 304 separately elected executive branch officials covering 12 major offices in the states. This compares to 306 elected officials in 1972. There were some shifts for certain statewide elective offices; however, as in 1992, there were five more elected comptrollers and four fewer elected superintendents of public instruction as well as three fewer elected commissioners of public utilities than in 1972.[1] But for a period in which there was much state governmental reform, including major reorganizations, the stability of the number of separately elected officials is noteworthy.[2]

This suggests that each office, as well as each incumbent in that office, has continuing clientele and sufficient support so that proposals to reduce the number of separately elected officials do not fare well. Further, these incumbents also have a political death grip on that office. For example, in the last six statewide elections for the 10 council of state offices in North Carolina (1972-92), only one of the 39 incumbents seeking re-election was beaten. These are lifetime offices.[3]

Only Maine, New Hampshire and New Jersey have a single statewide elected official, the governor. North Dakota has the most (12), followed by Georgia, North Carolina, Oklahoma, South Carolina and Washington, with more than nine each. Southern states tend to have more elected officials than states in other parts of the country.[4]

Lieutenant Governors

The relationship between lieutenant governors and governors continues to be of interest in the states. It begins when they are nominated and elected.[5] In 19 states, these candidates are nominated and elected separately. There has been, however, a trend toward joint nomination and joint election of these two officials. Since the 1950s, when only New York had a joint election, the number of states with joint elections has increased to 24.[6] In nine states, candidates for these offices run as a team in the primary or convention and then in the general election.[7] In three other states, after governors are selected in a party primary, a party convention selects the lieutenant governors.[8] In 12 other states, candidates for the two offices run as a team in the general election only.[9] When the lieutenant governor and governor are elected as a team, however, the lieutenant governor is less powerful and the office is "less often a launching pad for a race for governor."[10]

Several states have seen some difficult situations develop between the incumbents of the two offices. Arkansas Governor Jim Guy Tucker has discovered the problems of leaving the state and having an acting governor take action. After succeeding to the office made vacant by the election of Bill Clinton to the presidency, Tucker's visit to the Washington inaugural event was marred by the actions of the acting governor, Senate President Pro Tem Jerry Jewell (D) who granted two pardons and

---

Thad L. Beyle is a professor of political science, The University of North Carolina at Chapel Hill.

executive clemency to two prison inmates.[11] Then while Tucker was in Minnesota on a medical visit, Lt. Governor Mike Huckabee (R) signed a proclamation for a Christian Heritage Week after Tucker declined to do so earlier.[12]

The serious illness of Pennsylvania Governor Robert Casey (D) placed Lt. Governor Mark Singel in the acting governor role for an extended period of time in 1993. The uncertainty of Casey's health and recovery made for an uncertain tenure for Singel whose vote in the state Senate was also needed to ensure Democratic control over the body.[13]

Executive Branch Reorganization[14]

State government reorganization continues to be a suggested remedy to some of the problems facing a state. Born of the good government movement in the early 20th century, reorganization in the states is an intensely political issue to those with a direct interest in state government. The rationale for such actions range from enhancing the power of the governor, to the need to bring a range of agencies into a more rational structure, and, obviously, for economy and efficiency reasons.

There are four basic options when considering reorganization: (1) No reorganization. This is often the preferred option as it does not stir up unnecessary politics and indicates that the organizational structure is basically satisfactory or can be worked with. (2) Partial reorganization, where a few agencies' units are targeted for change into new departments, consolidated into existing departments or abolished as outdated. This often flows from a governor's specific agenda or a realization that the state is ill-structured for a particular situation or responsibility. (3) Reorganization affecting elected executive officials, where the method of separately electing other executive officials is curtailed in favor of providing the governor with more power. An ongoing debate in many states, the fact is that such reorganizations occur only occasionally for "typical" elected branch officials as noted earlier. (4) Comprehensive reorganization, where an attempt is made to completely overhaul the executive branch in order to bring it up-to-date and to provide the governor with more control

and power over it. Of the more than 170 comprehensive efforts undertaken, implementation has been successful in only one-third of them. These efforts have been successful in a series of four waves over the 20th century, with about half of the states undertaking such endeavors since the mid-1960s. States are currently between waves.[15]

While different goals predominate at different times in these reorganizations, the most common outcome in recent decades is to develop a form of the cabinet system. In this model, the number of agencies and departments are usually reduced, but more importantly agency heads are appointed by and responsible to the governor. In a 1992 survey, 38 states reported having some variation of cabinet system. The cabinet system model is the midpoint between two extreme options. At one end is the secretary model in which the regrouping of agencies is much more severe, often down to just five or so units coordinated by a super-secretary-coordinator appointed by the governor. At the other end is the traditional model in which there may be some, or even considerable, reduction in the number of agencies but no real change in who controls them.[16]

In the past two years there has been some activity to reform or reorganize state governments. The most comprehensive attempt, and startling to some observers, were the changes in South Carolina, which began the move from legislative government to executive government.[17] Following the report of the South Carolina Commission on Government Restructuring,[18] the governor and legislature abolished 75 state boards, folding them into 17 executive agencies. The governor gained control over 33 percent of the executive budget, including most of the important agencies, and was given authority to hire and fire the heads of 11 major state agencies. Much of state government is still outside the governor's control as 50 state governing boards remain, two-thirds of the state budget is out of the governor's reach (such as in education, the environment, law enforcement and road building), and some agency heads are appointed by other sources.[19] Still, it was a major step forward for a state with such a low ranking on gubernatorial powers.[20]

Performance-based Governance

In the 1990s, the states began to operate under the rubrics of reinventing government, performance-based governance, and total quality management. The National Governors' Association sponsored a year-long effort on this subject with separate task forces exploring and explaining performance-based governance, human service consolidation and coordination, privatization of government services and assets, and management systems reform.[21]

States have been exploring and executing changes in their organizational structures as well as in their management systems. These states have been most often driven by a difficult financial situation, such as Arizona with its Long-Term Improved Management Task Force (SLIM), Delaware's Maximizing Efficiency of Service Quality Program (MAX), Hawaii's Advisory Committee on Excellence (ACE), Nevada's Project Streamline, New Jersey's Management Review Commission and Washington's Cost Cutting and Efficiency Commission.[22] Other states exploring reorganization include California,[23] Colorado,[24] Florida,[25] Kentucky,[26] Oregon,[27] South Carolina,[28] South Dakota,[29] Tennessee,[30] Texas[31] and Wisconsin.[32] The most recent addition to this list is the report of the Kentucky Commission on Quality Government and Efficiency, which the governor partially implemented by executive order.[33]

Several states focused their attention on improving those who work in state government rather than just on structures and processes. Among them are Delaware, Hawaii, Kentucky, Oklahoma, Virginia[34] and New York.[35]

Another popular answer to a state's organizational and management problems is to privatize some of a state government's activities. Governor William Weld of Massachusetts has done this in the areas of health and mental health.[36] Steps also are being taken in this direction in Illinois.

As is so often the case in many of the individual states noted above, the initial action is to set up a blue ribbon committee or panel to investigate the possible need, and then build the case and blueprint for such action in a report. This report then is used as the basis to sell both the need for reform and the reforms. This "Blue-Ribbon" approach was used again in Illinois as the governor created a Private Enterprise Review and Advisory Board (PER-AB) to report in 1993, which mirrored previous efforts in 1917, 1950, 1965 and in 1976.

While some of these efforts work, quite a few do not. Why don't they work? From the Illinois perspective, Jim Nowlan argues that such endeavors are "extremely costly — in time, effort, political credits and opportunity costs — because of opposition that would be aroused among interest groups, bureaucrats and legislative patrons of agencies."[37]

Gender Equity

Over the past decade, women have become more a part of state government. While not yet achieving gender equity, an increasing number of women are serving in executive branch positions. As of 1994, three of the 50 governors were women (6 percent), 11 of the 42 lieutenant governors were women (26 percent) and 58 of the other 232 elected executive branch officials were women (22 percent).[38] A recent study of state government administrators finds that rather than breaking through the glass ceiling, which has stopped their upward mobility in the past, women are circumventing it and making gains in specific types of agencies. They have made most significant gains in the areas of aging, libraries, public assistance and state treasurers. Women also have made some gains in the areas of employment security, mental health, personnel, secretaries of state and social services.[39]

Ethics

The problems of ensuring ethical behavior among state officials continue to exist. Changes in what is now called into question as being ethical or unethical are part of the problem, as is aggressive federal law enforcement and media oversight. But there are also those who cross the line between ethical and unethical behavior.

State responses to the ethics issues are usually related to major ethical problems and situations. For example, in the three years around the Nixon Watergate episode (1973-75), 28 state ethics agencies, committees and commissions were created. In the four years in which federal officials were investigating state officials in several states (1989-92), 12 similar agencies, committees and commissions were created. In between these two peak periods, 19 such units were created.[40]

But creating ethics organizations is not all the states have been doing in recent years. Some of the other state legislation includes limits on gifts and honoraria (eight states), financial disclosure requirements (five states), restrictions on post state government employment to curb the revolving door effect (two states), ethics education efforts for legislators and lobbyists (two states), anti-nepotism laws (two states) and bans on political contributions during the legislative session (one state).[41]

Yet, ethical problems still persist. California's top public school official, Superintendent Bill Honig, was removed from office after being found guilty of a felony.[42] Former Missouri Attorney General William Webster pleaded guilty to federal charges of conspiracy and misapplication of state funds while in office.[43] The former head of the West Virginia state lottery was convicted of mail fraud and insider trading.[44] The chief justice of the Rhode Island Supreme Court, Thomas Fay, resigned a day after being charged with violating ethics laws.[45] The ethical problems of the governors were discussed earlier in "The Governors, 1992-93" on pages 36-49 of this volume.

In two unique situations, the Rhode Island Ethics Commission found that the many scandals it had to deal with had depleted its budget, and it was facing a $50 million deficit.[46] In South Carolina, ethics legislation was causing problems for academics as public employees "may not accept anything of value related to performance of . . . official duties."[47]

Footnotes

[1] Keon S. Chi, "State Executive Branch Reorganization: Options for the Future," *State Trends & Forecasts*, 1:1 (The Council of State Governments, December 1992), 8.

[2] Keon S. Chi, "Trends in Executive Reorganization," *Spectrum: The Journal of State Government*, 65:2 (The Council of State Governments, April-June 1992), 37.

[3] Thad Beyle, "North Carolina's Majority Party," *North Carolina DataNet*, No. 4 (May 1994). Those 21 incumbents who did not run for re-election were either constitutionally restricted to a single term, retired from office or for another office.

[4] Chi, "Trends in Executive Reorganization," 37.

[5] There is no lieutenant governor's office in Arizona, Maine, New Hampshire, New Jersey, Oregon, West Virginia and Wyoming.

[6] Laura M. Zaremba, "Governor and Lieutenant Governor On Same Ballot," *First Reading*, 9:1 (January 1994), 1,7, reprinted in *Comparative State Politics*, 15:1 (February 1994), 39-40.

[7] Florida, Kansas, Kentucky, Maryland, Minnesota, Montana, North Dakota and Ohio allow their candidates to be jointly nominated by party primary, while in Utah a party convention nominates both candidates jointly.

[8] Connecticut, Indiana and Michigan.

[9] Alaska, Colorado, Hawaii, Illinois, Iowa, Massachusetts, Nebraska, New Mexico, New York, Pennsylvania, South Dakota and Wisconsin.

[10] Malcolm Jewell, "Amendment Changes Elections," *Kentucky Journal*, 6:1 (March 1993), 16.

[11] "Just Never Leave Home," *The Hotline*, 7:93 (February 4, 1994), 2.

[12] "Arkansas: When the Gov's Away, the LG Will Play," *The Hotline*, ibid., 16.

[13] "Pennsylvania: GOP Takes Back Control of the State Senate," *The Hotline*, 7:119 (March 16, 1994), 18.

[14] Much of the following is taken from Keon S. Chi, "State Executive Branch Reorganization: Options for the Future," *State Trends & Forecasts*, 1:1 (The Council of State Governments, December 1992).

[15] Chi, "State Executive Branch Reorganization," 11-14.

[16] Ibid., 12.

[17] Alan Ehrenhalt, "Reinventing Government In the Unlikeliest Place," *Governing*, 6:11 (August 1993), 7-8.

[18] For a thorough review of the reorganization movement in the states see: States Reorganization Commission, "On Reorganization: An Overview of Theory, Practice and the South Carolina Experience," (Columbia: South Carolina General Assembly, April 1991).

[19] Cindi Ross Scoppe, "Win some, lose some" and "Piecing together a new government" in a Special Section, "Restructuring: The players and Politics," *The State* (Columbia), January 10 - July 1, 1993, 12.

[20] Ehrenhalt, 7.

[21] Reports of the State Management Task Force Strategy Groups, *An Action Agenda to Redesign State Government*, (Washington, D.C.: National Governors' Association, 1993).

[22] Lee Seglum, "Turning State Street Upside Down," *State Legislatures*, 18:7 (June 1992), 21-25.

[23] "Wilson creates Quality Task Force," *Governors' Bulletin*, 27:17 (August 30, 1993), 6.

[24] "Redesigning Government," *Governors' Bulletin*, 27:14 (July 19, 1993), 5.

[25] Bill Moss, "Government Reform, Florida-Style," *State Legislatures*, 18:7 (July 1992), 27-30, Lawton Chiles, "State Smarts," *State Government News*, 35:5 (May 1992), 14-15, and Barton Wechsler, "Florida's Civil Service Reform," *Spectrum: The Journal of State Government*, 66:1 (Winter 1993), 45-51.

[26] "Managing for Results," *State Government News*, 35:11 (November 1992), 44.

[27] Lanny Proffer, "Benchmarks to a Better Oregon," *State Legislatures*, 18:7 (July 1992), 33-35, "Managing for Results," *State Government News*, 35:11 (November 1992), 44, and "Redesigning Government," *Governors' Bulletin*, 27:14 (July 19, 1993), 5.

[28] "Managing for Results."

[29] "State Commissions to Help Cut Waste," *Governors' Bulletin*, 27:23 (November 22, 1993), 4.

[30] "Quality Improvement in Tennessee Government," *State Legislatures*, 18:8 (August 1992, 12.

[31] Dave McNeely, "The BIG Audit," *State Legislatures*, 19:6 (June 1993), 14-18.

[32] "State Commissions to Help Cut Waste," *Governors' Bulletin*, 27:23 (November 22, 1993), 4.

[33] "Reforms to Save Kentucky $900 Million," *Governors' Bulletin*, 28:1 (January 10, 1994), 6.

[34] Julie Olberding, "Marks of Quality," *State Government News*, 35:12 (December 1992), 13, 20.

[35] "Managing for Results."

[36] "Redesigning Government."

[37] Jackson Williams, "Another Blue-ribbon Panel Studies Illinois State Government," *Comparative State Politics*, 14:4 (September 1993), 27.

[38] "Where Women Serve Today," *State Legislatures*, 20:1 (January 1994), 31. Data are from the Center for the American Women and Politics, Eagleton Institute, Rutgers University.

[39] Deil S. Wright and Angela M. Bullard, "Circumventing the Glass Ceiling: Women Executives in American State Governments," *Public Administration Review*, 53:3 (May/June 1993), 189-202.

[40] "Peak years in the creation of state ethics agencies, committees and commissions," *State Government News*, 37:2 (February 1994), 13.

[41] "State Stats: Ethics Legislation (1991-92)," *Spectrum: The Journal of State Government*, 66:1 (Winter 1993), 58-59.

[42] "Calif. school chief gets probation," *USA Today* (February 25, 1993).

[43] Associated Press, "Ex-Mo. attorney general pleads guilty," *Durham Herald Sun* (June 3, 1993).

[44] "West Virginia," *USA Today* (September 30, 1993).

[45] Associated Press, "R.I. justice responds to ethics charge," *Durham Herald Sun* (August 26, 1993).

[46] "Rhode Island Ethics Commission is overspending its budget," *State Legislatures*, 18:4 (April 1992), 11.

[47] "South Carolina ethics law threatens scholars subsidies," *State Legislatures*, 18:4 (April 1992), 11.

Table 2.9
CONSTITUTIONAL AND STATUTORY PROVISIONS FOR LENGTH AND NUMBER OF TERMS OF ELECTED STATE OFFICIALS

State or other jurisdiction	Governor	Lt. governor	Secretary of state	Attorney general	Treasurer	Auditor	Comptroller	Education	Agriculture	Labor	Insurance	Other
Alabama	4/2	4/2	4/2	4/2	4/2	4/2	...	...	4/2 (a)	...	...	Bd. of Education—4/-; Public Service Comm.—4/-
Alaska	4/2 (b)	4/-	(c)	...	(d)	...	...	...	...	...	...	
Arizona	4/2	(e)	4/2	4/2	4/2	...	...	4/2	...	...	...	Corporation Comm.—6/-; Mine inspector—2/-
Arkansas	4/2	4/2	4/2	4/2	4/2	4/2	(f)	...	...	...	...	Land Cmsr.—4/2
California	4/2	4/2	4/2	4/2	4/2	...	4/2	4/2	...	...	4/-	Bd. of Equalization—4/-
Colorado	4/2	4/2	4/2	4/2	4/2	...	...	...	...	...	...	Regents of Univ. of Colo.—6/-; Bd. of Education—6/-
Connecticut	4/-	4/-	4/-	4/-	4/-	...	4/-	...	...	...	4/-	
Delaware	4/2 (g)	4/-	...	4/-	4/-	4/-	...	...	...	...	4/-	
Florida	4/(h)	4/(h)	4/(h)	4/(h)	4/(h,i)	...	4/(h)	4/(h)	4/(h)	...	(i)	
Georgia	4/2 (b)	4/-	4/-	4/-	(f)	...	(j)	4/-	4/-	4/-	4/- (j)	Public Service Comm.—6/-
Hawaii	4/2	4/2	(c)	...	(f)	...	(k)	4/-	...	...	...	
Idaho	4/-	4/-	4/-	4/-	4/-	4/-	(k)	4/-	...	...	...	
Illinois	4/-	4/-	4/-	4/-	4/-	...	4/-	...	...	...	...	Bd. of Trustees, Univ. of Ill.—6/-
Indiana	4/(l)	4/-	4/(l)	4/-	4/(l)	4/(l)	(k)	4/-	(c)	...	...	
Iowa	4/-	4/-	4/-	4/-	4/-	4/-	(f)	...	4/-	...	...	
Kansas	4/2	4/2	4/-	4/-	4/-	...	...	...	4/2	...	4/-	Bd. of Education—4/-
Kentucky	4/2	4/2	4/2	4/2	4/2	4/2	(f)	...	4/2	...	4/-	Railroad Comm.—4/-
Louisiana	4/2	4/-	4/-	4/-	4/-	...	(m)	...	4/-	...	4/-	Bd. of Education—4/-; Elections Cmsr.—4/-
Maine	4/2	(n)	...	...	...	...	...	...	...	...	...	
Maryland	4/2 (b)	4/-	...	4/-	...	...	4/-	...	...	...	...	
Massachusetts	4/-	4/-	4/-	4/-	4/-	4/-	..	...	...	...	...	Exec. Council—2/-; Univ. Regents—8/-;
Michigan	4/2	4/2	4/2	4/2	...	...	(f)	...	...	...	...	Bd. of Education—8/-
Minnesota	4/-	4/-	4/-	4/-	4/-	4/-	(f)	...	...	...	(o)	
Mississippi	4/2	4/2	4/-	4/-	4/-	4/-	(f)	...	4/-	...	4/-	
Missouri	4/2 (g)	4/-	4/-	4/-	4/2 (g)	4/-	...	...	...	...	...	
Montana	4/(p)	4/(p)	4/(p)	4/(p)	...	4/(p)	(m)	4/(p)	...	...	...	
Nebraska	4/2 (b)	4/2 (b)	4/2 (b)	4/2 (b)	4/2	4/2 (b)	...	...	...	...	...	Regents of Univ. of Neb.—6/2 (b); Bd. of Education—4/2 (b); Public Service Comm.—6/2 (b)
Nevada	4/2	4/-	4/-	4/-	4/-	...	4/-	...	...	...	...	Bd. of Regents—6/-; Bd. of Education—4/3
New Hampshire	2/-	(n)	...	...	...	...	...	...	...	...	...	Exec. Council—2/-
New Jersey	4/2 (b)	(n)	...	...	...	...	(f)	...	...	...	...	
New Mexico	4/2 (b)	4/2 (b)	4/2 (b)	4/2 (b)	4/2 (b)	4/2 (b)	(q)	...	...	...	...	Cmsr. of Public Lands—4/2 (b); Bd. of Education—4/-; Corporation Comm.—6/-
New York	4/-	4/-	...	4/-	...	(d)	4/-	...	...	...	...	
North Carolina	4/2	4/2	4/-	4/-	4/-	4/-	...	4/-	4/-	4/-	4/-	
North Dakota	4/-	4/-	4/-	4/-	4/2	4/-	...	4/-	4/- (r)	4/- (r)	4/-	Public Service Comm.—6/-; Tax Cmsr.—4/-
Ohio	4/2 (g)	4/2 (g)	4/2 (g)	4/2 (g)	4/2 (g)	4/2 (g)	(q)	...	...	...	...	Bd. of Education—6/-
Oklahoma	4/2	4/U	...	4/U	4/U	4/U	...	4/U	...	4/-	4/-	Corporation Comm.—6/-
Oregon	4/2	(e)	4/2	4/2	4/2	...	(q)	4/2	...	4/2	...	
Pennsylvania	4/2	4/2	...	4/2	4/2 (s)	4/2	...	...	...	...	...	
Rhode Island	2/- (t)	2/- (t)	2/- (t)	2/- (t)	2/- (t)	...	...	...	...	...	...	
South Carolina	4/2	4/-	4/-	4/-	4/-	...	4/-	4/-	4/-	...	...	Adjutant General—4/-

LENGTH AND NUMBER OF TERMS—Continued

State or other jurisdiction	Governor	Lt. governor	Secretary of state	Attorney general	Treasurer	Auditor	Comptroller	Education	Agriculture	Labor	Insurance	Other
South Dakota	4/2	4/2	4/2	4/2	4/2	4/2	(k)	...	...	...	...	Cmsr. of School & Public Lands—4/-; Public Utilities Comm.—6/-
Tennessee	4/2	(n)	...	...	...	(d)	...	...	...	...	...	Public Service Comm.—6/-
Texas..............	4/-	4/-	...	4/-	4/-	...	4/-	...	4/-	...	...	Bd. of Education—4/-; Cmsr. of General Land Off.—4/-; Railroad Comm.—6/-
Utah	4/3 (u)	4/3 (u)	(c)	4/3 (u)	4/3 (u)	4/3 (u)	(f)	...	...	...	...	Bd. of Education—4/-
Vermont	2/-	2/-	2/-	2/-	2/-	2/-	(f)	...	...	...	...	
Virginia...........	4/0	4/U	...	4/U	...	...	...	...	...	...	...	
Washington	4/(v)	4/(v)	4/-	4/-	4/-	4/-	(q)	4/-	...	...	4/-	Cmsr. of Public Lands—4/-
West Virginia	4/2 (w)	(n)	4/-	4/-	4/-	4/-	(k)	...	4/-	...	...	
Wisconsin..........	4/-	4/-	4/-	4/-	4/-	...	(f)	4/-	...	...	...	
Wyoming	4/(p)	(e)	4/(p)	...	4/(p)	4/(p)	(k)	4/(p)	...	...	...	
Dist. of Columbia....	4/- (x)		...	...	...	...	...	...		...	...	Chmn. of Council of Dist. of Col.—4/U
American Samoa ...	4/2 (y)	4/2	(c)	...	...	...	(q)	...	...	...	...	
Guam	4/2 (b)	4/2	(c)	...	...	...	(z)	...	...	...	(aa)	
No. Mariana Islands..	4/2 (g)	4/2		...	...	...	(q)	...	(bb)	...	(o)	
Puerto Rico	4/-	(e)	...	...	...	...	...	...	...	...	...	
U.S. Virgin Islands ...	4/2 (b)	4/2	(c)	...	(f)	...	(f)	...	...	...	(c)	

Note: First entry in a column refers to number of years per term. Entry following the slash refers to the maximum number of consecutive terms allowed. Blank cells indicate no specific administrative official performs function. Footnotes specify if a position's functions are performed by an appointed official under a different title. This table reflects a literal reading of the state constitutions and statutes.

Key:

- — No provision specifying number of terms allowed

0 — Provision specifying officeholder may not succeed self

U — Provision specifying individual may hold office for an unlimited number of terms

... — Position is appointed or elected by governmental entity (not chosen by electorate)

(a) Commissioner of agriculture and industries.
(b) After two consecutive terms, must wait four years before being eligible again.
(c) Lieutenant governor performs function.
(d) Comptroller performs function.
(e) Secretary of state is next in line of succession to the governorship.
(f) Finance administrator performs function.
(g) Absolute two-term limitation, but not necessarily consecutive.
(h) Eligible for eight consecutive years, beginning January 1995.
(i) State treasurer also serves as insurance commissioner.
(j) Insurance commissioner also serves as comptroller general.
(k) State auditor performs function.
(l) Eligible for eight out of 12 years.

(m) Head of administration performs function.
(n) President or speaker of the Senate is next in line of succession to the governorship. In Tennessee, speaker of the Senate has the statutory title "lieutenant governor."
(o) Commerce administrator performs function.
(p) Eligible for eight out of 16 years.
(q) State treasurer performs function.
(r) Constitution provides for a secretary of agriculture and labor. However, the legislature was given constitutional authority to provide for (and has provided for) a department of labor distinct from agriculture, and a commissioner of labor distinct from the commissioner of agriculture.
(s) Treasurer must wait four years before being eligible to the office of auditor general.
(t) Beginning January 1995, the term length will increase to four years.
(u) Eligible for 12 consecutive years beginning January 1995.
(v) Eligible for eight out of 14.
(w) A person who has been elected or who has served as governor during all or any part of two consecutive terms shall be eligible for the office of governor during any part of the term immediately following the second of the two consecutive terms.
(x) Mayor.
(y) Limit is statutory.
(z) General services administrator performs function.
(aa) Taxation administrator performs function.
(bb) Natural resources administrator performs function.

Table 2.10
SELECTED STATE ADMINISTRATIVE OFFICIALS: METHODS OF SELECTION

State	Governor	Lieutenant governor	Secretary of state	Attorney general	Treasurer	Adjutant general	Administration	Agriculture	Banking	Budget
Alabama	CE	CE	CE	CE	CE	GS	(a-16)	CE	GS	CS
Alaska	CE	CE	(a-1)	GB	(a-9)	GB	GB	A	A	(c)
Arizona	CE	(a-2)	CE	CE	CE	G	GS	GS	GS	G
Arkansas	CE	CE	CE	CE	CE	GS	(a-15)	B	BG	AG
California	CE	CE	CE	CE	CE	GS	(d)	GS	GS	(a-15)
Colorado	CE	CE	CE	CE	CE	GS	GS	GS	CS	G
Connecticut	CE	CE	CE	CE	CE	GE	GE	GE	GE	CS
Delaware	CE	CE	GS	CE	CE	GS	GS	GS	G	GS
Florida	CE	CE	CE	CE	CE	G	A	CE	(a-9)	G
Georgia	CE	CE	CE	CE	B	G	GS	CE	GS	G
Hawaii	CE	CE	(a-1)	GS	(a-6)	GS	(a-9)	GS	AG	GS
Idaho	CE	CE	CE	CE	CE	G	G	G	G	(a-15)
Illinois	CE	CE	CE	CE	CE	GS	GS	GS	GS	G
Indiana	CE	CE	CE	SE	CE	G	G	LG	G	G
Iowa	CE	CE	CE	CE	CE	GS	(a-16)	SE	GS	GS
Kansas	CE	CE	CE	CE	SE	GS	GS	G	GS	G
Kentucky	CE	CE	CE	CE	CE	G	AG	CE	AG	G
Louisiana	CE	CE	CE	CE	CE	GS	G	CE	GS	CS
Maine	CE	(t)	CL	CL	CL	G	GLS	GLS	ALS	A
Maryland	CE	CE	GS	CE	CL	G	(a-16)	GS	AG	GS
Massachusetts	CE	CE	CE	CE	CE	GLS	GLS	B	B	B
Michigan	CE	CE	CE	CE	GS	GS	(a-6)	B	GS	GS
Minnesota	CE	CE	CE	CE	CE	G	GS	GS	A	(a-15)
Mississippi	CE	CE	CE	CE	CE	GS	A	SE	G	(a-15)
Missouri	CE	CE	CE	CE	CE	G	GS	GS	AGS	A
Montana	CE	CE	SE	SE	AGS	AGS	(a-16)	AGS	A	AGS
Nebraska	CE	CE	CE	CE	CE	GS	GS	GS	GS	A
Nevada	CE	CE	CE	CE	CE	G	G	BA	A	(a-5)
New Hampshire	CE	(t)	CL	GC	CL	GC	GC	GC	GC	AGC
New Jersey	CE	(t)	GS	GS	GS	GS	(a-16)	BG	GS	GS
New Mexico	CE	CE	CE	CE	CE	G	(a-16)	N.A.	AG	AG
New York	CE	CE	GS	CE	(nn)	G	(a-16)	GS	GS	G
North Carolina	CE	CE	SE	SE	SE	G	G	SE	G	G
North Dakota	CE	CE	CE	CE	CE	G	G	CE	G	(pp)
Ohio	CE	CE	CE	CE	CE	G	G	G	G	G
Oklahoma	CE	CE	GS	CE	CE	GS	G	GS	GS	(a-15)
Oregon	CE	(a-2)	CE	SE	CE	G	GS	GS	A	A
Pennsylvania	CE	CE	GS	CE	CE	GS	G	GS	GS	G
Rhode Island	CE	CE	CE	CE	CE	G	G	AGS	AGS	AGS
South Carolina	CE	CE	CE	CE	CE	CE	A	CE	(a-4)	A
South Dakota	CE	CE	CE	CE	CE	G	G	G	A	(a-15)
Tennessee	CE	(p)	CL	CT	CL	G	(a-15)	G	G	A
Texas	CE	CE	GS	CE	CE	GS	(a-16)	SE	BS	A
Utah	CE	CE	(a-1)	CE	CE	GS	GS	GS	G	G
Vermont	CE	CE	CE	SE	CE	SE	GS	GS	GS	(a-15)
Virginia	CE	CE	GB	CE	GB	GB	GB	GB	B	GB
Washington	CE	CE	CE	CE	CE	GS	GS	GS	GS	(a-15)
West Virginia	CE	(p)	CE	CE	CE	GS	GS	CE	GS	CS
Wisconsin	CE	CE	CE	CE	CE	G	GS	B	GS	A
Wyoming	CE	(a-2)	CE	G	CE	G	GS	GS	A	A

Source: The Council of State Governments' survey of state personnel agencies, January 1994.

Note: The chief administrative officials responsible for each function were determined from information given by the states for the same function as listed in *State Administrative Officials Classified by Function, 1993-94*, published by The Council of State Governments.

Key:
N.A. — Not available
. . . — No specific chief administrative official or agency in charge of function
CE — Constitutional, elected by public
CL — Constitutional, elected by legislature
SE — Statutory, elected by public
SL — Statutory, elected by legislature
L — Selected by legislature or one of its organs
CT — Constitutional, elected by state court of last resort

Appointed by:
G — Governor
GS — Governor
GB — Governor
GE — Governor
GC — Governor
GD — Governor

Approved by:
Senate
Both houses
Either house
Council
Departmental board

Appointed by:
GLS — Governor

GOC — Governor & Council or cabinet
LG — Lieutenant Governor
LGS — Lieutenant Governor
AT — Attorney General
SS — Secretary of State
A — Agency head
AB — Agency head
AG — Agency head
AGC — Agency head
ALS — Agency head
ASH — Agency head
B — Board or commission
BG — Board
BGS — Board
BS — Board or commission
BA — Board or commission
CS — Civil Service
LS — Legislative Committee

Approved by:
Appropriate legislative committee & Senate

Senate

Board
Governor
Governor & Council
Appropriate legislative committee
Senate president & House speaker

Governor
Governor & Senate
Senate
Agency head

Senate

SELECTED OFFICIALS: METHODS OF SELECTION—Continued

State	Civil rights	Commerce	Community affairs	Comptroller	Consumer affairs	Corrections	Economic development	Education	Election administration	Emergency management
Alabama	...	G	G	CS	AT	G	(a-8)	B	CS	G
Alaska	G	GB	GB	A	AT	GB	A	GB	A	A
Arizona	A	GS	(a-7)	A	A	GS	(A-7)	CE	(a-2)	A
Arkansas	...	(a-11)	(a-27)	(a-15)	(a-3)	B	G	BG	(a-2)	G
California	GS	GS	G	CE	GS	GS	(a-7)	CE	CS	GS
Colorado	CS	...	CS	CS	A	GS	G	B	CS	CS
Connecticut	B	...	A	CE	CS	GE	GE	B	CS	A
Delaware	G	(a-2)	...	AG	AG	GS	GS	B	GS	AG
Florida	AB	GB	GB	CE	A	GB	A	CE	SS	A
Georgia	G	B	B	(a-4)	G	G	(a-7)	CE	A	G
Hawaii	B	GS	GS	GS	G	GS	GS	B	(a-1)	GS
Idaho	G	G	A	(a-23)	(a-3)	B	A	CE	SS	A
Illinois	GS	GS	(a-7)	CE	(a-3)	GS	(a-7)	B	B	GS
Indiana	G	(a-1)	LG	(a-23)	AT	G	LG	CE	G	G
Iowa	GS	GS	A	(a-6)	A	GS	GS	GS	(a-2)	CS
Kansas	B	GS	A	A	AT	GS	(p)	B	SS	CS
Kentucky	B	(a-11)	G	(a-15)	(a-3)	AG	B	B	G	AG
Louisiana	B	(a-11)	GS	(a-5)	AT	GS	GS	B	CE	A
Maine	B	(a-11)	...	A	ALS	GLS	GLS	GLS	A	A
Maryland	(w)	AG	A	CE	A	AGS	GS	B	G	AG
Massachusetts	B	(a-11)	GLS	GLS	GLS	B	GLS	B	GE	B
Michigan	B	GS	CS	CS	CS	GS	CS	B	(a-2)	CS
Minnesota	GS	GS	A	(a-15)	AT	GS	A	GS	(bb)	A
Mississippi	...	(a-1 1)	A	(a-15)	...	GS	G	G	A	G
Missouri	B	(a-11)	A	A	(a-3)	GS	GS	B	SS	A
Montana	B	AGS	A	AGS	A	AGS	A	SE	SS	A
Nebraska	B	(a-11)	A	A	A	GS	GS	B	(a-2)	A
Nevada	G	G	...	CE	A	G	G	B	SS	A
New Hampshire	CS	GC	G	AGC	(a-3)	GC	AGC	B	(a-2)	G
New Jersey	AT (kk)	GS	GS	(a-6)	GS	GS	AG	GS	(ll)	B
New Mexico	AG	(a-11)	AG	(a-4)	AT	GLS	GLS	B	SS	CS
New York	G	(a-11)	(a-2)	CE	G	GS	GS	B	A	A
North Carolina	AG	G	AG	GC	(a-3)	G	AG	SE	G	AG
North Dakota	(a-18)	(a-11)	A	G	A	A	G	CE	A	A
Ohio	G	G	G	(a-4)	G	G	G	G	G	G
Oklahoma	B	G	(a-7)	AG	B	B	(a-7)	CE	L	G
Oregon	A	...	G	(a-4)	...	GS	GS	SE	A	AG
Pennsylvania	BG	GS	GS	G	N.A.	GS	(a-7)	GS	A	G
Rhode Island	B	(a-11)	G	AGS	...	G	G	B	G	G
South Carolina	B	A	N.A.	CE	B	GS	(a-7)	CE	B	A
South Dakota	CS	G	(a-11)	(a-23)	AT	G	G	G	SS	A
Tennessee	B	(a-11)	(a-11)	CL	A	G	G	G	SS	A
Texas	B	B	GS	CE	(a-3)	B	(a-7)	BGS	A	A
Utah	A	G	(ddd)	(a-15)	A	G	A	B	...	A
Vermont	(ggg)	(a-11)	(a-11)	(a-15)	AT	AGS	AGS	BS	CS	AG
Virginia	GB	GB	GB	GB	CS	GB	(hhh)	GB	GB	GB
Washington	GS	GS	(a-7)	(a-4)	A	GS	(a-7)	CE	A	A
West Virginia	GS	GS	GS	CE	AT	GS	(a-8)	CE (kkk)	(a-2)	G
Wisconsin	A	GS	A	CS	(nnn)	GS	A	CE	B	GS
Wyoming	CS	GS	(a-11)	CE	A	GS	A	CE	(ppp)	AG

(a) Chief administrative official or agency in charge of function:
(a-1) Lieutenant Governor
(a-2) Secretary of state
(a-3) Attorney general
(a-4) Treasurer
(a-5) Administration
(a-6) Budget
(a-7) Commerce
(a-8) Community affairs
(a-9) Comptroller
(a-10) Consumer affairs
(a-11) Economic development
(a-12) Education (chief state school officer)
(a-13) Energy
(a-14) Environmental protection
(a-15) Finance
(a-16) General services
(a-17) Highways
(a-18) Labor
(a-19) Natural resources
(a-20) Parks and recreation
(a-21) Personnel
(a-22) Post audit
(a-23) Pre-audit
(a-24) Public utility regulation

(a-25) Purchasing
(a-26) Revenue
(a-27) Social services
(a-28) Tourism
(a-29) Transportation
(a-30) Welfare
(b) The Governor serves as Chairperson of this Board and makes the selection and appointment of the Commissioner.
(c) Responsibilities shared between Director, Office of Management and Budget (A); and Director, Division of Budget Review, same department (A).
(d) Responsibilities shared between Director, Department of General Services (GS); and Chief Deputy Director, same department (A).
(e) Responsibilities shared between Chief, Financial and Performance Audits, Department of Finance (CS); and Auditor General (GLS).
(f) Responsibilities shared between Director, Fisheries Division (CS); and Director, Wildlife Division (CS).
(g) Responsibilities shared between Commissioner, Department of Mental Retardation (GE); and Commissioner, Department of Mental Health (GE).
(h) Responsibilities shared between Director, Division of Alcoholism, Drug Abuse and Mental Health (AG); and Director, Division of Mental Retardation (GS).
(i) Method not specified.
(j) Responsibilities shared between Secretary, Department of Services for Children, Youth and Their Families (GS); and Secretary, Department of Health and Social Services (GS).

SELECTED OFFICIALS: METHODS OF SELECTION—Continued

State	Employment services	Energy	Environmental protection	Finance	Fish & wildlife	General services	Health	Higher education	Highways	Historic preservation
Alabama	CS	A	B	G	CS	CS	B	BS	G	B
Alaska	A	...	GB	A	GB	A	A	A	...	A
Arizona	A	CS	BS	A	B	A	GS	B	(a-29)	A
Arkansas	G	AG	BG	G	B	G	BG	B	B	A
California	GS	GS	GS	GS	GS	GS	GS	B	CS	G
Colorado	GS	G	CS	(a-9)	CS	(a-5)	GS	BG	(a-29)	A
Connecticut	A	A	GE	GE	(f)	CS	GE	B	A	BG
Delaware	(a-21)	A	GS	GS	AG	(a-5)	AG	B	AG	AG
Florida	A	A	GB	A	B	GB	A	AGC	GB	SS
Georgia	A	G	BG	(A-4)	A	A	N.A.	B	(a-29)	A
Hawaii	CS	CS	GS	(a-6)	CS	(a-25)	GS	B	CS	(a-19)
Idaho	G	A	A	G	B	(a-5)	G	B	(a-29)	B
Illinois	GS	GS	GS	(m)	(a-19)	(a-5)	GS	B	A	GS
Indiana	A	LG	G	(a-6)	A	(a-5)	G	G	(a-29)	A
Iowa	GS	A	A	(a-6)	A	GS	GS	(o)	A	GS
Kansas	GS	A	(q)	(r)	CS	(a-5)	G	B	(a-29)	CS
Kentucky	AG	AG	AG	G	(s)	(a-5)	AG	B	AG	B
Louisiana	GS	GS	GS	(a-5)	GS	(a-5)	GS	B	(a-29)	LGS
Maine	A	...	GLS	(a-5)	GLS	A	GLS	N.A.	(a-29)	B
Maryland	A	A	GS	GS	A	GS	GS	G	AG	A
Massachusetts	...	B	B	(a-5)	B	(a-5)	B	GLS	B	B
Michigan	CS	...	B	(a-6)	(aa)	CS	GS	CS	(a-29)	CS
Minnesota	A	A	A	GS	A	(a-5)	GS	B	A	N.A.
Mississippi	B	A	B	G	G	(a-5)	B	B	B	B
Missouri	A	A	A	...	(ee)	A	GS	B	B	A
Montana	A	A	A	AGS	(ff)	A	A	B	AGS	A
Nebraska	A	A	GS	(hh)	(ii)	A	GS	B	(a-29)	B
Nevada	A	(a-10)	A	(a-9)	AB	(a-5)	AG	B	(a-29)	A
New Hampshire	GC	G	GC	(a-5)	GC	(a-5)	AGC	B	(a-29)	GC
New Jersey	CS	GS	GS	(a-6)	BG	AG	GS	BG	(a-29)	(a-19)
New Mexico	(a-18)	AG	GLS	GLS	B	GLS	GLS	B	GLS	AG
New York	(a-18)	GS	GS	(a-9)	(a-14)	GS	GS	(a-12)	(a-29)	(a-20)
North Carolina	G	AG	AG	(a-6)	BG	(a-5)	AG	B	AG	AG
North Dakota	G	G	A	(rr)	G	(a-5)	G	B	(a-29)	A
Ohio	G	G	G	(a-6)	G	(a-5)	G	G	(a-29)	G
Oklahoma	(vv)	B	AG	G	AG	(a-5)	B	B	B	B
Oregon	GS	GS	B	(a-6)	B	(a-5)	AG	B	(a-29)	B
Pennsylvania	G	G	G	(a-6)	(xx)	GS	GS	G	G	B
Rhode Island	G	(a-24)	G	(a-6)	AGS	(a-5)	G	B	(a-29)	N.A.
South Carolina	B	A	A	B	B	(a-25)	B	B	(a-29)	A
South Dakota	CS	G	G	G	A	(a-5)	G	B	A	A
Tennessee	G	A	A	G	B	G	G	B	(a-29)	AB
Texas	B	(a-16)	A	(a-9)	B	B	B	B	(a-29)	B
Utah	B	A	G	A	A	(a-5)	(eee)	N.A.	(a-29)	A
Vermont	GS	GS	AGS	AGS	AGS	AGS	AGS	G	(a-29)	CS
Virginia	GB	GB	GB	GB	B	GB	GB	B	GB	GB
Washington	A	GS	GS	GS	GS	(a-5)	GS	B	(a-29)	A
West Virginia	GS	(a-14)	GS	(a-5)	CS	CS	(lll)	(mmm)	(a-29)	CS
Wisconsin	A	A	A	A	(ooo)	(a-5)	A	B	A	CS
Wyoming	A	CS	GS	(a-9)	GS	(a-5)	GS	BG	(a-29)	(a-20)

(k) Responsibilities shared between Director, Division of Licensing, Department of State (SS); and Secretary, Department of Professional Regulation (N.A.).

(l) Responsibilities shared between Deputy Director, Behavioral Health Services Administration, Department of Health (GS); and Mental Retardation Administrator, same department (GS).

(m) Responsibilities shared between Director, Bureau of the Budget, Office of the Governor (GS); and Director, Department of Revenue (GS).

(n) Responsibilities shared between Executive Director, Health Professions Bureau (N.A.); and Executive Director, Professional Licensing Agency (G).

(o) Responsibilities shared between Director, Department of Education (GS); and Executive Secretary, Board of Regents (B).

(p) Responsibilities shared between Secretary, Department of Commerce and Housing (GS); Director, Division of Existing Industry, same department (A); Director, Division of Industrial Development, same department (A); and President, Kansas Inc. (B).

(q) Responsibilities shared between Secretary, Department of Health and Environment (G); and Director, Division of the Environment, same department (A).

(r) Responsibilities shared between Director, Division of the Budget (G); and Secretary, Department of Administration (GS).

(s) Responsibilities shared between Director, Fisheries Division, Department of Fish and Wildlife (AG); and Director, Wildlife Division, same department (AG).

(t) In Maine, New Hampshire, New Jersey, Tennessee and West Virginia, the presidents (or speakers) of the Senate are next in line of succession to the Governorship. In Tennessee, the speaker of the Senate bears the statutory title of lieutenant governor.

(u) Subject to civil service examination.

(v) Responsibilities shared between Commissioner, Environmental Protection Department (GLS); and Commissioner, Department of Conservation (GLS).

(w) Appointed by Governor from a list of five names submitted by the Commissioners. The position is subject to removal by the Governor upon the recommendation of 2/3 of the Commissioners.

(x) Responsibilities shared between Director, Mental Hygiene Administration (A); and Director, Developmental Disabilities Administration, Department of Health and Mental Hygiene (GS).

(y) Responsibilities shared between Commissioner, Department of Mental Retardation (BA); and Commissioner, Department of Mental Health, Executive Office of Human Services (BA).

(z) Responsibilities shared between Director, Division of Forests and Parks, Department of Environmental Management (BA); and Director, Recreational Facilities, Metropolitan District Commission (BA).

(aa) Responsibilities shared between Chief, Wildlife Division, Department of Natural Resources (CS); and Chief, Fisheries Division, same department (CS).

(bb) Responsibilities shared between Secretary of State (CE); and Director, Election Division, Office of the Secretary of State (SS).

(cc) Responsibilities shared between State Auditor (CE); and Legislative Auditor (L).

SELECTED OFFICIALS: METHODS OF SELECTION—Continued

State	Information systems	Insurance	Labor	Licensing	Mental health & retardation	Natural resources	Parks & recreation	Personnel	Planning	Post audit
Alabama	CS	G	G	...	G	G	CS	B	A	LS
Alaska	A	A	GB	A	A	GB	A	A	...	CL
Arizona	A	GS	B	...	A	CS	B	A	(a-6)	L
Arkansas	G	BG	G	...	BA	G	G	AG	...	L
California	G	SE	GS	(a-10)	GS	GS	GS	GS	G	(e)
Colorado	CS	N.A.	GS	GS	CS	GS	CS	GS	(a-6)	L
Connecticut	A	GE	GE	...	(g)	CS	CS	A	(a-13)	...
Delaware	A	CE	GS	AG	(h)	(a-14)	AG	GS	(i)	CE
Florida	A	(a-4)	BGC	(k)	A	(a-14)	A	A	G	GOC
Georgia	A	CE	SE	A	A	BG	A	GS	(a-6)	SL
Hawaii	CS	AG	GS	(a-7)	(l)	GS	CS	GS	G	CS
Idaho	(a-5)	G	G	G	N.A.	...	B	B	(a-7)	A
Illinois	(a-5)	GS	GS	GS	GS	GS	(a-19)	A	G	SL
Indiana	A	G	G	(n)	G	G	A	G	G	G
Iowa	A	GS	GS	GS	A	GS	CS	GS	(a-11)	CE
Kansas	A	SE	A	...	A	(a-20)	GS	A	(a-6)	L
Kentucky	AG	AG	G	AG	AG	AG	AG	G	(a-6)	CE
Louisiana	CS	CE	GS	CS	GS	GS	LGS	CS	CS	SL
Maine	A	GLS	GLS	A (u)	GLS	(v)	A	A	G	CL
Maryland	A	GS	AG	GS	(x)	GS	A	GS	GS	ASH
Massachusetts	GLS	B	B	BA	(y)	BA	(z)	GLS	(a-11)	CE
Michigan	CS	GS	GS	CS	GS	B	CS	B	...	CL
Minnesota	A	(a-7)	GS	A	A	GS	A	GS	GS	(cc)
Mississippi	B	SE	...	(a-2)	(dd)	(a-14)	G	BS	A	CE
Missouri	A	GS	GS	A	BS	GS	A	G	A	CE
Montana	A	A	AGS	A	(gg)	AGS	A	A	(a-6)	L
Nebraska	A	GS	GS	A	(jj)	GS	B	A	GS	CE
Nevada	G	A	A	...	GD	G	A	G	(a-5)	L
New Hampshire	...	GC	GC	(a-2)	AGC	(a-7)	AGC	AGC	(a-8)	L
New Jersey	N.A.	GS	GS	AG	AG	AG	AG	GS	G	A
New Mexico	CS	B	GLS	GLS	(mm)	CS	AG	BG	...	CE
New York	(a-16)	GS	GS	(oo)	(pp)	(a-14)	GS	GS	(a-11)	(a-9)
North Carolina	AG	SE	SE	...	AG	G	AG	G	AG	SE
North Dakota	A	CE	SE	(a-2)	A	A	G	AB	(a-8)	(ss)
Ohio	G	G	G	...	(uu)	G	N.A.	G	(a-6)	CE
Oklahoma	(ww)	CE	CE	...	B	(a-28)	(a-28)	GS	...	CE
Oregon	A	GS	SE	...	AG	...	B	A	B	A
Pennsylvania	G	GS	GS	GS	(yy)	GS	A	G	G	CE
Rhode Island	A	A	G	A	G	(a-14)	A	A	A	(zz)
South Carolina	A	B	GS	(a-18)	B	A	GS	A	(a-21)	B
South Dakota	(a-5)	(a-7)	G	A	(aaa)	G	A	G	(a-15)	L
Tennessee	A	G	G	(bbb)	G	G	A	G	G	(a-9)
Texas	B	B	B	B	B	B	B	AS	(a-6)	L
Utah	A	G	G	A	A	G	A	G	(a-6)	(fff)
Vermont	A	GS	GS	SS	AGS	GS	AGS	AGS	G	CE
Virginia	GB	SL	GB	(iii)	GB	GB	GB	GB	(a-6)	SL
Washington	GS	CE	GS	GS	A	CE	B	G	(a-15)	CE
West Virginia	CS	GS	GS	...	(a-27)	GS	GS	GS	(a-5)	SL
Wisconsin	CS	GS	GS	GS	CS	B	CS	GS	(a-6)	L
Wyoming	A	GS	G	A	GS	GS	A	A	A	(a-9)

(dd) Responsibilities shared between Bureau Director, Mental Retardation Division, Department of Mental Health (A); and Executive Director, Department of Mental Health (B).

(ee) Responsibilities shared between Chief, Division of Fisheries, Department of Conservation (A); Chief, Division of Protection, same department (A); and Chief, Division of Wildlife, same department (A).

(ff) Responsibilities shared between Administrator, Wildlife Division, Department of Fish, Wildlife and Parks (A); and Administrator, Fisheries Division, same department (A).

(gg) Responsibilities shared between Administrator, Mental Health Division, Department of Institutions (A); and Administrator, Developmental Disabilities Division, Department of Social and Rehabilitative Services (A).

(hh) Responsibilities shared between State Tax Commissioner, Department of Revenue (GS); Administrator, Budget Division, Department of Administrative Services (A); and Auditor of Public Accounts (CE).

(ii) Responsibilities shared between Administrator, Wildlife Division, Game & Parks Commission (A); and Assistant Director, same commission (A).

(jj) Responsibilities shared between Director, Office of Community Mental Health, Department of Public Institutions (A); and Director, same department (GS).

(kk) Appointment must be approved by Governor and Commission on Civil Rights.

(ll) Responsibilities shared between Director, Election Division, Department of State (B); and Executive Director, Election Law Enforcement Commission, Department of Law & Public Safety (B).

(mm) Responsibilities shared between Director, Developmental Disabilities Division, Department of Health (AG); and Director, Division of Mental Health, same department (AG).

(nn) Responsibilities shared between Deputy Commissioner & Treasurer, Department of Taxation & Finance (A); and State Comptroller (CE).

(oo) Responsibilities shared between Executive Coordinator, State Boards for Professions, Department of State Education (A); and Secretary of State (GS).

(pp) Responsibilities shared between Commissioner, Department of Mental Retardation & Developmental Disabilities (GS); and Commissioner, Office of Mental Health (GS).

(qq) Responsibilities shared between Director, Office of Management and Budget (G); and Deputy Director, same department (A).

(rr) Responsibilities shared between Director of Accounting, Office of Management and Budget (A); and Director, same department (G).

(ss) Responsibilities shared between Legislative Budget Analyst/Auditor, Legislative Council (A); and State Auditor (CE).

(tt) Responsibilities shared between Associate Director, Field Services, Department of Human Services (A); and Associate director, Program and Policy Development, same department, (A).

(uu) Responsibilities shared between Director, Department of Mental Health (A); and Director, Department of Mental Retardation and Developmental Disabilities, (A).

(vv) Responsibilities shared between Secretary of Human Resources, Office of Personnel Management (G); and Executive Director, Employment Security Commission (GS).

(ww) Responsibilities shared between Director, Data Processing & Planning Division, Department of Transportation (A); and Manager, Information Services Division, Office of State Finance (A).

SELECTED OFFICIALS: METHODS OF SELECTION—Continued

State	Pre-audit	Public library development	Public utility regulation	Purchasing	Revenue	Social services	Solid waste management	State police	Tourism	Transportation	Welfare
Alabama	(a-9)	B	SE	CS	G	BG (b)	CS	CS	G	CS	(a-27)
Alaska	(a-15)	A	GB	(a-16)	A	GB	GS	A	GS	GS	A
Arizona	(a-9)	A	B	A	GS	GS	A	G	AG	(a-17)	(a-27)
Arkansas	AG	G	BG	AG	AG	G	AG	GS	G	GS	(a-27)
California	(a-9)	A	GS	G	B	GS	GS	CS	CS	GS	(a-27)
Colorado	(a-9)	A	A	CS	GS	GS	CS	CS	CS	GS	(a-27)
Connecticut	(a-9)	B	GE	(a-16)	GE	. . .	CS	GE	CS	GE	GE
Delaware	(a-22)	AG	AG	AG	AG	(j)	AG	AG	A	GS	GS
Florida	(a-26)	SS	L	A	GOC	A	A	BG	A	B	(a-27)
Georgia	(a-22)	B	SE	A	GS	A	A	BG	A	B	(a-27)
Hawaii	CS	GS	AG	CS	GS	GS	CS	. . .	(a-11)	GS	CS
Idaho	CE	A	GS	A	GS	GS	A	G	A	B	A
Illinois	(a-9)	SS	B	A	GS	GS	A	GS	(a-7)	GS	G
Indiana	CE	G	G	A	G	G	A	G	LG	G	G
Iowa	(a-26)	CS	GS	A	GS	A	CS	A	A	GS	CS
Kansas	(a-9)	GS	GS	A	GS	GS	A	GS	A	GS	A
Kentucky	AG	G	G	(a-5)	G	AG	CS	G	G	GS	AG
Louisiana	(a-5)	S	B	CS	GS	GS	GS	AS	LGS	GS	GS
Maine	(a-9)	B	GLS	A	A	GLS	GLS	ALS	A	GLS	A
Maryland	CS	A	GS	A	CE	A	A	GS	A	GS	(a-27)
Massachusetts	(a-9)	B	A	A	B	GLS	A	GLS	B	GLS	B
Michigan	CL	CL	GS	CS	CS	GS	CS	A	A	GS	(a-27)
Minnesota	A	A	A	A	GS	A	A	A	A	GS	A
Mississippi	. . .	B	B	A	G	A	A	GS	A	(a-13)	. . .
Missouri	(a-9)	B	GS	A	GS	GS	A	GS	B	(a-17)	A
Montana	. . .	B	G	A	AGS	AGS	A	AT	A	A	(a-27)
Nebraska	A	B	B	(a-16)	GS	GS	A	GS	A	GS	(a-27)
Nevada	(a-5)	G	G	A	G	G	A	A	GB	B	AG
New Hampshire	(a-9)	AGC	GC	CS	GC	GC	CS	AGC	CS	GC	AGC
New Jersey	(a-22)	A	A	A	(a-22)	GS	A	A	A	GS	AB
New Mexico	AG	. . .	G	AG	GLS	AG	CS	G	GLS	(a-17)	CS
New York	(a-9)	(a-12)	GS	(a-16)	GS	GS	(a-14)	G	(a-11)	GS	(a-27)
North Carolina	(a-22)	AG	AG	AG	G	AG	AG	G	AG	G	G
North Dakota	A	A	CE	(a-23)	CE	(tt)	A	G	G	G	(a-27)
Ohio	(a-22)	G	G	G	G	G	CS	GS	G	GS	(a-27)
Oklahoma	(a-15)	B	CE	A	CS	CS	A	GS	GS	BS	AG
Oregon	. . .	B	GS	A	GS	G	A	GS	A	GS,	GS
Pennsylvania	(a-4)	. . .	G	G	A	G	A	G	(a-7)	G	A
Rhode Island	. . .	G	G	A	A	G	A	A	A	B	(a-27)
South Carolina	(a-9)	B	B	A	B	GS	A	A	A	B	(a-27)
South Dakota	CE	A	B	A	G	G	CS	A	G	G	(a-27)
Tennessee	A	SS	CE	A	G	A	A	G	G	B	G
Texas	(a-9)	A	B	A	(a-9)	(a-30)	(ccc)	B	A	G	A
Utah	(a-15)	A	A	A	G	G	A	A	A	GS	AGS
Vermont	(a-15)	G	GB	CS	AGS	AGS	CS	A	AGS	GS	AGS
Virginia	(a-9)	GB	SL	CS	GB	GB	(a-14)	GB	CS	GB	(a-27)
Washington	(a-4)	(jjj)	B	A	GS	GS	A	GS	A	B	(a-27)
West Virginia	(a-5)	B	GS	CS	G	G	B	G	G	GS	(a-27)
Wisconsin	CS	CS	GS	CS	GS	GS	CS	GS	A	GS	A
Wyoming	(a-9)	A	GS	A	GS	GS	(a-30)	A	B	A	GS

(xx) Responsibilities shared between Executive Director, Fish Commission, (BG); and Executive Director, Game Commission (BG).

(yy) Responsibilities shared between Deputy Secretary, Mental Health, Department of Public Welfare (G); and Deputy Secretary, Mental Retardation, same department (G).

(zz) Responsibilities shared between Chief, General Audit Section, Office of Accounts and Control, Department of Administration, (A); and Auditor General (L).

(aaa) Responsibilities shared between Director, Division of Mental Health, Department of Human Services (A); and Secretary same department (G).

(bbb) Responsibilities shared between Director, Regulatory Boards, Department of Commerce & Insurance, (A); and Director, Health Related Boards (A).

(ccc) Responsibilities shared between Executive Director, Office of Waste Management, Natural Resources Conservation Commission (A); and Director, Municipal Solid Waste, same commission (A).

(ddd) Responsibilities shared between Director, Division of Business and Economic Development (A); and Lieutenant Governor (CE).

(eee) Responsibilities shared between Director, Division of Health Care Financing, Department of Health (A); and Director, Government and Community Relations (A).

(fff) Responsibilities shared between State Auditor (CE); and Audit Manager, Office of the Legislative Auditor General (N.A.)

(ggg) Responsibilities shared between Chief, Public Protection Division, Office of the Attorney General (AT); and Executive Director, Human Rights Commission (B).

(hhh) Responsibilities shared between Secretary, Commerce and Trade (GB); and Director, Department of Economic Development (GB).

(iii) Responsibilities shared between Director, Department of Health Professions (GB); and Director, Department of Professional and Occupational Regulation (GB).

(jjj) Responsibilities shared between State Librarian, Library Planning and Development Division, State Library (A); and State Librarian, State Library (B).

(kkk) Responsibilities shared between Secretary, Department of Education and the Arts (G); and Superintendent, Department of Education (B).

(lll) Responsibilities shared between Secretary, Department of Health & Human Resources (GS); and Commissioner, Bureau of Public Health (GS).

(mmm) Responsibilities shared between Secretary, Department of Education and the Arts (GS); Chancellor, State College System, Department of Education (B); and Chancellor, Board of Trustees for Higher Education, Department of Education and the Arts (B).

(nnn) Responsibilities shared between Administrator, Trade and Consumer Protection Division, Agriculture, Trade and Consumer Protection (A); and Director, Office of Consumer Protection, Department of Justice (CS).

(ooo) Responsibilities shared between Director, Bureau of Fish Management, Division of Resource Management (CS); and Director, Bureau of Wildlife Management, same division (CS).

(ppp) Responsibilities shared between Secretary of State (CE); and Director of Elections, Office of Secretary of State (CS).

Table 2.11
SELECTED STATE ADMINISTRATIVE OFFICIALS: ANNUAL SALARIES

State	Governor	Lieutenant governor	Secretary of state	Attorney general	Treasurer	Adjutant general	Administration	Agriculture	Banking	Budget
Alabama	$ 81,151	(b)	$ 57,204	$ 90,475	$ 57,204	$ 61,073	(a-16)	$ 56,806	$ 61,073 (c)	$ 72,514 (d)
Alaska	81,648	$ 76,188	(a-1)	86,760	(a-9)	83,844	$83,844	70,092	86,740	(f)
Arizona	75,000	(a-2)	47,735	76,440	54,600	73,706	91,000	82,240	73,706	86,000
Arkansas	60,000	29,000	37,500	50,000	37,500	66,318	(a-15)	59,675	79,001	62,466
California	114,286 (g)	90,000	90,000	102,000	85,714	107,879	(h)	101,343	95,052	(a-15)
Colorado	60,000	48,500	48,500	60,000	48,500	88,000	77,848	77,800	69,528	77,800
Connecticut	78,000	55,000	49,999	60,000	50,000	67,639 (d)	78,732 (d)	67,639 (d)	67,639 (d)	83,098 (d)
Delaware	95,000	38,400	80,700	88,900	71,600	66,300	75,200	69,300	74,600	86,400
Florida	97,850	93,728	96,861	96,490	96,861	87,959	69,850	96,490	(a-9)	91,155
Georgia	94,390	61,647	75,811	77,536	81,500	100,187	73,506	75,815	73,521	86,070
Hawaii	94,780	90,041	(a-1)	85,302	(a-6)	110,796	(a-9)	85,302	74,652	85,302
Idaho	75,000	20,000	62,500	67,500	62,500	81,099	65,125	66,747	68,390	(a-15)
Illinois	103,097	72,775	90,968	90,968	78,839	44,877	75,806	72,775	75,444	82,000
Indiana	77,200 (g)	64,000	46,000	59,200	46,000	61,672	71,084	47,814	66,196	81,120
Iowa	76,700	60,000	60,000	73,600	60,000	69,694	(a-16)	60,000	57,750	73,273
Kansas	76,476	71,642	59,112	68,328	59,400	63,900	76,920	65,880	57,000	72,180
Kentucky	81,647	69,412	67,378	69,412	69,412	70,000	59,370	69,412	61,383	N.A.
Louisiana	73,440	63,372	60,169	60,169	60,169	101,036	69,156	60,169	75,920	69,360
Maine	69,992	(w)	49,587	66,123	60,008	54,101	77,896	64,188	69,846	62,462
Maryland	120,000	100,000	70,000	100,000	100,000	72,896 (d)	(a-16)	85,027 (d)	62,497 (d)	99,175 (d)
Massachusetts	75,000	60,000	85,000	62,500	60,000	87,954	73,156	53,570	69,015	77,547
Michigan	112,025 (g)	84,315	109,000	109,000	87,300	89,650	(a-6)	87,300	75,000	87,300
Minnesota	109,053	59,981	59,981	85,194	59,981	87,947	67,500	67,500	67,500	(a-15)
Mississippi	75,600	40,800	59,400	68,400	59,400	50,400	51,656 (d)	59,400	59,200	(a-15)
Missouri	91,615	55,286	73,450	79,505	73,450	90,169	79,505	70,422	60,105	66,639
Montana	55,850	40,310	37,525	50,646	54,305	54,305	(a-16)	54,305	43,851	54,307
Nebraska	65,000	47,000	52,000	64,500	49,500	52,597	61,265	67,274	75,031	67,234
Nevada	90,000	20,000	62,000	85,000	62,000	68,796	80,950	60,000	60,655	(a-5)
New Hampshire	82,325 (g)	(w)	50,955 (d)	73,492	50,955 (d)	54,883 (d)	73,492	43,127 (d)	54,883 (d)	50,955 (d)
New Jersey	85,000	(w)	100,225	100,225	100,225	100,225	(a-16)	100,225	100,225	89,250
New Mexico	90,000	65,000	65,000	72,500	65,000	64,436	(a-16)	N.A.	50,999	59,991
New York	130,000 (g)	110,000	90,832	110,000	(nn)	(a-16)	(a-16)	90,832	90,832	100,528
North Carolina	93,777	77,289	77,289	77,289	77,289	69,005	77,289	77,289	74,389	94,070
North Dakota	68,280	56,112	51,744	58,416	51,744	89,628	68,724	51,744	52,992	(qq)
Ohio	110,250	57,011	81,445	85,517	85,517	76,586	89,253	78,749	68,099	93,896
Oklahoma	70,000	40,000	42,500	55,000	50,000	79,333	69,320	63,000	71,954	(a-15)
Oregon	80,000	(a-2)	61,500	66,000	61,500	69,180	88,296	76,332	69,180	76,332
Pennsylvania	105,000	83,000	72,000	84,000	84,000	72,000	(a-16)	72,000	72,000	80,000
Rhode Island	69,900	52,000	52,000	55,000	52,000	63,684	83,763	51,139	58,294	82,557
South Carolina	103,998	44,737	90,203	90,203	90,203	90,203	75,442 (d)	90,203	(a-4)	73,462 (d)
South Dakota	72,475	9,889 (aaa)	49,244	61,556	49,244	65,692	64,742	61,491	68,543	(a-15)
Tennessee	85,000	(w)	80,700	100,200	80,700	71,388	(a-15)	68,892	71,388	70,740
Texas	99,122	99,122	76,967	79,247	79,247	63,431	(a-16)	79,247	97,066	79,567
Utah	77,250	60,000	(a-1)	65,000	60,000	49,650 (d)	58,504 (d)	49,650 (d)	53,633 (d)	53,633 (d)
Vermont	80,724	33,654	50,793	61,027	50,793	56,680	63,003	58,406	56,659	(a-15)
Virginia	110,000	32,000	73,023	97,500	82,330	74,069	99,556	80,246	(a-24)	90,662
Washington	121,000 (kkk)	62,700	64,300	92,000	79,500	89,892	87,000	87,500	90,057	(a-15)
West Virginia	72,000	(w)	43,200	50,400	50,400	70,000	70,000	46,800	38,300	36,420 (d)
Wisconsin	92,823	49,673	45,088	82,706	45,088	75,400	92,281	86,537	63,461	70,495
Wyoming	70,000	(a-2)	55,000	71,298	55,000	68,202	64,087	66,201	54,504	63,036

Source: The Council of State Governments' survey of state personnel agencies, January 1994.

Note: The chief administrative officials responsible for each function were determined from information given by the states for the same function as listed in *State Administrative Officials Classified by Function, 1993-94*, published by The Council of State Governments.

Key:
N.A. — Not available
. . . — No specific chief administrative official or agency in charge of function
(a) Chief administrative official or agency in charge of function:
(a-1) Lieutenant governor
(a-2) Secretary of state
(a-3) Attorney general
(a-4) Treasurer
(a-5) Administration
(a-6) Budget
(a-7) Commerce
(a-8) Community affairs
(a-9) Comptroller
(a-10) Consumer affairs
(a-11) Economic development
(a-12) Education (chief state school officer)

(a-13) Energy
(a-14) Environmental protection
(a-15) Finance
(a-16) General services
(a-17) Highways
(a-18) Labor
(a-19) Natural resources
(a-20) Parks and recreation
(a-21) Personnel
(a-22) Post audit
(a-23) Pre-audit
(a-24) Public utility regulation
(a-25) Purchasing
(a-26) Revenue
(a-27) Social services
(a-28) Tourism
(a-29) Transportation
(a-30) Welfare
(b) $12/day seven days per week, $50/session day, $3,780/month for office expense and mileage.
(c) Filled by merit system employee at higher rate of pay.

SELECTED OFFICIALS: ANNUAL SALARIES—Continued

State	Civil rights	Commerce	Community affairs	Comptroller	Consumer affairs	Corrections	Economic development	Education	Election administration	Emergency management
Alabama	. . .	$ 91,340	$ 61,073	$ 62,400 (d)	$51,220	$ 78,000	(a-8)	$148,035	$29,068 (d)	$61,073
Alaska	$80,772	83,844	83,844	72,468	77,964	83,844	$72,468	83,844	75,144	80,772
Arizona	85,430	80,000	(a-7)	69,831	83,000	103,140	(a-7)	54,600	(a-2)	53,564
Arkansas	. . .	(a-11)	(a-27)	(a-15)	(a-3)	84,776	79,322	87,380	(a-2)	51,023
California	83,869	106,410	82,164	85,714	95,052	95,052	(a-7)	99,804	78,233	83,869
Colorado	69,528	. . .	69,528	69,528	67,000	77,800	77,800	94,478	77,000	63,000
Connecticut	67,639 (d)	. . .	67,639 (d)	50,000	67,639 (d)	78,732 (d)	72,681 (d)	78,732 (d)	54,054 (d)	60,805 (d)
Delaware	46,700	(a-2)	. . .	66,800	48,100	80,700	80,700	101,900	43,200	48,700
Florida	31,200 (d)	91,670	91,670	96,861	67,980	91,670	67,367	96,861	63,744	72,100
Georgia	60,456	84,852	84,834	(a-4)	66,816	73,512	(a-7)	77,536	68,136	75,330
Hawaii	68,412	85,302	74,880	85,302	74,655	85,302	85,302	90,041	(a-1)	76,404
Idaho	48,610	63,565	39,998	(a-23)	(a-3)	71,843	45,157	62,500	57,637	51,022
Illinois	63,071	72,775	(a-7)	78,839	(a-3)	85,000	(a-7)	133,076	73,500	48,825
Indiana	53,560	(a-1)	64,402	(a-23)	61,802	73,086	61,802	63,100	41,236	61,802
Iowa	50,586	59,850	63,440	(a-6)	70,096	70,500	94,500	99,900	(a-2)	47,700
Kansas	42,720	76,200	49,440	71,436	47,112	79,200	(s)	102,125	35,688	27,969
Kentucky	63,000	(a-11)	60,600	(a-15)	(a-3)	62,620	112,500	135,000	59,177	47,979
Louisiana	34,000	(a-11)	62,500	(a-5)	40,000	60,320	60,000	95,000	60,169	49,872
Maine	52,666	(a-11)	. . .	62,462	54,995	70,658	77,896	77,896	47,216	50,274
Maryland	67,496 (d)	62,497 (d)	62,497 (d)	100,000	62,497 (d)	72,896 (d)	99,175 (d)	91,828 (d)	62,497 (d)	53,581 (d)
Massachusetts	50,117	(a-11)	69,015	77,546	64,482	58,912	70,066	77,547	69,015	63,273
Michigan	87,300	87,300	74,980 (d)	51,803 (d)	68,131 (d)	87,300	74,980 (d)	87,300	(a-2)	48,880 (d)
Minnesota	60,000	67,500	65,500	(a-15)	74,300	67,500	51,553	78,500	(cc)	56,856
Mississippi	. . .	(a-11)	47,461 (d)	(a-15)	. . .	68,572	72,528 (d)	97,344 (d)	45,604 (d)	43,600
Missouri	52,056	(a-11)	66,612	60,119	(a-3)	70,422	70,422	80,280	34,992	54,183
Montana	37,794	54,307	46,195	54,305	38,896	54,305	52,836	44,009	21,936	39,826
Nebraska	73,894	(a-11)	44,148	72,336	46,992	67,298	81,882	96,372	(a-2)	41,976
Nevada	53,290	80,950	. . .	62,000	46,100	80,950	66,393	80,950	38,220	45,974
New Hampshire	34,593 (d)	73,492	59,410	45,088 (d)	(a-3)	56,842 (d)	43,127 (d)	73,492	(a-2)	58,336
New Jersey	78,750	100,225	100,225	(a-6)	78,000	100,225	65,000	100,225	(ll)	84,530
New Mexico	54,383	(a-11)	60,471	(a-4)	60,827	64,906	64,906	76,017	55,793	36,961
New York	82,614	(a-11)	(a-2)	110,000	76,421	102,335	90,832	136,500	82,614	94,951
North Carolina	45,412	77,289	62,133	112,301	(a-3)	77,289	66,300	77,289	41,871	41,399 (d)
North Dakota	(a-18)	(a-11)	44,604	68,724	33,732	49,200	80,004	52,788	26,880	39,960
Ohio	72,613	60,590 (d)	74,651	(a-4)	55,245	87,734	89,253	119,621	64,896	50,648
Oklahoma	48,228	93,450	(a-7)	62,585	47,920	72,180	(a-7)	55,000	65,962	40,553
Oregon	62,784	. . .	78,600	(a-4)	. . .	84,096	84,096	61,500	69,180	59,808
Pennsylvania	74,211	76,000	72,000	75,900	N.A.	80,000	(a-7)	80,000	49,174	74,211
Rhode Island	41,073	(a-11)	69,079	63,684	. . .	83,763	78,626	105,000	38,057	49,439
South Carolina	70,784 (d)	85,107 (d)	N.A.	90,203	70,784 (d)	99,314 (d)	(a-7)	90,203	52,207 (d)	40,823 (d)
South Dakota	24,170	64,642	(a-11)	(a-23)	52,000	66,486	64,742	64,472	34,143	49,858
Tennessee	60,756	(a-11)	(a-11)	80,700	43,368	75,732	76,992	80,076	57,300	58,728
Texas	54,768	79,536	92,000	79,246	(a-3)	94,420	(a-7)	135,239	71,767	55,697
Utah	33,659 (d)	53,663 (d)	(eee)	(a-15)	33,659 (d)	58,504 (d)	64,749	60,134 (d)	. . .	39,609 (d)
Vermont	(hhh)	(a-11)	(a-11)	(a-15)	61,027	60,590	50,003	70,304	34,673	45,988
Virginia	49,635	99,566	76,633	90,139	52,280	98,706	(iii)	111,059	53,581	67,894
Washington	67,542	90,057	(a-7)	(a-4)	90,600	90,057	(a-7)	86,600	57,732	59,196
West Virginia	40,000	70,000	95,000	46,800	39,900 (a-3)	45,000	(a-8)	(mmm)	(a-2)	32,000
Wisconsin	59,331	81,025	54,000	73,602	(ppp)	84,000	62,500	79,787	57,549	54,810
Wyoming	37,358	65,662	(a-11)	55,000	35,414	65,662	55,682	55,000	(rrr)	37,992

(d) Minimum figure in range: top of range follows:

Alabama: Budget, $110,318; Comptroller, $95,134; Elections administration, $44,070; Employment services, $70,720; Fish & wildlife, $70,720; General services, $65,598; Information services, $95,134; Mental Health & retardation, $110,318; Parks & recreation, $70,720; Purchasing, $76,154; Solid waste management, $70,720; State police, $56,550; Transportation, $51,220.

Connecticut: Adjutant general, $81,686; Administration, $95,155; Agriculture, $81,686; Banking, $81,686; Budget, $106,745; Civil rights, $81,686; Community affairs, $81,686; Consumer affairs, $81,686; Corrections, $95,100; Economic development, $88,034; Education, $95,155; Elections administration, $69,337; Emergency management, $77,995; Employment services, $81,686; Energy, $81,686; Environmental protection, $88,024; Finance, $95,155; General services, $91,248; Health, $95,155; Highways, 88,024; Historic preservation, 56,982; Information systems, $94,901; Insurance, $81,686; Labor, $88,024; Natural resources, $81,118; Parks & recreation, $87,735; Personnel, $88,024; Public library development, $72,100; Public utility regulation, $102,645; Revenue, $88,024; Solid waste management, $59,083; State police, $95,155; Tourism, $72,110; Transportation, $95,155; Welfare, $95,155.

Florida: Civil rights, $57,677; Social services, $96,166; Welfare, $78,107.

Kentucky: Solid waste management, $47,808

Maryland: Adjutant general, $89,654; Administration, $104,572; Agriculture, $104,572; Banking, $76,864; Budget, $121,973; Civil rights, $83,012; Commerce, $76,864; Community affairs, $76,864; Consumer affairs, $76,864;

Corrections, $89,654; Economic development, $121,973; Education, $112,937; Elections administration, $76,864; Emergency management, $65,899; Employment services, $71,171; Energy, $76,864; Environmental protection, $104,572; Finance, $121,973; Fish & wildlife, $58,104; General services, $104,572; Health, $121,973; Higher education, $112,937; Historic preservation, $76,864; Information systems, $76,864; Labor, $76,864; Licensing, $104,572; Natural resources, $112,9;37; Parks & recreation, $71,171; Personnel, $104,572; Planning, $83,012; Post audit, $96,827; Pre-audit, $29,362; Public library development, $76,864; Public utility regulation, $89,654; Purchasing, $53,800; Social services, $83,012; Solid waste management, $53,800; State police, $89,654; Tourism, $71,171; Transportation, $121,973; Welfare, $83,012.

Michigan: Community affairs, $85,942; Comptroller, $69,342; Consumer affairs, $91,892; Economic development, $85,942; Emergency management, $65,333; Employment services, $85,942; Environmental protection, $65,333; Higher education, $79,511; Historic preservation, $85,942; Information systems, $85,942; Licensing, $91,997; Parks & recreation, $85,942; Personnel, $93,387; Revenue, $91,997; Solid waste management, $85,942; Tourism, $85,942.

Mississippi: Administration, $77,391; Commerce, $92,147; Community affairs, $71,088; Economic development, $92,147; Education, $120,706; Elections administration, $53,765; Energy, $71,088; General services, $77,391; Health, $125,042; Planning, $75,095; Purchasing, $64,993; Social services, $58,816; Solid waste management, $51,928; Tourism, $71,088.

Nevada: Historic preservation, $46,577; Purchasing, $55,858; State police, $67,155.

SELECTED OFFICIALS: ANNUAL SALARIES—Continued

State	Employment services	Energy	Environmental protection	Finance	Fish & wildlife	General services	Health	Higher education	Highways	Historic preservation
Alabama............	$46,358 (d)	$55,008	$ 71,000	$ 61,073	$46,358 (d)	$43,004 (d)	$135,000	$106,500	$61,073 (c)	$64,500
Alaska.............	75,144	. . .	83,844	80,772	83,844	80,772	89,820	N.A.	. . .	65,508
Arizona............	71,000	62,000	96,000	76,000	80,772	75,000	105,000	115,700	(a-29)	46,000
Arkansas	83,703	67,682	69,831	88,647	73,658	72,795	126,353	89,833	95,720	48,611
California..........	95,052	95,403	101,343	101,343	95,052	95,052	99,805	111,750	67,788	64,896
Colorado	77,800	65,000	66,216	(a-9)	69,528	(a-5)	90,000	66,200	(a-29)	59,500
Connecticut	67,639 (d)	67,639 (d)	72,681 (d)	78,732 (d)	(j)	71,136 (d)	78,732 (d)	N.A.	72,681 (d)	44,426 (d)
Delaware	(a-21)	28,100	80,700	86,400	59,800	(a-5)	106,500	54,600	73,600	58,800
Florida	77,250	75,000	91,670	68,151	93,159	91,670	161,877	174,900	91,670	64,502
Georgia............	65,610	66,816	82,403	(a-4)	70,476	71,586	N.A.	134,000	(a-29)	55,122
Hawaii	74,028	85,116	76,404	(a-6)	71,376	(a-25)	85,302	150,000	83,580	(a-19)
Idaho	65,125	53,602	70,075	68,390	77,251	(a-5)	85,176	90,334	(a-29)	51,022
Illinois.............	78,839	63,071	72,775	(p)	(a-19)	(a-5)	78,839	132,000	84,876	61,320
Indiana............	38,558	42,484	75,218	(a-6)	38,558	(a-5)	89,856	113,728	(a-29)	38,142
Iowa	71,703	69,971	69,971	(a-6)	69,971	68,000	68,250	(r)	72,030	65,062
Kansas	73,200	29,988	(t)	(u)	50,928	(a-5)	78,000	105,370	(a-29)	41,892
Kentucky	59,777	52,839	60,600	70,000	(v)	(a-5)	112,000	91,692	70,708	46,000
Louisiana	47,413	55,728	68,000	(a-5)	60,320	(a-5)	75,000	104,000	(a-29)	45,600
Maine	57,138	. . .	64,188	(a-5)	44,221	62,462	74,110	N.A.	(a-29)	60,154
Maryland	57,868 (d)	62,497 (d)	85,027 (d)	99,175 (d)	44,236	85,027 (d)	99,175 (d)	91,828 (d)	93,500	62,497 (d)
Massachusetts	. . .	63,272	66,606	(a-5)	66,606	(a-5)	77,547	80,067	73,156	63,273
Michigan	74,980 (d)	. . .	87,300	(a-6)	(bb)	74,980 (d)	87,300	69,342 (d)	(a-29)	74,980 (d)
Minnesota	64,832	56,146	54,622	78,500	51,427	(a-5)	67,500	93,350	78,300	N.A.
Mississippi	61,600	47,461 (d)	71,005	75,760	71,005	(a-5)	98,304 (d)	N.A.	80,125	58,000
Missouri	67,000	43,969	63,735	. . .	(ff)	56,461	86,244	85,000	82,596	36,408
Montana...........	57,533	48,048	53,772	54,307	(gg)	46,600	51,942	87,499	54,305	32,427
Nebraska	57,372	52,452	78,409	(ii)	(jj)	58,926	93,045	68,598	(a-29)	62,500
Nevada	63,991	(a-10)	75,000	(a-9)	58,204	(a-5)	63,210	129,950	(a-29)	34,177 (d)
New Hampshire	50,955 (d)	46,575	56,842 (d)	(a-5)	53,127	(d) (a-5)	84,765	35,285 (d)	(a-29)	45,088 (d)
New Jersey	78,750	77,000	100,225	(a-6)	69,300	89,250	91,500	100,225	(a-29)	(a-19)
New Mexico.........	(a-18)	54,887	64,906	64,906	63,419	64,906	67,300	69,732	64,906	49,085
New York	(a-18)	90,832	95,635	(a-9)	(a-14)	95,635	102,335	(a-12)	(a-29)	(a-20)
North Carolina	74,389	51,431	69,938	(a-6)	64,205	(a-5)	94,372	145,370	98,550	53,707
North Dakota	59,016	41,040	60,864	(rr)	59,004	(a-5)	110,724	126,192	(a-29)	35,880
Ohio	89,971	64,501	84,011	(a-6)	66,269	(a-5)	97,698	126,194	(a-29)	58,489
Oklahoma	(vv)	64,493	70,000	68,732	68,100	(a-5)	95,620	155,000	73,100	55,020
Oregon	76,332	56,904	76,332	(a-6)	76,332	(a-5)	76,332	133,668	(a-29)	71,400
Pennsylvania	74,900	71,531	75,900	(a-6)	(xx)	76,000	80,000	74,900	75,900	66,993
Rhode Island	80,954	(a-24)	78,626	(a-6)	55,469	(a-5)	112,593	112,289	(a-29)	N.A.
South Carolina	95,137	57,120	71,004 (d)	99,314 (d)	69,329 (d)	(a-25)	99,314 (d)	82,429 (d)	(a-29)	33,552 (d)
South Dakota	33,613	67,742	73,784	76,503	55,598	(a-5)	64,742	104,210	56,634	46,300
Tennessee	71,388	44,004	70,836	80,700	71,364	68,892	75,732	127,800	(a-29)	42,120
Texas..............	82,432	(a-16)	82,027	(a-9)	80,204	73,520	148,681	N.A.	(a-29)	53,362
Utah	46,625 (d)	28,585 (d)	58,506 (d)	80,143	57,400	(a-5)	(fff)	N.A.	(a-29)	35,338 (d)
Vermont	55,016	61,984	55,494	56,680	52,998	57,990	71,468	N.A.	(a-29)	47,486
Virginia............	81,439	90,900	90,652	99,566	73,023	78,829	111,059	108,847	103,442	64,832
Washington	68,640	72,120	90,057	108,124	90,057	(a-5)	90,057	95,004	(a-29)	53,616
West Virginia	65,000	(a-14)	70,000	(a-5)	38,976 (d)	34,032 (d)	(nnn)	(ooo)	(a-29)	29,712 (d)
Wisconsin...........	73,145	58,884	83,309	74,000	(qqq)	(a-5)	71,616	141,298	79,760	57,021
Wyoming	53,604	33,204	59,884	(a-9)	64,927	(a-5)	65,662	64,260	(a-29)	(a-20)

(d) Minimum figure in range: top of range follows (continued):

New Hampshire: Secretary of State, $65,650; Treasurer, $65,650; Adjutant general, $69,583; Agriculture, $54,880; Banking, $69,583; Budget, $65,650; Civil rights, $41,242; Comptroller, $57,824; Corrections, $71,541; Economic development, $54,880; Employment services, $65,650; Environmental protection, $71,541; Fish & wildlife, $54,880; Higher education, $47,038; Historic preservation, $57,824; Mental health & retardation, $71,541; Parks & recreation, $54,880; Personnel, $65,650; Public library development, 54880; Purchasing, $43,095; Solid waste management, $43,095; State police, $65,650; Tourism, $43,095; Welfare, $57,824.

North Carolina: Emergency management, $67,439.

Ohio: Commerce, $86,965.

South Carolina: Administration, $102,068; Budget, $99,390; Civil rights, $95,766; Commerce, $115,145; Consumer affairs, $95,766; Corrections, $134,366; Economic development, $115,145; Elections administration, $70,633; Emergency management, $61,234; Environmental protection, $106,506; Finance, $134,366; Fish & wildlife, $93,797; General services, $66,236; Health, $134,366; Higher education, $111,521; Highways, $139,723; Historic preservation, $50,328; Information systems, $102,068; Insurance, $95,766; Labor, $86,471; Licensing, $86,471; Mental health & retardation, $117,823; Parks & recreation, $88,834; Personnel, $99,390; Planning, $99,390; Post audit, $99,390; Public library development, $73,008; Public utility regulation, $79,064; Purchasing, $66,2367; Revenue, $92,696; Social services, $117,823; Solid waste management, $68,683; State police, $92,696; Tourism, $66,236; Transportation, $139,723; Welfare, $117,823.

Utah: Adjutant general, $67,150; Administration, $79,000; Agriculture,

$67,150; Banking, $72,615; Budget, $72,615; Civil rights, $50,571; Commerce, $72,615; Consumer affairs, $50,571; Corrections, $79,000; Education, $81,307; Emergency management, $59,487; Employment services, $69,990; Energy, $42,971; Environmental protection, $79,010; Historic preservation, $53,390; Insurance, $67,150; Labor, $67,150; Licensing, $53,390; Natural resources, $79,010; Parks & recreation, $62,786; Personnel, $79,000; Public utility regulation, $56,355; Purchasing, $53,390; Revenue, $79,010; Social services, $79,010; State police, $62,786; Transportation $79,010.

West Virginia: Budget, $59,220; Consumer affairs, $47,250; Fish & wildlife, $63,372; General services, $55,344; Historic preservation, $48,336; Information systems, $67,812; Personnel, $63,372; Purchasing, $63,372

(e) This position's salary is paid by the federal government and reimbursed to state.

(f) Responsibilities shared between Director, Office of Management and Budget, $86,760; and Director, Division of Budget Review, same department, $70,092.

(g) Official salary: In California, Governor has taken a voluntary 5 percent cut; in Indiana, Governor accepts $66,000; in Michigan, Governor accepts $106,690; in New Hampshire, Governor accepts $71,587; in New York, Governor accepts $100,000.

(h) Responsibilities shared between Director, Department of General Services $95,052; and Chief Deputy Director, same department, $91,224.

(i) Responsibilities shared between Chief, Financial and Performance Audits, Department of Finance, $81,936; and Auditor General, $106,410.

(j) Responsibilities shared between Director, Fisheries Division, $65,768-84,357; and Director, Wildlife Division, $65,768-84,357.

SELECTED OFFICIALS: ANNUAL SALARIES—Continued

State	Information systems	Insurance	Labor	Licensing	Mental health & retardation	Natural resources	Parks & recreation	Personnel	Planning	Post audit
Alabama	$ 62,400 (d)	$ 61,073	$61,073	. . .	$ 72,514 (d)	$61,073	$46,358 (d)	$ 98,525	$55,008	$90,558
Alaska	80,772	77,964	83,844	$70,092	72,468	83,844	86,940	72,468	. . .	77,964
Arizona	80,000	82,091	80,772	. . .	77,000	54,524	80,772	76,000	(a-6)	86,964
Arkansas	80,191	68,410	72,961	. . .	68,303	51,000	67,610	62,466	. . .	89,879
California	90,876	90,526	101,343	(a-10)	95,052	101,343	95,052	95,052	95,052	(i)
Colorado	69,528	N.A.	77,800	77,800	69,528	77,800	66,216	77,800	(a-6)	84,400
Connecticut	74,372 (d)	67,639 (d)	72,681 (d)	. . .	(k)	63,238 (d)	68,396 (d)	72,681 (d)	(a-13)	. . .
Delaware	81,700	66,000	75,200	52,300	(l)	(a-14)	63,400	80,700	75,200	66,000
Florida	67,272	(a-4)	69,907	(n)	72,100	(a-14)	76,583	68,116	74,160	95,676
Georgia	72,252	73,950	75,810	61,218	96,000	81,333	81,512	84,870	(a-6)	75,241
Hawaii	75,120	74,655	85,302	(a-7)	(o)	85,302	58,932	85,302	85,302	77,976
Idaho	(a-5)	63,565	59,093	40,955	N.A.	. . .	68,390	65,125	(a-7)	56,264
Illinois	(a-5)	66,710	66,710	66,710	78,839	72,775	(a-19)	52,752	76,875	76,991
Indiana	62,816	54,106	55,718	(q)	82,394	73,190	51,948	66,950	70,096	64,584
Iowa	69,971	61,505	58,422	42,866	76,856	72,429	60,778	68,250	(a-11)	60,000
Kansas	65,544	59,406	54,396	. . .	63,360	(a-20)	73,200	68,808	(a-6)	74,568
Kentucky	65,291	63,000	70,000	46,371	N.A.	N.A.	60,600	70,000	(a-6)	67,378
Louisiana	78,732	60,169	60,328	61,380	160,000	58,451	45,600	86,616	51,768	75,000
Maine	68,557	63,461	70,658	30,742	77,896	(x)	61,256	62,462	68,557	55,661
Maryland	62,497 (d)	90,000	62,497 (d)	85,027 (d)	(y)	91,828 (d)	57,868 (d)	85,027 (d)	67,496 (d)	78,728 (d)
Massachusetts	70,601	66,000	55,648	63,273	(z)	77,547	(aa)	73,156	(a-11)	73,156
Michigan	74,980 (d)	74,980	87,300	85,942 (d)	87,236	87,300	74,980 (d)	85,942 (d)	. . .	90,350
Minnesota	66,210	(a-7)	67,500	66,649	76,734	67,500	58,026	67,500	67,500	(dd)
Mississippi	77,294	59,400	. . .	59,400	(ee)	(a-14)	71,005	73,614	50,133 (d)	59,400
Missouri	60,119	70,422	70,422	56,448	78,623	70,422	60,094	56,461	66,639	73,450
Montana	53,123	32,999	54,305	40,845	(hh)	41,099	43,091	50,014	(a-6)	67,727
Nebraska	68,820	65,106	55,967	55,692	(kk)	58,220	77,411	60,800	54,421	49,500
Nevada	68,000	69,997	47,284	. . .	75,348	80,950	57,000	68,000	(a-5)	67,010
New Hampshire	. . .	73,492	73,492	(a-2)	56,842 (d)	(a-7)	43,127 (d)	50,955 (d)	(a-8)	69,583
New Jersey	89,250	100,225	83,667	78,000	85,037	74,500	71,199	100,225	94,500	89,250
New Mexico	53,313	64,563	64,906	65,341	(mm)	43,163	58,025	59,277	. . .	65,080
New York	(a-16)	90,832	95,635	(oo)	(pp)	(a-14)	90,832	90,832	(a-11)	(a-9)
North Carolina	100,070	77,289	77,289	. . .	93,993	77,289	60,495	77,289	59,514	77,289
North Dakota	60,768	51,744	51,744	(a-2)	53,880	40,176	53,124	47,316	(a-8)	(ss)
Ohio	64,688	78,749	78,749	. . .	(uu)	85,051	N.A.	67,766	(a-6)	85,517
Oklahoma	(ww)	62,000	42,140	. . .	88,691	(a-28)	(a-28)	59,661	. . .	50,000
Oregon	72,696	76,332	61,500	. . .	84,096	. . .	76,332	76,332	69,180	76,332
Pennsylvania	80,000	72,000	82,060	N.A.	(yy)	80,000	68,440	75,900	80,000	84,000
Rhode Island	74,236	63,676	70,922	53,516	86,328	(a-14)	59,343	72,283	79,656	(zz)
South Carolina	75,442 (d)	70,784 (d)	63,913 (d)	(a-18)	87,087 (d)	51,000	65,660 (d)	73,462 (d)	(a-21)	73,462 (d)
South Dakota	(a-5)	(a-7)	58,329	28,911	(bbb)	64,742	52,944	64,742	(a-15)	64,744
Tennessee	73,536	71,388	68,892	(ccc)	79,956	75,732	59,028	71,388	47,844	(a-9)
Texas	80,204	150,000	53,515	62,494	93,868	85,288	80,204	48,552	(a-6)	90,176
Utah	58,756	49,600 (d)	49,650 (d)	35,538 (d)	64,979	58,506 (d)	41,823 (d)	58,504 (d)	(a-6)	(ggg)
Vermont	54,496	56,659	53,268	45,510	71,489	67,059	56,035	52,000	N.A.	50,793
Virginia	89,629	97,566	71,074	(jjj)	99,345	99,566	64,832	N.A.	(a-6)	94,294
Washington	90,057	77,200	87,500	87,500	79,596	86,600	83,629	90,057	(a-15)	89,100
West Virginia	41,712 (d)	47,800	35,700	. . .	(a-27)	65,000	65,000	38,976 (d)	(a-5)	N.A.
Wisconsin	65,233	81,203	91,120	64,325	47,773	92,281	65,346	77,160	(a-6)	91,471
Wyoming	60,395	54,500	47,861	55,383	65,662	65,808	54,027	50,000	52,849	(a-9)

(k) Responsibilities shared between Commissioner, Department of Mental Retardation, $78,732-95,155; and Commissioner, Department of Mental Health, $78,732-95,155.

(l) Responsibilities shared between Director, Division of Alcoholism, Drug Abuse and Mental Health, $91,300; and Director, Division of Mental Retardation, $72,800.

(m) Responsibilities shared between Secretary, Department of Services for Children, Youth and Their Families, $86,400; and Secretary, Department of Health and Social Services, $86,400.

(n) Responsibilities shared between Director, Division of Licensing, Department of State, $59,584; and Secretary, Department of Professional Regulation, $91,670.

(o) Responsibilities shared between Deputy Director, Behavioral Health Services Administration, Department of Health, $74,880; and Mental Retardation Administrator, same department; $74,880.

(p) Responsibilities shared between Director, Bureau of the Budget, $78,839; and Director, Department of Revenue, $78,839.

(q) Responsibilities shared between Executive Director, Health Professions Bureau, N.A.; and Executive Director, Professional Licensing Agency, $42,484-48,698.

(r) Responsibilities shared between Director, Department of Education, $99,000; and Executive Secretary, Board of Regents, $99,804.

(s) Responsibilities shared between Secretary, Department of Commerce and Housing, $76,200; Director, Division of Existing Industry, same department, $52,020; Director, Division of Industrial Development, same department, $57,576; and President, Kansas Inc., $79,223.

(t) Responsibilities shared between Secretary, Department of Health and Environment, $78,000; and Director, Division of the Environment, same department, $68,820.

(u) Responsibilities shared between Director, Division of the Budget, $72,180; and Secretary, Department of Administration, $76,920.

(v) Responsibilities shared between Director, Fisheries Division, Department of Fish and Wildlife, $50,835; and Director, Wildlife Division, same department, $48,690.

(w) In Maine, New Hampshire, New Jersey, Tennessee and West Virginia, the presidents (or speakers) of the Senate are next in line of succession to the governorship. In Tennessee, the speaker of the Senate bears the statutory title of lieutenant governor.

(x) Responsibilities shared between Commissioner, Environmental Protection Department, $64,189; and Commissioner, Department of Conservation, $67,330.

(y) Responsibilities shared between Director, Mental Hygiene Administration, $75,236-85,777; and Director, Developmental Disabilities Administration, Department of Health and Mental Hygiene, $62,497-76,864.

(z) Responsibilities shared between Commissioner, Department of Mental Retardation, $77,547; and Commissioner, Department of Mental Health, Executive Office of Human Services, $77,547.

(aa) Responsibilities shared between Director, Division of Forests and Parks, Department of Environmental Management, $70,666; and Director, Recreational Facilities, Metropolitan District Commission, $70,666.

(bb) Responsibilities shared between Chief, Wildlife Division, Department of Natural Resources, $74,980-85,942; and Chief, Fisheries Division, same department, $74,980-85,942.

SELECTED OFFICIALS: ANNUAL SALARIES—Continued

State	Pre-audit	Public library development	Public utility regulation	Purchasing	Revenue	Social services	Solid waste management	State police	Tourism	Transportation	Welfare
Alabama	(a-9)	$66,150	$51,482	$49,972 (d)	$ 61,073 (c)	(e)	$46,358 (d)	$37,128 (d)	$61,073	$ 33,618 (d)	(a-27)
Alaska	(a-15)	80,772	72,468	(a-16)	80,772	$83,844	60,864	80,772	67,800	83,844	$80,772
Arizona	(a-9)	43,025	79,000	66,313	94,000	98,000	62,000	91,535	74,485	100,000	71,000
Arkansas	41,653	61,807	68,745	62,466	68,508	91,817	69,831	64,116	49,284	(a-17)	(a-27)
California	(a-9)	85,714	100,173	82,164	104,796	95,052	N.A.	106,410	86,196	95,052	(a-27)
Colorado	(a-9)	66,120	58,400	69,528	77,800	77,800	66,216	69,528	69,528	86,300	(a-27)
Connecticut	(a-9)	56,217 (d)	80,015 (d)	(a-16)	72,681 (d)	. . .	48,317 (d)	78,732 (d)	56,217 (d)	78,732 (d)	78,732 (d)
Delaware	(a-22)	47,300	50,600	53,000	77,000	(m)	73,100	74,200	45,900	80,700	72,800
Florida	(a-26)	69,281	90,097	70,145	91,670	52,020 (d)	61,800	79,568	65,405	90,177	42,640 (d)
Georgia	(a-22)	78,363	72,972	60,744	74,352	70,000	58,512	80,690	80,472	105,000	(a-27)
Hawaii	74,028	85,302	77,964	50,364	85,302	85,302	61,572	. . .	(a-11)	85,302	76,092
Idaho	62,500	40,955	59,987	46,301	48,485	71,843	49,795	60,528	46,301	85,176	70,075
Illinois	(a-9)	74,100	72,881	55,656	78,839	76,991	59,964	72,775	(a-7)	78,839	78,839
Indiana	46,000	63,596	56,212	55,510	66,950	73,450	45,292	66,794	59,566	75,218	64,168
Iowa	(a-26)	60,778	68,194	50,482	78,837	76,856	60,778	73,320	64,293	82,206	52,749
Kansas	(a-9)	60,000	83,672	57,576	76,800	78,000	53,460	64,680	48,996	79,200	62,292
Kentucky	62,300	62,000	70,500	(a-5)	70,000	63,425	29,856 (d)	61,999	70,000	70,000	72,489
Louisiana	(a-5)	64,368	64,008	61,692	72,456	60,320	60,000	52,000	52,008	70,000	55,640
Maine	(a-9)	66,144	76,336	50,024	69,846	74,110	60,466	62,462	54,226	77,896	60,029
Maryland	22,360 (d)	62,497 (d)	72,896 (d)	40,959 (d)	100,000	67,496 (d)	40,959 (d)	72,896 (d)	57,868 (d)	99,175 (d)	(a-27)
Massachusetts	(a-9)	53,570	69,015	73,156	77,547	77,547	68,048	70,776	50,117	70,666	77,547
Michigan	90,350	N.A.	75,000	46,520 (d)	79,511 (d)	90,285	74,980 (d)	87,300	74,980 (d)	87,300	(a-27)
Minnesota	67,735	65,438	54,497	67,484	78,500	70,386	63,496	75,000	67,484	78,500	53,181
Mississippi	. . .	58,000	43,600	43,392 (d)	70,000	39,259 (d)	34,667 (d)	58,000	47,462 (d)	(a-13)	. . .
Missouri	(a-9)	65,496	70,422	56,461	79,505	73,450	43,830	60,792	56,448	(a-17)	63,778
Montana	. . .	47,208	41,590	35,996	54,305	54,305	45,261	47,761	43,780	47,667	(a-27)
Nebraska	72,336	57,662	46,968	(a-16)	75,315	62,778	54,996	60,302	44,952	80,500	(a-27)
Nevada	(a-5)	68,000	69,997	40,752 (d)	80,950	81,294	75,000	48,721 (d)	66,393	80,950	67,595
New Hampshire	(a-9)	43,127 (d)	73,492	36,134 (d)	73,492	73,492	36,133 (d)	50,955 (d)	36,133 (d)	73,492	45,088 (d)
New Jersey	(a-22)	89,250	83,472	86,100	(a-22)	100,225	73,980	77,712	80,000	100,225	83,391
New Mexico	59,991	. . .	61,940	49,314	64,906	57,208	49,655	60,305	64,906	(a-17)	46,303
New York	(a-9)	(a-12)	95,635	(a-16)	95,635	102,335	(a-14)	95,635	(a-11)	102,335	(a-27)
North Carolina	(a-22)	54,316	78,289	67,701	77,289	78,806	44,169	81,505	63,022	77,289	77,289
North Dakota	55,440	45,204	51,744	(a-23)	51,744	(tt)	42,720	54,552	41,412	65,712	84,996
Ohio	(a-22)	72,290	85,010	65,686	78,728	93,891	61,963	72,987	54,600	91,998	(a-27)
Oklahoma	(a-15)	52,227	52,000	53,140	69,371	85,000	45,150	63,160	63,441	72,934	(a-27)
Oregon	. . .	62,784	76,332	62,784	84,096	92,760	56,904	84,096	62,784	84,096	84,096
Pennsylvania	(a-4)	. . .	78,500	61,301	76,000	71,750	62,670	76,000	(a-7)	80,000	80,000
Rhode Island	. . .	65,789	77,165	78,191	86,142	105,383	42,724	92,915	52,189	99,159	77,306
South Carolina	(a-9)	53,962 (d)	58,438 (d)	44,157 (d)	61,798 (d)	87,087 (d)	42,456 (d)	61,798 (d)	44,157 (d)	103,273 (d)	(a-27)
South Dakota	49,244	46,434	50,315	55,307	64,742	77,278	48,500	58,492	61,384	74,507	(a-27)
Tennessee	67,824	72,828	80,700	55,284	75,732	50,916	60,024	68,892	71,388	75,732	75,732
Texas	(a-9)	57,925	72,101	56,238	(a-9)	(a-30)	(ddd)	84,660	68,173	93,558	89,116
Utah	(a-15)	55,248	37,521	35,538 (d)	58,506 (d)	58,506 (d)	68,212	41,823 (d)	58,443	58,506 (d)	66,294
Vermont	(a-15)	57,449	70,179	48,131	55,494	66,227	56,617	61,318	52,104	67,995	61,172
Virginia	(a-9)	82,870	97,566	83,459	90,652	90,156	(a-14)	84,639	76,345	99,566	(a-27)
Washington	(a-4)	(lll)	83,629	60,660	102,005	104,064	63,744	90,057	63,744	105,065	(a-27)
West Virginia	(a-5)	59,492	50,000	38,976 (d)	70,000	70,000	46,000	60,000	65,000	70,000	(a-27)
Wisconsin	46,174	56,576	68,000	59,193	89,379	92,281	73,947	56,442	58,965	89,318	71,869
Wyoming	(a-9)	44,417	61,233	47,500	65,662	(a-30)	52,860	52,836	59,301	70,704	70,380

(cc) Responsibilities shared between Secretary of State, $59,981; and Director, Election Division, Office of the Secretary of State, $44,078.

(dd) Responsibilities shared between State Auditor, $65,437; and Legislative Auditor, $72,474.

(ee) Responsibilities shared between Bureau Director, Mental Retardation Division, Department of Mental Health, $47,461-71,088; and Executive Director, Department of Mental Health, $72,152.

(ff) Responsibilities shared between Chief, Division of Fisheries, Department of Conservation, $61,656; Chief, Division of Protection, same department, $51,960; and Chief, Division of Wildlife, same department, $61,656.

(gg) Responsibilities shared between Administrator, Wildlife Division, Department of Fish, Wildlife and Parks, $46,600; and Administrator, Fisheries Division, same department, $46,600.

(hh) Responsibilities shared between Administrator, Mental Health Division, Department of Institutions, $52,008; and Administrator, Developmental Disabilities Division, Department of Social and Rehabilitative Services, $52,008.

(ii) Responsibilities shared between State Tax Commissioner, Department of Revenue, $75,315; Administrator, Budget Division, Department of Administrative Services, $67,234; and Auditor of Public Accounts, $49,500.

(jj) Responsibilities shared between Administrator, Wildlife Division, Game & Parks Commission, $44,280; and Assistant Director, same commission; $57,372.

(kk) Responsibilities shared between Director, Office of Community Mental Health, Department of Public Institutions, $54,276; and Director,

same department, $82,424.

(ll) Responsibilities shared between Director, Election Division, Department of State, $57,000; and Executive Director, Election Law Enforcement Commission, Department of Law & Public Safety, $86,051.

(mm) Responsibilities shared between Director, Developmental Disabilities Division, Department of Health, $59,893; and Director, Division of Mental Health, same department, $59,893.

(nn) Responsibilities shared between Deputy Commissioner & Treasurer, Department of taxation & Finance, $95,635; and State Comptroller, $110,000.

(oo) Responsibilities shared between Executive Coordinator, State Boards for Professions, Department of State Education, $94,951; and Secretary of State, $90,832.

(pp) Responsibilities shared between Commissioner, Department of Mental Retardation & Developmental Disabilities, $102,235; and Commissioner, Office of Mental Health, $102,235.

(qq) Responsibilities shared between Director, Office of Management and Budget, $68,724; and Deputy Director, same department, $40,728.

(rr) Responsibilities shared between Director of Accounting, Office of Management and Budget, $55,440; and Director, same department, $68,724.

(ss) Responsibilities shared between Legislative Budget Analyst/Auditor, Legislative Council, $69,000; and State Auditor, $51,744.

(tt) Responsibilities shared between Associate Director, Field Services, Department of Human Services, $70,044; and Associate director, Program and Policy Development, same department, $60,000.

SELECTED OFFICIALS: ANNUAL SALARIES—Continued

(uu) Responsibilities shared between Director, Department of Mental Health, $89,232; and Director, Department of Mental Retardation and Developmental Disabilities, $83,990.

(vv) Responsibilities shared between Secretary of Human Resources, Office of Personnel Management, $59,661; and Executive Director, Employment Security Commission, $75,038.

(ww) Responsibilities shared between Director, Data Processing & Planning Division, Department of Transportation, $49,493; and Manager, Information Services Division, Office of State Finance, $68,816.

(xx) Responsibilities shared between Executive Director, Fish Commission, $74,211; and Executive Director, Game Commission, $76,000.

(yy) Responsibilities shared between Deputy Secretary, Mental Health, Department of Public Welfare, $75,400; and Deputy Secretary, Mental Retardation, same department, $75,400.

(zz) Responsibilities shared between Chief, General Audit Section, Office of Accounts and Control, Department of Administration, $42,625; and Auditor General, $106,508.

(aaa) Annual salary for duties as presiding officer of the Senate.

(bbb) Responsibilities shared between Director, Division of Mental Health, Department of Human Services, $41,129; and Secretary same department, $73,784.

(ccc) Responsibilities shared between Director, Regulatory Boards, Department of Commerce & Insurance, $46,428; and Director, Health Related Boards, $32,952.

(ddd) Responsibilities shared between Executive Director, Office of Waste Management, natural Resources Conservation Commission, $78,007; and Director, Municipal Solid Waste, same commission, $62,406.

(eee) Responsibilities shared between Director, Division of Business and Economic Development, $39,609-59,487; and Lieutenant Governor, $60,000.

(fff) Responsibilities shared between Director, Division of Health Care Financing, Department of Health, $63-554-85,900; and Director, Government and Community Relations, $63,554-85,900.

(ggg) Responsibilities shared between State Auditor, $62,000; and Audit Manager, Office of the Legislative Auditor General, $51,970-78,008.

(hhh) Responsibilities shared between Chief, Public Protection Division, Office of the Attorney General, $61,027; and Executive Director, Human Rights Commission, $51,188.

(iii) Responsibilities shared between Secretary, Commerce and Trade, $99,566; and Director, Department of Economic Development, $76,345.

(jjj) Responsibilities shared between Director, Department of Health Professions, $63,884; and Director, Department of Professional and Occupational Regulation $66,000.

(kkk) Annually returns $31,000 of salary to general fund.

(lll) Responsibilities shared between State Librarian, Library Planning and Development Division, State Library, $51,060; and State Librarian, State Library, $83,629.

(mmm) Responsibilities shared between Secretary, Department of Education and the Arts, $70,000; and Superintendent, Department of Education, $70,000.

(nnn) Responsibilities shared between Secretary, Department of Health & Human Resources, $70,000; and Commissioner, Bureau of Public Health, $79,500.

(ooo) Responsibilities shared between Secretary, Department of Education and the Arts, $70,000; Chancellor, State College System, Department of Education, $105,000; and Chancellor, Board of Trustees for Higher Education, Department of Education and the Arts, $105,000.

(ppp) Responsibilities shared between Administrator, Trade and Consumer Protection Division, Agriculture, Trade and Consumer Protection, $65,000; and Director, Office of Consumer Protection, Department of Justice, $79,233.

(qqq) Responsibilities shared between Director, Bureau of Fish Management, Division of Resource Management, $56,357; and Director, Bureau of Wildlife Management, same division, $58,393.

(rrr) Responsibilities shared between Secretary of State, $55,000; and Director of Elections, Office of Secretary of State, $21,880.

Table 2.12
LIEUTENANT GOVERNORS: QUALIFICATIONS AND TERMS

State or other jurisdiction	Minimum age	State citizen (years) (a)	U.S. citizen (years)	State resident (years)	Qualified voter (years)	Length of term (years)	Maximum consecutive terms allowed
Alabama	30	7	10	7	...	4	2
Alaska	30	7	7	7	★	4	...
Arizona	---(b)---						
Arkansas	...	...	★	7	★	4	...
California	18	...	5	5	★	4	2
Colorado	30	...	★	2	...	4	2
Connecticut	30	...	...	...	★	4	...
Delaware	30	...	12	6	...	4	...
Florida	30	...	...	7	★	4	(c)
Georgia	30	6	15	6	...	4	...
Hawaii	30	...	★	5	★	4	2
Idaho	30	...	★	2	...	4	...
Illinois	25	...	★	3	...	4	...
Indiana	30	...	5	5	...	4	...
Iowa	30	...	2	2	...	4	...
Kansas	...	...	...	...	...	4	2
Kentucky	30	6	★	6	...	4	2
Louisiana	25	5	5	...	★	4	...
Maine	---(b)---						
Maryland	30	...	(d)	5	5	4	...
Massachusetts	...	...	...	7	...	4	...
Michigan	30	...	...	...	4	4	2
Minnesota	25	...	★	1	...	4	...
Mississippi	30	...	20	5	...	4	2
Missouri	30	...	15	10	...	4	...
Montana	25	...	★	2	...	4	(e)
Nebraska	30	5	5	5	...	4	2
Nevada	25	2	...	2	★	4	...
New Hampshire	---(b)---						
New Jersey	---(b)---						
New Mexico	30	5	★	5	★	4	2
New York	30	5	★	5	...	4	...
North Carolina	30	...	5	2	...	4	2
North Dakota	30	...	★	5	★	4	...
Ohio	...	...	★	...	★	4	2
Oklahoma	31	...	★	...	10	4	...
Oregon	---(b)---						
Pennsylvania	30	...	★	7	...	4	2
Rhode Island	18	...	★	★	★	4	...
South Carolina	30	5	★	5	...	4	...
South Dakota	...	...	2	2	...	4	2
Tennessee	---(b)---						
Texas	30	...	★	5	...	4	...
Utah	30	5	...	5	★	4	3 (f)
Vermont	...	...	...	4	...	2	...
Virginia	30	...	★	5	5	4	...
Washington	...	...	★	...	★	4	(g)
West Virginia	---(b)---						
Wisconsin	18	...	★	...	★	4	...
Wyoming	---(b)---						
American Samoa	35	...	★	5	...	4	2
Guam	30	...	5	5	★	4	2
No. Mariana Islands	35	7	...	7	7	4	2
Puerto Rico	---(b)---						
U.S. Virgin Islands	30	...	5	5	5	4	2

Source: The Council of State Governments' survey, February 1994.
Note: This table includes constitutional and statutory qualifications.
Key:
★ — Formal provision; number of years not specified.
. . . — No formal provision.
(a) Some state constitutions have requirements for "state citizenship." This may be different from state residency.
(b) No lieutenant governor. In Tennessee, the speaker of the Senate, elected from Senate membership, has statutory title of "lieutenant governor."

(c) Eligible for eight consecutive years.
(d) *Crosse v. Board of Supervisors of Elections* 243 Md. 555, 221 A.2d431 (1966)—opinion rendered indicated that U.S. citizenship was, by necessity, a requirement for office.
(e) Eligible for eight out of 16 years.
(f) Eligible for 12 consecutive years beginning January 1995.
(g) Eligible for eight out of 14 years.

Table 2.13
LIEUTENANT GOVERNORS: POWERS AND DUTIES

State or other jurisdiction	Presides over Senate	Appoints committees	Breaks roll-call ties	Assigns bills	Authority for governor to assign duties	Member of governor's cabinet or advisory body	Serves as acting governor when governor out of state
Alabama	★	★ (a)	★	★	. . .	. . .	★ (b)
Alaska	. . .	. . .	. . .	. . .	★	★	★ (c)
Arizona				--------- (d) ---------			
Arkansas	★	. . .	★	★	. . .	. . .	★
California	★	. . .	★	. . .	★	. . .	★
Colorado	. . .	. . .	. . .	. . .	★	★	★
Connecticut	★	. . .	★	★	★	★	★
Delaware	★	. . .	★	★	★	★	. . .
Florida	. . .	. . .	. . .	. . .	★	. . .	. . .
Georgia	★	★ (a)	. . .	★	★	. . .	. . .
Hawaii	. . .	. . .	. . .	. . .	★	★	★
Idaho	★	. . .	★	. . .	★	. . .	★
Illinois	. . .	. . .	. . .	. . .	★	. . .	. . .
Indiana (e)	★	. . .	★	. . .	★	★	. . .
Iowa	. . .	. . .	. . .	. . .	★	. . .	. . .
Kansas	. . .	. . .	. . .	. . .	. . .	. . .	★
Kentucky	. . .	. . .	. . .	. . .	★	★	. . .
Louisiana	. . .	. . .	. . .	. . .	★	. . .	★
Maine				--------- (f) ---------			
Maryland	. . .	. . .	. . .	. . .	★	★	★
Massachusetts	. . .	. . .	. . .	. . .	★	★	★
Michigan	★	. . .	★	. . .	★	★	★
Minnesota	. . .	. . .	. . .	. . .	★	★	. . .
Mississippi	★	★ (a)	★	★	. . .	. . .	★
Missouri	★	. . .	★	. . .	★	. . .	★
Montana	. . .	. . .	. . .	. . .	★	★	★ (b)
Nebraska	★ (g)	. . .	★ (h)	. . .	★	. . .	★
Nevada	★	. . .	★	. . .	. . .	. . .	★
New Hampshire				--------- (f) ---------			
New Jersey				--------- (f) ---------			
New Mexico	★	. . .	★	. . .	★	★	★
New York	★	. . .	★	. . .	★	★	★
North Carolina	★	. . .	★	. . .	★	★ (i)	★
North Dakota	★	. . .	★	★	★	★	★
Ohio	. . .	. . .	. . .	. . .	(j)	★	(k)
Oklahoma	★	. . .	★	. . .	★	★	★
Oregon				--------- (d) ---------			
Pennsylvania	★	. . .	★ (h)	★	★	★	. . .
Rhode Island	★	. . .	★	★	★	. . .	. . .
South Carolina	★	. . .	★	. . .	. . .	. . .	(l)
South Dakota	★	(m)	★	★	★	★	(n)
Tennessee				--------- (f) ---------			
Texas	★	★ (a)	★	★	. . .	. . .	★
Utah	. . .	. . .	. . .	. . .	★	★	. . .
Vermont	★	★ (a)	★	★	. . .	. . .	★
Virginia	★	. . .	★	. . .	★	★	. . .
Washington	★	(o)	★ (h)	. . .	★	. . .	★
West Virginia				--------- (f) ---------			
Wisconsin	. . .	. . .	. . .	. . .	★	★	(p)
Wyoming				--------- (d) ---------			
American Samoa	. . .	. . .	. . .	. . .	★	. . .	★
Guam	(g)	. . .	. . .	. . .	★	★	★
No. Mariana Islands	. . .	. . .	. . .	. . .	★	★	★
Puerto Rico				--------- (d) ---------			
U.S. Virgin Islands	. . .	. . .	. . .	. . .	★ (j)	★	★

LIEUTENANT GOVERNORS: POWERS AND DUTIES—Continued

Source: The Council of State Governments' survey, February 1994.
Key:
★ — Provision for responsibility.
. . . — No provision for responsibility.
(a) Appoints all standing committees. Alabama—appoints some special committees; Georgia—appoints all Senate members of conference committees and all senators who serve on interim study committees; Mississippi—appoints members of conference, joint and special committees; Texas—appoints members of standing subcommittees, conference, special, joint legislative and temporary committees; Vermont— appoints all committees as a member of the Committee on Committees.
(b) After 20 days absence. In Montana, after 45 days.
(c) Alaska constitution identifies two types of absence from state: (1) temporary absence during which the lieutenant serves as acting governor; and (2) continuous absence for a period of six months, after which the governor's office is declared vacant and lieutenant governor succeeds to the office.
(d) No lieutenant governor; secretary of state is next in line of succession to governorship.
(e) By statute, lieutenant governor serves as Director of Department of Commerce and Commissioner of Agriculture.

(f) No lieutenant governor; Senate president or speaker is next in line of succession to governorship. In Tennessee, speaker of the Senate bears the additional statutory title of "lieutenant governor."
(g) Unicameral legislative body. In Guam, that body elects own presiding officer.
(h) Except on final enactments.
(i) Member of *Council of State* per state constitution. Also sits on Governor's Cabinet, by invitation.
(j) Presides over cabinet meetings in absence of governor.
(k) Only if governor asks the lieutenant to serve in that capacity, in the former's absence.
(l) Only in emergency situations.
(m) Conference committees.
(n) Only in event of governor's continuous absence from state.
(o) In theory, lieutenant governor is responsible; in practice, appointments are made by majority caucus.
(p) Only in situations of an absence which prevents governor from discharging duties which need to be undertaken prior to his return.

Table 2.14
SECRETARIES OF STATE: QUALIFICATIONS FOR OFFICE

State or other jurisdiction	Minimum age	U.S. citizen (years)	State resident (years)	Qualified voter (years)	Method of selection to office
Alabama	25	★	★	★	E
Alaska			--------- (a) ---------		
Arizona	25	10	5	. . .	E
Arkansas	18	. . .	. . .	. . .	E
California	18	★	★	★	E
Colorado	25	★	2	25 days	E
Connecticut	18	. . .	. . .	★	E
Delaware	. . .	. . .	★	. . .	A
Florida	30	★	7	★	E
Georgia	25	10	4	. . .	E
Hawaii			--------- (a) ---------		
Idaho	25	★	2	. . .	E
Illinois	25	★	3	. . .	E
Indiana	. . .	. . .	. . .	. . .	E
Iowa	. . .	. . .	. . .	. . .	E
Kansas	18	★	★	★	E
Kentucky	30	★	2 (b)	★	E
Louisiana	25	5	5 (b)	★	E
Maine	. . .	. . .	. . .	. . .	(c)
Maryland	. . .	. . .	★	. . .	A
Massachusetts	18	★	5	★	E
Michigan	18	★	★	★	E
Minnesota	21	★	★	★	E
Mississippi	25	5	5 (b)	5	E
Missouri	. . .	★	. . .	★	E
Montana (d)	25	★	2	★	E
Nebraska (e)	19	★	. . .	. . .	E
Nevada	25	★	2	★	E
New Hampshire	. . .	★	★	★	(c)
New Jersey	. . .	★	★	★	A
New Mexico	30	★	5	★	E
New York	. . .	. . .	. . .	. . .	A
North Carolina	21	★	★	★	E
North Dakota	25	★	★	★	E
Ohio	. . .	. . .	★	★	E
Oklahoma	31	★	. . .	10	A
Oregon	18	★	★	★	E
Pennsylvania	. . .	. . .	. . .	. . .	A
Rhode Island	18	★	30 days	★	E
South Carolina	21	★	★	★	E
South Dakota	. . .	. . .	★	. . .	E
Tennessee	. . .	. . .	. . .	. . .	(c)
Texas	. . .	. . .	. . .	. . .	A
Utah			--------- (a) ---------		
Vermont	. . .	. . .	. . .	. . .	E
Virginia	. . .	. . .	. . .	. . .	A
Washington	18	★	★	★	E
West Virginia	18	★	30 days	30 days	E
Wisconsin	18	★	★	★	E
Wyoming	25	★	★	★	E
American Samoa			--------- (a) ---------		
Guam			--------- (a) ---------		
No. Mariana Islands			--------- (a) ---------		
Puerto Rico	. . .	5	5	. . .	A
U.S. Virgin Islands			--------- (a) ---------		

Source: The Council of State Governments' survey, February 1994.
Note: This table contains constitutional and statutory provisions. "Qualified voter" provision may infer additional residency and citizenship requirements.

Key:
★ — Formal provision; number of years not specified
. . . — No formal provision
A — Appointed by governor
E — Elected by voters

(a) No secretary of state.
(b) State citizenship requirement.
(c) Chosen by joint ballot of state senators and representatives. In Maine and New Hampshire, every two years. In Tennessee, every four years.
(d) No person convicted of a felony is eligible to hold public office until final discharge from state supervision.
(e) No person in default as a collector and custodian of public money or property shall be eligible to public office; no person convicted of a felony shall be eligible unless restored to civil rights.

Table 2.15
SECRETARIES OF STATE: ELECTION AND REGISTRATION DUTIES

State or other jurisdiction	Chief election officer	Determines ballot eligibility of political parties	Receives initiative and/or referendum petition	Files certificate of nomination or election	Supplies election ballots or materials to local officials	Files candidates' expense papers	Files other campaign reports	Conducts voter education programs	Registers charitable organizations	Registers corporations (a)	Processes and/or commissions notaries public	Registers securities	Registers trade names/marks
Alabama	★	★	★	★	★	★	★	★	...	★	...	...	★
Alaska (b)	★	★	★	★	★	...	...	★	...	...	★	...	...
Arizona	★	★	★	★	★	★	...	★	★	...	★	...	★
Arkansas	★	★	★	★	★	★	★	★	★	★	★	...	★
California	★	★	★	★	★	★	★	★	...	★	★	...	★
Colorado	★	★	★	★	★	★	★	★	★	★	★	...	★
Connecticut	★	★	...	★	★	★	★	★	★ (e)	★	★	...	★
Delaware	...	...	...	(c)	...	...	(d)	...	★ (e)	★	★	...	★
Florida	★	★	...	★	★	★	★	★	...	★	★	...	★
Georgia	★	★	...	★	★	★	★	★	★	★	★	★	★
Hawaii (b)	★	★	...	...	★	★	★	★	...	...	...	...	...
Idaho	★	★	★	★	★	★	★	★	...	★	★	★	★
Illinois	...	...	...	★	...	...	...	...	★	★	★	★	★
Indiana	★	...	...	★	...	...	...	...	...	★	★	★	★
Iowa	★	★	...	★	★	...	...	★	★	★	★	...	★
Kansas	★	★	...	★	★	★	★	★	★	★	★	...	★
Kentucky	★	★	...	★	★	★	★	★	...	★	★	...	★
Louisiana	★	★	...	★	★	★ (f)	★ (f)	★	...	★	★	...	★
Maine	★	★	★	★	★	...	...	★	...	★	★	...	★
Maryland	...	...	★	...	...	...	★		★	...	★	...	★ (g)
Massachusetts	★	★	★	★	★	(d)	(d)	★	...	★	★	★	...
Michigan	★	...	★	★	★	★	★	★	...	★	★	...	...
Minnesota	★	★	...	★	★	...	...	★	...	★	...	...	★
Mississippi	(h)	★	★	★	★	★	★	★	★	★	★	★	★
Missouri	★	★	★	★	★	...	★	★	...	★	★	★	★
Montana	★	★	★	★	★	...	...	★	...	★	★	...	★
Nebraska	★	★	★	★	★	...	...	★	★	★	★	...	★
Nevada	★	★	★	★	★	★	★	★	★	★	★	★	★
New Hampshire	★	★	★	★	★	★	★	★	★	★	★	...	★
New Jersey	★	★	...	★	★	★	★	★	...	★	★	...	★
New Mexico	★	★	★	★	★	★	★	★	...	...	★	...	★
New York	...	...	...	...	...	...	...	...	★	★	★	★	★
North Carolina	...	...	...	★	...	...	...	★	★	★	★	★	★
North Dakota	★	★	★	★	★	★	★	★	★	★	★	...	★
Ohio	★	★	★	★	★	★	★	★	...	★	★	...	★
Oklahoma	...	...	★	★ (i)	...	...	...	...	...	★	★	...	★
Oregon	★	★	★	★	★	★	★	★	★	★	★	...	★
Pennsylvania	★	★	...	★ (j)	★	★	★	★	★	★	★	...	★
Rhode Island	★	...	N.A.	★	★	(d)	(d)	★	★	★	★	...	★
South Carolina	...	...	...	...	...	...	...	...	★	★	★	★	★
South Dakota	★	★	★	★	★	★	★	★	...	★	★	...	★
Tennessee	(k)	★	...	★	★	...	...	...	★	★	★	...	★
Texas	★	★	...	★	★	...	...	★	...	★	★	...	★
Utah (b)	★	★	★	★	★	★	★	★	N.A.	N.A.	N.A.	N.A.	N.A.
Vermont	★	★	N.A.	★ (l)	★	★	★	★	...	★	...	...	★
Virginia	...	...	...	...	...	...	...	...	...	...	...	...	...
Washington	★	★	★	★	★	...	...	★	★	★	...	...	★
West Virginia	★	★	N.A.	★	★	★	★	★	★	★	...	...	★
Wisconsin	...	...	N.A.	N.A.	...	...	...	...	...	★ (m)	★	...	★
Wyoming	★	★	★	★	...	★	★	★	★	★	★	★	★
Guam (b)	...	...	...	...	...	...	...	...	...	...	★	...	...
Puerto Rico	...	...	...	...	...	...	...	...	...	★ (m)	★	...	★
U.S. Virgin Islands (b)	...	...	...	...	...	...	...	...	★	★ (m)	★	...	★

See footnotes at end of table.

SECRETARIES OF STATE: ELECTION AND REGISTRATION DUTIES—Continued

Source: The Council of State Governments' survey, February 1994.
Key:
★ — Responsible for activity
. . . — Not responsible for activity
N.A. — Not applicable.
(a) Unless otherwise indicated, office registers domestic, foreign and non-profit corporations.
(b) No secretary of state. Duties indicated are performed by lieutenant governor.
(c) Files certificates of election for publication purposes only; does not file certificates of nomination.
(d) Federal candidates only.
(e) Incorporated organizations only.

(f) Candidates for Congress only.
(g) Registers trade/service marks, but trade names are registered at a different agency.
(h) State Election Commission composed of governor, secretary of state and attorney general.
(i) Files certificates of national elections only; does not file certificates of nomination.
(j) Certificates of nomination are filed only for special elections or when vacancies in nominations occur.
(k) Secretary appoints state coordinator of elections.
(l) Files certificates of election for House of Representatives only.
(m) Both domestic and foreign profit; but only domestic non-profit.

Table 2.16
SECRETARIES OF STATE: CUSTODIAL, PUBLICATION AND LEGISLATIVE DUTIES

State or other jurisdiction	Custodial				Publication					Legislative			
	Archives state records and documents	Files state agency rules and regulations	Administers uniform commercial code provisions	Files other corporate documents	State manual or directory	Session laws	State constitution	Statutes	Administrative rules and regulations	Opens legislative sessions (a)	Enrolls or engrosses bills	Retains copies of bills	Registers lobbyists
Alabama	...	...	★	★	...	★	★	★	...	...	...	★	...
Alaska (b)	...	★	...	...	...	...	★	...	★	★	...	★	...
Arizona	...	★	★	...	★	...	★	★	★	...	...	★	...
Arkansas	...	★	★	★	★	★	★	★	...	...	...	★	★
California	★	★	★	★	★	...	...	...	...	...	...	★	★
Colorado	...	★	★	★	★	...	★	...	...	...	...	★	★
Connecticut	★	★	★	★	★	...	★	...	...	S	...	★	★
Delaware	★	★	★	★	...	...	...	...	★	...	...	...	...
Florida	★	★	★	★	...	★	★	...	★	...	...	...	...
Georgia	★	★	...	★	★	★	★	★	★	...	...	★	...
Hawaii (b)	...	★	...	...	★	...	...	...	...	...	...	...	...
Idaho	...	...	★	★	★	...	★	...	...	...	...	★	★
Illinois	★	★	★	★	★	★	★	...	★	H	...	★	★
Indiana	...	★	★	★	...	...	★	...	...	H	...	★	...
Iowa	...	...	★	★	★	...	★	...	...	...	...	★	...
Kansas	...	★	★	★	...	★	...	...	★	★	★	★	★
Kentucky	...	...	★	★	★	...	★	★	...	...	...	...	...
Louisiana	★	...	★	★	★	★	★	★	...	...	...	★	...
Maine	★	★	★	★	★	...	★	...	★	...	...	★	★
Maryland	...	★	...	...	...	...	...	...	★	...	...	...	...
Massachusetts	★	★	★	★	★	★	★	★	...	...	...	★	★
Michigan	★	★	★	...	...	...	...	...	★	...	★	★	★
Minnesota	...	★	★	★	★	...	★	...	...	H	...	★	...
Mississippi	★	★	★	★	★	★	★	★	★	...	★	★	★
Missouri	★	★	★	★	★	★	★	...	★	★	...	...	...
Montana	★	★	★	★	★	...	★	...	★	H	...	★	...
Nebraska	★	★	★	★	...	★	★	...	★	H	★	★	...
Nevada	...	★	★	★	...	...	★	...	...	H	...	★	...
New Hampshire	★	...	★	★	★	...	★	...	...	...	...	★	★
New Jersey	★	...	★	★	★	...	★	...	...	...	...	★	...
New Mexico	...	...	★	★	★	★	★	★	...	H	...	★	★
New York	★	★	★	★	★	...	★	...	★	...	...	...	...
North Carolina	...	...	★	★	★	★	★	...	...	...	...	★	★
North Dakota	...	★	★	★	...	...	...	...	...	★	...	...	★
Ohio	...	★	★	★	★	★	★	...	...	...	...	★	...
Oklahoma	...	★	...	★	...	★	...	...	★	...	...	★	...
Oregon	★	★	★	★	★	...	...	...	★	...	...	★	...
Pennsylvania	...	...	★	★	...	...	...	...	...	...	...	★	...
Rhode Island	★	★	★	★	★	...	★	...	★	...	★ (c)	★	★
South Carolina	...	...	★	★	...	...	...	...	...	...	...	...	...
South Dakota	...	★	★	★	★	...	★	...	...	H	...	★	★
Tennessee	★	★	★	★	★	★	★	★	★	...	...	★	...
Texas	...	★	★	★	★	★	...	...	★	H (d)	...	★	...
Utah (b)	...	...	...	...	...	...	...	...	...	...	...	★	★
Vermont	★	★	★	★	★	★	★	...	...	H (d)	...	★	★
Virginia	...	...	...	...	★	...	...	...	...	...	...	...	...
Washington	★	...	...	★	...	...	...	...	...	...	...	...	...
West Virginia	★	★	★	★	...	...	...	...	★	...	...	★	...
Wisconsin	★	★	★	★	...	...	...	...	...	...	...	...	...
Wyoming	...	★	★	★	★	...	★	...	...	H	...	★	★ (e)
Guam (b)	...	...	...	...	...	...	...	...	...	...	...	...	...
Puerto Rico	...	...	...	...	...	★	...	★	...	...	...	...	...
U.S. Virgin Islands (b)	...	★	★	★	...	...	...	★	...	...	★	★	...

Source: The Council of State Governments' survey, February 1994.
Key:
★ — Responsible for activity
... — Not responsible for activity
(a) In this column only: ★ — Both houses; H — House; S — Senate.
(b) No secretary of state. Duties indicated are performed by lieutenant governor.

(c) Senate only.
(d) Until speaker is elected.
(e) Only groups supporting or opposing legislation which was subject to a statewide initiative or referendum within the past four years.

Table 2.17
ATTORNEYS GENERAL: QUALIFICATIONS FOR OFFICE

State or other jurisdiction	Minimum age	U.S. citizen (years)	State resident (years)	Qualified voter (years)	Licensed attorney (years)	Membership in the state bar (years)	Method of selection to office
Alabama	25	7	5	...	...	...	E
Alaska	...	★	...	...	...	...	A
Arizona	25	10	5	...	...	...	E
Arkansas	18	★	★	★	(a)	(a)	E
California	18	...	...	...	...	...	E
Colorado	25	★	2	...	★	(b)	E
Connecticut	18	★	★	★	10	10	E
Delaware	...	...	...	★	...	...	E
Florida	30	...	7	★	5	5	E
Georgia	25	10	4	...	7	7	E
Hawaii	...	★	1	...	(c) ★	...	A
Idaho	30	★	2	...	★	★	E
Illinois	25	★	3	...	★	...	E
Indiana	...	...	(d)	...	...	...	E
Iowa	...	...	...	...	...	...	E
Kansas	...	...	...	...	...	...	E
Kentucky	30	2	2 (d)	...	8	2	E
Louisiana	25	5	5 (d)	★	5	5	E
Maine	...	...	...	...	...	...	(e)
Maryland	...	★ (f)	10 (d)	★	10	10 (c)	E
Massachusetts	...	...	5	...	...	★	E
Michigan	18	★	6 mos.	★	(a)	(a)	E
Minnesota	21	★	30 days	★	...	...	E
Mississippi	26	...	5 (d)	...	5	5	E
Missouri	...	★	1	...	...	...	E
Montana (g)	25	★	2	...	5	★	E
Nebraska (h)	...	...	...	...	...	...	E
Nevada	25	★	2 (d)	★	...	...	E
New Hampshire	...	...	...	...	★	★	A
New Jersey	18 (c)	...	★	...	...	...	A
New Mexico	30	...	5	...	(c)	...	E
New York	30	★	5	...	★	(c)	E
North Carolina	21	...	...	★	...	...	E
North Dakota	25	★	★	★	...	...	E
Ohio	18	★	★	★	...	...	E
Oklahoma	31	★	10	10	...	...	E
Oregon	18	★	6 mos.	★	...	...	E
Pennsylvania	30	★	7	...	★	★	E
Rhode Island	18	★	★	★	...	...	E
South Carolina	...	...	★	★	...	...	E
South Dakota	...	★	★	...	★	★	E (i)
Tennessee	...	...	...	...	...	...	E
Texas	...	...	...	...	★	★	E
Utah	25	...	5 (d)	★	★	★	E
Vermont	...	...	...	...	...	...	E
Virginia	30	★	5 (j)	...	...	5 (j)	E
Washington	...	...	...	...	...	★	E
West Virginia	25	★	5 (d)	★	...	...	E
Wisconsin	...	★	★	...	...	...	A
Wyoming	...	...	★	★	4	4	A
American Samoa	...	★	...	...	...	...	A
Guam	...	...	...	...	5	...	A
No. Mariana Islands	...	...	3	...	...	...	A
Puerto Rico	21 (c)	★	...	...	(c)	(c)	A
U.S. Virgin Islands	...	★	...	...	(k)	...	A

Source: The Council of State Governments' survey, February 1994.
Note: This table contains constitutional and statutory provisions. "Qualified voter" provision may infer additional residency and citizenship requirements.
Key:
★ — Formal provision; number of years not specified.
. . . — No formal provision.
A — Appointed by governor.
E — Elected by voters.
(a) No statute specifically requires this, but the State Bar act can be interpreted as making this a qualification.
(b) Licensed attorneys are not required to belong to the bar association.
(c) Implied.

(d) State citizenship requirement.
(e) Chosen biennially by joint ballot of state senators and representatives.
(f) *Crosse* v. *Board of Supervisors of Elections* 243 Md. 555, 2221A. 2d431 (1966)—opinion rendered indicated that U.S. citizenship was, by necessity, a requirement for office.
(g) No person convicted of felony is eligible to hold public office until final discharge from state supervision.
(h) No person in default as a collector and custodian of public money or property shall be eligible to public office; no person convicted of a felony shall be eligible unless restored to civil rights.
(i) Appointed by judges of state Supreme Court.
(j) Same as qualifications of a judge of a court of record.
(k) Must be admitted to practice before highest court.

Table 2.18
ATTORNEYS GENERAL: PROSECUTORIAL AND ADVISORY DUTIES

State or other jurisdiction	Authority to initiate local prosecutions	Authority in local prosecutions: May intervene in local prosecutions	May assist local prosecutor	May supersede local prosecutor	Issues advisory opinions: To state executive officials	To legislators	To local prosecutors	On the interpretation of statutes	On the constitutionality of bills or ordinances	Reviews legislation: Prior to passage	Before signing
Alabama	A	A,D	A,D	A	★	★	★	★	★	★	...
Alaska	(a)	(a)	(a)	(a)	★	★	...	★	★	★	★
Arizona	A,B,C,D,F	B,D	B,D	B	★	★	★	★	★	★	...
Arkansas	...	D	D	...	★	★	★	★	★	...	...
California	A,B,D,E,F	A,B,D,E	A,B,D,E	A,B,D,E	★	★	★	★	★	★	★
Colorado	B,F	B	D,F (b)	B	★	★	★	★	★	★	★
Connecticut	...	...	...	...	★	(c)	...	★	★	★	★
Delaware	(a)	(a)	(a)	(a)	★	★	(a)	★	★	★	★
Florida	F (b,d)	D (b,d)	D	...	★	★	★	★	...	★	★
Georgia	A,B,F	A,B,D,G	A,B,D,F	B	★	(e)	★	★	...	★	★
Hawaii	E	A,D,G	A,D	A,G	★	★	★	★	★	★	★
Idaho	A,D,F	A	A,D	A	★	★	★	★	...	★	★
Illinois	D,F	D,F	D,F	F	★	★ (f)	★	★	★	(g)	(g)
Indiana	F (b)	...	A,D,E	G	★	★	★	★	★	...	★
Iowa	D,F	D	D	...	★	★	★	★	★	★	★
Kansas	A,B,C,D,F	A,D	D	A,F	★	★	★	★	★	(g)	(g)
Kentucky	A,B,D,E,F,G	B,D,G	B,D,F	G	★	★	★	★	★	★	...
Louisiana	G	G	D	G	★	★	★	★	★	★	★
Maine	A	A	A	A	★	★	...	★	★	★	★
Maryland	B,C,F	B,C,D	B,C,D	B,C	★	★	★	★	★	★	★
Massachusetts	A	A	A,D	A	★	★ (h)	★	★	★	(g)	(g)
Michigan	A	A	D	A	★	★	★	★	★	★	★
Minnesota	B	B,D,G	A,B,D	B	★	★ (h)	★	★	...	...	(g)
Mississippi	B,D,E,F	D	B,D,F	E	★	★	★	★	★	(g)	(g)
Missouri	F	G	B	...	★	★	★	★	...	★	★
Montana	B,C,D,E,F	A,B,C,D,E	A,B,C,D,E,F	A,B,E,F	★	★ (c)	★	★	★	★	★
Nebraska	A	A	A,D	A	★	★	★	★	★	...	...
Nevada	D,F,G (d)	D (d)	(d,i)	★	★	...	★	★	★ (j)	...	...
New Hampshire	A	A	A	A	★	...	...	★	★	★	★
New Jersey	A	A,B,D,G	A,D	A,B,D,G	★	★	★	★	★	★	★
New Mexico	A,B,D,E,F	...	D	...	★	★	★	★	★	★	★
New York	B,F	B	D	B	★	★ (h)	...	★	...	...	★
North Carolina	...	D	D	...	★	★	★	★	★	★	...
North Dakota	A,G	A,D	A,D	A	★	★	★	★	...	(f)	(g)
Ohio	B,C,F	B,F	F	B,C	★	★ (k)	★	★	...	...	...
Oklahoma	B,C,F	B,C	B,C	...	★	★	★	★	★ (l)	★ (a)	★ (g)
Oregon	B,F	B,D	B,D	B	★	★	★	★	★	(g)	(g)
Pennsylvania	A,D,F,G	D,G	D	G	★	...	...	★	...	★	★
Rhode Island	A	A	A	...	★	★	...	★	★	...	...
South Carolina	A,D (b)	A,D	A,D	...	★	★	★	★	★	★	★
South Dakota	A (m)	A,D	A,D	A,E	★	★	★	★	...	...	...
Tennessee	D,F,G (b)	D,G (b)	D	...	★	★	★	★	★	(g)	(g)
Texas	F	...	D	...	★	★	★	★	★	★	★
Utah	A,B,D,E,F,G	E,G	D,E	E	★	★ (n)	★	★	★	(g)	(g)
Vermont	A	A	A	...	★	★	★	★	★	★	★
Virginia	B,F	A,B,D,F	B,D,F	B	★	★	★	★	★	★	★
Washington	B,D,G	B,D,G	D	B	★	★	★	★	★	★	★
West Virginia	...	...	D	...	★	(c)	★	★	★	(e)	(e)
Wisconsin	B,C,F	B,C,D	D	B	★	★	★	★	★ (l)	(e)	(e)
Wyoming	B,D (d),F	B,D	B,D	...	★	★	★	★	...	★	★
American Samoa	A,E	A,E	A,E	A,E	★	★	...	★	★	★	★
Guam	A	...	...	...	★	★	...	★	★	(g)	B
No. Mariana Islands	A	...	...	...	★	★	...	★	★	★	★
Puerto Rico	A,B,E	A,B,E	A,E	A,B,E	★	★	...	★	★	...	★
U.S. Virgin Islands	A (o)	(o)	(o)	(o)	★	★	...	★	★	...	★

Source: The Council of State Governments' survey, February 1994.
Key:
A — On own initiative.
B — On request of governor.
C — On request of legislature.
D — On request of local prosecutor.
E — When in state's interest.
F — Under certain statutes for specific crimes.
G — On authorization of court or other body.
★ — Has authority in area.
. . . . — Does not have authority in area.
(a) Local prosecutors serve at pleasure of attorney general.
(b) Certain statutes provide for concurrent jurisdiction with local prosecutors.
(c) To legislative leadership.

(d) In connection with grand jury cases.
(e) No legal authority, but sometimes informally reviews laws at request of legislature.
(f) Opinion may be issued to officers of either branch of General Assembly or to chairman or minority spokesman of committees or commissions thereof.
(g) Only when requested by governor or legislature.
(h) To legislature as a whole not individual legislators.
(i) Will prosecute as a matter of practice when requested.
(j) On the constitutionality of legislation.
(k) To either house of legislature, not individual legislators.
(l) Bills, not ordinances.
(m) Has concurrent jurisdiction with states' attorneys.
(n) Only when requested by legislature.
(o) The attorney general functions as the local prosecutor.

Table 2.19
ATTORNEYS GENERAL: CONSUMER PROTECTION ACTIVITIES, SUBPOENA POWERS AND ANTITRUST DUTIES

State or other jurisdiction	May commence civil proceedings	May commence criminal proceedings	Represents the state before regulatory agencies (a)	Administers consumer protection programs	Handles consumer complaints	Subpoena powers (b)	Antitrust duties
Alabama	★	★	★	★	★	•	A,B
Alaska	★	★	★	...	★	★	B,C
Arizona	★	...	...	★	★	★	A,B,D
Arkansas	★	...	★	★	★	★	B,C
California	★	★	★	★	★	★	A,B,C,D (c)
Colorado	★	★	★	★	★	•	A,B,C,D
Connecticut	★	(d)	★	★	...	...	A,B,D
Delaware	★	★	★	★	...	★	A,B,C
Florida	★	...	★	...	★	★	A,B,C,D (e)
Georgia	★	★	★	...	...	•	B,C
Hawaii	★	★	★	★ (d,f)	(f)	★	A,B,C,D
Idaho	★	...	★	★	★	•	D
Illinois	★	★	★	★	★	•	A,B,C,D
Indiana	★	...	★	★	★	...	B,D
Iowa	★	★	★	★	★	•	A,B,C,D
Kansas	★	★	★	★	★	★	A,B,C,D
Kentucky	★	★	★	★	★	★	A,B,D
Louisiana	★	★	★	★	★	★	A,B,C,D
Maine	★	★	★	★	★	★	A,B,C
Maryland	★	★	★	★	★	★	B,C,D
Massachusetts	★	★	★	★	★	•	A,B,C,D
Michigan	★	★	★	★	★	•	A,B,C,D
Minnesota	★	...	★	★	★	•	B,C,D
Mississippi	★	★	★	★	★	•	A,B,C,D
Missouri	★	★	★	★	★	•	A,B,C,D
Montana	★ (g)	★ (g)	★	...	...	★	A,B,C,D
Nebraska	★	...	★	★	★	•	A,B,C (h),D
Nevada	★	★	...	★	★	★	A,B,C,D
New Hampshire	★	★	★	...	★	•	B,C,D
New Jersey	★	★	★	★	★	★	A,B,C,D
New Mexico	★	★	★	★	★	•	A,B,C,D
New York	★	★	...	★	★	★	A,B,C,D
North Carolina	★	...	★	★	★	•	A,B,C,D
North Dakota	★	...	★	★	★	★	A,B,D
Ohio	★	★	★	★	★	★	A,B,C,D
Oklahoma	★	(d)	(d)	★	★	•	B,D
Oregon	★	★	★	★	★	•	A,B,C,D
Pennsylvania	★	★	★	★	★	•	A (i),B (j),C,D
Rhode Island	★	★	★	★	★	★	A,B,C,D
South Carolina	★	★	★	...	★	•	A,B,C,D
South Dakota	★	★	★	★	★	•	A,B,C,D
Tennessee	★	(e)	(d)	...	...	★	A,B,C,D
Texas	★	...	★	★	★	•	A,B,D
Utah	★ (h)	...	★ (h)	...	★ (f)	•	A (k),B,C,D (k)
Vermont	★	★	★	★	★	★	A,B,C
Virginia	★	(d)	★	★ (f)	★ (f)	•	A,B,C,D
Washington	★	(d)	★	★	★	•	A,B,D
West Virginia	★	...	★	★	★	★	A,B,D
Wisconsin	★	(d)	★	★	★	•	B,C
Wyoming	★	...	...	★	★	...	...
American Samoa	★	★	★	★	★	★	...
Guam	★	★	★	★	★	★	A,B,C,D
No. Mariana Islands	★	★	★	★	★	★	B,C,D
Puerto Rico	★	★	★	★ (d)	★ (d)	★	A,B,C
U.S. Virgin Islands	★	★ (l)	★	...	...	•	B (m),C

Source: The Council of State Governments' survey, February 1994.

Key:

A — Has *parens patriae* authority to commence suits on behalf of consumers in state antitrust damage actions in state courts.

B — May initiate damage actions on behalf of state in state courts.

C — May commence criminal proceedings.

D — May represent cities, counties and other governmental entities in recovering civil damages under federal or state law.

★ — Has authority in area.

... — Does not have authority in area.

(a) May represent state on behalf of: the "people" of the state; an agency of the state; or the state before a federal regulatory agency.

(b) In this column only: ★ broad powers and • limited powers.

(c) When permitted to intervene.

(d) To a limited extent.

(e) May commence criminal proceedings with local state attorney.

(f) Attorney general handles legal matters only with no administrative handling of complaints.

(g) Only when requested by the state department of commerce or by a county attorney.

(h) Attorney general has exclusive authority.

(i) In federal courts only.

(j) For bid rigging violations only.

(k) Opinion only, since there are no controlling precedents.

(l) May prosecute in inferior courts. May prosecute in district court only by request or consent of U.S. Attorney General.

(m) May initiate damage actions on behalf of jurisdiction in district court.

Table 2.20
ATTORNEYS GENERAL: DUTIES TO ADMINISTRATIVE AGENCIES AND OTHER RESPONSIBILITIES

State or other jurisdiction	Serves as counsel for state	Appears for state in criminal appeals	Issues official advice	Interprets statutes or regulations	Conducts litigation: On behalf of agency	Conducts litigation: Against agency	Prepares or reviews legal documents	Represents the public before the agency	Involved in rule-making	Reviews rules for legality
Alabama	A,B,C	★ (a)	★	★	★	★	★	(b)	(b)	★
Alaska	A,B,C	★	★	★	★	★	★	...	★	★
Arizona	A,B,C	(c,d)	★	★	★	★	★	...	★	★
Arkansas	A,B,C	★ (a)	★	★	★	(b)	★	★	★	★
California	A,B,C	★ (a)	★	★	★	★	★	...	...	...
Colorado	A,B,C	(b)	★	★	★	★	★	(e)	★	★
Connecticut	A,B,C	(b)	★	★	★	(b)	★	(b)	★	★
Delaware	A,B,C	★ (a)	★	★	★	★	★	★	★	...
Florida	A,B,C	★ (a)	★	★	★	...	★	★	★	★
Georgia	A,B,C	(b,c)	★	★	★	★	★	...	★	★
Hawaii	A,B,C	(b,c)	★	★	★	★	★	★	★	★
Idaho	A,B,C	★ (a)	★	★	★	★	★	...	★	★
Illinois	A,B,C	(b,c,f)	★	★	★	★	★	★	...	...
Indiana	A,B,C	★ (a)	★	★	★	...	★	...	★	★
Iowa	A,B,C	★ (a)	★	★	★	★	★	...	...	★
Kansas	A,B,C	★ (a)	★	★	★	★	★	...	...	★ (a)
Kentucky	A,B*,C	★	★	★	★	★	★	(e)	(b)	(b)
Louisiana	A,B,C	(c)	★	★	★	★	★	...	★	★
Maine	A,B,C	(d)	★	★	★	(b)	★	(b)	★	★
Maryland	A,B,C	★	★	★	★	(b)	★	★	★	★
Massachusetts	A,B,C	(b,c,d)	★	★	★	★	★	★	★	★
Michigan	A,B,C	(b,c,d)	★	★	★	★	★	★	...	★
Minnesota	A,B,C	(c,d)	★	★	(a)	★	★	★	★	★
Mississippi	A,B,C	★	★	★	★	★	★	★	★	★
Missouri	A,B,C	★	★	★	★	...	★	...	★	★
Montana	A,B,C	★	★	★	★	...	★	...	★	★
Nebraska	A,B,C	★	★	★	★	★	★	...	...	★
Nevada	A,B,C	★ (d)	★	★	★	...	★	★	★	★
New Hampshire	A,B,C	★ (a)	★	★	★	★	★	★	★	★
New Jersey	A,B,C	★ (d)	★	★	★	★	★	...	★	★
New Mexico	A,B,C	★ (a)	★	★	★	★	★	★	★	★
New York	A,B,C	(b)	...	★	★	(b)	★	(b)	...	...
North Carolina	A,B,C	★	★	★	★	★	★	(b)	★	★
North Dakota	A,B,C	(b)	★	★	★	...	★	...	★	★
Ohio	A,B,C	(b)	★	★	★	★	★	★	★	...
Oklahoma	A,B,C	(b)	★	★	★	(b)	★	(b)	★	★
Oregon	A,B,C	★	(a)	★	★	...	★	...	★	★
Pennsylvania	A,B,C	★	★	★	★	★	★	...	★	★
Rhode Island	A,B,C	★ (a)	★	★	★	★	★	★	★	★
South Carolina	A,B,C	★ (d)	★	★	★	...	★	...	★	★
South Dakota	A,B,C	★ (a)	★	★	★	...	★	...	...	...
Tennessee	A,B,C	★ (a)	★	★	★	...	★	...	...	★
Texas	A,B,C	(c)	★	★	★	★	★	...	★	★
Utah	A,B,C	★ (a)	★	★	★	★	★	(b)	★	★
Vermont	A,B,C	★	★	★	★	★	★	★	★	★
Virginia	A,B,C	★ (a)	★	★	★	★	★	★ (g)	★	★
Washington	A,B,C	(c,g)	★	★	★	★	★	★	★	★
West Virginia	A,B,C	★ (a)	★	★	★	(g)	★	★	★	...
Wisconsin	A,B,C	★	★	★	★	(b)	(b)	(b)	(b)	(b)
Wyoming	A,B,C	★ (a)	★	★	★	...	★	...	★	★
American Samoa	A,B,C	★ (a)	★	★	★	...	★	...	★	★
Guam	A,B	★	★	★	(b)	...	(b)	...	★	★
No. Mariana Islands	A,B,C	★	★	★	★	...	★	...	★	★
Puerto Rico	A,B,C	★	★	★	★	...	★	...	★	★
U.S. Virgin Islands	A,B,C (h)	★	★	★	★	★	★	...	★	★

Source: The Council of State Governments' survey, February 1994.
Key:
A — Defend state law when challenged on federal constitutional grounds.
B — Conduct litigation on behalf of state in federal and other states' courts.
C — Prosecute actions against another state in U.S. Supreme Court.
* — Only in federal courts.
★ — Has authority in area.
... — Does not have authority in area.

(a) Attorney general has exclusive jurisdiction.
(b) In certain cases only.
(c) When assisting local prosecutor in the appeal.
(d) Can appear on own discretion.
(e) Public Service Commission only.
(f) In certain courts only.
(g) If authorized by the governor.
(h) Except in cases in which the U.S. Attorney is representing the Government of the U.S. Virgin Islands.

Table 2.21
TREASURERS: QUALIFICATIONS FOR OFFICE

State or other jurisdiction	Minimum age	U.S. citizen (years)	State citizen (years)	Qualified voter (years)	Method of selection to office
Alabama	30	10	7	. . .	E
Alaska	. . .	. . .	. . .	. . .	A
Arizona	25	10	5	. . .	E
Arkansas	18	★	. . .	★	E
California	18	. . .	★	. . .	E
Colorado	25	★	2	. . .	E
Connecticut	21	★	. . .	★	E
Delaware	. . .	. . .	. . .	. . .	E
Florida	30	. . .	7	★	E
Georgia	. . .	. . .	. . .	. . .	(a)
Hawaii	. . .	★	1	. . .	A
Idaho	25	★	2	. . .	E
Illinois	25	★	3	. . .	E
Indiana	. . .	. . .	(b)	. . .	E
Iowa	18	. . .	. . .	. . .	E
Kansas	. . .	. . .	. . .	. . .	E
Kentucky	30	. . .	2 (c)	. . .	E
Louisiana	. . .	. . .	. . .	. . .	E
Maine	. . .	. . .	★	. . .	L
Maryland	. . .	. . .	. . .	. . .	L
Massachusetts	. . .	. . .	5	. . .	E
Michigan	. . .	. . .	. . .	. . .	A
Minnesota	. . .	. . .	. . .	. . .	E
Mississippi	25	★	5	★	E
Missouri	. . .	. . .	. . .	. . .	E
Montana	. . .	. . .	. . .	. . .	A
Nebraska	. . .	★	★	★	E
Nevada	25	★	2	★	E
New Hampshire	. . .	. . .	. . .	. . .	L
New Jersey	. . .	. . .	. . .	. . .	A
New Mexico	30	★	5	★	E
New York	. . .	. . .	. . .	. . .	A
North Carolina	21	★	★	★	E
North Dakota	25	★	★	★	E
Ohio	18	★	★	3 mos.	E
Oklahoma	31	10	10	10	E
Oregon	. . .	. . .	. . .	. . .	E
Pennsylvania	30	★	7	. . .	E
Rhode Island	18	★	★	30 days	E
South Carolina	. . .	★	★	★	E
South Dakota	. . .	. . .	. . .	. . .	E
Tennessee	. . .	. . .	. . .	. . .	L
Texas	18	★	1	. . .	E
Utah	18	★	5	★	E
Vermont	. . .	. . .	. . .	. . .	E
Virginia	. . .	. . .	. . .	. . .	A (d)
Washington	18	★	★	30 days	E
West Virginia	18	★	★	★	E
Wisconsin	. . .	. . .	. . .	. . .	E
Wyoming	25	★	★	★	E
Dist. of Columbia	. . .	. . .	. . .	. . .	(e)
Puerto Rico	. . .	. . .	. . .	. . .	A
U.S. Virgin Islands	. . .	. . .	. . .	. . .	A

Source: The Council of State Governments' survey, March 1994.
Note: "Qualified voter" provision may infer additional residency and citizenship requirements.
Key:
★ — Formal provision; number of years not specified
. . . — No formal provision
A — Appointed by the governor
E — Elected by the voters
L — Elected by the legislature

(a) Appointed by State Depository Board.
(b) Residency requirements while in office.
(c) State resident and citizen requirement.
(d) Subject to confirmation by the General Assembly.
(e) Appointed by the mayor.

Table 2.22
TREASURERS: DUTIES OF OFFICE

State or other jurisdiction	Investment of excess funds	Investment of retirement and/or trust funds	Management of bonded debt	Bond issue	Debt service	Arbitrage rebate	Unclaimed property	Deferred compensation	Linked deposits	College savers program
Alabama	★	★	...	★	★	★	...	...	★	★
Alaska	★	★	★	★	★	★	...	★	...	★
Arizona	★	★	...	...	...	★	...	...	...	...
Arkansas	★	★	...	...	...	...	...	...	...	...
California	★	...	★	★	★	...	...	...	...	N.A.
Colorado	★	...	...	...	...	...	★	...	...	...
Connecticut	★	★	★	★	★	★	★	...	...	★
Delaware	★	...	★	★	★	★	...	★	...	...
Florida	★	...	...	...	...	...	...	...	★	★
Georgia	★	...	...	...	...	...	...	...	...	...
Hawaii	★	...	★	★	★	★	★	...	...	★
Idaho	★	...	...	...	...	...	...	...	...	...
Illinois	★	★	★	...	★	★	...	...	★	★
Indiana	★	★	...	...	...	...	...	...	...	...
Iowa	★	...	★	★	...	...	★	...	★	★
Kansas	★	...	...	★	★	...	★ (a)	...	N.A.	...
Kentucky	★	...	...	...	...	...	★ (a)	...	N.A.	★
Louisiana	★	★	★	★	★	★	...	...	★	N.A.
Maine	★	...	★	★	★	★	★	...	N.A.	...
Maryland	★	...	★ (b)	★ (b)	...	★	...	...	★	...
Massachusetts	★	★	★	★	★	★	★	★	...	...
Michigan	★	★	★	★	★	...	★	...	★	★
Minnesota	...	...	★	...	★	...	★	...	...	...
Mississippi	★	...	★	★	★	★	★	...	...	...
Missouri	★	...	...	...	...	★	★	...	★	...
Montana	...	...	...	...	...	...	...	...	★	...
Nebraska	...	...	...	...	...	...	★	...	...	...
Nevada	★	★ (c)	★	★	★	...	...	...	...	★
New Hampshire	★	★	★	★	★	★	★	★	...	★
New Jersey	...	...	★	★	★	★	★	...	...	★
New Mexico	★	★ (d)	★	★	★	★	★	...	★	...
New York	★ (e)	...	...	...	...	...	...	...	...	★ (f)
North Carolina	★	★	★	★	★	★	★	...	...	...
North Dakota	★	...	...	...	...	...	...	...	...	...
Ohio	★	...	...	★	...	...	...	...	★	★
Oklahoma	★	...	...	...	...	...	...	...	★	...
Oregon	★	★	★	★	★	★ (g)	...	★ (h)	...	...
Pennsylvania	★	★	...	★	★	...	★	...	★	★
Rhode Island	★	★	★	★	★	...	★	...	★	N.A.
South Carolina	★	★	★	★	★	★	...	★	...	...
South Dakota	...	...	...	★	...	...	★	...	...	★
Tennessee	★	★	...	...	...	...	★	★	...	★
Texas	★	★	★	★	★	★	★	...	★	★
Utah	★	★	★	★	★	★	★	...	...	... (a)
Vermont	★	★	★	★	★	★	★	★	...	★
Virginia	★	★ (i)	★	★	★	★	★	...	...	N.A.
Washington	★	...	★	★	★	...	...	...	N.A.	★
West Virginia	...	...	...	...	...	...	★	...	N.A.	...
Wisconsin	...	...	...	...	...	...	★	...	...	...
Wyoming	★	★ (j)	★	★ (k)	★	★	★	★	...	★
Dist. of Columbia	★	...	★	★	★	★	...	...	...	...
Puerto Rico	★	...	...	...	★	...	...	...	...	...

Source: National Association of State Treasurers' survey, Fall 1993.
Note: For additional information on functions of the treasurers' offices, see Tables 6.5 - 6.7.
Key:
★ — Responsible for activity
. . . — Not responsible for activity
N.A. — Not available
(a) Portions.
(b) General obligation.
(c) Except for Public Employees Retirement System.
(d) Short term.

(e) Commissioner of Taxation and Finance invests funds of a number of state entities, but does not invest the state's general fund monies. Commissioner serves as joint custodian of the general fund, but the state comptroller invests general fund monies.
(f) Not administered by Treasury.
(g) Contract out for actual services.
(h) Investment only.
(i) Short term portfolio only.
(j) As board member only.
(k) With Farm Loan Board.

Chapter Three

STATE LEGISLATIVE BRANCH

An overview of state legislatures and legislative processes in the states, with special emphasis on activities during 1992-93. Includes basic information on the legislatures — such as legal provisions for legislative sessions and a variety of information on legislative procedures — along with legislative compensation, statistics on 1992 and 1993 bill introductions and enactments, committee appointments and procedures, and review of administrative regulations.

State Legislatures

As legislatures become more professional and modern, they are tackling issues that are thornier and more complicated.

by Rich Jones

State legislatures today are strong, effective and modern institutions. They are crafting innovative policies in areas as diverse as health-care reform, economic development, education and welfare reform. As programs have shifted from the federal government to the states, legislatures have taken on greater policy-making responsibilities and have become independent, equal branches of state government. However, this was not always true.

The modern legislature was born in the 1960s. At that time, a series of state and federal court decisions following the U.S. Supreme Court rulings in *Baker v. Carr* (1962) and *Reynolds v. Simms* (1964) required state legislative districts to be drawn with equal populations. At the same time studies conducted by universities, foundations, the Citizens Conference on State Legislatures and other citizen groups found legislatures to be weak, ineffectual, nonrepresentative bodies.

To correct these shortcomings, reformers advocated making legislatures more professional and more fully representative of the diverse populations in the states. The goal of these reforms was to create legislatures better able to handle the increasingly complex policy issues facing the states. Therefore, they recommended developing independent sources of information, attracting skilled and dedicated people to legislative service, and giving legislatures adequate time to deliberate on and craft public policies.

During the past three decades, state legislatures added professional staff, lengthened legislative sessions, increased lawmakers' salaries as their workloads increased and professionalized their operations. However, these reforms brought problems of their own — problems that are more subtle and less easily affected by changes in legislative operations and procedures. In fact, many of the problems lie outside the lawmakers' control and involve relationships among legislatures, the public and the media.

One of the more vexing concerns is that, despite the improvements of the past three decades, the general public has an increased disdain and low opinion of state legislatures. Voter anger with legislatures and politicians is manifested in the movement to limit lawmakers' terms and efforts to restrict the power and authority of legislatures. It is ironic that although legislatures of the 1990s are vastly improved over the 1960s model, they rate lower in public opinion polls. In some ways, the increased professionalization of legislatures is a subject of public disdain.

Public opinion of the legislatures' performance varies considerably among the states. Legislatures' actions — raising taxes, missing the deadline for passing the state budget or violating ethics laws — directly affect public opinion about their performance. Part of the drop in public support for legislatures also can be attributed to an overall decline in public trust in government. Using the University of Michigan's National Election Survey data, political scientist Arthur Miller found that public trust in government was at an all-time low in 1990.[1] These sentiments were reflected in a series of focus group discussions with citizens sponsored by the Kettering Foundation. Conducted throughout 1990 and 1991, the Kettering study found widespread public distrust and anger with the political system.[2]

Rich Jones is the director of Legislative Programs at the National Conference of State Legislatures.

In addition, opinion polls indicate that many citizens sometimes confuse actions taken by the federal government with those taken by state government. As a result, federal policies on controversial issues such as the budget deficit and taxes negatively affect public opinion about state government.

During the past three decades, legislatures significantly professionalized their operations. They evolved from institutions described as a "series of sometimes governments" into vital, healthy and successful institutions that are a leading source of policy innovations.[3] In the 1990s, state legislatures must balance the benefits that further professionalism brings to the policy-making process with the public's desire for part-time, citizen lawmakers.

Term Limits

One measure of the public's disdain for professional politicians is the movement to limit the terms of state legislators, members of Congress and state executive branch officials. For a full discussion of term limits, see the essay, "Term Limits in the States" on pages 28-33 of this volume.

Legislative Operations, Organization and Procedures

During the past two decades, legislatures have taken a more active policy-making role and are addressing increasingly complex issues. In addition, they are receiving greater attention from the public and the media. These factors have combined to expand legislative workloads. To meet these increased demands and complete their business within the prescribed time limits, legislatures have devoted considerable attention to streamlining and improving their operations. Legislatures are using technology and other means to increase public access to the legislative process. They are also eliminating unnecessary procedures and doing more work in the interim between legislative sessions.

In recent years legislatures have studied their operations and procedures. Rhode Island formed a blue ribbon citizens commission in 1992 that studied all aspects of the legislative process and made a series of recommendations to make the General Assembly a more independent institution. The commission recommended reducing the size of the House from 100 to 75 members and the Senate from 50 to 25 members. The commission argued the reduction will better balance local interests with the needs of the state. The commission also recommended increasing legislator salaries from $5 per session day to $10,000 per year, providing members with shared office space, adding more research staff to help analyze bills and improving the ability of legislative committees to develop policy expertise and play a larger role in crafting legislation.[4]

In North Dakota, a citizens' group is conducting a study of ways to improve the legislature. The study is being conducted under the auspices of the North Dakota Consensus Council and involves a group of former legislators, executive and judicial branch officials and lobbyists. It is focusing on ways for the legislature to effectively deal with the issues confronting the state while maintaining its tradition as a part-time citizen legislature. The issues being considered include the use of computer technology to provide citizens with better access to the legislative process, flexibility in scheduling the biennial session and reform of the initiative and referenda process.[5]

In 1993, Wisconsin conducted a review of its budget and bill drafting processes, and Tennessee conducted a study of its staff resources. In 1992, Maryland undertook a performance review of its legislative staff operations.

Length of Legislative Sessions

During the past three decades, states have relaxed session length limitations and restrictions on the legislatures' ability to call a special session. Currently, 13 states place no limit on session length, 31 states have constitutional limits and six have statutory limits, limits in legislative rules or indirect limitations based on cutoffs in legislators' salaries or per diem expense payments. All but seven states (Arkansas, Kentucky, Montana, Nevada, North Dakota, Oregon and Texas) meet annually. Following World War II, only four states held annual sessions. By 1966, this number increased to 20 states, and by 1974, 42 states were meeting annually. (See Table 3.2)

In the late 1980s and early 1990s, there was increased public sentiment to limit the length of legislative sessions. In 1984, Alaska went from unlimited sessions to a 120-day limit, and Colorado voters approved a constitutional amendment in 1988 that limited legislative sessions to 120 days. In 1989, Oklahoma voters approved a constitutional amendment specifying that the Legislature could only meet from February through May. Because of legislative scheduling, it limited time spent in session. Louisiana voters approved a constitutional amendment in 1993 that reduced the length of even-year sessions from 60 days to 30 days and limited the subject matter during the reduced session to fiscal issues.

Regardless of the restrictions and the intention of lawmakers to reduce time they spend in session, the legislatures' workloads continue to grow. As the length of regular sessions is restricted, legislatures have met in special sessions. From 1991 through 1993, budget problems and reapportionment forced legislatures to stay in session longer or to meet in special sessions. Nationwide, 31 states held more than 50 special sessions in 1991, 27 states held 52 special sessions in 1992 and 22 states held 40 special sessions in 1993. Arizona, for example, held five special sessions in 1992 and seven in 1993, and Florida held five in 1992 and two in 1993.[6] (See Table 3.20)

Full-time Legislatures and Legislators

Debates over the time legislatures spend in session often center on the desire to preserve the part-time citizen legislature versus the need to develop professional or full-time legislatures similar to Congress. The amount of time in session and compensation paid directly affect the type of person found in legislative bodies. States with longer sessions and higher salaries, for the most part, have a larger number of members who consider the legislature their career. The traditional argument is that legislatures benefit by having members who represent a variety of vocations, who come to the legislature for a short time and then return to their other occupations. In recent years, however, other lawmakers and legislative observers

have argued that the complexities of issues and the demands placed on legislatures have increased the need for full-time members. A National Conference of State Legislatures' (NCSL) task force of lawmakers and staffers who studied ways to strengthen legislatures recommended that legislatures, "consider carefully any changes in operations that will further professionalize the legislature." The task force urged legislatures to more consciously balance the benefits derived from being part-time citizen bodies with the need to professionalize their operations.[7]

Notwithstanding the desire for part-time citizen legislatures, the number of members who consider themselves to be full-time lawmakers continues to grow. In a 1993 National Conference of State Legislatures study, 15 percent of all legislators reported the legislature is their sole occupation. That is up from 3 percent in 1976 and 11 percent in 1986. If other categories such as retired, student and homemaker are included, full-time lawmakers would total 24 percent of all legislators. More than half of the members in Massachusetts, Michigan, New York, Pennsylvania and Wisconsin consider themselves full-time legislators. Full-time lawmaker is the most common occupational category in 12 states (the five states listed above plus Connecticut, Illinois, Minnesota, Ohio, California, Hawaii and Oregon). Full-time lawmakers are found primarily in the Eastern and Midwestern states.[8]

Attorney remains the most common occupational background, comprising 16 percent of all lawmakers, the same level as 1986. (In 1976, 22 percent of all lawmakers were attorneys.) The South has the largest composition of lawyers with 25 percent. Attorneys represent 14 percent of Eastern legislators, 13 percent of Midwestern legislators and 12 percent of Western legislators. It is the most common occupation in 23 states, and attorneys serve in every legislature. In order, the five largest occupational categories are attorney (16 percent), full-time lawmaker (15 percent), business owner (10 percent), agriculture (8 percent) and retired (7 percent).

In 1992, the National Conference of State Legislatures grouped the legislatures into three categories based on the extent to which they exhibit the characteristics of a full-time legislature — high salaries, large staffs and long sessions. California, Illinois, Massachusetts, Michigan, New Jersey, New York, Ohio, Pennsylvania and Wisconsin are considered to be full-time legislatures. At the other end of the spectrum are 17 states with clearly part-time legislatures. They meet in short sessions, have low salaries and small staffs. In between are 25 states whose legislatures have some, but not all, of the characteristics of full-time legislatures. Florida, for example, has a large legislative staff but meets in short session and ranks in the mid-range on legislative pay. Given the increased demands on legislatures, it is possible that states such as Florida and Missouri will move into the full-time category during the next decade. Others, such as Maine and Georgia, could evolve from being part-time bodies and begin to take on more of the characteristics of full-time legislatures.[9]

Demographics of Legislators

The number of minorities and women state lawmakers continued to grow following the 1992 election. In 1993, 1,516 or 20 percent of the nation's lawmakers were women. This represents a 12 percent increase over the 1991 total and a five-fold increase since 1969, when 301 or 4 percent of all legislators were women. The number of women holding leadership positions in state legislatures also is growing. In 1993, 27 women held positions as presiding officer, majority and minority leader compared to four women who held similar positions in 1979. The number of Hispanic lawmakers grew by 26 percent following the 1992 election, increasing to 161 or just over 2 percent of the total. In 1993, there were 514 African-American lawmakers (6.92 percent of the total), which represented a 20 percent increase over the 1991 total. In 1993, there were also 40 Native American lawmakers (0.54 percent of the total) and 54 Asian-American (0.73 percent of the total) lawmakers.[10]

The number of districts with a majority of minority citizens that were drawn up during the redistricting process following the 1990 census accounts for some of this increase.

African Americans gained 79 seats nationwide over the total they held following the 1990 election. Gains were impressive in the South where they won more than 15 percent of the elections in Alabama, Georgia, Louisiana (1991 elections), Maryland (1990 elections), Mississippi and South Carolina. Blacks now occupy nearly 7 percent of all legislative seats, up from 2 percent in 1970 and 6 percent after the 1990 elections. Some election experts argue that this change has improved Republican chances in states with large black populations. They theorize that by increasing the number of blacks in legislative districts, the surrounding, mostly suburban, districts become more Republican.[11]

Bill Introductions

In an attempt to deal with increased workloads, state legislatures have adopted a number of techniques to reduce the number of bills introduced and to consider them more efficiently. Limits on bill introductions and deadlines for introducing bills are two examples of techniques legislatures have adopted. The California, Colorado, Indiana, Louisiana, Michigan, Montana, Nevada and North Dakota legislatures and the Florida House, Hawaii House and Tennessee Senate limit the number of bills each member can introduce. For example, Colorado limits a member to five bills in each regular session of the General Assembly.

Forty-seven legislatures have deadlines for bill introductions, and 47 allow filing of bills before the session begins. (See Tables 3.14 and 3.15) These procedures are designed to encourage members to introduce bills earlier in the session so committees can begin work upon convening. In addition, 14 legislative chambers use proposed, short form or skeleton bills. If, after initial consideration, there is interest in pursuing policies embodied in the skeleton bills, a complete bill will be drafted. By using skeleton bills, legislatures reduce the number of bills introduced, ease the burden on bill drafters and give committees the opportunity to combine duplicate proposals into a single bill.[12]

From 1975 to 1990, state legislatures considered an average of 193,000 bills each biennium. The number introduced in each state during a biennium varied from a low of about 1,000 in Alaska, Colorado, North Dakota, Vermont and Wyoming to highs of more than 30,000 in New York and 18,000 in Massachusetts. During the same period legislatures passed an average of 23 percent of all bills introduced or about 43,000 in an average biennium.[13]

Legislative Compensation

Adequate pay for state lawmakers is a key ingredient in attracting qualified and dedicated people to serve in legislatures. It was a principal recommendation of legislative reformers three decades ago. In the mid-1960s legislative salaries were set by the constitutions in 26 states. Because of the difficulty in amending the constitution to revise salaries, legislative reformers recommended that salaries be removed from state constitutions. Currently, only five states retain constitutional limits on pay. These states pay relatively low salaries such as Alabama's $10 per day for 105 calendar day regular session, New Hampshire's $100 per year and Rhode Island's $5 per day for 60 session days. One recommendation in a blue ribbon citizens commission's study to improve the Rhode Island General Assembly was to raise the salaries of lawmakers to $10,000 per year. See Table 3.8 for further information on methods of setting legislative compensation.

In 1994, salaries range from a low of $100 per year in New Hampshire to a high of $57,500 per year in New York. Eleven states will pay lawmakers annual salaries of $30,000 or more in 1994, with five of these states paying in excess of $40,000 annually. All but five states pay legislators a per diem to cover living expenses. In at least 40 Houses and 32 Senates, presiding officers and majority or minority leaders receive additional compensation. In at least 13 states, additional pay is given to other leaders such as deputy leaders, assistant leaders, whips, caucus chairs, speakers pro tem and policy chairs. In at least 11 states committee chairs get extra pay. In eight states all chairs receive additional compensation; in the other states it is limited to chairs of specific committees such as finance or ways and means. (See Tables 3.9, 3.11 and 3.12)

In at least 41 states, lawmakers are eligible for retirement benefits in addition to their salaries. The 1990 citizen initiative adopted by California voters that limits legislators' terms also eliminated lawmakers' retirement benefits. Those elected in 1990 and beyond are barred from participating in the legislative retirement system. Those who currently are participating can remain in the system. (See Table 3.13)

Lawmakers in at least 43 states receive insurance benefits such as health, dental and optical coverage. In most of these states it is the same as provided for state employees. California and Pennsylvania provide monthly allowances to lease automobiles, and certain leaders in Louisiana, Missouri, New Jersey and New York are provided a state car.

Office expenses, staff allowances, or both are paid to legislators in at least 31 states. Some states provide relatively low allowances for expenses such as Idaho's $500 per year and Maine's "Constituent Service Allowance" of $750 per year for representatives and $1,000 per year for senators. Other states, such as California, New York and Texas, provide staffing allowances of more than $100,000 to pay district office employees. (See Table 3.10)

Legislative Staffing

The growth and development of professional staffs have helped make state legislatures more independent and effective institutions. Through their ability to gather, evaluate, process and synthesize information, staff members free lawmakers from their dependence on lobbyists and executive agencies for information.

The number of legislative staffers grew dramatically throughout the 1970s and 1980s. For example, the number of staff working in state legislatures grew by approximately 24 percent, from almost 27,000 total staff in 1979 to more than 33,000 total staff by 1988. Most of this growth came in the area of full-time professional staff, which grew by 5,400, or almost 65 percent. The number of session-only staff declined by 12 percent during the same period. The 1980s also saw the decentralization of legislative staff as legislatures added personal staff for individual lawmakers, party caucus staff and policy staff for legislative committees.[14]

The 1990s mark a new era for legislative staffing. Unlike the previous three decades in which there was a steady growth in the size of legislative staffs, the number is likely to remain constant throughout the 1990s. Tight budgets and a national focus on reinventing government are forcing legislative staff units to re-examine their missions, streamline their operations and change their organizational structures. Although few legislatures are cutting the number of legislative staff, lawmakers are asking staffers to demonstrate their value and to do more with less.[15]

California, however, is a state that drastically cut the number of legislative staff. Proposition 140, approved by the voters in 1990, limited lawmakers' terms and also set a $115 million ceiling on total legislative expenditures. This resulted in a 38 percent cut in the Legislature's budget, which forced more than 600 staffers out of work and a restructuring of several legislative staff agencies. For example, the Legislature made the auditor general's office part of the executive branch rather than the Legislature and mandated that it do specific legislative audits. The legislative analyst's office remained part of the Legislature. However, the number of staffers working there was cut by almost 60 percent, and the number of studies undertaken was reduced dramatically.

A 1992 NCSL survey of legislative staff directors revealed some of the changes wrought by these new conditions. Directors in 26 states indicated they have undertaken a "significant re-examination" of their operations ranging from complete reassessments of their organization to more limited evaluations of how to cut costs. In most cases, staff agencies are rethinking relationships with their key clients and setting new priorities for future operations.[16]

Oregon's nonpartisan Legislative Administration Committee undertook a self-assessment that resulted in a major reorganization. The agency created three units, each with a distinct objective to provide "one-stop shopping" for their customers. In addition, the traditional hierarchical management system was scrapped in favor of work teams. Virginia's Joint Legislative Audit and Review Commission streamlined its research process, re-evaluated the agency's

administrative functions, rewrote its style manual and developed a list of strategic issues for future computer upgrades as a result of an internal review of its operations. The Maine Legislature directed the Legislative Council staff to develop an operational plan based on Total Quality Management. Maine's Committee on Total Quality Management in the Legislature, composed of lawmakers and staff, recommended changes in joint committee procedures, modifications in the confirmation of gubernatorial nominations and proposals for providing better institutional information to people attending committee hearings. This committee is examining ways to expand and improve the orientation for new lawmakers, increase citizen access to the legislative process and change in the budget process.

During the past four years Delaware, Maryland and West Virginia completed studies of their legislative staff structures. The West Virginia Legislature reorganized its staff, hired an executive director and added staff to do performance audits. In Idaho, the Legislature also reorganized its staff by consolidating all the staff agencies within a new Legislative Services Office. The goals of this office include providing effective coordination among all staff, consolidating functions and avoiding duplication, designing and implementing a performance evaluation program, redesigning post-auditing procedures, and strengthening the institutional identity of the Legislature.

Legislative Facilities

Legislatures are modern institutions and need offices, committee rooms and access to communications and information technologies to conduct their business effectively. The number of staff and the public's desire to participate in the legislative process are some of the factors driving the demand for additional and more sophisticated office space. At the same time, legislators must balance the need for modern facilities with the need to preserve the architectural integrity of state capitols. In the late 1980s, Connecticut opened a new legislative office building, and Pennsylvania added a new wing to its main Capitol. Wisconsin moved staff and legislator offices into leased space outside the Capitol. In 1993, Texas completed construction on a new four-story underground office complex and parking garage behind the Capitol.

Michigan, Ohio, Texas and Wisconsin are renovating and restoring their capitols and legislative chambers. New Mexico completed a restoration of its capitol in 1992, and New Jersey reopened its restored Statehouse in 1993. Minnesota restored its Capitol to the way it was in 1905. Many of these restoration projects involve undoing renovations completed in the 1950s and 1960s that jeopardized the capitols' historical integrity.[17]

Disasters struck the capitols in Idaho and Oregon. A fire in the Idaho Capitol on New Year's Day 1992 damaged the rotunda and offices, blackened ornamental plasterwork and cracked the exterior sandstone. A team of architects, engineers, historians and designers was able to repair the damage. The Oregon Capitol suffered damage during a brief earthquake in 1993 that registered 5.7 on the Richter scale. The rotunda was cracked as were the concrete and steel beams that support the Capitol roof. Golden Pioneer, the 23-foot, 10-ton statue that tops the rotunda, was rocked free and twisted an eighth-inch to the east by the earthquake. The legislative session continued on schedule despite the damage as lawmakers moved to a hearing room in the basement until workers hung nets in the chambers to catch falling concrete.[18]

Technology

The evolution of computer technology — particularly the development of powerful, relatively inexpensive personal computers — has changed the operations of state legislatures significantly. Computers have enhanced the legislatures' policy-making capacity, increased the efficiency of legislative functions such as bill drafting and journal production, and expanded legislators' ability to provide constituent services. Through networking, legislative computer systems can be connected with executive agency systems and the legislatures' computers in different locations. North Carolina and Washington, for example, receive executive agency expenditure data when entered

into the agencies' systems. California, Florida and New Jersey link computers in the district offices with the legislatures' main information system at the capitol. Minnesota and Wisconsin are among the legislatures using advanced technology such as CD-ROM, thus enhancing public access to state statutes. California, Georgia, Hawaii, Maryland, Minnesota, Missouri, North Dakota, Oregon, Utah and Virginia provide free public access to legislative information via the Internet network.

The increase in members who are familiar with computers is driving the type and level of computer technology within legislatures. More lawmakers want access through the legislature's information system to commercial spreadsheet and word processing software packages they use in their private lives. The use of computer systems to answer and track constituent requests also is growing. The issues citizens are concerned about can be tracked and tickler files created to ensure requests are answered. The California Assembly and Louisiana and Washington legislatures are using these types of systems.

The emphasis in legislatures is shifting toward personal computers and local area networks and away from central, mainframe systems. Colorado, for example, has moved most of its computing functions off the state's mainframe onto a PC network. In 1990, the Michigan Senate installed computers on the floor for every senator that wanted one. Senators vote through the computers, review bills and amendments, receive messages via electronic mail and access the systems in their offices to draft correspondence and communicate with staff. In the 1991 session, 24 North Dakota legislators (16 House members and eight senators) participated in a project that placed terminals at their desks in the chamber. During the 1993 session, the number of legislators with terminals on their desks was increased to 50 — 33 House members and 17 senators. Members use the terminals to review bills, bill status, the journal and calendars. They also can send and receive messages on an e-mail system as well as draft correspondence. The legislature is considering increasing the number of computers placed on the floor and using personal computers rather than terminals attached to the state mainframe computer. During the 1992 session, the Florida House installed computers on the floor with capabilities similar to those in the Michigan Senate. Indiana is implementing a wireless computer network in the legislative chamber. Under this system, members will have a portable computer on their desks connected to a local area network via wireless communications technology.

Legislatures also are using other forms of technology to better communicate with the public and to improve public access to legislative information. In Alaska for example, citizens can send "public opinion messages" to their lawmakers via the computer system available in all Legislative Information Offices. In addition, for a small fee, anyone with a personal computer and modem can retrieve bills, bill status, the Alaska Constitution, statutes, committee minutes and legislative journals. At least 14 states place computer terminals in the capitol for the public to access legislative records such as bill status and bill summaries. Hawaii has installed public access terminals in shopping malls.[19]

A number of legislatures use video conferencing to make it easier for people to participate in legislative hearings. Alaska has been using audio teleconferencing since 1978. California, Nebraska and Wyoming have held interactive televised hearings in which citizens testified from remote locations in the state. Kentucky turned one of its committee rooms into a teleconferencing center that the General Assembly will use to beam committee hearings and other meetings to four sites around the state. Nevada uses teleconferencing to link hearing rooms in the Capitol in Carson City with Las Vegas, bringing the Legislature closer to the majority of its citizens.

Party Control

Democrats continue to control the majority of legislative seats, although Republicans made gains in the 1992 elections. Republicans controlled nine new legislative chambers following these elections, while Democrats gained control of two Senates previously controlled by Republicans. Nationwide, Democrats lost 150 seats in the 1992 election.[20] All New Jersey lawmakers and members of the Virginia House of Delegates were up for election in 1993. Republicans maintained control of both houses in New Jersey, but Democrats picked up three seats in the Senate and six in the House. Republicans gained six seats in the Virginia House, giving them 47 members to the Democrats 52. There is one independent in the Virginia House.[21] At the start of the 1994 sessions, Democrats controlled both chambers in 25 states, Republicans controlled both in eight states and 16 were split between the parties. Nebraska is unicameral and nonpartisan. Following the 1993 elections, there were 4,318 Democratic lawmakers, 3,022 Republicans, 15 independents, seven members of other parties and 13 vacant seats.[22]

During the 1980s and into the 1990s, Republicans have gained strength in the South. They now control 30 percent of the seats in that region compared to 10 percent 30 years ago and 17 percent in 1982. They are tied in the Florida Senate, and it is likely that Republicans will control at least one or more chambers in the South before the end of the 1990s.[23]

Two chambers, the Florida Senate and Michigan House, were tied following the 1992 elections. Two other chambers, the Pennsylvania Senate and the Wisconsin Senate, became tied due to party switches and vacancies. In Pennsylvania and Wisconsin, one party gained a majority and the tie was broken. The Florida Senate and Michigan House operated under power-sharing arrangements negotiated between the two parties.

In Florida, the leadership term was divided in half with the Republican Ander Crenshaw serving as Senate President the first year and Democrat Pat Thomas serving the second year. To ensure things went as planned, Crenshaw tendered a letter of resignation effective October 1993, and the Senate adopted a rule requiring the pro tem (Thomas' position) to automatically ascend to the presidency. A unanimous vote was required to amend the ascendancy rule. Committee membership was divided equally between the parties.[24]

Lawmakers in the Michigan House decided to have co-speakers, each one presiding for a month at a time throughout the session. Committees have an equal number of Republicans and Democrats, and each has co-chairs and co-vice chairs that rotate monthly. The committee co-chairs and co-vice chairs selected by the Democratic speaker will preside in those months when the House presiding officers are Republican and vice versa. Co-chief clerks were elected with the Republican clerk serving with the Democratic Speaker and vice versa. A written agreement between the parties that created this power-sharing arrangement can be amended with a majority vote.[25]

The Pennsylvania Senate became evenly divided between Republicans and Democrats when a senator originally elected as a Republican, but who voted with the Democrats and who ran for Congress as a Democrat, joined with Democrats to organize the Senate. This gave the tie-breaking vote to the Democratic lieutenant governor, who used it to elect a Democrat as president pro tem. Rather than wait until the beginning of the 1993 sessions, the Democrats seized control in the waning days of the 1992 session. In 1993, a special election was held to fill the seat of a Democratic member who died. The results of the election were disputed. After several recounts and court cases, the Democratic candidate, who was originally declared the winner and seated, was ordered removed from the Senate by a federal court because of voting fraud. Republicans regained partisan control of the Senate in March 1994 after the death of another Democratic senator gave them a majority.[26]

The Wisconsin Senate became tied when two Democratic senators were elected to Congress and a third was appointed to a post in the state Labor Department. Although Democrats organized the Senate in early 1993 before the two senators left for Congress, the rules were changed when the body became tied. An even number of Republicans and Democrats were appointed to all committees. While Democrats retained their positions as committee chairs, Republicans were named as vice chairs on all committees. Republicans gained control of the Senate in the spring of 1993 when they won two of the three special elections to fill the vacant seats.[27]

Future Changes in State Legislatures

Increasing the level of public trust in and support for the legislative institution are the major challenges facing state legislatures in the 1990s. To meet these challenges legislatures must preserve the integrity of the legislative process, improve public understanding of the role and function of state legislatures and discharge their constitutional responsibilities effectively.

Real or perceived unethical behavior by lawmakers and staff erodes public confidence in all legislators. Even though legislative behavior is subject to more stringent rules and more closely scrutinized now than at any time in recent history, public expectations are high. Standards of conduct have shifted over time, and actions that were once acceptable are now a cause for concern. Legislatures have reacted to this change in public attitudes by enacting ever more stringent ethics laws. In several states, such as Minnesota, South Carolina and Wisconsin, lawmakers are prohibited from receiving anything of value, including a cup of coffee. As the decade unfolds, lawmakers are likely to continue to take ethics seriously, adopt stricter ethics laws and focus greater attention on enforcing those ethics statutes on the books.

Public support for the legislative institution also depends on public understanding of the role and function of legislatures. Legislatures provide a wide variety of information to the public such as the status of bills, session schedules and summaries of bills. An increasing number of legislatures are using technology such as computer bulletin boards and video teleconferencing to make the legislative process more accessible to the public. This trend toward using technology to bring legislatures to the people is likely to continue. Legislatures also are likely to concentrate greater efforts at providing information about the legislative process to students. NCSL is working with the states to develop information that can be used to teach classes on legislatures.

Legislatures are also likely to continue efforts to increase their capacity to deal with policy issues. These efforts are likely to concentrate on ways to handle the increased workloads within current limits on session time. The trend toward increasing professionalization of state legislatures that was so apparent during the past three decades is moderating. Legislatures are not likely to add large numbers of new staff, extend the length of sessions or significantly increase lawmakers salaries. The focus on internal legislative operations that was so consuming during the past 30 years will have less of an effect on legislative performance. Most legislatures have the requisite staff, facilities and technology to be considered modern institutions. Only marginal gains in increased effectiveness will be achieved through improved internal procedures. In short, legislatures have been "modernized," and public support will be based primarily on how they use these resources to address the problems facing the states.

Footnotes

[1] Karl T. Kurtz, *The Public Standing of the Legislature.* A paper prepared for the Symposium on the Legislature in the Twenty-First Century, Williamsburg, Virginia, March 1990.

[2] The Harwood Group, *Citizens and Politics: A View from Main Street America* (Dayton, Ohio: The Kettering Foundation, 1991), p. 1-9.

[3] John Burns, *The Sometimes Governments* (New York: Bantam Books, 1971), p. 32.

[4] The Blue Ribbon Commission on the General Assembly, *The General Assembly in Rhode Island: A Blue Print for the 21st Century* (Providence, Rhode Island: The Blue Ribbon Commission on the General Assembly, 1994), pp. 4-12.

[5] Conversation with Bruce Levi, Counsel, North Dakota Consensus Council, March 11, 1994.

[6] Data compiled by the National Conference of State Legislatures and The Council of State Governments, March 1994.

[7] National Conference of State Legislatures, *Strengthening State Legislatures: A Report of NCSL's Legislative Institution Task Force* (Denver: National Conference of State Legislatures, 1994), p. 13.

[8] Eric Hirsch, *State Legislators Occupations: 1993 Update* (Denver: National Conference of State Legislatures, 1994).

[9] Karl T. Kurtz, *Understanding the Diversity of American State Legislatures*, National Conference of State Legislatures, June 1992.

[10] National Conference of State Legislatures, *A Compilation of Asian, Black, Hispanic, Native American and Women Legislators.* February 1993.

[11] Karl T. Kurtz, "The Election in Perspective," *State Legislatures*, January 1993, p. 17.

[12] American Society of Legislative Clerks and Secretaries and National Conference of State Legislatures, *Inside the Legislative Process* 1992 ed. (Denver: National Conference of State Legislatures, 1992).

[13] National Conference of State Legislatures. Compilation of bill introductions and passage rates, 1975-1990, updated in 1994.

[14] Brian Weberg, "Changes in Legislative Staff," *Journal of State Government* 61 (November/December 1988), pp. 191-197.

[15] Brian Weberg, "Change Ahead for Legislative Staffs," *State Legislatures*, February 1993, pp. 22-23.

[16] *Ibid.*

[17] Laura Loyacono, "Our Magnificent Monuments," *State Legislatures*, August 1992, pp. 16-17.

[18] "Earthquake Puts Oregon Legislature in the Cellar," *State Legislatures*, June 1993, p. 8.

[19] Citizen Education Task Force of the Legislative Staff Coordinating Committee, *Educating Citizens About the Legislature: Six Recommendations* (Denver: National Conference of State Legislatures, 1993), pp. 11-13.

[20] Kurtz, "The Election in Perspective," p. 16.

[21] "Voters Turn Out to Decide Taxes, Term Limits, Tuition," *State Legislatures*, January 1994, p. 6.

[22] National Conference of State Legislatures, *Partisan Composition of State Legislatures*, November 1993.

[23] Kurtz, "The Election in Perspective," p. 16.

[24] Bill Moss, "Sunshine State Detente," *State Legislatures*, July 1993, pp. 27-33.

[25] George Weeks and Don Weeks, "Taking Turns," *State Legislatures*, July 1993, pp. 19-25.

[26] National Conference of State Legislatures, *Leaders Letter*, February 1994, p. 1.

[27] "Special Election Will Decide Fate of Tied Wisconsin Senate," *State Legislatures*, April 1993, p. 11.

Table 3.1
NAMES OF STATE LEGISLATIVE BODIES AND CONVENING PLACES

State or other jurisdiction	Both bodies	Upper house	Lower house	Convening place
Alabama	Legislature	Senate	House of Representatives	State House
Alaska	Legislature	Senate	House of Representatives	State Capitol
Arizona	Legislature	Senate	House of Representatives	State Capitol
Arkansas	General Assembly	Senate	House of Representatives	State Capitol
California	Legislature	Senate	Assembly	State Capitol
Colorado	General Assembly	Senate	House of Representatives	State Capitol
Connecticut	General Assembly	Senate	House of Representatives	State Capitol
Delaware	General Assembly	Senate	House of Representatives	Legislative Hall
Florida	Legislature	Senate	House of Representatives	The Capitol
Georgia	General Assembly	Senate	House of Representatives	State Capitol
Hawaii	Legislature	Senate	House of Representatives	State Capitol
Idaho	Legislature	Senate	House of Representatives	State Capitol
Illinois	General Assembly	Senate	House of Representatives	State House
Indiana	General Assembly	Senate	House of Representatives	State House
Iowa	General Assembly	Senate	House of Representatives	State Capitol
Kansas	Legislature	Senate	House of Representatives	State Capitol
Kentucky	General Assembly	Senate	House of Representatives	State Capitol
Louisiana	Legislature	Senate	House of Representatives	State Capitol
Maine	Legislature	Senate	House of Representatives	State House
Maryland	General Assembly	Senate	House of Delegates	State House
Massachusetts	General Court	Senate	House of Representatives	State House
Michigan	Legislature	Senate	House of Representatives	State Capitol
Minnesota	Legislature	Senate	House of Representatives	State Capitol
Mississippi	Legislature	Senate	House of Representatives	New Capitol
Missouri	General Assembly	Senate	House of Representatives	State Capitol
Montana	Legislature	Senate	House of Representatives	State Capitol
Nebraska	Legislature	(a)		State Capitol
Nevada	Legislature	Senate	Assembly	Legislative Building
New Hampshire	General Court	Senate	House of Representatives	State House
New Jersey	Legislature	Senate	General Assembly	State House
New Mexico	Legislature	Senate	House of Representatives	State Capitol
New York	Legislature	Senate	Assembly	State Capitol
North Carolina	General Assembly	Senate	House of Representatives	State Legislative Building
North Dakota	Legislative Assembly	Senate	House of Representatives	State Capitol
Ohio	General Assembly	Senate	House of Representatives	State House
Oklahoma	Legislature	Senate	House of Representatives	State Capitol
Oregon	Legislative Assembly	Senate	House of Representatives	State Capitol
Pennsylvania	General Assembly	Senate	House of Representatives	Main Capitol Building
Rhode Island	General Assembly	Senate	House of Representatives	State House
South Carolina	General Assembly	Senate	House of Representatives	State House
South Dakota	Legislature	Senate	House of Representatives	State Capitol
Tennessee	General Assembly	Senate	House of Representatives	State Capitol
Texas	Legislature	Senate	House of Representatives	State Capitol
Utah	Legislature	Senate	House of Representatives	State Capitol
Vermont	General Assembly	Senate	House of Representatives	State House
Virginia	General Assembly	Senate	House of Delegates	State Capitol
Washington	Legislature	Senate	House of Representatives	Legislative Building
West Virginia	Legislature	Senate	House of Delegates	State Capitol
Wisconsin	Legislature	Senate	Assembly (b)	State Capitol
Wyoming	Legislature	Senate	House of Representatives	State Capitol
Dist. of Columbia	Council of the District of Columbia	(a)		District Building
American Samoa	Legislature	Senate	House of Representatives	Maota Fono Congress Building
Guam	Legislature	(a)		Civic Center Building
No. Mariana Islands	Legislature	Senate	House of Representatives	The Capitol
Puerto Rico	Legislative Assembly	Senate	House of Representatives	Capitol Building
U.S. Virgin Islands	Legislature	(a)		

(a) Unicameral legislature. Except in Dist. of Columbia, members go by the title Senator.

(b) Members of the lower house go by the title Representative.

Table 3.2
LEGISLATIVE SESSIONS: LEGAL PROVISIONS

State or other jurisdiction	Regular sessions				Special sessions		
	Year	Legislature convenes		Limitation on length of session (a)	Legislature may call	Legislature may determine subject	Limitation on length of session
		Month	Day				
Alabama	Annual	Jan. / Apr. / Feb.	2nd Tues. (b) / 3rd Tues. (c,d) / 1st Tues. (e)	30 L in 105 C	No	Yes (f)	12 L in 30 C
Alaska	Annual	Jan. / Jan.	3rd Mon. (c) / 2nd Mon. (e)	120 C (g)	By 2/3 vote of members	Yes (h)	30 C
Arizona	Annual	Jan.	2nd Mon.	(i)	By petition, 2/3 members, each house	Yes (h)	None
Arkansas	Biennial-odd year	Jan.	2nd Mon.	60 C (g)	No	Yes (f,j)	(j)
California	(k)	Jan.	1st Mon. (d)	None	No	No	None
Colorado	Annual	Jan.	2nd Wed.	120 C	By request, 2/3 members, each house	Yes (h)	None
Connecticut	Annual (l)	Jan. / Feb.	Wed. after 1st Mon. (m) / Wed. after 1st Mon. (n)	(o)	Yes (p)	(p)	None (q)
Delaware	Annual	Jan.	2nd Tues.	June 30	Joint call, presiding officers, both houses	Yes	None
Florida	Annual	Feb.	Tues. after 1st Mon. (d)	60 C (g)	Joint call, presiding officers, both houses	Yes	20 C (g)
Georgia	Annual	Jan.	2nd Mon.	40 L	By petition, 3/5 members, each house	Yes (h)	(r)
Hawaii	Annual	Jan.	3rd Wed.	60 L (g)	By petition, 2/3 members, each house	Yes	30 L (g)
Idaho	Annual	Jan.	Mon. on or nearest 9th day	None	No	No	20 C
Illinois	Annual	Jan.	2nd Wed.	None	Joint call, presiding officers, both houses	Yes (h)	None
Indiana	Annual	Jan.	2nd Mon. (d,s)	odd-61 L or Apr. 30; even-30 L or Mar. 15	No	Yes	30 L or 40 C
Iowa	Annual	Jan.	2nd Mon.	(t)	By petition, 2/3 members, both houses	Yes (h)	None
Kansas	Annual	Jan.	2nd Mon.	odd-None; even-90 C (g)	Petition to governor of 2/3 members, each house	Yes	None
Kentucky	Biennial-even yr.	Jan.	Tues. after 1st Mon. (d)	60 L (u)	No	No	None
Louisiana	Annual	Mar. / Apr.	last Mon. (d,m) / last Mon. (l, n)	odd-60 L in 85 C; even-30 L in 45 C	By petition, majority, each house	Yes (h)	30 C
Maine	(k,l)	Dec. / Jan.	1st Wed. (b) / Wed. after 1st Tues. (n)	3rd Wed. of June (g) / 3rd Wed. of April (g)	Joint call, presiding officers, with consent of majority of members of each political party, each house	Yes (h)	None
Maryland	Annual	Jan.	2nd Wed.	90 C (g)	By petition, majority, each house	Yes	30 C
Massachusetts	Annual	Jan.	1st Wed.	None	By petition (v)	Yes	None

See footnotes at end of table.

LEGISLATIVE SESSIONS: LEGAL PROVISIONS—Continued

State or other jurisdiction	Regular sessions				Special sessions		
	Legislature convenes			Limitation on length of session (a)	Legislature may call	Legislature may determine subject	Limitation on length of session
	Year	Month	Day				
Michigan	Annual	Jan.	2nd Wed. (d)	None	No	No	None
Minnesota	(w)	Jan.	Tues. after 1st Mon. (m)	120 L or 1st Mon. after 3rd Sat. in May (w)	No	Yes	None
Mississippi	Annual	Jan.	Tues. after 1st Mon.	125 C (g,x); 90 C (g,x)	No	No	None
Missouri	Annual	Jan.	Wed. after 1st Mon.	May 30	By petition, 3/4 members, each house	Yes	30 C (y)
Montana	Biennial-odd yr.	Jan.	1st Mon.	90 L (g)	By petition, majority, each house	Yes	None
Nebraska	Annual	Jan.	Wed. after 1st Mon.	odd-90 L (g); even-60 L (g)	By petition, 2/3 members, each house	Yes	None
Nevada	Biennial-odd yr.	Jan.	3rd Mon.	60 C (t)	No	No	20 C (t)
New Hampshire	Annual	Jan.	Wed. after 1st Tues. (d)	45 L	By 2/3 vote of members, each house	Yes	15 L (t)
New Jersey	Annual	Jan.	2nd Tues.	None	By petition, majority, each house	Yes	None
New Mexico	Annual (l)	Jan.	3rd Tues.	odd-60 C; even-30 C	By petition, 3/5 members, each house	Yes (h)	30 C
New York	Annual	Jan.	Wed. after 1st Mon.	None	By petition, 2/3 members, each house	Yes (h)	None
North Carolina	(w)	Jan.	3rd Wed. after 2nd Mon. (m)	None	By petition, 3/5 members, each house	Yes	None
North Dakota	Biennial-odd yr.	Jan.	Tues. after Jan. 3, but not later than Jan. 11 (d)	80 L (z)	No	Yes	None
Ohio	Annual	Jan.	1st Mon.	None	Joint call, presiding officers, both houses	Yes	None
Oklahoma	Annual	Feb.	1st Mon. (aa)	160 C	By 2/3 vote of members, each house	Yes (h)	None
Oregon	Biennial-odd yr.	Jan.	2nd Mon.	None	By petition, majority, each house	Yes	None
Pennsylvania	Annual	Jan.	1st Tues.	None	By petition, majority, each house	No	None
Rhode Island	Annual	Jan.	1st Tues.	60 L (t)	No	No	None
South Carolina	Annual	Jan.	2nd Tues. (d)	1st Thurs. in June (g)	No	Yes	None
South Dakota	Annual	Jan.	2nd Tues.	odd-40 L; even-35 L	No	No	None
Tennessee	(w)	Jan.	(bb)	90 L (t)	By petition, 2/3 members, each house	Yes	30 L (t)
Texas	Biennial-odd yr.	Jan.	2nd Tues.	140 C	No	No	30 C
Utah	Annual	Jan.	2nd Mon.	45 C	No	No	30 C
Vermont	(w)	Jan.	Wed. after 1st Mon. (m)	None	No	Yes	None
Virginia	Annual	Jan.	2nd Wed.	odd-30 C (g); even-60 C (g)	By petition, 2/3 members, each house	Yes	None

LEGISLATIVE SESSIONS: LEGAL PROVISIONS—Continued

State or other jurisdiction	Regular sessions				Special sessions		
	Legislature convenes			Limitation on length of session (a)	Legislature may call	Legislature may determine subject	Limitation on length of session
	Year	Month	Day				
Washington.........	Annual	Jan.	2nd Mon.	odd-105 C; even-60 C	By vote, 2/3 members, each house	Yes	30 C
West Virginia.......	Annual	Feb. Jan.	2nd Wed. (c,d) 2nd Wed. (e)	60 C (g)	By petition, 3/5 members, each house	Yes (cc)	None
Wisconsin..........	Annual (dd)	Jan.	1st Mon. (m)	None	No	No	None
Wyoming	Annual (l)	Jan. Feb.	2nd Tues. (m) 3rd Mon. (n)	odd-40 L; even-20 L	No	Yes	None
Dist. of Columbia	(ee)	Jan.	2nd day	None			
American Samoa	Annual	Jan. July	2nd Mon. 2nd Mon.	45 L 45 L	No	No	None
Guam	Annual	Jan.	2nd Mon. (ff)	None	No	No	None
No. Mariana Islands .	Annual	(gg)	(d,gg)	90 L (gg)	Upon request of presiding officers, both houses	Yes (h)	10 C
Puerto Rico........	Annual	Jan.	2nd Mon.	Apr. 30 (g)	No	No	20 C
U.S. Virgin Islands	Annual	Jan.	2nd Mon.	75 L	No	No	15 C

Sources: State constitutions and statutes.

Note: Some legislatures will also reconvene after normal session to consider bills vetoed by governor. Connecticut—if governor vetoes any bill, secretary of state must reconvene General Assembly on second Monday after the last day on which governor is either authorized to transmit or has transmitted every bill with his objections, whichever occurs first; General Assembly must adjourn *sine die* not later than three days after its reconvening. Hawaii—legislature may reconvene on 45th day after adjournment *sine die*, in special session, without call. Louisiana—legislature meets in a maximum five-day veto session on the 40th day after final adjournment. Missouri—if governor returns any bill on or after the fifth day before the last day on which legislature may consider bills (in even-numbered years), legislature automatically reconvenes on first Wednesday following the second Monday in September for a maximum 10 C session. New Jersey—legislature meets in special session (without call or petition) to act on bills returned by governor on 45th day after *sine die* adjournment of the regular session; if the second year expires before the 45th day, the day preceding the end of the legislative year. Utah—if 2/3 of the members of each house favor reconvening to consider vetoed bills, a maximum five-day session is set by the presiding officers. Virginia—legislature reconvenes on sixth Wednesday after adjournment for a maximum three-day session (may be extended to seven days upon vote of majority of members elected to each house). Washington—upon petition of 2/3 of the members of each house, legislature meets 45 days after adjournment for a maximum five-day session.

Key:
C — Calendar day
L — Legislative day (in some states, called a session day or workday; definition may vary slightly, however, generally refers to any day on which either house of the legislature is in session)
(a) Applies to each year unless otherwise indicated.
(b) General election year (quadrennial election year).
(c) Year after quadrennial election.
(d) Legal provision for organizational session prior to stated convening date. Alabama—in the year after quadrennial election, on the second Tuesday in January for 10 C. California—in the even-numbered, general election year, on first Monday in December for an organizational session, recess until the first Monday in January of the odd-numbered year. Florida—in general election year, 14th day after election. Indiana—third Tuesday after first Monday in November. Kentucky—in odd-numbered year, Tuesday day after first Monday in January for 10 L. Louisiana—in year after general election, second Monday

in January, not to exceed 3 L. Michigan—held in odd-numbered year. New Hampshire—in even-numbered year, first Wednesday in December. North Dakota—in December. South Carolina—in even-numbered year, Tuesday after certification of election of its members for a maximum three-day session. West Virginia—in year after general election, on second Wednesday in January. No. Mariana Islands—in year after general election, second Monday in January.
(e) Other years.
(f) By 2/3 vote each house.
(g) Session may be extended by vote of members in both houses. Alaska: 2/3 vote for 10-day extension. Arkansas: 2/3 vote. Florida: 3/5 vote. Hawaii: petition of 2/3 membership for maximum 15-day extension. Kansas: 2/3 vote. Maine: 2/3 vote for maximum 10 L. Maryland: 3/5 vote for maximum 30 C. Mississippi: 2/3 vote for 30 C extension, no limit on number of extensions. Nebraska: 4/5 vote. South Carolina: 2/3 vote. Virginia: 2/3 vote for 30 C extension. West Virginia: 2/3 vote (or if budget bill has not been acted upon three days before session ends, governor issues proclamation extending session). Puerto Rico: joint resolution.
(h) Only if legislature convenes itself. Special sessions called by the legislature are unlimited in scope in Arizona, Georgia, Maine, and New Mexico.
(i) No constitutional or statutory provision; however, legislative rules require that regular sessions adjourn no later than Saturday of the week during which the 100th day of the session falls.
(j) After governor's business has been disposed of, members may remain in session up to 15 C by a 2/3 vote of both houses.
(k) Regular sessions begin after general election, in December of even-numbered year. In California, legislature meets in December for an organizational session, recesses until the first Monday in January of the odd-numbered year and continues in session until Nov. 30 of next even-numbered year. In Maine, session which begins in December of general election year runs into the following year (odd-numbered); second session begins in next even-numbered year.
(l) Second session limited to consideration of specific types of legislation. Connecticut—individual legislators may only introduce bills of a fiscal nature, emergency legislation and bills raised by committees. Louisiana—fiscal matters. Maine—budgetary matters; legislation in the governor's call; emergency legislation; legislation referred to committees for study. New Mexico—budgets, appropriations and revenue bills; bills drawn pursuant to governor's message; vetoed bills. Wyoming—budget bills.
(m) Odd-numbered years.

LEGISLATIVE SESSIONS: LEGAL PROVISIONS—Continued

(n) Even-numbered years.

(o) Odd-numbered years—not later than Wednesday after first Monday in June; even-numbered years—not later than Wednesday after first Monday in May.

(p) Constitution provides for regular session convening dates and allows that sessions may also be held ". . .at such other times as the General Assembly shall judge necessary." Call by majority of legislators is implied.

(q) Upon completion of business.

(r) Limited to 40 L unless extended by 3/5 vote and approved by the governor, except in cases of impeachment proceedings.

(s) Legislators may reconvene at any time after organizational meeting; however, second Monday in January is the final date by which regular session must be in process.

(t) Indirect limitation; usually restrictions on legislator's pay, per diem, or daily allowance.

(u) May not extend beyond April 15.

(v) Joint rules provide for the submission of a written statement requesting special session by a specified number of members of each chamber.

(w) Legal provision for session in odd-numbered year; however, legislature may divide, and in practice has divided, to meet in even-numbered years as well.

(x) 90 C sessions every year, except the first year of a gubernatorial administration during which the legislative session runs for 125 C.

(y) 30 C if called by legislature; 60 C if called by governor.

(2) No legislative day is shorter than a natural day.

(aa) Odd number years will include a regular session commencing on the first Tuesday after the first Monday in January and recessing not later than the first Monday in February of that year. Limited constitutional duties can be performed.

(bb) Commencement of regular session depends on concluding date of organizational session. Legislature meets, in odd-numbered year, on second Tuesday in January for a maximum 15 C organizational session, then returns on the Tuesday following the conclusion of the organizational session.

(cc) According to a 1955 attorney general's opinion, when the legislature has petitioned to the governor to be called into session, it may then act on any matter.

(dd) The legislature, by joint resolution, establishes the session schedule of activity for the remainder of the biennium at the beginning of the odd-numbered year.

(ee) Each Council period begins on January 2 of each odd-numbered year and ends on January 1 of the following odd-numbered year.

(ff) Legislature meets on the first Monday of each month following its initial session in January.

(gg) 60 L before April 1 and 30 L after July 31.

Table 3.3
THE LEGISLATORS: NUMBERS, TERMS AND PARTY AFFILIATIONS
(As of April 1994)

State or other jurisdiction	Senate						House						Senate and House totals
	Democrats	Republicans	Other	Vacancies	Total	Term	Democrats	Republicans	Other	Vacancies	Total	Term	
All states	1,139	794	2	...	1,984	...	3,193	2,219	20	8	5,440	...	7,424
Alabama............	27	8	...	...	35	4	82	23	...	...	105	4	140
Alaska..............	10	10	...	...	20	4	20	18	2 (a)	...	40	2	60
Arizona.............	12	18	...	...	30	2	25	35	...	...	60	2	90
Arkansas	30	5	...	...	35	4	88	11	1 (b)	...	100	2	135
California...........	22	16	2 (b)	...	40	4	47	33	...	...	80	2	120
Colorado	16	19	...	...	35	4	31	34	...	...	65	2	100
Connecticut	19	17	...	...	36	2	86	65	...	...	151	2	187
Delaware	15	6	...	...	21	4	18	23	...	...	41	2	62
Florida	20	20	...	...	40	4	71	49	...	...	120	2	160
Georgia............	39	17	...	...	56	2	128	52	...	...	180	2	236
Hawaii	22	3	...	...	25	4	47	4	...	...	51	2	76
Idaho	12	23	...	...	35 (c)	2	20	50	...	...	70 (c)	2	105
Illinois.............	27	32	...	...	59	4 (d)	67	51	...	...	118	2	177
Indiana	22	28	...	...	50	4	55	45	...	...	100	2	150
Iowa	27	23	...	...	50	4	49	51	...	...	100	2	150
Kansas	13	27	...	...	40	4	59	66	...	...	125	2	165
Kentucky	24	14	...	...	38	4	71	29	...	...	100	2	138
Louisiana	33	6	...	...	39	4	88	16	1 (b)	...	105	4	144
Maine	20	15	...	...	35	2	91	60	...	...	151	2	186
Maryland	38	9	...	...	47	4	117	24	...	...	141	4	188
Massachusetts	31	9	...	...	40	2	122	35	1 (b)	2	160	2	200
Michigan	16	22	...	...	38	4	55	55	...	...	110	2	148
Minnesota	45 (e)	22 (f)	...	...	67	4	85 (e)	49 (f)	...	...	134	2	201
Mississippi	39	13	...	...	52	4	96	24	2 (b)	...	122	4	174
Missouri	20	14	...	...	34	4	98	65	...	...	163	2	197
Montana............	30	20	...	...	50	4 (g)	47	53	...	...	100	2	150
Nebraska...........	---------- Nonpartisan election ----------				49	4	------------------------- Unicameral -------------------------						49
Nevada	10	11	...	...	21	4	27	12	...	3	42	2	63
New Hampshire	11	13	...	...	24	2	138	254	5 (h)	3	400	2	424
New Jersey..........	16	24	...	...	40	4 (i)	27	53	...	...	80	2	120
New Mexico.........	27	15	...	...	42	4	52	18	...	...	70	2	112
New York	26	35	...	...	61	2	100	50	...	...	150	2	211
North Carolina	39	11	...	...	50	2	78	42	...	...	120	2	170
North Dakota	25	24	...	...	49 (j)	4	33	65	...	...	98 (j)	2	147
Ohio	13	20	...	...	33	4	53	46	...	...	99	2	132
Oklahoma	37	11	...	...	48	4	68	33	...	...	101	2	149
Oregon	16	14	...	...	30	4	28	32	...	...	60	2	90
Pennsylvania	24	26	...	...	50	4	105	98	...	...	203	2	253
Rhode Island	39	11	...	...	50	2	85	15	...	...	100	2	150
South Carolina	30	16	...	...	46	4	73	50	1 (b)	...	124	2	170
South Dakota	20	15	...	...	35	4	28	42	...	...	70	2	105
Tennessee	19	14	...	...	33	4	63	36	...	...	99	2	132
Texas..............	18	13	...	...	31	4	92	58	...	...	150	2	181
Utah	18	11	...	...	29	4	26	49	...	...	75	2	104
Vermont	14	16	...	...	30	2	87	57	6 (k)	...	150	2	180
Virginia............	22	18	...	...	40	4	52	47	1 (b)	...	100	2	140
Washington	28	21	...	...	49	4	65	33	...	...	98	2	147
West Virginia	32	2	...	...	34	4	79	21	...	...	100	2	134
Wisconsin	16	17	...	...	33	4	52	47	...	...	99	2	132
Wyoming	10	20	...	...	30	4	19	41	...	...	60 (l)	2	90
Dist. of Columbia (m) .	12	...	1 (b)	...	13	4	------------------------------ Unicameral ------------------------------						13
American Samoa	---------- Nonpartisan selection ----------				18	4	----------- Nonpartisan election -----------			21	2		39
Guam	14	7	...	...	21	2	------------------------------ Unicameral ------------------------------						21
No. Mariana Islands...	3	6	...	...	9	4	6	10	2 (b)	...	18	2	27
Puerto Rico	8 (n)	20 (o)	1 (p)	...	29 (q)	4	15 (n)	37 (o)	1 (p)	...	53	4	82
U.S. Virgin Islands	8	4	3 (r)	...	15	2	------------------------------ Unicameral ------------------------------						15

See footnotes at end of table.

THE LEGISLATORS: NUMBERS, TERMS AND PARTY AFFILIATIONS—Continued

Source: The Council of State Governments, compiled from various sources.

(a) Independent; Alaskan Independent.

(b) Independent.

(c) As a result of redistricting, membership of the legislature decreased: Senate-from 42 to 35 members, House-from 84 to 70 members.

(d) The entire Senate is up for election every 10 years, beginning in 1972. Senate districts are divided into three groups. One group elects senators for terms of 4 years, 4 years and 2 years, the second group for terms of 4 years, 2 years and 4 years, the third group for terms of 2 years, 4 years, and 4 years.

(e) Democrat-Farmer-Labor.

(f) Independent-Republican.

(g) After each decennial reapportionment, lots are drawn for half of the senators to serve an initial 2-year term. Subsequent elections are for 4-year terms.

(h) Independent (1); Libertarian (4).

(i) Senate terms beginning in January of second year following the U.S. decennial census are for 2 years only.

(j) As a result of redistricting, membership of the legislature decreased: Senate-from 53 to 49 members, House-from 106 to 98 members.

(k) Independent (4); Progressive (2).

(l) As a result of redistricting, membership of the House decreased from 64 to 60 members.

(m) Council of the District of Columbia.

(n) New Progressive Party.

(o) Popular Democratic Party.

(p) Puerto Rico Independent Party.

(q) As a result of redistricting, membership of the Senate increased from 27 to 29.

(r) Independent (2); Indepependent Citizens Movement (1).

Table 3.4
MEMBERSHIP TURNOVER IN THE LEGISLATURES: 1992

State	Senate			House		
	Total number of members	Number of membership changes	Percentage change of total	Total number of members	Number of membership changes	Percentage change of total
Alabama	35 (a)	2	6	105 (a)	2	2
Alaska	20	14	70	40	23	58
Arizona	30	11	37	60	29	48
Arkansas	35	4	11	100	19	19
California	40	9	23	80	32	40
Colorado	35	8	23	65	23	35
Connecticut	36	12	33	151	57	38
Delaware	21	1	5	41	8	20
Florida	40	19	48	120	48	40
Georgia	56	24	43	180	67	37
Hawaii	25	5	20	51	10	20
Idaho	35 (b)	(b)	(b)	70 (b)	(b)	(b)
Illinois	59	23	39	118	49	42
Indiana	50	9	18	100	24	24
Iowa	50	12	24	100	37	37
Kansas	40	22	55	125	47	38
Kentucky	38	6	16	100	19	19
Louisiana	39 (c)	15	38	105 (c)	41	39
Maine	35	16	46	151	52	34
Maryland	47 (a)	2	4	141 (a)	7	5
Massachusetts	40	15	38	160	36	23
Michigan	38 (a)	3	8	110	29	26
Minnesota	67	17	25	134	33	25
Mississippi	52 (c)	28	54	122 (c)	50	41
Missouri	34	8	24	163	48	29
Montana	50	12	24	100	31	31
Nebraska	49	15	31	--------------------------Unicameral--------------------------		
Nevada	21	5	24	42	17	40
New Hampshire	24	8	33	400	154	39
New Jersey	40 (c)	13	33	80 (c)	33	41
New Mexico	42	17	40	70	12	17
New York	61	8	13	150	31	21
North Carolina	50	13	26	120	43	36
North Dakota	49 (d)	(d)	(d)	98 (d)	(d)	(d)
Ohio	33	4	12	99	21	21
Oklahoma	48	6	13	101	18	18
Oregon	30	8	27	60	19	32
Pennsylvania	50	2	4	203	37	18
Rhode Island	50	16	32	100	38	38
South Carolina	46	17	37	124	43	35
South Dakota	35	16	46	70	29	41
Tennessee	33	5	15	99	19	19
Texas	31	9	29	150	41	27
Utah	29	8	28	75	31	41
Vermont	30	12	40	150	53	35
Virginia	40 (c)	15	38	100 (c)	25	25
Washington	49	16	33	98	38	39
West Virginia	34	6	18	100	31	31
Wisconsin	33	7	21	99	26	26
Wyoming	30	14	47	60 (e)	(e)	(e)

Note: Turnover calculated after 1992 legislative elections. Data were obtained by comparing the 1991-92 and 1993-94 editions of *State Elective Officials and the Legislatures*, published by The Council of State Governments.

(a) No election in 1992.

(b) As a result of redistricting, membership of the Idaho Legislature decreased: Senate — from 42 to 35 members, House — from 84 to 70 members. Turnover cannot be determined using method employed here.

(c) Election held in 1991.

(d) As a result of redistricting, membership of the North Dakota Legislative Assembly decreased: Senate — from 53 to 49 members, House — from 106 to 98 members. Turnover cannot be determined using method employed here.

(e) As a result of redistricting, membership of the Wyoming House decreased from 64 to 60 members. Turnover cannot be determined using method employed here.

Table 3.5
THE LEGISLATORS: QUALIFICATIONS FOR ELECTION

State or other jurisdiction	House					Senate				
	Minimum age	U.S. citizen (years)	State resident (years)	District resident (years)	Qualified voter (years)	Minimum age	U.S. citizen (years)	State resident (years)	District resident (years)	Qualified voter (years)
Alabama	21		3 (a)	1		25		3 (a)	1	
Alaska	21		3	1	★	25		3	1	★
Arizona	25	★	3	1		25	★	3	1	
Arkansas	21	★	2	1		25	★	2	1	
California	18	3	3	1	★	18	3	3	1	★
Colorado	25	★		1		25	★		1	
Connecticut	18			★	★	18			★	★
Delaware	24		3 (a)	1		27		3 (a)	1	
Florida	21		2 (a)	★	★	21		2 (a)	★	★
Georgia	21	★	2 (a)	1		25	★	2 (a)	1	
Hawaii	18	★	3	(b)	★	18	★	3	(b)	★
Idaho	18	★		1	★	18	★		1	★
Illinois	21	★		2 (c)		21	★		2 (c)	
Indiana	21	★	2	1		25	★	2	1	
Iowa	21		1	60 days		25		1	60 days	
Kansas	18		2 (a)	★	★	18			★	★
Kentucky	24		2	1		30		6 (a)	1	
Louisiana	18	5	2	1		18	5	2	1	
Maine	21			3 mo.		25		1	3 mo.	
Maryland	21		1 (a)	6 mo. (d)	★	25		1 (a)	6 mo. (d)	★
Massachusetts	18			1		18		5	★	
Michigan	21	★		(b)	★	21	★		(b)	★
Minnesota	21		1	6 mo.	★	21		1	6 mo.	★
Mississippi	21			2	★	25			2	★
Missouri	24		4 (a)	1 (e)	2	30			1 (e)	3
Montana	18			6 mo. (f)		18		1	6 mo. (f)	
Nebraska	U	U	U	U	U	21		1 (a)	1	★
Nevada	21		1 (a)	1	★	21		1 (a)	1	★
New Hampshire	18		2 (a)	★		30		7 (a)	★	
New Jersey	21		2 (a)	1	★	30		4 (a)	1	★
New Mexico	21	★		★	★	25	★		1 (g)	★
New York	18	★	5	1 (g)	★	18	★	5	1	★
North Carolina	(h)	★	1	(b)	★	25	★	2 (a)	(b)	★
North Dakota	18		1	(b)	★	18		1	1	★
Ohio	18			1		18			1	
Oklahoma	21			(b)	★	25	★		(b)	★
Oregon	21	★		1		21	★		1	
Pennsylvania	21		4 (a)	1		25			1	
Rhode Island	18					18				
South Carolina	21			(b)	★★	25	★	4 (a)	(b)	★★
South Dakota	25	★	2	(b)	★	25	★	2	(b)	★
Tennessee	21	★	3 (a)	1 (b)	★	30	★	3	1 (b)	★
Texas	21	★	2	1	★	26	★	5	1	★
Utah	25	★	3	6 mo. (b)	★	25	★	3	6 mo. (b)	★
Vermont	18		2	1		18		2	1	

THE LEGISLATORS: QUALIFICATIONS FOR ELECTION—Continued

State or other jurisdiction	House					Senate				
	Minimum age	U.S. citizen (years)	State resident (years)	District resident (years)	Qualified voter (years)	Minimum age	U.S. citizen (years)	State resident (years)	District resident (years)	Qualified voter (years)
Virginia	21	...	1	★	★	21	...	1	★	★
Washington	18	★	5 (a)	(b)	★	18	★	5 (a)	(b)	★
West Virginia	18	...	1	1	★	25	...	1	1	★
Wisconsin	18	...	1	(b)	...	18	...	(a)	(b)	...
Wyoming	21	★	(a)	1	...	25	★	(a)	1	...
Dist. of Columbia ...	U	U	U	U	U	18	★ (i)	1	★	U
American Samoa	25	★ (i)	5	1	...	30 (j)	★	5	1	...
Guam	U	U	U	U	U	25	...	5	...	U
No. Mariana Islands ..	21	...	3	...	★	25	...	2	1 (l)	...
Puerto Rico (k)	25	★	2	1 (l)	...	30	★	3	...	U
U.S. Virgin Islands ..	U	U	U	U	U	21	★	(a)	...	★

Sources: State constitutions and statutes.

Note: Many state constitutions have additional provisions disqualifying persons from holding office if they are convicted of a felony, bribery, perjury or other infamous crimes.

Key:

U — Unicameral legislature; members are called senators, except in District of Columbia.

★ — Formal provision; number of years not specified.

... — No formal provision.

(a) State citizenship requirement.

(b) Must be a qualified voter of the district; number of years not specified.

(c) Following redistricting, a candidate may be elected from any district that contains a part of the district in which he resided at the time of redistricting, and reelected if a resident of the new district he represents for 18 months prior to reelection.

(d) If the district was established for less than six months, residency is length of establishment of district.

(e) Only if the district has been in existence for one year; if not, then legislator must have been a one year resident of the district(s) from which the new district was created.

(f) Shall be a resident of the county if it contains one or more districts or of the district if it contains all or parts of more than one county.

(g) After redistricting, must have been a resident of the county in which the district is contained for one year immediately preceding election.

(h) A conflict exists between two articles of the constitution, one specifying age for House members (i.e., "qualified voter of the state") and the other related to general eligibility for elective office (i.e., "every qualified voter ... who is 21 years of age ... shall be eligible for election").

(i) Or U.S. national.

(j) Must be registered matai.

(k) Read and write the Spanish or English language.

(l) When there is more than one representative district in a municipality, residence in the municipality shall satisfy this requirement.

Table 3.6
SENATE LEADERSHIP POSITIONS—METHODS OF SELECTION

State or other jurisdiction	President	President pro tem	Majority leader	Assistant majority leader	Majority floor leader	Assistant majority floor leader	Majority whip	Majority caucus chairman	Minority leader	Assistant minority leader	Minority floor leader	Assistant minority floor leader	Minority whip	Minority caucus chairman
Alabama	(a)	ES	EC						EC					
Alaska	ES	AP	EC				EC	EC	EC	EC			EC	
Arizona	ES	AP	EC				EC	EC	EC	EC			EC	EC
Arkansas	(a)	ES												
California	(a)		EC		EC		EC	EC	EC	EC	EC	EC	EC	EC
Colorado (b)	ES	ES	EC	EC				EC	EC	EC	EC		EC	EC
Connecticut (b)	(a)	ES	EC	AT,AL/3			AT,AL	EC	EC	AL/4			EC	EC
Delaware	(a)	EC (c)	EC	EC			EC	AP	EC (d)	EC (e)	EC/2	EC	EC	
Florida	ES	ES	AP				EC	EC	EC	AL/5	EC		EC	EC
Georgia	(a)	ES	EC				EC	EC	EC	EC	EC	EC	EC	EC
Hawaii	ES	ES (f)	EC	EC	EC		EC	EC (g)	EC	EC	EC		EC	EC
Idaho	(a)	ES	EC	EC	AT	AT	AT	AP	EC	AL/5	EC		EC	AL
Illinois	ES (h)		(h)	AP/6			EC	AP	EC	EC	EC	EC	EC	EC
Indiana	(a)	ES	EC	EC	AT		AT	EC	EC	EC	EC	EC	EC	EC
Iowa	ES	ES	EC	EC				EC	EC	EC	EC	EC	EC	
Kansas (i)	ES (f)	ES (f)	EC	EC (j)	EC (j)		EC (k)	(j)	EC	EC	EC		EC	EC
Kentucky	ES	ES					EC	EC	EC	EC	EC		EC	EC
Louisiana	ES	ES	EC (m)	EC (m)	(m)	(m)			EC	EC	EC	EC	EC	
Maine (n)	AP (l)	AP (l)	AP (o)	AP,AL (p)	(o)	(p)	AP,AL		EC (m)	EC (m)	(m)	(m)	EC	
Maryland (n)	ES	ES							EC					
Massachusetts	EC (q)	ES	AP	AP/2					EC (q)	AL/3			ES	(q)
Michigan	(a)	ES	AP	EC			EC	(q)	EC	EC/4	EC	EC	EC	EC
Minnesota	ES	ES	EC	EC			AL/4		EC				EC (r)	
Mississippi	(a)	EC							EC				EC	
Missouri	(a)		EC	EC/3				EC	EC	EC/3	EC	EC	EC	EC
Montana	ES	ES	EC		ES	EC	ES		ES	AL/3	ES	EC	ES	
Nebraska (U)	(a)	ES (s)	EC				EC	EC	EC	EC	EC	EC	EC	EC
Nevada	(a)	ES					EC		EC				EC	
New Hampshire (t)	ES		EC					EC	EC	EC	EC	EC	EC	EC
New Jersey (u)	ES	ES	EC	EC/3				EC	EC	EC/3	EC	EC	EC	EC
New Mexico	(a)	ES	EC				EC	EC	EC	EC	EC		EC	(q)
New York (v)	(a)	ES (w)	ES (w)	AT/2			AT	AT (x)	EC	AL/3	EC	EC	AL	EC
North Carolina (y)	(a)	ES					AT		EC	EC	EC		EC	AL (x)
North Dakota	(a)	ES	EC	EC			EC	EC	EC	ES	EC	EC	EC	EC
Ohio (z)	ES (q)	ES	ES (q)				ES	(q)	ES (q)	ES	EC		ES	(q)
Oklahoma	(a)	ES	EC	EC	EC	EC	EC	EC	EC	EC	EC	EC	EC	EC
Oregon	ES	ES	ES (q)	AL/5			AL	(q)	ES (q)	AL/3	EC	EC	AL	(q)
Pennsylvania	(a)	ES	EC	EC	EC	EC	AL	EC	EC	EC	EC	EC	AL	EC
Rhode Island (y)	(a)	ES	EC	AL/6 (aa)			AL		EC	AL/2 (aa)			AL	EC
South Carolina	(a)	ES												

SENATE LEADERSHIP POSITIONS—METHODS OF SELECTION—Continued

State or other jurisdiction	President	President pro tem	Majority leader	Assistant majority leader	Majority floor leader	Assistant majority floor leader	Majority whip	Majority caucus chairman	Minority leader	Assistant minority leader	Minority floor leader	Assistant minority floor leader	Minority whip	Minority caucus chairman
South Dakota	(a)	ES	EC	EC			EC/2		EC	EC			EC/2	EC (bb)
Tennessee	ES (s)	AP (bb)	EC (bb)					EC (bb)	EC (bb)					EC (bb)
Texas	(a)	ES												
Utah	ES		EC	EC (cc)			EC (cc)		EC	EC (cc)			(cc)	
Vermont	(a)	ES	EC											
Virginia	(a)	EC	EC (dd)		(dd)		EC	EC	EC (dd)		(dd)			EC
Washington (ee)	(a)	ES	EC	EC	EC		AP	EC	EC (ff)	EC	EC (ff)	EC (ff)	AL	EC (ff)
West Virginia	ES	AP	AP				EC	EC	EC	EC			EC	EC
Wisconsin	ES	ES	EC	EC	EC			EC	EC	EC	EC			EC
Wyoming	ES	ES (f)					EC							
Dist. of Columbia (U)	(gg)	(hh)												
American Samoa	ES	ES		EC			EC		EC	EC			EC	
Guam (U)	ES (s)	ES (f)	EC					(q)	EC					(q)
No. Mariana Islands	ES (h)		(h)											
Puerto Rico	ES (q)	ES (f)	EC		ES (ii)				EC/2 (q)					
U.S. Virgin Islands (U)	ES	ES (f)	ES		EC (jj)						EC (jj)			

Source: The Council of State Governments' legislative survey, March 1994.

Note: In some states, the leadership positions in the Senate are not empowered by the law or by the rules of the chamber, but rather by the party members themselves. Entry following slash indicates number of individuals holding specified position.

Key:
ES — Elected or confirmed by all members of the Senate
EC — Elected by party caucus
AP — Appointed by president
AT — Appointed by president pro tempore
AL — Appointed by party leader
(U) — Unicameral legislative body
. . . — Position does not exist or is not selected on a regular basis

(a) Lieutenant governor is president of the Senate by virtue of the office.
(b) Additional positions include deputy president pro tem, two deputy majority leaders (EC), minority leader pro tem, and two deputy minority leaders (appointed by minority leader and approved by party caucus).
(c) Approved by Senate members.
(d) Preferred title is Republican leader.
(e) Official title is minority leader pro tempore.
(f) Official title is vice president. In Guam, vice speaker.
(g) Official title is majority caucus leader.
(h) President also serves as majority leader.
(i) Additional positions include minority caucus policy chair (EC).
(j) Assistant majority leader also serves as majority party caucus chairperson.
(k) Official title is assistant majority leader/whip.
(l) Appointed only in the president's absence.
(m) Majority leader also serves as majority floor leader; minority leader also serves as minority floor leader; assistant majority leader also serves as assistant majority floor leader; assistant minority leader also serves as assistant minority floor leader.
(n) Other positions include deputy majority whip and assistant deputy majority whip; both positions are appointed by president and majority leader.
(o) Majority leader also serves as majority floor leader.
(p) Official title is deputy majority leader. Also serves as assistant majority floor leader.

(q) President and minority floor leader are also caucus chairmen. In Ohio and Puerto Rico, president and minority leader. In Oregon, majority leader and minority leader.
(r) Official title is assistant minority leader/minority whip.
(s) Official title is speaker. In Tennessee, official also has the statutory title of "lieutenant governor."
(t) Additional positions include a Republican leader and a Democratic leader.
(u) Additional positions include deputy majority leader (EC), two deputy assistant minority leaders (EC), and minority leader pro tem (EC).
(v) Additional positions include vice-president pro tem (AT), deputy majority leader (AT), majority program development chairman (AT), deputy minority leader (AL), senior assistant majority leader (AT), majority conference vice-chairman (AT), minority conference vice-chairman (AL), majority conference secretary (AT), deputy majority whip (AT), majority steering committee chairman (AT), minority conference secretary (AL), assistant majority whip (AT), and assistant minority whip (AL).
(w) President pro tempore is also majority leader.
(x) Majority caucus chairman: official title is majority conference chairman. Minority caucus chairman: official title is minority conference chairman.
(y) Additional positions include deputy president pro tempore.
(z) Additional positions include assistant president pro tempore (ES) and assistant minority whip (ES).
(aa) Assistant majority leader: official title is deputy majority leader. Assistant minority leader: official title is deputy minority leader.
(bb) President pro tem: official title is speaker pro tem. Official titles of majority party leaders: Democratic; official titles of minority party leaders: Republican.
(cc) Assistant majority leader also serves as majority floor leader. Assistant minority leader also serves as minority whip.
(dd) Majority leader also serves as majority floor leader. Minority leader also serves as minority floor leader.
(ee) Additional positions include vice president pro tem (ES), majority assistant whip (EC), and Republican assistant whip (EC).
(ff) Customary title of minority party leaders is the party designation (Republican).
(gg) Chairman of the Council, which is an elected position.
(hh) Appointed by the chairman; official title is chairman pro tem.
(ii) Official title is floor leader.
(jj) Official title is alternate floor leader.

Table 3.7
HOUSE LEADERSHIP POSITIONS—METHODS OF SELECTION

State or other jurisdiction	Speaker	Speaker pro tem	Majority leader	Assistant majority leader	Majority floor leader	Assistant majority floor leader	Majority whip	Majority caucus chairman	Minority leader	Assistant minority leader	Minority floor leader	Assistant minority floor leader	Minority whip	Minority caucus chairman
Alabama	EH	EH	EC						EC					
Alaska	EH	AS	EC				EC		EC	EC			EC	
Arizona	EH	AS	EC	EC			EC	EC	EC	EC			EC	EC
Arkansas	EH	EH							EC	AL/10 (e)			AL/2 (b)	EC
California	EH	EH			AS (a)				EC		EC	EC		EC
Colorado	EH	AS	EC	EC			EC	EC	EC	EC			EC	EC
Connecticut (c)	EH	AS/3 (d)	EC	(e)					EC					EC (g)
Delaware	EC (f)	EH	AS		AS (g)	AS (g)	AS	EC	EC	EC (g)	AL (g)		EC	EC
Florida	EH	EH	EC	AS (g)	AS (g)	AS (g)	EC	EC	EC (g)		AL (g)	AL (g)	EC	
Georgia	EH	EH	AS						EC					
Hawaii	EH (d)	EH (d)	EC	EC	EC		EC	EC	EC	EC	EC	EC	EC	EC
Idaho	EH		EC	AS/6	AS/2 (h)	EC/9		AS (h)	EC	AL/6	AL/2 (h)			AL (h)
Illinois	EH		AS		EC			EC	EC		EC	(i)	(i)	(i)
Indiana	EH	AS	EC	EC					EC	EC				EC
Iowa	EH	EH	EC						EC	EC	EC			EC
Kansas (j)	EH	EH	EC		EC		EC		EC		EC	EC	EC	
Kentucky	EH	EH	EC		EC		EC		EC		EC	EC	EC	
Louisiana	EH	EH	EC	EC/4					EC	AL/7				
Maine	EH	AS (k)	AS (n)		(m)	AS		(p)	EC (q)	AL	EC	EC	EC	(p)
Maryland (l)	EH	EH	AS (m)	AS (n)	AS	EC (q)	AS	EC (q)	EC (q)	EC (q)	EC	EC	EC (q)	EC (q)
Massachusetts	EC (p)	EH (q)	AS	AS/2	EC (q)				EC (r)	AL	EC (q)	EC (q)		
Michigan	EH (q)	AS	EC (r)	EC/4	(r)		EC (q)	EC		EC (q)			EC	EC
Minnesota	EH	EH			EC					EC (r)	EC	EC		
Mississippi	EH	EH			EC						EC	EC		
Missouri	EH	EH			EH		EH		EH (p)		EH	EH	EH	
Montana	EH	EH			EH		EH	(s)			EC			
Nebraska														
Nevada	EH	AS (d)	AS	AS	EC	EC	EC	EC (v)	AS (t)	AL (t)	EC	EC	EC	EC (v)
New Hampshire	EH	EH	EC	EC/3	EC		EC	EC	EC	EC/3	EC		AL	AL (x)
New Jersey	EH	EH	EC				EC	AS (x)	EC	EC/3			EC	
New Mexico	EH	AS	EC	AS	EC	EC	EC	EC	EC		EC	EC	EC	EC
New York (w)	EH	AS	AS	AS			AS	AS	EC	AL/2			AL	AL
North Carolina	EH	AS	AS				EC	AS (x)	EC				EC	EC
North Dakota	EH	EH	EC	EC	EH	EH		EC (p)	EC	EC	EH	EC/3		(p)
Ohio (y)	EH (p)	EH			EH		EH	(p)	EH (p)	EH			EH	(p)
Oklahoma (z)	EH	EH	EH (aa)	AL/5	AS	AS/7	AS/2	EC (aa)	EH (aa)	AL/5	EC	EC/3	EC/2	(aa)
Oregon	EH	EH	EC	EC			AL	EC	EC (bb)				EC (bb)	EC
Pennsylvania	EH	EH	EC	EC			EC		EC				EC	
Rhode Island (cc)	EH	AS (dd)	EC	EC/11 (n)	EC	EC	EC	EC	EC	EC/3 (ee)	EC	EC/3 (ee)	EC	
South Carolina (ff)	EH	EH	EC	EC	EC		EC (gg)		EC	EC	EC	EC	EC	
South Dakota (hh)	EH	EH	EC	EC	EC	EC	EC	EC	EC	EC	EC	EC/3	EC/3	EC
Tennessee	EH	EH	EC	EC	EC	EC	EC		EC	EC	EC	EC	EC	
Texas	EH	AS	AS						EC					
Utah (ii)	EH		EC	EC (jj)	EC	EC (jj)	(jj)	EC	EC	EC (jj)	EC	EC (jj)	(jj)	EC
Vermont	EH		EC		EC				EC		EC			

HOUSE LEADERSHIP POSITIONS—METHODS OF SELECTION—Continued

State or other jurisdiction	Speaker	Speaker pro tem	Majority leader	Assistant majority leader	Majority floor leader	Assistant majority floor leader	Majority whip	Majority caucus chairman	Minority leader	Assistant minority leader	Minority floor leader	Assistant minority floor leader	Minority whip	Minority caucus chairman
Virginia	EH	EH	EC (r)	EC	(r)	...	EC	EC	EC (r)	...	(r)	...	EC	EC
Washington (kk)	EH	EH	EC	EC	EC	EC/4 (ll)	...	EC	EC	...	EC	EC/2	EC	EC
West Virginia	EH	AS	AS	...	...	...	AS	...	EC	AL	...	...	AL	AL
Wisconsin	EH	EH	EC	EC	EC	...	EC	EC	EC	EC	EC	EC	EC	EC
Wyoming	EH	EH	...	...	...	...	...	EC	...	...	...	...	...	EC
Dist. of Columbia	...	...	...	...	...	...	...	(s)	...	...	...	...	...	...
American Samoa	EH	EH (d)	EH (d)	...	...	...	...	...	...	...	...	...	...	...
Guam	...	...	...	...	...	...	...	(s)	...	...	...	...	...	...
No. Mariana Islands	EH (mm)	EH (d)	(mm)	...	EH (nm)	...	...	...	EC	...	(oo)	...	...	...
Puerto Rico	EH (p)	EH (d)	EH (d)	...	EC (oo)	...	...	(p)	EC/2 (p)	...	...	...	...	(p)
U.S. Virgin Islands	...	...	...	...	...	...	...	(s)	...	...	...	...	...	...

Source: The Council of State Governments' legislative survey, March 1994.

Note: In some states, the leadership positions in the House are not empowered by the law or by the rules of the chamber, but rather by the party members themselves. Entry following slash indicates number of individuals holding specified position.

Key:
EH — Elected or confirmed by all members of the House
EC — Elected by party caucus
AS — Appointed by speaker
AL — Appointed by party leader
. . . — Position does not exist or is not selected on a regular basis.

(a) Appointed by speaker, after consultation with members of supporting majority.
(b) Appointed by minority floor leader.
(c) Additional positions include four deputy majority leaders (appointed by majority leader) and three deputy minority leaders (appointed by minority leader and approved by party caucus).
(d) Official title is deputy speaker. In Hawaii, American Samoa and Puerto Rico, vice speaker.
(e) Eleven assistant majority leaders are appointed by speaker and approved by party caucus. Ten assistant minority leaders are appointed by minority leader.
(f) Approved by house members.
(g) Official titles: assistant majority leader is deputy majority leader, majority floor leader is majority floor whip, assistant majority floor leader is freshman majority whip, assistant minority leader is Republican leader pro tem. Other titles of minority floor leaders are designated by party affiliation (Republican).
(h) Official titles: majority floor leader is deputy majority leader, majority caucus chairman is majority conference chairperson, minority floor leader is deputy minority leader, and minority caucus chairman is minority conference chairperson.
(i) Appointed by minority floor leader.
(j) Additional positions include minority agenda chair (EC) and minority policy chair (EC).
(k) Appointed only in the speaker's absence.
(l) Additional positions include 10 deputy majority whips.
(m) Majority leader also serves as majority floor leader.
(n) Official title is deputy majority whip.
(o) Official title is assistant minority whip.
(p) Speaker and minority leader are also caucus chairmen.
(q) Due to an equal partisan split, a shared power agreement provides for the election of co-speakers, co-speakers pro tem and co-clerks. For the 1993-94 biennium, the official titles for the other leadership positions omit the designation of "majority" and "minority."
(r) Majority leader also serves as majority floor leader; minority leader also serves as minority floor leader.

(s) Unicameral legislature; see entries in Table 3.6, "Senate Leadership Positions — Methods of Selection."
(t) Official titles: minority leader is Democratic leader and assistant minority leader is deputy Democratic leader.
(u) Additional positions include four deputy speakers (EC), three assistant majority whips (EC), majority budget officer (EC), minority leader pro tem (EC), and three deputy minority leaders (EC).
(v) Official titles: majority caucus chairman is majority conference leader and minority caucus chairman is conference chairman.
(w) Additional positions: deputy speaker (AS), assistant speaker (AS), assistant speaker pro tem (AS), minority leader pro tem (AL), assistant minority leader pro tem (AL), deputy majority leader (AS), deputy minority leader (AL), assistant minority whip (AS), deputy minority whip (AL), assistant majority whip (AL), assistant majority whip (AS), minority conference vice-chairman (AL), majority conference secretary (AS), minority conference secretary (AL), majority steering committee chairman (AL), majority steering committee vice-chairman (AS), minority steering committee vice-chairman (AL), majority program committee chairman (AS), and minority program committee chairman (AL).
(x) Official titles: majority caucus chairman is majority conference chairman; minority caucus chairman is minority conference chairman.
(y) Additional positions include assistant majority whip (EH) and assistant minority whip (EH).
(z) Additional positions include assistant majority whip and minority caucus secretary.
(aa) Majority leader also serves as assistant majority caucus chairman; minority leader also serves as minority caucus chairman.

(bb) Official titles: minority leader is Republican leader and minority whip is Republican whip.
(cc) Additional positions include first deputy speaker (AS).
(dd) Official title is senior speaker pro tem.
(ee) Official title is deputy minority leader.
(ff) Additional positions include two deputy majority whips, three assistant majority whips, and two freshman whips.
(gg) Official title is chief deputy majority whip.
(hh) Additional positions include three assistant majority whip and assistant minority whip.
(ii) Additional positions include assistant majority whip and assistant minority whip.
(jj) Assistant majority leader also serves as majority whip; assistant minority leader also serves as minority whip (AL).
(kk) Additional positions include three assistant minority whips (AL).
(ll) Official title is assistant majority whip.
(mm) Speaker also serves as majority leader.
(oo) Official title is alternate floor leader.

Table 3.8
METHOD OF SETTING LEGISLATIVE COMPENSATION
(As of April 1994)

State or other jurisdiction	Constitution	Legislature	Compensation commission	Legislators' salaries tied or related to state employees' salaries
Alabama	★	. . .	★	. . .
Alaska	. . .	★	★ (a)	Tied to state employees' salary schedule for non-salaried employees.
Arizona	. . .	. . .	★ (b)	. . .
Arkansas	. . .	★	. . .	. . .
California	. . .	★	. . .	. . .
Colorado	. . .	. . .	★	. . .
Connecticut	. . .	. . .	★	. . .
Delaware	. . .	★	★ (c)	. . .
Florida	. . .	★	. . .	Tied to average percentage increase of state career service employees for the fiscal year just concluded.
Georgia..............	. . .	★	. . .	Automatic cost-of-living increases equal to 1/2 of percentage approved for state employees.
Hawaii	. . .	. . .	★ (d)	. . .
Idaho	. . .	★	★ (e)	. . .
Illinois..............	. . .	. . .	★	. . .
Indiana	. . .	★	. . .	. . .
Iowa	. . .	. . .	★	. . .
Kansas	. . .	★	. . .	Legislators receive same margin of increase given to all state employees.
Kentucky	. . .	★	. . .	. . .
Louisiana	. . .	★	. . .	. . .
Maine	. . .	★	. . .	. . .
Maryland	. . .	. . .	★ (f)	. . .
Massachusetts	. . .	★	★	. . .
Michigan	. . .	. . .	★ (g)	. . .
Minnesota	. . .	★	. . .	. . .
Mississippi	. . .	★	. . .	. . .
Missouri	. . .	★	. . .	Legislators receive all cost-of-living increases given to state employees.
Montana..............	. . .	★	. . .	Tied to state employee pay schedule.
Nebraska	★	★	. . .	. . .
Nevada	. . .	. . .	★	. . .
New Hampshire	★	. . .	. . .	. . .
New Jersey...........	. . .	★	. . .	. . .
New Mexico..........	. . .	. . .	★	. . .
New York	. . .	★	. . .	. . .
North Carolina	. . .	★	. . .	Amount increased equal to the average increase received by state employees.
North Dakota	. . .	★	★	. . .
Ohio	. . .	★	. . .	. . .
Oklahoma	. . .	★	★	. . .
Oregon	. . .	★	. . .	. . .
Pennsylvania	. .	★	. . .	. . .
Rhode Island	★	. . .	. . .	. . .
South Carolina	. . .	★	. . .	. . .
South Dakota	. . .	★	. . .	. . .
Tennessee	. . .	★	. . .	. . .
Texas................	★	. . .	. . .	. . .
Utah	. . .	. . .	★	. . .
Vermont	. . .	★	. . .	. . .
Virginia..............	. . .	★	. . .	. . .
Washington	. . .	. . .	★	. . .
West Virginia	. . .	. . .	★	. . .
Wisconsin.............	. . .	★ (h)	. . .	Tied to pay plan of classified non-represented employees.
Wyoming	. . .	★	. . .	. . .
Dist. of Columbia	. . .	★	. . .	. . .

Source: National Conference of State Legislatures.
Key:
★ — Method used to set compensation.
. . . — Method not used to set compensation.
(a) Alaska commission makes recommendations but does not have the force of law.
(b) Arizona commission recommendations are put on ballot for a vote of the people.
(c) Delaware legislature must reject recommendations within 30 days by joint resolution or pay recommendation becomes effective.

(d) Hawaii commission recommendations effective unless legislature or governor disapproves by official action.
(e) Idaho commission recommendations adopted unless rejected by the legislature prior to 25th day.
(f) Maryland commission meets before each four-year term of office and presents recommendations to General Assembly for its action.
(g) Michigan commission recommendations take effect unless rejected by 2/3 vote in each house.
(h) Approved by Joint Committee on Employment Relations.

Table 3.9
LEGISLATIVE COMPENSATION: REGULAR SESSIONS
(As of January 1994)

State or other jurisdiction	Salaries — Regular sessions — Per diem salary (a)	Salaries — Regular sessions — Limit on days	Annual salary	Travel allowance (as of January 1993) — Cents per mile	Travel allowance (as of January 1993) — Round trips home to capital during session	Per diem living expenses
Alabama	$10	105C	. . .	(b)	One	$2,280/m plus $50 three times/w for committee meetings attended (V). Out-of-state travel, actual expenses.
Alaska	. . .	. . .	$24,012	25.5	. . .	$151 ($113 for legislators living within 50 miles of capitol) (U) (c).
Arizona	. . .	. . .	$15,000	25.5 (d)	. . .	$35/C during session ($65/C during session for out-of-Maricopa Cty. members) (U).
Arkansas*	. . .	. . .	$12,500	25-Senate 27.5-House	Weekly	$82 for members more than 50 miles from capitol. Senate (U); House (V).
California	. . .	. . .	$52,500	18	. . .	$101 (U).
Colorado	. . .	. . .	$17,500	20 (24 for 4-wheel drive)	. . .	$45 ($99 for members outside Denver metro area) (V).
Connecticut	. . .	. . .	$16,760	21	. . .	None.
Delaware	. . .	. . .	$24,900	20	. . .	$5,000/annum for all expenses.
Florida (e)	. . .	. . .	$22,560	28	. . .	$75 for first 40 days (V); $75 for last 20 days (U).
Georgia	. . .	. . .	$10,641	21	. . .	$59 (committee and session days) plus $4,800/y expense allowance (V).
Hawaii	. . .	. . .	$32,000	. . .	. . .	$80 for members living outside Oahu. $130 for official business out-of-state. When in recess more than 3 days, Oahu legislators receive $10; non-Oahu legislators, $80 (V).
Idaho	. . .	. . .	$12,000	(f)	. . .	$70 ($40 for legislators who do not establish a second residence in Boise and up to $25 mileage) (U except mileage). $500/y expense allowance (U).
Illinois	. . .	. . .	$38,420	25	. . .	$81 (V).
Indiana	. . .	. . .	$11,600	25	. . .	$105 (U); tied to federal per diem.
Iowa	. . .	. . .	$18,100 (g)	21	. . .	$50 ($35 for Polk Cty. members) (U) (h). Limited to 110 C in odd y; 100 C in even y.
Kansas	$62	. . .	. . .	26	. . .	$73 (U).
Kentucky*	$100	. . .	. . .	25	. . .	$74.80/C (U).
Louisiana	. . .	. . .	$16,800	26	. . .	$75 (U) for session and committee work. Conference travel: (V).
Maine (e)	. . .	. . .	$7,125 (1994) $9,975 (1995)	22	. . .	For legislative session days and authorized committee meetings (V): $38 lodging or mileage in lieu of lodging. $32 meals.
Maryland	. . .	. . .	$28,000	26	. . .	$98 (V). Out-of-state travel $141 (V).
Massachusetts	. . .	. . .	$30,000	. . .	. . .	$5-50 depending on distance from capitol (U) plus $2,400/y (U) expense allowance.
Michigan	. . .	. . .	$47,723	. . .	. . .	None.
Minnesota	. . .	. . .	$27,979	28	. . .	House: $48 (U); up to $600/m housing during session. Senate: $50 (U); up to $500/m housing during session.
Mississippi	. . .	. . .	$10,000	20	. . .	$82 expense allowance (V).
Missouri	. . .	. . .	$22,862.52	20.5	. . .	$35 (U); however, must answer daily roll call.
Montana*	$57.062	90 L (odd y)	. . .	28	. . .	$50 (U).
Nebraska	. . .	. . .	$12,000	24	. . .	$73 ($26 if member resides within 50 miles of capitol) (V).
Nevada*	$130	60C	. . .	28	. . .	$66/C (U). Actual travel expenses reimbursed, subject to an overall limit of $6,800.
New Hampshire	. . .	. . .	$100	38 for first 45 miles, 19 thereafter	. . .	None.
New Jersey	. . .	. . .	$35,000	. . .	. . .	None.
New Mexico	. . .	. . .	. . .	25	One	$75 (V). Limit of 60 L in odd y.
New York	. . .	. . .	$57,500	26	. . .	$89 ($130 in New York City metro area and out-of-state travel); $45/partial L (V).
North Carolina	. . .	. . .	$13,026	25	. . .	$92 subsistence allowance (U) plus $522/m expense allowance.
North Dakota*	$90/C	. . .	$2,160	20	. . .	$35 housing allowance; maximum of $600/m during session (V).
Ohio	. . .	. . .	$42,426.90	20.5; 22.5	. . .	None.
Oklahoma	. . .	. . .	$32,000	20.5	One (i)	$35 for those unable to reside at home (U).
Oregon*	. . .	. . .	$13,104	22	. . .	$75 (U).
Pennsylvania	. . .	. . .	$47,000	22	. . .	Senate: $88/L (V). House: $109/L (V).
Rhode Island	$5	60L	. . .	8 (j)	One/L (V) (j)	
South Carolina	. . .	. . .	$10,400	25.5	. . .	$83 (V).

See footnotes at end of table.

LEGISLATIVE COMPENSATION: REGULAR SESSIONS—Continued

| State or other jurisdiction | Salaries | | | Travel allowance (as of January 1993) | | |
| | Regular sessions | | Annual salary | Cents per mile | Round trips home to capital during session | Per diem living expenses |
	Per diem salary (a)	Limit on days				
South Dakota	...	...	$4,267 (odd y) $3,733 (even y)	(k)	(k)	$75 (U).
Tennessee	...	...	$16,500	22	...	$82 (U).
Texas*	...	...	$7,200	27.5	...	$90 (U).
Utah	$85	45L	...	27	...	$35 (U).
Vermont	...	...	$7,680 (1993) $8,160 (1994)	25	...	$50 for rent and $37.50 for meals; commuters: $32 for meals (U).
Virginia.	...	...	Senate-$18,000 House-$17,640	24	(l)	$93/C (U); subject to taxation if member lives within 50 miles of capitol.
Washington	...	...	$25,900	28	...	$66 (U).
West Virginia	...	...	$6,500 (m)	20	...	$40 lodging plus $30 meals (V) (m).
Wisconsin.......... ...	...	...	$35,070	26 (n)	Weekly	$75 (U).
Wyoming .... $75 (o) ...	$75 (o)	...	...	35	...	$60 (U), not to exceed 40L during odd y or a total of 60 d over two y.
Dist. of Columbia.... ...	...	...	$71,885	(p)	...	$118 (V) when out-of-town.

Source: National Conference of State Legislatures.

Note: In many states, legislators who receive an annual salary or per diem salary also receive an additional per diem amount for living expenses. Consult appropriate columns for a more complete picture of legislative compensation during sessions. For information on interim compensation and other direct payments and services to legislators, see Table 3.10, "Legislative Compensation: Interim Payments and Other Direct Payments."

* — Biennial session. In Arkansas, Oregon and Texas, legislators receive an annual salary.

Key:
C — Calendar day
L — Legislative day
(U) — Unvouchered
(V) — Vouchered
d — day
w — week
m — month
y — year
. . . — Not applicable

(a) Legislators paid on a per diem basis receive the same rate during a special session.

(b) Tied to state employee mileage rate.

(c) Some legislators have opted to accept a lower per diem at $100; $75 for those living within 50 miles of capitol.

(d) Out-of-Maricopa County members only.

(e) Additional compensation during a special session: Florida, $50; Maine, $100.

(f) Up to $25 during the session.

(g) Annual salary will increase to $18,800 in 1995.

(h) Per diem living expenses will increase to $60 ($45 for Polk County members) in 1995.

(i) For those unable to reside at home during the session.

(j) Limit of 60 L.

(k) One round trip/weekend at .05/mile; .24/mile for the remaining weekends during session.

(l) Senators also receive one round trip/w and one round trip/session at .24/mile.

(m) The West Virginia Legislature voted in April 1994 to raise legislators' salaries in 1995 to $15,000 per year and the per diem living expenses to $85 per day. However, the constitutionality of the measure is in question.

(n) Mileage at .26/mile anytime legislature is in session fewer than three days/month.

(o) Includes non-business days.

(p) $50 per month.

Table 3.10
LEGISLATIVE COMPENSATION: INTERIM PAYMENTS AND OTHER DIRECT PAYMENTS

State or other jurisdiction	Per diem compensation and living expenses for committee or official business during interim (as of January 1994)	Other direct payments or services to legislators (as of January 1993)
Alabama	$40	$1,900/m for district expenses (U).
Alaska	$65 for legislative business.	District office space, telephones, supplies, travel and staff allocated by presiding officers (no set dollar amount).
Arizona	$35 ($60 for out-of-Maricopa Cty. members plus one round trip/w at .25½/mile).	None.
Arkansas	$82 for committee meetings + .28/mile (U) for members more than 50 miles from capitol.	$600/m for office, travel, meals, lodging and clerical staff.
California	$101 for authorized travel; may receive more if lodging portion exceeds $101.	$279,380/y in Assembly for both capitol and district office expenses; Senate allowances vary.
Colorado	$99 plus all actual and necessary travel and subsistence expenses (V).	None.
Connecticut	None.	Office allowance: Senate, $4,500/y; House, $3,500/y. No staffing allowance.
Delaware	None.	$5,500/y unspecified allowance.
Florida	$50 (U). Members may choose actual hotel plus $21/d meal allowance (V).	$1,500/m for district office and staffing; $250/m additional for Senate president, speaker and members with three or more district staff. Senate: $7,500/y for postage, telephone, in-state travel, etc. (V); House: $7,100/y for mailing newsletters. Staff salaries paid directly by legislature.
Georgia	$59 plus .21/mile for in-state travel (V); actual expenses for out-of-state travel (V).	$4,800/y expense allowance (includes district office expenses); some legislators provided with one paid aide during session.
Hawaii	$10 on island residence; $80 on another island; $130 for out-of-state travel (V).	Staffing allowance during session: Senate, $310/d; House, $4,500/m. Additional $5,000/y expense allowance for incidental expenses.
Idaho	None.	$500/y expense allowance.
Illinois	$81 (V). Senate: two round trips/m; House: one round trip/yr. Mileage at .25/mile for one additional round trip each session.	Rent, utilities, supplies, mailings and staff: Senate, $57,000/y; House, $47,000/y.
Indiana	$105 (V).	Office expense allowance of $25/d seven days/w during interim only.
Iowa	$50 salary ($60 in 1995) plus .21/mile for one round trip each week (except Polk Cty. members).	$75/m for postage, travel, telephone, and district constituent relations. Staff salaries paid by legislature.
Kansas	$62 salary; $73 expenses + .26/mile (V).	$600/m during interim; secretarial staff provided during session.
Kentucky	Actual expenses (V).	District office allowance of $950/m.
Louisiana	$75 (V).	District office allowance of $625/m. Staffing allowance of $1,500-$2,500/m.
Maine	$55 salary; $32 maximum for meals; actual mileage and tolls; actual expenses for lodging (V).	Constituent service allowance: Senate, $1,000/y; House, $750/y.
Maryland	$102 or $148 out-of-state (V).	District office expenses: Senate, $16,765/fiscal y; House, $15,507/fiscal y. $250/y (U) for in-district travel.
Massachusetts	$5-50 depending on distance from capitol.	None.
Michigan	None.	Unspecified allowance of $8,925/y for 1994.

See footnotes at end of table.

LEGISLATIVE COMPENSATION: INTERIM PAYMENTS AND OTHER DIRECT PAYMENTS—Continued

State or other jurisdiction	Per diem compensation and living expenses for committee or official business during interim (as of January 1994)	Other direct payments or services to legislators (as of January 1993)
Minnesota	.28/mile. House: $48 (V), Senate: $50 (V); meals cannot be claimed if per diem is taken.	None.
Mississippi	$40 salary; $82 plus mileage. $800/m expense allowance (U).	None.
Missouri	None.	District office expenses: Senate, $6,000/y; House, $600/m. Staffing allowance during interim: Senate, $48,195 to $62,370; House, $300/m.
Montana	Actual expenses (V) up to statutory limit.	None.
Nebraska	Actual expenses for travel, meals, lodging.	Two full-time staff provided to each member.
Nevada	$130/authorized meeting day. Actual travel expenses. $58 for in-state meetings (U); $24 (U) plus lodging (V) for out-of-state travel.	None.
New Hampshire	None.	None.
New Jersey	Some reimbursement for authorized conference travel.	$750/y for supplies.
New Mexico	$75 + .25/mile for committee meetings.	None.
New York	$89 ($130 for New York City and out-of-state travel); $45/half session d (V).	$1,600/y for incidental expenses. Major office expenses are covered by the legislature. Approximately $130,000 to $250,000 for district and capitol staff, depending on member and district.
North Carolina	.25/mile plus $92 subsistence allowance (U).	May use $522/m expense allowance for office expenses. $1,500/biennium allowance for telephone and postage. One clerical staff provided by legislature.
North Dakota	$62.50/actual days spent on committee work. Mileage, lodging and meals; based on state employee rate.	None.
Ohio	Actual travel expenses.	None.
Oklahoma	$25 for meeting (U); mileage for interim meetings.	None.
Oregon	$75 for committees and task force meetings (V). Interim expense allowance of $400-$500/m depending on district size.	May use $400-500/m expense allowance for office expenses during interim. Staffing allowance: $3,465/m during session; $1,100/m during interim.
Pennsylvania	Senate: $88, House: $109 for meals and lodging (V).	District expenses: Senate, $22,500/y; House, $800/m for rent, equipment and utilities + $10,000/y for additional district expenses. No separate staffing allowance.
Rhode Island	None.	None.
South Carolina	$35 (Senate - V; House uses roll call); mileage reimbursed.	$300/m for in-district expenses; $500/y for postage and mailings. Senate: $2,400/y for postage and telephone and additional $1,000 for committee chairs. House: $1,800/y for telephone; $600/y for postage.
South Dakota	$75/meeting d (U); travel expenses at state rates (V).	None.
Tennessee	$78 (U in-state; V out-of-state).	District office expenses of $525/m. No staffing allowance.
Texas	$90 when in capital; limited to 10 days/m (V).	$20,000/m for staff salaries.
Utah	$35 (V) (outside Salt Lake and Davis Cty. members, additional $50 if overnight stay).	None.
Vermont	Actual expenses (V).	None.

LEGISLATIVE COMPENSATION: INTERIM PAYMENTS AND OTHER DIRECT PAYMENTS—Continued

State or other jurisdiction	Per diem compensation and living expenses for committee or official business during interim (as of January 1994)	Other direct payments or services to legislators (as of January 1993)
Virginia	$100 salary. Actual expenses (V).	Office expenses of $6,000/y. Staffing allowance of $16,740/y.
Washington	$66 (U); if high cost area, expenses over $66 reimbursed with receipts.	Senate: $1,350/quarter; one staff during interim, two during session. House: $450/m for legislative expenses; no staffing allowance.
West Virginia	$50 (U).	None.
Wisconsin	$73 (U); .26/mile anytime legislature is in session fewer than three days/m.	Senators may establish district offices; general office budget up to $26,858 for biennium includes rent, utilities and telephone.
Wyoming	$75 salary; $60 (V) + .35/mile.	None.
Dist. of Columbia	$118 for out-of-town travel (V).	None.

Source: National Conference of State Legislatures.
Note: For more information on legislative compensation, see Table 3.9, "Legislative Compensation: Regular Sessions."
Key:
(U) — Unvouchered
(V) — Vouchered
d — day
m — month
w — week
y — year

Table 3.11
ADDITIONAL COMPENSATION FOR SENATE LEADERS
(As of January 15, 1993)

State	President	President pro tem	Majority leader	Minority leader	Other
Alabama	(a)	0	. . .	. . .	
Alaska	$500/y	. . .	0	0	
Arizona	0	0	0	0	
Arkansas	(a)	$1,500/y	0	0	
California	(a)	$10,500/y	$5,250/y	$5,250/y	
Colorado	0	0	0	0	
Connecticut	(a)	$6,400/y	$5,290/y	$5,290/y	Dep. Maj. Ldr., Dep. Min. Ldr.: $3,860/y; Asst. Maj. Ldr., Asst. Min. Ldr.: $2,540/y.
Delaware	(a)	$9,828/y	$7,644/y	$7,644/y	Maj. Whip, Min. Whip: $4,914/y.
Florida	$8,772/y	0	0	0	
Georgia	(a)	$4,800/y	0	0	
Hawaii	$5,000/y	0 (b)	0	0	
Idaho	(a)	$3,000/y	0	0	
Illinois	$16,000/y (c)	. . .	(c)	$16,000/y	Asst. Maj. Ldr. (6): $12,000/y; Asst. Min. Ldr. (5): $12,000/y; Maj. Caucus Chair, Min. Caucus Chair: $12,000/y.
Indiana	(a)	$6,500/y	$5,000/y	$5,000/y	Asst. Pres. Pro Tem: $4,000/y; Maj. Caucus Chair: $5,000/y; Maj. Whip: $1,500/y; Asst. Maj. Floor Ldr.: $4,500/y; Min. Caucus Chair: $4,500/y; Min. Whip: $1,500/y.
Iowa	$9,800/y	$1,000/y	$9,800/y	$9,800/y	
Kansas	$816.25/m	$416.58/m (b)	$736.33/m	$736.33/m	Asst. Maj. Ldr., Asst. Min. Ldr.: $416.58/m.
Kentucky	$25/d	$15/d	$20/d	$20/d	Maj. Caucus Chair, Min. Caucus Chair, Maj. Whip, Min. Whip: $15/d.
Louisiana	$32,000/y	0	. . .	. . .	
Maine	$5,250/y (odd y) $3,750/y (even y)	0	$2,625/y (odd y) $1,875/y (even y)	$1,312.50/y (odd y) $937.50/y (even y)	
Maryland	0	0	0	0	
Massachusetts	0	. . .	0	0	
Michigan	(a)	0	0	0	
Minnesota	0	0	$11,191.56/y	$11,191.56/y	
Mississippi	(a)	0	. . .	. . .	
Missouri	(a)	$2,500/y	$1,500/y	$1,500/y	
Montana	$5/d	0	. . .	. . .	
Nebraska	(a)	0	. . .	. . .	
Nevada	(a)	$2/d	. . .	. . .	
New Hampshire	$25/y	. . .	0	0	
New Jersey	$11,667/y	0	0	0	
New Mexico	(a)	0	0	0	
New York	(a)	$30,000/y (c)	(c)	$25,000/y	Vice Pres. Pro Tem: $24,500/y; other leadership positions: between $9,500/y and $24,500/y; cmte. chairs: between $9,000/y and $24,500/y.
North Carolina	(a)	$35,622/y plus $1,320/m expense allowance	$15,918/y plus $622/m expense allowance	$15,918/y plus $622/m expense allowance	Dep. Pres. Pro Tem: $20,298/y plus $780/m expense allowance.
North Dakota	(a)	$10/d	$10/d	$10/d	
Ohio	$23,706.83/y	$17,913.80/y	. . .	$17,913.80/y	Asst. Pres. Pro Tem: $14,411.53/y; Maj. Whip: $10,913.46/y; Asst. Min. Ldr., $12,663.90/y; Min. Whip: $7,415.41/y; Asst. Min. Whip: $1,958.68/y.
Oklahoma	(a)	$1,245/m	$858/m	$858/m	
Oregon	$989/m	0	0	0	
Pennsylvania	(a)	$26,370/y	$21,097/y	$21,097/y	Maj. Whip, Min. Whip: $16,011; Maj. Caucus Chair: $9,983; Maj. Caucus Secy., Min. Caucus Secy.: $6,593/y; Maj. Caucus Admnr., Min. Caucus Admnr.: $6,593.
Rhode Island	(a)	0	0	0	
South Carolina	$1,575/y (a)	$7,500/y	. . .	. . .	
South Dakota	(a)	0	0	0	
Tennessee	$750/session plus $5,700 local office expenses (a)	0	0	0	
Texas	(a)	0	. . .	. . .	
Utah	$1,000/y	. . .	$500/y	$500/y	
Vermont	(a)	0	0	0	
Virginia	(a)	0	0	0	
Washington	(a)	0	$4,000/y	$4,000/y	
West Virginia	$50/d plus $100/d for 80 days/ calendar y	0	$25/d	$25/d	
Wisconsin	0	0	0	0	
Wyoming	$78/d	0 (b)	$75/d	$75/d	

ADDITIONAL COMPENSATION FOR SENATE LEADERS—Continued

Source: National Conference of State Legislatures.
Note: This table reflects the amount paid the leadership in addition to their regular legislative compensation.
Key:
L — Legislative day
C — Calendar day in session
d — day
m — month
w — week
y — year
. . . — Position does not exist or is not selected on a regular basis

(a) Lieutenant governor is president of the Senate. In Tennessee, speaker of the Senate also has the statutory title of lieutenant governor.
(b) Official title is vice president.
(c) In Illinois, president also serves as majority leader. In New York, president pro tem also serves as majority leader.

Table 3.12
ADDITIONAL COMPENSATION FOR HOUSE LEADERS
(As of January 15, 1993)

State	Speaker	Speaker pro tem	Majority leader	Minority leader	Other
Alabama	$2/d, 60 d limit	. . .	. . .	. . .	
Alaska	$500/y	. . .	0	0	
Arizona	0	0	0	0	
Arkansas	$1,500/y	0	0	0	
California	$10,500/y	0	$5,250/y	$5,250/y	
Colorado	0	0	0	0	
Connecticut	$6,400/y	$3,860 (a)	$5,290/y	$5,290/y	Dep. Maj. Ldr., Dep. Min. Ldr.: $3,860/y; Asst. Maj. Ldr., Asst. Min. Ldr.: $2,540/y. Maj. Whip, Min. Whip: $4,914/y.
Delaware	$9,828/y	. . .	$7,644/y	$7,644/y	
Florida	$8,722/y	0	0	0	
Georgia	$63,582/y	$4,800/y	0	0	
Hawaii	$5,000/y	0 (a)	0	0	
Idaho	$3,000/y	. . .	0	0	
Illinois	$16,000/y	. . .	$13,500/y	$16,000/y	Dep. Maj. Ldr. (2): $11,500; Dep. Min. Ldr. (2): $11,500; Asst. Maj. Ldr. (6): $10,500; Asst. Min. Ldr.: $10,500; Maj. Conference Chair, Min. Conference Chair: $6,000/y.
Indiana	$6,500/y	$5,000/y	$5,000/y	$5,500/y	
Iowa	$9,800/y	$1,000/y	$9,800/y	$9,800/y	
Kansas	$816.25/m	$416.58/m	$736.33/m	$736.33/m	Asst. Maj. Ldr., Asst. Min. Ldr.: $416.58/m. Maj. Caucus Chair, Min. Caucus Chair, Maj. Whip, Min. Whip: $15/d.
Kentucky	$25/d	$15/d	$20/d	$20/d	
Louisiana	$32,000/y	0	0	. . .	
Maine	$5,250 (odd y) $3,750 (even y)	0	$2,625 (odd y) $1,875 (even y)	$1,312.50 (odd y) $937.50 (even y)	
Maryland	0	0	0	0	
Massachusetts	0	. . .	0	0	
Michigan	0 (b)	0	0	0	
Minnesota	$11,191.56/y	0	$11,191.56/y	$11,191.56/y	
Mississippi	0	0	. . .	. . .	
Missouri	$2,500/y	$1,500/y	$1,500/y	$1,500/y	
Montana	$5/d	0	0	0	
Nebraska	------------------------------ Unicameral Legislature ------------------------------				
Nevada	$2/d	0	0	0	
New Hampshire	$25/y	0 (a)	0	0	
New Jersey	$11,667/y	0	0	0	
New Mexico	0	. . .	0	0	
New York	$30,000/y	$18,000/y	$25,000/y	$25,000/y	Dep. Spkr., Asst. Spkr.: $18,000/y; other leadership positions: between $10,000/y and $16,000/y; cmte. chairs: between $9,000/y and $24,500/y.
North Carolina	$22,596/y	$7,272/y	$2,892/y	$2,892/y	
North Dakota	$10/d	. . .	$10/d	$10/d	
Ohio	$23,706.83/y	0	0	0	
Oklahoma	$3,912/m	$3,525.33/m	$3,525.33/m	$3,525.33/m	
Oregon	$989/m	0	0	0	
Pennsylvania	$26,370/y	. . .	$21,097/y	$21,097/y	Maj. Whip, Min. Whip: $16,011/y; Maj. Caucus Chair, Min. Caucus Chair: $9,983/y; Maj. Caucus Secy., Min. Caucus Secy., Maj. Caucus Admnr., Min. Caucus Admnr.: $6,593/y.
Rhode Island	$5/d, 60 d limit	0 (a)	0	0	
South Carolina	$11,000/y	$3,600/y	0	0	
South Dakota	0	0	0	0	
Tennessee	$750/session plus $5,700 local office expenses	0	0	0	
Texas	0	0	. . .	. . .	
Utah	$1,000/y	. . .	$500/y	$500/y	
Vermont	$8,200/y	. . .	0	0	
Virginia	$10,200/y	. . .	0	0	
Washington	$8,000/y	0	0	$4,000/y	
West Virginia	$50/d plus $100/d for 80 days/calendar y	0	$25/d	$25/d	
Wisconsin	$25/m	0	0	0	
Wyoming	$78/d	0	$75/d	$75/d	

ADDITIONAL COMPENSATION FOR HOUSE LEADERS—Continued

Source: National Conference of State Legislatures.

Note: This table reflects the amount paid the leadership in addition to their regular legislative compensation.

Key:

L — Legislative day
C — Calendar day in session
d — day
m — month
w — week
y — year
. . . — Position does not exist or is not selected on a regular basis

(a) Official title is deputy speaker; in Hawaii, vice speaker; in Rhode Island, senior speaker pro tem.

(b) Additional expense allowance of $5,000.

TABLE 3.13
STATE LEGISLATIVE RETIREMENT BENEFITS
(As of January 15, 1993)

State or other jurisdiction	Participation	Requirements for regular retirement	Contribution rate	Monthly benefit estimates			Benefit formula	Same as state employees
				4 yrs	12 yrs	20 yrs		
Alaska	Optional	Age 60, 30 yrs service; 5 yrs vested	Employee 6.75%; employer 14.92%	Not yet vested	$480.24	$800.40	2% x avg. of 3 highest consecutive yrs of salary x yrs service	Yes
Arizona	Mandatory	Age - N.A., 5 yrs service	7%	Not yet vested	48% final annual salary or $7,200/yr	80% final annual salary or $12,000/yr	4% x yrs service x final annual salary	No
Arkansas	Mandatory	Age 65, 10 yrs service; age 55, 35 yrs service	Non-contributory	Not eligible	$270	$450	1.8% x 5 yr avg. salary x 2 x yrs service	No
California (a)								
Colorado	Mandatory	Age 60, 5 yrs service	8% of gross				N.A.	Yes
Connecticut	Mandatory	Age 60, 25 yrs service; age 62, 10 yrs service; age 70, 5 yrs service	0	Not eligible	$223	$372	[(.0133 x avg. annual salary) + [.005 x avg. annual salary in excess of breakpoint (specified dollar amount for each yr)] x yrs credited service	Yes
Delaware	Mandatory	Age 65, 5 yrs service; age 60, 15 yrs service	3% of monthly compensation in excess of $500 + 2% of portion exceeding the amount determined by dividing social security wage base by 12				1⅔% of 5 yr avg. x yrs service (minimum benefit of $17.60 x yrs service)	No
Florida	Optional	Age 62, 10 yrs service; 30 yrs service at any age; 8 yrs for members	22.62%	Not eligible	$677	$1,128	3% x yrs service x highest 5 yr avg. salary	Similar
Georgia	Optional	Age 65, 8 yrs service (including service not with General Assembly); 62, 8 yrs membership (as legislator or designated staff)	Employee 8.5%; employer 7%	$112	$336	$560	$28 x yrs service. Employee is penalized 5% for each yr below age 62	No
Hawaii	Optional	No age minimum; 10 yrs legislative service	7.80%	0	$19,364/yr	$24,000/yr	.035 x avg. final compensation x yrs service + (total contributions divided by actuarial value of member's age at retirement)	No
Idaho	Mandatory	Age 62 with early retirement options; no service requirement	Employee 5.84%; employer 9.75%	$80/month	$240/month	$400/month	Avg. monthly salary for base period x multiplier percentage factor x number of months of service	Similar
Illinois	Optional	Age 55, 8 yrs service; age 62, 4 yrs service	8½% for retirement; 2% for survivors; 1% for automatic increases for 11½% total	12% of final salary	57% of final salary	85% of final salary	3% for each of 1st 4 yrs; 3½% for each of next 2 yrs; 4% for each of next 2 yrs; 4½% for next 4 yrs; 5% for each yr above 12; 85% maximum	No

STATE LEGISLATIVE RETIREMENT BENEFITS—Continued

State or other jurisdiction	Participation	Requirements for regular retirement	Contribution rate	Monthly benefit estimates			Benefit formula	Same as state employees
				4 yrs	12 yrs	20 yrs		
Indiana	Mandatory	None	Employee 5% of taxable income; employer 20%	Minimum $11,600/yr	Minimum $34,800/y	Minimum $58,00/yr	Defined contribution, paid in one lump sum at age 65	No
Iowa	Optional	Age 62, 30 yrs service	Employee 3.7%; employer 5.75%	$172	$336	$559	56% of avg. of highest 3 yrs of covered wages x yrs service divided by 30	Yes
Kansas	Optional	Age 55, 10 yrs service	4%				Final avg. salary of highest 4 yrs x a rate (1%, 1.25%, 1.4%, or 1.5%) based on yrs service	N.A.
Kentucky	Mandatory	No age minimum and 5 yrs as legislator; 8 yrs if legislator and other service credit	5% of estimated gross of $27,500	0	$962.40	$1,374.96	Final compensation (last 60 month avg.) x yrs service x 2.75%	No
Louisiana	Optional	Any age, 16 yrs service; age 50, 12 legislative yrs service; age 55, 12 yrs service	11.50%				Yrs service x 3.5% x avg. compensation + $300	Similar
Maine	Mandatory	Age 62, 10 yrs vested service	Employee 4.5% of gross salary; employer 16.87%	$60	$180	$300	1/50 x avg. of highest 3 yrs x yrs service	No
Maryland	Optional	Age 60, 8 yrs service	5% of gross monthly salary				N.A.	No
Massachusetts*	Optional	Age 65, 6 yrs service	Before 1975: 5%; 1975-83: 7%; 1983-1/88:8%; after 1/88: 8% of first $30,000 salary and 10% of additional salary	Not eligible	$750	$1,250	2.5% x 3 yr avg. salary x yrs service	Yes (b)
Michigan*	Optional	Age 55, 5 yrs service; age 50, 20 yrs service	9%	Not eligible	$1,818	$2,576	20% x final salary x yrs of service after 5 yrs service; 4% of highest salary per yr for yrs 6-15; 1% per yr for yrs 16-20 (maximum 64%)	No
Minnesota	Mandatory	Age 62 (reduced annuity available at age 60), 6 yrs service	9%	0	$759	$1,645	2.5% x 5 yr avg. salary/yr service, except yrs served before 1979 earn 5% up to 8 yrs	No
Mississippi	Mandatory	Age 55, 25 yrs service	7.25%				N.A.	Yes
Missouri	Mandatory	Age 55, 3 biennial assemblies	None	0	$630	$1,300	3-4 bienniums served = $80/biennium; 5-9 bienniums served = $105/biennium; 10 or more served = $130/biennium	No
Montana	Optional	Age 50, 5 yrs service	6.48%				1/50 x yrs service x final avg. salary	Similar

See footnotes at end of table.

STATE LEGISLATIVE RETIREMENT BENEFITS—Continued

State or other jurisdiction	Participation	Requirements for regular retirement	Contribution rate	Monthly benefit estimates			Benefit formula	Same as state employees
				4 yrs	12 yrs	20 yrs		
Nevada..............	Mandatory	Age 60, 8 yrs legislative service with credit before 7/1/85; 10 yrs for legislators with no service credit before 7/1/85	15% of salary during session	0	$300	$500	$25/month x yrs service to a maximum of 30 yrs	No
New Jersey..........	Mandatory	Age 60	5%	$350	$1,050	$1,750	3% x highest 3 yr avg. salary x yrs service	Yes
New York	Mandatory	Depends on tier set by date of initial membership; from between 55 to 62. Minimum 10 yrs service	Varies (0-3%); depends on tier	0			1.66 x final 3 yr avg. salary x yrs service	Yes
North Carolina	Mandatory	Age 65, 5 yrs service	7%	0	$502	$781.50	Highest annual compensation x 4.02% x yrs service. Monthly benefit maximum 75% of salary	Similar
Ohio	Optional	Age 60, 5 yrs service	Employee 8½%; employer 13.71%				2.1% of final avg. salary x first 30 yrs service and 2.5% of final avg. salary for each yr service over 30 yrs	Yes
Oklahoma	Optional	Age 60, 6 yrs service	4½%-10%	0			At 4½% legislators receive $50.67/month/yr service; at 10%, receive $106.67/month/yr service	No
Oregon	Optional	Age 55, 30 yrs service. May retire at 58 with reduced benefits	15.11% of subject wages				1.67% x yrs service and final avg. monthly salary	Yes
Pennsylvania	Optional	Age 50 or 21 yrs service for those serving prior to 3/1/74. Others: age 50, 3 yrs service	Service prior to 3/1/74: 18.75%; after 3/1/74 but before 7/22/83: 5%; after 7/22/83: 6.25%	$313	$940	$1,565	Service after 3/1/74: 3.75 x 2% x avg. salary of 3 highest yrs x yrs service. All others: 2% x avg. salary of 3 highest yrs x yrs service	Similar
Rhode Island*.......	Optional	Age 55, 8 yrs service	30% or $90/yr	Not eligible	$600	$1,000	$600/yr of service (maximum $12,000/yr at 20 yrs of service)	No (c)
South Carolina	Mandatory	Age 60, 30 yrs service	10% of $10,400 + $3,600	Not vested	$674.40	$1,124	4.82% of annual compensation x yrs service	No
Tennessee	Optional	Age 55, 4 yrs service	0	$280	$840	$1,400	$70 x yrs service (monthly benefit)	No
Texas..............	Optional	Age 50, 8 yrs service	8% ($48/month)	0	$1,488	$2,480	2 x length of service (based on current salary of state district judges)	No
Utah...............	Optional	Age 65, 4 yrs service	Varies — determined by yearly appropriation				$10/yr of service	No
Virginia............	Mandatory	Age 55, 30 yrs service early retirement; age 65 normal retirement	5%	0	$250	$462	1.5% of first $13,200 of avg. final compensation + 1.65% of avg. final compensation in excess of $13,200 x yrs service	Yes
Washington	Optional	Age 65, 5 yrs service; age 55, at least 20 yrs service. Early retirement reduces benefits	N.A.				2% x service credit yrs x avg. final compensation	No

STATE LEGISLATIVE RETIREMENT BENEFITS—Continued

State or other jurisdiction	Participation	Requirements for regular retirement	Contribution rate	Monthly benefit estimates			Benefit formula	Same as state employees
				4 yrs	12 yrs	20 yrs		
West Virginia	Optional	Age 60 if actively employed; 62, 5 yrs service	4.50%	0	$130	$216.67	2% x yrs service x avg. highest 3 yrs out of last 10	Yes
Wisconsin..............	Mandatory	Age 62, no service requirement	5.50%	$233.80	$701.40	$1,169	2%/yrs service x statutory salary of $35,070	Yes (d)
Dist. of Columbia ...	Mandatory	Age 55, 30 yrs service	7% of gross income				Formula based on federal retirement	Yes

Source: National Conference of State Legislatures. All data from 1993 except as noted by * where data are from 1991.

Note: The following states do not have legislative retirement benefits: Alabama, Nebraska, New Hampshire, New Mexico, North Dakota, South Dakota, Vermont and Wyoming.

Key:
N.A. — Not available

(a) California proposition 140 (passed November 1990) terminated participation by legislators elected after January 1, 1991, in the Legislator's Retirement System.
(b) Plans are the same except that state employees are vested for 10 yrs.
(c) State employees contribute 7.5 percent of their annual salaries.
(d) Same as executive salary group.

Table 3.14
BILL PRE-FILING, REFERENCE, AND CARRYOVER

State or other jurisdiction	Pre-filing of bills allowed (a)	Bills referred to committee by: Senate	Bills referred to committee by: House	Bill referral restricted by rule Senate	Bill referral restricted by rule House	Bill carryover allowed (b)
Alabama	★ (c)	President (d)	Speaker	★	...	...
Alaska	★ (e)	President	Speaker	★	★	★
Arizona	★	President	Speaker	...	...	...
Arkansas	★	President	Speaker	★	★	...
California	(f)	Rules Cmte.	Rules Cmte.	★	...	★ (g)
Colorado	★	President	Speaker	...	...	...
Connecticut	★	Pres. Pro Tempore	Speaker	★	★	...
Delaware	★	President (d)	Speaker	...	...	★
Florida	★	President	Speaker	★	★	...
Georgia	...	President (d)	Speaker	...	...	★
Hawaii	(h)	President	Speaker	★	★	★
Idaho	(i)	President (d)	Speaker	...	...	...
Illinois	★	Rules Cmte.	Cmte. on Assignment	...	...	★
Indiana	★	Pres. Pro Tempore	Speaker	...	...	★
Iowa	★	President	Speaker	...	...	★
Kansas	★	President	Speaker	★	★	★
Kentucky	★	Cmte. on Cmtes.	Cmte. on Cmtes.	★	★	★
Louisiana	★	President (j)	Speaker (j)	★	★	...
Maine	★ (k)	-------- Secy. of Senate and Clerk of House (l) --------		...		★
Maryland	★	President	Speaker	(m)	(m)	...
Massachusetts	★	Clerk (j)	Clerk (j)	★	★	...
Michigan	...	Majority Ldr.	Speaker	...	...	★
Minnesota	★ (n)	President	Speaker	(m)	(m)	★
Mississippi	★	President (d)	Speaker	...	...	...
Missouri	★	Pres. Pro Tempore	Speaker	★	★	...
Montana	★	President	Speaker	...	...	...
Nebraska	★	Reference Cmte.	U	★	U	★
Nevada	★	(o)	(n)	★	...	...
New Hampshire	★	President	Speaker	...	...	★
New Jersey	★ (k)	President	Speaker	...	...	★
New Mexico	★	(p)	Speaker	(m)	(m)	...
New York	★	Pres. Pro Tempore (q)	Speaker	★	...	★
North Carolina	★	Clerk (r)	Speaker	(m)	(m)	★
North Dakota	★	President (d)	Speaker	(m)	(m)	...
Ohio	★	Reference Cmte.	Reference Cmte.	...	...	★
Oklahoma	★	Pres. Pro Tempore	Speaker	(m)	...	★
Oregon	★	President	Speaker	★	★	...
Pennsylvania	★	President (d)	Speaker	...	...	★
Rhode Island	★	President (d)	Speaker	★	...	★
South Carolina	★	(s)	Speaker	...	...	★
South Dakota	★	President (d)	Speaker	...	...	...
Tennessee	★	Speaker	Speaker	★	...	★
Texas	★	President (d)	Speaker	...	★	...
Utah	★	President	Speaker	...	...	...
Vermont	★	President (d)	Speaker	★	★	★
Virginia	★	Clerk	Clerk (t)	★	...	★
Washington	★	(s)	(s)	...	...	★
West Virginia	★	President	Speaker	...	★	★
Wisconsin	...	President	Speaker	...	...	★ (u)
Wyoming	★ (k)	President	Speaker	...	...	...
No. Mariana Islands	★	President (v)	Speaker	★	★	...

BILL PRE-FILING, REFERENCE, AND CARRYOVER—Continued

Source: State legislative rule books and manuals.

Key:

★ — Yes

. . . — No

U — Unicameral legislature

(a) Unless otherwise indicated by footnote, bills may be introduced prior to convening each session of the legislature. In this column only: ★—pre-filing is allowed in both chambers (or in the case of Nebraska, in the unicameral legislature); . . . — pre-filing is not allowed in either chamber.

(b) Bills carry over from the first year of a legislature to the second (does not apply in Arkansas, Kentucky, Montana, Nevada, North Dakota, Oregon and Texas, where legislatures meet biennially). Bills generally do not carry over after an intervening legislative election.

(c) Except between the end of the last regular session of the legislature in any quadrennium and the organizational session following the general election.

(d) Lieutenant governor is the president of the Senate.

(e) Maximum 10 bills per member.

(f) California has a continuous legislature. Members may introduce bills at any time during the biennium.

(g) Bills introduced in the first year of the regular session and passed by the house of origin on or before January 30 of the second year are "carryover bills."

(h) House only in even-numbered years.

(i) House members may prefile bills after the first Thursday in December before the next regular legislative session.

(j) Subject to approval or disapproval. Louisiana—majority of members present. Massachusetts—by presiding officer and Committee on Steering and Policy.

(k) Prior to convening of first regular session only.

(l) For the joint standing committee system. Secretary of Senate and clerk of House, after conferring, suggest an appropriate committee reference for every bill, resolve and petition offered in either house. If they are unable to agree, the question of reference is referred to a conference of the president of the Senate and speaker of the House. If the presiding officers cannot agree, the question is resolved by the Legislative Council.

(m) Not restricted, except: Maryland—local bills; Minnesota—in House, bills referred to Appropriations, Governmental Operations and Gambling, and Taxes Committees; in Senate, bills referred to Finance and Governmental Operations Committees. New Mexico—in House, bills referred to Appropriations and Finance Committee; in Senate, bills referred to Finance Committee. North Carolina—bills referred to Appropriations, Finance, and Ways and Means committees. North Dakota—bills referred to Appropriations Committee. Oklahoma—in Senate, bills referred to Appropriations Committees.

(n) Prior to convening of second regular session only.

(o) Motion for referral can be made by any member.

(p) Senator introducing the bill endorses the name of the committee to which the bill is referred. If an objection is made, the Senate determines the committee to which the bill is referred.

(q) Also serves as majority leader.

(r) Under the supervision of the chairman of the Senate Committee on Rules and Operation.

(s) By the membership of the chamber.

(t) Under the direction of the speaker.

(u) Any bill, joint resolution on which final action has not been taken at the conclusion of the last general-business floor period in the odd-numbered year shall be carried forward to the even-numbered year.

(v) With the advice of the Committee on Rules and Procedure.

Table 3.15
TIME LIMITS ON BILL INTRODUCTION

State	Time limit on introduction of bills	Procedure for granting exception to time limits
Alabama	Senate: 24th L day of regular session (a). House: no limit.	Majority vote after consideration by Rules Committee.
Alaska	35th C day of 2nd regular session (b).	2/3 vote of membership (concurrent resolution).
Arizona	29th day of regular session; 10th day of special session.	Permission of Rules Committee.
Arkansas	55th day of regular session (50th day for appropriations bills).	2/3 vote of membership of each house.
California	March 8 of odd-year session; Feb. 21 of even-year session (c).	Approval of Committee on Rules and 2/3 vote of membership.
Colorado	House: 22nd L day of regular session. Senate: 17th L day of regular session (d).	House, Senate Committees on Delayed Bills may extend deadline.
Connecticut	Depends on schedule set out by joint rules adopted for biennium (e).	2/3 vote of members present.
Delaware	House: no introductions during last 30 C days of 2nd session. Senate: no limit.	
Florida	House: noon 1st day of regular session (b,d). Senate: noon 4th L day of regular session (d,f).	Committee on Rules and Calendar determines whether existence of emergency compels bill's consideration.
Georgia	House: 30th L day of regular session because of Senate ruling. Senate: 33rd L day of regular session.	House: unanimous vote. Senate: 2/3 vote of membership.
Hawaii	Actual dates established during session.	Majority vote of membership.
Idaho	House: 20th day of session (g); 45th day of session (h). Senate: 12th day of session (g); 35th day of session (h).	
Illinois	House: March 10 of odd-year session (d,g). Senate: determined by president.	House: rules governing limitations may not be suspended except for bills determined by a majority of members of the Rules Committee to be an emergency bill. Senate: rules may be suspended by affirmative vote of majority of members; suspensions approved by Rules Committee, adopted by majority of members present.
Indiana	House: 16th day of 1st regular session; 4th day of 2nd regular session. Senate: 10th day of 1st regular session; 4th day of 2nd regular session.	House: 2/3 vote of membership. Senate: consent of Rules and Legislative Procedures Committee.
Iowa	House: Friday of 7th week of 1st regular session (g,i,j); Friday of 2nd week of 2nd regular session (g,i,j). Senate: Friday of 7th week of 1st regular session (g,i); Friday of 2nd week of 2nd regular session (g,i).	Constitutional majority.
Kansas	26th C day in 1993 and 1994 regular sessions; 38th day of regular session for committees (k).	Resolution adopted by majority of members of either house may make specific exceptions to deadlines.
Kentucky	House: 38th L day of regular session. Senate: no introductions during last 20 L days of session.	Majority vote of membership each house.
Louisiana	30th C day of odd-year session; 10th C day of even-year session.	2/3 vote of elected members of each house.
Maine	3rd Friday in December of 1st regular session; deadlines for 2nd regular session established by Legislative Council.	Approval of majority of members of Legislative Council.
Maryland	No introductions during last 35 C days of regular session.	2/3 vote of elected members of each house.
Massachusetts	1st Wednesday in December even numbered years, preceding regular session (l). 1st Wednesday in November odd numbered years, preceding regular session (l).	2/3 vote of members present and voting.
Michigan	No limit.	
Minnesota	House: Actual date established during session (g,m). Senate: no limit.	2/3 vote of members.
Mississippi	No introductions during last 3 C days of session (d,n).	2/3 vote of members present and voting.
Missouri	60th L day of regular session (d).	Majority vote of elected members each house; governor's request for consideration of bill by special message.
Montana	Individual introductions: 14th L day; revenue bills: 21st L day; committee bills and resolutions: 40th L day; committee bills: 78th L day; committee revenue bills: 66th L day (d,o).	2/3 vote of members.
Nebraska	10th L day of any session (d,p).	3/5 vote of elected membership for standing or special committees to introduce bills after 10th L day.
Nevada	10th C day of regular session (q).	Affirmative vote of majority of members elected.

TIME LIMITS ON BILL INTRODUCTION—Continued

State	Time limit on introduction of bills	Procedure for granting exception to time limits
New Hampshire	Actual dates established during session. 1993 — House: Jan. 14 (d), Senate: Jan 11 (d).	2/3 vote of members present.
New Jersey	Assembly: No printing of bills after September 1 during 2nd session. Senate: no limit.	Majority vote of members.
New Mexico	28th C day of odd-year session (d,r); 13th C day of even-year session (d,r).	2/3 vote of membership of each house.
New York	Assembly: for unlimited introduction of bills, 1st Tuesday in March; for introduction of 10 or fewer bills, last Tuesday in March (s,t). Senate: 1st Tuesday of March (t,u).	Unanimous vote.
North Carolina	House: 3rd Wednesday in February of 1st biennial session (v). Senate: June 24 for 1st biennial session.	House: 2/3 of members present and voting. Senate: 2/3 vote of membership.
North Dakota	House: 10th L day (w). Senate: 15th L day (w); resolutions: 18th L day (x); bills requested by executive agency or Supreme Court: Dec. 10 prior to regular session.	2/3 vote or approval of majority of Committee on Delayed Bills.
Ohio	House: after March 15 of 2nd regular session, majority vote of members may end bill introductions (d).	House majority vote on recommendation of bill by Reference Committee.
Oklahoma	January 28 for house of origin in 1st session (y); February 3 for 2nd session (z).	2/3 vote of membership.
Oregon	House: 36th C day of session (aa). Senate: 36th C day following election of Senate president (bb).	2/3 vote of membership.
Pennsylvania	No limit (cc).	
Rhode Island	Actual dates established during session: 1994-public bills, February 17.	House: 2/3 vote of members present. Senate: majority present and voting.
South Carolina	House: April 15 of regular session; May 1 for bills first introduced in Senate (d). Senate: May 1 of regular session for bills originating in House (d).	House: 2/3 vote of members present and voting. Senate: 2/3 vote of membership.
South Dakota	40-day session: 15th L day; committee bills and joint resolutions, 16th L day. 35-day session: 10th L day; committee bills and joint resolutions, 11th L day; bills introduced at request of department, board, commission or state agency: 1st L day (d,dd).	2/3 vote of membership.
Tennessee	House: general bills, 10th L day of regular session (ee). Senate: general bills, 10th L day of regular session; resolutions, 40th L day (ee).	Unanimous consent of Committee on Delayed Bills.
Texas	60th C day of regular session (ff).	4/5 vote of members present and voting.
Utah	House: 42nd day of regular session (d). Senate: 22nd day.	2/3 vote of members.
Vermont	House, individual introductions: 1st session, March 1; 2nd session, Feb. 1. Committees: 10 days after 1st Tuesday in March (gg). Senate, individual and committee: 1st session, 53rd C day; 2nd session, sponsor requests bill drafting 25th C day before session (hh).	Approval by Rules Committee.
Virginia	Deadlines may be set during session.	
Washington	(Constitutional limit) No introductions during final 10 days of regular session (d,ii).	2/3 vote of elected members of each house.
West Virginia	House: 50th day of regular session (d). Senate: 41st day of regular session (d,g).	2/3 vote of members present.
Wisconsin	No limit.	
Wyoming	House: 15th L day of session (d). Senate: 12th L day of session (d).	2/3 vote of elected members of either house.

See footnotes at end of table.

TIME LIMITS ON BILL INTRODUCTION—Continued

Source: State legislative rule books and manuals.

Key:

C — Calendar

L — Legislative

(a) Not applicable to local bills, advertised or otherwise.

(b) Not applicable to bills sponsored by any joint committees. In Florida, also does not apply to short-form bills.

(c) Not applicable to constitutional amendments or bills referred to committees under Joint Rule 26.5.

(d) Not applicable to appropriations bills. In West Virginia, supplementary appropriations bills or budget bills.

(e) Not applicable to (1) bills providing for current government expenditures; (2) bills the presiding officers certify are of an emergency nature; (3) bills the governor requests because of emergency or necessity; and (4) the legislative commissioners' revisor's bills and omnibus validating act.

(f) Not applicable to local bills and joint resolutions.

(g) Not applicable to standing committee bills.

(h) Not applicable to House State Affairs, Appropriations, Education, Revenue and Taxation, or Ways and Means committees, nor to Senate State Affairs, Finance, or Judiciary and Rules committees.

(i) Unless written request for drafting bill had been filed before deadline.

(j) Not applicable to bills co-sponsored by majority and minority floor leaders.

(k) Not applicable to Senate Ways and Means; Federal and State Affairs and the select committees of either house; or House committees on Calendar and Printing, Appropriations and Taxation.

(l) Not applicable to messages from governor, reports required or authorized to be made to legislature, petitions filed or approved by voters of cities or towns (or by mayors and city councils) for enactment of special legislation and which do not affect the powers and duties of state departments, boards, or commissions.

(m) Not applicable to bills recommended by conference committee reports, Rules and Legislative Administration Committee, the Senate, or the governor.

(n) Not applicable to revenue, local and private bills.

(o) Not applicable to interim study resolutions or joint resolutions concerning administration.

(p) Not applicable to "A" bills and those introduced at the request of the governor.

(q) Requests submitted to legislative counsel for bill drafting. Does not apply to standing committees or to member who had requested bill drafting before 11th C day of session.

(r) Not applicable to bills to provide for current government expenses;

bills referred to legislature by governor by special message setting forth emergency necessitating legislation.

(s) Does not apply to bills introduced by Rules Committee, by message from the Senate, with consent of the speaker or by members elected at special election who take office on or after the first Tuesday of March.

(t) In no case may a bill be introduced on Fridays, unless submitted by governor or introduced by Rules Committee or by message from Senate.

(u) Bills recommended by state department or agency must be submitted to office of temporary president not later than March 1. Bills proposed by governor, attorney general, comptroller, department of education or office of court administration must be submitted to office of temporary president no later than first Tuesday in April.

(v) Not applicable to local and public bills or bills establishing districts for Congress or state or local entities.

(w) No member other than majority and minority leaders may introduce more than five bills in House after the 5th L day; three bills in Senate after 10th L day.

(x) Not applicable to resolutions proposing amendments to U.S. Constitution or directing Legislative Council to carry out a study (deadline, 34th L day).

(y) Final date for consideration on floor in house of origin during first session. Bills introduced after date are not placed on calendar for consideration until second session.

(z) Not applicable to reapportionment bills.

(aa) Not applicable to measures approved by Committee on Legislative Rules and Reorganization or by speaker; appropriation or fiscal measures sponsored by committees on Appropriations; true substitute measures sponsored by standing, special or joint committees; or measures drafted by legislative counsel.

(bb) Not applicable to measures approved by Rules Committee, appropriation or fiscal measures sponsored by Committee on Ways and Means or measures requested for drafting by legislative counsel.

(cc) Resolutions fixing the last day for introduction of bills in the House are referred to the Rules Committee before consideration by the full House.

(dd) Not applicable to governor's bills.

(ee) Not applicable to certain local bills.

(ff) Not applicable to local bills, resolutions, emergency appropriations or all emergency matters submitted by governor in special messages to the legislature.

(gg) Not applicable to Appropriations or Ways and Means committees.

(hh) Not applicable to Appropriations or Finance committees.

(ii) Not applicable to substitute bills reported by standing committees for bills pending before such committees.

Table 3.16
ENACTING LEGISLATION: VETO, VETO OVERRIDE AND EFFECTIVE DATE

State or other jurisdiction	Governor may item veto appropriation bills — Amount	Other (b)	Days allowed governor to consider bill (a): During session — Bill becomes law unless vetoed	After session — Bill becomes law unless vetoed	After session — Bill dies unless signed	Votes required in each house to pass bills or items over veto (c)	Effective date of enacted legislation (d)
Alabama	★	★	6	20P	10A	Majority elected	Immediately (e)
Alaska	★ (f)	…	15	10A		2/3 elected (g)	90 days after enactment
Arizona	★	…	5	10A		Majority elected	90 days after adjournment
Arkansas	★ (f)	★	5	20A (h)		2/3 elected	90 days after adjournment
California	★ (f)	…	12 (i)	(i)		2/3 elected	(j)
Colorado	★	★	10 (h)	30A (h)		2/3 elected	Immediately (k)
Connecticut	★	★	5	15P (h)		2/3 elected	Oct. 1
Delaware	★	★	10		30A (h)	3/5 elected	Immediately
Florida	★	★	7 (h)	15P (h)		2/3 elected	60 days after adjournment
Georgia (l)	★	…	6 (h)	40A (h,m)		2/3 elected	July 1 (m)
Hawaii (l)	★ (f)	…	10 (o,p)	45A (o,p)	(p)	2/3 elected	Immediately
Idaho	★	★	5	10A		2/3 elected	60 days after adjournment
Illinois (l)	★ (f)	…	60 (h)	60P (h)		3/5 elected (g)	(n)
Indiana	…	…	7	7P (h)		Majority elected	(q)
Iowa	★	★	3	(r)	(r)	2/3 elected	July 1 (m)
Kansas	★	…	10 (h)	10P		2/3 elected	Upon publication
Kentucky	★ (f)	★	10	10A		Majority elected	90 days after adjournment
Louisiana (l)	★ (f)	★	10 (h)	20P (h)		2/3 elected	60 days after adjournment
Maine	…	★	10	(m)		2/3 present	90 days after adjournment
Maryland (l)	★	★	6	30P (m)		3/5 elected	June 1 (s)
Massachusetts	★ (f)	★	10	10P	10P	2/3 present	90 days after enactment
Michigan	★ (f)	★	14 (h)	10A	14P (h)	2/3 elected and serving	90 days after adjournment
Minnesota	★	…	3	20P (h)	14A	2/3 elected	Aug. 1 (t)
Mississippi	★	★	5	15P (m)		2/3 elected	60 days after enactment
Missouri	★	★	15 (h)	45P (h,m)		2/3 elected	90 days after adjournment (t,u)
Montana	★	★	5 (h)	25A (h)		2/3 present	Oct. 1 (t)
Nebraska	★ (v)	…	5	5A		3/5 elected	3 months after adjournment
Nevada	…	…	5	10A		2/3 elected	Oct. 1
New Hampshire	…	…		(w)	5P (w)	2/3 elected	60 days after enactment
New Jersey	★ (f)	…	45 (h,w)	(w)		2/3 present	July 4; other dates usually specified
New Mexico	★	…	3	15A	20A	2/3 elected	90 days after adjournment (t)
New York	★	…	10	10A	30A	2/3 elected	20 days after enactment
North Carolina	…	★	(x)				30 days after adjournment
Ohio	★	★	10	10A		3/5 elected	90 days after filed with secretary of state
Oklahoma	★	★	5 (o)	30A (o)	15A	2/3 elected (g)	90 days after adjournment
Oregon	★	★	5 (o)	30A (h)		2/3 present	90 days after adjournment
Pennsylvania	★	★	10 (h)	10A (h)		3/5 elected	60 days after enactment
Rhode Island	…	…	6			3/5 present	Immediately
South Carolina	★	★	5	(m)		2/3 present	20 days after enactment
South Dakota	★	★	5 (h)	15A (h)		2/3 elected	90 days after adjournment
Tennessee	★ (f)	…	10	10A		Majority elected	40 days after enactment
Texas	★	…	10	20A		2/3 present	90 days after adjournment
Utah	★	…	10	20A (h)		2/3 elected	60 days after adjournment
Vermont	…	★	5		3A	2/3 present	July 1

See footnotes at end of table.

VETO, VETO OVERRIDE AND EFFECTIVE DATE—Continued

State or other jurisdiction	Days allowed governor to consider bill (a)			Governor may item veto appropriation bills		Votes required in each house to pass bills or items over veto (c)	Effective date of enacted legislation (d)
	During session — Bill becomes law unless vetoed	After session — Bill becomes law unless vetoed	After session — Bill dies unless signed	Amount	Other (b)		
Virginia	7 (h)		30A (h)	★	★	2/3 present (z)	July 1 (aa)
Washington	5	20A		★ (f)	★	2/3 present	90 days after adjournment
West Virginia	5	15A (bb)		★	★	Majority elected (g)	90 days after enactment
Wisconsin	6		60P	★	★	2/3 elected	Day after publication date
Wyoming	3	15A (h)				2/3 elected	Immediately
American Samoa	10		30A	★	. . .	2/3 elected	60 days after adjournment (cc)
Guam	10		30P	★	★	2/3 elected	Immediately (dd)
No. Mariana Islands	40 (h,ee)			★	. . .	2/3 elected	Immediately
Puerto Rico	10		30P (h)	★ (f)	★	2/3 elected	Specified in act
U.S. Virgin Islands	10		30P (h)	★	★	2/3 elected	Immediately

Sources: State constitutions and statutes.

Note: Some legislatures reconvene after normal session to consider bills vetoed by governor. Connecticut—if governor vetoes any bill, secretary of state must reconvene General Assembly on second Monday after the last day on which governor is either authorized to transmit or has transmitted every bill with his objections, whichever occurs first; General Assembly must adjourn *sine die* not later than three days after its reconvening. Hawaii—legislature may reconvene on 45th day after adjournment *sine die,* in special session, without call. Louisiana—legislature meets in a maximum five-day veto session on the 40th day after final adjournment. Missouri—if governor returns any bill on or after the fifth day before the last day on which legislature may consider bills (in even-numbered years), legislature automatically reconvenes on first Wednesday following the second Monday in September for a maximum 10-calendar day session. New Jersey—legislature meets in special session (without call or petition) to act on bills returned by governor on 45th day after *sine die* adjournment of the regular session; if the second year expires before the 45th day, the day preceding the end of the legislative year. Utah—if 2/3 of the members of each house favor reconvening to consider vetoed bills, a maximum five-day session is set by the presiding officers. Virginia—legislature reconvenes on sixth Wednesday after adjournment for a maximum three-day session (may be extended to seven days upon vote of majority of members elected to each house). Washington—upon petition of 2/3 of the members of each house, legislature meets 45 days after adjournment for a maximum five-day session.

Key:
★ — Yes
. . . — No
A — days after adjournment of legislature
P — days after presentation to governor
(a) Sundays excluded, unless otherwise indicated.
(b) Includes language in appropriations bill.
(c) Bill returned to house of origin with governor's objections.
(d) Effective date may be established by the law itself or may be otherwise changed by vote of the legislature. Special or emergency acts are usually effective immediately.
(e) Penal acts, 60 days.
(f) Governor can also reduce amounts in appropriations bills. In Hawaii, governor can reduce items in executive appropriations measures, but cannot reduce nor item veto amounts appropriated for the judicial or legislative branches.
(g) Different number of votes required for revenue and appropriations bills. Alaska—3/4 elected. Illinois—appropriations reductions, majority elected. Oklahoma—emergency bills, 3/4 vote. West Virginia—budget and supplemental appropriations, 2/3 elected.
(h) Sundays included.
(i) A bill presented to the governor that is not returned within 12 days (excluding Saturdays, Sundays and holidays) becomes a law; provided that any bill passed before Sept. 1 of the second calendar year of the biennium of the legislative session and in the possession of the governor on or after Sept. 1 that is not returned by the governor on or before Sept. 30 of that year becomes law. The legislature may not present to the governor any bill after Nov. 15 of the second calendar year of the biennium of the session. If the legislature, by adjournment of a special session prevents the return of a bill with the veto message, the bill becomes law unless the governor vetoes the bill within 12 days by depositing it and the veto

message in the office of the secretary of state.
(j) For legislation enacted in regular sessions: Jan. 1 next following 90-day period from date of enactment. For legislation enacted in special sessions: 91 days after adjournment. Does not apply to statutes calling elections, statutes providing for tax levies or appropriations for the usual current state expenses or urgency statutes, all of which take effect immediately.
(k) An act takes effect on the date stated in the act, or if no date is stated in the act, then on its passage.
(l) Constitution withholds right to veto constitutional amendments.
(m) Bills vetoed after adjournment are returned to the legislature for reconsideration. Georgia: bills vetoed during last three days of session and not considered for overriding, and all bills vetoed after *sine die* adjournment may be considered at next session. Maine: returned within three days after the next meeting of the same legislature which enacted the bill or resolution. Maryland: reconsidered at the next meeting of the same General Assembly. Mississippi: returned within three days after the beginning of the next session. Missouri: bills returned on or after the 5th day before the last day to consider bills—legislature automatically reconvenes on the first Wednesday following the second Wednesday in September; be not to exceed 10 calendar days. South Carolina: within two days after the next meeting.
(n) Effective date for bills which become law on or after July 1. Georgia—Jan. 1, unless a specific date has been provided for in legislation. Illinois—a bill passed after June 30 does not become effective prior to July 1 of the next calendar year unless legislature by a 3/5 vote provides for an earlier effective date. Iowa—if governor signs bill after July 1, bill becomes law on Aug. 15; for special sessions, 90 days after adjournment. South Dakota—91 days after adjournment.
(o) Except Sundays and legal holidays. In Hawaii, except Saturdays, Sundays, holidays and any days in which the legislature is in recess prior to its adjournment. In Oregon, except Saturdays and Sundays.
(p) The governor must notify the legislature 10 days before the 45th day of his intent to veto a measure on that day. The legislature may convene on the 45th day after adjournment to consider the vetoed measures. If the legislature fails to reconvene, the bill does not become law. If the legislature reconvenes, it may pass the measure over the governor's veto or it may amend the law to meet the governor's objections. If the law is amended, the governor must sign the bill within 10 days after it is presented to him in order for it to become law.
(q) No act takes effect until it has been published and circulated in the counties, by authority, except in cases of emergency.
(r) Governor must sign or veto all bills presented to him. Any bill submitted to the governor for his approval during the last three days of a session must be deposited by him in the secretary of state's office within 30 days after adjournment with his approval or objections.
(s) Bills passed over governor's veto are effective in 30 days or on date specified in bill, whichever is later.
(t) Different date for fiscal legislation. Minnesota—July 1. Missouri, New Mexico—immediately.
(u) In event of a recess of 30 days or more, legislature may prescribe, by joint resolution, that laws previously passed and not effective shall take effect 90 days from beginning of recess.
(v) No appropriation can be made in excess of the recommendations contained in the governor's budget except by a 3/5 vote. The excess is subject to veto by the governor.
(w) On the 45th day after the date of presentation, a bill becomes law unless the governor returns it with his objections, except that (1) if the legislature is in adjournment *sine die* on the 45th day, a special session is convened (without petition or call) for the sole purpose of acting upon bills returned by

VETO, VETO OVERRIDE AND EFFECTIVE DATE—Continued

the governor; (2) any bill passed between the 45th day and the 10th day preceding the end of the second legislative year must be returned by the governor by the day preceding the end of the second legislative year; (3) any bill passed or reenacted within 10 days preceding the expiration of the second legislative year becomes law if signed prior to the seventh day following such expiration, or the governor returns it to the house of origin and 2/3 elected members agree to pass the bill prior to such expiration.

(x) Governor has no approval or veto power.

(y) August 1 after filed with secretary of state; if enacted between August 1 and January 1 of following year, 90 days after its filing. Appropriations and tax bills: July 1.

(z) Must include majority of elected members.

(aa) Special sessions—first day of fourth month after adjournment.

(bb) Five days for appropriations bills.

(cc) Laws required to be approved only by the governor. An act required to be approved by the U.S. Secretary of the Interior only after it is vetoed by the governor and so approved takes effect 40 days after it is returned to the governor by the secretary.

(dd) U.S. Congress may annul.

(ee) Twenty days for appropriations bills.

Table 3.17
LEGISLATIVE APPROPRIATIONS PROCESS: BUDGET DOCUMENTS AND BILLS

State or other jurisdiction	Legal source of deadline		Budget document submission					Budget bill introduction		
			Submission date relative to convening							Not until committee review of budget document
	Constitutional	Statutory	Prior to session	Within one week	Within two weeks	Within one month	Over one month	Same time as budget document	Another time	
Alabama	...	★	...	5th day	...	...	...	★	...	...
Alaska	...	★	...	★	...	...	...	★	...	...
Arizona	...	★	...	★	...	...	...	...	...	...
Arkansas	...	★	(a)	...	...	...	...	...	...	★
California	★	...	...	...	★	...	...	★	...	★
Colorado	...	★	★ (b)	...	...	...	...	...	...	★
Connecticut	...	★	...	(a)	...	...	...	★	...	...
Delaware	...	★	...	...	...	by Feb. 1	...	★ (c)	...	...
Florida	...	★	45 days	...	...	...	...	...	...	★ (c)
Georgia	★	...	...	★	...	...	...	★	...	...
Hawaii	...	★	20 days	...	...	...	...	...	★	...
Idaho	...	★	...	★	...	...	...	...	...	★
Illinois	...	★	...	...	...	...	★	...	★	...
Indiana	...	★	7 days (d)	...	...	...	...	★	★	...
Iowa	...	★	...	...	...	★ (a)	...	...	...	★ (c)
Kansas	...	★	...	...	★ (e)	...	...	...	★	...
Kentucky	...	★	...	...	★ (a,e)	...	...	...	...	...
Louisiana	...	★	(a)	(a)	...	...	...	(f)	(f)	...
Maine	...	★	...	★ (a,e)	...	...	...	★	...	...
Maryland	★	...	...	★ (e)	...	...	...	★ (g)	...	...
Massachusetts	...	★	...	...	...	★	...	★ (h)	...	...
Michigan	...	★	...	...	...	★ (e)	...	★	...	...
Minnesota	...	★	...	...	...	★ (a)	...	...	...	...
Mississippi	...	★	...	1st day	...	...	...	...	...	★
Missouri	★	...	...	...	...	★	...	...	★	...
Montana	...	★	★	...	...	...	...	...	★	...
Nebraska	...	★	...	...	...	★ (a,e)	...	★ (c)	...	...
Nevada	...	★	...	...	★	...	...	...	...	...
New Hampshire	...	★	...	...	...	...	★ (a)	★	...	...
New Jersey	...	★	...	...	...	★ (e)	...	...	...	★ (i)
New Mexico	...	★	...	...	...	(j)	...	★	...	...
New York	★	...	...	...	★ (e)	...	...	★ (k)	...	...
North Carolina	...	...	...	(i)	...	...	...	★	...	...
North Dakota	...	★	(l)	...	...	...	...	★	...	...
Ohio	...	★	...	...	...	★ (e)	...	★	...	...
Oklahoma	...	★	...	★	...	...	...	★	...	...
Oregon	...	★	Dec. 1 (e)	...	...	...	...	...	★ (a)	...
Pennsylvania	...	★	...	...	...	...	★ (e,m)	...	...	★
Rhode Island	...	★	...	...	...	...	★	★	...	★
South Carolina	...	★	(a,b)	...	...	...	...	...	...	★
South Dakota	...	★	★ (a)	...	...	...	...	...	...	★
Tennessee	...	★	...	...	★ (a,e)	...	...	★	...	...
Texas	...	★	...	5th day	...	...	...	...	★ (a)	...
Utah	...	...	(n)	★	...	...	...	...	...	...
Vermont	...	★	...	...	...	★ (a)	...	...	...	★
Virginia	...	★	...	Dec. 20	...	...	...	...	★ (a)	...
Washington	...	★	Dec. 20 (o)	...	...	...	...	...	(p)	...
West Virginia	★	...	...	1st day (e)	...	...	...	★	...	...
Wisconsin	...	★	...	...	...	★ (q)	...	★	...	...
Wyoming	...	★	Dec. 1	...	...	...	...	...	...	★
No. Mariana Islands	...	★	(a)	...	...	...	...	...	(r)	★
Puerto Rico	...	★	...	...	...	...	...	...	(r)	★
U.S. Virgin Islands	...	★	...	...	...	★ (s)	...	★	...	...

LEGISLATIVE APPROPRIATIONS PROCESS—Continued

Source: The Council of State Governments' legislative survey, March 1994.

Key:

★ — Yes

. . . — No

(a) Specific time limitations: Arkansas—50 days; Connecticut—odd numbered years—no later than the first session day following the third day in February, in even numbered years—on the day the General Assembly convenes; Iowa—no later than February 1; Kentucky—10th legislative day; Louisiana—operating budget to Joint Budget Committee 30 days prior to session and to full legislature on first day of session; Maine—by Friday following the first Monday in January; Minnesota—fourth Monday in January during biennial session; Nebraska—by January 15; New Hampshire—by February 15; Oregon—Dec. 15; South Carolina—first Tuesday in January; South Dakota—first Tuesday after the first Monday in December; Tennessee—on or before February 1; Texas—within seven days; Vermont—within three weeks; Virginia—first day of session; No. Mariana Islands—no later than 6 months before the beginning of the fiscal year.

(b) Copies of agency budgets to be presented to the legislature by November 1. Governor's budget usually is presented in January.

(c) Executive budget bill is introduced and used as a working tool for committee. Delaware—after hearings on executive bill, a new bill is then introduced; the committee bill is considered by the legislature.

(d) Budget document submitted prior to session does not necessarily reflect budget message which is given sometime during the first three weeks of session.

(e) Later for first session of a new governor: Kansas—21 days; Kentucky—15th legislative day; Maine—by Friday following first Monday in February; Maryland—10 days after convening; Michigan—within 60 days; Nebraska—

February 1; New Jersey—March 15; New York—February 1; Ohio—by March 15; Oregon—February 1; Pennsylvania—first full week in March; Tennessee—March 1; West Virginia—10 days, in odd-numbered years.

(f) Operating budget bills subject to general constitutional limitations controlling introduction of legislation. Preliminary capital budget submitted to legislature by March 1; submission of capital budget and bill no later than eighth legislative day.

(g) Appropriations bills other than the budget bill (supplementary) may be introduced at any time. They must provide their own tax source and may not be enacted until the budget bill is enacted.

(h) General appropriations bills only.

(i) By custom only. No statutory or constitutional provisions.

(j) Statutes provide for submission by the 25th legislative day; however, the executive budget is usually presented by the first day of the session.

(k) Governor has 30 days to amend or supplement the budget; he may submit any amendments to any bills or submit supplemental bills.

(l) For whole legislature. The Legislative Council only receives budget on December 1.

(m) Submitted by governor as soon as possible after General Assembly organizes, but not later than the first full week in February.

(n) Must submit to fiscal analyst 30 days prior to session.

(o) Even-numbered years.

(p) No set time.

(q) Last Tuesday in January. A later submission date may be requested by the governor.

(r) By enacting annual appropriations legislation.

(s) Organic Act specifies at opening of each regular session; statute specifies on or before May 30.

Table 3.18
FISCAL NOTES: CONTENT AND DISTRIBUTION

| | Content | | | | | | Distribution | | | | | | |
| | | | | | | | Legislators | | | Appropriations committee | | | |
State or other jurisdiction	Intent or purpose of bill	Cost involved	Projected future cost	Proposed source of revenue	Fiscal impact on local government	Other	All	Available on request	Bill sponsor	Members	Chairman only	Fiscal staff	Executive budget staff
Alabama	...	★	...	★	★		★ (a)	...	...	...	...	...	...
Alaska	...	★	★	★ (b)	★ (c)		★ (d)	...	...	...	...	★	★
Arizona	★	★	★	★	★		★	★	...	...	...	★	★
Arkansas	...	★	★	...	★		★	★	...	...	...	...	...
California	★	★	★	★	★		★	...	...	...	...	★	★
Colorado	★	★	★	★	★		★	...	...	...	...	...	...
Connecticut	...	★	★	...	★		★	...	...	...	...	★	...
Delaware	...	★	★	...	...	★ (e)	...	★	...	★	...	★	★
Florida	...	★	★	★	★	★ (f)	★	...	...	...	...	...	...
Georgia	...	★	★	★	★	★ (f)	★	★	...	...	...	...	...
Hawaii	...	...	...	...	...		★	...	...	...	...	★	★
Idaho	★	★	★	...	★		★	...	...	...	...	...	...
Illinois	...	★	★	★	★		...	★ (g)	★ (g)	...	...	...	...
Indiana	★	★	★	★	★		★	...	...	...	...	★	★
Iowa	...	★	★	★	★		★	...	...	...	...	...	...
Kansas	★	★	★	★	★		...	★	...	...	★ (h)	★	★
Kentucky	★	★	★	★	★	★ (i)	...	★	★	★ (h)	...	★	...
Louisiana	...	★	★	...	★		...	★	★	...	...	★ (j)	...
Maine	...	★	★	★	★		★	...	...	...	...	...	...
Maryland	...	★	★	★	★		...	★	★	★ (h)	...	★	...
Massachusetts	...	★ (k)	★	...	...		★	★	...	...	...	★	...
Michigan	★	★	★	★	★	★ (l)	★ (m)	★	...	...	...	★	...
Minnesota	...	★	★	...	★	★ (f)	...	...	★	...	★	★	...
Mississippi	★	★	★	...	★		...	★	...	...	★	...	...
Missouri	...	★	★	★	★		★	...	...	...	...	...	...
Montana	...	★	★	...	...	★ (f)	★	...	...	...	...	...	...
Nebraska	...	★	★	...	...	★ (f)	★	...	...	...	...	★	...
Nevada	★	★	★	★	★		★	...	...	...	...	★	★
New Hampshire	★	★	★	★	★		★	...	...	...	...	★	★
New Jersey	★	★	★	★	★	★ (l)	★	...	...	...	...	...	...
New Mexico	★	★	★	...	(n)	★ (o)	...	★ (p)	...	...	★ (p)	...	...
New York	...	★	★	...	★	★ (i)	...	★	★	★	...	★	...
North Carolina	...	★	★	...	★	★ (f)	★	...	...	...	...	...	...
North Dakota (q)	★	★	★ (r)	★	★	★ (i)	...	★	...	...	★	★	★
Ohio	★	★	★	★	★		★ (s)	★	★	★ (t)	(t)	★	...
Oklahoma (u)	★	★	...	★	...	★ (e)	...	★	★	...	★	★	...
Oregon	...	★	★	★	★		★	...	...	...	...	...	...
Pennsylvania	...	★	★	★	★	★ (i)	★	...	...	...	...	★	★
Rhode Island	...	★	★	...	★	★ (v)	...	★	...	...	★	★	★
South Carolina	...	★	★	★	★		...	★	★	...	...	★	...
South Dakota	...	★	★	★	★	★ (i)	...	★	...	...	...	...	...
Tennessee	★	★	★	★	★	★ (w)	★	...	...	...	...	★	★
Texas	...	★	★	★	★		...	★	★	★ (h)	...	...	★
Utah	...	★	★	★	★		★	...	...	...	...	...	...
Vermont	★	★	★	★	...		...	★	...	...	★	...	...
Virginia	★	★	★	★ (x)	★	★	...	★	★	★	...	...	...
Washington	...	★	★	★	★		...	★	...	...	★	★	★
West Virginia	★	★	★	★	★		...	...	...	★ (h)	...	...	...
Wisconsin	...	★	★	★	★		★	...	...	...	...	...	...
Wyoming	...	★	★	★	...		★	...	...	...	...	...	...
No. Mariana Islands	★	★	★	★	★		★	...	...	...	...	★	★
Puerto Rico	...	★	...	...	★		★	...	...	...	...	...	...

FISCAL NOTES: CONTENT AND DISTRIBUTION—Continued

Source: The Council of State Governments' legislative survey, March 1994.

Note: A fiscal note is a summary of the fiscal effects of a bill on government revenues, expenditures and liabilities.

Key:

★ — Yes

. . . — No

(a) Fiscal notes are included in bills for final passage calendar.

(b) Contained in the bill and in the fiscal note.

(c) Information on fiscal impact on municipalities is requested by the last committee to which the bill is referred on the day it is introduced. This provision will be repealed July 1, 1998.

(d) Fiscal notes are attached to the bill before it is reported from the first committee of referral. Governor's bills must have fiscal note before introduction. Once fiscal notes are submitted, they are copied and available to all.

(e) Relevant data and prior fiscal year cost information.

(f) Mechanical defects in bill.

(g) A summary of the fiscal note is attached to the summary of the relevant bill in the Legislative Synopsis and Digest. Fiscal notes are prepared for the sponsor of the bill and are attached to the bill on file in either the office of the clerk of the House or the Secretary of the Senate.

(h) Or to the committee to which referred.

(i) Bill proposing changes in retirement system of state or local government must have an actuarial note.

(j) Prepared by the Legislative Fiscal Office; copies sent to House and Senate staff offices respectively.

(k) Fiscal notes are prepared only if cost exceeds $100,000 or matter has not been acted upon by the Joint Committee on Ways and Means.

(l) Other relevant data.

(m) Analyses prepared by the Senate Fiscal Agency are distributed to Senate members only; analyses prepared by the House Fiscal Agency are distributed to House members only.

(n) Occasionally.

(o) The impact of revenue bills is reviewed by the Legislative Finance Committee and executive agencies.

(p) Legislative Finance Committee staff prepare fiscal notes for Appropriations Committee chairman; other fiscal impact statements prepared by Legislative Finance Committee and executive agencies are available to anyone upon request.

(q) Notes required only if impact is above $5,000.

(r) A four-year projection.

(s) If a bill comes up for floor consideration.

(t) Fiscal notes are prepared for bills being voted on in any standing committee and are distributed to the chairman and all committee members.

(u) Fiscal notes are prepared only in the House.

(v) Technical or mechanical defects may be noted.

(w) Effects of revenue bills.

(x) The Department of Taxation prepares revenue impact notes, including the intent and revenue impact.

Table 3.19
BILL AND RESOLUTION INTRODUCTIONS AND ENACTMENTS:
1992 AND 1993 REGULAR SESSIONS

State or other jurisdiction	Duration of session*	Introductions		Enactments		Measures vetoed by governor	Length of session
		Bills	Resolutions	Bills	Resolutions		
Alabama...........	Feb. 4-May 18, 1992	1,532	668	341	560	8	30L
	Feb. 2-May 17, 1993	1,683	712	433	679	4	30L
Alaska.............	Jan. 13-May 13, 1992	400	101	137	51	12 (a)	122L
	Jan. 11-May 11, 1993	522	121	83	26	2	121L
Arizona...........	Jan. 13-July 1, 1992	1,142	84	361	17	8	171C
	Jan. 11-April 17, 1993	826	43	259	12	2	97C
Arkansas	No regular session in 1992						
	Jan. 11-May 14, 1993	1,981	26	1,319	3	45	88C
California..........	Jan. 6-Nov. 30, 1992	2,383	209	1,374	147	334	150L
	Dec. 7, 1992-Sept. 11, 1993	3,664	282	1,307	123	240	130L
Colorado	Jan. 8-May 6, 1992	586	14	352	2	13	120C
	Jan. 13-May 12, 1993	617	10	340	1	5	120C
Connecticut	Feb. 5-May 6, 1992	1,446	172	289	149	11 (a)	92C
	Jan. 6-June 9, 1993	3,432	239	477	152	12 (a)	155C
Delaware	Jan. 14-June 30, 1992	472	188	126	91	8	(b)
	Jan. 12-June 30, 1993	610	213	98	109	7	(b)
Florida	Jan. 14-Mar. 13, 1992	2,348	168	282	136	20	60C
	Feb. 2-April 4, 1993	2,191	207	398	163	16	62C
Georgia............	Jan. 14-Mar. 31, 1992	2,429	1,070	870	807	27	40L
	Jan. 11-Mar. 23, 1993	1,559	1,020	632	851	16	40L
Hawaii	Jan. 15-April 30, 1992	2,971	1,423	323	519	37	63L
	Jan. 20-May 3, 1993	4,086	1,448	365	318	18	60L
Idaho	Jan. 6-April 3, 1992	728	102	343	39	8	89C
	Jan. 11-Mar. 27, 1993	752	97	418	48	14	76C
Illinois.............	Jan. 8, 1992-Jan. 12, 1993	2,162	90	436	64	53 (a)	(b)
	Jan. 12, 1993-Jan. 12, 1994	3,694	195	527	108	33 (a)	(b)
Indiana	Nov. 19, 1991-Feb. 14, 1992	902	10	156	0	3 (a)	30L
	Nov. 17, 1992-April 29, 1993	1,616	34	273	3	4 (a)	60L
Iowa	Jan. 13-May 4, 1992	892	24	252	3	27 (c)	113C
	Jan. 11-May 2,1993	1,105	39	180	4	9 (c)	112C
Kansas	Jan. 13-May 26, 1992	917	53	327	19	27 (a,c)	102C
	Jan. 11-June 7, 1993	991	40	292	13	17 (a,c)	92C
Kentucky	Jan. 7-April 14, 1992	1,378	544	427	470	4 (a)	58L
	No regular session in 1993						
Louisiana	Mar. 30-June 22, 1992 (d)	3,389	679	1,137	403	32	56L
	Mar. 29-June 10, 1993	3,234	660	1,039	505	21 (a)	52L
Maine	Jan. 8-Mar. 31, 1992	472	3	317	3	1	38L
	Dec. 2, 1992-July 14, 1993	1,567	1	580	1	13	(b)
Maryland	Jan. 8-April 10, 1992	2,351	49	652	10	89	94C
	Jan. 13-April 12, 1993	2,548	50	642	6	100	90C
Massachusetts	Jan. 8, 1992-Jan. 5, 1993	7,353	0	414	0	39 (a)	(b)
	Jan. 6, 1993-Jan. 4, 1994	7,667	0	498	0	53 (a)	(b)
Michigan	Jan. 8-Dec. 20, 1992	1,365	18	309	1	13	92L
	Jan. 13-Dec. 13, 1993	2,232	52	362	2	16	117L
Minnesota	Jan. 6-April 17, 1992	2,537	12 (e)	246	10 (e)	16	42L
	Jan. 5-May 17, 1993	3,476	7	345	6	30	61L
Mississippi	Jan. 7-May 16, 1992	2,693	535	676	221	0	125C
	Jan. 5-April 2, 1993	4,346	343	406	155	17	90C
Missouri	Jan. 8-May 15, 1992	1,471	2,200	161	1,300	19	128C
	Jan. 6-May 14, 1993	1,401	2,100	197	1,200	6	129C
Montana...........	No regular session in 1992						
	Jan. 4-April 24, 1993	1,213	83	707	65	4	90L
Nebraska	Jan. 8-April 14, 1992	437	14	144	2	3 (a)	60L
	Jan. 6-June 8, 1993	845	20	345	0	2	90L

INTRODUCTIONS AND ENACTMENTS: REGULAR SESSIONS—Continued

State or other jurisdiction	Duration of session*	Introductions Bills	Resolutions	Enactments Bills	Resolutions	Measures vetoed by governor	Length of session
Nevada	No regular session in 1992						
	Jan. 18-July 2, 1993	1,365	243	669	191	5	166C
New Hampshire	Jan. 8-June 17, 1992	594	63	290	1	4 (a)	29L
	Jan. 6-June 30, 1993	670	12	361	3	7 (a)	36L
New Jersey.........	Jan. 14, 1992-Jan. 12, 1993	3,532	359	215	6	41 (a)	105L
	Jan. 12, 1993-Jan. 11, 1994	1,721	228	386	8	32 (a)	67L
New Mexico........	Jan. 21-Feb. 20, 1992	974	35	135	3	17	30C
	Jan. 19-Mar. 20, 1993	1,905	37	460	11	93	60C
New York	Jan. 8-July 30, 1992	17,667	3,731	846	3,731	51 (c)	151L
	Jan. 6-July 7, 1993	14,596	3,607	720	3,607	93 (c)	152L
North Carolina	May 26-July 25, 1992	500	183 (f)	283	46	0	61C
	Jan. 27-July 24, 1993	2,693	105	558	31	0	179 C
North Dakota	No regular session in 1992						
	Jan. 5-April 24, 1993	1,062	154	648	122	20 (c)	77L
Ohio	Jan. 7-Dec. 31, 1992	424	58	202	36	4	(b)
	Jan. 4-Dec. 30, 1993	841	70	78	30	0	(b)
Oklahoma	Feb. 3-May 29, 1992	1,194	50	404	11	17 (a)	71L
	Jan. 5-May 28, 1993	1,416	57	366	9	14 (a)	71L
Oregon	No regular session in 1992						
	Jan. 11-August 5, 1993	2,955	195	819	59	12 (a)	207C
Pennsylvania	Jan. 7-Nov. 30, 1992	1,257	266	228	180	9	(b)
	Jan. 5-Dec. 15, 1993	3,816	307	131	199	0	(b)
Rhode Island	Jan. 7-July 14, 1992	3,946	415	538	194	18	(b)
	Jan. 5-July 23, 1993	4,093	341	528	178	39	(b)
South Carolina	Jan. 14-June 4, 1992	877	556	326	436	13	65L
	Jan. 12-June 25, 1993	1,531	609	213	410	6	67L
South Dakota	Jan. 14-Mar. 17, 1992	623	30	365	18	8 (a)	35L
	Jan. 12-Mar. 23, 1993	668	38	379	27	9	40L
Tennessee	Jan. 30-May 6, 1992	2,482	639	622	567	0	(b)
	Jan. 12-May 19, 1993	3,356	772	640	668	0	(b)
Texas..............	No regular session in 1992						
	Jan. 12-May 31, 1993	4,380	2,601	1,075	2,217	24	140C
Utah	Jan. 13-Feb. 26, 1992	716	107	307	68	5	45C
	Jan. 18-Mar. 3, 1993	754	97	310	28	7	45C
Vermont	Jan. 7-April 26, 1992	564	104	165	80	0	112C
	Jan. 6-May 16, 1993	799	110	115	82	2	131C
Virginia............	Jan. 8-Mar. 7, 1992	1,724	625	897	522	20	60L
	Jan. 3-Feb. 27, 1993	1,784	708	998	616	15	45L
Washington	Jan. 13-Mar. 12, 1992	1,255	54	247	6	33 (c)	60C
	Jan. 11-April 25, 1993	2,127	102	536	17	35 (c)	105C
West Virginia	Jan. 8-Mar. 14, 1992	1,676	198	216	82	2	67C
	Jan. 13-April 24, 1993	1,410	164	180	92	7 (a)	74C
Wisconsin..........	Jan. 7, 1991-Jan. 4, 1993	1,676	276	318	122	46	99L
	Jan. 4, 1993-(still active) (g)	1,584 (g)	187 (g)	121 (g)	67 (g)	0 (g)	56L (g)
Wyoming	Feb. 10-Mar. 17, 1992	346	22	101	1	3	29L
	Jan. 12-Mar. 5, 1993	611	21	236	2	7 (a)	39L
No. Mariana Islands ...	(h)	227	74	20	66	5	90C
	(h)	127	265	17	220	0	90C
Puerto Rico	Jan. 13-May 31, 1992	247	697	38	298	48	47L
	Jan. 11-June 30, 1993	967	632	67	138	32	63L
	Sept. 13-Oct. 30, 1993	471	691	51	273	35	18L
U.S. Virgin Islands	Jan. 14, 1991-Jan. 11, 1993 (i)	337 (i)	36 (i)	128 (i)	36 (i)	24 (a,i)	50C (i)
	Jan. 26-Dec. 21, 1993	1,022	24	117	17	10 (a)	23C

See footnotes at end of table.

INTRODUCTIONS AND ENACTMENTS: REGULAR SESSIONS—Continued

Source: The Council of State Governments' legislative survey, March 1994.

* Actual adjournment dates are listed regardless of constitutional or statutory limitations. For more information on provisions, see Table 3.2, "Legislative Sessions: Legal Provisions."

Key:

C — Calendar day

L — Legislative day (in some states, called a session or workday; definition may vary slightly; however, it generally refers to any day on which either chamber of the legislature is in session.)

(a) Number of vetoes overridden: Alaska: 1; Connecticut: 1992—7, 1993—4; Illinois: 1992—1, 1993—4; Indiana: 1992—1, 1993—1; Kansas: 1992—9 bills and 4 line items, 1993—3 bills and 3 line items; Kentucky: 2; Louisiana: 1; Massachusetts: 1992—7, 1993—6; Nebraska: 2; New Hampshire: 1992—1, 1993—1; New Jersey: 1992—6, 1993—6; Oklahoma: 1992—1; 1993—2; Oregon: 1; South Dakota: 1; West Virginia: 2; Wyoming: 2; U.S. Virgin Islands: 1991-1992 session—2, 1993-6.

(b) Length of session: Delaware: 1992—Senate 41L and House 43L, 1993—Senate 46L and House 49L; Illinois: 1992—Senate 58L and House 55L, 1993—Senate 87L and House 81L; Maine: 1993—Senate 74L and House 75L; Massachusetts: 1992—Senate 37L and House 144L, 1993—Senate 49L and House 150L; Ohio: 1992—Senate 125L and House 96L,

1993—Senate 119L and 109L; Pennsylvania: 1992—Senate 58L and House 62L, 1993—Senate 49L and House 66L; Rhode Island:1992—Senate 87L and House 89L, 1993—Senate 92L and House 98L; Tennessee: 1992—Senate 38L and 40L, 1993—3 organizational days plus Senate 49L and House 48L.

(c) Line item or partial vetoes: Iowa—1992: includes 15 line item vetoes; 1993: includes 7 line item vetoes. Kansas—1992: plus 12 line items vetoed; 1993: plus 41 line items vetoed. New York—includes line item vetoes in appropriation bills. North Dakota—includes 3 line item vetoes. Washington—1992: includes 26 bills partially vetoed; 1993: includes 27 bills partially vetoed.

(d) In addition, an organizational session was held on January 13, 1992.

(e) Resolutions for 1991-92.

(f) Joint resolutions for 1991-92 session.

(g) Data as of Dec. 18, 1993.

(h) The legislature meets each year for 60 legislative days during January-March and 30 legislative days beginning in August. During the two-year session of the Eighth Legislature (Jan. 13, 1992-Jan. 7, 1994), the House of Representatives met in five regular sessions; the Senate, four regular sessions.

(i) Data are total bills and resolutions from the two-year session.

Table 3.20
BILL AND RESOLUTION INTRODUCTIONS AND ENACTMENTS:
1992 AND 1993 SPECIAL SESSIONS

State or other jurisdiction	Duration of session*	Introductions		Enactments		Measures vetoed by governor	Length of session
		Bills	Resolutions	Bills	Resolutions		
Alabama	Jan. 27-Feb. 3, 1992	44	56	7	45	0	8L
	Sept. 21-Oct. 1, 1992	211	138	46	127	5	7L
	Aug. 12-24, 1993	202	134	72	115	2	7L
Alaska	May 13-16, 1992	11	1	5	1	0	4L
	June 15-22, 1992	6	4	1	2	0	8L
	No special session in 1993						
Arizona	Feb. 17-20, 1992	9	1	2	0	0	4C
	Feb. 17-May 7, 1992	3	0	0	0	0	81C
	Mar. 17-31, 1992	8	0	4	0	0	10C
	April 8-June 27, 1992	13	0	3	0	0	81C
	May 4-July 1, 1992	6	4	2	4	0	59C
	Feb. 23-Mar. 4, 1993	1	0	1	0	0	10C
	Mar. 11-16, 1993	18	0	9	0	0	6C
	June 7-11, 1993	10	4	0	0	0	5C
	Sept. 2, 1993	2	0	1	0	0	1C
	Sept. 27-28, 1993	2	1	1	0	0	2C
	Nov. 5-11, 1993	10	4	3	2	0	7C
	Dec. 17, 1993	4	0	2	0	0	1C
Arkansas	Feb. 24-Mar. 4, 1992	98	0	76	0	3	4C
	Dec. 14-18, 1992	26	0	7	0	0	5C
	No special session in 1993						
California	Jan. 6-Nov. 30, 1992	51	3	26	1	2	67L
	Oct. 8-Nov. 30, 1992	9	2	0	1	0	2L
	Jan. 4-Sept. 11, 1993	4	1	3	1	0	39L
Colorado	No special session in 1992						
	Sept. 7-11, 1993	36	2	10	0	0	5C
Connecticut	May 12-June 1, 1992	24	6	20	6	1	21C
	June 22-July 6, 1992	7	13	4	13	0	15C
	June 29-July 6, 1992	1	5	1	5	0	8C
	June 10-17, 1993	3	5	3	5	0	8C
	July 12, 1993	1	5	1	5	0	1C
	Sept. 22-27, 1993	1	5	1	5	0	6C
	Oct. 20, 1993	6	7	6	7	0	1C
Delaware	(a)	9	13	79 (b)	18 (b)	4	(c)
	(a)	16	10	63 (b)	13 (b)	0	(c)
Florida	Mar. 23-April 1, 1992	39	6	4	6	0	10C
	April 1, 1992	3	2	2	2	0	1C
	April 2-10, 1992	2	2	1	1	0	9C
	June 1-July 10, 1992	273	58	67	57	6	40C
	Dec. 9-11, 1992	23	15	9	15	0	3C
	May 24-28, 1993	58	8	12	7	0	5C
	Nov. 1-10, 1993	54	15	16	9	0	10C
Georgia	No special sessions in 1992/1993						
Hawaii	No special session in 1992						
	Aug. 23-Sept. 13, 1993	15	15	8	10	0	11L
Idaho	July 27-28, 1992	4	7	3	1	0	2C
	No special session in 1993						
Illinois	Nov. 17-Dec. 2, 1992	2	0	0	0	0	5L
	Sept. 2-Nov. 14, 1993	4	15	1	12	0	29L
Indiana	No special session in 1992						
	June 9-30, 1993	28	0	2	0	1 (d)	18L
Iowa	May 20-22, 1992	16	0	4	0	0	3L
	June 25, 1992	2	0	1	0	0	1L
	No special session in 1993						
Kansas	No special sessions in 1992/1993						
Kentucky	No special session in 1992						
	Feb. 1-17, 1993	9	83	3	77	0	13L
	May 10-27, 1993	16	96	2	91	1 (d)	14L
	Aug. 6, 1993	0	24	0	21	0	1L
Louisiana	No special session in 1992						
	Mar. 7-26, 1993	178	73	0	52	0	15L

See footnotes at end of table.

INTRODUCTIONS AND ENACTMENTS: SPECIAL SESSIONS—Continued

State or other jurisdiction	Duration of session*	Introductions		Enactments		Measures vetoed by governor	Length of session
		Bills	Resolutions	Bills	Resolutions		
Maine	Oct. 1-6, 1992	3	0	3	0	0	5L
	Oct. 16, 1992	1	0	1	0	0	1L
	No special session in 1993						
Maryland	April 10, 1992	11	0	5	0	0	1C
	No special session in 1993						
Massachusetts	No special sessions in 1992/1993						
Michigan	No special sessions in 1992/1993						
Minnesota	No special session in 1992						
	May 27, 1993	10	0	6	0	1	1L
Mississippi	Sept. 16, 1992	2	1	2	1	0	1C
	Aug. 9, 1993	2	1	2	1	0	1C
Missouri	No special session in 1992						
	Sept. 15-23, 1993	14	4	4	2	1	9C
Montana...........	Jan. 6-17, 1992	28	2	21	2	0	11L
	July 6-18, 1993	81	3	22	3	2	12L
	Nov. 29-Dec. 18, 1993	161	12	50	6	0	18L
Nebraska	July 31-Aug. 12, 1992	16	0	5	0	0	7L
	Sept. 21-Oct. 2, 1992	30	0	16	0	0	10L
	Nov. 5-12, 1992	8	0	2	0	0	7L
	No special session in 1993						
Nevada	No special sessions in 1992/1993						
New Hampshire	No special sessions in 1992/1993						
New Jersey.........	No special sessions in 1992/1993						
New Mexico........	Jan. 3-6, 1992	16	0	2	0	0	4C
	No special session in 1993						
New York	No special sessions in 1992/1993						
North Carolina	No special sessions in 1992/1993						
North Dakota	No special sessions in 1992/1993						
Ohio	No special sessions in 1992/1993						
Oklahoma	No special sessions in 1992/1993						
Oregon	July 1-3, 1992	3	5	0	2	0	3C
	No special session in 1993						
Pennsylvania	Oct. 5-Nov. 30, 1992	4	1	0	1	0	3L
	No special session in 1993						
Rhode Island	Sept. 17, 1992	0	0	0	0	0	1L
	Oct. 23, 1992	18	4	0	4	0	1L
	Dec. 21, 1992	1	0	1	0	0	1L
	No special session in 1993						
South Carolina	No special sessions in 1992/1993						
South Dakota	No special session in 1992						
	May 25, 1993	5	0	5	0	0	1L
Tennessee	Jan. 14-30, 1992	95	76	0	50	0	8L
	No special session in 1993						
Texas..............	Jan. 2-8, 1992	50	208	4	198	0	7C
	Nov. 10-Dec. 3, 1992	33	313	0	288	0	23C
	No special session in 1993						
Utah	May 19, 1992	6	3	6	3	0	1C
	Mar. 31, 1993	1	0	1	0	0	1C
	Oct. 11-12, 1993	30	3	17	1	0	2C
Vermont	No special session in 1992						
	July 20-21, 1993	1	3	1	3	0	2C
Virginia............	April 15, 1992	6	31	5	29	1	1L
	April 7, 1993	6	21	3	21	0	1L

INTRODUCTIONS AND ENACTMENTS: SPECIAL SESSIONS—Continued

State or other jurisdiction	Duration of session*	Introductions		Enactments		Measures vetoed by governor	Length of session
		Bills	Resolutions	Bills	Resolutions		
Washington	No special session in 1992						
	April 26-May 6, 1993	3	2	25 (f)	1	8 (e)	11C
West Virginia	Mar. 14, 1992	4	7	4	7	0	1C
	May 16-27, 1993	19	8	10	7	0	12C
	Oct. 17-18, 1993	6	9	3	9	0	2C
Wisconsin...........	April 14-June 4, 1992	7	3	2	3	0	19L
	June 1, 1992	0	2	0	2	0	1L
	Aug. 25-Sept. 15, 1992	1	3	1	3	0	7L
	No special session in 1993						
Wyoming	May 11-13, 1992	18	0	1	0	0	3L
	No special session in 1993						
No. Mariana Islands ...	(g)	132	28	3	19	0	(c)
	(g)	60	32	2	28	0	(c)
Puerto Rico	June 8-27, 1992	8	1	8	1	0	14L
	July 6-24, 1992	41	158	23	149	1	14L
	July 30-Aug. 18, 1992	26	9	11	5	0	13L
	Sept. 17-Oct. 6, 1992	17	84	12	84	0	20C
	Oct. 8-28, 1992	6	10	3	10	8	20C
	July 1-20, 1993	12	7	3	4	0	11L
	Aug. 11-30, 1993	11	1	10	1	1	20C
	Nov. 29-Dec. 17, 1993	12	119	8	118	1	19C
U.S. Virgin Islands	No special session in 1992						
	March 25, 1993	1	0	1	0	0	1 C

Source: The Council of State Governments' legislative survey, March 1994.

* Actual adjournment dates are listed regardless of constitutional or statutory limitations. For more information on provisions, see Table 3.2, "Legislative Sessions: Legal Provisions."

Key:
C — Calendar day
L — Legislative day (in some states, called a session or workday; definition may vary slightly; however, it generally refers to any day on which either chamber of the legislature is in session.)
(a) Dates of sessions: 1992—Senate and House: July 1, July 14; Senate only: August 3. 1993—Senate and House: February 9, July 1 and November 4; Senate only: September 21.

(b) Includes carryover bills and resolutions introduced in the regular session and passed during the special session on July 1 of each year.
(c) Length of session: Delaware: 1992—Senate 3L and House 2L, 1993—Senate 4L and House 3L; No. Mariana Islands: 1992—Senate 6L and House 5L, 1993—Senate 8L and House, 3L.
(d) Veto overridden.
(e) Partial vetoes.
(f) Includes carryover bills introduced in the regular session and passed during the special session.
(g) The legislature met in special session between April and July in 1992 and 1993.

Table 3.21
STAFF FOR INDIVIDUAL LEGISLATORS

State or other jurisdiction	Senate Capitol Personal	Shared	District	House Capitol Personal	Shared	District
Alabama	YR	YR/2	...	...	YR/10	...
Alaska	YR	...	...	YR	...	...
Arizona	...	YR/2 (a)	...	...	YR/7 (a)	...
Arkansas	...	YR	...	...	YR	...
California	YR	YR/4 (b)	YR	YR	YR/2.7 (b)	YR
Colorado	(c)	YR (b)	...	(c)	YR (b)	...
Connecticut	YR	YR/.5 (d)	...	...	YR/3 (d)	...
Delaware	SO	YR/2	...	SO	YR/2	...
Florida	YR (e)	...	(e)	YR (e)	...	(e)
Georgia	...	YR/3 (b)	...	...	YR/5 (b)	...
Hawaii	YR	...	...	YR	...	...
Idaho	...	SO/.75	...	...	SO/1.5	...
Illinois	YR	YR/2 (f)	YR (g)	YR	YR/1 (f)	YR (g)
Indiana	...	YR/3	...	...	YR/3	...
Iowa	SO	...	...	SO	...	...
Kansas	SO (b)	...	...	...	SO/3 (b)	...
Kentucky	...	YR/12	...	...	YR/12	...
Louisiana	(h)	YR (i)	YR (h)	(h)	YR (i)	YR (h)
Maine	...	SO/15 (b)	...	...	SO/45 (b)	...
Maryland	YR	...	...	SO	SO/3	(g)
Massachusetts	YR	...	...	YR	...	...
Michigan	YR	...	...	YR	...	...
Minnesota	YR (j)	IO/2 (j)	...	...	YR/3	...
Mississippi	...	YR	...	...	YR	...
Missouri	YR	...	YR	YR	IO/1	...
Montana	...	SO	...	...	SO	...
Nebraska	YR	...	...	---------- Unicameral ----------		
Nevada	SO	YR	...	SO	YR	...
New Hampshire	...	SO	...	...	YR	...
New Jersey	YR (e)	...	(e)	YR (e)	...	(e)
New Mexico	SO	SO/3	...	SO	SO/7	...
New York	YR	...	YR	YR	YR	YR
North Carolina	SO (b)	YR	...	SO (b)	YR	...
North Dakota	...	SO/10 (b)	...	...	SO/12 (b)	...
Ohio	YR (k)	YR	(l)	YR (m)	YR (m)	(l)
Oklahoma	SO (b,c)	IO	...	SO (b,c)	IO/7	...
Oregon	YR	...	...	YR	...	...
Pennsylvania	YR	...	YR	YR	YR	YR
Rhode Island	...	YR/8	...	...	YR/7	...
South Carolina	YR	YR/(n)	...	SO	SO/1	...
South Dakota	...	...	...	...	...	...
Tennessee	YR	...	...	YR	...	...
Texas	YR	...	YR	YR	...	YR
Utah	(o)	SO/1	...	(o)	SO/1	...
Vermont	...	YR/15 (b)	...	...	YR/90 (b)	...
Virginia	SO (e)	...	(e)	YR (e)	SO/2	(e)
Washington	YR (p)	...	(q)	YR	...	(q)
West Virginia	SO	...	...	...	SO/17	...
Wisconsin	YR (r)	...	(r)	YR	...	...
Wyoming	...	...	...	...	...	...
No. Mariana Islands	YR (s)	(s)	...	YR (s)	(s)	...
Puerto Rico	YR (s)	...	(r)	YR (s)	...	(r)

Source: The Council of State Governments' legislative survey, March 1994.

Note: For entries under column heading "Shared," figures after slash indicate approximate number of legislators per staff person, where available.

Key:
... — Staff not provided for individual legislators
YR — Year-round
SO — Session only
IO — Interim only
(a) Includes only majority and minority policy staff, not secretarial staff.
(b) Secretarial staff.
(c) Majority and minority leadership have a year-round secretarial staff.
(d) Each senator is provided with one constituent case worker; all Senate and House members receive support from a centralized caucus staff.
(e) Personal and district staff are the same.
(f) Majority and minority offices provide staff year-round.
(g) District office expenses allocated per year from which staff may be hired.
(h) Each legislator may hire as many assistants as desired, but pay from public funds is capped at $2,500 per month per legislator. Assistant(s) generally work in the district office but may also work at the capitol during the session.

(i) The six caucuses are assigned one full-time position each (potentially 24 legislators per one staff person).
(j) Each majority party senator has one year-round secretary; some minority party senators share secretarial staff (YR/2).
(k) One secretary and one legislative aide per senator. Senate president and other leaders have one or more additional staff members.
(l) Some legislators have established district offices at their own expense.
(m) One secretary per house member. Members in the minority caucus share constituent aides and legislative research assistants.
(n) Some legislators share secretaries for 32 of the members; one secretary per one senator for 14 of the members.
(o) Legislators are provided student interns during session.
(p) Leadership, caucus chair, and Ways and Means Committee chair have two full-time staff each. All other legislators have one full-time staff year-round and one additional staff session only.
(q) Full-time staff may move to the district office during interim period.
(r) Some of personal staff may work in the district office. Total of all staff salaries for each senator must be within limits established by the Senate.
(s) Individual staffing and staff pool arrangements are at the discretion of the individual legislator.

Table 3.22
STAFF FOR LEGISLATIVE STANDING COMMITTEES

State or other jurisdiction	Committee staff assistance				Source of staff services*							
	Senate		House		Joint central agency (a)		Chamber agency (b)		Caucus or leadership		Committee or committee chairman	
	Prof.	Cler.	Prof.	Cler.	Prof.	Cler.	Prof.	Cler.	Prof.	Cler.	Prof.	Cler.
Alabama	...	★	...	★	B	...	...	B	...	...	...	...
Alaska	★	★	★	★	...	...	...	...	...	...	...	...
Arizona	★	★	★	★	B	...	...	B	B	...	B	B
Arkansas	★	★	★	★	B	B	...	...	...	...	...	...
California	★	★	★	★	...	...	...	...	...	...	...	...
Colorado	★	...	★	...	B	...	...	...	...	...	...	...
Connecticut	★ (c)	★ (c)	★ (c)	(c)	B (c)	...	...	...	...	B (c)	...	...
Delaware	•	★	•	★	B	...	B	...	...	B	B	B
Florida	★	★	★	★	...	...	...	...	...	...	...	...
Georgia	...	★ (d)	...	★ (d)	B	...	B	...	...	...	...	...
Hawaii	•	★	★	★	B	B	B	B	B	B	B	B
Idaho	★	★	★	★	B	B	...	...	...	...	B	B
Illinois	★	★	★	★	...	...	B	B	B	B	...	...
Indiana	★	•	★	(e)	B	...	...	S	...	S	...	...
Iowa	★	...	★	...	B	...	...	B (f)	B	...	...	B (f)
Kansas	★	★	★	★	B	B (g)	...	...	...	...	...	...
Kentucky	★	★	★	★	B	B	...	...	...	...	...	...
Louisiana	★ (h)	★	★ (h)	★	B	B	B	B	B	B	B (i)	B (i)
Maine	★ (c)	★ (c,j)	★ (c)	(c,j)	B	...	...	...	...	...	...	...
Maryland	★ (k)	★ (k)	★ (k)	★ (k)	B	...	...	...	...	...	...	...
Massachusetts	★	★	★	★	...	...	...	...	...	...	...	...
Michigan	★	★	★	★	B	...	...	H	B	...	B	S
Minnesota	★	★	★	★	...	...	B	...	H	H	B	B
Mississippi	•	★	•	★	...	...	B	B	...	...	B	B
Missouri	★	★	★	...	B	...	B	B	...	...	...	B
Montana	★	★	★	★	B	...	...	B	...	...	...	...
Nebraska	★	★	-----Unicameral-----		...	...	...	B	...	...	U	U
Nevada	★	★	★	★	B	...	...	...	...	...	...	...
New Hampshire	•	★	★	★	B	...	...	...	B	...	...	...
New Jersey	★	★	★	★	B	B	...	...	...	...	...	...
New Mexico	★	★	★	★	...	...	...	...	B	B	B	...
New York	★	★	★	★	B	B	B	B	B	B	B	B
North Carolina	★	★ (l)	★	★ (l)	B	...	...	...	...	...	...	★ (l)
North Dakota	(h)	★	(h)	★	B	...	...	B	...	...	...	...
Ohio	★	★	★	★	B	...	...	...	B	B	B (m)	B (m)
Oklahoma	★	★	★	★ (l)	...	...	B	B	H	B	...	H
Oregon	★	★	★	★	B	B	...	...	...	...	B	B
Pennsylvania	★	★	★	★	B	B	...	...	B	B	B	B
Rhode Island	★	★	★	★	B	B	B	B	B	B	B	B
South Carolina	★	★	★	★	...	...	B	B	H	H	B	B
South Dakota	★	★	★	★	B	...	...	...	...	B	S	...
Tennessee	★	★	★	★	B	...	B (n)	...	...	...	S	B
Texas	★	★	★	★	B	...	...	B	...	...	B	B
Utah	★	★	★	★	B	B	...	B	...	...	...	...
Vermont	★	★	★	★	B	B	...	...	...	...	B	B
Virginia	★	★	★	★	B	...	B	B	...	...	...	(i)
Washington	★	★	★	★	...	...	...	...	...	...	...	...
West Virginia	★	★	★	★	B	B	B	B	B	B	B	B
Wisconsin	★	★	★	★	B	...	B	...	...	...	B	B
Wyoming	★	★	★	★	B	...	...	B	...	B	...	B
No. Mariana Islands	★	★	★	★	B (o)	B (o)	B (o)	B (o)	B (o)	B (o)	B (o)	B (o)
Puerto Rico	★	★	★	★	B (o)	B (o)	...	...	...	...	...	...

See footnotes at end of table.

STAFF FOR LEGISLATIVE STANDING COMMITTEES—Continued

Source: The Council of State Governments' legislative survey, March 1994.

* Multiple entries reflect a combination of organizational location of services.

Key:

★ — All committees
• — Some committees
. . . — Services not provided
B — Both chambers
H — House
S — Senate
U — Unicameral

(a) Includes legislative council or service agency or central management agency.

(b) Includes chamber management agency, office of clerk or secretary and House or Senate research office.

(c) Standing committees are joint House and Senate committees.

(d) Provided on a pool basis.

(e) Provided on an ad hoc basis.

(f) The Senate secretary and House clerk maintain supervision of committee clerks. During the session each committee selects its own clerk.

(g) Senators select their secretaries and notify the central administrative services agency; all administrative employee matters handled by the agency.

(h) House and Senate Appropriations Committees have Legislative Council fiscal staff at their hearings.

(i) Staff is assigned to each committee but work under the direction of the chairman.

(j) Clerical staff hired during session only.

(k) Committees hire additional staff on a contractual basis during session only under direction of chairman.

(l) Member's personal secretary serves as a clerk to the committee or subcommittee that the member chairs.

(m) Member's personal legislative aide and secretary serve as staff to the committee that the member chairs. House Finance and Appropriations Committee—one additional fiscal analyst; Senate Finance Committee—one additional aide.

(n) Bill clerks during session only.

(o) In general, the legislative service agency provides legal and staff assistance for legislative meetings and provides associated materials. Individual legislators hire personal or committee staff as their budgets provide and at their own discretion.

Table 3.23
STANDING COMMITTEES: APPOINTMENT AND NUMBER

State or other jurisdiction	Committee members appointed by:		Committee chairpersons appointed by:		Number of standing committees during regular 1993 session (a)	
	Senate	House	Senate	House	Senate	House
Alabama	P (b)	S	P (b)	S	25	26
Alaska	CC (c)	CC (c)	CC (c)	CC (c)	9 (d)	9 (d)
Arizona	P	S	P	S	11 (d)	15 (d)
Arkansas	CC	S	CC	(e)	10 (d)	10 (d)
California	CR	S (f)	CR	S	23 (d)	24 (d)
Colorado	MjL,MnL	S,MnL	MjL	S	10	10
Connecticut	PT	S	PT	S	(g)	(g)
Delaware	PT	S (h)	PT	S	24 (d)	20 (d)
Florida	P	S	P	S	20 (d)	22 (d)
Georgia	P (b)	S	P (b)	S	26	28
Hawaii	P (i)	(j)	P (i)	(j)	14	20
Idaho	PT (k)	S	PT	S	10	14
Illinois	P,MnL	S,MnL	P	S	14	29
Indiana	PT	S	PT	S	18	25
Iowa	MjL,MnL (l)	S	MjL,MnL (l)	S	16 (d)	17 (d)
Kansas	(m)	S	(m)	S	15 (d)	17 (d)
Kentucky	CC	CC	CC	CC	13	16
Louisiana	P	S (n)	P	S	17	16
Maine	P	S	P	S	4 (g)	6 (g)
Maryland	P	S	P	S	6 (d)	7 (d)
Massachusetts	P	S,MnL	P	S	8 (g)	6 (g)
Michigan	MjL	S	MjL	S	18	28
Minnesota	(o)	S	(o)	S	18	21
Mississippi	P (b,p)	S (p)	P (b,p)	S (p)	30 (d)	27 (d)
Missouri	PT (q)	S,MnL	PT	S	22 (d)	42 (d)
Montana	CC	S	CC	S	16	15
Nebraska	CC	U	(r)	U	14	U
Nevada	(s)	S	(s)	S	9	11
New Hampshire	P (t)	S (u)	P (t)	S	18 (d)	24 (d)
New Jersey	P	S	P	S	17 (d)	21 (d)
New Mexico	CC	S	CC	S	9	15
New York	PT (v)	S	PT (v)	S	32 (d)	37 (d)
North Carolina	PT,MnL	S	PT	S	27	24
North Dakota	CC	S	CC	S	11 (d)	11 (d)
Ohio	(w)	S	(w)	S	14	27
Oklahoma	PT,MnL	S	PT	S	17 (d)	23 (d)
Oregon	P	S	P	S	15 (d)	11 (d)
Pennsylvania	PT	CC (x)	PT	S	22	21
Rhode Island	MjL	S	MjL	S	6 (d)	6 (d)
South Carolina	E (y)	S	E	E	14	11
South Dakota	(z)	S	(z)	S	13	13
Tennessee	S	S	S	S	9 (d)	11 (d)
Texas	P (b)	S (aa)	P (b)	S	10	31
Utah	P	S	P	S	10 (d)	10 (d)
Vermont	CC	S	CC	S	12 (d)	15 (d)
Virginia	E	S (bb)	(cc)	S	11	20
Washington	P (b,dd)	S (ee)	P (b,dd)	S (ff)	14	21
West Virginia	P	S	P	S	17 (d)	13 (d)
Wisconsin	(gg)	S	(gg)	S	13 (d)	32 (d)
Wyoming	P (hh)	S (hh)	P (hh)	S (hh)	12	12
Dist. of Columbia	(ii)	U	(ii)	U	12	U
No. Mariana Islands	P	S	P	S	8	8
U.S. Virgin Islands	P	U	P	U	10	U

See footnotes at end of table.

STANDING COMMITTEES: APPOINTMENT AND NUMBER—Continued

Sources: State legislative rule books and manuals.

Note: Standing committees are those which regularly consider legislation during the legislative session.

Key:

CC — Committee on Committees
CR — Committee on Rules
E — Election
MjL — Majority Leader
MnL — Minority Leader
P — President
PT — President pro tempore
S — Speaker
U — Unicameral Legislature

(a) According to survey conducted for *State Legislative Leadership, Committees & Staff, 1993-94,* a publication of The Council of State Governments; and state legislative rule books.

(b) Lieutenant governor is president of the Senate.

(c) Report of Committee on Committees is subject to approval by majority vote of chamber's membership.

(d) Also, joint standing committees. Alaska, 2; Arizona, 5 (joint statutory); Arkansas, 5; California, 9; Delaware, 2; Florida, 4; Iowa, 1; Kansas, 11; Maryland, 3 (and 12 joint statutory); Mississippi, 4; Missouri, 8; New Hampshire, 6; New Jersey, 2; New York, 16 (joint commissions); North Dakota, 1; Oklahoma, 3; Oregon, 1; Rhode Island, 7; Tennessee, 3 (joint statutory); Utah, 10; Vermont, 4; West Virginia, 5; Wisconsin, 7.

(e) Chair of the standing committee is the ranking member of the committee on seniority basis.

(f) Except membership of the Committee on Rules. Speaker considers recommendation of party caucuses when appointing members of standing committees.

(g) Substantive standing committees are joint committees. Connecticut, 17; Maine, 19; Massachusetts, 21.

(h) Shall include members of two political parties.

(i) President appoints committee members and chairs; minority members on committees are nominated by minority party caucus.

(j) By resolution, with members of majority party designating the chair, vice-chairs and majority party members of committees, and members of minority party designating minority party members.

(k) Committee members appointed by the Senate leadership under the direction of the president pro tempore, by and with the Senate's advice.

(l) Appointments made after consultation with the president.

(m) Committee on Organization, Calendar and Rules.

(n) Speaker appoints only 11 of the 19 members of the Committee on Appropriations.

(o) Subcommittee on Committees of the Committee on Rules and Administration.

(p) Senate: except Rules Committee; House: except Rules and Management Committees.

(q) Membership shall be composed of majority and minority party members in the same proportion as in the total membership of the Senate.

(r) Appointed by the legislature.

(s) Committee composition and leadership usually determined by party caucus.

(t) Appointments made after consultation with the minority leader.

(u) Speaker appoints minority members with advice of the minority floor leader.

(v) President pro tempore is also majority leader.

(w) Appointed by Senate.

(x) Makes recommendation to the House.

(y) Seniority system is retained in process.

(z) Presiding officer announces committee membership after selection by president pro tempore, majority and minority leaders.

(aa) A maximum of one-half of the membership on each standing committee, exclusive of the chair and vice chair, is determined by seniority; the remaining membership is appointed by the speaker.

(bb) Unless otherwise specially directed by the House, in which case they shall be appointed by ballot and a plurality of votes shall prevail.

(cc) Senior member of the majority part on the committee is the chair.

(dd) Confirmed by the Senate.

(ee) By each party caucus.

(ff) By majority caucus.

(gg) Committee on Senate Organization.

(hh) With the advice and consent of the Rules and Procedures Committee.

(ii) Chair of the Council.

Table 3.24
STANDING COMMITTEES: PROCEDURE

State or other jurisdiction	Uniform rules of committee procedure Senate	House	Joint	Public access to committee meetings Open to public Senate	House	Advance notice required (number of days) Senate	House	Recorded roll call on vote to report bill to floor Senate	House
Alabama	★	★		★	★	...	2	Al	Sm
Alaska	...	...		★	★	...	...	Sm	Sm
Arizona	★	★		★	★	(a)	(a)	Sm	Al
Arkansas	★	★	★	★	★	2	1	Sm	Sm
California	★	★	★	★	★	(a)	(a)	Al	Al
Colorado	★	★		★	★	...	...	Al	Al
Connecticut			★	★	★	1	1	Al	Al
Delaware	★	★		★	★ (b)	(a)	(a)	Al	Al
Florida	★	★		★	★	4 hrs (c)	2 (d)	Al	Al
Georgia	...	...		★	★	1	...	Sm	Nv
Hawaii	★	★		★ (b)	★	2	2	Al	Al
Idaho	★	★		★ (b)	★	...	...	Sm	Sm
Illinois	★	★		★ (b)	★ (b)	6	6.5	Al	Al
Indiana	...	...		★	★	2	(a)	Al	Al
Iowa	★	★		★	★	(a)	1	Al	Al
Kansas	★	★		★	★	...	1	Sm	Al
Kentucky	★	★		★	★	...	...	Al	Al
Louisiana	★	★		★	★	(a)	(a)	Sm	Al
Maine			★	★	★	(a)	(a)	Sm	Sm
Maryland	★	★		★	★	(a)	(a)	Al	Al
Massachusetts	...	★	...	★	★ (b)	...	2	Nv	Sm
Michigan	★	★		★	★	...	...	Al	Al
Minnesota	★	★		★	★	3	3	Sm	Sm
Mississippi	...	...	...	★	★ (b)	(a)	(a)	Sm	Sm
Missouri	★	★	★	★	★	...	1	Al	Al
Montana	...	...		★	★	3	...	Al	Al
Nebraska	★	U		★ (b)	U	7	U	Al	U
Nevada	★	★		★	★	(a)	5 (e)	Al	Al
New Hampshire	...	★		★	★	5	4	Al	Al
New Jersey	★	★		★	★	5	5	Al	Al
New Mexico	★	★		★	★	...	...	Sm	Sm
New York	★	★		★ (b)	★ (b)	7	7	Al	Nv
North Carolina	★	★		★ (b)	★	(a)	(a)	Sm	Sm
North Dakota	★	★		★	★	(f)	(f)	Al	Al
Ohio	★	★		★	★	2	(a)	Al	Al
Oklahoma	★	★		★	★	(a)	(a)	Al	Sm
Oregon	★	★		★	★	1 (g)	1 (h)	Al	Al
Pennsylvania	★	★		★ (b)	★	(a)	5	Al	Al
Rhode Island	★	★		★ (b)	★ (b)	2	...	Al	Al
South Carolina	★	★		★ (b)	★ (b)	1	1	Sm	Sm
South Dakota	★	★	★	★	★	1	1	Al	Al
Tennessee	★	★		★	★	(i)	(i)	Al	Al
Texas	★	★		★	★ (b)	1	5	Sm	Al
Utah	★	★	★	★	★	1	1	Al	Al
Vermont	★	★	★	★ (b)	★	...	...	Al	Al
Virginia	★	★		★ (b)	★ (j)	(a)	(a)	Al	Al
Washington	★	★		★	★	5	5	Al	Al
West Virginia	★	★	★	★ (b)	★ (b)	...	...	Al	Al
Wisconsin	★	★	★	★	★	7	7	Al	Al
Wyoming	★	★		★	★	...	...	Al	Al
No. Mariana Islands	★	★		★	★	...	...	Sm	Al

Sources: State legislative rule books and manuals.

Key:
★ — Yes
... — No
Al — Always
Sm — Sometimes
Nv — Never
U — Unicameral legislature

(a) No specified time. Maryland—"from time to time," usually seven days. Nevada—"adequate notice." North Carolina—notice must be given in the House or Senate; two methods to waive notice in the Senate. Ohio—"due notice." Virginia—notice published in the daily calendar.

(b) Certain matters specified by statute can be discussed in executive session. Illinois—upon a vote of 2/3 elected. North Carolina—appropriations committees are required to sit jointly in open session. Guam—hearings are open to the public, but meetings may be closed.

(c) During session—four-hour notice for first 50 days, two hours thereafter.

(d) During session—two days notice for first 45 days, two hours thereafter.

(e) Public hearings on bills or resolutions of "high public importance" must receive five calendar days notice. All other committee meetings must have 24 hours notice.

(f) Rules require posting of bills and resolutions to be considered at each meeting and provide deadlines for such posting depending upon the schedules for particular committees.

(g) Except in case of meeting to resolve conflicts or inconsistencies among two or more measures, in which case posting and notice to the public shall be given immediately upon call of the meeting, and notice of the meeting shall be announced on the floor if the Senate is in session.

(h) In case of actual emergency, a meeting may be held upon such notice as is appropriate to the circumstances.

(i) Committees meet on a fixed schedule during sessions. Senate: five days notice required during interim. House: 72 hours notice required during interim.

(j) Committee meetings are required to be open for final vote on bill.

Table 3.25
LEGISLATIVE REVIEW OF ADMINISTRATIVE REGULATIONS: STRUCTURES AND PROCEDURES

State	Type of reviewing committee	Rules reviewed	Time limits in review process
Alabama	Mbrs. Legislative Council	P	60 days for action by committee.
Alaska	Joint bipartisan	P,E	. . .
Arizona	--(a)--		
Arkansas	Joint bipartisan	P,E	. . .
California	--(a)--		
Colorado (b)	Joint bipartisan	E	Every newly adopted or amended rule expires on June 1 of the following year. Each year the committee sponsors a bill before the General Assembly which extends the adopted or amended rules due to expire.
Connecticut	Joint bipartisan	P	65 days for action by committee.
Delaware	--(a)--		
Florida	Joint bipartisan	P,E	. . .
Georgia (b)	Standing committee	P	The agency notifies the Legislative Counsel 30 days prior to the effective dates of proposed rules.
Hawaii	--(a)--		
Idaho	Germane joint subcommittees	P,E	All rules expire one year after adoption and must be reauthorized through legislative action.
Illinois	Joint bipartisan	P,E	If the committee objects to a rule, the agency has 90 days to modify or withdraw the rule. If the agency refuses to act during that period, the committee may prohibit adoption of the rule for 180 days.
Indiana (b)	Joint bipartisan	E	The legislature is not involved in the rules review process.
Iowa	Joint bipartisan	P,E	. . .
Kansas	Joint bipartisan	E	New rules become effective 45 days following publication in the *Kansas Register*.
Kentucky	Joint bipartisan subcommittee	P	. . .
Louisiana (b)	Standing committee	P	All proposed rules and fees are submitted to designated standing committees of the legislature. If a rule is unacceptable, the committee sends a written report to the governor. The governor has 10 days to disapprove the committee report. If both Senate and House committees fail to find the rule acceptable, or if the governor disapproves the action of a committee within 10 days, the agency may adopt the rule change.
Maine	Jt. standing cmtes. & Executive Dir. of the Legislative Council	E	Any group of 100 or more registered voters, or any person directly, substantially, or adversely affected by a rule may file an application for review with the executive director of the Legislative Council. One-third or more of the appropriate standing committee must request a review within 15 days of receipt of the application.
Maryland (b)	Joint bipartisan	P,E	
Massachusetts (b)	Jt. standing cmtes. & Commissioner of Administration and Finance	P	Rules review applies to capitol facilities only. If the rule is not approved by the General Court and the governor within 90 days of filing, it is deemed to have been disapproved.
Michigan	Joint bipartisan	P	Joint Committee on Administrative Rules has two months (three months by vote of committee) to approve/disapprove proposed rule.
Minnesota	Joint Legislative Commission	E	The commission may not take action until the standing committees of both houses report to the commission or after 60 days have lapsed.
Mississippi	--(a)--		
Missouri	Joint bipartisan	P,E	. . .
Montana	Joint bipartisan	P,E	. . .
Nebraska	--(a)--		
Nevada	Joint bipartisan	P	If the committee objects to a rule, the agency has 10 days to revise it.
New Hampshire	Joint bipartisan	P	Within 45 days of the filing, the committee may approve or object.
New Jersey	--(a)--		
New Mexico	--(a)--		
New York	Joint bipartisan commission	P,E	. . .
North Carolina	Public membership appointed by legislature	P	Generally 30 days for action by committee. Majority vote of the committee delays the rule's effective date for a period not to exceed 90 days.
North Dakota	Interim committee with possible public membership	P,E	Within 14 days the agency must respond in writing to the committee's objection. Objections are published in the supplement to the *North Dakota Code*.
Ohio	Joint bipartisan	P,E	All proposed rules are submitted to the committee 60 days prior to adoption.
Oklahoma (b)	Standing cmte. or cmte. appointed by leadership of both houses	E	. . .
Oregon	Joint bipartisan	P,E	. . .
Pennsylvania	Standing committee	P	Standing committee has 20 days to review the final form regulation.
Rhode Island	--(a)--		
South Carolina	Standing committees	P	120 days for action by committee or legislature. If the committee does not approve the rule, the agency must resubmit or withdraw it within 30 days.

STRUCTURES AND PROCEDURES—Continued

State	Type of reviewing committee	Rules reviewed	Time limits in review process
South Dakota	Joint bipartisan	P	A proposed or provisional rule can be suspended until July 1 following the next legislative session if five of the committee's six members agree.
Tennessee	Joint standing committee	P	All permanent rules take effect 45 days after filing with the secretary of state. Rules filed in a calendar year expire on June 30 of the following year unless extended by the General Assembly.
Texas	Appropriate standing committees	P	. . .
Utah	Joint bipartisan	P	Each rule in effect on January 1 of each year expires on May 1 of that year unless it is reauthorized by the legislature.
Vermont	Joint bipartisan	P,E	All final proposed rules must be submitted to the committee, which has 30 days to review them. Within 14 days of receiving an objection the agency must respond in writing. If the committee still objects it may file its objection with the secretary of state.
Virginia (b)	Standing committee	P,E	Legislative review is optional. Within 21 days after the receipt of an objection, the agency shall file a response with the registrar, the objecting legislative committee and the governor. After an objection is filed, the regulation unless withdrawn by the agency shall become effective on a date specified by the agency which shall be after the 21-day extension period.
Washington (b)	Joint bipartisan	P,E	If the committee determines that a proposed rule does not comply with legislative intent, it notifies the agency, which must schedule a public hearing within 30 days of notification. The agency notifies the committee of its action within seven days after the hearing. If a hearing is not held or the agency does not amend the rule, the objection may be filed in the state register and referenced in the state code. The committee's powers, other than publication of its objections, are advisory.
West Virginia	Joint bipartisan	P	. . .
Wisconsin	Joint bipartisan	P	The standing committee has 30 days to conduct its review.
Wyoming (b)	Joint bipartisan	P,E	. . .

Source: National Conference of State Legislatures.
Key:
P — Proposed rules
E — Existing rules
. . . — No formal time limits

(a) No formal mechanism for legislative review of administrative rules.
(b) Review of rules is performed by both legislative and executive branches.

Table 3.26
LEGISLATIVE REVIEW OF ADMINISTRATIVE REGULATIONS: POWERS

State	Reviewing committee's powers:			Legislative powers:
	Advisory powers only (a)	No objection constitutes approval of proposed rule	Committee may suspend rule	Method of legislative veto of rules
Alabama	...	★	★	Joint resolution (b)
Alaska	(c)	(c)	...	Statute (c)
Arizona	----------------------------------(d)---------------------------			
Arkansas	(e)	N.A.	N.A.	N.A.
California	----------------------------------(d)---------------------------			
Colorado	...	★	...	Statute (f)
Connecticut	...	★	★	Resolution (g)
Delaware	----------------------------------(d)---------------------------			
Florida	★	N.A.	N.A.	(h)
Georgia	...	★	...	Resolution (i)
Hawaii	----------------------------------(d)---------------------------			
Idaho	...	★	...	Concurrent resolution (j)
Illinois	...	...	★	Joint resolution
Indiana	★ (k)	...	N.A.	(l)
Iowa	...	★	★	Joint resolution
Kansas	...	★	...	Concurrent resolution
Kentucky	...	★	...	Statute
Louisiana	...	★	(m)	Concurrent resolution
Maine	★	N.A.	N.A.	(n)
Maryland	(o)	★	...	N.A.
Massachusetts	...	(p)	...	Joint resolution
Michigan	...	...	(q)	Concurrent resolution (r)
Minnesota	...	...	★	Statute
Mississippi	----------------------------------(d)---------------------------			
Missouri	...	★	★	(s)
Montana	...	...	...	Statute
Nebraska	----------------------------------(d)---------------------------			
Nevada	★	★	N.A.	N.A.
New Hampshire	★	★	N.A.	(t)
New Jersey	----------------------------------(d)---------------------------			
New Mexico	----------------------------------(d)---------------------------			
New York	★	★	N.A.	N.A.
North Carolina	...	...	★	Statute (u)
North Dakota	★	★ (v)	N.A.	(w)
Ohio	...	(x)	★	Concurrent resolution (y)
Oklahoma	...	★	...	Joint resolution (z)
Oregon	★ (aa)	N.A.	N.A.	(bb)
Pennsylvania	...	★	...	Concurrent resolution (cc)
Rhode Island	----------------------------------(d)---------------------------			
South Carolina	...	★	...	Joint resolution (dd)
South Dakota	...	★	★	Statute
Tennessee	...	N.A.	...	Statute (ee)
Texas	★ (ff)	N.A.	N.A.	N.A.
Utah	...	N.A.	...	Statute (ee)
Vermont	★ (t)	★	N.A.	None
Virginia (d)	★ (gg)	N.A.	N.A.	N.A.
Washington	★ (hh)	N.A.	(ii)	N.A.
West Virginia	★	...	N.A.	(jj)
Wisconsin	...	★	★	Statute (kk)
Wyoming	... (ll)	N.A.	...	Statute (mm)

POWERS—Continued

Source: National Conference of State Legislatures.

Key:

★ — Yes

. . . — No

N.A. — Not applicable

(a) This column is defined by those legislatures or legislative committees that can only recommend changes to rules but have no power to enforce a change.

(b) A rule disapproved by the reviewing committee is reinstated at the end of the next session if a joint resolution in the legislature fails to sustain committee action.

(c) Committee powers are advisory. Veto authority of the committee was ruled unconstitutional. However, the legislature can pass legislation for presentment to the executive to annul a rule.

(d) No formal mechanism for legislative review of administrative rules. In Virginia, legislative review is optional.

(e) Committee reports findings only to Legislative Council. Council acts in an advisory capacity to General Assembly and may submit appropriate legislation.

(f) All newly adopted or amended rules expire on June 1 of the year following adoption or amendment. The legislature exercises sunset control over rules. Each year a bill is filed that extends all rules promulgated the previous year, except for those rules specifically designated by the committee.

(g) By February 15 of each regular session, the committee submits for study to the General Assembly a copy of all disapproved regulations. The General Assembly may by resolution sustain or reverse a vote of disapproval.

(h) Committee is required to report annually to the legislature to recommend needed legislation.

(i) The reviewing committee must introduce a resolution to override a rule within the first 30 days of the next regular session of the General Assembly. If the resolution passes by less than a two-thirds majority of either house, the governor has final authority to affirm or veto the resolution.

(j) All rules are terminated one year after adoption unless the legislature reauthorizes the rule.

(k) Governor can veto rules with or without cause.

(l) Legislature has authority to intervene only after a rule is adopted. The committee meets during the interim but can affect a rule only through recommending a change in statute.

(m) If the committee determines that a proposed rule is unacceptable, it submits a report to the governor who then has 10 days to accept or reject the report. If the governor rejects the report, the rule change may be adopted by the agency. If the governor accepts the report, the committee can block agency action.

(n) If the legislature determines a rule is inappropriate or unnecessary, it may direct the Office of Policy and Legal Analysis to draft legislation to amend the statutory authority of the agency to amend the rule.

(o) In six specific instances, the legislature has added language to the enabling statutes giving it veto power over regulations.

(p) If a rule is not approved by the General Court and the governor with-

in 90 days of filing, it is considered disapproved.

(q) Committee can suspend rules during interim only.

(r) Must be passed within 60 days of its introduction in the legislature.

(s) In many statutes, the committee has the authority to rescind a rule or any part of a rule.

(t) Filing an objection to a rule shifts the burden of proof to the agency in any action for judicial review.

(u) If an agency does not amend a rule to address an objection of the commission, the commission may send written notice to leadership in both houses. The General Assembly may enact legislation disapproving the rule.

(v) Unless formal objections are made, rules are considered approved.

(w) Objection to a rule can lead to legislation affecting statutory authority of agency.

(x) Committee does not approve rules. Committee can recommend invalidation only of all or part of a rule. Inaction on a rule is not considered approval or consent of legality of a rule.

(y) Must be adopted within 60 days. Any rule promulgated during the interim goes into effect, but a concurrent resolution may be passed within the first 60 days of the next session to disapprove the rule.

(z) Failure of the legislature to adopt a joint resolution within 30 legislative days results in automatic approval.

(aa) Neither the governor nor the legislature has veto authority over rules.

(bb) The committee reports to the legislature during each regular session on the review of rules by the committee.

(cc) The committee has 14 days to introduce a concurrent resolution, which then must be passed by both chambers within 10 legislative days or 30 calendar days.

(dd) Must be passed within 120-day review period and presented to the governor for signature.

(ee) The legislature exercises sunset control over rules. Each year a bill is filed that extends all rules promulgated the previous year, except for those rules specifically designated by the committee.

(ff) On a vote of a majority of the committee, the committee may send a statement supporting or opposing the proposed rule.

(gg) Rules objected to become effective 21 days after receipt of objection by the Registrar of Regulations.

(hh) Objections are published in the *Washington State Register*.

(ii) By a two-third's vote, the committee may request the governor to approve suspension of a rule. If the governor approves, the suspension is effective until 90 days after the end of the next regular session.

(jj) State agencies have no power to promulgate rules without first submitting proposed rules to the legislature which must enact a statute authorizing the agency to promulgate the rule. If the legislature fails to enact a statute during a regular session, the agency may not issue the rule nor take action to implement all or part of the rule unless authorized to do so.

(kk) Bills are introduced simultaneously in both houses.

(ll) Legislative Management Council can recommend action be taken by the full legislature.

(mm) Action must be taken before the end of the next succeeding legislative session to nullify a rule.

Table 3.27
SUMMARY OF SUNSET LEGISLATION

State	Scope	Preliminary evaluation conducted by	Other legislative review	Other oversight mechanisms in bill	Phase-out period	Life of each agency (in years)	Other provisions
Alabama	C	Select Jt. Cmte.	Dept. of Examiners of Public Accounts	Zero-base budgeting	180	4	One-hour time limit on floor debate on each bill.
Alaska	C	Legis. Auditor	Standing cmtes.	Perf. audit	1/y	Varies (usually 4)	...
Arizona	S	Off. of the Auditor General	Legislative cmtes. of reference	Perf. audit	6/m	10	Jt. Legis. Audit Cmte. selects agencies for review and assigns responsibilities for hearings to the legis. cmtes. of reference.
Arkansas	(a)	...		...	...	...	...
California	(b)	...		...	...	...	...
Colorado	R	Dept. of Regulatory Agencies	Joint Legislative Sunrise Sunset Review Cmte.	...	1/y	up to 10	Advisory cmtes. are reviewed at least once after establishment; all regulatory functions of the state are reviewed.
Connecticut	(c)	...		...	...	...	...
Delaware	C	Agencies under review submit reports to Del. Sunset Comm. based on criteria for review and set forth in statute. Comm. staff conducts separate review	...	Perf. audit	Dec. 31 of next succeeding calendar year	4	Yearly sunset review schedules must include at least nine agencies. If the number automatically scheduled for review or added by the General Assembly is less than a full schedule, additional agencies shall be added in order of their appearance in the Del. Code to complete the review schedule.
Florida	R	House Regulatory Reform Cmte. and appropriate substantive cmte. in the Senate	Subject area committees handle some sunset review	Perf. audit, progress review	...	10	Automatic repeal if legislature fails to reenact legislation by a specific date.
Georgia	R	Dept. of Audits	Standing cmtes.	Perf. audit	1/y	1-6	A performance audit of each regulatory agency must be conducted upon the request of the Senate or House standing committee to which an agency has been assigned for oversight and review (d).
Hawaii	R	Legis. Auditor	Consumer Protection Cmte. of each house	Perf. eval.	None	6-10	Schedules the various professional and vocational licensing programs for repeal according to a specified timetable. Proposed new regulatory measures must be referred to the Auditor for sunrise analysis.
Idaho	(b)	...		...	...	...	...
Illinois	R	Bur. of the Budget	...	...	1	10	...
Indiana	C	Off. of Fiscal and Management Analysis	...	Perf. audit, Perf. eval.	...	10	...
Iowa				No program			

Key:
C — Comprehensive
R — Regulatory
S — Selective
D — Discretionary
d — day
m — month
y — year
... — Not applicable

SUNSET LEGISLATION—Continued

State	Scope	Preliminary evaluation conducted by	Other legislative review	Other oversight mechanisms in bill	Phase-out period	Life of each agency (in years)	Other provisions
Kansas	(e)	...	...	No program	...	...	...
Kentucky	...						
Louisiana	C	Standing cmtes. of the two houses with subject matter jurisdiction	...	Zero budget review (f), Perf. eval.	1/y	Up to 9	Act provides for termination of a department and all agencies and offices in a department. Also permits committees to select particular agencies or offices for more extensive evaluation. Provides for review by Jt. Legis. Cmte. on Budget of programs that were not funded during the prior fiscal year for possible repeal.
Maine	C	Jt. Standing Cmte. on Audit & Program Review	...	Perf. eval., Perf. audit	1/y	Subject to review every 11/y	...
Maryland	R	Dept. of Fiscal Services	Standing cmtes.	Perf. eval.	2/y	10	Sunset cycle reviews completed in 1993 and will resume again in 1999.
Massachusetts				No program			
Michigan	(b)	...	...	...	...	...	...
Minnesota	(b)	...	...	...	...	...	...
Mississippi	(g)	...	...	...	...	...	...
Missouri				No program			
Montana	(b)	...	...	...	...	...	...
Nebraska	(b)	...	...	...	...	...	...
Nevada	(b)	...	...	...	...	...	...
New Hampshire	(h)	...	...	...	...	...	...
New Jersey	(b)	...	...	...	...	...	...
New Mexico	R	Legis. Finance Cmte.	...	Perf. eval., Progress review	(i)	5-7	Legis. Finance Cmte. is responsible for introducing legislation to continue any agency reviewed.
New York	(b)	...	...	...	...	...	...
North Carolina	(j)	...	...	No program	...	...	...
North Dakota							
Ohio	(b)	...	...	Prog. review	...	...	...
Oklahoma	R,C	Jt. Cmte. on Sunset Review	Appropriations and Budget Cmte.	Prog. review	...	6	...
Oregon	(k)	...	(k)	...	1/y	...	...

See footnotes at end of table.

Key:
C — Comprehensive
R — Regulatory
S — Selective
D — Discretionary
d — day
m — month
y — year
. . . — Not applicable

SUNSET LEGISLATION—Continued

State	Scope	Preliminary evaluation conducted by	Other legislative review	Other oversight mechanisms in bill	Phase-out period	Life of each agency (in years)	Other provisions
Pennsylvania (l)...	S	Legis. Budget and Finance Cmte.	Standing cmtes.	Perf. audit	6/m	10	...
Rhode Island	(m)	...	...	...	...	...	...
South Carolina ..	R	Legis. Audit Council	Reorganization Comm., Standing cmtes.	Perf. audit	1/y	6	...
South Dakota ..	(n)	...	...	...	...	...	...
Tennessee	C	Jt. Government Operations Cmte.	...	Perf. audit	1/y	1-8	Sunrise review provision 1/y after creation of entity.
Texas	S	Sunset Advisory Comm.	...	Perf. eval.	1/y	12	The Sunset Advisory Comm. chair and vice-chair rotate every two years between the House and Senate. Members can serve a total of six years and are not eligible for reappointment.
Utah	R	Interim study cmte.	Off. of Legis. Research & General Counsel	Interim cmte's discretion	1/y	Up to maximum of 10/y	Legis. Audit Cmte. may at its discretion coordinate the audit of state agencies with the interim cmte.'s sunset review.
Vermont	S	Legis. Council staff	Senate and House Government Operations Cmtes.	...	None	...	Reviews only focus on the need for regulation of professions and occupations. Statutory preference is for the least restrictive form of regulation necessary to protect the public.
Virginia..........	(o)	...	...	...	...	...	...
Washington	C	Legis. Budget Cmte.	Standing cmtes.	...	1/y	Varies	...
West Virginia ...	S	Jt. Cmte. on Govt. Operations	Legis. Post Audit Div.	Perf. audit	1/y	6	Jt. Cmte. on Govt. Operations composed of five House members, five Senate members and five citizens appointed by governor. Agencies may be reviewed more frequently.
Wisconsin	(b)	...	...	...	...	...	...
Wyoming	(p)	...	...	...	...	...	...

Source: The Council of State Governments' legislative survey, March 1994.

Key:
C — Comprehensive
R — Regulatory
S — Selective
D — Discretionary
d — day
m — month
y — year
. . — Not applicable

(a) A one-time review of selected programs ended in 1983.
(b) While they have not enacted sunset legislation in the same sense as the other states with detailed information in this table, the legislatures in California, Idaho, Michigan, Minnesota, Montana, Nebraska, Nevada, New Jersey, New York, Ohio, and Wisconsin have included sunset clauses in selected programs or legislation.
(c) Sunset legislation suspended in 1983. Next review cycle is scheduled for 1995.
(d) The automatic sunsetting of an agency every six years was eliminated in 1992. The legislature must pass a bill in order to sunset a specific agency.
(e) Sunset legislation terminated July 1992. Legislative oversight of designated state agencies, consisting of audit, review and evaluation, continues.

(f) No longer applicable because zero-based budgeting is no longer part of the budget process.
(g) Sunset Act terminated December 31, 1984.
(h) New Hampshire's Sunset Committee was repealed July 1, 1986.
(i) Agency termination is scheduled on July 1 of the year prior to the scheduled termination of statutory authority for that agency.
(j) North Carolina's sunset law terminated on July 30, 1981. Successor vehicle, the Legislative Committee on Agency Review, operated until June 30, 1983.
(k) Sunset legislation was repealed in 1993. Joint Legislative Audit Committee still serves as legislative review body.
(l) Sunset act terminated December 22, 1991.
(m) Sunset activity is currently inactive.
(n) South Dakota suspended sunset legislation in 1979.
(o) By joint resolution, Senate and House of Delegates establish a schedule for review of "functional areas" of state government. Program evaluation is carried out by Joint Legislative Audit and Review Commission. Agencies are not scheduled for automatic termination. Commission reports are made to standing committees which may conduct public hearings.
(p) Wyoming repealed sunset legislation in 1988.

Chapter Four

STATE JUDICIAL BRANCH

An exploration of the current status of state judicial systems, with a focus on efforts to make the judiciary more accessible to the public and on long-term planning goals for state courts. Includes information on the state courts of last resort, intermediate appellate courts and general trial courts, as well as the selection and compensation of judges and judicial administrators.

Accessing the Judicial System: The States' Response

State courts are trying new ways to improve the quality of justice handed down from the bench.

by Erick B. Low

The watchword in state courts in the 1990s is *access*. Issues concerning individual access to justice, access to the courts and access to court information and services permeate the public discourse of judges, court managers, members of the bar and private citizens. Access is at the center of discussion of judicial issues, whether the specific topic is technology, the effects of drug cases on civil delay, mass tort litigation or court security.

Equal Access to Justice

Equal access to justice for all citizens is one of the most compelling issues facing state courts today. Programs for private judging such as EnDispute Inc., Judicial Arbitration & Mediation Services (JAMS), Judicate and U.S. Arbitration and Mediation (USA) raise legitimate concerns about whether a two-tiered system of justice is evolving in the states.[1] Corporations and private citizens who can afford private dispute resolution can bypass delays in civil litigation in public courts and may be able to resolve matters of legitimate public interest in private hearings.

The private judging phenomenon appears to be spreading rapidly. In California, the state in which private judging originated under a 100-year-old statute, JAMS employs 160 retired judges, more than the number of judges hearing civil cases in the Los Angeles Superior Court, where over 100,000 civil cases are filed annually.[2] In New Jersey, a private dispute resolution provider is advertised as the "state's first private court system."[3] Given the general lack of understanding of the courts and the distrust of public institutions in today's society, it is little wonder that court leaders express

concern that strategies to avoid delay in civil litigation benefit all consumers of justice services, not only the fortunate and commercial interests.

In August 1987, the National Center for State Courts and the Bureau of Justice Assistance of the U.S. Department of Justice began the Trial Court Performance Standards Project to develop measurable performance standards for the nation's general jurisdiction state trial courts. The *Trial Court Performance Standards*, published in 1990 by the National Center for State Courts, and its supplement, *Measurement of Trial Court Performance: 1990 Supplement to the Trial Court Performance Standards with Commentary* (1990), represent the diverse experience of a wide range of court leaders and shift the focus of judicial administration from resource management to performance measurement.

The Trial Court Performance Standards are in use in selected jurisdictions in the states of California, Florida, Illinois, Ohio, New Jersey, Virginia, Washington and Arizona, to name a few.[4] Standards 1.1 through 1.5 of the Trial Court Performance Standards concern access to justice. These standards require trial courts to be open and accessible and to eliminate unnecessary barriers to justice services, whether economic, physical or procedural.[5] The following sections discuss issues that are related to the accessibility portion of the standards and that directly or indirectly affect the ability of civil and criminal participants in the judicial process to gain effective access to justice.

Erick B. Low is director of Library Services for the National Center for State Courts.

Indigent Defense

The issue of adequate and constitutional representation of indigent defendants is the subject of study in a number of states. Courts in several states, including Arizona, Arkansas, Louisiana, North Carolina, Ohio, Oregon and Washington, have established statewide task forces to examine indigent defense. In 1988, Washington established an Indigent Defense Task Force to recommend improvements in that state's indigent defense system. The Task Force determined that Washington had the highest number of indigent cases in the nation. In 1990, an Indigent Defense Advisory Group was established to examine indigent defense issues within the context of the larger criminal justice system.

State courts also are examining the various methods by which counsels are appointed to represent indigent criminal defendants. New York has developed an experimental three-year pilot program, the Neighborhood Public Defender Program of Harlem, to demonstrate that public defender organizations can provide better services to their clients by restructuring the manner in which legal representation is provided. Several jurisdictions in Florida are examining procedures to appoint counsel when there is a conflict of defendant representation within the public defender's office.

Issues of compensation inevitably arise when states contemplate assignment of private attorneys to indigent defense. In 1992, the New Jersey Supreme Court upheld the practice of several local jurisdictions of assigning attorneys to take pro bono assignments in municipal courts. The court found that this practice does not violate an attorney's constitutional due process, equal protection or property rights, nor does it deprive indigent defendants of effective counsel.[6]

Court Interpreters

The influx of individuals into the United States in recent years without English language skills calls access to justice into question in courts that lack competent interpreters. Court interpretation requires not only full command of two languages, but also a strong legal vocabulary, knowledge of courtroom procedures and a professional commitment to exact interpretation without emendation or amendment.

Arizona, California, Florida, Massachusetts, New Jersey, New Mexico and Washington have been in the forefront in developing standards and programs for training, certifying and using court interpreters. These programs include training courses and specifications for qualification, certification, appointment, compensation and ethics of court interpreters.

Individuals with Disabilities

Enforcement of the Americans with Disabilities Act (ADA) will have a significant impact on the courts and other governmental institutions. The ADA, a comprehensive federal anti-discrimination statute that prohibits discrimination against disabled individuals in employment, public accommodations and in state and local government programs, activities and services, began to take effect on January 26, 1992.

Title II of the ADA requires court managers and judges to examine the methods and manner in which services, programs and activities are provided to litigants, victims, witnesses, attorneys, jurors, judges and court employees with disabilities, and to take affirmative steps to accommodate court users who qualify under the provisions of the act. Title I of the ADA prohibits public entities from discriminating against qualified disabled individuals in the workplace with regard to employment application, hiring, advancement, compensation, job training, discharge and other terms, conditions and privileges of employment. Courts were required to conduct a self-assessment of compliance with the act by January 26, 1993.

The term "disability" is broadly defined by the ADA. Litigation has been initiated against courts or court systems on the basis of the ADA in several states, including Hawaii, Missouri and Utah, but none of these actions has reached the trial stage.[7] Issues in contention include lack of appropriate elevators and parking spaces for handicapped individuals at court facilities. Although none of these cases has been adjudicated, court managers are concerned about how governmental entities should proceed to conform to the broad coverage of the act, especially since the public sector is still suffering the effects of recessionary pressures and cutback management.

Kansas has examined the potential fiscal effects of ADA compliance. As a matter of public policy, the chief justice has made it clear that the judiciary is concerned with fairness and equal protection under the law and is ready to assume its responsibilities under the comprehensive disabilities legislation. He has noted, however, that implementation of the act's provisions will have a substantial fiscal impact upon all branches and levels of state government.[8]

In order to ensure compliance with the ADA, the chief justice issued an order on June 4, 1992, establishing a Supreme Court Commission on Access to Justice. The mission of the commission is to "study and identify physical, communication and procedural barriers to justice and to recommend means to improve access to the court system for all Kansans."[9] Steps have already been taken to bring the facilities of the Kansas Judicial Center into minimum compliance with the ADA.

Jury Participation

State courts continue to broaden the participation of the public in the jury process by using expanded source lists, eliminating exemptions from jury service and reducing the number of days a juror must serve. Multiple source lists are used statewide in 25 states and in local jurisdictions in other states. Four states use the driver's license list as the sole source of prospective jurors. This avoids the duplication of names when both the driver's list and the voter's list are used. In these states, the driver's license list has been shown to be more current, more representative of the population, and available in computer form, thus facilitating automated random selection procedures.

The Americans with Disabilities Act provides individuals with disabilities increased opportunities to serve on juries and to remain on lists of eligible jurors. Blind or hearing-impaired persons have successfully served as jurors throughout the country. State courts are discovering that a hearing impairment does not disqualify a juror nor does an interpreter's presence during jury deliberations deprive the defendant of a fair trial. This means sight- or hearing-impaired jurors can be challenged only for cause and not automatically eliminated from initial consideration.

To reduce the financial burden placed on persons serving as jurors, the courts and employers are redefining jury fees and terms of service. One day/one trial jury service is now in place in 34 states, representing approximately 25 percent of the U.S. population. Advantages associated with one day/one trial include a decrease in excuses requested, more certainty in serving, and reduced waiting time. Although reduced terms of service mean that more people must be called to serve, which increases administrative workloads, shorter terms of service have a positive effect on the willingness of citizens to serve.

The root cause of many complaints about jury duty is the length of time required away from work and the potential loss of income. One answer to this dilemma has been to change the method of juror compensation. In Massachusetts, for example, the juror fee has been eliminated for the first three days of service, but employers are required to pay a juror's salary starting on the fourth day of service. Colorado and Connecticut have adopted similar compensation methods.[10]

Racial/Ethnic Bias in the Courts

The treatment of minorities in the courts continues to be an issue of major concern to the judiciary, especially since futurists predict that minority populations will increase and constitute a majority of the population in the next century. Task forces on racial/ethnic bias in the courts have been established by supreme courts or bar associations in Arizona, Arkansas, California, Connecticut, Delaware, District of Columbia, Florida, Georgia, Hawaii, Idaho, Iowa, Kentucky, Louisiana, Massachusetts, Michigan, Minnesota, Nevada, New Jersey, New York, Ohio, Oregon and Washington.[11]

In 1993, the Delaware Supreme Court issued an administrative directive instructing presiding judges to submit comprehensive written reports to the chief justice concerning the need for, and feasibility of, task force studies of bias within each court. The Supreme Court of Iowa has established a Committee for Equality in the Courts, and the Hawaii Supreme Court has formed a Committee on Fairness in the Courts. These committees have been charged to examine the treatment of both women and minorities in the courts. The Colorado Bar Association/Denver Bar Association Minorities in the Profession Committee and the New Mexico State Bar Task Force on Minorities in the Profession have been established by bar associations in both states to study the treatment and involvement of minority attorneys.

Final reports from a number of state race/ethnic bias task forces have concluded that racial and ethnic bias exists in the legal profession, the criminal justice system and the state courts. Racial and ethnic bias is manifested in discriminatory practices in law enforcement, prosecutorial discretion, bail, legal representation, jury selection, interpreter training and availability, sentencing and the treatment of minority juveniles. The task forces also found bias in employment of minority attorneys and non-judicial personnel and selection of minority judges.

Race/ethnic task forces advocate adoption of affirmative actions plans for hiring and promoting minority law enforcement officers, attorneys and non-judicial personnel, and recommend increased minority representation on judicial nominating commissions. In addition, task forces urge passage of court interpreter certification legislation, development of curricula to educate judges and court personnel on hate crimes and racial bias in the courts, adoption of techniques to increase the diversity of jury pools, establishment of effective criteria to ensure fair and equal exposure to mandatory and minimum sentencing statutes, and the expansion of community-based programs, pre-trial intervention programs and probation.

Gender Bias in the Courts

Thirty-nine states, the District of Columbia and Puerto Rico have established task forces on gender bias in the courts.[12] In addition, the states of New Hampshire and North Carolina have demonstrated substantial interest in the issue of gender fairness. Although the New Hampshire Supreme Court has not established its own task force, the Administrative Office of the Courts works closely with representatives of the New Hampshire Bar Association Committee on Women in the Profession and has reviewed task force reports from the judiciaries of other states. Similarly, North Carolina is assembling an advisory committee on gender issues in lieu of a formal task force. The committee will review materials published by other states and examine which of their recommendations should be implemented in North Carolina.

Task forces established by the courts or state bar associations in Colorado, Connecticut, Florida, Georgia, Hawaii, Illinois, Kansas, Maryland, Massachusetts, Michigan, Minnesota, Nevada, New Hampshire, New Jersey, New York, Rhode Island, Utah, Vermont, Washington and Wisconsin have issued final reports that include findings and recommendations on gender bias in the courts.

The task forces in Colorado and Michigan were disbanded following publication of their final reports. In both states, the responsibility for implementation of task force findings and recommendations rests with the courts' administrative offices in conjunction with committees of the state bar associations. (Gender bias task forces in most states are established under the authority of the supreme courts. In states with committees authorized by bar associations, the supreme courts commonly endorse, participate in or fund the bar's task force activities.)

The states of California, Connecticut, Florida, Hawaii, Maryland, Massachusetts, Michigan, Minnesota, New Jersey, New York, New Mexico, Rhode Island, Utah, Vermont and Washington have moved into the implementation phase of gender bias task force efforts. Work continues on legislative, procedural and educational projects in response to final report recommendations. Task forces in the implementation phase are also developing and distributing materials that will guide the courts toward bias-free behavior in the courts and provide direction for bias-free treatment in areas of substantive law. Some of the handbooks and manuals for judges and court personnel on gender fairness include *Court Conduct Handbook: Gender Equality in the Courts* (Massachusetts Supreme Judicial Court Committee for Gender Equality 1990), "Court Conduct Handbook: Gender Fairness in the Courts — A Handbook for the Kentucky Court of Justice," *56 Kentucky Bench and Bar 49* (Fall 1992), *Court Conduct Handbook: Fairness and Equality in the Courts* (Idaho Supreme Court, June 1992), and *And Justice For All: Guide to Bias-Free Behavior in the Courts* (Michigan State Court Administrative Office, 1993, draft).

An issue of central concern to many of the gender bias task forces is domestic violence. As the judicial community has focused its attention on gender and domestic issues, many courts have adopted innovative uses of protective orders to provide sanctuary to victims of spousal abuse and family violence. The emphasis of some court initiatives has been on speeding up access to court protection and offering immediate relief in the face of imminent danger. Judges in Kentucky have begun to develop procedures that allow abuse victims to receive protective orders 24 hours a day.[13] A recent Massachusetts statute authorizes judges to communicate protective orders by telephone, day or night, to police officers on the scene of a domestic violence incident. Massachusetts law also now protects individuals who "are or have been in a substantive dating or engagement relationship" from abuse.

In Texas, the Legislature repealed a state law exempting spouses from rape charges. Spouses may now be prosecuted for sexual assault where there is a showing of bodily injury or the threat of serious bodily injury. Utah's Legislature has approved a similar bill. A new Iowa law increases the criminal penalties for domestic violence by imposing a two-day jail term on those convicted of spousal abuse. Repeat offenders serve additional time, and defendants who violate "no contact" orders serve mandatory seven-day jail terms. Convicted abusers also are required to enter treatment programs.[14]

Increasing judges' and court officials' awareness of abuse issues through education and training has been a focus of recent legislation on domestic violence. A domestic violence bill passed in New Jersey in 1991 mandates training in domestic violence matters for judges, court staff and law enforcement personnel.[15] The courts themselves also are increasing the number and scope of training programs on domestic violence. The Arkansas Administrative Office of the Courts hosted a two-day conference for trial court judges on domestic violence in September 1992. The Connecticut Gender, Justice and the Courts Implementation Committee also has responded to the issue of domestic violence through education and training programs for judicial and nonjudicial personnel. In Michigan, the Administrative Office of the Courts has developed a forms packet to be used for *pro se* temporary restraining orders and conducts education programs on domestic violence issues for judges. Judicial education programs on domestic violence and acquaintance rape have been developed in Minnesota. The New Jersey Supreme Court Task Force on Women in the Courts has emphasized a focus on judicial education. The Administrative Office of the Courts conducts numerous domestic violence training programs for judges and court personnel who handle domestic violence matters. Topics addressed at these training programs have included information about the dynamics of abuse, the cycle of domestic violence and the laws and procedures applicable to domestic violence cases. In addition, a New Jersey working group has developed a manual for judges and staff on domestic violence.[16]

Court-created gender bias task forces have recommended other strategies to enhance access to the courts to victims of gender-based violence or to extend new protections to women who find themselves targets of abuse. In California, the Judicial Council Advisory Committee on Gender Bias in the Courts developed a comprehensive set of recommendations from which the California Legislature passed Civil Code §4351.6, which allows persons in a supportive role to accompany domestic violence victims to court and mediation sessions, and Civil Code §4359, which prohibits mutual restraining orders in domestic violence cases unless mutual application and proof can be demonstrated.[17]

The Florida Domestic Violence Act incorporates virtually all the recommendations contained in the Florida Gender Bias Study Commission's Final Report, including directing the Florida Court Education Council to establish standards for instruction of county court judges with respect to domestic violence cases, and redefining the term "domestic violence" to include "family or household members."[18] The Massachusetts Gender Bias Study Committee's c.209A/Domestic Violence Subcommittee has published *Opening Doors: Model Projects Providing Advocacy to Victims of Domestic Violence Seeking Relief in Eastern Massachusetts Courts* (1991) and created resource centers in all of the district and probate courts that collaborate with county bars and local shelters.[19]

Access to the Courts

Family Courts

Some states have enhanced access to families in need of supervision and court services by establishing a family court that consolidates all family matters in a single forum. Family courts generally have jurisdiction over all divorce and dissolution matters, including marital property distribution, child custody and support, Uniform Reciprocal Enforcement Support (URESA), adoption, paternity, and domestic violence. Family court jurisdiction also frequently includes child dependency, neglect and abuse cases.

The first family court was established in Rhode Island in 1961. Since that time, Delaware, Hawaii, Louisiana, New York and South Carolina have established family courts. Several other jurisdictions are considering incorporation of all family matters, including divorce, custody and child support, into a single court to reduce duplication and to promote a more comprehensive view of "the family" in the criminal justice system.

Virginia recently completed a two-year pilot family court project and evaluation process. The culmination of years of planning and study occurred in 1993 with the passage of a family court bill. This legislation established a single court to handle all matters involving children and families by combining the jurisdiction of the juvenile and domestic relations district courts with jurisdiction over cases concerning divorce, annulment, affirmation of marriage and adoption. This new court is designed to provide a more effective forum for the resolution of problems of children and families in Virginia and is scheduled to begin operations on January 1, 1995. The judiciary's attention has now turned to ensuring that sufficient resources are provided to implement the family court system.[20]

The Judicial Conference of Missouri also has endorsed the concept of a family court. The state's judicial leaders believe that problems of broken homes, juvenile law-breakers, modifications of child support orders, and failure to pay child support and maintenance obligations are interdependent. In the past, judicial efforts to assist families often have failed because courts have treated family problems as though they were unconnected.[21]

The expansion of judicial responsibilities in response to increasingly complex societal problems is particularly evident in measures taken by the courts to address the needs of children and families. These matters place enormous strains on the courts because they require repeated monitoring after disposition.

Often these cases require coordination with other courts when family members are enmeshed in multiple actions. It is not unusual for a dysfunctional family to be involved in a divorce court on a child support matter, a juvenile court on a delinquency matter and a criminal court on a domestic violence matter. These cases also require extensive intervention and coordination with social service agencies. Courts are often the last resort for dysfunctional families. Judges and other court professionals are becoming service coordinators as well as adjudicators and service providers, matching individuals at risk to appropriate services in the community so that family stress can be contained if not alleviated.

Drugs and the Courts

In large cities, as many as 75 percent of those arrested for felonies test positive for drug use at the time of arrest. In an attempt to reduce case delay and overcrowding in prisons and jails, state courts continue to seek and implement innovative case processing and sentencing strategies for the handling of drug-related cases. These strategies include use of specialized drug courts, application of various case management principles and methods, and use of drug treatment programs as an alternative to incarceration.

Drug courts, such as those in New York City, N.Y.; Jersey City, N.J.; Dade County, Fla.; Milwaukee County, Wis.; and Cook County, Ill.; are designed to combat caseload pressures associated with the increase in drug prosecutions. Using a tracking system approach, several courts have found that faster processing of drug cases is possible without case segregation. In Washington state's Pierce County Superior Court, simple and complex drug cases are separated, and judicial procedures and time limits are matched to the cases to expedite case disposition and to efficiently use court resources. Because of jail and prison space forecasts and the belief that rehabilitation and treatment can be effective for those addicted to drugs, many courts are turning to the use of residential drug treatment facilities, self-help drug treatment programs (i.e., Narcotics Anonymous and Alcoholics Anonymous), literacy programs, boot camps, day reporting centers, intensive supervision programs (i.e., electronic monitoring or house arrest), and acupuncture programs for those convicted of drug offenses.

Night Court Programs

Another way access to courts is enhanced is by establishing special courts such as commerce courts, landlord-tenant courts and night courts. Night court may be defined as any time that a court remains open for appearances after normal closing hours. Reasons for establishing night court programs range from reducing the delay between arrest and release on bail, reducing jail overcrowding, maximizing the use of courtroom space, spreading the court's workload over more hours or convenience for the public and other participants. The most common courts to extend their hours to night time or weekends are municipal courts, traffic courts and small claims courts. General jurisdiction trial courts generally do not extend their hours outside of regular business hours.

Examples of courts that have been established for the convenience of public officials and private citizens include the Birmingham, Ala., Municipal Court, initially established to provide an alternative court time for prosecution witnesses, particularly police officers assigned to afternoon or evening shifts,[22] and the Fulton County, Ga., State Court, where sessions in landlord-tenant cases start at 4 p.m., since many tenants have trouble getting time off from their jobs to appear in court. A 1987 California statute requires a municipal court district with four or more judges in a county with a population of at least 2 million to schedule at least one night traffic court session a week. Night courts are held in California jurisdictions including the Los Angeles Municipal Court, the North Orange County Municipal Court and the Sacramento County Municipal Court, among many others.[23]

Weekend and night courts often are unable to take advantage of clerical, security, probation office and data processing support available during normal business hours. Administrative issues of inefficient operation of night courts must be weighed against concerns of public convenience, especially of low-income wage earners, and access to court services.

Access Through Applied Technology

Video Court Reporting

Applied technology also enhances access to court processes through increased efficiency and convenience. The use of operatorless video recording equipment to make the trial record continues to spread throughout the nation's trial courts. About 60 state courts were known to use video court reporting in 1991. In 1992, this number swelled to over 140. The most rapid rate of expansion of video court reporting can be seen in Michigan, where videotapes are routinely transcribed for appellate review. The approach originally devised by Jefferson Audio Video Systems Inc., of Louisville, Ky., is now being replicated by three other vendors, and a few systems are found in the federal district courts.

Technology development and refinement efforts, meanwhile, are also focused on hardware and software to make the process of review of videotapes faster and more convenient. Many vendors are now competing to integrate video recording and PC technology to produce records where the video images and a written transcript produced with computer-aided transcription are indexed to each other and where both can be searched and played back very quickly on a PC monitor.

Closed-Circuit Television

The use of two-way audio-video links between courts and detention facilities for first appearances, arraignments, bond hearings and sentencing continues to spread. Video systems between the courthouse and other facilities are in use in both general and limited jurisdiction courts all across the country. In some court systems, video arraignments have been used successfully for so long that they are now considered routine. Many courts are now using split-screen technology to allow all participants to see each other. Oakland County (Mich.) Circuit Court has broken new ground by becoming the first court to offer an integrated video arraignment/video court reporting system.

While start-up costs are substantial, closed circuit systems have proven to be cost-effective because they save the expense of transporting defendants to and from court, and because the audio-visual recording can provide the record without the necessity of a court reporter. Other advantages include eliminating security problems connected with transportation, avoiding bringing shackled prisoners through public corridors in old courthouses, shortening pre-arraignment detention time and eliminating waiting periods in crowded holding cells at the courthouse. Court staffs have found that defendants prefer the option of audio-video links: They have more time to confer with counsel, the atmosphere is more relaxed and the proceedings take less time.

Access to Court Information

Information retrieval is another example of the access debate. The creation of electronic, "paperless" libraries was predicted in the 1970s with the advent of computer-assisted legal research, but data base services still only supplement, not replace, book collections in court libraries. One reason for this is public access. Court libraries in many states are required by statute to provide services to the general public. It is questionable, however, whether data base access alone satisfies public access requirements, especially since many *pro se* litigants and other members of the public lack searching and computer skills. Effective access to legal information was the cornerstone of recommendations adopted in November 1992 at the first National Conference on State Court Libraries in Columbus, Ohio, where court leaders concluded that the availability of legal information is an essential element of access to the powers of the courts.

Technological advances also have created a growing demand for public access to electronic court records and information. Courts have invested millions of dollars in sophisticated information systems, and are receiving increasing numbers of requests to provide electronic data linkages from private citizens, attorneys and corporations. It is not clear, however, what steps the courts must take to ensure the accuracy of the data they manage as custodians of public and confidential information.

Increasingly sophisticated judicial information systems continue to enhance the capabilities of courts to collect, store, massage and distribute information about cases and individuals. As the courts' data management capabilities increase, however, so do demands for public access to court information. It is unclear, however, whether public access is the same thing as commercial access. More and more companies are retrieving court data electronically to provide information services to the public, the bar and other segments of the information industry. The courts are caught in the middle of a battle between proponents of the right of privacy and advocates of the right of public access.

Alternative Dispute Resolution (ADR)

Access to justice may not necessarily require access to a courtroom. The Trial Court Performance Standards recognize "the establishment of appropriate alternative methods for resolving disputes," including mediation, court-annexed arbitration and early neutral evaluation, as measures courts may take to provide affordable access to justice.[24]

For nearly 20 years, a wide variety of programs have developed across the country for the resolution of disputes outside the courtroom. These programs offer disputing parties informal alternatives to expensive and time-consuming adjudicative procedures. Initially, informal programs to resolve disputes evolved at the neighborhood and local levels without formal recognition by the courts. More recently, the trend has been toward an integration of dispute resolution and adjudicative procedures.

Many courts have recognized or annexed alternative dispute resolution (ADR) programs and woven them into the fabric of civil and, to a more limited extent, criminal justice. New York was the first state to adopt a comprehensive dispute resolution statute. The law was aimed at criminal cases but included funding for programs in civil and family matters as well. The Dispute Resolution Act was enacted in 1981 creating a Dispute Resolution Centers Program under the authority of the Unified Court System.[25]

Despite budgetary setbacks during the recent recession, there has been a continuing trend in trial and appellate courts toward the assimilation of alternative dispute resolution programs into the mainstream of court processes. As the courts adapt to management techniques and structures such as total quality management that promote awareness of the needs of consumers of justice services, it is inevitable that the incorporation of ADR into the judicial matrix will continue unabated.[26]

In 1992, the American Bar Association's Standing Committee on Dispute Resolution began the process of becoming a section of the ABA, a change that would memorialize the maturation of the dispute resolution movement in the United States. The new Section of Dispute Resolution held its organizational meeting in conjunction with the 1993 Annual Meeting in New York City. One of the section's first important projects was to draft "Standards of Conduct for Mediators in Civil Disputes"

in cooperation with the American Arbitration Association and the Society of Professionals in Dispute Resolution. The draft standards will be presented to the ABA House of Delegates for adoption in August 1994.[27] Armed with the support of the organized bar as well as the majority of judicial leaders, ADR is unlikely to become a passing phenomenon.

However, the recent recession and governmental budget crises in many states have reduced the amount of funding available to support court-sponsored ADR programs. Consequently, some established programs have had to cutback or cease operations, and some planned programs have had to be postponed. Still, recessionary pressures have awakened interest in ADR among other courts as judicial leaders and court administrators explore new ways to reduce costs and delay in dispute resolution and to increase participant satisfaction. So far, studies on ADR in the courts have shown mixed results with respect to these goals. The December 1990 *Report to the Membership of the Committee on Alternative Dispute Resolution of the Conference of State Court Administrators* (COSCA) summarizes the current state of knowledge on the efficacy of ADR: "Research findings to date indicate that for certain types of cases and in certain jurisdictions alternative processes such as mediation and arbitration can provide speedy disposition, greater levels of compliance with agreements, and participant satisfaction. No single alternative dispute resolution process or program model is, however, suitable for all cases and all jurisdictions."[28]

In October 1993, the National Center for State Courts conducted the National Symposium on Court Connected Dispute Resolution Research under a cooperative agreement with the State Justice Institute. Its purpose was to enhance the value of present evaluation research for court policy-makers and ADR practitioners and to promote greater utility of future studies.

Five interrelated themes emerged from the symposium proceedings:

• Judicial planners need a broader understanding of the dynamics of the litigation process and of the expectations of litigants about the place of ADR in an adjudicative framework. This knowledge would enable courts to integrate ADR into their case management systems more effectively, to assess which matters are most amenable to ADR and to determine which ADR processes are best suited to particular cases.

• Courts need more reliable findings on the benefits of ADR, including cost avoidance or reduction, not only to improve ADR programs, but also to obtain political and financial support for successful programs.

• In court-based programs, quality assurance is the responsibility of the court. To establish reliable standards and to monitor the performance of ADR service providers, courts need empirical information about the most effective methods to select, qualify and train ADR providers.

• Innovative measures of participant satisfaction must be developed since most litigants are one-time users of the justice system and lack a frame of reference to compare the dispute resolution processes they experience with other ADR and adjudicative procedures.

• Finally, courts need access to practical guides for implementing, operating and evaluating ADR programs as well as exposure to basic and applied research findings.[29]

Futures and Strategic Planning

Long range planning has been an established practice in state courts since the emphasis placed on comprehensive planning as a component of the Law Enforcement Assistance Administration's funding programs in the 1970s and '80s. A radical development in court planning, however, has recently taken shape. Courts are not only planning five or 10 years ahead but are envisioning the distant future, forecasting to 2020 and beyond. The process of futures planning in the courts is consistent with the widespread judicial concern with providing access to justice to all citizens. One of the driving forces behind futures planning in the courts is an awareness of major demographic shifts in the nation's population and the increasing impact of cultural diversity upon access to justice.

The impetus towards examining the future of the courts began in 1972, when the Hawaii judiciary sponsored the Citizens Conference on the Administration of Justice. Hawaii's efforts to envision the provision of justice in the future paved the way for other states to examine the needs of their courts and their citizens in the 21st century. In 1990, the State Justice Institute funded the first national conference on futures planning in the judiciary. The Future and the Courts Conference was designed to encourage judges, court personnel, and concerned citizens to "look over the rim," 30 years into the future, in order to seize their destiny and provide fair and responsive justice to all Americans.

California is an example of a court system that is committed to futures and strategic planning. The chief justice appointed a Commission on the Future of the Courts in 1992 and asked it to identify long-term trends affecting California's courts and to help the courts prepare for the future. In cooperation with the Commission, a five-year strategic plan has been designed by the California Judicial Council. Equal access to justice and a commitment to fairness and diversity in the courts are the central themes of the strategic plan, which was made public on February 17, 1994. The council has created a committee on access and fairness that will develop proposals to increase access for the poor, the middle class and individuals engaged in family court proceedings. It will also study the impact of criminal caseloads on access to the courts in other areas of litigation.[30]

Table A summarizes state court initiatives to prepare for the future though strategic and futures planning.

State-Federal Judicial Councils

As state courts confront their immediate and pressing problems and focus on the uncertainties of the future as well, the complexities of modern litigation increasingly call upon them to include federal issues in their planning process. It is no longer possible for state and federal courts to pursue separate paths or to be insensitive to conditions in corresponding systems. Changes in procedure in federal

Table A
SELECTED RECENT STATE COURT STRATEGIC PLANNING EFFORTS

State	Year Initiated	Description of Strategic Planning Activity (a)
Arizona	1985	Commission on the Future of Virginia's Judicial System ("Courts in Transition," May 1989)
California	1992 1994	Commission on the Future of the Courts Judicial Council's Strategic Plan
Colorado	1989	Vision 2020: Colorado Courts of the Future Commission
Delaware	N.A.	Delaware Courts 2000 Commission
Georgia	1989	Georgia's Court Futures Vanguard
Hawaii	1972	Citizen's Conference on the Administration of Justice
New Hampshire	1989	Supreme Court Long-Range Planning Task Force ("As New Hampshire Approaches the Twenty-First Century," July 1990)
Maine	N.A.	The Commission to Study the Future of Maine's Courts ("New Dimensions for Justice," 1993)
Massachusetts	N.A.	Chief Justice's Commission on the Future of the Courts ("Reinventing Justice: 2020," June 1992)
Michigan	N.A.	Commission on the Courts in the 21st Century ("Michigan's Courts in the 21st Century," December 1990)
Utah	N.A.	Commission on Justice in the Twenty-First Century ("The Final Report: Commission on Justice in the Twenty-First Century and Executive Summary," December 1991)
Virginia	1987	Commission on the Future of Virginia's Judicial System ("Courts in Transition," May 1989)

Key:
N.A. — Not available
(a) Information appearing in parenthesis refers to title and date of publication of report issued.

courts inevitably influence modes of operation in state courts and may affect state court caseloads as well. Rules adopted in federal courts, for example, to sanction litigants who abuse court processes, have been widely adopted in state courts.[31] Conversely, experimental procedures adopted in many states, such as sentencing guidelines, influence federal practice. The Federal Sentencing Guidelines, which took effect November 1, 1987, amid continuing controversy, owed much to state models developed in the late 1970s and early 1980s that relied on data analysis of prior sentencing patterns to derive guidelines for future sentencing practices. The Federal Sentencing Commission did not adhere strictly to existing sentencing practices as it developed its guidelines, but its guidelines represent "an approach that begins with, and builds upon, empirical data."[32] Simi-

larly, the Administrative Office of the United States Courts conducted a review of long-range planning practices in the state courts before embarking upon the development of a long-range planning process for the federal judiciary.[33]

In 1991, Chief Justice William H. Rehnquist stated that the nation's court systems stand at a crossroads and that decisions must be made about the balance between state and federal courts. Abolishing, with limited exceptions, federal diversity jurisdiction, curtailing federal drug prosecutions, habeas corpus procedures, especially in capital cases, and asbestos cases are all issues of concern to the federal courts.

Fortunately, these issues arise at a time of increasing cooperation between federal and state judges. A National Federal State Judicial Council was formed recently, composed of state and federal court judges, to discuss and review matters of mutual concern. Many states have also recently created state-federal judicial councils within their own jurisdictions. As of June 1992, active councils were in operation in 19 states including Alabama, Alaska, California, Connecticut, Delaware, Florida, Georgia, Hawaii, Iowa, Louisiana, Maine, Maryland, Massachusetts, Missouri, Montana, New York, North Carolina, Virginia and Washington.

The Georgia state-federal judicial council meets twice a year. The executive committee consists of eight state court judges, five federal court judges, the president-elect of the Georgia State Bar and the immediate past-president of the bar. In addition to the executive committee, the Georgia state-federal judicial council maintains nine special committees that examine a wide range of common issues including professional responsibility, continuing education, professionalism and lawyer competence, bar discipline, bar polling, rules of evidence and civil procedure, cross filings in state and federal court, and calendar conflicts.

The New Hampshire council was established by statute in 1977, but has not met recently. The Texas state-federal judicial council was formally organized 22 years ago, but has not met for several years. The Illinois council was formed in 1991, but did not meet during its first year of existence. Formal state-federal judicial councils do not exist in the states of Idaho, Indiana, Kentucky or North Dakota, but informal meetings between state and federal judges occur periodically. Federal judges in North Dakota often attend state education programs and judicial conferences. Issues under examination of interest to both state and federal court judges include habeas corpus, state certification, shared facilities and courtrooms, conflict scheduling, attorney discipline and judicial education.[34]

In April 1992, bridges between the state and federal judiciaries were cemented in Orlando, Fla., by a historic summit of state and federal judicial leaders. The first National Conference on State-Federal Judicial Relationships was funded by the State Justice Institute and co-sponsored by the Federal Judicial Center, the Conference of Chief Justices, the National Center for State Courts, the National Judicial Council of State and Federal Courts, and the Federal-State Jurisdiction Planning Committee of the U.S. Judicial Conference.

In addition to addressing major issues that affect both state and federal courts, the participants discussed ways that state and federal courts can assist each other on administrative matters such as coordinating bar admissions and attorneys' schedules, and sharing jury lists and facilities. The conference also served to revitalize state-federal judicial councils in the various states that had ceased to meet on a regular basis. The conference made it clear once again that issues such as habeas corpus, capital punishment, drugs, mass tort litigation and diversity jurisdiction require an unprecedented scale of cooperation between the state and federal courts, not only at the appellate level, but at the trial level as well.[35]

Conclusion

State courts are responding to sweeping changes in the composition and cohesiveness of American society by opening their doors to more of the nation's citizens. Access to the powers of the judiciary is increasing in part through innovations within the courts and in part through judicial recognition of programs outside the courts that provide a marketplace of justice services such as mediation, early neutral evaluation and other forms of alternative dispute resolution.

As courts are turning outward, they are also turning inward to assess their capabilities to provide quality justice services to the public. Through futures and strategic planning and the application of national time and performance standards, courts are submitting themselves to an unprecedented degree of examination and self-discipline as they prepare for an uncertain future in the coming century.

At the same time, members of the judiciary are engaging as individuals in new programs of performance evaluation. About 20 states, Puerto Rico and the Navajo Nation have established or are developing judicial performance evaluation programs. The primary purpose of these programs is to help judges improve their judicial performance. State programs that conform to the *Guidelines for the Evaluation of Judicial Performance* approved by the American Bar Association[36] are planned to promote more effective assignment of judges, enhanced design of judicial education programs and increased accountability in judicial retention procedures.

The courts also are beginning to assess their internal procedures and operational philosophies through the application of modern management techniques such as total quality management, which is slowly moving from the private to the public sector. Maine has attracted national attention by becoming the first state to adopt total quality management (TQM) throughout its judicial system in conjunction with statewide strategic and futures planning. The introduction of TQM in the courts is particularly significant because of the consumer emphasis of total quality management planning and analysis. Judges and court managers are becoming increasingly aware of litigants and participants in court-ordered programs as consumers of justice services. As programs for private judging and other forms of alternative dispute resolution proliferate outside of the courtroom, it is becoming more apparent that the courts must increase the quality and accessibility of their services to the consuming public if they are to remain the cornerstone of justice in America. As the leader of a state court system that has undergone extensive self-examination recently observed, "The task of finding new and better ways to serve the users of the court system will continue to demand our attention for as long as the courts exist."[37]

Notes

[1] Janice A. Roehl, *Private Dispute Resolution: A Working Paper for the National Symposium on Court-Connected Dispute Resolution Research*, October 15-16, 1993, at 1.

[2] Id. At 5.

[3] Id.

[4] Unless otherwise noted, the information provided in this chapter is derived from the files of the Information Service of the National Center for State Courts. For further information, contact: Director, Information Service, National Center for State Courts, 300 Newport Avenue, Williamsburg, Virginia 23187, (804) 253-2000, (804) 220-0449 (fax).

[5] The following standards comprise the Access to Justice portion of the Trial Court Performance Standards. (Presented here without commentary.)

Standard 1.1 Public Proceedings — The court conducts its proceedings and other public business openly.

Standard 1.2 Safety, Accessibility, and Convenience — Court facilities are safe, accessible and convenient to use.

Standard 1.3 Effective Participation — All who appear before the court are given the opportunity to participate effectively without undue hardship or inconvenience.

Standard 1.4 Courtesy, Responsiveness, and Respect — Judges and other trial court personnel are courteous and responsive to the public and accord respect to all with whom they come into contact.

Standard 1.5 Affordable Costs of Access — The costs of access to the trial court's proceedings and records — whether measured in terms of money, time or the procedures that must be followed — are reasonable, fair and affordable.

[6] Several states have removed caps on fees paid in capital cases, including Arkansas, Mississippi, Missouri, Oklahoma and West Virginia. The Mississippi Supreme Court interpreted the fee statute to allow judges to reimburse "actual expenses" in addition to the $1,000 maximum fee paid to each attorney. The Court of Appeals in Kentucky ruled in November 1991 that a capital case automatically is a special circumstance case under state law, allowing for attorney fee compensation beyond the statutory maximum. The Arkansas Supreme Court found the cap on fees for death penalty cases to be the unconstitutional taking of property, and the mixed public defense system, in which attorneys in counties without public defenders were required to "financially subsidize the State's responsibility of indigent representation," violated an attorney's due process rights. In February 1992

a New Orleans judge struck down Louisiana's indigent defense system as unconstitutional. The court found the statute's funding provisions to be so inadequate that the local public defender's office could not hire sufficient personnel nor provide the necessary research tools. The system denied criminal defendants their constitutional right to qualified counsel, according to the court.

[7] Further information about the Americans with Disabilities Act and the courts may be obtained from the National Center for State Courts, Court Services Division in Denver, Colo. The Court Services Division maintains a National ADA Clearinghouse and Resource Center for State and Local Court Systems under a grant from the State Justice Institute.

[8] Honorable Richard W. Holmes, *State of the Judiciary, Annual Report of the Chief Justice of the Kansas Supreme Court*, January 14, 1993, at 12.

[9] Id.

[10] For further information concerning modern techniques of jury management, see *Standards Relating to Juror Use and Management* (American Bar Association Judicial Administration Division Committee on Jury Standards (1993).

[11] Up-to-date information about the status of race/ethnic bias commissions and task forces may be obtained from the National Center for State Courts' Information Service, which provides staff assistance to the National Consortium of Task Forces and Commissions on Racial and Ethnic Bias in the Courts. In addition to state commissions and task forces on race/ethnic bias, the American Bar Association has established the Commission on Opportunities in the Legal Profession, and the Commission on Systematic Racism in the Ontario Criminal Justice System has been established in Canada as well as a similar commission in British Columbia.

[12] Task forces on gender bias in the courts have been established in the following jurisdictions: Alaska, Arizona, Arkansas, California, Colorado, Connecticut, Delaware, District of Columbia, Florida, Georgia, Hawaii, Idaho, Illinois, Indiana, Iowa, Kansas, Louisiana, Maine, Maryland, Massachusetts, Michigan, Minnesota, Missouri, Montana, Nebraska, Nevada, New Jersey, New Mexico, New York, North Dakota, Ohio, Puerto Rico, Rhode Island, South Dakota, Tennessee, Texas, Utah, Vermont, Washington and Wisconsin. Up-to-date information about the status of gender bias commissions and task forces may be obtained from the National Center for State Courts' Information Service.

[13] Rae Lovko, "State Court Activity Regarding Gender-Based Violence," National Center for State Courts' Information Service, Memorandum REF. No. S93.0004, February 9, 1993, at 5.

[14] National Center for State Courts' Information Service, Memorandum REF. No. S93.0004, February 9, 1993, at 5.

[15] Id. At 7.

[16] Further information on training programs for judges and non-judicial personnel in gender and domestic violence matters may be obtained from the National Center for State Courts' Information Service.

[17] Rae Lovko, "State Court Activity Regarding Gender-Based Violence," National Center for State Courts' Information Service, Memorandum REF. No. S93.0004, February 9, 1993, at 2.

[18] Id. At 4.

[19] Id. At 6.

[20] Honorable Harry L. Carrico, Chief Justice, Supreme Court of Virginia, State of the Judiciary Message, Judicial Conference of Virginia, May 17, 1993, at 1.

[21] Honorable Edward D. Robertson, Jr., Chief Justice, Supreme Court of Missouri, The State of the Judiciary Address, First Regular Session of the 87th General Assembly, Thursday, January 7, 1993, at 8.

[22] *A Study for the Birmingham Municipal Court* (National Center for State Courts, undated).

[23] For further information on night courts in California, see *Report to the California Legislature on Alternative Sessions* (Judicial Council of California, November 8, 1991).

[24] Commentary, Standard 1.5, Affordable Costs of Access, Trial Court Performance Standards with Commentary (National Center for State Courts 1990), at 9.

[25] Cassandra Howard, *State Trends in Alternative Dispute Resolution* (Dispute Resolution Information Center 1986), at 2.

[26] Martin L. Haines, "Inside the Courts: TQM: Maine Leads the Nation; N.J. Should Follow," *New Jersey Law Journal 21* (December 21, 1992). Maine has attracted national attention by becoming the first state to adopt total quality management (TQM) throughout its judicial system.

[27] Section of Dispute Resolution, Informational Report to the House of Delegates, Informational Reports to the House of Delegates: American Bar Association, 1994 Midyear Meeting, Kansas City, Missouri, February 7-8, 1994, at 6.

[28] *Report to the Membership* of the Committee on Alternative Dispute Resolution of the Conference of State Court Administrators (COSCA).

[29] See Susan Keilitz, *Civil Dispute Resolution Processes: A Working Paper for the National Symposium on Court Connected Dispute Resolution Research*, October 15-16, 1993. This working paper critiques research that has been performed on a broad range of dispute resolution processes including civil case mediation, case evaluation (early neutral evaluation), summary jury trial, medical malpractice mediation, small claims mediation and appellate mediation. The paper analyzes the results of studies in each of these areas in terms of case processing times, court workloads, settlement rates, litigant costs, participant satisfaction, implications for court management and integration into case management systems. The State Justice Institute has funded a large number of alternative dispute resolution projects since 1987. Some of the recent projects include: "Evaluation of Rural Alternative Dispute Resolution Projects," Alaska Judicial Council, "Impact of State Court-Annexed Arbitration on Civil Justice in Nevada," Nevada Supreme Court, and "Dispute Resolution for Children of Domestic Violence," Florida Supreme Court/Sixth Circuit Court.

[30] For further information on futures commissions and strategic planning in state courts, contact the National Center for State Courts' Information Service. Under a grant from the State Justice Institute, the National Center for State Courts, the Institute for Alternative Futures and the Hawaii Research Center for Future Studies recently completed a major project on futures planning and filmed a 45-minute videotape entitled, *Envisioning Justice: Reinventing Courts for the 21st Century*. The video is accompanied by a guidebook on futures planning that outlines a court visioning process and describes how vision development can be incorporated into ongoing court planning and management activities. For additional information on strategic planning in the courts, see John A. Martin, *An Approach to Long Range Strategic Planning for the Courts* (Center for Public Policy Studies, May 29, 1992). See also James A. Dator & Sharon J. Rodgers, *The Future and the Courts Conference: Executive Summary* (American Judicature Society, November 1990), at 5.

[31] See Appendix A, "State Laws," in Jerold S. Solovy, Laura A. Kaster, Norman M. Hirsch, and James L. Thompson, *Sanctions In Federal Litigation* (Butterworth Legal Publishers 1991).

[32] *Sentencing Guideline Manual* (U.S. Sentencing Commission, October 1987), at 1.4.

[33] *Long Range Planning in the State Courts: Selected Features for the Federal Judiciary: A Staff Study Supervised by an Academy Panel for the Administrative Office of the U.S. Courts* (National Academy of Public Administration, June 1992), at iii.

[34] The information in this and the preceding paragraphs is based on a survey conducted in 1992 by the National Center for State Courts' Information Service. The Information Service surveyed 50 state (and the District of Columbia) administrative offices of the courts to secure information on states that have formal state-federal judicial councils. The Information Service's findings are available in tabular form. To obtain a copy of the table, request: Rae Lovko & Karen Way, "State/Federal Judicial Councils," National Center for State Courts' Information Service, Memorandum REF. No. S92.0009, June 9, 1992.

[35] "State, Federal Judicial Leaders Attend 'Working Summit,' " 19 *National Center for State Courts Report 1* (May 1992). See also symposium issue on the National Conference

on State-Federal Judicial Relationships, 78 *Virginia Law Review* no. 8 (November 1992).

[36] *Guidelines for the Evaluation of Judicial Performance* (American Bar Association, Special Committee on Evaluation of Judicial Performance 1985).

[37] Honorable Harry L. Carrico, Chief Justice, Supreme Court of Virginia, State of the Judiciary Message, Judicial Conference of Virginia, May 17, 1993, at 3.

Table 4.1
STATE COURTS OF LAST RESORT

State or other jurisdiction	Name of court	Justices chosen (a) At large	Justices chosen (a) By district	No. of judges (b)	Term (in years) (c)	Chief justice Method of selection	Term of service as chief justice
Alabama	S.C.	*		9	6	Popular election	6 years
Alaska	S.C.	*		5	10	By court	3 years (d)
Arizona	S.C.	*		5	6	By court	5 years
Arkansas	S.C.	*		7	8	Popular election	8 years
California	S.C.	*		7	12	Appointed by governor (e)	12 years
Colorado	S.C.	*		7	10	By court	At pleasure of court
Connecticut	S.C.	*		7	8	Nominated by governor, appointed by General Assembly	8 years
Delaware	S.C.	*		5	12	Appointed by governor with consent of Senate	12 years
Florida	S.C.	*		7	6	By court	2 years
Georgia	S.C.	*		7	6	By court	4 years
Hawaii	S.C.	*		5	10	Appointed by governor, with consent of Senate	10 years
Idaho	S.C.	*		5	6	By court	4 years
Illinois	S.C.		*	7	10	By court	3 years
Indiana	S.C.	*		5	10 (f)	Selected by Judicial Nominating Commission from S.C. members	5 years
Iowa	S.C.	*		9	8	By court	Remainder of term or 8 years
Kansas	S.C.	*		7	6	By seniority of service (g)	Remainder of term
Kentucky	S.C.		**	7	8	By court	4 years
Louisiana	S.C.		**	7	10	By seniority of service	Remainder of term
Maine	S.J.C.	*		7	7	Appointed by governor, with consent of Senate	7 years
Maryland	C.A.		*	7	10	Designated by governor	Remainder of term
Massachusetts	S.J.C.	*		7	To age 70	Appointed by governor	To age 70
Michigan	S.C.	*		7	8	By court	2 years
Minnesota	S.C.	*		7	6	Popular election	6 years
Mississippi	S.C.		*	9	8	By seniority of service	Remainder of term
Missouri	S.C.	*		7	12	By court	2 years
Montana	S.C.	*		7	8	Popular election	8 years
Nebraska	S.C.	* (h)		7	6	Appointed by governor from Judicial Nominating Commission	Remainder of term
Nevada	S.C.	*		5	6	Rotation by seniority (i)	1-2 years
New Hampshire	S.C.	*		5	To age 70	Appointed by governor and Council	To age 70
New Jersey	S.C.	*		7	7 (j)	Appointed by governor, with consent of Senate	Remainder of term
New Mexico	S.C.	*		5	8	By court	2 years
New York	C.A.	*		7	14 (j)	Appointed by governor from Judicial Nomination Commission, with consent of Senate	14 years (j)
North Carolina	S.C.	*		7	8	Popular election	8 years
North Dakota	S.C.	*		5	10	By Supreme and district court judges	5 years (k)
Ohio	S.C.	*		7	6	Popular election	6 years
Oklahoma	S.C.		**	9	6	By court	2 years
	C.C.A.		**	5	6	By court	2 years
Oregon	S.C.	*		7	6	By court	6 years
Pennsylvania	S.C.	*		7	10	Rotation by seniority	Remainder of term
Rhode Island	S.C.	*		5	Life	By legislature	Life
South Carolina	S.C.	*		5	10	Joint public vote of General Assembly	10 years

STATE COURTS OF LAST RESORT—Continued

State or other jurisdiction	Name of court	Justices chosen (a) At large	Justices chosen (a) By district	No. of judges (b)	Term (in years) (c)	Chief justice Method of selection	Chief justice Term of service as chief justice
South Dakota	S.C.		★ (l)	5	8	By court	4 years
Tennessee	S.C.	★		5	8	By court	18 months
Texas	S.C.	★		9	6	Popular election	6 years
	C.C.A.	★		9	6	Popular election (m)	6 years (m)
Utah	S.C.	★		5	10 (n)	By court	4 years
Vermont	S.C.	★		5	6	Appointed by governor from Judicial Nomination Commission with consent of Senate	6 years
Virginia	S.C.	★		7	12	By seniority of service	Remainder of term
Washington	S.C.	★		9	6	By seniority of service	2 years
West Virginia	S.C.A.	★		5	12	Rotation by seniority	1 year
Wisconsin	S.C.	★		7	10	By seniority of service (o)	Remainder of term or until declined
Wyoming	S.C.	★		5	8	By court	2 years
Dist. of Columbia	C.A.	★		9	15	Designated by Mayor from Judicial Nominating Commission	4 years
American Samoa	H.C.	★		8 (p)	(q)	Appointed by Secretary of the Interior	(q)
Puerto Rico	S.C.	★		7	To age 70	Appointed by Governor with consent of Senate	To age 70

(e) Subsequently, must run on record for retention.
(f) Initial two years; retention 10 years.
(g) If two or more qualify, then senior in age.
(h) Chief justice chosen statewide; associate judges chosen by district.
(i) If two or more chosen statewide, then determined by lot.
(j) May be reappointed to age 70.
(k) Or expiration of term, whichever is first.
(l) Initially chosen by district; retention determined statewide.
(m) Presiding judge of Court of Criminal Appeals.
(n) Initial three years; retention 10 years.
(o) If two or more qualify, then justice with least number of years remaining in term.
(p) Chief judges and associate judges sit on appellate and trial divisions.
(q) For good behavior.

Sources: National Center for State Courts, State Court Caseload Statistics: Annual Report 1992 (released 1994) and State Court Organization 1993; state constitutions and statutes.
Key:
S.C. — Supreme Court
S.C.A. — Supreme Court of Appeals
S.J.C. — Supreme Judicial Court
C.A. — Court of Appeals
C.C.A. — Court of Criminal Appeals
H.C. — High Court
(a) See Table 4.4, "Selection and Retention of Judges," for details.
(b) Number includes chief justice.
(c) The initial term may be shorter. See Table 4.4, "Selection and Retention of Judges," for details.
(d) A justice may serve more than one term as chief justice, but may not serve consecutive terms in that position.

Table 4.2
STATE INTERMEDIATE APPELLATE COURTS AND GENERAL TRIAL COURTS: NUMBER OF JUDGES AND TERMS

State or other jurisdiction	Intermediate appellate court			General trial court		
	Name of court	No. of judges	Term (years)	Name of court	No. of judges	Term (years)
Alabama	Court of Criminal Appeals	5	6	Circuit Court	127	6
	Court of Civil Appeals	3	6			
Alaska	Court of Appeals	3	8	Superior Court	30 (a)	6
Arizona	Court of Appeals	21	6	Superior Court	125	4
Arkansas	Court of Appeals	6	8	Chancery Court and Circuit Court	99 (b)	(b)
California	Court of Appeals	88	12	Superior Court	789 (c)	6
Colorado	Court of Appeals	16	8	District Court	114 (d)	6
Connecticut	Appellate Court	9	8	Superior Court	150	8
Delaware	. . .	. . .	. . .	Superior Court and Court of Chancery	20 (e)	12
Florida	District Courts of Appeals	57	6	Circuit Court	421	6
Georgia	Court of Appeals	9	6	Superior Court	159	4 (f)
Hawaii	Intermediate Court of Appeals	3	10	Circuit Court	25 (g)	10
Idaho	Court of Appeals	3	6	District Court	34 (h)	4
Illinois	Appellate Court	40 (i)	10	Circuit Court	820	6
Indiana	Court of Appeals	15 (j)	10 (k)	Superior Court, Probate Court and Circuit Court	242	6
Iowa	Court of Appeals	6	6	District Court	332 (l)	6
Kansas	Court of Appeals	10	4	District Court	149 (m)	4
Kentucky	Court of Appeals	14	8	Circuit Court	91	8
Louisiana	Court of Appeals	54	10	District Court	207 (n)	6
Maine	. . .	. . .	. . .	Superior Court	16	7
Maryland	Court of Special Appeals	13	10	Circuit Court	123	15
Massachusetts	Appeals Court	14	(o)	Trial Court	320	(o)
Michigan	Court of Appeals	24	6	Circuit Court	206	6
Minnesota	Court of Appeals	16	6	District Court	242	6
Mississippi	. . .	. . .	. . .	Chancery Court	39	4
				Circuit Court	40	4
Missouri	Court of Appeals	32	12	Circuit Court	134 (p)	6
Montana	. . .	. . .	. . .	District Court	37 (q)	6
Nebraska	Court of Appeals	6	6	District Court	50	6
Nevada	. . .	. . .	. . .	District Court	38	6
New Hampshire	. . .	. . .	. . .	Superior Court	29 (r)	(o)
New Jersey	Appellate Division of Superior Court	28	7	Superior Court	374 (s)	7
New Mexico	Court of Appeals	10	8	District Court	61	6
New York	Appellate Division of Supreme Court	48	5 (o)	Supreme Court and County Court	597	14 (o)
	Appellate Terms of Supreme Court	15	5 (o)			
North Carolina	Court of Appeals	12	8	Superior Court	77 (t)	8
North Dakota	Court of Appeals (temporary)	3	. . .	District Court	24	6
Ohio	Court of Appeals	65	6	Court of Common Pleas	355	6
Oklahoma	Court of Appeals	12	6	District Court	71 (u)	4
Oregon	Court of Appeals	10	6	Circuit Court	92	6
				Tax Court	1	6
Pennsylvania	Superior Court	15	10	Court of Common Pleas	366	10
	Commonwealth Court	9	10			
Rhode Island	. . .	. . .	. . .	Superior Court	22 (v)	Life
South Carolina	Court of Appeals	6	6	Circuit Court	40 (w)	6

STATE INTERMEDIATE APPELLATE COURTS AND GENERAL TRIAL COURTS—Continued

State or other jurisdiction	Intermediate appellate court			General trial court		
	Name of court	No. of judges	Term (years)	Name of court	No. of judges	Term (years)
South Dakota	. . .	. . .	. .	Circuit Court	36 (x)	8
Tennessee	Court of Appeals	12	8	Chancery Court	33	8
	Court of Criminal Appeals	9	8	Circuit Court	108	8
Texas	Court of Appeals	80	8	District Court	386	4
Utah	Court of Appeals	7	6	District Court	35	6
Vermont	. . .	. . .	10 (y)	Superior Court and District Court	31 (z)	6
Virginia	Court of Appeals	10	8	Circuit Court	135	8
Washington	Court of Appeals	17	6	Superior Court	153	4
West Virginia	. . .	. . .	. .	Circuit Court	60	8
Wisconsin	Court of Appeals	13	6	Circuit Court	223	6
Wyoming	. . .	. . .	. . .	District Court	17	6
Dist. of Columbia	. . .	. . .	. . .	Superior Court	59	15
Puerto Rico	. . .	. . .	. . .	Superior Court	111	12

Sources: National Center for State Courts, *State Court Caseload Statistics: Annual Report 1992* (released 1994) and *State Court Organization 1993;* state statutes and court administration offices.

Key:

. . . — Court does not exist in jurisdiction or not applicable

(a) Plus 5 masters.
(b) At the general trial court level, Arkansas has three types of courts: chancery, circuit and chancery probate courts. There are 32 chancery court judges and 34 circuit court judges who serve four-year terms. Chancery probate court, a hybrid of both chancery and circuit, consists of 33 judges (20 of whom serve in the juvenile division of chancery court) who serve six-year terms.
(c) Plus 114 commissioners and 24 referees.
(d) Plus 3 magistrates.
(e) Superior court: president judge, three resident judges and 11 associate judges; court of chancery: 5 chancellors.
(f) For judges of the Superior Court of the Atlanta Judicial Court, term of office is eight years.
(g) Plus 13 family court judges.
(h) Plus 75 lawyer and 2 non-lawyer magistrates.
(i) Plus 11 supplemental judges.
(j) Plus 1 tax court judge.

(k) Two years initial; 10 years retention.
(l) Includes 8 chief judges, 101 district judges, 46 district associate judges, 17 senior judges, 11 associate juvenile judges and 149 part-time magistrates.
(m) Plus 69 district magistrates.
(n) Plus 7 commissioners.
(o) To age 70.
(p) Plus 175 associate circuit judges.
(q) Plus 6 judges for Water Court and 1 for Workers' Compensation Court.
(r) Plus 9 full-time and 2 part-time marital masters.
(s) Plus 21 surrogates.
(t) Plus 100 clerks who hear uncontested probate.
(u) Plus 77 associate judges and 63 special judges.
(v) Includes 2 masters in the Superior Court; plus 10 judges for Workers' Compensation Court.
(w) Plus 20 masters-in-equity.
(x) Plus 17 law magistrates, 7 part-time law magistrates, 83 full-time clerk magistrates, and 49 part-time clerk magistrates.
(y) Three years initial; 10 years retention.
(z) Plus 4 magistrates. District court judges also serve as family court judges.

Table 4.3
QUALIFICATIONS OF JUDGES OF STATE APPELLATE COURTS
AND GENERAL TRIAL COURTS

State or other jurisdiction	U.S. citizenship (years)		Years of minimum residence				Minimum age		Member of state bar (years)		Other	
			In state		In district							
	A	T	A	T	A	T	A	T	A	T	A	T
Alabama	5	5	(a)	(a)	...	1	25	25	★	★	...	...
Alaska	★	★	5 (a)	5 (a)	...	...	...	...	★ (b)	★ (b)	...	...
Arizona	...	...	10 (c)	5	1 (d,e)	...	30 (d)	30	10 (c)	5	(f,g)	(f,g)
Arkansas	★	★	2	2	...	...	30	28	(h,i)	(h,i)	(f)	(f)
California	...	...	...	...	...	...	...	...	10 (i)	10 (i)	...	...
Colorado	...	...	(e)	...	...	(e)	...	...	5	5	(g)	(g)
Connecticut	...	...	...	...	...	...	18	...	10	10	...	...
Delaware	...	...	(a)	(a)	...	...	...	...	(h)	(h)	...	...
Florida	...	...	(e)	(e)	★	★	...	...	10	5	(g)	(g)
Georgia	3	3	★	(a)	...	...	★	30	7	7	...	...
Hawaii	★	★	★ (a)	★ (a)	...	...	...	...	10	10	...	...
Idaho	★	★	2	1	...	(e)	30	30	★	10	...	...
Illinois	★	★	...	...	★	★	...	...	★	★	...	...
Indiana	★	★	...	...	★	★	...	...	10 (i)	★	...	...
Iowa	...	...	...	...	...	...	...	...	★	★	...	...
Kansas	...	...	...	...	...	★	30	★	★ (i)	★ (i)	...	...
Kentucky	★	★	2	2	2	2	...	...	8	8	...	...
Louisiana	...	...	2	2	2	2	25	...	5	5	...	...
Maine	...	...	...	...	...	...	...	...	(h)	(h)	(f)	(f)
Maryland	...	...	5 (a,e)	5 (a,e)	6 mo.	6 mo.	30	30	★	★	(f)	(f)
Massachusetts	...	...	...	...	...	...	...	...	...	...	...	...
Michigan	...	...	(e)	...	(e)	(e)	...	...	★	★	(g,j)	(g,j)
Minnesota	...	...	...	...	...	...	...	...	(h)	(h)	...	...
Mississippi	...	...	(a)	(a)	...	...	30	26	5	5	...	...
Missouri	15	10	(e)	(e)	★	1	★	30	★	★	...	...
Montana	★	★	2	2	...	...	...	...	5	5	...	...
Nebraska	★	★	3	...	★ (e)	★	30	30	5 (i)	5 (i)	...	...
Nevada	...	...	2 (e)	2 (e)	...	...	25	25	★	★	(k)	(k)
New Hampshire	...	...	...	...	...	...	...	...	...	...	(l)	(l)
New Jersey	...	...	...	...	...	...	...	...	10	10	...	...
New Mexico	...	...	3	3	...	★	35	35	10 (h,i)	6 (h,i)	...	...
New York	...	...	...	...	...	...	18	18	10	10	...	...
North Carolina	...	...	★	...	...	...	21	...	★	★	...	...
North Dakota	★	★	★	★	...	...	...	...	★ (h)	★ (h)	...	...
Ohio	...	...	...	...	...	★	...	...	6 (i)	6 (i)	(g)	(g)
Oklahoma	...	...	(e)	...	(e)	(e)	30	...	5 (i)	4 (i)	...	...
Oregon	★	★	3	3	(e)	1	...	...	★	★	...	...
Pennsylvania	★	★	1 (a)	(a)	...	1	...	...	★	★	...	...
Rhode Island	...	...	...	...	...	...	21	...	...	...	...	...
South Carolina	★	★	5 (a)	5 (a)	...	★ (e)	26	26	5	5	...	...
South Dakota	★	★	★	★	★ (e)	★ (e)	...	...	★	★	...	...
Tennessee	...	...	5 (a)	5	...	1	35 (m)	30	★ (h)	★ (h)	...	...
Texas	★	★	(a)	(a)	(d)	2	35	★	★ (i)	★ (i)	...	...
Utah	...	...	5 (n)	3	...	★	30 (o)	25	★ (i)	★ (i)	...	...
Vermont	...	...	5	5	...	...	...	...	★ (i)	★ (i)	...	...
Virginia	...	...	★	★	...	...	...	...	5	5	...	...
Washington	...	...	1	1	1	1	...	...	★ (p)	★	...	...
West Virginia	...	...	5	5	...	...	30	30	10 (i)	★ (i)	...	...
Wisconsin	...	...	10 days	10 days	10 days	10 days (e)	...	...	5	5	...	...
Wyoming	★	★	3	2	...	...	30	28	9 (h,i)	1 (h)	...	...
Dist. of Columbia	★	★	...	...	90 days	10 days	...	...	5 (i)	5 (i)	...	...
American Samoa	★	★	...	...	...	...	...	...	★	★	...	...
Guam	...	★	...	...	...	...	...	...	...	(h)	...	...
No. Mariana Islands	...	★	...	...	...	...	...	30	...	(h)	...	...
Puerto Rico	★	★	5	...	...	...	...	25	10	★ (i)	...	...

QUALIFICATIONS OF JUDGES—Continued

Sources: National Center for State Courts, *State Court Organization 1993;* state constitutions and statutes.

Note: The information in this table is based on a literal reading of the state constitutions and statutes. Requirements that an individual be a member of the state bar or a qualified elector may imply additional requirements.

Key:

A — Judges of courts of last resort and intermediate appellate courts.

T — Judges of general trial courts.

★ — Provision; length of time not specified.

. . . — No specific provision.

(a) Citizen of the state. In Alabama, Mississippi and Tennessee (court of criminal appeals), five years; in Georgia, three years.

(b) Must have been engaged in active practice of law for specific number of years. Alaska: appellate — eight years; trial—five years.

(c) For court of appeals, five years.

(d) For court of appeals judges only.

(e) Qualified elector. For Arizona court of appeals, must be elector of county of residence. For Michigan Supreme Court, elector in state; court of appeals, elector of appellate circuit. For Missouri Supreme and appellate courts, electors for nine years; for circuit courts, electors for three years. For Oklahoma Supreme Court and Court of Criminal Appeals, elector for one year; court of appeals and district courts, elector for six months. For Oregon court of appeals, qualified elector in county.

(f) Specific personal characteristics. Arizona, Arkansas—good moral character. Maine—sobriety of manners. Maryland—integrity, wisdom and sound legal knowledge.

(g) Nominee must be under certain age to be eligible. Arizona—under 70. Colorado—under 72, except when name is submitted for vacancy. Florida—under 70, except upon temporary assignment or to complete a term. Michigan, Ohio—under 70.

(h) Learned in law.

(i) Years as a practicing lawyer and/or service on bench of court of record in state may satisfy requirement. Arkansas—appellate: eight years; trial: six years. Indiana—10 years admitted to practice or must have served as a circuit, superior or criminal court judge in the state for at least five years. Kansas—appellate: 10 years; trial: five years (must have served as an associate district judge in state for two years). Texas—appellate: 10 years; trial: four years. Vermont—five of 10 years preceding appointment. West Virginia—appellate: 10 years; trial: five years. Puerto Rico—appellate: 10 years; trial: five years.

(j) A person convicted of a felony or breach of public trust is not eligible to the office for a period of 20 years after conviction.

(k) May not have been previously removed from judicial office.

(l) Except that record of birth is required.

(m) Thirty years for judges of court of appeals and court of criminal appeals.

(n) Supreme Court is five; court of appeals is three.

(o) Supreme Court is 30 years; court of appeals is 25 years.

(p) For court of appeals, admitted to practice for five years.

Table 4.4
SELECTION AND RETENTION OF JUDGES

State or other jurisdiction	How selected and retained
Alabama............	Appellate, circuit, district and probate judges elected on partisan ballots. Municipal court judges appointed by the governing body of the municipality (majority vote of its members).
Alaska.............	Supreme Court, court of appeals, superior court and district court judges appointed by governor from nominations submitted by Judicial Council. Supreme Court, court of appeals and superior court judges approved or rejected at first general election held more than three years after appointment. Reconfirmation every 10, eight and six years, respectively. District court judges approved or rejected at first general election held more than one year after appointment. Reconfirmation every four years. District court magistrates appointed by and serve at pleasure of presiding judge of superior court in each judicial district.
Arizona............	Supreme Court justices and court of appeals judges appointed by governor from a list of not less than three nominees submitted by a nine-member Commission on Appellate Court Appointments. Superior court judges (in counties with population of at least 150,000) appointed by governor from a list of not less than three nominees submitted by a nine-member commission on trial court appointments. Judges initially hold office for term ending 60 days following next regular general election after expiration of two-year term. Judges who file declaration of intention to be retained in office run at next regular general election on non-partisan retention ballot. Superior court judges in counties having population less than 150,000 elected on non-partisan ballot; justices of the peace elected on partisan ballot; police judges and magistrates selected as provided by charter or ordinance; Tucson city magistrates appointed by mayor and council from nominees submitted by non-partisan Merit Selection Commission on magistrate appointments.
Arkansas	All elected on partisan ballot.
California..........	Supreme Court and courts of appeal judges appointed by governor, confirmed by Commission on Judicial Appointments. Judges run unopposed on non-partisan retention ballot at next general election after appointment. Superior court judges elected on non-partisan ballot or selected by method described above; judges elected to full term at next general election on non-partisan ballot. Municipal court and justice court judges initially appointed by governor and county board of supervisors, respectively, retain office by election on non-partisan ballot.
Colorado	Supreme Court and court of appeals judges appointed by governor from nominees submitted by Supreme Court Nominating Commission. Other judges appointed by governor from nominees submitted by Judicial District Nominating Commission. After initial appointive term of two years, judges run on record for retention. Municipal judges appointed by municipal governing body. Denver County judges appointed by mayor from list submitted by nominating commission; judges run on record for retention.
Connecticut	All nonelected judges appointed by legislature from nominations submitted by governor exclusively from candidates submitted by the Judicial Selection Commission. Judicial Review Council makes recommendations on nominations for reappointment. Probate judges elected on partisan ballots.
Delaware	All appointed by governor from list submitted by a judicial nominating commission (which is established by executive order) with consent of majority of Senate.
Florida	Supreme Court and district courts of appeal judges appointed by governor from nominees submitted by appropriate judicial nominating commission. Judges run for retention at next general election preceding expiration of term. Circuit and county court judges elected on non-partisan ballots.
Georgia............	Supreme Court, court of appeals and superior court judges elected on non-partisan ballots. Probate judges and justices of peace elected on partisan ballots. Other county and city court judges appointed.
Hawaii	Supreme Court and intermediate court of appeals justices and circuit court judges nominated by Judicial Selection Commission (on list of at least six names) and appointed by governor with consent of Senate. Judges reappointed to subsequent terms by the Judicial Selection Commission. District court judges nominated by Commission (on list of at least six names) and appointed by chief justice.
Idaho	Supreme Court and court of appeals justices and district court judges elected on non-partisan ballot. Magistrates appointed on non-partisan merit basis by District Magistrates Commission and run for retention in first general election next succeeding the 18-month period following initial appointment; thereafter, run every four years.
Illinois.............	Supreme Court, appellate court and circuit court judges nominated at primary elections or by petition and elected at general or judicial elections on partisan ballot. Judges run in uncontested retention elections for subsequent terms. Circuit court associate judges, once appointed by circuit judges for four-year terms, are being converted to full circuit judges.
Indiana	Supreme Court justices, court of appeals judges and tax court judges are appointed by governor from list of three nominees submitted by seven-member Judicial Nominating Commission. Judges serve until next general election after two years from appointment date; thereafter, run for retention on record. Circuit, superior and county judges in most counties run on partisan ballot. Marion County municipal judges appointed by governor from nominees submitted by county nominating commission.
Iowa	Supreme Court, court of appeals and district court judges appointed by governor from lists submitted by nominating commissions. Judges serve initial one-year term and until January 1 following next general election, then run on records for retention. Full-time judicial magistrates appointed by district judges in judicial election district from nominations submitted by county judicial magistrate appointing commission. Part-time magistrates appointed by county judicial magistrate appointing commission.
Kansas	Supreme Court and court of appeals judges appointed by governor from nominations submitted by Supreme Court Nominating Commission. Judges serve until second Monday in January following first general election after one year in office; thereafter run on record for retention every six (Supreme Court) and four (court of appeals) years. District judges in most judicial districts selected by non-partisan commission plan.
Kentucky	All judges elected on non-partisan ballot.
Louisiana	All justices and judges elected on non-partisan basis, but state has open primary which requires all candidates to appear on a single ballot.
Maine	All appointed by governor with confirmation of the senate, except probate judges who are elected on partisan ballot.

SELECTION AND RETENTION OF JUDGES—Continued

State or other jurisdiction	How selected and retained
Maryland	Court of Appeals and Court of Special Appeals judges nominated by Judicial Nominating Commission, and appointed by governor with advice and consent of Senate. Judges run on record for retention after one year of service. Judges of circuit courts and Supreme Bench of Baltimore City nominated by Commission and appointed by governor. Judges run in first general election after year of service (may be challenged by other candidates). District court judges nominated by Commission and appointed by governor, subject to Senate confirmation.
Massachusetts	All nominated and appointed by governor with advice and consent of Governor's Council. Judicial Nominating Commission, established by executive order, submits names on non-partisan basis to governor.
Michigan	All elected on non-partisan ballot, except remaining municipal judges who are selected in accordance with local procedures for selecting public officials.
Minnesota	All elected on non-partisan ballot.
Mississippi	All elected on partisan ballot, except municipal court judges who are appointed by governing authority of each municipality.
Missouri	Judges of Supreme Court, court of appeals and several circuit courts appointed initially by governor from nominations submitted by judicial selection commissions. Judges run for retention after one year in office. All other judges elected on partisan ballot.
Montana	All elected on non-partisan ballot. Judges unopposed in reelection effort, run for retention. Water court judges are appointed by chief justice; Workers' compensation judges are appointed by the governor.
Nebraska	All judges appointed initially by governor from nominees submitted by judicial nominating commissions. Judges run for retention on non-partisan ballot in general election following initial three-year term; subsequent terms are six years.
Nevada	All elected on non-partisan ballot.
New Hampshire	All appointed by governor and confirmed by majority vote of elected five-member Executive Council.
New Jersey	All appointed by governor with advice and consent of Senate, except judges of municipal courts serving a single municipality who are appointed by the governing body. Judges are reappointed by the governor (to age 70) with the advice and consent of Senate.
New Mexico	Supreme Court, Court of Appeals, district and municipal judges appointed by governor from list submitted by a judicial nominating commission. At next general election, after appointment, judges run for full terms in partisan, contested election. If appointed judge wins the contested election, the judge runs for subsequent terms in uncontested retention elections.
New York	All elected on partisan ballot, except judges of Court of Appeals who are appointed by governor with advice and consent of Senate. Governor also appoints judges of court of claims and designates members of appellate division of supreme court. Mayor of New York City appoints judges of criminal and family courts in the city from list submitted by a judicial nominating commission, established by mayor's executive order.
North Carolina	All elected on partisan ballot, except special judges of superior court who are appointed by governor.
North Dakota	All elected on non-partisan ballot.
Ohio	All elected on non-partisan ballot, except court of claims judges who may be appointed by chief justice of Supreme Court from ranks of Supreme Court, court of appeals, court of common pleas or retired judges.
Oklahoma	Supreme Court justices and Court of Criminal Appeals judges appointed by governor from lists of three submitted by Judicial Nominating Commission. Judges run for retention on non-partisan ballot at first general election following completion of one year's service. Judges of court of appeals, and district and associate district judges elected on non-partisan ballot. Special judges appointed by district judges within judicial administrative districts. Municipal judges appointed by governing body of municipality.
Oregon	All judges elected on non-partisan ballot for six-year terms, except municipal judges who are generally appointed and serve as prescribed by city council.
Pennsylvania	All initially elected on partisan ballot and thereafter on non-partisan retention ballot, except magistrates (Pittsburgh) who are appointed by mayor.
Rhode Island	Supreme Court justices elected by legislature. Superior, district and family court judges appointed by governor with advice and consent of Senate. Probate and municipal court judges appointed by city or town councils.
South Carolina	Supreme Court, court of appeals, circuit court and family court judges elected by legislature from names submitted on a non-partisan basis by judiciary committee of legislature. Probate judges elected on partisan ballot. Magistrates appointed by governor with advice and consent of Senate. Municipal judges appointed by mayor and alderman of city.
South Dakota	Supreme Court justices appointed by governor from nominees submitted by Judicial Qualifications Commission. Justices run for retention at first general election after three years in office. Circuit court judges elected on non-partisan ballot. Magistrates appointed by presiding judge of judicial court with approval of Supreme Court.
Tennessee	Judges of intermediate appellate courts appointed initially by governor from list of three nominees submitted by Appellate Court Nominating Commission. Judges run for election to full term at biennial general election held more than 30 days after occurrence of vacancy. Supreme Court judges and all other judges elected on partisan ballot, except some municipal judges who are appointed by governing body of city.
Texas	All elected on partisan ballot (method of selection for municipal judges determined by city charter or local ordinance).
Utah	Supreme Court, district court, circuit court and juvenile court judges appointed by governor from list of at least three nominees submitted by Judicial Nominating Commission. Judges run unopposed for retention in general election following initial three-year term; thereafter run on record for retention every 10 (Supreme Court) and six (other courts of record) years.

See footnotes at end of table.

SELECTION AND RETENTION OF JUDGES—Continued

State or other jurisdiction	How selected and retained
Vermont	Supreme Court justices, superior court and district and family court judges nominated by Judicial Nominating Board and appointed by governor with advice and consent of Senate. Judges retained in office unless legislature votes for removal.
Virginia	All full-time judges elected by majority vote of legislature.
Washington	All elected on non-partisan ballot (municipal judges are appointed by mayor).
West Virginia	Supreme Court of Appeals judges, circuit court judges and magistrates elected on partisan ballot.
Wisconsin	Supreme Court, court of appeals and circuit court judges elected on non-partisan ballot.
Wyoming	Supreme Court justices, district and county court judges appointed by governor from list of three nominees submitted by judicial nominating commission. Judges run for retention on non-partisan ballot at first general election occurring more than one year after appointment. Justices of the peace elected on non-partisan ballot. Municipal (police) judges appointed by mayor with consent of Council.
Dist. of Columbia	Court of appeals and superior court judges nominated by president of the United States from a list of persons recommended by District of Columbia Judicial Nominating Commission; appointed upon advice and consent of U.S. Senate.
American Samoa	Chief justice and associate justice(s) appointed by the U.S. Secretary of the Interior pursuant to presidential delegation of authority. Associate judges appointed by governor of American Samoa on recommendation of the chief justice, and subsequently confirmed by the Senate of American Samoa.
Guam	All appointed by governor with consent of legislature from list of nominees submitted by Judicial Council; thereafter, run on record for retention every seven years.
No. Mariana Islands . . .	All appointed by governor with advice and consent of Senate.
Puerto Rico	All appointed by governor with advice and consent of Senate.
U.S. Virgin Islands	All appointed by governor with advice and consent of legislature.

Sources: Warrick, Judicial Selection in the United States: A Compendium of Provisions, 2nd Edition (Chicago: American Judicature Society), 1993; Donna Vandenberg, "Judicial Merit Selection: Current Status," American Judicature Society; National Center for State Courts, *State Court Organization 1993*; and state constitutions and statutes.
Note: Unless otherwise specified, judges included in this table are in the state courts of last resort and intermediate appellate and general trial courts.

Table 4.5
METHODS FOR REMOVAL OF JUDGES AND FILLING OF VACANCIES

State or other jurisdiction	How removed	Vacancies: how filled
Alabama	Judicial Inquiry Commission investigates, receives or initiates complaints concerning any judge. Complaints are filed with the Court of the Judiciary which is empowered to remove, suspend, censure or otherwise discipline judges in the state.	By gubernatorial appointment. At next general election held after appointee has been in office one year, office is filled for a full term. In some counties, vacancies in circuit and district courts are filled by gubernatorial appointment on nominations made by judicial commission.
Alaska	Justices and judges subject to impeachment for malfeasance or misfeasance in performance of official duties. On recommendation of Judicial Qualifications Commission or on its own motion, Supreme Court may suspend judge without salary when judge pleads guilty or no contest or is found guilty of a crime punishable as felony under state or federal law or of any other crime involving moral turpitude under that law. If conviction is reversed, suspension terminates and judge is paid salary for period of suspension. If conviction becomes final, judge is removed from office by Supreme Court. On recommendation of Judicial Qualifications Commission, Supreme Court may censure or remove a judge for action (occurring not more than six years before commencement of current term) which constitutes willful misconduct in office, willful and persistent failure to perform duties, habitual intemperance or conduct prejudicial to the administration of justice that brings the judicial office into disrepute. The Court may also retire a judge for a disability that seriously interferes with the performance of duties and is (or is likely to become) permanent.	By gubernatorial appointment, from nominations submitted by Judicial Council.
Arizona	Judges subject to recall election. Electors, equal in number to 25% of votes cast in last election for judge, may petition for judge's recall. All Supreme Court, court of appeals and superior court judges (judges of courts of record) are subject to impeachment. On recommendation of Commission on Judicial Qualifications or on its own motion, Supreme Court may suspend without salary, a judge who pleads guilty or no contest or is found guilty of a crime punishable as felony or involving moral turpitude under state or federal law. If conviction is reversed, suspension terminates and judge is paid salary for period of suspension. If conviction becomes final, judge is removed from office by Supreme Court. Upon recommendation of Commission on Judicial Qualifications, Supreme Court may remove a judge for willful misconduct in office, willful and persistent failure to perform duties, habitual intemperance or conduct prejudicial to the administration of justice that brings the office into disrepute. The Court may also retire a judge for a disability that seriously interferes with performance of duties and is (or is likely to become) permanent.	Vacancies on Supreme Court, court of appeals and superior courts (in counties with population over 150,000) are filled as in initial selection. Vacancies on superior courts in counties of less than 150,000 may be filled by gubernatorial appointment until next general election when judge is elected to fill remainder of unexpired term. Vacancies on justice courts are filled by appointment by county board of supervisors.
Arkansas	Supreme, appellate, circuit and chancery court judges are subject to removal by impeachment or by the governor upon the joint address of 2/3 of the members elected to each house of General Assembly. On recommendation of Judicial Discipline & Disability Commission, the Supreme Court may suspend, with or without pay, or remove a judge for conviction of any offense punishable as a felony under the laws of Arkansas or the United States; for conviction of a criminal act that reflects adversely on the judge's honesty, trustworthiness, or fitness as a judge in other respects; for conduct involving dishonesty, fraud, deceit, or misrepresentation; for conduct that is prejudicial to the administration of justice; for a willful violation of the Code of Judicial Conduct or the Rules of Professional Responsibility; for willful and persistent failure to perform the duties of office; or for habitual intemperance in the use of alcohol or other drugs.	By gubernatorial appointment. Appointee serves remainder of unexpired term if it expires at next general election.
California	All judges subject to impeachment for misconduct. All judges subject to recall election. On recommendation of the Commission on Judicial Performance or on its own motion, the Supreme Court may suspend a judge without salary when the judge pleads guilty or no contest or is found guilty of a crime punishable as a felony or any other crime that involves moral turpitude under that law. If conviction is reversed, suspension terminates and judge is paid salary for period of suspension. If conviction becomes final, judge is removed from office by Supreme Court. Upon recommendation of Commission on Judicial Performance, Supreme Court may remove judge for willful misconduct in office, persistent failure or inability to perform duties, habitual intemperance or conduct prejudicial to the administration of justice that brings the office into disrepute. The Court may also retire a judge for disability that seriously interferes with performance of duties and is (or is likely to become) permanent.	Vacancies on appellate courts are filled by gubernatorial appointment with approval of Commission on Judicial Appointments until next general election at which appointee has the right to become a candidate. Vacancies on superior courts are filled by gubernatorial appointment for remainder of unexpired term; on justice courts by appointment of county board of supervisors or by nonpartisan special election.
Colorado	Supreme, appeals and district court judges are subject to impeachment for high crimes and misdemeanors or malfeasance in office by 2/3 vote of Senate. Supreme Court, on its own motion or upon petition, may remove a judge from office upon final conviction for a crime punishable as felony under state or federal law or of any other crime involving moral turpitude under that law. Upon recommendation of Commission on Judicial Discipline, Supreme Court may remove or discipline a judge for willful misconduct in office, willful or persistent failure to perform the duties of office, intemperance or violation of judicial conduct, or for disability that seriously interferes with performance and is (or is likely to become) permanent. Denver county judges are removed in accordance with charter and ordinance provisions.	By gubernatorial appointment (or mayoral appointment in case of Denver county court) from names submitted by appropriate judicial nominating commission.

METHODS FOR REMOVAL OF JUDGES—Continued

State or other jurisdiction	How removed	Vacancies: how filled
Connecticut	Supreme and superior court judges are subject to removal by impeachment or by the governor on the address of 2/3 of each house of the General Assembly. On recommendation of Judicial Review Council or on its own motion, the Supreme Court may remove or suspend a judge of the Supreme or superior court after an investigation and hearing. If the investigation involves a Supreme Court justice, such judge is disqualified from participating in the proceedings. If a judge becomes permanently incapacitated and cannot adequately fulfill the duties of office, the judge may be retired for disability by the Judicial Review Council on its own motion or on application of the judge.	If General Assembly is in session, vacancies are filled as in initial selection. Otherwise vacancies are filled temporarily by gubernatorial appointment.
Delaware	Judges are subject to impeachment for treason, bribery or any high crime or misdemeanor. The Court on the Judiciary may (after investigation and hearing) censure or remove a judge for willful misconduct in office, willful and persistent failure to perform the duties of office or an offense involving moral turpitude or other persistent misconduct in violation of judicial ethics. The Court may also retire a judge for permanent mental or physical disability interfering with the performance of duties.	Vacancies are filled as in initial selection.
Florida	Supreme Court, district courts of appeal and circuit court judges are subject to impeachment for misdemeanors in office. On recommendation of Judicial Qualifications Commission, Supreme Court may discipline or remove a judge for willful or persistent failure to perform duties or for conduct unbecoming to a member of the judiciary, or retire a judge for a disability that seriously interferes with the performance of duties and is (or is likely to become) permanent.	By gubernatorial appointment, from nominees recommended by appropriate judicial nominating commission.
Georgia	Judges are subject to impeachment for cause. Upon recommendation of the Judicial Qualifications Commission (after investigation of alleged misconduct), the Supreme Court may retire, remove or censure any judge.	By gubernatorial appointment (by executive order) on nonpartisan basis from names submitted by Judicial Nominating Commission.
Hawaii	Upon recommendation of the Commission on Judicial Discipline (after investigation and hearings), the Supreme Court may reprimand, discipline, suspend (with or without salary), retire or remove any judge as a result of misconduct or disability.	Vacancies on Supreme, intermediate court of appeals and circuit courts are filled by gubernatorial appointment (subject to consent of Senate) from names submitted by Judicial Selection Committee. Vacancies on district courts are filled by appointment by chief justice from names submitted by Committee.
Idaho	Judges are subject to impeachment for cause. Upon recommendation by Judicial Council, Supreme Court (after investigation) may remove judges of Supreme Court, court of appeals and district court judges. District court judges (or judicial district sitting en banc), by majority vote in accordance with Supreme Court rules, may remove magistrates for cause. District Magistrate's Commission may remove magistrates without cause during first 18 months of service.	Vacancies on Supreme Court, court of appeals and district courts are filled by gubernatorial appointment from names submitted by Judicial Council for unexpired term. Vacancies in magistrates' division of district court are filled by District Magistrate's Commission for remainder of unexpired term.
Illinois	Judges are subject to impeachment for cause. The Judicial Inquiry Board receives (or initiates) and investigates complaints, and files complaints with the Courts Commission which may remove, suspend without pay, censure or reprimand a judge for willful misconduct in office, persistent failure to perform duties or other conduct prejudicial to the administration of justice or that brings the judicial office into disrepute. The Commission may also suspend (with or without pay) or retire a judge for mental or physical disability.	Vacancies on Supreme, appellate and circuit courts are filled by appointment by Supreme Court until general election. Associate judge vacancies on circuit courts are filled as in initial selection.
Indiana	Upon the recommendation of the Judicial Qualifications Commission or on its own motion, the Supreme Court may suspend or remove an appellate judge for pleading guilty or no contest to a felony or crime involving moral turpitude. The Supreme Court may also retire, censure or remove a judge for other matters. The Supreme Court may also discipline or suspend without pay a non-appellate judge.	Appellate vacancies are filled as in initial selection. Vacancies on circuit courts are filled by gubernatorial appointment until general election. Vacancies on most superior courts are filled by gubernatorial appointment.
Iowa	Supreme and district court judges are subject to impeachment for misdemeanor or malfeasance in office. Upon recommendation of Commission on Judicial Qualifications, the Supreme Court may retire a Supreme, district or associate district judge for permanent disability, or remove such judge for failure to perform duties, habitual intemperance, willful misconduct, conduct which brings the office into disrepute or substantial violations of the canons of judicial ethics. Judicial magistrates may be removed by a tribunal in the judicial election district of the magistrate's residence.	Vacancies are filled as in initial selection.

METHODS FOR REMOVAL OF JUDGES—Continued

State or other jurisdiction	How removed	Vacancies: how filled
Kansas	All judges are subject to impeachment for treason, bribery or other high crimes and misdemeanors. Supreme Court justices are subject to retirement upon certification to the governor (after a hearing by the Supreme Court nominating commission) that such justice is so incapacitated as to be unable to perform adequately the duties of office. Upon recommendation of the Judicial Qualifications Commission, the Supreme Court may retire for incapacity, discipline, suspend or remove for cause any judge below the Supreme Court level.	Vacancies on Supreme Court and court of appeals are filled as in initial selection. Vacancies on district courts (in areas where commission plan has not been adopted) are filled by gubernatorial appointment until next general election, when vacancy is filled for remainder of unexpired term; in areas where commission plan has been adopted, vacancies are filled by gubernatorial appointment from names submitted by judicial nominating commission.
Kentucky	Judges are subject to impeachment for misdemeanors in office. Retirement and Removal Commission, subject to rules of procedure established by Supreme Court, may retire for disability, suspend without pay or remove for good cause any judge. The Commission's actions are subject to review by Supreme Court.	By gubernatorial appointment (from names submitted by appropriate judicial nominating commission) or by chief justice if governor fails to act within 60 days. Appointees serve until next general election after their appointment at which time vacancy is filled.
Louisiana	Judges are subject to impeachment for commission or conviction of felony or malfeasance or gross misconduct. Upon investigation and recommendation by Judiciary Commission, Supreme Court may censure, suspend (with or without salary), remove from office or retire involuntarily a judge for misconduct relating to official duties, willful and persistent failure to perform duties, persistent and public conduct prejudicial to the administration of justice that brings the office into disrepute, or conduct while in office which would constitute a felony or conviction of felony. The Court may also retire a judge for disability which is (or is likely to become) permanent.	Vacancies are filled by Supreme Court appointment if remainder of unexpired term is six months or less; if longer than six months, vacancies are filled in special election.
Maine	Judges are subject to removal by impeachment or by governor upon the joint address of the legislature. Upon recommendation of the Committee on Judicial Responsibility and Disability, the Supreme Judicial Court may remove, retire or discipline any judge.	Vacancies are filled as in initial selection.
Maryland	Judges are subject to impeachment. Judges of Court of Appeals, court of special appeals, trial courts of general jurisdiction and district courts are subject to removal by governor on judge's conviction in court of law, impeachment, or physical or mental disability. Judges are also subject to removal upon joint address of the legislature. Upon recommendation of the Commission on Judicial Disabilities (after hearing), the Court of Appeals may remove or retire a judge for misconduct in office, persistent failure to perform duties, conduct prejudicial to the proper administration of justice, or disability that seriously interferes with the performance of duties and is (or is likely to become) permanent. Elected judges convicted of felony or misdemeanor relating to public duties and involving moral turpitude may be removed from office by operation of law when conviction becomes final.	Vacancies are filled as in initial selection.
Massachusetts	Judges are subject to impeachment. The governor, with the consent of the Executive Council, may remove judges upon joint address of the legislature, and may also (after a hearing and with consent of the Council) retire a judge because of advanced age or mental or physical disability. The Commission on Judicial Conduct, using rules of procedure approved by the Supreme Judicial Court, may investigate the action of any judge that may, by consequence of willful misconduct in office, willful or persistent failure to perform his duties, habitual intemperance or other conduct prejudicial to the administration of justice, bring the office into disrepute.	Vacancies are filled as in initial selection.
Michigan	Judges are subject to impeachment. With the concurrence of 2/3 of the members of the legislature, the governor may remove a judge for reasonable cause insufficient for impeachment. Upon recommendation of Judicial Tenure Commission, Supreme Court may censure, suspend (with or without salary), retire or remove a judge for conviction of a felony, a physical or mental disability, or a persistent failure to perform duties, misconduct in office, habitual intemperance or conduct clearly prejudicial to the administration of justice.	Vacancies in all courts of record are filled by gubernatorial appointment from nominees recommended by a bar committee. Appointee serves until next general election at which successor is selected for remainder of unexpired term. Vacancies on municipal courts are filled by appointment by city councils.

METHODS FOR REMOVAL OF JUDGES—Continued

State or other jurisdiction	How removed	Vacancies: how filled
Minnesota	Supreme and district court judges are subject to impeachment. Upon recommendation of Board of Judicial Standards, Supreme Court may censure, suspend (with or without salary), retire or remove a judge for conviction of a felony, physical or mental disability, or persistent failure to perform duties, misconduct in office, habitual intemperance or conduct prejudicial to the administration of justice.	Statutory plan to fill vacancies on district courts requires governor to appoint from nominees recommended by a judicial nominating commission. Vacancies on other levels of court filled by gubernatorial appointment (no nominating commission). Appointee serves until general election occurring more than one year after appointment at which time a successor is elected to serve a full term.
Mississippi	Judges are subject to impeachment. For reasonable cause which is not sufficient for impeachment, the governor may, on joint address of legislature, remove judges of Supreme and inferior courts. Upon recommendation of Commission on Judicial Performance, Supreme Court may remove, suspend, fine, publicly censure or reprimand a judge for conviction of a felony (in a court outside the state), willful misconduct, willful and persistent failure to perform duties, habitual intemperance or conduct prejudicial to the administration of justice which brings the office into disrepute. The Commission may also retire any judge for physical or mental disability that seriously interferes with performance of duties and is (or is likely to become) permanent.	By gubernatorial appointment, from names submitted by a nominating commission. The office is filled for remainder of unexpired term at next state or congressional election held more than seven months after vacancy.
Missouri	Upon recommendation of Commission on Retirement, Removal and Discipline, Supreme Court may retire, remove or discipline any judge.	Vacancies on Supreme Court, court of appeals and circuit courts which have adopted commission plan are filled as in initial selection. Vacancies on other circuit courts and municipal courts are filled, respectively, by special election and mayoral appointment.
Montana	All judges are subject to impeachment. Upon recommendation of Judicial Standards Commission, Supreme Court may suspend a judge and remove same upon conviction of a felony or other crime involving moral turpitude. The Supreme Court may retire any judge for a disability that seriously interferes with the performance of duties, and that is (or may become) permanent. The Court may also censure, suspend, or remove any judge for willful misconduct in office, willful and persistent failure to perform duties, violation of canons of judicial ethics adopted by the Supreme Court, or habitual intemperance.	Vacancies on Supreme and district courts are filled by gubernatorial appointment (with confirmation by Senate) from names submitted by judicial nominating commission. Vacancies on municipal and city courts are filled by appointment by city councils for remainder of unexpired term.
Nebraska	Judges are subject to impeachment. In case of impeachment of Supreme Court justice, judges of district court sit as court of impeachment with 2/3 concurrence required for conviction. In case of other judicial impeachments, Supreme Court sits as court of impeachment. Upon recommendation of the Commission on Judicial Qualifications, the Supreme Court may reprimand, discipline, censure, suspend or remove a judge for willful misconduct in office, willful failure to perform duties, habitual intemperance, conviction of crime involving moral turpitude, disbarment or conduct prejudicial to the administration of justice that brings the office into disrepute. The Supreme Court also may retire a judge for physical or mental disability that seriously interferes with performance of duties and is (or is likely to become) permanent.	Vacancies are filled as in initial selection.
Nevada	All judges, except justices of peace, are subject to impeachment. Judges are also subject to removal by legislative resolution and by recall election. The Commission on Judicial Discipline may censure, retire or remove a Supreme Court justice or district judge for willful misconduct, willful or persistent failure to perform duties or habitual intemperance, or retire a judge for advanced age which interferes with performance of duties or for mental or physical disability that is (or is likely to become) permanent.	Vacancies on Supreme or district courts are filled by gubernatorial appointment from among three nominees submitted by Commission on Judicial Selection. Vacancies on justice courts are filled by appointment by board of county commissioners or by special election.
New Hampshire	Judges are subject to impeachment. Governor, with consent of Executive Council, may remove judges upon address of both houses of legislature.	Vacancies are filled as in initial selection.
New Jersey	Supreme and superior court judges are subject to impeachment by the legislature. Except for Supreme Court justices, judges are subject to a statutory removal proceeding that is initiated by the filing of a complaint by the Supreme Court on its own motion or the governor or either house of the legislature acting by a majority of its total membership. Prior to institution of the formal proceedings, complaints are usually referred to the Supreme Court's Advisory Committee on Judicial Conduct, which conducts a preliminary investigation, makes findings of fact and either dismisses the charges or recommends that formal proceedings be instituted. The Supreme Court's determination is based on a plenary hearing procedure, although the Court is supplied with a record created by the Committee. The formal statutory removal hearing may be either before the Supreme Court sitting en banc or before three justices or judges (or combination thereof) specifically designated by chief justice. If Supreme Court certifies to governor that it appears a Supreme Court or superior court judge is so incapacitated as to substantially prevent the judge from performing the duties of office, the governor appoints a commission of three persons to inquire into the circumstances. On their recommendation, the governor may retire the justice or judge from office, on pension, as may be provided by law.	Vacancies on Supreme, superior, appellate division of superior, county, district, tax and municipal courts are filled as in initial selection.

METHODS FOR REMOVAL OF JUDGES—Continued

State or other jurisdiction	How removed	Vacancies: how filled
New Mexico.........	Judges are subject to impeachment. Upon recommendation of the Judicial Standards Commission, the Supreme Court may discipline or remove a judge for willful misconduct in office, willful and persistent failure or inability to perform duties or habitual intemperance, or retire a judge for disability that seriously interferes with performance of duties and is (or is likely to become) permanent.	Vacancies on Supreme, Court of Appeals and district courts are filled by gubernatorial appointment from names submitted by judicial nominating commission.
New York	All judges are subject to impeachment. Court of Appeals and supreme court judges may be removed by 2/3 concurrence of both houses of legislature. Court of claims, county court, surrogate's court, family court, civil and criminal court (NYC) and district court judges may be removed by 2/3 vote of the Senate on recommendation of governor. Commission on Judicial Conduct may determine that a judge be admonished, censured or removed from office for cause, or retired for disability, subject to appeal to the Court of Appeals.	Vacancies on Court of Appeals and appellate division of supreme court are filled as in initial selection. Vacancies in elective judgeships (outside NYC) are filled at the next general election for full term; until election, governor makes appointment (with consent of Senate if in session).
North Carolina	Upon recommendation of Judicial Standards Commission, Supreme Court may censure or remove a court of appeals or trial court judge for willful misconduct in office, willful and persistent failure to perform duties, habitual intemperance, conviction of a crime involving moral turpitude, conduct prejudicial to the administration of justice that brings the office into disrepute, or mental or physical incapacity that interferes with the performance of duties and is (or is likely to become) permanent. Upon recommendation of Judicial Standards Commission, a seven-member panel of the court of appeals may censure or remove (for the above reasons) any Supreme Court judge.	Vacancies on Supreme, appeals and superior courts are filled by gubernatorial appointment until next general election.
North Dakota	Supreme and district court judges are subject to impeachment for habitual intemperance, crimes, corrupt conduct, malfeasance or misdemeanor in office. Governor may remove county judges after hearing. All judges are subject to recall election. On recommendation of Commission on Judicial Qualifications or on its own motion, Supreme Court may suspend a judge without salary when judge pleads guilty or no contest or is found guilty of a crime punishable as a felony under state or federal law or any other crime involving moral turpitude under that law. If conviction is reversed, suspension terminates and judge is paid salary for period of suspension. If conviction becomes final, judge is removed by Supreme Court. Upon recommendation of Commission on Judicial Qualifications, Supreme Court may censure or remove a judge for willful misconduct, willful failure to perform duties, willful violation of the code of judicial conduct or habitual intemperance. The Court may also retire a judge for disability that seriously interferes with the performance of duties and is (or is likely to become) permanent.	Vacancies on Supreme and district courts are filled by gubernatorial appointment from nominees submitted by Judicial Nominating Committee until next general election, unless governor calls for a special election to fill vacancy for remainder of term. Vacancies on county courts are filled by appointment by board of county commissioners from names submitted by nominating commission.
Ohio	Judges are subject to impeachment. Judges may be removed by concurrent resolution of 2/3 members of both houses of legislature or removed for cause upon filing of a petition signed by 15% of electors in preceding gubernatorial election. The Board of Commissioners on Grievances and Discipline of the Judiciary may disqualify a judge from office when judge has been indicted for a crime punishable as felony under state or federal law. Board may also remove or suspend a judge for willful and persistent failure to perform duties, habitual intemperance, conduct prejudicial to the administration of justice or which would bring the office into disrepute, or suspension from practice of law, or retire a judge for physical or mental disability that prevents discharge of duties. Judge may appeal action to Supreme Court.	Vacancies are filled by gubernatorial appointment until next general election when successor is elected to fill unexpired term. If unexpired term ends within one year following such election, appointment is made for unexpired term.
Oklahoma	Judges are subject to impeachment for willful neglect of duty, corruption in office, habitual intemperance, incompetency or any offense involving moral turpitude. Upon recommendation of Council on Judicial Complaints, chief justice of Supreme Court may bring charges against any judge in the Court on the Judiciary. Court on the Judiciary may order removal of judge for gross neglect of duty, corruption in office, habitual drunkenness, an offense involving moral turpitude, gross partiality in office, or oppression in office. Judge may also be retired (with or without salary) for mental or physical disability that prevents performance of duties, or for incompetence to perform duties.	Vacancies on Supreme Court and Court of Criminal Appeals are filled as in initial selection. Vacancies on court of appeals and district courts are filled by gubernatorial appointment from nominees submitted by Judicial Nominating Commission. For court of appeals vacancies, judge is elected to fill unexpired term at next general election.
Oregon	On recommendation of Commission on Judicial Fitness, Supreme Court may remove a judge for conviction of a felony or crime involving moral turpitude, willful misconduct in office, willful or persistent failure to perform judicial duties, habitual intemperance, illegal use of narcotic drugs, willful violation of rules of conduct prescribed by Supreme Court or general incompetence. A judge may also be retired for mental or physical disability after certification by Commission. Judge may appeal action to Supreme Court.	Vacancies on Supreme Court, court of appeals and circuit courts are filled by gubernatorial appointment, until next general election when judge is selected to fill unexpired term.
Pennsylvania	All judges are subject to impeachment for misdemeanor in office. Upon recommendation of Judicial Inquiry and Review Board, a judge may be suspended, removed or otherwise disciplined by Supreme Court for specific forms of misconduct, neglect of duty or disability.	By gubernatorial appointment (with advice and consent of Senate), from names submitted by appropriate nominating commission. Appointee serves until next election if the election is more than 10 months after vacancy occurred.

METHODS FOR REMOVAL OF JUDGES—Continued

State or other jurisdiction	How removed	Vacancies: how filled
Rhode Island	All judges are subject to impeachment. The Supreme Court on its own motion may suspend a judge who pleaded guilty or no contest or was found guilty of a crime punishable as felony under state or federal law or any other crime involving moral turpitude. Upon recommendation of the Commission on Judicial Tenure and Discipline, the Supreme Court may censure, suspend, reprimand or remove from office a judge guilty of a serious violation of the canons of judicial ethics or for willful or persistent failure to perform duties, a disabling addiction to alcohol, drugs or narcotics, or conduct that brings the office into disrepute. The Supreme Court may also retire a judge for physical or mental disability that seriously interferes with performance of duties and is (or is likely to become) permanent. Whenever the Commission recommends removal of a Supreme Court justice, the Supreme Court transmits the findings to the speaker of the House of Representatives, recommending the initiation of proceedings for the removal of the justice by resolution of the legislature.	Vacancies on Supreme Court are filled by the two houses of the legislature in grand committee until the next election. In case of a judge's temporary inability, governor may appoint a person to fill vacancy. Vacancies on superior, family and district courts are filled by gubernatorial appointment (with advice and consent of Senate).
South Carolina	Judges are subject to removal by impeachment or by governor on address of 2/3 of each house of legislature. Upon review of the findings of fact, conclusions of law, and recommendation of the Board of Commissioners on Judicial Standards, the Supreme Court can discipline, suspend, remove, retire, or hold in contempt a judge who has been convicted of a crime of moral turpitude, has violated the Code of Judicial Conduct or the Rules of Professional Conduct, persistently fails to perform his judicial duties or is persistently incompetent or neglectful in the performance of his judicial duties, or is habitually intemperate, consistently fails to timely issue his official orders, decrees, or opinions or otherwise perform his official duties without just cause or excuse, or for disability.	Vacancies are filled as in initial selection for remainder of unexpired term; if remainder is less than one year, vacancy is filled by gubernatorial appointment. Vacancies on probate courts are filled by gubernatorial appointment until next general election.
South Dakota	Supreme Court justices and circuit court judges are subject to removal by impeachment. Upon recommendation of Judicial Qualifications Commission, Supreme Court may remove a judge from office.	Vacancies on Supreme and circuit courts are filled by gubernatorial appointment from names submitted by Judicial Qualifications Commission for balance of unexpired term.
Tennessee	Judges are subject to impeachment for misfeasance or malfeasance in office. Upon recommendation of the Court on the Judiciary, the legislature (by concurrent resolution) may remove a judge for willful misconduct in office or physical or mental disability.	Vacancies on Supreme, circuit, criminal and chancery courts are filled by gubernatorial appointment until next biennial election held more than 30 days after vacancy occurred. At election, successor is chosen as in initial selection. Vacancies on court of appeals and court of criminal appeals are filled as in initial selection.
Texas..............	Supreme Court, court of appeals and district court judges are subject to removal by impeachment or by joint address of both houses. Supreme Court may remove district judges from office. District judges may remove county judges and justices of the peace. Upon charges filed by the State Commission on Judicial Conduct, the Supreme Court may remove a judge for willful or persistent violation of the code of judicial conduct, and willful or persistent conduct that is clearly inconsistent with the proper performance of duties, or casts public discredit upon the judiciary or administration of justice. The Court may also retire a judge for disability.	Vacancies on appellate and district courts are filled by gubernatorial appointment until next general election, at which time a successor is chosen. Vacancies on county courts are filled by appointment by county commissioner's court until next election when successor is chosen. Vacancies on municipal courts are filled by governing body of municipality for remainder of unexpired term.
Utah	All judges, except justices of the peace, are subject to impeachment. Following investigations and hearings, the Judicial Conduct Commission may order the reprimand, censure, suspension, removal, or involuntary retirement of any judge for willful misconduct, final conviction of a crime punishable as a felony under state or federal law, willful or persistent failure to perform judicial duties, disability that seriously interferes with performance, or conduct prejudicial to the administration of justice that bring the judicial office into disrepute. Prior to implementation, the Supreme Court reviews the order. Lay justices of the peace may be removed for willful failure to participate in judicial education program.	Vacancies on Supreme, district and circuit courts are filled by gubernatorial appointment from candidates submitted by appropriate nominating commission.
Vermont	Upon review of the findings of the Judicial Conduct Board, all judges are subject to impeachment. Supreme Court may discipline, impose sanctions on, or suspend from duties any judge in the state.	Vacancies on Supreme, superior and district courts are filled as in initial selection if Senate is in session. Otherwise, by gubernatorial appointment from nominees submitted by judicial nominating board.
Virginia............	All judges are subject to impeachment. Upon certification of charges against judge by Judicial Inquiry and Review Commission, Supreme Court may remove a judge.	Vacancies are filled as in initial selection if General Assembly is in session. Otherwise, by gubernatorial appointment, with appointee serving until 30 days after commencement of next legislative session.

METHODS FOR REMOVAL OF JUDGES—Continued

State or other jurisdiction	How removed	Vacancies: how filled
Washington	A judge of any court of record is subject to impeachment. After notice, hearing and recommendation of Judicial Qualifications Commission, Supreme Court may censure, suspend or remove a judge for violating a rule of judicial conduct. The Supreme Court may also retire a judge for disability that seriously interferes with the performance of duties and is (or is likely to become) permanent.	Vacancies on appellate and general trial courts are filled by gubernatorial appointment until next general election when successor is elected to fill remainder of term.
West Virginia	Judges are subject to impeachment for maladministration, corruption, incompetency, gross immorality, neglect of duty or any crime or misdemeanor. Upon review of recommendations of the Judicial Hearing Board, the Supreme Court of Appeals may censure or suspend a judge for any violation of the judicial code of ethics or retire a judge who is incapable of performing duties because of advancing age, disease or physical or mental infirmity.	Vacancies on appellate and general trial courts are filled by gubernatorial appointment. If unexpired term is less than two years (or such additional period not exceeding three years), appointee serves for remainder of term. If unexpired term is more than three years, appointee serves until next general election, at which time successor is chosen to fill remainder of term.
Wisconsin	All judges are subject to impeachment. Supreme Court, court of appeals and circuit court judges are subject to removal by address of both houses of legislature with 2/3 of members concurring, and by recall election. As judges of courts of record must be licensed to practice law in state, removal of judge may also be by disbarment. Upon review of the findings of fact, conclusions of law, and recommendation of the Judicial Commission, the Supreme Court may reprimand, censure, suspend, or remove for cause or disability any judge or justice for a willful violation of a rule of the Code of Judicial Ethics, willful or persistent failure to perform official duties, habitual intemperance, due to consumption of intoxicating beverages or use of dangerous drugs, which interferes with the proper performance of judicial duties, or conviction of a felony.	Vacancies on Supreme Court, court of appeals and circuit courts are filled by gubernatorial appointment from nominees submitted by nominating commission.
Wyoming	All judges, except justices of peace, are subject to impeachment. Upon recommendation of Judicial Supervisory Commission, the Supreme Court may retire or remove a judge. After a hearing before a panel of three district judges, the Supreme Court may remove justices of the peace.	Vacancies are filled as in initial selection. Vacancies on justice of the peace courts are filled by appointment by county commissioners until next general election.
Dist. of Columbia	Commission on Judicial Disabilities and Tenure may remove a judge upon conviction of a felony (including a federal crime), for willful misconduct in office, willful and persistent failure to perform judicial duties or for other conduct prejudicial to the administration of justice which brings the office into disrepute.	Vacancies are filled as in initial selection, unless president of the United States fails to nominate candidate within 60 days of receipt of list of nominees from D.C. Judicial Nominating Commission; then Commission nominates and appoints, wth advice and consent of U.S. Senate.
American Samoa	U.S. Secretary of the Interior may remove chief and associate justices for cause. Upon recommendation of governor, chief justice may remove associate judges for cause.	Vacancies are filled as in initial selection.
Guam	On recommendation of Judicial Qualifications Commission, a special court of three judges may remove a judge for misconduct or incapacity.	By gubernatorial appointment.
No. Mariana Islands	Judges are subject to impeachment for treason, commission of a felony, corruption or neglect of duty. Upon recommendation of an advisory commission on the judiciary, the governor may remove, suspend or otherwise sanction a judge for illegal or improper conduct.	By gubernatorial appointment.
Puerto Rico	Supreme Court justices are subject to impeachment for treason, bribery, other felonies and misdemeanors involving moral turpitude. Supreme Court may remove other judges for cause (as provided by judiciary act) after a hearing on charges brought by order of chief justice, who disqualifies self from final proceedings.	Vacancies are filled as in initial selection.

Source: American Judicature Society (Spring 1992) (used with permission).

Table 4.6
COMPENSATION OF JUDGES OF APPELLATE COURTS
AND GENERAL TRIAL COURTS

State or other jurisdiction	Appellate courts				General trial courts	Salary
	Court of last resort	Salary	Intermediate appellate court	Salary		
Alabama	Supreme Court	$107,125	Court of Criminal Appeals	$106,125	Circuit courts	$ 72,500
			Court of Civil Appeals	106,125 (b)		
Alaska	Supreme Court	(a,d)	Court of Appeals	98,688	Superior courts	(d)
Arizona	Supreme Court	91,728 (a)	Court of Appeals	89,544	Superior courts	87,360
Arkansas	Supreme Court	93,349 (a,e)	Court of Appeals	90,379 (b,e)	Chancery courts	87,439 (e)
					Circuit courts	87,439 (e)
California	Supreme Court	127,267 (a)	Court of Appeals	119,314	Superior courts	104,262
Colorado	Supreme Court	84,000 (a)	Court of Appeals	79,500 (b)	District courts	75,000
Connecticut	Supreme Court	106,553 (a,f)	Appellate Court	99,077 (b,f)	Superior courts	94,647 (f)
Delaware	Supreme Court	105,100 (a)	. . .	. . .	Superior courts	99,900 (b)
Florida	Supreme Court	103,457	District Court of Appeals	98,284	Circuit courts	93,111
Georgia	Supreme Court	96,118	Court of Appeals	95,509	Superior courts	73,344 (c)
Hawaii	Supreme Court	93,780 (a)	Intermediate Court	89,780 (b)	Circuit courts	86,780
Idaho	Supreme Court	79,183 (a)	Court of Appeals	78,183	District courts	74,214
Illinois	Supreme Court	103,097	Appellate Court	97,032	Circuit courts	82,977 (b)
Indiana	Supreme Court	81,000 (g)	Court of Appeals	76,500 (g)	Circuit courts	61,740 (c)
					Superior courts	61,740 (c)
Iowa	Supreme Court	90,300 (a)	Court of Appeals	86,800 (b)	District courts	82,500 (b)
Kansas	Supreme Court	84,465 (a)	Court of Appeals	81,451 (b)	District courts	(h)
Kentucky	Supreme Court	78,273 (a)	Court of Appeals	75,078 (b)	Circuit courts	71,883 (i)
Louisiana	Supreme Court	94,000	Court of Appeals	89,000	District courts	84,000
Maine	Supreme Judicial Court	83,616 (a)	. . .	. . .	Superior court	79,073 (b)
Maryland	Court of Appeals	99,000 (a)	Court of Special Appeals	92,500 (b)	Circuit courts	89,000
Massachusetts	Supreme Judicial Court	90,450 (a)	Appeals Court	83,708 (b)	Trial court (j)	80,360 (b)
Michigan	Supreme Court	111,941	Court of Appeals	107,463	Circuit courts	61,565 (c)
					Recorder's court (Detroit)	102,986
Minnesota	Supreme Court	94,395 (a)	Court of Appeals	88,945 (b)	District courts	83,494 (b)
Mississippi	Supreme Court	90,800 (a,e)	. . .	. . .	Chancery courts	81,200 (e)
					Circuit courts	81,200 (e)
Missouri	Supreme Court	92,910 (a)	Court of Appeals	86,755	Circuit courts	70,810 (b)
					Municipal division of circuit courts	up to 70,810
Montana	Supreme Court	64,452 (a)	. . .	. . .	District courts	63,178
Nebraska	Supreme Court	88,157	Court of Appeals	83,749	District courts	81,546
Nevada	Supreme Court	85,000 (k)	. . .	. . .	District courts	79,000 (k)
New Hampshire	Supreme Court	95,623 (a,e)	. . .	. . .	Superior courts	89,628 (b,e)
New Jersey	Supreme Court	115,000 (a)	Appellate division of Superior Court	108,000	Superior courts	100,000 (l)
New Mexico	Supreme Court	77,250 (a)	Court of Appeals	73,388 (b)	District courts	69,719
New York	Court of Appeals	125,000 (a,e)	Appellate divisions of Supreme Court	(b,e,m)	Supreme courts	113,000 (e)
North Carolina	Supreme Court	91,855 (a,n)	Court of Appeals	86,996 (b,n)	Superior courts	77,289 (b,n)
North Dakota	Supreme Court	71,555 (a)	. . .	. . .	District courts	65,970 (b)
Ohio	Supreme Court	101,150 (a)	Court of Appeals	94,200	Courts of common pleas	72,650 (c)
Oklahoma	Supreme Court	83,871 (a)	Court of Appeals	78,660	District courts	71,330 (o)
Oregon	Supreme Court	83,700 (a)	Court of Appeals	81,700 (b)	Circuit courts	76,200
					Tax Court	78,600
Pennsylvania	Supreme Court	108,045 (a)	Superior Court	104,444 (b)	Courts of common pleas	92,610 (b)
			Commonwealth Court	104,444 (b)		
Rhode Island	Supreme Court	99,431 (a,p)	. . .	. . .	Superior courts	89,521 (b,p)
South Carolina	Supreme Court	92,986 (a)	Court of Appeals	88,338 (b)	Circuit courts	88,338
South Dakota	Supreme Court	72,079 (a)	. . .	. . .	Circuit courts	67,314 (b)
Tennessee	Supreme Court	96,348	Court of Criminal Appeals	91,860	Chancery courts	87,900
					Circuit courts	87,900
					Criminal courts	87,900
Texas	Supreme Court	94,685 (a)	Court of Appeals	89,952 (b,c)	District courts	85,217 (c)
Utah	Supreme Court	89,300 (a)	Court of Appeals	85,250 (b)	District courts	81,200
Vermont	Supreme Court	73,890 (a)	. . .	. . .	Superior courts	70,188 (b)
					District courts	70,188 (b)
Virginia	Supreme Court	102,700 (a,q)	Court of Appeals	97,565 (b,q)	Circuit courts	95,340
Washington	Supreme Court	107,200	Court of appeals	101,900	Superior courts	96,600
West Virginia	Supreme Court of Appeals	72,000	. . .	. . .	Circuit courts	65,000
Wisconsin	Supreme Court	94,906 (a)	Court of Appeals	89,358	Circuit courts	83,773
Wyoming	Supreme Court	85,000	. . .	. . .	District courts	77,000

COMPENSATION OF JUDGES—Continued

State or other jurisdiction	Appellate courts				General trial courts	Salary
	Court of last resort	Salary	Intermediate appellate court	Salary		
Dist. of Columbia ..	Court of Appeals	141,700 (a)	...	...	Superior courts	133,600 (b)
American Samoa ...	High Court	74,303 (a)	...	...	(r)	(r)
Guam	...	...	...	...	Superior courts	100,000 (b)
No. Mariana Islands .	Commonwealth Supreme Court	126,000 (a)	...	...		120,000 (b)
Puerto Rico	Supreme Court	80,000 (a)	Appellate Court	70,000	Superior courts	58,000
					District courts	50,000
U.S. Virgin Islands ...	...	...	...	...	Territorial courts	75,000 (b)

Source: National Center for State Courts, *Survey of Judicial Salaries* (January 1994).

Note: Compensation is shown according to most recent legislation, even though laws may not yet have taken effect.

(a) These jurisdictions pay the following additional amounts to the chief justice or presiding judge of court of last resort:

Alabama, Hawaii, Utah—$1,000.
Alaska—$516.
Arizona—$2,184.
Arkansas—$7,701 (effective July 1994).
California—$6,192.
Colorado, Missouri—$2,500.
Connecticut—$9,929.
Delaware—$3,700.
Idaho—$1,500.
Iowa—$3,400.
Kansas—$2,341.
Kentucky, New Jersey—$5,000.
Maine—$4,173.
Maryland—$16,000.
Massachusetts—$3,258.
Minnesota—$9,440.
Mississippi—chief justice, $3,200; presiding judge, $600.
Montana—$1,270.
New Hampshire—$2,988 (effective July 1994).
New Mexico—$2,000.
New York—$4,000 (effective October 1994).
North Carolina—$1,992.
North Dakota—$2,040.
Ohio—$6,500.
Oklahoma—$2,920.
Oregon—$1,900.
Pennsylvania—$3,087.
Rhode Island—$9,943.
South Carolina—$4,894.
South Dakota—$2,000.
Texas—$2,785.
Vermont—$3,585.
Virginia—$6,791 (plus $6,500 in lieu of travel expenses).
Wisconsin—$8,000.
District of Columbia—$500.
American Samoa—plus non-foreign post differentials where applicable.
No. Mariana Islands—$4,000.
Puerto Rico—$600.

(b) Additional amounts paid to various judges:

Alabama—presiding judge, $500.
Arkansas—chief judge, $1,495 (effective July 1994).
Colorado—chief judge, $2,500.
Connecticut—chief judge, $6,117.
Delaware—presiding judge, $3,800.
Hawaii—chief judge, $1,500.
Illinois—chief judge, $6,064.
Iowa—chief judges of court of appeals and district court, $3,400.
Kansas—chief judge, $2,221.
Kentucky—chief judge, $3,000.
Maine—chief justice, $3,939.
Maryland—chief judge, $2,500.

Massachusetts—chief justice of appeals court, $3,259; superior court chief justice, $3,348.
Minnesota—chief judge of the court of appeals, $4,447; chief judge of district court, $4,175.
Missouri—chief judge, $9,546.
New Hampshire—chief judge, $5,995 (effective July 1994).
New Mexico—chief judge, $1,900.
New York—presiding judges of appellate divisions of supreme court, $3,000 (effective October 1994).
North Carolina—chief judge of court of appeals, $1,934; senior judge of superior court, $2,534.
North Dakota—presiding judge, $1,581.
Oregon—chief judge, $2,000.
Pennsylvania—presiding judges of superior court and commonwealth court, $1,543; president judges of courts of common pleas, additional amounts to $2,573, depending on number of judges and population.
Rhode Island—presiding judge, $5,567.
South Carolina—chief judge, $3,718.
South Dakota—presiding circuit judge, $2,000.
Texas—chief judge, $530.
Utah, Virginia—chief judge, $1,000.
Vermont—administrative judges of superior and district courts, $3,702.
District of Columbia—chief judge, $500.
Guam—presiding judge, $25,000.
No. Mariana Islands—presiding judge of superior court, $3,000.
U.S. Virgin Islands—presiding judge of territorial court, $5,000.

(c) Plus local supplements, if any.

(d) Salaries range from $104,472 to $105,876 for supreme court; $96,600 to $103,596 for superior court, depending on location and cost-of-living differentials.

(e) Effective as of July 1994. In New York, October 1994.

(f) Plus 3 percent semiannually after 25 or more years, 3/4 of 3 percent after 20-25 years, 1/2 of 3 percent after 15-20 years, and 1/4 of 3 percent after 10-15 years.

(g) Plus $3,000 subsistence allowance for associate judges; for chief judges, $5,500.

(h) District judge designated as administrative judge, $74,268; district judge, $73,430; district magistrate judge, $34,670.

(i) Chief regional judges receive $72,883.

(j) Superior court department of the trial court.

(k) Plus 6 percent at 7 years and an additional 1 percent each year thereafter for a maximum of 22 percent.

(l) Assignment judges receive $105,001.

(m) Intermediate Appellate Court, Appellate Division of the Supreme Court (1st, 2nd, 3rd and 4th departments): $119,000 (effective October 1994); Appellate Terms of the Supreme Court (1st, 2nd, 9th, 10th, 11th, and 12th districts): $115,000 (effective October 1994).

(n) Plus 4.8 percent after 5 years, 9.6 percent after 10 years, 14.4 percent after 15 years, and 19.2 percent after 20 years.

(o) District judges, $71,330; associate district judges paid on basis of population ranges: over 30,000—$67,281; 10,000 to $30,000—$59,859; under 10,000—$56,146.

(p) Plus 5 percent after 5 years, 10 percent after 11 years, 15 percent after 15 years, 17.5 percent after 20 years, and 20 percent after 25 years.

(q) Plus $6,500 in lieu of travel, lodging and other expenses.

(r) General trial court responsibilities handled by the chief justice or associate judges of the High Court.

Table 4.7
SELECTED DATA ON COURT ADMINISTRATIVE OFFICES

State or other jurisdiction	Title	Established	Appointed by (a)	Salary
Alabama............	Administrative Director of Courts (b)	1971	CJ	$ 90,558
Alaska..............	Administrative Director	1959	CJ (b)	102,468
Arizona.............	Administrative Director of Courts	1960	SC	90,000
Arkansas	Director, Administrative Office of the Courts	1965	CJ (c)	64,457
California..........	Administrative Director of the Courts	1960	JC	119,314
Colorado	State Court Administrator	1959	SC	76,500
Connecticut	Chief Court Administrator (d)	1965	CJ	111,290 (e)
Delaware	Director, Administrative Office of the Courts	1971	CJ	70,000
Florida	State Courts Administrator	1972	SC	84,872
Georgia............	Director, Administrative Office of the Courts	1973	JC	75,842
Hawaii	Administrative Director of the Courts	1959	CJ (b)	85,302
Idaho	Administrative Director of the Courts	1967	SC	70,000
Illinois............	Administrative Director of the Courts	1959	SC	97,032
Indiana	Executive Director, Division of State Court Administration	1975	SC	70,122
Iowa	Court Administrator	1971	SC	70,000 to 99,900
Kansas	Judicial Administrator	1965	CJ	73,430
Kentucky	Administrative Director of the Courts	1976	CJ	71,884
Louisiana	Judicial Administrator	1954	SC	84,000
Maine	Court Administrator	1975	CJ	68,784
Maryland	State Court Administrator (b)	1955	CJ	81,200
Massachusetts	Administrator, Supreme Judicial Court (b)	1978	SC	86,967
Michigan	State Court Administrator	1952	SC	93,605
Minnesota	State Court Administrator	1963	SC	not to exceed 83,494
Mississippi	Court Administrator	1974	SC	76,200
Missouri	State Courts Administrator	1970	SC	70,433
Montana............	State Court Administrator	1975	SC	49,655
Nebraska	State Court Administrator	1972	CJ	71,440
Nevada	Director, Office of Court Administration	1971	SC	63,118
New Hampshire	Director of Administrative Services	1980	SC	73,643
New Jersey..........	Administrative Director of the Courts	1948	CJ	100,000
New Mexico.........	Director, Administrative Office of the Courts	1959	SC	65,000
New York	Chief Administrator of the Courts (f)	1978	CJ (g)	114,750
North Carolina	Director, Administrative Office of the Courts	1965	CJ	79,823 (e)
North Dakota	Court Administrator (h)	1971	CJ	61,284
Ohio	Administrative Director of the Courts	1955	SC	89,252
Oklahoma	Administrative Director of the Courts	1967	SC	78,660
Oregon	Court Administrator	1971	CJ	81,700
Pennsylvania	Court Administrator	1968	SC	98,784
Rhode Island	State Court Administrator	1969	CJ	76,424 (e)
South Carolina	Director of Court Administration	1973	CJ	72,911
South Dakota	State Court Administrator	1974	SC	43,139 to 64,230
Tennessee	Executive Secretary of the Supreme Court	1963	SC	91,860
Texas..............	Administrative Director of the Courts (i)	1977	SC	82,209
Utah	Court Administrator	1973	SC	81,200
Vermont	Court Administrator (j)	1967	SC	70,188
Virginia............	Executive Secretary to the Supreme Court	1952	SC	95,340
Washington	Administrator for the Courts	1957	SC (k)	91,770
West Virginia	Administrative Director of the Supreme Court of Appeals	1975	SC	66,000
Wisconsin...........	Director of State Courts	1978	SC	89,358
Wyoming	Court Coordinator	1974	SC	46,294
Dist. of Columbia	Executive Officer, Courts of D.C.	1971	(l)	133,600
American Samoa	Court Administrator	1977	CJ	27,092
Guam	Administrative Director of Superior Court	N.A.	CJ (m)	82,025
Puerto Rico	Administrative Director of the Court	1952	CJ	72,500
U.S. Virgin Islands	Court/Administrative Clerk	N.A.	N.A.	55,700

Source: Salary information was taken from National Center for State Courts, *Survey of Judicial Salaries* (January 1994).
Key:
SC—State court of last resort.
CJ—Chief justice or chief judge of court of last resort.
JC—Judicial council.
N.A.—Not available.
(a) Term of office for all court administrators is at pleasure of appointing authority.
(b) With approval of Supreme Court.
(c) With approval of Judicial Council.

(d) Administrator is an associate judge of the Supreme Court.
(e) Base pay supplemented by increments for length of service.
(f) If incumbent is a judge, the title is Chief Administrative Judge of the Courts.
(g) With advice and consent of Administrative Board of the Courts.
(h) Serves as executive secretary to Judicial Council.
(i) Serves as executive director of Judicial Council.
(j) Also clerk of the Supreme Court.
(k) Appointed from list of five submitted by governor.
(l) Joint Committee on Judicial Administration.
(m) Presiding judge of Superior Court (general trial court).

Chapter Five

STATE ELECTIONS, CAMPAIGN FINANCE & INITIATIVES

A review of election legislation and developments in campaign financing and initiatives across the states in recent years. Includes information on which state offices will be up for election in the years 1994-2003, formulas for election dates, voting statistics, campaign finance laws, and procedures for initiatives, referenda and recalls.

Election Legislation, 1992-93

States are adapting to new technologies and new federal laws to streamline voting and registration.

by Richard G. Smolka and Ronald D. Michaelson

In many ways, election legislation in the states during 1992-1993 was a response to federal law and federal court decisions. For the first time, Congress directly intervened in the general process of election administration by passing the National Voter Registration Act of 1993 (NVRA). Although Congress had previously passed election laws, traditionally they were designed to protect voting rights of specific groups such as minorities, handicapped, military personnel and their dependents, and overseas citizens.

The NVRA was passed even though the states were rapidly easing voter registration requirements and procedures. During the time the law was being considered, at least 29 states, with a substantial majority of the national population, permitted voters to register by mail. More than 25 states offered voters an opportunity to register at the same time they obtain or renew a driver's license. Many states also permitted members of political parties and interest groups to serve as deputy registrars and/or provided voter registration opportunities at state and local government offices serving the public. Moreover, states reported that voter registration and voter turnout hit all-time highs in the 1992 election, before the federal law passed.

Presently, almost half a million public officials are elected under state law, and only 537 are elected under federal law. Under the NVRA, which takes effect January 1, 1995, the registration laws and some voting laws now applicable to electing the 537 soon will apply to those elected under state law.

The NVRA not only directs the states to register voters but mandates the state agencies that must do so and specifies the procedures states must follow. It also makes some people

eligible to vote in federal elections who would not have been eligible to vote for state officials under state law.

Four states are not covered by the NVRA. Minnesota, Wisconsin and Wyoming are exempt from the law because they had Election Day registration in effect on March 11, 1993. North Dakota is exempt because it did not require voters to register at all. Both Minnesota and Wisconsin have had Election Day registration laws in effect since the 1970s, but Wyoming's law was passed conditionally in 1993 to allow the state to escape regulation if the federal voting act was passed.

The NVRA mandates the other 46 states to offer people the opportunity to vote when they apply for or renew a driver's license; apply for or receive certain types of public assistance or other services; at military recruiting offices; and by mail. People who decline registration must submit a written refusal.

States must accept a voter registration form the Federal Election Commission will devise and, for federal elections, may not require more information on the state registration form than is required on the federal form. The law also prohibits the states from removing voters' names from the registration lists solely for failure to vote and requires a program to confirm the accuracy and currency of the voter list.

One of the major changes states must adopt will allow certain people who are not registered at their current address to cast a ballot for federal officers. The "fail-safe" provisions

Richard G. Smolka is professor emeritus of Political Science at American University and editor, Election Administration Reports. *Ronald D. Michaelson is executive director, Illinois State Board of Elections.*

of the federal law mandate the states to allow registrants, who changed residence within the registrar's jurisdiction but remain within the same congressional district, to vote for candidates for federal office. It also requires states to allow voting for residents who fail to respond to confirmation notices, and registrants who have not moved but whose records were changed to show that they had. In brief, the state must allow anyone to vote who is registered in the jurisdiction, still claims residence in the jurisdiction even though not at the same address and has not been disqualified from voting for reasons other than residence. States are allowed various options to implement these provisions, so many state legislatures will be considering these issues during 1994 sessions.

States are permitted to continue their current laws on voter registration for state elections but such an option would require distinguishing between voters eligible to vote in all elections and those registered to vote only in federal elections. It is expected that the 46 states will adopt laws to make state voter registration practices the same as federal elections.

The NVRA also requires the Federal Election Commission in odd-numbered years to submit a report assessing the impact of the act on election administration during the preceding two years and recommending improvements in federal and state procedures, forms and other matters the act affects. As a result, local and state election officials will be required to compile statistics related to all aspects of the federal law — including the number of applications received by each method the law specifies. The FEC also is expected to require states to track confirmation mailings, responses to these mailings, purge practices, the number of redundant or duplicate registration applications and postal costs. Congress appropriated no funds to implement this federal mandate, and there is no indication that the FEC will attempt to obtain state information on the cost of implementing the law.

The act also requires each state to "designate a State officer or employee as the chief state election official" to be responsible for coordination of state responsibilities. The designated election officer has the duty of making national and state mail registration forms available for distribution through governmental and private entities. Finally, the law also designates the state election official as the recipient of U.S. attorneys' notices on felony convictions in federal courts of people who claimed residence in the state.

Election Technology

States may find that the revised recordkeeping requirements under the NVRA present a timely opportunity to adopt some new election technologies. During the past two years the number of jurisdictions using electronic means to capture and store voters' signatures has increased sharply. Many states laws require polling place workers to identify the voter by checking the signature on a polling book with the original signature in a binder card or registry at the polls. New York and some other states now allow original signatures to be electronically stored and reproduced for use at the polls. Digitized signatures for verification of petition signatures also have been used under new laws and regulations, and more state legislatures are considering such laws.

Although ballots were sent by electronic transmission (fax) during the 1990 general election because of the Gulf War, there has been little initiative to continue this practice. However, some states and local jurisdictions have accepted ballot applications by fax, and several will even send ballots electronically. Indiana law permits faxing absentee ballots to and from circuit court clerks offices if mandated by federal law. Missouri permits absentee ballots to be sent and returned by fax if the president declares a national emergency. The Department of Defense Federal Voting Assistance Program supports federal legislation that would mandate the states to accept electronically transmitted ballots from military and overseas citizens, but Congress has not passed this legislation. Such proposals have already found resistance in some states.

Beginning in 1994, candidates for public office in New Mexico may file reports of contributions and expenditures on a computer disk. Candidates may request software from the Bureau of Elections. The software sent to candidates contains encrypted identification notations to ensure that only the candidate who requested the software is submitting the material.

New Mexico, like many other states, requires that campaign finance statements be signed and notarized. To comply with this requirement, the software is written to print out a summary page, which must be signed and notarized and submitted with the computer disk. Software is available only for candidates' campaign finance reports; although New Mexico now is developing software for political action committees, and will follow that with software for lobbyist filings.

As state laws attempt to accommodate new voting technologies, some states are looking at the records of older systems. Wisconsin, in September 1993, held a hearing to consider decertifying punch-card voting. Testimony showed that more invalid ballots were cast with punch cards than with other systems used in the state. Election statistics also showed that while some towns that use punch cards had a high number of invalid ballots, sometimes in excess of 10 percent, other towns with punch cards had almost no invalid ballots. The state election board placed a two-year moratorium on the adoption of punch card voting by any jurisdiction that did not have it, and called for those jurisdictions with the high percentages of invalid ballots to provide greater voter instruction and pay attention to required voting device maintenance procedures.

Absentee Voting

The trend toward liberalization of absentee voting procedures continues unabated despite numerous instances of vote fraud with this practice. Washington state expanded a law for elderly and disabled individuals to be placed on a permanent absentee voter list to allow any voter to be placed on the permanent absentee voter list. These voters automatically receive a mailed ballot each election. If the ballot is returned as undeliverable, the person's name is removed from the permanent absentee list.

Hawaii now allows any voter to cast an absentee ballot. A Minnesota experimental law

in certain counties allowed any eligible voter to vote absentee in the 1992 primary and general election without specifying any one of the several reasons previously required. States that require reasons for requesting an absentee ballot also are easing up on some requirements. For example, people in Missouri who request an absentee ballot because of illness or disability no longer need to obtain a notary's signature and seal.

Federal law enforcement authorities continued to warn state officials to be alert to unusual patterns of absentee ballot requests, multiple absentee ballots sent to a single address, and high percentages of absentee ballots coming from small geographic areas.

Electioneering

State laws that establish a campaign-free zone to prevent electioneering at the polls are being upheld against the charge that they infringe upon free speech. Louisiana passed a law prohibiting electioneering within 600 feet of the polls, and Tennessee's 100-foot limit was upheld by the Supreme Court (*Burson v. Freeman* 112 S. Ct. 1846, 119 L. ed. 2d 5 (1992)).

Term Limits

In 1990, voters adopted term limits in three states — California, Colorado and Oklahoma. By 1992, voters in 13 more states — Arizona, Arkansas, Florida, Michigan, Missouri, Montana, Nebraska, North Dakota, Ohio, Oregon, South Dakota, Washington and Wyoming — had adopted similar proposals. And most recently, in November 1993, Maine voters adopted term limits for state legislators and state executives. Most of the laws apply to state officials and/or Congress.

For a more complete discussion of this issue, see "Term Limits in the States" by Thad Beyle and Rich Jones on pages 28-33 of this volume.

General Administration

Reflecting the increasing complexity of election administration, more states are passing laws to require training of election officials. A Washington law requires training of election administrators, and Ohio introduced a bill in 1994, considered likely to pass, that would require training for election board members.

A shortage of poll workers, which has been worsening for several years, continues. Political parties that once jealously guarded and enshrined in law their right to name poll workers have been unable to meet the need. The pool of potential poll workers that meet the legal requirements has diminished almost everywhere. Many who had worked at the polls for years quit when Congress passed a law requiring that Social Security tax be deducted from the election workers' already meager earnings. In some jurisdictions, poll workers are paid less than the federal minimum wage.

Reacting to the poll worker shortage, several states — beginning with Hawaii — began allowing persons too young to vote to staff the polls. Other states are doing the same. A new Minnesota law allows 16- and 17-year olds to serve at polls, and a new Nevada law permits high school students to do so.

Ballot Access

Several states recently changed laws to make it easier for candidates and political parties to qualify for the ballot. Oregon lowered the number of signatures required for new parties to gain ballot access from 2.5 percent to 1.5 percent of the votes cast in the previous gubernatorial election. Missouri reduced the number of signatures required of independent and third-party statewide candidates by at least one-third when it changed its requirement from 1 percent of the votes cast in the previous gubernatorial election to 10,000. Nevada lowered the number of signatures for a new party from 3 percent to 1 percent of the total congressional vote in the state. Virginia expanded the range of petition circulators, allowing them to collect petitions for statewide offices in congressional districts adjacent to their own district. South Dakota made it easier for individual candidates of a new party to get on the ballot and lowered the vote a party needs to remain on the ballot from 10 percent to 2.5 percent. New York reduced the number of signatures needed on statewide petitions from 20,000 to 15,000 and eased procedural requirements that used to be strictly enforced.

In an important decision, the U.S. Supreme Court in 1992 upheld a Hawaii law that prohibited write-in voting in all elections. The court decided: "When a state's ballot access laws pass constitutional muster in imposing only reasonable burdens on First and Fourteenth Amendment rights — as do Hawaii's election laws — a prohibition on write-in voting will be presumptively valid, since any burden on the right to vote for the candidate of one's choice will be light and normally will be counterbalanced by the very state interests supporting the ballot access scheme" (*Burdick v. Takushi*, 112 S. Ct. 2059, 119 L. ed. 2d 245 (1992)).

Military and Overseas Voting

State legislatures also responded to voting needs of military personnel, their dependents, and overseas citizens by passing laws making it easier for those people to register and vote. Seven states passed laws accepting a single postcard application for an absentee ballot as an application for ballots for all elections in a calendar year. Two states that had laws limiting absentee ballot applications to certain dates removed "not earlier than" restrictions. Four states passed laws providing for a special state write-in ballot to complement the federal write-in ballot used in case of emergencies. Four states granted chief election officials authority to respond to emergencies in elections that will enable them to act if it appears military and overseas citizens will not be able to vote by traditional methods.

Presidential Primaries

Presidential primary dates are moving in one direction — forward. California and Ohio moved their presidential primaries to March beginning in 1996. New York is expected to do so as well. Maine, which has not conducted presidential primary elections, passed a law in 1993 requiring political parties that choose to have a primary to conduct it on the same day as the New Hampshire primary, or if New Hampshire has no presidential primary, in the first week in March. New Hampshire law, however, provides that its presidential primary be held one week earlier than that in any other state. The net effect of changes in state presidential primary schedules will be that more than three-fourths of all delegates to national party conventions will be selected before the end of March 1996.

References:

Alexander, Herbert E., Eugene A. Goss, and Jeffrey A. Schwartz, *Public Funding of State Elections: A Databook on Tax-Assisted Funding of Political Parties and Candidates in Twenty-Four States*, Los Angeles: Citizens' Research Foundation, 1992.

Alexander, Herbert E., and Jeffrey A. Schwartz, "Laboratories for Reform," *National Voter*, September-October 1993, pp. 9-11.

Amy, Douglas, *Real Choices, New Voices*, New York: Columbia University Press, 1993.

Federal Election Commission. *Implementing The National Voter Registration Act of 1993, Requirements, Issues, Approaches, and Examples*. First ed. September 1993.

Feigenbaum, Ed and James A. Palmer, *Campaign Finance Law 92*, Washington, D.C.: National Clearinghouse on Election Administration, Federal Election Commission, 1993.

Feigenbaum, Ed, James A. Palmer and David T. Skelton, *Election Case Law 93*, Washington, D.C.: National Clearinghouse on Election Administration, Federal Election Commission, 1993.

Pildes, Richard and Richard G. Niemi, "Expressive Harms, 'Bizarre Districts', and Voting Rights: Evaluating Election District Appearances After Shaw." Ann Arbor: *Michigan Law Review*, December 1993.

Smith Burck, ed. *Policy Alternatives on Citizen Participation — a State Report*, Vol. 5, No. 1, Washington, D.C.: Center for Policy Alternatives, 1991.

Smolka, Richard G., *Election Administration Reports*, a biweekly newsletter for election officials. Washington, D.C.

Table 5.1
STATE EXECUTIVE BRANCH OFFICIALS TO BE ELECTED: 1994-2003

State	1994	1995	1996	1997	1998
Alabama	G,LG,AG,AR,A,SS,T				G,LG,AG,AR,A,SS,T
Alaska (a)	G,LG				G,LG
Arizona	G,AG,SS,SP,T (b)				G,AG,SS,SP,T (b)
Arkansas	G,LG,AG,A,SS,T (c)				G,LG,AG,A,SS,T (c)
California	G,LG,AG,C,SS,SP,T (d)				G,LG,AG,C,SS,SP,T (d)
Colorado (e)	G,LG,AG,SS,T				G,LG,AG,SS,T
Connecticut	G,LG,AG,C,SS,T				G,LG,AG,C,SS,T
Delaware	AG,A,T		G,LG (e)		AG,A,T
Florida	G,LG,AG,AR,C,SS,SP,T				G,LG,AG,AR,C,SS,SP,T
Georgia	G,LG,AG,AR,C,SS,SP, (f)		(f)		G,LG,AG,AR,C,SS,SP (f)
Hawaii	G,LG (g)		(g)		G,LG (g)
Idaho	G,LG,AG,A,SS,SP,T				G,LG,AG,A,SS,SP,T
Illinois (h)	G,LG,AG,C,SS,T				G,LG,AG,C,SS,T
Indiana	A,SS,T		G,LG,AG,SP		A,SS,T
Iowa	G,LG,AG,AR,A,SS,T				G,LG,AG,AR,A,SS,T
Kansas	G,LG,AG,SS,T (i)		(i)		G,LG,AG,SS,T (i)
Kentucky		G,LG,AG,AR,A,SS,SP,T (j)			
Louisiana (k)		G,LG,AG,AR,SS,T			
Maine	G				G
Maryland	G,LG,AG,C				G,LG,AG,C
Massachusetts	G,LG,AG,A,SS,T				G,LG,AG,A,SS,T
Michigan (l)	G,LG,AG,SS				G,LG,AG,SS
Minnesota	G,LG,AG,A,SS,T				G,LG,AG,A,SS,T
Mississippi		G,LG,AG,AR,A,SS,T (m)			
Missouri	A		G,LG,AG,A,SS,T		A
Montana			G,LG,AG,A,SS,SP		
Nebraska (n)	G,LG,AG,C,SS,T (o)		(o)		G,LG,AG,C,SS,T (o)
Nevada	G		G		G
New Hampshire	G		G	G	G
New Jersey				G	
New Mexico (p)	G,LG,AG,A,SS,T				G,LG,AG,A,SS,T
New York	G,LG,AG,C				G,LG,AG,C
North Carolina			G,LG,AG,AR,A,SS,SP,T (q)		
North Dakota (r)			G,LG,AG,AR,A,SS,SP,T		
Ohio	G,LG,AG,A,SS,T (s)		(s)		G,LG,AG,A,SS,T (s)
Oklahoma (t)	G,LG,AG,A,SP,T		AG,SS,T		G,LG,AG,A,SP,T
Oregon	G,SP (u)		AG,A,T		G,SP (u)
Pennsylvania	G,LG				G,LG
Rhode Island	G,LG,AG,SS,T				G,LG,AG,SS,T
South Carolina	G,LG,AG,AR,C,SS,SP,T (v)				G,LG,AG,AR,C,SS,SP,T (v)

See footnotes at end of table.

Key:
... — No regularly scheduled elections
G — Governor
LG — Lieutenant governor
AG — Attorney general
AR — Agriculture
A — Auditor
C — Comptroller
SS — Secretary of state
SP — Superintendent of public instruction (bb)
T — Treasurer

STATE EXECUTIVE BRANCH OFFICIALS TO BE ELECTED—Continued

State	1994	1995	1996	1997	1998
South Dakota (w)	G,LG,AG,A,SS,T	...	...	...	G,LG,AG,A,SS,T
Tennessee (x)	G	...	...	...	G
Texas (y)	G,LG,AG,AR,C,T	...	G,LG,AG,A,T (z)	...	G,LG,AG,AR,C,T
Utah	(z)	...	G,LG,AG,A,SS,T	...	(z)
Vermont	G,LG,AG,A,SS,T	...	G,LG,AG,A,SS,T	...	G,LG,AG,A,SS,T
Virginia	...	...		G,LG,AG	...
Washington	...	...	G,LG,AG,A,SS,SP,T (aa)	...	...
West Virginia	...	...	G,AG,AR,A,SS,T	...	...
Wisconsin	G,LG,AG,SS,T	...	...	SP	G,LG,AG,SS,T
Wyoming	G,A,SS,SP,T	...	...	...	G,A,SS,SP,T
Totals for year					
Governor	36	3	11	2	36
Lieutenant Governor .	30	3	9	1	30
Attorney General ...	29	3	10	1	29
Agriculture	6	3	3	0	6
Auditor	16	2	8	0	16
Comptroller	10	0	0	0	10
Secretary of State ...	26	3	8	0	26
Supt. of Public Inst. (bb)	9	1	5	1	9
Treasurer	27	3	9	0	27

Key:
... — No regularly scheduled elections
G — Governor
LG — Lieutenant governor
AG — Attorney general
AR — Agriculture
A — Auditor
C — Comptroller
SS — Secretary of state
SP — Superintendent of public instruction (bb)
T — Treasurer

STATE EXECUTIVE BRANCH OFFICIALS TO BE ELECTED—Continued

State	1999	2000	2001	2002	2003
Alabama	...	...	...	G,LG,AG,AR,A,SS,T	...
Alaska (a)	...	...	...	G,LG	...
Arizona	...	...	...	G,AG,SS,SP,T (b)	...
Arkansas	...	...	...	G,LG,AG,A,SS,T	...
California	...	...	...	G,LG,AG,C,SS,SP,T (d)	...
Colorado (e)	...	...	...	G,LG,AG,SS,T	...
Connecticut	...	...	...	G,LG,AG,C,SS,T	...
Delaware	...	G,LG (e)	...	AG,A,T	...
Florida	...	(f)	...	G,LG,AG,AR,C,SS,SP,T	...
Georgia	...	(f)	...	G,LG,AG,AR,C,SS,SP	...
Hawaii	...	(g)	...	G,LG	...
Idaho	...	...	...	G,LG,AG,A,SS,SP,T	...
Illinois (h)	...	...	...	G,LG,AG,C,SS,T	...
Indiana	...	G,LG,AG,SP	...	A,SS,T	...
Iowa	...	...	...	G,LG,AG,A,SS,T	...
Kansas	G,LG,AG,AR,A,SS,SP,T (j)	(i)	...	G,LG,AG,SS,T	...
Kentucky	G,LG,AG,AR,SS,T	...	...	...	G,LG,AG,AR,A,C,SS,SP,T
Louisiana (k)	...	...	...	...	G,LG,AG,AR,SS,T
Maine	...	...	...	G	...
Maryland	...	...	...	G,LG,AG,C	...
Massachusetts	...	...	...	G,LG,AG,A,SS,T	...
Michigan (l)	...	...	...	G,LG,AG,SS	...
Minnesota	...	...	...	G,LG,AG,A,SS,T	...
Mississippi	G,LG,AG,AR,A,SS,T (m)	...	...	G,LG,AG,AR,A,SS,T (m)	...
Missouri	...	G,LG,AG,SS,T	...	A	...
Montana	...	G,LG,AG,A,SS,SP	...	G,LG,AG,A,SS,T	...
Nebraska (n)	...	(o)	...	G,LG,AG,C,SS,T	...
Nevada	...	G	...	G	...
New Hampshire	...	...	G	...	...
New Jersey	...	...	G	...	...
New Mexico (p)	...	G,LG,AG,AR,A,SS,SP,T (q)	...	G,LG,AG,A,SS,T	...
New York	...	G,LG,AG,AR,A,SS,SP,T	...	G,LG,AG,C	...
North Carolina	...	(s)	...	...	...
North Dakota (r)	...	...	...	...	...
Ohio	...	...	...	G,LG,AG,AR,A,SS,T (s)	...
Oklahoma (l)	...	AG,SS,T	...	G,LG,AG,C,SP,T	...
Oregon	...	AG,A,T	...	G,SP (u)	...
Pennsylvania	...	...	...	G,LG	AG,A,T
Rhode Island	...	...	...	G,LG,AG,SS,T	...
South Carolina	...	...	...	G,LG,AG,A,C,SS,SP,T (v)	...

See footnotes at end of table.

Key:
... — No regularly scheduled elections
G — Governor
LG — Lieutenant governor
AG — Attorney general
AR — Agriculture
A — Auditor
C — Comptroller
SS — Secretary of state
SP — Superintendent of public instruction (bb)
T — Treasurer

STATE EXECUTIVE BRANCH OFFICIALS TO BE ELECTED—Continued

State	1999	2000	2001	2002	2003
South Dakota (w)	...	...	...	G,LG,AG,A,SS,T	...
Tennessee (x)	...	...	...	G	...
Texas (y)	...	...	...	G,LG,AG,A,C,T	...
Utah	...	G,LG,AG,A,T (z)	...	...	...
Vermont	...	G,LG,AG,A,SS,T	...	G,LG,AG,A,SS,T	...
Virginia	...	...	G,LG,AG	...	G,LG,AG
Washington	...	G,LG,AG,A,SS,SP,T (aa)	...	...	...
West Virginia	...	G,AG,AR,A,SS,T	...	...	...
Wisconsin	...	...	SP	G,LG,AG,SS,T	SP
Wyoming	...	...	...	G,A,SS,SP,T	...
Totals for year					
Governor	3	11	2	37	3
Lieutenant Governor	3	9	1	31	3
Attorney General	3	10	1	30	4
Agriculture	3	3	0	5	2
Auditor	2	8	0	18	2
Comptroller	0	0	0	10	1
Secretary of State	3	8	0	26	2
Supt. of Public Inst. (bb)	1	5	1	9	2
Treasurer	3	9	0	28	3

Sources: State election administration offices, except information on Maine which is from *The Book of the States 1992-93.*

Note: This table shows the executive branch officials up for election in given year. Footnotes indicate other offices (e.g., commissioners of labor, insurance, public service, etc.) also up for election in a given year. The data contained in this table reflect information available at press time.

Key:

. . . — No regularly scheduled elections
G—Governor
LG—Lieutenant governor
AG—Attorney general
AR—Agriculture
A—Auditor
C—Comptroller
SS—Secretary of state
SP—Superintendent of public instruction (bb)
T—Treasurer

(a) Election of school boards established to maintain system of state dependent public school systems established in areas of the unorganized borough and military reservations not served by other public school systems.
(b) Mine inspector—2 year term; corporation commissioners (3)—2 year terms.
(c) Commissioner of state lands—4 year term.
(d) Insurance commissioner.
(e) State board of education (7)—6 year terms; University of Colorado regents (9)—6 year terms.
(f) Public service commissioners (5)—6 year terms; 1994—2, 1996—2, 1998—1, 2000—2. Commissioner of labor—4 year term, 1994, 1998.
(g) State board of education (13)—4 year terms; 1994-6, 1996—7, 1998—6, 2000—7.
(h) University of Illinois trustees (9)—6 year terms.
(i) Commissioner of insurance 1994; 1998. Board of education members (10)—4 year terms, 1994—5, 1996—5, 1998—5, 2000—5.

(j) Railroad commissioners (3).
(k) Commissioner of elections—4 year term; commissioner of insurance—4 year term; board of elementary and secondary education (8)—4 year terms; public service commissioners (5)—6 year terms.
(l) Michigan State University trustees (8)—8 year terms; University of Michigan regents (8)—8 year terms; Wayne State University governors (8)—8 year terms; board of education (8)—8 year terms, 1994—2, 1996—2, 1998—2, 2000—2.
(m) Commissioner of insurance, highway commissioners (3), public service commissioners (3).
(n) Public service commissioners (5)—6 year terms; state board of education (8)—4 year terms; state university regents (8)—6 year terms.
(o) State board of education (11)—4 year terms, 1994—6, 1996—5, 1998—6, 2000—5.
(p) Commissioner of public lands—4 year terms, 1994, 1998; board of education (10)—6 year terms; corporation commissioners (3)—6 year terms.
(q) Commissioner of labor; commissioner of insurance.
(r) Commissioner of labor—4 year term, 1994, 1998; commissioner of insurance—4 year term, 1994, 1998; tax commissioner—4 year term, 1994, 1998; public service commissioners (3)—6 year terms.
(s) State board of education (19)—6 year terms, 1994—6; 1996—6; 1998—7; 2000—6.
(t) Corporation commissioner (3)—6 year terms, 1992, 1994, 1996, 1998, 2000; commissioner of insurance—4 year term, 1994, 1998; commissioner of labor—4 year term, 1994, 1998.
(u) Commissioner of labor and industries—4 year term.
(v) Adjutant general—4 year term.
(w) Commissioner of school and public lands; public utility commissioners (3)—6 year terms; board of education (15)—6 year terms, 1994, 1996,1998, 2000.
(x) Public service commissioners (3)—6 year terms.
(y) Commissioner of general land office—4 year term; railroad commissioners (3)—6 year terms; board of education (15)—6 year terms.
(z) State board of education (9) 4 year terms, 1994—7, 1996—8, 1998—7, 2000—8.
(aa) Insurance commissioner, commissioner of public lands.
(bb) Superintendent of public instruction or commissioner of education.

Table 5.2
STATE LEGISLATURES: MEMBERS TO BE ELECTED, 1994-2003

State	Total legislators Senate	Total legislators House	1994 Senate	1994 House	1995 Senate	1995 House	1996 Senate	1996 House	1997 Senate	1997 House	1998 Senate	1998 House
Alabama	35	105	35	105	..	..	..	..	..	..	35	105
Alaska	20	40	10	40	..	..	10	40	..	..	10	40
Arizona	30	60	30	60	..	..	30	60	..	..	30	60
Arkansas	35	100	18	100	..	..	17	100	..	..	18	100
California	40	80	20	80	..	..	20	80	..	..	20	80
Colorado	35	65	17	65	..	..	18	65	..	..	17	65
Connecticut	36	151	36	151	..	..	36	151	..	..	36	151
Delaware	21	41	10	41	..	..	11	41	..	..	10	41
Florida	40	120	20	120	..	..	20	120	..	..	20	120
Georgia	56	180	56	180	..	..	56	180	..	..	56	180
Hawaii	25	51	12	51	..	..	13	51	..	..	12	51
Idaho	35	70	35	70	..	..	35	70	..	..	35	70
Illinois	59 (b)	118	20	118	..	..	39	118	..	..	40	118
Indiana	50	100	25	100	..	..	25	100	..	..	25	100
Iowa	50	100	25 (c)	100	..	..	25 (d)	100	..	..	25 (c)	100
Kansas	40	125	..	125	..	..	49	125	..	..	..	125
Kentucky	38	100	19	100	..	..	19	100	..	..	19	100
Louisiana	39	105	..	..	39	105	..	..	..	..	..	..
Maine	35	151	35	151	..	..	35	151	..	..	35	151
Maryland	47	141	47	141	..	..	..	..	..	..	47	141
Massachusetts	40	160	40	160	..	..	40	160	..	..	40	160
Michigan	38	110	38	110	..	..	..	110	..	..	38	110
Minnesota	67	134	..	134	..	..	67	134	..	..	..	134
Mississippi	52	122	..	122	52	122	..	..	..	..	..	..
Missouri	34	163	17	163	..	..	17	163	..	..	17	163
Montana	50	100	25	100	..	..	25	100	..	..	25	100
Nebraska	49	U	24	U	..	..	25	U	..	..	24	U
Nevada	21	42	11	42	..	..	10	42	..	..	11	42
New Hampshire	24	400	24	400	..	..	24	400	..	..	24	400
New Jersey	40	80	..	80	..	80	..	..	40	80	..	..
New Mexico	42	70	..	70	..	..	42	70	..	..	..	70
New York	61	150	61	150	..	..	61	150	..	..	61	150
North Carolina	50	120	50	120	..	..	50	120	..	..	50	120
North Dakota	49	98	25 (c)	98	..	..	24 (d)	98	..	..	25 (c)	98
Ohio	33	99	17	99	..	..	16	99	..	..	17	99
Oklahoma	48	101	24	101	..	..	24	101	..	..	24	101
Oregon	30	60	15	60	..	..	15	60	..	..	15	60
Pennsylvania	50	203	25	203	..	..	25	203	..	..	25	203
Rhode Island	50	100	50	100	..	..	50	100	..	..	50	100
South Carolina	46	124	..	124	..	..	46	124	..	..	..	124
South Dakota	35	70	35	70	..	..	35	70	..	..	35	70
Tennessee	33	99	17	99	..	..	16	99	..	..	17	99
Texas	31	150	31 (e)	150	..	..	15	150	..	..	16	150
Utah	29	75	15	75	..	..	14	75	..	..	15	75
Vermont	30	150	30	150	..	..	30	150	..	..	30	150

See footnotes at end of table.

STATE LEGISLATURES: MEMBERS TO BE ELECTED—Continued

State	Total legislators		1994		1995		1996		1997		1998	
	Senate	House	Senate	House	Senate	House	Senate	House	Senate	House	Senate	House
Virginia	40	100	...	...	40	100	...	...	...	100	...	...
Washington	49	98	24	98	...	...	25	98	...	...	24	98
West Virginia	34	100	17	100	...	...	17	100	...	...	17	100
Wisconsin	33	99	17	99	...	...	16	99	...	...	17	99
Wyoming	30	60	15	60	...	...	15	60	...	...	15	60
Totals	1,984	5,440	1,117	5,033	131	407	1,193	4,787	40	180	1,122	5,033

STATE LEGISLATURES: MEMBERS TO BE ELECTED—Continued

State	1999 Senate	1999 House	2000 Senate	2000 House	2001 Senate	2001 House	2002 Senate	2002 House	2003 Senate	2003 House
Alabama	...	...	...	...	...	...	35	105	...	...
Alaska	...	...	10	40	...	...	10	40	...	...
Arizona	...	...	30	60	...	...	30	60	...	...
Arkansas	...	...	17	100	...	...	35	100	...	...
California	...	...	20	80	...	...	20	80	...	...
Colorado	...	...	18	65	...	...	18	65	...	...
Connecticut	...	...	36	151	...	...	36	151	...	...
Delaware	...	...	11	41	...	...	10	41	...	...
Florida	...	...	20	120	...	...	20 (a)	120	...	...
Georgia	...	...	56	180	...	...	56	180	...	...
Hawaii	...	...	13	51	...	...	12	51	...	...
Idaho	...	...	35	70	...	...	35	70	...	...
Illinois	...	...	19	118	...	...	59	118	...	...
Indiana	...	...	25	100	...	...	25	100	...	...
Iowa	...	...	25 (d)	100	...	...	25 (c)	100	...	...
Kansas	...	...	40	125	...	...	...	125	...	...
Kentucky	39	...	19	100	...	...	19	100	39	...
Louisiana	...	105	...	...	...	...	...	...	...	105
Maine	...	...	35	151	...	...	35	151	...	...
Maryland	...	...	...	...	...	...	47	141	...	...
Massachusetts	...	...	40	160	...	...	40	160	...	...
Michigan	...	...	110	...	...	...	38	110	...	...
Minnesota	...	...	67	134	...	...	...	134	...	...
Mississippi	52	122	...	...	...	...	...	...	52	122
Missouri	...	...	17	163	...	...	17	163	...	...
Montana	...	...	25	100	...	...	25	100	...	...
Nebraska	...	...	25	U	...	...	24	U	...	...
Nevada	...	...	10	42	...	...	11	42	...	...
New Hampshire	...	...	24	400	...	...	24	400	...	...
New Jersey	...	80	...	...	40	80	...	...	40	80
New Mexico	...	...	42	70	...	...	...	70	...	...
New York	...	...	61	150	...	...	61	150	...	...
North Carolina	...	...	50	120	...	...	50	120	...	...
North Dakota	...	...	24 (d)	98	...	...	25 (c)	98	...	...
Ohio	...	...	16	99	...	...	17	99	...	...
Oklahoma	...	...	24	101	...	...	24	101	...	...
Oregon	...	...	15	60	...	...	15	60	...	...
Pennsylvania	...	...	25	203	...	...	25	203	...	...
Rhode Island	...	...	50	100	...	...	50	100	...	...
South Carolina	...	...	46	124	...	...	...	124	...	...
South Dakota	...	...	35	70	...	...	35	70	...	...
Tennessee	...	...	16	99	...	...	17	99	...	...
Texas	...	...	15	150	...	...	31	150	...	...
Utah	...	...	14	75	...	...	15	75	...	...
Vermont	...	...	30	150	...	...	30	150	...	...

See footnotes at and of table.

STATE LEGISLATURES: MEMBERS TO BE ELECTED—Continued

State	1999 Senate	1999 House	2000 Senate	2000 House	2001 Senate	2001 House	2002 Senate	2002 House	2003 Senate	2003 House
Virginia	40	100	...	...	...	100	...	...	40	100
Washington	...	...	25	98	...	...	25	98	...	...
West Virginia	...	...	17	100	...	...	17	100	...	...
Wisconsin	...	...	16	99	...	...	17	99	...	...
Wyoming	...	...	15	60	...	...	15	60	...	...
Totals	131	407	1,283	4,677	40	180	1,175	5,033	171	407

Sources: State elections administration offices, except information on Maine which is from *The Book of the States 1992-93.*

Note: This table shows the number of legislative seats up for election in a given year. As a result of redistricting, states may adjust some elections. The data contained in this table reflect information available at press time. See Table 3.3, "The Legislators: Numbers, Terms, and Party Affiliations," for specific information on legislative terms.

Key:

. . . — No regularly scheduled elections

U—Unicameral legislature

(a) In the year following reapportionment, if the Florida Legislature deems it necessary, all 40 Senate seats may have to run—20 for two-year terms and 20 for four-year terms.

(b) The entire Senate is up for election every 10 years, beginning in 1972. Senate districts are divided into three groups. One group of senators is elected for terms of four years, four years and two years; two years four years and four years.

(c) Odd-numbered Senate districts.

(d) Even-numbered Senate districts.

(e) Due to redistricting, elections for all Texas Senate seats were held in 1992. Fifteen of those elected served a two-year term instead of a four-year term. Those fifteen seats are again up for election in 1994.

Table 5.3
METHODS OF NOMINATING CANDIDATES FOR STATE OFFICES

State or other jurisdiction	*Method(s) of nominating candidates*
Alabama	Primary election; however, the state executive committee or other governing body of any political party may choose instead to hold a state convention for the purpose of nominating candidates (meetings must be held at least 60 days prior to the date on which primaries are conducted).
Alaska	Primary election.
Arizona	Primary election.
Arkansas	Primary election.
California	Primary election or independent nomination procedure.
Colorado	Assembly/primary; however, a political party may hold a pre-primary assembly (at least 65 days before the primary) for the designation of candidates. Each candidate who receives at least 30 percent of the delegates' vote of those present and voting is listed on the primary ballot, with the candidate receiving the most votes listed first. If no candidate receives at least 30 percent of the vote, a second ballot shall be taken on all candidates, and the two candidates with the highest number of votes will be the candidate placed on the primary ballot. If any candidate receives less than 10 percent of the votes from the assembly, they are precluded from petitioning further.
Connecticut	Convention/primary election. Major political parties hold state conventions (convening not earlier than the 68th day and closing not later than the 50th day before the date of the primary) for the purpose of endorsing candidates. If no one challenges the endorsed candidate, no primary election is held. However, if anyone (who received at least 15 percent of the delegate vote on any roll call at the convention) challenges the endorsed candidate, a primary election is held to determine the party nominee for the general election.
Delaware	Convention/primary election; political parties hold state conventions for purpose of selecting delegates and candidates. If candidate unopposed no primary is held.
Florida	Primary election.
Georgia	Primary election.
Hawaii	Primary election.
Idaho	Primary election.
Illinois	Primary election; however, state conventions are held for the nomination of candidates for trustees of the University of Illinois.
Indiana	Primary election held for the nomination of candidates for governor and U.S. senator; state party conventions held for the nomination of candidates for other state offices.
Iowa	Primary election; however, if there are more than two candidates for any nomination and none receives at least 35 percent of the primary vote, the primary is deemed inconclusive and the nomination is made by party convention.
Kansas	Primary election; however, candidates of any political party whose secretary of state did not poll at least 5 percent of the total vote cast for all candidates for that office in the preceding general election are restricted to nomination by delegate or mass convention.
Kentucky	Primary election.
Louisiana	Primary election. Open primary system requires all candidates, regardless of party affiliation, to appear on a single ballot. Candidate who receives over 50 percent of the vote in the primary is elected to office; if no candidate receives a majority vote, a runoff election is held between the two candidates who received the most votes.
Maine	Primary election.
Maryland	Primary election.
Massachusetts	Primary election.
Michigan	Primary election held for the nomination of candidates for governor, U.S. congressional seats, state senators and representatives; court of appeals, circuit and district courts; state conventions held for the nomination of candidates for lieutenant governor, secretary of state and attorney general. State convention also held to nominate candidates for Justice of Supreme Court, State Board of Education, Regents of University of Michigan, Trustees of Michigan State University, Governors of Wayne State University.
Minnesota	Primary election.
Mississippi	Primary election.
Missouri	Primary election.
Montana	Primary election.
Nebraska	Primary election.
Nevada	Primary election.
New Hampshire	Primary election.
New Jersey	Primary election.
New Mexico	Convention/primary election.

METHODS OF NOMINATING CANDIDATES FOR STATE OFFICES —Continued

State or other jurisdiction	Method(s) of nominating candidates
New York	Committee meeting/primary election. The person who receives the majority vote at the state party committee meeting becomes the designated candidate for nomination; however, all other persons who received at least 25 percent of the convention vote may demand that their names appear on the primary ballot as candidates for nomination. Other candidates not receiving 25 percent of the vote may use a designating petition to put their names on the primary ballot as candidates for nomination
North Carolina	Primary election.
North Dakota	Convention/primary election. Political parties hold state conventions for the purpose of endorsing candidates. Endorsed candidates are automatically placed on the primary election ballot, but other candidates may also petition their name on the ballot.
Ohio	Primary election.
Oklahoma	Primary election.
Oregon	Primary election.
Pennsylvania	Primary election.
Rhode Island	Primary election.
South Carolina	Primary election for Republicans and Democrats; party conventions held for three minor parties. All must file with proper election commission by varying dates depending on office.
South Dakota	Primary election. Any candidate who receives a plurality of the primary vote becomes the nominee; however, if no individual receives at least 35 percent of the vote for the candidacy for the offices of governor, U.S. senator, or U.S. congressman, a runoff election is held two weeks later.
Tennessee	Primary election.
Texas	Primary election.
Utah	Convention/primary election. Delegates from the county primary conventions are elected to the state primary convention for the purpose of selecting the political party nominees to run at the regular primary election.
Vermont	Primary election.
Virginia	Primary election; however, the state executive committee or other governing body of any political party may choose instead to hold a state convention for the purpose of nominating candidates (party opting for convention can only do so within 32 days prior to date on which primary elections are normally held).
Washington	Primary election.
West Virginia	Primary election; however, executive committees may make nomination in case of certain vacancies on ballot.
Wisconsin	Primary election.
Wyoming	Primary election.
Dist. of Columbia	Primary election.

Sources: State election administration offices, except information on Maine which is from *The Book of the States 1992-93.*
Note: The nominating methods described here are for state offices; procedures may vary for local candidates. Also, independent candidates may have to petition for nomination.

Table 5.4
ELECTION DATES FOR NATIONAL, STATE AND LOCAL ELECTIONS (Formulas)

State	National			State			Local		
	Primary	Runoff	General	Primary	Runoff	General	Primary	Runoff	General
Alabama	June, 1st T	...	Nov., ★	State	June, Last T	Nat.	State	State	Oct., 1st T
Alaska	Aug., 4th T	...	Nov., ★	(a)	...	Nat.	(a)	...	Nat. or May, 1st M (d)
Arizona	8 T Prior	June, 2nd T (b)	Nov., ★	Nat.	...	Nat.	Nat.	Nat.	Nat. (a)
Arkansas	2 wks. Prior	...	Nov., ★	V	Nat.	Nat.	V	...	Nat.
California	June, ★	...	Nov., ★		...			...	Nat.
Colorado	Aug., 2nd T	...	Nov., ★	State	...	Nat. (c)	State	...	(a)
Connecticut	56th day Prior (N) (c); March, T After 4th M (P)	...	Nov., ★		...	Nat.	State	...	Nat. (c)
Delaware	Sept., 1st S After 1st M	...	Nov., ★	Nat.	...	Nat. (c)	...	...	Nat. (c)
Florida	9th T Prior	5th T Prior	Nov., ★	Nat.	Nat.	Nat. (c)	Nat.	21 days AP	(a)
Georgia	July, 3rd T	...	Nov., ★	July, 3rd T	21 days AP	Nat. (c)	July, 3rd T	21 days AP	Nat. (c)
Hawaii	Sept., 2nd Last S	...	Nov., ★	Nat.	...	Nat.	Nat.	...	Nat.
Idaho	May, 4th T	...	Nov., ★	Nat.	...	Nat.	Nat.	...	Nat.
Illinois	March, 3rd T	...	Nov., ★	February, Last T	...	Nat.	February, Last T	...	April, 1st T (d)
Indiana	May, ★	...	Nov., ★	Nat.	...	Nat. (c)	Nat.	...	Nat.
Iowa	June, ★	...	Nov., ★	Nat. (e)	...	Nat. (c)	Nat. (e)	...	Nat. (e)
Kansas	Aug, 1st T	...	Nov., ★	5 wks. Prior (f)	...	Nat. (a)	5 wks. Prior (f)	...	April, 1st T (f)
Kentucky	May, ★	...	Nov., ★	Nat.	...	Nat.	Nat.	...	Nat.
Louisiana (g)	Oct., 1st S	...	Nov., ★	V	...	4th S AP	V	...	V
Maine	June, 2nd T	...	Nov., ★	Nat.	...	Nat.	Nat.	...	V
Maryland	Sept., 2nd T After 1st M	...	Nov., ★	Nat.	...	Nat.	Nat.	...	Nat.
Massachusetts	7th T Prior	...	Nov., ★	V	...	Nat.	V	...	V
Michigan	Aug., ★ (h)	...	Nov., ★	Nat. (a)	...	Nat. (c)	Nat. (a)	...	Nat. (c)
Minnesota	Sept.,	...	Nov., ★	Nat. (a)	...	Nat.	Nat. (a)	...	Nat. (a)
Mississippi	June, 1st T (i)	3rd T AP	Nov., ★	May, 1st T (a)	3rd T AP	Nat. (a)	May, 1st T (a)	2 T AP	June, ★ (a)
Missouri	Aug., ★	...	Nov., ★	Nat.	...	Nat.	Nat.	...	Nat.
Montana	June, ★	...	Nov., ★	Nat.	...	Nat.	Nat.	...	Nat. (f)
Nebraska	May, 1st T After 2nd M	...	Nov., ★	Sept., 1st T after 2nd M (a)	...	Nat.	Sept., 1st T after 2nd M (a).	...	Nat.
Nevada	Sept., 1st T	...	Nov., ★	Nat.	...	Nat.	Nat.	...	Mar., 2nd T or May, 2nd T
New Hampshire	Sept., 2nd T (c)	...	Nov., ★	Nat.	...	Nat.	Nat.	...	Nat.
New Jersey	June, ★	...	Nov., ★	Nat.	...	Nat.	Nat.	...	Nat. (f)
New Mexico	June, 1st T (j)	...	Nov., ★	Nat.	...	Nat.	Nat.	...	Nat.
New York	April, 1st T (P)	...	Nov., ★	State	4 wks. AP	State	State	Sept., 2 wks. AP (a)	Nat. (c)
North Carolina	May, 3rd T	...	Nov., ★	V	...	V	V	V	Nat. (a)
North Dakota	June, 2nd T	...	Nov., ★	Nat. (a)	...	Nat.	Nat. (a)	...	V
Ohio	March, 3rd T (P)	...	Nov., ★	Nat. (a)	...	Nat.	Nat. (a)	...	April 1st T or June 2nd T
Oklahoma	Aug., 4th T (j)	Sept., 3rd T	Nov., ★	Nat.	Nat.	Nat. (c)	Nat.	Nat.	Nat. (a)
Oregon	May, 3rd T	...	Nov., ★	Nat.	...	Nat.	Nat.	...	Nat. (c)
Pennsylvania	April, 4th T (P) (k)	...	Nov., ★	Nat.	...	Nat.	Nat.	...	Nat.
Rhode Island	Sept., 2nd T After 1st M	2nd T AP	Nov., ★	Nat. (a)	Nat.	Nat.	Nat. (a)	Nat.	Nat.
South Carolina	June, 2nd T	...	Nov., ★	Nat. (a)	Nat.	Nat.	Nat. (a)	...	Nat. (a)

See footnotes at end of table.

Key:
★ — first Tuesday after first Monday
M — Monday
T — Tuesday
TH — Thursday
S — Saturday
Nat. — Same date as national elections
State — Same date as state elections
Prior — Prior to general election
(P) — Presidential election years
(N) — Non-presidential election years
AP — After primary
V — Varies

ELECTION DATES FOR NATIONAL, STATE AND LOCAL ELECTIONS—Continued

State	National			State			Local		
	Primary	Runoff	General	Primary	Runoff	General	Primary	Runoff	General
South Dakota	June, 1st T	2nd T AP	Nov., ★	June, 1st T	2nd T AP	Nat.	State	...	Nat. (l)
Tennessee	Feb., Last T (P); Aug, 1st TH	...	Nov., ★	Aug, 1st TH	...	Nat.	May, 1st T (m); March, 2nd T (P)	...	Aug, 1st TH
Texas	March, 2nd T	Apr., 2nd T (c)	Nov., ★ (c)	March, 2nd T	Nat.	Nat.	Nat.	Nat.	Nat.
Utah	June, 4th T	... (c)	Nov., ★ (c)	June, 4th T	...	Nat.	Nat.	...	Nat.
Vermont (n)	Sept., 2nd T	...	Nov., ★	Sept., 2nd T	...	Nat. ★	March, 1st T	...	March, 1st T
Virginia	June, 2nd T	...	Nov., ★	Nat.	...	Nat.	Nat. or March, 1st T	...	Nat. or May, 1st T
Washington	Sept. 3rd T (o)	...	Nov., ★	Nat.	...	Nat.	Nat.	...	Nat.
West Virginia	May, 2nd T	...	Nov., ★	Nat.	...	Nat.	Nat.	...	Nat.
Wisconsin	Sept., 2nd T	...	Nov., ★	Nat.	...	Nat. (p)	Feb, 3rd T	...	April, 1st T (p)
Wyoming	Aug, 1st T After 3rd M	...	Nov., ★	Nat.	...	Nat.	Nat.	...	Nat.

Sources: State election administration offices, except information on Maine which is from *The Book of the States 1992-93*.

Note: This table describes the basic formulas for determining when national, state and local elections will be held in each state and is meant to be used as a general guideline for comparing when state elections will be held. For specific information on a particular state, the reader is advised to contact the specific state election administration office. National elections are defined as elections for President, U.S. Senate and U.S. House of Representatives. In some cases, states have elected to provide specific data on variations between national elections in presidential and non-presidential years. Where provided, these variations have been noted.

Key:
★ — first Tuesday after first Monday
M — Monday
T — Tuesday
TH — Thursday
S — Saturday
Nat. — Same date as national elections
State — Same date as state elections
Prior — Prior to general election
(P) — Presidential election years
(N) — Non-presidential election years
AP — After primary
V — Varies

(a) In Arizona, municipalities—not less than 30 days prior to general election. In Delaware, elections are determined by city charter. In Iowa, partisan election only. In Kansas, state and county elections. In Minnesota, county elections only. In Mississippi, state and county elections are held together; municipal elections are held in separate years. In Montana, municipalities only. In New York, runoff in New York City only. In Ohio, municipalities and towns in odd years and counties in even years. In South Carolina, school boards vary.

(b) In Arkansas, a general primary is scheduled for the second Tuesday in June. A preferential primary is held two weeks before the general primary; should no candidate receive a majority vote, the general (runoff) primary is held.

(c) Even years.

(d) Unless that date conflicts with Passover, then 1st Tuesday following last day of Passover.

(e) County, township offices, and city elections are held in odd-numbered years on Nov. ★. School elections are held annually on Sept., 2T.

(f) Odd years.

(g) Louisiana has an open primary which requires all candidates, regardless of party affiliation, to appear on a single ballot. If a candidate receives over 50 percent of the vote in the primary, that candidate is elected to the office. If no candidate receives a majority vote, then a single election is held between the two candidates receiving the most votes. For national elections, the first vote is held on the first Saturday in October of even numbered years with the general election held on the first Tuesday after the first Monday in November. For state elections, the election is held on the second to last Saturday in October with the runoff being held on the fourth Saturday after first election. Local elections vary depending on the location and the year.

(h) Applies to federal, state, county and township offices. Cities may hold their primaries and elections at different times depending on charter or governing statutes. Villages generally hold primary in February and elections in March on an annual basis. Schools for the most part hold annual elections in June.

(i) Except in presidential election year when congressional races correspond to Super Tuesday.

(j) The primary election is held the 4th Tuesday in August in each even-numbered year, including presidential election years. The presidential preferential primary is held on the 2nd Tuesday in March during presidential election years.

(k) Except the 1994 election which would have landed on a Jewish holiday. It was held on May 10, 1994.

(l) County officials.

(m) County party has the option of having a county primary in conjunction with the presidential primary in March or the regular May date.

(n) In Vermont, if there is a tie in the general election, the legislature decides winner. In state primary runoffs, the runoff election must be proclaimed within 7 days after time in primary; after proclamation, election is held 15-22 days later. Local elections are held by annual town meetings which may vary depending on town charter.

(o) Other election dates for special elections include: Feb. ★, March 2T, April ★, May, 4T or date of Presidential Primary.

(p) Superintendent of Public Instruction, Supreme Court, Court of Appeals and Circuit Court Justices are elected with local officials.

Table 5.5
POLLING HOURS: GENERAL ELECTIONS

State or other jurisdiction	Polls open	Polls close	Notes on hours (a)
Alabama	No later than 8 a.m.	Between 6 and 8 p.m.	Polls must be open at least 10 consecutive hours; hours set by county commissioner.
Alaska	7 a.m.	8 p.m.	
Arizona	6 a.m.	7 p.m.	
Arkansas	7:30 a.m.	7:30 p.m.	
California	7 a.m.	8 p.m.	
Colorado	7 a.m.	7 p.m.	
Connecticut	6 a.m.	8 p.m.	
Delaware	7 a.m.	8 p.m.	
Florida	7 a.m.	7 p.m.	
Georgia	7 a.m.	7 p.m.	
Hawaii	7 a.m.	6 p.m.	
Idaho	8 a.m.	8 p.m.	Polls may open earlier at option of county clerk, but not earlier than 7 a.m. Polls may close earlier if all registered electors in a precinct have voted.
Illinois	6 a.m.	7 p.m.	
Indiana	6 a.m.	6 p.m. local time	
Iowa	7 a.m.	9 p.m.	
Kansas	Between 6 and 7 a.m.	Between 7 and 8 p.m.	Hours may be changed by county election officer, but polls must be open at least 12 consecutive hours between 6 a.m. and 8 p.m.
Kentucky	6 a.m.	6 p.m. (prevailing time)	Persons in line may vote only until 7 p.m.
Louisiana	6 a.m.	8 p.m.	
Maine	Between 6 and 9 a.m.	8 p.m.	Towns with population less than 100 may close after all registered voters have voted.
Maryland	7 a.m.	8 p.m.	
Massachusetts	7 a.m.	8 p.m.	
Michigan	7 a.m.	8 p.m.	
Minnesota	7 a.m.	8 p.m.	Municipalities of less than 500 may establish hours of no later than 10 a.m. to 8 p.m.
Mississippi	7 a.m.	7 p.m.	
Missouri	6 a.m.	7 p.m.	
Montana	7 a.m. noon	8 p.m. 8 p.m.	In precincts of over 200 registered voters. In precincts of less than 200 registered voters, polls may close when all registered electors have voted.
Nebraska	7 a.m. 8 a.m.	7 p.m. (MST) 8 p.m. (CST)	
Nevada	7 a.m.	7 p.m.	
New Hampshire	Varies 11 a.m.	Varies (cities) 7 p.m. (towns)	All polls open not later than 11 a.m. and close not earlier than 7 p.m. In cities, city council shall determine polling hours at least 30 days prior to state elections.
New Jersey	7 a.m.	8 p.m.	
New Mexico	7 a.m.	7 p.m.	
New York	6 a.m.	9 p.m.	
North Carolina	6:30 a.m.	7:30 p.m.	In precincts where voting machines are used, county board of elections may permit closing at 9:30 p.m., provided that all precincts in the county remain open until 9:30 p.m.
North Dakota	Between 7 and 9 a.m.	Between 7 and 9 p.m.	In precincts where less than 75 votes were cast in previous election, polls may open at noon.
Ohio	6:30 a.m.	7:30 p.m.	

See footnotes at end of table.

POLLING HOURS: GENERAL ELECTIONS—Continued

State or other jurisdiction	Polls open	Polls close	Notes on hours (a)
Oklahoma	7 a.m.	7 p.m.	
Oregon	7 a.m.	8 p.m.	
Pennsylvania	7 a.m.	8 p.m.	
Rhode Island	Between 6 a.m. and 9 a.m.	9 p.m.	Opening hours vary across cities and towns.
South Carolina	7 a.m.	7 p.m.	
South Dakota	7 a.m. 8 a.m.	7 p.m. (MST) 8 p.m. (CST)	
Tennessee	No standard opening time	7 p.m. (CST) 8 p.m. (EST)	Must be open at least 10 hours and no more than 13 hours.
Texas................	7 a.m.	7 p.m.	
Utah	7 a.m.	8 p.m.	
Vermont	Between 6 and 10 a.m.	7 p.m.	
Virginia..............	6 a.m.	7 p.m.	
Washington	7 a.m.	8 p.m.	
West Virginia	6:30 a.m.	7:30 p.m.	
Wisconsin.............	7 a.m. Between 7 and 9 a.m.	8 p.m. 8 p.m.	1st, 2nd, 3rd class cities. 4th class cities, towns and villages.
Wyoming	7 a.m.	7 p.m.	
Dist. of Columbia	7 a.m.	8 p.m.	

Sources: State election administration offices, except information on Maine which is from *The Book of the States 1992-93.*
Note: Hours for primary, municipal and special elections may differ from those noted.

(a) In all states, voters standing in line when the polls close are allowed to vote; however, provisions for handling those voters vary across jurisdictions.

Table 5.6
VOTER REGISTRATION INFORMATION

State or other jurisdiction	Mail registration allowed for all voters	Closing date for registration before general election (days)	Persons eligible for absentee registration (a)	Automatic cancellation of registration for failure to vote for _____ years
Alabama	. . .	10	M/O	—
Alaska	★	30	(b)	2
Arizona	★	29	(b)	4 (c)
Arkansas	. .	20	(b)	4
California	★	29	(b)	—
Colorado	. . .	25	B,D,C,E,O,P,R,S,T	2 general elections
Connecticut	★	14 (d)	(b)	—
Delaware	★	3rd Sat. in Oct. (c)	(b)	4
Florida	. . .	30	B,D,E,R,S,T	5 (c)
Georgia	. . .	30	P,C,D,O,A	3 (c)
Hawaii	★	30	(e)	2 elections
Idaho	. . .	17/10 (f)	T	4
Illinois	. . .	29	M/O	6 (c)
Indiana	★	29 (g)	B,D,S,T	4
Iowa	★	10	(b)	4
Kansas	★	14	(b)	2 general elections
Kentucky	★	28	(b)	—
Louisiana	. . .	24	D	—
Maine	★	Election day	(b)	—
Maryland	★	29	(b)	5
Massachusetts	. . .	28	D	—
Michigan	. . .	30	D,T	5
Minnesota	★	Election day (h)	(b)	4
Mississippi	★	30	M/O	4
Missouri	. . .	28	B,D,E,R,S,T	—
Montana	★	30	(b)	1 presidential election
Nebraska	★	(i)	(b)	—
Nevada	★	30	M/O	(j)
New Hampshire	. . .	10	B,D,E,R,S,T	3 elections
New Jersey	★	29	(b)	4
New Mexico	★	28	T	8
New York	★	25	(b)	5 (c)
North Carolina	★	16 (k)	(b)	2 presidential elections
North Dakota			(l)	
Ohio	★	30	(b)	4
Oklahoma	. . .	10	M/O	8
Oregon	★	20	(b)	2 general elections
Pennsylvania	★	30	B,D,M/O,O,P,R,S,T	2
Rhode Island	. . .	30	D	5
South Carolina	★	30	(b)	2 general elections
South Dakota	. . .	15	M/O	4
Tennessee	★	30	(b)	4
Texas	★	30	(b)	—
Utah	★	5 (m)	D,O,T	4
Vermont	★	17	(e)	—
Virginia	. . .	2 (n)	T	4
Washington	★	30	M/O	2 (j)
West Virginia	★	30	(b)	(o)
Wisconsin	★	Election day (m)	(b)	4 (c)
Wyoming	. . .	(h)	(b)	1 general election
Dist. of Columbia	★	30	(b)	2
American Samoa	★	30	M/O	2 general elections
Guam	★	10	(b)	1 general election
Puerto Rico	. . .	50	(b)	1 general election
U.S. Virgin Islands	. . .	30	(p)	2 general elections

Sources: State election administration offices, except Maine which is from *The Book of the States 1992-93.*

Note: In many cases, existing state registration laws will be superceded and/or changed in January 1995 by the National Voter Registration Act. Many states will be considering legislation in response to the NVRA throughout 1994.

Key:
★ — Mail registration allowed
. . . — Mail registration not allowed
— — No automatic cancellation
(a) In this column: B—Absent on business; C—Senior citizen; D—Disabled persons; E—Not absent, but prevented by employment from registering; M/O—No absentee registration except military and oversees citizens as required by federal law; O—Out of state; P—Out of precinct; R—Absent for religious reasons; S—Students; T—Temporarily out of jurisdiction.
(b) All voters. See column on mail registration.
(c) In Arizona and Wisconsin, registration is suspended for failure to vote after four years and after no response to notification. In Florida, suspended after two years and canceled after five years. In Illinois, suspended after four years and canceled after six years. In Georgia, registration is

canceled only if no voting in three years and failure to return card requesting confirmation of registration. In New York, suspended following a five-year period ending with a presidential election.
(d) Closing date differs for primary election. In Connecticut, 1 day; Delaware, 21 days.
(e) Anyone unable to register in person.
(f) With precinct registrar, 17 days before; with county clerk, 10 days.
(g) Absent uniformed services voters and overseas voters may be registered until the final poll list is prepared—up to 10 days before election day.
(h) Minnesota — 21 days or election day; Wyoming — 30 days or primary election day.
(i) 2nd Friday before election day.
(j) Four years if person voted in presidential election.
(k) Business days.
(l) No voter registration.
(m) By mail: Utah, 20 days; Wisconsin, 13 days.
(n) Six-13 days for special elections.
(o) Two general elections and two primary elections.
(p) No one is eligible to register absentee.

Table 5.7
VOTING STATISTICS FOR GUBERNATORIAL ELECTIONS

State	Primary election			General election						
	Republican	Democrat	Total votes	Republican	Percent	Democrat	Percent	Other	Percent	Total votes
Alabama........	122,190	741,710	863,900	633,519	52.1	582,106	47.9	625	0.1	1,216,250
Alaska...........	-----(a)-----									
Arizona..........	372,324	253,057	625,381	492,569	52.4	448,168	47.6	0	0.0	940,737 (b)
Arkansas	86,977	491,146	578,123	295,925	42.5	400,386	57.5	101	0.0	696,412
California........	2,121,728	2,604,853	4,726,581	3,791,904	49.2	3,525,197	45.8	382,366	5.0	7,699,467
Colorado	unopposed	unopposed	0	358,403	35.4	626,032	61.9	26,837	2.7	1,011,272
Connecticut (c)	(d)	131,065	131,065	427,840	37.5	236,641	20.7	476,641	41.8	1,141,122
Delaware ‡......	unopposed	unopposed	0	169,733	70.7	70,236	29.3	0	0.0	239,969
Florida	668,181	1,074,056	1,742,237	1,535,068	43.5	1,995,206	56.5	597	0.0	3,530,871
Georgia..........	118,118	1,052,315 (e)	1,170,433	645,625	44.5	766,662	52.9	37,395	2.6	1,449,682
Hawaii	43,104	202,747	245,851	131,310	38.6	203,491	59.8	5,331	1.6	340,132
Idaho	101,725	unopposed	101,725	101,937	31.8	218,673	68.2	0	0.0	320,610
Illinois..........	767,695	unopposed	767,695	1,653,126	50.7	1,569,217	48.2	35,067	1.1	3,257,410
Indiana *	457,246	390,938	848,184	822,533	36.9	1,382,151	62.0	24,432	1.1	2,229,116
Iowa	unopposed	200,305	200,305	591,852	60.6	379,372	38.9	5,259	0.5	976,483
Kansas	309,560	172,228	481,788	333,589	42.6	380,609	48.6	69,127	8.8	783,325
Kentucky †.......	164,570	506,646	673,519	237,069	42.1	616,558	48.5	20,260	0.2	873,887
Louisiana †	-----(f)-----									
Maine	unopposed	unopposed	0	243,766	46.7	230,038	44.0	48,688	9.3	522,492
Maryland	-----(g)-----									
Massachusetts	446,922	1,052,432	1,499,354	1,175,817	50.2	1,099,878	46.9	67,232	2.9	2,342,927
Michigan	473,223	unopposed	473,223	1,276,134	49.8	1,258,539	49.1	29,890	1.2	2,564,563
Minnesota	342,879	393,571	736,450	895,988	49.6	836,218	46.3	74,571	4.1	1,806,777
Mississippi †	63,561	726,465	790,026	361,500	50.8	338,435	47.6	11,253	1.6	711,188
Missouri ‡	unopposed	460,973	460,973	1,339,531	64.2	724,919	34.8	21,478	1.0	2,085,928
Montana *	99,051	132,276	231,327	-----(g)-----						407,822
Nebraska	190,941	167,109	358,050	288,741	49.2	292,771	49.9	5,030	0.9	586,542
Nevada	76,028	88,297	164,325	95,789	29.9	207,878	64.8	17,076	5.3	320,743
New Hampshire *..	115,142	87,339	204,224	289,170	43.7	206,232	31.2	20,663	4.0	516,065
New Jersey §	387,018	369,323	756,341	838,553	37.2	1,379,937	61.2	35,274	1.6	2,253,764
New Mexico.......	80,971	181,240	262,211	185,692	45.2	224,564	54.6	980	0.2	411,236
New York	unopposed	unopposed	0	865,948	21.3	2,157,087	53.2	1,033,861	25.5	4,056,896
North Carolina ‡ ..	unopposed	506,073	506,073	1,222,338	56.1	957,687	43.9	0	0.0	2,180,025
North Dakota ‡ ...	unopposed	unopposed	0	119,986	40.1	179,094	59.9	0	0.0	299,080
Ohio	unopposed	815,496	815,496	1,938,103	55.7	1,539,416	44.3	131	0.0	3,477,650
Oklahoma	189,450 (e)	543,006 (e)	732,456	297,584	32.7	523,196	57.4	90,534	9.9	911,314
Oregon	288,040	unopposed	288,040	444,646	40.0	508,749	45.7	159,452	14.3	1,112,847
Pennsylvania	589,799	820,959	1,410,758	987,516	32.3	2,065,244	67.7	0	0.0	3,052,760
Rhode Island	10,801	167,916	178,717	92,177	25.8	264,411	74.1	84	0.0	356,672
South Carolina	unopposed	193,900	193,900	528,831	69.5	212,034	27.9	20,100	2.6	760,965
South Dakota	unopposed	unopposed	0	151,198	58.9	105,525	41.1	0	0.0	256,723
Tennessee	172,001	unopposed	172,001	288,904	36.6	479,990	60.8	20,174	2.6	789,068
Texas............	855,231	1,487,260 (e)	2,342,491	1,826,431	46.9	1,925,670	49.5	140,645	3.6	3,892,746
Utah *	(d)	(d)	(d)	321,713	47.0	177,181	23.0	255,753	34.0	965,211
Vermont	44,869	16,930	61,959 (h)	109,540	51.8	97,321	46.0	4,561 (h)	2.2	211,422
Virginia §	401,887	(d)	401,887	890,195	49.8	896,936	50.1	1,947	0.1	1,789,078
Washington *	661,124	481,768	1,142,892	1,086,216	47.8	1,184,315	52.2	0	0.0	2,270,531
West Virginia *	120,519	333,327	453,846	240,399	36.6	368,302	56.0	48,873	7.4	657,565
Wisconsin........	217,723	unopposed	217,723	802,321	58.2	576,280	41.8	1,126	0.1	1,379,727
Wyoming	76,076	43,473	119,549	55,471	34.6	104,638	65.4	0	0.0	160,109

Sources: State election administration offices, except information on Maine which is from *The Book of the States 1992-93.*

Note: Figures are for 1990 except where indicated: ‡ 1988; § 1989; † 1991; * 1992.

(a) Alaska will not have current voting statistics for the gubernatorial election until 1995. The state recognizes two other political parties and one "limited" party.

(b) In 1990, neither major-party candidate won an absolute majority, therefore a runoff election was held on February 26, 1991; the vote shown is for the February runoff.

(c) In 1990, Lowell P. Weicker, A Connecticut Party candidate, polled 460,576 votes (40.4 percent of the total vote) and won the election with a 32,736 plurality.

(d) Candidate nominated by convention.

(e) Total shown is for first primary. Total votes for runoff elections: Georgia, 956,027; Oklahoma Republican, 186,241; Oklahoma Democratic, 479,849; Texas, 1,122,734.

(f) Louisiana has an open primary which requires all candidates, regardless of party affiliation, to appear on a single ballot. If a candidate receives over 50 percent of the vote in the primary, he is elected to the office. If no candidate receives a majority vote, then a single election is held between the two candidates receiving the most votes.

(g) Information is not available.

(h) Includes Libertarian Party (major party) candidate for governor.

Table 5.8
VOTER TURNOUT IN NON-PRESIDENTIAL ELECTION YEARS: 1982, 1986 AND 1990
(In thousands)

	1990			1986			1982		
State	Voting age population (a)	Number registered (b)	Number voting (c)	Voting age population (a)	Number registered (b)	Number voting (c)	Voting age population (a)	Number registered (b)	Number voting (c)
Alabama	3,060	2,375	1,216	3,010	2,362	1,236	2,812	2,136	1,128
Alaska	381	300	198	377	292	183	309	266	199
Arizona	2,591*	1,860	1,095	2,241*	1,698	890	2,090*	1,141	743
Arkansas	1,780	1,219	696	1,761	1,189	695	1,650	1,116	789
California	21,709	13,478	7,699	20,878	12,834	7,444	18,277	11,559	7,876
Colorado	2,475	1,922	1,022	2,489	1,822	1,061	2,225	1,456	956
Connecticut	2,516	1,701	1,141	2,440	1,671	994	2,353	1,648	1,084
Delaware	514	299	180	490	296	161	443	286	191
Florida	10,150	6,031	3,531	9,614	5,631	3,430	8,169	4,866	2,689
Georgia	4,751	2,773	1,450	4,665	2,576	1,225	4,040	2,317	1,169
Hawaii	854	453	350	824	420	334	716	405	312
Idaho	698	540	321	693	550	387	668	541	327
Illinois	8,682	6,032	3,257	8,550	6,004	3,144	8,346	5,965	3,691 (d)
Indiana	4,008	2,765	1,513	4,032	2,878	1,556	3,938	2,937	1,817
Iowa	2,100	1,580	984	2,068	1,622	911	2,094	1,586	1,038
Kansas	1,864	1,205	805	1,829	1,173	841	1,759	1,186	763
Kentucky	2,707*	1,854	916	2,685*	1,999	677	2,633*	1,827	700
Louisiana	2,994	2,123	1,396	3,082	2,179	1,370	3,016	1,965	(e)
Maine	931	872	522	893	790	427	831	766	460
Maryland	3,622	2,135	1,111	3,491	2,140	1,113	3,190	1,968	1,139
Massachusetts	4,598	3,214	2,343	4,535	3,006	1,684	4,394	3,027	2,051
Michigan	6,870	5,892	2,565	6,791	5,791	2,397	6,554	5,625	3,040
Minnesota	3,249	2,871	1,808	3,161	2,615	1,416	2,988	2,668	1,805
Mississippi	1,877	1,593	369	1,867	1,652	524	1,745	1,508	645
Missouri	3,893	2,748	1,353	3,821	2,769	1,477	3,640	2,749	1,544
Montana	577	436	327	587	444	326	579	446	328
Nebraska	1,181	891	594	1,167	850	564	1,144	832	548
Nevada	858	516	321	780	368	262	661	322	240
New Hampshire	861	659	295	823	551	251	697	462	285
New Jersey	5,986	3,718	1,938	5,943	3,777	1,554	5,544	3,681	2,194
New Mexico	1,091	658	411	1,101	633	395	936	583	407
New York	13,582	8,202	4,057	13,480	8,071	4,294	13,153	7,635	5,222
North Carolina	5,071	3,348	2,071	4,913	3,081	1,591	4,417	2,675	1,321
North Dakota	473	(f)	240	464	(f)	295	462	(f)	273
Ohio	8,119	5,834	3,478	7,970	5,987	3,121	7,793	5,674	3,395
Oklahoma	2,337	2,011	911	2,404	2,018	910	2,299	1,614	883
Oregon	2,123	1,477	1,113	2,441	1,502	1,060	1,944	1,517	1,042
Pennsylvania	9,221	5,659	3,053	9,060	5,847	3,388	8,883	5,703	3,684
Rhode Island	771	537	364	764	525	323	726	534	343
South Carolina	2,620	1,360	794	2,475	1,304	771	2,161	1,231	688
South Dakota	479	420	260	498	428	296	485	427	279
Tennessee	3,660*	2,460	789 (g)	3,517*	2,446	1,210 (g)	3,383*	2,273	1,260
Texas	12,156	7,701	3,893	12,270	7,287	3,441	10,793	6,415	3,191
Utah	1,084	781	458	1,078	763	445	986	749	537
Vermont	419	350	215	393	328	199	379	316	169
Virginia	4,755	2,738	1,153	4,544	2,610	1,043	4,078	2,234	1,415
Washington	3,597	2,225	1,313	3,417	2,230	1,337	3,154	2,106	1,368
West Virginia	1,339	885	426	1,398	946	396	1,419	948	565
Wisconsin	3,617	(f)	1,380	3,563	(f)	1,527	3,464	(f)	1,580
Wyoming	329	222	160	349	235	235	354	230	169

Sources: State election administration offices and where indicated (*) U.S. Department of Commerce, Bureau of the Census, *State Population Estimates By Age and Sex: 1980-1992*, except information on Maine which is from *The Book of the States 1992-93.*

(a) Estimated as of November 1 of the year indicated. Includes armed forces stationed in each state, aliens and institutional population but does not include Americans abroad.

(b) Registration figures include (nationally) about 10 percent component of those who have died or moved but are still maintained on the voter registration rolls.

(c) Number represents highest total vote cast in general election for either senatorial, gubernatorial or combined U.S. House of Representatives for that year, except where noted.

(d) Total votes for largest race—secretary of state.

(e) Under Louisiana's election law, candidates of all parties run together on a single non-partisan ballot in September. If no candidate wins a majority of the vote, the top two finishers, regardless of party, oppose each other in a November runoff. In 1982, the congressional incumbents were reelected in the September race.

(f) No required statewide registration.

(g) In Tennessee, refers to the gubernatorial election.

Table 5.9
VOTER TURNOUT FOR PRESIDENTIAL ELECTIONS: 1984, 1988 AND 1992
(In thousands)

State	1992 Voting age population (a)	1992 Number registered	1992 Number voting (b)	1988 Voting age population (a)	1988 Number registered	1988 Number voting (b)	1984 Voting age population (a)	1984 Number registered	1984 Number voting (b)
Alabama	2,999	2,380	1,687	3,010	2,380	1,378	2,892	2,343	1,442
Alaska	404	315	261	370	293	203	350	305	213
Arizona	2,749	1,965	1,516	2,605	1,798	1,204	2,268	1,463	1,051
Arkansas	1,768	1,318	950	1,761	1,203	828	1,607	1,268	884
California	20,864	15,101	11,374	20,875	14,004	9,887	19,181	13,074	9,505
Colorado	2,501	2,002	1,569	2,489	2,030	1,372	2,353	1,621	1,295
Connecticut	2,535	1,962	1,616	2,492	1,795	1,443	2,401	1,809	1,467
Delaware	525	340	290	490	318	250	459	314	255
Florida	10,586	6,542	5,439	9,614	6,047	4,302	8,665	5,547	4,180
Georgia	4,750	3,177	2,321	4,665	2,941	1,810	4,231	2,372	1,776
Hawaii	889	465	382	824	444	354	758	419	336
Idaho	740	611	482	701	572	409	686	582	411
Illinois	8,568	6,600	5,164	8,550	6,357	4,559	8,438	6,470	4,819
Indiana	4,108	3,180	2,347	4,068	2,866	2,169	3,993	3,050	2,233
Iowa	2,075	1,704	1,355	2,068	1,690	1,226	2,120	1,729	1,320
Kansas	1,881	1,366	1,162	1,829	1,266	993	1,798	1,291	1,022
Kentucky	2,779	2,076	1,493	2,746	2,026	1,323	2,697	2,023	1,369
Louisiana	2,992	2,247	1,790	3,010	2,232	1,628	3,069	2,212	1,707
Maine	944	975	679	893	855	555	854	811	553
Maryland	3,719	2,463	1,985	3,491	2,310	1,714	3,260	2,253	1,676
Massachusetts	4,607	3,346	2,774	4,535	3,275	2,633	4,443	3,254	2,559
Michigan	6,884	6,147	4,275	6,791	5,953	3,669	6,566	5,889	3,802
Minnesota	3,278	2,711	2,356	3,161	2,917	2,097	3,058	2,893	2,084
Mississippi	1,826	1,640	1,008	1,867	1,596	932	1,802	1,670	941
Missouri	3,858	3,057	2,391	3,821	2,942	2,094	3,708	2,969	2,123
Montana	586	530	418	586	506	379	591	527	395
Nebraska	1,167	951	744	1,167	899	661	1,172	903	652
Nevada	1,013	650	506	780	445	350	691	356	287
New Hampshire	830	661	545	823	650	451	734	544	389
New Jersey	5,943	4,060	3,344	5,943	4,011	3,100	5,687	4,073	3,218
New Mexico	1,150	707	591	1,101	675	521	1,002	651	514
New York	13,609	9,196	7,069	13,480	8,612	6,486	13,301	9,044	6,807
North Carolina	5,217	3,817	2,612	4,913	3,432	2,134	4,593	3,271	2,715
North Dakota	463	(c)	315	483	(c)	309	471	(c)	324
Ohio	8,146	6,358	5,043	7,970	6,323	4,394	7,841	6,358	4,548
Oklahoma	2,328	2,302	1,390	2,404	2,199	1,171	2,408	1,950	1,256
Oregon	2,210	1,775	1,461	2,044	1,528	1,202	1,962	1,609	1,227
Pennsylvania	9,129	5,993	4,961	9,060	5,876	4,536	8,975	6,194	4,845
Rhode Island	776	554	453	764	549	405	735	542	410
South Carolina	2,566	1,537	1,236	2,565	1,447	1,047	2,417	1,404	1,019
South Dakota	500	448	336	507	440	313	485	443	318
Tennessee	3,861	2,726	1,982	3,598	2,417	1,636	3,450	2,580	1,712
Texas	12,524	8,440	6,154	12,270	8,202	5,427	11,436	7,900	5,398
Utah	1,159	965	780	1,078	807	662	1,023	840	642
Vermont	420	383	293	407	348	247	392	322	235
Virginia	4,842	3,054	2,583	4,544	2,877	2,192	4,235	2,552	2,147
Washington	3,818	2,814	2,324	3,417	2,499	1,865	3,228	2,458	1,884
West Virginia	1,350	956	684	1,398	969	653	1,433	1,025	741
Wisconsin	3,677	(d)	2,531	3,536	(d)	2,192	3,485	(d)	2,112
Wyoming	322	235	201	351	226	177	354	240	189

Sources: 1988 and 1984 data provided by Committee for the Study of the American Electorate, with update by state election administration offices. 1992 base data provided by state election offices, as available; remaining data provided by Committee for the Study of the American Electorate.

(a) Estimated population, 18 years old and over. Includes armed forces in each state, aliens, and institutional population.
(b) Number voting is number of ballots cast in presidential race.
(c) Information not available.
(d) No statewide registration required. Excluded from totals for persons registered.

Financing State and Local Elections: Recent Developments

Campaign finance reform is experiencing a great resurgence.
Contribution limits, public financing and disclosure laws
are among the steps that states are taking to prevent misuse.

by Frederick M. Herrmann and Ronald D. Michaelson

Of the more than half million elected officials who run for office in the United States, the Federal Election Campaign Act covers only one-tenth of 1 percent. The rest, ranging from governor to school board member, are subject to regulation by 50 different sets of state laws as well as numerous local ones. No two of these jurisdictions are exactly alike in how they monitor such activity. Consequently, it is a daunting task to comprehend how our states and localities regulate the financing of political campaigns.

Although state and local candidates spend millions of dollars seeking office, most observers of the political scene concentrate on the national level. A prime reason for this federal fixation is that it is much easier to study one national system than 50 state and numerous local ones. While significant national reform of campaign finance laws has stagnated since the period just after Watergate, many state and some local governments have been experimenting recently to strengthen their campaign finance regulations. Indeed, many of the most important regulatory innovations have occurred in these "laboratories for reform."[1]

Today, campaign finance reform at the state and local levels may be experiencing its greatest resurgence since the mid-1970s. Real and potential scandals across the nation increase public cynicism with the way the electoral process is financed. The public's pressure to change "business as usual" is leading state and local lawmakers to experiment with old and new methods for more open and competitive contests that will prevent misused campaign dollars from debasing democracy.

Limiting Contributions

Contribution limits are one of the most popular tools of campaign finance regulation. Most states use them in one form or another. Colorado, Florida, Illinois, Kansas, Kentucky, Massachusetts, Missouri, Nebraska, New Jersey, Oregon, South Dakota and Wisconsin are considering introducing such limits or modifying existing schemes. In addition, a new Arizona law requires a candidate who exceeds the contribution limit on personal monies to give written notice within 24 hours to all other candidates for the same office (and to the filing officer of that jurisdiction). The other candidates may enjoy a temporary lifting of the limit until they can match the higher amount. The law also allows those in compliance to receive an additional $500 for each day the notice is delinquent.[2] A new law in the District of Columbia greatly reduces its contribution limits,[3] while the Los Angeles City Charter has established an aggregate limit per contributor for giving to all candidates in an election.[4]

Public Financing

Public finance regulation continues as a means for change and experimentation. States considering public financing proposals for statewide office and/or the legislature are: Connecticut, Illinois, Massachusetts, Missouri

Frederick M. Herrmann is executive director of the New Jersey Election Law Enforcement Commission, and Ronald D. Michaelson is executive director of the Illinois Board of Elections.

and Nebraska. In one proposed experiment, a Michigan bill would modify the state public funding law by not matching with taxpayer dollars any contributions a candidate receives from outside the state or from political action committees (PACs), independent committees and political party committees. It also would raise the amount of the taxpayer checkoff that funds the program, simplify the method for establishing candidate spending limits and establish a new standard for returning leftover dollars in the public financing fund to the general treasury.[5] Minnesota (in addition to its existing program) now provides first-time, publicly financed candidates with a 10 percent increase in their spending limits and allows a candidate whose opponent refuses to participate in the program to receive the opponent's share of the public funds.[6]

A Wisconsin bill would raise spending limits and restore an inflationary adjustment mechanism that was repealed in 1987.[7] It also would allow challengers to spend more than incumbents, permit candidates to exceed their spending limits to the extent that their opponents receive support from independent expenditures, prevent out-of-state and bundled contributions from being matched, reduce the amount of public money a candidate may receive by the bundled funds accepted and restrict the amount of money that may be carried over to the next election.

A Florida Supreme Court decision held as violative of the First Amendment a law requiring various political committees to pay a 1.5 percent assessment of their contributions to a fund to help support the races of gubernatorial and cabinet-position candidates.[8] A complaint filed in that state challenges the law that automatically provides supplementary financing from general revenues once the public financing fund is depleted.

In addition to contribution limits and public financing, the imposition of various fund-raising limits also is an active area. For example, many states are moving to restrict the time frame in which a candidate may accept donations. Alabama, Arkansas, Colorado, Florida, Minnesota, New Mexico, Washington and Wisconsin are reviewing bans on accepting money during legislative sessions or in a specified period before or after an election. A new Minnesota statute prohibits legislative caucus fundraising when the Legislature is in session.[9]

Many states are busy with proposals to prevent or restrict corporate, union and PAC contributions. Legislation being considered in Kansas would limit candidates to receiving no more than 30 percent of their contributions from PACs.[10] Kentucky law limits a candidate's total PAC contributions to 35 percent of receipts or $5,000, whichever is larger. Leftover PAC money carried into the next election would not count against the limit.[11] An Oregon voter initiative would prohibit all contributions from corporations, professional corporations, nonprofit corporations and labor organizations.[12] In Washington, a new law restricts out-of-state contributions from PACs, unions and corporations and requires an annual re-authorization of employee checkoffs to their companies' PACs.[13]

A growing concern in many states is the fund-raising relationship between public officials and the private entities they regulate or with which they have contact. The Georgia Supreme Court has upheld a law prohibiting an insurer from making a campaign contribution to a candidate for the office of commissioner of insurance,[14] while a bill in Kansas would prohibit candidates for that same office from accepting campaign contributions from insurance companies or agents.[15] In Illinois, a bill would prohibit a person from making aggregate contributions exceeding $2,500 in a reporting period to one or more political committees of an executive branch officer with whom the person has done business during the most recent reporting period or any of the three previous ones. Contributions in excess of this limit would revert to the state.[16] Another piece of Illinois legislation under consideration would make it unlawful for a person having a state contract or a pecuniary interest in one to contribute more than $1,000 to any constitutional officer or legislator,[17] and a New Mexico law bans candidates and officeholders from soliciting contributions from any industry their office regulates.[18]

Table A
DISTRIBUTION OF POLITICAL ACTION COMMITTEE (PAC) FUNDS IN SELECTED STATES
1987 OR 1988 STATE LEGISLATIVE ELECTIONS

Average Dollar ($) and Percent Amounts (a)

State	Incumbents		Challengers		Open Seats		Totals
California	217,020	(73)	28,407	(70)	80,809	(6)	122,925
	39%		13%		23%		26%
Idaho	4,367	(32)	863	(31)	2,308	(20)	2,362
	57%		12%		28%		31%
Minnesota	6,021	(118)	1,204	(117)	4,583	(16)	3,684
	24%		8%		18%		16%
Missouri	5,343	(54)	490	(51)	2,148	(41)	2,750
	21%		6%		9%		12%
Montana	904	(53)	283	(59)	512	(37)	561
	28%		17%		9%		18%
North Carolina	6,729	(65)	1,890	(65)	2,325	(10)	4,168
	49%		16%		16%		31%
New Jersey	19,671	(65)	7,657	(74)	12,446	(12)	13,209
	28%		15%		15%		21%
Oregon	30,724	(37)	9,890	(37)	39,064	(22)	24,605
	63%		21%		48%		43%
Pennsylvania	16,559	(107)	1,626	(110)	8,513	(44)	8,909
	53%		19%		29%		35%
Washington	14,688	(73)	4,409	(73)	13,571	(24)	9,942
	37%		31%		26%		33%
Wisconsin	4,177	(59)	836	(60)	3,080	(21)	2,581
	22%		5%		14%		13%

Source: William E. Cassie, Joel A. Thompson and Malcolm E. Jewell, "The Pattern of PAC Contributions in Legislative Elections: An Eleven State Analysis," Paper delivered at the Annual Meeting of the American Political Science Association, 1992, Chicago, (as it appears in *State Trends & Forecasts: Campaign Finance Reform*, The Council of State Governments, 1993).
(a) Dollar amounts represent the average total PAC contribution per candidate. Figures in parentheses are the total number of candidates in the category. The percentages represent the PAC funds as a proportion of the candidates' total revenues.

Disclosure

Many jurisdictions are moving to enhance disclosure. Uniformity in reporting is an important innovation. A Florida bill,[19] a North Dakota law[20] and a Virginia law require various committees to file on the same dates,[21] and an Arkansas law mandates equal reporting thresholds for state, district, county and municipal candidate committees.[22] Acts in both Kentucky and Maine, and bills in Nevada and West Virginia, increase reporting by reducing the thresholds at which committees must itemize their contributors. Better disclosure of PAC activity is furthered by an Arkansas bill that would require more frequent reporting by PACs[23] and a law in South Dakota that requires certain committees to report all PAC contributions by eliminating the threshold for itemization.[24] In similar fashion, a New Jersey statute establishes a PAC registration requirement that calls for the name of the PAC, a descriptive statement giving the name, address, occupation and employer of each person organizing or controlling the PAC and the general category of interests the PAC represents.[25]

A number of states are adding to their reporting requirements. An Alabama bill would require a political committee receiving a contribution from another political committee to report to the secretary of state within 10 days,[26]

New Jersey law adds a 48-hour requirement for last-minute expenditures by a PAC or a political committee,[27] and both Idaho and Oregon bills would add pre-election reports.[28] In New Mexico, a statute requires more pre-election reporting in election years and annual reporting in non-election years,[29] while Nebraska now requires non-election year reporting and candidates and political committees to report receipts and expenditures on a cumulative basis for the primary and general elections (instead of separately).[30] Lobbyists and political committees that solicit contributions of more than $5,000 a year for candidates and legislative caucuses must file special reports under a new Minnesota law,[31] and Rhode Island now requires state vendors who provide goods or services worth more than $5,000 to report contributions of $250 or more to candidates and political parties.[32] A Nebraska Accountability and Disclosure Commission advisory opinion determined that an out-of-state entity has to file campaign finance reports because: 1) it had lobbyists registered with the legislative clerk for the previous seven years, 2) the substance of its in-state activities was part of its ordinary business, and 3) its participation in elections, ballot questions and lobbying activities constituted a continuous rather than an isolated presence in the state.

Various jurisdictions have been paying attention to the disclosure of occupation and employer information about contributors. A Florida bill, a New Jersey law, a New Mexico law and a District of Columbia law require reporting this kind of data. In Maine, contributors to political party committees must now report their occupations and places of business; and in Virginia, a new act has lowered the reporting threshold for similar information.[33] Meanwhile, the governor of Connecticut vetoed legislation to require the disclosure of the occupation, employer and labor union affiliation of contributors in excess of $150 to any candidate or PAC. The basis of the veto was the labor union affiliation disclosure, which the governor claimed impermissibly burdened the rights of union members to free association under the First Amendment.[34] In related legislation, Arizona requires that both the

chair and treasurer of a political committee list their occupations and employers.

Technology and Disclosure

The use of technology to enhance disclosure is an exciting trend that is probably only in its infancy. A bill in Florida and a law in Idaho allow reporting by fax machines.[35] At the same time, a Wyoming statute allows reports to be filed by fax provided an original copy is mailed the same day a transmission is made.[36] The Connecticut Legislature has approved a bond authorization to fund the purchase of computer hardware for campaign disclosure records on file with the secretary of state, while a Michigan bill requires the secretary of state to establish standards for computerization of campaign finance records.[37]

Surplus Funds

One of the major problem areas for many states is how to use and dispose of surplus campaign funds. Common approaches include a clear ban on personal use with guidelines allowing the money to be given to other candidates, political parties and charities. Some states specify that unused money may be returned to contributors or even applied to the ordinary expenses of holding public office. Alabama, Arizona, Florida, Illinois, Iowa, Kentucky, New Jersey and Oregon are considering or have enacted such initiatives.

Besides the traditional approaches for regulating surplus funds, some states are looking at more innovative solutions. For example, an Alabama bill would require a candidate who does not qualify for the next election to return money to contributors on a pro-rata basis after the deduction of verifiable expenses,[38] a bill in Florida would mandate that any surplus funds exceeding a statutory cap must be given to a candidate's political party,[39] and an Arkansas act directs candidates to disclose their method of disposing surplus funds after an election.[40] An Illinois bill would provide that a political committee may use campaign funds only for personnel, services, materials, facilities or other things of value purchased to further the candidate's nomination or election to office;[41] and a Kentucky law limits the

Table B
USE OF SURPLUS FUNDS BY CANDIDATES AFTER AN ELECTION

Types of Use	Number of States
Transfer to a political organization	4
Transfer to a political committee	6
Reimburse candidate for candidate's contributions	7
Pay officeholder expenses	13
Transfer to the state's general revenue fund or other state funds	13
Transfer to another candidate's committee	14
Spend on a future campaign	16
Transfer to a political party committee	25
Return to contributors	28
Give to charity	29

Sources: Compiled from Edward D. Feigenbaum and James A. Palmer, *Campaign Finance Law 92*, Washington, D.C.: National Clearinghouse on Election Administration, Federal Election Commission, 1992; and Ronald D. Michaelson, *1992 Campaign Finance Update: Legislation and Litigation in the 50 States, the District of Columbia and the Federal Government*, prepared for the Council on Governmental Ethics Laws Annual Conference, September 1992, (as the information appears in *State Trends & Forecasts: Campaign Finance Reform*, The Council of State Governments, 1993).

use of leftover campaign money for campaign purposes instead of broader "political" purposes.[42] Laws in Minnesota and Washington ban the transfer of campaign funds from one candidate to another, and the secretary of state's office in Michigan ruled that a candidate committee may only make expenditures that assist the election of the candidate and may not make contributions to other candidates.

Enforcement

Many states are moving toward tougher penalties and enhanced enforcement. Alabama, Arizona, Arkansas, Connecticut, Florida, Idaho, Indiana, Massachusetts, New Mexico, New Jersey and West Virginia are at various stages of increasing or adding penalties for late, incorrect, false or incomplete reporting. One Florida bill would require a candidate to provide a written statement that certain fines have been paid before qualifying for candidacy,[43] and a second bill would prohibit a political party committee that violates candidate contribution limits from giving to candidates during the next election cycle. An Alabama bill would direct the attorney general or district attorney to remove from the ballot or office a candidate who fails to file or pay a fine.[44]

Initiative, Referendum and Recall

The initiative, referendum and recall process has led to disclosure experimentation in some states and significant problems in others. An act in Wyoming increases the financial information reporting for any committee formed to support or oppose an initiative or referendum question to include: the total amount expended to obtain petition signatures, the number of people paid, the rate paid per signature and the period of time during which the signatures were obtained.[45] In Arizona, a law extends the initiative, ballot question and referendum financial disclosure statutes to committees operating at the district, county and municipal levels as well as the state level. This enactment also lowers reporting thresholds and expands the definitions of such committees to include people and entities outside the state.[46] A Mississippi bill would create a constitutional initiative process but does not address how ballot committees would disclose financial activity.

New Jersey voters approved a recall ballot question that has raised an important campaign financing question. Should an officeholder who is the target of a recall drive be subject to the contribution limits that affect all other candidates? If so, an unbalanced playing field

Table C
AGENCY EXPENDITURE BUDGETS (AS OF 1992)

Jurisdiction/Agency	Actual Expenditures					1992 Annual Budget
	Fiscal Year 1987	Fiscal Year 1988	Fiscal Year 1989	Fiscal Year 1990	Fiscal Year 1991	
Alaska						
Alaska Public Offices Commission	562,600	571,700	595,400	726,700	704,300	607,700
Arkansas						
Arkansas Ethics Commission	(a)	(a)	(a)	(a)	51,915 (a)	271,685
California						
California Fair Political Practices Commission	4,700,000	5,100,000	5,400,000	5,700,000	6,000,000	5,189,000
Los Angeles City Ethics Commission	. . .	. . .	. . .	. . .	115,000	1,675,000
Connecticut						
Connecticut State Elections Enforcement Commission	262,637	338,852	377,841	416,486	411,240	431,812
Florida						
Florida Department of State, Division of Elections	1,531,239	1,775,398	2,674,036	2,782,698	3,187,769	4,414,089
Georgia						
State Ethics Commission	150,014	192,059	191,956	171,219	193,212	179,601
Hawaii						
Campaign Spending Commission	26,001	34,120	29,059	29,254	31,720	28,844
Idaho						
Secretary of State's Office	52,000	54,000	56,000	58,800	61,700	64,800
Illinois						
Illinois State Board of Elections	4,535,000	4,335,000	5,157,000	4,952,943	5,645,957	5,192,798
Indiana						
Indiana State Elections Board	. . .	. . .	. . .	280,000	209,000	318,481
Iowa						
Iowa Campaign Finance Disclosure Commission	. . .	. . .	. . .	235,305	260,110	264,927
Kansas						
Commission on Governmental Standards & Conduct	176,765	187,717	198,114	232,386	248,934	322,069
Kentucky						
Kentucky Registry of Election Finance	296,300	309,800	369,300	374,500	618,500	589,400
Louisiana						
Louisiana Ethics Administration Program	420,322	432,858	404,417	409,000	647,318	676,494
Maine						
Commission on Governmental Ethics & Election Practices	12,265	10,345	46,287	61,868	96,702	88,082
Massachusetts						
Office of Campaign and Political Finance	424,000	424,000	424,000	438,750	434,528	434,528
Michigan						
Michigan Department of State, Bureau of Elections	1,650,000	1,920,000	1,900,000	2,120,000	1,950,00	2,400,000

Table C
AGENCY EXPENDITURE BUDGETS (AS OF 1992)

Jurisdiction/Agency	Actual Expenditures					
	Fiscal Year 1987	Fiscal Year 1988	Fiscal Year 1989	Fiscal Year 1990	Fiscal Year 1991	1992 Annual Budget
Minnesota						
Minnesota Ethical Practices Board	221,076	233,336	233,955	292,571	322,047	346,400
Mississippi						
Secretary of State's Office	. . .	. . .	. . .	. . .	4,880,452	4,670,000 (b)
Montana						
Commissioner of Political Practices	132,442	83,771	101,505	106,111	113,433	168,483 (c)
Nebraska						
Nebraska Accountability & Disclosure Commission	191,051	223,575	214,176	264,565	332,263	305,084
New Jersey						
New Jersey Election Law Enforcement Commission	1,059,000	1,127,000	1,235,000	1,208,000	1,062,000	965,000
New York						
New York City Campaign Finance Board	. . .	. . .	604,652	2,407,553	671,910	4,321,000
New York State Board of Elections	2,315,300	2,352,700	3,578,885	2,461,196	2,823,150	2,450,100
North Dakota						
Secretary of State's Office	1,008,211	1,016,307	1,016,307	1,039,275	855,405	1,046,140
Ohio						
Secretary of State's Office	6,436,368	5,910,411	6,793,736	7,743,138	7,850,335	7,626,062
Oklahoma						
Ethics Commission of the State of Oklahoma	93,513	114,071	188,783	236,106	235,784	362,519
Rhode Island						
Rhode Island State Board of Elections	1,900,000	1,800,000	2,000,000	1,600,000	2,103,000	1,800,000
Tennessee						
Registry of Election Finance	. . .	. . .	. . .	118,616	238,226	223,871
Texas						
Texas Ethics Commission	(d)	(d)	(d)	(d)	(d)	(d)
Utah						
Lieutenant Governor's Office	429,000	295,000	475,000	408,501	571,122	500,000
Vermont						
Secretary of State's Office	1,249,564	1,325,327	1,583,235	1,552,853	1,987,880	2,160,969
Washington						
Washington State Public Disclosure Commission	483,514	575,628	665,015	642,278	705,438	925,868
West Virginia						
Secretary of State's Office	857,856	719,802	719,800	757,105	802,524	882,018

Source: The Council of State Governments, COGEL Blue Book, Ninth Edition, 1993.
(a) Agency came into existence in May 1991. Fiscal year 1991 expenditures are for a partial year ($260,090 appropriated).
(b) Includes corporations, securities regulation and public lands.
(c) Includes biennial appropriations of legal, court costs and $13,530 (audit, part-time help) the unspent portions of which carry over to 1992-93.
(d) Texas Ethics Commission began operations in January 1992.

would result because the First Amendment prohibits contribution limits for a recall ballot question committee. Complicating the problem is the recall question's setup. In addition to deciding whether or not to recall an official, voters must choose a candidate to fill the created vacancy. This nuance might allow the imposition of contribution limits for recall ballot question committees.

Fiscal Realities

It shouldn't be suprising that there is continuing concern in the states about agency budgets and the use of filing fees to fill revenue gaps. An Alabama bill would require certain political committees to pay an annual fee to the secretary of state, who would then deposit the money into the state general fund;[47] and a bill in Alaska would direct state and local candidates and groups to pay 3 percent of the funds they collect in contributions to support the state's Public Offices Commission.[48] In New Jersey, a bill would provide for PAC and political party filing fees based on amounts raised and spent and for candidate filing fees based on the office sought. These fees would be used as a supplement to the appropriation of the Election Law Enforcement Commission.[49] The Oklahoma Supreme Court has declined to assume original jurisdiction over the Ethics Commission's action challenging the constitutionality of a legislative resolution and related statutes that cut the agency's budget while expanding its jurisdiction. Under the constitution of that state, the commission is guaranteed "an annual appropriation sufficient to . . . perform its duties."[50]

In Michigan, a bill would create a computerization fund and require the collection of filing fees from PACs and candidates to finance it. The PAC fee would be based on the total contributions to, and independent expenditures made on behalf of, all candidates in the previous two-year cycle. It would be paid each calendar year when the first report is filed. Candidate committees pay a flat rate of $100 when a statement of organization is filed.[51]

Administration

The restructuring of the governmental en-

tities and processes involved in the regulation of campaign financing is an important development in some of the states. An Arkansas bill would transfer all ethics and disclosure filings from the secretary of state to the ethics commission,[52] while a Wisconsin bill would transfer jurisdiction over lobbyists' campaign contributions from the State Ethics Board to the State Elections Board.[53] An act in Missouri moves the secretary of state's campaign finance division to the newly created State Ethics Commission. Administration of the campaign finance disclosure law still is handled by the secretary of state, but enforcement falls to the new commission.[54] Meanwhile, the Oklahoma Supreme Court has ruled that under the state constitution the Legislature could modify but not rewrite the campaign finance rules of the State Ethics Commission.[55]

An interesting trend seen in many states is decreasing regulation in selected areas. A bill in Arkansas would grant a $1,000 exemption from the contribution limit for donations covering the cost of hosting a fund-raiser;[56] a Florida bill would provide that contribution limit requirements do not cover a political party's polling and research services, technical assistance and voter mobilization efforts if they are equally available to all candidates of the party;[57] and an Iowa law increases the contribution limit for a political party giving to a candidate to 10 times the limit for other categories of contributors. Arkansas now eases the frequency of reporting requirements for all candidates,[58] and Virginia exempts all political party committees from filing a first post-election report as candidates are required to do.[59] An Iowa law raises the candidate filing threshold from $200 to $500,[60] and a bill in Illinois would raise the threshold for determining what minimum contribution or expenditure is necessary to constitute a political committee from $1,000 to $2,000.[61] New Jersey has enacted a law that raises the reporting threshold for contributor disclosure from more than $100 to more than $200 and for last-minute contributors on 48-hour notices from more than $250 to more than $500. These and other thresholds in the law are to be adjusted for inflation every four years.[62]

Other Important Activities

Finally, there are a number of proposals and actions that defy easy categorization but are important. An Alabama bill would prohibit a lobbyist from serving as the chairperson or treasurer of a campaign for a state or local candidate,[63] a law in Arkansas allows a former candidate with a campaign debt to raise funds to retire the debt[64] and a Kansas bill would give a tax credit of up to $100 per year to individuals who make campaign contributions to candidates for state office.[65] In Kentucky, a law prohibits legislators or legislative leaders from forming PACs,[66] while in New Jersey a new enactment creates four legislative leadership committees for the party leaders in both houses. These committees have the same ability to raise and spend money as New Jersey's two state political party committees. Unlike candidate committees that are rigidly restricted in raising and spending funds, the leadership committees may accept contributions as high as $25,000 and have no limits on their expenditures in support of candidates.[67]

Both a voter initiative in Oregon and a bill in West Virginia propose voluntary expenditure limits for candidates.[68] The West Virginia measure couples the limits with higher filing fees for those who do not accept them.[69] Washington state has passed a voter initiative restricting legislators' free mailings, and Wisconsin has a bill that would prohibit a PAC from contributing to another PAC. A Tennessee law tightens the statute on the inspection of campaign finance disclosure statements. People inspecting reports must notify candidates within three business days (instead of 30) of their home and business telephone numbers and their driver's license numbers or other appropriate identification, as well as their names and addresses.[70]

Conclusion

State and local governments across the United States have continued with their experimentation in campaign finance reform. Some of their ideas and innovations will be crucial to preserving and enhancing our democratic form of government. Many jurisdictions, however, still do not have an adequate disclosure of campaign funding sources, thus inhibiting the public from being able to judge the extent of influence on its elected officials. Moreover, the campaign finance systems in most states still foster non-competitive environments in which many experts have observed that "an incumbent has a better chance of dying than of losing." As regrettable as the remaining loopholes in campaign finance laws across the country are, the inability of some state and local governmental ethics agencies to administer and enforce workable and equitable laws is equally of concern.

It should be heartening that there is an emerging national consciousness that thinks governmental bodies charged with oversight of campaign finance laws must be strengthened. Two recent studies, one by the Center for Responsive Politics and the other by The Council of State Governments (CSG), make the points that "an independent and effective campaign finance regulatory agency [in each state is central] to the integrity of the campaign finance laws and public confidence in the electoral process" and that "reporting and disclosure is meaningless unless designated state agencies can do their jobs and prosecute campaign finance violators."[71] Both studies agree that the governmental bodies that oversee campaign finance must be given autonomy, funding and enforcement authority. The situation of "insufficient budgets, limited enforcement authority and partisan political pressures" must be changed.[72]

Not all governmental entities that regulate campaign financing have sufficient autonomy. According to the CSG study, "reformers prefer the independent agency model" over the use of a department headed by a partisan official.[73] However, among the bodies and officials that administer and enforce state campaign finance laws, only 31 are regulatory commissions while 23 are secretaries of state, one is an attorney general and one is a lieutenant governor.[74]

The funding picture is no better. Of the 34 state and local regulatory entities reviewed in the most recent *COGEL Blue Book*, about one-half had their budgets reduced from 1987 to 1992, with the New Jersey Election Law Enforcement Commission suffering the greatest budget cut in the nation (losing 22 percent of its funding).[75] The staffing of such bodies

Table D
ENFORCEMENT AUTHORITY OF SURVEYED AGENCIES

Jurisdiction/Agency	Authorized to Investigate	Authorized to Conduct Hearings	Authorized to Impose Fines	Authorized to Impose Fees for Late Reports	Authorized to Audit Randomly	Authorized to Render Advisory Opinions
Alaska Public Offices Commission	★	★	★	★	★	★
California Fair Political Practices Commission	★	★	★	★	★	★
Connecticut State Elections Enforcement Commission	★	★	★	. . .	★	★
Delaware State Election Commission	. . .	. . .	. . .	★	. . .	★
Georgia State Ethics Commission	★	★	★	. . .	★	★
Hawaii Campaign Spending Commission	★	★	. . .	. . .	. . .	★
Illinois State Board of Elections	★	★	★	. . .	. . .	. . .
Indiana State Elections Board	★	. . .	. . .	. . .	★	. . .
Iowa Campaign Finance Disclosure Commission	★	★	★	★	★	. . .
Kansas Commission on Governmental Standards & Conduct	★	★	★	★	★	★
Kentucky Registry of Election Finance	★	★	★	. . .	★	★
Los Angeles City Ethics Commission	★	★	. . .	. . .	★	. . .
Louisiana Ethics Administration Program	★	★	. . .	. . .	★	. . .
Maine Commission on Governmental Ethics	★	★	★	. . .	★	★
Maryland State Administrative Board of Election Laws	. . .	. . .	. . .	★	★	. . .
Minnesota Ethical Practices Board	★	★	★	★	★	★
Missouri Campaign Finance Review Board	★	★	. . .	★	★	★
Montana Commissioner of Political Practices	★	. . .	. . .	. . .	★	★
Nebraska Accountability & Disclosure Commission	★	★	★	. . .	★	★
New Jersey Election Law Enforcement Commission	★	★	★	★	★	★
New York City Campaign Finance Board	★	. . .	. . .	. . .	★	★

Table D
ENFORCEMENT AUTHORITY OF SURVEYED AGENCIES

Jurisdiction/Agency	Authorized to Investigate	Authorized to Conduct Hearings	Authorized to Impose Fines	Authorized to Impose Fees for Late Reports	Authorized to Audit Randomly	Authorized to Render Advisory Opinions
New York State Board of Elections	★	★	★	. . .	★	★
North Carolina State Board of Elections	★	. . .	. . .	★	. . .	★
Ohio Elections Commission	★	★	★	. . .	. . .	★
Oklahoma Ethics Commission	★	. . .	. . .	★	. . .	★
Rhode Island State Board of Elections	★	★	★	. . .	. . .	★
South Carolina State Ethics Commission	★	★	★	. . .	. . .	★
Tennessee Registry of Election Finance	★	★	★	★	. . .	★
Texas Ethics Commission	★	★	★	★	★	★
Virginia State Board of Elections	. . .	. . .	. . .	★	. . .	. . .
Washington State Public Disclosure Commission	★	★	★	. . .	★	★
Wisconsin State Elections Board	★	. . .	. . .	. . .	★	★
Dist. of Columbia Office of Campaign Finance	★	★	★	★	★	★
Totals (a)	30	24	20	15	23	26

Source: The Center for Responsive Politics, *Enforcing the Campaign Finance Laws*, 1993.
(a) Number indicates total number of agencies with authority in the designated area.

is also inadequate, with the majority of them having fewer than 10 full-time employees.[76] Finally, according to the Center for Responsive Politics, enforcement of campaign finance laws is still a major problem. Of the 33 state and local regulatory agencies reviewed, three are not authorized to investigate, nine cannot conduct hearings, 12 do not have the power to impose fines, 18 are not able to charge penalties for late reports, 10 cannot conduct random audits and six are not even authorized to render advisory opinions.[77]

It would seem a tragic irony at this point in history — just as politically less fortunate nations are moving to embrace a more democratic future — that Americans would allow their birthright of free government to erode. An improvement throughout the United States

in the way campaign financing is regulated must continue to succeed. As part of this crucial effort, governmental bodies that regulate the financing of campaigns must be given the ability and the authority to perform their ethical missions. Reform without empowering these bodies will be the same as no reform at all.

Selected State Court Cases

City of Talladega v. Pettus, 602 So. 2d 357 (Alabama) (1992) — The failure to file campaign disclosure forms of contributions and expenditures within five days of declaring candidacy is not "misconduct, fraud or corruption" as defined by state law and thus the court lacked jurisdiction to annul or revoke a mayoral election.

Griset v. Fair Political Practices Commis-

sion, 12 Cal Rptr. 2d 249 (California) (1992) — State law that prohibited candidate anonymity by requiring candidate mass mailings to contain name, street address and city upheld as promoting a compelling interest of the state (an informed electorate) and not violative of the First Amendment.

Service Employees International Union AFL-CIO, CLC v. Fair Political Practices Commission, 995 F. 2d 1312 (California) (1992) — A ban on candidate transfers, as contained in California's Proposition 73, was held unconstitutional on First Amendment grounds. Also held unconstitutional was formula limiting contributions that discriminated in favor of incumbents by limiting contributions during each fiscal year rather than during each election cycle.

State by Butterworth v. Republican Party of Florida, 604 So. 2d 477 (Florida) (1992) — State law requiring political committees to pay a 1.5 percent assessment of all contributions to a special fund to be used by qualifying candidates for governor and cabinet offices held unconstitutional.

Gwinn v. State Ethics Commission, 426 S.E. 2d 890 (Georgia) (1993) — State law that prohibited an insurance company from making contributions to any candidate for the office of commissioner of insurance was upheld as the state had a compelling interest to preserve the integrity of its democratic process.

State v. Carter, 480 N.W. 2d 850 (Iowa) (1992) — Candidate was not entitled to claim an exemption from campaign disclosure requirements sometimes afforded to minor political parties absent a showing the candidate's ties to atheist groups were political in nature, rather than religious or philosophical.

Cicoria v. State, 598 A. 2d 771 (Maryland) (1992) — The Court of Special Appeals of Maryland held that the authorized election campaign committee and not the treasurer or the candidate, was the "owner" of contributions for purposes of state law. Thus, the state was authorized to prosecute the candidate for theft from the Citizens for Cicoria, his election campaign committee, and the conviction of the Prince Georges' County Circuit Court was upheld.

Weber v. Heaney, 995 F 2d 872 (Minnesota) (1993) — Held that the Federal Election Campaign Act preempted Minnesota state law, which allowed for its congressional candidates to agree to expenditure limits in exchange for state funding for their campaigns. Whether these limits were voluntary or involuntary under state laws was considered irrelevant in considering whether state law was preempted.

Guy v. City of St. Louis, 829 s.W. 2d 66 (Missouri) (1992) — A St. Louis City Charter provision was held unenforceable as it prevented fire fighters from making contributions to local, state and federal candidates.

Salem Committee v. Secretary of State, 819 P. 2d 752 (Oregon) (1992) — The fact that a petitioner had not collected enough signatures on an initiative petition within a prescribed time period did not absolve him from responsibility to file a contributions and expenditures statement as required by state law.

Vote Choice, Inc. v. De Stefano, 814 F. Supp. 195 (Rhode Island) (1993) — State law that prohibited corporations from making independent expenditures to influence the outcome of ballot questions held unconstitutional as violative of corporate rights under the First and Fourteenth Amendments.

Also held that incentive provisions contained in state law designed to encourage candidates to accept public funding by increasing aggregate contribution limits and providing free television time did not violate the First Amendment in that the incentives furthered rather than burdened First Amendment values.

Selected Federal Court Cases

Buckley v. Valeo, 424 U.S. 1 (1976) — This landmark U.S. Supreme Court case involved the constitutionality of the Federal Election Campaign Act of 1971, as amended in 1974. The court upheld limits on contributions, the disclosure and recordkeeping provisions and public financing of presidential elections. It declared unconstitutional the limits on expenditures (except for presidential candidates who accept public funding), limits on independent expenditures, limits on expenditures by candidates from their personal funds (except for presidential candidates who accept public funding) and the method of appointing members of the Federal Election Commission.

First National Bank of Boston v. Bellotti, 435 U.S. 765 (1978) — The U.S. Supreme Court struck down a Massachusetts statute that severely restricted the participation of banks and corporations in state ballot measures. The court found that the state law abridged the First Amendment rights of corporations, noting that freedom of expression for communications by businesses needed to be protected to ensure the free flow of information and ideas to the public.

FEC v. NCPAC and FCM, consolidated with *Democratic National Committee v. NCPAC,* 578 F. Supp. 797; 470 U.S. 480 (1985) — In these cases, the U.S. Supreme Court resolved with finality that statutory attempts to limit independent expenditures in any federal election violated First Amendment rights of free speech and association. Speaking with particular reference to presidential elections, the court noted that restrictions on campaign speech are allowable "only to prevent corruption or its appearance," and that independent expenditures produce little evidence of either.

FEC v. Massachusetts Citizens for Life, Inc. (MCFL), 589 F. Supp. 646 (D.Mass, 1984), aff'd 769 F. 2d 13 (1st Cir. 1985), aff'd 479 U.S. 238 (1986) — The Supreme Court found that the federal law's prohibition on corporate expenditures in connection with federal campaigns was unconstitutional as applied to independent expenditures made by a narrowly defined type of nonprofit corporation. The court delineated the type of corporation that would be permitted to make independent expenditures under this ruling.

Austin v. Michigan State Chamber of Commerce, 856 F. 2d 783 (6th Cir. 1988), rev'd 494 U.S. 652, 110 S. Ct. 1391 (1990) — The U.S. Supreme Court ruled that a Michigan state law prohibiting independent expenditures by corporations was constitutional. The decision reversed a Sixth Circuit U.S. Court of Appeals decision, which had found the prohibition unconstitutional as applied to the state chamber.

Common Cause v. FEC, 729 F. Supp. 148 (D.D.C. 1990), & FEC v. National Republican

Senatorial Committee, 2 Fed. Elec. Camp. Fin. guide (CCH) ¶ 9302 (D.D.C. 1991), ¶ 9316 (D.C. Cir. 1992) — The U.S. Court of Appeals found that the National Republican Senatorial Committee (NRSC) did not exceed its statutory contribution limits through its exercise of "direction or control" over earmarked contributions. The court noted that every solicitation "pre-selects" candidates to some degree, and that it was unrealistic to believe that national political committees of any party would expend their resources merely to urge individuals to contribute to the candidate of their choice.

Notes

[1] Herbert E. Alexander, *Reform and Reality: The Financing of State and Local Elections* (New York: Priority Press Publications, 1991), pp. 1-2; Herbert E. Alexander and Jeffrey A. Schwartz, "Laboratories for Reform: The States Experience with Public Funding of Elections," *National Voter* (September - October), 1992, p. 9.

[2] SB 1039 (1993).

[3] Initiative Measure No. 41 (1993).

[4] Los Angeles City Charter, Section 312 (1993).

[5] SB 595 (1993).

[6] House File 201 (1993).

[7] SB 529 (1993).

[8] *State by Butterworth v. Republican Party of Florida,* 604 So. 2d 477 (1992).

[9] House file 201 (1993).

[10] No bill introduced as of the end of 1993.

[11] SB 7 (1993).

[12] To be submitted to Oregon voters in 1994.

[13] Approved as Initiative No. 134 in November 1992.

[14] *Gwinn v. State Ethics Commission,* 426 S.E. 2d 890 (1993).

[15] HB 2454 (1993).

[16] HB 49 (1993).

[17] HB 103 (1993).

[18] HB 105 (1993).

[19] HB 2201 (1993).

[20] SB 2470 (1993).

[21] Amendment to the Fair Elections Practices Act.

[22] HB 1100 (1993).

[23] HB 1098 (1993).

[24] HB 1008 (1993).

[25] Assembly Bill 100 (1993).

[26] Act 93762 (1993).

[27] Assembly Bill 100 (1993).

[28] The Oregon Proposal, SB 416, did not pass.

[29] HB 105 (1993).

[30] The Legislature amended the Nebraska Political Accountability and Disclosure Act.

[31] House File 201 (1993).

[32] 93-H 6543, an Act Relating to Political Contributions by State Vendors.

[33] Amendment to the Fair Elections Practices Act.

[34] It is anticipated this bill will be reintroduced in the 1994 session without the labor union affiliation component.

[35] Florida bill HB 2201 (1993); Idaho bill HB 165 (1993).

[36] HB 14 (1993).

[37] SB 1084 would amend the Michigan Campaign Finance Act.

[38] Act 93762 (1993).

[39] HB 603 (1993).

[40] Act 1209 (1993).

[41] HB 147 (1993).

[42] SB 7 (1993).

[43] HB 2201 (1993).

[44] Act 93762 (1993).

[45] HB 99 (1993).

[46] SB 1039 (1993).

[47] Act 93762 (1993).

[48] HB 219 (1993).

[49] Assembly Bill 100 (1993).

[50] *Ethics Commission v. Cullison et al.*, Case No. 79, 903, P. 2d, 64 OBAJ 978 (Okl. 1993).

[51] SB 1084 (1993).

[52] Act 1114 (1993).

[53] SB 529 (1993).

[54] SB 262 (1993).

[55] *Ethics Commission v. Cullison et al.*, Case No. 79, 903, P. 2d, 64 OBAJ 978 (Okl. 1993).

[56] Introduced but failed to pass.

[57] HB 957 (1993).

[58] Introduced but failed to pass.

[59] Amendment to the Fair Elections Practices Act.

[60] House File 576 (1993).

[61] HB 278 (1993).

[62] Assembly Bill 100 (1993).

[63] Act 93762 (1993).

[64] Act 1196 (1993).

[65] Recommended by the Governor's Task Force on Ethical Reform for introduction in the 1994 legislative session.

[66] SB 7 (1993).

[67] Assembly Bill 100 (1993).

[68] To be submitted in 1994.

[69] SB 278 (1993).

[70] For greater detail on recent state and local campaign financing activity, see Ronald D. Michaelson, *1993 Campaign Finance Update: Legislation and Litigation in the 50 States, the District of Columbia and the Federal Government*, prepared for the Council on Governmental Ethics Laws Annual Meeting, September 1993.

[71] Carol Mallory and Elizabeth Hedlund, *Enforcing the Campaign Finance Laws: An Agency Model* (Washington, D.C.: Center for Responsive Politics, 1993), p. 53; Keon S. Chi, "Campaign Finance Reform," *State Trends & Forecasts*, Vol. 2, No. 1 (April, 1993), 10. For similar views, see Alexander, *Reform and Reality*, pp. 3-4, 54-58; Frederick M. Herrmann, "How to Structure an Ethics Agency: A Blueprint fot Reform," *COGEL Guardian*, Vol. 11, No. 6 (December 31, 1990), 8; Frederick M. Herrmann, "Campaign Spending: What Kind of Reform?" *State Government News*, Vol. 31, No. 4 (April, 1988), 18-19; Frederick M. Herrmann, "Budget Crunch — Living With A Larger Mandate and a Smaller Budget," *COGEL Guardian*, Vol. 14, No. 1 (February, 1993), 1, 3-4.

[72] Mallory and Hedlund, *Agency Model*, p. 1.

[73] Chi, "Reform," pp. 31-33.

[74] *Ibid.*, pp. 31-33.

[75] Joyce Bullock, ed., *COGEL Blue Book*, Ninth Edition, (Lexington, Ky.: The Council of State Governments, 1993), pp. 21-24; Table C.

[76] Chi, "Reform," p. 10.

[77] Mallory and Hedlund, *Agency Model*, pp. 21-22; Table D.

Selected References

Ad Hoc Commission on Legislative Ethics and Campaign Finance. *Findings and Rec-*

ommendations. Trenton, N.J.: Office of Legislative Services, 1990.

Adamany, David W. *Campaign Finance in America*. North Scituate, Mass.: Duxbury Press, 1972.

Adamany, David W. *Political Money: A Strategy for Campaign Financing in America*. Baltimore: Johns Hopkins University Press, 1975.

Alexander, Herbert E., ed. *Campaign Money: Reform and Reality in the States*. New York: Free Press, 1976.

Alexander, Herbert E. *Financing Politics: Money, Elections, and Political Reform*. Fourth Edition. Washington, D.C. CQ Press, 1992.

Alexander, Herbert E. "Hidden Costs of Campaign Reform." *State Government News*. Vol. 33, No. 4 (April 1990), 16-18.

Alexander, Herbert E. *Money in Politics*. Washington, D.C.: Public Affairs Press, 1972.

Alexander, Herbert E. "The Resurgence of Election Reform in the States and Cities." *Comparative State Politics Newsletter*. Vol. 9., No. 6 (December, 1988), 30-32.

Alexander, Herbert E.; Goss, Eugene R.; and Schwartz, Jeffrey A. *Public Financing of State Elections: A Data Book on Tax-Assisted Funding of Political Parties and Candidates in Twenty-Four States*. Los Angeles: Citizens' Research Foundation, 1992.

Beyle, Thad. "The Governor's Chair: It Costs a Lot to Get There." *State Government News*. Vol. 34, No. 11 (November, 1991), 10-18.

Brindle, Jeffrey M. *Is There a PAC Plaque in New Jersey?* ELEC White Paper Series, No. 7. Trenton, N.J.: New Jersey Election Law Enforcement Commission, 1991.

Brindle, Jeffrey M. *Legislative Candidates: How They Spend Their Money*. ELEC White Paper Series, No. 9. Trenton, N.J.: New Jersey Election Law Enforcement Commission, 1994.

Brindle, Jeffrey M. *Technology in the Future: Strengthening Disclosure*. ELEC White Paper Series, No. 8. Trenton, N.J.: New Jersey Election Law Enforcement Commission, 1992.

California Commission on Campaign Financing. *The New Gold Rush: Financing California's Legislative Campaigns*. Los Angeles: Center for Responsive Government, 1985.

Cherry, Christopher. "State Campaign Finance Law: The Necessity and Efficiency of Reform." *Journal of Law and Politics*. Vol. III, No. 3 (Winter, 1987), 567-595.

COGEL Guardian. Newsletter of the Council on Governmental Ethics Laws, Los Angeles: The Center for Governmental Studies.

Common Cause. *Campaign Finance Reform in the States*. Washington D.C.: Common Cause, 1993.

Drew, Elizabeth. *Politics and Money: The New Road to Corruption*. New York: Macmillan and Company, 1983.

Feigenbaum, Edward D.; Larsen, John L.; and Reynolds, Betty J. *A Model Law for Campaign Finance, Ethics, and Lobbying Regulation*. Lexington, Ky.: Council on Governmental Ethics Laws, 1990.

Garfield, Jeffrey B. And Stern, Robert M. "Limiting Campaign Costs." *State Government News*. Vol. 33, No. 10 (October, 1990), 27.

Gordon, Nicole A. and Wagner, Hyla Pottharst. "The New York City Campaign Finance Program: A Reform that is Working." *Fordham Urban Law Journal*. Vol. XIX, No. 3 (1992), 605-630.

Gross, Kenneth A. "The Enforcement of Campaign Finance Rules: A System in Search of Reform." *Yale Law and Policy Review*. Vol. 9, No. 2 (Fall, 1991), 229-300.

Guear, Christopher. "Walking Around Money: What It Is, What It Does, and What Can Be Done?" M.P.A. Dissertation, Pennsylvania State University, 1992.

Hall, Janet A. "When Political Campaigns Turn to Slime: Establishing a Virginia Fair Campaign Practices Committee." *Journal of Law and Politics*. Vol. VII, No. 2 (Winter, 1991), 353-377.

Haughee, Chris. "The Florida Election Campaign Financing Act: A Bold Approach to Public Financing of Elections." *Florida State University Law Review*. Vol. 14, No. 3 (Fall, 1986), 585-605.

Heard, Alexander. *The Costs of Democracy*. Chapel Hill, N.C.: University of North Carolina Press, 1960.

Herrmann, Frederick M. *COGEL Campaign Financing and Lobbying Bibliography*. Lexington, Ky.: The Council of State Governments, 1992.

Herrmann, Frederick M. *1990 Campaign Finance Update: Legislation and Litigation*.

Los Angeles: Citizens' Research Foundation, 1990.

Herrmann, Frederick M. "Public Funding Lesson: Taxpayer-Financed Gubernatorial Elections Work in New Jersey." *Campaigns and Elections*. Vol. 8, No. 2 (July-August, 1987), 53-54.

Huckshorn, Robert J. "Who Gave It? Who Got It?: The Enforcement of Campaign Finance Laws in the States." *Journal of Politics*. Vol. 47, No. 3 (August, 1985), 773-789.

Huwa, Randy. "Political Action Committees: Creating a Scandal." *Business Forum*. (Winter, 1984), 11-14.

Illinois State Board of Elections. *Money and Elections in Illinois 1992*. Springfield, Ill.: Illinois State Board of Elections, 1993.

Jackson, Brooks. *Broken Promise: Why the Federal Election Commission Failed*. New York: Priority Press Publications, 1990.

Jackson, Brooks. *Honest Graft: Big Money and the American Political Process*. New York: Alfred A. Knopf, 1988.

Jacobson, Gary C. "Practical Consequences of Campaign Finance Reform: An Incumbent Protection Act?" *Public Policy*. Vol. 24, No. 1 (Winter, 1976), 1-32.

Jones, Ruth S. "State Public Campaign Finance: Implications for Partisan Politics." *American Journal of Political Science*. Vol., 25, No. 2 (May, 1980), 342-361.

Jones, Ruth S. and Hopkins, Anne H. "State Campaign Fund Raising: Targets and Response." *Journal of Politics*. Vol. 47 (1985), 433-449.

Kebschull, Kim; Kersey, Marianne; and Coble, Ran. *Campaign Disclosure Laws: An Analysis of Campaign Finance Disclosure in North Carolina and a Comparison of 50 State Campaign Reporting Laws*. Raleigh, N.C.: North Carolina Center for Public Policy Research, 1990.

Kehler, David. "Why Initiative and Referendum Contributions and Expenditures Cannot Be Limited." *Initiative and Referendum Analysis*. No. 1 (January, 1992). Princeton, N.J.: Public Affairs Research Institute of New Jersey, 1992.

Lowenstein, Daniel Hays. "Campaign Spending and Ballot Propositions: Recent Experience, Public Choice Theory and the First Amendment." *UCLA Law Review*. Vol. 29, No. 3 (February, 1982), 505-641.

Lowenstein, Daniel Hays. "On Campaign Finance Reform: The Root of All Evil Deeply Rooted." *Hofstra Law Review*. Vol. 18, No. 2 (Fall, 1989), 301-367.

Malbin, Michael J. "Looking Back at the Future of Campaign Finance Reform." *Commonsense*. Vol. 6, No. 1 (December, 1983), 50-70.

Malbin, Michael J., ed. *Money and Politics in the United States: Financing Elections in the 1980's*. Chatham, N.J.: American Enterprise Institute/Chatham House Publishers, 1984.

Malbin, Michael J. *Parties, Interest Groups, and Campaign Finance Laws*. Washington, D.C.: American Enterprise Institute, 1980.

Malbin, Michael J. "What Should Be Done About Independent Expenditures?" *Regulation*. Vol. 6, No. 1, (January-February, 1982), 41-46.

Massar, Nedda Gold. *New Jersey Gubernatorial Public Financing Revised: 1989 and Beyond*. Trenton, N.J.: New Jersey Election Law Enforcement Commission, 1992.

Michaelson, Ronald D. *1992 Campaign Finance Update: Legislation and Litigation in the 50 States, the District of Columbia, and the Federal Government*. Lexington, Ky.: The Council of State Governments, 1993.

Michaelson, Ronald D. "The State of the States in 1991." *COGEL Guardian*. Vol. 12, No. 6 (December, 1991), 1, 34.

Michaelson, Ronald D. *The State of the States in 1991: Financing Political Campaigns*. Lexington, Ky.: The Council of State Governments, 1991

Michaelson, Ronald D. "The State of the States in 1992 — Financing Political Campaigns." *COGEL Guardian*. Vol. 14, No. 1 (February, 1993), 4-6.

Michaelson, Ronald D. "The State of the States in 1993: Financing Political Campaigns." *COGEL Guardian*. Vol. 14, No. 6 (December, 1993), 1, 3-4.

Mutch, Robert E. "Corporate Money and Elections: The New Look of State Laws." *State Legislatures*. Vol. 9, No. 2 (February, 1983), 22-25.

New York Commission on Government Integrity. *The Albany Money Machine: Campaign Financing for New York State Legislative Races*. New York: State of New York, 1988.

Noragon, Jack L. "Political Finance and Political Reform: The Experience with State Income Tax Check-offs." *American Political Science Review*. Vol. 75, No. 3 (September, 1981), 667-687.

Overacker, Louise. *Money in Elections*. New York: Macmillan Company, 1932.

Palmer, James A. and Feigenbaum, Edward D. *Campaign Finance Law 92: A Summary of State Campaign Finance Laws with Quick Reference Charts*. Washington, D.C.: National Clearinghouse on Election Administration, 1992.

Sabato, Larry J. "Campaign Finance Reform: Bad Reform Ideas that Sound Good." *Campaigns and Elections*. Vol. 14, No. 1 (April - May, 1993), 25, 80.

Sabato, Larry J. *PAC Power: Inside the World of Political Action Committees*. New York: W.W. Norton and Company, 1984.

Sabato, Larry J. *Paying for Elections: The Campaign Finance Thicket*. New York: Priority Press Publications, 1989.

Salmore, Stephen A. and Salmore, Barbara G. *Candidates, Parties, and Campaigns: Electorial Politics in America*. Second Edition. Washington, D.C.: CQ Press, 1992.

Scarinci, Donald. "The New Jersey Campaign Contribution and Expenditures Reporting Act: Is It Reform?" *Seton Hall Legislative Journal*. Vol. 18, No. 1 (1993), 161-205.

Schlossstein, Steven. *The End of the American Century*. Chapters 8 and 9. New York and Chicago: Congdon and Weed, 1989.

Schwartz, A.P. and Stern, Robert M. "Are Campaign Funds for Personal Use?" *State Government News*. Vol. 34, No. 3 (March 1991), 16-17.

Singer, Sandra. "The Arms Race of Campaign Financing." *State Legislatures*. Vol. 14, No. 6 (July, 1988), 24-28.

Smolka, Richard G. "New York City Campaign Finance Board Hits Dinkins with $320,000 Penalty." *Election Administration Reports*. Vol. 23, No. 21 (October 25, 1993), 6.

Sorauf, Frank J. *Inside Campaign Finance: Myths and Realities*. New Haven: Yale University Press, 1992.

Sorauf, Frank J. *Money in American Elections*. Glenview, Ill.: Scott, Foresman, and Company, 1988.

Sorauf, Frank J. *What Price PACs?* New York: Twentieth Century Fund, 1984.

Stern, Robert M. "California's New Campaign Finance Laws: Reforms Still Needed." *COGEL Guardian*. Vol. 10, No. 3 (June 30, 1989), 4-6.

Thayer, George. *Who Shakes the Money Tree? American Campaign Financing Practices from 1789 to the Present*. New York: Simon and Schuster, 1973.

Verniero, Peter. "Commentary — Money and Politics: Time to Act." *New Jersey Reporter*. Vol. 21, No. 1 (May-June, 1991), 40-42.

Wagner, Holly. "Costly Campaigns Attract Special Interest Dollars." *State Government News*. Vol. 29, No. 9 (September, 1986), 19-20.

Wertheimer, Fred. "The PAC Phenomenon in American Politics." *Arizona Law Review*. Vol. 22, No. 2 (Summer, 1980), 603-626.

Wollock, Andrea J. "Public Financing of State Elections: The Minnesota Experience." *State Legislatures*. Vol. 5, No. 5 (June, 1979), 12-14.

Zuckerman, Edward. "Intended Consequences: The Dark Side of Reform." *PACs and Lobbies*. Vol. XII, No. 5 (March 6, 1991), 1-3.

Table 5.10
CAMPAIGN FINANCE LAWS: GENERAL FILING REQUIREMENTS
(As of January 1992)

State or other jurisdiction	Statements required from	Statements filed with	Time for filing
Alabama	Political committees.	Secy. of state: for statewide and judicial offices, state Senate, House of Representatives and district attorney. Secy. of state and probate judge in counties of district: for state Senate or House of Representatives, and county offices.	45 days before and between 10 and 5 days before an election; annually on January 31.
Alaska	State candidates and municipal candidates in municipalities of more than 1,000 residents; ongoing organizations; a business entity, labor organization, or municipality making a contribution/expenditure; groups and individuals contributing more than $250 to any group or candidate.	Alaska Public Office Commission (central office).	30 days and one week before election; 10 days after election; and annually on January 15 for contributions and expenditures not reported the prior year. (a)
Arizona	Candidates, committees, and continuing political organizations.	Secy. of state: for state offices and state measures (including state legislature). Clerk of board of supervisors: for judges seeking retention and county offices. City or town clerk: for city or town offices or measures.	10-15 days before primary and 20 days after a primary; 10-15 days before and 20 days after a general or special election; supplemental reports annually by April 1 for contributions and expenditures subsequent to post-election reports.
Arkansas	Candidates whose cumulative contributions exceed $500; exploratory committees; approved political action committees.	Secy. of state and county clerk of county where candidate resides.	Generally, a monthly report due within 15 days after the end of each month; pre-election report due 7 days before any election; quarterly supplemental report due within 15 days of the end of each quarter.
California	Candidates, committees and elected officeholders. (b)	Secy. of state, registrar of Los Angeles and San Francisco and clerk of country of residence; legislative candidates, board of equalization, court of appeals and superior court judges file with Secy. of state, clerk of county with largest number of registered voters in the district and clerk of county of domicile. (c)	Semi-annual: July 31 and January 31 for all candidates and committees, whether or not they received contributions or made expenditures, and all elected officers, except judges, whose salary is less than $100 per month, and judges file only if they received contributions or made expenditures. Periodic: for elections in June or November of even-numbered years: March 22, 12 days before June election, October 5, and 12 days before the November election. (d)
Colorado	Candidates; political committees (except those which spend or receive less than $250 in a calendar year and are organized to support or oppose a ballot issue); and persons making independent expenditures more than $100.	Non-municipal elections: either Secy. of state (statewide, legislative, district, or multi-county candidates) or appropriate county clerk and recorder (other officers). Municipal elections: municipal clerk. Non-statewide multi-county issues: county clerk and recorder of each appropriate county.	11 days before and 30 days after elections. (e) Supplemental reports are required annually on the anniversary of the election until a report shows no unexpended balance or deficit.
Connecticut	Candidates, political committees, and party committees spending or receiving more than $1,000 in any election.	Generally with Secy. of state, with local candidates and referendum committees filing with town clerks.	Generally: 2nd Thursday of January, April, July and October; 7th day before each regular state election; 45 days after election and 30 days after primary. State central committees: January 30, April 10, July 10; 12 days before any election. Supplemental reports: 7 days after distribution of surplus, or, if deficit, 90 days after primary or election, then 30 days after increase in deficit.
Delaware	Candidates and committees.	State Election Commissioner.	20 days before election; December 31 of year of election; December 31 of year after election, and annually on December 31 until contributions and expenditures are balanced and the fund is closed.

GENERAL FILING REQUIREMENTS—Continued

State or other jurisdiction	Statements required from	Statements filed with	Time for filing
Florida	Candidates, political committees, committees of continuous existence, political party executive committees and persons making independent expenditures of $100 or more unless no funds have been received or reportable expenditures made during reporting period.	Candidates file with officer before whom candidate qualifies, with copy to supervisor of elections in candidate's county of residence for other than statewide candidates. Statewide committees file with division of elections, while other committees file with county supervisor of elections.	Generally by the 10th day of each calendar quarter after treasurer is appointed through last day of qualifying for office and on the 4th, 18th and 32nd days preceding first and second primaries; and on the 4th and 18th days immediately preceding the general election for an opposed candidate, political committee or committee of continuous existence. Candidates receiving public funds file on the 4th, 11th, 18th, 25th and 32nd days prior to first primary and general election, and on the 4th, 11th, 18th, and 25th days prior to the second primary. Any candidate who becomes unopposed files within 90 days of that date.
Georgia	Generally, those making or accepting contributions in excess of $500 on behalf of a candidate for election, a referendum, or recall.	Secy. of state for statewide candidates and referenda. Secy. of state with copy to superintendent of elections in county of candidate's residence for general assembly candidates. Local superintendent of elections for other offices and elections.	45 days and 15 days before and 15 days after primary, 15 days before general or special election, 6 days before general and nonpartisan runoff election and December 31 of election year; following December 31 for winning candidates.
Hawaii	Candidates, parties and committees; committees that form within 10 days before an election and spend $1,000 or more.	Original and a copy with Campaign Spending Commission. In counties of less than 200,000 voters, file original and two copies with either Commission or clerk in county where candidate resides.	Generally 10 working days before each election, 20 days after primary, and 30 days after a general or special election. Supplemental reports in the event of surplus or deficit over $250 are filed on the 5th day after the last day of election year, and every 6 months thereafter.
Idaho	Candidates, political committees, organizations that contribute more than $500 to a political committee, and any person who makes an expenditure of more than $50.	Secy. of state.	By 7 days before and 30 days after election. Supplemental reports in the event of an unexpended balance or expenditure deficit are filed annually on January 31.
Illinois	Treasurers of state and local political committees.	State Board of Elections for state political committees; county clerk for local political committees; State Board of Elections and county clerk for political committees acting as both state and local political committee.	Reports of campaign contributions: 15 days before each election. Semi-annual reports of contributions and expenditures: January 31 and July 31.
Indiana	Political committees, candidate committees, regular party committees, and political action committees.	State Election Board. Local candidates and committees file with county election board of each county in district. General Assembly candidates file duplicate with board of candidate's county of residence.	14 days (postmarked) or 11 days (hand-delivered) before election or convention; 20 days after convention if no pre-convention report was filed; annually by January 15 (by March 1 for political party committee).
Iowa	Candidates and committees receiving contributions or making expenditures in excess of $250 ($500 for candidates for city or school office).	Statewide office: Campaign Finance Disclosure Commission. County, city or school office: county election commissioner. State statutory political committee: Commission. Other statutory political committee: county election commissioner and copy to Commission.	May 20, July 20, October 20, and January 20 annually, except for committees for city and school office candidates who file 5 days before the election and the first of the month thereafter. In years in which no primary or general election is held, a state or city committee is not required to file the May, July, and October reports in a year in which the candidate is not standing for election.
Kansas	Candidates, political committees, party committees, constitutional amendment committees, and persons making independent expenditures of more than $100.	State offices elected statewide: with Secy. of state. Constitutional amendments: Kansas Commission on Governmental Standards and Conduct. State offices elected on less than statewide basis: with Secy. of state and county election officer of residence. Local offices: county election officer.	Generally, 8 days before election, and January 10 each year. Constitutional amendment committees file each February 15 and 15 days before and 15 days after elections.

See footnotes at end of table.

GENERAL FILING REQUIREMENTS—Continued

State or other jurisdiction	Statements required from	Statements filed with	Time for filing
Kentucky	Candidates, campaign committees, permanent committees, and political party executive committees.	Kentucky Registry of Election Finance. Duplicate reports filed with clerk in county where candidate resides. Campaign committee files with appropriate central campaign committees.	Candidates/campaign committees: 32nd and 12th day before an election, and 30 days after an election. Candidates have five days from filing deadline to file with Registry. Party executive committees: 30 days after an election. Permanent committees: last day of each calendar quarter. Semi-annual supplemental reports required June 30 and December 31 until fund shows a zero balance.
Louisiana	Candidates for major or district office; candidates for other office who receive contributions of more than $200 from any one source or make expenditures of more than $5,000; political committees, persons not a candidate who make independent expenditures or accept contributions other than to or from a candidate or committee more than $500; persons who make contributions or make expenditures more than $200 to support or oppose propositions.	Supervisory Committee on Campaign Finance Disclosure.	Candidates and committees: 180th, 90th, 30th and 10th day before primary; 10th day before and 40th day after general election. Annual reports by February 15 for most surpluses/deficits. (f)
Maine	Candidates, political committees, political action committees, and persons making independent expenditures in excess of $50.	Commission on Governmental Ethics and Election Practices.	6 days before and 42 days after each election; gubernatorial candidates also file January 15 and July 15 in non-election years if they received or spent more than $1,000 in that year, and 42 days before an election.
Maryland	Candidates receiving contributions of $300 or more; political committees; party central committees; slates.	Candidates and their noncontinuing committees and slates file with the board with which candidate filed statement of candidacy. Party central committees and all continuing committees file with the State Administrative Board of Election Laws. Government contractors file with Secy. of state.	4th Tuesday before primary, 2nd Friday before any election, and earlier of the 3rd Tuesday after general election or before taking office. Central and continuing committees also file annually on the date of the last general election. If there is a surplus or deficit, 6 months after general election, one year after general election, and annually on the election anniversary until the surplus or deficit is eliminated.
Massachusetts	Candidates and political committees.	City or town candidates and committees: with city or town clerk. Other candidates: with Director of Campaign and Political Finance.	Candidates for General Assembly: 8 days before primary, 8 days before general election, and January 10 of year after general election. Candidates for other than non-city or town offices and political committees: 3rd business day after designating depository and January 10 of year after general election.
Michigan	Candidates, political and independent committees, party committees, and ballot question committees; certain persons making independent expenditures.	Secy. of state: candidates for state elective office, judicial office and all political party committees. County clerk: candidates for local office.	Candidate committees, party committees, ballot question committees: 11 days before and 30 days after election; committees other than independent committees: not later than January 31 of each year; political or independent committees (PACs) filing on state level: January 31, July 25, October 25.
Minnesota	Candidates, party committees, political committees, and persons making independent expenditures of more than $100.	Ethical Practices Board; Board files a duplicate of legislative candidate reports with the auditor in each county of the district.	Candidates for statewide, legislative, and high court offices file 10 days before a primary and general election and January 31 annually. (g)
Mississippi	Candidates and political committees.	Secy. of state if candidate for statewide, state district or legislative office; circuit clerk of appropriate county for all others.	For years other than 1995 and every 4th year thereafter: 7 days before any election; January 31 to cover the entire prior calendar year. For 1995 and every 4th year thereafter, detailed reporting dates are specified.

GENERAL FILING REQUIREMENTS—Continued

State or other jurisdiction	Statements required from	Statements filed with	Time for filing
Missouri	Committees, candidates who spend or receive more than $1,000 or receive a single contribution of more than $250, and persons making independent expenditures of $500 or more.	(h)	40th and 7th day before and 30th day after election with minor exception. (i) Supplemental reports are required each January 15 if contributions or expenditures of $1,000 or more were made or received since the last report. A supplemental report is required if post-election report shows outstanding debts greater than $5,000; this report must be filed until the deficit is less than $5,000.
Montana	Candidates and political committees (except in certain school districts and special district elections).	Commissioner of Political Practices and election administrator of county where candidate is resident or political committee has headquarters.	Statewide office candidates and related political committees: pre-election year quarterly reports on the 5th day after each quarter; March 10th and September 10th in an election year; 15 and 25 days before an election; not more than 20 days after an election; March 10th and September 10th of each year following an election until closing report is filed. State district office candidates and related political committees: 10th day before election, not more than 20 days after election, and whenever closing report is filed. Other public office candidates and related political committees: same as for state district office if contributions or expenditures to campaign exceed $500. Statewide ballot issue committee: pre-election year reports on the 5th day of each quarter; March 10th, and 10th day of subsequent month through September; 15 and 25 days before election; within 20 days after election. Independent committees: 10th day before election, not more than 20 days after election, and when closing report at the end of the calendar year is due. (j)
Nebraska	Candidate committees, political party committees, independent committees, and ballot question committees upon raising, receiving, or spending more than $2,000 in a calendar year.	Nebraska Accountability and Disclosure Commission. Copies to be filed with election commissioner or county clerk, as appropriate, depending on the type of committee.	By 30th day and 10th day before a primary or general election, and 40th day after each election. Annual statement due by January 31 for preceding year if statements not required to be filed during previous years or did not receive or expend more than $200 during previous year. (k)
Nevada	State, district, county, township, and city office candidates; persons that make candidate-related independent expenditures if any contributions received (except political party) or individual/cumulative expenditures exceed $500; ballot question advocacy persons and groups if any contributions received or individual/cumulative expenditures exceed $500; and committees for the recall of a public officer if individual/cumulative contributions or expenditures exceed $500. Persons include individuals, corporations, business and voluntary associations, labor unions, political action committees, and political party committees.	Secy. of state: candidate for statewide office, state senator, or assemblyman in multi-county district, or any other office with multi-county district; person making independent expenditures for a candidate elected from other than a single city or county; committee for the recall of a public officer; and ballot question advocacy group for a question voted on in other than a single county or city. County clerk: candidate for state senator or assemblyman voted on in a single county; county or township office; person making independent expenditures for a candidate elected only from the county; and ballot question advocacy group for a question voted on only in the county. City clerk: candidate for city office; person making independent expenditures for a candidate elected only from the city; and ballot question advocacy group for a question voted on only in the city.	Candidate at primary or general election: 15 days before primary, 15 days before general election, and 15th day of 2nd month after general election. City office candidate: 15 days before city primary, 15 days before city general election, and 15th day of 2nd month after city general election. Candidate at recall election: contributions report 30 days after election and expenses report 60 days after election. Candidate at special district office election: 15 days before election, contributions report 30 days after election, and expenses report 60 days after election. Recall committee: if petition for recall not filed, 30 days after notice of intent to circulate petition expired; if court does not order special recall election, 30 days after court decision; and if court orders special recall election, 15 days before and 30 days after election. Person making candidate-related independent expenditures and ballot question advocacy group: 15 days before primary election or city primary election, as appropriate; 15 days before general election or city general election, as appropriate; and 15th day of second month after election.
New Hampshire	Candidates for governor, councilor, state senator, representative to General Court, and county office whose expenditures exceed $500, and political committees (including political party committees) whose receipts or expenditures exceed $500.	Secy. of state.	Wednesday 12 weeks before primary (except political committee of candidate or political party), Wednesday 3 weeks before election, and 2nd Wednesday after election. Every 6 months after election until obligations satisfied or surplus depleted. (l)

See footnotes at end of table.

GENERAL FILING REQUIREMENTS—Continued

State or other jurisdiction	Statements required from	Statements filed with	Time for filing
New Jersey	Candidates, political committees, and continuing political committees (including political party committees). Detailed reports are not required if the total amount expended on behalf of a candidacy does not exceed $2,000; however, aggregate contributions over $100 from a single source must be reported by candidate. Reporting exemptions are provided for political committees and continuing political committees.	New Jersey Election Law Enforcement Commission. In case of candidates for municipal, county-wide, or school district office, a copy is filed with the county clerk of county of candidate's residence.	Candidates and political committees: 29th day and 11th day before election and 20th day after election, and if post-election report is not the final report, every 60 days thereafter until certification of winding up of business (final report) is filed. Continuing political committees: by April 15th, July 15th, October 15th, and January 15th of each calendar year. Aggregate contributions, expenditures, or testimonial affair or public solicitation proceeds over $100 to be reported within 20 days after $100 aggregate exceeded, starting with 19th day after election. (m)
New Mexico	Candidates (except candidates who file a statement that they anticipate receiving or spending less than $500 per primary or general election), special purpose political committees (except committees authorized by a candidate and included in the candidate's report), and general purpose political committees.	Secy. of state: statewide elective offices, multi-county state legislative offices, judicial offices (except magistrates), multi-county district offices, and general purpose political committees. County Clerk: county elective offices, magistrates, and single-county state legislative offices. Special purpose political committees, if supporting or opposing candidate, file with same filing officer as candidate, or with Secy. of state, if involved with constitutional amendment or question.	Candidates and special purpose political committees: by 10 days before and 30 days after an election, 6 months after an election if contributions remain unexpended or debts unpaid, and every 12 months after an election as long as unpaid debts remain. General purpose political committee: by 10 days before and 30 days after an election.
New York	Candidates and political committees; however, filing is not required for candidates or their authorized political committees (1) that do not expend more than $50 in a calendar year or $1,000 in a reporting period, (2) before an uncontested primary election, or (3) for an election in a city, town, or village of less than 10,000 unless total receipts or expenditures exceed $1,000.	Candidates: presidential electors, state executive or legislative offices, supreme court justices, constitutional convention delegates, and multi-county party positions (if not wholly within New York City), with State Board of Elections; other public offices (except village offices and party positions in a single county or New York City), with city or county board of elections, as appropriate; and village offices if election not on general election day, with county board of elections. Political Committees: with State Board of Elections, except committees taking part solely in an election for a candidate required to file with a local board of elections, are also required to file with local board. County political party committees file with the county board of elections. Committees are required to file with other boards in certain instances.	Primary elections: 32nd and 11th day before and 10th day after contested primary election. Runoff primary: 4th day before and 10th day after primary. General election: 32nd day and 11th day before and 27th day after the election. Periodic statements are also required by January 15 and July 15 in each subsequent year until activities terminated. (n)
North Carolina	Candidates, political committees, referendum committees, and individuals making independent contributions or expenditures over $100; however, municipal and county offices in municipalities and counties under 50,000 are not required to file reports. Candidates and political party committees whose contributions, expenditures, and loans will not exceed $1,000 can be exempted from reporting.	State Board of Elections: candidates, political committees, and persons making independent contributions or expenditures over $100 with respect to candidates for state and multi-county offices and referendum committees with respect to statewide referenda. County Board of Elections: candidates, political committees, and persons making independent contributions or expenditures over $100 with respect to candidates for single-county district, county and municipal offices.	Primary election: by 10th day before primary (and 10th day after primary if candidate eliminated); if there is a second primary, by the 10th day after the primary if the candidate was eliminated. General election: by 10th day before election. Annual report if contributions are received or expenditures are made during the calendar year for which no reports are otherwise required, by last Friday in January of following year. Candidates and political committees in elections in municipalities over 50,000 must submit reports according to the schedule for the particular method under which the election is conducted. Individuals making independent contributions or expenditures over $100 must report within 10 days after the contribution or expenditure is made.

GENERAL FILING REQUIREMENTS—Continued

State or other jurisdiction	Statements required from	Statements filed with	Time for filing
North Dakota	Candidates for statewide or legislative office who receive any contributions more than $100 during a calendar year; political parties that receive contributions of more than $100 and contribute money to a statewide or legislative office candidate of more than $100; political committees administering PACs; and persons who solicit or accept contributions aggregating more than $100 in a calendar year concerning statewide referenda and initiatives.	Secy. of state: state office candidates, political parties, political committees, and statewide initiative/referendum group or person. State legislative candidates file with the county auditor in the candidate's county of residence.	Candidates: by 10th day before primary and general election and January 30 of following calendar year. (o) Political committees: by October 15th, with supplemental statement by January 30. Referendum/initiative group or persons: by 10th day before election and by January 30.
Ohio	Committees and political parties.	Secy. of state: statewide and state board of education offices, state political committees, and state and national political parties. County board of elections: offices within county and multi-county district (file in county with greatest population), county political committees, and county political parties.	12th day before and 38th day after an election: annual statement on the last business day of January except in year post-general election statement is filed.
Oklahoma	Candidates, candidate committees, and other committees accepting contributions or making expenditures.	State Ethics Commission: state and county candidates/candidate committees and other non-local committees. Clerk of political subdivision: municipal and school board candidates/committees and supporting/opposing committees.	10th day before primary, runoff and general election, and 40th day after general election. Supplemental report if contributions received or expenditures made within 6 months after general election to be filed within 6 months and 10 days after election; if contributions received or expenditures made after 6-month period, on January 15 of each year thereafter. Separate comprehensive reporting schedule applies to committees for or against a state question.
Oregon	Candidates (or their principal campaign committees) and political committees.	Secy. of state: statewide, state, and congressional district office. County Clerk: non-city office within a county, County clerk in county where the chief administrative officer is located: multi-county district office. Chief city election officer: city office.	29-39 days and 5-8 days before election and 30 days after election. (p) If the post-election statement shows an unexpended balance of contributions or expenditure deficit, a post-election annual supplemental statement is required until there is no balance or deficit.
Pennsylvania	Candidates and political committees if amount received or expended or liabilities incurred exceed $250 during a reporting period.	Report concerning candidate: office with which a candidate files nomination documents, either the Secy. of the Commonwealth or appropriate county board of elections. If report concerns both candidates who file nomination documents with the Secy. and those who file with county boards, then with the Secy. of the Commonwealth.	Statewide office candidates and political committees influencing statewide election: by 6th Tuesday and 2nd Friday before primary and general election. All other committees: 2nd Friday before primary and general election. All candidates and political committees: 30 days after election and annual report on January 31 of each year until no balance or debt; then termination report may be filed.
Rhode Island	Candidates, political action committees, and state and municipal party committees that receive contributions of over $200 from one source in a calendar year, or spend more than $5,000 in the aggregate on behalf of a candidate or question.	State Board of Elections.	28th and 7th day before a primary, general or special election, and 28th day after an election (final report). Political party committee must file annual report by March 1. Ongoing reports due 120 days after election and at 90-day intervals thereafter until dissolution of campaign fund or completion of a committee's business regarding the past election.
South Carolina	Candidates and committees.	State Ethics Commission: non-legislative candidates and non-legislative committees. State Senate or House of Representatives ethics committee, as appropriate: legislative candidates and caucus committees.	Initial report: if receipt or expenditures of contributions exceeds $500, 10 days after threshold amount met; if $500 threshold not met, 15 days before an election. Subsequent reports: 10 days after calendar quarter in which contributions are received or expenditures are made, whether before or after an election. Independent expenditure by committee within 20 days before an election to be reported immediately if more than $10,000 for statewide office candidate, or $2,000 for any other candidate. Final report may be filed at any time when contributions no longer received or expenditures made or incurred.

See footnotes at end of table.

GENERAL FILING REQUIREMENTS—Continued

State or other jurisdiction	Statements required from	Statements filed with	Time for filing
South Dakota	State executive, state legislative, and county office candidates or candidate's committees; political action committees that participate in an election; political party committees; persons or ballot question committees involved with a question or constitutional amendment at a statewide election; and persons and political committees involved with a question at a non-statewide election.	Secy. of state: state office and legislative office candidates and candidate's committees, political party committees, political action committees, and persons involved with a statewide question. County auditor: county office candidates and candidate's committees. Person in charge of an election: persons and committees involved with a non-statewide question.	State office candidates: last Tuesday prior to primary and general election, and by February 1 for preceding calendar year or remainder not covered by previous report. (q) Legislative and county office candidates: by July 1 and December 31 of election year. Person or committee involved with a statewide election: by July 1 of election year and last Tuesday before election; annually thereafter by February 1. (q) Person or committee involved with non-statewide question: 10 days before and 30 days after election.
Tennessee	Candidates and political campaign committees.	Registry of Election Finance: state office candidates and political campaign committees in state elections. Appropriate county election commission: local office candidates and committees for local elections. General Assembly candidates and their political committees file a copy with the county election commission where the candidate resides.	Candidates, single-candidate political campaign committees, and single-measure political campaign committees: if political treasurer appointed more than one year before election, by February 1 each year through year of election; in election year, 7 days before and 48 days after each election. If unexpended balance, continuing obligations or expenditure deficit exists after the post-election statement is filed, a supplemental annual statement must be filed. Multi-candidate political campaign committees: within 10 days after each quarter. (r)
Texas	Candidates, officeholders and political committees (except political party county executive committees with aggregate contributions and expenditures of $5,000 or less in a calendar year).	Secy. of state, county clerk or clerk or secretary of non-county subdivision. (s)	Candidates, officeholders and political committees: semi-annual reports by July 15 and January 15. Opposed candidates and political committees in an election year: pre-election reports by 30th and 8th day before each election day (and by 8th day before runoff election day, if applicable). General purpose political committee may elect to file monthly by 5th day of each month in lieu of semi-annual and pre-election reports. Opposed candidates and specific purpose political committees may elect to file only semi-annual reports if aggregate contributions and expenditures do not exceed $500 in an election. Local officeholders not required to file for a reporting period in which aggregate contributions and expenditures do not exceed $500.(t)
Utah	Candidates for governor, lieutenant governor, state auditor, state treasurer, attorney general, state senator, state representative; candidates for county office and for city offices in cities of the first or second class; political action committees and political issues committees that receive contributions or make political expenditures of $750 or more in a calendar year; and corporations that make political expenditures of $750 or more in a calendar year.	Lieutenant Governor: state executive and legislative office candidates, political action committees, political issues committees, and corporations. County clerk: county office candidates. City recorder: city office candidates.	State executive/legislative office candidates: interim reports due 7 days before party convention if contest, 7 days before primary if candidate involved, 7 days before general election; summary report due December 31st of general election year; statement of dissolution and final summary report may be submitted at any time. County and city office candidates: if candidate loses at primary, report due 30 days after primary, otherwise, due 30 days after general election. political action committees, political issues committees, and corporations: annually by December 31st, 7 days before primary, and 7 days before general election.
Vermont	State executive office candidates, state legislative, county and local office candidates who have accepted contributions or made expenditures of $500 or more; political parties; and political committees that have accepted contributions or made expenditures of $500 or more in a calendar year.	Secy. of state: state executive office candidates, political committees, and political parties. Officer with whom candidate files nomination papers: state legislative, county, and local office candidates.	State executive office candidates, political committees, and political parties: 40 and 10 days before primary and general election; 10 days after general election; and July 15 and annually thereafter or when all contributions and expenditures have been accounted for and any indebtedness and surplus funds eliminated. Political committees and political parties involved in a local election also file 10 days before and 10 days after the election with the municipal clerk. State legislative and county office candidates: 10 days before primary and general election, and within 30 days after the general election; annual reporting as for state executive office candidates. Local office candidates: 10 days before and 10 days after the election.

GENERAL FILING REQUIREMENTS—Continued

State or other jurisdiction	Statements required from	Statements filed with	Time for filing
Virginia	Candidates or campaign treasurers (other than in elections for office in towns of less than 25,000, or for director of soil or water conservation districts); political action committees, state political party committees, and other committees (except district, county, and city political party committees) that expend over $500 for a statewide election or over $100 for any other election; political party committees that receive over $500 for a statewide election or over $100 for any other election; political party committees that receive earmarked contributions of over $100; and inauguration fund committees.	State Board of Elections: all statewide candidates, political action committees, political party committees, inauguration fund committees, and other committees. State Board of Elections and electoral board where candidate resides; candidates for General Assembly and a constitutional office shared by two or more counties and cities. Electoral board where candidate resides: all candidates for local office.	Candidates: all candidates except local office candidates in May general election: May 1 of election year; 8th day before primary, July 15, August 15, October 1, 8th day before general election, and December 1; January 15 and July 15 of next year; and January 15 in subsequent years. Candidates for state executive or state legislative office also file by January 15 a pre-election year annual report, if applicable, beginning with first year (other than election year) when a contribution is accepted or expenditure made. Local office candidates in May general election: 8th day before primary and general election, June 15 and July 15 in election year, and January 15 of the next and subsequent years. A final report is required and reporting terminates whenever final report is filed regardless of filing schedule. (u) Political action committees, political party committees, and other committees: January 15 (annual report), 8 days before 1st Tuesday in March and May, 8 days before 2nd Tuesday in June, 8 days before Tuesday after first Monday in November, and 30th day after November general election; final report is required. (u) Inauguration fund committees: March 15 after inauguration; July 15 of inauguration year; January 15 each year until final report is filed.
Washington	Candidates and political committees except in election campaigns for federal elective office and precinct committee officer. Candidates and political committees concerning an office whose constituency covers less than an entire county and contains less than 5,000 voters and in jurisdictions with less than 1,000 voters are exempted unless the exemption is voided.	Public Disclosure Commission and auditor or elections officer of county in which the candidate resides. Continuing political committees file reports with the Public Disclosure Commission and auditor or elections officer of county in which the committee maintains its office or headquarters.	At time campaign treasurer is designated; 21st and 7th day before and by the 10th day of the month following an election; 10th day of each month in which no other reports are required if a contribution is received or expenditure made in the previous month provided total contributions or expenditures since last report exceed $200; and at time campaign fund is closed and campaign concluded (final report). Post-primary report not required for candidate whose name will appear on general election ballot, or from continuing political committee. Continuing political committees also file monthly reports by 10th day if total contributions or expenditures since last report exceed $200. Candidates and political committees may file only post-election reports if they qualify for abbreviated campaign reporting or candidates may file only the registration statement if they qualify for mini-campaign reporting. (v)
West Virginia	Candidates, financial agents, party committee treasurers, and persons, associations of persons and organizations (including corporations) that support or oppose a candidate or issue, and their treasurers or equivalent officer.	Secy. of state: state and multi-county political subdivision offices. Clerk of the county commission: all other offices.	Last Saturday in March or within 15 days thereafter before the primary; 7-10 days before and 25-30 days after a primary, general or special election; and annually on last Saturday in March or within 15 days thereafter if contributions or expenditures exceed $5,000 or any loan is outstanding.

See footnotes at end of table.

GENERAL FILING REQUIREMENTS—Continued

State or other jurisdiction	Statements required from	Statements filed with	Time for filing
Wisconsin	Candidates and personal campaign committees, political committees, political groups, individuals, and conduits that meet minimum criteria concerning contributions, disbursements, obligations, or transfers. A political committee, political group, or individual, if other than a candidate or personal campaign committee, is exempted from registration and reporting if it does not make or accept contributions, make disbursements, or incur obligations of over $25 in a calendar year. Elections for presidential elector, convention delegate, and precinct committeeman are exempted from registration and reporting. Persons, political committees, and political groups (except political committees and individuals required to file a statement under oath concerning independent candidate-related disbursements) that do not anticipate aggregate contributions, disbursements, or obligations of over $1,000 in a calendar year and receipt of single-source contributions of over $100 in a calendar year are exempt from reporting.	State Elections Board: political party committees, state office candidates and committees, committees and individuals in both state and local office elections, and political groups and individuals involved with statewide referenda. Clerk of the most populous jurisdiction: local office candidates and committees (and duplicates of certain reports required to be filed with State Elections Board) and committees and individuals involved with local referenda only. City Clerk: city school district elections. School district clerk: other district school elections.	8-14 days before a primary or general election; continuing semi-annual reports between January 1 and 31 and July 1 and 10 until a termination report is filed. (w)
Wyoming	Candidates, candidates' campaign committees, political action committees, state and county political party central committees, and referendum/initiative organizations.	Secy. of state: statewide office candidates, state and county political party central committees, state legislative, and district judge candidates and their supporting committees. County clerk: state legislative and district judge candidates and supporting committees, other office candidates and supporting committees, and political party county central committees.	Candidates: within 10 days after an election. Non-party committees: within 10 days after an election; political action committees and candidates' campaign committes formed after an election to defray campaign expenses and any ongoing committees also report semi-annually on July 1 and December 31 of each odd-numbered year until committee terminates. Party committees: 10 days after general or special election. Initiative or referendum organizations: within 10 days after petition submitted. Ballot proposition organizations: within 10 days after election.
Dist. of Columbia	Candidates spending more than $250 in any one election; political committees; persons making independent expenditures of $50 or more.	Director of Campaign Finance.	Each year: January 31. Election years: 10th day of March, June, August, October and December; 8 days before an election. Non-election years: July 31. (x)

GENERAL FILING REQUIREMENTS—Continued

Sources: Edward D. Feigenbaum and James A. Palmer, *Campaign Finance Law '92* (Washington, D.C.: National Clearinghouse on Election Administration, Federal Election Commission, 1992); 1994 information will be available from the FEC in August 1994.

Note: This table deals with filing requirements for state and local offices in general terms. For detailed legal requirements, state statutes should be consulted.

(a) Contributions exceeding $250 made within one week before election must be reported within 24 hours.

(b) Short forms may be used by candidates and officeholders who raise and spend less than $1,000 in calendar year. There are three types of committees: (1) recipient committees receive $1,000 in contributions in a year; (2) independent expenditure committees make independent expenditures of $1,000 in a year; and (3) major donor committees make contributions of $10,000 in a year.

(c) Statewide officers, candidates, and committees: Original and one copy with the Secy. of state, two copies with the Registrar-Recorder of Los Angeles Country, two copies with the Registrar of Voters of the County of San Francisco, and two copies with the filer's county of domicile. State legislature, Board of Equalization, Appellate and Superior Court elections: Original and one copy with Secy. of state, two copies with the country clerk with the largest number of registered voters in the district affected, and two copies with the filer's county of domicile. Other multi-county elections (offices in jurisdiction other than legislative, Board of Equalization, or appellate court district that contain parts of two or more counties); original and one copy with the county clerk with the largest number of registered voters in the jurisdiction, two copies with the filer's county of domicile. County offices and municipal courts: original and one copy with the county clerk, two copies with the filer's county of domicile. City offices: original and one copy with the city clerk.

(d) Late contributions received or made and late independent expenditures of $1,000 or more made during the 16 days before an election must be reported by telegram within 24 hours.

(e) Contributions received more than $500 within 16 days before the election must be reported by the recipient within 48 hours after receipt.

(f) Special report required within 48 hours after receipt of a contribution of certain amounts, or expenditures on certain persons from 20 days before election through election day.

(g) Any contribution or loan to a statewide candidate of $2,000, or more than $400 to any legislative or district court candidate received between the closing date and the last pre-election report and the election must be reported within 48 hours after receipt.

(h) As of January 1, 1993, the filing officer became the Missouri Ethics Commission. Statements filed with the Missouri Ethics Commission for statewide office candidates and committees, and candidates for the supreme or appellate courts. Candidates for legislative office, circuit court and county clerk file with the Commission and election authority of the candidate's place of residence. Varied requirements for other candidates.

(i) Contributions of more than $1,000 received by a statewide office candidate ($500 for any other committee) after the closing date of the last pre-election disclosure report but before election day must be reported within 48 hours after receipt.

(j) Report required for all candidates and related political committees within 24 hours if contribution of $500 or more received for statewide or statewide ballot issue, or $100 for state district offices.

(k) Report of contributions of $500 or more received within 14 days before election is required to be filed within 5 days after receipt.

(l) Notice of a contribution more than $500 received after 2nd Wednesday before election is to be filed within 24 hours. Report of independent expenditures to be filed within 24 hours after expenditure more than $500 is made, and thereafter each time $500 more is spent.

(m) Single-source contribution of over $250 received by a continuing political committee after final day of quarterly reporting period and on or before election day to be reported within 48 hours. Single-

source contributions received by a candidate or political committee between the 13th day and election day to be reported within 48 hours.

(n) Contributions of more than $1,000 received after close of pre-election filing period must be reported within 24 hours of receipt.

(o) Supplemental statement for contribution of $500 or more received in 15-day period before an election must be filed within 48 hours by statewide or legislative office candidate and by referendum/initiative group or person.

(p) If $500 in contributions received after 9th day and before the day preceding the election, a pre-election supplemental statement is due on the day before the election.

(q) If a contribution of $500 or more is received within 9 days prior to an election, statement must be filed within 48 hours.

(r) If large contribution, loan or transfer of funds received within 10 days of election ($5,000 if it concerns a state office candidate; $2,500 if it concerns a local office candidate), report must be filed within 72 hours.

(s) Secy. of state: candidate for statewide office, district office filled by voters of more than one county, state senator or representative, or state board of elections, specific purpose committee supporting or opposing candidate filing with Secy. of state; officeholder and special purpose committee for assisting an officeholder for the office files with the Secy. of state; specific purpose committee involved with a statewide measure; specific purpose committee required to file with more than one filing officer; and a general purpose committee. County clerk: candidate for county office, precinct office, or an office filled by voters of one county; specific purpose committees supporting or opposing a candidate who files with the county clerk; officeholder and specific purpose committee for assisting an officeholder if a candidate for the office files with the county clerk; and specific purpose committee involved with a county measure. Clerk or secretary of non-county political subdivision: candidates for local office; specific purpose committee supporting or opposing a local office candidate; officeholder and specific purpose committee for assisting an officeholder if a candidate for the office files with the clerk/secretary; and specific purpose committee involved with a local measure.

(t) Certain large aggregate pre-election contributions or direct campaign expenditures between 9th and 2nd day before an election must be reported to Secy. of state within 48 hours.

(u) Candidate: Single contribution of more than $1,000 for statewide office or more than $500 for other office received between 11th day before and election day must be reported in writing within 72 hours or day before election, if received within 72 hours of election). Political action committees, political party committees and other committees: Contributions given or expenditures made by non-party committee of more than $1,000 for statewide office, or more than $500 for any other office after 11th day before 1st Tuesday in March and May, after 11th day before 2nd Tuesday in June, or after 11th day before Tuesday following 1st Monday in November must be reported within 72 hours (or not later than Monday before designated Tuesday if made within 24 hours of designated Tuesday).

(v) Contributions of over $500 received by a candidate or political committee or made by a political committee after the last pre-primary report or within 21 days of the general election are to be reported within 24 hours (contribution made) or 48 hours (contribution received).

(w) An unreported cumulative contribution of $500 or more by a state office candidate, committee, or individual within 15 days before an election must be reported within 24 hours of receipts. A candidate-related disbursement of more than $20 cumulatively within 15 days before an election must be reported within 24 hours of making.

(x) Contributions of $200 or more received after closing date for last pre-election report must be reported within 24 hours.

Table 5.11
CAMPAIGN FINANCE LAWS: LIMITATIONS ON CONTRIBUTIONS BY ORGANIZATIONS
(As of January 1992)

State or other jurisdiction	Corporate	Labor union	Separate segregated fund—political action committee (PAC)	Regulated industry	Political party
Alabama	Limited to $500 to any candidate, political committee or political party per election.	Unlimited.	Unlimited.	Public utility regulated by Public Service Commission may only contribute through a PAC.	Unlimited.
Alaska (a)	Limited to $1,000 per office per year. Corporations and their subsidiaries collectively limited to $1,000 for a single candidate.	Limited to $1,000 per office per year.	Same as labor union.	Same as labor union.	Unlimited.
Arizona	Prohibited.	Prohibited.	Limited to $2,750 for statewide candidates and $1,100 for other candidates.	Prohibited.	Unlimited.
Arkansas (a)	Limited to $1,000 per candidate per election.	Same as corporate.	Limited to $1,000 per candidate per election from approved political action committee.	Same as corporate.	Limited to $2,500 per candidate per election.
California (a)	Limits of $5,000 for a broad-based political committee; $2,500 for a political committee; and $1,000 per person per candidate per special election or special runoff election only. Certain jurisdictions have local limits on contributions to general election candidates.	Same as corporate.	Same as corporate.	Same as corporate.	Limits of $5,000 per candidate per special election or special runoff election only.
Colorado (a)	Unlimited.	Unlimited.	Unlimited.	Unlimited.	Unlimited.
Connecticut (a)	Prohibited.	Prohibited.	Corporate PAC: limited to aggregate of $100,000/election and twice limits per candidate as individuals. Labor PAC: limited to aggregate of $50,000 per election and same limits per candidate as individuals.	Prohibited.	Unlimited.
Delaware (a)	Limited to $1,200 per statewide candidate per election and $600 per non-statewide candidate per election.	Same as corporate.	Same as corporate.	Same as corporate.	Limited by office.
Florida (a)	Limited to $500 per candidate.	Same as corporate.	Same as corporate.	Limited to $500 per candidate; investment and law firms and their officers, directors, and employees making contributions or engaged in fundraising for state-level candidates cannot compete for business from Florida Housing Finance Agency.	Party may not contribute to candidate for judicial office. Party limited in contributions to candidates receiving public financing. Generally, $50,000 limit, with no more than $25,000 in last 28 days before general election.
Hawaii (a)	Limited to $2,000 in any election period.	Same as corporate.	Same as corporate.	Same as corporate.	Limited to a sliding scale percentage limit based upon candidate expenditure limits.
Idaho	Unlimited.	Unlimited.	Unlimited.	Unlimited.	Unlimited.

LIMITATIONS ON CONTRIBUTIONS BY ORGANIZATIONS—Continued

State or other jurisdiction	Corporate	Labor union	Separate segregated fund—political action committee (PAC)	Regulated industry	Political party
Illinois	Unlimited.	Unlimited.	Unlimited.	Unlimited.	Unlimited.
Indiana	Limited to an aggregate of $5,000 for statewide candidates, an aggregate of $5,000 for state party central committees, an aggregate of $2,000 for other offices, and an aggregate of $2,000 for other offices.	Same as corporate.	Unlimited.	No contributions to statewide candidates by major lottery vendors. Limited to an aggregate of $5,000 for statewide candidates, an aggregate of $5,000 for state party central committees, an aggregate of $2,000 for other offices, and an aggregate of $2,000 for other offices.	Unlimited.
Iowa	Prohibited.	Unlimited if through a union PAC.	Unlimited.	Prohibited for banks, savings & loans, and credit unions.	Unlimited.
Kansas (a)	Limited to $2,000 per statewide candidate per election; $1,000 per election for Senate seats; $500 per election for House seats and local office.	Same as corporate.	Same as corporate.	Same as corporate.	Unlimited in uncontested primaries and general election.
Kentucky (a)	Prohibited.	Limited to $4,000 per candidate per election.	Same as labor union.	Prohibited. No contributions by major lottery vendors.	Unlimited.
Louisiana (a)	Limited to $5,000 for major office candidates, $2,500 for district office candidates, and $1,000 for any other offices, per candidate, per election. During any four-year period, may not contribute greater than $100,000 to any political committee other than a candidate committee.	Same as corporate.	Limited to $5,000 for major office candidates, $2,500 for district office candidates, and $1,000 for any other offices, per candidate, per election. During any four-year period, may not contribute greater than $100,000 to any political committee other than a candidate committee. PACs with greater than 250 members who contributed at least $50 to the PAC during the preceding calendar year may give twice the limits. Aggregate limits from all PACs combined that candidates may receive for primary and general elections: $50,000 for major office; $35,000 for district office; $10,000 for other office.	Limited to $5,000 for major office candidates, $2,500 for district office candidates, and $1,000 for any other offices, per candidate, per election.	Unlimited.
Maine	Limited to $5,000 per candidate per election.	Same as corporate.	Same as corporate.	Same as corporate.	Same as corporate.
Maryland (a)	Limited to an aggregate of $10,000 per four-year election cycle and $4,000 per candidate or political committee.	Same as corporate.	Limited to an aggregate of $6,000 per four-year election cycle per candidate or political committee.	Same as corporate.	Unlimited.
Massachusetts (a)	Prohibited.	Unlimited.	Unlimited.	Prohibited.	State party cmte. $3,000 per calendar year and city party limited to $1,000 per calendar year.

See footnotes at end of table.

LIMITATIONS ON CONTRIBUTIONS BY ORGANIZATIONS—Continued

State or other jurisdiction	Corporate	Labor union	Separate segregated fund—political action committee (PAC)	Regulated industry	Political party
Michigan (a)	Prohibited for candidate elections.	Limited to $3,400 for a statewide office, $1,000 for state Senate and $500 for state representative candidates per election cycle.	Limited to $3,400 for a statewide office, $1,000 for state Senate and $500 for state representative candidates per election cycle. A PAC that qualifies as an independent committee may contribute ten times these amounts.	Prohibited except through a PAC.	State central: $68,000 for governor/lt. governor, $10,000 for Senate, $5,000 for House, $68,000 for all other state elective offices.
Minnesota	Prohibited.	Governor/Lt. governor: limited to $20,000 per election year and $3,000 in a non-election year. Attorney General: limited to $10,000 per election year and $2,000 in a non-election year. Other statewide offices: limited to $5,000 per election year and $1,000 in a non-election year. State Senate: limited to $1,500 per election year and $500 in a non-election year. State representative: limited to $750 per election year and $250 in a non-election year.	Same as labor union.	Prohibited; including for insurance companies.	Governor/lt. governor: limited to $100,000 per election year and $15,000 in a non-election year. Attorney general: limited to $50,000 per election year and $10,000 in a non-election year. Other statewide offices: limited to $25,000 per election year and $5,000 in a non-election year. State Senate: limited to $7,500 per election year and $2,500 in a non-election year. State representative: limited to $3,750 per election year and $1,250 in a non-election year.
Mississippi	Limited to $1,000 per candidate per election.	Unlimited.	Unlimited.	Generally prohibited.	Unlimited.
Missouri (a)	Unlimited.	Unlimited.	Unlimited.	Unlimited.	Unlimited.
Montana	Prohibited.	As an independent committee, limited for all elections in a campaign to $8,000 for governor/lt. governor, $2,000 for other statewide candidates, $1,000 for public service commissioner, district court judge, $600 for state senator, and $300 for other candidates. State legislative campaigns also subject to limits on receipt of non-party, political committee contributions.	Same as labor union.	Prohibited.	As an independent committee, limited for all elections in a campaign to $8,000 for governor/lt. governor, $2,000 for other statewide candidates, $1,000 for public service commissioner, district court judge, $600 for state senator, and $300 for other candidates. Contributions to judicial candidates prohibited.
Nebraska (a)	Unlimited, but may not receive contributions unless establishes a PAC.	Same as corporate.	Unlimited.	Same as corporate.	Unlimited.
Nevada	Statewide office: $20,000 per election cycle. City, county, state, or judicial office: $10,000 per election cycle.	Same as corporate.	Same as corporate.	Same as corporate.	Unlimited.
New Hampshire	Prohibited.	Prohibited.	Limited to $5,000 per candidate, per election, except limited to $1,000 per election if to candidate or political committee working on behalf of a candidate who does not voluntarily agree to limit campaign expenditures.	Prohibited.	. . .

LIMITATIONS ON CONTRIBUTIONS BY ORGANIZATIONS—Continued

State or other jurisdiction	Corporate	Labor union	Separate segregated fund—political action committee (PAC)	Regulated industry	Political party
New Jersey (a)	Generally unlimited. Limited to $1,500 for governor in any primary or general election.	Same as corporate.	Same as corporate.	Prohibited for insurance corporations or associations.	Generally unlimited, except state committee is limited to $1,500 for governor in a general election and political committee may not contribute to party candidates until after primary.
New Mexico	Unlimited.	Unlimited.	Unlimited.	Unlimited.	Unlimited.
New York (a)	Limited to an aggregate of $5,000 per calendar year.	Unlimited.	Unlimited.	Unlimited if not corporation; if corporation: limited to aggregate of $5,000 per calendar year. Public utilities may not contribute from public service revenues unless cost is charged to shareholders.	Unlimited.
North Carolina (a)	Prohibited.	Prohibited.	Limited to $4,000 per committee or candidate per election.	Prohibited.	Unlimited.
North Dakota	Prohibited.	Prohibited.	Unlimited.	Prohibited.	Unlimited.
Ohio (a)	Prohibited.	Unlimited.	Unlimited.	Prohibited.	Unlimited.
Oklahoma (a)	Prohibited.	Limited per person or family to $5,000 to a political party or organization in a calendar year, $5,000 to a candidate/ candidate committee for state office or municipal office in a municipality of 250,000 or more, and $1,000 to any other local candidate/candidate committee. Inter-PAC transfers not limited if established by common organization.	Limited per person or family to $5,000 to a political party or organization in a calendar year, $5,000 to a candidate/candidate committee for state office or municipal office in a municipality of 250,000 or more, and $1,000 to any other local candidate/ candidate committee.	Prohibited.	Limited to $5,000 to a political party or organization in a calendar year, $5,000 to a candidate/candidate committee for state office or municipal office in a municipality of 250,000 or more, and $1,000 to any other office candidate/candidate committee.
Oregon	Unlimited.	Unlimited.	Unlimited.	Unlimited.	Unlimited.
Pennsylvania (a)	Prohibited.	Prohibited.	Unlimited.	Prohibited.	Unlimited.
Rhode Island	$2,000 per calendar year.	Same as corporate.	Same as corporate.	Same as corporate.	Unlimited.
South Carolina (a)	Limited to $3,000 per statewide candidate per election; $1,000 per other candidate per election; $3,500 per committee per calendar year. Corporation or corporate committee may solicit contributions to the corporation or corporate committee only from shareholders, employees, and families.	Limited to $3,000 per statewide candidate per election; $1,000 per other candidate per election; $3,500 per committee per calendar year. Organization or organization committee may solicit contributions to the organization only from members and families.	Limited to $3,000 per statewide candidate per election; $1,000 per other candidate per election; $3,500 per committee per calendar year.	Limited to $3,000 per statewide candidate per election; $1,000 per other candidate per election; $3,500 per committee per calendar year. Public utility may not include contributions or expenditures to influence election or operate PAC in its operating expenses. Lobbyist and contractors may not contribute.	Limited to $50,000 per statewide candidate per election, $5,000 per other candidate per election.
South Dakota	Prohibited.	Prohibited if union is corporation; permitted if an association but not out of dues or treasury funds.	Unlimited.	Prohibited.	Unlimited.

See footnotes at end of table.

LIMITATIONS ON CONTRIBUTIONS BY ORGANIZATIONS—Continued

State or other jurisdiction	Corporate	Labor union	Separate segregated fund—political action committee (PAC)	Regulated industry	Political party
Tennessee	Prohibited.	Unlimited.	Unlimited.	Prohibited; public service commissioner or candidate for that office may not accept a contribution from a regulated party during contested case.	Unlimited.
Texas (a)	Prohibited.	Prohibited, except to political party, but during 60 days before general election.	Unlimited, but may not be made from mandatory assessments from corporation employees or labor organization members. Contributions from an out-of-state political committee are subject to special notification and reporting requirements.	Prohibited.	Unlimited.
Utah	Unlimited.	Unlimited.	Unlimited.	Insurers are generally prohibited from making political contributions.	Unlimited.
Vermont (a)	Limited to $1,000 per candidate or committee per election.	Same as corporate.	Same as corporate.	Same as corporate.	Unlimited.
Virginia	Unlimited.	Unlimited.	Unlimited.	Pari-mutuel betting licensees cannot contribute to candidates.	Unlimited.
Washington (a)	Aggregate contributions of more than $50,000 for a statewide office campaign or $5,000 for any other campaign may not be made to a candidate or political committee within 21 days of a general election.	Same as corporate.	Same as corporate.	Aggregate contributions of more than $50,000 for a statewide office campaign or $5,000 for any other campaign may not be made to a candidate or political committee within 21 days of a general election. Insurer or fraternal benefit society may not contribute to insurance commissioner candidate.	Unlimited.
West Virginia(a)	Prohibited.	Limited to $1,000 per candidate, per primary or general election.	Same as labor union.	Prohibited.	Same as labor union.
Wisconsin (a)	Prohibited, except concerning a referendum.	Prohibited if it is a chapter 185 association, except concerning a referendum.	Limited to 4% of authorized disbursement level for state office candidate, $1,000 for state senator, $500 for representative, varying amounts for other offices, and $6,000 in a calendar year for a political party.	Prohibited; also may not offer special privileges to candidates, political committees, and individuals making independent disbursements.	Unlimited; however, a political party or legislative campaign committee that files a statement under oath concerning independent candidate-related disbursements becomes subject to the limits for PACs. A candidate may not receive more than 65% of authorized disbursement level from all political committees. Political party may not receive more than $150,000 in any biennium from all political committees other than political party and legislative campaign committees. Contributions from committees (other than political party or legislative campaign committees) limited to $6,000 in a calendar year.
Wyoming	Prohibited.	Prohibited.	Unlimited.	Prohibited.	Prohibited in primary elections; otherwise unlimited.

LIMITATIONS ON CONTRIBUTIONS BY ORGANIZATIONS—Continued

State or other jurisdiction	Corporate	Labor union	Separate segregated fund—political action committee (PAC)	Regulated industry	Political party
Dist. of Columbia ...	Limited to an aggregate of $4,000 per election and $2,000 for mayor; $1,500 for council chair; $1,000 for council member at-large; $400 for council member from a district or board of education member at-large; $200 for board of education member from a district or party official; and $25 for a neighborhood advisory committee member.	Same as corporate.	Same as corporate.	Same as corporate.	...

Source: Edward D. Feigenbaum and James A Palmer. *Campaign Finance Law 92.* (Washington, D.C.: National Clearinghouse on Election Administration, Federal Election Commission, 1992); 1994 information will be available from the FEC in August 1994.

Note: For detailed legal requirements, state statutes should be consulted.

Key:

. . . — No reference to contribution in the law.

(a) Restrictions on cash contributions. In Oklahoma, cash contributions are prohibited. In Alaska, Arkansas, Colorado, Florida, Kansas, Kentucky, Maine, Missouri, New York and North Carolina eliminated to $100 or less. In California, less than $100. In Connecticut, Delaware, Maryland, Massachusetts, Nebraska, Vermont and West Virginia, limited to $50 or less. Michigan limits cash contributions to $20 or less. In Wisconsin, must be $10 or less. In Hawaii, contributions greater than $100 require a receipt to the donor and a record of the transaction. In Louisiana, contributions greater than $100 must be by written instrument and all contributions by corporations, labor organizations, and associations must be by check. In New Jersey, cash contributions prohibited unless in response to public solicitation or a written contributor statement is filed (maximum up to $100 cumulatively). In Ohio, must be $100 or less per election. In Pennsylvania, must be $100 or less in the aggregate if to or for a candidate. In South Carolina, prohibited if over $25 from an individual. In Texas, must be $100 or less in the aggregate per each reporting period, except no limit for general purpose political committee. In Washington, limited to greater of one percent of total accumulated contributions received or $300.

Table 5.12
CAMPAIGN FINANCE LAWS: LIMITATIONS ON CONTRIBUTIONS BY INDIVIDUALS
(As of January 1992)

State or other jurisdiction	Individual	Candidate	Candidate's family member	Government employees	Anonymous or in name of another
Alabama	Unlimited.	Unlimited.	Unlimited.	No solicitation of state employees for state political activities. City employees may contribute to county/state political activities; county employees may contribute to city/state political activities.	Contribution in the name of another prohibited.
Alaska (a)	Limited to $1,000 per office per year.	Unlimited.	Same as individual.	Contribution may not be required of state employees.	Prohibited.
Arizona	Limited to $550 per statewide candidate; $220 per other offices; and a maximum of $2,200 in total contributions per calendar year.	Unlimited.	Same as individual.	. . .	. . .
Arkansas (a)	Limited to $1,000 per candidate per election.	Unlimited.	Same as individual.	Certain state employees are prohibited from soliciting, as are certain judges (for campaigns other than their own). Contribution may not be required of state employees.	Anonymous contribution must be less than $50 per year. Contribution in the name of another prohibited.
California (a)	Limits of $5,000 for a broad-based political committee; $2,500 for a political committee; and $1,000 per person per candidate per special election or special runoff election only. Certain jurisdictions have local limits on contributions to general election candidates.	Unlimited.	Same as individual.	Local agency employees may not solicit employees of agency except incidentally through a large solicitation. Contribution must be less than $100.	Anonymous contribution must not exceed $100. Contribution in the name of another prohibited.
Colorado (a)	Unlimited.	Unlimited.	Unlimited.	. . .	Anonymous contribution must be maximum of $25. Contribution in the name of another prohibited.
Connecticut (a)	Limited to an aggregate of $15,000; per election and $2,500 for governor; $1,500 for other statewide office; $1,000 for sheriff or local chief executive; $500 for state Senate, probate judge, or any other local office; $250 for state representative; and $5,000 per year to state party.	Unlimited.	Same as individual.	State department heads and deputies may not solicit. Contribution may not be required.	Anonymous contribution must be less than $15. Contribution in the name of another prohibited.
Delaware (a)	Limited to $1,200 per statewide candidate per election and $600 per non-statewide candidate per election.	Same as individual.	Same as individual.	. . .	Prohibited.
Florida (a)	Limited to $500 per candidate. Unemancipated child under 18 limited to $100 per candidate.	Unlimited, except candidates accepting public financing are limited to $25,000 to their own campaigns.	Limited to $500 per candidate.	Solicitation generally prohibited for state employees. Judges may not solicit contributions. Judges not elected in contested public elections may not make contributions.	Contribution in the name of another prohibited.
Georgia	Limited to $3,500 per election.	Same as individual.	Same as individual.	Prohibited for state employee to coerce another state employee.	Anonymous contribution prohibited.

LIMITATIONS ON CONTRIBUTIONS BY INDIVIDUALS—Continued

State or other jurisdiction	Individual	Candidate	Candidate's family member	Government employees	Anonymous or in name of another
Hawaii (a)	Limited to $2,000 in any election period.	Same as individual.	Same as individual.	Solicitation of contributions prohibited. Contributions to other employees are prohibited.	Prohibited.
Idaho	Unlimited.	Unlimited.	Unlimited.	Prohibited for state employee to coerce another state employee. Contribution permitted.	Anonymous contribution must be $50 or less. Contribution in the name of another prohibited.
Illinois	Unlimited.	Unlimited.	Unlimited.	Solicitation and contribution by employees prohibited under certain circumstances.	Prohibited.
Indiana	Unlimited.	Unlimited.	Unlimited.	Certain law enforcement personnel/firefighters may not solicit on duty or in uniform; state employees cannot solicit (1) when on duty, (2) acting in official capacity, (3) from those employees known to have a business relationship with the employee's agency, and (4) from state employees directly supervised by the employee. Judges may not personally solicit. Contribution may not be required. Judges should not contribute.	Contribution in the name of another prohibited.
Iowa	Unlimited.	Unlimited.	Unlimited.	Prohibited for state employee to coerce another state employee.	Prohibited.
Kansas (a)	Limited to $2,000 per statewide candidate per election; $1,000 per election for Senate seats; $500 per election for House seats and local office.	Unlimited.	Same as individual.	Certain employees cannot compel contributions.	Anonymous contribution must be $10 or less. Contribution in the name of another prohibited.
Kentucky (a)	Limited to $4,000 per candidate per election, and to PAC. Limited to $6,000 to all state/local political parties.	Unlimited (direct). Loans are limited.	Limited to $4,000 per candidate per election. Minors limited to $100.	Assessments and coercion of state employees prohibited. Contribution may not be required of state employees.	Anonymous contribution must be $100 or less. Contribution in the name of another prohibited. (b)
Louisiana (a)	Limited to $5,000 for major office candidates, $2,500 for district office candidates, and $1,000 for any other offices, per candidate, per election. During any four-year period, may not contribute more than $100,000 to any political committee other than a candidate committee.	. . .	Same as individual.	Solicitation and contribution generally prohibited.	Anonymous contribution generally prohibited. Contribution in the name of another prohibited.
Maine	Limited to an aggregate of $25,000 in a calendar year and $1,000 per candidate per election.	Unlimited.	Unlimited for spouse.	Prohibited for state employee to coerce another state employee.	Contribution in the name of another prohibited.
Maryland (a)	Limited to an aggregate of $10,000 per four-year election cycle and $4,000 per candidate or political committee.	Unlimited.	Unlimited for spouse.	Contribution may not be required.	Prohibited.

See footnotes at end of table.

LIMITATIONS ON CONTRIBUTIONS BY INDIVIDUALS—Continued

State or other jurisdiction	Individual	Candidate	Candidate's family member	Government employees	Anonymous or in name of another
Massachusetts (a)	Limited to $1,000 per candidate per year. Minors limited to $25 per year.	Unlimited.	Same as individual.	Solicitation generally prohibited. Contribution may not be required.	Prohibited.
Michigan (a)	Limited to $3,400 for a statewide office, $1,000 for state Senate, and $500 for state representative candidates per election cycle.	Unlimited, except to $50,000 per gubernatorial campaign from candidate and family per election cycle.	Unlimited, except to $50,000 per gubernatorial campaign per election cycle.	Contribution may not be required.	Prohibited.
Minnesota	Governor/lt. governor: limited to $20,000 per election year and $3,000 in a non-election year. Attorney general: limited to $10,000 per election year and $2,000 in a non-election year. Other statewide offices: limited to $5,000 per election year and $1,000 in a non-election year. State Senate: limited to $1,500 per election year and $500 in a non-election year. State representative: limited to $750 per election year and $250 in a non-election year.	Unlimited.	Same as individual.	Solicitation prohibited during hours of employment. Contribution may not be required.	Anonymous contributions must be less than $20. Contribution in the name of another prohibited.
Mississippi	Unlimited.	Unlimited.	Unlimited.	Solicitation prohibited for employees of certain specified agencies. Contribution may not be required. Employees of certain specified agencies may not contribute.	. . .
Missouri (a)	Unlimited.	Unlimited.	Unlimited.	Members of the Missouri Ethics Commission may not contribute.	Anonymous contribution must be $25 or less. Contribution in the name of another prohibited.
Montana	Limited for all elections in a campaign to $1,500 for governor/lt. governor, $750 for other statewide candidates, $400 for public service commissioner, district court judge, or state senator, and $250 for other candidates.	Unlimited.	Same as individual.	Solicitation by municipal government employees prohibited. Contributions by municipal employees in city with municipal commission form of government is prohibited.	Prohibited.
Nebraska (a)	Unlimited.	Unlimited, except that candidate committee cannot contribute to another candidate committee other than in fundraising event.	Unlimited.	Contribution unlimited.	Anonymous contribution prohibited. Contribution in the name of another prohibited, except earmarked contributions permitted if disclosure requirements met.
Nevada	Statewide office: $10,000 per election cycle. City, county, state, or judicial office: $2,000 per election cycle.	Same as individual.	Same as individual.	Judges and judicial candidates should not solicit contributions for political organizations and other candidates.	If anonymous contribution $100 or more, must be delivered to state treasurer or donated to nonprofit entity.
New Hampshire	Limited to $5,000 per candidate, per election, except limited to $1,000 per election if to candidate or political committee working on behalf of a candidate who does not voluntarily agree to limit campaign expenditures.	Unlimited.	Same as individual.	Cannot coerce classified state employee to contribute.	Prohibited.

LIMITATIONS ON CONTRIBUTIONS BY INDIVIDUALS—Continued

State or other jurisdiction	Individual	Candidate	Candidate's family member	Government employees	Anonymous or in name of another
New Jersey (a)	Generally limited. Limited to $1,500 for governor in any primary or general election. Contributor's spouse may contribute up to $1,500 for governor in a primary or general election.	Unlimited, except if receiving public funds for governor, limited to $25,000 per election from own funds.	Same as individual.	Prohibited to demand from other public employees.	Prohibited.
New Mexico	Unlimited.	Unlimited.	Unlimited.	Judges may not solicit from litigants in pending cases or attorneys or for other candidates. Non-probationary state employees cannot be dismissed for failure to contribute.	Anonymous contributions permitted; if in excess of $50 must be reported.
New York (a)	Limited to an aggregate of $150,000 in calendar year and maximum aggregate per office: statewide office nomination or statewide party position election: 2.5¢ x voters in party in state; statewide office election: 2.5¢ x voters in state; non-statewide party position election: 2.5¢ x voters in party in district (minimum $1,000/ maximum $50,000); non-statewide office election: 5¢ x voters in district (minimum $1,000/maximum $50,000); state senator/assembly member nomination: 5¢ x voters in party in district (senator: minimum $4,000/maximum $50,000; assembly member: minimum $2,500/maximum $50,000); senator/assembly member election: 5¢ x voters in district (senator: minimum $4,000/maximum $50,000; assembly member: minimum $2,500/maximum $50,000).	Unlimited.	Candidate's spouse is unlimited. Other family members together are limited to maximum aggregate per office: statewide office nomination or statewide party position election: 2.5¢ x voters in party in state; statewide office election: 2.5¢ x voters in state; non-statewide office nomination or non-statewide party position election: 25¢ x voters in party in district (minimum $1,250/maximum $100,000); non-statewide office election: 25¢ x voters in district (minimum $1,250/maximum $100,000); state senator/assembly member nomination: 25¢ x voters in party in district (senator: minimum $20,000/maximum $100,000); assembly member: minimum $12,500/maximum $100,000); senator/assembly member election: 25¢ x voters in district (senator: minimum $20,000/maximum $100,000; assembly member: minimum $12,500/maximum $100,000).	Solicitation prohibited for police force members and judicial candidates. Contribution permitted, but may not be required. Contribution by judicial candidates prohibited.	Prohibited.
North Carolina (a) ...	Limited to $4,000 per committee or candidate per election.	Unlimited.	Unlimited.	Judge or judicial candidate may not solicit contributions.	Prohibited.
North Dakota	Unlimited.	Unlimited.	Unlimited.	Full-time judge may not solicit contributions. Contribution unlimited.	Prohibited.
Ohio (a)	Unlimited.	Unlimited.	Unlimited.	May not solicit or be solicited if in classified service. Court employees should not be solicited for a judge. A judge should not contribute to a political party in the year judge is a candidate.	Prohibited.

See footnotes at end of table.

LIMITATIONS ON CONTRIBUTIONS BY INDIVIDUALS—Continued

State or other jurisdiction	Individual	Candidate	Candidate's family member	Government employees	Anonymous or in name of another
Oklahoma (a)	Limited per person or family to $5,000 to a political party or organization in a calendar year, $5,000 to a candidate/candidate committee for state office or municipal office in a municipality of 250,000 or more, and $1,000 to any other local candidate/candidate committee.	Unlimited to own campaign; otherwise subject to limits for individuals.	Same as individual.	State officials and employees may not solicit or receive contributions. Judges should not solicit. Contribution prohibited for state highway patrol members and supernumerary tax consultants. Judges should not contribute.	Prohibited.
Oregon	Unlimited.	Unlimited.	Unlimited.	Solicitation prohibited during hours of employment. Contribution may not be demanded to pay a political assessment.	Prohibited.
Pennsylvania (a)	Unlimited.	Unlimited.	Unlimited.	Public officers and employees may not demand a political assessment. Judges should not solicit state funds. State classified service, state crime commission, public utility commission, community action agency, and county board of health personnel may not solicit. Workplace contributions by state classified service employees are restricted. Judges and judicial candidates should not make candidate contributions.	Prohibited.
Rhode Island	$2,000 per calendar year.	Unlimited.	Same as individual.	State classified employees may not solicit. State or municipal official may not solicit contribution with understanding that official will be influenced. Judge or candidate for judicial office should not solicit. State classified employees may not be solicited.	Prohibited. Must be returned to donor if identity can be ascertained; if it cannot, escheats to state.
South Carolina (a) ...	Limited to $3,000 per statewide candidate per election; $1,000 per other candidate per election; $3,500 per committee per calendar year.	Unlimited.	Same as individual.	Employer cannot give preference to employees who contribute; must inform them of right to refuse without penalty. No one may solicit uniformed law enforcement officer, judge, judicial candidate, solicitor and staff, and attorney general and staff. Judge and judicial candidate should not solicit. Contribution prohibited by state ethics commission personnel; judges and judicial candidates should not contribute, except in competitive office may contribute to a political party.	Anonymous contribution prohibited generally. Must give to children's trust fund.
South Dakota	Limited to any calendar year to $1,000 for a statewide office candidate; $250 for a legislative or county office candidate; and $3,000 to a political party.	Unlimited.	Unlimited.	Judge or judicial candidate should not solicit. Judge or judicial candidate should not pay an assessment to a political organization or candidate, but a judge or judicial candidate for competitive office may contribute to a political party.	...

LIMITATIONS ON CONTRIBUTIONS BY INDIVIDUALS—Continued

State or other jurisdiction	Individual	Candidate	Candidate's family member	Government employees	Anonymous or in name of another
Tennessee	Unlimited.	Unlimited.	Unlimited.	Prohibited for state government superiors to solicit their employees. Prohibited to solicit persons who receive government benefits. State career service employees may not solicit. Judges should not solicit. Employees of sheriff's department under civil service law may not solicit. Judges expressly permitted to contribute only to political party or candidate.	...
Texas (a)	Unlimited.	Unlimited.	Unlimited.	...	Contribution in the name of another prohibited, unless there is disclosure.
Utah	Unlimited.	Unlimited.	Unlimited.	Prohibited to solicit executive branch employees during hours of employment. Judges should not solicit funds. Judges are not permitted to make contributions to a political party or organization.	...
Vermont (a)	Limited to $1,000 per candidate or committee per election.	Unlimited, except federal office candidate limited to $1,000 to another candidate or committee per election.	Unlimited.	Solicitation prohibited.	...
Virginia	Unlimited.	Unlimited.	Unlimited.	Contribution by judges prohibited.	...
Washington (a)	Aggregate contributions of more than $50,000 for a statewide office campaign or $5,000 for any other campaign may not be made to a candidate or political committee within 21 days of a general election.	Same as individual.	Same as individual.	Solicitation on government property is prohibited. Judges may not solicit. Contribution prohibited if city with commission form of government. Judges may not contribute to a political party, political organization, or non-judicial candidate.	Anonymous contribution limited to greater of one percent of total accumulated contributions received or $300. Contribution in the name of another prohibited.
West Virginia (a)	Limited to $1,000 per candidate, per primary or general election.	Same as individual.	Same as individual.	Contribution may not be solicited.	Anonymous contribution prohibited. Contributor disclosure required for contribution in the name of another.
Wisconsin (a)	Limited to an aggregate of $10,000 in a calendar year. Limits for campaign: $10,000 for statewide office, $1,000 for state senator, $500 for state representative, $2,500 or $3,000 for court of appeals judge (depending on population of district), $1,000 or $3,000 for circuit judge (depending on population of circuit), and for local office, the greater of $250 or 1¢ x number of inhabitants ($3,000 maximum).	Unlimited as to candidate's own personal funds and property or personal funds and property owned jointly or as marital property with spouse. State office candidate who receives election campaign fund grant is limited to 200% of the amount that an individual may contribute.	Limited to same amounts as individual, except in the case of property and personal funds owned jointly or as marital property by a candidate and spouse.	Solicitation and contribution prohibited during hours of employment or while engaged in official duties. Judges may not solicit or contribute for political party.	Anonymous contribution must be $10 or less. Contribution in the name of another prohibited.

See footnotes at end of table.

LIMITATIONS ON CONTRIBUTIONS BY INDIVIDUALS—Continued

State or other jurisdiction	Individual	Candidate	Candidate's family member	Government employees	Anonymous or in name of another
Wyoming	Limited to an aggregate of $25,000 and to $1,000 per candidate, per primary, general, or special election in any general election year and the preceding year.	Unlimited.	Unlimited.	Judges may not solicit funds for candidates.	. . .
Dist. of Columbia	Limited to an aggregate of $4,000 per election and $2,000 for mayor; $1,500 for council chair; $1,000 for council member at-large; $400 for council member from a district or board of education member at-large; $200 for board of education member from a district or party official; and $25 for a neighborhood advisory committee member.	Same as individual.	Same as individual.	Contribution permitted but employees may not solicit or collect political contributions.	Anonymous contributions prohibited.

Source: Edward D. Feigenbaum and James A. Palmer *Campaign Finance Law 92.* (Washington, D.C.: National Clearinghouse on Election Administration, Federal Election Commission, 1992); 1994 information will be available from the FEC in August 1994.

Note: For detailed legal requirements, state statutes should be consulted.

Key:

. . . — No reference to contribution in the law.

(a) Restrictions on cash contributions. In Oklahoma, cash contributions are prohibited. In Alaska, Arkansas, Colorado, Florida, Kansas, Kentucky, Maine, Missouri, New York and North Carolina limited to $100 or less. In California, less than $100. In Connecticut, Delaware, Maryland, Massachusetts, Nebraska, Vermont and West Virginia, limited to $50 or less. Michigan limits cash contributions to $20 or less. In Wisconsin, must be $10 or less. In Hawaii, contributions greater than $100 require a receipt to the donor and a record of the transaction. In Louisiana, contributions greater than $100 must be by written instrument. In New Jersey, cash contributions prohibited unless in response to public solicitation or a written contributor statement is filed (maximum up to $100 cumulatively). In Ohio, must be $100 or less per election. In Pennsylvania, must be $100 or less in the aggregate if to or for a candidate. In South Carolina, prohibited if over $25 from an individual. In Texas, must be $100 or less in the aggregate per reporting period, except no limit for general purpose political committee. In Washington, limited to greater of one percent of total accumulated contributions received or $300.

(b) Language has been held to be unconstitutionally vague. *Kentucky v. E.O. Associates.*

Table 5.13
CAMPAIGN FINANCE LAWS: LIMITATIONS ON EXPENDITURES
(As of January 1992)

State or other jurisdiction	Who may make expenditures	Total expenditures allowed	Expenditures prior to first filing	For certain purposes	Use of surplus funds (a)
Alabama (b)	Only committee named and designated by candidate	...	...	...	Unlimited as to officeholder expenses, contributions to charity, transfers to another committee, or uses for other lawful purposes.
Alaska	Candidate, treasurer, or deputy treasurer	...	No expenditures permitted before filing date except for personal travel expenses and public opinion polls/surveys.	...	May be given to charity, used to repay contributors, spent on a future campaign, used to repay candidate or used as income, contributed to another committee, or transferred to office allowance fund. Surplus funds may be taken as income by candidate.
Arizona	...	...	No expenditures permitted until registration form is properly filed.	...	May be retained for a future campaign; returned to contributors; donated to a party committee, charitable organization, political organization, or other candidate (after 12/31/92 may not be donated to another candidate's committee or used for candidate's personal use).
Arkansas	...	...	...	...	After setting aside any funds needed to pay debts, and an amount equal to the yearly salary for the office sought, surplus funds must either be turned over to the state treasurer for the benefit of the general revenue fund, to an organized political party, or to contributors to the candidate's campaign (c).
California (b)	...	...	...	Must be directly related to political, legislative, or governmental purpose if candidate or elected officer receives substantial personal benefit. Certain expenditures must be directly related regardless of benefit received.	May be used for debts or charitable contributions; contributed to a political party, candidate for federal office or ballot measure; contributed to an out-of-state campaign; or used to defray certain legal or professional expenses associated with the election and aftermath. Personal use of funds by candidate generally prohibited; must be directly related to political, legislative, or governmental purpose if candidate or elected officer receives substantial personal benefit. Certain expenditures must be directly related regardless of benefit received.

See footnotes at end of table.

LIMITATIONS ON EXPENDITURES—Continued

State or other jurisdiction	Who may make expenditures	Total expenditures allowed	Expenditures prior to first filing	For certain purposes	Use of surplus funds (a)
Colorado (b)	...	...	...	Must be reasonably related to an election, voter registration, or political education. May not be used to encourage another candidate's withdrawal from race.	May be contributed to a nonprofit or charitable organization, or to the state or a political subdivision of the state, but not to a political party or to a candidate.
Connecticut (b)	Treasurer or those authorized by treasurer.	...	No expenditures permitted until treasurer and campaign depository have been designated.	Polls, meeting halls, rally expenses, printing and advertising, professional service fees, travel, staff salaries, rent, supplies, voter transportation, communications, petition-related expenses, and other expenses permitted by the commission.	Surplus may be donated to another committee (except one established to further the candidate's future campaigns), distributed pro rata to contributors, or used for transition expenses. Ballot question committees may also distribute surplus to government agencies or tax-exempt organizations. Personal use of funds by candidate prohibited.
Delaware	Candidate committee	...	...	Staff salaries, travel expenses, filing fees, communications and printing, food, office supplies, voter lists and canvasses, poll watchers, rent, advertising, rallies, legal counsel.	May be contributed to a tax-exempt religious, charitable, educational, or scientific organization, volunteer fire department, or a successful committee.
Florida (b)	...	Public financed candidates and those agreeing to voluntary limits: $5 million for governor and lt. governor; $2 million for cabinet. Limits may be increased under certain circumstances.	...	Expenditures may only be used to influence the results of an election.	Funds remaining after an election are to be used to pay remaining obligations incurred prior to or on election day. Surplus funds may be used to reimburse a candidate for candidate's contributions; transferred to a public officeholder account in various amounts dependent upon office; given to a candidate's contributors; given to a nonprofit or charitable organization; or given to the state for the general fund or the election campaign financing trust fund (by a state candidate) or political subdivision (by a local candidate). Personal use of funds by candidate permitted if disclosed at the time of first filing.
Georgia............	...	...	...	May only be used to defray ordinary and necessary campaign expenses.	Personal use of funds by candidate prohibited.
Hawaii	Only campaign treasurer or deputy treasurer.	Voluntary election year limits: governor—$1.25 x qualified voters; lt. governor—70¢ x qualified voters; mayor—$1.00 x qualified voters; House/Senate/council/prosecutor—70¢ x qualified voters; others—10¢ x qualified voters.	...	Must be related to a campaign purpose, including donations to community, youth, social or recreational organizations; reports, surveys, and polls.	Surplus may be used for fundraising; candidate-sponsored, politically related activity; ordinary and necessary officeholder expenses; donations to any community service, scientific, education, youth, recreation, charitable, or literary organization. Personal use of funds by candidate prohibited.

LIMITATIONS ON EXPENDITURES—Continued

State or other jurisdiction	Who may make expenditures	Total expenditures allowed	Expenditures prior to first filing	For certain purposes	Use of surplus funds (a)
Idaho	...	...	...	...	...
Illinois	Must be authorized by chair, treasurer, or their designated agents.	...	...	Only for nomination or election or retention of a person in public office or in connection with a public policy question.	...
Indiana	Only treasurer may make expenditures.	...	...	Must be used for campaign, for continuing political activity, activity related to service in an elected office, or contributions to party committees or other candidate committees.	May be transferred to political committees or state election board, unless otherwise provided in committee statement of organization. Personal use of funds by candidate prohibited.
Iowa	...	...	...	Generally prohibited. Public funds may only be used for legitimate campaign purposes in general elections, including salaries, rent, advertising, supplies, travel, campaign paraphernalia, contributions to other candidates or committees, and the like.	Public funds may not be used to lease or purchase any item whose benefits extend beyond the time in which the funds must be spent. Campaign funds may not generally be used to pay civil/criminal penalties; personal debts or expenses; for personal services unrelated to the campaign; most motor vehicle leases and payments; professional organization and most service organization memberships; mortgage or rental payments for the candidate; meals, groceries, and other food not for campaign uses; payments clearly in excess of the fair market value of the service or item. Personal use of funds by candidate prohibited.
Kansas	Must be by or through treasurer.	...	No expenditures permitted until registration form properly filed.	Must be for legitimate campaign or officeholding expenses.	Personal use of funds by candidate prohibited.
Kentucky (b)	Treasurer must make or authorize all expenditures on behalf of a candidate.	...	No expenditures permitted until primary campaign depository is designated.	Political parties receiving tax money may use these funds to support their party's candidates in a general election, and for administrative costs of maintaining a party headquarters.	Any unexpended balance may be returned pro rata to all contributors, transferred to the candidate's party executive committee, retained for election to the same office, or escheat to the state treasury.
Louisiana (b)	...	...	No expenditures aggregating in excess of $500 may be made by a political committee until statement of organization is properly filed.	Must be related to a political campaign or holding of office.	May be returned pro rata to contributors; given to a charitable organization; spent for or against a candidate, political party, or a proposition; used in future political campaigns; or activity related to a future campaign. Personal use of funds by candidate prohibited except to replace items stolen, lost, or damaged in connection with a campaign.

See footnotes at end of table.

LIMITATIONS ON EXPENDITURES—Continued

State or other jurisdiction	Who may make expenditures	Total expenditures allowed	Expenditures prior to first filing	For certain purposes	Use of surplus funds (a)
Maine	…	PAC is limited to expenditures of $5,000 per candidate or political committe in any election.	…	…	Returned pro rata to contributors, used for the candidate's future campaigns or transferred to other committees.
Maryland	Public funds may only be spent upon authority of candidate or treasurer. Other expenditures must be made through treasurer.	Publicly financed candidates for governor/lt. governor limited to 20¢ x qualified voters.	No expenditures permitted until registration form is properly filed.	Public contributions may only be used to further the candidate's nomination or election, for legal purposes, and for expenses not incurred later than 30 days after the election.	Surplus public funds must be repaid not later than 60 days after the election for which the funds are granted. Other surplus funds must be returned on a pro rata basis to contributors; paid to a party central committee; donated to a local board of education, recognized non-profit educational or charitable organization; or given to a higher education institution for scholarships.
Massachusetts (b)	…	…	…	…	…
Michigan (b)	An expenditure may only be made with the authorization of the treasurer or the treasurer's designee.	Gubernatorial candidates who accept public funds limited to $1.5 million per election; except up to $300,000 more can be spent to solicit contributions, and additional expenditures are authorized in response to editorials, endorsements, etc.	…	Public funds may only be spent on services, facilities, materials, or other things of value to further the candidate's election during the election year.	Surplus public funds must be promptly repaid and may not be used in a subsequent election. Other funds may be transferred to another committee (with restrictions), party, or tax-exempt charitable institution or returned to contributors. Public funds cannot be used to pay a candidate.
Minnesota (b)	Must be authorized by treasurer or deputy treasurer of committee or fund.	Candidates accepting public subsidies are limited as follows in election years (to be adjusted each election year based on Consumer Price Index): governor/lt. governor: $1,626,691; attorney general: $271,116; other statewide office: $135,559; state Senate: $40,660; state representative: $20,335. Limits in non-election years are 25% of applicable election year limits.	…	Limited to salaries, wages, and fees; communications, mailing, and transportation and travel; advertising and printing; office space and furnishings; supplies; and other expenses reasonably related to the election.	…
Mississippi	…	…	…	…	…
Missouri (b)	All expenditures must be made by or through the treasurer.	…	…	…	May only be used to defray campaign or officeholder expenses, returned pro rata to contributors, or contributed to a political or charitable organization or candidate committee. Personal use of funds by candidate prohibited.
Montana (b)	Campaign treasurers and deputy campaign treasurers.	…	…	…	…

LIMITATIONS ON EXPENDITURES—Continued

State or other jurisdiction	Who may make expenditures	Total expenditures allowed	Expenditures prior to first filing	For certain purposes	Use of surplus funds (a)
Nebraska (b)	Treasurers or treasurers' designees; however, candidates and their agents are also permitted to make expenditures.	. . .	Expenditure may not be made by a committee raising, receiving, or disbursing more than $2,000 in a calendar year until it files a statement of organization and has a treasurer.	A committee other than a political party may not expend or transfer funds except for goods, materials, services, or facilities to assist or oppose a candidate for a ballot question.	After an election, a committee may expend or transfer funds for continued operation of campaign offices; social events for workers, volunteers, and constituents; obtaining public input and opinion; repayment of campaign loans; newsletters and other political communications; gifts of acknowledgment; and officeholder-related meals, lodging and travel. After termination of a candidate committee, unexpended funds may be transferred to another candidate committee, a political party committee, or a tax-exempt charitable organization, or returned to contributors. A committee may not make expenditures for the payment of a candidate's clothes, or medical or dental expenses; mortgage or rental payments for the candidate's permanent residence; installment payments for an auto owned by the candidate; satisfaction of personal debts (excluding reportable campaign loans); or personal services (such as legal or accounting services).
Nevada	. . .	. . .	. . .	. . .	Elected and defeated candidates and non-candidate officeholders are required to dispose of unspent contributions in a statutorily authorized manner, including return to contributors, contribution for political purpose, and donation to tax-exempt nonprofit entity. Elected candidates may use for present or future campaign expenses or public office expenses. Personal use of funds by candidate prohibited.
New Hampshire	Candidate or candidate's fiscal agent.	Candidate may agree to limit campaign expenditures made by candidate and by committees, political party and immediate family on candidate's behalf in a primary or general election in accordance with a maximum expenditure schedule.	Before nonparty political committee may make expenditures, a registration statement must be filed, and if the political committee is organized to support a candidate, written consent of the candidate or candidate's fiscal agent must have been secured and filed. Political committee making independent expenditures must declare in registration statement it will abide by $1,000 expenditure limit per candidate per election.	. . .	. . .

See footnotes at end of table.

LIMITATIONS ON EXPENDITURES—Continued

State or other jurisdiction	Who may make expenditures	Total expenditures allowed	Expenditures prior to first filing	For certain purposes	Use of surplus funds (a)
New Jersey	Treasurer or deputy treasurer of a candidate, political party committee, political committee, and continuing political committee.	Maximum amount to aid candidate for governor (excluding travel expenses) in 1989 primary: $2.2 million; in 1989 general election: $5 million. Spending limits are subject to adjustment prior to gubernatorial election year to reflect changes in campaign costs. Gubernatorial candidate receiving public funding is limited to $25,000 in primary and $25,000 in general election from candidate's personal funds.	. . .	. . .	. . .
New Mexico	Treasurer of candidate or political committee.	Treasurer must be appointed before candidate or political committee may make an expenditure.		. . .	Judicial candidates must return unused funds to contributors or donate to charitable organization.
New York (b)	Treasurer of candidate or political committee.	. . .	Expenditures may not be made by a political committee until the designation of a treasurer and depository have been filed.	Contributions may be expended for any lawful purpose.	May be used for any lawful purpose, including transfer to political party committee, return to donor, or holding for use in subsequent campaign. Contributions may not be converted to personal use of candidate not related to political campaign or holding public office or party position.
North Carolina (b)	Except for independent expenditures, candidate-related expenditures may be made only through the treasurer or assistant treasurer of a candidate or political committee.	Candidates for state constitutional office in general election who qualify for and receive public matching funds are subject to expenditure limit depending on office involved.	Except for independent expenditures, candidate-related expenditures may not be made until a treasurer is appointed and certified.	. . .	. . .
North Dakota	. . .	. . .			
Ohio (b)	For a campaign committee, only the campaign treasurer and deputy campaign treasurer.	. . .	Candidate must designate a treasurer before candidate's campaign committee may receive contributions or make expenditures.	Candidate expenditures must be legitimate, verifiable, ordinary, and necessary.	Personal use of funds by candidate prohibited.
Oklahoma	Agents and subagents in the case of candidates/candidate committees and other committees.	. . .	. . .	Candidates may use contributions only to defray campaign expenditures or ordinary and necessary expenses incurred in connection with duties of public officeholder.	Excess funds of candidate/candidate committee available within 48 months of general election must be disposed of by return to contributors, donation to another campaign or political party, donation to charitable organization, or retention for a future campaign. Personal use of funds by candidate prohibited.
Oregon (b)	Expenditures must be made by or through the treasurer of a political committee.	No expenditure may be made until the political committee appoints and certifies the treasurer.	. . .	. . .	. . .

LIMITATIONS ON EXPENDITURES—Continued

State or other jurisdiction	Who may make expenditures	Total expenditures allowed	Expenditures prior to first filing	For certain purposes	Use of surplus funds (a)
Pennsylvania (b)	For a political committee, the treasurer.	. . .	No expenditure may be made by a political committee until a chair and treasurer have been appointed.	No candidate, political committee chair, or treasurer may make an expenditure except as provided by law.	After financial activity is terminated, residual funds may be used for lawful expenditures, or returned pro rata to contributors. Judicial candidate should not use contributions for private benefit.
Rhode Island	Campaign treasurer or deputy campaign treasurer.	Unlimited, except for gubernatorial candidate who accepts public funding.	No expenditures may be made before the appointment of a treasurer and the filing of such designation.	. . .	Judicial office candidate should not use contributions for private benefit.
South Carolina (b)	Candidates or duly authorized officer of a committee.	. . .	. . .	. . .	Disposition of excess funds of a candidate or committee is restricted to specific recipients and uses. Personal use of funds by candidate prohibited.
South Dakota	. . .	. . .	. . .	Necessary expenditure of money for ordinary or usual expense of conducting a political campaign unless expressly forbidden.	Judicial office candidate should not use for private benefit.
Tennessee	Political treasurer of candidate and political campaign committee.	. . .	Candidate and political committee are required to certify name and address of political treasurer before making an expenditure in an election.	Clerical/office force; dissemination of literature; public speakers; newspaper announcements of candidacy; and transportation of voters unable to go to the polls.	Judicial office candidate should not use for private benefit.
Texas	Candidate for candidate's own election; political committee; campaign treasurer or assistant campaign treasurer acting in an official capacity; and an individual who makes independent, unreimbursed expenditures.	. . .	No expenditure may be made or authorized unless a campaign treasurer appointment is in effect. Campaign treasurer appointment of a political committee must be filed by 30th day before making or authorizing expenditures affecting a candidate for statewide office, multi-county district office, state senator or representative, or state board of education.	Use of public funds for political advertising prohibited. Payment from contributions for personal services of candidate, officeholder, or family restricted. Reimbursement of personal funds for expenditures by and repayment of loans made by relatives of a candidate to a candidate or officeholder limited to an aggregate of $500,000 per election for governor and $250,000 per election for other statewide office.	Contributions may not be converted to the personal use of a candidate or officeholder. Specific purpose political committee also may not convert contributions to the personal use of a former candidate or officeholder. Expenditures from personal funds may be reimbursed from contributions.
Utah	Candidate and the secretary of a personal campaign committee in the case of a candidate for state executive office. A committee member may not make an expenditure over $1,000 without written authorization by candidate or committee secretary.	. . .	State office candidate must file a statement of appointment of personal campaign committee before the committee may make expenditures.	Expenditures prohibited by law may not be made.	Judicial candidates may not use contributions for candidate's private benefit.

See footnotes at end of table.

LIMITATIONS ON EXPENDITURES—Continued

State or other jurisdiction	Who may make expenditures	Total expenditures allowed	Expenditures prior to first filing	For certain purposes	Use of surplus funds (a)
Vermont (b)	Designated treasurer.	. . .	. . .	Existing surplus may be contributed and existing debts assigned to new fund.	Conversion of surplus funds to personal use of candidate is prohibited, but the candidate may use such funds to reduce personal campaign debts.
Virginia (b)	. . .	. . .	Candidate must appoint one campaign treasurer not later than upon acceptance of a contribution, expenditure of any funds, or qualification as a candidate, whichever comes first.	Prohibited.	After filing of final report, surplus funds may be used in a succeeding election; returned to contributors; donated to a Section 170 organization; contributed to other candidates or committees, including a political party committee; or used to defray unreimbursable elective office expense of candidate. Personal use of funds by candidate prohibited.
Washington (b)	Campaign treasurer, candidate, or person on authority of campaign treasurer or candidate.	. . .	. . .	. . .	May be disposed of by return to the contributors in an amount not to exceed the original contributions, transfer to the candidate's personal account for reimbursement for lost earnings during the campaign, donation to a charitable organization, transmittal to the state, or retention for a future campaign, political activity, or community activity, or for non-reimbursable public office-related expenditures. Contributions may be transferred to the personal account of a candidate or expended for candidate's personal use for reimbursement for loans to cover lost earnings while campaigning or performing services for the political committee and for direct out-of-pocket expenses for repayment of loans made to political committee.
West Virginia (b)	Candidates, financial agents, and political committee treasurers.	. . .	No person may act as treasurer or financial agent before filing designation. Political party may not disburse money for election expenses unless treasurer is appointed.	Generally, lawful payments for political expenses; rent, maintenance, and furnishing of political headquarters or office; payment of support staff; political advertising and advertising agency services; public meeting-related expenses; travel, lodging and administrative expenses; nominating petition costs; prevention of unlawful registration of voters; voter transportation; and public polls.	Excess campaign assets may be disposed of by transfer to new candidate committee; contribution to political party committee or candidate; or returned to contributors on a pro rata basis. Personal use of funds by candidate prohibited, except for reimbursement of election expenses. Use of excess campaign assets for personal economic benefit is prohibited.

LIMITATIONS ON EXPENDITURES—Continued

State or other jurisdiction	Who may make expenditures	Total expenditures allowed	Expenditures prior to first filing	For certain purposes	Use of surplus funds (a)
Wisconsin (b)	Treasurer of a candidate, political committee, political group, or individual.	State office candidates who receive election campaign fund grant may not expend more for a campaign than amount specified in the authorized disbursement schedule unless opponents not accepting grant do not agree to comply with the limit voluntarily.	Disbursements may not be made by candidate or personal campaign committee, political committee, political group, or individual before registration statement is filed and campaign depository account established.	Expenditures may be made for any lawful purpose. Contributions must be used for a political purpose.	...
Wyoming	...	...	...	...	Candidate for judicial office may not use contributions for private benefit of candidate.
Dist. of Columbia (b)	Only the chair, treasurer, or designated agents may make an expenditure.	...	...	...	May be donated to a political party for political purposes; returned to donors; transferred to a scientific, technical, or literacy or educational organization; or used for constituent services with certain limits.

expenditures from petty cash fund may not exceed $50; aggregate calendar year expenditures may not exceed the lesser of ten percent of the committee's total calendar year expenditures. Montana, petty cash fund may pay for office supplies, transportation expenses, postage stamps, and other necessities of less than $25, but may not be used for purchase of time, space, or services from any communications medium. In Ohio, permitted; if over $25, must be vouched for by a receipted bill. In Pennsylvania vouchers for all expenditures over $25 must be by written instrument—petty cash fund may not exceed $100 and independent cash expenditure may not exceed $25. In Vermont expenditures by a candidate who has made expenditures or received contributions of $500 or more and by a political committee must be paid by the treasurer by check from a single checking account. In Virginia, petty cash expenditures of less than $25 permitted; otherwise only by check. In West Virginia payments to campaign election workers and paid staff must be by check. In Wisconsin prohibited; disbursements must be made by negotiable instrument. District of Columbia must be $50 or less to any one person in connection with a single transaction and must be fully documented.

(c) Unopposed candidate may not take any campaign funds for personal use or for income for spouse or dependent children after the date of winning the nomination (or if opposed in the primary but not in the general election, after the date of winning the nomination).

Source: Edward D. Feigenbaum and James A. Palmer, *Campaign Finance Law 92.* (Washington, D.C.: National Clearinghouse on Election Administration, Federal Election Commission, 1992); 1994 information will be available from the FEC in August 1994.

Note: For detailed legal requirements, state statutes should be consulted.

Key:

... — No reference in the law.

(a) Post election.

(b) Restrictions on cash expenditures. California, Colorado and New York (otherwise by check) may not exceed $100. Arkansas (except for properly receipted filing fees), Massachusetts, Michigan, Nebraska, North Carolina (for non-media expenses excluding postage), Oregon and Washington (if no receipt) may not exceed $50. Alabama and Connecticut may not exceed $100 from petty cash. Florida, must be less than $30 petty cash, and may not be used to pay for the purchase of time, space, or services from the communications media. In Kentucky expenditures of $25 or more must be made by check. In Louisiana cash expenditures of up to $100 may be made from petty cash for items other than personal services and voter transportation if complete records are maintained. In Minnesota petty cash expenditures limited to $100 per week for statewide elections; $20 per week for legislative elections. In Missouri single cash

Table 5.14
FUNDING OF STATE ELECTIONS: TAX PROVISIONS AND PUBLIC FINANCING
(As of January 1992)

State	Credit	Deduction	Checkoff	Surcharge	Source of funds	Public financing — Distribution of funds
Alabama	...	...	...	$1 (a)	Surcharge	To political party designated by taxpayer.
Alaska	...	...	...	...	...	...
Arizona	...	$100 (a). Money designated as surcharge is deductible.	...	$2, $5, or $10 (b)	Surcharge and donated amounts	To political party designated by taxpayer.
Arkansas	...	...	...	...	...	...
California	...	$100	...	$1, $5, $10, or $25 (c)	Surcharge and an equal amount matched by state.	To political parties for party activities and distribution to statewide general election candidates.
Colorado	...	...	...	...	...	...
Connecticut	...	...	...	...	...	...
Delaware	...	...	...	...	...	...
Florida	...	...	...	$5 (d)	Direct appropriations; assessments on contributions received by certain political committees; candidate filing fees; donated surplus funds; and voluntary surcharge on intangibles tax return, motor vehicle registration, driver's license applications, boat registration, and annual reports for corporations.	To candidates for governor and lieutenant governor and members of the cabinet.
Georgia	...	...	...	...	...	...
Hawaii	...	$100 for contributions to central or county party committees, or $500 for contributions to candidates who abide by expenditure limits, with deductible maximum of $100 of a total contribution to a single candidate.	$2 (a)	...	Checkoff, appropriated funds, other moneys.	To candidates for all non-federal elective offices.
Idaho	...	...	$1	...	Checkoff	To political party designated by taxpayer.
Illinois	...	...	...	...	...	...
Indiana	...	...	...	...	Revenues from personalized motor vehicle plates.	Percentage divided equally between the qualified political parties for state and county party use.
Iowa	...	...	$1.50 (a)	...	Checkoff	To political party designated by taxpayer or divided among qualified parties as specified by taxpayer.
Kansas	...	...	...	...	...	...
Kentucky	...	...	$2 (a)	...	Checkoff	To political party designated by taxpayer for party activities and distribution to general election candidates.
Louisiana	...	...	...	...	...	...
Maine	...	...	...	Any amount	Surcharge	To political party designated by taxpayer.
Maryland	...	...	...	...	Direct appropriations	To candidates for governor and lieutenant governor only (program is scheduled to end in 1995).

FUNDING OF STATE ELECTIONS—Continued

State	Tax provisions relating to individuals				Public financing	
	Credit	Deduction	Checkoff	Surcharge	Source of funds	Distribution of funds
Massachusetts	...	...	...	$1 (a)	Surcharge	To candidates in statewide primary and general elections.
Michigan	...	...	$2 (a)	...	Checkoff and an equal amount matched by state.	To candidates in gubernatorial primaries and candidates for governor and lieutenant governor in general election.
Minnesota	Refund of up to $50 for contributions made to political parties and qualified candidates (a)	...	$5 (a)	...	Checkoff and excess anonymous contributions; direct appropriations for qualifying candidates in a special election and for contributor tax refunds.	To qualifying candidates for governor, lieutenant governor, attorney general, other statewide offices, state senator and state representative after primary and general elections, and to the state committee of a political party for multi-candidate expenditures.
Mississippi	...	...	...	...	...	...
Missouri	...	$100 (a)	...	...	...	...
Montana	...	...	...	$1 (a)	Surcharge	To candidates opposed in elections for governor and lieutenant governor and chief justice and justice of the Supreme Court.
Nebraska	...	...	...	...	...	...
Nevada	...	...	...	...	...	...
New Hampshire	...	...	...	...	...	...
New Jersey	...	...	$1 (a)	...	Direct appropriations and checkoff	To qualified gubernatorial candidates.
New Mexico	...	...	...	...	...	...
New York	...	...	...	...	...	...
North Carolina	...	$25 for political contribution or newsletter fund contribution. Income tax surcharge for candidates is intended to be deductible.	$1 (a)	Up to an amount of income tax refund due	Checkoff for political parties funds; surcharge for candidates fund.	Political parties fund divided among political parties according to registration. In non-general election years, not more than 50% in election campaign fund. In general election year 50% to state party and 50% to presidential election year candidates fund. In general election year, 100% in election campaign fund to state party (with 50% to special party committee). If presidential election year, 100% in presidential election year candidates fund to state party (with 50% to special party committee). Candidates fund divided among opposed candidates for state constitutional office who agree to abide by the expenditure limit and raise matching funds equal to 5% of expenditure limit. Matching funds are provided on a one-to-one basis for general election campaign.
North Dakota	...	...	...	...	...	...
Ohio	...	...	$1 (a)	...	Checkoff	Divided equally among major political parties each calendar quarter. Party allocation divided: 50% to state executive committee of party, and 50% to county executive committees of party according to proportion of income from tax return checkoffs in each county to total checkoff income.
Oklahoma	Lessor of (1) total contributions with a maximum of $50 (a), or (2) the taxpayer's liability	$100	...	...	...	...
Oregon	...	...	...	Amount designated by taxpayer from income tax refund	Surcharge	To political party designated by taxpayer. State central committees allocate funds. Major political party: not less than 50% of county central committees and not less than 50% of remainder to party candidates; not less than 50% of funds to each county committee is to go to party candidates. Minor political party: not less than 50% to party candidates.
Pennsylvania	...	...	...	...	...	...
Rhode Island	...	...	$5 (a)	...	Checkoff ("credit")	First $2 ($4 for a joint return) of checkoff allocated to major political parties. Distributed to eligible political party designated by taxpayer. If a party is not designated, 5 percent of the amount is allocated to each party for each state officer elected, and the remainder to each party in proportion to the votes its candidate for governor received in previous election. Maximum of $200,000 allocated to all political parties. Remainder to qualifying candidates for governor as state matching funds (maximum for 1990 was $750,000).
South Carolina	...	...	...	...	...	...

See footnotes at end of table.

FUNDING OF STATE ELECTIONS—Continued

State	Tax provisions relating to individuals				Public financing	
	Credit	Deduction	Checkoff	Surcharge	Source of funds	Distribution of funds
South Dakota	...	...	...	...	...	...
Tennessee	...	...	...	...	...	...
Texas	...	...	$1	...	Checkoff (although funds actually are from revenue from sales and use taxes).	To political party designated by taxpayer: 50% to state central committee, and 50% to county central committee in proportion to the number of taxpayers designating the party in each county to the total number of taxpayers in the state who designate the party.
Vermont	...	...	...	...	...	...
Virginia	...	...	...	$2 (a) of income tax refund	Surcharge	To designated political party.
Washington	...	...	...	...	...	...
West Virginia	...	...	...	...	...	...
Wisconsin	...	...	$1 (a)	...	Checkoff	According to formula, to state executive office, state legislative office and state Supreme Court candidates in a spring, general, or special election (e).
Wyoming	...	...	...	...	...	...

(a) For joint returns, amount indicated may be doubled.
(b) Additional amounts may be donated.
(c) And a separate designation of $1, $5, $10, or $25.
(d) On intangibles tax return.
(e) Candidates must meet certain qualifications.

Source: Edward D. Feigenbaum and James A. Palmer, *Campaign Finance Law 1992* (Washington, D.C., National Clearinghouse on Election Administration, Federal Election Commission, 1992); 1994 information will be available from the FEC in August 1994.

Note: Table details only those states that have a tax provision relating to individuals or a provision for public financing of state elections. Credits and deduction may be allowed only for certain types of candidates and/or political parties. Consult state statutes for further details.

Key:

. . . — No provision

Initiatives in the 1980s and 1990s

More states are letting voters make the laws — a process that can give individuals more power, but can result in single-issue politics.

by David Kehler and Robert M. Stern

The number of initiatives appearing on statewide ballots is on the rise — a symptom of increasing turbulence in state politics and government. In 1992, voters in 19 states decided 69 initiative questions, more than in any year since 1932. From 1981 to 1992, a total of 346 initiatives appeared on state ballots, compared to 248 from 1940 to 1980 and 253 from 1900 to 1939. The increasing complexity, dynamism and contentiousness of the conventional legislative process has encouraged a greater number of issue advocates to view the initiative process as a favorable alternative.

Currently, 24 states and the District of Columbia have adopted procedures for statewide initiatives. Initiatives provide for any person, organization, coalition or company with an idea for a policy change to circulate petitions in an effort to put the proposal on a state ballot. With enough valid signatures, the proposal qualifies to go before the voters. If a majority of those voting favor the proposal, it becomes (depending on the state) law or part of the state's constitution.

No two states have identical initiative systems. "These differences from one state to the next emerged naturally, as a result of the unique American federal system, which allows for substantial differences in most categories of law, including initiative and referendum provisions. The practical result of this creative system, of course, is a sometimes difficult-to-follow array of procedures." (McGuigan, 1985)

Alaska, Idaho, Maine, Utah, Washington and Wyoming permit only statutory initiatives. Florida permits only constitutional initiatives. Most of the remaining states have procedures for both statutory and constitutional initiatives, with the latter requiring more signatures to qualify for the ballot. Washington is one of the states that has both direct and indirect initiative procedures. In a direct system, the collection of the requisite number of valid signatures of registered voters places a measure on the ballot. In an indirect system, the legislature is asked by petitioners to enact a measure which otherwise is placed on the ballot if the legislature fails to approve the proposal or something similar.

Petitioning

Petitioning triggers the initiative process. Petitioning measures the breadth and intensity of popular support for a policy idea to determine whether a proposal merits a place on the ballot.

States vary on the petition requirements for qualifying a proposal. Each state determines the number of requisite valid signatures to qualify a measure to go before the voters. Some requirements are more difficult than others. For instance, a petitioner seeking to collect signatures equal to 10 percent of the total number voting in the previous election will have a tougher time than those needing only 5 percent. The formulas also differ. Some states require that the number of signatures match a predetermined percentage of the registered voters for the state. Others require a percentage of a previous vote for a designated office (for example, 5 percent of the number who voted at the last gubernatorial election) to qualify.

The ratio, of itself, is a misleading guide to the degree of difficulty of qualifying an initiative in a particular state. One reason is that

David Kehler is the former president of the Public Affairs Research Institute of New Jersey. Robert Stern is co-director and general counsel of the Center for Governmental Studies, California.

Table A
STATUTORY INITIATIVE PETITION SIGNATURE GEOGRAPHIC DISTRIBUTION REQUIREMENTS, BY STATE: 1992

Alaska — At least one signature must be provided by voters resident in each of at least two-thirds of Alaska's 27 election districts.

Arkansas — Signatures equal to 4 percent of the total votes cast for governor in the previous gubernatorial general election must be gathered in each of at least 15 counties. Arkansas has a total of 75 counties.

Massachusetts — No more than 25 percent of the requisite number of signatures can be provided by voters of any single county.

Missouri — Signatures equal to 5 percent of the total votes cast for governor in the previous gubernatorial general election must be gathered in each of at least six congressional districts. Missouri has a total of nine congressional districts.

Montana — Signatures equal to 5 percent of the total votes cast for governor in the previous gubernatorial general elections must be gathered in each of at least 34 legislative districts. Montana has a total of 100 legislative districts.

Nebraska — Signatures equal to 5 percent of the total votes cast for governor in the previous gubernatorial general election must be gathered in each of at least 38 counties. Nebraska has 93 counties.

Nevada — Signatures equal to 10 percent of the total votes cast in the previous general election held in an even numbered year must be gathered in each of at least 13 counties. Nevada has a total of 17 counties.

Ohio — Signatures equal to 1½ percent of the total votes cast for governor in the previous gubernatorial general election must be gathered in each of at least 44 counties. Ohio has a total of 88 counties.

Utah — Signatures equal to 10 percent of the total votes cast for governor in the previous gubernatorial general election must be gathered in each of at least 15 counties. Utah has a total of 29 counties.

Wyoming — At least one signature must be provided by voters that are a resident in each of at least eight of Wyoming's 23 counties.

Source: Public Affairs Research Institute of New Jersey.
Note: Florida does not provide for statutory initiatives, but it does impose a signature distribution requirement for constitutional initiative petitions.

any registered voter, not just those who voted in the identified election, may sign an initiative petition. A more meaningful indicator is the percentage of total registered voters (PTRV) who must sign a petition to put an initiative on the ballot. Again, the PTRV in each state varies. In Massachusetts, the lowest, it is 2.55 percent. It is 10.8 percent in Wyoming, the highest, based on 1990 voter registration figures.

How petitions are circulated factors into the formidability of an initiative system's signature threshold. Volunteers, paid circulators or a combination of both may circulate them. In most states, the person gathering signatures must attest that he or she witnessed each signing. In California, however, signatures may be collected by mail; and in Washington, petitions may be printed as advertisements in newspapers for voters to clip, sign and mail to the measure's sponsor. According to a study by the privately funded California Commission on Campaign Financing, these two methods of signature gathering are not cost-effective compared to the conventional commercial approach of employing paid in-person circulators. Nine states — Alaska, Arkansas, Colorado, Florida, Maine, Massachusetts, Montana, Oklahoma and Washington — do not require that an initiative petition be signed in the presence of a circulator. In these states, it is possible to obtain signatures by stapling a petition to a bulletin board any place where people congregate. This method, however, produces a particularly high number of invalid signatures.

The most important factor in qualifying an initiative for the ballot is the number of people who are asked to sign. Other observers of the initiative process concur. Researchers Daniel Hays Lowenstein and Robert M. Stern conclude " . . . the significance of the popularity of the [initiative] measure is minor relative to the significance of the number of people who can be solicited." (*Hastings Constitutional Law Quarterly*, fall 1989)

Another consideration is the length of time permitted for gathering signatures. Several states have no time limit for signature gathering. Ohio requires a two-stage petition drive, with the first one of unlimited duration and the second phase 90 days in length. On the other hand, Oklahoma, California and Massachusetts have brief signature-gathering periods. Like Ohio, Massachusetts has a two-stage procedure. Of particular note, in six states — Arizona, Colorado, Massachusetts, Missouri, Nevada and Washington — all initiative petitions must circulate simultaneously. This means every initiative campaign must compete with every other initiative campaign for volunteers; and signature-gathering firms may be able to charge premium rates if there is sufficient demand.

Ten states with statutory initiative procedures require some form of geographic distribution of signatures on ballot measure petitions. The ostensible goal of a geographic distribution requirement in these states is to ensure that a proposal has broad support across the state. The practical effect, in several of the states, however, is the injection of an anti-urban bias into the signature gathering process, an unsurprising result, considering that the original advocates of the initiative, the Progressives, wanted to use the device to curb the power of the big city political machines of the day.

Initiatives and Money

The Progressive reformers who originally championed the initiative concept in this country did so, in part, to counter the pervasive influence of corporations on the state legislatures of that era. Railroad interests, in particular, dominated a number of state legislatures. The initiative was intended to be a grassroots countervailing power through which the public could write its own laws and skirt the compromised or corrupted legislature. The intent was to reduce the significance of money in state lawmaking.

Over time, campaign circumstances, strategies and technologies have changed markedly. In some states, initiative campaigns have become very costly, undermining one of the key goals of Progressive reformers. Several states with initiative systems have minimal campaign finance reporting requirements, so comprehensive data on the nationwide cost of initiative campaigns unfortunately do not exist.

In California, where extensive reporting is required, there have been a number of very expensive initiative campaigns. To take the most egregious example, over $129 million was spent on initiative contests in California in 1988, where 12 measures (six of which were initiatives) were before the voters in the June 7 primary, and 29 (12 of which were initiatives) were on the Nov. 8 general election ballot. More money was spent in the 1988 California initiative contests than was spent in the presidential election that year. Lobbying expenditures on state government in 1988 in California (which has a broad definition of lobbying) totalled just under $83 million. So in California that year, more was spent in initiative campaigns than was spent on lobbying. That was not the only year in which large expenditures were made in California initiative campaigns, and the Golden State has not been the sole locus of multi-million dollar spending on ballot measures.

Major contributors or loans to initiative campaigns, either pro or con, vary depending upon the issue at hand. Funding may come from businesses, labor unions, associations, political candidates and their campaigns, political parties, political action committees, public interest organizations, religious organizations, foundations, agricultural entities and individuals. A "special interest" is often in the eye of the beholder, but there are obvious circumstances where the passage of an initiative would provide a direct benefit or a clear harm to a contributor on one side or the other of a ballot question. There are also instances where large sums are contributed to initiative campaigns with no direct stake clearly evident. As in all initiative matters, California examples are instructive.

On occasion, a single entity will provide virtually all of the funding to support an initiative campaign, as in the case of Proposition 37 on the California 1984 general election ballot, which proposed the creation of a state lottery. The proposition was drafted and sponsored by Scientific Games, an Atlanta-based company that provides services, such as tickets, to state lotteries. Scientific Games spent $2,155,501 in support of Proposition 37 and also provided a $100,000 loan to the campaign. The Proposition 37 campaign spent $1,188,553 to qualify the question for the ballot (through, for example, paid petition circulators) and $1,374,654 to encourage voters to approve the measure. Scientific Games' loans and contributions represented 88 percent of the total spent supporting Proposition 37. The voters approved Proposition 37.

Why did Scientific Games propose the initiative and help fund the campaign? Tom Edwards Thomas' unpublished 1989 University of California-Berkeley, doctoral dissertation, "Corporate Political Strategy and Influence in the California Initiative Process," provides one answer. Thomas observed, "Leaving nothing to chance, Prop. 37 contained certain provisions that virtually guaranteed that the firm [Scientific Games] would be awarded the lucrative contract to supply the state's lottery tickets [as no other existing company could comply with those provisions]. The company revealed its intention by beginning an advertising campaign directed toward the contract even before the lottery initiative came to vote. . . . Company officials were so certain of victory that they secretly spent $6 million on a ticket printing plant in Gilroy, California prior to the election. . . . As expected, the lottery's first 'instant winner' was its sponsor, Scientific Games. The company was awarded a $40 million contract to supply lottery tickets, immediately giving it a substantial return on its political investment."

During the campaign on Proposition 37, the opposition, which had a spending advantage, attacked Scientific Games directly to no avail. As in some initiative campaigns, there were direct stakes on both sides of the issue; horse racing interests provided the majority of the opposition's campaign contributions, with three of the contributions of more than $750,000 each. As a postscript, the Legislature eventually amended the lottery law to open the marketplace, and contracts were awarded to some other firms.

Another initiative on the 1984 California general election ballot provides an example of a clash of interests, this one of political interests. Proposition 39 was a legislative reapportionment scheme backed by then-Gov. George Deukmejian, a Republican. Proponents and

opponents, combined, spent over $10 million on this initiative, at that time one of the costliest ballot question battles in California history. Much of the funding came from campaign committees controlled by various political figures, political parties and PACs. For example, a Deukmejian campaign committee lent the Proposition 39 support committee $1,575,000, while the California Republican Party contributed over $900,000, and the California Business PAC contributed over $200,000.

For the opposition campaign, Assembly Speaker Willie Brown, a Democrat, was the largest donor at $319,200, while other major elected Democratic officials David Roberti and Gray Davis contributed from funds at their disposal $217,909 and $192,500, respectively. A number of union PACs contributed to the opposition campaign, with the largest of these contributions provided by a Teamsters committee at a bit over $100,000. Some companies contributed five-figure sums in support of Proposition 39, while others made major contributions to the opposition.

The campaign itself was a classic California initiative battle, complete with television commercials featuring entertainment celebrities. In the end, the Deukmejian initiative was defeated.

While "special interests" may be of many varieties and their contributions may result in great spending disparities between initiative proponents and opponents (when there are opponents), it is important to recognize that some ballot measure campaigns attract large contributions from individuals without a financial stake in the result. Two initiatives on the 1982 California general election ballot provide examples: Proposition 12, concerning a nuclear weapons ban, and Proposition 15, a gun control initiative. Between them, these two initiatives were supported by two dozen or so contributions from individuals in amounts of $10,000 or more, the largest being $80,000 in support of Proposition 12 from entertainment executive Norman Lear and his wife.

A great disparity in expenditures between proponents and opponents in initiative campaigns does not always result in victory for the higher spenders. Several scholars have studied the relationship between campaign expenditures and voting results across a number of years in states with initiative procedures (and where campaign finance data are reported). Their general conclusion is that great disparities in expenditures are more effective in defeating a ballot question than in passing one. This pattern is likely found when the proponents of an initiative measure are consumer or environmental organizations, and the opposition is funded by commercial interests.

There are important exceptions, however, that cloud the issue. In the 1988 California general election, five competing auto insurance initiatives were before the voters in the most expensive ballot measure showdown in the history of America. The only one approved, Proposition 103, had vastly less campaign expenditure support than some of the losing measures sponsored by insurance companies. Particularly helpful for Proposition 103 at the ballot box, according to a *Los Angeles Times* poll, was an endorsement by consumer activist Ralph Nader. In another example, from the 1986 California general election, Proposition 65, an environmental initiative regarding toxic discharges, was approved by voters despite a well-funded opposition campaign to which 109 business and agricultural interests contributed $10,000 or more, including two contributions of well above $200,000. Proponents of Proposition 65 (who received six-figure contributions from the Sierra Club; Assembly member Tom Hayden; Hayden's then-wife, actress Jane Fonda; and the Hayden-allied organization, the Campaign For Economic Democracy) spent $368,844 to qualify the measure for the ballot and $1,850,628 for the electoral campaign, while the unsuccessful opposition spent more than twice as much, $4,883,529. Proponents effectively used the amounts and corporate sources of the opposition's spending to convince voters to approve the initiative. It is relatively uncommon for the proponents and opponents of an initiative to spend roughly equal amounts, and analysis of California data reveals that large disparities are not rare.

Finance Restrictions

As one might expect, the financial aspects of initiative campaigns have not escaped notice in the states in which ballot question procedures are in place. A wave of campaign finance reform measures washed across the United States in the years after the revelations of improprieties in the effort to re-elect President Richard Nixon. At the state and municipal levels, measures were adopted in a number of jurisdictions to limit contributions to, or spending in, ballot measure campaigns.

Legislation to this effect was adopted in California, Montana, Florida and Massachusetts. The California limitation was actually imposed by an initiative, Proposition 9, on the 1974 primary ballot. However, these state statutes were overturned as courts found them to be infringements on the U. S. Constitution's First Amendment protection of freedom of speech.

It is important to recognize that the multimillion dollar initiative campaigns in California and elsewhere cannot be restricted by state legislation limiting contributions or expenditures. There are several key cases.

In *Meyer v. Grant*, 486 U.S. 414 (1988), the U.S. Supreme Court held that a Colorado statute prohibiting payment of initiative petition circulators was an abridgement of free speech and violated the First and Fourteenth Amendments of the federal Constitution. The court ruled, "The circulation of an initiative petition of necessity involves both the expression of a desire for political change and a discussion of the merits of the proposed change. . . . that is appropriately described as 'core political speech.' " This case is important because some entities wishing to place an initiative before the voters may lack the necessary volunteer force to do so. By paying a company to gather the requisite signatures, the lack of a volunteer base is overcome.

In *Citizens Against Rent Control v. Berkeley*, 454 U.S. 290 (1981), the U.S. Supreme Court held that a California city's ordinance to impose a limit on contributions to committees formed to support or oppose ballot measures violated the First Amendment. The court determined that the Berkeley ordinance imposed " . . . a significant restraint on the freedom of expression of groups and those individuals who wish to express their views through committees," and that "The tradition of volunteer

Table B
NUMBER OF STATEWIDE INITIATIVES
APPEARING ON THE BALLOT,
BY STATE: 1981-1992

State	Initiatives on Ballot	Initiatives Approved by Voters
Alaska	10	5
Arizona	20	7
Arkansas	11	6
California	65	30
Colorado	24	10
Florida	6	4
Idaho	6	4
Illinois	0	0
Maine	16	10
Massachusetts	15	7
Michigan	9	3
Missouri	9	5
Montana	17	7
Nebraska	6	3
Nevada	7	3
North Dakota	18	4
Ohio	13	3
Oklahoma	6	4
Oregon	44	17
South Dakota	14	8
Utah	6	0
Washington	20	9
Wyoming	4	4
Total	**346**	**153**

Source: Public Affairs Research Institute of New Jersey.

Table C
NUMBER OF STATEWIDE INITIATIVES
ON THE BALLOT, BY YEAR: 1981-92

Year	Initiatives on Ballot
1981	3
1982	54
1983	4
1984	41
1985	1
1986	41
1987	3
1988	55
1989	3
1990	64
1991	6
1992	69
Total	**346**

Source: Public Affairs Research Institute of New Jersey.
Note: Many states do not place initiatives on the ballot in odd-numbered years.

committees for collective action has manifested itself in myriad community and public activities; in the political process it can focus on a candidate or on a ballot measure."

In a forceful passage, the court said, "Whatever may be the state interest or degree of that interest in regulating and limiting contributions to or expenditures of a candidate or a candidate's committees there is no significant state or public interest in curtailing debate and discussion of a ballot measure. Placing limits on contributions which in turn limit expenditures plainly impairs freedom of expression. The integrity of the political system will be adequately protected if contributions are identified in a public filing revealing the amounts contributed . . . "

A third key case is *First National Bank of Boston v. Bellotti*, 435 U.S. 765 (1978) in which the U.S. Supreme Court invalidated a Massachusetts statute prohibiting business corporations from making contributions or expenditures " . . . for the purpose of . . . influencing or affecting the vote on any question submitted to the voters, other than one materially affecting any of the property, business or assets of the corporation." In viewing the Massachusetts legislation, the court said, "If the speakers here were not corporations, no one would suggest that the state could silence their proposed speech. It is the type of speech indispensable to decision making in a democracy, and this is no less true because the speech comes from a corporation rather than an individual. The inherent worth of the speech in terms of its capacity for informing the public does not depend on the identity of its source. . . . "

The court rejected the Commonwealth of Massachusetts' claim that the statute preserved the integrity of the electoral process and public confidence in democratic government with this key passage: "The risk of corruption perceived in cases involving candidate elections . . . simply is not present in a popular vote on a public issue. To be sure, corporate advertising may influence the outcome of the vote; this would be its purpose. But the fact that advocacy may persuade the electorate is hardly a reason to suppress it. . . . Moreover, the people in our democracy are entrusted with the responsibility for judging and evaluating the relative merits of conflicting arguments. They may consider, in making their judgment, the source and credibility of the advocate."

Campaigns

Like statewide campaigns for office, initiative elections can be complex, multi-faceted struggles. The converse, however, may also be true: sometimes an initiative may have no organized opposition, and the election is uncontested. Where initiative campaigns are contested, professional campaign consultants have become an increasing influence. Some consultants have specialized in initiative contests, providing every conceivable service to advocates and foes of ballot measures.

These consultants are collectively known as the "initiative industry," and are seen by critics of direct democracy as hired guns who manipulate public opinion and shop potential initiative questions to prospective sponsors as a means of obtaining business. Some signature-gathering firms practically guarantee that, for a fee, they can qualify virtually any measure for almost any state's ballot. Interest in the role of the initiative industry in direct democracy has become so great in recent years that Patrick McGuigan, in his 1985 book, *The Politics of Direct Democracy in the 1980s*, included a section on the leading consultants.

Generally, the judiciary is more involved in initiative matters than in campaigns for office. Opponents of a measure have little disincentive to mount a variety of legal challenges on such matters as the sufficiency of petition signatures, the description of the question to appear on the ballot, whether the measure addresses a single subject or is an impermissible omnibus proposal, and other fundamental matters.

Some campaign techniques are applicable only to initiative contests. While campaigns for office are contested by identifiable persons frequently running as members of political parties, initiatives are essentially policy ideas, and the advocacy of, or opposition to, a concept often involves different sorts of campaigning. While some initiatives involve simple proposals, complex policy may also be put before the electorate.

Critics of direct democracy particularly point to advertising that greatly reduces sophisticated proposals to slogans and sound bites as "bumper sticker democracy." While some states provide, prior to elections, voter guides printed at government expense that includes arguments for and against initiative questions, sometimes these documents are too sophisticated for most voters. Advocates of the initiative process, however, believe in the goodwill and innate wisdom of the electorate and hold that the variety of information sources — advertising, voter guides, press coverage, endorsements and the like — provide a wealth and variety of information on which a rational choice can be made. They believe that the deliberately deceptive advertising that sometimes occurs in initiative campaigns can be detected by the public, a point of view that is sometimes naive.

One important new campaign strategy developed in California, the "counter initiative," merits special mention because of its effectiveness. The counter initiative is a strategy to defeat an initiative which, if the measure were to be adopted, would be harmful to the counter initiative's sponsors. The intent of the counter initiative is to confuse the voter. Suppose environmentalists qualified an initiative measure for the ballot that would impose stricter water quality standards in a state. Opponents of the proposal might qualify a different proposal — a counter initiative — on water quality, not with the primary intent of getting it adopted, but to create confusion about the measure proposed by the environmentalists. The strategy behind the counter initiative is that voters are more inclined to vote against initiatives when the issues are confusing. Employed several times in recent years in California, the counter initiative strategy has been successful most of the time.

While initiatives are state-specific, similar measures sometimes appear on a number of states' ballots. That was the case in 1992, when 14 states adopted term limit measures of one sort or another. However, little is written about the financial and campaign roles of national organizations in such elections. Clearly, the various pro-term limits initiative sponsors in several states benefitted from the assistance of national pro-term limit organizations. Sometimes, press attention is devoted to the participation of such groups. Washington voters defeated a term limit initiative in 1991, in part due to an expose by a Tacoma newspaper on the participation of a national organization in the campaign in support of the measure. Gay and lesbian activists have documented and decried the influence of several national organizations in recent initiative proposals to restrict homosexuals' rights. Several years ago, an organization headquartered in Michigan, U.S. English, had a hand in initiatives adopted in four states to declare English the official state language. In the mid-1970s, a number of anti-nuclear power initiatives were proposed by a multistate alliance called the Western Bloc.

Issue Areas

As a device, the initiative is ideologically neutral. Many initiatives have been adopted to enact liberal policies and many to enact conservative proposals. Initiatives have been adopted in recent years to cut taxes and, in other states, to hike taxes. Initiatives have been adopted to restrict personal liberties in a number of states, but initiatives also have been enacted to expand personal freedoms. Generalities about initiative subject matter are difficult to make. However, common initiative subjects include tax policy, fiscal limitations such as spending caps, utility policy and nuclear energy, environmental issues, business regulation, gambling, moral issues, minority rights (particularly restrictions of them), criminal justice, political reform and reapportionment, and education.

The November 1992 elections provide an excellent overview of the issue areas addressed by initiatives. In 1992, 69 initiatives appeared on the ballot in 19 states.[1] Of these, 36 were approved by the voters and 33 were turned down. Surprisingly, California did not have the most initiatives on the November ballot. Colorado led the nation, and its voters had to consider 10 initiatives, three of which allowed limited gambling in certain communities and counties. All three were defeated overwhelmingly. California tied Oregon for runner-up

honors with seven initiatives each.

By far, the most popular subject on the 1992 ballot was term limits. Fourteen states adopted 17 initiatives limiting terms; in addition, three state legislatures (Florida, Mississippi and Rhode Island) put term limits on the ballot. Not one term limit measure was defeated, and almost all of them passed overwhelmingly. Many of the states that did not consider term limits in 1992 will have a term limit initiative on the 1994 ballot, and several states approved term limit initiatives in 1990. (For a more complete discussion on term limits, see "Term Limits in the States," by Thad Beyle and Rich Jones on pages 28-33 of this volume.)

The next biggest area of interest in 1992 concerned taxes. Seven states either lowered taxes or refused to raise them. The only state that increased taxes was Massachusetts, which raised its cigarette taxes, despite a heavily financed campaign against the increase mounted by the tobacco industry.

Two states addressed gay rights issues, with Colorado enacting restrictions forbidding special laws establishing gay rights, and Oregon defeating proposed restrictions. Subsequently, the Colorado law was declared unconstitutional, although the case is on appeal.

The most unusual initiative was in Colorado, which placed on the ballot a measure that prohibits taking of black bears out of season by dogs or bait. The voters approved the measure. Oregon voters, however, turned down a measure that restricted fishing on the lower Columbia River. Finally, Arizona approved a Martin Luther King Jr., Holiday initiative after several previous attempts had failed. The state was under intense pressure to enact the holiday after a Super Bowl, which had been scheduled to be played in Arizona, was moved to California.

Is The Initiative A Good Idea?

In most states without initiative procedures, proposals are made from time to time to create an initiative system. For example, in New Jersey in 1992, debate over a proposal to adopt initiative procedures was one of the three leading issues before the Legislature. Despite endorsement by Democratic Governor Jim Florio, many leading Republican legislators in the overwhelmingly GOP-dominated Senate, and support in the General Assembly, the proposals failed. Virtually every New Jersey lobbying organization opposed the initiative proposals, and they mounted an unprecedented joint lobbying effort. A number of critical analyses of initiative actions in other states were published, citing the increasing role of large contributions in initiative campaigns, the use of the initiative in a number of states to attack minority rights, the diminution of the importance of the legislature in states in which initiative activity is extensive, the ease of qualifying a measure for the ballot under the provisions of the proposed bills, and the undesirability of single-issue politics.

What are the advantages and disadvantages in considering adopting the initiative process? Supporters of the device cite the following:

• Initiatives allow the public to circumvent a recalcitrant governor and legislature;

• Initiatives neutralize the power of special interests;

• Initiatives make governmental reforms (such as campaign financing and term limits) possible;

• Initiatives stimulate public involvement in state issues; and

• Initiatives exert pressure on the legislature to act responsibly.

The initiative process, however, can be abused as critics note:

• Initiatives undermine legislative power and procedures;

• Initiatives too often generate poorly drafted and ill-conceived proposals;

• Initiatives encourage high-spending, deceptive campaigns;

• Initiatives encourage single-issue politics;

• Initiatives undermine the political parties and weaken the political process;

• Money has become too dominant in initiative campaigns;

• Initiatives generate voter confusion and overload; and

• Initiatives discourage compromise.

Despite the many reasons cited against this form of direct democracy, once a state adopts the initiative process, it is never repealed. Thus, it is important to discuss a potentially ideal process for states that are considering adopting this form of direct democracy.

Three groups in California, one appointed by the Legislature and the governor, recently reviewed the initiative process as it now exists in California. All three concluded that California's initiative process should be retained but significantly improved.[2] Their findings should be examined by any state that is either considering adopting any form of direct democracy or modifying its current laws.

The process recommended by the California studies has not been adopted by any state that has the initiative process. It is an amalgam of processes now existing in many different states. The California groups believe, however, that this recommended process would be more flexible than any now in place in any state in the nation or government in the world. The reforms cover all aspects of the ballot initiative process — including drafting, amendability, circulation, qualification, voting requirements, voter information and financial disclosures. If adopted, these reforms would provide a sophisticated and modernized ballot initiative process.

Some of the key recommendations include:

• Allowing the initiative proponent to correct errors or omissions or make other changes to the initiative's text before it is placed on the ballot, provided the amendments further the "purposes and intent" of the initiative;

• Creating a 45-day "cooling-off period" to allow the proponents and the legislature to negotiate compromise legislation that would then permit the proponents to withdraw the initiative from the ballot;

• Requiring the legislature to vote on each initiative before it appears on the ballot, and publishing each legislator's vote in the ballot pamphlet;

• Allowing the legislature to correct errors and amend any successful initiative after enactment by a 60 percent supermajority vote of each house, if the amendments further the initiative's "purposes and intent;"

• Requiring any constitutional amendment to be enacted by a 60 percent vote at one elec-

---

A Brief History

The initiative is largely the product of the Progressive Era. First proposed in this country by a handful of reformers in 1885, early advocates were inspired by Switzerland's process. These reformers regarded state legislatures, courts and urban political machines as hopelessly corrupt, and they advocated direct legislation as an antidote.

In 1904, Oregon passed the first initiative system. South Dakota and Utah quickly followed. Within 10 years, 12 states adopted initiative procedures. Massachusetts adopted the initiative in 1918, and Alaska adopted it in 1956. Since then, only Florida (1968), Wyoming (1968), Illinois (1970), and Mississippi (1993), have adopted statewide initiative procedures.

Bills have been introduced in recent years to create initiative systems in most of the remaining states.

Source: Public Affairs Research Institute

---

tion or by a simple majority in two successive elections;

- Making the petition circulation period 180 days to allow volunteers to compete more equally with paid signature gatherers;
- Identifying the names and affiliations of the top two contributors to each side of an initiative campaign at the top of all signature petitions and in all broadcast, print, and slate mail advertising; and
- Publishing a short version summary ballot pamphlet that would be sent to all voters three weeks before the election in addition to the regular ballot pamphlet. Highlights of this pamphlet include a simple chart which the voter could easily scan, a list of major contributors, major supporters and opponents, and the legislative vote on the measure, broken down by Democrats and Republicans.

Today's initiative process in nearly all the states, with the exceptions of Massachusetts and Ohio, puts proponents into a straightjacket. Once a measure is titled, not a word can be changed, even though the proponent may discover that it contains outright mistakes or omissions. The measure must be circulated, placed on the ballot, defended in a campaign and, if approved by the voters, put into effect — without the possibility of a single word being changed. Even after enactment, some state laws prohibit legislative amendments — unless the text of the initiative allows them. The result can be catastrophic for the state. Poorly drafted measures with errors or omissions can be frozen into the statute books.

A unique feature of the California reform recommendations is to make the initiative process more flexible and amendable. Because the initiative process has turned the electorate into a "fourth and new branch of government" in some states, the electorate should be given some of the same powers available to a legislator moving a bill through the legislative process.

Tremendously dynamic, the initiative process is likely to continue to be a major factor in the political life of many states.

Selected Court Cases

Bilofsky v. Deukmejian, 124 Cal. App. 3d 825 (1981) — California statute that prevents any use of names gathered on initiative petition is constitutional.

Chemical Specialties Manufacturers v. Deukmejian, 227 Cal. App. 3d 663 (1991) — The California Appellate Court finds Proposition 105, which requires disclosure in a wide variety of areas (campaigns, hospitals, South African contracts, etc.) violates the single subject rule of the state constitution. This is the only California initiative found to be in violation of the single subject rule.

Citizens Against Rent Control v. City of Berkeley, 454 U.S. 290, 102 S. Ct. 434 (1981) — The U.S. Supreme Court rules that Berkeley's $250 limit on contributions to ballot measure campaigns is unconstitutional.

Citizens for Jobs and Energy v. Fair Political Practices Commission, 16 Cal. 3d 671 (1976) — The California Supreme Court declares that the Political Reform Act may not limit expenditures by ballot measure committees.

Finn v. McCuen, 303 Ark. 418, 798 S.W. 2d 34 (1990) — Since the title of a lottery measure is misleading, the Supreme Court finds that the measure should be allowed on the ballot.

First National Bank of Boston v. Bellotti, 435 U.S. 765, 99 S. Ct. 1407 (1978) — The U.S.

Supreme Court rules that a criminal statute prohibiting corporate contributions to ballot measures is unconstitutional.

HCHH Associates v. Citizens for Representative Government, 193 Cal. App. 3d 1193 (1987) — The California Appellate Court finds that an indoor shopping mall can ban petition gatherers during the Christmas season and impose reasonable rules on circulators.

Hardie v. Eu, 18 Cal. 3d 371 (1977) — The California Supreme Court finds unconstitutional the Political Reform Act's cap on expenditures for qualifying ballot measures since it violates First Amendment rights.

Insurance Industry Initiative Campaign Committee v. Eu, 203 Cal. App. 3d 961 (1988) — An initiative measure can be prevented from being circulated if it violates the single subject rule.

Meyer v. Grant, 486 U.S. 414, 108 S. Ct. 1886 (1988) — The U.S. Supreme Court rules that Colorado may not ban paid circulators.

Michigan Chamber of Commerce v. Austin, 832 F. 2d 947 (1987) — The federal appellate court rules that Michigan's provisions limiting corporate contributions to ballot measure campaigns violates the right of association and free speech guarantees of the First Amendment.

Missourians to Protect Initiative Process v. Blunt, 799 S.W. 824 (1990) — The Missouri Supreme Court rules an initiative off the ballot because it is a violation of the single subject rule for a ballot measure to establish an ethics committee that regulates both the executive and the legislative branches.

Pruneyard Shopping Center v. Robins, 447 U.S. 74, 100 S. Ct. 2035 — The U.S. Supreme Court rules that state constitutional provisions that permit political activity at a privately-owned shopping center does not violate federal constitutional private property rights of owner.

Stanson v. Mott, 17 Cal. 3d 206 (1976) — The California Supreme Court rules that the use of public funds for election campaigning to promote or oppose a ballot measure is illegal.

State ex. rel. Nelson v. Jordan, 104 Ariz. 193 (1969) — The Arizona Supreme Court finds that where two initiatives conflict, it is the duty of the court to harmonize both.

Taxpayers to Limit Campaign Spending v. FPPC, 51 Cal. 3d 744 (1990) — The California Supreme Court finds that where two initiatives covering the same topic (campaign financing) appear on the same ballot, the one initiative receiving the most votes supersedes the other measure in all respects, even though some of the provisions of the one initiative with fewer voters do not conflict with the provisions of the other measure receiving the higher number of votes.

Notes

[1] "Vital Signs: 1992 Election Returns: Statewide Initiatives and Referenda," *Campaign Magazine*, March 1993, pp. 28-31.

[2] California Commission on Campaign Financing, *Democracy By Initiative: Shaping California's Fourth Branch of Government*, Center for Responsive Government, 1992; Citizen's Commission on Ballot Initiatives, *Report and Recommendations on the Statewide Initiative Process*, 1994; Dubois, Philip L., and Floyd F. Feeney, *Improving the California Initiative Process: Options for Change*, California Policy Seminar, University of California, 1992.

Selected References

Substantial literature on initiative and referendum exists, dating from the late 19th century. In addition to the references listed below, researchers may wish to review the constitutional and statutory provisions on initiative and referendum in the states in which these procedures are permitted. Some of these states, such as Nevada and Utah, publish official guides to their initiative and referendum systems. Also helpful are ballot pamphlets published by some states, such as California and Washington, disseminated to voters prior to elections and containing analysis of questions being put before the electorate. Perhaps the most complete archive of recent writing on initiative and referendum is housed at the library of the Institute of Governmental Studies at the University of California-Berkeley. Included in that collection are a complete set of three important, but now discontinued, newsletters: *Initiative and Referendum Report, Initiative News*

Report, and *Initiative Quarterly*. The Public Affairs Research Institute of New Jersey, located in Princeton, has an archive of initiative voting results. Valuable bibliographies are included in the books by Cronin, Magleby, Schmidt and Zisk, listed below. Of particular interest to researchers is the literature review by Whitehall, listed below.

Books

Butler, David, and Austin Ranney, eds. *Referendums: A Comparative Study of Practice and Theory*, Washington, D.C.: American Enterprise Institute for Public Policy Research, 1978.

Cronin, Thomas E. *Direct Democracy: The Politics of Initiative, Referendum, and Recall*, Cambridge, Mass.: Harvard University Press. 1989.

Democracy By Initiative: Shaping California's Fourth Branch of Government, Report and Recommendations of the California Commission on Campaign Financing (Los Angeles), 1992.

Magleby, David B. *Direct Legislation: Voting on Ballot Propositions in the United States*, Baltimore: The John Hopkins University Press, 1984.

McGuigan, Patrick B. *The Politics of Direct Democracy in the 1980s: Case Studies in Political Decision Making*, Washington, D.C.: The Free Congress Research and Education Foundation, 1985.

Schmidt, David D. *Citizen Lawmakers: The Ballot Initiative Revolution*, Philadelphia: Temple University Press, 1989.

Zisk, Betty H. Money, *Media and the Grass Roots: State Ballot Issues and the Electoral Process*, Newbury Park, Calif.: Sage Publications, 1987.

Reports and Articles on Various Topics

Arrow, Dennis W., "Representative Government and Popular Distrust: The Obstruction/Facilitation Conundrum Regarding State Constitutional Amendment by Initiative Petition," *Oklahoma City University Law Review*, Vol. 17 (1992), 3-88.

Barnes, James A., "Losing the Initiative," *National Journal* (September 1, 1990), 2046-2053.

Bell, Charles and Charles Price, "Lawmakers and Initiatives: Are Ballot Measures the Magic Ride to Success?" *California Journal* (September, 1988), 380-384.

Berg, Larry L. and C. B. Holman, "The Initiative Process and its Declining Agenda-setting Value," *Law & Policy*, Vol. 11 (1989), 451-469.

Bowler, Shaun, Todd Donovan, and Trudy Happ, "Ballot Propositions and Information Costs: Direct Democracy and the Fatigued Voter," *The Western Political Quarterly*, Vol. 45 (1992), 559-568.

Castello, James E., "The Limits of Popular Sovereignty: Using the Initiative Power to Control Legislative Procedure," *California Law Review*, Vol. 74 (1986), 491-563.

Cronin, Thomas E., "Public Opinion and Direct Democracy," *PS: Political Science and Politics*, Vol. 21 (1988), 612-619.

Entin, Jonathan L., "Innumeracy and Jurisprudence: The Surprising Difficulty of Counting Petition Signatures," *Jurimetrics*, Vol. 33 (1993), 223-246.

Eule, Julian N., "Judicial Review of Direct Democracy," *The Yale Journal*, Vol. 99 (1990), 1502-1590.

Farrell, Michael J., "The Judiciary and Popular Democracy: Should Courts Review Ballot Measures Prior to Elections?" *Fordham Law Review*. Vol. 53 (1985), 919-935.

Fountaine, Cynthia L., "Lousy Lawmaking: Questioning the Desirability and Constitutionality of Legislating by Initiative," *Southern California Law Review*, Vol. 61 (1988), 735-776.

Gordon, James E., III, and David B. Magleby, "Pre-Election Judicial Review of Initiatives and Referendums," *Notre Dame Law Review*, Vol. 64 (1989), 298-320.

Initiative and Referendum: It's Not the Answer, New Jersey Citizen Action, (Hackensack, N.J.), July, 1992.

Initiatives and Voter Turnout, Public Affairs Research Institute of New Jersey (Princeton, N.J.), July, 1992.

Initiative Petitions, Public Affairs Research Institute of New Jersey (Princeton, N.J.), July, 1992.

Initiative Petitions, Public Affairs Research Institute of New Jersey (Princeton, N.J.), June, 1992.

Lee, Eugene C., "Representative Government and the Initiative Process," John J. Kirlin and Donald R. Winkler, eds., *California Policy Choices*, Vol. 6, Los Angeles: School of Public Administration, University of Southern California, 1990.

Linde, Hans A., "When Initiative Lawmaking Is Not 'Republican Government': The Campaign Against Homosexuality," *Oregon Law Review*, Vol. 72, (1993), 19-45.

Magleby, David B., "Ballot Access for Initiatives and Popular Referendums: The Importance of Petition Circulation and Signature Validation Procedures," *Journal of Law & Politics*, Vol. 2 (1985), 278-311.

Magleby, David B., "Taking the Initiative: Direct Legislation and Direct Democracy in the 1980s," *PS: Political Science and Politics*, Vol. 21 (1988), 600-611.

Mason, David M., ed. *Term Limits: Sweeping the States?* Washington, D.C.: The Heritage Foundation, 1992.

Matsusaka, John G., "Economics of Direct Legislation," *The Quarterly Journal of Economics*, Vol. 107 (1992), 541-572.

McNellie, Elizabeth A., "The Use of Extrinsic Aids in the Interpretation of Popularly Enacted Legislation," *Columbia Law Review*, Vol. 89 (1989), 157-179.

Neiman, Max and M. Gottdiener, "The Relevance of the Qualifying State of Initiative Politics: The Case of Petition Signing," *Political Science Quarterly*, Vol. 63 (1982), 582-588.

Schmidt, David D., "Winning an Initiative Big: How They Whipped 'Whoops' in Washington State," *Campaigns & Elections* (Fall, 1983), 4-19.

Sirko, Louis J. Jr., "The Constitutionality of the Initiative and Referendum," *Iowa Law Review*, Vol. 65 (1980), 637-677.

Stern, Robert M., "Salvaging the Initiative Process," *State Government News* (September 1992), 24-25.

The Popular Interest Versus the Public Interest . . . : A Report on the Popular Initiative, New York Senate Research Service (Albany, NY), May, 1979.

Thomas, Tom E., "Has Business 'Captured' the California Initiative Agenda?," *California Management Review* (fall 1990), 131-147.

Tweedy, John Jr., "Coalition Building and the Defeat of California's Proposition 128," *Stanford Environmental Law Journal*, Vol. 11 (1992), 114-148.

Wheeler, Douglas P. and Bill Owens, "Is the Initiative Process a Good Idea?" *State Government News* (July 1991), 14-15.

Whitehall, Lisa, "Direct Legislation: A Survey of Recent Literature," *Legal Reference Services Quarterly*, Vol. S (1985), 3-45.

Listings of Ballot Questions

Allswang, John M. *California Initiatives and Referendums 1912-1990: A Survey and Guide to Research*, Los Angeles: Edmund G. "Pat" Brown Institute of Public Affairs, California State University, Los Angeles, 1991.

Carlisle, John. *1992 State Ballot Listing: Post-Election Analysis*, Washington, D.C.: The Free Congress Foundation, 1992.

Miller, Matthew M. *1990 Ballot Measures: Post-Election Survey*, Washington, D.C.: The Free Congress Foundation, 1991.

Statewide Initiatives 1981-90, Public Affairs Research Institute of New Jersey (Princeton, N.J.), June 1992.

Campaign Finance Issues

Garrison, Michael J., "Corporate Political Speech, Campaign Spending and First Amendment Doctrine," *American Business Law Journal*, Vol. 27 (1989), 163-213.

Hall, Adam P., "Regulating Corporate 'Speech' in Public Elections," *Case Western Reserve Law Review*, Vol. 39 (1988-89), 1313-1342.

Holman, C.B. and Matthew T. Stodder, "The Fairness Fund: Addressing Spending Initiatives in Ballot Initiative Campaigns," paper delivered at the Annual Meeting of the American Political Science Association, August 1991, Washington, D.C.

Lowenstein, Daniel Hays and Robert M. Stern, "The First Amendment and Paid Initiative Petition Circulators: A Dissenting View and a Proposal," *Hastings Constitutional Law Quarterly*, Vol. 17 (1989), 175- 224.

Mastro, Randy M., Deborah C. Costlow and Heidi P. Sanchez, "Taking the Initiative: Corporate Control of the Referendum Process Through Media Spending and What to Do

About It," *Federal Communications Bar Journal*, Vol. 32 (1980), 315-359.

Merrick, Michael J., "The Saga Continues — Corporate Political Free Speech and the Constitutionality of Campaign Finance Reform: Austin v. Michigan Chamber of Commerce," *Creighton Law Review*, Vol, 24 (1990), 195-237.

Price, Charles M., "Initiative Campaigns: Afloat on a Sea of Cash," *California Journal* (November 1988), 481-486.

Reich, Kenneth, "The 64-Million Dollar Question," *Campaigns & Elections* (March/April 1989), 15-20.

Shockley, John S., "Direct Democracy, Campaign Finance and the Courts: Can Corruption, Undue Influence, and Declining Voter Confidence Be Found?" *University of Miami Law Review*, Vol. 39 (1985), 377-428.

Thomas, Tom E., "Corporate Campaign Spending and Initiative Outcomes in California" *Working Papers*, Institute of Governmental Studies, University of California, Berkeley, March 1988.

Why Initiative and Referendum Contributions and Expenditures Cannot Be Limited, Public Affairs Research Institute of New Jersey (Princeton, N.J.), January 1992.

California Initiative Issues

Eu, March Fong. *A History of the California Initiative Process*, Sacramento: California Secretary of State, December 1989.

Eule, Julian N., "Checking California's Plebiscite," *Hastings Constitutional Law Quarterly*, Vol, 17 (1989), 151-173.

Goldberg, Joseph, "Raven v. Deukmejian: A Modern Guide to the Voter Initiative Process and State Constitutional Independence," *San Diego Law Review*, Vol. 28 (1991), 729-744.

Initiative and Referendum in California: A Legacy Lost, League of Women Voters of California (Sacramento), 1984.

Labarre, Bob, "Initiatives Inc.," *Golden State Report* (October 1985), 13-14.

Lowenstein, Daniel H., "California Initiatives and the Single-Subject Rule," *UCLA Law Review*, Vol. 30 (1983), 936-975.

Minger, Marilyn E., "Putting the 'Single' Back in the Single-Subject Rule: a Proposal for Initiative Reform in California," *U.C. Davis Law Review*, Vol. 24 (1991), 879-930.

Peterson, Larry, "Call These Political Persuaders," *Golden State Report* (June 1987), 16-23.

Price, Charles and Robert Waste, "Initiatives: Too Much of a Good Thing," *California Journal* (March 1991), 117-120.

Ray, Steven W., "The California Initiative Process: The Demise of the Single-Subject Rule," *Pacific Law Journal*, Vol. 14 (1983), 1095-1111.

Rose, Roger, ed. *The California Initiative Process: Current Controversies and Prescriptions*, Davis, Calif.: University of California, Davis, March 1990.

Salvato, Greg M., "New Limits on the California Initiative: An Analysis and Critique," *Loyola of Los Angeles Law Review*, Vol. 19 (1986), 1045-1096.

Initiative Issues in Other States

Albury, Cherie B., "Amendment Nine and the Initiative Process: A Costly Trip to Nowhere," *Stetson Law Review*, Vol. 14 (1985), 349-373. (Florida)

Bradley, M. Katheryn and Deborah L. Williams, "Be It Enacted by the People of Alaska . . . a Practitioner's Guide to Alaska's Initiative Law," *Alaska Law Review*, Vol. 9 (1992), 279-303.

Chesley, Richard A., "The Current Use of the Initiative and Referendum in Ohio and Other States," *University of Cincinnati Law Review*, Vol. 52 (1984), 541-560.

Gillette, Michael, "The Legislative Function: Initiative and Referendum," *Oregon Law Review*, Vol. 67 (1988), 55-64. (Oregon)

Gray, Alexander G., Jr., and Thomas R. Kiley, "The Initiative and Referendum in Massachusetts," *New England Law Review*, Vol. 26 (1991), 27-109.

Guerin, Stan P., "Pre-Election Judicial Review: The Right Choice," *Oklahoma City University Law Review*, Vol. 17 (1992), 221-240.

Horvat, Robert, "The Oregon Initiative Process: A Critical Appraisal," *Oregon Law Review*, Vol. 65 (1986), 169-184.

Hurley, Sheila M., "The Constitutionality of the Massachusetts County Distribution Requirement for Initiative Petition Signatures," *Suffolk University Law Review*, Vol. 13 (1979), 113-123.

Leary, Patricia, "Power to the People? A Critique of the Florida Supreme Court's Interpretation of the Referendum Power," *Florida State University Law Review*, Vol. 15 (1987), 673-686.

Lowe, Robert J. Jr., "Solving the Dispute Over Direct Democracy in Florida: Are Ballot Summaries Half-Empty or Half-Full?," *Stetson Law Review*, Vol. 21 (1992), 565-602.

Lummings, Daniel L., "Coping With Confusion: A Unitary Procedure For Judicial Review of the Referendum Process," *Maine Law Review*, Vol. 41 (1989), 113-135.

Medina, J. Michael, "The Emergency Clause and the Referendum in Oklahoma: Current Status and Needed Reform," *Oklahoma Law Review*, Vol. 43 (1990), 401-428.

Rahm, David A., "Citizens Versus Legislators — The Continuing Fight to Ensure the Rights of Initiative and Referendum in Nebraska," *Creighton Law Review*, Vol. 26 (1992), 195-220.

Shipley, Michael S., "The Initiative Process in Missouri: A Call For Statutory Change," *Missouri Law Review*, Vol. 51 (1986), 215-238.

Teague, William Lawton Jr., "Pre-Election Constitutional Review of Initiative Petitions: A Pox on Vox Populi?" *Oklahoma City University Law Review*, Vol. 17 (1992), 201-220. (Oklahoma)

Williams, Stephanie Rae, "Voter Initiatives in Illinois: Where Are We After Chicago Bar Association v. State Board of Elections?" *Loyola University Chicago Law Journal*, Vol. 22 (1991), 1119-1138.

Table 5.15
STATEWIDE INITIATIVE AND REFERENDUM

	Changes to Constitution			Changes to Statutes			
	Initiative		Referendum	Initiative		Referendum	
State	Direct (a)	Indirect (a)	Legislative (b)	Direct (c)	Indirect (c)	Legislative	Citizen Petition (d)
Alabama	. . .	. . .	. . .	. . .	. . .	. . .	. . .
Alaska	. . .	. . .	★	★	. . .	★	★
Arizona	★	. . .	★	★	. . .	★	★
Arkansas	★	. . .	★	★	. . .	★	★
California	★	. . .	★	★	. . .	★	★
Colorado	★	. . .	★	★	. . .	. . .	. . .
Connecticut	. . .	. . .	★	. . .	. . .	. . .	. . .
Delaware	. . .	. . .	★	. . .	. . .	★	. . .
Florida	★	. . .	★	. . .	. . .	. . .	. . .
Georgia	. . .	. . .	★	. . .	. . .	. . .	. . .
Hawaii	. . .	. . .	★	. . .	. . .	. . .	. . .
Idaho	. . .	. . .	★	★	. . .	★	★
Illinois	★	. . .	★	★	. . .	★	. . .
Indiana	. . .	. . .	★	. . .	. . .	. . .	. . .
Iowa	. . .	. . .	★	. . .	. . .	. . .	. . .
Kansas	. . .	. . .	★	. . .	. . .	. . .	. . .
Kentucky	. . .	. . .	★	. . .	. . .	★	★
Louisiana	. . .	. . .	★	. . .	. . .	. . .	. . .
Maine	. . .	. . .	★	. . .	★	★	★
Maryland	. . .	. . .	★	. . .	. . .	★	★
Massachusetts	. . .	★	★	. . .	★	★	★
Michigan	★	. . .	★	. . .	★	★	★
Minnesota	. . .	. . .	★	. . .	. . .	. . .	. . .
Mississippi	. . .	★	★	. . .	. . .	. . .	. . .
Missouri	★	. . .	★	★	. . .	★	★
Montana	★	. . .	★	★	. . .	★	★
Nebraska	★	. . .	★	★	. . .	★	★
Nevada	★	. . .	★	★	★	★	★
New Hampshire	. . .	. . .	★	. . .	. . .	. . .	. . .
New Jersey	. . .	. . .	★	. . .	. . .	. . .	. . .
New Mexico	. . .	. . .	★	. . .	. . .	★	★
New York	. . .	. . .	★	. . .	. . .	. . .	. . .
North Carolina	. . .	. . .	★	. . .	. . .	. . .	. . .
North Dakota	★	. . .	★	★	. . .	★	★
Ohio	★	. . .	★	★	★	★	★
Oklahoma	★	. . .	★	★	. . .	★	★
Oregon	★	. . .	★	★	. . .	★	★
Pennsylvania	. . .	. . .	★	. . .	. . .	. . .	. . .
Rhode Island	. . .	. . .	★	. . .	. . .	. . .	. . .
South Carolina	. . .	. . .	★	. . .	. . .	. . .	. . .
South Dakota	★	. . .	★	★	. . .	★	★
Tennessee	. . .	. . .	★	. . .	. . .	. . .	. . .
Texas	. . .	. . .	★	. . .	. . .	. . .	. . .
Utah	. . .	. . .	★	★	★	★	★
Vermont	. . .	. . .	★	. . .	. . .	. . .	. . .
Virginia	. . .	. . .	★	. . .	. . .	. . .	. . .
Washington	. . .	. . .	★	★	★	★	★
West Virginia	. . .	. . .	★	. . .	. . .	. . .	. . .
Wisconsin	. . .	. . .	★	. . .	. . .	. . .	. . .
Wyoming	. . .	. . .	★	. . .	★	. . .	★

Sources: State election administration offices, state constitutions and statutes, except information on Maine which is from the *The Book of the States 1992-93.*

Note: This table summarizes state provisions for initiatives and referenda. *Initiatives* may propose constitutional amendments or develop state legislation and may be formed either directly or indirectly. The *direct initiative* allows a proposed measure to be placed on the ballot after a specific number of signatures have been secured on a citizen petition. The *indirect initiative* must be submitted to the legislature for a decision after the required number of signatures has been secured on a petition and prior to placing the proposed measure on the ballot.

Referendum refers to the process whereby a state law or constitutional amendment passed by the legislature may be referred to the voters before it goes into effect. Three forms of referendum exist: (1) citizen petition, whereby the people may petition for a referendum on legislation which

has been considered by the legislature; (2) submission by the legislature (designated in table as "Legislative"), whereby the legislature may voluntarily submit laws to the voters for their approval; and (3) constitutional requirement, whereby the state constitution may require that certain questions be submitted to the voters.

Key:
★ — State provision
. . . — No state provision
(a) See Table 1.3, "Constitutional Amendment Procedure: By Initiative," for more detail.
(b) See Table 1.2, "Constitutional Amendment Procedure: By the Legislature," for more detail.
(c) See Tables 5.16 through 5.19 on *State Initiatives*, for more detail.
(d) See Tables 5.20 through 5.23 on *State Referendums*, for more detail.

Table 5.16

STATE INITIATIVES: REQUESTING PERMISSION TO CIRCULATE A PETITION

State	Applied to (a): Const. amdt.	Applied to (a): Statute	Signatures required to request a petition (b): Const. amdt.	Signatures required to request a petition (b): Statute	Request submitted to	Request form furnished by (c)	Restricted subject matter (d)	Individual responsible for petition: Title	Individual responsible for petition: Summary	Financial contributions reported (e)	Deposit required (f)
Alabama	...	...	...	...	...	...	...	...	...	...	...
Alaska	...	D	...	100	LG	SP	Y	LG	LG	Y	$100
Arizona	D	D	15% (g)	10% (g)	SS	ST	N	...	...	Y	...
Arkansas	D	D	...	...	AG	SP	N	AG	AG	Y	...
California	D	D	...	...	AG	SP	N	AG	AG	Y	$200
Colorado	D	D	...	...	...	...	N	(h)	(h)	Y	...
Connecticut	...	...	...	...	...	...	...	...	...	...	...
Delaware	...	...	...	...	...	...	...	...	...	...	...
Florida	D	...	...	...	SS	SP	N	P	P	Y	...
Georgia	...	...	...	...	...	...	...	...	...	...	...
Hawaii	...	...	...	...	...	...	...	...	...	...	...
Idaho	...	D	...	20	SS	SP	N	AG	AG	Y	...
Illinois	D	...	...	...	...	...	Y	...	...	...	...
Indiana	...	...	...	...	...	...	...	...	...	...	...
Iowa	...	...	...	...	...	...	...	...	...	...	...
Kansas	...	...	...	...	...	...	...	...	...	...	...
Kentucky	...	...	...	...	...	...	...	...	...	...	...
Louisiana	...	...	...	...	...	...	...	...	...	...	...
Maine	...	I	...	5 (i)	...	SP	Y	P	P	Y	...
Maryland	...	...	...	...	...	...	...	...	...	...	...
Massachusetts	I	I	10	10	AG	ST	Y	AG	AG	Y	...
Michigan	D	I	...	...	...	...	Y	...	...	Y	...
Minnesota	...	...	...	...	...	...	...	...	...	...	...
Mississippi	I	...	...	...	SS	...	Y	AG	AG	Y	...
Missouri	D	D	...	...	SS	SP	Y	SS,AG	...	Y	...
Montana	D	D	...	...	SS	SP	Y	AG	AG	Y (j)	N
Nebraska	D	D	...	...	SS	SP	Y	AG	AG	Y	N
Nevada	D	I	...	...	SS	SP	Y	P	P	N	N
New Hampshire	...	...	...	...	...	...	...	...	...	...	...
New Jersey	...	...	...	...	...	...	...	...	...	...	...
New Mexico	...	...	...	...	...	...	...	...	...	...	...
New York	...	...	...	...	...	...	...	...	...	...	...
North Carolina	...	...	...	...	...	...	...	...	...	...	...
North Dakota	D	D	25	25 (k)	SS	SP	N	SS,AG	SS,AG	Y (e)	...
Ohio	D	I	...	...	SS	SP	Y	...	AG	Y	...
Oklahoma (l)	D	D	...	...	SS	SP	N	AG	AG	Y	...
Oregon	D	D	25	25	SS	ST	N	AG	AG	Y	...
Pennsylvania	...	...	...	...	...	...	...	...	...	...	...
Rhode Island	...	...	...	...	...	...	...	...	...	...	...
South Carolina	...	...	...	...	...	...	...	...	...	...	...
South Dakota	D	D	...	...	SS	SP	N	P	...	Y	...
Tennessee	...	...	...	...	...	...	...	...	...	...	...
Texas	...	...	...	...	...	...	...	...	...	...	...
Utah	...	I,D	...	5	LG	SP	N	LG	LG	Y (m)	N
Vermont	...	...	...	...	...	...	...	...	...	...	...
Virginia	...	...	...	...	...	...	...	...	...	...	...
Washington	...	I,D	...	1	SS	SP	N	AG	AG	Y	N
West Virginia	...	...	...	...	...	...	...	...	...	...	...
Wisconsin	...	...	...	...	...	...	...	...	...	...	...
Wyoming	...	D	...	100	SS	SS	Y	AG,SS	AG,SS	Y	$500

Sources: State election administration offices, except information on Maine which is from *The Book of the States 1992-93.*

Key:

... — Not applicable
D — Direct initiative
I — Indirect initiative
EV — Eligible voters
LG — Lieutenant Governor
SS — Secretary of State
AG — Attorney General
P — Proponent
ST — State
SP — Sponsor
Y — Yes
N — No

(a) An initiative may provide a constitutional amendment or develop a new statute, and may be formed either directly or indirectly. The direct initiative allows a proposed measure to be placed on the ballot after a specific number of signatures have been secured on a petition. The indirect initiative must first be submitted to the legislature for decision after the required number of signatures have been secured on a petition, prior to placing the proposed measure on the ballot.

(b) Prior to circulating a statewide petition, a request for permission to do so must first be submitted to a specified state officer.

(c) The form on which the request for petition is submitted may be the responsibility of the sponsor or may be furnished by the state.

(d) Restrictions may exist regarding the subject matter to which an initiative may be applied. The majority of these restrictions pertain to the dedication of state revenues and appropriations, and laws that maintain the preservation of public peace, safety, and health. In Illinois, amendments are restricted to "structural and procedural subjects contained in" the legislative article.

(e) In some states, a list of financial contributors and the amount of their contributions must be submitted to the specified state officer with whom the petition is filed. In North Dakota, if over $100 in aggregate for calendar year.

(f) A deposit may be required after permission to circulate a petition has been granted. This amount is refunded when the completed petition has been filed correctly.

(g) The total number of votes cast for governor in last election.

(h) Title Setting Board—secretary of state, attorney general, director of legislative legal services.

(i) The name and address of five voters.

(j) Contributions reported to Commissioner of Political Practices; petitions filed with Secretary of State.

(k) Petition needs 25 people who act as a sponsoring committee. Their names and addresses appear on the front of the petition.

(l) In Oklahoma, a person is not required to obtain permission to circulate a petition. Information provided by Oklahoma refers to procedural requirements for filing a petition only.

(m) Political issues committees must report if contributions or expenditures exceed $750 in a calendar year.

Table 5.17
STATE INITIATIVES: CIRCULATING THE PETITION

State	Basis for signatures (see key below) Const. amdt.	Statute	Maximum time period allowed for petition circulation (a)	Can signatures be removed from petition (b)	Completed petition filed with	Days prior to election Const. amdt.	Statute
Alabama	...	...					
Alaska	15% VG	10% TV from 2/3 ED	1 yr.	Y	LG	4 mos.	4 mos.
Arizona	10% VG	10% VG	2 yr.	Y	SS	4 mos.	4 mos.
Arkansas	8% VG	8% VG			SS		
California	8% VG	5% VG	150 days	Y	SS	131 days	131 days
Colorado	5% VSS	5% VSS	6 mos.	Y	SS	3 mos.	3 mos.
Connecticut	...	...					
Delaware	...	...					
Florida	8% VEP, 8% from 1/2 CD	...	4 yr.		SS	91 days	
Georgia	...	...					
Hawaii	...	...					
Idaho	8% VG	10% VG			SS		
Illinois	8% VG	...	2 yr.	Y	SS	6 mos.	4 mos.
Indiana	...	...					
Iowa	...	...					
Kansas	...	...					
Kentucky	...	...					
Louisiana	...	...					
Maine	10% VG	10% VG	1 yr.		SS		
Maryland	...	...					
Massachusetts	3% VG, no more than 25% from 1 county	3% VG, no more than 25% from 1 county (c)		Y	SS		
Michigan	10% VG	8% VG	(d)		SS	(e)	(e)
Minnesota	...	...					
Mississippi	12% VG	...	1 yr.		SS (f)	90 days prior to LS	
Missouri	8% VG, 8% each from 2/3 CD	5% VG, 5% each from 2/3 CD	20 mos.	Y	SS	4 mos.	4 mos.
Montana	10% VG, 10% each from 2/5 SLD	5% VG, 5% each from 1/3 SLD	1 yr.	Y	SS	(g)	(g)
Nebraska	10% EV, 5% each from 2/5 counties	7% EV, 5% each from 2/5 counties		Y	SS	4 mos.	4 mos.
Nevada	10% TV, 10% each from 3/4 counties	10% TV, 10% each from 3/4 counties	(h)		SS	90 days	30 days prior to LS
New Hampshire	...	...					
New Jersey	...	...					
New Mexico	...	...					
New York	...	...					
North Carolina	...	...					
North Dakota	4% resident population	2% resident population	1 yr.		SS	90 days	90 days
Ohio	10% VG, 1.5% each from 1/2 counties	3% VG, 1.5% each from 1/2 counties (i)			SS	90 days	90 days
Oklahoma	15% VH	8% VH	90 days	N	SS		
Oregon	8% VG	6% VG		N (j)	SS	4 mos.	4 mos.
Pennsylvania	...	...					
Rhode Island	...	...					
South Carolina	...	...					
South Dakota	10% VG	5% VG	1 yr.	Y	SS	1 yr.	182 days
Tennessee	...	...					
Texas	...	...					
Utah	10% VG, 10% each from 1/2 counties	10% VG, 10% each from 1/2 counties		Y	LG		
Vermont	...	...					120 days

STATE INITIATIVES: CIRCULATING THE PETITION—Continued

State	Basis for signatures (see key below)		Maximum time period allowed for petition circulation (a)	Can signatures be removed from petition (b)	Completed petition filed with	Days prior to election	
	Const. amdt.	Statute				Const. amdt.	Statute
Virginia	...	...	(i)	...	...	...	...
Washington	...	8% VG	...	Y	SS	...	(k)
West Virginia	...	...	...	...	...	...	...
Wisconsin	...	...	...	Y	SS	...	...
Wyoming	...	15% TV, from 2/3 counties	18 mos.	...	SS	...	60 days

Sources: State election administration offices, except information on Maine which is from *The Book of the States 1992-93.*

Key:
... — Not applicable
VG — Total votes cast for the position of governor in the last election
EV — Eligible voters
VH — Total votes cast for the office receiving the highest number of votes in last general election
TV — Total voters in last general election
VSS — Total votes cast for all candidates for the office of secretary of state at the previous general election
VEP — Total votes cast in the state as a whole in the last presidential election
ED — Election district
CD — Congressional district
SLD — State legislative district
LG — Lieutenant Governor
SS — Secretary of State
LS — Legislative session
Y — Yes
N — No

(a) The petition circulation period begins when petition forms have been approved and provided to sponsors. Sponsors are those individuals granted permission to circulate a petition, and are therefore responsible for the validity of each signature on a given petition.
(b) Should an individual wish to remove his/her name from a petition, a request to do so must be submitted in writing to the state officer with whom the petition is filed.
(c) First Wednesday in December.
(d) In Michigan, signatures dated more than 180 days prior to the filing date are ruled invalid.
(e) Constitutional amendment—not less than 120 days prior to the next general election; statute—approximately 160 days prior to the next general election.
(f) Petitions first must be submitted to county circuit clerks for signature certification.
(g) Second Friday of the fourth month prior to election (3½ months).
(h) Constitutional amendment—276 days; Amend or create a statute—291 days.
(i) Direct—6 months; Indirect—10 months.
(j) Not after petition has been filed.
(k) Direct—4 months; Indirect—2 weeks prior to legislative session.

Table 5.18
STATE INITIATIVES: PREPARING THE INITIATIVE TO BE PLACED ON THE BALLOT

State	Signatures verified by: (a)	Within how many days after filing	Number of days to amend/appeal a petition that is: Incomplete (b)	Not accepted (c)	Penalty for falsifying petition (denotes fine, jail term)	Petition certified by: (d)
Alabama						
Alaska	Director of elections	60 days	30 days		Class B misdemeanor	LG
Arizona	County recorder	10 days			Class 1 misdemeanor	SS
Arkansas	SS	30 days	30 days	15 days	$50-$100, 1-5 yrs.	SS
California	Clerk or registrar of voters	50 days				SS
Colorado	SS	30 days	15 days		(e)	SS
Connecticut						
Delaware						
Florida	Supervisor of elections					SS
Georgia						
Hawaii						
Idaho	County clerk	14 days		10 days	$5,000, 2 yrs.	SS
Illinois	SBE and election authority					SBE
Indiana						
Iowa						
Kansas						
Kentucky						
Louisiana						
Maine	Registrars of voters	25 days				SS
Maryland						
Massachusetts	Local board of registrar	2 weeks	4 weeks (f)			
Michigan	City and township clerks					BSC
Minnesota						
Mississippi	Circuit clerk				$1,000, 1 yr.	SS
Missouri	SS, local election authority		Prior to filing deadline		Class A misdemeanor	SS
Montana	County clerk and recorder	4 weeks			$500, 6 mos.	SS
Nebraska	County clerk or election commissioner	40 days		10 days	Class IV felony	SS
Nevada	County clerk or registrar	20-50 days			$10,000, 1-10 yrs.	SS
New Hampshire						
New Jersey						
New Mexico						
New York						
North Carolina	SS					
North Dakota	SS	35 days	20 days			SS
Ohio	County board of elections		10 days		$1,000, 6 mos.	SS
Oklahoma	SS, county elections official				$1,000, 1 yr.	SS
Oregon		15 days			Class C felony (possible)	SS
Pennsylvania						
Rhode Island						
South Carolina						
South Dakota	SS					SS
Tennessee						SS
Texas						
Utah	County clerk				$500, 2 yrs.	LG
Vermont						

STATE INITIATIVES: PREPARING THE INITIATIVE—Continued

State	Signatures verified by: (a)	Within how many days after filing	Number of days to amend/appeal a petition that is:		Penalty for falsifying petition (denotes fine, jail term)	Petition certified by: (d)
			Incomplete (b)	Not accepted (c)		
Virginia	SS	...	...	...	...	SS
Washington	...	(g)	...	10 days (h)	...	...
West Virginia	...	...	...	...	...	...
Wisconsin	SS	...	...	...	...	...
Wyoming		60 days	30 days	30 days	$1,000, 1 yr.	

Sources: State election administration offices, except information on Maine which is from *The Book of the States 1992-93.*

Key:
::: — Not applicable
SS — Secretary of State
LG — Lieutenant Governor
BSC — Board of State Canvassers
SBE — State Board of Elections

(a) The validity of the signatures, as well as the correct number of required signatures must be verified before the initiative is allowed on the ballot.

(b) If an insufficient number of signatures are submitted, sponsors may amend the original petition by filing additional signatures within a given number of days after filing. If the necessary number of signatures have not been submitted by this date, the petition is declared void.

(c) In some cases, the state officer will not accept a valid petition. In such a case, sponsors may appeal this decision to the Supreme Court, where the sufficiency of the petition will be determined. If the petition is determined to be sufficient, the initiative is required to be placed on the ballot.

(d) A petition is certified for the ballot when the required number of signatures have been submitted by the filing deadline, and are determined to be valid.

(e) No more than $500, one-year in county jail, or both.

(f) Applies to statutory initiatives.

(g) Direct—no specific limit; Indirect—45 days.

(h) In Washington, a petition that is not accepted may be *appealed* within 10 days.

Table 5.19
STATE INITIATIVES: VOTING ON THE INITIATIVE

State	Ballot (a) Title by:	Summary by:	Election where initiative voted on	Effective date of approved initiative (b) Const. amdt.	Statute	Days to contest election results (c)	Can an approved initiative be: Amended?	Vetoed?	Repealed?	Can a defeated initiative be refiled?
Alabama	...	...	...	...	...	...	...	...	...	...
Alaska	LG	...	(d)	...	...	5	Y	N	after 2 yrs.	Y
Arizona	...	...	GE	IM (e)	IM (e)	5	Y (f)	N (e)	Y (f)	Y
Arkansas	AG	AG	GE	30 days	30 days	60	Y	N	N	...
California	AG	AG	GE	1 day (b)	IM (b)	5	Y (g)	N	Y	Y
Colorado	SS,AG,LSS	SS,AG,LSS	next biennial election	30 days	30 days	...	...	N	...	Y
Connecticut	...	...	...	...	...	...	...	...	...	...
Delaware	...	...	...	...	...	...	...	...	...	...
Florida	P,AG	P,AG	GE	(h)	...	10	Y	N	N	Y
Georgia	...	...	...	...	...	...	...	...	...	...
Hawaii	...	...	...	...	...	...	...	...	...	...
Idaho	AG	AG	GE	...	30 days	20	Y	N	Y	Y
Illinois	SBE	SBE	GE	20 days	...	15	...	...	...	...
Indiana	...	...	...	...	...	...	...	...	...	...
Iowa	...	...	...	...	...	...	...	...	...	...
Kansas	...	...	...	...	...	...	...	...	...	...
Kentucky	...	...	...	...	...	...	...	...	...	...
Louisiana	...	...	...	...	...	...	...	...	...	...
Maine	...	...	REG or SP	...	30 days (e)	...	N	N	N	...
Maryland	...	...	...	...	...	...	...	...	...	...
Massachusetts	AG	AG	GE	30 days (b)	30 days (b)	10	Y	Y	Y	after 2 biennial elections
Michigan	BSC	BSC	GE	45 days (b)	10 days (b)	2 (i)	Y	N	Y	Y
Minnesota	...	...	...	...	...	...	...	...	...	...
Mississippi	AG	AG	GE	30 days	...	...	Y	N	Y	after 2 yr.
Missouri	SS	LC	GE or SP	30 days	IM	30	Y (j)	N	Y (k)	Y
Montana	...	AG	GE	July 1	Oct. 1	...	...	N	...	Y
Nebraska	AG	AG	GE 4 mos. after filing	10 days (b)	10 days (b)	40	...	N	...	after 3 yrs.
Nevada	SS,AG	SS,AG	GE	10 days (l)	10 days (l)	3	N	N	N	Y
New Hampshire	...	...	...	...	...	...	...	...	...	...
New Jersey	...	...	...	...	...	...	...	...	...	...
New Mexico	...	...	...	...	...	...	...	...	...	...
New York	...	...	...	...	...	...	...	...	...	...
North Carolina	...	...	...	...	...	...	...	...	...	...
North Dakota	AG,SS	AG,SS	PR,SP or GE	30 days	30 days	14	w/i 7 yrs. (m)	N	w/i 7 yrs. (m)	Y
Ohio	SS	Ohio Ballot Board	(n)	30 days	30 days	15	...	N	...	Y
Oklahoma	AG	AG	...	IM	IM	...	...	N	Y	after 3 yrs.
Oregon	AG	AG	GE even yrs.	30 days	30 days	40	N	N	Y	Y
Pennsylvania	...	...	...	...	...	...	...	...	...	...
Rhode Island	...	...	...	...	...	...	...	...	...	...
South Carolina	...	...	...	...	...	...	...	...	...	...
South Dakota	P	AG	GE	1 day	1 day	10	Y	N	Y	Y
Tennessee	...	...	...	...	...	...	...	...	...	...
Texas	...	...	...	...	...	...	...	...	...	...
Utah	LC	LC	GE	...	5 days (o)	40	Y	N	...	Y
Vermont	...	...	...	...	...	...	...	...	...	...
Virginia	...	...	...	...	...	...	...	...	...	...
Washington	AG	AG	GE	...	IM	5	after 2 yrs.	...	after 2 yrs.	Y
West Virginia	...	...	...	...	...	...	...	...	...	...
Wisconsin	...	...	...	...	...	...	...	...	...	...
Wyoming	SS	SS,AG	GE 120 days after LS	...	90 days	...	Y	N	after 2 yrs.	after 5 yrs.

Sources: State election administration offices, except information on Maine which is from *The Book of the States 1992-93*.

Key:
... — Not applicable
LG — Lieutenant Governor
SS — Secretary of State
AG — Attorney General
P — Proponent
LC — Legislative Council
LSS — Legislative Legal Services
BSC — Board of State Canvassers
SBE — State Board of Elections

PR — Primary election
GE — General election
REG — Regular election
SP — Special election
IM — Immediately
LS — Legislative session
Y — Yes
N — No
w/i — Within

(a) In some states, the ballot title and summary will differ from that on the petition.
(b) A majority of the popular vote is required to enact a measure. In Massachusetts and Nebraska, apart from satisfying the requisite majority vote, the measure must receive, respectively, 30% and 35% of the total votes cast in favor. An initiative approved by the voters may be put into effect immediately after the approving votes have been canvassed. In California and Nebraska, the measure may specify an enacting date.
(c) Individuals may contest the results of a vote on an initiative within a certain number of days after the election including the measure proposed.
(d) First statewide election at least 120 days after the legislative session.
(e) Upon governor's proclamation.
(f) Unless measure was approved by a majority vote of qualified electors.
(g) As specified.
(h) First Tuesday after the first Monday in January following the general election.
(i) After election is certified.
(j) By vote of people for constitutional change.
(k) By legislative act.
(l) Fourth Wednesday in November.
(m) Except by a two-thirds vote by both houses of the legislature.
(n) General election at least 90 days after filing.
(o) Effective date may be written in the initiative, otherwise it takes place within five days.

Table 5.20
STATE REFERENDUMS: REQUESTING PERMISSION TO CIRCULATE A CITIZEN PETITION

State	Citizen petition (a)	Signatures required to request a petition (b)	Request submitted to:	Request forms furnished by: (c)	Restricted subject matter (d)	Individual responsible for petition — Title	Individual responsible for petition — Summary	Financial contributions reported (e)	Deposit required (f)
Alabama	...	...	...	...	...	...	...	...	...
Alaska	Y	100	LG	SP	Y	LG	LG	Y	$100
Arizona	Y	5% VG	SS	ST	N	Y	Y	Y	...
Arkansas	Y	...	AG	SP	N	AG	AG	Y	...
California	Y	...	AG	SP	N	AG	AG	Y	N
Colorado	Y	...	...	...	N	(g)	(g)	Y	...
Connecticut	...	...	...	...	...	...	...	...	...
Delaware	...	...	...	...	...	...	...	...	...
Florida	...	...	...	...	...	...	...	...	...
Georgia	...	...	...	...	...	...	...	...	...
Hawaii	...	...	...	...	...	...	...	...	...
Idaho	Y	20	SS	SP	N	AG	AG	Y	...
Illinois	...	...	...	...	Y	...	...	...	...
Indiana	...	...	...	...	...	...	...	...	...
Iowa	...	...	...	...	...	...	...	...	...
Kansas	...	...	...	...	...	...	...	...	...
Kentucky	Y	...	SS	...	Y	...	...	...	...
Louisiana	...	...	...	...	...	...	...	...	...
Maine	Y	5 (h)	SS	SP	Y	SS	SS	Y	...
Maryland	Y	...	SS	...	...	...	...	...	...
Massachusetts	Y	10	SS	ST	...	AG	AG	Y	...
Michigan	Y	...	...	...	Y	...	...	Y	...
Minnesota	...	...	...	...	...	...	...	...	...
Mississippi	...	...	...	...	...	...	...	...	...
Missouri	Y	...	SS	SP	Y	SS,AG	...	Y	...
Montana	Y	...	SS	SP	N	AG	AG	Y	N
Nebraska	Y	5% EV	SS	SP	Y	AG	AG	Y	N
Nevada	Y	...	SS	SP	N	P	P	(i)	N
New Hampshire	...	...	...	...	...	...	...	...	...
New Jersey	...	...	...	...	...	...	...	...	...
New Mexico	Y	...	SS	...	...	SS	SS	...	...
New York	...	...	...	...	...	...	...	...	...
North Carolina	...	...	...	...	...	...	...	...	...
North Dakota	Y	25 EV	SS	SP	N	SS,AG	SS,AG	Y (e)	N
Ohio	Y	...	SS	SP	Y	...	AG	Y	N
Oklahoma (j)	Y	...	SS	SP	N	SS	SS	Y	...
Oregon	Y	...	SS	ST	N	AG	AG	Y	...
Pennsylvania	...	...	...	...	...	...	...	...	...
Rhode Island	...	...	...	...	...	...	...	...	...
South Carolina	...	...	...	...	...	...	...	...	...
South Dakota	Y	...	SS	SP	Y	P	...	Y	...
Tennessee	...	...	...	...	...	...	...	...	...
Texas	...	...	...	...	...	...	...	...	...
Utah	Y	5	LG	SP	N	LG	LG	Y (k)	...
Vermont	...	...	...	...	...	...	...	...	...
Virginia	...	...	...	...	...	...	...	...	...
Washington	Y	1	SS	SP	Y	AG	AG	Y	N
West Virginia	...	...	...	...	...	...	...	...	...
Wisconsin	...	...	...	...	...	...	...	...	...
Wyoming	Y	100	SS	SS	Y	SS	SS	Y	$500

Sources: State election administration offices, except information on Maine which is from *The Book of the States 1992-93.*

Key:
... — Not applicable
EV — Eligible voters
VG — Total votes cast for the position of governor in the last election
LG — Lieutenant Governor
SS — Secretary of State
AG — Attorney General
P — Proponent
ST — State
SP — Sponsor
Y — Yes
N — No

(a) Three forms of referendum exist: citizen petition, submission by the legislature, and constitutional requirement. This table outlines the steps necessary to enact a citizen's petition.

(b) Prior to circulating a statewide petition, a request for permission to do so must first be submitted to a specified state officer. Some states require that signatures only be those of eligible voters.

(c) The form on which the request for petition is submitted may be the responsibility of the sponsor or may be furnished by the state.

(d) Restrictions may exist regarding the subject matter to which a referendum may be applied. The majority of these restrictions pertain to the dedication of state revenues and appropriations, and laws that maintain the preservation of public peace, safety and health. In Kentucky, referendums are only permitted for the establishment of soil and water and watershed conservation districts.

(e) In some states, a list of individuals who contribute financially to the referendum campaign must be submitted to the specified state officer with whom the petition is filed. In North Dakota, if over $100 in aggregate for calendar year.

(f) A deposit may be required after permission to circulate a petition has been granted. This amount is refunded when the completed petition has been filed correctly.

(g) Title Setting Board—secretary of state, attorney general, director of legislative legal services.

(h) The name and address of five voters.

(i) Expenditures advocating defeat or passage of the question in excess of $500 must be reported.

(j) In Oklahoma, a person is not required to receive permission to circulate a petition. The individual must, however, file the petition with the Secretary of State. The circulation period is 90 days.

(k) If more than $750 is spent to influence the vote.

Table 5.21
STATE REFERENDUMS: CIRCULATING THE CITIZEN PETITION

State	Basis for signatures	Maximum time period allowed for petition circulation (a)	Can signatures be removed from petition (b)	Completed petition filed: With	Completed petition filed: Days after legislative session
Alabama	. . .	. . .	. . .	. . .	. . .
Alaska	10% TV, from 2/3 ED	w/i 90 days of LS	Y	LG	90 days
Arizona	5% VG	w/i 90 days after LS	Y	SS	90 days
Arkansas	6% VG	. . .	. . .	SS	90 days
California	5% VG	90 days	Y	SS	90 days
Colorado	5% VSS	6 mos.	. . .	SS	90 days
Connecticut	. . .	. . .	. . .	. . .	. . .
Delaware	. . .	. . .	. . .	. . .	. . .
Florida	. . .	. . .	. . .	. . .	. . .
Georgia	. . .	. . .	. . .	. . .	. . .
Hawaii	. . .	. . .	. . .	. . .	. . .
Idaho	10% VG	w/i 60 days after LS	. . .	SS	60 days
Illinois	. . .	. . .	. . .	. . .	. . .
Indiana	. . .	. . .	. . .	. . .	. . .
Iowa	. . .	. . .	. . .	. . .	. . .
Kansas	. . .	. . .	. . .	. . .	. . .
Kentucky	5% VG	. . .	. . .	SS	4 mos.
Louisiana	. . .	. . .	. . .	. . .	. . .
Maine	10% VG	90 days of LS (c)	. . .	SS	90 days
Maryland	3% VG	. . .	. . .	SS	. . .
Massachusetts	3% VG	90 days	. . .	. . .	90 days
Michigan	5% VG	. . .	N	SS	90 days
Minnesota	. . .	. . .	. . .	. . .	. . .
Mississippi	. . .	. . .	. . .	. . .	. . .
Missouri	5% VG from 2/3 ED	. . .	Y	SS	90 days
Montana	5% VG, from 1/3 ED	1 yr.	Y	SS	6 mos.
Nebraska	5% VG, from 2/5 county	. . .	. . .	SS	90 days
Nevada	10% EV last GE	approx. 6 mos.	. . .	SS	120 prior to next GE
New Hampshire	. . .	. . .	. . .	. . .	. . .
New Jersey	. . .	. . .	. . .	. . .	. . .
New Mexico	10% EV last GE, from 3/4 county	. . .	. . .	. . .	4 mos. prior to next GE
New York	. . .	. . .	. . .	. . .	. . .
North Carolina	. . .	. . .	. . .	. . .	90 days (d)
North Dakota	2% total population	90 days	. . .	SS	90 days after receiving
Ohio	6% EV, 3% each from 1/2 county	. . .	. . .	SS	90 days
Oklahoma	5% VH	w/i 90 days of LS	N	SS	w/i 90 days of LS
Oregon	4% VG	w/i 90 days of LS	N	SS	90 days
Pennsylvania	. . .	. . .	. . .	. . .	. . .
Rhode Island	. . .	. . .	. . .	. . .	. . .
South Carolina	. . .	. . .	. . .	. . .	. . .
South Dakota	5% VG	. . .	N	SS	90 days
Tennessee	. . .	. . .	. . .	. . .	. . .
Texas	. . .	. . .	. . .	. . .	. . .
Utah	10% VG	. . .	Y	LG	60 days
Vermont	. . .	. . .	. . .	. . .	. . .
Virginia	. . .	. . .	. . .	. . .	. . .
Washington	4% VG	w/i 90 days after LS	Y	SS	90 days
West Virginia	. . .	. . .	. . .	. . .	. . .
Wisconsin	. . .	. . .	. . .	. . .	. . .
Wyoming	15% TV, from 2/3 county	18 mos.	Y	SS	90 days

Sources: State election administration offices, except information on Maine which is from *The Book of the States 1992-93.*

Key:
. . . — Not applicable
VG — Total votes cast for the position of governor in the last election
EV — Eligible voters
TV — Total voters in the last general election
VH — Total votes cast for the office receiving the highest number of votes in last general election
VSS — Total votes cast for all candidates for the office of secretary of state at the previous general election.
ED — Election district
GE — General election
LS — Legislative session
LG — Lieutenant Governor
SS — Secretary of State
Y — Yes
N — No
w/i — Within

(a) The petition circulation period begins when petition forms have been approved and provided to or by the sponsors. Sponsors are those individuals granted permission to circulate a petition, and are therefore responsible for the validity of each signature on a given petition.
(b) Should an individual wish to remove his/her name from a petition, a request to do so must first be submitted in writing to the state officer with whom the petition is filed.
(c) Request for petition must be submitted within 10 days of adjournment of legislative session.
(d) Within 90 days of being filed with the secretary of state.

Table 5.22
STATE REFERENDUMS: PREPARING THE CITIZEN PETITION REFERENDUM TO BE PLACED ON THE BALLOT

State	Signatures verified by: (a)	Within how many days after filing	No. of days to amend/appeal petition that is: Incomplete (b)	No. of days to amend/appeal petition that is: Not accepted (c)	Penalty for falsifying petition (denotes fine, jail term)	Petition certified by: (d)
Alabama	. . .	. . .	. . .	. . .	. . .	. . .
Alaska	Director of elections	60	10 (e)	. . .	Class B misdemeanor	LG
Arizona	SS, county recorder	20 (f)	. . .	10	Class 1 misdemeanor	SS
Arkansas	SS	. . .	30	15	$50-$100, 1-5 yrs.	SS
California	County clerk or registrar of voters	. . .	. . .	. . .	. . .	SS
Colorado	SS	30	. . .	. . .	(g)	SS
Connecticut	. . .	. . .	. . .	. . .	. . .	. . .
Delaware	. . .	. . .	. . .	. . .	. . .	. . .
Florida	. . .	. . .	. . .	. . .	. . .	. . .
Georgia	. . .	. . .	. . .	. . .	. . .	. . .
Hawaii	. . .	. . .	. . .	. . .	. . .	. . .
Idaho	County clerk	. . .	. . .	. . .	$5,000, 2 yrs.	. . .
Illinois	. . .	. . .	. . .	. . .	. . .	. . .
Indiana	. . .	. . .	. . .	. . .	. . .	. . .
Iowa	. . .	. . .	. . .	. . .	. . .	. . .
Kansas	. . .	. . .	. . .	. . .	. . .	. . .
Kentucky	. . .	. . .	. . .	. . .	. . .	. . .
Louisiana	. . .	. . .	. . .	. . .	. . .	. . .
Maine	SS, registrars of voters	. . .	. . .	. . .	. . .	. . .
Maryland	County board of elections	. . .	. . .	. . .	. . .	. . .
Massachusetts	. . .	. . .	. . .	. . .	. . .	. . .
Michigan	City and township clerks	. . .	. . .	. . .	. . .	BSC
Minnesota	. . .	. . .	. . .	. . .	. . .	. . .
Mississippi	. . .	. . .	. . .	. . .	. . .	. . .
Missouri	SS, local election authorities	. . .	. . .	. . .	Class A misdemeanor	SS
Montana	County clerk, recorder	28	. . .	. . .	$500, 6 mos.	SS
Nebraska	SS, county clerk, election commr.	40	. . .	. . .	Class IV felony	SS
Nevada	County clerk, registrar	20-50	. . .	. . .	$10,000, 1-10 yrs.	SS
New Hampshire	. . .	. . .	. . .	. . .	. . .	. . .
New Jersey	. . .	. . .	. . .	. . .	. . .	. . .
New Mexico	. . .	. . .	30	15	. . .	. . .
New York	. . .	. . .	. . .	. . .	. . .	. . .
North Carolina	. . .	. . .	. . .	. . .	. . .	. . .
North Dakota	SS	. . .	20 (h)	. . .	. . .	SS
Ohio	County board of elections	. . .	10	. . .	$1000, 6 mos.	SS
Oklahoma	. . .	. . .	. . .	. . .	$500, 2 yrs.	. . .
Oregon	SS, county elections officials	15	. . .	. . .	Class C felony (possible)	SS
Pennsylvania	. . .	. . .	. . .	. . .	. . .	. . .
Rhode Island	. . .	. . .	. . .	. . .	. . .	. . .
South Carolina	. . .	. . .	. . .	. . .	. . .	. . .
South Dakota	SS	. . .	. . .	. . .	. . .	SS
Tennessee	. . .	. . .	. . .	. . .	. . .	. . .
Texas	. . .	. . .	. . .	. . .	. . .	. . .
Utah	County clerks	60	. . .	. . .	$500, 2 yrs.	LG
Vermont	. . .	. . .	. . .	. . .	. . .	. . .
Virginia	. . .	. . .	. . .	. . .	. . .	. . .
Washington	SS	(i)	. . .	10 (j)	. . .	SS
West Virginia	. . .	. . .	. . .	. . .	. . .	. . .
Wisconsin	. . .	. . .	. . .	. . .	. . .	. . .
Wyoming	SS	60	60	60	$1,000, 1 yr.	. . .

Sources: State election administration offices, except information on Maine which is from *The Book of the States 1992-93.*

Key:
. . . — Not applicable
SS — Secretary of State
LG — Lieutenant Governor
BSC — Board of State Canvassers
SBE — State Board of Elections
(a) The validity of the signatures, as well as the correct number of required signatures must be verified before the referendum is allowed on the ballot.
(b) If an insufficient number of signatures are submitted, sponsors may amend the original petition by filing additional signatures within a given number of days after filing. If the necessary number of signatures have not been submitted by this date, the petition is declared void.
(c) In some cases, the state officer will not accept a valid petition. In

such cases, sponsors may appeal this decision to the Supreme Court, where the sufficiency of the petition will be determined. If the petition is determined to be sufficient, the referendum is required to be placed on the ballot.
(d) A petition is certified for the ballot when the required number of signatures have been submitted by the filing deadline, and are determined to be valid.
(e) If within 90 days of the legislative session.
(f) In Arizona, the secretary of state has 48 hours to count signatures and 15 days to complete random sample; the county recorder then has 10 days to verify signatures.
(g) Not more than $500 or one year in city jail, or both.
(h) No additional signatures may be added. Sponsors have 20 days to correct insufficient signatures which already have been gathered.
(i) No specified time.
(j) In Washington, a petition that is not accepted may be appealed in 10 days.

Table 5.23
STATE REFERENDUMS: VOTING ON THE CITIZEN PETITION REFERENDUM

State	Ballot (a) Title by:	Summary by:	Election where referendum voted on	Effective date of approved referendum (b)	Days to contest election results (c)
Alabama	. . .	. . .	. . .	. . .	. . .
Alaska	LG,AG	LG,AG	1st statewide election 180 days after LS	30 days	5
Arizona	. . .	. . .	GE	IM	5
Arkansas	AG	AG	GE or SP	30 days	60
California	AG	AG	GE or SP 31 days after LS	IM	. . .
Colorado	SS,AG,LSS	SS,AG,LSS	GE	30 days	. . .
Connecticut	. . .	. . .	. . .	. . .	. . .
Delaware	. . .	. . .	. . .	. . .	. . .
Florida	. . .	. . .	. . .	. . .	. . .
Georgia	. . .	. . .	. . .	. . .	. . .
Hawaii	. . .	. . .	. . .	. . .	. . .
Idaho	AG	AG	Biennial or REG	30 days	. . .
Illinois	. . .	. . .	. . .	. . .	. . .
Indiana	. . .	. . .	. . .	. . .	. . .
Iowa	. . .	. . .	. . .	. . .	. . .
Kansas	. . .	. . .	. . .	. . .	. . .
Kentucky	. . .	. . .	GE or SP	IM	. . .
Louisiana	. . .	. . .	. . .	. . .	. . .
Maine	. . .	. . .	GE or SP more than 60 days but less than 6 mos. after LS	30 days	. . .
Maryland	SS,AG,SBE	. . .	GE	30 days	. . .
Massachusetts	. . .	. . .	GE more than 60 days after filing	30 days	. . .
Michigan	BSC	BSC	GE	10 days	2 (d)
Minnesota	. . .	. . .	. . .	. . .	. . .
Mississippi	. . .	. . .	. . .	. . .	. . .
Missouri	SS	LC	GE or SP called by legislation	IM	30
Montana	AG	AG	GE	Oct. 1 (e)	. . .
Nebraska	AG	AG	GE not less than 30 days after filing	10 days	40
Nevada	SS,AG	SS,AG	GE	Nov., 4th Wed.	10
New Hampshire	. . .	. . .	. . .	. . .	. . .
New Jersey	. . .	. . .	. . .	. . .	. . .
New Mexico	SS	. . .	GE	IM	. . .
New York	. . .	. . .	. . .	. . .	. . .
North Carolina	. . .	. . .	. . .	. . .	. . .
North Dakota	SS,AG	SS,AG	PR,SP or GE	30 days	14 (d)
Ohio	. . .	Ohio Ballot Bd.	GE more than 60 days after filing	30 days	15
Oklahoma	SS	. . .	GE or SP	IM	. . .
Oregon	AG	. . .	GE (f)	30 days	40
Pennsylvania	. . .	. . .	. . .	. . .	. . .
Rhode Island	. . .	. . .	. . .	. . .	. . .
South Carolina	. . .	. . .	. . .	. . .	. . .
South Dakota	P	AG	GE	1 day	10
Tennessee	. . .	. . .	. . .	. . .	. . .
Texas	. . .	. . .	. . .	. . .	. . .
Utah	LC	LC	GE	5 days (e)	40
Vermont	. . .	. . .	. . .	. . .	. . .
Virginia	. . .	. . .	. . .	. . .	. . .
Washington	AG	AG	GE	IM	5
West Virginia	. . .	. . .	. . .	. . .	. . .
Wisconsin	. . .	. . .	. . .	. . .	. . .
Wyoming	SS	SS,AG	GE more than 180 days after LS	30 days	30

Sources: State election administration offices, except information on Maine which is from *The Book of the States 1992-93.*

Key:
. . . — Not applicable
LG — Lieutenant Governor
AG — Attorney General
SS — Secretary of State
BSC — Board of State Canvassers
LC — Legislative Counsel
LSS — Legislative Legal Services
SBE — State Elections Board
GE — General election
PR — Primary election
REG — Regular election
SP — Special election
IM — Immediately
LS — Legislative session

(a) In some states, the ballot title and summary will differ from that on the petition.
(b) A majority of the popular vote is required to enact a measure in every state. In Arizona, a referendum approved by the voters becomes effective upon the governor's proclamation. In Nebraska, a referendum may be put into effect immediately after the approving votes have been canvassed by the governor or after a certain number of days have passed following the vote for a successful referendum. In Massachusetts the measure must also receive at least 30 percent of the total ballots cast in the last election.
(c) Individuals may contest the results of a vote on a referendum within a certain number of days after the election including this matter. In Alaska, five days to request recount with appeal to the court within five days after recount.
(d) After election is certified.
(e) Unless otherwise specified.
(f) In Oregon, a state referendum initiated by citizen petition can only be voted on in a general election. A referral by the legislature can be voted on in a general election, a primary, or on any date determined necessary.

Table 5.24
STATE RECALL PROVISIONS: APPLICABILITY TO STATE OFFICIALS AND PETITION CIRCULATION

State	Officers to whom recall is applicable (a)	No. of times recall can be attempted	Recall may be initiated after official has been in office	Recall may not be initiated with days remaining in term	Basis for signatures (b) (see key below)		Maximum time period allowed for petition circulation (c)
					Statewide officers	Others	
Alabama	All but judicial officers	…	120 days	180 days	25% VO	25% VO	…
Alaska	All	(d)	6 mos./5 days legislators	…	25% VO	25% VO	120 days
Arizona	All	(e)	No limit	…	12% VO, 1% from 5 counties	20% VO	160 days
California	All	…	…	…	25% VO	25% VO	60 days
Colorado	All	(f)	6 mos./5 days general assembly	…	…	…	…
Connecticut	…	…	…	…	…	…	…
Delaware	…	…	…	…	…	…	…
Florida	…	…	…	…	…	…	…
Georgia	All	…	180 days	180 days	15% VO, 1/15 from each congressional district	30% VO	90 days (g)
Hawaii	…	…	…	…	…	…	…
Idaho	All but judicial officers	(d)	90 days	…	20% EVg	20% EV	60 days
Illinois	…	…	…	…	…	…	…
Indiana	…	…	…	…	…	…	…
Iowa	…	…	…	…	…	…	…
Kansas	All but judicial officers	1 time	120 days	200 days	40% VO	40% VO	90 days
Kentucky	…	…	…	…	…	…	…
Louisiana	All but judicial officers of records	(h)	…	6 mos.	33 1/3% EV (i)	33 1/3% EV (i)	180 days
Maine	…	…	…	…	…	…	…
Maryland	…	…	…	…	…	…	…
Massachusetts	…	…	…	…	…	…	…
Michigan	All but judicial officers of records	…	6 mos.	6 mos.	25% VG	25% VG	(j)
Minnesota	…	…	…	…	…	…	…
Mississippi	…	…	…	…	…	…	…
Missouri	…	…	…	…	…	…	…
Montana	All public officers elected or appt.	(d)	2 mos.	…	15% EV	(k)	3 mos.
Nebraska	All public officers	(d)	6 mos. (l)	…	25% EV in given jurisdiction	25% EV in given jurisdiction	60 days
Nevada	…	…	…	…	…	…	…
New Hampshire	…	…	…	…	…	…	…
New Jersey	…	…	…	…	…	…	…
New Mexico	…	…	…	…	…	…	…
New York	…	…	…	…	…	…	…
North Carolina	All	1 time	…	…	…	…	…
North Dakota	…	…	…	…	25% EVg	25% EVg	…
Ohio	…	…	…	…	…	…	…
Oklahoma	All but U.S. Congress	(d)	6 mos./5 days general assembly	…	15% (m)	15% (m)	90 days
Oregon	…	…	…	…	…	…	…
Pennsylvania	G,LG,SS,AG,T	…	…	…	15% (n)	…	90 days
Rhode Island	…	…	…	1 yr.	…	…	…
South Carolina	…	…	6 mos.	…	…	…	…

See footnotes at end of table.

STATE RECALL PROVISIONS: APPLICABILITY TO STATE OFFICIALS—Continued

State	Officers to whom recall is applicable (a)	No. of times recall can be attempted	Recall may be initiated after official has been in office	Recall may not be initiated with days remaining in term	Basis for signatures (b) (see key below)		Maximum time period allowed for petition circulation (c)
					Statewide officers	Others	
South Dakota	Municipal only (1st & 2nd class)	...	...	...	...	15% EV	...
Tennessee	...	...	...	...	...	...	...
Texas	...	...	...	...	...	...	...
Utah	...	...	...	...	...	...	...
Vermont	...	...	...	...	...	...	...
Virginia	...	...	...	...	...	...	...
Washington	All but judges of courts of records	...	1M	180 days	25% VO	35% VO	(o)
West Virginia	...	...	...	...	...	...	...
Wisconsin	All	1 time	1 yr. (p)	...	25% VG (q)	25% VP (r)	60 days (s)
Wyoming	...	...	...	...	...	...	...

Sources: State election administration offices, except information on Maine which is from *The Book of the States 1992-93.*

Key:

... — Not applicable
All — All elective officials
VO — Number of votes cast in the last election for the office or official being recalled
EV — Number of eligible voters in the last general election for governor
VG — Total votes cast for the position of governor in the last election.
VP — Total votes cast for position of president in last presidential election
IM — Immediately

(a) An *elective* official may be recalled by qualified voters entitled to vote for the recalled official's successor. An *appointed* official may be recalled by qualified voters entitled to vote for the successor(s) of the elective officer(s) authorized to appoint an individual to the position.

(b) Signature requirements for recall of those other than state elective officials are based on votes in the jurisdiction to which the said official has been elected.

(c) The petition circulation period begins when petition forms have been approved and provided to sponsors. Sponsors are those individuals granted permission to circulate a petition, and are therefore responsible for the validity of each signature on a given petition.

(d) Additional recall attempts can be made provided that the state treasury is reimbursed the cost of the previous recall attempt(s).

(e) Must wait until 6 months after the first recall attempt.

(f) If signatures are obtained at least equal in number to 50% of those voting in the last general election.

(g) 90 days for statewide, others vary by number of signatures required.

(h) Must wait at least until 18 months after the first recall attempt.

(i) Basis for signatures — 33 1/3% if over 1,000 EV; 40% if under 1,000 EV.

(j) In Michigan, signatures dated more than 90 days prior to the filing deadline are ruled invalid.

(k) 15% EV for district or county officials, 10% EV for municipal or school officials.

(l) Six months or 10 days after legislative session begins for legislators.

(m) 15% of the total votes cast in the public officer's electoral district for all candidates for governor at the election next preceding the filing of the petition at which a candidate for governor was elected for a four-year term.

(n) In Rhode Island, a recall may be instituted by filing with the state board of elections an application for issuance of a recall petition against said general officer which is signed by duly qualified electors equal to three percent of the total number of votes cast at the last preceding general election for that office. If, upon verification, the application is determined to contain signatures of the required number of electors, the state board of elections shall issue a recall petition for circulation amongst the electors of the state. Within 90 days of issuance, recall petitions containing the signatures of duly qualified electors consisting of 15% of the total number of votes cast in the last preceding general election for said office must be filed with the state elections board.

(o) Statewide officials—270 days; others—180 days.

(p) Petition may be filed after official has been in office one year.

(q) State, congressional, judicial, legislative and county offices.

(r) For city, village, town and school district elected officials.

(s) For statewide offices, 30 days for local offices (city, town and village).

Table 5.25
STATE RECALL PROVISIONS: PETITION REVIEW, APPEAL AND ELECTION

State	Signatures verified (a) by:	Days to amend/appeal a petition that is: Incomplete (b)	Days to amend/appeal a petition that is: Not accepted (c)	Penalty for falsifying petition (denotes fines, jail time)	Days allowed for petition to be certified (d)	Days to step down after certification (e)	Voting on the recall (f): Election held	Voting on the recall (f): Election type	Days to contest election results (g)
Alabama	Director of elections	20	20	Class B misdemeanor	30	...	60-90 days after cert.	SP, GE or PR	5
Alaska	SS, county recorder	...	...	Class 1 misdemeanor	75	5	100-120 days after cert.	SP	5
Arizona		...	...	...	...	...	...	...	...
Arkansas		...	...	...	...	...	...	...	...
California	County clerk/registrar of voters	...	...	...	...	...	60-80 days after cert.	SP	...
Colorado	SS	60	...	...	30-60	5	60-90 days after cert.	SP or GE	...
Connecticut		...	...	...	...	...	...	...	...
Delaware		...	...	...	...	...	...	...	...
Florida	Election supervisor	...	10	$1,000, 12 mos.	30-45	...	30-45 days after cert.	SP, PR or GE	5
Georgia		Not allowed	...	...	...	...	...	...	...
Hawaii		...	...	...	...	...	45+ days after cert. (h)	SP or GE (h)	...
Idaho	SS, county clerk	30	10	$5,000, 2 yrs.	10	5	...	...	...
Illinois		...	...	...	...	...	...	...	...
Indiana		...	...	...	...	...	...	...	...
Iowa		...	...	...	...	...	...	...	...
Kansas	County election officer	...	...	...	30	...	60-90 days after cert.	SP or GE	30
Kentucky		...	...	...	...	5	(i)	SP	30
Louisiana	Registrar of voters	...	...	$100-1,000, 30-90 days	10	...	...	...	...
Maine		...	...	...	...	...	...	...	...
Maryland		...	...	...	...	...	...	...	...
Massachusetts	SS	...	...	...	35	...	w/i 60 days after cert.	SP	2 (j)
Michigan		...	...	...	...	...	...	...	...
Minnesota		...	...	...	...	...	...	...	...
Mississippi		...	...	...	...	...	...	...	...
Missouri		...	...	...	...	...	...	...	...
Montana	County clerk, recorder	20	...	$500, 6 mos.	30	5	3 mos. after cert.	SP or GE	...
Nebraska		...	...	...	...	...	...	...	...
Nevada	County clerk, registrar	...	...	$10,000, 1-10 yrs.	20-50	5	(k)	SP	10
New Hampshire		...	...	...	...	...	...	...	...
New Jersey		...	...	...	...	...	...	...	...
New Mexico		...	...	...	...	...	...	...	...
New York		...	...	...	...	...	...	...	...
North Carolina	SS	20 (l)	...	...	35	...	...	...	...
North Dakota	SS		...	...		...	...	...	...
Ohio		...	...	...	...	10 (m)	...	SP, GE or PR	14 (n)
Oklahoma		...	...	...	...	...	...	...	...
Oregon	SS or county clerk	...	...	Class C felony (possible)	10	5	w/i 40 days after cert.	SP	40
Pennsylvania		...	...	...	...	...	...	...	...
Rhode Island		...	...	...	...	...	...	...	...
South Carolina		...	...	...	...	...	...	...	...
South Dakota	Municipal finance officer	...	...	...	...	...	(k)	SP	...
Tennessee		...	...	...	...	...	...	...	...
Texas		...	...	...	...	...	...	...	...
Utah		...	...	...	...	...	...	...	...
Vermont		...	...	...	...	...	...	...	...

See footnotes at end of table.

STATE RECALL PROVISIONS: PETITION REVIEW—Continued

State	Signatures verified (a) by:	Days to amend/appeal a petition that is: Incomplete (b)	Not accepted (c)	Penalty for falsifying petition (denotes fines, jail time)	Days allowed for petition to be certified (d)	Days to step down after certification (e)	Voting on the recall (f) Election held	Election type	Days to contest election results (g)
Virginia	...	...	...	...	...	...	...	...	...
Washington	SS, county auditor	...	10 (o)	Felony	w/i 10	IM	45-60 days after cert.	SP	10
West Virginia	...	...	...	...	...	...	...	SP (r)	...
Wisconsin	Filing offices (p)	5	7 (q)	Not more than $10,000, not more than 3 yrs. or both	31	10	6 weeks after cert.	SP (r)	3 (s)
Wyoming	...	...	...	...	...	...	...	...	...

Sources: State election administration offices, except information on Maine which is from *The Book of the States 1992-93.*

Key:
... — Not applicable
SS — Secretary of State
SP — Special election
GE — General election
PR — Primary election
IM — Immediate and automatic removal from office
w/i — Within

(a) The validity of the signatures, as well as the correct number of required signatures must be verified before the recall is allowed on the ballot.
(b) If an insufficient number of signatures are submitted, sponsors may amend the original petition by filing additional signatures within a given number of days. If the necessary number of signatures have not been submitted by this date, the petition is declared void.
(c) In some cases, the state officer will not accept a valid petition. In such a case, sponsors may appeal this decision to the Supreme Court, where the sufficiency of the petition will be determined. When this is declared, the recall is required to be placed on the ballot.
(d) A petition is certified for the ballot when the required number of signatures have been submitted by the filing deadline, and are determined to be valid.
(e) The official to whom a recall is proposed has a certain number of days to step down from his position before a recall election is initiated, if he desires to do so.
(f) A majority of the popular vote is required to recall an official in each state.

(g) Individuals may contest the results of a vote on a recall within a certain number of days after the results are certified. In Alaska, an appeal to courts must be filed within five days of the recount.
(h) In Idaho, the dates on which elections may be conducted are the first Tuesday in February, the fourth Tuesday in May, the first Tuesday in August, or the Tuesday following the first Monday in November. In addition, an emergency election may be called upon motion of the governing board of a political subdivision. Recall elections conducted by any political subdivision shall be held on the nearest of these dates which falls more than 45 days after the clerk of the political subdivision orders that the recall election shall be held.
(i) The election must be held on the next available date of six dates per year allowed by the election committee.
(j) After election is certified.
(k) In Nevada, a recall election is held 10-20 days after the court determines a recall election is to be held. In South Dakota, a recall election is held 30-50 days after the governing board orders a recall election. The governing board must meet within 10 days after the petition is filed.
(l) Only signatures already collected can be amended such as adding addresses or correcting some other flaw which makes the signature unverifiable.
(m) After petition is filed with the secretary of state.
(n) Fourteen days after the canvas board has certified the results.
(o) In Washington, a petition that is not accepted may be appealed in 10 days.
(p) Where declaration of candidacy is filed.
(q) After certificate.
(r) May be held on general election but is still considered special election.
(s) Business days.

Chapter Six

STATE FINANCES

A focus on the states' financial situation, with an update on recent trends in taxation and tax collections, and federal spending in the states. Includes information on state budgetary procedures and fund management activities, their revenue sources, expenditures and debt for 1991 and 1992, and tax rates for 1994.

The Road to Recovery?

The recession might be over, but states still face an uncertain fiscal road ahead.

by Douglas J. Olberding

The state financial data contained in this chapter are from the U.S. Department of Commerce, Bureau of the Census, and cover fiscal years 1991 and 1992. The tax rate information in this chapter is from the Federation of Tax Administrators and are tax rates for selected sources as of January 1, 1994. This essay uses other available sources to present an overview and discussion of the current fiscal condition of the states, including fiscal years 1993 and 1994.

Overview

Although the recession that began in July 1990 officially ended in March 1991, economic growth since then has been uneven, and states have struggled to keep the books balanced amid a period of fiscal uncertainty. During this period, state expenditures for Medicaid and corrections have continued to soar, eroding the traditional base of state spending; revenue growth has been uneven; and federal program cutbacks and mandates have placed additional burdens on state finances. Also, many experts have argued that state tax systems have failed to keep pace with the structural changes in the U.S. economy and are in need of serious overhaul.

To combat these challenges, states have raised taxes and fees, cut spending and have even begun to experiment with alternative forms of revenue generation. According to some recent data, these efforts may have put some states on the right track, but many still have a ways to go.

Fiscal 1992 went on record as the year with the largest total revenue increase in history as states raised more than $15 billion in new revenue (see Table A).[1] By and large, these revenue increases supported the continuation of

current programs, rather than funding new or expanded programs. On the other side of the ledger, 35 states cut nearly $4.5 billion from their enacted budgets in order to balance books at the end of fiscal 1992. These cuts were widespread, although some states exempted entitlement programs such as Aid to Families with Dependent Children (AFDC) and Medicaid. These actions helped balance state budgets but did not do much to increase low fund balances. Year-end budget reserves averaged only 1.5 percent of expenditures.

States began to turn the corner in fiscal 1993 as total revenue increases and budget cuts both dropped dramatically. Compared to fiscal 1991 when states raised $10 billion in new revenue and fiscal 1992 when states raised $15 billion, fiscal year 1993 was almost static. States enacted only $3 billion in combined increases. States also cut less from enacted fiscal 1993 budgets than in the past two fiscal years. Cuts in fiscal 1993 totaled only $1.8 billion with elementary and secondary education and higher education absorbing a large share of reductions while cuts in fiscal 1991 and 1992 enacted budgets totaled $7.5 billion and $4.4 billion respectively.

Year-end fund balances also showed signs of improvement from the previous two fiscal years. Year-end fund balances averaged 3 percent in fiscal 1993, and seven states reported balances of less than 1 percent. In fiscal 1991, fund balances averaged only 1.8 percent and 21 states had balances of less than 1 percent; and in fiscal 1992, balances averaged a mere

Douglas J. Olberding is a policy analyst with the State Policy and Innovations group of The Council of State Governments.

Table A
SUMMARY OF STATE BUDGET ACTIONS, FY 1992 TO FY 1994
(In thousands of dollars except as noted)

	FY 1992	FY 1993	FY 1994
Expenditures			
State budget increases (%)			
Nominal	5.1	3.3 (a)	4.6 (a)
Real	1.5	−0.2 (a)	1.1 (a)
State spending growth (b)		*Number of states*	
Negative	10	5	8
0.0% to 4.9%	21	26	15
5.0% to 9.9%	11	12	21
10% or higher	5	7	6
Total budget cuts (c)	$4,457.8	$1,836.4	. . .
Revenues (d)			
State revenue increases	$15 billion	$3 billion	$3 billion
Increases by source			
Sales	$3,849.5	$1,423.6	$965.5
Personal income	$5,429.9	$912.3	$552.6
Corporate income	$1,439.4	$429.9	$204.5
Cigarette/tobacco	$245.7	$189.4	$634.3
Motor fuels	$628.7	$213.8	$255.4
Alcohol	$203.9	$121.5	$45.7
Other tax	$3,232.1	$1,784.3	$64.7
Fees	. . .	. . .	$296.4
Year-end balances			
Total balance	$2.5 billion	$9.5 billion (a)	$8.1 billion (a)
As % of expenditures	1.5	3	2.5
		Number of states	
Less than 1.0%	16	7	14
1.0% to 2.9%	10	14	15
3.0% to 4.9%	11	10	6
5% or more	13	19	15

Source: National Association of State Budget Officers, *Fiscal Survey of the States.*
Key:
. . . — Not available
(a) Figures are estimates.
(b) Based on FY 1993 preliminary actual and FY 1994 appropriated.
(c) Cuts made after fiscal year budget was passed.
(d) FY 1994 based on enacted budget.

0.3 percent with 18 states below 1 percent (see Figure A).

Preliminary information for fiscal year 1994 indicates that states may be on solid footing, although some of the signals are mixed. On the brighter side, states are only enacting approximately $3 billion dollars in new taxes and fees. However, much of this "new" revenue is actually tax increases from previous fiscal years that were scheduled to expire, or rate reductions that have been temporarily postponed.

Because states vary in how they interpret revenue action, it is unclear at this point how much new revenue is actually being raised.

State spending is scheduled to grow modestly in fiscal year 1994 as the shifts in the overall pattern of state spending that began in the 1990s continues. Overall, state budgets are scheduled to increase nominally by approximately 4.6 percent from the previous year. Medicaid is expected to continue absorbing a larger share of state spending, which will be offset in part by continued cuts in elementary and secondary education and higher education.

Year-end fund balances tell the other side of the story. Balances are expected to be at 2.5 percent of total state expenditures, down from 3 percent in fiscal year 1993. In addition, the number of states with a balance below 1 percent increased from seven in fiscal year 1993 to 14 in fiscal year 1994.

Economic Recovery

The economic recovery that is underway differs from previous recoveries in several ways. Growth of personal income and gross domestic product in this post-recession period have not followed the patterns of previous periods of economic expansion. Also, a series of natural disasters have strained budgets in many states and lingering unemployment following the recession has caused concerns among state policy-makers.

First, personal income growth in the 50 states during the past two years or so has not been as vigorous as growth seen after previous recessions. State personal income, or the income received by, or on behalf of, all the residents of a state, increased at an annual rate of 4.6 percent in the first eight quarters of the recovery which began in March 1991.[2] By contrast, in the three previous recoveries that lasted at least as long as the current one, personal income increased at an average rate of 9.8 percent. In this recovery, states in the Rockies, the Plains and the Southeast lead the nation in personal income growth, while Mideast and New England states, along with Florida and California exhibit the slowest growth.

A second difference in the current recovery versus previous ones is that gross domestic product growth has been erratic (see Figure B). The gross domestic product (GDP) is a measure of goods and services produced in the United States and is used to chart expansion of the economy. The range of growth since the recession ended in March 1991 has been from 0.5 percent in the fourth quarter of 1991 to 7.5 percent in the fourth quarter of 1993. There

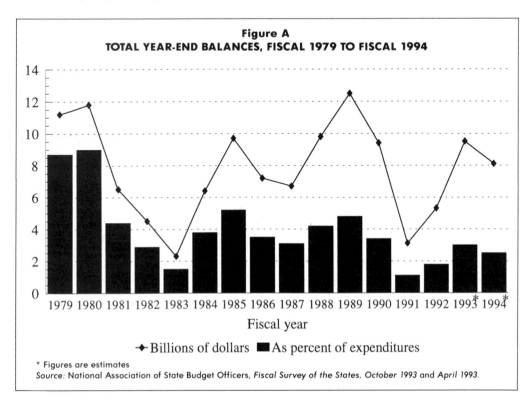

Figure A
TOTAL YEAR-END BALANCES, FISCAL 1979 TO FISCAL 1994

Fiscal year

→ Billions of dollars ■ As percent of expenditures

* Figures are estimates
Source: National Association of State Budget Officers, *Fiscal Survey of the States, October 1993 and April 1993.*

were even fears of a double-dip recession in the fourth quarter of 1991 as the GDP dipped to only 0.5 percent growth. By contrast, GDP growth following the 1981-82 and 1973-75 recessions followed a steady, upward path.

Further complicating the picture is the series of natural disasters since the recovery began, including flooding in the Midwest, earthquakes in California and hurricanes in Florida, Louisiana and Hawaii. While the full impact of some of these disasters is not yet known, recent data suggest that declining personal income in the Midwest in the second and third quarters of 1993 is partly attributable to farm losses as a result of flooding in summer 1993.[3] In addition, the Bureau of Economic Analysis has estimated uninsured losses as a result of destruction caused by Hurricane Andrew in Florida and Louisiana at $55 billion. These losses directly impact state personal income.[4]

Finally, in previous recessions the unemployment rate was higher during the recession and fell sooner after the recession than the one that ended in March 1991. According to the Bureau of Labor Statistics, the civilian unemployment rate was at 6.5 percent in the final quarter of the recession and peaked at 7.6 percent in the third quarter of 1992, over a year after the recession officially ended.[5] However, during the 1981-82 recession, the unemployment rate peaked just below 11 percent in the final quarter of the recession and then fell sharply immediately after the recession ended. The same is true for the 1973-75 recession where unemployment reached a high of 8.8 percent, peaked one quarter after the recession at 9 percent, then fell dramatically afterwards. Those expecting the rapid job growth that has occurred in most post-recession periods have been extremely disappointed.

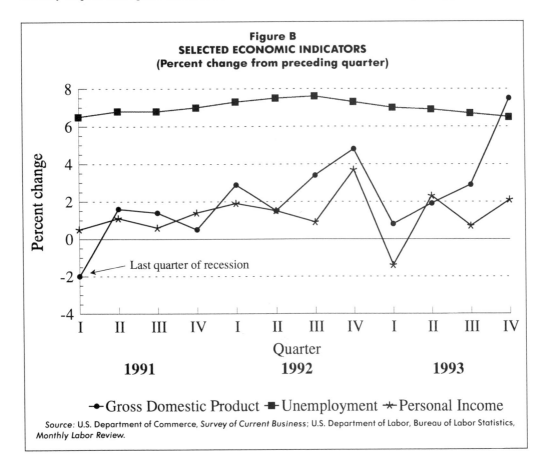

Figure B
SELECTED ECONOMIC INDICATORS
(Percent change from preceding quarter)

Source: U.S. Department of Commerce, *Survey of Current Business*; U.S. Department of Labor, Bureau of Labor Statistics, *Monthly Labor Review*.

Developments in State Finances

Each of these factors has contributed to a climate of uncertainty facing state policy-makers. Furthermore, states are facing spending pressures in the areas of health and corrections, as well as pressure from the courts to equalize state support in education financing.

Leading the way in the school finance reform arena is Michigan, where in March 1994 voters elected to cut residential property taxes by 33 percent while increasing the state sales tax from 4 percent to 6 percent and increasing the excise tax on cigarettes from 25 cents to 75 cents a pack. This represents a major development in education finance in the United States where the property tax has been the staple of education support for over 300 years. At issue in many states is the increased reliance on property taxes since 1986, the regressive nature of the tax and the inability for poorer districts to support local schools. The action in Michigan opens the possibility of education finance reform in other states where similar problems exist.

State spending for Medicaid continues to erode spending for non-mandated state programs like education and transportation. Unlike the trend in the 1980s of rapid growth in state education spending, Medicaid has been steadily eating away at state budgets in the 1990s (see Figure C). According to the National Association of State Budget Officers, state spending for Medicaid replaced spending for higher education as the second largest expenditure category in fiscal 1992. While higher education spending has remained constant at 12 percent, relying mainly on tuition and fee increases for new support, Medicaid spending has jumped from 10 percent of total state spending in fiscal 1987 to 18.4 percent in fiscal 1993.

State corrections spending has also increased in recent years as new prisons have opened. Corrections spending reflects state spending to build and operate prison systems and may also include spending on juvenile justice programs and on alternatives to incarceration such

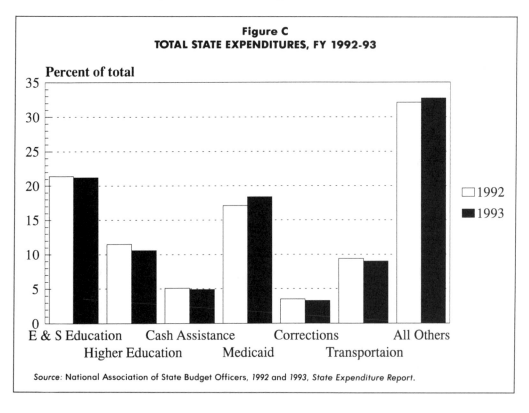

Figure C
TOTAL STATE EXPENDITURES, FY 1992-93

Source: National Association of State Budget Officers, 1992 and 1993, State Expenditure Report.

as probation and parole. As public sentiment has increased for mandatory sentences, less generous parole, longer sentences and higher sentencing rates for certain crimes, state government has responded by increasing resources in this area. And as states are finding out, these responses are costly. Although state spending for corrections has remained around 3.5 percent of total state expenditures, from 1990 to 1991 total state corrections spending increased 13.5 percent — from $16.9 billion to $19.2 billion — and from $19.2 billion to $20.6 billion or 7.7 percent in the period 1991 to 1992.[6]

Conclusion

Although the recession has ended, states are facing continued challenges. While states have been able to meet fiscal pressures in recent years through program cutbacks and revenue increases, underlying structural problems still exist and must be dealt with in a serious manner. Among these challenges are controlling expenditure growth in critical areas like health and corrections, developing fair and equitable revenue systems that reflect the long-term shifts in the U.S. economy from a manufacturing base to a service base and developing programs and services that meet the needs of their citizens.

Footnotes

[1] Data presented in Table A are from the *Fiscal Survey of the States, 1991-93*, which is published twice annually by the National Association of State Budget Officers and the National Governors' Association.

[2] Friedenberg, Howard L. and Duke D. Tran "Personal Income by State and Region: First Quarter 1993." *Survey of Current Business*, U.S. Department of Commerce, Washington, D.C., July 1993.

[3] Friedenberg, Howard L. and Duke D. Tran "Personal Income by State and Region: Third Quarter 1993." *Survey of Current Business*, U.S. Department of Commerce, Washington, D.C., January 1994.

[4] Larkins, Daniel, "The Business Situation," *Survey of Current Business*, U.S. Department of Commerce, Washington, D.C., September 1993.

[5] *Monthly Labor Review*, U.S. Department of Labor, Washington, D.C., March 1992, 93, 94.

[6] *1992 Fiscal Survey of the States*, National Association of State Budget Officers, Washington, D.C., April 1993.

Table 6.1
STATE BUDGETARY CALENDARS

State	Budget guidelines to agencies	Agency requests submitted to governor	Agency hearings held	Governor's budget sent to legislature	Legislature adopts budget	Fiscal year begins	Frequency of legislative/budget cycles
Alabama	September	Nov/Dec	January	February	Feb/May	October	Annual/Annual
Alaska	August	October	November	December	May	July	Annual/Annual
Arizona	May	September	Nov/Dec	January	June	July	Annual/Annual
Arkansas	March	July	August	Sept/Dec	Jan/April	July	Biennial/Biennial
California	July/Nov	Aug/Sept	Aug/Nov	January	June	July	Annual/Annual
Colorado	June	August	September	November (a)	June	July	Annual/Annual
Connecticut	July	September	February	February	May/June (b)	July	Annual/Annual
Delaware	August	Oct/Nov	Oct/Nov	January	June	July	Annual/Annual
Florida	June	September	November	February	June	July	Annual/Biennial (c)
Georgia	May	September	Nov/Dec	January	March	July	Annual/Annual
Hawaii	July/Aug	Aug/Sept	November	January (d)	April	July	Annual/Biennial
Idaho	June	August	. . .	January	March	July	Annual/Annual
Illinois	August	Nov/Dec	Nov/Dec	March	June	July	Annual/Annual
Indiana	June	September	. . .	January	April/May	July	Annual/Annual
Iowa	June	September	Nov/Dec	January	April/May	July	Annual/Annual
Kansas	June	September	Oct/Nov	January	April/May	July	Annual/Annual
Kentucky	July	October	Oct/Dec	January	March/April	July	Biennial/Biennial
Louisiana	September	December	February	April	July	July	Annual/Annual
Maine	July	August	Oct/Dec	January	June	July	Biennial/Biennial
Maryland	July	Aug/Sept	Oct/Nov	January	April	July	Annual/Annual
Massachusetts	August	October	October	January	June	July	Annual/Annual
Michigan	September	Oct/Nov	Dec/Jan	February	June	October	Annual/Annual
Minnesota	August	October	November	January	May	July	Annual/Biennial
Mississippi	June	August	. . .	November	March/April	July	Annual/Annual
Missouri	July	October	. . .	January	April/May	July	Annual/Annual
Montana	June	August	Nov/Dec	December	April	July	Biennial/Biennial
Nebraska	July	September	January	January	April	July	Annual/Biennial
Nevada	July	September	Sept/Dec	January	June	July	Biennial/Annual
New Hampshire	June	October	November	February	June	July	Annual/Biennial
New Jersey	May	October	. . .	January	June	July	Annual/Annual
New Mexico	July	September	Oct/Dec	January	Feb/March	July	Annual/Annual
New York	July	September	Oct/Nov	January	March	April	Annual/Annual
North Carolina	January	August	November	February	June	July	Biennial/Biennial (e)
North Dakota	March	June/July	July/Oct	December	Jan/April	July	Biennial/Biennial
Ohio	September (f)	October (f)	Sept/Nov	Jan/March (g)	June	July	Annual/Biennial
Oklahoma	July	September	Sept/Nov	February	May	July	Annual/Annual
Oregon	Jan/June	September	Oct/Nov	December	Jan/June	July	Biennial/Biennial
Pennsylvania	August	October	Dec/Jan	February (h)	June	July	Annual/Annual
Rhode Island	June/July	October	November	February	May/June	July	Annual/Annual
South Carolina	June	September	October	January	June	July	Annual/Annual
South Dakota	June/July	September	Oct/Nov	December	March	July	Annual/Annual
Tennessee	August	October	November	January	April/May	July	Annula/Annual
Texas	March	July/Nov	July/Sept	January	May	September	Biennial/Biennial
Utah	July/August	Sept/Oct	November	January	February	July	Annual/Annual
Vermont	September	October	Nov/Dec	January	May	July	Biennial/Annual
Virginia	May (f)	June/Sept (f)	Sept/Oct	January	March	July	Annual/Biennial (i)
Washington	April	September	October	December	May	July	Annual/Biennial (j)
West Virginia	July/August	September	Oct/Dec	January	March	July	Annual/Annual
Wisconsin	June	October	March	January	June	July	Annual/Biennial
Wyoming	May	Oct/Nov	November	January	May	July	Biennial/Annual

Sources: National Association of State Budget Officers, *Budgetary Process in the States* (July 1992); updated April 1994 by The Council of State Governments. Update reflects literal reading of state constitutions and statutes.

Key:
. . . — Not applicable
(a) Governor submits approved department budgets to legislature November 1. Final statewide budget is submitted in January.
(b) Legislature adopts budget during June of odd years, May of even years.
(c) Biennial budget submission but annual appropriation.
(d) Budget document due to legislature at end of December. Appropriations bill due in January.

(e) With annual updates.
(f) These dates are for the operating expense budget. For the capital budget, guidelines are sent to agencies in December, with requests due by March 1.
(g) Budget is submitted in January except during inauguration, then submitted in March. Appropriations are annual.
(h) Budget is submitted in March when governor has been elected for first full term.
(i) Virginia adopts a biennial budget in the even-numbered year. It is amended by the General Assembly in the odd-numbered year.
(j) There are annual updates of the budget.

Table 6.2
OFFICIALS OR AGENCIES RESPONSIBLE FOR BUDGET PREPARATION, REVIEW AND CONTROLS

State or other jurisdiction	Official/agency responsible for preparing budget document	Special budget review agency in legislative branch	Agency(ies) responsible for budgetary and related accounting controls
Alabama	State Budget Off., Dept. of Finance	Legislative Fiscal Off.	Dept. of Finance
Alaska	Director, Off. of Mgt. & Budget, Off. of the Governor	Div. of Legislative Audit; Div. of Legislative Finance; Administrative Services Div., Legislative Affairs Agcy.	Div. of Finance, Dept. of Admn.
Arizona	Director, Off. of Strategic Planning & Budgeting	Jt. Legislative Budget Cmte.	Finance Div., Dept. of Admn.
Arkansas	Administrator, Off. of Budget, Dept. of Finance & Admn.	Fiscal & Tax Research Services, Bur. of Legislative Research	Dept. of Finance & Admn.
California	Director, Dept. of Finance	Senate Cmte. on Budget & Fiscal Review; Assembly Ways & Means Cmte.; Off. of Legislative Analyst	Dept. of Finance
Colorado	Director, Off. of State Planning & Budgeting	Jt. Budget Cmte.; Legislative Council	Div. of Accounts & Control, Dept. of Admn.
Connecticut	Executive Budget Officer, Budget & Finance Div., Off. of Policy & Mgt.	Off. of Fiscal Analysis	Off. of Policy & Mgt.
Delaware	Director, Off. of the Budget	Off. of Controller General,	Dept. of Finance
Florida	Director, Off. of Planning & Budgeting, Off. of the Governor	Senate, House Appropriations Cmtes.	Finance Div., Dept. of Banking & Finance
Georgia	Director, Off. of Planning & Budget	Legislative Budget Analyst, Legislative Budget Off.	Off. of Treasury & Fiscal Services
Hawaii	Director, Dept. of Budget & Finance	Senate Ways & Means Cmte.; House Finance Cmte.	Dept. of Budget & Finance
Idaho	Administrator, Div. of Financial Mgt., Off. of the Governor	Legislative Budget Off.	Div. of Financial Mgt., Off. of the Governor
Illinois	Director, Bur. of the Budget, Off. of the Governor	Economic & Fiscal Comm.	Dept. of Revenue; Bur. of the Budget, Off. of the Governor
Indiana	Director, Budget Agcy.	Off. of Fiscal & Mgt. Analysis, Legislative Services Agcy.	Budget Agcy.
Iowa	Director, Dept. of Mgt.	Legislative Fiscal Bur.	Dept. of Mgt.
Kansas	Director, Div. of the Budget., Dept. of Admn.	Legislative Research Dept.	Div. of the Budget, Dept. of Admn.
Kentucky	State Budget Director, Governor's Off. for Policy & Mgt.	Budget Review Off., Legislative Research Comm.	Finance & Admn. Cabinet
Louisiana	Budget Director, Div. of Admn., Off. of the Governor	Legislative Fiscal Off.; Fiscal Services, Senate Research Services	Div. of Admn.
Maine	State Budget Officer, Bur. of the Budget, Dept. of Admn. & Financial Services	Off. of Fiscal & Program Review, Legislative Council	Dept. of Admn. & Financial Services
Maryland	Secretary, Dept. of Budget & Fiscal Planning	Div. of Fiscal Research, Dept. of Fiscal Services	Dept. of Budget & Fiscal Planning
Massachusetts	Budget Director, Executive Off. for Admn. & Finance	Senate, House Ways & Means Cmtes.	Executive Off. for Admn. & Finance
Michigan	Director, Dept. of Mgt. & Budget	Senate, House Fiscal Agencies	Dept. of Mgt. & Budget
Minnesota	Commissioner, Dept. of Finance	Legislative Coordinating Comm.	Dept. of Finance
Mississippi	Executive Director, Dept. of Finance & Admn.	Jt. Legislative Budget Off.	Dept. of Finance & Admn.
Missouri	Commissioner, Div. of Budget & Planning, Off. of Admn.	Oversight Div.; Cmte. on Legislative Research	Off. of Admn.
Montana	Director, Budget & Program Planning Off.	Off. of Legislative Fiscal Analyst	Budget & Program Planning Off.

See footnotes at end of table.

BUDGET OFFICIALS OR AGENCIES—Continued

State or other jurisdiction	Official/agency responsible for preparing budget document	Special budget review agency in legislative branch	Agency(ies) responsible for budgetary and related accounting controls
Nebraska	Administrator, Budget Div., Dept. of Administrative Services	Legislative Fiscal Off.	Budget Div., Dept. of Administrative Services; Auditor of Public Accounts; Dept. of Revenue
Nevada	Director, Budget Div., Dept. of Admn.	Fiscal Analyst Div., Legislative Counsel Bur.	Controller
New Hampshire	Commissioner, Dept. of Administrative Services	Legislative Budget Assistant's Off.	Dept. of Administrative Services
New Jersey	Director, Off. of Mgt. & Budget; Dept. of Treasury	Legislative Budget & Finance Off.; Central Mgt. Unit, Off. of Legislative Services	Dept. of Treasury
New Mexico	Director, Budget Div., Dept. of Finance & Admn.	Legislative Finance Cmte.; Legislative Council Service	Dept. of Finance & Admn.
New York	Director, Div. of Budget, Executive Dept.	Senate Finance Cmte.; Assembly Ways & Means Cmte.; Jt. Legislative Comm. on Expenditure Review	Off. of the State Comptroller
North Carolina	State Budget Officer, Off. of State Budget	Fiscal Research Div., Legislative Services Off.	Off. of State Budget
North Dakota	Director, Off. of Mgt. & Budget	Legislative Budget Analyst & Auditor, Legislative Council	Off. of Mgt. & Budget
Ohio	Director, Off. of Budget & Mgt.	Legislative Budget Off.	Off. of Budget & Mgt.
Oklahoma	Director, Off. of State Finance	House of Rep., Fiscal Div.; Appropriations Coordinator, Senate Fiscal Staff	Off. of State Finance
Oregon	Administrator, Budget & Mgt. Div., Executive Dept.	Legislative Fiscal Off.	Budget & Mgt. Div., Executive Dept.
Pennsylvania	Secretary, Off. of Budget, Off. of the Governor	Senate, House Appropriations Cmtes.; Legislative Budget & Finance Cmte.	Secretary of the Budget, Off. of the Governor
Rhode Island	Budget Officer; Off. of the Budget, Dept. of Admn.	Senate, House Fiscal Advisory Staffs	Dept. of Admn.
South Carolina	Director, Budget Div., Budget & Control Bd.	Senate Finance Cmte.; House Ways and Means Cmte.	Budget & Control Bd.
South Dakota	Commissioner, Bur. of Finance & Mgt.	Legislative Research Council	Bur. of Finance & Mgt.
Tennessee	Assistant Commissioner, Budget Div., Dept. of Finance & Admn.	Fiscal Review Cmte.	Dept. of Finance & Admn.
Texas	Director, Governor's Off. of Budget & Planning	Legislative Budget Bd.	Comptroller of Public Accounts
Utah	Director, Off. of Planning & Budget	Off. of Legislative Fiscal Analyst	Div. of Finance, Dept. of Admn.
Vermont	Commissioner, Dept. of Finance & Mgt.; Agency of Admn.	Jt. Fiscal Cmte.	Dept. of Finance & Mgt., Agency of Admn.
Virginia	Director, Dept. of Planning & Budget	Senate Finance Cmte.; House Appropriations Cmte.	Secretary of Finance, Governor's Cabinet
Washington	Director, Off. of Financial Mgt.	Legislative Budget Cmte.	Off. of Financial Mgt.
West Virginia	Director, Budget Div., Dept. of Finance & Admn.	Off. of Legislative Auditor	Dept. of Finance & Admn.
Wisconsin	Administrator, State Executive Budget & Planning, Dept. of Admn.	Legislative Fiscal Bur.	State Finance & Program Mgt., Dept. of Admn.
Wyoming	Administrator, Budget Div.	Legislative Services Off.	Off. of State Auditor
Dist. of Columbia	Director, Off. of the Budget	Accounting Unit, Off. of the Secretary of Council	Financial Mgt.
American Samoa	Director, Program Planning & Budget Development	Legislative Fiscal Off.	Dept. of Treasury
Guam	Director, Bur. of Budget & Mgt. Research	Ways & Means Cmte.	Dept. of Admn.

BUDGET OFFICIALS OR AGENCIES—Continued

State or other jurisdiction	Official/agency responsible for preparing budget document	Special budget review agency in legislative branch	Agency(ies) responsible for budgetary and related accounting controls
No. Mariana Islands	Planning & Budget, Off. of the Governor	Senate Fiscal Affairs Cmte.; House Ways & Means Cmte.	Finance & Accounting Dept.
Puerto Rico	Director, Off. of Budget & Mgt.	Off. of Legislative Services; Senate Budget Off.; House Budget & Finance Off.	Off. of Budget & Mgt.
U.S. Virgin Islands	Director, Off. of Mgt. & Budget	Post Audit Div.	Dept. of Finance

Sources: The Council of State Governments, *State Legislative Leadership, Committees and Staff: 1993-94* and *State Administrative Officials Classified by Function: 1993-94.*

Table 6.3
STATE BALANCED BUDGETS: CONSTITUTIONAL AND STATUTORY PROVISIONS, GUBERNATORIAL AND LEGISLATIVE AUTHORITY

State	Constitutional and Statutory Provisions				Gubernatorial Authority				Legislative Authority	
	Governor must submit a balanced budget	Legislature must pass a balanced budget	Governor must sign a balanced budget	May carry over deficit	Governor has line item veto	Can reduce budget without legislative approval	Restrictions on budget reductions	Votes required to override gubernatorial veto	Votes required to pass revenue increase	Votes required to pass budget
Alabama	S	S			★	★	ATB	Majority elected (a)	Majority	Majority
Alaska	S	S	S		★	★		2/3 elected (a)	Majority	Majority elected
Arizona	C,S	C,S	C,S		★	★	(c)	2/3 elected	Majority	Majority
Arkansas	S	S	S		★			Majority elected	3/4 elected	3/4 elected
California	C	C		★ (b)	★			2/3 elected	2/3 elected	2/3 elected
Colorado	C	C	C	★	★	★		2/3 elected	Majority	Majority present
Connecticut	S	C,S	C,S	★	★	★ (e)	MR	2/3 elected	Majority (d)	Majority present (d)
Delaware	C,S	C,S	C,S		★	★ (f)	★	2/3 elected	3/5 elected	Majority elected
Florida	C,S	C	C		★	★	MR	2/3 elected	Majority	Majority
Georgia	C		C,S		★	★	ATB	2/3 elected	Majority	Majority
Hawaii	C,S		C,S		★	★		2/3 elected	Majority elected	Majority elected (g)
Idaho	C	C			★	★		2/3 elected	Majority	Majority
Illinois	C,S	C,S	C,S		★			3/5 elected	Majority elected	3/5 elected
Indiana	C	C	C	★				Majority	Majority	Majority
Iowa	C,S	C,S		★	★	★	ATB	2/3 elected	Majority	Majority
Kansas	C	C,S	C,S		★		ATB (h)	2/3 elected	Majority elected	Majority
Kentucky	C,S	C,S	C,S		★	★	MR	Majority	2/3 elected	Majority present
Louisiana	C,S	C	C,S		★	★	ATB (i)	2/3 present	2/3 elected	2/3 present
Maine	C,S	C	C,S		★		★	2/3 present	Majority elected	Majority (j)
Maryland	C	C		★	★	★		(k)	Majority	Majority
Massachusetts	C	C	C	★	★	★		2/3 present	Majority	Majority (l)
Michigan	C,S	C	C,S	★	★	★		2/3 elected	Majority elected	Majority elected
Minnesota	S	S	C,S		★	★		2/3 elected	Majority elected	Majority elected
Mississippi	C	S			★	★	MR	2/3 elected	3/5 elected	Majority elected
Missouri	C		C		★	★		2/3 elected	Majority elected	Majority elected
Montana	S				★	(m)	MR	2/3 present	Majority	Majority
Nebraska	C	C	C		★	★	★	3/5 elected	3/5 elected	3/5 elected
Nevada	S	S			★	★	MR	2/3 elected	Majority	Majority
New Hampshire	S	S	C			(n)		2/3 elected	Majority	Majority present
New Jersey	C	C	C		★	★		2/3 elected	Majority	Majority
New Mexico	C	C	C		★	(o)	(o)	2/3 present	Majority	Majority
New York	C	C	C		★	(o)		2/3 elected	Majority	Majority
North Carolina	C	S	S			★			Majority	Majority
North Dakota	C		C		★	★	ATB	2/3 elected	Majority (p)	Majority (p)
Ohio	(q)	(q)	C		★	★	★	(r)	2/3 both houses	2/3 both houses
Oklahoma	C,S	C	C		★	★	ATB,MR	2/3 elected (s)	3/4 elected	Majority (s)
Oregon	C	C	C		★	★		2/3 elected	Majority	Majority
Pennsylvania	C,S	C,S	S		★	★	★	2/3 elected	Majority elected	Majority elected
Rhode Island	C			★ (t)		★		3/5 elected	Majority	2/3 both houses
South Carolina	(u)	C	C		★	★	★	2/3 present	Majority	Majority

STATE BALANCED BUDGETS—Continued

State	Constitutional and Statutory Provisions				Gubernatorial Authority				Legislative Authority		
	Governor must submit a balanced budget	Legislature must pass a balanced budget	Governor must sign a balanced budget	May carry over deficit	Governor has line item veto	Can reduce budget without legislative approval	Restrictions on budget reductions	Votes required to override gubernatorial veto	Votes required to pass revenue increase	Votes required to pass budget
South Dakota	C	C	C	...	★	★	...	2/3 elected	2/3 elected	Majority elected
Tennessee	C	C,S	C	...	★	★	...	Majority elected	Majority elected	Majority elected
Texas	C,S	C,S	S	★	★	★	ATB	2/3 elected	Majority	Majority elected
Utah	C,S	C	S	...	★	★	★	2/3 elected	Majority	Majority
Vermont	...	...	...	★	...	★	★	2/3 present	Majority	Majority
Virginia	S	...	...	...	★	★	MR (v)	2/3 elected	Majority elected	Majority elected
Washington	S	...	C	...	★	★	ATB	2/3 elected	Majority present	Majority present
West Virginia	... C	C	...	★	★	★ (w)	★	2/3 elected	majority	Majority
Wisconsin	C	C	...	...	★	...	...	2/3 elected	Majority	Majority present
Wyoming	...	...	...	...	★	★	ATB	2/3 elected	Majority	Majority

Sources: National Association of State Budget Officers, *Budgetary Processes in the States* (July 1992); updated April 1994 by The Council of State Governments. Update reflects literal reading of state constitutions and statutes.

Key:
C — Constitutional
S — Statutory
ATB — Across the board
MR — Maximum reduction dictated
★ — Yes
... — No

(a) Joint session.
(b) May carry over "casual deficits," i.e., not anticipated.
(c) Governor may reduce budgets of administration-appointed agencies only.
(d) Must have quorum.
(e) Budget reductions are limited to executive branch only.
(f) The Governor and elected cabinet may reduce the budget. The reductions must be reported to the legislature and advice as to proposed reductions may be offered.
(g) If general fund expenditure ceiling is exceeded, 2/3 vote required; otherwise majority of elected members.
(h) Reductions allowed only to get back to a balanced budget.
(i) Governor may expend funds up to one year. Certain restrictions apply to ATB reductions.
(j) For emergency enactment, 2/3 votes required.

(k) Governor has no veto power over the budget bill, but vote of 3/5 elected required to override veto on other bills.
(l) For capital budget, 2/3 votes required.
(m) May reduce appropriations by 15 percent except debt service, legislative and judicial branch appropriations, school foundation programs, and salaries of elected officials.
(n) May not reduce debt service.
(o) May reduce budget without approval only for state operations; only restriction on reductions is that reductions in aid to localities cannot be made without legislative approval.
(p) Emergency measures and measures that amend a statute that has been referred or enacted through an initiated measure within the last seven years must pass both houses by a 2/3 majority.
(q) There is no constitutional or statutory requirement that the Governor submit or the legislature enact a balanced budget. There is a constitutional requirement that the legislature provide sufficient revenues to meet state expenses. The Governor is required by statute to examine monthly the relationship between appropriations and estimated revenues and to reduce expenditures to prevent imbalance.
(r) 2/3 if appropriation or tax, 3/5 for all others.
(s) Emergency measures require a 3/4 vote for passage.
(t) May carry over deficit into subsequent year only.
(u) Formal budget submitted by Budget and Control Board, not Governor.
(v) The Governor has power to withhold allotments of appropriations, but cannot reduce legislative appropriations.
(w) May reduce spending authority.

Table 6.4
REVENUE ESTIMATING PRACTICES

State or other jurisdiction	Primary authority for revenue estimate	Estimates bind the budget	Frequency of estimate updates	Multi-year forecasting	Economic Advisory Boards
Alabama	C	★	As necessary	CY+1	(a)
Alaska	E	. . .	Semi-annual	CY+20	. . .
Arizona	C	★	Quarterly	CY+2	. . .
Arkansas	E	★	Quarterly	CY+2	Council of Economic Advisors
California	E	. . .	Semi-annual	CY+1	Department of Finance Semi-annual Review Conference
Colorado	L	. . .	Quarterly	CY+3	Governor's Revenue Estimating Advisory Group
Connecticut	E	★	Monthly	CY+4	Economic Conference Board
Delaware	C	★ (b)	Bi-monthly	CY+4	. . .
Florida	C	★	Semi-annual, or as needed	CY+1 or 9	. . .
Georgia	E	★	Semi-annual, or as needed	CY+1	House and Senate Appropriations Committees
Hawaii	C	. . .	Quarterly	CY+6	Council on Revenues
Idaho	E	. . .	Semi-annual	CY+3	. . .
Illinois	E	★	Quarterly	CY+1	. . .
Indiana	C	. . .	Semi-annual	CY+2	Economic Forum; Revenue Technical Forecast Committee
Iowa	C	★	Quarterly	CY+1	Economic Forecasting Council
Kansas	C	★	Semi-annual	CY+1	. . .
Kentucky	E	★	Bi-annually	CY+2	Economic Roundtable
Louisiana	C	★	Quarterly	CY+4	Revenue Estimating Conference; Economic Estimating Conference
Maine	C	★	Semi-annual	CY+2	Consensus Economic Forecasting Commission
Maryland	E	. . .	Semi-annual, or as needed	CY+1	Business Advisory Panel
Massachusetts	E	★	Semi-annual	CY+2	. . .
Michigan	C	. . .	Semi-annual	CY+1	Governor's Council of Economic Advisors
Minnesota	E	★	Semi-annual	CY+4 or 5	Council of Economic Advisors
Mississippi	C	★	Semi-annual	CY+10 (c)	. . .
Missouri	E	★	Semi-annual	CY+4	. . .
Montana	L	★	As necessary	CY+4	. . .
Nebraska	C	★	Semi-annual	CY+2	Economic Forecasting Advisory Board
Nevada	E	. . .	As necessary	CY+2	. . .
New Hampshire	L	★	Quarterly	CY+6	. . .
New Jersey	E	★	Semi-annual	CY+1	. . .
New Mexico	C	. . .	Semi-annual	CY+3	. . .
New York	E	★	Quarterly	CY+2	. . .
North Carolina	L	★	Quarterly	CY+4	. . .
North Dakota	E	★	Semi-annual	CY+2	. . .
Ohio	E	★	Semi-annual	CY+2	The Economic Advisory Council to the Governor
Oklahoma	E	★	Informal semi-annual revision	CY+1	. . .
Oregon	E	★	Quarterly	CY+5	Governor's Council of Economic Advisors
Pennsylvania	E	★	Semi-annual	CY+5	. . .
Rhode Island	C	★	Quarterly	CY+1	. . .
South Carolina	E	★	Quarterly	CY+1	Board of Economic Advisors
South Dakota	L	★	(d)	CY+2	The Governor's Council of Economic Advisors
Tennessee	E	★	Semi-annual or as needed	CY+1	. . .
Texas	I (e)	★	As necessary	CY . 2	. . .
Utah	C	★	Quarterly	CY+10	The Economic Coordinating Committee
Vermont	E	. . .	Semi-annual	CY+1	. . .
Virginia	E	★	Varies, 2 or 3 times per FY	CY+2 or 3	Governor's Advisory Board of Economists; Governor's Advisory Council on Revenue Estimates; Governor's Economic Advisory Council
Washington	C	★	Quarterly	CY+4	Governor's Council of Economic Advisors
West Virginia	E	★	Annual (f)	CY+3	Center for Economic Research; Bureau of Employment Programs; West Virginia Research League; West Virginia Development Office
Wisconsin	(g)	★	Annual	CY+3	(h)
Wyoming	C	★	Semi-annual	CY+5	. . .
Dist. of Columbia	E	★	Three times a year	CY+5	. . .
Puerto Rico	E	★	Semi-annual	CY+1	. . .

Source: The Council of State Governments' survey, 1993.
Key:
★ — Yes
. . . — No
C — Consensus
E — Executive
L — Legislative
I — Independent
CY — Current year
(a) Various groups advise the Consensus Committee.
(b) There is no formal statute which obligates the legislature to use Delaware Economic & Financial Advisory Council estimates. However, since its inception, DEFAC estimates have been used exclusively.

(c) University Research Center forecasts 10 years out. Office of Policy Development forecasts 12 quarters out.
(d) Semi-annual by executive, annual by legislature.
(e) Texas vests authority for revenue estimation in an independently elected comptroller.
(f) Unofficial estimates revised quarterly.
(g) The executive branch is required by statute to prepare revenue estimates. The Legislature's Joint Committee on Finances has final approval of revenue estimates used in the state budget.
(h) A technical forecast advisory group consisting of economists from various state agencies reviews national and state economic forecasts. It does not review revenue estimating.

State Government Finances, 1992

State governments, which are significant economic entities, are hampered by increasing local and federal demands.

by Henry S. Wulf

State governments play a pivotal role in the intergovernmental finance system. What we now think of as a tripartite federal system — federal, state and local — was originally a division of power and responsibilities between the national government and the state governments. As our national system of federalism matured, the states developed a variety of roles to handle the tasks with which they were confronted. These intergovernmental relationships are continuously in flux and often the changes, confrontations and compromises occur on the financial battlefield.

We find wide variation in how states and local governments deal with one another — for example, from New Hampshire relying on local revenue sources for about 90 percent of elementary and secondary education to Hawaii relying on no local government revenue for this service. As our federal system developed, each state devolved varying types and degrees of responsibilities on their local governments. Though the organization has changed some over time, in most instances the connections between states and local governments retain the mark of the originally established relationships. But nearly all these relationships come together in the financial role that each state has chosen for itself.

At the same time, however, state government finances, as with any large business corporation, are tied closely to prevailing economic conditions.[1] The recession of 1990-91 created considerable fiscal stress for all levels of government — federal, state and local. State governments found themselves buffeted in their central financial role. Not only did they suffer reduced revenue capability and extra demands for their own services, but there were extra demands from hard-hit local governments for

help and a reluctance by the federal government — with a significant build up of the national debt in the prior decade — to assume any more financial burden than absolutely necessary.

There are three major roles that state governments play in the intergovernmental fiscal system. First, they create and finance local government services. Many states, for example, have programs for funding various types of social services, and every state (except Hawaii) has some mechanism for funding local government education programs. Second, states serve as a conduit and redistributor of federal funds for programs such as social services block grants, low income home energy assistance and food stamps. Finally, the states provide some important services directly such as hospitals, highways and corrections. These varied activities place state governments in the center of any discussion about fiscal federalism.

Foremost to recognize when discussing state government finances is just how significant states are as economic entities. In the latest study comparing state government financial activity with Fortune magazine's ranking of the 500 largest industrial corporations, California would rank fourth between Ford and IBM, while New York would be eighth between General Electric and Philip Morris. South Dakota, with the least amount of financial activity among the states, would rank 343rd, ahead of such significant corporations as American Greetings and E.W. Scribbs.[2]

This essay on state finances is divided into six sections. First is a summary of the primary

---

Henry S. Wulf is special assistant for Programs, Governments Division, Bureau of the Census, U.S. Department of Commerce.

aspects of finances — revenue, expenditure, indebtedness, and cash and securities. The next four sections provide an in-depth discussion of each of these primary financial components. The concluding section provides an examination of some important financial issues in state governments.[3]

Summary of State Finances

State government revenues totaled $742 billion in 1992, an increase of 12.2 percent over 1991.[4] In the past 5 years, the year-to-year percentage increases in total revenues have varied markedly, from growth of less than 5 percent to more than 12 percent (1987 to 1988, 4.9 percent; 1988 to 1989, 8.4 percent; 1989 to 1990, 7.8 percent; and 1990 to 1991, 4.5 percent). Four major revenue sources accounted for 90 percent of the total: taxes (44 percent), funds from the federal government (21 percent), insurance trust revenue (18 percent) and current charges (7 percent).

The 1992 expenditures were $701 billion. In contrast to the wide year-to-year fluctuations in revenues, expenditure increases during the past five years have been rising steadily: 1987 to 1988, 4.9 percent; 1988 to 1989, 8.3 percent; 1989 to 1990, 9.0 percent; 1990 to 1991, 9.9 percent; and 1991 to 1992, 11.5 percent. The states' role in financing activities of their subordinate governments is highlighted by the fact that about $3 of every $10 they expended went to local governments in support of local services. Education and public welfare outlays together comprised more than half of all state expenditures, accounting for 30.2 percent and 22.3 percent, respectively. Insurance trust expenditures were 11.3 percent, followed by highways with 7.7 percent. Most of the other individual activities accounted for small pieces, with most amounting to 3 percent or less of the total.

Indebtedness is a relatively less important aspect of the state government financial picture when compared with the federal and local aggregates. The state amount of $372 billion at the end of 1992 was only about 60 percent of the local government total and less than 10 percent of the federal amount.

States held $1.1 trillion in cash and investments at the end of 1992. However, most of this money — about 88 percent — is pledged by the state for specific purposes such as redemption of long-term debt and employee retirement programs. States held the single largest portion of their assets, $657 billion, in state employee retirement trust systems, making this accumulation of funds a major source of investment capital. The next largest holdings were in long-term debt offsets ($217 billion), reducing the net debt to slightly over $150 billion.

State Government Revenue

Table A shows there was significant variation in the year-to-year changes among the various state revenue sources. The three major revenues are about 83 percent of the total — taxes (44.2 percent), revenue from the federal government (21.4 percent) and insurance trust revenue (17.5 percent). Two of these (insurance trust and federal revenue) were considerably above the average for all revenue (12.2 percent) and the largest — taxes — far below. It is interesting that of the two above average, the revenue for one is both dedicated and generally untouchable (insurance trust), and the other is largely directed to specific programs (federal money). Thus, the most rapidly rising revenues were of limited value in helping the states cover most of their major expenses.

The major restraint on tax collections continued to be economic conditions. Although rising slowly, the year-to-year change was still better than 1990 to 1991 when taxes were up only 3.3 percent. The increases were muted across the board. Of the major taxes, motor fuel sales was the top performer and that increased only 7.6 percent.

The primary driving force for revenue from the federal government was in the public welfare category, which increased almost 27 percent and comprised nearly $1 out of every $8 of state revenues. In 1988 this was about one out of every $11 in state revenue. Since 1990, the year-to-year increases in federal money for welfare have been 14, 21 and 27 percent, respectively. The two best known public welfare programs are Aid to Families with Dependent Children (AFDC) and Medicaid, and it is the latter where the major increases have occurred.

Table A
SOURCES OF STATE REVENUE AND
CHANGE FROM 1991 TO 1992

	Percent change, 1991 to 1992	Percent of total revenue
Insurance trust revenue	26.2	17.5
Revenue from local governments	26.2	1.5
Revenue from federal government	17.9	21.4
Total Revenue	**12.2**	**100.0**
Current charges	11.8	7.1
Miscellaneous general revenue	8.7	7.4
Taxes	5.6	44.2
State liquor store revenue	1.8	0.4
Utility revenue	1.5	0.5

Source: U.S. Department of Commerce, Bureau of the Census

Federal aid for education — up almost 11 percent from 1991 to 1992 — also has shown strong growth since 1988, averaging 9.5 percent growth each year over that span. Education revenues comprise the second largest type of federal revenue received by the states. Without the public welfare and education money, revenue from the federal government went up only about 6 percent from 1991 to 1992.

The striking rise in insurance trust revenue was due to a variety of reasons. Employee retirement revenue had shown a significant drop from 1990 to 1991 (-8.3 percent) and the 22.0 percent jump from 1991 to 1992 probably reflected improved post-recession investment opportunities. The unemployment compensation revenues, showing a 50 percent increase, were tied to the continued high unemployment rates.

There were four major contributors to taxes — general sales, individual income, motor fuel sales and corporate income taxes. Of the $328 billion total, these four sources supplied about 78 percent. Table B shows the effect of the economic downturn on these major state revenue sources — especially in 1990 and 1991 — and the improvement in 1992. Corporate net income taxes are very sensitive to economic changes and the nearly 6 percent increase in 1992, after two consecutive years of lower yields, should be a good portent.

The yearly growth rate of current charges since 1988 has been very steady, varying little from the average annual increase of 11.4 percent during that time. This pace would double the total amount in a little more than 6 years. Current charges continue to be a focus of discussion about government finances because of the debate about instituting more pay-for-service fees and the desire to lower tax burdens. State government current charges are concentrated in education — primarily tuition from public post-secondary education institutions — and state hospitals. Almost $4 out of every $5 received by states in current charges derives from these two sources.

It is extremely difficult to predict what direction and magnitude the changes in current charges will take. Forcing them up will be the issues that make them such a hot topic — pay-for-service and the potential for some tax relief. With such a large percentage coming from education, mostly higher education, and hospitals, the key might be what happens with a national health-care plan and the effect of the business cycle on public higher education. States increased tuition considerably when faced with lower levels of state support for higher education.[5] If tax revenues rise with improving economic conditions, there could be more political pressure to mute increases in higher education charges and replace those revenues with state subsidies.

Table B
GROWTH RATES FOR MAJOR TAX SOURCES

Year	General sales	Individual income	Motor fuel sales	Corporate net income
1988 to 1989	+7.4	+10.8	+5.2	+10.5
1989 to 1990	+6.6	+8.2	+7.0	−8.9
1990 to 1991	+3.2	+3.3	+6.5	−6.4
1991 to 1992	+4.3	+5.2	+7.6	+5.9

Source: U.S. Department of Commerce, Bureau of the Census

Table C
STATE EXPENDITURES BY CHARACTER AND OBJECT

Type of expenditure	1991 to 1992	Average, 1988 to 1992	1992 Percent of total expenditure
Insurance benefits and repayments	23.6	16.0	11.3
Current operations other than salaries and wages	17.7	13.7	30.1
Total Expenditures	**11.5**	**9.7**	**100.0**
Assistance and subsidies	10.1	8.4	3.0
Intergovernmental expenditure	7.9	7.3	28.7
Interest on debt	5.3	6.0	3.6
Salaries and wages	4.7	6.7	16.1
Capital outlay	4.6	5.4	7.2

Source: U.S. Department of Commerce, Bureau of the Census

State Government Expenditure

The pattern of state government expenditure growth has been steadily upward during the past few years. Since 1988 the increases have been: 1988 to 1989, 8.3 percent; 1989 to 1990, 9.0 percent; 1990 to 1991, 9.9 percent; and 1991 to 1992, 11.5 percent. The increases during this period are similar to the higher patterns of growth that marked the interval from 1980 to 1985 when the annual rise averaged 8.7 percent. The average annual increase from 1988 to 1992 was 9.7 percent, a rate that, if maintained, would double state expenditures in seven years.

Table C shows the considerable span of growth for various expenditures. Two types exceeded the average growth considerably from 1991 to 1992, insurance benefits and repayments (23.6 percent) and current operations other than salaries and wages (17.7 percent). Three types, on the other hand, increased less than 6 percent: interest on debt (5.3 percent),

salaries and wages (4.7 percent) and capital outlay (4.6 percent). The pattern from 1991 to 1992 repeats, for the most part, the long-term pattern that existed from 1988 to 1992.

The three largest categories of state expenditures show a definite divergence in trends from 1991 to 1992. The biggest, current operations other than salaries and wages, was up nearly 18 percent. Although this was a significant spurt, it was in line with the continuing upward trend of the prior four years. The nearly 8 percent increase in intergovernmental expenditures was very close to the four-year trend. Salaries and wages, up only 4.7 percent, was not only considerably below the four-year trend, but it was the lowest year-to-year increase in the past four decades by nearly two percentage points.

The major implication of these trends is that it appears local governments and state employees are losing in competition with obligations and services that states pay for directly.

The most significant of the pieces in this direct payment category are public welfare expenditures for vendor services and cash assistance. In 1992 these expenditures amounted to nearly 52 percent of the current operations other than salaries and wages category, up from about 42 percent in 1982. As recently as 1990, the figure was 44 percent. The analysis below examines this growth phenomenon in public welfare.

Capital outlays show a continuing pattern of very low increases. Since 1985, when the change from 1984 was a substantial 20.3 percent, the year-to-year increases have — with one exception — become smaller each year. From 1991 to 1992 it was the lowest it has been (4.6 percent) since 1983.

It is very difficult to interpret the meaning of this trend for both economic growth and infrastructure development. The greatest impact is in highways because that spending accounts for about half the money states spend on capital outlay. The trend for 1992 seems especially at odds with the general availability of funds for capital projects from debt issuance. This is the normal source of funds for capital projects, and in 1991 and 1992 low interest rates made capital markets quite accessible to governments. It is possible that the competition from other current spending has made the states delay or put aside their capital project plans. The competition for the limited state dollars among education, public welfare and other social service activities promises to become more intense. If this is true, there may be significant long-term consequences of these low increases in capital expenditures for economic growth.[6]

Two functional areas of state spending continue to dominate — education and public welfare. They comprised, respectively, 30 and 22 percent of all state government spending in 1992. Along with the four next most significant activities — expenditures for insurance trust programs (11.3 percent), highways (7 percent), hospitals (3.7 percent) and interest on general debt (3.5 percent) — these six functions accounted for nearly $4 out of every $5 spent by states.

Education outlays totaled $212 billion in 1992, up 6.6 percent over the previous year. This was below the average annual rise that has occurred since 1988 (7.3 percent), but the increases over that time have fallen in a relatively narrow band between 6.6 and 8.6 percent. State education expenditures have two primary thrusts. First is financial support, through intergovernmental payments, to local government education programs ($125 billion). The second is direct payments for higher education programs ($71 billion).

The annual increase in the intergovernmental payment category was 7.6 percent in 1992. In 1990 this had fallen to 4.4 percent. The 1992 change, however, is much more in line with the 1985 to 1990 average annual increase of 7.9 percent.

The situation concerning these education intergovernmental payments — primarily for elementary and secondary education support — is extremely unsettled. There are still numerous states involved in court cases and discussions concerning equalizing elementary and secondary education expenditures. As of March 1994, there is the example of Michigan's substitution of state sales tax revenues for local property taxes, a solution to equity questions that a number of other states are considering. In the next few years, there is the potential for rapid and dramatic changes in the financing of local education payments. If other states follow Michigan, there will be a marked rise in state intergovernmental payments to support local government elementary and secondary education spending.

Though there was some thought that the recession might slow state spending for higher education,[7] this did not occur. Instead, the increase from 1991 to 1992, a robust 8.9 percent, was preceded by increases of 7.5 and 8.2 percent. The outlays for higher education, in fact, increased at a higher rate than during the economically more vibrant period from 1985 to 1990 when the average annual increase was 6.9 percent. It seems likely that one of the rules-of-thumb used by education analysts — that during recessionary times students find public higher education more attractive despite tuition increases — was definitely a factor.

Public welfare remains a fairly distant second to education spending. The past few years, however, have seen changes in public welfare that have brought dramatic transformations to the states' entire financial landscape.[8] What fueled this rise was Medicaid costs. From 1985 to 1990, public welfare expenditures were growing an average annual rate of 9.3 percent. From 1990 to 1991, the costs jumped 18.6 percent and from 1991 to 1992 another 25.6 percent. The share of total state expenditures for public welfare rose from 18.4 percent in 1990 to 22.3 percent in 1992.

The rapid rise in Medicaid costs has been attributed in part to changes in the federal handling of so-called "disproportionate share" payments. These payments to state governments are reimbursement for the states' subsidization of low-income hospital patients. The program generated controversy because, as one analyst stated, there were, "manipulations by state governments of the Medicaid open-ended entitlement system to generate what was essentially general revenue sharing for states."[9]

It seems clear that welfare costs will continue upward, but the rate probably will abate some. A report from the National Conference of State Legislatures, for example, indicated that Medicaid growth continued into 1994, but was generally under control because the costs had stabilized some and a number of states, "budgeted for substantial Medicaid increases."[10] Further, more than half the states had received or requested waivers from the federal government to experiment with other welfare programs to try to reduce costs.[11] The major unknown, of course, is how proposed federal welfare reforms will rewrite the rules, responsibilities and relationships in welfare federalism.

For the other major functional activities of states, insurance trust expenditures jumped nearly 24 percent, on top of an 18 percent boost from 1990 to 1991. Unemployment compensation expenditures drove this trend. Highways were up 3.6 percent, hospitals 6.8 percent and interest on general debt 5.3 percent. Highway increases have been very muted since the mid-1980s, averaging less than 5 percent a year. Thus, the small increase from 1991 to 1992 of 3.6 percent is in line with recent history.

State Government Indebtedness

The state government indebtedness at the end of fiscal year 1992 was up 7.6 percent over the prior year to a total of $372 billion. As noted previously, debt activity has been of less importance for state government finances than what occurs with their revenues, expenditures and assets. Since 1986, the year-to-year increases in total debt have hovered between 6.8 and 8.6 percent, with one exception when it was slightly under 5 percent. The three factors that influence the direction of state indebtedness are interest rates, financial condition and need to finance infrastructure (in particular highways). Interest rates, which had been at their lowest point in the past two decades, have bottomed out. If borrowing costs go up, the arguments for incurring debt because of the low rates will become secondary to the other factors. Though credit ratings for states — and governments in general — have improved in the past few years, a cautious attitude toward debt remains.

As noted above, state capital expenditures in the past few years has been particularly muted. Although occasional reports indicate a continuing — or coming — infrastructure problem, the evidence seems to be that either the states don't perceive one or don't have the financial capability to solve it. If interest rates don't climb too high and an improving economy allows the states greater financial flexibility, those factors might be just the type of climate that will induce the states to use debt instruments for solving some long-term problems.[12]

State Government Cash and Investments

State government cash and investments totaled nearly $1.1 trillion in fiscal year 1992. This included $657 billion in employee retirement trust funds, $217 billion in funds held as offsets to long-term debt and $210 billion in miscellaneous insurance trust funds, bond funds and others.

A high percentage of these assets are reserved for very specific purposes not related to the general operations of state governments. About three-fifths is dedicated for employee retirement, nearly one-fifth for redemption of long-term debt, about 5 percent for insurance trust purposes such as unemployment or workers' compensation and 2 percent as unspent proceeds of bond issues.

Only 12 percent of the assets, about $132 billion, are available for financing general government activities. Normally these are found in the states' general accounts and specialized accounting reserves such as the so-called rainy day funds.

It is misleading, however, to imply that the entire $132 billion is available for any purpose. Most often, state constitutions or laws severely restrict access to these monies. Two of the best examples of this — and also among the largest of these specially restricted funds — are the Texas Permanent School Fund and the Alaska Permanent Fund.

The growth in these assets normally reflects general economic conditions because they differ from other financial investments only in their source and size. The increase from fiscal 1991 to 1992 was 6.5 percent. Preceding this were a 5.7 percent increase from 1990 to 1991 and a 12.4 percent rise from 1989 to 1990. This last noted increase reflected the positive financial climate prior to the recession. If the investment climate improves in 1994, so will the fortunes of the assets.

The relationship between the returns on assets and the general financial condition of the states is very direct. The best example of this is in the state retirement systems. There are only three sources of funds for retirement systems; investment earnings, state contributions and employee contributions. If investment earnings don't provide long-term financial stability for the systems, states need to increase their contributions or ask the employees to pay more.

Issues in State Finances

This discussion will touch briefly on three major financial issues facing the states that have not been examined previously. They are: the economic recovery, national health-care reform and unfunded mandates. Each of these is related to the others.

After the 1990-91 national recession, analyses are finding that there is considerable unevenness in the economic fortunes in different states. The recoveries in California and the Northeast are lagging considerably, while the Rocky Mountain states appear to be doing much better than average.[13] A major effect of the recession derives not from this unevenness,

which occurs with every economic change, but from which states are lagging.

This is important because of the major new national initiatives in health, welfare and educational reform. These areas are where the states have their heaviest financial involvement. Because some of our largest states still have very sluggish economies, they are less likely to be amenable to any changes in programs that place additional financial requirements on them. It is also in the very large states where the greatest financial burdens are likely to occur when these programs finally emerge. With the large states having fewer financial resources but considerable political influence, this appears to be a built-in conflict. However, the result might well be a better sorting out of the federal and state roles in these areas as a political compromise is achieved.

The national health-care reform debate has very important implications for state governments. The key provision related to state and local government finances is whether there will be a spending cap on the amount states must pay for health insurance coverage for their employees, similar to what's suggested for private industry. Without this, the states — and local governments also — fear they could be open to significant financial liability.[14]

Finally, the issue of unfunded mandates imposed by the federal government has become a rallying cry for state and local officials trying to gain better control of their financial resources. For the states, however, this issue is a double-edged sword as local officials pressure the state governments not to impose unfunded state mandates. The issue has many dimensions,[15] but the most positive result of this controversy would be a broader systemization of the administrative and financial responsibilities among the different levels of government, one that would take advantage of the strengths of each level.

Footnotes

[1] For example, as private business and personal incomes change, so do the revenues that states derive from income taxes. As sales rise and fall, so does the income that states derive from general or selective sales taxes. In good times, there are fewer persons that need social

service and income maintenance programs. If economic conditions turn sour, there is an upsurge in the demand for these activities. As consumers of services, state governments' negotiating positions shift when land and construction prices fluctuate.

[2] Robert D. Behn, "The Fortune 500 and the 50 States: A Combined Ranking," Institute of Policy Sciences and Public Affairs, Duke University (February 1993).

[3] This analysis uses information primarily from the U.S. Bureau of the Census surveys of state and local government finances. It is intended to show financial occurrences in relation to the recent past and the past few decades. It does this by using data from 1992 and comparing it with 1991 and previous periods. The reference point for the state information is fiscal year 1992, noted in this discussion as 1992. For all states except four, this is the period from July 1, 1991 to June 30, 1992. The four with a different reference period are (reference period end in parentheses): Alabama and Michigan (Sept. 30, 1992); New York (March 31, 1992); and Texas (Aug. 31, 1992).

[4] The Census Bureau data are a statistical compilation of information, not an accounting balance sheet. The practical application of this is that total revenues nearly always exceed total expenditures, but this cannot be equated with a budget or accounting "surplus" or "deficit." The reasons for this are manifold, but have to do with varying treatments of items such as debt, capital expenditures, accruals and insurance trust system transactions.

[5] "Bad Times Force Universities to Rethink What They Are," *The New York Times*, Feb. 3, 1992.

[6] See, *Public Investment and Private Sector Growth* by David Alan Aschauer, Economic Policy Institute, 1990. Aschauer's argument is that investment in physical public infrastructure stimulates private sector activity.

[7] See for example, "The College of Hard Times," by Kathleen Sylvester in *Governing*, September 1991 and "Bad Times Force Universities to Rethink What They Are," *The New York Times*, Feb. 3, 1992.

[8] For a useful analysis of different ways to view welfare spending by the states, see "Wel-

fare Spending in State Budgets," by Sarah Ritchie, Center for the Study of the States, June 1993.

[9] Quote from Victor Miller, Health Care Policy Alternatives Inc. in "Small Provisions Turns into a Golden Goose," *The Washington Post*, Jan. 31, 1994. See also, "Louisiana Took Every Federal Dollar We Could Get Our Hands On," *The Washington Post*, Jan. 31, 1994.

[10] "State Fiscal Outlook for 1994," National Conference of State Legislatures, Legislative Finance Paper No. 90, January 1994.

[11] See, for example, "Setting Limits on Welfare," *City and State*, Nov. 22 - Dec. 5, 1993 and "Putting Welfare on the Clock," by Penelope Lemov, *Governing*, November 1993, pp. 29-30.

[12] For a good example of the inter-relationships among debt, infrastructure needs and financial condition, see, "Higher Taxes Are Likely in California As Officials Debate Financing of Repairs," *The Wall Street Journal*, Jan. 21, 1994.

[13] See, for example: "Northeastern States and California Trail Nation in Income Growth," *The Bond Buyer*, Nov. 19, 1993; "Fed Study Finds Economy Rising in Most Regions," *The Wall Street Journal*, Dec. 9, 1993; and "Update on the Second District Economy," by Rae D. Rosen in *Federal Reserve Bank of New York Quarterly Review*, Autumn 1993, pp. 37-46. For a more theoretical analysis on constructing state indexes for measuring how business cycles differ from state to state see, "New Indexes Track the State of the States," by Theodore M. Crone in *Business Review*, Federal Reserve Bank of Philadelphia, January-February 1994, pp. 19-31.

[14] "Governors Group Approves States' Roles in Clinton Health Plan," *The Bond Buyer*, Nov. 5, 1993; "States May Need to Borrow Big If Health Reform Cost Estimates Are Off, Officials Say," *The Bond Buyer*, Nov. 17, 1993; and "Health-System Cure No Rx for State and Local Budgets," *City and State*, Nov. 22 - Dec. 5, 1993, p. 1.

[15] A good introduction to this issue with state case studies can be found in *Mandates: Cases in State-Local Relations*, Advisory Commission on Intergovernmental Relations, M-173, September 1990. For examples of some

of the issues involved, see: "Financing National Policy Through Mandates," by Joseph F. Zimmerman in *National Civic Review*, Summer-Fall 1992, pp. 366-373; "Fighting Mandates in the States," by John E. Berthoud in *Comparative State Politics*, Illinois Legislative Study Center; " . . . and Federal Mandates Crush States," *The Wall Street Journal*, Jan. 31, 1994; and "A New Approach to an Old Problem: State Mandates," by Janet M. Kelly in *Government Finance Review*, December 1993, pp. 27-29.

Table 6.5
ALLOWABLE STATE INVESTMENTS

State or other jurisdiction	Certificates of deposits (in state)	Certificates of deposits (nationally)	Other time deposits	Bankers acceptances	Commercial paper	Corporate notes/bonds	Mutuals	State and local government obligations	U.S. Treasury obligations	U.S. agency obligations	Eurodollars (CDs or TDs)	Repurchase agreements
Alabama	N.A.	N.A.	★	N.A.	N.A.	N.A.	N.A.	N.A.	★	★	N.A.	★
Alaska (a)	N.A.	★	N.A.	★	★	★	★	N.A.	N.A.	N.A.	N.A.	N.A.
Arizona	★							★	★	★		★
Arkansas	★	★	★	★				★	★	★		★
California	★	★	★	★	★	★	★	★	★	★		★
Colorado	N.A.	N.A.	N.A.	N.A.	N.A.	N.A.	N.A.	N.A.	N.A.	N.A.	N.A.	N.A.
Connecticut	N.A.			N.A.	N.A.	★		★	★	★	★	★
Delaware	★		★	★	★	★	★	★	★	★		★
Florida	★	★	★	★	★	★	★	★	★	★		★
Georgia	★						★	★	★	★		★
Hawaii	★						★	★	★	★		★
Idaho	★	★		★	★	★	★	★	★	★		★
Illinois	★				★		★	★	★	★		★
Indiana	★	★	★	★	★	★	★	★	★	★	★	★
Iowa	★	★	★	★	★	★	★	★	★	★		★
Kansas	★								★	★		★
Kentucky	★	★	★	★				★	★	★		★
Louisiana	★			★			★	★	★	★		★
Maine	★	★	★	★	★	★	★	★	★	★	★	★
Maryland	★	★	★	★	★	★	★	★	★	★		★
Massachusetts	★	★	★	★	★	★	★	★	★	★	★	★
Michigan	★			★	★	★	★	★	★	★		★
Minnesota	★	★	★	★	★	★	★	★	★	★		★
Mississippi	★			★	★	★	★	★	★	★		★
Missouri	★	★	★	★	★	★	★	★	★	★		★
Montana	★	★		★	★ (b)	★	★	★	★	★		★
Nebraska	★			★	★	★	★	★	★	★	★	★
Nevada	★	★	★	★	★	★	★	★	★	★		★
New Hampshire	★		★	★	★	★	★	★	★	★		★
New Jersey	★	★	★	★	★	★	★	★	★	★		★
New Mexico	★	★	★	★	★	★	★	★	★	★		★
New York	★	★	★	★	★	★	★	★	★	★		★
North Carolina	★	★	★	★	★	★		★	★	★		★
North Dakota	★			★			★		★	★		
Ohio	★	★	★	★	★	★	★	★	★	★	★	★
Oklahoma	★							★	★	★		★
Oregon	★	★	★	★	★	★	★	★	★	★		★
Pennsylvania	★	★	★	★	★	★	★	★	★	★		★
Rhode Island	★	★	★	★	★	★	★	★	★	★	★	★
South Carolina	★							★	★	★		★
South Dakota	★	★	★	★	★	★	★	★	★	★		★
Tennessee	★		★	★	★	★	★	★	★	★	★	★
Texas	★	★	★	★	★	★	★ (c)	★	★	★		★
Utah	★		★	★					★	★		★
Vermont	★	★							★	★ (d)	★	★

ALLOWABLE STATE INVESTMENTS—Continued

State or other jurisdiction	Certificates of deposits (in state)	Certificates of deposits (nationally)	Other time deposits	Bankers acceptances	Commercial paper	Corporate notes/bonds	Mutuals	State and local government obligations	U.S. Treasury obligations	U.S. agency obligations	Eurodollars (CDs or TDs)	Repurchase agreements
Virginia	★	...	...	★	★	★	★	★	★	★	...	★
Washington	★	★	★	★	★	★	★	★	★	★	★	★
West Virginia (e)	N.A.	N.A.	N.A.	N.A.	N.A.	N.A.	N.A.	N.A.	N.A.	N.A.	N.A.	N.A.
Wisconsin	★	★	★	★	★	★	★	★	★	★	★	★
Wyoming	★ (f)	★ (f)	★	★	★	★	...	★	★	★	...	★
Dist. of Columbia	★	...	...	...	...	...	...	★	★	★	...	★
Puerto Rico	★	★	★	...	...	★	...	★	★	★	...	★

Source: National Association of State Treasurers' survey, Fall 1993.

Key:
★ — Investment allowed
... — Investment not allowed
N.A. — Not available

(a) Any investment meeting prudent expert standard is allowable.
(b) A./P. only.
(c) Money market mutual funds, only.
(d) Limited.
(e) Treasurer's office does not have investment function.
(f) Must be collateralized 100 percent.

Table 6.6
CASH MANAGEMENT PROGRAMS AND SERVICES

State or other jurisdiction	Reviews of cash management programs: Banking relations — Reviewing agency	Frequency of review	Investment practices — Reviewing agency	Frequency of review	Lock boxes	Wire transfers	Agency preparing cash management services: Zero balance accounts	Information services	Account reconciliation services	Automated clearinghouse
Alabama	SE	(a)	SE	(a)	OF	OF	N.A.	N.A.	N.A.	IH
Alaska	SE	Annually	SE	Annually	OF	OF,IH	OF	OF	OF,IH	OF,IH
Arizona	SE	Annually	SE	Ongoing	OF	IH	OF	IH	IH	N.A.
Arkansas	SE	Quarterly/Annually	SE	Quarterly/Annually	N.A.	OF	N.A.	N.A.	N.A.	N.A.
California	SE	Annually	SE	Quarterly	OF,IH	OF,IH	OF	OF	OF,IH	OF
Colorado	SE/OF	3 years	SE/OF	Ongoing	OF	OF	IH,OF	IH,OF	IH,OF	IH,OF
Connecticut	SE	Quarterly	SE	Quarterly	OF,IH	OF,IH	OF	IH	OF,IH	OF
Delaware	SE	4-6 years	SE/OF	5+ years	OF	IH,OF	OF	OF	OF	IH,OF
Florida	SE/OF	(b)	SE	Annually	IH,OF	OF	N.A.	N.A.	IH	OF
Georgia	SE	As needed	SE	As needed	N.A.	IH,OF	N.A.	IH	N.A.	N.A.
Hawaii	SE	Annually	SE	Annually	N.A.	OF	N.A.	OF	IH	OF
Idaho	SE	Ongoing	SE	Ongoing	N.A.	OF	N.A.	IH	IH	OF
Illinois	SE/OF	Bi-annually	SE/OF	Monthly	OF	IH,OF	OF	IH,OF	IH,OF	IH,OF
Indiana	SE	Ongoing	SE	Ongoing	OF	OF	OF	IH	N.A.	OF
Iowa	SE	4 years	SE	Monthly	OF	IH,OF	OF	N.A.	IH	IH,OF
Kansas	SE	Annually	SE/OF	Monthly/Annually	OF	IH,OF	OF	OF	N.A.	IH,OF
Kentucky	N.A.	2 years	N.A.	N.A.	N.A.	IH	OF	IH	N.A.	OF
Louisiana	SE	As needed	SE	As needed	OF	OF	OF	OF	OF	OF
Maine	SE	Annually	SE	Annually	N.A.	OF	N.A.	N.A.	OF	OF
Maryland	SE	Monthly	SE	Annually	OF	OF	OF	N.A.	IH,OF	OF
Massachusetts	SE	Quarterly	SE	Quarterly	OF	IH,OF	OF	IH,OF	IH,OF	IH,OF
Michigan	SE	Annually	SE	Monthly	OF	OF	OF	IH,OF	IH	OF
Minnesota	SE	3 years	SE	Quarterly	OF	IH	OF	IH	IH	IH
Mississippi	SE	Annually	SE	Quarterly	N.A.	OF	N.A.	OF	N.A.	OF
Missouri	SE	4 years	SE	4 years	IH	OF	OF	IH,OF	OF	OF
Montana	SE/OF	Monthly	SE	Monthly/Annually	N.A.	IH,OF	N.A.	IH	IH	IH
Nebraska	SE	3-5 years	SE/OF	Ongoing/Annually	N.A.	OF	N.A.	N.A.	IH	IH,OF
Nevada	SE	Monthly	SE	Monthly	OF	IH	IH	IH	OF	OF
New Hampshire	SE	Quarterly	SE	Quarterly	OF	IH	OF	IH	IH,OF	OF
New Jersey	SE	Ongoing	SE	Daily	OF	IH,OF	OF	IH,OF	IH,OF	IH,OF
New Mexico	SE	Daily	SE	Monthly	OF	OF	OF	IH	IH	IH
New York	SE	N.A.	SE	Annually (c)	OF	OF	OF	N.A.	IH,OF	N.A.
North Carolina	SE	Daily	SE	Daily	IH	IH,OF	OF	IH	IH,OF	IH,OF
North Dakota	SE	Ongoing	SE	Ongoing	N.A.	OF	OF	N.A.	IH,OF	IH,OF
Ohio	SE	Bi-annually	N.A.	N.A.	N.A.	OF	OF	N.A.	IH,OF	OF
Oklahoma	SE	Annually	SE	Annually	OF	N.A.	N.A.	IH	N.A.	IH
Oregon	SE	Ongoing	SE	Ongoing	IH,OF	IH	OF	IH,OF	OF	IH
Pennsylvania	SE	N.A.	SE	N.A.	★	★	★	★	★	★
Rhode Island	SE	Monthly	SE	Monthly	IH,OF	IH,OF	IH,OF	IH,OF	IH,OF	IH,OF
South Carolina	SE	Monthly	SE	Semi-annual	OF	OF	OF	IH,OF	IH,OF	IH,OF
South Dakota	N.A.	N.A.	SE/OF	Annually	OF	IH,OF	OF	IH,OF	N.A.	OF
Tennessee	SE	Monthly	SE	Quarterly	IH	N.A.	N.A.	IH	IH	IH
Texas	SE	Ongoing	SE	Ongoing	IH	IH,OF	OF	OF	OF	OF
Utah	SE	Ongoing	SE	Annually	OF	IH	N.A.	OF	IH	IH
Vermont	SE	Annually	SE	Annually	OF	OF	OF	OF	OF	OF

CASH MANAGEMENT PROGRAMS AND SERVICES—Continued

State or other jurisdiction	Reviews of cash management programs				Agency preparing cash management services					
	Banking relations		Investment practices		Lock boxes	Wire transfers	Zero balance accounts	Information services	Account reconciliation services	Automated clearinghouse
	Reviewing agency	Frequency of review	Reviewing agency	Frequency of review						
Virginia	SE	Annually	SE/OF (c)	Varies	IH,OF (d)	OF	OF	OF	IH,OF (e)	OF
Washington	SE	Monthly/Ongoing	SE	Annually	OF	OF	IH	IH,OF	IH	IH,OF
West Virginia	N.A.	N.A.	N.A.	N.A.	N.A.	N.A.	N.A.	N.A.	N.A.	N.A.
Wisconsin	SE	6 years	SE	Monthly	OF	OF	OF	OF	OF	OF
Wyoming	SE	Quarterly	SE	Ongoing	N.A.	★	★	N.A.	N.A.	★
Dist. of Columbia	SE	N.A.	SE	N.A.	IH,OF	OF	OF	N.A.	IH	OF
Puerto Rico	SE	Weekly	SE	Monthly	N.A.	OF	OF	IH	OF	OF

(a) No formal review, but ongoing informal.
(b) Contract expiration.
(c) Sooner if required by changing conditions.
(d) Two agencies in-house.
(e) Bank provides partial reconciliation.

Source: National Association of State Treasurers' survey, Fall 1993.
Key:
SE — State employee or board
OF — Outside firm
IH — Within treasurer's office
★ — Service utilized; agency preparing service not specified
∴ — Service not utilized
N.A. — Not available

Table 6.7
DEMAND DEPOSITS

State or other jurisdiction	Method for selecting depository							Selection of depository made by	Compensation for demand deposits		Collateralization required above the federal insurance level	Percentage requiring collateral
	Competitive bid	Application	Negotiation	Depositor's convenience	Compensating balances	Agency's convenience	Agencies request		Procedure used	Method for determining compensation		
Alabama	...	★	...	★	...	★	...	Treasurer	Account analysis	CB	Yes	100
Alaska	★	★	...	...	...	...	...	Commissioner of Revenue	Competitive bid, account analysis	CB	Yes	100
Arizona	★	...	...	★	...	...	...	Board	Competitive bid	CB,FS	Yes	102
Arkansas	...	...	...	...	...	...	...	Treasurer	Competitive bid	CB	Yes	102-120
California	...	...	★	...	★	...	...	Treasurer	Annual negotiation	CB	Yes	110
Colorado	★	...	...	★★	...	...	...	Treasurer (a)	Competitive bid	FS	Yes	100,000
Connecticut	★	...	...	★★	★	★	...	Treasurer, various agencies	Annual negotiating, account analysis, competitive bid	CB	Yes	(b)
Delaware	★★	...	...	...	...	...	...	Board	Account analysis	CB,FS	No	N.A.
Florida	★	...	...	...	...	...	...	Treasurer	Competitive bid	CB	Yes	25-200
Georgia	...	...	...	...	...	★	...	Board	Account analysis	CB	Yes	0
Hawaii	...	★	...	★★	...	★	...	Treasurer	Account analysis	CB,FS	Yes	100
Idaho	★	★	★	★★	...	...	...	Treasurer	Annual negotiation	FS	No	N.A.
Illinois	...	...	★	...	...	★	...	Treasurer	Competitive bid, account analysis	FS,CB	Yes	100
Indiana	...	...	★★	★★	...	★★	...	Treasurer	Competitive bid	CB	No	0
Iowa	★	...	★★	★★	...	★★	...	Treasurer	Annual negotiation, competitive bid, account analysis	CB,FS	Yes	110
Kansas	★ (c)	...	...	...	...	...	...	Board	Competitive bid	FS	Yes	100
Kentucky	★★	...	...	★	...	...	...	(d)	Competitive bid	FS	Yes	100
Louisiana	...	★★	...	★	...	...	...	Treasurer	Competitive bid	FS	Yes	100
Maine	★	...	...	★	...	★	...	Treasurer	Competitive bid	CB	N.A.	N.A.
Maryland	...	...	...	★	...	...	...	Treasurer	Competitive bid	FS	Yes	102
Massachusetts	★ (e)	...	...	★	...	★	...	Treasurer and agency	Annual negotiation, competitive bid, account analysis	CB,FS,MB	No	0
Michigan	...	...	★	★	...	★	...	Agency (f)	Annual negotiation	CB	Yes	85
Minnesota	★	...	...	...	...	...	...	Board	Competitive bid	CB,FS	Yes	110
Mississippi	...	...	★★	★	...	...	...	Treasurer	Annual negotiation	CB	Yes	105
Missouri	...	★	...	★	...	...	...	Treasurer	Competitive bid	CB	Yes	100
Montana	★ (g)	...	...	...	...	★	...	Treasurer	Competitive bid, account analysis	CB,FS	Yes	50
Nebraska	...	...	★	★	★	...	...	Treasurer	Account analysis	CB	Yes	75 (h)
Nevada	...	...	...	...	...	...	...	Treasurer	Competitive bid	CB	Yes	100
New Hampshire	★	★	...	★	...	...	...	Treasurer	Account analysis	FS	Yes	N.A.
New Jersey	★	...	...	★	...	★	...	Treasurer	Competitive bid, account analysis	CB,FS	Yes	100-120
New Mexico	★	★	...	★	...	★	...	Treasurer, Board	Competitive bid	CB,FS	Yes	50-100
New York	★	...	★	...	...	...	...	Treasurer	Account analysis	CB,FS	Yes	100
North Carolina	...	...	★★	★★	...	...	...	Treasurer	Account analysis	CB	Yes	100
North Dakota	...	★	★	...	...	...	...	Treasurer	Competitive bid	No fee	No	100
Ohio	...	★	...	...	...	...	...	Board	Biennial negotiation	CB,FS	Yes	115

DEMAND DEPOSITS—Continued

State or other jurisdiction	Method for selecting depository						Selection of depository made by	Compensation for demand deposits			
	Competitive bid	Application	Negotiation	Depositor's convenience	Compensating balances	Agency's convenience		Procedure used	Method for determining compensation	Collateralization required above the federal insurance level	Percentage requiring collateral
Oklahoma	...	...	...	★	...	...	Treasurer	Account analysis	FS	Yes	110
Oregon	...	...	...	...	...	★	(i) Treasurer	Negotiation, account analysis	CB,FS	Yes	25
Pennsylvania	...	★	★	...	...	...	Treasurer, Bd. of Finance/Revenue	Negotiation, account analysis	CB	Yes	120
Rhode Island	...	★	★	...	...	...	Treasurer	Negotiation, account analysis	CB	Yes	(j)
South Carolina	...	...	★	★	...	...	Treasurer	Negotiation	CB	Yes	100
South Dakota	★	...	...	...	...	...	Treasurer	Competitive bid	CB	Yes	110
Tennessee	...	★	...	...	...	...	Treasurer	Account analysis	CB,FS	Yes	105
Texas	...	★	...	...	...	...	Board	Account analysis	CB,FS	Yes	105 (k)
Utah	...	...	...	★	...	...	Treasurer (l)	Negotiation, competitive bid, account analysis	CB,FS	No	0
Vermont	...	...	...	...	★	...	Treasurer	Competitive bid	FS	Yes	(m)
Virginia	★	★	...	★	...	★	Manager of cash and banking	Account analysis (n)	CB,FS	Yes	(o)
Washington	★	...	★	...	...	★	Treasurer, State agencies	Negotiation, competitive bid, account analysis	CB,FS	Yes	10
West Virginia	(p)	...	...	...	...	...	(p)	N.A.	N.A.	N.A.	N.A.
Wisconsin	★	...	...	...	...	...	Board	Competitive bid	CB,FS	No	N.A.
Wyoming	★	...	...	...	...	...	Treasurer	Negotiation, competitive bid, account analysis	CB,FS	Yes	100
Dist. of Columbia	★	...	...	...	...	...	N.A.	Account analysis	CB	Yes	100
Puerto Rico	...	...	...	...	...	★	Treasurer	Account analysis	CB	Yes	91

Source: National Association of State Treasurers' survey, Fall 1993.
Key:
★ — Method utilized
N.A. — Method not utilized
... — Not available
CB — Compensating balances
FS — Fee for service
MB — Minimum balance
(a) And various agencies and departments of state.
(b) Depends upon Risk Based Capital Ratio.
(c) Competitive bid for primary depository; depositors convenience for imprest accounts.
(d) Finance Cabinet Division of Purchases (based on valuation committee recommendation for primary depository).
(e) And Treasurer's approval.

(f) Agency picks bank, explains why selected. Receipts Processing Division has final decision.
(g) Competitive bid for 10 largest accounts; agency convenience for remaining accounts.
(h) Require collateral pledged at 110 percent of deposits over FDIC.
(i) Treasury approval of agency request.
(j) Requires 125 percent if mortgage backed securities are pledged.
(k) When bank does not meet minimum capitalization standards; past; 60 days—investments.
(l) Agencies select financial institutions for local deposit of revenue collections.
(m) Renewing agreements and terms.
(n) Large applications are competitively bid.
(o) 50 percent, all banks pool risk for remaining 50 percent; 100 percent for savings banks and those banks rated low.
(p) Function outside of Treasurer's office.

Table 6.8
SUMMARY FINANCIAL AGGREGATES, BY STATE: 1991
(In millions of dollars)

State	Revenue				Expenditure				Debt outstanding at end of fiscal year	Cash and security holdings at end of fiscal year
	Total	General	Utilities and liquor store	Insurance trust	Total	General	Utilities and liquor store	Insurance trust		
United States	$661,192	$551,722	$6,474	$102,996	$628,804	$554,901	$9,721	$64,182	$345,554	$1,018,480
Alabama	9,767	8,173	150	1,445	8,855	8,050	136	669	4,214	14,630
Alaska	6,355	5,673	13	669	4,941	4,493	111	337	5,291	23,435
Arizona	9,016	7,544	15	1,457	8,041	7,287	22	732	2,540	13,091
Arkansas	4,810	4,307	0	503	4,649	4,315	0	334	1,764	6,884
California	90,784	72,676	162	17,946	85,640	75,033	68	10,539	31,956	129,271
Colorado	7,863	6,226	0	1,637	6,992	6,089	2	901	2,659	14,152
Connecticut	9,816	8,745	18	1,053	11,115	9,807	169	1,139	13,006	16,197
Delaware	2,443	2,227	4	212	2,318	2,152	18	149	3,215	5,200
Florida	25,754	22,080	5	3,670	25,168	23,628	24	1,515	11,084	34,918
Georgia	13,866	11,864	0	2,003	13,286	12,280	0	1,006	3,652	18,284
Hawaii	4,916	4,348	0	567	4,510	4,174	0	336	4,202	8,349
Idaho	2,584	2,148	40	396	2,305	2,055	32	218	1,122	3,564
Illinois	25,092	21,801	0	3,291	24,619	22,168	0	2,451	18,238	35,824
Indiana	12,288	11,222	0	1,066	11,734	11,153	0	581	4,624	13,740
Iowa	7,137	6,200	82	854	6,820	6,384	57	379	1,620	7,999
Kansas	5,249	4,724	0	525	5,126	4,699	0	427	337	5,532
Kentucky	9,951	8,706	0	1,245	9,048	8,248	5	795	6,024	13,885
Louisiana	10,764	9,410	0	1,354	10,537	9,592	0	945	10,729	16,735
Maine	3,222	2,902	73	248	3,515	3,095	52	368	2,585	4,369
Maryland	12,479	10,605	70	1,804	12,576	10,776	375	1,425	7,528	17,754
Massachusetts	18,727	17,460	52	1,216	20,349	18,265	67	2,016	21,102	18,881
Michigan	24,505	20,891	443	3,171	24,037	20,749	375	2,913	10,109	30,633
Minnesota	13,701	11,642	0	2,059	12,730	11,688	0	1,042	3,941	19,134
Mississippi	5,794	4,949	116	729	5,171	4,680	93	398	1,413	7,603
Missouri	10,002	8,661	0	1,341	9,254	8,478	0	776	5,775	15,680
Montana	2,359	1,886	35	439	2,384	2,058	26	300	1,611	4,365
Nebraska	3,436	3,219	0	217	3,266	3,192	0	74	1,596	3,673
Nevada	3,553	2,463	60	1,029	3,436	2,557	64	814	1,708	6,481
New Hampshire	2,088	1,702	196	191	2,135	1,749	157	229	4,127	5,224
New Jersey	24,743	20,056	369	4,319	23,250	19,399	920	2,932	19,039	43,297
New Mexico	4,913	4,332	0	580	4,527	4,204	0	323	1,752	11,307
New York	65,715	54,935	1,917	8,864	64,321	53,916	4,507	5,898	51,804	103,481
North Carolina	15,266	12,927	0	2,339	15,036	13,805	0	1,231	3,490	23,755
North Dakota	1,998	1,755	0	243	1,793	1,653	0	140	964	2,695
Ohio	31,721	21,379	373	9,970	27,791	22,324	287	5,180	11,367	67,455
Oklahoma	7,819	6,655	215	949	7,267	6,271	245	751	3,730	10,426
Oregon	8,201	6,353	162	1,686	7,249	6,292	102	855	6,451	19,006
Pennsylvania	27,086	22,155	642	4,289	26,710	22,879	619	3,212	11,640	40,940
Rhode Island	3,104	2,592	6	505	3,288	2,750	37	501	4,393	5,992
South Carolina	9,413	7,408	554	1,451	8,970	7,698	584	688	4,189	14,864
South Dakota	1,597	1,412	0	186	1,417	1,356	0	60	1,754	3,435
Tennessee	9,544	8,385	0	1,160	9,238	8,596	0	642	2,790	12,077
Texas	33,773	28,819	0	4,954	29,526	27,026	0	2,500	7,687	53,455
Utah	4,344	3,662	68	614	4,108	3,692	50	366	1,911	6,780
Vermont	1,703	1,548	28	127	1,736	1,607	27	102	1,486	2,292
Virginia	14,523	12,431	259	1,833	13,352	12,390	207	755	6,500	20,262
Washington	16,394	12,750	247	3,397	15,666	13,170	209	2,287	6,520	25,195
West Virginia	4,896	4,152	71	673	4,741	3,996	48	696	2,770	4,899
Wisconsin	14,137	11,825	0	2,312	12,448	11,340	0	1,108	6,625	26,344
Wyoming	1,979	1,741	29	209	1,813	1,638	26	149	922	5,039

Source: U.S. Department of Commerce, Bureau of the Census, *State Government Finances 1991.*
Note: Detail may not add to totals due to rounding. Data presented are statistical in nature and do not represent an accounting statement. Therefore, a difference between an individual government's total revenues and expenditures does not necessarily indicate a budget surplus or deficit.

Table 6.9
SUMMARY FINANCIAL AGGREGATES, BY STATE: 1992
(In millions of dollars)

| State | Revenue | | | | Expenditure | | | | Debt outstanding at end of fiscal year | Cash and security holdings at end of fiscal year |
	Total	General	Utilities and liquor store	Insurance trust	Total	General	Utilities and liquor store	Insurance trust		
United States	$741,853	$605,334	$6,579	$129,940	$700,894	$611,922	$9,613	$79,359	$371,901	$1,084,187
Alabama............	10,536	8,910	153	1,473	9,651	8,788	137	725	4,129	14,594
Alaska..............	6,327	5,343	26	958	5,255	4,788	76	391	4,942	24,529
Arizona.............	9,551	7,975	17	1,559	9,096	8,236	29	831	2,849	13,310
Arkansas	5,864	5,190	0	674	5,478	5,062	0	417	1,942	7,517
California...........	100,154	79,399	179	20,576	97,079	83,360	88	13,631	37,824	138,561
Colorado	9,079	7,016	0	2,063	7,492	6,494	3	995	2,977	15,943
Connecticut	11,784	10,137	18	1,629	11,627	9,957	134	1,535	11,957	15,551
Delaware	2,824	2,456	4	363	2,475	2,241	15	218	3,542	5,787
Florida	28,311	23,652	5	4,654	27,089	24,851	27	2,211	12,295	36,762
Georgia............	14,761	12,377	0	2,384	14,054	12,781	0	1,273	4,471	20,599
Hawaii	5,299	4,568	0	731	5,301	4,903	0	399	4,687	8,915
Idaho	2,902	2,447	44	411	2,604	2,316	35	253	1,292	3,906
Illinois.............	27,865	23,103	0	4,761	26,832	23,639	0	3,192	18,742	36,832
Indiana	13,490	12,265	0	1,225	12,341	11,691	0	649	5,172	15,620
Iowa	7,520	6,519	84	917	7,227	6,711	58	457	1,884	8,689
Kansas	5,794	4,968	0	826	5,484	5,052	0	432	486	5,412
Kentucky	10,640	9,222	0	1,418	10,154	9,235	4	915	6,619	13,710
Louisiana	11,842	10,362	0	1,480	11,750	10,683	0	1,067	9,994	16,745
Maine	3,755	3,312	73	369	3,722	3,232	51	439	2,637	4,480
Maryland	13,730	11,320	70	2,340	13,004	11,012	352	1,640	8,335	18,922
Massachusetts	20,456	18,234	60	2,162	20,368	17,812	118	2,438	24,008	22,295
Michigan	26,298	22,079	444	3,775	25,522	21,840	381	3,301	10,357	31,202
Minnesota	15,090	12,347	0	2,744	13,526	12,322	0	1,205	4,143	20,881
Mississippi	6,177	5,290	123	765	5,762	5,217	99	446	1,626	7,473
Missouri	11,619	9,872	0	1,747	10,446	9,513	0	933	6,301	17,774
Montana............	2,661	2,121	36	504	2,460	2,108	34	318	1,868	4,767
Nebraska	3,751	3,526	0	225	3,624	3,535	0	88	1,754	3,848
Nevada	3,948	2,715	65	1,169	3,826	2,953	69	804	1,934	6,863
New Hampshire	2,727	2,303	206	218	2,871	2,453	161	257	4,313	5,421
New Jersey	28,922	23,400	366	5,156	29,316	24,109	1,011	4,196	19,786	44,421
New Mexico........	5,582	4,743	0	839	4,972	4,594	0	378	1,605	11,761
New York	74,931	60,412	1,915	12,604	73,153	60,869	4,194	8,090	55,868	108,098
North Carolina	17,664	14,981	0	2,683	16,046	14,671	0	1,374	3,819	26,019
North Dakota	2,072	1,810	0	262	2,001	1,834	0	167	1,027	2,879
Ohio	35,590	22,990	374	12,226	30,425	24,106	296	6,022	12,193	76,279
Oklahoma	8,379	6,941	218	1,219	8,183	7,063	238	883	3,657	10,528
Oregon	10,025	7,297	169	2,559	7,979	6,842	104	1,033	6,295	16,158
Pennsylvania	36,699	29,859	667	6,173	35,095	30,338	638	4,118	12,962	42,920
Rhode Island	3,609	2,849	7	753	3,968	3,331	40	597	5,151	6,279
South Carolina	9,897	7,862	563	1,473	9,433	7,969	636	828	4,685	16,667
South Dakota	1,756	1,518	0	238	1,565	1,490	0	75	1,889	3,933
Tennessee	11,126	9,624	0	1,502	10,406	9,633	0	773	2,806	13,266
Texas...............	36,763	31,346	0	5,418	33,894	30,744	0	3,150	8,001	53,435
Utah	4,917	4,060	69	787	4,481	4,057	52	371	2,153	7,440
Vermont	1,898	1,701	29	168	1,841	1,690	29	122	1,543	2,261
Virginia............	15,292	13,087	258	1,947	13,921	12,694	212	1,014	7,403	22,446
Washington	17,366	13,434	260	3,672	17,316	14,724	223	2,369	7,192	25,867
West Virginia	5,452	4,559	46	848	5,262	4,396	40	826	2,594	5,492
Wisconsin...........	17,131	12,107	0	5,024	13,596	12,258	0	1,338	7,299	29,315
Wyoming	2,026	1,723	32	272	1,925	1,725	27	173	895	11,811

Source: U.S. Department of Commerce, Bureau of the Census, *State Government Finances 1992.*
Note: Detail may not add to totals due to rounding. Data presented are statistical in nature and do not represent an accounting statement. Therefore, a difference between an individual government's total revenues and expenditures does not necessarily indicate a budget surplus or deficit.

Table 6.10
NATIONAL TOTALS OF STATE GOVERNMENT FINANCES FOR SELECTED YEARS: 1980-92

Item	Amount (in millions)										Percentage change 1991 to 1992	Percentage change 1990 to 1991	Per capita 1992	Per capita 1991
	1992	1991	1990	1989	1988	1987	1986	1984	1982	1980				
Revenue total	$741,853	$661,192	$632,462	$586,931	$541,426	$516,793	$481,307	$397,087	$330,899	$276,962	12.0	5.0	$2,915.00	$2,628.00
General revenue	605,334	551,722	517,720	482,721	445,138	419,063	393,503	330,740	275,111	233,592	9.7	6.6	2,378.60	2,193.00
Taxes	327,822	310,561	300,779	284,413	264,146	246,510	228,082	196,795	162,607	137,075	5.6	3.3	1,288.10	1,234.40
Intergovernmental revenue	169,902	143,534	126,329	115,765	107,241	102,381	98,574	81,450	69,166	64,326	18.4	13.6	667.60	570.50
From Federal Government	159,041	134,926	118,353	108,235	100,478	95,463	92,666	76,140	66,026	61,892	17.9	14	624.90	536.30
Public welfare	91,091	71,961	59,397	51,934	47,908	44,828	41,802	35,423	31,510	24,681	26.6	21.2	357.90	286.00
Education	25,867	23,337	21,271	19,547	17,970	16,883	16,523	13,975	13,149	12,765	10.8	9.7	101.60	92.80
Highways	14,367	14,098	13,931	14,404	13,467	12,963	12,963	10,380	8,304	8,860	1.9	1.2	56.50	56.00
Employment security administration	3,747	3,235	3,013	2,968	2,896	2,794	2,790	2,606	2,352	2,050	15.8	7.4	14.70	12.90
Other	23,969	22,295	20,742	19,384	18,237	17,993	17,696	13,757	10,711	13,536	7.5	7.5	94.20	88.60
From local governments	10,861	8,607	7,976	7,530	6,763	6,918	5,908	5,310	3,139	2,434	26.2	7.9	42.70	34.20
Charges and miscellaneous revenue	107,610	97,627	90,612	82,543	73,751	70,173	66,848	52,495	43,338	32,190	10.2	7.7	422.80	388.10
Liquor stores revenue	3,067	3,013	2,907	2,788	2,767	2,833	2,807	2,759	2,854	2,765	1.8	3.6	12.10	12.10
Utility revenue	3,512	3,460	3,305	3,248	3,030	2,964	2,907	2,638	2,085	1,304	1.5	4.7	13.80	13.80
Insurance trust revenue	129,940	102,996	108,530	98,174	90,491	91,933	82,090	60,950	50,848	39,301	26.2	-5.1	510.60	409.40
Unemployment compensation	26,921	17,952	18,370	19,640	17,187	18,839	18,173	16,671	16,854	13,468	50.0	-2.3	105.80	71.40
Employee retirement	88,281	72,356	78,898	67,964	63,556	64,660	56,820	38,564	29,035	21,146	22.0	-8.3	346.90	287.60
Other	14,738	12,688	11,262	10,571	9,749	8,435	7,097	5,715	4,959	4,686	16.2	12.7	57.90	50.40
Expenditure and debt redemption	736,095	650,460	592,213	546,254	505,507	476,116	439,810	361,546	316,844	263,328	13.2	9.8	2,892.30	2,585.30
Debt redemption	35,201	21,656	19,895	21,177	20,840	20,416	15,577	10,364	6,715	5,516	62.5	8.9	138.30	86.10
Expenditure total	700,894	628,804	572,318	525,077	484,667	455,700	424,233	351,182	310,129	257,812	11.5	9.9	2,754.10	2,499.40
General expenditure	611,922	554,901	508,284	469,269	432,179	403,942	376,457	309,775	269,327	228,223	10.3	9.2	2,404.50	2,205.70
Education	211,570	196,648	184,935	173,184	159,500	149,901	140,189	116,058	102,984	87,939	7.6	6.3	831.30	781.70
Intergovernmental expenditure	124,920	116,180	109,438	104,601	95,391	88,253	81,929	67,485	60,684	52,688	7.5	6.2	490.90	461.80
State institutions of higher educations	70,904	65,560	60,978	55,988	52,410	50,710	47,928	40,016	34,296	27,927	8.2	7.5	278.60	260.60
Other education	13,524	12,911	12,720	11,177	10,302	9,636	9,173	7,599	6,951	6,360	4.7	1.5	53.10	51.30
Public welfare	156,364	124,456	104,971	92,750	84,235	78,454	72,464	62,749	55,257	44,220	25.6	18.6	614.40	494.70
Intergovernmental expenditure	29,512	24,341	21,635	19,614	17,665	17,184	16,298	13,628	13,744	10,977	21.2	12.5	116.00	96.80
Cash assistance, categorical programs	28,295	25,306	22,643	21,103	20,759	20,320	19,715	17,748	15,549	14,349	11.8	11.8	111.20	100.60
Cash assistance, other	1,269	1,376	1,299	1,256	1,153	1,140	1,161	1,154	875	687	-7.8	5.9	5.0	5.50
Other public welfare	112,070	86,773	71,364	61,956	55,614	50,540	45,728	39,671	33,301	25,725	29.2	21.6	440.40	344.90
Highways	48,747	47,038	44,249	42,694	40,681	38,273	36,661	28,840	25,131	25,044	3.6	6.3	191.50	187.00
Regular state highway facilities	37,193	36,179	34,121	33,039	31,509	29,713	28,598	21,874	19,078	19,652	2.8	6.0	146.10	143.80
State toll highway facilities	3,073	2,733	2,344	2,279	2,222	1,776	1,593	1,278	1,025	1,009	12.4	16.6	12.10	10.90
Intergovernmental expenditure	8,481	8,126	7,784	7,376	6,949	6,785	6,470	5,687	5,028	4,383	4.4	4.4	33.30	32.30
Health and hospitals	48,123	45,878	42,666	38,602	34,872	32,131	30,160	24,982	22,121	17,855	4.9	7.5	189.10	182.40
State hospitals and institutions for handicapped	25,904	24,279	22,445	21,206	19,489	17,862	16,990	15,068	13,681	11,015	6.7	8.2	101.80	96.50
Other	21,998	21,412	20,029	17,188	15,202	14,083	12,980		8,440	6,485	2.7	6.9	86.40	85.10
Natural resources	10,521	10,256	9,909	9,070	8,310	7,816	7,312	5,945	5,485	4,449	2.6	3.5	41.30	40.80
Corrections	20,120	19,240	17,266	15,018	13,303	11,704	10,771		5,889	3,031	4.6	11.4	79.10	76.50
Financial administration	9,751	9,101	8,616	7,672	6,969	6,459	5,855	4,517	2,278	2,001	7.1	5.6	38.30	36.20
Employment security administration	3,702	3,238	3,003	2,937	2,842	2,741	2,697	2,546	2,730	2,263	14.3	7.8	14.50	12.90
Police protection	5,489	5,506	5,166	4,746	4,508	4,048	3,714	3,140			-0.3	6.6	21.60	21.90
Interest on general debt	24,622	23,393	21,532	20,355	19,367	18,587	16,876	13,137	9,015	6,763	5.3	8.6	96.70	93.00
Veterans' services	170	157	152	146	134	129	122	99			8.3	3.3	0.70	0.60
Utility expenditure	7,036	7,217	7,131	6,410	6,229	5,971	5,530	4,817	3,730	2,401	-2.5	1.2	27.60	28.70
Insurance trust expenditure	79,359	64,182	54,452	46,995	43,881	43,116	39,828	34,277	34,664	24,981	23.6	17.9	311.80	255.10
Employee retirement	35,628	32,264	29,562	26,966	24,196	22,189	19,878	16,112	13,133	10,257	10.4	9.1	140.00	128.20
Unemployment compensation	32,761	22,017	16,423	12,791	13,024	15,174	14,821	13,987	18,027	12,006	48.8	34.1	128.70	87.50
Other	10,969	9,902	8,467	7,237	6,661	5,952	5,131	4,178	3,503	2,719	10.8	16.9	43.10	39.40

NATIONAL TOTALS OF STATE GOVERNMENT FINANCES—Continued

Item	Amount (in millions)										Percentage change 1991 to 1992	Percentage change 1990 to 1991	Per capita 1992	Per capita 1991
	1992	1991	1990	1989	1988	1987	1986	1984	1982	1980				
Total expenditure by character and object	700,893	628,804	572,319	525,076	484,667	455,700	424,233	351,182	310,129	257,812	11.5	9.9	2,754.05	2,499.27
Direct expenditure	499,580	442,264	397,291	359,661	333,005	314,421	292,267	242,809	211,386	173,308	13	11.3	1,963.00	1,758.00
Current operation	323,830	287,079	258,046	232,964	213,249	199,806	186,098	156,922	133,152	108,131	12.8	11.3	1,272.50	1,141.10
Capital outlay	50,126	47,937	45,524	43,121	40,667	37,209	34,578	25,486	23,303	23,325	4.6	5.3	197.00	190.50
Construction	39,001	37,647	34,803	33,612	31,421	28,174	26,557	19,507	19,397	19,736	3.6	8.2	153.20	149.60
Purchase of land and existing structures	3,822	3,401	3,471	2,715	3,082	2,594	2,205	1,883	1,316	1,345	12.4	-2.0	15.00	13.50
Equipment	7,303	6,889	7,250	6,795	6,164	6,440	5,816	4,096	2,590	2,243	6.0	-5.0	28.70	27.40
Assistance and subsidies	20,784	18,876	16,902	15,421	15,000	14,705	14,162	12,386	10,867	9,818	10.1	11.7	81.70	75.00
Interest on debt	25,482	24,189	22,367	21,160	20,208	19,385	17,601	13,738	9,400	7,053	5.3	8.1	100.10	96.10
Insurance benefits and repayments	79,359	64,182	54,452	46,995	43,881	43,316	39,828	34,277	34,664	24,981	23.6	17.9	311.80	255.10
Intergovernmental expenditure	201,313	186,540	175,028	165,415	151,662	141,279	131,966	108,373	98,743	84,504	7.9	6.6	791.00	741.50
Cash and security holdings at end of fiscal year	1,084,187	1,018,480	963,342	880,994	783,362	697,390	611,023	443,366	338,274	272,397	6.5	5.7	4,260.20	4,048.40
Unemployment fund balance in U.S. Treasury	27,390	33,088	37,167	34,342	27,398	22,431	18,019	5,708	6,789	11,945	-17.2	-11.0	107.60	131.50
Securities, total by purpose	656,761	611,774	565,641	505,664	434,870	403,895	341,867	255,697	191,926	144,031	7.4	8.2	2,580.70	2,431.70
Insurance trust	216,528	201,759	189,966	175,028	166,624	120,827	116,990	81,527	56,655	40,011	7.3	6.2	850.80	802.00
Debt offsets														

Source: U.S. Department of Commerce, Bureau of the Census, annual reports on State Government Finances.

Table 6.11
STATE GENERAL REVENUE, BY SOURCE AND BY STATE: 1991
(In thousands of dollars)

State	Total general revenue (a)	Taxes Total (b)	Sales and gross receipts Total (b)	General	Motor fuels	Licenses Total (b)	Motor vehicle	Individual income	Corporation net income	Intergovernmental revenue	Charges and miscellaneous general revenue
United States	$551,721,744	$310,561,109	$153,534,721	$103,165,478	$20,638,959	$19,418,622	$10,131,352	$99,278,910	$20,356,868	$143,533,607	$97,627,028
Alabama	8,173,252	3,942,565	2,022,653	1,049,526	290,447	382,073	141,015	1,174,230	168,253	2,362,160	1,868,527
Alaska	5,673,482	1,806,131	96,674	0	39,917	82,624	20,760	0	253,649	715,392	3,151,959
Arizona	7,543,585	4,710,745	2,677,036	2,005,801	362,018	287,793	209,350	1,245,645	192,325	1,789,506	1,043,334
Arkansas	4,306,727	2,366,105	1,258,163	876,900	224,929	150,859	74,193	793,880	122,240	1,197,842	742,780
California	72,675,540	44,874,424	18,721,452	14,339,942	2,002,287	2,130,937	1,239,599	16,817,244	4,440,479	18,150,980	9,650,098
Colorado	6,225,665	3,213,833	1,366,667	844,572	331,515	221,528	99,353	1,466,285	114,514	1,611,107	1,400,725
Connecticut	8,745,397	4,983,328	3,407,057	2,438,653	329,815	269,917	165,318	474,609	515,879	2,132,602	1,629,467
Delaware	2,226,730	1,165,492	170,477	0	66,216	358,510	20,508	461,723	122,457	376,238	685,000
Florida	22,079,594	13,764,055	10,884,691	8,138,690	821,776	937,132	533,113	0	582,149	4,826,682	3,488,857
Georgia	11,863,592	7,154,525	3,497,055	2,656,792	451,169	194,328	78,734	2,947,681	416,558	3,455,792	1,253,275
Hawaii	4,348,045	2,639,152	1,598,490	1,278,737	53,188	34,048	20,935	872,734	116,380	734,349	974,544
Idaho	2,147,617	1,204,607	587,765	404,164	112,305	106,171	56,402	446,148	59,712	553,947	389,063
Illinois	21,800,813	13,291,517	6,632,507	4,163,801	1,024,492	817,275	597,981	4,538,545	940,759	4,923,880	3,585,416
Indiana	11,222,425	6,182,409	3,385,256	2,538,335	581,740	215,351	165,706	2,183,972	310,394	2,684,747	2,355,269
Iowa	6,200,457	3,447,460	1,506,257	977,056	330,530	323,165	220,730	1,343,571	201,929	1,519,439	1,233,558
Kansas	4,724,172	2,796,415	1,348,119	918,211	234,725	170,841	106,728	880,740	212,950	1,149,319	778,438
Kentucky	8,705,621	5,043,183	2,150,471	1,299,665	350,369	272,440	141,080	1,693,339	319,351	2,232,815	1,429,623
Louisiana	9,409,886	4,309,467	2,125,805	1,308,090	443,770	385,408	78,273	803,592	326,659	2,856,778	2,243,641
Maine	2,901,540	1,558,231	744,774	497,069	130,005	93,019	47,904	580,748	76,053	757,361	585,948
Maryland	10,604,748	6,401,428	2,641,718	1,540,887	443,563	239,729	144,195	2,931,020	255,488	2,284,169	1,919,151
Massachusetts	17,459,634	9,683,597	2,946,443	1,909,438	464,222	389,477	243,568	5,343,387	719,569	4,455,486	3,320,551
Michigan	20,891,046	11,103,151	4,513,241	3,190,647	733,501	696,207	490,222	3,787,197	1,593,109	5,412,629	4,375,266
Minnesota	11,642,450	7,050,698	3,037,426	1,963,433	457,571	521,215	363,922	2,974,554	458,271	2,602,191	1,989,561
Mississippi	4,948,942	2,460,836	1,600,978	1,120,155	305,100	159,276	64,248	479,602	139,823	1,840,948	647,158
Missouri	8,660,697	4,996,388	2,503,050	1,863,374	364,998	371,753	194,014	1,829,224	224,759	2,243,693	1,420,616
Montana	1,885,816	817,679	183,377	0	110,246	96,568	37,007	282,960	70,784	625,026	443,111
Nebraska	3,219,076	1,767,368	959,370	624,259	222,715	110,526	55,175	603,112	81,948	767,607	684,101
Nevada	2,463,276	1,682,602	1,436,754	826,288	120,487	174,199	56,982	0	0	440,835	339,839
New Hampshire	1,701,548	624,627	312,063	0	90,820	98,759	50,457	36,949	122,205	499,840	577,081
New Jersey	20,055,805	11,644,652	6,363,602	4,042,805	400,186	585,154	316,855	3,391,026	1,030,620	4,407,155	4,003,998
New Mexico	4,332,211	2,085,690	1,250,442	939,242	175,944	132,651	103,468	369,455	48,989	991,481	1,255,040
New York	54,934,621	28,299,769	9,686,126	5,751,832	506,704	935,643	537,935	14,482,059	2,030,332	19,205,336	7,429,516
North Carolina	12,927,231	7,850,043	3,126,370	1,689,871	825,425	510,649	214,325	3,534,474	499,958	3,353,941	1,723,247
North Dakota	1,754,991	755,054	419,793	235,225	75,917	58,151	37,866	114,273	50,911	511,672	488,265
Ohio	21,378,542	11,555,584	5,803,212	3,574,539	1,035,492	824,988	399,016	4,217,200	630,183	5,755,502	4,067,456
Oklahoma	6,654,808	3,861,985	1,658,748	963,548	330,819	374,600	279,644	1,218,279	137,582	1,555,232	1,237,591
Oregon	6,353,331	3,029,829	424,301	0	258,969	376,623	243,259	1,983,705	149,074	1,857,741	1,465,761
Pennsylvania	22,154,850	13,021,344	6,544,459	4,197,700	722,713	1,369,409	446,355	3,274,656	1,011,966	5,633,430	3,500,086
Rhode Island	2,592,301	1,256,652	676,966	448,402	74,602	72,742	51,934	429,247	45,966	783,104	552,545
South Carolina	7,407,573	3,933,214	2,093,427	1,437,473	340,112	242,102	72,463	1,386,648	151,433	2,133,314	1,341,045

STATE GENERAL REVENUE, BY SOURCE AND BY STATE: 1991—Continued

State	Total general revenue (a)	Taxes								Intergovernmental revenue	Charges and miscellaneous general revenue
		Total (b)	Sales and gross receipts			Licenses		Individual income	Corporation net income		
			Total (b)	General	Motor fuels	Total (b)	Motor vehicle				
South Dakota	1,411,633	528,248	400,595	247,974	78,686	65,000	38,174	0	38,578	505,291	378,094
Tennessee	8,384,829	4,310,573	3,299,700	2,363,252	635,248	454,329	152,357	97,033	345,542	2,772,431	1,301,825
Texas	28,818,616	16,016,913	12,877,251	8,294,921	1,509,285	1,657,332	725,608	0	0	7,632,301	5,169,402
Utah	3,662,138	1,860,817	943,438	739,633	131,057	75,061	41,497	714,915	82,463	1,015,897	785,424
Vermont	1,548,168	684,519	313,268	125,611	52,213	54,229	35,353	257,517	27,387	454,298	409,351
Virginia	12,431,333	6,852,365	2,791,294	1,558,873	617,586	376,559	245,912	3,236,011	285,106	2,520,128	3,058,840
Washington	12,749,674	7,989,522	5,994,394	4,758,204	584,960	432,318	193,546	0	0	2,842,312	1,917,840
West Virginia	4,151,718	2,328,132	1,235,863	817,368	205,981	138,826	83,676	576,340	191,214	1,083,802	739,784
Wisconsin	11,825,069	7,016,734	3,084,971	2,026,711	546,508	333,442	158,643	3,003,381	440,918	2,725,371	2,082,964
Wyoming	1,740,957	637,452	230,812	177,779	36,116	57,686	35,994	0	0	590,508	512,997

Source: U.S. Department of Commerce, Bureau of the Census, *State Government Finances 1991.*
Note: Detail may not add to totals due to rounding.
(a) Total general revenue equals total taxes plus intergovernmental revenue plus charges and miscellaneous revenue.

(b) Total includes other taxes not shown separately in this table.

Table 6.12
STATE GENERAL REVENUE, BY SOURCE AND BY STATE: 1992
(In thousands of dollars)

State	Total general revenue (a)	Taxes Total (b)	Sales and gross receipts Total (b)	Sales and gross receipts General	Sales and gross receipts Motor fuels	Licenses Total (b)	Licenses Motor vehicle	Individual income	Corporation net income	Intergovernmental revenue	Charges and miscellaneous general revenue
United States	$605,333,551	$327,821,571	$162,308,450	$107,578,897	$22,197,941	$21,690,507	$10,766,482	$104,400,506	$21,565,953	$169,902,072	$107,609,908
Alabama	8,910,315	4,217,916	2,218,884	1,115,516	330,895	395,202	145,769	1,233,824	164,779	2,737,180	1,955,219
Alaska	5,342,507	1,602,937	101,286	0	43,247	80,704	24,219	0	200,025	773,106	2,966,464
Arizona	7,975,484	4,826,755	2,781,851	2,088,288	369,946	279,700	193,389	1,240,372	210,824	2,110,356	1,038,373
Arkansas	5,190,388	2,748,292	1,517,788	1,032,536	307,534	195,634	115,316	850,111	125,525	1,635,962	806,134
California	79,399,033	46,128,169	19,548,658	14,924,766	2,248,089	2,287,864	1,358,935	17,029,575	4,518,418	23,429,204	9,841,660
Colorado	7,015,963	3,533,180	1,483,720	913,599	360,498	242,004	103,328	1,611,954	123,458	1,918,574	1,564,209
Connecticut	10,136,861	6,058,854	3,072,870	2,090,143	361,770	284,763	173,429	1,865,711	593,720	2,274,928	1,803,079
Delaware	2,456,338	1,339,752	195,341	0	72,874	447,643	18,441	497,589	128,737	412,211	704,375
Florida	23,651,927	14,411,775	11,284,828	8,325,978	1,084,611	997,465	533,357	0	695,114	5,711,452	3,528,700
Georgia	12,377,277	7,266,981	3,503,083	2,687,346	449,782	211,443	84,135	3,081,708	375,286	3,770,676	1,339,620
Hawaii	4,567,848	2,709,518	1,659,493	1,294,723	72,106	54,831	39,540	906,982	67,768	848,559	1,009,771
Idaho	2,447,293	1,390,585	647,370	439,173	132,019	115,332	48,878	535,482	68,171	643,738	412,970
Illinois	23,103,286	13,463,435	6,739,404	4,241,572	1,030,266	800,708	612,073	4,582,387	970,531	5,740,717	3,899,134
Indiana	12,265,017	6,476,135	3,588,981	2,779,108	542,470	206,076	155,642	2,202,545	386,371	3,203,811	2,585,071
Iowa	6,519,228	3,601,571	1,570,624	1,010,228	333,425	343,235	226,548	1,410,926	192,818	1,651,321	1,266,336
Kansas	4,967,838	2,801,692	1,418,591	958,165	250,999	174,975	109,739	833,756	198,998	1,359,425	806,721
Kentucky	9,221,972	5,080,971	2,227,986	1,366,872	360,058	281,006	148,517	1,678,526	271,027	2,609,286	1,531,715
Louisiana	10,361,962	4,250,245	2,161,652	1,268,695	470,116	412,425	86,569	867,478	232,061	3,695,255	2,416,462
Maine	3,312,483	1,664,359	853,351	573,418	143,483	98,228	50,845	591,487	69,921	931,856	716,268
Maryland	11,319,918	6,502,494	2,739,685	1,579,785	462,777	266,302	151,855	2,907,450	216,946	2,662,442	2,154,982
Massachusetts	18,234,258	9,903,246	3,100,368	1,978,654	541,069	412,046	250,986	5,336,957	756,781	4,626,979	3,704,033
Michigan	22,079,192	11,279,170	4,988,579	3,665,541	745,000	730,604	514,341	3,241,549	1,729,549	6,134,453	4,665,569
Minnesota	12,346,845	7,449,787	3,358,838	2,190,676	464,916	573,240	393,416	2,999,091	422,812	2,909,750	1,987,308
Mississippi	5,289,771	2,494,392	1,677,133	1,182,356	317,098	155,912	62,691	439,577	146,308	2,077,281	718,098
Missouri	9,872,284	5,131,360	2,588,639	1,916,680	384,342	407,396	200,840	1,844,004	229,730	2,956,376	1,784,548
Montana	2,120,857	950,724	202,157	0	121,493	120,083	40,943	321,538	57,683	685,573	484,560
Nebraska	3,525,758	1,889,877	998,913	663,159	222,145	122,367	54,631	652,638	103,617	897,151	738,730
Nevada	2,714,759	1,817,208	1,532,460	892,721	132,963	217,369	67,740	0	0	547,402	350,149
New Hampshire	2,303,247	856,179	530,469	0	92,534	106,976	51,514	69,167	95,635	799,809	647,259
New Jersey	23,400,274	12,802,662	7,007,550	4,049,282	410,625	573,085	315,419	4,101,895	845,823	5,337,844	5,259,708
New Mexico	4,743,342	2,237,656	1,306,764	982,572	182,739	135,610	106,314	445,303	77,786	1,202,897	1,302,789
New York	60,412,276	30,110,341	10,658,851	6,005,503	495,208	939,761	561,678	14,913,380	2,518,790	22,142,003	8,159,932
North Carolina	14,980,885	9,009,742	3,972,981	2,171,041	861,487	601,150	279,959	3,583,018	643,865	4,017,596	1,953,547
North Dakota	1,809,691	754,555	441,109	256,583	75,245	67,732	35,031	119,497	38,610	580,195	474,941
Ohio	22,989,818	12,114,788	6,069,518	3,751,523	1,128,832	899,932	481,465	4,407,036	641,701	6,468,864	4,406,166
Oklahoma	6,940,935	3,874,272	1,576,216	971,331	340,208	507,118	407,009	1,218,181	149,142	1,779,458	1,287,205
Oregon	7,297,350	3,313,496	438,629	0	271,561	401,223	244,920	2,221,297	152,161	2,062,649	1,921,205
Pennsylvania	29,859,039	16,269,988	7,265,895	4,499,734	694,408	1,769,602	447,173	4,689,139	1,623,774	8,016,454	5,572,597
Rhode Island	2,849,495	1,276,391	636,448	388,987	94,074	73,857	50,787	478,461	48,502	988,262	584,842
South Carolina	7,861,740	3,935,500	2,051,830	1,452,014	287,393	279,459	79,127	1,410,893	141,895	2,443,841	1,482,399

STATE GENERAL REVENUE, BY SOURCE AND BY STATE: 1992—Continued

State	Total general revenue (a)	Taxes Total (b)	Sales and gross receipts Total (b)	Sales and gross receipts General	Sales and gross receipts Motor fuels	Licenses Total (b)	Licenses Motor vehicle	Individual income	Corporation net income	Intergovernmental revenue	Charges and miscellaneous general revenue
South Dakota	1,518,437	565,032	449,237	289,325	82,685	55,710	25,176	0	35,222	549,243	404,162
Tennessee	9,624,174	4,525,662	3,515,642	2,514,798	656,573	500,876	158,693	93,360	295,266	3,427,157	1,671,355
Texas	31,345,670	17,030,546	13,609,648	8,575,890	1,953,453	2,266,080	692,888	0	0	8,577,914	5,737,210
Utah	4,060,030	1,987,793	1,017,959	802,439	136,352	82,054	45,472	781,383	76,375	1,150,310	921,927
Vermont	1,701,217	763,391	367,723	157,030	55,854	56,083	35,637	271,430	30,954	509,744	428,082
Virginia	13,086,581	7,025,345	2,857,652	1,570,789	629,104	390,242	255,805	3,321,243	273,258	2,725,900	3,335,336
Washington	13,434,299	8,467,932	6,309,551	5,022,574	627,136	430,822	203,538	0	0	2,994,704	1,971,663
West Virginia	4,558,622	2,351,858	1,222,148	796,889	207,992	141,056	79,462	612,619	182,081	1,490,087	716,677
Wisconsin	12,106,898	6,911,133	3,001,201	1,958,348	520,161	430,670	204,792	2,899,987	438,135	3,015,338	2,180,427
Wyoming	1,722,869	645,929	238,895	182,547	38,326	66,832	38,511	0	0	666,779	410,161

Source: U.S. Department of Commerce, Bureau of the Census, State Government Finances 1992.
Note: Detail may not add to totals due to rounding.
(a) Total general revenue equals total taxes plus intergovernmental revenue plus charges and miscellaneous revenue.
(b) Total includes other taxes not shown separately in this table.

Table 6.13
STATE EXPENDITURE, BY CHARACTER AND OBJECT AND BY STATE: 1991
(In thousands of dollars)

State	Intergovernmental expenditure	Total	Direct expenditure Current operation	Capital outlay Total	Construction	Land and existing structures	Equipment	Assistance and subsidies	Interest on debt	Insurance benefits and repayments	Exhibit: Total salaries and wages
United States	$186,540,238	$442,264,102	$287,079,068	$47,937,389	$37,647,332	$3,400,729	$6,889,328	$18,875,874	$24,189,437	$64,182,334	$107,621,814
Alabama	2,042,035	6,813,225	4,972,250	678,910	527,346	30,236	121,328	218,070	275,353	668,642	1,947,162
Alaska	930,327	4,010,698	2,707,959	365,307	280,843	10,981	73,483	94,301	505,866	337,265	885,466
Arizona	2,575,296	5,466,074	3,484,829	800,570	614,353	111,728	74,489	255,385	193,531	731,759	1,204,997
Arkansas	1,259,279	3,389,911	2,466,248	338,986	258,348	16,945	63,693	120,370	130,201	334,106	997,278
California	36,387,815	49,252,161	32,508,277	3,274,074	2,283,087	455,854	535,133	735,287	2,195,669	10,538,854	11,457,630
Colorado	1,956,314	5,035,974	3,229,345	622,698	465,020	62,098	95,580	48,183	235,167	900,581	1,449,668
Connecticut	1,993,721	9,121,000	5,440,266	1,321,359	1,147,412	54,129	119,818	477,598	742,603	1,139,174	2,082,785
Delaware	384,710	1,933,362	1,212,827	308,538	248,435	32,087	28,016	56,152	207,242	148,603	569,423
Florida	8,292,704	16,875,075	11,956,156	1,807,440	1,484,262	83,807	239,371	901,964	694,414	1,515,101	5,099,656
Georgia	3,757,866	9,528,465	6,380,976	1,488,340	1,187,435	110,002	190,903	418,587	234,536	1,006,026	2,421,367
Hawaii	104,219	4,405,815	2,763,873	971,210	678,131	166,191	126,888	104,839	230,308	335,585	1,385,987
Idaho	665,736	1,639,404	1,021,293	269,563	209,497	10,814	49,252	36,261	94,574	217,713	364,804
Illinois	6,508,465	18,110,696	10,776,274	2,047,368	1,686,083	110,443	250,842	1,543,634	1,292,228	2,451,192	3,490,889
Indiana	3,779,085	7,955,180	5,963,148	940,820	730,279	47,897	162,644	150,333	320,008	580,871	2,052,795
Iowa	2,116,655	4,703,161	3,310,177	626,185	504,838	28,170	93,177	240,639	146,895	379,265	1,390,328
Kansas	1,406,963	3,718,896	2,591,746	499,100	393,672	3,953	101,475	169,674	31,114	427,262	1,153,534
Kentucky	2,221,186	6,826,587	4,511,472	870,438	676,075	43,819	150,544	270,614	378,733	795,330	1,755,572
Louisiana	2,467,214	8,069,941	5,161,914	861,540	673,549	48,463	139,528	271,679	830,016	944,792	2,190,067
Maine	701,731	2,812,902	1,883,389	221,213	165,153	29,067	26,993	168,978	171,670	367,652	562,359
Maryland	2,682,227	9,894,058	6,149,094	1,348,939	1,151,740	72,870	124,329	508,277	463,139	1,424,609	2,369,448
Massachusetts	4,497,141	15,851,734	10,056,633	1,393,681	1,201,227	82,742	109,712	991,136	1,394,092	2,016,192	2,704,803
Michigan	6,586,640	17,449,942	11,185,120	1,086,024	838,391	67,002	180,631	1,605,194	660,449	2,913,155	4,333,048
Minnesota	4,882,754	7,847,602	5,526,842	809,563	606,066	46,599	156,898	184,429	284,496	1,042,272	2,460,769
Mississippi	1,627,186	3,544,098	2,492,964	453,375	375,071	15,355	62,949	103,375	96,407	397,977	1,012,197
Missouri	2,671,247	6,582,942	4,520,921	632,646	495,234	40,638	96,774	289,709	363,602	776,064	1,911,256
Montana	589,106	1,795,237	1,033,769	312,940	292,532	3,286	17,122	54,925	93,512	300,091	387,709
Nebraska	891,619	2,374,584	1,736,842	352,889	285,200	9,191	58,498	86,305	124,148	74,400	801,288
Nevada	1,037,053	2,398,450	1,137,505	272,119	217,371	10,666	44,082	36,942	137,619	814,265	548,196
New Hampshire	257,088	1,878,075	1,230,067	123,699	98,915	10,842	13,942	51,484	243,709	229,116	447,390
New Jersey	6,145,398	17,105,056	10,934,817	1,641,691	1,348,620	46,663	246,408	184,519	1,412,321	2,931,708	4,098,293
New Mexico	1,552,216	2,974,545	2,046,836	378,458	295,862	20,435	62,161	109,210	116,936	323,105	822,362
New York	20,560,925	43,759,935	28,308,864	5,213,995	4,092,733	457,994	663,268	689,423	3,649,834	5,897,819	9,849,045
North Carolina	5,447,610	9,588,605	6,576,807	1,119,880	837,833	87,995	194,052	436,203	224,668	1,231,047	2,665,523
North Dakota	388,431	1,404,410	988,227	167,208	133,929	810	32,469	31,514	77,812	139,649	418,618
Ohio	7,769,101	20,021,658	10,827,577	1,918,688	1,537,389	56,946	324,353	1,298,396	797,471	5,179,526	4,317,504
Oklahoma	1,931,607	5,335,172	3,469,232	637,464	458,928	54,263	124,273	204,006	273,758	750,712	1,495,726
Oregon	1,600,306	5,648,616	3,367,377	730,252	620,777	9,973	99,502	230,343	465,565	855,079	1,463,690
Pennsylvania	6,896,859	19,812,654	12,155,435	1,788,994	1,533,959	53,316	201,719	1,713,544	943,134	3,211,547	3,588,010
Rhode Island	447,817	2,839,808	1,581,967	323,377	260,373	38,607	24,397	143,967	289,186	501,311	586,657
South Carolina	2,007,109	6,963,235	5,048,748	692,390	503,470	73,697	115,223	166,040	367,849	688,208	2,012,432

STATE EXPENDITURE, BY CHARACTER AND OBJECT AND BY STATE: 1991—Continued

State	Inter-governmental expenditure	Direct expenditure									Exhibit: Total salaries and wages
		Total	Current operation	Capital outlay				Assistance and subsidies	Interest on debt	Insurance benefits and repayments	
				Total	Construction	Land and existing structures	Equipment				
South Dakota	270,004	1,146,509	747,757	171,364	136,535	4,345	30,484	28,996	138,066	60,326	291,688
Tennessee	2,460,175	6,777,612	4,623,892	1,044,358	865,859	79,546	98,953	269,056	198,556	641,750	1,868,810
Texas	8,288,581	21,237,407	14,470,535	2,603,965	1,872,806	322,981	408,178	1,064,316	598,499	2,500,092	4,822,609
Utah	1,060,590	3,047,749	2,100,773	316,883	200,828	16,444	99,611	123,587	140,594	365,912	884,471
Vermont	297,218	1,438,668	1,026,835	109,864	79,287	9,929	20,648	89,207	110,966	101,796	348,751
Virginia	3,492,960	9,859,011	6,911,212	1,221,245	1,067,805	6,280	147,160	493,025	478,340	755,189	3,079,501
Washington	4,263,416	11,402,631	6,527,373	1,487,966	1,050,576	194,457	242,933	693,379	407,388	2,286,525	2,568,852
West Virginia	1,179,220	3,561,336	2,228,843	324,779	261,850	5,322	57,607	134,813	176,898	696,003	736,847
Wisconsin	4,598,923	7,849,518	5,048,288	680,881	478,330	41,646	160,905	537,331	474,970	1,108,048	1,944,613
Wyoming	608,390	1,204,718	675,497	264,153	234,018	3,205	26,930	40,675	75,325	149,068	319,941

Source: U.S. Department of Commerce, Bureau of the Census, State Government Finances 1991.
Note: Detail may not add to totals due to rounding.

Table 6.14
STATE EXPENDITURE, BY CHARACTER AND OBJECT AND BY STATE: 1992
(In thousands of dollars)

State	Inter-governmental expenditure	Total	Direct expenditure — Current operation	Capital outlay — Total	Construction	Land and existing structures	Equipment	Assistance and subsidies	Interest on debt	Insurance benefits and repayments	Exhibit: Total salaries and wages
United States	$201,313,434	$499,580,274	$323,829,720	$50,125,540	$39,000,537	$3,822,488	$7,302,515	$20,784,152	$25,482,343	$79,358,519	$112,685,119
Alabama	2,143,312	7,507,203	5,564,374	664,748	464,013	62,394	138,341	273,050	280,179	724,852	2,097,747
Alaska	1,048,860	4,206,065	2,846,879	389,682	308,641	9,373	71,668	106,839	472,114	390,551	880,018
Arizona	2,996,879	6,098,902	4,027,781	698,704	509,405	108,913	80,386	347,934	193,298	831,185	1,282,892
Arkansas	1,465,060	4,013,433	2,896,061	444,873	353,890	18,642	72,341	125,273	130,387	416,839	1,084,056
California	39,402,316	57,676,834	37,292,266	3,501,400	2,223,144	717,964	560,292	758,994	2,493,551	13,630,623	12,003,701
Colorado	1,969,365	5,522,558	3,659,108	585,807	441,273	54,629	89,905	56,857	226,105	994,681	1,618,721
Connecticut	2,090,932	9,536,269	5,730,088	1,051,739	929,951	40,556	81,232	494,130	724,969	1,535,343	2,096,748
Delaware	390,542	2,084,344	1,277,082	299,643	254,280	19,595	25,768	61,562	227,957	218,100	573,586
Florida	8,405,800	18,683,492	12,404,979	2,266,801	1,572,318	396,448	298,035	1,060,478	740,022	2,211,212	5,270,941
Georgia	3,723,502	10,330,078	7,019,185	1,289,662	1,057,336	73,859	158,467	467,982	280,715	1,272,534	2,387,790
Hawaii	127,640	5,173,696	3,123,408	1,225,593	909,219	207,676	108,698	149,441	276,544	398,710	1,518,237
Idaho	780,742	1,823,365	1,170,495	258,447	210,694	1,730	46,023	42,565	98,592	253,266	467,534
Illinois	6,706,663	20,124,996	12,048,053	2,075,088	1,723,935	61,449	289,704	1,549,229	1,260,329	3,192,297	3,532,678
Indiana	3,677,893	8,662,829	6,523,585	970,708	741,540	48,371	180,797	164,481	354,703	649,352	2,154,978
Iowa	2,160,539	5,066,269	3,496,682	711,905	604,448	27,511	79,946	268,281	132,253	457,148	1,638,938
Kansas	1,440,836	4,043,286	2,706,654	674,153	560,699	13,254	100,200	189,200	40,908	432,371	1,187,891
Kentucky	2,392,289	7,761,910	5,118,942	996,454	822,516	45,994	127,944	297,357	434,180	914,977	2,009,040
Louisiana	2,634,974	9,114,616	6,124,989	911,795	718,991	49,106	143,698	277,636	733,312	1,066,884	2,438,250
Maine	711,798	3,009,714	2,016,805	199,041	163,478	5,332	30,231	168,993	185,569	439,306	603,582
Maryland	2,558,591	10,445,759	6,882,619	922,492	743,935	59,150	119,407	528,406	471,998	1,640,244	2,330,900
Massachusetts	4,047,945	16,319,709	9,927,341	1,574,666	1,349,612	132,535	92,519	949,003	1,430,372	2,438,327	2,823,466
Michigan	6,970,998	18,550,694	12,130,839	1,053,852	814,807	60,853	178,192	1,426,744	637,860	3,301,399	4,498,828
Minnesota	4,733,385	8,792,792	5,876,867	789,399	603,183	42,030	144,186	627,373	294,517	1,204,636	2,503,110
Mississippi	1,765,089	3,996,996	2,852,119	477,498	398,070	19,813	59,615	105,325	115,741	446,313	986,032
Missouri	2,773,013	7,672,836	5,311,631	712,495	535,845	63,087	113,563	321,312	394,592	932,806	1,914,685
Montana	610,277	1,849,257	1,124,492	233,948	209,397	199	24,352	59,340	113,806	317,671	427,380
Nebraska	1,047,544	2,576,224	1,901,333	365,268	297,154	8,418	59,696	93,233	127,914	88,476	836,290
Nevada	1,107,607	2,718,324	1,402,123	333,472	283,341	12,312	37,819	50,116	128,407	804,206	586,980
New Hampshire	293,668	2,577,383	1,797,183	142,341	109,967	20,408	11,966	83,329	297,478	257,052	476,190
New Jersey	7,859,234	21,456,983	13,496,190	2,160,051	1,885,585	78,980	195,486	210,140	1,394,755	4,195,847	4,285,141
New Mexico	1,619,075	3,352,840	2,386,069	349,303	267,072	14,224	68,007	135,659	103,474	378,335	908,125
New York	24,711,442	48,441,915	30,974,869	4,840,656	3,761,733	549,834	529,089	774,309	3,761,704	8,090,377	9,744,357
North Carolina	5,523,219	10,522,295	7,241,610	1,123,760	924,074	8,948	190,738	509,146	273,409	1,374,370	2,707,150
North Dakota	402,727	1,597,888	1,112,798	203,827	170,739	1,444	31,644	39,844	74,478	166,941	434,720
Ohio	7,999,399	22,425,215	11,863,466	2,192,738	1,879,686	47,785	265,267	1,492,076	854,526	6,022,409	4,529,244
Oklahoma	2,166,336	6,016,877	3,996,533	641,984	501,291	22,919	117,774	233,852	261,777	882,731	1,600,527
Oregon	1,613,334	6,365,198	3,725,052	547,176	439,863	6,139	101,174	255,422	804,793	1,032,755	1,558,880
Pennsylvania	8,616,122	26,473,691	17,065,820	2,379,438	1,460,351	60,996	858,091	1,840,608	1,074,788	4,118,037	4,576,908
Rhode Island	500,667	3,467,228	2,054,330	352,347	304,278	17,785	30,284	157,622	306,275	596,654	586,047
South Carolina	2,031,830	7,401,255	5,066,353	886,740	668,763	50,862	167,115	221,927	397,940	828,295	2,107,818

STATE EXPENDITURE, BY CHARACTER AND OBJECT AND BY STATE: 1992—Continued

| State | Inter-governmental expenditure | Total | Current operation | Capital outlay | | | | Assistance and subsidies | Interest on debt | Insurance benefits and repayments | Exhibit: Total salaries and wages |
				Total	Construction	Land and existing structures	Equipment				
South Dakota	280,445	1,284,437	853,259	183,017	148,155	1,687	33,175	33,081	139,731	75,349	337,902
Tennessee	2,288,949	8,116,619	5,658,680	1,192,638	1,023,325	97,442	71,871	290,022	202,680	772,599	1,829,908
Texas	9,365,415	24,528,382	16,947,642	2,600,803	1,921,125	262,231	417,447	1,214,312	615,624	3,150,001	4,994,814
Utah	1,140,214	3,340,575	2,333,785	349,000	237,292	11,052	100,656	136,887	150,072	370,831	944,010
Vermont	303,258	1,538,185	1,092,944	107,501	75,310	4,829	27,362	102,239	113,052	122,449	362,453
Virginia	3,489,912	10,430,735	7,268,259	1,113,277	928,586	4,392	180,299	556,378	478,499	1,014,322	3,032,098
Washington	4,578,587	12,737,771	7,558,592	1,643,209	1,355,996	170,362	116,851	733,118	434,223	2,368,629	2,832,003
West Virginia	1,149,496	4,112,299	2,596,757	370,284	292,137	1,677	76,470	147,077	172,304	825,877	734,489
Wisconsin	4,845,330	8,750,290	5,591,741	771,504	577,228	20,134	174,142	550,527	498,978	1,337,540	2,043,091
Wyoming	650,384	1,274,763	691,008	294,613	262,866	7,165	24,582	45,443	70,889	172,810	304,245

Source: U.S. Department of Commerce, Bureau of the Census, *State Government Finances 1992.*
Note: Detail may not add to totals due to rounding.

Table 6.15
STATE GENERAL EXPENDITURE, BY FUNCTION AND BY STATE: 1991
(In thousands of dollars)

State	Total general expenditure (a)	Education	Public welfare	Highways	Hospitals	Natural resources	Health	Corrections	Financial administration	Employment security administration	Police
United States	$554,900,684	$196,648,164	$124,455,584	$47,037,783	$24,465,507	$10,256,134	$21,411,822	$19,239,732	$9,100,736	$3,238,133	$5,506,357
Alabama	8,050,247	3,508,818	1,356,970	679,371	705,923	152,596	342,850	176,812	104,603	55,583	76,653
Alaska	4,493,231	1,098,062	434,961	501,887	31,609	242,492	142,270	129,827	93,540	23,554	43,067
Arizona	7,287,499	2,807,281	1,034,440	1,094,076	75,230	126,784	282,181	347,329	165,781	27,269	114,981
Arkansas	4,315,084	1,840,883	953,593	459,403	165,407	103,721	128,557	99,568	70,708	32,910	37,021
California	75,033,397	27,217,855	18,990,798	3,888,891	2,377,993	1,659,523	3,427,654	2,982,713	1,453,660	304,384	832,254
Colorado	6,089,428	2,653,866	1,131,940	670,712	187,080	127,586	197,509	256,967	136,465	47,140	40,136
Connecticut	9,806,921	2,334,659	2,068,735	1,019,058	687,910	73,402	341,777	459,799	155,298	70,114	99,256
Delaware	2,151,640	758,217	256,892	257,350	43,596	28,960	103,227	82,709	53,897	7,985	36,500
Florida	23,628,437	9,096,937	4,556,120	1,778,850	491,279	690,528	1,457,379	924,210	403,197	35,797	251,709
Georgia	12,280,305	5,199,458	2,672,806	1,019,880	529,250	256,184	484,224	628,057	113,364	83,873	110,779
Hawaii	4,174,449	1,268,863	478,011	276,620	171,610	109,483	198,137	91,877	77,883	18,112	8,086
Idaho	2,055,374	862,416	285,200	278,597	30,442	88,312	56,787	52,688	36,418	15,707	25,025
Illinois	22,167,969	7,206,280	4,860,235	2,375,834	652,516	278,112	877,710	661,982	393,427	194,882	234,794
Indiana	11,153,394	4,591,219	2,271,725	1,044,286	461,749	138,129	301,396	295,942	173,069	66,246	89,725
Iowa	6,383,519	2,581,131	1,171,292	866,714	457,525	164,599	118,513	150,815	99,903	44,058	46,324
Kansas	4,698,597	1,945,407	816,831	633,246	285,331	149,598	137,029	208,646	90,152	17,646	30,147
Kentucky	8,247,566	3,309,670	1,936,684	826,158	277,843	210,807	195,324	208,584	144,019	45,156	105,093
Louisiana	9,592,363	3,464,812	1,831,817	842,546	697,136	235,753	300,405	258,672	81,568	56,533	114,214
Maine	3,095,441	960,894	877,679	286,969	73,553	75,568	104,482	68,009	50,498	23,009	29,951
Maryland	10,776,479	3,353,612	2,107,771	1,187,070	351,043	228,142	544,860	506,282	222,087	26,985	272,558
Massachusetts	18,265,374	3,299,520	5,784,674	699,095	841,011	146,345	762,023	708,076	360,633	108,139	121,887
Michigan	20,748,884	6,948,119	5,125,229	1,436,775	1,092,771	254,145	1,284,400	815,372	207,374	152,467	191,369
Minnesota	11,688,084	4,501,100	2,375,445	1,011,745	536,654	273,637	356,518	167,194	190,309	82,190	88,390
Mississippi	4,680,374	1,902,486	868,399	496,226	228,720	127,640	146,126	91,211	46,689	34,843	32,496
Missouri	8,478,125	3,454,018	1,771,716	902,654	409,013	195,700	306,142	197,081	134,118	61,821	97,133
Montana	2,058,039	752,810	331,119	272,279	40,536	116,574	74,086	45,601	53,400	10,391	21,146
Nebraska	3,191,803	1,161,219	594,398	434,941	213,008	107,960	112,979	66,098	39,167	21,894	33,610
Nevada	2,556,872	997,787	262,459	242,575	48,677	49,612	56,461	125,696	69,082	21,339	23,751
New Hampshire	1,748,813	404,343	398,299	175,348	43,854	28,822	98,808	43,257	28,919	16,989	24,179
New Jersey	19,398,772	5,830,322	4,185,677	1,372,131	813,156	169,743	500,009	633,398	301,179	70,904	239,138
New Mexico	4,203,656	1,777,914	537,590	364,475	209,973	81,073	161,635	123,341	65,427	45,517	47,139
New York	53,916,492	14,580,528	17,015,247	2,569,144	3,431,920	352,635	1,920,611	2,203,720	845,155	337,336	319,577
North Carolina	13,805,168	6,258,105	2,361,902	1,389,936	613,921	286,206	471,143	526,724	137,648	51,342	142,297
North Dakota	1,653,192		255,754	196,408	63,502	74,635	29,671	15,181	18,744	4,702	6,908
Ohio	22,324,368	8,008,509	5,712,108	2,046,757	1,072,703	242,266	678,654	642,984	480,144	147,724	145,855
Oklahoma	6,270,902	2,597,006	1,263,277	778,673	316,717	101,195	229,586	201,807	143,656	41,931	41,969
Oregon	6,292,079	1,891,945	1,144,097	783,904	333,374	195,083	240,548	237,256	153,990	34,300	63,280
Pennsylvania	22,879,014	6,892,290	6,115,065	2,362,726	1,018,528	386,620	828,192	541,069	337,697	140,677	298,807
Rhode Island	2,749,576	724,989	651,329	194,402	112,944	28,386	141,678	92,086	43,066	22,837	27,030
South Carolina	7,698,481	3,021,894	1,538,128	510,991	487,973	145,065	429,404	314,469	114,342	49,788	83,763

STATE GENERAL EXPENDITURE, BY FUNCTION AND BY STATE: 1991—Continued

State	Total general expenditure (a)	Education	Public welfare	Highways	Hospitals	Natural resources	Health	Corrections	Financial administration	Employment security administration	Police
South Dakota	1,356,187	409,004	212,120	209,354	36,235	58,625	55,827	28,258	22,892	13,023	13,903
Tennessee	8,596,037	3,074,195	1,977,532	1,060,615	391,388	110,973	312,102	393,752	102,002	61,779	62,139
Texas	27,025,896	12,310,342	5,393,405	2,612,497	1,312,703	386,552	802,863	1,064,135	295,281	213,233	206,626
Utah	3,692,298	1,804,567	533,666	300,314	212,173	87,602	116,754	91,610	64,257	41,716	30,003
Vermont	1,606,774	540,115	345,516	169,872	22,971	60,092	41,453	30,319	34,228	9,192	23,164
Virginia	12,389,500	4,868,391	1,814,379	1,696,901	881,507	172,285	430,685	567,343	271,623	70,455	274,623
Washington	13,170,331	5,748,501	2,451,817	1,104,748	437,731	487,506	550,856	309,694	191,007	80,217	164,297
West Virginia	3,996,068	1,721,050	708,271	500,904	87,688	109,860	100,270	40,470	75,370	22,488	25,095
Wisconsin	11,340,393	3,948,375	2,480,359	829,118	364,506	205,552	364,954	307,794	114,535	59,522	42,131
Wyoming	1,637,792	535,714	152,107	324,757	35,625	73,466	65,113	23,248	39,265	12,434	16,379

Source: U.S. Department of Commerce, Bureau of the Census, *State Government Finances 1991.*
Note: Detail may not add to totals due to rounding.

(a) Does not represent state figures because total includes miscellaneous expenditures not shown separately.

Table 6.16
STATE GENERAL EXPENDITURE, BY FUNCTION AND BY STATE: 1992
(In thousands of dollars)

State	Total general expenditure (a)	Education	Public welfare	Highways	Hospitals	Natural resources	Health	Corrections	Financial administration	Employment security administration	Police
United States	$611,921,919	$211,569,798	$156,363,573	$48,746,992	$26,125,186	$10,520,664	$21,998,367	$20,119,779	$9,750,993	$3,702,371	$5,488,853
Alabama	8,788,293	3,570,524	1,853,436	694,874	780,815	151,432	394,119	182,698	111,858	63,001	77,789
Alaska	4,788,127	1,200,990	507,655	547,162	34,411	236,426	170,885	135,804	109,502	27,800	52,292
Arizona	8,235,841	2,929,886	1,811,875	954,360	70,853	148,651	360,340	343,958	181,538	39,638	111,084
Arkansas	5,061,654	2,122,905	1,176,619	576,635	180,485	117,150	179,361	105,591	76,817	35,618	38,512
California	83,360,138	28,284,998	25,247,530	4,374,948	2,609,358	1,519,328	2,649,728	3,226,256	1,533,237	413,145	894,794
Colorado	6,493,768	2,709,235	1,437,575	652,462	166,544	158,367	206,028	265,445	130,703	54,358	47,853
Connecticut	9,957,439	2,506,350	2,434,040	822,768	755,195	62,148	303,026	420,815	186,577	78,031	79,616
Delaware	2,241,388	789,489	291,746	233,778	43,470	28,185	120,462	109,140	59,071	8,528	37,735
Florida	24,851,056	8,814,361	5,333,949	2,175,460	507,514	840,390	1,416,490	1,036,611	430,546	46,874	224,694
Georgia	12,781,046	5,184,261	3,313,204	875,483	531,163	244,118	494,102	601,073	114,917	100,635	101,449
Hawaii	4,902,626	1,344,015	597,925	359,249	183,888	121,579	226,619	104,655	78,360	11,884	8,503
Idaho	2,315,712	986,673	352,315	290,629	32,677	100,764	61,743	57,671	38,338	13,620	28,782
Illinois	23,639,362	7,295,009	6,261,356	2,461,626	668,792	261,464	935,684	625,412	412,731	212,024	232,584
Indiana	11,691,370	4,652,761	2,621,020	1,078,475	519,914	135,944	333,319	321,025	180,005	86,357	90,726
Iowa	6,711,337	2,649,186	1,305,649	949,347	473,312	180,637	116,473	166,751	83,524	46,741	44,335
Kansas	5,051,751	2,197,864	890,373	649,159	290,204	125,394	148,918	189,460	97,030	20,482	34,108
Kentucky	9,235,218	3,572,415	2,382,835	933,960	290,631	236,480	203,176	209,874	162,776	42,236	105,438
Louisiana	10,682,706	3,687,009	2,544,821	879,977	729,533	237,919	342,706	275,992	114,135	63,955	119,440
Maine	3,231,655	1,010,112	1,003,035	272,669	63,164	79,694	104,129	67,339	53,456	26,737	25,893
Maryland	11,011,767	3,448,754	2,677,218	971,632	336,625	266,984	571,483	555,635	220,158	30,555	179,805
Massachusetts	17,811,534	3,271,297	5,302,997	1,020,836	781,637	123,079	792,392	645,378	406,780	98,769	131,252
Michigan	21,839,665	7,415,632	5,574,552	1,482,396	1,104,211	238,690	1,343,071	854,828	306,265	183,048	200,145
Minnesota	12,321,541	4,556,323	3,022,239	1,043,000	542,849	282,290	392,684	193,832	180,577	82,643	94,852
Mississippi	5,216,887	1,993,166	1,210,496	538,749	241,776	125,371	153,976	87,310	41,567	41,358	36,894
Missouri	9,513,043	3,529,312	2,516,484	958,218	388,183	213,410	333,158	201,873	134,836	71,451	97,446
Montana	2,107,991	770,502	333,833	283,277	38,447	94,666	84,636	37,479	66,372	8,841	23,040
Nebraska	3,535,292	1,258,940	706,022	442,543	235,982	107,954	143,469	73,336	43,475	23,123	35,646
Nevada	2,952,987	1,113,095	449,175	295,087	50,256	52,735	55,698	127,967	87,975	25,346	28,513
New Hampshire	2,452,808	467,794	937,208	192,968	37,370	32,175	101,077	45,698	36,555	19,201	24,196
New Jersey	24,109,399	7,017,892	6,048,477	1,835,212	921,095	224,852	474,848	659,074	278,788	93,981	233,751
New Mexico	4,593,580	1,919,305	710,830	383,802	233,171	79,409	181,599	128,427	67,601	45,679	51,487
New York	60,869,111	17,972,006	20,307,423	2,478,453	3,377,503	332,618	1,978,690	2,008,174	849,205	363,645	300,169
North Carolina	14,671,144	6,312,907	2,948,994	1,448,093	640,018	279,626	513,656	551,411	138,372	66,693	148,812
North Dakota	1,833,674	685,148	338,256	228,278	55,509	71,042	39,384	16,118	21,705	7,029	8,018
Ohio	24,106,118	8,489,030	6,493,661	2,286,803	1,142,110	241,823	738,828	691,342	503,461	166,990	154,244
Oklahoma	7,062,982	3,026,061	1,539,537	815,685	333,028	105,807	262,327	200,789	148,949	45,358	44,241
Oregon	6,841,896	1,935,358	1,326,612	672,363	382,678	216,263	290,155	209,026	225,465	43,918	71,087
Pennsylvania	30,338,335	9,973,242	9,599,604	2,191,425	1,406,827	363,354	993,155	588,169	400,250	156,024	308,727
Rhode Island	3,331,245	813,449	771,274	181,412	104,803	23,285	146,268	101,022	41,826	28,236	23,513
South Carolina	7,968,594	3,070,613	1,617,805	530,144	564,637	133,692	402,620	297,225	121,505	54,757	81,591
South Dakota	1,489,533	430,517	290,455	210,619	42,337	66,853	45,020	29,928	23,658	14,174	13,524
Tennessee	9,632,969	3,100,593	2,816,658	1,134,464	417,108	154,836	318,768	380,028	97,310	69,206	65,338
Texas	30,743,796	13,283,188	7,410,273	2,472,785	1,581,840	416,612	894,568	1,336,280	337,310	238,138	215,192
Utah	4,057,498	1,950,521	667,567	324,258	232,405	92,095	110,084	96,951	71,752	33,748	32,865
Vermont	1,690,440	562,724	380,804	176,313	22,337	55,682	42,225	33,664	29,953	9,365	27,325

STATE GENERAL EXPENDITURE, BY FUNCTION AND BY STATE: 1992—Continued

State	Total general expenditure (a)	Education	Public welfare	Highways	Hospitals	Natural resources	Health	Corrections	Financial administration	Employment security administration	Police
Virginia	12,694,076	4,930,767	2,094,146	1,521,447	959,503	163,418	464,732	579,591	279,584	78,057	258,671
Washington	14,724,379	6,224,137	2,809,043	1,154,322	499,173	560,473	763,019	544,770	181,985	106,624	152,133
West Virginia	4,395,674	1,753,193	1,094,068	510,002	89,277	103,038	107,815	36,491	94,808	24,510	23,850
Wisconsin	12,258,080	4,191,273	2,809,436	853,627	392,025	238,610	439,166	338,479	123,605	68,484	53,072
Wyoming	1,725,394	595,016	191,468	325,758	38,549	73,852	52,490	23,914	34,150	11,756	13,827

Source: U.S. Department of Commerce, Bureau of the Census, *State Government Finances 1992.*
Note: Detail may not add to totals due to rounding.

(a) Does not represent sum of state figures because total includes miscellaneous expenditures not shown separately.

Table 6.17
STATE DEBT OUTSTANDING AT END OF FISCAL YEAR, BY STATE: 1991
(In thousands of dollars, except per capita amounts)

State	Total	Per capita	Long-term Total	Full faith and credit	Nonguaranteed	Short-term	Net long-term (a) Total	Full faith and credit
United States	$345,554,047	$1,374	$342,164,446	$84,749,448	$257,414,998	$3,389,601	$140,405,030	$73,220,302
Alabama	4,213,842	1,031	4,213,694	1,065,553	3,148,141	148	1,791,929	1,014,383
Alaska	5,290,972	9,282	5,287,972	606,165	4,681,807	3,000	701,717	210,854
Arizona	2,539,685	677	2,539,685	0	2,539,685	0	2,048,237	0
Arkansas	1,764,450	744	1,763,013	67,085	1,695,928	1,437	280,882	67,085
California	31,956,108	1,052	31,956,108	7,940,155	24,015,953	0	13,485,135	7,883,309
Colorado	2,659,408	788	2,659,408	28,925	2,630,483	0	290,629	28,925
Connecticut	13,006,152	3,952	12,430,852	5,735,016	6,695,836	575,300	5,508,926	4,977,516
Delaware	3,215,375	4,728	3,203,268	495,424	2,707,844	12,107	866,345	493,421
Florida	11,083,642	835	11,074,300	1,291,595	9,782,705	9,342	5,923,221	574,866
Georgia	3,651,646	551	3,651,646	2,361,120	1,290,526	0	2,490,978	2,318,182
Hawaii	4,201,628	3,702	4,156,806	2,274,846	1,881,960	44,822	2,873,897	2,236,678
Idaho	1,122,423	1,080	1,122,423	0	1,122,423	0	170,913	0
Illinois	18,238,449	1,580	18,233,523	5,388,300	12,845,223	4,926	6,229,018	5,134,512
Indiana	4,623,993	824	4,617,738	0	4,617,738	6,255	1,759,230	0
Iowa	1,620,256	580	1,611,235	0	1,611,235	9,021	384,516	0
Kansas	336,964	135	336,964	0	336,964	0	260,079	0
Kentucky	6,024,486	1,623	6,024,486	57,705	5,966,781	0	3,183,120	4,171
Louisiana	10,728,679	2,523	10,628,963	3,468,991	7,159,972	99,716	4,486,767	2,874,128
Maine	2,584,646	2,093	2,488,657	395,420	2,093,237	95,989	424,727	393,847
Maryland	7,527,848	1,549	7,527,848	2,043,240	5,484,608	0	3,731,966	2,034,302
Massachusetts	21,101,790	3,519	20,955,674	9,737,527	11,218,147	146,116	10,375,767	9,629,801
Michigan	10,109,004	1,079	10,107,977	667,000	9,440,977	1,027	2,075,297	667,000
Minnesota	3,940,713	889	3,940,713	1,574,056	2,366,657	0	1,655,689	1,308,581
Mississippi	1,412,925	545	1,412,925	670,521	742,404	0	578,054	538,268
Missouri	5,775,342	1,120	5,718,932	780,115	4,938,817	56,410	941,751	686,984
Montana	1,611,458	1,994	1,594,540	70,050	1,524,490	16,918	292,913	70,050
Nebraska	1,595,738	1,002	1,595,550	0	1,595,550	188	367,785	0
Nevada	1,708,027	1,330	1,703,880	749,210	954,670	4,147	926,501	732,484
New Hampshire	4,126,744	3,735	4,126,744	640,139	3,486,605	0	686,393	506,069
New Jersey	19,039,169	2,454	19,021,915	3,140,616	15,881,299	17,254	8,559,241	3,135,986
New Mexico	1,751,531	1,131	1,741,587	105,709	1,635,878	9,944	307,491	105,709
New York	51,804,160	2,869	50,607,760	6,459,704	44,148,056	1,196,400	22,417,865	4,561,189
North Carolina	3,489,720	518	3,489,720	577,545	2,912,175	0	890,598	565,070
North Dakota	963,767	1,518	960,447	0	960,447	3,320	47,350	0
Ohio	11,367,331	1,039	11,275,705	2,754,040	8,521,665	91,626	4,623,549	2,754,040
Oklahoma	3,729,656	1,175	3,729,129	20,945	3,708,184	527	1,915,286	20,945
Oregon	6,450,578	2,208	6,360,578	5,403,689	956,889	90,000	1,941,744	1,665,327
Pennsylvania	11,640,349	973	11,246,589	4,742,428	6,504,161	393,760	6,296,719	4,705,105
Rhode Island	4,392,975	4,375	4,142,822	434,079	3,708,743	250,153	1,063,203	434,079
South Carolina	4,189,096	1,177	4,069,096	828,838	3,240,258	120,000	2,556,924	707,960
South Dakota	1,753,731	2,495	1,753,565	0	1,753,565	166	252,412	0
Tennessee	2,789,937	563	2,722,644	688,662	2,033,982	67,293	926,802	688,109
Texas	7,686,504	443	7,686,395	3,419,503	4,266,892	109	4,125,060	1,569,735
Utah	1,911,495	1,080	1,900,618	239,295	1,661,323	10,877	316,764	215,043
Vermont	1,485,874	2,621	1,483,356	392,300	1,091,056	2,518	450,006	392,300
Virginia	6,500,254	1,034	6,499,853	476,436	6,023,417	401	1,108,330	476,436
Washington	6,519,718	1,299	6,519,274	3,983,296	2,535,978	444	4,051,115	3,938,140
West Virginia	2,769,644	1,538	2,721,704	420,000	2,301,704	47,940	1,142,187	410,367
Wisconsin	6,624,538	1,337	6,624,538	2,553,545	4,070,993	0	2,554,676	2,488,686
Wyoming	921,627	2,004	921,627	660	920,967	0	65,326	660

Source: U.S. Department of Commerce, Bureau of the Census, *State Government Finances 1991*.
Note: Detail may not add due to rounding.

(a) Long-term debt outstanding minus long-term debt offsets.

Table 6.18
STATE DEBT OUTSTANDING AT END OF FISCAL YEAR, BY STATE: 1992
(In thousands of dollars, except per capita amounts)

State	Total	Per capita	Long-term Total	Long-term Full faith and credit	Long-term Nonguaranteed	Short-term	Net long-term (a) Total	Net long-term (a) Full faith and credit
United States	$371,900,683	$1,461	$368,951,380	$96,598,016	$272,353,364	$2,949,303	$158,896,895	$85,258,416
Alabama...........	4,128,724	998	4,128,697	1,026,439	3,102,258	27	1,709,054	952,946
Alaska.............	4,941,602	8,418	4,935,602	595,495	4,340,107	6,000	637,412	154,952
Arizona...........	2,848,842	743	2,848,842	0	2,848,842	0	2,328,708	0
Arkansas	1,942,169	810	1,938,018	155,370	1,782,648	4,151	365,026	155,370
California..........	37,823,709	1,225	37,342,433	11,516,745	25,825,688	481,276	18,826,800	11,425,581
Colorado	2,977,116	858	2,977,116	25,527	2,951,589	0	253,026	25,527
Connecticut	11,956,502	3,644	11,951,202	6,566,526	5,384,676	5,300	6,207,791	5,665,650
Delaware	3,541,920	5,141	3,535,869	511,736	3,024,133	6,051	997,658	467,125
Florida	12,295,486	912	12,294,744	1,415,095	10,879,649	742	6,652,382	642,635
Georgia............	4,470,781	662	4,470,781	2,885,970	1,584,811	0	3,004,472	2,831,475
Hawaii	4,686,763	4,040	4,641,560	2,328,546	2,313,014	45,203	3,240,031	2,319,514
Idaho	1,292,022	1,211	1,291,987	0	1,291,987	35	164,176	0
Illinois.............	18,741,630	1,611	18,733,734	5,701,790	13,031,944	7,896	6,368,450	5,273,520
Indiana	5,171,670	913	5,158,423	0	5,158,423	13,247	1,632,139	0
Iowa	1,883,987	670	1,872,632	0	1,872,632	11,355	652,817	0
Kansas	485,787	193	485,787	0	485,787	0	411,001	0
Kentucky	6,618,526	1,763	6,618,526	44,155	6,574,371	0	3,846,222	0
Louisiana	9,994,058	2,331	9,921,756	3,527,356	6,394,400	72,302	4,300,862	2,959,725
Maine	2,637,052	2,135	2,637,052	429,680	2,207,372	0	456,295	428,371
Maryland	8,334,681	1,698	8,334,681	2,182,620	6,152,061	0	4,072,292	2,175,548
Massachusetts	24,008,036	4,003	23,734,212	11,427,721	12,306,491	273,824	11,958,134	11,206,039
Michigan	10,356,583	1,097	10,353,207	1,185,200	9,168,007	3,376	3,221,259	1,185,200
Minnesota	4,143,203	925	4,143,203	1,634,327	2,508,876	0	1,704,889	1,363,307
Mississippi	1,625,737	622	1,625,737	676,152	949,585	0	596,034	547,526
Missouri	6,301,143	1,213	6,230,943	804,225	5,426,718	70,200	1,036,805	717,817
Montana...........	1,867,677	2,267	1,855,308	205,066	1,650,242	12,369	429,867	205,066
Nebraska	1,754,223	1,092	1,754,059	0	1,754,059	164	340,739	0
Nevada	1,934,144	1,458	1,933,165	872,601	1,060,564	979	1,081,418	856,356
New Hampshire	4,313,471	3,883	4,313,471	683,694	3,629,777	0	715,880	528,889
New Jersey..........	19,786,201	2,540	19,771,722	3,316,391	16,455,331	14,479	9,248,855	3,309,615
New Mexico.........	1,605,048	1,015	1,595,787	92,591	1,503,196	9,261	418,423	92,591
New York	55,868,432	3,083	54,969,282	8,288,205	46,681,077	899,150	25,770,332	6,445,206
North Carolina	3,819,102	558	3,819,102	668,124	3,150,978	0	1,037,179	665,341
North Dakota	1,027,158	1,615	1,027,158	0	1,027,158	0	37,205	0
Ohio	12,193,154	1,107	12,105,467	2,826,720	9,278,747	87,687	4,778,070	2,826,720
Oklahoma	3,656,622	1,138	3,656,193	16,285	3,639,908	429	1,916,735	16,285
Oregon	6,295,080	2,115	6,295,080	5,245,590	1,049,490	0	2,155,672	1,855,787
Pennsylvania	12,962,120	1,079	12,448,794	4,840,163	7,608,631	513,326	5,273,219	4,827,365
Rhode Island	5,150,733	5,125	5,067,269	1,182,504	3,884,765	83,464	1,923,701	1,182,504
South Carolina	4,684,627	1,300	4,529,277	845,143	3,684,134	155,350	2,832,846	781,800
South Dakota	1,889,222	2,657	1,888,622	0	1,888,622	600	200,399	0
Tennessee	2,806,366	559	2,653,939	624,390	2,029,549	152,427	813,007	614,994
Texas..............	8,001,178	453	8,001,146	3,417,302	4,583,844	32	4,732,797	1,875,762
Utah	2,153,233	1,188	2,139,812	330,900	1,808,912	13,421	450,956	313,474
Vermont	1,542,571	2,706	1,539,321	426,195	1,113,126	3,250	497,815	426,195
Virginia............	7,402,641	1,161	7,402,272	514,796	6,887,476	369	1,051,352	514,796
Washington	7,191,988	1,400	7,190,427	4,436,506	2,753,921	1,561	4,496,276	4,375,582
West Virginia	2,594,324	1,432	2,594,324	371,600	2,222,724	0	1,078,496	367,419
Wisconsin...........	7,298,851	1,458	7,298,851	2,752,575	4,546,276	0	2,895,126	2,678,841
Wyoming	894,788	1,920	894,788	0	894,788	0	76,795	0

Source: U.S. Department of Commerce, Bureau of the Cenus, *State Government Finances 1992*.
Note: Detail may not add to totals due to rounding.

(a) Long-term debt outstanding minus long-term debt offsets.

Trends in State Taxation, 1992-93

State tax trends followed familiar business-cycle pattern except for excises taxes — as many states raised at least one of three major excise taxes.

by Ronald Alt

State tax trends during the past two years followed patterns typical of the normal economic business cycle. During recessions, state revenue typically falls while demand for many services rises. In order to meet balanced budget requirements, it is not surprising to see state policy-makers increasing taxes. On the other hand, strong revenue growth brought on by an economic recovery can lead some states to cut taxes.

The economic recession of 1990 and the slow recovery left state budgets weak, and as a result, many states raised income and sales taxes rates during the first years of the 1990s. Although some of these tax increases expired during 1992 or 1993, many states raised taxes during this period because of continued economic weakness or to fund new programs. But, as the economy showed signs of strength in 1993, fewer states increased tax rates.

A different trend developed for excise taxes as numerous states raised at least one of the three major excise taxes during this period, while very few states reduced rates. This can be attributed to increased spending on various projects funded by these tax sources (i.e., highways, health care). Also, the per unit bases on which excise taxes are levied require state officials to periodically increase the rate so that revenues from the sources can keep pace with inflation.

Individual Income Taxes

Only six states made any changes to their individual income tax structures to raise additional revenues. Kansas revised its individual income tax structure changing from a two-rate system (4.5 and 5.95 percent) to a three-rate system (4.4, 7.5, and 7.75 percent). Maine imposed a temporary surcharge of 5 percent to 10 percent for tax years beginning in 1991 and 1992. Maryland added a temporary fifth bracket, which will sunset beginning with tax year 1995, that imposes a 6 percent tax rate on incomes of more than $100,000. New York once again suspended the scheduled drop in the top marginal rate until April 1993. Ohio added an additional tax bracket equal to 7.5 percent of taxable income greater than $200,000. Pennsylvania permitted a scheduled drop in the income tax rate from 3.1 percent to 2.8 percent to become effective on July 1, 1992 (a blend rate of 2.95 could be used for the entire year). Rhode Island, which levies its tax as a percentage of federal liability, temporarily implemented a two rate structure. For the 1993 tax year, the state tax will be calculated as 27.5 percent of federal liability up to $15,000, and 32 percent of the liability over this amount. For 1992, a blend rate of 29.75 percent can be used. This provision expires for the 1994 tax year.

Eight states made some type of change to their individual income tax structure during 1993, three of those changes being tax reductions. Nebraska was the only state to make substantial revisions to its income tax structure. State lawmakers replaced the personal exemption allowances with tax credits. The net effect was to increase the progressivity of the tax to assist poorer taxpayers while raising additional revenue.

Several states implemented previously approved tax cuts, and two states suspended

Ronald Alt is a senior research associate for the Federation of Tax Administrators.

scheduled tax reductions. New York once again suspended the scheduled reduction in the top marginal rate until April 1, 1994, and Illinois continued indefinitely a higher personal income tax rate. Meanwhile, Maine permitted a temporary surcharge to expire beginning with the 1993 tax year. Rhode Island and Vermont, which apply their income tax as a percentage of federal liability, implemented a scheduled tax decrease returning the rates to their pre-1992 levels. Both states had imposed a multi-tiered rate structure where higher income taxpayers applied a higher percentage to their federal liability. In addition, the Rhode Island tax administrator, as required by state law, administratively adjusted some of the tax rate downward for the 1993 tax year to account for the federal tax increases enacted with the Omnibus Reconciliation Act of 1993. The impact was revenue neutral.

Two other states made changes to their income tax structures without affecting the nominal rate structure. Arizona increased the personal exemption amount from $2,100 to $2,300 and accelerated the increase in the allowable medical expense deductions. In tax year 1993, medical expenses greater than 2 percent of adjusted gross income (AGI) are deductible, while all expenses in 1994 will be deductible. Formerly, the full deduction was not to be reached until 1995. Also, Missouri capped the federal taxes paid deduction amount at $10,000 ($5,000 for single filers).

Corporate Income Taxes

In 1992, four states made changes to their corporate income tax structure with three of these changes being scheduled tax reductions approved by previous legislatures. Colorado permitted a scheduled rate reduction to go into effect for tax years beginning after July 1, 1992, by reducing the top marginal rate from 5.2 percent to 5.1 percent. North Carolina permitted a scheduled reduction in the surtax, decreasing from 4 percent to 3 percent. Another scheduled reduction was a drop in the West Virginia corporate tax rate from 9.3 percent to 9.15 percent for the tax years beginning July 1, 1991, and another drop to 9 percent for the tax year beginning in July 1, 1992. In 1992, the

Kansas Legislature lowered the corporate tax rate from 4.5 percent to 4 percent, while raising the surtax on income greater than $50,000 to 3.35 percent.

Ten states made changes to their corporate income tax structure in 1993, but only two states enacted legislation that changed the statutory rate. Effective September 1, 1993, Missouri raised its flat corporate income tax rate from 5 percent to 6.25 percent. New Hampshire lowered the income tax rate from 8 percent to 7.5 percent for tax periods ending on or after July 1, 1993; and 7 percent after July 1, 1994. In addition, the state also implemented a 0.25 percent business enterprise tax imposed on total compensation, interest and dividends paid by a business.

Illinois extended indefinitely the corporate tax rate at 3 percent (scheduled to fall to 2.75 percent), and New York temporarily extended the 15 percent surcharge on corporate income tax liability. New Mexico imposed a temporary 18 percent surcharge on corporations with net income greater than $1 million. California repealed the filing fee for multi-national corporations using total U.S. income (water's edge) instead of apportioning worldwide income (worldwide combination). This eliminated the domestic disclosure spreadsheet requirement for multi-national corporations.

Three states acted to decrease the effective tax on corporations. Rhode Island accelerated the expiration of an 11 percent surtax scheduled to expire in 1996 to the 1994 tax year. Colorado permitted a scheduled drop in the corporate income tax rate so that for tax years beginning on or after July 1, 1993, the tax rate is a flat 5 percent on all taxable income. North Carolina permitted a scheduled reduction in the surtax, which fell from 3 percent to 2 percent for 1993. The surtax will fall to 1 percent for the 1994 tax year.

In Montana, a citizen's petition forced state officials to suspend a legislatively approved increase in the corporate income tax. The law would have imposed a two-rate income tax on corporations of 7.08 percent of the first $500,000, and 7.57 percent of the rest for tax year 1993. In 1994 and thereafter, the rates would fall to 6.75 percent and 7.25 percent.

Higher rates would apply for corporations making a water's edge election. However, voters must approve this tax change in the next general election before it can be implemented.

Sales Taxes

Five states made changes to their general sales tax rates in 1992. Iowa raised the rate from 4 percent to 5 percent; Kansas increased the rate from 4.25 percent to 4.9 percent; Mississippi increased its rate from 6 percent to 7 percent; and Tennessee increased its rate from 5.5 percent to 6 percent. New Jersey was the only state to lower its general sales tax rate during 1992, when state officials lowered the rate one percentage point to 6 percent.

While only three states actually changed their general sales tax rates in 1993, legislation affecting the sales tax was enacted in nine states. Five states referred tax proposals to the voters. Voters in three states — Michigan, Montana and Oregon — rejected the tax increases. (The Montana and Oregon measures would have enacted new sales taxes while also making other tax changes.) Meanwhile, California residents approved the permanent extension of a 0.5 percent sales tax increase, and Arkansas residents will vote in November 1994 on whether to impose a 0.125 percent additional sales tax.

The Tennessee and Maine legislatures approved provisions making permanent a temporary 1 percent sales tax increase that was scheduled to expire in 1993. The sales tax rate in both states will remain indefinitely at 6 percent. Louisiana increased the sales tax applicable to food by 1 percent, raising it to the same rate applied to other tangible goods, and Vermont permitted a temporary 1 percent sales tax increase to expire on schedule July 1, 1993, before permanently re-imposing it September 1.

Motor Fuels

Ten states made changes to their motor fuel tax rates during 1992. However, the median tax rate for gasoline, diesel and gasohol remained unchanged at 18 cents per gallon. States raising their tax rate on gasoline include Alabama, a 5-cent-per-gallon increase; California, 1 cent; Connecticut, 2 cents; Kansas, 1 cent; Maryland, 5 cents; Missouri, 2 cents; Nevada, 2.5 cents; and Oregon, 2 cents.

Eight states have variable tax rates that are subject to periodic adjustments depending on current market conditions and state revenue needs. Four of these states impose a tax based upon the average wholesale price, with the gallonage rate adjusted periodically according to the average price. The actual tax rates are 9 percent in Kentucky, 10 percent in Massachusetts, 13 percent in Rhode Island, and 17 cents per gallon plus 7 percent in North Carolina. The current rates are at the statutory minimum amounts in Massachusetts and Rhode Island. Meanwhile, the tax rates in Michigan, Nebraska, Ohio and Wisconsin are adjusted annually based on a formula taking into account highway maintenance costs and the volume of sales. Only two states administratively adjusted their motor fuel tax rate through statutory procedures in 1992. The excise tax rate in Nebraska changed each quarter, reaching a high of 24.6 cents per gallon in the current quarter. North Carolina lowered the rate to 21.9 cents per gallon for the second half of 1992, before increasing it to the current rate. While the motor fuel excise tax rate in Wisconsin was calculated to increase 0.3 cents per gallon in 1992, the Legislature froze the rate at 22.2 cents per gallon through April 1, 1993.

All states except Connecticut, Maryland and Oregon made similar changes to the excise tax rates on diesel fuel and gasohol. Connecticut decreased its diesel fuel tax rate by 8 cents per gallon. In May 1992, Maryland raised its diesel fuel tax rate to 19.25 cents per gallon. Meanwhile, Oregon reduced the tax rate on gasohol to 5 cents below the motor fuel rate in January 1992.

In 1993, motor fuel tax rates were changed in 12 states, increasing the median state tax rate for gasoline and gasohol. The median tax rate for gasoline increased from 18 cents to 19 cents per gallon, while gasohol increased by one-half cent from 18 cents to 18.5 cents per gallon. The median state diesel fuel tax rate remained at 18 cents per gallon.

Six states enacted new legislation raising the state gasoline excise tax rate. They include

Delaware, a 3-cent-per-gallon increase; Montana, 4 cents; New Mexico, 6 cents; Rhode Island, 2 cents; and West Virginia, 5 cents. In addition, North Dakota passed legislation authorizing the tax commissioner to adjust the fuel tax rate upward by as much as 2 cents per gallon if necessary to match federal highway funding. On December 1, 1993, the excise tax rate increased from 17 cents to 18 cents per gallon. This adjustment procedure will sunset after December 31, 1995. Meanwhile, three states implemented tax rate increases enacted during previous legislative sessions. They are: California, 1 cent per gallon; Connecticut, 2 cents; and Ohio, 1 cent.

In addition to North Dakota, only three other states with adjustable tax rates made administrative adjustments to their motor fuel tax rates during 1993. The tax rate in Nebraska changed each quarter, falling to 22.7 cents during the second quarter before increasing to its current rate of 26 cents per gallon. The tax rate in North Carolina fell to the current rate of 22 cents per gallon on July 1993. Wisconsin raised the motor fuel tax rate by 1 cent per gallon in April.

All these states, except one, made corresponding changes to their gasohol tax rate. Effective August 31, 1993, Oregon repealed the lower tax rate applicable to gasohol. This leaves only seven states with a preferential rate for gasohol. They are: Alaska, Iowa, Minnesota, New Jersey, South Carolina, South Dakota and Wyoming.

In four states, the changes applied to diesel fuel differed from those made to gasoline. Connecticut and Delaware did not apply the tax increase to diesel fuel. Maryland, which did not increase its gasoline tax, raised the diesel fuel rate by 2.5 cents per gallon. Montana added an another 0.75 cents per gallon tax on diesel fuel only, in addition to the 4 cent increase applicable to all motor fuels.

Tobacco

Only six states and the District of Columbia increased their cigarette tax rates in 1992, raising the median state tax rate to 24.5 cents per pack: District of Columbia, a 20-cent-per-pack increase; Maryland, 20 cents; Massachusetts,

25 cents as approved by the voters; Minnesota, 5 cents; Montana, 1.26 cents; Ohio, 6 cents; and Wisconsin, 20 cents.

Two more states enacted an excise tax on other tobacco products (OTP) in 1992, bringing the total to 40 states. Ohio and Rhode Island implemented new OTP taxes with a rate of 17 percent and 20 percent of the wholesale price, respectively. Montana temporarily imposed a 7 percent surtax through August 1993. Meanwhile, California and New Hampshire administratively adjusted the OTP rate down.

Sixteen states made changes to their cigarette excise tax rate during 1993, raising the median state tax rate from 24.5 cents to 25.75 cents per pack. All but two of these changes were the result of legislation approved during the year. Arkansas implemented a temporary increase from 22 cents to 34.5 cents per pack, effective February 1-June 30, 1993. As of July 1, 1993, the tax rate is 31.5 cents per pack. Montana permitted a temporary surtax to expire on August 14, 1993, when the rate fell by 1.26 cents.

During 1993, legislatures in 13 states and the District of Columbia approved cigarette tax increases. They are California, 2 cents per pack; Connecticut, 2 cents; Illinois, 14 cents; Maine, 2 cents; Missouri, 4 cents; Nebraska, 7 cents; New Mexico, 6 cents; New York, 17 cents; North Dakota, 15 cents; Oregon, 10 cents; Rhode Island, 7 cents; Washington, 20 cents; and the District of Columbia, 15 cents. Hawaii converted its ad valorem (percentage) based tax to a tax applied per package. This resulted in an increase from an average per package rate of 51 cents to a fixed 60 cents per pack.

Two more states enacted OTP excise taxes in 1993, bringing the total to 42 states. In October, Illinois and Missouri began collecting OTP taxes at the rates of 20 percent and 10 percent of wholesale value, respectively.

Meanwhile, seven states made changes to their OTP tax rates in 1993. Three states enacted legislation to increase their tax rates. They are New York, from 15 percent to 20 percent; North Dakota, from 22 percent to 28 percent; and Washington, from 64.9 percent to 74.9 percent. Arkansas implemented a previously approved legislative change raising the tax rate from 16 percent to 25 percent in February, then falling to 23 percent on July 1, 1993. Montana permitted a scheduled decrease in the tax rate from 13.38 to 12.5 percent after August 14, 1993.

Two states have provisions whereby the tax administrator must adjust the tax rate to make it equivalent to the cigarette tax in terms of a percentage of price. In California, the Board of Equalization calculates the OTP tax annually; it lowered the tax rate from 26.82 percent to 23.03 percent on July 1, 1993. The New Hampshire tax commissioner must adjust the OTP rate twice a year. In July 1993, the New Hampshire OTP rate fell from 21.5 to 20.8 percent. And on January 1, 1994, the tax rate was increased from 20.8 percent to 26.9 percent. The tax rate in both states will be adjusted again on July 1, 1994.

Alcoholic Beverages

In 1992, only four states changed their tax rates on alcoholic beverages, leaving the median state excise tax rates unchanged. The median rates are $3.25 per gallon for distilled spirits, 73 cents per gallon for wine and 18 cents per gallon for beer. New Jersey permitted a scheduled increase to become effective and eliminated the wholesale sales tax; Ohio raised all alcoholic beverage tax rates on January 1, 1993; the District of Columbia raised the sales tax rate applicable to off-premise sales by two percentage points; and Montana imposed a temporary 7 percent surtax.

Few changes were made to alcoholic beverage excise tax rates in 1993, leaving the median state tax rate for distilled spirits and wine unchanged. However, the median tax rate for beer increased from 18 cents to 18.5 cents per gallon.

New Mexico was the only state to raise the excise taxes applicable to all three beverage types. Effective July 1, 1993, the tax rate on spirits increased from $1.04 to $1.50 per liter ($5.68 per gallon); wine from $0.25 to $0.34 per liter ($1.29 per gallon); and beer from 18 cents to 35 cents per gallon. The rate will increase again on July 1, 1994, to $1.60 per liter for spirits, 45 cents per liter for wine and 41 cents per gallon for beer. Washington was the only other state to raise alcoholic beverage taxes, imposing an additional 96 cents per barrel tax applicable to beer.

Table 6.19
AGENCIES ADMINISTERING MAJOR STATE TAXES
(As of January 1994)

State or other jurisdiction	Income	Sales	Gasoline	Motor vehicle
Alabama	Dept. of Revenue	Dept. of Revenue	Dept. of Revenue	Dept. of Revenue
Alaska	Dept. of Revenue	. . .	Dept. of Revenue	Dept. of Public Safety
Arizona	Dept. of Revenue	Dept. of Revenue	Dept. of Transportation	Dept. of Transportation
Arkansas	Dept. of Fin. & Admin.	Dept. of Fin. & Admin.	Dept. of Fin. & Admin.	Dept. of Fin. & Admin.
California	Franchise Tax Bd.	Bd. of Equalization	Bd. of Equalization	Dept. of Motor Vehicles
Colorado	Dept. of Revenue	Dept. of Revenue	Dept. of Revenue	Dept. of Revenue
Connecticut	Dept. of Revenue & Serv.	Dept. of Revenue & Serv.	Dept. of Revenue & Serv.	Dept. of Motor Vehicles
Delaware	Div. of Revenue	. . .	Dept. of Public Safety	Dept. of Public Safety
Florida	Dept. of Revenue	Dept. of Revenue	Dept. of Revenue	Dept. of Motor Vehicles
Georgia	Dept. of Revenue	Dept. of Revenue	Dept. of Revenue	Dept. of Revenue
Hawaii	Dept. of Taxation	Dept. of Taxation	Dept. of Taxation	County Treasurer
Idaho	Dept. of Revenue & Tax.	Dept. of Revenue & Tax.	Dept. of Revenue & Tax.	Dept. of Transportation
Illinois	Dept. of Revenue	Dept. of Revenue	Dept. of Revenue	Secretary of State
Indiana	Dept. of Revenue	Dept. of Revenue	Dept. of Revenue	Bur. of Motor Vehicles
Iowa	Dept. of Revenue & Finance	Dept. of Revenue & Finance	Dept. of Revenue & Finance	Local (a)
Kansas	Dept. of Revenue	Dept. of Revenue	Dept. of Revenue	Local (a)
Kentucky	Revenue Cabinet	Revenue Cabinet	Revenue Cabinet	Transportation Cabinet
Louisiana	Dept. of Revenue & Tax.	Dept. of Revenue & Tax.	Dept. of Revenue & Tax.	Dept. of Public Safety
Maine	Bur. of Taxation	Bur. of Taxation	Bur. of Taxation	Secretary of State
Maryland	Comptroller	Comptroller	Comptroller	Dept. of Transportation
Massachusetts	Dept. of Revenue	Dept. of Revenue	Dept. of Revenue	Reg. of Motor Vehicles
Michigan	Dept. of Treasury	Dept. of Treasury	Dept. of Treasury	Secretary of State
Minnesota	Dept. of Revenue	Dept. of Revenue	Dept. of Revenue	Dept. of Public Safety
Mississippi	Tax Comm.	Tax Comm.	Tax Comm.	Tax Comm.
Missouri	Dept. of Revenue	Dept. of Revenue	Dept. of Revenue	Dept. of Revenue
Montana	Dept. of Revenue	. . .	Dept. of Revenue	Local (a)
Nebraska	Dept. of Revenue	Dept. of Revenue	Dept. of Revenue	Dept. of Motor Vehicles
Nevada	. . .	Dept. of Taxation	Dept. of Taxation	Dept. of Motor Vehicles
New Hampshire	Dept. of Revenue & Admin.	. . .	Dept. of Safety	Dept. of Safety
New Jersey	Dept. of Treasury	Dept. of Treasury	Dept. of Treasury	Dept. of Law & Public Safety
New Mexico	Tax & Revenue Dept.	Tax & Revenue Dept.	Tax & Revenue Dept.	Tax & Revenue Dept.
New York	Dept. of Tax. & Finance	Dept. of Tax. & Finance	Dept. of Tax. & Finance	Dept. of Motor Vehicles
North Carolina	Dept. of Revenue	Dept. of Revenue	Dept. of Revenue	Dept. of Transportation
North Dakota	Tax Commr.	Tax Commr.	Tax Commr.	Dept. of Transportation
Ohio	Dept. of Taxation	State Treasurer	Dept. of Taxation	Bur. of Motor Vehicles
Oklahoma	Tax Comm.	Tax Comm.	Tax Comm.	Tax Comm.
Oregon	Dept. of Revenue	. . .	Dept. of Transportation	Dept. of Transportation
Pennsylvania	Dept. of Revenue	Dept. of Revenue	Dept. of Revenue	Dept. of Transportation
Rhode Island	Dept. of Administration	Dept. of Administration	Dept. of Administration	Dept. of Transportation
South Carolina	Dept. of Revenue & Tax.	Dept. of Revenue & Tax.	Dept. of Revenue & Tax.	Dept. of Revenue & Tax.
South Dakota	. . .	Dept. of Revenue	Dept. of Revenue	Dept. of Motor Vehicles
Tennessee	Dept. of Revenue	Dept. of Revenue	Dept. of Revenue	Dept. of Revenue
Texas	. . .	Tax Comm.	Tax Comm.	Dept. of Hwys. & Public Trans.
Utah	Tax Comm.	Tax Comm.	Tax Comm.	Tax Comm.
Vermont	Commr. of Taxes	Commr. of Taxes	Commr. of Motor Vehicles	Commr. of Motor Vehicles
Virginia	Dept. of Taxation	Dept. of Taxation	Dept. of Motor Vehicles	Dept. of Motor Vehicles
Washington	. . .	Dept. of Revenue	Dept. of Licensing	Dept. of Licensing
West Virginia	Dept. of Tax & Revenue	Dept. of Tax & Revenue	Dept. of Tax & Revenue	Dept. of Motor Vehicles
Wisconsin	Dept. of Revenue	Dept. of Revenue	Dept. of Revenue	Dept. of Transportation
Wyoming	. . .	Dept. of Revenue & Tax.	Dept. of Revenue & Tax.	Dept. of Revenue & Tax.
Dist. of Columbia	Dept. of Fin. & Revenue	Dept. of Fin. & Revenue	Dept. of Fin. & Revenue	Dept. of Fin. & Revenue

See footnotes at end of table.

AGENCIES ADMINISTERING MAJOR STATE TAXES—Continued

State or other jurisdiction	Tobacco	Death	Alcoholic beverage	Number of agencies administering taxes
Alabama	Dept. of Revenue	Dept. of Revenue	Alcoh. Bev. Control Bd.	2
Alaska	Dept. of Revenue	Dept. of Revenue	Dept. of Revenue	2
Arizona	Dept. of Revenue	Dept. of Revenue	Dept. of Revenue	2
Arkansas	Dept. of Fin. & Admin.	Dept. of Fin. & Admin.	Dept. of Fin. & Admin.	1
California	Bd. of Equalization	Controller	Bd. of Equalization	4
Colorado	Dept. of Revenue	Dept. of Revenue	Dept. of Revenue	1
Connecticut	Dept. of Revenue & Serv.	Dept. of Revenue & Serv.	Dept. of Revenue & Serv.	2
Delaware	Div. of Revenue	Div. of Revenue	Div. of Revenue	2
Florida	Dept. of Business Reg.	Dept. of Revenue	Dept. of Business Reg.	3
Georgia	Dept. of Revenue	Dept. of Revenue	Dept. of Revenue	1
Hawaii	Dept. of Taxation	Dept. of Taxation	Dept. of Taxation	2
Idaho	Dept. of Revenue & Tax.	Dept. of Revenue & Tax.	Dept. of Revenue & Tax.	2
Illinois	Dept. of Revenue	Attorney General	Dept. of Revenue	3
Indiana	Dept. of Revenue	Dept. of Revenue	Dept. of Revenue	2
Iowa	Dept. of Revenue & Finance	Dept. of Revenue & Finance	Dept. of Revenue & Finance	2
Kansas	Dept. of Revenue	Dept. of Revenue	Dept. of Revenue	2
Kentucky	Revenue Cabinet	Revenue Cabinet	Revenue Cabinet	2
Louisiana	Dept. of Revenue & Tax.	Dept. of Revenue & Tax.	Dept. of Revenue & Tax.	2
Maine	Bur. of Taxation	Bur. of Taxation	Liquor Comm.	3
Maryland	Comptroller	Local	Comptroller	3
Massachusetts	Dept. of Revenue	Dept. of Revenue	Dept. of Revenue	2
Michigan	Dept. of Treasury	Dept. of Treasury	Liquor Control Comm.	3
Minnesota	Dept. of Revenue	Dept. of Revenue	Dept. of Revenue	2
Mississippi	Tax Comm.	Tax Comm.	Tax Comm.	1
Missouri	Dept. of Revenue	Dept. of Revenue	Dept. of Revenue	1
Montana	Dept. of Revenue	Dept. of Revenue	Dept. of Revenue	2
Nebraska	Dept. of Revenue	Dept. of Revenue	Liquor Control Comm.	3
Nevada	Dept. of Taxation	Dept. of Taxation	Dept. of Taxation	2
New Hampshire	Dept. of Revenue & Admin.	Dept. of Revenue & Admin.	Liquor Comm.	3
New Jersey	Dept. of Treasury	Dept. of Treasury	Dept. of Treasury	2
New Mexico	Tax & Revenue Dept.	Tax & Revenue Dept.	Tax & Revenue Dept.	1
New York	Dept. of Tax. & Finance	Dept. of Tax. & Finance	Dept. of Tax. & Finance	2
North Carolina	Dept. of Revenue	Dept. of Revenue	Dept. of Revenue	2
North Dakota	Tax Commr.	Tax Commr.	Treasurer	3
Ohio	Dept. of Taxation	Dept. of Taxation	State Treasurer	3
Oklahoma	Tax Comm.	Tax Comm.	Tax Comm.	1
Oregon	Dept. of Revenue	Dept. of Revenue	Liquor Control Comm.	3
Pennsylvania	Dept. of Revenue	Dept. of Revenue	Dept. of Revenue	2
Rhode Island	Dept. of Administration	Dept. of Administration	Dept. of Administration	2
South Carolina	Dept. of Revenue & Tax.	Dept. of Revenue & Tax.	Dept. of Revenue & Tax.	1
South Dakota	Dept. of Revenue	Dept. of Revenue	Dept. of Revenue	2
Tennessee	Dept. of Revenue	Dept. of Revenue	Dept. of Revenue	1
Texas	State Treasurer	Tax Comm.	State Treasurer	3
Utah	Tax Comm.	Tax Comm.	Tax Comm.	1
Vermont	Commr. of Taxes	Commr. of Taxes	Commr. of Taxes	2
Virginia	Dept. of Taxation	Dept. of Taxation	Alcoh. Bev. Control	3
Washington	Dept. of Revenue	Dept. of Revenue	Liquor Control Board	3
West Virginia	Dept. of Tax & Revenue	Dept. of Tax & Revenue	Dept. of Tax & Revenue	2
Wisconsin	Dept. of Revenue	Dept. of Revenue	Dept. of Revenue	2
Wyoming	Dept. of Revenue & Tax.	Dept. of Revenue & Tax.	Liquor Comm.	2
Dist. of Columbia	Dept. of Fin. & Revenue	Dept. of Fin. & Revenue	Dept. of Fin. & Revenue	1

Source: The Federation of Tax Administrators.
Key:
. . . — Not applicable

(a) Joint state and local administration. State level functions are performed by the Dept. of Transportation in Iowa and Montana, and the Dept. of Revenue in Kansas.

Table 6.20
STATE TAX AMNESTY PROGRAMS
November 22, 1982 - Present

State or other jurisdiction	Amnesty Period	Legislative authorization	Major taxes covered	Accounts receivable included	Collections ($ Millions) (a)	Installment arrangements permitted (b)
Alabama............	01/20/84 - 04/01/84	No (c)	All	No	3.2	No
Arizona............	11/22/82 - 01/20/83	No (c)	All	No	6.0	Yes
Arkansas	09/01/87 - 11/30/87	Yes	All	No	1.7	Yes
California..........	12/10/84 - 03/15/85	Yes Yes	Individual income Sales	Yes No	154.0 43.0	Yes Yes
Colorado	09/16/85 - 11/15/85	Yes	All	No	6.4	Yes
Connecticut	09/01/90 - 11/30/90	Yes	All	Yes	54.0	Yes
Florida	01/01/87 - 06/30/87 01/01/88 - 06/30/88	Yes Yes (d)	Intangibles All	No No	13.0 8.4 (e)	No No
Georgia............	10/01/92 - 12/05/92	Yes	All	Yes	51.3	Yes
Idaho	05/20/83 - 08/30/83	No (c)	Individual income	No	0.3	No
Illinois.............	10/01/84 - 11/30/84	Yes	All	Yes	160.5	No
Iowa	09/02/86 - 10/31/86	Yes	All	Yes	35.1	N.A.
Kansas	07/01/84 - 09/30/84	Yes	All	No	0.6	No
Kentucky	09/15/88 - 09/30/88	Yes (c)	All	No	61.1	No
Louisiana	10/01/85 - 12/31/85 10/01/87 - 12/15/87	Yes Yes	All All	No No	1.2 0.3	Yes (f) Yes (f)
Maine	11/01/90 - 12/31/90	Yes	All	Yes	29.0	Yes
Maryland	09/01/87 - 11/02/87	Yes	All	Yes	34.6 (g)	No
Massachusetts	10/17/83 - 01/17/84	Yes	All	Yes	86.5	Yes (h)
Michigan	05/12/86 - 06/30/86	Yes	All	Yes	109.8	No
Minnesota	08/01/84 - 10/31/84	Yes	All	Yes	12.1	No
Mississippi	09/01/86 - 11/30/86	Yes	All	No	1.0	No
Missouri	09/01/83 - 10/31/83	No (c)	All	No	0.9	No
New Jersey.........	09/10/87 - 12/08/87	Yes	All	Yes	186.5	Yes
New Mexico........	08/15/85 - 11/13/85	Yes	All (i)	No	13.6	Yes
New York	11/01/85 - 01/31/86	Yes	All (j)	Yes	401.3	Yes
North Carolina	09/01/89 - 12/01/89	Yes	All (k)	Yes	37.6	No
North Dakota	09/01/83 - 11/30/83	No (c)	All	No	0.2	Yes
Oklahoma	07/01/84 - 12/31/84	Yes	Income, Sales	Yes	13.9	No (l)
Rhode Island	10/15/86 - 01/12/87	Yes	All	No	0.7	Yes
South Carolina	09/01/85 - 11/30/85	Yes	All	Yes	7.1	Yes
Texas..............	02/01/84 - 02/29/84	No (c)	All (m)	No	0.5	No
Vermont	05/15/90 - 06/25/90	Yes	All	Yes	1.0 (e)	No
Virginia............	02/01/90 - 03/31/90	Yes	All	Yes	32.2	No
West Virginia	10/01/86 - 12/31/86	Yes	All	Yes	15.9	Yes
Wisconsin..........	09/15/85 - 11/22/85	Yes	All	Yes (n)	27.3	Yes
Dist. of Columbia.....	07/01/87 - 09/30/87	Yes	All	Yes	24.3	Yes

Source: The Federation of Tax Administrators.
Key:
N.A. — Not available
(a) Where applicable, figure includes local portions of certain taxes collected under the state tax amnesty program.
(b) "No" indicates requirement of full payment by the expiration of the amnesty period. "Yes" indicates allowance of full payment after the expiration of the amnesty period.
(c) Authority for amnesty derived from pre-existing statutory powers permitting the waiver of tax penalties.
(d) Does not include intangibles tax and drug taxes. Gross collections totaled $22.1 million, with $13.7 million in penalties withdrawn.
(e) Preliminary figure.
(f) Amnesty taxpayers were billed for the interest owed, with payment due within 30 days of notification.
(g) Figure includes $1.1 million for the separate program conducted by the Department of Natural Resources for the boat excise tax.
(h) The amnesty statute was construed to extend the amnesty to those who applied to the department before the end of the amnesty period, and permitted them to file overdue returns and pay back taxes and interest at a later date.
(i) The severance taxes, including the six oil and gas severance taxes, the resources excise tax, the corporate franchise tax, and the special fuels tax were not subject to amnesty.
(j) Availability of amnesty for the corporation tax, the oil company taxes, the transportation and transmissions companies tax, the gross receipts oil tax and the unincorporated business tax restricted to entities with 500 or fewer employees in the United States on the date of application. In addition, a taxpayer principally engaged in aviation, or a utility subject to the supervision of the State Department of Public Service was also ineligible.
(k) Local taxes and real property taxes were not included.
(l) Full payment of tax liability required before the end of the amnesty period to avoid civil penalties.
(m) Texas does not impose a corporate or individual income tax. In practical effect, the amnesty was limited to the sales tax and other excises.
(n) Waiver terms varied depending upon the date of tax liability was accessed.

Table 6.21
STATE EXCISE TAX RATES
(As of January 1, 1994)

State or other jurisdiction	General sales and gross receipts tax (percent)	Cigarettes (cents per pack of 20)	Distilled spirits (a) ($ per gallon)	Motor fuel (b) (cents per gallon) Gasoline	Diesel
Alabama	4	16.5	. . .	16	17
Alaska	. . .	29	5.60	8	8
Arizona	5	18	3.00	18	18
Arkansas	4.5	31.5	2.50 (c)	18.5	18.5
California	6 (d)	37	3.30	18	18
Colorado	3	20	2.28	22	20.5
Connecticut	6	47 (e)	4.50	30 (e)	18
Delaware	. . .	24	5.46	22	19
Florida	6	33.9	6.50 (f)	4 (g)	4 (g)
Georgia	4	12	3.79	7.5	7.5
Hawaii	4	60	5.75	16	16
Idaho	5	18	. . .	21	21
Illinois	6.25 (h)	44	2.00	19	21.5
Indiana	5	15.5	2.68	15	16
Iowa	5	36	. . .	20	22.5
Kansas	4.9	24	2.50 (i)	18	20
Kentucky	6	3 (j)	1.92 (k)	15 (l)	12 (l)
Louisiana	4	20	2.50	20	20
Maine	6	39	. . .	19	20
Maryland	5	36	1.50	23.5	24.25
Massachusetts	5	51	4.05	21 (l)	21 (l)
Michigan	4	25	. . .	15 (l)	15 (l)
Minnesota	6.5 (h)	48	5.03 (m)	20	20
Mississippi	7	18	. . .	18	18
Missouri	4.225	17	2.00	13 (e)	13 (e)
Montana	. . .	18	. . .	24 (e)	24.75 (e)
Nebraska	5	34	3.00	26 (l)	26 (l)
Nevada	6.5 (h)	35	2.05	22.25	27
New Hampshire	. . .	25	. . .	18	18
New Jersey	6	40	4.40	10.5	13.5
New Mexico	5	21	5.68 (e)	22	18
New York	4	56	6.44	8	10
North Carolina	4	5	. . .	22 (l)	22 (l)
North Dakota	5	44	2.50	18	18
Ohio	5	24	. . .	22	22
Oklahoma	4.5	23	5.56 (n)	17	14
Oregon	. . .	38	. . .	24	24
Pennsylvania	6	31	. . .	12	12
Rhode Island	7	44	3.75	28 (l)	28 (l)
South Carolina	5	7	2.72 (o)	16	16
South Dakota	4	23	3.93 (p)	18	18
Tennessee	6	13 (j)	4.00 (q)	21	18
Texas	6.25	41	2.40 (r)	20	20
Utah	5	26.5	. . .	19	19
Vermont	5	20	. . .	15	16
Virginia	3.5	2.5	. . .	17.5	16
Washington	6.5	54 (e)	. . .	23	23
West Virginia	6	17	. . .	20.5	20.5
Wisconsin	5	38	3.25	23.2 (l)	23.2 (l)
Wyoming	4	12	. . .	9	9
Dist. of Columbia	6	65	1.50	20	20

STATE EXCISE TAX RATES—Continued

Source: The Federation of Tax Administrators, compiled from various sources.

Key:

. . . — Tax is not applicable.

(a) Eighteen states have liquor monopoly systems. In Alabama, Idaho, Iowa, Maine, Michigan, Mississippi, Montana, New Hampshire, Ohio, Oregon, Pennsylvania, Utah, Vermont, Virginia, Washington, West Virginia and Wyoming, the state operates retail/wholesale liquor outlets. In North Carolina, liquor stores are operated by county boards. Tax rates in these states cannot be compared to others, since revenue is generated from various taxes, fees and net liquor profits. Only gallonage taxes imposed by states with a license system are reported in the table.

(b) In some states, different tax rates apply to liquefied petroleum gas, compressed natural gas and gasohol. Connecticut, New York and Pennsylvania have gross receipts or franchise taxes on oil companies, which are not covered in this table.

(c) Additional 20 cents per case and 3 percent off-premise or 14 percent on-premise sales taxes are imposed.

(d) Includes a 0.5 percent temporary tax pending a judicial ruling on school finance.

(e) Several states have approved tax increases which will become effective during the year. Effective April 1, 1994, Missouri will raise the motor fuel tax rate to 15 cents per gallon. On July 1, 1994, the cigarette tax will increase to 50 cents in Connecticut and 56.5 cents in Washington. Also, the liquor tax rate will increase to $6.06 per gallon in New Mexico. The motor fuel tax rates are scheduled to increase to 31 cents (gasoline) in Connecticut, and 27 cents (gasoline) and 27.75 cents (diesel) in Montana on July 1, 1994.

(f) An additional 10 cent per ounce on-premise tax is imposed.

(g) Additional 7.8 cents per gallon sales tax and an enhanced transportation tax equal to two-thirds of the local rate (6 cents maximum) are imposed.

(h) Tax includes an uniform statewide local levy. The local component is 1.25 percent in Illinois, 0.5 percent in Minnesota, and 3.75 percent in Nevada.

(i) Plus two additional taxes: an 8 percent enforcement tax on all sales and a 10 percent on-premise gross receipts tax.

(j) Dealers pay an additional enforcement and administrative fee of 0.1 cent per pack in Kentucky and 0.05 cents per pack in Tennessee.

(k) Additional 5 cents per case and 9 percent wholesale taxes are imposed.

(l) The motor fuel rate varies in some states. The statutes in four states impose a tax rate based on wholesale price and is adjusted periodically. The actual rates are 9 percent in Kentucky, 19.1 percent in Massachusetts, 17 cents plus 7 percent in North Carolina, and 13 percent in Rhode Island. The tax rates in Michigan, Nebraska and Wisconsin vary according to a formula incorporating maintenance costs, sales volume or cost of fuel to the state.

(m) An additional one cent per bottle tax is imposed on all liquor except miniatures.

(n) Additional $1.00 per bottle and 12 percent gross receipts taxes are imposed on all on-premise sales.

(o) Additional $5.36 per case tax and a 9 percent surtax are imposed on all liquor sales.

(p) An additional 2 percent wholesale tax is imposed.

(q) Additional 15 cents per case and 15 percent (on-premise sales) taxes are imposed.

(r) Additional 14 percent (on-premise sales) and 5 cents per drink (airline sales) taxes are also imposed.

Table 6.22
FOOD AND DRUG SALES TAX EXEMPTIONS
(As of January 1, 1994)

State or other jurisdiction	Tax rate (percentage)	Exemptions		
		Food (a)	Prescription drugs	Nonprescription drugs
Alabama	4	. . .	★	. . .
Alaska	none	. . .	. . .	. . .
Arizona	5	★	★	. . .
Arkansas	4.5 (b)	. . .	★	. . .
California	6	★	★	. . .
Colorado	3	★	★	. . .
Connecticut	6	★	★	. . .
Delaware	none	. . .	. . .	. . .
Florida	6	★	★	★
Georgia	4	. . .	★	. . .
Hawaii	4	. . .	★	. . .
Idaho	5	. . .	★	. . .
Illinois	6.25 (c)	(d)	(d)	(d)
Indiana	5	★	★	. . .
Iowa	5	★	★	. . .
Kansas	4.9	. . .	★	. . .
Kentucky	6	★	★	. . .
Louisiana	4	. . .	★	. . .
Maine	6	★	★	. . .
Maryland	5	★	★	★
Massachusetts	5	★	★	. . .
Michigan	4	★	★	. . .
Minnesota	6.5 (c)	★	★	★
Mississippi	7	. . .	★	. . .
Missouri	4.225	. . .	★	. . .
Montana	none	. . .	. . .	. . .
Nebraska	5	★	★	. . .
Nevada	6.5	★	★	. . .
New Hampshire	none	. . .	. . .	. . .
New Jersey	6	★	★	★
New Mexico	5	. . .	. . .	. . .
New York	4	★	★	★
North Carolina	4	. . .	★	. . .
North Dakota	5	. . .	★	. . .
Ohio	5	★	★	. . .
Oklahoma	4.5	. . .	★	. . .
Oregon	none	. . .	. . .	. . .
Pennsylvania	6	★	★	★
Rhode Island	7	★	★	★
South Carolina	5	. . .	★	. . .
South Dakota	4	. . .	★	. . .
Tennessee	6	. . .	★	. . .
Texas	6.25	★	★	. . .
Utah	5	. . .	★	. . .
Vermont	5	★	★	. . .
Virginia	3.5	. . .	★	(e)
Washington	6.5	★	★	. . .
West Virginia	6	. . .	★	. . .
Wisconsin	5	★	★	. . .
Wyoming	4	. . .	★	. . .
Dist. of Columbia	6	★	★	★

Source: The Federation of Tax Administrators, compiled from various sources.

Key:
★ — Yes
. . . — No

(a) Some states tax food, but allow an (income) tax credit to compensate poor households. They are: Hawaii, Idaho, Kansas, South Daktoa, Vermont and Wyoming.

(b) Includes a 0.5 percent temporary tax pending a judicial ruling on school finance.

(c) 1.25 percent of the tax in Ilinois and 0.5 percent in Minnesota is distributed to local governments.

(d) Not fully exempt but taxable at 1 percent.

(e) Fully exempt after June 30, 1994.

Table 6.23
STATE INDIVIDUAL INCOME TAXES
(As of January 1, 1994)

State or other jurisdiction	Tax rate range (in percents) Low		High	Number of brackets	Income brackets Lowest		Highest	Personal exemptions Single		Married	Dependents	Federal income tax deductible
Alabama	2.0	-	5.0	3	500 (a)	-	3,000 (a)	1,500		3,000	300	★
Alaska					--------------------------(b)----------------------							
Arizona	3.8	-	7.0	5	10,000 (a)	-	150,000 (a)	2,300		4,600	2,300	
Arkansas	1.0	-	7.0 (c)	6	3,000	-	25,000	20 (d)		40 (d)	20 (d)	
California (e)	1.0	-	11.0	8	4,666 (a)	-	207,200 (a)	64 (d)		128 (d)	64 (d)	
Colorado	5.0			1	--------------Flat rate--------------			--------------------None----------------------				
Connecticut	4.5				--------------Flat rate--------------			12,000 (f)		24,000 (f)	0	
Delaware	0.0	-	7.7	8	2,000	-	40,000	1,250		2,500	1,250	
Florida					--------------------------(b)----------------------							
Georgia	1.0	-	6.0	6	750 (g)	-	7,000 (g)	1,500		3,000	1,500	
Hawaii	2.0	-	10.0	8	1,500 (a)	-	20,500 (a)	1,040		2,080	1,040	
Idaho	2.0	-	8.2	8	1,000 (g)	-	20,000 (g)	2,450 (h)		4,900 (h)	2,450 (h)	
Illinois	3.0			1	--------------Flat rate--------------			1,000		2,000	1,000	
Indiana	3.4			1	--------------Flat rate--------------			1,000		2,000	1,000	
Iowa (e)	0.4	-	9.98	9	1,060	-	47,700	20 (d)		40 (d)	15 (d)	★
Kansas	4.4	-	7.75	3	20,000 (i)	-	30,000 (i)	2,000		4,000	2,000	
Kentucky	2.0	-	6.0	5	3,000	-	8,000	20 (d)		40 (d)	20 (d)	
Louisiana	2.0	-	6.0	3	10,000 (a)	-	50,000 (a)	4,500 (j)		9,000 (j)	1,000 (j)	★
Maine (e)	2.0	-	8.5	5	4,150 (a)	-	16,500 (a)	2,100		4,200	2,100	
Maryland	2.0	-	6.0	5	1,000	-	100,000 (k)	1,200		2,400	1,200	
Massachusetts	5.95 (l)			1	--------------Flat rate--------------			2,200		4,400	1,000	
Michigan	4.6			1	--------------Flat rate--------------			2,100		4,200	2,100	
Minnesota (e)	6.0	-	8.5	3	14,780 (m)	-	48,550 (m)	2,450 (h)		4,900 (h)	2,450 (h)	
Mississippi	3.0	-	5.0	3	5,000	-	10,000	6,000		9,500	1,500	
Missouri	1.5	-	6.0	10	1,000	-	9,000	1,200		2,400	400	★ (n)
Montana (e)	2.0	-	11.0	10	1,700	-	61,100	2,400		2,800	1,400	★
Nebraska (e)	2.62	-	6.99	4	2,400 (o)	-	26,500 (o)	69 (d)		138 (d)	69 (d)	
Nevada					--------------------------(b)----------------------							
New Hampshire					--------------------------(p)----------------------							
New Jersey	2.0	-	7.0	5	20,000 (q)	-	75,000 (q)	1,000		2,000	1,500	
New Mexico	1.8	-	8.5	7	5,200 (r)	-	41,600 (r)	2,450 (h)		4,900 (h)	2,450 (h)	
New York	4.0	-	7.875 (s)	5	5,500 (a)	-	13,000 (a)	0		0	1,000	
North Carolina	6.0	-	7.75	3	12,750 (t)	-	60,000 (t)	2,000		4,000	2,000	
North Dakota	2.67	-	12.0 (u)	8	3,000	-	50,000	2,450 (h)		4,900 (d)	2,450 (d)	★ (u)
Ohio	0.743	-	7.5	9	5,000	-	200,000	650 (v)		1,300 (v)	650 (v)	
Oklahoma	0.5	-	7.0 (w)	8	1,000	-	10,000	1,000		2,000	1,000	★ (w)
Oregon (e)	5.0	-	9.0	3	2,050 (a)	-	5,150 (a)	113 (d)		226 (d)	113 (d)	★ (x)
Pennsylvania	2.8			1	--------------Flat rate--------------			--------------------None----------------------				
Rhode Island					--------------27.5% Federal tax liability--------------							
South Carolina (e)	2.5	-	7.0	6	2,170	-	10,850	2,450 (h)		4,900 (h)	2,450 (h)	
South Dakota					--------------------------(b)----------------------							
Tennessee					--------------------------(p)----------------------							
Texas					--------------------------(b)----------------------							
Utah	2.55	-	7.2	6	750 (a)	-	3,750 (a)	1,838 (h)		3,675 (h)	1,838 (h)	★ (y)
Vermont					---------------- 28%-34% Federal tax liability (z) ----------------							
Virginia	2.0	-	5.75	4	3,000	-	17,000	800		1,600	800	
Washington					--------------------------(b)----------------------							
West Virginia	3.0	-	6.5	5	10,000 (a)	-	60,000 (a)	2,000		4,000	2,000	
Wisconsin	4.9	-	6.93 (aa)	3	7,500	-	15,000	0		0	50 (d)	
Wyoming					--------------------------(b)----------------------							
Dist. of Columbia	6.0	-	9.5	3	10,000	-	20,000	1,370		2,740	1,370	

See footnotes at end of table.

STATE INDIVIDUAL INCOME TAXES—Continued

Source: The Federation of Tax Administrators (based on legislation enacted at 1993 sessions).

Note: This table excludes the following states' taxes: New Hampshire, taxes interest and dividends at 5 percent; Tennessee, taxes interest and dividends at 6 percent.

(a) For joint returns, the tax is twice the tax imposed on half the income.

(b) No state income tax.

(c) A special tax table is available for low income taxpayers reducing their tax payments.

(d) Tax credits.

(e) Seven states have statutory provision for automatic adjustment of tax brackets, personal exemption or standard deductions to the rate of inflation. Nebraska indexes the personal exemption amounts only.

(f) Combined personal exemptions and standard deduction. An additional tax credit is allowed ranging from 75 percent to 0 percent based on state adjusted gross income. Exemption amounts are phased out for higher income taxpayers until they are eliminated for households earning over $71,000.

(g) The tax brackets reported are for single individuals and married households filing jointly. For married households filing separately, the same rates apply to income brackets ranging from $500 to $5,000.

(h) These states allow personal exemption or standard deductions as provided in the IRC. Utah allows a personal exemption equal to three-fourths the federal exemptions. Amounts reported include the 1994 index adjustment.

(i) The tax brackets reported are for single individual and married households filing jointly. For married household filing jointly, the rates range from 3.5 percent for income under $30,000 to 6.45 percent for income over $60,000.

(j) Combined personal exemption and standard deduction.

(k) The tax brackets reported are for single individuals. For married taxpayers filing jointly, the top tax rate applies to income over $150,000. The upper tax bracket expires on January 1, 1995.

(l) A 12 percent tax rate applies to interest, dividends and capital gains.

(m) The tax brackets reported are for single individuals and married taxpayers filing separately. For married taxpayers filing jointly, the same rates apply to income brackets ranging from $2,600 to $85,830. An addition 0.5 percent tax is applied to certain income levels.

(n) Limited to $10,000 for joint returns and $5,000 for individuals.

(o) The tax brackets reported are for single individual. For married couples, the tax rates range from 2.62 percent for income under $4,000 to 6.99 percent over $46,750.

(p) State income tax is limited to dividends and interest income only.

(q) The tax brackets reported are for single individuals. A separate schedule is provided for married households filing jointly which ranges from 2 percent under $20,000 to 7 percent for income over $150,000.

(r) The tax brackets reported are for single individuals. For married individuals, the rate ranges from 2.4 percent under $8,000 to 8.5 percent over $64,000. Married households filing separately pay twice the tax imposed on half the income.

(s) Effective April 1, 1994, the top tax bracket is scheduled to fall to 7.5 percent. A blend rate of 7.59375 percent is used for the entire year.

(t) The tax brackets reported are for single individuals. For married taxpayers, the same rates apply to income brackets ranging from $21,250 to $100,000.

(u) Taxpayers have the option of paying 14 percent of the adjusted federal income tax liability, without a deduction of federal taxes. An additional $300 personal exemption is allowed for joint returns or unmarried head of households.

(v) Plus an additional $20 per exemption tax credit.

(w) The rate range reported is for single persons not deducting federal income tax. For married persons filing jointly, the same rates apply to income brackets ranging from $2,000 to $21,000. Separate schedules, with rates ranging from 0.5 percent to 10 percent, apply to taxpayers deducting federal income taxes.

(x) Limited to $3,000.

(y) One half of the federal income taxes are deductible.

(z) If Vermont tax liability for any taxable year exceeds the tax liability determinable under federal tax law in effect on January 1, 1992, the taxpayer will be entitled to a credit of 106 percent of the excess tax.

(aa) The tax brackets reported are for single individuals. For married taxpayers, the same rates apply to income brackets ranging from $10,000 to $20,000.

Table 6.24
STATE PERSONAL INCOME TAXES: FEDERAL STARTING POINTS

State or other jurisdiction	Relation to Internal Revenue Code	Tax base
Alabama	. . .	. . .
Alaska	(a)	. . .
Arizona	1/1/93	Federal adjusted gross income
Arkansas	. . .	. . .
California	1/1/93	Federal adjusted gross income
Colorado	Current	Federal taxable income
Connecticut	Current	Federal adjusted gross income
Delaware	Current	Federal adjusted gross income
Florida	(a)	. . .
Georgia	1/1/93	Federal adjusted gross income
Hawaii	12/31/92	Federal taxable income
Idaho	1/1/93	Federal taxable income
Illinois	Current	Federal adjusted gross income
Indiana	1/1/93	Federal adjusted gross income
Iowa	1/1/93	Federal adjusted gross income
Kansas	Current	Federal adjusted gross income
Kentucky	12/31/91	Federal adjusted gross income
Louisiana	Current	Federal adjusted gross income
Maine	12/31/92	Federal adjusted gross income
Maryland	Current	Federal adjusted gross income
Massachusetts	1/1/88	Federal adjusted gross income
Michigan	Current (b)	Federal adjusted gross income
Minnesota	12/31/92	Federal taxable income
Mississippi	. . .	. . .
Missouri	Current	Federal adjusted gross income
Montana	Current	Federal adjusted gross income
Nebraska	Current	Federal adjusted gross income
Nevada	(a)	. . .
New Hampshire	(c)	. . .
New Jersey	. . .	. . .
New Mexico	Current	Federal adjusted gross income
New York	Current	Federal adjusted gross income
North Carolina	1/1/93	Federal taxable income
North Dakota	Current	Federal liability (d)
Ohio	Current	Federal adjusted gross income
Oklahoma	Current	Federal adjusted gross income
Oregon	Current	Federal taxable income
Pennsylvania	. . .	. . .
Rhode Island	Current	Federal liability
South Carolina	12/31/92	Federal taxable income
South Dakota	(a)	. . .
Tennessee	(c)	. . .
Texas	(a)	. . .
Utah	Current	Federal taxable income
Vermont	Current (e)	Federal liability
Virginia	12/31/92	Federal adjusted gross income
Washington	(a)	. . .
West Virginia	1/1/93	Federal adjusted gross income
Wisconsin	12/31/92	Federal adjusted gross income
Wyoming	(a)	. . .
Dist. of Columbia	11/5/91	Federal adjusted gross income

Source: The Federation of Tax Administrators, compiled from various sources.
Key:
. . . — State does not employ a federal starting point.
Current — State has adopted Internal Revenue Code as currently in effect. Dates indicate state has adopted IRC as amended to that date.
(a) No state income tax.

(b) Or 1/1/87, taxpayer's option.
(c) On interest and dividends only.
(d) Or federal taxable income based on current Internal Revenue Code.
(e) Not to exceed tax computed using Internal Revenue Code as of 1/1/92.

Table 6.25
RANGE OF STATE CORPORATE INCOME TAX RATES
(As of January 1, 1994)

State or other jurisdiction	Tax rate (percent)	Tax brackets Lowest	Highest	Number of brackets	Tax rate (a) (percent) financial institution	Federal income tax deductible
Alabama	5.0	------------------ Flat Rate ------------------		1	6.0	★
Alaska	1.0 - 9.4	10,000	90,000	10	1.0 - 9.4	. . .
Arizona	9.3 (b)	------------------ Flat Rate ------------------		1	9.3 (b)	. . .
Arkansas	1.0 - 6.5	3,000	100,000	6	1.0 - 6.5	. . .
California	9.3 (c)	------------------ Flat Rate ------------------		1	10.668 (c)	. . .
Colorado	5.0	------------------ Flat Rate ------------------		1	5.0	. . .
Connecticut	11.5 (d)	------------------ Flat Rate ------------------		1	11.5 (d)	. . .
Delaware	8.7	------------------ Flat Rate ------------------		1	8.7 - 2.7 (e)	. . .
Florida	5.5 (f)	------------------ Flat Rate ------------------		1	5.5 (f)	. . .
Georgia	6.0	------------------ Flat Rate ------------------		1	6.0	. . .
Hawaii	4.4 - 6.4 (g)	25,000	100,000	3	7.92 (g)	. . .
Idaho	8.0 (h)	------------------ Flat Rate ------------------		1	8.0 (h)	. . .
Illinois	7.3 (i)	------------------ Flat Rate ------------------		1	7.3 (i)	. . .
Indiana	7.9 (j)	------------------ Flat Rate ------------------		1	7.9 (j)	. . .
Iowa	6.0 - 12.0	25,000	250,000	4	5.0	★ (k)
Kansas	4.0 (l)	------------------ Flat Rate ------------------		1	4.5 (l)	. . .
Kentucky	4.0 - 8.25	25,000	250,000	5	(a)	. . .
Louisiana	4.0 - 8.0	25,000	200,000	5	(a)	★
Maine	3.5 - 8.93 (m)	25,000	250,000	4	1.0	. . .
Maryland	7.0	------------------ Flat Rate ------------------		1	7.0	. . .
Massachusetts	9.5 (n)	------------------ Flat Rate ------------------		1	12.54 (n)	. . .
Michigan		------------------ (o) ------------------				
Minnesota	9.8 (p)	------------------ Flat Rate ------------------		1	9.8 (p)	. . .
Mississippi	3.0 - 5.0	5,000	10,000	3	(a)	. . .
Missouri	6.52	------------------ Flat Rate ------------------		3	7.0	★ (k)
Montana	6.75 (q)	------------------ Flat Rate ------------------		1	6.75 (q)	. . .
Nebraska	5.58 - 7.81 (s)	50,000		2	(a)	. . .
Nevada		------------------ (r) ------------------				
New Hampshire	7.5 (s)	------------------ Flat Rate ------------------		1	7.5 (s)	. . .
New Jersey	9 (t)	------------------ Flat Rate ------------------		1	3 (t)	. . .
New Mexico	4.8 - 7.6 (u)	500,000	1 million	3	4.8 - 7.6 (u)	. . .
New York	9.0 (v)	------------------ Flat Rate ------------------		1	9.0 (v)	. . .
North Carolina	7.75 (w)	------------------ Flat Rate ------------------		1	7.75 (w)	. . .
North Dakota	3.0 - 10.5 (x)	3,000	50,000	6	7.0 (x)	★
Ohio	5.1 - 8.9 (y)	50,000		2	(y)	. . .
Oklahoma	6.0	------------------ Flat Rate ------------------		1	6.0	. . .
Oregon	6.6 (b)	------------------ Flat Rate ------------------		1	6.6 (b)	. . .
Pennsylvania	12.25	------------------ Flat Rate ------------------		1	(a)	. . .
Rhode Island	9.0	------------------ Flat Rate ------------------		1	8.0 (z)	. . .
South Carolina	5.0	------------------ Flat Rate ------------------		1	4.5 (aa)	. . .
South Dakota	. . .	. . .		. . .	6.0 (b)	. . .
Tennessee	6.0	------------------ Flat Rate ------------------		1	6.0	. . .
Texas		------------------ (bb) ------------------				
Utah	5.0 (b)	------------------ Flat Rate ------------------		. . .	5.0 (b)	. . .
Vermont	5.5 - 8.25 (b)	10,000	250,000	4	5.5 - 8.25 (b)	. . .
Virginia	6.0	------------------ Flat Rate ------------------		1	6.0 (cc)	. . .
Washington		------------------ (r) ------------------				
West Virginia	9.0	------------------ Flat Rate ------------------		1	9.0	. . .
Wisconsin	7.9 (dd)	------------------ Flat Rate ------------------		1	7.9	. . .
Wyoming		------------------ (r) ------------------				
Dist. of Columbia	10.0 (ee)	------------------ Flat Rate ------------------			10.0 (ee)	. . .

RANGE OF STATE CORPORATE INCOME TAX RATES—Continued

Source: The Federation of Tax Administrators, compiled from various sources.

Key:

★ — Yes

. . . — No

(a) Rates listed include the corporate tax rate applied to financial institutions or excise taxes based on income. Some states have other taxes based upon the value of deposits or shares.

(b) Minimum tax is $50 in Arizona, $10 in Oregon, $250 in Rhode Island, $200 per location in South Dakota (banks), $100 in Utah and $150 in Vermont.

(c) Minimum tax is $800. The tax rate on S-Corporations is 1.5 percent (4.67 percent for banks).

(d) Or 3.1 mills per dollar of capital stock and surplus (maximum tax $1 million) or $250.

(e) The marginal rate decreases over 4 brackets ranging from $20,000 to $30,000 million in taxable income. Building and loan associations are taxed at a flat 8.7 percent.

(f) Or 3.3 percent Alternative Minimum Tax. An exemption of $5,000 is allowed.

(g) Capital gains are taxed at 4 percent.

(h) Minimum tax is $20. An additional tax of $10 is imposed on each return.

(i) Includes a 2.5 percent personal property replacement tax.

(j) Consists of 3.4 percent on income from sources within the state plus a 4.5 percent supplemental income tax.

(k) Fifty percent of the federal income tax is deductible.

(l) Plus a surtax of 3.35 percent (2.125 percent for banks) taxable income in excess of $50,000 ($25,000).

(m) Or a 27 percent tax on Federal Alternative Minimum Taxable Income.

(n) Rate includes a 14 percent surtax, as does the following: an additional tax of $2.60 per $1,000 on taxable tangible property (or net worth allocable to state, for intangible property corporations); minimum tax of $456.

(o) Michigan imposes a single business tax (sometimes described as a business activities tax or value added tax) of 2.35 percent on the sum of federal taxable income of the business, compensation paid to employees, dividends, interest, royalties paid and other items.

(p) Plus a 5.8 percent tax on any Alternative Minimum Taxable Income over the base tax.

(q) A 7 percent tax on taxpayers using water's edge combination. Minimum tax is $50; for small business corporations, $10. If approved by the voters, the 1994 tax rates will increase to 7.08 percent of the first $500,000

in income and 7.57 percent of the remainder. For water's edge election, the rates are 7.33 percent and 7.82 percent, respectively.

(r) No state coporate income tax.

(s) Plus a 0.25 percent tax on the enterprise base (total compensation, interest and dividends paid). Business profits tax imposed on both corporations and unincorporated associations. The rate is scheduled to fall to 7.0 percent for tax years begining after July 1, 1994.

(t) Plus a 0.375 percent surcharge effective through July 1, 1994. The rate reported in the table is the business franchise tax rate; there is also a net worth tax at rates ranging from 0.2 to 2 mills. The minimum tax is $25 for domestic corporations, $50 for foreign corporations. Corporations not subject to the franchise tax are subject to a 7.25 percent income tax. Banks other than savings institutions are subject to the franchise tax.

(u) Plus-for tax year beginning in 1993-a temporary surtax for all corporations with a net income over $1 million, which is equal to 18 percent of the tax due (with a $200,000 cap).

(v) For tax years beginning before July 1, 1994, a 15 percent surcharge is applied. For tax years beginning after June 30, 1994 but before July 1, 1995, a 10 percent surcharge is applied. Or 1.78 (0.1 for banks) mills per dollar of capital (up to $350,000); or 5 percent (3 percent for banks) of the minimum taxable income; or a minimum of $1,500 to $325 depending on payroll size ($250 plus 2.5 percent surtax for banks); if any of these is greater than the tax computed on net income. An addition tax of 0.9 mills per dollar of subsidiary capital is imposed on corporations.

(w) Plus a 1 percent surtax. Financial institutions are also subject to a Franchise tax equal to $30 per one million in assets.

(x) Or 6 percent Alternative Minimum Tax. The bank tax rate includes a 2 percent privilege tax. Minimum tax is $50.

(y) Or 5.82 mills time the value of the taxpayer's issued and outstanding share of stock; minimum tax $50. An additional litter tax is imposed equal to 0.11 percent on the first $25,000 of taxable income, 0.22 percent on income over $25,000; or 0.14 mills on net worth. Corporations manufacturing or selling litter stream products are subject to an additional 0.22 percent tax on income over $25,000 or 0.14 mills on net worth.

(z) For banks, the alternative tax is $2.50 per $10,000 of capital stock ($100 minimum).

(aa) Savings and Loans are taxed at a 6 percent rate.

(bb) Texas imposes a franchise tax of 4.5 percent of earned surplus.

(cc) State and national banks subject to the state's franchise tax on net capital is exempt from the income tax.

(dd) Plus a surtax set annually by the Department of Revenue to finance a special recycling fund.

(ee) A 2.5 percent surtax is also imposed. Minimum tax is $100.

Table 6.26
STATE SEVERANCE TAXES: 1993

State	Title and application of tax (a)	Rate
Alabama	Iron Ore Mining Tax	$.03/ton
	Forest Products Severance Tax	Varies by species and ultimate use
	Oil and Gas Conservation & Regulation of Production Tax	2% of gross value at point of production
	Oil and Gas Production Tax	8% of gross value at point of production; 4% of gross value at point of incremental production resulting from a qualified enhanced recovery project; 4% if wells produce 25 bbl. or less oil per day or 200,000 cu. ft. or less gas per day; 6% of gross value at point of production for certain on-shore and off-shore wells; 2% of gross value of occluded natural gas from coal seams at point of production for well's first five years
	Coal Severance Tax (b)	$.135/ton
	Coal and Lignite Severance Tax	$.20/ton in addition to Coal Severance Tax
Alaska	Fisheries Business Tax	3% to 5% of fish value based on type of fish
	Fishery Resource Landing Tax	3.3% of the value of the fishery resource at the place of landing
	Oil and Gas Production Tax	The greater of $.60/bbl. for old crude oil ($.80 for all other) or 15% of gross value at production point (multiplied by economic limit factor); the greater of $.064/1,000 cu. ft. of gas or 10% of gross value at production point (multiplied by economic limit factor). Additional $.00125/bbl. of oil and $.00125/50,000 cu. ft. of gas (oil and gas conservation tax)
	Salmon Marketing Tax	1% of the value of salmon that is removed or transferred
Arizona	Severance Tax (c)	2.5% of net severance base for mining; 1.5% of value for timbering
Arkansas	Natural Resources Severance Tax	Separate rate for each substance
	Oil and Gas Conservation Tax	Maximum 25 mills/bbl. of oil and 5 mills/1,000 cu. ft. of gas (d)
California	Oil and Gas Production Tax	Rate determined annually by Department of Conservation (e)
Colorado	Severance Tax (f)	Separate rate for each substance
	Oil and Gas Conservation Tax	Maximum 1.5 mills/$1 of market value at wellhead (g)
Florida	Oil, Gas and Sulfur Production Tax	5% of gross value for small well oil and 8% of gross value for all other; additional 12.5% for escaped oil and $12.4/mcf of gas produced and sold or used during the month. $2.31/long-ton produced or recovered sulfur
	Solid Minerals Tax (h)	5% of market value at point of severance, except $1.35/ton phosphate rock and $1.84/ton heavy minerals times the change in the producer price index
Georgia	Tax on Phosphates	$1/ton
Idaho	Ore Severance Tax	2% of net value
	Oil and Gas Production Tax	Maximum of 5 mills/bbl. of oil and 5 mills/50,000 cu. ft. of gas (d)
	Additional Oil and Gas Production Tax	2% of market value at site of production
Illinois	Timber Fee	4% of purchase price (i)
Indiana	Petroleum Production Tax (j)	1% of value
Kansas	Severance Tax (k)	8% of gross value of oil and gas; $1/ton of coal
	Oil and Gas Assessments	21 mills/bbl. crude oil or petroleum marketed or used; 5.5 mills/1,000 cu. ft. of gas produced, sold, marketed or used
	Mined-Land Conservation & Reclamation Tax	$50, plus per ton fee of between $.03 and $.10
Kentucky	Oil Production Tax	4.5% of market value
	Coal Severance Tax	4.5% of gross value
	Natural Resource Severance Tax (l)	4.5% of gross value, less transportation expenses
Louisiana	Natural Resources Severance Tax	Rate varies according to substance
	Oil Field Site Restoration Fee	Rate varies according to type of well, condition of site and production
Maine	Mining Excise Tax	The greater of a tax on facilities and equipment or a tax on gross proceeds
Maryland	Mine Reclamation Surcharge	$.09/ton (as per state authority) and $.06/ton (as per county authority) of coal removed by open-pit or strip method
	Coal and Gas Severance Taxes	$.30/ton of surface-mined coal
Michigan	Gas and Oil Severance Tax	5% (gas), 6.6% (oil) and 4% (oil from stripper wells and marginal properties) of gross cash market value of the total production. Maximum additional fee of 1% of gross cash market value on all oil and gas produced in state in previous year
Minnesota	Taconite, Iron Sulphides and Agglomerate Taxes	$2.054/ton ($.05/ton for agglomerates)
	Semi-Taconite Tax	$.10/ton ($.05/ton if agglomerated or sintered in state), plus $.001/ton depending on percentage of iron content
	(m)	
Mississippi	Oil and Gas Severance Tax	6% of value at point of production; 3.5% of gross value of occluded natural gas from coal seams at point of production for well's first five years; also, maximum 30 mills/bbl. oil or 4 mills/1,000 cu ft. gas (Oil and Gas Board maintenance tax)
	Timber Severance Tax	Varies depending on type of wood and ultimate use
	Salt Severance Tax	3% of value of entire production in state

STATE SEVERANCE TAXES—Continued

State	Title and application of tax (a)	Rate
Missouri	Surface Coal Mining Permittee Assessment	$.45/ton for first 50,000 tons sold (shipped, or otherwise disposed of) in calendar year, and $.30/ton for next 50,000 tons. After September 1, 1998, rate subject to increase if Coal Mine Reclamation Fund falls below $2 million
Montana	Coal Severance Tax	Varies by quality of coal and type of mine
	Metalliferous Mines License Tax (n)	Progressive rate, taxed on amounts in excess of $250,000. For concentrate shipped to smelter, mill or reduction work, 1.81%. Gold, silver or any platinum group metal shipped to refinery, 1.61%
	Oil or Gas Producers' Severance Tax	5% of total gross value of petroleum and other mineral or crude oil (o), and 2.65% of total gross value of natural gas (license tax); maximum 0.2% of market value/bbl. of oil and of each 10,000 cu. ft. of gas (conservation tax) (d)
	Micaceous Minerals License Tax	$.05/ton
	Cement License Tax (p)	$.22/ton of cement, $.05/ton of cement, plaster, gypsum or gypsum products
	Mineral Mining Tax	$25 plus 0.5% of gross value over $5,000
		$25 plus 0.4% of gross value for talc
Nebraska	Oil and Gas Severance Tax	3% of value of nonstripper oil and natural gas; 2% of value of stripper oil
	Oil and Gas Conservation Tax	Maximum 4 mills/$1 of value at wellhead
	Uranium Tax	2% of gross value over $5 million
Nevada	Net Proceeds of Mine Tax	Minimum 2%, maximum 5%. Based on ratio of net proceeds to gross proceeds of whole operation.
	Oil and Gas Conservation Tax	50 mills/bbl. of oil and 50 mills/50,000 cu. ft. of gas
		$50 for drilling each well
New Hampshire	Refined Petroleum Products Tax	0.1% of fair market value
New Mexico	Resources Excise Tax (q)	Varies according to substance
	Severance Tax (q)	Varies according to substance
	Oil and Gas Severance Tax	3.75% of value of oil, other liquid hydrocarbons and carbon dioxide
	Oil and Gas Privilege Tax	3.15% of value
	Natural Gas Processor's Tax	0.45% of value of products
	Oil and Gas Ad Valorem Production Tax	Varies, based on property tax in district of production
	Oil and Gas Conservation Tax (r)	Percentage varies (s)
North Carolina	Oil and Gas Conservation Tax	Maximum 5 mills/bbl. of oil and 0.5 mill/1,000 cu. ft. of gas (h)
	Primary Forest Product Assessment Tax	$.40 or $.50/1,000 board ft. and $.12 or $.20/cord depending on type of wood and use
North Dakota	Oil and Gas Gross Production Tax	5% of gross value at well
	Coal Severance Tax	$.75/ton plus $.02/ton (t)
	Oil Extraction Tax	6.5% of gross value at well (with exceptions due to price and date of well completion)
Ohio	Resource Severance Tax	$.10/bbl. of oil; $.025/1,000 cu. ft. of gas; $.04/ton of salt; $.02/ton of sand, gravel, limestone and dolomite; $.07/ton of coal
Oklahoma	Oil, Gas and Mineral Gross Production Tax (u)	Separate rate for each substance
	Natural Gas and Casinghead Gas Conservation Excise Tax	$.07/1,000 cu. ft., less 7% of gross value of each 1,000 cu. ft. of gas
Oregon	Forest Products Harvest Tax	$.05/1,000 board ft. (privilege tax) (v); $.50/1,000 board ft. (harvest tax)
	Oil and Gas Severance Tax	6% of gross value at well
	Severance Tax on Eastern Oregon Timber	5% of immediate harvest value and additional severance tax on reforestation land
	Severance Tax on Western Oregon Timber	6.5% of value and additional severance tax on reforestation land except from July 1, 1991 through December 31, 1993
South Dakota	Precious Metals Severance Tax	2% of gross yield from sale of metals plus 8% on net profits or royalties from sale of precious metals
	Energy Minerals Severance Tax	4.5% of taxable value of any energy minerals
	Conservation Tax	2.4 mills of taxable value of any energy minerals
Tennessee	Oil and Gas Severance Tax	3% of sales price
	Coal Severance Tax (w)	$.20/ton
Texas	Natural Gas Production Tax	7.5% of market value
	Oil Production Tax	The greater of 4.6% of market value or $.046/bbl.
	Sulphur Production Tax	$1.03/long ton or fraction thereof
	Cement Production Tax	$.0275/100 lbs. or fraction thereof
	Oil Field Cleanup Regulatory Fees	5/16 of $.01/barrel; 1/13 of $.01/1000 cubic feet of gas (x)
Utah	Metalliferous Minerals Tax	2.6% of gross value for metals
	Oil and Gas Tax	3% of the value of the well for the first $13 per barrel of oil, 5% from $13.01 and above; 3% of the value at the well for first $1.50/mef, 5% from $1.51 and above
	Oil and Gas Conservation Tax	2 mills/$1 of market value at wellhead
Virginia	Forest Products Tax	Varies by species and ultimate use
	Coal Surface Mining Reclamation Tax	Varies depending on balance of Coal Surface Mining Reclamation Fund
	Oil Severence Tax (y)	0.5% of gross receipts from sale

See footnotes at end of table.

STATE SEVERANCE TAXES—Continued

State	Title and application of tax (a)	Rate
Washington	Uranium and Thorium Milling Tax	$.05/lb.
	Enhanced Food Fish Tax	0.07% to 5% of value (depending on species) at point of landing
West Virginia	Natural Resource Severence Tax	Coal, 5% plus 0.35% for counties and municipalities. timber, 3.22% (z)
Wisconsin	Metalliferous Minerals Occupation Tax	Progressive net proceeds tax from 3% to 15%
	Oil and Gas Severance	7% of markey value
Wyoming	Oil and Gas Production Tax	Maximum 0.8 mill/$1 of value at wellhead (h,aa)
	Mining Excise and Severance Taxes	Varies by substance from 1.5% to 3.34% of value; some additional excise taxes of 2% to 3%

Source: Commerce Clearing House Inc., *State Tax Guide.*

(a) Application of tax is same as that of title unless otherwise indicated by a footnote.

(b) Tax scheduled to terminate upon the redemption of, and payment of all accrued interest on, bonds issued by the Alabama State Docks Department.

(c) Timber, metalliferous minerals.

(d) Actual rate set by administrative actions.

(e) For 1993, $.01673/bbl. of oil or per 10,000 cu. ft. of gas. $.02522.

(f) Metallic minerals, molybdenum ore, coal, oil shale, oil and gas.

(g) Currently set at 1.1 mill.

(h) Clay, gravel, phosphate rock, lime, shells, stone, sand, heavy minerals and rare earths.

(i) Buyer deducts amount from payment to grower; amount forwarded to Department of Conservation.

(j) Petroleum, oil, gas and other hydrocarbons.

(k) Coal, salt, oil and gas.

(l) Coal and oil excepted.

(m) State also has two related taxes; Mining Occupation Tax and Proceeds Tax. Also selected counties must impose an Aggregate Materials Tax of $.10/cubic yard or $.07/ton on materials produced in the county.

(n) Metals, precious and semi-precious stones and gems.

(o) Except 2.5 percent of gross value of incremental petroleum and other mineral or crude oil produced in tertiary recovery projects. Over $250,000 gross value to over $1 million.

(p) Cement and gypsum or allied products.

(q) Natural resources except oil, natural gas, liquid hydrocarbons or carbon dioxide.

(r) Oil, coal, gas, liquid hydrocarbons, geothermal energy, carbon dioxide and uranium.

(s) Currently, rate is .18 percent.

(t) Rate reduced by 50 percent if burned in cogeneration facility using renewable resources as fuel to generate at least 10 percent of its energy output.

(u) Asphalt, oil, gas, uranium and metals.

(v) Additional $.25 for the fiscal years beginning July 1, 1991 and July 1, 1992.

(w) Counties and municipalities also authorized to levy severence taxes on sand, gravel, sandstone, chert, and limestone and a privilege tax on nuclear materials.

(x) Fees will not be collected when fund reaches $10 million, but will again be collected when fund falls below $6 million.

(y) May be levied by counties and cities, until July 1, 1995.

(z) Tax rates for other natural resources will vary each year until 1994, when they will be taxed at 5 percent of gross value.

(aa) Currently, rate is .2 mill/$1.

State Tax Collections in 1992

State coffers are relying more on income taxes and less on taxes from sales and gross receipts.

by Gerard T. Keffer

State tax collections totaled $328 billion in fiscal 1992, an increase of 5.6 percent from the $311 billion collected in fiscal 1991. The states received 44.3 percent of their fiscal 1992 total revenue of $742 billion from taxes. Major non-tax revenue sources included intergovernmental payments from the federal government of $159 billion, and $130 billion from insurance trust sources (mainly employee retirement contributions). This article presents data on revenue from state government taxes only. In fiscal 1992, as in previous years, these state tax collections exceeded locally imposed collections ($328 billion versus $221 billion).

The distribution of state tax collections by major tax category remained fairly constant over the previous decade. However, in the 20 years (1960-1980) prior to that, a major realignment of tax revenue sources occurred. The primary reason was the increase in the number of states collecting individual and corporate income taxes. In 1960, 33 states collected individual income taxes, and 37 states collected corporation net income taxes; by 1972, these numbers rose to 43 and 46, respectively. With two exceptions, those same states continue to collect individual and corporate income taxes today. (Alaska in 1980 repealed its individual income tax retroactively to January 1, 1979. Connecticut in 1991 adopted a broad-based tax on individual income; prior to that, individuals paid only a tax on capital gains and dividends.) With the additional states imposing income taxes, the percentage of these taxes of total taxes nearly doubled from 1960 (18.8 percent) to 1980 (36.8 percent). As Table A reflects, this caused a relative decrease over the same period in sales and gross receipts taxes, license taxes and other taxes.

General sales and gross receipts taxes were the largest source of state tax revenue at $108 billion, up 4 percent from 1991. Individual income taxes accounted for $105 billion, up 5 percent. Together, the yield from general sales and gross receipts taxes and individual income taxes accounted for nearly two-thirds (65 percent) of all state tax revenue in fiscal 1992. Following two consecutive years of decline, corporate net income taxes rose 6 percent to $22 billion.

Selective sales taxes totaled $55 billion, an increase of 8 percent since 1991. Motor fuel taxes climbed 8 percent to $22 billion, the largest share of selective sales taxes. Increased motor fuel tax rates in 24 states during fiscal years 1991 and/or 1992, contributed significantly to the overall rate of tax increase. Three states had rate increases in both years. The sale of motor fuel also is taxable under the general sales tax provisions (in addition to the motor fuel excise tax) in six states: California, Florida, Illinois, Indiana, Michigan and New York.

Tobacco product taxes showed a 2 percent increase to $6 billion. Ten states increased the cigarette tax rate in either fiscal years 1991 or 1992. These increases offset any decline in consumption. Alcoholic beverage taxes registered a 3 percent growth and stood at $4 billion.

Severance taxes, after rising in 1990 (+13 percent) and 1991 (+16 percent), declined 14 percent in 1992 to $5 billion. This is the fifth yearly decline in this revenue source in the eight years beginning with 1985. During the 1985-1987 period, the decline in severance tax revenues (mostly related to oil and gas) was

Gerard T. Keffer is chief of the Finance and Taxation Branch, Governments Division, Bureau of the Census, U.S. Department of Commerce.

Table A
PERCENT DISTRIBUTION OF STATE TAX COLLECTIONS
BY MAJOR TAX CATEGORY

Year	Sales & Gross Receipts Taxes	Income Taxes	License Taxes	Other Taxes
1960	58.3	18.8	13.8	9.1
1965	57.7	21.4	12.3	8.6
1970	56.8	27.0	9.6	6.6
1975	54.1	31.8	7.8	6.3
1980	49.4	36.8	6.3	7.5
1985	48.8	37.8	6.3	7.1
1990	49.0	39.2	6.3	5.5
1992	49.5	38.4	6.6	5.5

Table B
SELECTED STATES' TAX COLLECTIONS: 1992

Name	Amount of Taxes (in millions)	Per Capita Amount (Dollars)	Per Capita Rank
California	$46,128	$1,494	10
New York	30,110	1,662	6
Texas	17,031	965	46
Pennsylvania	16,270	1,355	15
Florida	14,412	1,068	41
Illinois	13,463	1,158	30
New Jersey	12,803	1,644	9
Ohio	12,115	1,100	37
Michigan	11,279	1,195	27

so drastic in several states that it resulted in an overall decrease in total tax revenues in those states. The states affected by this were Alaska, Louisiana, Oklahoma and Texas.

Individual State Tax Collections

State government per capita taxes reached a record high of $1,287 in 1992. Nine states collected $10 billion or more in taxes in 1992. Table B ranks these states by dollars and per capita amounts.

Taxes for the nine states listed were nearly $174 billion or 53 percent of the total. Their collective estimated 1992 populations were 132 million, or 52 percent of the U.S. total. Their per capita tax burden as a group was $1,315, about 2 percent above the national average of $1,288. Of this group, only New York ($1,662), New Jersey ($1,644), California ($1,494) and Michigan ($1,355) exceeded the national per capita tax average.

Nine states reported state tax collections in 1992 that exceeded a 10 percent increase from the previous year: New Hampshire (37.1 percent), Pennsylvania (24.9 percent), Connecticut (21.6 percent), Arkansas (16.2 percent), Idaho (15.4 percent), Delaware (15.1 percent), Vermont (11.5 percent), North Carolina (10.7 percent) and South Dakota (10.2 percent) (see Table 6.28). Six states had increases of this magnitude between 1990 and 1991. None of the states was in this category for both periods.

At the other end of the spectrum, three states experienced a decrease in 1992 tax collections. This compares with eight states that had tax revenue declines the previous year, and five states that had decreases in 1990. Only Maine had year-to-year tax revenue decreases in more than one of these three years (−0.2 percent in 1991, and −1.9 percent in 1990). The three states affected in 1992 and their percentage changes are shown on page 377.

Alaska . . . . −11.3 percent
Louisiana . . . . − 1.4 percent
North Dakota . . . − 0.1 percent

A decrease in corporate net income tax revenues in all three of these states was the primary reason for the decrease in their total tax collections.

Tax Burden

While all states rely on various types of selective sales taxes, Alaska, Delaware, Montana, New Hampshire and Oregon do not levy a general sales tax. Seven states — Alaska, Florida, Nevada, South Dakota, Texas, Washington and Wyoming — do not impose individual income taxes. Four states — Nevada, Texas, Washington and Wyoming — exclude corporation net income from taxation. Therefore, the burden of state taxation varies from state to state. Identifying the actual taxpayer is even more complicated in states with a high degree of tourism or "exported" severance taxes. For

these and reasons of state versus local tax authority and distribution of responsibility for services, caution should be exercised in comparing per capita tax revenue and rankings of states.

Compared to a national state per capita average of $1,287, Alaska still leads with $2,731 in 1992. Hawaii was second ($2,336) and Delaware third ($1,946). However, Massachusetts had the highest per capita personal income tax, $890 compared to an average of $410; Tennessee with $19, had the lowest among states imposing this type of tax. Note, though, that Massachusetts ranked 37th in per capita general sales tax revenues.

Because states utilize a variety of revenue sources to support their programs, one should be cautious in making comparisons or drawing conclusions without a background analysis of their general economy and changes in demography.

Table 6.27
NATIONAL SUMMARY OF STATE GOVERNMENT TAX REVENUE,
BY TYPE OF TAX: 1990 TO 1992

Tax source	Amount (in thousands of dollars)			Percent change year-to-year		Percent distribution, 1992	Per capita, 1992 (in dollars)
	1992	1991	1990	1991 to 1992	1990 to 1991		
Total collections	$328,381,766	$311,050,614	$300,721,397	5.6%	3.4%	100.0%	$1,287.36
Sales and gross receipts	162,665,967	153,824,685	147,350,894	5.7	4.4	49.5	637.70
General	107,756,864	103,185,236	99,928,683	4.4	3.3	32.8	422.44
Selective	54,909,103	50,639,449	47,422,211	8.4	6.8	16.7	215.26
Motor fuels	22,246,709	20,638,958	19,379,385	7.8	6.5	6.8	87.21
Public utilities	7,760,221	6,752,407	6,520,714	14.9	3.6	2.4	30.42
Insurance	7,863,137	7,698,315	7,369,651	2.1	—	2.4	30.83
Tobacco products	6,103,608	5,980,154	5,540,620	2.1	7.9	1.9	23.93
Alcoholic beverages	3,513,149	3,401,249	3,191,130	3.3	6.6	1.1	13.77
Other...................	7,422,279	6,168,366	5,420,711	20.3	13.8	2.3	29.10
Licenses	21,681,981	19,522,288	18,845,537	11.1	3.6	6.6	85.00
Motor vehicles.............	10,769,188	10,256,479	9,841,176	5.0	4.2	3.3	42.22
Corporations in general.....	4,104,183	3,110,503	3,099,175	31.9	0.4	1.2	16.09
Motor vehicle operators	1,006,263	864,521	834,298	16.4	3.6	0.3	3.94
Hunting and fishing........	880,158	829,387	792,801	6.1	4.6	0.3	3.45
Alcoholic beverages	259,997	276,234	265,290	−5.9	4.1	0.1	1.02
Other.....................	4,662,192	4,185,164	4,012,797	11.4	4.3	1.4	18.28
Individual income...........	104,642,730	99,323,888	96,076,243	5.4	3.4	31.9	410.23
Corporation net income	21,565,507	20,344,834	21,751,119	6.0	−6.5	6.6	84.54
Severance	4,647,479	5,424,499	4,691,119	−14.3	15.6	1.4	18.22
Property	6,593,958	6,230,473	5,775,098	5.8	7.9	2.0	25.85
Death and gift..............	4,448,533	4,283,723	3,831,781	3.8	11.8	1.4	17.44
Other......................	2,135,611	2,096,224	2,399,606	1.9	−12.6	0.7	8.37

Source: U.S. Department of Commerce, Bureau of the Census, *State Government Tax Collections 1992.*
Note: Because of rounding, detail may not add to totals. Population figures as of July 1, 1991 were used to calculate per capita amounts; see Table 6.32.

Table 6.28
SUMMARY OF STATE GOVERNMENT TAX REVENUE, BY STATE: 1990 TO 1992

State or other jurisdiction	Amount (in thousands of dollars)			Percent change year-to-year		Per capita, 1992 (in dollars)
	1992	1991	1990	1991 to 1992	1990 to 1991	
United States	$328,381,766	$311,050,614	$300,721,397	5.6%	3.4%	$1,287.36
Alabama...............	4,217,916	3,942,565	3,819,513	7.0	3.2	1,019.81
Alaska.................	1,602,937	1,806,332	1,546,441	−11.3	16.8	2,730.73
Arizona...............	4,826,755	4,710,745	4,376,761	2.5	7.6	1,259.59
Arkansas	2,748,292	2,366,105	2,260,980	16.2	4.6	1,145.60
California.............	46,128,169	44,874,424	43,419,164	2.8	3.4	1,494.42
Colorado	3,520,866	3,239,336	3,069,428	8.7	5.5	1,014.66
Connecticut	6,058,854	4,983,328	5,268,014	21.6	−5.4	1,846.65
Delaware	1,341,005	1,165,492	1,130,061	15.1	—	1,946.31
Florida	14,411,775	13,764,055	13,307,625	4.7	3.4	1,068.49
Georgia...............	7,266,981	7,154,525	7,078,197	1.6	1.1	1,076.43
Hawaii	2,709,518	2,639,152	2,334,797	2.7	13.0	2,335.79
Idaho	1,390,585	1,204,607	1,138,491	15.4	5.8	1,303.27
Illinois...............	13,463,435	13,232,569	12,890,512	1.7	2.7	1,157.55
Indiana	6,476,135	6,182,409	6,101,619	4.8	1.3	1,143.79
Iowa	3,601,571	3,453,721	3,313,094	4.3	4.2	1,280.79
Kansas	2,801,692	2,796,415	2,668,998	0.2	4.8	1,110.46
Kentucky	5,080,971	5,043,183	4,260,691	0.7	18.4	1,353.12
Louisiana	4,250,245	4,309,467	4,086,693	−1.4	5.5	991.43
Maine	1,664,359	1,558,231	1,560,869	6.8	−0.2	1,347.66
Maryland	6,502,494	6,401,428	6,450,139	1.6	−0.8	1,324.88
Massachusetts	9,903,246	9,683,597	9,369,108	2.3	3.4	1,651.09
Michigan	11,279,470	11,103,151	11,343,403	1.6	−2.1	1,195.24
Minnesota	7,449,787	7,108,483	6,829,169	4.8	4.1	1,662.90
Mississippi	2,494,392	2,481,597	2,397,321	0.5	3.5	954.24
Missouri	5,131,360	4,996,387	4,939,169	2.7	1.2	988.31
Montana...............	950,724	865,150	775,345	9.9	11.6	1,153.79
Nebraska	1,889,877	1,767,368	1,512,928	6.9	16.8	1,176.76
Nevada	1,817,208	1,682,602	1,597,338	8.0	5.3	1,369.41
New Hampshire	856,179	624,627	602,498	37.1	3.7	770.64
New Jersey.............	12,802,662	11,644,652	10,425,060	9.9	11.7	1,643.68
New Mexico............	2,237,656	2,085,690	2,016,122	7.3	3.5	1,415.34
New York	30,110,341	28,317,365	28,614,593	6.3	−1.0	1,661.81
North Carolina	9,009,742	8,138,964	7,864,737	10.7	3.5	1,316.64
North Dakota	754,555	755,054	694,120	−0.1	8.8	1,186.41
Ohio	12,114,788	11,555,584	11,436,367	4.8	1.0	1,099.74
Oklahoma	3,991,148	3,970,466	3,472,328	0.5	14.3	1,242.57
Oregon	3,313,496	3,029,829	2,782,459	9.4	8.9	1,113.03
Pennsylvania	16,269,988	13,021,344	13,219,655	24.9	−1.5	1,354.82
Rhode Island	1,276,391	1,256,652	1,233,478	1.6	1.9	1,270.04
South Carolina	3,935,500	3,933,214	3,934,383	—	0.0	1,092.28
South Dakota	565,032	512,631	505,428	10.2	1.4	794.70
Tennessee	4,525,662	4,310,573	4,245,024	5.0	1.5	900.81
Texas.................	17,030,546	16,017,785	14,716,513	6.3	8.8	964.58
Utah	1,987,793	1,860,814	1,776,625	6.8	4.7	1,096.41
Vermont	763,391	684,519	686,703	11.5	−0.3	1,339.28
Virginia...............	6,992,351	6,840,331	6,827,236	2.2	0.2	1,096.50
Washington	8,476,932	7,989,522	7,423,096	6.1	7.6	1,650.49
West Virginia	2,351,858	2,328,132	2,229,745	1.0	4.4	1,297.93
Wisconsin..............	7,389,207	7,018,990	6,557,746	5.3	7.0	1,475.78
Wyoming	645,929	637,452	611,613	1.3	4.2	1,386.11
Dist. of Columbia........	2,439,667	2,414,022	2,320,610	1.1	4.0	4,142.05

Source: U.S. Department of Commerce, Bureau of the Census, *State Government Tax Collections 1992.*

Note: Detail may not add to totals due to rounding. Population figures as of July 1, 1991 were used to calculate per capita amounts; see Table 6.32.

TAXES

Table 6.29
STATE GOVERNMENT TAX REVENUE, BY TYPE OF TAX: 1992
(In thousands of dollars)

State or other jurisdiction	Total	Sales and gross receipts	Licenses	Individual income	Corporation net income	Severance	Property	Death and gift	Documentary and stock transfer	Other
Number of states using tax	50	50	50	43	46	34	42	50	30	17
United States	$328,381,766	$162,665,967	$21,681,981	$104,642,730	$21,565,507	$4,647,479	$6,593,958	$4,448,533	$1,836,524	$299,087
Alabama	4,217,916	2,218,884	395,202	1,233,824	164,779	61,864	98,027	30,279	15,057	...
Alaska	1,602,937	101,286	80,704	...	200,025	1,150,605	69,048	1,029	...	240
Arizona	4,826,755	2,781,851	279,700	1,240,372	210,824	14,996	288,356	25,652	...	...
Arkansas	2,748,292	1,517,788	195,634	850,111	125,525	29,309	11,089	8,587	7,070	17,492
California	46,128,169	19,548,658	2,287,864	17,029,575	4,518,418	...	2,266,501	447,844	...	...
Colorado	3,520,866	1,472,888	240,522	1,611,954	123,458	16,046	7,382	34,325	51,119	14,291
Connecticut	6,058,854	3,072,870	284,763	1,865,711	593,720	...	12	190,659	30,728	...
Delaware	1,341,005	195,341	448,896	497,589	128,737	...	...	38,297	595,927	1,417
Florida	14,411,775	11,284,828	997,465	...	695,114	67,000	490,073	281,368	14,023	...
Georgia	7,266,981	3,503,083	211,443	3,081,708	375,286	...	27,758	37,584	...	16,096
Hawaii	2,709,518	1,659,493	54,831	906,982	67,768	...	...	16,416	4,028	...
Idaho	1,390,585	647,370	115,352	535,482	68,171	792	12	21,706	...	...
Illinois	13,463,435	6,739,404	800,708	4,582,387	970,531	...	223,973	120,553	25,879	1,700
Indiana	6,476,135	3,588,981	206,076	2,202,545	386,371	762	4,431	86,969	...	...
Iowa	3,601,571	1,570,624	343,235	1,410,926	192,818	...	...	78,030	5,938	...
Kansas	2,801,692	1,418,591	174,975	833,756	198,998	88,789	34,043	52,540	...	...
Kentucky	5,080,971	2,227,986	281,006	1,678,526	271,027	203,329	338,548	77,355	3,194	...
Louisiana	4,250,245	2,161,652	412,425	867,478	232,061	487,887	42,584	46,158	...	...
Maine	1,664,359	853,351	98,228	591,487	69,921	...	35,324	8,551	7,497	...
Maryland	6,502,494	2,739,685	266,302	2,907,450	216,946	...	193,770	80,331	60,261	37,749
Massachusetts	9,903,246	3,100,368	412,046	5,336,957	756,781	...	195	260,215	36,684	...
Michigan	11,279,470	4,988,579	730,604	3,241,549	1,729,549	41,331	321,346	207,774	63,488	18,738
Minnesota	7,449,787	3,358,838	573,240	2,999,091	422,812	2,045	7,961	22,312	...	...
Mississippi	2,494,392	1,677,133	155,912	439,577	146,308	41,994	22,617	10,851	...	...
Missouri	5,131,360	2,588,639	407,396	1,844,004	229,730	109	12,896	46,711	...	1,875
Montana	950,724	202,157	120,083	321,538	57,683	123,795	98,052	11,338	...	16,078
Nebraska	1,889,877	998,913	122,367	652,638	103,617	2,631	207	6,619	2,885	...
Nevada	1,817,208	1,532,460	217,369	...	...	17,847	41,099	8,433	...	...
New Hampshire	856,179	530,469	106,976	69,167	95,635	40	319	19,101	34,472	...
New Jersey	12,802,662	7,007,550	573,085	4,101,895	845,823	...	14,158	224,854	35,297	...
New Mexico	2,237,656	1,306,764	135,610	445,303	77,786	239,170	21,400	11,623	...	...
New York	30,110,341	10,658,851	939,761	14,913,380	2,518,790	...	112,183	747,639	331,920	...
North Carolina	9,009,742	3,972,981	601,150	3,583,018	643,865	1,621	1,908	94,924	...	...
North Dakota	754,555	441,109	67,732	119,497	38,610	83,305	...	2,394	...	...
Ohio	12,114,788	6,069,518	899,932	4,407,036	641,701	9,143	11,581	75,877	...	...
Oklahoma	3,991,148	1,693,092	507,118	1,218,181	149,142	354,988	...	46,873	4,485	17,269
Oregon	3,313,496	438,629	401,223	2,221,297	152,161	63,788	136	20,427	15,835	...
Pennsylvania	16,269,988	7,265,895	1,769,602	4,689,139	1,623,774	...	210,818	537,731	173,029	...
Rhode Island	1,276,391	636,449	73,857	478,461	48,502	...	17,858	17,730	3,351	183
South Carolina	3,935,500	2,051,830	279,459	1,410,893	141,895	...	12,585	26,145	12,693	...

STATE GOVERNMENT TAX REVENUE, BY TYPE OF TAX: 1992—Continued

State or other jurisdiction	Total	Sales and gross receipts	Licenses	Individual income	Corporation net income	Severance	Property	Death and gift	Documentary and stock transfer	Other
South Dakota	565,032	449,237	55,710	...	35,222	5,768	...	18,996	99	...
Tennessee	4,525,662	3,515,642	500,876	93,360	295,266	1,199	...	42,414	54,204	22,701
Texas	17,030,546	13,609,648	2,266,080	...	...	1,013,811	...	141,007	...	...
Utah	1,987,793	1,017,959	82,054	781,383	76,375	25,776	271	3,975	...	...
Vermont	763,391	367,723	56,083	271,430	30,954	...	9,754	6,948	10,209	10,290
Virginia	6,992,351	2,857,652	390,242	3,321,243	273,258	1,426	15,351	48,791	1,426	82,962
Washington	8,476,932	6,318,551	430,822	...	...	64,768	1,386,622	34,456	211,325	30,388
West Virginia	2,351,858	1,222,148	141,056	612,619	182,081	180,833	2,053	7,410	3,658	...
Wisconsin	7,389,207	3,243,674	422,373	3,142,211	437,689	1,275	53,960	57,664	20,743	9,618
Wyoming	645,929	238,895	66,832	...	...	249,437	87,697	3,068	...	...
Dist. of Columbia	2,439,667	671,832	47,864	627,800	120,898	...	903,319	29,922	38,032	...

Source: U.S. Department of Commerce, Bureau of the Census, *State Government Tax Collections 1992.*
Key:
. . . — Not applicable

Table 6.30
STATE GOVERNMENT SALES AND GROSS RECEIPTS TAX REVENUE: 1992
(In thousands of dollars)

State or other jurisdiction	Total	General sales or gross receipts	Selective sales and gross receipts Total	Motor fuels	Public utilities	Tobacco products	Insurance	Alcoholic beverages	Parimutuels	Amusements	Other
Number of states using tax	50	45	50	50	41	50	50	50	35	31	37
United States	$162,665,967	$107,756,864	$54,909,103	$22,246,709	$7,760,221	$6,103,608	$7,863,137	$3,513,149	$595,308	$822,246	$6,004,725
Alabama	2,218,884	1,115,516	1,103,368	330,895	299,164	67,346	221,685	110,997	4,698	103	68,480
Alaska	101,286	...	101,286	43,247	2,101	16,972	25,451	12,034	...	1,479	2
Arizona	2,781,851	2,088,288	693,563	369,946	105,152	52,548	115,857	41,091	8,085	884	...
Arkansas	1,517,788	1,032,536	485,252	307,534	...	65,948	51,952	27,441	18,634	...	13,743
California	19,548,658	14,924,766	4,623,892	2,248,089	40,222	717,624	1,173,297	296,811	121,255	...	26,594
Colorado	1,472,888	913,599	559,289	360,498	5,260	61,599	90,513	21,520	8,496	1,179	10,224
Connecticut	3,072,870	2,090,143	982,727	361,770	158,303	118,713	160,843	43,443	54,689	20,120	64,846
Delaware	195,341	...	195,341	72,874	21,057	19,662	44,686	10,875	144	...	26,043
Florida	11,284,828	8,325,978	2,958,850	1,084,611	391,380	420,876	311,977	448,356	93,540	2,336	205,774
Georgia	3,503,083	2,687,346	815,737	449,782	...	84,261	166,827	114,867	...	...	...
Hawaii	1,659,493	1,294,723	364,770	72,106	82,255	27,384	61,551	41,492	...	...	79,982
Idaho	647,370	439,173	208,197	132,019	1,616	22,995	46,108	5,459	...	...	...
Illinois	6,739,404	4,241,572	2,497,832	1,030,266	717,660	310,187	197,720	59,434	44,046	26,361	112,158
Indiana	3,588,981	2,779,108	809,873	542,470	...	111,196	122,788	33,419	...	...	...
Iowa	1,570,624	1,010,228	560,396	333,425	...	97,433	97,447	12,631	4,754	14,706	...
Kansas	1,418,591	958,165	460,426	250,999	355	55,549	88,613	54,791	...	899	9,220
Kentucky	2,227,986	1,366,872	861,114	360,058	...	14,045	206,917	54,163	6,852	278	218,801
Louisiana	2,161,652	1,268,695	892,957	470,116	21,826	86,783	208,193	62,112	10,464	2,495	30,968
Maine	853,351	573,418	279,933	143,483	477	52,127	46,376	36,400	1,070	...	...
Maryland	2,739,685	1,579,785	1,159,900	462,777	122,240	91,867	138,719	25,277	2,843	2,120	314,057
Massachusetts	3,100,368	1,978,654	1,121,714	541,069	...	139,856	284,809	64,675	26,089	9,353	55,863
Michigan	4,988,579	3,665,541	1,323,038	745,000	...	245,937	178,304	122,309	19,972	...	11,516
Minnesota	3,358,838	2,190,676	1,168,162	464,916	...	164,767	130,617	53,368	...	55,327	279,429
Mississippi	1,677,133	1,182,356	494,777	317,098	17,941	51,778	90,154	34,207	1,797	1,540	...
Missouri	2,588,639	1,916,680	671,959	384,342	1,395	79,683	182,969	23,570	...	...	...
Montana	202,157	...	202,157	121,493	13,983	13,397	27,768	14,853	142	...	10,521
Nebraska	998,913	663,159	335,754	222,145	1,855	38,751	35,892	15,725	567	8,333	12,486
Nevada	1,532,460	892,721	639,739	132,963	5,085	48,292	67,107	14,854	...	366,136	5,302
New Hampshire	530,469	...	530,469	92,534	27,376	38,140	37,747	11,181	7,810	1,895	313,786
New Jersey	7,007,550	4,049,282	2,958,268	410,625	1,701,161	269,465	206,458	80,547	6,955	257,023	26,034
New Mexico	1,306,764	982,572	324,192	182,739	6,327	18,408	41,000	17,425	1,135	810	56,348
New York	10,658,851	6,005,503	4,653,348	495,208	1,572,830	593,580	610,046	235,004	76,770	696	1,069,214
North Carolina	3,972,981	2,171,041	1,801,940	861,487	248,274	40,363	202,157	155,515	...	...	294,144
North Dakota	441,109	256,583	184,526	75,245	12,824	13,770	18,745	4,905	...	5,701	53,336
Ohio	6,069,518	3,751,523	2,317,995	1,128,832	605,503	224,199	281,301	64,205	13,955	...	...
Oklahoma	1,693,092	971,331	721,761	340,208	14,004	68,854	109,998	56,744	7,261	...	124,692
Oregon	438,629	...	438,629	271,561	4,859	87,528	59,506	10,741	4,406	28	...
Pennsylvania	7,265,895	4,499,734	2,766,161	694,408	660,117	336,244	404,806	144,665	11,799	382	513,740
Rhode Island	636,449	388,987	247,462	94,074	60,673	36,545	33,751	9,131	9,408	152	3,728
South Carolina	2,051,830	1,452,014	599,816	287,393	37,418	28,461	66,733	109,870	...	19,796	50,145

STATE GOVERNMENT SALES AND GROSS RECEIPTS TAX REVENUE: 1992—Continued

State or other jurisdiction	Total	General sales or gross receipts Total	Selective sales and gross receipts Motor fuels	Public utilities	Tobacco products	Insurance	Alcoholic beverages	Parimutuels	Amusements	Other
South Dakota	449,237	289,325	159,912	82,685	694	13,952	28,566	9,381	569	...	24,065
Tennessee	3,515,642	2,514,798	1,000,844	656,573	5,587	80,105	183,326	63,234	...	21,479	12,019
Texas	13,609,648	8,575,890	5,033,758	1,953,453	217,599	582,793	516,081	386,848	...	...	1,355,505
Utah	1,017,959	802,439	215,520	136,352	4,893	26,100	31,085	17,090	...	...	...
Vermont	367,723	157,030	210,693	55,854	14,614	13,996	16,723	13,961	207	...	95,338
Virginia	2,857,652	1,570,789	1,286,863	629,104	100,917	15,315	174,788	97,155	5,899	65	269,519
Washington	6,318,551	5,031,574	1,286,977	627,136	190,610	146,930	110,016	119,885	8,650	21	86,480
West Virginia	1,222,148	796,889	425,259	207,992	11,319	32,088	55,964	8,582	12,093	41	100,623
Wisconsin	3,243,674	2,127,315	1,116,359	568,929	253,295	153,564	88,306	39,664	254	508	...
Wyoming	238,895	182,547	56,348	38,326	...	5,632	10,894	1,242	...	...	...
Dist. of Columbia	671,832	442,496	229,336	28,586	115,297	17,065	31,785	5,835	...	...	30,768

Source: U.S. Department of Commerce, Bureau of the Census, *State Government Tax Collections 1992.*
Key:
. . . — Not applicable

Table 6.31
STATE GOVERNMENT LICENSE TAX REVENUE: 1992
(In thousands of dollars)

State or other jurisdiction	Total	Motor vehicle	Motor vehicle operators	Corporations in general	Occupations and businesses, n.e.c.	Hunting and fishing	Alcoholic beverages	Public utilities	Amusements	Other
Number of states using tax	50	50	48	48	50	50	49	30	37	49
United States	$21,681,981	$10,769,188	$1,006,263	$4,104,183	$3,879,135	$880,158	$259,997	$292,432	$225,298	$265,327
Alabama	395,202	145,769	14,142	121,586	91,283	17,452	2,323	2,647		
Alaska	80,704	24,219	680	930	41,568	11,459	1,689		109	50
Arizona	279,700	193,389	8,828	4,000	32,299	13,510	2,167		27	25,480
Arkansas	195,634	115,316	8,659	8,122	36,079	17,111	1,025	8,517	303	502
California	2,287,864	1,358,935	97,207	50,200	614,857	62,678	31,267	66,023	70	6,627
Colorado	240,522	103,328	13,195	981	57,863	51,576	3,347		254	9,978
Connecticut	284,763	173,429	23,595	9,829	63,880	2,538	5,766		564	5,162
Delaware	448,896	18,441	1,500	297,004	127,337	901	671	2,382	87	573
Florida	997,465	533,357	97,250	48,832	223,136	15,181	24,925	22,517	8,525	23,742
Georgia	211,443	84,135	19,773	23,748	37,823	18,014	1,930			26,020
Hawaii	54,831	39,540		1,815	10,066	247		2,996		167
Idaho	115,352	48,878	4,332	283	23,791	19,054	924	16,612		1,478
Illinois	800,708	612,073	44,507	82,947	39,996	15,248	2,868		936	2,133
Indiana	206,076	155,642		3,954	22,369	12,976	9,677	40		1,418
Iowa	343,235	226,548	16,471	30,600	37,504	14,506	8,234	5,447	2,506	1,419
Kansas	174,975	109,739	9,465	14,437	24,428	9,590	2,696	2,687	179	1,754
Kentucky	281,006	148,517	5,221	82,087	27,186	11,766	1,819	1,950	433	2,027
Louisiana	412,425	86,569	6,315	265,035	35,621	11,769	2,433	3,511		1,172
Maine	98,228	50,845	6,642	2,087	26,309	8,426	2,399		644	876
Maryland	266,302	151,855	16,998	3,982	82,062	9,364	327		14	1,700
Massachusetts	412,046	250,986	63,577	18,576	69,426	4,295	1,176		794	3,216
Michigan	730,604	514,341	37,486	14,506	76,483	38,968	11,516	17,085	603	19,616
Minnesota	573,240	393,416	19,998	3,013	109,380	35,773	476		399	10,785
Mississippi	155,912	62,691	9,057	46,920	24,488	8,889	2,269	1,491		107
Missouri	407,396	200,840	16,481	63,436	82,274	19,902	2,467	12,190	985	8,821
Montana	120,083	40,943	3,092	849	17,196	22,325	1,503	1,345	32,685	145
Nebraska	122,367	54,631	4,636	10,077	31,427	8,071	208			13,317
Nevada	217,369	67,740	6,904	8,455	58,424	7,456	20		64,870	3,500
New Hampshire	106,976	51,514	7,678	7,713	24,145	5,940	2,828	4,461	543	2,154
New Jersey	573,085	315,419	25,218	98,451	60,539	9,766	3,238	16	57,203	3,235
New Mexico	135,610	106,314	4,954	1,191	13,421	8,463	470	101	154	542
New York	939,761	561,678	54,200	23,655	200,000	31,594	29,812	35,969	31	2,822
North Carolina	601,150	279,959	55,159	161,398	79,800	13,644	4,727		5,003	1,460
North Dakota	67,732	35,031	3,382		15,697	5,104	237		243	8,038
Ohio	899,932	481,465	21,359	180,364	165,586	22,557	24,600	442		3,559
Oklahoma	507,118	407,009	7,397	35,131	37,312	12,854	2,889	4	4,185	337
Oregon	401,223	244,920	14,349	4,013	98,179	26,854	1,586	7,485	1,773	2,064
Pennsylvania	1,769,602	447,173	55,484	943,904	223,502	43,272	13,663	35,713	72	6,819
Rhode Island	73,857	50,787	1,244	5,973	13,456	1,054	239		217	887
South Carolina	279,459	79,127	14,703	27,446	83,570	11,341	9,099		26,672	27,501

STATE GOVERNMENT LICENSE TAX REVENUE: 1992—Continued

State or other jurisdiction	Total	Motor vehicle	Motor vehicle operators	Corporations in general	Occupations and businesses, n.e.c.	Hunting and fishing	Alcoholic beverages	Public utilities	Amusements	Other
South Dakota	55,710	25,176	2,063	564	18,029	8,916	231	...	180	551
Tennessee	500,876	158,693	27,117	230,776	56,419	20,353	1,627	4,081	...	1,810
Texas	2,266,080	692,888	71,259	1,116,796	295,707	44,639	17,885	7,535	6,197	13,174
Utah	82,054	45,472	8,991	...	9,863	16,624	529	...	...	575
Vermont	56,083	35,637	4,532	648	7,718	4,783	362	...	161	2,242
Virginia	390,242	255,805	23,956	23,799	62,108	15,436	5,983	15,399	11	3,144
Washington	430,822	203,538	20,040	9,015	140,941	27,156	7,746	12,333	4,313	2,674
West Virginia	141,056	79,462	4,383	5,356	19,861	13,512	5,934	20	...	215
Wisconsin	422,373	207,498	21,667	7,397	126,937	45,929	182	1,433	3,353	9,390
Wyoming	66,832	38,511	1,117	2,302	1,790	21,322	8	...	...	349
Dist. of Columbia	47,864	18,494	1,919	5,750	16,782	...	3,342	...	...	1,577

Source: U.S. Department of Commerce, Bureau of the Census, State Government Tax Collections 1992.
Key:
... — Not applicable

Table 6.32

FISCAL YEAR, POPULATION AND PERSONAL INCOME, BY STATE

State or other jurisdiction	Date of close of fiscal year in 1992	Total population (excluding armed forces overseas) (in thousands)		Personal income, calendar year 1991 (a)		State government portion of state-local tax revenue in fiscal 1990-91 (d) (percent)
		July 1, 1992 (b)	July 1, 1991 (c)	Amount (in millions)	Per capita (in dollars)	
United States	. . .	254,492	251,579	$4,800,098	$19,149	59.4%
Alabama	September 30	4,136	4,089	63,458	15,518	70.7
Alaska	June 30	587	570	12,015	21,067	71.8
Arizona	June 30	3,832	3,750	62,166	16,579	62.7
Arkansas	June 30	2,399	2,372	34,698	14,629	74.6
California	June 30	30,867	30,380	633,326	20,847	64.7
Colorado	June 30	3,470	3,377	65,365	19,358	48.6
Connecticut	June 30	3,281	3,291	85,642	26,022	56.8
Delaware	June 30	689	680	14,154	20,816	82.4
Florida	June 30	13,488	13,277	252,146	18,992	56.6
Georgia	June 30	6,751	6,623	115,473	17,436	60.1
Hawaii	June 30	1,160	1,135	24,045	21,190	81.1
Idaho	June 30	1,067	1,039	15,935	15,333	72.3
Illinois	June 30	11,631	11,543	239,293	20,713	54.0
Indiana	June 30	5,662	5,610	96,365	17,179	63.4
Iowa	June 30	2,812	2,795	48,347	17,296	63.3
Kansas	June 30	2,523	2,495	45,706	18,322	58.1
Kentucky	June 30	3,755	3,713	58,027	15,626	78.5
Louisiana	June 30	4,287	4,252	63,970	15,046	61.3
Maine	June 30	1,235	1,235	21,548	17,454	62.1
Maryland	June 30	4,908	4,860	107,836	22,189	57.7
Massachusetts	June 30	5,998	5,996	137,924	23,003	65.4
Michigan	September 30	9,437	9,368	174,750	18,655	56.3
Minnesota	June 30	4,480	4,432	84,769	19,125	67.8
Mississippi	June 30	2,614	2,592	34,545	13,325	72.9
Missouri	June 30	5,193	5,158	92,470	17,928	60.7
Montana	June 30	824	808	12,673	15,675	64.4
Nebraska	June 30	1,606	1,593	28,220	17,718	56.8
Nevada	June 30	1,327	1,284	25,398	19,783	67.5
New Hampshire	June 30	1,111	1,105	24,038	21,760	29.5
New Jersey	June 30	7,789	7,760	199,181	25,666	54.0
New Mexico	June 30	1,581	1,548	22,665	14,646	78.3
New York	March 31	18,119	18,058	405,765	22,471	47.0
North Carolina	June 30	6,843	6,737	113,536	16,853	69.7
North Dakota	June 30	636	635	9,903	15,605	68.6
Ohio	June 30	11,016	10,939	194,384	17,770	57.0
Oklahoma	June 30	3,212	3,175	49,340	15,541	72.8
Oregon	June 30	2,977	2,922	51,353	17,575	51.4
Pennsylvania	June 30	12,009	11,961	230,917	19,306	57.7
Rhode Island	June 30	1,005	1,004	19,291	19,207	58.7
South Carolina	June 30	3,603	3,560	55,055	15,467	70.8
South Dakota	June 30	711	703	11,303	16,071	50.5
Tennessee	June 30	5,024	4,953	81,651	16,486	61.7
Texas	August 31	17,656	17,349	298,928	17,230	52.5
Utah	June 30	1,813	1,770	25,890	14,625	65.7
Vermont	June 30	570	567	10,198	17,997	56.9
Virginia	June 30	6,377	6,286	126,237	20,087	55.6
Washington	June 30	5,136	5,018	97,766	19,484	71.2
West Virginia	June 30	1,812	1,801	25,754	14,301	79.3
Wisconsin	June 30	5,007	4,955	88,891	17,939	63.6
Wyoming	June 30	466	460	7,783	16,937	61.5
Dist. of Columbia	September 30	585	594	14,397	24,063	. . .

Source: U.S. Department of Commerce, Bureau of the Census, *State Government Tax Collections 1992.*

Note: United States totals exclude the District of Columbia. Detail may not add to totals due to rounding.

Key:

. . . — Not applicable.

(a) U.S. Department of Commerce, *Survey of Current Business,* August 1992.
(b) Represents resident U.S. population (50 states) as of July 1, 1992 from the Bureau of the Census, *Current Population Reports,* Series P-25, July 1992.
(c) Bureau of the Census, *Current Population Reports,* Series P-25, July 1991.
(d) Bureau of the Census, *Government Finances: 1990-91,* February 1993.

Passing the Bucks: A Look at Federal Spending Programs in 5 States

Changes in spending for discretionary programs have a bigger effect in areas where they are concentrated than changes in formula-driven programs do.

by Robert McArthur

In an essay in the *1992-93 Book of the States*[1], David Kellerman remarked on the general equitability found in the geographic distribution of federal dollars, particularly when looked at on a per capita basis. He found that per capita differences among the states primarily were due to the presence or absence of significant federal installations, a sizable federal work force relative to overall employment and/or major industries doing business with the federal government.

As Kellerman noted, the federal government, with 4 million military and civilian employees and $200 billion per year in contracts with private businesses, is a major national economic activity. How and where federal funds are distributed are of great interest in both the public and private sectors.

Some differences in the geographic distribution of federal funds among the states can be ascribed to program formulas that target demographic features such as age or income level, which vary from one area to another. Other differences, however, are due to special discretionary programs of the government that are carried out in certain geographic areas. Changes in spending priorities on these programs often have a much more dramatic effect on the economies of the areas where they are concentrated than do changes in formula-driven programs.

This essay examines the nature of federal investment in five states where the per capita differences from the national average, due to a special federal presence, are the greatest. It identifies the federal agencies and spending programs with the largest outlays and indicates whether the spending is concentrated in one or a few localities, or is dispersed throughout the state. The states chosen for the study were those whose overall ranking in terms of per capita federal spending was higher than and differed the most from their ranking in per capita federal entitlement outlays, categorized as direct payments for individuals. Entitlements were excluded from the study because in most cases such payments are determined by formulas uniformly applied regardless of the location of the recipient.

Tracking Federal Spending

Since 1981, the Census Bureau has produced annual reports and data files detailing domestic federal spending by program and geographic location. Five broad categories of expenditure[2] are covered:

- Grants to states and localities;
- Federal salaries and wages;
- Direct payments for individuals;
- Procurement; and,
- Other direct payments (mainly research grants and agricultural subsidies).

Each record in the data files contains a two-character "object code" designating the category of federal expenditure to which the record belongs. In most cases, records in the grants and direct payments categories appear in the files identified by their Catalog of Federal Domestic Assistance (CFDA) program number. As a result, data for most such spending

Robert McArthur is chief of the Federal Programs Branch, Governments Division, Bureau of the Census, U.S. Department of Commerce.

programs are presented individually in the files. Information on federal procurement orders and payroll, however, are not part of the CFDA. For these data, Census has assigned pseudo-CFDA codes to distinguish defense outlays from postal service and other non-defense spending. However, in most instances, procurement and payroll data could not be identified by specific military service or civilian department using the pseudo-CFDA number.

Commencing with the 1993 reports, The Bureau of the Census has added an agency identifier field to each record in the federal spending files. This field contains the four-character Federal Information Processing Standards (FIPS) agency identification code issued by the National Institute of Standards and Technology. The two left-most characters form a component data element, called the Treasury Agency Symbol (TAS), which is identical to the two-digit numerical code used in the budgetary process to identify major federal agencies. The FIPS agency code has greatly increased the proportion of the data file made up of procurement and payroll information. In past years there was one record for each unique combination of geographic place of performance and pseudo-CFDA code. Beginning with the 1993 files there is one record for each unique combination of geographic place of performance, pseudo-CFDA code and FIPS agency code. Each spending program now has three program-related identifiers: a CFDA code, an object category code and an agency identification code.

States Most Affected by Special Federal Presence

Direct payments for individuals form the largest object category of federal per capita spending. Social Security, Medicare, federal retirement and disability, food stamps, and other entitlement programs are included in this category, which nationally accounts for more federal spending than the combined totals of federal grants, procurement, payroll and other direct payments. This is also true in most of the states individually. Nevertheless, a sizable portion of domestic federal outlays is for purposes other than entitlements,

and these other outlays can contribute significantly to the rank order of states in their per capita receipt of federal funds.

The five states with the greatest per capita effect in 1993 from special federal investment were Alaska, Colorado, New Mexico, Hawaii and Virginia, in that order. In each case, defense installations were a leading influence. In all but Virginia the military presence was coupled with relatively small state populations to magnify the per capita effect. Each state also was helped by nondefense outlays.

Alaska

Alaska provides the most striking example of a state where federal spending priorities lie in areas other than entitlements. Alaska, which received the highest per capita amount of federal funds, was last in direct payments for individuals. Alaska ranked No. 1 in per capita federal salaries and wages at $2,712, more than 4 times greater than the national average of $635. Per capita defense pay was $1,812, more than 6 times the national average.

The Army accounted for more than half the defense pay, followed by the Air Force with about 40 percent. Over 90 percent of both the Army and Air Force payroll amounts were in the Anchorage and Fairbanks areas, where about half the state's population lives.

Per capita nondefense pay in Alaska was about 2.8 times higher than the national average. The Department of Transportation (DOT), including the U.S. Coast Guard, was Alaska's largest nondefense federal employer ($280 per capita), followed by the Postal Service ($182 per capita) and the Department of Interior ($163 per capita). Roughly 40 percent of DOT's payroll was in the Anchorage area, 22 percent on Kodiak Island and about 10 percent in the Fairbanks area. About 84 percent of Interior's pay was in the Anchorage and Fairbanks areas, while the Postal Service distribution was more proportional. DOT, USPS and Interior payrolls taken together provided Alaska with a per capita amount nearly equal to the national average for all federal agencies combined.

After salaries and wages, procurement orders were Alaska's next largest per capita category of federal outlays, at $1,622. Defense procurement ($924 per capita) exceeded the national per capita average for all agencies combined ($769). Nationally, the Air Force and the Navy were the top agencies in procurement order amounts, but in Alaska the Army took the lead for procurement at $378 per capita. Army procurement orders were distributed among 20 of the state's 26 boroughs and Census areas, with heaviest concentrations in the Anchorage and Fairbanks areas.

The second leading agency for procurement orders was the Public Health Service (PHS), an agency in the Department of Health and Human Services, at $338 per capita. Most of the PHS money was for health services contracts in 17 boroughs around the state. The Air Force was third from the top, at $243 per capita, with orders in 10 boroughs. Over half the Air Force procurement amounts were in the Anchorage area, which includes Elmendorf Air Force Base. Nationally, Alaska ranked No. 3 in per capita federal procurement spending in 1993.

Alaska ranked No. 1 in per capita federal grants to states and localities in 1993 at $1,583, which is more than double the national average of $746. The Highway Trust Fund provided the largest grant amount, at $372 per capita, with distributions to most boroughs. Airport and Airway Trust Fund grants, at $122 per capita in Alaska, were 17 times higher than the national average per capita amount of $7. Most of this money went to the Anchorage area.

Colorado

In Colorado, the category of federal spending with the highest per capita dollar amount was direct payments for individuals, as it was in almost all other states. Direct payments amounted to $2,092 per capita in the state. However, Colorado still ranked near the bottom at No. 48 in this category. The payroll and procurement categories, in both of which Colorado ranked sixth, had the greatest effect in raising the overall ranking for the state to No. 12.

Federal procurement orders were $1,193 per capita in Colorado, about 55 percent higher than the national average. The Air Force had the largest amount of any agency, at $573 per

capita, primarily in contracts with the Martin Marietta Corporation in Denver. The Energy Department was second, at $275 per capita, with several large contracts in Golden.

Federal pay in Colorado was $968 per capita, or more than 50 percent higher than the national average. The top federal employer was the Air Force at $187 per capita, followed by the Postal Service at $178. Two-thirds of the Air Force payroll was in the Colorado Springs area and one-fourth was in Denver. Postal Service pay was spread throughout the state and appeared to be regionally proportional to the population distribution. The Army had the third highest payroll at $139 per capita, with 73 percent of the amount going to the Colorado Springs area and 19 percent to Adams County. Interior was fourth at $119 per capita, with 83 percent of the amount concentrated in Jefferson County.

New Mexico

New Mexico placed second overall in per capita federal spending, but was 35th in direct payments for individuals. Procurement orders provided the greatest per capita amount, at $2,504. A large part of this amount, $1,772, was due to Department of Energy contracts divided mainly between the Albuquerque and Los Alamos areas, which got 55 percent and 42 percent, respectively. The Air Force and Army also had sizable procurement orders in the state. The Air Force spent $204 per capita, of which 70 percent went to Kirtland Air Force Base and the Albuquerque area (Bernalillo County), and 20 percent went to Holloman Air Force Base (Otero County). The Army amount was $170 per capita, with about 50 percent going to the White Sands area (Dona Ana County), 20 percent to the Cannon Air Force Base (Curry County), and 15 percent to Albuquerque.

In fifth place for federal salaries and wages per capita at $973, New Mexico's amount was 53 percent higher than the national average for this category. The Air Force was by far the largest federal employer in the state ($307 per capita), followed by the Army and the Postal Service ($126 each), then Interior ($120). These four agencies alone put New Mexico's federal payroll per capita above the national average for all agencies combined. Air Force employment was divided primarily among three county areas: Bernalillo (43 percent), Curry (26 percent) and Otero (29 percent). Army payroll was mostly concentrated in Dona Ana County (69 percent), with smaller amounts in Bernalillo and elsewhere. Postal Service and Interior Department salaries were distributed roughly proportionate to the population.

Hawaii

Hawaii ranked 33rd in direct payments for individuals. The outstanding feature putting the state in fifth place for total federal per capita spending is the huge military presence there. Defense salaries, at $1,768 per capita, were over six times greater than the national average of $283. Navy pay alone was $958 per capita, more than 50 percent higher than the national average for *total* federal salaries and wages ($635). The Army payroll was also large, at $581 per capita. Together, the Army and Navy accounted for three-fourths of federal pay in Hawaii, almost all of it on the island of Oahu.

The only other spending category in which Hawaii's per capita figure was substantially higher than the national average was grants to states and localities. At $840, the per capita federal grants total for Hawaii exceeded the national average of $746 by 13 percent. On a per capita basis, Hawaii placed high for housing assistance grants, Highway Trust Fund grants and Federal Emergency Management Agency disaster relief grants.

Virginia

Virginia, which ranked 24th in the category of direct payments for individuals, was third overall in per capita federal spending. Although Virginia received more funds in the form of direct payments for individuals than in any other category ($2,478 per capita), the amount was slightly below the national average ($2,487). While lower than the direct payments figure, the state's per capita amount of $1,761 in federal procurement orders ranked second after Alaska. Defense procurement accounted for $1,132 per capita federal spending, about double the national average for that category. Almost half of the defense procurement

total in Virginia was due to Navy contracts. There were major shipbuilding contracts in the state's Tidewater area and other large Navy contracts in the Northern Virginia suburbs of Washington, D.C.

The Army ($249 per capita) and Air Force ($113 per capita) each had larger procurement totals in Virginia than did any single nondefense agency. Still, nondefense procurement in Virginia amounted to $629 per capita, 2.3 times higher than the $273 national average. The leading nondefense agencies were the General Services Administration ($103 per capita), the Department of Energy ($101 per capita), and the National Aeronautics and Space Administration ($79 per capita). The GSA contracts were concentrated in the Washington suburbs; Energy contracts were greatest in the Washington suburbs, Tidewater and Lynchburg areas; and NASA contracts were heaviest in the Washington suburbs, Tidewater and Wallops Island areas.

Virginia's $1,902 per capita federal pay ranked the state third behind Alaska and Hawaii in that category. The Northern Virginia and Tidewater regions each had about 43 percent of the total, but the defense/nondefense ratios differed markedly between the two areas. The Tidewater area accounted for 52 percent of all defense and 17 percent of all nondefense salaries in Virginia, compared to Northern Virginia's 39 percent of defense and 54 percent of nondefense pay in the state.

Virginia's high ranking among the states in the salaries and wages category was due primarily to defense employment, which accounted for three-fourths of federal pay in the state. Among federal employers, the Navy's payroll was the largest, at $826 per capita, with the Army a distant second, at $328. About 70 percent of the Navy payroll was concentrated in the Tidewater area, and 25 percent was in the Washington suburbs. The Postal Service was the third largest federal employer in the state, at $156 per capita. Defense Department civilian and Air Force salaries were fourth and fifth largest, respectively.

Defense spending was directly related to the high per capita ranking of the five states discussed above. However, larger than average per capita defense outlays did not always boost states' rankings above the norm. Utah and North Carolina provide two examples. Both ranked in the top 10 in terms of per capita defense salaries and wages. Most of Utah's total was centered in Davis County at Hill Air Force Base. North Carolina's defense payroll was divided primarily among the Army at Fort Bragg in the Fayetteville area, the Navy at Camp Lejeune in Onslow County and the Air Force at Seymour Johnson Air Force Base in Wayne County. But even with the defense presence in these states, both ranked among the bottom 10 in total federal spending per capita.

Federal dollars may have a multiplier effect on local economies by boosting private sector employment, for example; they also may produce liabilities, such as an increased burden on the local infrastructure. This article did not attempt a cost/benefit analysis of the outlays, though that is certainly a topic worthy of research. It would also be useful to look at the other states, whatever their per capita ranking, to determine how federal spending priorities affect them.

Notes

[1] David Kellerman, "Federal Expenditures in the States and Other U.S. Jurisdictions: Fiscal 1990," in *The Book of the States 1992-93*, pp. 419-421.

[2] Excluding international transactions and interest payments on the public debt.

Table 6.33
SUMMARY DISTRIBUTION OF FEDERAL FUNDS, BY STATE AND TERRITORY: FISCAL YEAR 1993
(In millions of dollars)

State or other jurisdiction	Total	Grants to state and local governments	Salaries and wages	Direct payments for individuals	Procurement	Other programs
United States	$1,260,200	$195,201	$166,189	$650,952	$201,369	$46,489
Alabama	21,180	3,081	3,085	11,135	3,333	545
Alaska	4,611	948	1,624	886	972	181
Arizona	18,376	2,640	2,250	9,804	3,181	501
Arkansas	10,843	1,855	969	6,848	533	637
California	147,364	21,635	19,239	70,952	31,483	4,056
Colorado	18,159	2,109	3,452	7,461	4,253	883
Connecticut	16,447	2,691	1,368	8,671	3,277	439
Delaware	2,833	455	438	1,687	186	67
Florida	68,523	7,579	7,351	43,391	8,982	1,220
Georgia	30,139	4,408	5,832	14,505	4,670	725
Hawaii	7,052	984	2,385	2,732	743	208
Idaho	4,825	712	615	2,365	924	209
Illinois	47,559	7,845	5,306	29,368	3,189	1,851
Indiana	22,111	3,732	2,066	12,908	2,116	1,288
Iowa	12,131	1,737	864	7,163	658	1,709
Kansas	11,886	1,608	1,790	6,438	986	1,064
Kentucky	16,797	3,041	2,535	9,376	1,461	384
Louisiana	20,204	4,817	2,099	9,965	2,601	722
Maine	6,664	1,166	810	3,349	1,222	118
Maryland	33,775	3,310	7,227	12,743	7,745	2,750
Massachusetts	34,300	5,520	3,020	17,014	7,062	1,684
Michigan	36,830	6,654	2,725	24,177	2,243	1,031
Minnesota	18,017	3,297	1,525	9,549	2,034	1,612
Mississippi	13,080	2,285	1,469	6,825	2,014	488
Missouri	29,278	3,566	3,293	13,967	6,641	1,811
Montana	4,376	831	612	2,074	254	606
Nebraska	7,613	1,108	966	3,918	559	1,061
Nevada	5,766	767	738	3,147	1,031	83
New Hampshire	4,128	652	404	2,478	465	130
New Jersey	35,885	6,189	3,671	21,631	3,740	655
New Mexico	11,197	1,534	1,572	3,750	4,046	295
New York	87,442	21,166	7,241	49,121	7,438	2,477
North Carolina	27,210	4,498	4,727	15,350	1,868	767
North Dakota	3,642	640	559	1,586	235	623
Ohio	45,985	7,716	4,353	27,825	5,114	976
Oklahoma	14,799	2,111	2,609	8,420	1,022	638
Oregon	12,379	2,099	1,389	7,928	562	401
Pennsylvania	57,742	8,517	5,741	37,032	4,738	1,714
Rhode Island	5,287	1,107	610	2,972	467	130
South Carolina	16,367	2,521	2,537	8,275	2,734	299
South Dakota	3,627	654	553	1,730	240	450
Tennessee	23,778	3,925	2,600	12,544	4,285	425
Texas	75,268	11,035	9,887	38,653	12,755	2,938
Utah	7,461	1,173	1,504	3,263	1,279	242
Vermont	2,320	557	246	1,338	122	58
Virginia	44,295	2,945	12,346	16,086	11,432	1,487
Washington	24,832	3,722	4,105	12,584	3,461	961
West Virginia	8,928	1,884	756	5,663	463	163
Wisconsin	18,911	3,397	1,383	11,902	1,367	862
Wyoming	2,217	645	357	996	143	76
Dist. of Columbia	20,250	1,961	10,236	2,435	4,012	1,606
American Samoa	98	59	3	18	11	6
Guam	952	161	472	137	166	17
No. Mariana Islands ...	54	47	3	4	1	1
Puerto Rico	8,796	3,130	619	4,484	410	153
U.S. Virgin Islands	382	183	36	125	33	5
Adjustments or undistributed to states	25,227	592	20	206	24,408	0

Source: U.S. Department of Commerce, Bureau of the Census, *Federal Expenditures by State for Fiscal Year 1993*.
   Note: Detail may not add to totals due to rounding. For additional information on categories and distributions shown, see footnotes to Tables 6.34 through 6.38.

Table 6.34
FEDERAL GOVERNMENT GRANTS TO STATE AND LOCAL GOVERNMENTS BY AGENCY AND FOR SELECTED PROGRAMS, BY STATE AND TERRITORY: FISCAL YEAR 1993
(In thousands of dollars)

State or other jurisdiction	Total	Child nutrition programs	Food stamp administration (a)	Special supplemental food program (WIC)	Special milk program	State and private forestry	Economic development administration	Corporation for public broadcasting	National Guard centers —construction
United States (c) ...	$195,200,765	$6,340,005	$3,106,088	$2,838,720	$18,266	$82,452	$208,841	$313,422	$235,879
Alabama	3,081,234	136,318	64,068	58,447	33	2,221	5,885	1,487	3,663
Alaska	948,229	18,296	7,938	8,981	7	1,115	2,565	4,053	613
Arizona	2,640,230	111,397	20,661	50,311	151	720	2,114	2,482	10,202
Arkansas	1,854,928	85,544	12,911	36,045	21	1,080	7,401	992	2,720
California	21,634,772	813,854	335,614	316,607	933	7,688	11,351	20,332	9,424
Colorado	2,109,293	70,833	8,486	27,274	84	938	2,197	2,766	133
Connecticut	2,690,545	51,678	12,772	33,960	589	554	619	2,092	1,906
Delaware	455,281	18,835	3,818	7,857	1	233	40	0	360
Florida	7,578,676	339,370	52,317	105,328	137	1,398	1,488	9,905	5,699
Georgia	4,408,372	199,921	45,319	90,884	17	1,622	5,134	2,893	547
Hawaii	983,960	24,722	7,121	15,463	7	525	370	1,422	3,461
Idaho	712,276	25,328	4,222	15,441	187	1,430	3,669	1,422	10,522
Illinois	7,845,179	239,069	45,962	113,796	2,905	2,538	8,286	8,026	5,472
Indiana	3,732,487	100,481	23,465	61,843	347	1,023	4,877	4,795	1,540
Iowa	1,736,552	59,246	8,201	27,066	222	1,423	3,471	2,402	13,350
Kansas	1,607,885	79,861	7,681	24,832	264	575	1,376	2,110	4,125
Kentucky	3,040,509	113,475	25,045	51,523	164	1,179	5,920	3,151	1,396
Louisiana	4,817,050	187,716	31,429	68,417	69	1,820	6,964	2,492	4,404
Maine	1,166,081	27,195	5,489	11,975	128	1,196	2,583	1,795	1,197
Maryland	3,309,611	85,639	298,571	39,421	382	2,347	396	3,293	2,522
Massachusetts	5,520,291	104,554	19,862	42,907	514	804	3,182	7,263	1,200
Michigan	6,653,913	160,895	60,650	80,353	1,323	2,985	10,180	6,376	2,264
Minnesota	3,297,195	121,024	61,450	38,326	849	826	5,861	14,618	15,721
Mississippi	2,284,603	135,927	18,073	40,765	11	2,041	4,526	1,132	8,178
Missouri	3,565,884	113,152	26,248	53,718	464	1,410	5,480	3,241	10,537
Montana	830,732	21,896	5,008	9,816	67	1,122	2,028	642	920
Nebraska	1,108,448	45,718	5,613	15,236	230	545	476	2,916	1,790
Nevada	766,813	19,889	5,272	10,109	93	1,406	314	1,301	326
New Hampshire	651,746	13,300	2,753	8,535	176	909	171	887	0
New Jersey	6,189,385	116,118	46,377	62,668	1,081	816	2,520	1,900	11
New Mexico	1,533,749	72,175	59,223	23,237	18	833	2,059	2,196	5,374
New York	21,165,769	378,856	119,750	226,145	1,431	2,642	11,456	25,212	3,961
North Carolina	4,497,708	182,846	32,063	73,468	132	4,257	3,936	3,433	4,450
North Dakota	639,834	22,160	3,729	8,995	66	457	1,569	1,407	8,028
Ohio	7,716,434	204,571	104,001	108,413	1,056	12	4,204	8,050	263
Oklahoma	2,110,813	93,861	19,533	38,479	119	433	3,242	1,945	2,893
Oregon	2,099,267	62,659	23,127	27,491	212	1,445	3,488	2,800	2,118
Pennsylvania	8,516,588	195,418	99,563	115,301	805	2,968	5,869	11,125	2,325
Rhode Island	1,107,470	15,787	5,273	10,653	132	530	218	496	55
South Carolina	2,521,314	114,527	16,846	56,491	0	3,570	6,472	4,551	1,383
South Dakota	654,355	23,927	3,925	11,804	48	596	657	1,407	1,542
Tennessee	3,924,795	131,097	27,631	58,269	15	1,329	6,821	3,580	7,180
Texas	11,035,112	613,147	119,038	216,442	125	1,970	15,456	8,180	34,189
Utah	1,173,441	61,535	10,595	24,151	89	719	447	2,438	5,932
Vermont	556,885	11,498	7,622	8,709	173	1,042	110	992	2,084
Virginia	2,945,168	97,078	38,094	55,167	108	3,598	3,045	31,127	8,091
Washington	3,722,068	105,778	75,307	41,642	285	692	6,030	4,655	2,341
West Virginia	1,883,792	51,440	5,907	23,829	34	7,788	9,412	1,686	727
Wisconsin	3,396,867	82,414	25,036	45,350	1,918	1,556	2,490	4,316	13,138
Wyoming	644,614	11,762	3,117	6,040	19	782	287	483	3,600
Dist. of Columbia	1,960,840	18,022	8,066	6,776	17	259	910	7,058	163
American Samoa ...	59,460	5,807	0	0	0	0	170	364	0
Guam	160,564	3,210	1,989	3,490	0	0	10	374	93
No. Mariana Islands ..	46,642	490	3,539	0	0	156	70	0	0
Puerto Rico	3,130,170	130,633	1,018,582	115,746	0	260	5,518	1,634	1,436
U.S. Virgin Islands ...	182,626	4,907	2,135	4,728	9	69	3,435	391	310

See footnotes at end of table.

FEDERAL GOVERNMENT GRANTS—Continued

State or other jurisdiction	School improvement programs	Construction of wastewater treatment facilities	FEMA-disaster relief	Support payments (AFDC)	Low income home energy assistance	Medicaid	Supplemental security income	Section 8 housing assistance grants (b)
United States (c)	$1,902,676	$2,126,004	$1,155,247	$15,641,147	$1,346,026	$75,774,060	$33,500	$9,239,379
Alabama	32,835	22,542	12,062	110,882	11,778	1,203,939	717	95,726
Alaska	9,290	6,294	1,440	66,030	8,670	168,012	25	16,253
Arizona	25,859	16,666	20,758	234,979	6,688	975,989	612	79,187
Arkansas	19,071	16,075	2,638	57,177	8,683	782,350	56	71,136
California	204,379	137,176	153,572	3,329,219	62,968	7,413,922	2,363	1,266,886
Colorado	22,362	14,005	1,209	124,079	21,570	728,125	182	111,195
Connecticut	20,536	29,421	6,094	216,852	28,166	1,103,057	307	182,683
Delaware	9,319	6,034	1,939	30,676	3,789	132,490	85	26,321
Florida	80,006	76,678	390,672	588,124	17,942	2,857,407	1,094	329,192
Georgia	49,981	24,357	20,025	350,135	14,191	1,762,277	125	169,736
Hawaii	9,360	22,492	62,791	82,155	1,429	220,700	87	57,336
Idaho	9,380	4,400	411	27,553	8,394	221,286	208	30,468
Illinois	84,782	126,663	18,572	539,188	76,704	2,544,787	1,359	437,311
Indiana	39,326	32,998	11,399	188,201	34,741	1,796,915	920	150,258
Iowa	19,674	20,640	8,410	121,749	24,600	617,261	510	75,609
Kansas	17,489	19,547	6,471	101,206	11,686	666,566	266	46,465
Kentucky	29,141	33,062	4,295	195,715	18,075	1,297,607	877	125,223
Louisiana	37,431	22,794	78,545	166,183	11,597	2,820,173	279	116,915
Maine	9,468	18,888	4,967	84,067	18,184	524,797	163	68,070
Maryland	31,792	53,209	10,208	225,526	22,458	1,092,892	672	199,377
Massachusetts	38,548	166,348	13,815	467,379	56,757	2,016,770	1,409	489,638
Michigan	70,306	88,687	6,096	793,054	73,801	2,546,524	1,485	255,299
Minnesota	30,620	32,980	18,123	286,976	52,550	1,275,610	1,050	174,351
Mississippi	24,892	16,167	5,314	83,825	9,749	933,006	230	85,162
Missouri	36,400	51,610	13,015	216,124	30,671	1,403,709	754	158,126
Montana	9,339	10,836	431	43,063	10,097	231,600	199	22,986
Nebraska	11,554	7,690	4,031	78,277	12,158	361,715	167	42,171
Nevada	9,345	22,443	537	38,442	2,806	217,419	21	36,965
New Hampshire	9,343	19,691	1,712	39,286	10,522	210,299	45	44,300
New Jersey	52,518	59,886	28,861	446,614	54,767	2,820,194	571	399,004
New Mexico	12,942	8,758	1,149	97,083	6,441	438,178	16	42,035
New York	136,127	245,371	42,652	1,856,408	171,633	10,228,329	3,700	1,027,276
North Carolina	45,557	42,597	13,070	329,779	25,053	1,926,138	1,181	173,469
North Dakota	9,312	7,414	736	26,539	10,738	197,406	0	25,621
Ohio	77,473	123,586	10,537	733,854	68,453	3,230,049	1,551	396,054
Oklahoma	23,080	13,570	11,771	175,359	10,778	796,851	376	89,740
Oregon	19,570	28,873	6,538	163,508	16,686	642,305	539	102,612
Pennsylvania	81,973	70,897	29,773	616,408	92,531	3,320,631	1,755	398,700
Rhode Island	9,380	6,909	2,878	80,671	9,237	480,049	86	87,998
South Carolina	26,969	14,791	12,091	107,293	9,047	1,210,029	276	96,466
South Dakota	9,290	13,580	2,741	21,785	8,708	194,368	334	23,113
Tennessee	36,105	29,687	14,261	206,597	18,320	1,858,605	577	136,483
Texas	133,235	98,468	13,441	511,263	29,942	4,736,398	3,035	434,915
Utah	15,884	6,758	690	77,321	9,819	357,084	110	32,411
Vermont	9,295	7,567	1,965	45,845	7,925	167,424	44	25,070
Virginia	41,407	35,058	8,082	171,002	25,871	921,500	1,236	195,814
Washington	32,426	55,571	25,612	435,678	28,038	1,371,891	659	134,234
West Virginia	13,885	15,654	3,766	111,930	11,947	917,311	250	67,675
Wisconsin	34,948	85,838	7,523	334,646	47,999	1,303,774	868	141,631
Wyoming	9,281	4,125	294	26,369	3,973	102,756	31	12,810
Dist. of Columbia	9,372	11,133	884	82,112	4,908	344,741	38	65,884
American Samoa	2,706	0	136	0	29	1,450	0	0
Guam	6,233	578	16,423	5,578	64	2,293	0	6,311
No. Mariana Islands . . .	1,566	573	83	0	22	695	0	4,447
Puerto Rico	42,021	17,408	9,220	87,655	1,598	73,692	0	155,264
U.S. Virgin Islands	5,156	991	10,662	3,727	61	2,715	0	-4

FEDERAL GOVERNMENT GRANTS—Continued

State or other jurisdiction	Public housing grants	Office of Justice Assistance-justice programs	State unemployment insurance & services	Highway trust fund	State justice institute grants	FAA-airport trust fund	Urban mass transportation administration	All other grants
United States (c)	$3,198,769	$670,653	$3,436,068	$16,151,706	$10,924	$1,931,239	$3,515,859	$45,923,835
Alabama............	58,276	9,864	40,072	307,316	109	23,849	16,108	863,037
Alaska.............	36,772	2,395	29,368	222,717	101	73,448	2,232	261,614
Arizona............	68,264	11,913	40,742	244,586	174	46,560	17,526	651,689
Arkansas...........	21,329	6,508	28,381	203,775	11	14,081	8,831	468,112
California..........	115,308	90,619	536,693	1,379,548	372	125,845	488,318	4,811,781
Colorado	29,102	9,255	38,544	245,702	141	89,063	31,084	530,964
Connecticut	68,290	7,651	70,627	328,820	7	15,065	57,654	451,145
Delaware	10,197	3,948	9,037	57,375	91	852	2,714	129,270
Florida	75,409	31,327	119,085	630,069	129	103,831	124,611	1,637,458
Georgia............	81,924	13,620	60,090	409,562	216	50,706	58,232	996,859
Hawaii	23,989	4,184	16,042	192,702	0	13,427	22,908	201,267
Idaho	5,296	3,238	21,475	104,040	0	11,550	2,491	199,865
Illinois.............	295,834	23,266	151,096	544,413	131	132,188	369,075	2,073,755
Indiana............	32,406	10,628	49,107	382,779	8	32,182	26,591	745,656
Iowa	10,682	7,315	29,593	216,083	129	17,911	13,737	437,268
Kansas	18,924	7,006	22,705	162,167	0	19,627	8,125	378,812
Kentucky	63,061	8,425	32,049	215,145	44	46,402	17,779	751,756
Louisiana	43,139	9,965	35,300	292,266	8	44,339	28,937	805,867
Maine	17,067	3,059	24,275	87,146	77	11,408	4,917	237,971
Maryland	60,565	10,938	47,502	257,547	48	14,707	80,158	769,442
Massachusetts	50,958	15,923	100,118	773,253	164	35,834	125,065	988,026
Michigan	87,308	20,048	146,064	436,556	372	69,435	80,405	1,653,447
Minnesota	62,013	9,718	50,928	316,966	128	21,536	19,273	685,693
Mississippi	22,197	5,591	24,986	190,047	6	9,032	8,733	655,013
Missouri	43,233	14,225	58,578	339,151	41	23,497	123,762	838,738
Montana...........	15,543	3,357	13,229	161,118	1	14,821	2,248	250,365
Nebraska	21,637	5,584	20,078	137,138	50	11,575	9,386	312,713
Nevada	15,431	3,899	24,545	99,983	1,031	34,309	4,329	216,598
New Hampshire	13,848	3,972	14,138	97,673	43	12,750	3,218	144,174
New Jersey.........	111,954	14,271	117,202	440,126	55	15,096	158,233	1,238,543
New Mexico........	27,907	5,695	18,528	218,166	116	27,622	4,609	459,389
New York	672,038	43,659	268,622	854,549	240	102,340	576,603	4,166,768
North Carolina	62,192	13,524	60,499	425,236	330	32,940	23,979	1,017,579
North Dakota	10,701	3,073	13,008	108,635	52	10,011	2,906	167,272
Ohio	124,051	25,119	111,128	529,229	187	67,832	81,020	1,705,741
Oklahoma	45,492	8,726	29,419	159,261	0	25,664	9,283	550,938
Oregon	11,947	9,641	49,369	169,531	78	19,172	68,372	667,186
Pennsylvania	145,487	28,242	177,231	659,110	240	62,171	243,260	2,154,805
Rhode Island	27,695	3,420	21,646	131,513	0	3,760	18,184	190,901
South Carolina	20,657	7,918	33,605	213,521	169	13,261	9,341	542,040
South Dakota	20,712	2,951	9,608	120,523	0	7,304	2,539	172,893
Tennessee	56,266	17,171	43,848	244,428	55	44,211	29,998	952,261
Texas..............	116,252	52,457	164,553	1,060,705	14	173,975	119,776	2,378,136
Utah	8,720	6,501	31,793	153,997	49	28,260	28,128	310,010
Vermont	3,563	3,743	10,764	116,044	44	1,020	3,847	120,495
Virginia............	45,607	16,597	53,356	225,782	239	67,217	27,974	872,118
Washington	55,703	15,350	84,188	366,542	118	37,903	29,787	811,637
West Virginia	12,435	4,789	18,701	141,383	20	6,818	5,907	450,498
Wisconsin..........	36,644	11,342	62,040	347,798	229	22,937	33,285	749,147
Wyoming	2,020	2,066	10,447	118,610	1	14,064	1,731	309,946
Dist. of Columbia....	5,513	5,485	17,638	51,800	0	226	251,278	1,068,557
American Samoa	0	1,300	20	4,439	0	727	0	42,312
Guam	377	791	505	7,217	0	2,589	573	101,866
No. Mariana Islands...	5,438	801	0	4,123	0	2,957	0	21,682
Puerto Rico	72,929	7,115	26,805	68,331	1	15,467	20,618	1,258,237
U.S. Virgin Islands	26,740	1,385	2,332	8,054	0	5,647	582	98,594

Source: U.S. Department of Commerce, Bureau of the Census, *Federal Expenditures by State for Fiscal Year 1993.*

Note: Detail may not add to totals due to rounding. All amounts in this table represent actual expenditures of the federal government during the fiscal year.

(a) For Puerto Rico, amount shown is for nutritional assistance grant program. All other amounts are grant payments for food stamp administration.

(b) Section 8 payments to public agencies; Section 8 payments to non-public agencies are included in Table 6.36.

(c) Includes undistributed monies: $65,336 for corporation for public broadcasting, $144,766 for state unemployment insurance & services, $167,410 for the highway trust fund, and $211,744 for other programs.

Table 6.35
FEDERAL GOVERNMENT EXPENDITURES FOR SALARIES AND WAGES,
BY STATE AND TERRITORY: FISCAL YEAR 1993
(In thousands of dollars)

State or other jurisdiction	Total	Department of Defense Total	Military Total	Military Active	Military Inactive	Civilian	Postal service	All other federal agencies
United States	$166,189,234	$73,947,670	$43,631,622	$39,141,047	$4,490,575	$30,316,048	$39,849,979	$52,391,585
Alabama	3,084,786	1,646,232	746,282	584,943	161,339	899,950	478,573	959,981
Alaska	1,624,408	1,085,136	890,989	870,564	20,425	194,147	108,964	430,308
Arizona	2,249,944	928,954	609,651	551,205	58,446	319,303	507,624	813,366
Arkansas	969,454	359,125	220,358	166,594	53,764	138,767	290,935	319,394
California	19,238,701	10,555,446	6,491,647	6,180,809	310,838	4,063,799	4,530,166	4,153,089
Colorado	3,452,201	1,514,773	1,091,084	974,972	116,112	423,689	635,875	1,301,553
Connecticut	1,368,348	461,247	286,083	257,075	29,008	175,164	615,445	291,656
Delaware	438,349	190,781	140,358	110,226	30,132	50,423	188,972	58,596
Florida	7,351,167	3,594,558	2,531,713	2,403,334	128,379	1,062,845	2,070,262	1,686,347
Georgia	5,831,518	3,268,343	2,149,593	1,940,082	209,511	1,118,750	962,840	1,600,335
Hawaii	2,384,999	2,071,888	1,432,957	1,393,828	39,129	638,931	137,395	175,716
Idaho	614,529	197,968	153,346	128,342	25,004	44,622	125,394	291,167
Illinois	5,305,850	1,453,565	821,238	694,660	126,578	632,327	2,215,360	1,636,925
Indiana	2,066,153	865,560	342,391	129,467	212,924	523,169	742,505	458,088
Iowa	863,936	109,704	62,293	14,339	47,954	47,411	480,478	273,754
Kansas	1,789,553	919,464	720,289	629,541	90,748	199,175	416,376	453,713
Kentucky	2,535,374	1,542,157	1,137,868	1,064,803	73,065	404,289	439,855	553,362
Louisiana	2,098,718	955,200	695,041	591,977	103,064	260,159	516,339	627,179
Maine	809,644	475,205	194,370	171,135	23,235	280,835	206,212	128,227
Maryland	7,227,142	2,517,751	1,024,517	909,265	115,252	1,493,234	835,944	3,873,447
Massachusetts	3,020,391	725,018	335,029	214,097	120,932	389,989	1,240,605	1,054,768
Michigan	2,724,590	638,306	238,026	147,388	90,638	400,280	1,364,999	721,285
Minnesota	1,524,773	213,131	116,398	32,849	83,549	96,733	769,070	542,572
Mississippi	1,468,754	840,123	495,351	424,336	71,015	344,772	271,885	356,746
Missouri	3,292,539	1,203,521	582,747	468,782	113,965	620,774	981,754	1,107,264
Montana	612,454	169,453	130,406	109,782	20,624	39,047	125,108	317,893
Nebraska	966,342	456,004	332,718	304,330	28,388	123,286	283,315	227,023
Nevada	738,216	293,948	230,380	216,972	13,408	63,568	180,400	263,868
New Hampshire	403,532	92,571	43,179	27,167	16,012	49,392	186,829	124,132
New Jersey	3,670,988	1,299,250	400,173	296,156	104,017	899,077	1,580,727	791,011
New Mexico	1,572,274	743,667	433,308	409,924	23,384	310,359	203,545	625,062
New York	7,241,088	1,447,884	897,127	718,454	178,673	550,757	3,315,142	2,478,062
North Carolina	4,727,138	3,161,271	2,685,885	2,588,361	97,524	475,386	876,615	689,252
North Dakota	558,771	297,469	242,901	223,413	19,488	54,568	112,345	148,957
Ohio	4,353,182	1,721,373	521,394	400,301	121,093	1,199,979	1,598,785	1,033,024
Oklahoma	2,608,758	1,566,507	909,926	822,600	87,326	656,581	451,142	591,109
Oregon	1,388,859	183,584	80,154	32,096	48,058	103,430	402,804	802,471
Pennsylvania	5,740,504	1,993,312	482,531	246,646	235,885	1,510,781	2,113,183	1,634,009
Rhode Island	610,046	336,980	182,675	165,015	17,660	154,305	184,019	89,047
South Carolina	2,537,342	1,874,305	1,341,821	1,245,224	96,597	532,484	368,276	294,761
South Dakota	552,759	203,419	165,682	147,532	18,150	37,737	117,060	232,280
Tennessee	2,599,643	509,646	297,687	198,785	98,902	211,959	716,027	1,373,970
Texas	9,886,561	4,488,403	2,782,255	2,541,417	240,838	1,706,148	2,388,724	3,009,434
Utah	1,503,543	847,053	223,437	158,113	65,324	623,616	196,306	460,184
Vermont	245,731	42,912	24,053	5,414	18,639	18,859	109,916	92,903
Virginia	12,345,986	9,151,674	5,060,670	4,941,609	119,061	4,091,004	1,014,649	2,179,663
Washington	4,104,770	2,360,412	1,361,524	1,242,312	119,212	998,888	695,358	1,049,000
West Virginia	755,686	106,995	52,233	15,302	36,931	54,762	244,978	403,713
Wisconsin	1,383,143	254,859	160,802	38,966	121,836	94,057	720,799	407,485
Wyoming	357,377	132,815	100,937	89,133	11,804	31,878	61,959	162,603
Dist. of Columbia	10,236,174	1,235,975	579,208	541,908	37,300	656,767	281,743	8,718,456
American Samoa	2,528	36	0	0	0	36	476	2,016
Guam	471,523	451,626	280,767	279,188	1,579	170,859	6,905	12,992
No. Mariana Islands . . .	2,548	6	6	6	0	0	571	1,971
Puerto Rico	619,164	186,872	117,643	79,875	37,768	69,229	164,160	268,132
U.S. Virgin Islands	36,420	4,233	521	433	88	3,712	14,287	17,900

Source: U.S. Department of Commerce, Bureau of the Census, *Federal Expenditures by State for Fiscal Year 1993.*
    Note: Detail may not add to totals due to rounding. U.S. total includes $20.4 million undistributed monies for all other federal agencies.

Table 6.36
FEDERAL GOVERNMENT DIRECT PAYMENTS FOR INDIVIDUALS BY PROGRAM, STATE AND TERRITORY: FISCAL YEAR 1993
(In thousands of dollars)

State or other jurisdiction	Total	Social Security Retirement insurance payments	Social Security Survivors insurance payments	Social Security Disability insurance payments	Medicare Hospital insurance payments	Medicare Supplementary medical insurance payments	Federal retirement & disability payments Civilian	Federal retirement & disability payments Military	Payments for unemployment compensation
United States (a)....	$650,952,250	$203,803,980	$60,336,808	$33,804,687	$100,593,684	$54,127,869	$35,573,050	$25,752,104	$34,929,997
Alabama...........	11,135,232	2,971,145	1,169,165	740,396	1,573,453	737,653	836,872	634,381	264,317
Alaska.............	886,041	171,369	60,934	39,516	57,675	30,232	110,487	83,934	169,058
Arizona...........	9,803,860	3,357,973	821,421	532,699	1,156,940	738,724	675,087	672,951	279,752
Arkansas..........	6,848,449	1,971,081	670,098	506,294	962,413	568,277	332,675	319,912	251,749
California..........	70,951,543	19,883,860	5,231,169	3,127,364	10,786,358	7,387,829	3,447,194	3,413,016	5,749,492
Colorado	7,460,581	2,172,043	650,061	437,393	968,007	471,112	617,249	683,301	262,545
Connecticut	8,671,487	3,287,653	741,339	351,982	1,404,201	769,996	227,299	152,290	871,355
Delaware	1,686,802	602,917	161,301	85,199	223,033	128,143	88,514	81,642	87,404
Florida	43,391,122	15,067,065	3,517,842	1,826,707	6,461,997	4,194,603	2,656,441	2,692,993	1,218,973
Georgia...........	14,504,709	3,983,991	1,397,904	996,137	1,717,630	1,063,194	990,569	943,355	465,352
Hawaii	2,731,781	842,849	171,894	80,193	261,288	169,500	377,383	214,800	222,835
Idaho	2,365,355	817,672	224,959	123,797	282,056	152,917	150,430	125,963	121,845
Illinois............	29,368,261	9,603,464	2,865,588	1,366,470	5,696,747	2,474,241	957,960	391,248	1,803,535
Indiana	12,908,369	4,885,201	1,487,002	813,879	2,033,806	956,171	450,034	238,105	191,950
Iowa	7,162,691	2,723,699	811,254	324,708	1,242,084	549,068	274,847	103,861	247,897
Kansas	6,438,317	2,213,856	640,006	261,074	1,161,417	474,940	326,118	243,514	269,344
Kentucky	9,375,869	2,588,921	1,052,070	795,776	1,418,278	483,337	401,750	268,422	319,722
Louisiana	9,965,284	2,524,365	1,225,746	708,321	1,524,471	603,554	358,439	365,647	262,984
Maine	3,348,930	1,026,902	292,824	184,891	536,693	233,039	191,093	143,677	192,103
Maryland	12,743,360	3,281,060	1,005,116	441,940	1,805,712	943,546	2,391,845	664,598	592,856
Massachusetts	17,013,915	5,280,574	1,350,704	814,789	3,250,634	1,640,431	736,218	268,236	1,300,810
Michigan	24,177,087	8,065,004	2,512,312	1,411,822	4,295,786	2,359,568	554,359	266,818	1,642,321
Minnesota	9,548,961	3,496,993	979,844	445,127	1,510,868	731,908	366,540	163,616	486,523
Mississippi	6,825,470	1,710,651	672,923	522,634	966,347	457,453	315,857	294,872	165,381
Missouri	13,967,003	4,525,057	1,382,120	782,832	2,680,264	877,051	724,952	405,613	515,129
Montana..........	2,073,696	673,513	204,524	126,343	288,717	145,646	146,588	82,779	73,315
Nebraska	3,918,244	1,385,997	404,768	163,712	673,746	288,082	192,088	167,827	60,667
Nevada	3,146,855	1,066,496	237,865	172,240	320,372	194,578	233,662	304,533	198,059
New Hampshire	2,478,043	925,042	216,717	129,499	369,142	169,251	170,149	136,597	67,931
New Jersey........	21,630,524	7,416,343	1,864,156	926,528	3,731,986	2,047,518	899,487	306,661	2,103,601
New Mexico........	3,749,931	1,024,407	331,440	207,742	395,715	244,744	357,466	299,542	93,688
New York	49,120,520	15,908,173	4,133,591	2,468,539	8,595,808	5,136,823	1,502,452	396,404	3,641,357
North Carolina	15,350,151	5,198,769	1,502,702	1,114,547	1,838,816	1,021,231	755,380	877,658	481,245
North Dakota	1,585,592	511,186	176,386	61,962	331,057	130,866	74,480	35,868	38,697
Ohio	27,825,266	9,113,410	3,143,460	1,522,129	4,637,579	2,236,151	1,157,211	475,137	1,188,062
Oklahoma	8,419,760	2,526,748	843,927	420,796	1,304,619	560,085	700,116	417,805	201,474
Oregon	7,928,066	2,770,832	687,813	368,668	1,142,340	521,982	464,764	274,342	582,840
Pennsylvania	37,031,992	12,155,272	3,656,567	1,451,060	6,721,986	3,503,506	1,596,043	565,481	2,569,443
Rhode Island	2,972,138	994,165	221,794	139,315	438,418	254,857	147,755	88,102	292,414
South Carolina	8,274,746	2,529,569	793,299	604,476	940,337	421,039	513,190	670,444	272,777
South Dakota	1,729,957	590,999	186,523	78,928	292,158	116,990	109,921	57,321	14,699
Tennessee	12,543,763	3,722,605	1,285,431	877,904	1,840,094	853,078	628,878	519,467	387,438
Texas	38,652,645	10,507,291	3,887,765	1,752,626	5,396,681	3,149,893	2,074,027	2,549,106	1,742,375
Utah	3,263,107	1,047,521	292,582	151,454	289,119	181,130	476,847	146,743	110,606
Vermont	1,337,729	456,447	128,084	75,717	209,097	91,399	57,764	38,824	80,084
Virginia...........	16,085,746	4,058,202	1,293,954	782,192	1,787,389	955,889	2,399,767	2,076,454	387,527
Washington	12,583,927	4,031,317	1,024,472	594,665	1,385,798	824,243	942,357	959,862	1,057,516
West Virginia	5,662,619	1,545,460	676,024	430,156	845,050	353,608	190,109	109,795	215,763
Wisconsin	11,902,226	4,538,412	1,236,982	632,051	2,010,040	991,427	325,004	165,283	545,783
Wyoming	996,435	330,992	97,560	53,490	129,738	61,319	66,850	48,830	35,847
Dist. of Columbia.....	2,435,407	326,505	102,902	55,125	413,515	211,507	705,155	50,390	204,421
American Samoa	18,249	5,283	5,382	3,385	0	0	149	1,754	0
Guam	136,608	25,784	14,525	4,678	3,351	2,734	26,972	22,383	0
No. Mariana Islands...	3,541	0	0	0	0	0	0	337	0
Puerto Rico	4,483,643	1,321,392	575,940	704,821	275,526	257,239	90,362	67,789	319,166
U.S. Virgin Islands	124,703	40,483	14,058	7,996	7,335	4,569	5,166	1,821	7,970

See footnotes at end of table.

FEDERAL GOVERNMENT DIRECT PAYMENTS—Continued

State or other jurisdiction	Veterans benefits programs	Supplemental security income payments	Food stamps	Housing assistance	Pell grants	Excess earned income tax credit	National guaranteed student loan interest subsidies	Federal workers compensation payemts	All other
United States (a)...	$17,481,858	$21,137,159	$22,033,488	$10,496,222	$5,871,809	$10,182,950	$1,311,357	$1,821,631	$43,118,220
Alabama..........	409,902	536,778	457,946	117,020	120,250	292,761	11,447	48,914	212,832
Alaska............	42,507	20,249	44,927	22,559	9,295	8,540	169	9,507	5,083
Arizona..........	322,667	242,430	397,094	106,534	93,497	188,442	18,229	40,002	159,418
Arkansas	313,714	289,719	210,023	88,602	54,861	142,258	6,186	21,068	139,519
California.........	1,369,908	3,104,186	2,054,344	2,119,740	567,978	1,668,477	76,072	288,757	675,799
Colorado	266,852	186,711	226,136	118,449	78,949	108,061	29,054	29,493	155,165
Connecticut	141,936	157,552	142,448	252,644	33,877	40,806	8,126	9,497	78,486
Delaware	41,721	34,084	46,294	32,301	9,485	24,444	564	5,613	34,143
Florida	1,283,971	1,107,984	1,335,354	386,749	249,363	611,790	58,904	117,370	603,016
Georgia..........	552,351	671,568	657,321	235,491	133,262	386,393	8,630	53,356	248,205
Hawaii	69,085	64,044	131,887	63,948	9,086	20,446	1,846	20,028	10,669
Idaho	72,546	51,408	56,858	27,500	31,046	40,949	5,479	8,628	71,302
Illinois...........	424,539	1,056,980	1,069,037	293,736	217,531	402,958	48,073	32,670	663,484
Indiana	281,803	317,075	405,229	155,774	137,283	181,126	35,628	18,721	319,582
Iowa	157,149	132,653	149,216	82,637	76,310	66,051	24,670	7,141	189,446
Kansas	171,123	115,786	141,083	52,531	66,164	69,013	13,582	8,672	210,094
Kentucky	320,147	525,744	421,907	118,980	93,900	146,097	12,294	27,427	381,097
Louisiana	341,298	631,319	654,851	151,284	124,559	294,847	13,414	24,230	155,955
Maine	141,976	75,950	112,838	64,507	20,844	30,740	7,293	9,054	84,506
Maryland	281,172	281,318	338,165	195,352	74,214	153,402	7,175	78,912	206,977
Massachusetts	472,371	462,315	324,752	635,068	125,927	93,736	56,054	35,193	166,103
Michigan	444,026	752,955	840,211	229,455	221,039	231,437	29,912	27,525	292,532
Minnesota	258,673	195,652	233,575	178,425	119,148	84,507	6,862	16,334	274,366
Mississippi	272,090	460,148	417,531	101,638	82,432	248,537	11,242	19,031	106,703
Missouri	370,600	378,490	477,341	189,511	122,783	186,121	22,153	20,610	306,376
Montana..........	70,598	42,243	54,073	5,669	25,061	27,700	7,058	8,662	91,207
Nebraska	118,127	68,024	81,543	48,668	41,762	46,257	25,486	5,368	146,122
Nevada	103,448	57,584	85,420	44,622	14,784	51,453	232	14,533	46,974
New Hampshire	91,260	31,814	46,494	43,268	17,568	21,015	2,396	7,860	32,040
New Jersey.......	362,011	480,339	464,733	410,334	111,932	224,217	10,570	48,495	221,613
New Mexico.......	159,038	142,153	195,505	44,458	46,167	93,801	8,272	23,629	82,164
New York	912,995	1,932,340	1,789,184	780,085	628,153	537,930	135,154	87,788	533,744
North Carolina	576,862	597,200	482,210	180,343	107,224	367,745	13,951	34,846	199,422
North Dakota	41,384	27,580	36,292	15,601	23,724	15,883	7,696	2,429	54,501
Ohio	631,708	873,455	1,098,545	410,273	242,447	300,960	70,497	50,391	673,851
Oklahoma	415,100	237,971	294,098	115,826	94,351	137,837	9,171	36,004	103,832
Oregon	235,766	157,520	238,192	137,071	71,104	94,597	1,860	26,075	152,300
Pennsylvania	727,699	877,678	963,056	369,386	236,359	283,034	80,596	74,609	1,200,217
Rhode Island	81,294	65,942	72,345	87,049	27,389	22,397	8,703	6,323	23,876
South Carolina	293,558	357,711	307,454	124,794	74,340	229,009	13,828	22,726	106,195
South Dakota	65,706	41,316	42,864	26,732	23,579	23,281	27,738	3,802	27,400
Tennessee	423,029	587,370	617,123	152,189	95,077	256,134	12,043	55,307	230,596
Texas	1,369,842	1,244,737	2,240,887	563,512	344,152	1,068,358	79,081	133,933	548,379
Utah	87,717	67,808	97,672	40,342	82,254	53,015	15,874	17,486	104,937
Vermont	42,425	36,162	37,918	21,071	11,842	12,661	6,785	1,896	29,553
Virginia	534,528	399,860	430,390	164,250	114,105	223,904	22,866	67,753	386,716
Washington	407,249	309,486	380,536	184,724	98,701	130,412	4,748	54,113	193,728
West Virginia	186,679	226,648	261,403	84,863	40,871	65,419	3,979	9,070	417,722
Wisconsin	286,900	325,760	225,983	155,048	97,687	111,635	36,319	13,008	204,904
Wyoming	31,291	18,510	26,469	12,013	13,670	14,917	2,061	3,367	49,511
Dist. of Columbia....	54,237	74,366	80,086	50,616	14,805	35,662	3,719	15,392	36,982
American Samoa ...	1,801	0	0	15	377	0	26	45	32
Guam	4,717	0	17,316	11,607	1,019	0	0	887	635
No. Mariana Islands..	200	2,483	0	0	501	0	0	0	20
Puerto Rico	337,513	0	0	180,717	297,048	0	3,296	10,786	42,048
U.S. Virgin Islands ...	3,049	0	19,328	10,641	674	0	6	140	1,467

Source: U.S. Department of Commerce, Bureau of the Census, *Federal Expenditures by State for Fiscal Year 1993.*
Note: Detail may not add to totals due to rounding. Amounts represent actual expenditures during the fiscal year.

(a) Includes undistributed monies amounting to $206 million.

Table 6.37
FEDERAL GOVERNMENT PROCUREMENT CONTRACTS—VALUE OF AWARDS, BY STATE AND TERRITORY: FISCAL YEAR 1993
(In thousands of dollars)

State or other jurisdiction	Total	Department of Defense	Postal service	All other federal agencies
United States	$201,369,188	$129,996,047	$7,759,139	$63,614,002
Alabama	3,333,445	1,739,466	93,143	1,500,836
Alaska	971,502	553,440	21,207	396,855
Arizona	3,181,035	2,587,911	98,797	494,327
Arkansas	533,278	329,614	56,624	147,040
California	31,483,092	22,788,845	882,040	7,812,207
Colorado	4,253,355	2,614,097	123,758	1,515,500
Connecticut	3,277,143	2,878,268	119,782	279,093
Delaware	185,686	135,492	36,779	13,415
Florida	8,981,523	6,452,128	402,928	2,126,467
Georgia	4,670,225	3,973,386	187,531	509,308
Hawaii	742,528	624,366	26,741	91,421
Idaho	924,167	65,517	24,405	834,245
Illinois	3,188,682	1,335,789	431,395	1,421,498
Indiana	2,115,894	1,752,546	144,511	218,837
Iowa	658,384	363,016	93,514	201,854
Kansas	986,347	655,001	81,062	250,284
Kentucky	1,461,422	817,123	85,608	558,691
Louisiana	2,600,569	1,548,264	100,493	951,812
Maine	1,222,113	1,106,986	40,134	74,993
Maryland	7,744,505	3,950,995	162,697	3,630,813
Massachusetts	7,061,736	5,938,786	241,455	881,495
Michigan	2,243,058	1,357,745	265,665	619,648
Minnesota	2,034,045	1,486,359	149,681	398,005
Mississippi	2,013,523	1,573,935	52,916	386,672
Missouri	6,640,882	5,292,227	191,076	1,157,579
Montana	253,586	78,992	24,349	150,245
Nebraska	559,215	301,258	55,141	202,816
Nevada	1,031,462	224,021	35,111	772,330
New Hampshire	464,629	392,117	36,362	36,150
New Jersey	3,739,739	2,563,088	307,834	868,817
New Mexico	4,046,053	808,223	39,615	3,198,215
New York	7,437,799	4,605,262	645,215	2,187,322
North Carolina	1,868,317	1,193,127	170,613	504,577
North Dakota	235,106	171,378	21,865	41,863
Ohio	5,113,517	3,450,042	311,166	1,352,309
Oklahoma	1,022,130	627,681	87,804	306,645
Oregon	561,823	158,164	78,396	325,263
Pennsylvania	4,738,479	2,948,252	411,282	1,378,945
Rhode Island	466,927	384,076	35,815	47,036
South Carolina	2,734,295	710,935	71,676	1,951,684
South Dakota	239,619	94,651	22,783	122,185
Tennessee	4,284,663	911,517	139,358	3,233,788
Texas	12,755,082	8,956,566	464,909	3,333,607
Utah	1,278,844	532,269	38,206	708,369
Vermont	121,963	61,767	21,393	38,803
Virginia	11,431,638	7,349,384	199,829	3,882,425
Washington	3,460,634	1,863,041	135,335	1,462,258
West Virginia	463,096	130,649	47,679	284,768
Wisconsin	1,367,354	833,458	140,287	393,609
Wyoming	142,981	57,782	12,059	73,140
Dist. of Columbia	4,011,913	1,286,436	54,835	2,670,642
American Samoa	11,258	4,827	93	6,338
Guam	166,136	162,460	1,344	2,332
No. Mariana Islands ...	1,039	0	111	928
Puerto Rico	410,381	260,623	31,950	117,808
U.S. Virgin Islands	33,075	29,892	2,781	402

Source: U.S. Department of Commerce, Bureau of the Census, *Federal Expenditure by State for Fiscal Year 1993.*
Note: United States total includes undistributed funds of $24.4 billion with $16.9 billion occurring in the Department of Defense and $7.5 billion in all other federal agencies.

Table 6.38
FEDERAL GOVERNMENT EXPENDITURES FOR OTHER PROGRAMS,
BY STATE AND TERRITORY: FISCAL YEAR 1993
(In thousands of dollars)

| | | | | | | | Grants | | | |
| | | | | | NASA—space | National Endowment | | | |
State or other jurisdiction	Total	Total	Department of Health & Human Services research grants	National Science Foundation	program research grants	for the Arts Arts	Humanities	ACTION (a)	All other programs
United States (b)....	$46,488,659	$15,822,302	$8,060,103	$2,769,963	$609,688	$167,396	$161,472	$132,964	$3,920,716
Alabama............	544,932	216,945	114,143	18,167	18,593	1,047	1,066	3,044	60,885
Alaska.............	180,530	163,339	129,124	10,199	8,998	1,146	848	577	12,447
Arizona............	500,909	246,097	100,147	90,893	15,091	1,649	2,225	1,390	34,702
Arkansas...........	637,244	64,943	11,914	6,560	477	818	1,126	2,184	41,864
California..........	4,056,299	2,004,092	1,131,651	385,296	91,153	16,511	17,579	7,713	354,189
Colorado	883,225	368,700	126,162	154,928	18,991	1,354	2,039	1,991	63,235
Connecticut	439,373	274,518	177,565	34,289	1,728	2,399	4,612	2,070	51,855
Delaware	67,047	37,612	3,002	13,697	2,209	917	1,630	806	15,351
Florida	1,220,143	264,098	109,568	58,682	13,645	1,898	2,617	6,456	71,232
Georgia............	724,623	237,361	110,917	38,642	11,357	5,765	4,874	3,291	62,515
Hawaii	208,354	77,473	19,446	16,836	5,757	1,127	1,316	771	32,220
Idaho	208,841	23,170	1,849	4,371	-427	695	615	1,195	14,872
Illinois............	1,850,849	521,674	230,488	161,671	11,891	6,079	5,853	4,116	101,576
Indiana	1,288,026	198,689	79,212	56,313	4,573	1,364	2,446	2,742	52,039
Iowa	1,709,460	134,406	78,800	21,947	3,352	1,273	1,186	2,352	25,496
Kansas	1,064,228	81,635	30,908	12,805	6,348	917	1,518	2,020	27,119
Kentucky	384,167	81,324	31,287	13,303	851	2,563	1,037	2,073	30,210
Louisiana	722,042	138,938	52,830	17,829	2,351	1,648	1,161	2,296	60,823
Maine	117,720	56,605	23,903	12,334	573	998	1,058	1,051	16,688
Maryland	2,750,058	726,400	542,852	65,367	42,923	2,652	3,328	2,003	67,275
Massachusetts	1,683,601	1,291,172	815,648	196,567	34,349	5,952	10,979	3,261	224,416
Michigan	1,031,271	545,858	234,392	105,445	30,127	3,083	4,683	4,004	164,124
Minnesota	1,612,355	310,742	184,836	39,341	2,179	7,280	2,023	2,112	72,971
Mississippi	487,803	72,767	20,580	14,017	3,683	1,010	1,059	1,929	30,489
Missouri	1,811,276	247,839	176,956	23,322	4,833	3,452	2,690	3,123	33,463
Montana...........	605,953	40,073	6,897	18,065	947	968	881	1,210	11,105
Nebraska	1,060,838	58,484	31,456	12,044	1,060	1,219	923	1,654	10,128
Nevada	82,807	38,356	13,122	5,927	660	730	448	764	16,705
New Hampshire	130,218	84,832	33,019	11,631	6,231	1,078	1,651	995	30,227
New Jersey	654,603	232,198	87,683	53,839	6,679	2,697	3,655	3,193	74,452
New Mexico........	294,506	143,063	42,018	19,716	6,653	2,852	1,106	1,457	69,261
New York	2,477,169	1,408,059	803,135	280,099	26,552	37,347	23,634	9,429	227,863
North Carolina......	766,853	479,642	310,228	71,137	6,332	2,604	4,470	3,624	81,247
North Dakota	622,607	40,224	10,630	2,510	260	763	666	648	24,747
Ohio	976,385	385,189	216,717	53,109	33,321	3,834	2,837	4,925	70,446
Oklahoma	638,014	127,225	71,271	10,212	1,046	949	1,387	2,065	40,295
Oregon	400,769	172,772	70,801	31,522	3,536	1,996	1,407	1,976	61,534
Pennsylvania	1,714,056	934,760	523,861	146,749	23,258	6,539	8,431	6,324	219,598
Rhode Island	130,115	79,772	33,117	22,140	3,621	831	1,340	928	17,795
South Carolina	299,333	87,410	23,086	14,454	1,379	1,218	1,088	1,689	44,496
South Dakota	450,487	39,751	18,973	9,164	425	812	547	927	8,903
Tennessee	424,718	117,711	51,613	10,231	24,807	1,701	843	2,756	25,760
Texas..............	2,938,172	793,334	391,911	96,175	37,418	6,025	4,811	6,347	250,647
Utah	242,425	118,517	60,236	23,517	3,646	1,195	717	1,447	27,759
Vermont	58,109	39,671	25,566	6,029	235	1,142	1,111	1,059	4,529
Virginia............	1,486,885	337,579	140,378	77,339	21,040	1,494	6,548	4,020	86,760
Washington	961,084	404,793	261,195	57,033	8,915	3,977	1,273	2,508	69,892
West Virginia	163,040	119,017	8,534	39,515	34,123	974	532	1,686	33,653
Wisconsin..........	861,790	278,355	165,476	47,901	9,561	1,891	2,838	2,500	48,188
Wyoming	75,695	22,632	1,675	5,338	528	760	1,200	712	12,419
Dist. of Columbia.....	1,605,624	776,024	101,698	57,403	10,919	6,077	6,211	991	592,725
American Samoa	6,346	348	0	15	0	277	0	0	56
Guam	17,028	2,786	383	449	0	296	228	0	1,430
No. Mariana Islands...	634	420	0	0	0	203	217	0	0
Puerto Rico	152,509	70,930	16,661	13,725	933	1,105	667	2,335	35,504
U.S. Virgin Islands	5,412	1,874	593	162	0	281	268	226	344

FEDERAL GOVERNMENT EXPENDITURES FOR OTHER PROGRAMS—Continued

State or other jurisdiction	Total	Direct payments — other than for individuals					
		Department of Agriculture					
		Feed grain production stabilization payments	Conservation reserve program	Crop insurance claims & payments	Wheat production stabilization payments	Other agricultural programs	All other programs
United States (b)....	$30,666,357	$5,092,636	$1,650,595	$904,577	$1,911,381	$4,277,443	$16,829,731
Alabama............	327,987	6,673	22,681	1,899	4,629	86,584	205,521
Alaska.............	17,191	133	938	0	0	7,539	8,581
Arizona............	254,812	3,185	0	0	5,506	113,448	132,673
Arkansas	572,301	12,537	10,835	573	33,402	427,139	87,815
California	2,052,207	14,858	8,303	1,716	30,059	518,650	1,478,621
Colorado	514,525	70,264	78,348	1,197	73,034	41,554	250,128
Connecticut	164,855	960	0	8,224	0	1,566	154,105
Delaware	29,435	3,809	60	85	425	735	24,321
Florida	956,045	3,768	5,014	6,505	764	60,453	879,541
Georgia............	487,262	25,256	24,573	11,746	16,442	118,833	290,412
Hawaii	130,881	0	0	0	0	2,778	128,103
Idaho	185,671	20,338	36,760	377	70,665	31,083	26,448
Illinois.............	1,329,175	748,217	54,412	29,085	34,256	36,413	426,792
Indiana	1,089,337	334,123	30,325	1,575	15,450	15,763	692,101
Iowa	1,575,054	971,511	165,292	316,754	408	16,538	104,551
Kansas	982,593	254,399	150,543	42,990	334,079	124,156	76,426
Kentucky	302,843	57,520	24,948	791	8,260	6,895	204,429
Louisiana	583,104	7,821	6,083	1,396	5,230	279,037	283,537
Maine	61,115	903	1,715	57	2	15,715	42,723
Maryland	2,023,658	15,797	1,393	67	1,880	2,549	2,001,972
Massachusetts	392,429	327	1	524	0	2,294	389,283
Michigan	485,413	149,399	15,264	28	18,078	65,695	236,949
Minnesota	1,301,613	440,231	99,367	123,662	88,762	71,009	478,582
Mississippi	415,036	6,215	32,988	1,976	8,983	274,922	89,952
Missouri	1,563,437	143,516	100,349	12,064	43,090	119,763	1,144,655
Montana...........	565,880	42,836	100,999	192,058	146,403	52,986	30,598
Nebraska	1,002,354	634,642	75,306	5,809	72,301	74,530	139,766
Nevada	44,451	226	76	49	683	10,576	32,841
New Hampshire	45,386	257	0	18	0	1,476	43,635
New Jersey..........	422,405	3,915	34	46	435	3,035	414,940
New Mexico........	151,443	14,612	18,174	172	9,656	28,317	80,512
New York	1,069,110	41,389	3,130	1,662	4,000	25,790	993,139
North Carolina	287,211	41,967	6,325	5,734	7,352	58,154	167,679
North Dakota	582,383	107,320	103,056	21,344	284,120	43,644	22,899
Ohio	591,196	202,950	22,323	823	26,597	19,857	318,646
Oklahoma	510,789	16,427	49,221	37,206	174,886	56,442	176,607
Oregon	227,997	6,092	25,301	10	42,672	29,596	124,326
Pennsylvania	779,296	26,987	5,830	1,386	1,318	28,592	715,183
Rhode Island	50,343	3	0	5	0	165	50,170
South Carolina	211,923	18,606	11,033	1,713	9,108	46,029	125,434
South Dakota	410,736	174,406	67,707	14,390	82,707	52,515	19,011
Tennessee	307,007	23,773	22,974	495	8,838	77,890	173,037
Texas..............	2,144,838	210,062	154,163	35,838	116,485	906,603	721,687
Utah	123,908	3,588	9,011	42	5,567	19,472	86,228
Vermont	18,438	857	12	61	1	2,494	15,013
Virginia............	1,149,306	18,323	3,801	128	4,232	17,985	1,104,837
Washington	556,291	23,020	50,571	1,840	112,625	96,571	271,664
West Virginia	44,023	2,512	29	0	118	4,367	36,997
Wisconsin..........	583,435	182,248	41,599	20,085	2,172	109,573	227,758
Wyoming	53,063	3,859	9,703	173	5,701	23,072	10,555
Dist. of Columbia	829,600	0	0	0	0	38,977	790,623
American Samoa	5,998	0	0	0	0	5,979	19
Guam	14,242	0	0	0	0	237	14,005
No. Mariana Islands...	214	0	0	0	0	192	22
Puerto Rico	81,579	0	24	198	0	1,199	80,158
U.S. Virgin Islands	3,538	0	0	0	0	17	3,521

Source: U.S. Department of Commerce, Bureau of the Census, *Federal Expenditures by State for Fiscal Year 1993.*
Note: Detail may not add to totals due to rounding. Amounts represent a mix of value of awards and actual expenditures during the fiscal year. Grant amounts are other than those for state and local governments which are shown in Table 6.34.

(a) ACTION grants include the following federal domestic assistance programs: the Foster Grandparent Program; Retired Senior Volunteer Program; Volunteers in Service to America (VISTA); Student Community Service Program; Senior Companion Program; Mini-Grant Program; Volunteer Demonstration Program; Drug Alliance; and Literacy Corps.
(b) Includes undistributed monies.

Table 6.39
FEDERAL GOVERNMENT LOAN AND INSURANCE PROGRAMS—VOLUME OF
ASSISTANCE PROVIDED, BY STATE AND TERRITORY: FISCAL YEAR 1993
(In thousands of dollars)

State or other jurisdiction	Total	Direct loans				
		Commodity loans-price supports	Farmers Home Administration rural housing loans	Water & waste disposal system loans	Housing for the elderly or handicapped	Other direct loans
United States	$15,332,659	$9,065,463	$3,092,512	$647,140	$347,540	$2,180,004
Alabama..........	166,554	78,452	65,902	13,825	0	8,375
Alaska............	16,219	0	12,004	1,450	0	2,765
Arizona...........	70,604	26,179	28,276	1,615	1,853	12,681
Arkansas	762,523	634,308	64,997	55,296	0	7,922
California	1,238,295	824,564	136,640	10,901	19,963	246,227
Colorado	248,073	197,328	29,514	5,528	3,419	12,284
Connecticut	29,830	31	16,094	2,514	0	11,191
Delaware	55,015	1,927	9,708	41,656	1,624	100
Florida	1,073,970	275,158	111,462	12,296	30,245	644,809
Georgia...........	321,803	150,750	143,402	11,622	5,641	10,388
Hawaii	209,133	566	10,286	0	2,596	195,685
Idaho	69,399	27,484	34,181	3,764	0	3,970
Illinois...........	794,161	579,879	78,195	16,388	49,118	70,581
Indiana	408,376	288,582	81,833	10,885	9,371	17,705
Iowa	1,121,350	950,431	78,070	19,031	3,042	70,776
Kansas	194,495	119,527	48,360	3,912	0	22,696
Kentucky	396,476	264,310	85,348	30,126	2,215	14,477
Louisiana	437,799	315,077	61,014	16,827	0	44,881
Maine	84,427	123	59,107	14,528	0	10,669
Maryland	82,358	13,929	57,709	7,085	0	3,635
Massachusetts	76,783	113	46,054	20,564	653	9,399
Michigan	292,232	160,010	92,883	12,565	8,952	17,822
Minnesota	904,908	752,871	106,364	16,307	0	29,366
Mississippi	789,632	671,403	85,758	15,975	2,743	13,753
Missouri	442,128	231,881	70,228	5,641	2,073	132,305
Montana..........	80,977	60,788	16,772	628	0	2,789
Nebraska	569,484	508,346	50,017	3,468	1,000	6,653
Nevada	11,986	12	9,739	400	0	1,835
New Hampshire	33,253	0	19,949	8,878	3,988	438
New Jersey........	106,909	2,752	25,367	12,545	14,645	51,600
New Mexico........	50,196	8,801	29,056	1,242	5,890	5,207
New York	330,928	17,016	87,042	21,850	81,581	123,439
North Carolina	282,732	102,302	121,514	39,123	2,642	17,151
North Dakota	277,976	240,271	27,247	707	0	9,751
Ohio	289,506	147,106	105,999	21,482	3,274	11,645
Oklahoma	155,104	39,984	49,385	12,098	0	53,637
Oregon	67,607	7,473	40,387	6,941	4,707	8,099
Pennsylvania	221,670	13,645	117,674	27,181	34,162	29,008
Rhode Island	15,385	0	10,673	250	0	4,462
South Carolina	110,461	14,499	64,191	17,145	6,081	8,545
South Dakota	225,420	169,941	37,183	3,695	0	14,601
Tennessee	374,096	255,995	86,205	17,736	4,522	9,638
Texas.............	862,178	607,820	166,109	20,960	16,288	51,001
Utah	204,610	173,802	23,161	1,682	0	5,965
Vermont	23,335	114	16,566	4,544	0	2,111
Virginia...........	162,585	32,132	100,285	19,352	5,194	5,622
Washington	112,615	32,177	58,602	5,830	3,436	12,570
West Virginia	62,268	1,580	46,800	10,836	783	2,269
Wisconsin.........	174,745	61,980	74,903	2,909	6,786	28,167
Wyoming	22,770	2,043	19,524	380	0	823
Dist. of Columbia....	473	0	0	0	0	473
American Samoa ...	1,124	0	0	0	0	1,124
Guam	87,692	0	5,550	0	0	82,142
No. Mariana Islands..	1,577	0	58	0	0	1,519
Puerto Rico	114,457	0	59,142	34,979	9,053	11,283
U.S. Virgin Islands ...	12,029	0	10,030	0	0	1,999

FEDERAL GOVERNMENT LOAN AND INSURANCE PROGRAMS—Continued

State or other jurisdiction	Total	Guaranteed loans Mortgage insurance for homes	Guaranteed student loans	Veterans housing guaranteed & insured loans (a)	Mortgage insurance condominiums	Farmers Home Administration programs	Small business loans	Other guaranteed loans	Total insurance
United States	$105,198,594	$60,765,828	$17,872,072	$6,623,585	$5,310,399	$1,703,958	$5,451,002	$7,471,750	$270,107,625
Alabama	1,023,065	580,595	99,733	105,763	11,719	12,699	89,509	123,047	1,909,527
Alaska............	520,257	415,700	0	40,058	9,357	400	39,499	15,243	179,899
Arizona...........	3,773,961	2,979,578	323,769	251,048	87,241	1,338	61,058	69,929	1,596,177
Arkansas	831,606	485,768	96,878	54,744	3,240	34,079	52,779	104,118	551,738
California	11,613,413	6,471,450	1,411,642	913,062	1,409,016	34,723	945,626	427,894	23,264,899
Colorado	4,611,115	3,369,802	325,973	250,406	310,667	33,123	136,238	184,906	1,059,822
Connecticut	1,099,031	537,012	129,572	29,403	163,873	3,120	72,067	163,984	2,279,339
Delaware	165,656	102,096	25,831	17,591	1,351	1,675	9,767	7,345	1,123,967
Florida	4,838,545	3,278,859	444,866	483,447	182,120	100,967	203,256	145,030	107,223,237
Georgia...........	3,500,997	2,427,420	236,717	250,988	63,828	68,020	203,027	250,997	3,648,023
Hawaii	471,255	96,004	24,649	11,110	315,358	883	7,928	15,323	2,115,101
Idaho	667,654	464,387	56,968	42,288	2,818	26,750	53,173	21,270	281,064
Illinois...........	3,991,567	2,444,207	598,902	136,267	314,812	62,151	162,633	272,595	4,627,658
Indiana	4,987,169	1,280,531	3,430,543	88,691	22,586	27,265	49,846	87,707	1,376,231
Iowa	790,771	217,616	294,099	19,553	3,624	100,088	97,573	58,218	1,911,874
Kansas	887,417	554,760	0	67,096	4,169	56,999	106,100	98,293	1,217,648
Kentucky	1,022,314	440,219	159,396	56,105	13,178	32,955	36,983	283,478	869,558
Louisiana	1,326,898	820,075	130,150	66,384	6,050	87,408	81,259	135,572	20,800,631
Maine	301,503	125,828	79,029	16,746	3,942	12,868	38,940	24,150	470,605
Maryland	3,424,278	2,106,394	189,200	331,135	461,280	7,306	35,838	293,125	3,172,352
Massachusetts	1,733,679	601,315	729,964	66,560	64,985	9,216	82,339	179,300	2,983,420
Michigan	2,097,627	1,239,897	440,862	89,002	36,214	50,967	86,343	154,342	1,373,299
Minnesota	4,876,719	3,427,556	640,672	182,507	185,223	81,326	102,890	256,545	1,409,803
Mississippi	806,911	434,948	142,961	38,323	256	57,144	66,514	66,765	2,354,006
Missouri	2,328,776	1,608,903	245,356	96,611	56,654	41,860	132,518	146,874	1,320,765
Montana	602,488	338,715	76,212	22,635	5,482	20,699	79,199	59,546	368,246
Nebraska	824,723	307,156	294,847	56,381	342	68,160	40,957	56,880	1,311,562
Nevada	1,080,466	845,084	0	106,958	61,323	2,064	24,504	40,533	616,376
New Hampshire	448,780	183,683	85,917	31,146	27,188	2,261	86,235	32,350	250,316
New Jersey.........	1,791,415	1,083,742	278,562	76,220	164,125	3,497	92,484	92,785	14,467,326
New Mexico........	671,060	384,523	74,588	61,385	6,621	20,308	59,415	64,220	417,109
New York	4,291,661	1,756,242	1,309,208	67,896	18,749	37,870	282,885	818,811	7,853,468
North Carolina	2,119,523	1,298,755	144,107	212,163	57,513	52,741	82,543	271,701	5,529,333
North Dakota	476,458	239,880	63,746	12,957	7,123	40,617	35,758	76,377	1,012,940
Ohio	2,535,069	1,484,835	402,421	148,824	74,740	27,287	107,443	289,519	1,420,702
Oklahoma	1,287,222	721,444	195,637	92,558	10,864	69,889	57,728	139,102	966,359
Oregon	973,259	574,795	157,785	44,588	10,357	9,984	72,297	103,453	763,945
Pennsylvania	3,208,945	1,227,079	1,523,555	81,040	60,269	35,773	125,442	155,787	3,475,255
Rhode Island	324,706	150,539	83,310	12,472	9,842	403	34,577	33,563	888,751
South Carolina	910,964	400,422	151,533	140,049	18,780	16,118	45,637	138,425	8,397,557
South Dakota	406,545	149,131	81,824	15,967	937	54,721	41,582	62,383	394,297
Tennessee	2,221,483	1,577,125	223,378	137,349	37,699	20,130	76,452	149,350	700,937
Texas..............	7,230,369	4,803,252	814,487	447,904	51,627	129,038	532,027	452,034	22,932,214
Utah	2,168,707	1,694,323	145,058	76,150	75,513	5,850	54,620	117,193	115,082
Vermont	185,105	25,640	80,131	3,734	1,652	16,620	48,731	8,597	150,157
Virginia...........	4,155,322	2,230,114	332,869	657,926	628,021	9,991	59,202	237,199	4,902,613
Washington	2,612,187	1,594,811	274,464	259,456	134,164	24,828	168,080	156,384	1,311,773
West Virginia	158,766	98,928	0	12,367	461	10,656	25,365	10,989	607,326
Wisconsin..........	1,517,196	240,929	798,048	108,636	6,003	59,870	150,390	153,320	644,026
Wyoming	238,529	164,892	0	15,679	968	15,220	18,385	23,385	112,950
Dist. of Columbia ..	197,925	69,011	0	5,913	15,846	0	8,771	98,384	130,843
American Samoa ...	0	0	0	0	0	0	0	0	904
Guam	1,023	0	0	44	101	0	878	0	8,528
No. Mariana Islands..	0	0	0	0	0	0	0	0	0
Puerto Rico	852,030	604,455	21,276	10,056	88,816	4,039	81,339	42,049	1,038,518
U.S. Virgin Islands ...	14,498	5,403	1,376	245	1,709	0	4,370	1,395	196,833

Source: U.S. Department of Commerce, Bureau of the Census, *Federal Expenditures by State for Fiscal Year 1993.*
Note: Detail may not add to totals due to rounding. Amounts represent dollar volume of direct loans made and loans guaranteed, or the face value of insurance coverage provided during the fiscal year.

(a) Represents only the federal government's contingent liability which is the lesser of $36,000 or 40 percent of the loan value (minimum $22,500). Amount shown does not represent the full value of closed loans, as shown in the federal budget.

Chapter Seven

STATE MANAGEMENT, REGULATION & PERSONNEL

An overview of several components of state administration and regulation, including recent reforms in state management, personnel, and lobby laws. Includes information on state personnel systems, information resource management, and regulatory activities. Statistics on state government employment and payrolls, as well as public employee retirement systems, are presented for 1991 and 1992.

Reforming State Management and Personnel Systems

New technologies and management models are being implemented for personnel, budget and social spending programs to improve services and cut costs.

by Julie Cencula Olberding

In recent years, deteriorating revenue bases and growing public distrust of government have sparked efforts to reform the way government traditionally has been operated and managed. Fanned by "reinventing government" literature and politicking to change government-as-usual, this spark caught on quickly in a few states and has spread like wildfire during the past few years. While some dismiss "reinventing government" as rhetoric of change that will fade away soon, opponents argue that these reform efforts will fundamentally change the culture of government agencies.

Recently, several governors have developed commissions and initiated studies to help identify better and less expensive ways of running state government. About a dozen commissions have been created to study the efficiency and quality of state government during the past three to four years, according to a recent Council of State Governments' survey. Shortly after inauguration, President Bill Clinton brought the reform fever to Washington, D.C., directing Vice President Al Gore to conduct a performance audit of the federal government. State officials looked with great interest to the National Performance Review's recommendations — both to see how some may affect state government and how others could be adopted to make state agencies work better and cost less.

While the motivation for reform may differ among various government organizations, these efforts generally have two primary goals in common: to improve the performance of government agencies and to reduce the cost of doing business. Commonly used strategies to achieve these goals include instilling a cus-

tomer focus in employees, becoming outcome-oriented rather than process-oriented, reducing bureaucracy and streamlining government, encouraging competition through privatization, decentralizing decision-making and using technology.

Putting Customers First

In recent years, elected officials and agency managers in a number of states have experimented with new paradigms for managing personnel, programs and budgets. Two management models tried by several states and adopted as the norm by a few are Total Quality Management and performance-based management.

Total Quality Management is broadly defined as a comprehensive system of developing and maintaining the organizational capacity to improve the quality of work constantly, and to meet and exceed customer needs.[1] After Japanese and American businesses reported that TQM improved product quality and customer service, state managers adopted this strategy to instill a service orientation in their employees. One TQM success story is in Arizona, where teams of state employees have been evaluating organizational structures, management systems, service delivery, resource utilization and areas of potential privatization. Changes initiated through the TQM process have saved Arizona about $24 million during its first year of implementation.[2] Inspired by

---

Julie Cencula Olberding is a research associate with the Center for Management and Administration at The Council of State Governments.

positive results in Arizona as well as in Arkansas, New York and Texas, more and more states are initiating their own quality management programs. At least 25 states are involved in TQM, according to a recent survey by the National Association of State Directors of Administration and General Services.[3]

Another model adopted by some states to improve effectiveness and efficiency is performance-based management. Emphasizing the importance of results over inputs, performance management generally involves a long-term strategic plan for the state, which includes goals or benchmarks; performance measures for each program to indicate progress toward the established goals; and performance-based budgeting, which relies on the state's goals and priorities and allocates funds based on outcomes.

At the forefront of performance-based management is Oregon Benchmarks, which requires agencies to develop business plans that identify strategies to attain statewide goals, indicators of progress toward those goals and specific results that will be obtained with budget requests. Governor Barbara Roberts incorporated performance budgeting in the 1995-97 biennium by directing agencies to base their budget requests on the state's benchmarks. As the process unfolds, agencies in Oregon also will begin to identify services and expenditures that are not critical to fulfilling their missions and target them for elimination. Other states have followed suit with similar performance-based efforts, such as Iowa's Futures Agenda, Minnesota Milestones, Montana's Future, Puerto Rico 2005 and performance management programs in Idaho and Ohio.[4]

Restructuring and Reducing Bureaucracy

Another strategy to streamline state government is reorganization of the executive branch. Goals for changing the structure of government include reducing the number of departments and agencies, eliminating duplication of services among agencies, cutting the costs of operating state government and improving communication, service delivery and customer satisfaction.

Executive branch reorganization often is discussed by state officials, but only a few governors have committed to significant restructuring in recent years. Obstacles to restructuring include resistance by managers to being moved into a different agency, political support of the existing structure, the great amount of time and resources necessary to carry out such an effort, and difficulty measuring the actual cost savings.[5] In those states where governors have initiated reorganization in recent years, most have opted for a cabinet model of government by collapsing agencies, eliminating boards and commissions and grouping programs along functional lines into cabinet-level departments. Since 1965, the number of states with some kind of cabinet model has grown from 26 to 38 states.[6]

One of the most comprehensive reorganizations of state government in recent years was in Iowa, where the number of departments was reduced from 68 to 20, state employment was cut by 1,700 and operating costs were slashed by $60 million.[7] In South Carolina, Governor Carroll Campbell, Jr. initiated a plan in 1991 to grant the executive branch more responsibility for managing day-to-day government operations. In 1993, Campbell signed a bill that will reduce the number of state agencies from 79 to 17 and will eliminate many of the state's governing boards and commissions.[8]

A majority of states have taken a more incremental approach by implementing structural or functional change in one agency or a group of targeted agencies, boards and commissions. For example, in New Mexico, Governor Bruce King created the Children, Youth and Families Department in 1992 and gradually is transferring existing children and family services programs under this umbrella department.[9]

Changing the Rules

Many states are trying to streamline government by granting managers more authority and by making established systems more flexible. One important area in which such reform has been occurring is state civil service systems. Thirty-three states are undergoing or planning to initiate civil service reform, according to a recent survey by the National Association of State Personnel Executives. Of the 33 states, seven survey respondents reported that their merit systems were undergoing wholesale reform while others said changes were incremental. (see Table 7.6)

Blue-ribbon commissions, such as the National Commission on the State and Local Public Service, also known as the Winter Commission, have recommended that governments decentralize merit systems so that personnel departments provide clear guidelines and consultation, but departments and agencies have authority to make staffing decisions.[10] Another common recommendation for civil service reform is "broad banding," in which hundreds and often thousands of job classifications in state government are collapsed to only a few dozen with distinction between levels of expertise, or bands.

A few states already have begun implementing or have initiated systematic changes in human resource management. In Florida, Governor Lawton Chiles and the Legislature have agreed to revamp the civil service system by establishing a broad-band job classification system, eliminating cumbersome rules and procedures, establishing greater consultation between agencies and the centralized personnel department, and increasing agencies' authority to manage personnel.[11] In Iowa, Governor Terry Branstad consolidated personnel staff from agencies into a Department of Personnel for policy development and implementation and granted greater responsibility to agency managers, including more responsibility for hiring, disciplinary action and other personnel decisions. Iowa's reform also included cutting the number of job classifications in half and instituting pay-for-performance activities.[12]

In addition to granting more responsibility for human resource decisions, some states have delegated greater authority for purchasing to department and agency managers. According to a recent survey by the National Association of State Purchasing Officials, during the past few years, many states have raised the dollar threshold allowing agencies to purchase their goods and services. Since 1988, at least 32 states have raised the competitive bidding threshold, thereby increasing the authority of state managers to obtain quotations or competitively bid for goods and services. Of these 32 states, several have significantly increased this threshold: in California, from $960 to $10,000; in Illinois, from $2,500 to $50,000; in Indiana, from $50 to $5,000; in Nevada, from $500 to $5,000; and in Ohio from $1,000 to $10,000. (See Table A) As with a competitive bidding process, many states require managers to request more than one quotation and to maintain public records of bids and contract awards.[13]

Working with the Private Sector

In the search for better services at lower costs, many states have begun to privatize some services that traditionally have been provided by government agencies. In most cases, privatization in state government means contracting with a company to provide specified services, although some states have used, in a limited way, other forms of privatization, such as vouchers, grants and public-private partnerships. (See Table B)

At least 30 states are implementing some type of privatization, according to a recent survey of state personnel executives. Services that a number of states have privatized include custodial services (21 states), food services (15 states), clerical services (13 states) and security (10 states).[14]

In addition to administrative and trade services, states are beginning to privatize certain professional services, such as telecommunications and engineering. About one-third of government procurement officials are purchasing professional services from the private sector, including architects, engineers and land surveyors, according to a recent survey by the National Institute of Government Procurement.[15] Also, 29 states have privatized one or more information services during the past five years, according to a report by the National Association of State Information Resource Executives. At least nine states have considered privatizing the entire information services function, but no state has done so.[16]

Privatization of state services will likely continue during the next few years. Several state legislatures have passed resolutions encouraging executive branch agencies to study

Table A
PURCHASING THRESHOLDS: DOLLAR AMOUNT BELOW WHICH AGENCIES PERMITTED TO OBTAIN OWN QUOTATIONS

State	1988 (a)	1993 (b)
Alabama	$100	$250
Alaska	5,000	5,000
Arizona	750	5,000
Arkansas	5,000	5,000
California	960	10,000
Colorado	500	1,000
Connecticut	400	3,000
Delaware	5,000	10,000
Florida	3,000	10,000
Georgia	(c)	3,000
Hawaii	(d)	4,000
Idaho	500 (e)	500 (e)
Illinois	2,500	50,000
Indiana	50	5,000
Iowa	500	500
Kansas	2,000	2,000
Kentucky	1,000	1,000
Louisiana	(f)	5,000
Maine	250	1,000
Maryland	1,000	1,000/2,500/5,000 (g)
Massachusetts	500	1,000
Michigan	1,000	2,500/5,000/10,000 (g)
Minnesota	100/1,500 (h)	1,500/5,000 (h)
Mississippi	500	500
Missouri	2,000	2,000
Montana	500	2,000
Nebraska	35	100
Nevada	500	5,000
New Hampshire	100	100
New Jersey	1,500	8,000
New Mexico	250	500
New York	5,000	10,000
North Carolina	5,000	10,000
North Dakota	300	500
Ohio	1,000	10,000
Oklahoma	500	2,500
Oregon	500	2,500
Pennsylvania	5,000	5,000
Rhode Island	100	1,000
South Carolina	2,500	2,500
South Dakota	500	1,000
Tennessee	1,000	1,000
Texas	1,500	5,000
Utah	1,000	2,000
Vermont	200	500

(continued on page 410)

Table A (continued)		
State	1988 (a)	1993 (b)
Virginia	$1,200	$5,000
Washington	2,500	2,500
West Virginia	5,000	10,000
Wisconsin	5,000	5,000
Wyoming	1,000	1,500

(a) *State and Local Government Purchasing, Third Edition.* National Association of State Purchasing Officials. 1988.
(b) *State and Local Government Purchasing, Fourth Edition.* National Association of State Purchasing Officials. 1994.
(c) Four major universities have delegated purchasing authority up to $5,000.
(d) In 1988, state agencies in Hawaii were not mandated to procure goods through Central Purchasing.
(e) In Idaho, some agencies are delegated purchasing authority of $1,000, $2,000 or $5,000 and must follow certain requirements including monthly reports.
(f) Amount varied from $250 to 5,000, depending on the agency.
(g) Three levels of delegated purchasing authority.
(h) Two levels of delegated purchasing authority.

the feasibility of initiating privatization efforts, and a number of governors have established or are considering the establishment of permanent organizations to help identify and evaluate programs and services for privatization.[17]

Expanding the Role of Technology

States recently have accelerated efforts to integrate technology in the government structure to improve information management and storage, the efficiency and quality of service delivery, and communication among agencies and with the public. About 10 years ago, states began using an integrated strategy, called information resource management, or IRM, to coordinate hardware, software, services, personnel, training and other components of government's information technology activities. At the state level, IRM has evolved from an end in itself to a means for achieving broader government objectives and managing critical state resources.[18]

The use of computers and other technology in state government has resulted in paperwork reduction and cost savings. Automation of the procurement process is one area where some states have enjoyed particular success. Oregon's Vendor Information Program, the only fully automated bid information system in the nation, has saved hundreds of thousands of dollars in staff time, copying and postage. In addition, because the computerized system makes the bidding process easier, significantly

more vendors are bidding on state goods and services, which has increased competition and saved the state $17 million in purchases during the first five quarters the system was on-line.

New technology also has been used to improve the delivery of state services. For example, states are beginning to utilize cards with magnetic stripes that can be encoded with information and "smart cards" with computer chips. Maryland has the first statewide system that electronically transfers food stamps via smart cards, which clients can use to purchase pre-approved food at participating stores, as well as Aid to Families with Dependent Children, child support and general assistance payments, which clients can access at authorized terminals.[19] A number of other states are in the pilot or planning stages of electronic benefit transfer (EBT) systems. Evaluations of EBT programs and pilot projects have found that clients believe cards are more convenient, more flexible and safer than paper vouchers, and state employees believe cards reduce waste, fraud and abuse.

State agencies also are applying technology to enhance internal and external communications. Several states have acquired telecommunications equipment to facilitate statewide meetings and employee training and to make government more accessible to citizens. Colorado Governor Roy Romer placed interactive computers in shopping malls to get feedback on state programs and spending from the public, and Roberts, Oregon's governor, utilized

Table B
FORMS OF PRIVATIZATION AND FREQUENCY OF USE
IN STATE PROGRAMS AND SERVICES

Form of privatization	Admin. (a)	Corrections	Education	Health	Mental health (b)	Social services	Transportation	Agency totals
Contracting out	91.67%	92.09%	81.29%	69.57%	64.67%	71.32%	83.51%	78.06%
Grants	0.56%	1.19%	8.63%	14.13%	15.63%	12.48%	4.50%	8.48%
Vouchers	3.06%	0.40%	0.72%	4.89%	5.35%	9.31%	0.43%	4.11%
Volunteerism	1.39%	3.56%	1.44%	3.26%	3.64%	2.98%	5.35%	3.32%
Public-private partnerships	1.67%	2.37%	5.04%	5.43%	3.85%	2.23%	2.57%	2.95%
Private donation	0.56%	0.40%	0.72%	.00%	2.57%	0.19%	1.28%	0.96%
Franchise	0.28%	.00%	1.44%	1.09%	1.71%	0.37%	1.50%	0.91%
Service shedding	0.28%	.00%	0.72%	1.09%	0.86%	0.74%	0.43%	0.58%
Deregulation	.00%	.00%	.00%	0.54%	1.50%	0.37%	0.21%	0.46%
Asset sales	0.56%	.00%	.00%	.00%	0.21%	.00%	0.21%	0.17%
Agency totals	14.96%	10.51%	5.77%	7.64%	19.40%	22.31%	19.40%	100.00%

Source: The Council of State Governments, *State Trends & Forecasts: Privatization*, Vol. 2, Issue 2, November 1993.
(a) Administration/General services.
(b) Mental health/retardation.

her state's telecommunications network to solicit opinions from 10,000 citizens about government and tax issues. Other states such as California and Hawaii have set up interactive, electronic kiosks in shopping malls, libraries and other public areas so citizens can request government information and conduct transactions at their convenience.

Many of the information technology systems designed for specific programs have been successful in improving efficiency and service delivery. But, because most of these systems have been developed independently, they often are not compatible with other systems within their state as well as systems in other states and the federal government. To overcome this problem, state officials have begun working with each other and with federal officials to move away from program-specific technology systems toward an information infrastructure that can be accessed by government employees and the public. President Clinton recently created a commission to help develop policies for the national information infrastructure, or the "information superhighway," and has appointed state leaders, as well as federal officials and corporate representatives, to this commis-

sion. In addition, state legislative and executive officials formed the State Information Policy Consortium in 1991 to improve communication and coordinate action on information policy issues through CSG, the National Governors' Association and the National Conference of State Legislatures. Both the state consortium and the national information infrastructure commission seek to advance state and federal governments' electronic delivery of services.

Notes

[1] S. Cohen and R. Brand. *Total Quality Management in Government: A Practical Guide to the Real World*. 1993.

[2] *An Action Agenda to Redesign State Government: Reports of the State Management Task Force Strategy Groups*. National Governors' Association. 1993. p. 72.

[3] *Profiles of Administration and General Services: Departments and Leaders*. National Association of State Directors of Administration and General Services. 1994.

[4] *An Action Agenda*, pp. 6-12.

[5] Keon Chi, "Reorganization." *State Trends & Forecasts*. The Council of State Governments. December 1992. p. 3.

[6] Ibid., p. 13.

[7] Ibid., pp. 15-16.

[8] *An Action Agenda*, p. 31.

[9] Ibid., p. 32.

[10] *Hard Truths/Tough Choices: An Agenda for State and Local Governments*. The National Commission on the State and Local Public Service, The Nelson A. Rockefeller Institute of Government. 1993. p. 25

[11] *An Action Agenda*, p. 73.

[12] Ibid., p. 74.

[13] *State and Local Government Purchasing, Fourth Edition*. National Association of State Purchasing Officers. 1994. p. 16.

[14] *Civil Service Reform Survey Results 1993*. National Association of State Personnel Executives. January 1993. pp. 22-23.

[15] *State and Local Government Purchasing, Fourth Edition*, p. 63.

[16] *Outsourcing Information Services in the Public Sector*. National Association of State Information Resource Executives. January 1994. p. 1.

[17] *Restructuring and Innovations in State Management: Some Recent Examples*. National Association of State Budget Officers. July 1993. p. 37.

[18] *Making Government Work: Electronic Delivery of Federal Services*. U.S. Congress, Office of Technology Assessment. September 1993. pp. 124-125.

[19] Ibid., p. 94.

Table 7.1
THE OFFICE OF STATE PERSONNEL EXECUTIVE: SELECTION, PLACEMENT AND STRUCTURE

State or other jurisdiction	Method of selection	Reports to: Governor	Reports to: Personnel board	Reports to: Other	Directs departmental employees	Legal basis for personnel department	Organizational status: Separate agency	Organizational status: Part of a larger agency
Alabama	B	...	★	...	★	C,S	★	...
Alaska	D	...	...	★ (a)	...	S	★	...
Arizona	D	...	...	★ (b)	★	S	...	★
Arkansas	D,G (c)	...	...	★ (d)	★	S	...	★
California								
State Personnel Bd.	B	...	★	...	★ (e)	C	★	★
Dept. of Personnel Admin.	G (f)	★	...	...	★ (g)	S	★	...
Colorado	G	★	...	...	★	C,S	★	...
Connecticut	G	...	...	★ (a)	★	S	...	★
Delaware	G	★	...	...	★	S	★	...
Florida	G	★	...	...	★ (h)	S	★	...
Georgia	G	★	...	...	★	C,S	★	...
Hawaii	G (f)	★	...	...	★	S	★	...
Idaho	B	...	★	...	★	S	...	★
Illinois	G	★	...	...	★	S	...	★
Indiana	G	★	...	...	N.A.	S	★	...
Iowa	G (i)	★	...	...	★	S	★	...
Kansas	D (j)	...	...	★ (a)	★	S	...	★
Kentucky	G	...	...	★ (k)	★	S	★	...
Louisiana	(l)	...	...	★ (m)	★	C	...	★
Maine	D (n)	...	...	★ (a)	★ (o)	S	...	★
Maryland	G	★	...	...	★	S	★	...
Massachusetts	G (p)	...	...	★ (a)	★	S	★	...
Michigan	B (q)	...	★	...	★	C	★	...
Minnesota	G	★	...	...	★	S	★	...
Mississippi	B	...	★	...	★	S	★	...
Missouri	G (r)	...	...	★ (s)	...	C,S	...	★
Montana	(t)	...	...	★ (b)	★	S	...	★
Nebraska	G (u)	★	...	...	★	S	★	...
Nevada	G	★	...	...	★	S	★	...
New Hampshire	(v)	...	...	(a)	★ (w)	S	...	★
New Jersey	G (x)	★	...	...	★	S	★	...
New Mexico	B (y)	★	★	...	★	C,S	★	...
New York	G	★	...	...	★	S	★	...
North Carolina	G	★	★	...	★	S	★	...
North Dakota	D	...	...	★ (z)	★	S	...	★
Ohio	G	...	...	★ (a)	★	S	...	★
Oklahoma	G	★	...	...	★	S	★	...
Oregon	D (aa)	...	...	★ (bb)	★	S	...	★
Pennsylvania	G	...	...	★ (a)	★	E	...	★
Rhode Island	D	...	...	★ (cc)	★	S,C	...	★
South Carolina	(dd)	...	...	★ (ee)	★	S	...	★
South Dakota	G	★	...	...	...	S	...	★
Tennessee	G	★	...	...	★	S	★	...
Texas				----(ff)----				
Utah	G (e)	★	...	★ (gg)	★ (hh)	S	★	...
Vermont	G	...	...	★ (a)	★	S	...	★
Virginia	G	...	...	★ (a)	★	S	★	...
Washington	G	...	★	...	★	S	★	...
West Virginia	D (ii)	...	...	(jj)	★	C,E	...	★
Wisconsin	G	★	...	...	★	S	★	...
Wyoming	D	...	...	★ (kk)	...	S	...	★
Puerto Rico	G	★	...	...	★	S	★	...

See footnotes at end of table.

THE OFFICE OF STATE PERSONNEL EXECUTIVE—Continued

Source: National Association of State Personnel Executives, *State Personnel Office: Roles and Functions, Second Edition*, 1992.

Note: See above referenced source for more detailed information.

Key:

★ — Yes

. . . — No

B — Appointment by personnel board

D — Appointment by department head

G — Appointment by governor

C — Constitution

S — Statute

E — Executive Order

N.A. — Not available

(a) Head of administration/administrative services. Alaska: Commissioner, Administrative Services; Connecticut: Commissioner, Administrative Services; Kansas: Secretary of Administration; Maine: Commissioner, Department of Administration; Massachusetts: Secretary, Administration and Finance; New Hampshire: Commissioner, Administrative Services; Ohio: Director, Administrative Services; Pennsylvania: Secretary of Administration; Vermont: Secretary, Agency of Administration; Virginia: Secretary of Administration.

(b) Reports to a department director who is appointed by the governor.

(c) Dual appointment. Individual is selected by the department head and confirmed by the Governor.

(d) Department head (Finance and Administration) and Governor.

(e) Employees of the State Personnel Board only.

(f) Appointed by the Governor with the consent of the Senate.

(g) Only those employees in the Department of Personnel Administration.

(h) Employees of the Department of Administration only.

(i) Must be confirmed every four years by 60 percent of the Senate.

(j) Appointed by the Secretary of Administration who is a Cabinet level official.

(k) Secretary of the Governor's Executive Cabinet.

(l) Classified state employee, not an appointed position.

(m) Board of Commissioners.

(n) Director makes decision after consultation with the Policy Review Board (an eight-member advisory board to the Bureau of Human Resources comprised of five Commissioners of other state Departments, a representative from the Governor's office, and two private sector members).

(o) The state personnel executive is the Director of the Bureau of Human Resources.

(p) Four-year appointments, effective July 1.

(q) Civil Service Commission appointed by Governor for eight-year terms. No more than two can be members of the same political party. Executive is appointed after competitive exam.

(r) Five candidates are recommended by the personnel board and then appointed by the Governor to a four-year term with consent of the Senate.

(s) Reports to the department head on most issues and to the personnel board on some issues.

(t) A division administrator who must compete for the position through the customary application/interview process.

(u) Subject to confirmation by Legislature.

(v) Appointed by the Governor and Executive Council.

(w) Only in some areas does the executive direct employees.

(x) All cabinet officers are appointed by the Governor.

(y) Appointed by the State Personnel Board with concurrence of the Governor.

(z) Reports to the Director of the Office of Management and Budget.

(aa) Appointed by the Director of the Executive Department with the approval of the Governor.

(bb) Reports to the Director of the Executive Department.

(cc) Reports to Associate Director of Human Resources.

(dd) Appointed by the State Budget and Control Board which includes the following: the Governor, Comptroller General, State Treasurer, Chairman, House Ways and Means Committee and the Chairman, Senate Finance Committee.

(ee) Reports to the Executive Director of the Budget and Control Board.

(ff) Texas does not have a centralized personnel system.

(gg) Reports to the Executive Committee along with the Governor.

(hh) Directors in the Department of Human Resource Management.

(ii) Exempt employees are hired by cabinet-level Secretary of Administration.

(jj) Regulations approved by the Board, policies and day-to-day decisions by the Secretary of Administration.

(kk) Reports to the Cabinet-level agency director.

Table 7.2
STATE PERSONNEL ADMINISTRATION: FUNCTIONS

State or other jurisdiction	Administers merit tests (a)	Establishes qualifications	Provides human resource information system (a)	Human resource planning	Classification	Compensation (a)	Recruitment	Selection	Performance evaluation (a)	Position audits	Employee promotion	Employee assistance & counseling	Human resource development training	Employee health & wellness program	Affirmative action
Alabama	C,D	C,D	C,D	D	C,D	C,D (b)	C,D	C,D	C,D	C,D	C,D	O,D	C,D		C,D
Alaska	C	C,D			C	C	C,D	C,D	C	C	C	D	C,D	C,D	C,D
Arizona	C	C	C	D	C	C	C,D	C	C	C	C	D	C,D		C,O
Arkansas		C			C	C	C,D	C	C	C	C		C,D	C,D	C,D
California															
State Personnel Bd.	C,D	C	C		C (f),O	O	C,D	C,D	O	O	C,D	O	O	O	C,D
Dept. of Personnel Admin.	O,D	O		O,D	C	C	O,D	O,D	C,D	C	O,D	C	C		O,D
Colorado	D	C,D	C,D	D	D	C	C,D	C,D	C	C	D	O,D	C	C	C,D
Connecticut	C	C,D	C,D	C (n),D	C	C	C (n),D	C (n),D	D	C	D	C (n),O	D	D	C (n),D
Delaware	C	C	C	D	C	C	C,D	C,D	C	D	D	C,D	C	C,D	C
Florida	C	C	C	C,D	C,D	C,D	C,D	C,D	C,D	C,D	C,D	D	C,D	C,D	C,D
Hawaii	C	C	O	D	C	C	C	C	C	C	C	C	C	C	C
Idaho	C	C	O	D	C	C	C	C	D	C	D	D (r)	D		O,D
Illinois	C,D	C	O	D	C	C	C	C	D	D	D	C	C		C,D
Indiana	C	C	C	C,D	C	C	C	D	C	C	C	C	C	C	C,O,D
Iowa	C	C		C	C	C	C	C	C	C	C	C	C		C,O,D
Kansas	C,D	C	O	D	C,D	C	C	C,D	C,D	C	D	C	C,D	O	C,D
Kentucky	C	C	O	D,D	C	C	C	D	C	C	D	C	C,O	O	C,O,D
Louisiana	C,D	C	O	O,D	C	C	C	C,O,D	C,O,D	D	O,D	C,D	C,D	C,D	C,O,D
Maine	C,D	C	O	C	C	C,O,D	C	C	C	C	C	C	C		C,O,D
Maryland	C,D	C		C	C,D	C,D	C	C,D	C	C,D	C	O,D	C,D		C,O,D
Massachusetts	C,D	C	C	C,D	C,D	C	C	C,D	C (x),O	C,D	D		C,D	O	O,D
Michigan	C	C		D	C,D	C	C	C	D	C	D	C	O	O	C
Minnesota	C,D	C		D	C,D	C,O	C	C,D	C (aa),O	C,D	D	O	C,D	C,D	C
Mississippi	C	C		D	C	C	C		D	C	C	O	C		C
Missouri	C	C			C	C	C (n),D (n)		C (aa),D (n)	C	C		C (n),D (n)		O,D
Montana		D	C	D	C	C	D	D	D	D	D	O	C	C	C
Nebraska	C	C			C,D	C	C	C,D	C (ff)	C	D	C	C	C	C,D
Nevada		C	O	D,D	C,D	C,D	C,D	C,D	C,D	D	D	D	C,D	D	C
New Hampshire		C			C		D		C,D	C	C	C	C	D	D
New Jersey	C	C		D	C	C	C	D	C	C	C	D	C	D	O,D
New Mexico		D	C,O	C,D	C,D	C,O	C,D	C,D	C (ff),D (jj)	C	D	C	C		O,D
New York		C		C,O	C	C	D	C,D	O,D (gg)	C	D	O	O,D	D	C,D
North Carolina		C,D	O		C,D	C,D	D	C,D	D (ll),D	C (oo)	D	O	C,D	D	D
North Dakota	C	D	O	D	C	C	C,D	D	C (mm),D	C (oo),D (pp)	C	O,D		D	D
Ohio	C	C		D	C	C	C,D	D	C (nn),D	C	D	O	C	O	O,D

See footnotes at end of table.

STATE PERSONNEL ADMINISTRATION: FUNCTIONS—Continued

State or other jurisdiction	Administers merit tests (a)	Establishes qualifications	Provides human resource information system (a)	Human resource planning	Classification	Compensation (a)	Recruitment	Selection	Performance evaluation (a)	Position audits	Employee promotion	Employee assistance & counseling	Human resource development training	Employee health & wellness program	Affirmative action
Oklahoma	C	C	C	C,D	C	C	C,D	C,D	C,D	C,D	C,D	C,D	C	C,D	C,D
Oregon	C	C	C	C	C	C	C	C	D	D	D	C	D	D	C
Pennsylvania	C	C	C	C,D	C	C	O	D	C	C	D	. . .	C	C	C
Rhode Island	C	C	C	. . .	C	C	C	C	D	C	C,D	. . .	. . .	C	C,D
South Carolina	C	C	C	C,D	C	C	C,D	C,D	C	C	C	C,D	C,D	C	C,D
South Dakota	C	C	C	C	C	C	C,D	. . .,C,D	C,D	C,D	C,D	C	C,D	O	C
Tennessee	D	D	C	C	C	C	O	C	C	C,D	C	O	C	O	C
Texas (rr)	D	D	O	O,D	O,D	C	C,D	D	D	O	D	O,D	O,D	C,D	C,D
Utah	C	C	C	D	C	O	C,D	D	D	C	C	O,D	D	C,D	C,D
Vermont	C	C	C	C	C	C	C	C,D	D	C	C	O,D	C	O	C
Virginia	D	D	C	D	C,D	C,D	C,D	C,D	C,D	C,D	C,D	C,D	C,D	C,D	C,D
Washington	C	C	C	C,D	C	C	C	C,D	C (mm)	C	D	C	C,D	C	C,D
West Virginia	C	C,D	C	D	C,D	C,D	C,D	O,D	D	C	D	. . .,C,D	C,D	. . .	C
Wisconsin	C	C	O	. . .	C	C	C	C,D	C,D	C	D	. . .	C	. . .	C,D
Wyoming	C	C	. . .	. . .	. . .	C	. . .	C,D	C,D	C	D	. . .	. . .	. . .	D
Puerto Rico	C,D	C,D	. . .	C,D	C,D	C,D	C,D	D	C,D	C,D	C,D	C,D	C,D	D	C,D

Key:
C — Functions performed in centralized personnel agency
O — Functions performed in another centralized agency
D — Functions decentralized
. . . — Not applicable

STATE PERSONNEL ADMINISTRATION: FUNCTIONS—Continued

State or other jurisdiction	Labor & employee relations	Collective bargaining/labor negotiations	Grievance & appeals	Retirement	Employee incentive & productivity system	Employee attitude survey	Child care	Workers compensation	Group health insurance	Flexible benefits	Deferred compensation	Drug testing	Budget recommendations to legislature	Legislative liaison	Other
Alabama	C,D	O	C,D	O,D	O	…	…	O,D	O	O	O,D	…	C,O,D	C	O (c)
Alaska	O	O	O,D	C,O	…	…	C,O	O	O	O	O	…	C (d)	C	D (e)
Arizona	C	…	C	C,O	C	D	…	O	O	O	O	…	O	…	…
Arkansas	…	…	…	…	…	…	…	…	…	…	…	…	…	…	…
California															
State Personnel Bd.	O	O	C (g),O (h)	O	…	…	O	O	O	O	O	C,O,D	C	(i)	C (j)
Dept. of Personnel Admin.	C,D	C	C	O	C	C	C	C,O	O	C	C	C,D	O,D	C,D	…
Colorado	C,D	C	C,D	O,D	O	C	C (i),D	O,D	O	O	O	D	C,D	C,D	C (m)
Connecticut	C,D	…	C (n),D	O,D	C (k),D	C,D	C	C,D	O	C	O	…	C,D	C,D	C (o),D (p)
Delaware	C	C	C,O (g),D	O,D	C	…	C,D	O	O	C	O,D	…	O,D	C	…
Florida	C,D	C	C,D	O,D	O	D	C	O,D	O	O	O,D	C,D	O,D	C	…
Georgia	C,D	…	C,D	O,D	O	C	O	O,D	O	O	O	…	C,O	C	…
Hawaii	C	C	C,D	O	C	O	…	O	O	O	O	C	O	C	C (s)
Idaho	C	C,D	C,D	O	…	…	…	O	O	D	O,D	D	O	C,D	C (u)
Illinois	C	C	C,D	O	O	D	C	O	O	O	O	C,D	O,D	C	…
Indiana	C	O	C,D	O,D	O	…	…	O,D	O	O	O	…	…	…	C (w)
Iowa	C	…	O	O	C,D	…	C,D	O,D	O,D	…	O	…	C,D	C	…
Kansas	C,D	C,D	C,D	O	…	C,D	…	O	O	O	O,D	O,D	C,O,D	C,O,D	…
Kentucky	…	…	C,O (t)	O	O	…	…	C,O	C,O	O	O	D	O,D	C,O,D	…
Louisiana	O,D	O	C,O (g),D	O,D	…	D	C,D	C,D	C,D	…	O,O	C,D	…	C (v)	C (x),O (z)
Maryland	C,D	…	O	O	C,D	…	O	C,O	O	D	O	…	C (cc),O	C,O	C (dd)
Massachusetts	O	O	(y)	O	…	O	O	O	O	C	O	…	C	…	…
Michigan	C,D	O	C	O	C	C	…	O	C,D	…	O	…	C (ee),D	C,D	C (ee),D
Minnesota	C,D	…	C,D	O	…	D	…	O	C	C	O	…	C,O	C,O	…
Mississippi	C	…	C,D	O	C,D	D	C,D	O,D	O	C	C,O	D	C,D	C,D	C (hh),D (ii)
Missouri	…	…	O	O	…	…	O	O	O	O	C,O	…	C,D	C,D	…
Montana	C	C	C,D	O	O	…	…	O	O	O	O	…	C (kk),D	C	C (kk),D
Nebraska	C	C	C,D	O	C	D	…	O	O	C	O	C	C,O	…	C
Nevada	C	C	C,D	O	…	D	O	O	O	…	C,D	…	C,D	C,D	…
New Hampshire	C,D	C (gg)	C,D	O	…	…	O	O	O	C	O	…	C,O	C,D	…
New Jersey	C,D	…	O	O	C,D	O,D	…	O,D	O,D	C,O	C,O	D	C (mm)	C,D	…
New Mexico	C	D	C,D	O	C	…	…	O	O	O	O	…	C,O	C	…
New York	O,D	…	C,O	O	O	D	…	O	O	O	O	D	O	O	…
North Carolina	D	…	C	O	O	…	…	C,D	O,D	O	O,D	…	C (mm)	C	…
North Dakota	O,D	…	O,D	O	C	O,D	…	O	O	O	O	…	C,O	C,D	…
Ohio	O,D	O	O,D	O	…	O	C	C	O	O	O	D	O	C,D	C (u)

See footnotes at end of table.

STATE PERSONNEL ADMINISTRATION: FUNCTIONS—Continued

State or other jurisdiction	Labor & employee relations	Collective bargaining/labor negotiations	Grievance & appeals	Retirement	Employee incentive & productivity system	Employee attitude survey	Child care	Workers compensation	Group health insurance	Flexible benefits	Deferred compensation	Drug testing	Budget recommendations to legislature	Legislative liaison	Other
Oklahoma	C	...	O,D	O	C	...	C	O	O	C	O	...	C,O,D	C,D	...
Oregon	C	C	C (h),O (g)	O	C	D	C	O	O	C	O	D	C,O,D	C,D	...
Pennsylvania	C	C	D	...	C	C	C	O	O	...	O	D	C,O,D	C	C (qq)
Rhode Island	...	...	C	...	C	C	C	...	O	...	O	D	C	C	...
South Carolina	C	...	C	...	C	C	D	...	O	...	O	D	C	C	...
South Dakota	C	C	C,D	O	C	C	...	O	O	C	O	C	C,O,D	C	...
Tennessee (rr)	D	D	C	O	C	...	...	O	O	O	O	...	O,D	O	O (ss)
Utah	D	...	O,D	O	D	O	O,D	O	O	C	O	D	C,D	D	...
Vermont	C	C	C	...	D	D	D	O	O	C	O	C	C	C	...
Virginia	C	...	O,D	O	...	...	...	O	C,D	C	O	...	...	D	C (tt),D (uu)
Washington	C,D	C	C,D	O	O	C	C	O,D	C,D	C,D	O	D	C,D	C,D	C (vv),O (ww)
West Virginia	C,D	...	O,D	O,D	D	D	C	O,D	O,D	O	O	O,D	O	...	...
Wisconsin	C,D	...	C,D	...	...	C	C	O,D	...	O	O	...	...	...	...
Wyoming	C	...	C	...	D	...	...	...	...	...	O	...	...	...	...
Puerto Rico	C,D	O,D	...	O,D	D	...	C,D	O	C,D	C,O,D	O,D	D	O	...	C (xx)

Source: National Association of State Personnel Executives, *State Personnel Office: Roles and Functions, Second Edition,* 1992.

Note: See above referenced source for more detailed information.

Key:
C — Functions performed in centralized personnel agency
O — Functions performed in another centralized agency
D — Functions decentralized
... — Not applicable

(a) These functions have been computerized in the following states. **Testing Certification:** Alabama, Arizona, Arkansas, California, Colorado, Connecticut, Georgia, Illinois, Indiana, Iowa, Kansas, Kentucky, Maine, Maryland, Massachusetts, Michigan, Minnesota, Mississippi, Missouri, Nevada, New Jersey, New Mexico, New York, Ohio, Oregon, Pennsylvania, Rhode Island, South Carolina, South Dakota, Tennessee, Washington, West Virginia, Wyoming, Puerto Rico; **Human Resource Information System:** Arizona, Arkansas, California, Colorado, Connecticut, Delaware, Florida, Georgia, Hawaii, Idaho, Illinois, Indiana, Kansas, Louisiana, Maine, Maryland, Massachusetts, Michigan, Minnesota, Mississippi, Missouri, Montana, Nebraska, Nevada, New Hampshire, New Jersey, New Mexico, North Carolina, North Dakota, Oregon, Pennsylvania, Rhode Island, South Dakota, Tennessee, Texas, Utah, Virginia, Washington, Wyoming, Puerto Rico; **Payroll:** Alabama, Alaska, Arizona, Arkansas, California, Colorado, Connecticut, Delaware, Florida, Georgia, Hawaii, Idaho, Illinois, Iowa, Kansas, Kentucky, Maine, Maryland, Massachusetts, Michigan, Minnesota, Mississippi, Missouri, Nevada, New Jersey, New Mexico, New York, Ohio, Oregon, Pennsylvania, Rhode Island, South Carolina, South Dakota, Washington, West Virginia, Wyoming, Puerto Rico; **Fringe Benefits Summaries:** California (Dept. of Personnel Administration), Connecticut, Florida, Indiana, Maine, Massachusetts, Mississippi, Montana, New York, Rhode Island, South Carolina; **Job Evaluation:** Arkansas, Connecticut, Florida, Indiana, Maine, Massachusetts, Mississippi, Montana, New York, Rhode Island, South Carolina.
(b) Administrative as opposed to policy and regulation.
(c) Sign up employees for retirement and benefit programs.
(d) For adjustments to the salary and benefits plans only.
(e) Personnel managers and professional staff assigned to the agencies are employees of the central personnel authority.

(f) Establish and revise classes.
(g) Appeals only.
(h) Grievances only.
(i) Each agency has its own legislative liaison.
(j) Information practices—certification of court and administrative hearing interpreters; establish merit personnel standards for local government agencies as required by federal or state statutes.
(k) For managers.
(l) Indirect (startup support for child care facilities).
(m) Health Care Cost Containment Committee Management Relations.
(n) Shared.
(o) Other benefits (e.g., group life insurance, dental insurance, etc); personnel policies and procedures.
(p) Personnel files and records; personnel transactions.
(q) The central personnel office has system responsibility.
(r) Central Management Services serves as central coordinating agency.
(s) State Civil Service Board, Service Recognition Award, Employee Suggestions Award.
(t) Personnel Board responsible for appeals.
(u) Payroll.
(v) Through Department of Administration.
(w) Responsible for rules and regulations that govern the State Civil Service System.
(x) Management positions only.
(y) Department of Personnel Administration handles appeals of classification and civil service issues; grievances and other types of appeals handled by Office of Employee Relations; cases denied may be appealed to Civil Service Commission.
(z) Non-management positions only.
(aa) System development and supervisory training.
(bb) Disciplinary appeals only.
(cc) Pay plan only.
(dd) Leave benefit administration, personnel management consultation, Fair Labor Standards Act liaison.
(ee) With regard to compensation.

STATE PERSONNEL ADMINISTRATION: FUNCTIONS—Continued

(ff) System.
(gg) Labor negotiations only.
(hh) Work performance standards.
(ii) Payroll, employee records, personnel rules.
(jj) Individual.
(kk) Policy and procedure.
(ll) Establishes policy only.
(mm) Salaries and State Personnel Office Budget.
(nn) Development of evaluation forms.
(oo) For employees exempt from collective bargaining.
(pp) For bargaining unit employees.
(qq) Human resource management and total quality management consulting services, productivity studies, executive leadership, agency head pay, higher education administration and faculty pay, conditions of employment, service awards, suggestion program, technology training, reduction in force, employee relations policy interpretation.
(rr) Decentralized personnel system.
(ss) Interpretation of all leave, State Classification Office. Interpretation of longevity, merit increases and payroll, Comptroller of Public Accounts.
(tt) Meritorious service award program; policy development.
(uu) Meritorious service award program.
(vv) Career executive program.
(ww) Dependent Care Assistance Program, Committee for Deferred Compensation.
(xx) Legal representation for centralized agencies or as required by the Board of Appeal.

Table 7.3
CLASSIFICATION AND COMPENSATION PLANS

State or other jurisdiction	Legal basis for classification	Current number of classifications in state	Requirement for periodic comprehensive classification review plan	Date of most recent comprehensive review of classification	Legal basis for compensation plan	Compensation schedules determined by:
Alabama	S	1,600	★	1982	S	P
Alaska	S	1,050	. . .	1960	S	L
Arizona	S,R	1,500	. . .	N.A.	N.A.	L
Arkansas	S	1,900	. . .	1988-1990	S	L
California Dept. of Personnel Admin.	C,S	4,324	. . .	N.A.	S,CB	P (a)
Colorado	C,S,R	1,348	. . .	1991	S,R	P
Connecticut	S	2,600	★	1990	CB	P
Delaware	S	1,434	★	1987	S	L
Florida	S	1,596	★	1985	S	L
Georgia	S	1,570	. . .	1978	S	P
Hawaii	S	1,660	. . .	N.A.	S	(a)
Idaho	S	1,550	★	1991	S	L
Illinois	S	1,680	. . .	1969	S,R,CB	P
Indiana	S,R	1,500	. . .	1974-76 (b)	S,R	P
Iowa	S	1,250	★ On-going	On-going	S,R,EO,CB	P
Kansas	S,R,EO	1,142	★	On-going (c)	S,R,EO	P (d)
Kentucky	S	1,614	. . .	1982	S,R	P
Louisiana	C	3,800	. . .	1987	C	P
Maine	S	1,500	★	On-going	S,R,CB	P,L (e)
Maryland	S,R	3,000 (approx.)	. . .	On-going	S,R	P,L
Massachusetts	S	1,150 (approx.)	. . .	1980	S,CB	P (f),L (g), (h)
Michigan	C	2,700	★	1991	C	P
Minnesota	S	2,140	. . .	1978	S,CB	P (a)
Mississippi	S	2,053	★	1990	S	P
Missouri	S	1,100	. . .	1946	S	P
Montana	S	1,350 (approx.)	. . .	1990	S,CB	L
Nebraska	S	1,300	. . .	(i)	S,CB	P
Nevada	S,R	1,300	★	On-going	S	P
New Hampshire	R	1,490	★	1991	CB	L
New Jersey	S	6,400	. . .	1990	S,CB	P (j)
New Mexico	S,R	1,200	. . .	1989	S,R	P,L
New York	S	7,300	. . .	1984-1985	S,CB	(k)
North Carolina	S	3,500	. . .	(l)	S	(m)
North Dakota	S	1,075	. . .	1987-1988	S	(n)
Ohio	S	1,804	★	1987-1990	S,CB	L (a)
Oklahoma	S	1,418	. . .	1981	S	L
Oregon	S	1,100	. . .	1984-1990	S,CB	P (o)
Pennsylvania	S	2,782	. . .	1989	S	P
Rhode Island	S	1,500	★	1989	S	P
South Carolina	S	2,318	★	1991	S	(p)
South Dakota	S	551	. . .	1985-1986	S	P
Tennessee	S	2,258	. . .	1984	S	P,L
Texas	S (q)	1,339	★	(r)	S (q)	L
Utah	S	2,500	★	On-going	S	L
Vermont	S	1,280	. . .	1986	S,CB	(s)
Virginia	S	1,888	★	On-going	S	P,L
Washington	S,R	2,100	. . .	On-going	S,R	L
West Virginia	S,R	2,000 (approx.)	. . .	1984	S,R	P
Wisconsin	C,S	2,000	★	On-going	C,S,CB	N.A.
Wyoming	S	774	★	1989	S	P
Puerto Rico	S	1,107	. . .	On-going	S	(t)

CLASSIFICATION AND COMPENSATION PLANS—Continued

Source: National Association of State Personnel Executives, *State Personnel Office: Roles and Functions, Second Edition*, 1992.

Note: See above referenced source for more detailed information.

Key:
C — Constitution
L — Legislature
P — Personnel Department
S — Statute
R — Regulation
CB — Collective Bargaining
EO — Executive Order
. . . — Not applicable
N.A. — Not available
(a) Collective bargaining.
(b) Reviewed in 1989-90; results not yet implemented. Current classification plan implemented in 1977-78.
(c) The review of all classified jobs is to be completed by the beginning of fiscal year 1992. The review is on-going.
(d) Approval by governor; agencies with decentralized classification authority are audited annually by the centralized personnel department.
(e) Wages and salaries for majority of state employees are negotiated.

(f) Management compensation schedules.
(g) All department compensation schedules approved by legislation.
(h) Office of Employee Relations determines non-management compensation schedules.
(i) No single comprehensive review; periodic review of components.
(j) Department of Personnel assigns salary ranges; increases to ranges are negotiated.
(k) Salary schedules are set through negotiations for represented employees; management salary schedules are set by law.
(l) There has been no review of the classification system since it was established.
(m) State Personnel Commission (with funding from the legislature).
(n) The Personnel Division recommends schedules within legislative appropriations. The State Personnel Board has approval authority.
(o) Collective bargaining with approval of legislature.
(p) State Budget and Control Board.
(q) Appropriations Act.
(r) Reviewed each biennium in conjunction with budget and appropriation process.
(s) Collective bargaining or executive approval.
(t) Prepared by Personnel Department and approved by the legislature.

Table 7.4
SELECTED EMPLOYEE LEAVE POLICIES

State or other jurisdiction	Annual leave			Sick leave					
	Accrual (in days/year)		Carryover allowed	Accrual (in days/year)	Carryover allowed	Leave used for other purposes (a)	Leave bank/ program offered	Parental leave treated as:	Child care on-site
	One year	Five years							
Alabama............	13	16.08	★	13	★	★	I	M	...
Alaska.............	15	21	★	N.A.	★	★	I	M	...
Arizona............	12	15	★ (b)	12	★	★ (c)	I	(d)	★
Arkansas	12	15	★	12	★	★	B	M	...
California	10.5	15	★	12	★	★	I	U	★
Colorado	12	12	★	10	★ (e)	★	I,B	(f)	...
Connecticut	12	15	★	15	★	★	I,B	S	★
Delaware	15	15	★	15	★	★	...	U	★
Florida	13	16.25	★	13	★	★	B	(g)	...
Georgia............	15	15	★	15	★	★	...	A	...
Hawaii	21	21	★	21	★	★	...	A,S (h)	...
Idaho	12	15	★	12	★	★	...	M	...
Illinois.............	10	10	★	12	★	★	...	U	...
Indiana	12	15	★	6	★	...	...	...	...
Iowa	10	15	★	18	★	★ (i)	...	A,S	★
Kansas	12	15	★	12	★	★	...	(d)	★
Kentucky	12	15	(j)	12	★	★	I	U	...
Louisiana	(k)	(l)	★	varies	...	...	...	U (m)	...
Maine	12	15	★	12	★	★	...	U	★
Maryland	10	10	★	15	★	★	B	U	★ (n)
Massachusetts	10	15	★	15	★	★	...	U (o)	★ (p)
Michigan	13	15	★	13	★	★	...	U	★
Minnesota	13	16.25	★	13	★	★	...	U	...
Mississippi	18	21	★	(q)	★	...	...	M	...
Missouri	15	15	★	15	★	★	...	U	...
Montana...........	15	15	★ (r)	12	★	★	B	(d)	...
Nebraska	12	12	★	(s)	★	★	...	(t)	...
Nevada	15	15	★	15	★	★	I,B	U	...
New Hampshire	...	15	★	7.5	★	★	...	(u)	★
New Jersey.........	12	15	★	15	★	★	...	U	★
New Mexico........	10	12	★	12	★	★	I	(v)	...
New York	13-14 (w)	18	★	8,10 or 13 (w)	★	★	...	(x)	★
North Carolina	11.75	16.75	★	12	★	★	I	A (u)	...
North Dakota	12	15	★	12	★	★	...	(y)	...
Ohio	14	25	★	10	★	★	...	A,M (z)	★
Oklahoma	15	18	★	15	★	★	I	(aa)	...
Oregon	12	15	★	12	★	★ (bb)	I	(d)	★
Pennsylvania	5.5	10.4	★	13	★	★	...	(cc)	★
Rhode Island	14	15	★	15	★	★ (dd)	...	U (ee)	★
South Carolina	15	15	★	15	★	★ (ff)	B	(gg)	★
South Dakota	15	15	★	14	★	★ (hh)	I	M (ii)	...
Tennessee	12	16.95	★	12	★	★	B	(d)	★
Texas..............	10.5	13.5	★	12	★	★	B	(d)	★ (jj)
Utah	13	13	★	13	★	★	I,B	M	...
Vermont	12	15	★	12-21	★	★	B	A (kk)	★
Virginia............	12	15	★	12	★	★	...	S,M	★
Washington	12	15	★	12	★	★	I	(ll)	★
West Virginia	15	18	...	18	★	★ (hh)	...	(mm)	★
Wisconsin	10	15	★	13	★	★	...	A	...
Wyoming	12	15	★	12	★	★	I	(d)	★
Puerto Rico	30	30	★	18	★	...	...	M (nn)	★

SELECTED EMPLOYEE LEAVE POLICIES—Continued

Source: National Association of State Personnel Executives, *State Personnel Office: Roles and Functions, Second Edition,* 1992.

Note: See above referenced source for more detailed information.

Key:

★ — Yes

. . . — No

A — Annual leave without pay

B — Donation to a leave bank

I — Donation of leave directly to individual

M — Maternity leave only

S — Sick leave without pay

U — Unpaid leave of absence

N.A. — Not available

(a) Purposes vary across the states and individual jurisdictions should be consulted for specifics. However, sick leave typically may be used for family illness in these cases. Other purposes include medical appointments, funeral/bereavement leave, births, adoption and workers' compensation disability.

(b) Up to 30 days. Any additional carryover must be approved by Dept. of Administration director.

(c) Industrial disability, parental leave and limit of 40 hours for family member's illness.

(d) Annual leave, sick leave, compensatory credits or leave without pay.

(e) Up to 45 day maximum.

(f) Employee may use sick leave if physically unable to work, remainder of family leave is annual leave and leave without pay.

(g) Maternity leave without pay and annual, sick and compensatory leave with pay.

(h) Vacation.

(i) Emergency family care and death in the family up to 40 hours for non-contractual employees.

(j) Total amount of accrued leave and months of service determine whether carryover is allowable. Excess leave is converted to sick leave.

(k) Accrual rate is 1.8440 hours per month.

(l) Accrual rate is 2.7688 hours per month.

(m) Handled differently by each agency, usually annual leave with pay.

(n) Certain locations only.

(o) Up to eight weeks without pay.

(p) Child care program is privately owned and operates facility on state-owned property.

(q) First year employees—12 days; fifth year employees—10.5 days.

(r) Not more than two times maximum annual earned.

(s) 12 to 30 days depending on length of service.

(t) Pregnancies treated as temporary disabilities; additional leave without pay may be applied for.

(u) Annual leave

(v) No statewide policy.

(w) Depending on bargaining unit.

(x) Leave for pregnancy, childbirth and child care; child care leave for adoptive parents.

(y) Medical needs of family; limit of 40 hours per year.

(z) Sick leave to care for child.

(aa) Up to 12 weeks of sick, annual leave.

(bb) Up to five days.

(cc) Up to 183 days childbirth leave without pay with benefits.

(dd) 10 days per year.

(ee) Except where expending sick or vacation leave.

(ff) Five days for illness in immediate family; six weeks for adoption.

(gg) Up to six weeks sick leave with pay; annual leave or leave without pay for adoption

(hh) 40 hours maximum.

(ii) Father may use annual leave or 40 hours of personal leave.

(jj) At School for the Blind and Visually Impaired.

(kk) Paid and unpaid leave for parental leave.

(ll) Paid sick leave for period of disability only; paid annual leave; additional leave is without pay.

(mm) Unpaid family leave up to 12 weeks per year.

(nn) Adoption maternity leave.

Table 7.5
STATE EMPLOYEES: PAID HOLIDAYS*

State or other jurisdiction	Major holidays (a)	Martin Luther King's Birthday (b)	Lincoln's Birthday	President's Day (c)	Washington's Birthday (c)	Good Friday	Memorial Day (d)	Columbus Day (e)	Veteran's Day	Day after Thanksgiving	Day before or after Christmas	Day before or after New Year's	Election Day (f)	Other (g)
Alabama	★	★ (h)			★ (i)		★	★	★					★
Alaska	★	★		★			★		★	★				★
Arizona (k)	★	★		★	★		★		★					
Arkansas	★	★	★		★		★		★					★
California	★	★	★		★		★	★	★		Before		★	★
Colorado (l)	★	★		★			★	★	★					★
Connecticut	★	★	★		★	★	★	★	★	★				★
Delaware	★	★		★		★	★		★	★				★
Florida (k)	★	★		★			★		★					
Georgia (k)	★	★		★	(m)		★		★	(m)	(m)			
Hawaii	★	★		★		★	★		★					★
Idaho	★	★		★	★		★	★	★					★
Illinois	★	★ (o)	★ (n)	★	★ (n,l)		★	★	★	(n)	(n)			
Indiana	★	★					★	★	★	★ (n)				★
Iowa	★	★		★			★		★	★				★ ★
Kansas	★	★		★		★ (p)	★ (o)		★	★ (o)	★ (o)	★ (o)	(q)	★
Kentucky (k)	★	★	★	★		★	★	★	★	★	★	★	★	★
Louisiana	★	★		★	★	(j)	★	★	★	★ (o)	★ (o)	★ (o)	★	★
Maine (k)	★	★					★		★					★
Maryland	★	★		★	★		★	★	★				★	★
Massachusetts	★	★		★			★	★	★		Before	Before		★
Michigan	★	★		★			★		★	★				★
Minnesota	★	★		★			★		★	★				★
Mississippi (k)	★			★	★		★		★	★				★
Missouri	★	★	★	★			★	★	★	(o)			★	★
Montana (k)	★	★		★			★		★	★				★
Nebraska (k)	★	★		★	★		★		★	★ (o)				★
Nevada (k)	★	★			★	★	★	★	★				★	★
New Hampshire	★			★			★		★					★
New Jersey	★	★		★	★	★	★	★	★	★			★	★
New Mexico (k)	★	★	(o)	(r)			★		★	(r)				★
New York	★	★	★	★			★	★	★				★	★
North Carolina	★	★					★	★	★	★	★	★		★
North Dakota (k)	★	★		★			★		★	★				★
Ohio (k)	★				★		★		★		(s)		(o)	
Oklahoma	★	★	(o)	★			★		★	★	★	★		★
Oregon	★	★		★	★	★	★		★		After	After	★	★
Pennsylvania	★	★		★			★	★	★		(o)			
Rhode Island	★	★					★	★	★					★
South Carolina (k)					★		★		★	★	★		★ (q)	★

STATE EMPLOYEES: PAID HOLIDAYS* —Continued

State or other jurisdiction	Major holidays (a)	Martin Luther King's Birthday (b)	Lincoln's Birthday	President's Day (c)	Washington's Birthday (c)	Good Friday	Memorial Day (d)	Columbus Day (e)	Veteran's Day	Day after Thanksgiving	Day before or after Christmas	Day before or after New Year's	Election Day (f)	Other (g)
South Dakota	★	★		★			★		★	★				★
Tennessee (u)	★	★			★	(v)	★	(i)	★	(i)	★			
Utah (k)	★	★ (w)		★			★		★					★
Vermont (k)	★	(j)	(j)	★			★	★	★	(o)	(o)	(o)		★
Virginia	★	★ (x)			★		★	★	★	★				★
Washington	★	★		★			★		★	★				★
West Virginia	★	★	★				★	★	★	★	(y)	(y)	★	★
Wisconsin (aa)	★	★ (bb)				★ (p)	★		★		Before	Before	(z)	★
Wyoming	★	★					★							★
Dist. of Columbia	★	★		★	★		★	★	★					

* Holidays in addition to any other authorized paid personal leave granted state employees.

Source: The Council of State Governments' survey of state personnel offices, March 1994.

Note: In some states, the governor may proclaim additional holidays or select from a number of holidays for observance by state employees. In some states, the list of paid holidays is determined by the personnel department at the beginning of each year; as a result, the number of holidays may change from year to year. Number of paid holidays may also vary across some employee classifications. Dates are given for 1994 and may change slightly for 1995. If a holiday falls on a weekend, generally employees get the day preceding or following.

Key:

★ — Paid holiday granted

. . — Paid holiday not granted

(a) New Year's Day, Independence Day, Labor Day, Thanksgiving Day, and Christmas Day.

(b) Third Monday in January.

(c) Generally, third Monday in February; Washington's Birthday or President's Day. In some states the holiday is called President's Day or Washington-Lincoln Day. Most frequently, this day recognizes George Washington and Abraham Lincoln.

(d) Last Monday in May in all states indicated, except New Hampshire and Vermont where holiday is observed on May 30. Generally, states follow the federal government's observance (last Monday in May) rather than the traditional Memorial Day (May 30).

(e) Second Monday in October.

(f) General election day only, unless otherwise indicated.

(g) Additional holidays:

Alabama—Mardi Gras Day (day before Ash Wednesday) in Baldwin and Mobile Counties only; in other counties, state employees receive one floating holiday. Confederate Memorial Day (fourth Monday in April), Jefferson Davis' Birthday (first Monday in June).

Alaska—Seward's Day (last Monday in March), Alaska Day (October 18). Employee's birthday may be taken as a floating holiday under one collective bargaining agreement.

Arkansas—Employee's birthday.

California—One personal day.

Delaware—Return Day, after 12 noon (Thursday after a general election) in Sussex County only.

Florida—One personal day.

Georgia—Confederate Memorial Day (April 26).

Hawaii—Prince Jonah Kuhio Kalanianaole Day (March 26), King Kamehameha I Day (June 11), Admissions Day (third Friday in August).

Iowa—Two floating holidays.

Kansas—Discretionary day (taken whenever employee chooses with supervisor's approval).

Louisiana—Mardi Gras Day (day before Ash Wednesday), Inauguration Day (every four years, in Baton Rouge only).

Maine—Patriot's Day (third Monday in April).

Maryland—Maryland Day (March 25) and Defender's Day (September 12) are floating holidays; state offices remain open.

Massachusetts—Patriot's Day (third Monday in April), Evacuation Day (March 17) and Bunker Hill Day (June 17).

Minnesota—One floating holiday.

Mississippi—Confederate's Memorial Day (last Monday in April).

Missouri—Harry Truman's Birthday (May 8).

Nebraska—Arbor Day (last Friday in April).

Nevada—Nevada Day (October 31).

Rhode Island—Victory Day (second Monday in August).

South Carolina—One floating holiday.

South Dakota—Native American's Day (second Monday in October).

Texas—Confederate Heroes Day (January 19), Texas Independence Day (March 2), San Jacinto Day (April 21), Emancipation Day (June 19) and Lyndon Johnson's Birthday (August 27). A state employee may observe Rosh Hashanah, Yom Kippur and Good Friday in lieu of any state holiday on which the employee's agency is required to be open.

Utah—Pioneer Day (July 24).

Vermont—Town Meeting Day (first Tuesday in March), Battle of Bennington Day (August 16).

Washington—One floating holiday.

West Virginia—West Virginia Day (June 20).

District of Columbia—Inauguration Day (January 20, every four years).

(h) Also for Robert E. Lee's Birthday.

(i) Also for Thomas Jefferson's Birthday.

(j) Floating holiday; employee may take the holiday on another day. State offices are open.

(k) If a holiday falls on a Saturday, it is observed on the Friday before. If it falls on a Sunday, observed on the following Monday.

(k) In Colorado, agencies have the discretion to observe an alternate holiday schedule in lieu of statutory holidays.

STATE EMPLOYEES: PAID HOLIDAYS—Continued

(m) In Georgia, Robert E. Lee's Birthday is observed on the day after Thanksgiving, and Washington's birthday is observed the day after Christmas (in 1994, December 27).

(n) In Indiana, Lincoln's Birthday is observed on the day after Thanksgiving, and Washington's birthday is observed the day before Christmas.

(o) At the discretion of the governor.

(p) Half day.

(q) In Kentucky, state employees are granted four hours on election day. In South Carolina, election day is a holiday in even-numbered years.

(r) In New Mexico, President's Day is observed on the day after Thanksgiving.

(s) In North Dakota, if the day before Christmas is a weekday, state offices close at noon.

(t) In Tennessee, state employees have selected by ballot to observe Columbus Day on the day after Thanksgiving during the past few years.

(u) In Texas, a holiday is not observed if it falls on Saturday or Sunday.

(v) In Texas, a state employee may observe Good Friday in lieu of any state holiday on which the employee's agency is required to be open.

(w) Called Human Rights Day; celebrates Martin Luther King, Jr. and others who worked for human rights.

(x) Called Lee/Jackson/King Day, after Robert E. Lee, Andrew Jackson and Martin Luther King, Jr.

(y) Half day on Christmas Eve and New Year's Eve if they fall on Monday, Tuesday, Wednesday or Thursday.

(z) In West Virginia, both general and primary elections are holidays.

(aa) Any holiday that falls on a Saturday is a floating holiday. A holiday that falls on a Sunday is observed on the following Monday.

(bb) Called Martin Luther King, Jr./Wyoming Equality Day.

Table 7.6
CIVIL SERVICE REFORM IN THE STATES

State or other jurisdiction	Extent of reform	Initiator of reform	Merit testing	Classification	Compensation	Recruitment	Selection	Performance evaluation	Training	Employee relations	Benefits	Layoffs
Alabama	I	N.A.	...	...	★	...	...	...	...	...	...	...
Alaska	I	N.A.	...	★	★	★	★	★	★	★	★	★
Arizona	I	G (a)	...	★	★	★	★	★	★	★	★	★
Arkansas	I	G	...	★	★	★	...	★	★	...	★	...
California	I	N.A.	★	★	★	...	★	...	...	...	...	...
Colorado	I	G,L,P	...	★	★	...	★	★	...	...	★	★
Connecticut	I	L,P	★	★	★	...	★	★	...	...	★	...
Delaware						---------- (b) ----------						
Florida	W	G,P	★	★	★	★	★	★	★	★	★	★
Georgia	I	N.A.	...	...	★	...	...	...	...	...	...	...
Hawaii	I	P	★	★	★	★	★	★	★	★	★	...
Idaho	I	(a)	★	★	★	★	...	...	...	...	...	...
Illinois	(c)	G	★	★	★	★	★	...	★	★	★	...
Indiana	I	G,P	★	★	...	★	★	★	★	★	★	...
Iowa	I	G,L,P	★	★	★	...	★	★	★	...	...	★
Kansas	I	N.A.	...	★	...	...	...	...	...	...	...	...
Kentucky					No reform underway/planned							
Louisiana					No reform underway/planned							
Maine	I	G,L,P	★	★	...	★	★	★	★	...	★	★
Maryland	I	G,P	★	★	★	★	★	★	★	★	★	★
Massachusetts	W	G,P (a)	★	★	★	★	★	★	★	★	★	...
Michigan	I	G,P	★	★	★	★	★	★	★	★	★	★
Minnesota	W	G,P (a)	...	★	★	...	...	...	★	...	...	★
Mississippi					---------- (d) ----------							
Missouri					No reform underway/planned							
Montana	I	N.A.	...	★	★	★	★	★	...	★	...	★
Nebraska					No reform underway/planned							
Nevada	I	G	★	★	...	★	★	★	★	...	★	★
New Hampshire					---------- (d) ----------							
New Jersey	W	G,P	★	★	★	...	...	★	★	...	★	★
New Mexico					No reform underway/planned							
New York	I	G	★	★	...	...	...	★	...	★	...	...
North Carolina					---------- (b) ----------							
North Dakota	I	N.A.	...	★	...	...	...	...	...	...	...	...
Ohio	W	G,P	★	★	★	★	★	★	★	★	★	...
Oklahoma	W	G	★	★	★	★	★	★	★	★	★	...
Oregon	I	G,P	★	★	★	...	...	★	...	...	★	★
Pennsylvania	I	N.A.	...	...	...	...	...	...	...	...	...	...
Rhode Island					No reform underway/planned							
South Carolina	I	G,L,P (a)	...	★	...	...	...	...	...	...	...	...
South Dakota					No reform underway/planned							
Tennessee	I	N.A.	...	...	...	...	★	...	...	...	...	...
Texas					---------- (d) ----------							
Utah	I	P	...	★	★	★	★	★	★	...	...	...
Vermont	I	P	★	★	★	★	★	★	★	★	★	...
Virginia	I	P	★	★	★	★	...	★	...	...	★	★
Washington	I	N.A.	★	★	★	★	★	★	...	...	...	...
West Virginia					---------- (d) ----------							
Wisconsin	I	G,P	★	★	★	★	★	...	...	...	...	...
Wyoming					No reform underway/planned							
Dist. of Columbia	I	G	...	...	★	...	...	★	★	★	★	★
U.S. Virgin Islands	W	P	★	★	★	★	★	★	★	★	★	★

Source: National Association of State Personnel Executives, Civil Service Reform Survey, 1993.

Key:
★ — Function is being reformed or considered for reform
... — No reform
I — Incremental reform
W — Wholesale reform
G — Governor
L — Legislature
P — Personnel agency
N.A. — Not available

(a) Other initiators: Arizona, Idaho—various state agencies; Massachusetts—various groups dedicated to improving the effectiveness and efficiency of the delivery of state government services; Minnesota—Governor's Commission on Reform and Efficiency; South Carolina—citizens and customers.
(b) Reform is being planned or under consideration by the state personnel executives in Delaware and North Carolina; no further information available.
(c) Extent of reform unknown until review process has been completed.
(d) Data not available.

Table 7.7
DOWNSIZING: STATE WORK FORCE REDUCTION

State or other jurisdiction	Agencies must follow state reduction plan	Reductions based on seniority only	Employee displacement/ "bumping" (a)	Difference between downsizing and reorganization (b)	Plans for future reductions
Alabama	★	...	★	★ (c)	...
Alaska	...	...	★	★	...
Arizona	★	...	★	...	★
Arkansas	...	...	★	...	★
California	★	...	★	★ (d)	★
Colorado	★	...	★	...	...
Connecticut	...	...	★	★	★
Delaware	★	★	★	N.A.	...
Florida	★	...	★	★	...
Georgia	★ (e)	...	★	★	★
Hawaii	★	★	★	★ (d)	(f)
Idaho	★	...	★	...	...
Illinois	★	...	★	★	(f)
Indiana	...	...	★	★	...
Iowa	... (g)	...	★	★ (d)	...
Kansas	... (h)	...	★	★ (d)	★ (i)
Kentucky	★	...	...	★ (d)	...
Louisiana	★	★	★	★	...
Maine	★	★	★	★	★
Maryland	... (j)	★	★	★ (d)	...
Massachusetts	... (g)	...	★	★	N.A.
Michigan	...	★	★	★ (d)	...
Minnesota	----------(k)----------				
Mississippi	★	...	N.A.	★	...
Missouri	----------(k)----------				
Montana	...	...	...	...	★
Nebraska	...	★	★	...	...
Nevada	...	...	★	★	★ (l)
New Hampshire	----------(k)----------				
New Jersey	★	N.A.	★	★	N.A.
New Mexico	★	...	...	★ (d)	...
New York	...	★	★	★	★
North Carolina	... (g,m)	...	...	★	★ (n)
North Dakota	... (g)	...	...	...	★
Ohio	★	...	★	...	...
Oklahoma	... (g)	★	★	...	★
Oregon	★	...	★	...	★
Pennsylvania	★	N.A.	★	★ (d)	...
Rhode Island	----------(k)----------				
South Carolina	...	...	★	★	...
South Dakota	... (g)	...	...	...	...
Tennessee	★	...	★	...	★
Texas	...	...	...	★ (d)	(o)
Utah	★	...	★	★	★
Vermont	★	...	★	★ (d)	★
Virginia	★	...	★	★	...
Washington	... (g)	★	★	★	★
West Virginia	★	★	★	★	★
Wisconsin	... (g)	...	★	★	...
Wyoming	... (g)	★	★ (p)	★	...
Dist. of Columbia	★	...	★	★	★

Source: National Association of State Personnel Executives, Civil Service Reform Survey, 1993.

Key:
★ — Yes
... — No
N.A. — Not available

(a) If "bumping" is allowed during downsizing, a more senior employee in a position slated for elimination may displace an employee with lesser seniority.

(b) ... (No) in this column means that downsizing occurs during reorganization.

(c) Reorganization at management's discretion; layoffs are by formula.

(d) Reductions, by definition, eliminate positions and reduce the work force; reorganizations do not necessarily reduce the work force and can increase programs and personnel.

(e) Agencies do not have to follow plan for unclassified service.

(f) Not wholesale reduction, but as needed.

(g) Agencies develop own plans but must follow state policies or guidelines.

(h) Plans must be approved by the secretary for administration and the director of personnel services.

(i) Legislature passed law that will reduce the state work force by 25 percent through retirement of employees.

(j) Agencies that are independent personnel authorities must devise their own plans.

(k) Data not available.

(l) Legislature is considering proposal to reorganize state government.

(m) Each agency is required to develop a plan and file it with the office of state personnel.

(n) Legislature is considering proposal to eliminate some state positions.

(o) The determination to reduce the number of employees is made by each agency based on appropriations for the next biennium.

(p) Permanent employees may bump probationary employees.

Table 7.8
INFORMATION RESOURCE MANAGEMENT: CHIEF INFORMATION OFFICERS

State	Chief information officer's title and division (a)	Officer's decisions are binding	State IRM plans	State IRM policies	State IRM standards	State-level IRM acquisitions
			Has authority to approve:			
Alabama	Director, Data Systems Management Division	★	★	★	...	★
Alaska	----------(b)----------					
Arizona	Assistant Director, Data Management Division	(c)	★	★	...	★
Arkansas	Director, Department of Computer Services	★	...	★	★	★
California	Director, Office of Information Technology	★	...	★	★	★
Colorado	Staff Director, Commission on Information Management		...	...	...	...
Connecticut	----No chief information officer----					
Delaware	Executive Director, Office of Information Systems	★	★	★	...	★
Florida	Executive Administrator, Information Resource Commission	...	...	...	★	...
Georgia	----No chief information officer----					
Hawaii	Deputy Director of Finance, Information and Communication Services Division	N.A.	★	★	N.A.	...
Idaho	Statewide Data Processing Coordinator, Information Resource Management	(c)	★	★	★	★
Illinois	Director, Department of Central Management Services	★	★	★	...	★
Indiana	----No chief information officer----					
Iowa	----No chief information officer----					
Kansas	Director, Division of Information Systems & Communication	★	★	★	...	★
Kentucky	Commissioner, Department of Information Systems	★ (c)	...	★	★	★
Louisiana	----No chief information officer----					
Maine	Director, Bureau of Information Services	★	...	...	...	★
Maryland	Chief of Information Technology, Department of Budget and Fiscal Planning	★	★	★	...	...
Massachusetts	----No chief information officer----					
Michigan	----No chief information officer----					
Minnesota	Assistant Commissioner, Information Policy Office	★	...	★	...	★
Mississippi	Executive Director, Central Data Processing Authority	★	★	★	★	★
Missouri	----No chief information officer----					
Montana	Administrator, Information Services Division	(c)	★	★	★	★
Nebraska	Central Data Processing	N.A.	★	★	★	★
Nevada	Director, Department of Data Processing	(c)	★	★	★	★
New Hampshire	----No chief information officer----					
New Jersey	Administrator, Office of Telecommunications and Information Systems	N.A.	...	★	★	★
New Mexico	Director, Information Systems Division	★ (c)	★	★	★	...
New York	----No chief information officer----					
North Carolina	Deputy State Controller for IRM, Office of the State Controller	(c)	★	★	★	★
North Dakota	Director, Information Systems Division	(c)	...	...	★	★
Ohio	Deputy Director, Division of Computer and Information System Services	★	★	★	...	★
Oklahoma	----No chief information officer----					
Oregon	Administrator, Information Systems Division	★	★	★	★	★
Pennsylvania	Special Assistant to the Governor for Computer Information Systems	★	★	★	...	★
Rhode Island	----No chief information officer----					
South Carolina	Deputy Director, Office of Information Technology Policy & Management	★	★	★	★	★
South Dakota	Director, Information Systems	★	...	★	★	★
Tennessee	Chief of Information Systems	★	★	★	...	★
Texas	Executive Director, Department of Information Resources	★	★	★	★	...
Utah	Director, Division of Information Technology Services	N.A.	★	★	★	★
Vermont	----No chief information officer----					
Virginia	Director, Department of Information Technology	(c)	...	...	★	★
	Staff Director, Council on Information Management	(c)	★	★	★	...
Washington	Director, Department of Information Services	★	★	★	★	★
West Virginia	Director, Information Services and Communications	N.A.	★	★	★	★
Wisconsin	Division Administrator	★	★	★	★	★
Wyoming	Administrator, Computer Technology Division	N.A.	★	★	★	★

See footnotes at end of table.

CHIEF INFORMATION OFFICERS—Continued

Source: National Association of State Information Resource Executives, *State Information Resource Management Organizational Structures: 1992 NASIRE Biennial Report*, 1992.

Key:

★ — Yes

. . . — No

(a) The state's chief information officer is the individual with the highest level of authority for managing information resources and services.

(b) Data not available.

(c) Decisions are binding in some cases, but not in others. In Idaho, agency director can override unless purchasing laws could be violated. In Kentucky, decisions are binding for centralized service only. In New Mexico, there are six departments in the executive branch that are statutorily exempt from this provision. In North Carolina, departmental actions must comply with state IRM standards, policies and the strategic direction of the Information Technology Commission. Within those constraints, departmental IRM management may exercise considerable latitude in decision making.

Table 7.9
INFORMATION RESOURCE MANAGEMENT: STATE COMMISSIONS, CENTRAL ORGANIZATIONS AND BUDGETS

State	State commissions IRM commission (a)	Authority to approve:	Central IRM organization (b)	IRM budget as a percentage of total state budget (c)
Alabama	...	...	★	N.A.
Alaska	---------------------------------	(d)	---------------------------------	
Arizona	★	A,B	...	1.6
Arkansas	...	...	★	N.A.
California	...	...	...	1.3
Colorado	★	A,B,C	...	1.9 (e)
Connecticut	★	A,B,C,D	★	3.9
Delaware	★	B	★	7.5 (e)
Florida	★	A,B,C,D	★	0.9 (e)
Georgia	★	B	★	1.6
Hawaii	...	...	★	N.A.
Idaho	★	B,C	★	N.A.
Illinois	...	...	★	N.A.
Indiana	★	D	...	25.0
Iowa	...	...	...	1.5 (e)
Kansas	...	...	★	N.A.
Kentucky	★	A,B,C	★	1.7 (e,f)
Louisiana	...	...	...	N.A.
Maine	★	B,C	★	1.0
Maryland	★	none (g)	...	2.2 (f)
Massachusetts	★	B,C,D	★	N.A.
Michigan	...	...	★	1.0
Minnesota	...	...	★	N.A.
Mississippi	★	A,B,C,D	★	1.7 (f)
Missouri	...	...	★	1.0
Montana	★	none	...	1.9 (e)
Nebraska	★	none	★	N.A.
Nevada	★	none	★	0.5
New Hampshire	★	none	...	N.A.
New Jersey	...	...	★	N.A.
New Mexico	★	A,B,C,D	★	N.A. (h)
New York	...	...	...	1.3 (f)
North Carolina	★	A,B,C	★	0.8
North Dakota	...	...	★	N.A. (h)
Ohio	...	...	★	1.1
Oklahoma	...	...	...	3.4
Oregon	★	A,B,C	★	1.2 (f)
Pennsylvania	...	...	★	1.1
Rhode Island	...	...	★	N.A. (h)
South Carolina	...	...	...	2.8 (e,f)
South Dakota	...	...	★	1.0
Tennessee	★	A,B,D	★	0.6 (e)
Texas	★	A,B,C	...	1.7 (e,f)
Utah	★	A,B,C,D	★	N.A.
Vermont	...	...	...	N.A.
Virginia	★	A,B,C	★	1.7 (f)
Washington	★	A,B,C,D	★	3.4 (e,f)
West Virginia	★	A,C,D	★	N.A.
Wisconsin	★	A,B,C,D	★	1.4 (f)
Wyoming	★	B,C	★	N.A.

Source: National Association of State Information Resource Executives, *State Information Resource Management Organizational Structures: 1992 NASIRE Biennial Report,* 1992.

Key:
★ — Organization exists in the state
... — Organization does not exist in the state
A — State IRM plans
B — State IRM policies
C — State IRM standards
D — State-level IRM acquisitions
N.A. — Not available
(a) Formal board, commission, committee or authority established for the purpose of directing or managing the planning and implementation of information processing resources, policies, standards and services within the state.
(b) A department or agency with state-level authority over information management; usually sets policy and standards; possibly subject to approval of an IRM commission; and may have influence over day-to-day IRM operations.
(c) Budget includes information for the executive department only, except in Connecticut and where noted.
(d) Data not available.
(e) In addition to the executive department, budget includes information for the legislative and judicial branches, except in Tennessee—legislative only; Washington, Florida and Texas—judicial only.
(f) In addition to the executive department, budget includes information for universities.
(g) Advises state's chief information officer.
(h) Total amount of IRM budget in millions of dollars: New Mexico, $25.8 for executive department, universities, and legislative and judicial branches; North Dakota, $18.0 for executive department and legislative and judicial branches; Rhode Island, $7.5 for executive department.

Table 7.10
STATE AID FOR PUBLIC LIBRARIES

State	Total state aid (in thousands of dollars) (a)			Per capita state aid in dollars, 1992 (b)	Number of public libraries, 1991 (c)
	Fiscal 1992 expenditures	Fiscal 1993 appropriations	Fiscal 1994 appropriations		
Alabama	$ 4,790	$ 4,842	$ 4,646	$1.16	206
Alaska	1,003	985	985	1.35	83
Arizona	300	482	502	0.08	89
Arkansas	2,828	2,828	2,828	1.12	36
California	26,532	25,468	31,178	0.86	168
Colorado	3,009	3,009	3,009	0.04	119
Connecticut	3,723	4,074	1,210	0.42	194
Delaware	1,986	1,420	852	1.16	29
Florida	18,326	20,336	26,265	1.29	112
Georgia	26,444	22,226	26,816	3.92	53
Hawaii	0	0	0	0.00	1
Idaho	0	0	0	0.00	107
Illinois	43,233	57,930	74,555	0.81	602
Indiana	3,017	3,017	3,017	0.11	238
Iowa	0	0	980	0.00	513
Kansas	1,503	2,687	1,980	0.45	338
Kentucky	2,812	3,161	2,443	0.52	115
Louisiana	0	0	0	0.00	64
Maine	285	288	288	0.03	225
Maryland	19,377	20,042	20,052	3.22	24
Massachusetts	23,049	27,554	21,483	1.94	374
Michigan	17,292	16,812	16,662	1.80	377
Minnesota	6,645	8,345	8,376	1.24	133
Mississippi	2,768	2,854	3,483	1.06	47
Missouri	1,084	1,499	1,499	0.21	150
Montana	473	432	489	0.43	82
Nebraska	875	1,114	1,123	0.20	270
Nevada	0	0	0	0.00	26
New Hampshire	49	95	80	0.00	230
New Jersey	13,002	13,112	13,112	0.98	311
New Mexico	200	200	250	0.13	63
New York	69,992	69,182	73,106	3.01	761
North Carolina	11,083	10,920	11,135	1.56	73
North Dakota	501	491	447	0.00	91
Ohio	1,968	1,850	1,951	0.04	250
Oklahoma	1,710	1,710	1,593	0.53	108
Oregon	384	384	346	0.13	124
Pennsylvania	28,447	28,258	28,847	2.04	448
Rhode Island	3,168	3,326	2,994	0.33	51
South Carolina	3,275	3,240	3,498	0.91	40
South Dakota	0	0	0	0.00	118
Tennessee	5,702	6,029	5,831	1.08	190
Texas	4,863	4,938	4,715	0.28	482
Utah	616	610	610	0.34	70
Vermont	0	0	0	0.00	204
Virginia	10,664	10,636	10,645	1.60	90
Washington	0	0	0	0.00	70
West Virginia	5,255	5,557	5,710	2.90	98
Wisconsin	11,592	11,945	12,435	2.14	379
Wyoming	0	0	0	0.00	23

Source: Chief Officers of State Library Agencies, State Library Agencies Financial Survey, 1993, except where noted.
(a) Funds derived from state taxation for various public libraries; does not include state funds used to administer a state library agency.

(b) Based on fiscal year 1992 expenditures and U.S. Bureau of the Census population data.
(c) Source for this column: National Center for Education Statistics, 1991.

Table 7.11
STATE PURCHASING: BUY-AMERICAN LAWS AND OTHER PRACTICES

State	Buy-American laws affecting public procurement	Preference to specified products				
		Small business	Recycled plastic	Recycled paper	Other products with recycled content	Other
Alabama	...	...	...	...	...	...
Alaska	...	...	...	★	★	...
Arizona	...	★	...	★	...	...
Arkansas	...	...	...	★	...	...
California	★ (a)	★	...	★	★	...
Colorado	...	...	★	★	...	...
Connecticut	★ (b)	★	★	★	★	...
Delaware	...	...	...	...	...	...
Florida	...	★	★	★	★	...
Georgia	...	...	...	★	...	...
Hawaii	★ (c)	...	...	...	...	★ (d)
Idaho	...	...	...	...	...	...
Illinois	★ (e)	★	...	...	...	...
Indiana	...	★	★	★	★	★ (f)
Iowa	★ (a)	...	...	★	...	...
Kansas	★ (g)	...	...	★	...	...
Kentucky	...	★	★	★	★	...
Louisiana	★ (a)	...	★	★	★	★ (h)
Maine	...	...	...	★	...	★ (h)
Maryland	★ (e)	★	★	★	★	...
Massachusetts	...	★	★	★	★	...
Michigan	...	...	★	★	★	★ (h)
Minnesota	★ (i)	★	★	★	★	...
Mississippi	★ (j)	...	★	★	★	...
Missouri	★	...	★	★	★	...
Montana	...	★	...	...	...	...
Nebraska	...	...	★	★	★	...
Nevada	...	...	★	★	★	...
New Hampshire	...	...	...	★	...	...
New Jersey	★ (k)	★	★	★	★	...
New Mexico	★ (a)	...	★	★	★	...
New York	★ (e)	...	★	★	★	★ (h)
North Carolina	...	...	...	...	...	...
North Dakota	...	...	...	...	...	...
Ohio	★	...	...	...	...	...
Oklahoma	★ (c)	...	...	...	...	...
Oregon	...	...	★	★	★	★ (h)
Pennsylvania	★	...	★	★	...	...
Rhode Island	★ (e)	...	...	★	...	...
South Carolina	★	...	★	★	★	...
South Dakota	...	...	...	★	...	...
Tennessee	...	★ (l)	...	...	...	...
Texas	...	...	★	★	★	...
Utah	...	...	...	★	...	...
Vermont	...	...	★	★	★	...
Virginia	...	...	...	★	...	...
Washington	...	...	★	★	★	...
West Virginia	★	...	★	★	★	★
Wisconsin	★ (m)	...	...	...	...	★ (h)
Wyoming	★ (n)	...	...	★	★	...

Source: National Association of State Purchasing Officials, *State and Local Government Purchasing*, 4th Edition (1994).
Key:
★ — Yes
... — No
(a) Automobiles only.
(b) Textiles only.
(c) The law is too vague to apply.
(d) Hawaiian products, printing, software.
(e) Steel. In Illinois, domestically produced products receive a 10 percent preference for steel used in public works projects. In Maryland, 10,000 pounds or more for public works projects. In New York, steel for public works projects only.

(f) Five percent price preference to Indiana businesses.
(g) The law is permissive, not mandatory.
(h) Products or services of sheltered or rehabilitation workshops. Also in Michigan, prison industries. Also in New York, products of the special employment program of the state office of mental health.
(i) Five percent preference to American-made products and services.
(j) Specifications shall be written so as not to exclude comparable equipment of domestic manufacturer.
(k) Materials used in conjunction with public works contracts.
(l) Only in tie bids for products/services.
(m) The state will purchase materials that are manufactured to the greatest extent in the U.S. in case of tie bids.
(n) Beef.

Table 7.12
STATE PURCHASING OF RECYCLED PRODUCTS

State	Purchases of recycled products required by law	State purchases				Restrictions on purchasing:	
		Recycled oil	Recycled fuel	Alternative fuel vehicles	Soybean ink	Foam cups and plates	Products with CFCs
Alabama	...	...	...	...	...	...	...
Alaska	★	...	...	...	★	...	...
Arizona	...	...	...	...	...	...	...
Arkansas	★	...	...	...	★	...	★
California	★	★	★	★	...	...	...
Colorado	...	...	★	★	...	...	★
Connecticut	...	...	★	★	...	★	★
Delaware	★	...	...	...	...	...	...
Florida	...	...	...	...	...	...	...
Georgia	★	...	...	...	...	...	...
Hawaii	...	★	...	...	...	...	...
Idaho	...	...	...	...	...	...	...
Illinois	★	★	★	★	★	...	...
Indiana	★	★	...	★	★	...	...
Iowa	★	...	★	★	★	★	★
Kansas	★	...	★	★	★	...	...
Kentucky	...	★	...	...	★	...	...
Louisiana	★	...	...	★	★	...	...
Maine	★	★	★	...	★	★	★
Maryland	...	...	★	★	★	...	...
Massachusetts	...	...	★	★	★	★	★
Michigan	★	★	...	...	★	★	★
Minnesota	...	★	★	★	★	...	...
Mississippi	...	...	...	...	...	...	...
Missouri	★	★	...	★	★	★	★
Montana	...	★	★	...	...	...	...
Nebraska	...	★	★	★	★	...	...
Nevada	...	...	★	★	★	...	...
New Hampshire	★	...	...	...	...	★	...
New Jersey	★	★	★	★	★	...	★
New Mexico	...	★	★	...	...	...	...
New York	...	★	★	★	★	...	★
North Carolina	...	...	★	...	...	...	...
North Dakota	...	...	...	...	...	...	...
Ohio	...	...	★	★	★	...	...
Oklahoma	...	...	★	★	★	...	...
Oregon	★	★	★	★	...	★	...
Pennsylvania	★	★	...	★	★	...	...
Rhode Island	...	...	★	...	...	★	...
South Carolina	...	...	...	...	★	...	...
South Dakota	...	★	★	...	★	...	...
Tennessee	★	★	...	...	★	...	...
Texas	...	★	★	★	★	...	...
Utah	...	★	★	★	...	...	...
Vermont	★	★	★	...	★	★	...
Virginia	...	...	...	(a)	★	...	...
Washington	★	...	...	...	★	...	...
West Virginia	...	...	★	★	★	...	...
Wisconsin	...	...	★	★	★	...	★
Wyoming	...	...	★	...	...	...	...

Source: National Association of State Purchasing Officials, *State and Local Government Purchasing*, 4th Edition (1994).

(a) Used in test vehicles only.

Key:
★ — Yes
... — No

Government Employment in 1992

The size of the state and local workforce increased between 1982 and 1992, particularly in the areas dealing with corrections.

by Meredith De Hart

State governments employed nearly 4.6 million workers in their executive, legislative and judicial agencies and institutions (including higher education institutions) as of October 1992. Approximately 1.2 million of these employees, or 26 percent, work on a part-time basis. Since 1982, when the total state government workforce was 3.1 million, the number of state workers has grown by an average annual rate of 2.3 percent.

Salaries and wages paid to all state government employees in October 1992 totaled $9.8 billion, up from $5 billion in October 1982, or an average annual increase of 6.9 percent. Average gross pay for full-time state workers was $2,621 for the month of October 1992, reflecting an average annual increase of 4.9 percent since October 1982 when the average was $1,626.

Public Sector Employment Changes, 1982-1992

State governments' proportion of total public sector civilian employment was nearly 25 percent in 1992, up from 24 percent in 1982 and 22 percent in 1972. Federal government civilian employment (3 million in October 1992) accounted for slightly more than 16 percent, and local government employment (11.1 million in October 1992) accounted for slightly more than 59 percent of public sector civilian employment.

More than 41.5 percent of state government workers are employed in higher education, 12.1 percent in hospitals, and 7.6 percent in correction activities, for a total of 61.2 percent of all state government workers. Between 1982 and 1992, the number of state hospital workers decreased by nearly 10,000, or 1.7 percent.

Higher education employees increased by 409,489 or 27.3 percent. Higher education employment increased an average of 2.4 percent annually during this 10-year period, only slightly less than the average of 2.5 percent annually between 1972 and 1982.

The most notable increases in state government employment occurred in correction and judicial and legal activities. The number of state government correction employees increased by 164,781 or 89.9 percent during this 10-year period. The average annual increase in correction employees was 6.6 percent. The increase in employment in judicial and legal activities was less spectacular, but with an increase of 38,883 employees or 52.1 percent, the increase is notable. The average annual increase for this 10-year period was 4.3 percent. Table A presents state government employment, percent distribution and rates of change for selected functions.

As in previous years, elementary and secondary education accounted for slightly more than half of all local government workers in 1992. Police protection (6.2 percent), hospitals (5.5 percent), highways (2.7 percent) and public utilities (3.9 percent) represent a combined total of 18.2 percent of total local government employment, down from 22 percent in 1990. Local government correction activities continued as the fastest growing activity of local governments between 1982 and 1992, followed by health and judicial and legal activities. Local government employees engaged in correction activities increased by 93,184

Meredith De Hart heads the public employment data program in the Employment and Education Branch, Governments Division, Bureau of the Census, U.S. Department of Commerce.

Table A
TOTAL STATE GOVERNMENT EMPLOYMENT: OCTOBER 1992, 1982, 1972

	1992 Total Employment	Percent of Total	Change 1982-92	% Change 1982-92	1982 Total Employment	Percent of Total	1972 Total Employment	Percent of Total	Average Annual Rate of Change 1972 to 1982	1982 to 1992	1972 to 1992
Total State	4,594,635	100.00%	850,570	22.72%	3,744,065	100.00%	2,957,000	100.00%	2.39%	2.07%	2.23%
Higher Education	1,909,022	41.55%	409,489	27.31%	1,499,533	40.05%	1,168,000	39.50%	2.53%	2.44%	2.49%
Hospitals	554,560	12.07%	(9,712)	-1.72%	564,272	15.07%	467,000	15.79%	1.91%	-0.17%	0.86%
Health	166,888	3.63%	49,413	42.06%	117,475	3.14%	70,000	2.37%	5.31%	3.57%	4.44%
Social Insurance Admin.	118,143	2.57%	6,193	5.53%	111,950	2.99%	63,000	2.13%	5.92%	0.54%	3.19%
Highways	261,362	5.69%	17,003	6.96%	244,359	6.53%	290,000	9.81%	-1.70%	0.67%	-0.52%
Police	86,606	1.88%	10,514	13.82%	76,092	2.03%	63,000	2.13%	1.91%	1.30%	1.60%
Correction	347,985	7.57%	164,781	89.94%	183,204	4.89%	106,000	3.58%	5.62%	6.63%	6.12%
Natural Resources	164,333	3.58%	9,216	5.94%	155,117	4.14%	158,000	5.34%	-0.18%	0.58%	0.20%
Financial Admin.	150,612	3.28%	32,755	27.79%	117,857	3.15%	100,000	3.38%	1.66%	2.48%	2.07%
Judicial and Legal	113,548	2.47%	38,883	52.08%	74,665	1.99%	NA			4.28%	
Other Government	51,753	1.13%	8,649	20.07%	43,104	1.15%	59,000	2.00%	-3.09%	1.85%	-0.65%

Note: Prior to the 1982 Census of Governments, judicial and legal activities were included in the general government category. Consequently the 1972 count of employees on the "Other Government" line also includes judicial and legal employees.
Key:
NA — Not available.

Table B
TOTAL LOCAL GOVERNMENT EMPLOYMENT: OCTOBER 1992, 1982, 1972

	1992 Total Employment	Percent of Total	Change 1982-92	% Change 1982-92	1982 Total Employment	Percent of Total	1972 Total Employment	Percent of Total	Average Annual Rate of Change 1972 to 1982	1982 to 1992	1972 to 1992
Total Local	11,103,221	100.00%	1,854,140	20.05%	9,249,081	100.00%	8,007,000	100.00%	1.45%	1.84%	1.65%
Elementary and Secondary Education	5,727,103	51.58%	996,018	21.05%	4,731,085	51.15%	4,216,000	52.65%	1.16%	1.93%	1.54%
Police	683,468	6.16%	89,520	15.07%	593,948	6.42%	487,000	6.08%	2.01%	1.41%	1.71%
Fire	343,985	3.10%	46,149	15.49%	297,836	3.22%	279,000	3.48%	0.66%	1.45%	1.05%
Corrections	194,697	1.75%	93,184	91.80%	101,513	1.10%	63,000	0.79%	4.89%	6.73%	5.80%
Highways	299,763	2.70%	18,013	6.39%	281,750	3.05%	306,000	3.82%	-0.82%	0.62%	-0.10%
Hospitals	608,476	5.48%	9,403	1.57%	599,073	6.48%	475,000	5.93%	2.35%	0.16%	1.25%
Parks and Recreation	275,600	2.48%	64,673	30.66%	210,927	2.28%	177,000	2.21%	1.77%	2.71%	2.24%
Judicial and Legal	209,295	1.88%	74,630	55.42%	134,665	1.46%	NA			4.51%	
Health	214,288	1.93%	83,880	64.32%	130,408	1.41%	95,000	1.19%	3.22%	5.09%	4.15%
Utilities	430,459	3.88%	68,482	18.92%	361,977	3.91%	274,000	3.42%	2.82%	1.75%	2.28%
Water Supply	155,988	1.40%	29,489	23.31%	126,499	1.37%	110,000	1.37%	1.41%	2.12%	1.76%
Electric Power	78,451	0.71%	12,059	18.16%	66,392	0.72%	58,000	0.72%	1.36%	1.68%	1.52%
Gas Supply	10,561	0.10%	1,465	16.11%	9,096	0.10%	9,000	0.11%	0.11%	1.50%	0.80%
Transit	185,459	1.67%	25,469	15.92%	159,990	1.73%	97,000	1.21%	5.13%	1.49%	3.29%

Table C
AVERAGE PAY OF FULL-TIME EMPLOYEES: OCTOBER 1992

Region, Division and State	Total state & local	State only	Total local
United States	2,562	2,621	2,539
Northeast	2,954	2,951	2,955
New England	2,763	2,782	2,753
Maine	2,216	2,437	2,101
New Hampshire	2,444	2,416	2,456
Vermont	2,357	2,514	2,240
Massachusetts	2,736	2,645	2,775
Rhode Island	2,826	2,817	2,832
Connecticut	3,205	3,286	3,160
Middle Atlantic	3,010	3,015	3,008
New York	3,146	3,143	3,147
New Jersey	3,073	3,100	3,062
Pennsylvania	2,642	2,696	2,622
Midwest	2,542	2,688	2,487
East North Central	2,641	2,812	2,581
Ohio	2,485	2,691	2,417
Indiana	2,290	2,506	2,199
Illinois	2,665	2,642	2,672
Michigan	2,971	3,134	2,906
Wisconsin	2,754	3,216	2,594
West North Central	2,326	2,454	2,271
Minnesota	2,785	3,101	2,673
Iowa	2,393	2,895	2,179
Missouri	2,115	2,075	2,133
North Dakota	2,252	2,231	2,269
South Dakota	1,950	2,166	1,833
Nebraska	2,195	2,185	2,198
Kansas	2,151	2,191	2,133
South	2,156	2,254	2,115
South Atlantic	2,266	2,268	2,265
Delaware	2,562	2,463	2,669
Maryland	2,834	2,720	2,892
District of Columbia	3,175	(X)	3,175
Virginia	2,305	2,270	2,322
West Virginia	1,990	1,969	2,002
North Carolina	2,185	2,413	2,092
South Carolina	2,018	2,098	1,970
Georgia	1,998	2,075	1,968
Florida	2,272	2,202	2,294
East South Central	1,980	2,204	1,875
Kentucky	2,113	2,349	1,980
Tennessee	2,047	2,153	2,004
Alabama	1,968	2,243	1,830
Mississippi	1,725	2,000	1,608
West South Central	2,082	2,264	2,012
Arkansas	1,892	2,195	1,724
Louisiana	1,947	2,227	1,800
Oklahoma	1,951	2,044	1,903
Texas	2,165	2,351	2,107
West	2,926	2,911	2,932
Mountain	2,362	2,422	2,335
Montana	2,090	2,300	1,995
Idaho	2,050	2,265	1,943
Wyoming	2,156	2,055	2,202
Colorado	2,592	3,016	2,450
New Mexico	2,011	2,253	1,858
Arizona	2,504	2,361	2,557
Utah	2,158	2,100	2,204
Nevada	2,762	2,738	2,772
Pacific	3,157	3,139	3,164
Washington	2,746	2,760	2,738
Oregon	2,601	2,607	2,599
California	3,312	3,420	3,281
Alaska	3,413	3,258	3,590
Hawaii	2,661	2,554	3,031

(91.8 percent or an average annual increase of 6.7 percent), those in health increased by 83,880 (64.3 percent or an average annual increase of 5.1 percent) and those in judicial and legal activities increased by 74,630 (55.4 percent or an average annual increase of 4.5 percent). Table B presents total local government employment, percent distribution, and rates of change for selected functions.

Employee Average Earnings

The range in average gross pay for full-time state employees ran from a low of $1,969 in West Virginia to a high of $3,420 in California for the month of October 1992. Average earnings are influenced by factors which include the following: (1) compensation levels of private sector workers, (2) local cost of living, (3) the occupational mix of the work force, and (4) administrative practices. Some state governments prepare comparative studies ranking their own state government employment levels and payrolls against those of neighboring states. Grouping states by region reveals the effect of the various factors above. Table C provides October 1992 average earnings of full-time employees.

Sources of Additional Data

Data on government employment and pay are contained in the U.S. Bureau of the Census annual report, *Public Employment*, which provides summary federal, state and local government statistics by government function. Detailed state and local government data also are presented on a state-by-state basis. More extensive and detailed data on this subject are contained in the 1992 Census of Governments, Vol. 3, No. 2, *Compendium of Public Employment*, due for release in late 1994.

Table 7.13
SUMMARY OF STATE GOVERNMENT EMPLOYMENT: 1952-1992

Year (October)	Employment (in thousands)						Monthly payrolls (in millions of dollars)			Average monthly earnings of full-time employees		
	Total, full-time and part-time			Full-time equivalent								
	All	Education	Other	All	Education	Other	All	Education	Other	All	Education	Other
1952............	1,060	293	767	958	213	745	$ 260.3	$ 65.1	$ 195.2	$ 271	$ 298	$ 262
1953............	1,082	294	788	966	211	755	278.6	73.5	205.1	289	320	278
1954............	1,149	310	839	1,024	222	802	300.7	78.9	221.8	294	325	283
1955............	1,199	333	866	1,081	244	837	325.9	88.5	237.4	302	334	290
1956............	1,268	353	915	1,136	250	886	366.5	108.8	257.7	321	358	309
1957 (April)	1,300	375	925	1,153	257	896	372.5	106.1	266.4	320	355	309
1958............	1,408	406	1,002	1,259	284	975	446.5	123.4	323.1	355	416	333
1959............	1,454	443	1,011	1,302	318	984	485.4	136.0	349.4	373	427	352
1960............	1,527	474	1,053	1,353	332	1,021	524.1	167.7	356.4	386	439	365
1961............	1,625	518	1,107	1,435	367	1,068	586.2	192.4	393.8	409	482	383
1962............	1,680	555	1,126	1,478	389	1,088	634.6	201.8	432.8	429	518	397
1963............	1,775	602	1,173	1,558	422	1,136	696.4	230.1	466.3	447	545	410
1964............	1,873	656	1,217	1,639	460	1,179	761.1	257.5	503.6	464	560	427
1965............	2,028	739	1,289	1,751	508	1,243	849.2	290.1	559.1	484	571	450
1966............	2,211	866	1,344	1,864	575	1,289	975.2	353.0	622.2	522	614	483
1967............	2,335	940	1,395	1,946	620	1,326	1,105.5	406.3	699.3	567	666	526
1968............	2,495	1,037	1,458	2,085	694	1,391	1,256.7	477.1	779.6	602	687	544
1969............	2,614	1,112	1,501	2,179	746	1,433	1,430.5	554.5	876.1	655	743	597
1970............	2,755	1,182	1,573	2,302	803	1,499	1,612.2	630.3	981.9	700	797	605
1971............	2,832	1,223	1,609	2,384	841	1,544	1,741.7	681.5	1,060.2	731	826	686
1972............	2,957	1,267	1,690	2,487	867	1,619	1,936.6	746.9	1,189.7	778	871	734
1973............	3,013	1,280	1,733	2,547	887	1,660	2,158.2	822.2	1,336.0	843	952	805
1974............	3,155	1,357	1,798	2,653	929	1,725	2,409.5	932.7	1,476.9	906	1,023	855
1975............	3,271	1,400	1,870	2,744	952	1,792	2,652.7	1,021.7	1,631.1	964	1,080	909
1976............	3,343	1,434	1,910	2,799	973	1,827	2,893.7	1,111.5	1,782.1	1,031	1,163	975
1977............	3,491	1,484	2,007	2,903	1,005	1,898	3,194.6	1,234.4	1,960.1	1,096	1,237	1,031
1978............	3,539	1,508	2,032	2,966	1,016	1,950	3,483.0	1,332.9	2,150.2	1,167	1,311	1,102
1979............	3,699	1,577	2,122	3,072	1,046	2,026	3,869.3	1,451.4	2,417.9	1,257	1,399	1,193
1980............	3,753	1,599	2,154	3,106	1,063	2,044	4,284.7	1,608.0	2,676.6	1,373	1,523	1,305
1981............	3,726	1,603	2,123	3,087	1,063	2,024	4,667.5	1,768.0	2,899.5	1,507	1,671	1,432
1982............	3,747	1,616	2,131	3,083	1,051	2,032	5,027.7	1,874.0	3,153.7	1,625	1,789	1,551
1983............	3,816	1,666	2,150	3,116	1,072	2,044	5,345.5	1,989.0	3,357.0	1,711	1,850	1,640
1984............	3,898	1,708	2,190	3,177	1,091	2,086	5,814.9	2,178.0	3,637.0	1,825	1,991	1,740
1985............	3,984	1,764	2,220	2,990	945	2,046	6,328.6	2,443.7	3,884.9	1,935	2,155	1,834
1986............	4,068	1,800	2,267	3,437	1,256	2,181	6,801.4	2,583.4	4,226.9	2,052	2,263	1,956
1987............	4,115	1,804	2,310	3,491	1,264	2,227	7,297.8	2,758.3	4,539.5	2,161	2,396	2,056
1988............	4,236	1,854	2,381	3,606	1,309	2,297	7,842.3	2,928.6	4,913.7	2,260	2,490	2,158
1989............	4,365	1,925	2,440	3,709	1,360	2,349	8,443.1	3,175.0	5,268.1	2,372	2,627	2,259
1990............	4,503	1,984	2,519	3,840	1,418	2,432	9,083.0	3,426.0	5,657.0	2,472	2,732	2,359
1991............	4,521	1,999	2,522	3,829	1,375	2,454	9,437.0	3,550.0	5,887.0	2,479	2,530	2,433
1992............	4,595	2,050	2,545	3,856	1,384	2,472	9,828.0	3,774.0	6,054.0	2,562	2,607	2,521

Source: U.S. Department of Commerce, Bureau of the Census, annual
Public Employment reports.
Note: Detail may not add to totals due to rounding.

Table 7.14
EMPLOYMENT AND PAYROLLS OF STATE AND LOCAL GOVERNMENTS, BY FUNCTION: OCTOBER 1991

Functions	All employees, full-time and part-time (in thousands)			October payrolls (in millions of dollars)			Average October earnings of full-time employees
	Total	State governments	Local governments	Total	State governments	Local governments	
All functions	15,452	4,521	10,931	$31,550	$9,437	$22,113	$2,479
Education:							
Higher Education	2,297	1,858	439	3,901	3,241	660	2,859
Instructional personnel only ...	816	600	216	1,954	1,574	380	3,930
Elementary/Secondary schools...	5,669	35	5,635	11,545	73	11,473	2,450
Instructional personnel only ...	3,802	24	3,778	9,103	59	9,044	2,746
Libraries.....................	132	1	131	171	1	169	1,966
Other education	106	106	0	236	236	0	2,438
Selected Functions:							
Highways.....................	564	259	305	1,220	613	607	2,253
Public welfare................	492	217	275	948	464	485	2,060
Hospitals	1,146	559	587	2,404	1,208	1,196	2,263
Health.......................	368	165	203	768	376	391	2,314
Police protection.............	762	87	674	1,948	250	1,699	2,819
Police officers only	553	56	497	1,611	181	1,430	3,043
Fire protection	341	0	341	771	0	771	3,059
Firefighters only	316	0	316	723	0	723	3,093
Natural resources	200	162	39	418	349	70	2,416
Correction	531	338	193	1,239	788	451	2,386
Social insurance administration ..	107	107	0	253	253	0	2,451
Financial administration	361	149	212	719	343	376	2,238
Judicial and legal administration.	312	112	200	780	338	442	2,682
Other government administration	366	53	313	550	126	424	2,402
Utilities......................	456	28	428	1,254	94	1,160	2,879

Source: U.S. Department of Commerce, Bureau of the Census, *Public Employment 1991.*
Note: Statistics for local governments are estimates subject to sampling variation. Detail may not add to totals due to rounding.

Table 7.15
EMPLOYMENT AND PAYROLLS OF STATE AND LOCAL GOVERNMENTS, BY FUNCTION: OCTOBER 1992

Functions	All employees, full-time and part-time (in thousands)			October payrolls (in millions of dollars)			Average October earnings of full-time employees
	Total	State governments	Local governments	Total	State governments	Local governments	
All functions	15,698	4,595	11,103	$33,183	$9,828	$23,355	$2,562
Education:							
Higher Education	2,356	1,909	447	4,155	3,457	698	2,959
Instructional personnel only ...	841	623	218	2,094	1,695	400	4,108
Elementary/secondary schools ...	5,762	35	5,727	12,124	75	12,049	2,522
Instructional personnel only ...	3,859	25	3,825	9,557	61	9,496	2,838
Libraries.....................	132	1	131	178	1	177	2,057
Other education	106	106	0	242	242	0	2,496
Selected functions:							
Highways.....................	561	261	300	1,252	626	626	2,326
Public welfare................	496	215	281	1,015	471	544	2,179
Hospitals	1,163	555	608	2,518	1,224	1,294	2,327
Health.......................	381	167	214	822	389	433	2,395
Police protection.............	770	87	683	2,061	247	1,814	2,947
Police officers only	558	55	503	1,698	177	1,521	3,179
Fire protection	344	0	344	825	0	825	3,260
Firefighters only	319	0	319	776	0	776	3,297
Natural resources	204	164	40	431	355	76	2,436
Correction	543	348	194	1,308	844	464	2,454
Social insurance administration ..	118	118	0	275	275	0	2,433
Financial administration	355	151	205	751	351	400	2,320
Judicial & legal administration ..	323	114	209	832	350	482	2,765
Other government administration	370	52	318	568	125	443	2,491
Utilities......................	459	29	430	1,293	105	1,188	2,951

Source: U.S. Department of Commerce, Bureau of the Census, *Public Employment 1992.*
Note: Statistics for local governments are estimates subject to sampling variation. Detail may not add to totals due to rounding.

Table 7.16
STATE AND LOCAL GOVERNMENT EMPLOYMENT, BY STATE: OCTOBER 1991

State or other jurisdiction	All employees (full-time and part-time)		Full-time equivalent employment					
			Number			Number per 10,000 population		
	State	Local	Total	State	Local	Total	State	Local
United States	4,521,385	10,930,387	13,185,746	3,829,442	9,356,304	523	152	371
Alabama............	94,390	166,126	260,516	81,505	150,932	568	199	369
Alaska..............	24,995	25,850	50,845	22,360	21,618	772	392	379
Arizona.............	61,184	156,400	217,584	51,141	138,306	505	136	369
Arkansas	50,737	94,470	145,207	43,320	79,812	519	183	336
California..........	366,497	1,322,453	1,708,950	325,037	1,104,112	470	107	363
Colorado	71,736	159,750	231,486	53,266	132,626	551	158	393
Connecticut	66,262	110,531	176,793	58,015	97,703	473	176	297
Delaware	23,826	18,538	42,364	19,959	17,038	544	294	251
Florida	184,595	566,824	751,419	163,450	494,010	495	123	372
Georgia............	123,475	297,642	421,117	111,839	271,451	579	169	410
Hawaii	60,311	14,510	74,821	50,758	13,632	567	447	120
Idaho	23,659	47,988	71,647	18,587	38,577	550	179	371
Illinois.............	167,947	519,738	687,685	140,645	424,513	490	122	368
Indiana	111,775	232,723	344,498	89,895	198,894	515	160	355
Iowa	60,331	139,778	200,109	55,719	108,333	587	199	388
Kansas	57,678	133,313	190,991	49,334	105,411	620	198	422
Kentucky	87,999	132,272	220,271	76,351	119,212	527	206	321
Louisiana	102,878	173,947	276,825	87,696	156,368	574	206	368
Maine	26,315	54,289	80,604	21,772	42,810	523	176	347
Maryland	100,122	182,724	282,846	86,943	159,010	506	179	327
Massachusetts	103,664	215,933	319,597	87,865	190,966	465	147	318
Michigan	173,163	406,076	579,239	138,973	341,429	513	148	364
Minnesota	83,842	220,013	303,855	66,313	168,745	530	150	381
Mississippi	53,502	118,479	171,981	46,511	105,453	586	179	407
Missouri	86,927	203,478	290,405	74,478	171,956	478	144	333
Montana	23,639	44,969	68,608	16,737	35,269	644	207	436
Nebraska	35,919	94,805	130,724	29,450	68,769	617	185	432
Nevada	20,697	49,087	69,784	18,836	43,844	488	147	341
New Hampshire	21,171	43,566	64,737	16,188	34,858	462	146	315
New Jersey.........	126,616	341,687	468,303	112,580	305,333	539	145	393
New Mexico........	51,792	65,716	117,508	40,684	59,918	650	263	387
New York	291,232	987,446	1,278,678	269,051	853,993	622	149	473
North Carolina	125,248	297,097	422,345	107,545	253,299	536	160	376
North Dakota	20,701	33,966	54,667	15,029	20,552	560	237	324
Ohio	177,246	469,102	646,348	140,802	389,345	485	129	356
Oklahoma	79,759	135,038	214,797	68,000	117,106	583	214	369
Oregon	64,132	129,427	193,559	54,558	103,084	540	187	353
Pennsylvania	148,123	415,924	564,047	124,427	361,309	406	104	302
Rhode Island	23,457	29,859	53,316	19,705	26,965	465	196	269
South Carolina	88,590	132,160	220,750	80,678	119,555	562	227	336
South Dakota	17,429	37,775	55,204	13,482	24,572	541	192	350
Tennessee	88,569	190,593	279,162	76,111	173,786	505	154	351
Texas..............	266,737	792,860	1,059,597	228,001	723,387	548	131	417
Utah	45,189	68,410	113,599	38,800	51,927	513	219	293
Vermont	14,521	22,295	36,816	12,783	17,453	533	225	308
Virginia............	139,989	251,731	391,720	114,134	224,344	538	182	357
Washington	117,779	193,608	311,387	96,077	170,213	531	191	339
West Virginia	38,999	63,824	102,823	33,558	57,774	507	186	321
Wisconsin..........	93,033	237,345	330,378	69,302	186,720	517	140	377
Wyoming	13,008	30,995	44,003	11,172	24,608	778	243	535
Dist. of Columbia.....	0	57,257	57,257	0	55,404	926	0	926

Source: U.S. Department of Commerce, Bureau of the Census, *Public Employment 1991.*
Note: Statistics for local governments are estimates subject to sampling variation. Detail may not add to totals due to rounding.

Table 7.17
STATE AND LOCAL GOVERNMENT EMPLOYMENT, BY STATE: OCTOBER 1992

State or other jurisdiction	All employees (full-time and part-time)		Full-time equivalent employment					
			Number			Number per 10,000 population		
	State	Local	Total	State	Local	Total	State	Local
United States	4,594,635	11,103,221	13,365,686	3,856,222	9,509,464	524	151	373
Alabama	94,907	170,062	235,412	81,101	154,311	569	196	373
Alaska	27,485	26,134	46,027	24,246	21,781	784	413	371
Arizona	64,804	163,044	199,138	54,064	145,074	520	141	379
Arkansas	53,364	95,854	128,584	46,596	81,988	536	194	342
California	385,807	1,326,155	1,429,841	321,860	1,107,981	463	104	359
Colorado	72,424	159,020	185,140	53,004	132,136	534	153	381
Connecticut	63,843	110,133	151,167	54,154	97,013	461	165	296
Delaware	24,385	19,025	37,687	20,179	17,508	547	293	254
Florida	187,813	577,289	664,070	164,501	499,569	492	122	370
Georgia	127,075	309,546	397,053	114,464	282,589	588	170	419
Hawaii	61,786	15,196	64,539	50,657	13,882	556	437	120
Idaho	25,586	50,122	60,096	20,250	39,846	563	190	373
Illinois	164,182	525,396	567,178	136,623	430,555	488	117	370
Indiana	115,618	238,414	297,585	95,157	202,428	526	168	358
Iowa	60,418	140,176	155,793	47,354	108,439	554	168	386
Kansas	56,168	138,701	157,064	47,882	109,182	623	190	433
Kentucky	85,605	132,719	197,016	76,254	120,762	525	203	322
Louisiana	103,048	178,632	249,344	88,767	160,577	582	207	375
Maine	26,961	54,298	65,148	22,006	43,142	528	178	349
Maryland	97,529	179,538	239,627	82,072	157,555	488	167	321
Massachusetts	101,646	218,173	277,246	84,983	192,263	462	142	321
Michigan	172,502	407,519	460,471	137,853	322,618	488	146	342
Minnesota	83,922	226,558	239,943	67,332	172,611	536	150	385
Mississippi	55,388	121,253	155,159	47,433	107,726	594	181	412
Missouri	90,424	206,132	247,711	74,049	173,662	477	143	334
Montana	23,693	47,017	54,229	17,095	37,134	658	207	451
Nebraska	34,545	87,827	99,631	28,746	70,885	620	179	441
Nevada	20,961	52,264	66,001	19,142	46,859	497	144	353
New Hampshire	21,328	43,207	51,803	16,296	35,507	466	147	320
New Jersey	131,841	337,996	417,409	115,770	301,639	536	149	387
New Mexico	53,317	67,036	102,368	42,159	60,209	647	267	381
New York	290,433	988,512	1,147,540	267,429	880,111	633	148	486
North Carolina	127,279	301,532	368,847	109,046	259,801	539	159	380
North Dakota	21,964	34,088	37,515	16,468	21,047	590	259	331
Ohio	176,781	484,789	539,719	140,305	399,414	490	127	363
Oklahoma	79,346	141,272	187,811	67,071	120,740	585	209	376
Oregon	63,229	131,854	155,211	49,704	105,507	521	167	354
Pennsylvania	173,030	422,212	510,169	143,438	366,731	425	119	305
Rhode Island	24,225	30,851	47,629	19,890	27,739	474	198	276
South Carolina	90,504	137,661	201,698	77,754	123,944	560	216	344
South Dakota	17,631	39,549	39,172	13,517	25,655	551	190	361
Tennessee	90,593	196,760	253,944	75,930	178,014	505	151	354
Texas	278,281	820,720	987,993	239,702	748,291	560	136	424
Utah	46,491	70,398	92,955	39,618	53,337	513	219	294
Vermont	14,474	22,923	30,546	12,923	17,623	536	227	309
Virginia	141,664	259,277	344,975	115,817	229,158	541	182	359
Washington	120,368	201,393	275,419	98,016	177,403	536	191	345
West Virginia	40,280	64,927	92,232	33,597	58,635	509	185	324
Wisconsin	96,533	242,206	261,595	72,674	188,921	522	145	377
Wyoming	13,154	31,442	36,581	11,274	25,307	785	242	543
Dist. of Columbia . . .	0	56,419	54,655	0	54,655	928	0	928

Source: U.S. Department of Commerce, Bureau of the Census, *Public Employment 1992.*
Note: Statistics for local governments are estimates subject to sampling variation. Detail may not add to totals due to rounding.

Table 7.18
STATE AND LOCAL GOVERNMENT PAYROLLS AND AVERAGE EARNINGS
OF FULL-TIME EMPLOYEES, BY STATE: OCTOBER 1991

State or other jurisdiction	Amount of payroll (in thousands of dollars)			Percentage of October payroll		Average earnings of full-time state and local government employees (dollars)		
	Total	State government	Local governments	State government	Local governments	All	Education employees	Other
United States	$31,550,467	$9,437,078	$22,113,389	29.9	70.1	$2,479	$2,530	$2,433
Alabama..........	442,888	173,640	269,247	39.2	60.8	1,941	1,989	1,895
Alaska............	147,531	73,983	73,547	50.1	49.9	3,481	3,541	3,441
Arizona...........	446,201	111,043	335,158	24.9	75.1	2,509	2,591	2,433
Arkansas..........	216,950	84,243	132,707	38.8	61.2	1,807	1,900	1,697
California..........	4,407,267	1,047,687	3,359,581	23.8	76.2	3,234	3,225	3,239
Colorado	463,727	157,987	305,739	34.1	65.9	2,524	2,561	2,488
Connecticut	460,973	178,287	282,685	38.7	61.3	3,048	3,189	2,913
Delaware	85,121	45,173	39,948	53.1	46.9	2,371	2,600	2,169
Florida	1,438,591	358,559	1,080,032	24.9	75.1	2,240	2,170	2,295
Georgia...........	740,490	226,160	514,330	30.5	69.5	1,954	1,999	1,915
Hawaii	159,078	122,319	36,758	76.9	23.1	2,533	2,605	2,481
Idaho	109,342	39,103	70,239	35.8	64.2	1,998	1,954	2,049
Illinois...........	1,386,250	350,468	1,035,781	25.3	74.7	2,555	2,600	2,514
Indiana	618,903	210,306	408,597	34.0	66.0	2,238	2,558	1,878
Iowa	344,760	128,135	216,625	37.2	62.8	2,282	2,329	2,227
Kansas	308,481	101,325	207,155	32.8	67.2	2,067	2,106	2,022
Kentucky	388,006	163,120	224,886	42.0	58.0	2,051	2,178	1,893
Louisiana	454,022	181,329	272,693	39.9	60.1	1,887	1,965	1,809
Maine	138,871	52,974	85,897	38.1	61.9	2,222	2,199	2,250
Maryland	655,351	224,036	431,315	34.2	65.8	2,760	3,079	2,501
Massachusetts	710,125	221,572	488,554	31.2	68.8	2,621	2,663	2,589
Michigan	1,218,787	385,351	833,435	31.6	68.4	2,838	3,001	2,646
Minnesota	606,148	182,832	423,315	30.2	69.8	2,742	2,867	2,614
Mississippi	248,395	86,620	161,776	34.9	65.1	1,660	1,688	1,629
Missouri	494,969	144,132	350,837	29.1	70.9	2,074	2,195	1,956
Montana..........	102,652	36,129	66,523	35.2	64.8	2,070	2,169	1,941
Nebraska	203,019	60,364	142,655	29.7	70.3	2,148	2,138	2,156
Nevada	159,451	47,243	112,208	29.6	70.4	2,643	2,606	2,670
New Hampshire	114,115	36,662	77,453	32.1	67.9	2,329	2,424	2,223
New Jersey........	1,207,502	349,453	858,049	28.9	71.1	2,955	3,258	2,682
New Mexico........	193,337	85,024	108,314	44.0	56.0	1,995	1,976	2,015
New York	3,232,974	802,023	2,430,951	24.8	75.2	2,964	3,115	2,877
North Carolina	764,501	247,698	516,803	32.4	67.6	2,177	2,338	2,017
North Dakota	73,675	31,263	42,412	42.4	57.6	2,193	2,453	1,892
Ohio	1,215,313	337,070	878,243	27.7	72.3	2,383	2,546	2,228
Oklahoma	335,128	126,986	208,142	37.9	62.1	1,863	1,875	1,851
Oregon	364,431	123,691	240,740	33.9	66.1	2,441	2,490	2,397
Pennsylvania	1,194,983	323,904	871,079	27.1	72.9	2,541	2,740	2,353
Rhode Island	121,920	49,445	72,475	40.6	59.4	2,707	2,963	2,470
South Carolina	374,470	153,620	220,850	41.0	59.0	1,942	2,093	1,795
South Dakota	68,796	26,354	42,442	38.3	61.7	1,889	1,992	1,769
Tennessee	487,544	156,928	330,616	32.2	67.8	1,993	2,072	1,927
Texas.............	1,949,938	525,277	1,424,661	26.9	73.1	2,088	2,081	2,096
Utah	186,383	81,845	104,537	43.9	56.1	2,159	2,122	2,210
Vermont	66,645	29,851	36,793	44.8	55.2	2,285	2,317	2,241
Virginia...........	739,064	250,564	488,500	33.9	66.1	2,267	2,302	2,231
Washington	663,036	231,047	431,989	34.8	65.2	2,611	2,524	2,682
West Virginia	172,325	63,862	108,463	37.1	62.9	1,919	2,107	1,660
Wisconsin..........	622,122	188,084	434,037	30.2	69.8	2,596	2,824	2,335
Wyoming	73,065	22,304	51,301	30.3	69.7	2,154	2,336	1,988
Dist. of Columbia.....	172,312	0	172,312		100.0	3,142	3,025	3,175

Source: U.S. Department of Commerce, Bureau of the Census, *Public Employment 1991*

Note: Statistics for local governments are estimates subject to sampling variation. Detail may not add to totals due to rounding.

Table 7.19
STATE AND LOCAL GOVERNMENT PAYROLLS AND AVERAGE EARNINGS
OF FULL-TIME EMPLOYEES, BY STATE: OCTOBER 1992

State or other jurisdiction	Amount of payroll (in thousands of dollars)			Percentage of October payroll		Average earnings of full-time state and local government employees (dollars)		
	Total	State government	Local governments	State government	Local governments	All	Education employees	Other
United States	$33,011,649	$9,828,247	$23,183,402	0.3	0.7	2,562	2,607	2,521
Alabama	456,438	176,929	279,510	0.4	0.6	1,968	1,979	1,958
Alaska..............	151,925	76,792	75,133	0.5	0.5	3,413	3,227	3,555
Arizona.............	472,557	121,955	350,602	0.3	0.7	2,504	2,569	2,446
Arkansas	237,404	99,385	138,019	0.4	0.6	1,892	1,990	1,777
California..........	4,510,316	1,062,204	3,448,111	0.2	0.8	3,312	3,271	3,340
Colorado	476,398	165,021	311,377	0.3	0.7	2,592	2,616	2,589
Connecticut	469,559	174,518	295,042	0.4	0.6	3,205	3,304	3,107
Delaware	94,727	49,451	45,276	0.5	0.5	2,562	2,845	2,309
Florida	1,483,639	354,591	1,129,048	0.2	0.8	2,272	2,173	2,346
Georgia............	783,123	233,831	549,292	0.3	0.7	1,998	2,035	1,966
Hawaii	172,235	130,808	41,427	0.8	0.2	2,661	2677	2,650
Idaho	118,412	43,387	75,025	0.4	0.6	2,050	2,022	2,080
Illinois.............	1,448,754	346,998	1,101,756	0.2	0.8	2,665	2,707	2,627
Indiana	654,036	227,829	426,207	0.3	0.7	2,290	2,618	1,926
Iowa	359,657	136,016	223,642	0.4	0.6	2,393	2,463	2,312
Kansas	325,583	100,811	224,772	0.3	0.7	2,151	2,191	2,103
Kentucky	399,197	166,307	232,889	0.4	0.6	2,113	2,233	1,963
Louisiana	476,862	190,313	286,548	0.4	0.6	1,947	2,032	1,861
Maine	139,395	51,870	87,525	0.4	0.6	2,216	2,207	2,226
Maryland	662,057	223,037	439,021	0.3	0.7	2,834	3,146	2,568
Massachusetts	740,776	223,416	517,360	0.3	0.7	2,736	2,760	2,716
Michigan	1,276,871	401,837	875,034	0.3	0.7	2,971	3,157	2,745
Minnesota	626,869	190,889	435,980	0.3	0.7	2,785	2,881	2,688
Mississippi	263,839	93,589	170,250	0.4	0.6	1,725	1,744	1,703
Missouri	512,505	153,212	359,293	0.3	0.7	2,115	2,243	1,992
Montana............	108,117	37,577	70,540	0.3	0.7	2,090	2,170	1,981
Nebraska	209,200	59,849	149,351	0.3	0.7	2,195	2,210	2,180
Nevada	176,095	49,783	126,311	0.3	0.7	2,762	2,575	2,908
New Hampshire	121,667	38,410	83,257	0.3	0.7	2,444	2,529	2,347
New Jersey	1,249,578	351,750	897,829	0.3	0.7	3,073	3,370	2,796
New Mexico........	198,785	88,128	110,657	0.4	0.6	2,011	1,998	2,024
New York	3,521,278	832,608	2,688,671	0.2	0.8	3,146	3,324	3,036
North Carolina	788,619	257,507	531,112	0.3	0.7	2,185	2,304	2,064
North Dakota	78,779	33,979	44,801	0.4	0.6	2,253	2,524	1,955
Ohio	1,279,873	352,935	926,939	0.3	0.7	2,485	2,606	2,370
Oklahoma	358,012	133,413	224,600	0.4	0.6	1,951	2,008	1,890
Oregon	391,572	130,410	261,162	0.3	0.7	2601	2,636	2,569
Pennsylvania	1,323,316	400,895	922,421	0.3	0.7	2,642	2,876	2,409
Rhode Island	130,637	54,871	75,767	0.4	0.6	2,826	3,028	2,636
South Carolina	395,952	157,742	238,209	0.4	0.6	2,018	2,155	1,884
South Dakota	73,412	28,512	44,901	0.4	0.6	1,950	2,000	1,888
Tennessee	512,752	160,337	352,415	0.3	0.7	2,047	2,120	1,986
Texas	2,101,154	552,537	1,548,616	0.3	0.7	2,165	2,158	2,172
Utah	191,647	80,955	110,692	0.4	0.6	2,158	2,091	2,246
Vermont	69,051	31,270	37,781	0.5	0.5	2,357	2,360	2,353
Virginia............	769,247	252,987	516,260	0.3	0.7	2,305	2,356	2,254
Washington	719,780	249,095	470,685	0.3	0.7	2,746	2,627	2,843
West Virginia	180,767	64,883	115,884	0.4	0.6	1,990	2,191	1,709
Wisconsin..........	674,175	210,669	463,507	0.3	0.7	2,754	2,942	2,538
Wyoming	75,046	22,149	52,897	0.3	0.7	2,156	2,312	2,008
Dist. of Columbia ...	171,441	0	171,441	0.0	1.0	3,175	3,000	3,225

Source: U.S. Department of Commerce, Bureau of the Census, *Public Employment 1992.*
Note: Statistics for local governments are estimates subject to sampling variation. Detail may not add to totals due to rounding.

Table 7.20
STATE GOVERNMENT EMPLOYMENT (FULL-TIME EQUIVALENT), FOR SELECTED FUNCTIONS, BY STATE: OCTOBER 1991

State	All functions	Education Higher education (a)	Education Other education (b)	Highways	Public welfare	Hospitals	Corrections	Police protection	Natural resources	Financial and other governmental administration	Judicial and legal administration
United States	3,829,442	1,276,547	98,382	254,782	212,934	531,830	335,490	86,707	146,628	193,387	108,955
Alabama	81,505	29,885	4,073	4,166	4,468	12,985	4,332	1,111	3,375	3,052	2,661
Alaska	22,360	4,083	483	2,901	1,636	417	1,280	431	2,608	1,329	1,089
Arizona	51,141	19,131	2,476	3,190	2,589	1,010	5,925	1,691	2,060	3,514	994
Arkansas	43,320	13,085	2,624	3,942	3,255	4,302	2,762	858	2,429	2,292	336
California	325,037	108,645	4,617	18,893	3,203	36,004	35802	11,060	14,692	1,7190	2,418
Colorado	53,286	27,871	1,122	2,969	1,401	4,932	3,402	1,017	1,607	2,475	2,767
Connecticut	58,015	12,748	2,887	4,141	4,305	11,911	5,366	1,579	920	3,861	3,153
Delaware	19,959	6,268	235	1,292	1,534	2,252	1,634	741	447	1,010	1,121
Florida	163,450	38,018	2,663	10,217	8,845	16,693	28,623	4,225	6,941	8,584	8,980
Georgia	111,839	31,773	4,692	6,089	7,552	14,756	13,415	2,019	4,657	3,323	1,133
Hawaii	50,758	7,759	142	828	1,126	2,806	1,886	0	1,519	1,592	2,039
Idaho	18,587	6,943	560	1,741	1,248	380	1,085	430	1,676	1,365	356
Illinois	140,645	48,469	3,022	9,015	12,913	20,885	11,758	4,046	3,468	9,187	2,519
Indiana	89,895	42,757	4,322	4,842	5,186	11,096	6,141	1,785	2,908	4,376	1,069
Iowa	55,719	25,923	1,157	2,799	3,354	8,778	2,192	816	3,097	1,866	2,142
Kansas	49,334	19,509	1,076	3,743	3,642	7,548	3,290	988	1,971	2,008	1,804
Kentucky	76,351	26,810	4,271	6,261	5,016	5,899	5,235	1,804	4,011	4,376	3,655
Louisiana	87,696	26,519	3,474	5,474	6,231	18,540	6,592	1,052	4,740	3,556	1,265
Maine	21,772	5,471	1,135	2,819	1,855	1,955	1,160	589	1,484	1,399	563
Maryland	86,943	24,876	2,011	5,131	6,777	7,592	8,874	2,412	2,310	5,209	3,657
Massachusetts	87,865	22,011	822	4,927	7,587	18,628	5,300	1,990	1,985	6,364	5,264
Michigan	138,973	63,454	1,983	4,141	13,019	15,971	14,288	3,105	3,923	3,849	2,610
Minnesota	66,313	32,391	1,595	5,089	1,733	7,684	2,251	903	3,414	3,220	1,104
Mississippi	46,511	13,293	1,854	3,224	3,251	7,903	3,088	939	4,002	1,608	355
Missouri	74,478	22,089	2,150	6,277	6,195	13,080	6,325	1,892	2,342	3,175	3,097
Montana	16,737	5,450	727	1,811	1,203	1,270	812	376	1,488	1,355	149
Nebraska	29,450	10,655	692	2,326	2,827	4,184	1,728	679	1,817	985	617
Nevada	18,836	5,985	267	1,436	7,92	950	2,301	505	1,078	1,271	359
New Hampshire	16,188	5,169	312	1,950	1,149	1,050	950	345	476	719	761
New Jersey	112,580	24,569	3,139	8,290	5,901	19,287	9,608	3,651	2,029	7,807	4,663
New Mexico	40,684	16,289	829	2,593	2,022	5,437	2,548	521	1,650	2,631	1,579
New York	269,051	46,460	5,421	14,165	7,180	64,622	31,720	5,567	3,381	1,6777	16,106
North Carolina	107,545	38,452	3,028	11,657	1,239	15,354	12,420	3,010	4,018	3,436	4,630
North Dakota	15,029	6,225	423	1,134	144	1,654	370	218	1,393	517	311
Ohio	140,802	65,454	2,405	8,836	2,163	19,634	10,772	2,248	3,963	5,732	1,961
Oklahoma	68,000	23,881	1,953	3,641	7,957	8,230	4,910	1,742	2,745	2,831	1,670
Oregon	54,558	17,252	999	3,825	4,189	7,225	2,756	1,108	3,695	4,276	2,080
Pennsylvania	124,427	30,166	2,768	12,625	9,868	21,896	8,250	5,086	5,551	9,819	2,478
Rhode Island	19,705	5,980	1,054	963	1,549	976	1,777	236	635	1,419	905
South Carolina	80,678	28,317	2,983	5,187	5,095	10,805	7,530	1,788	2,487	3,435	548
South Dakota	13,482	4,312	438	1,256	1,081	1,533	575	281	897	705	517
Tennessee	76,111	29,256	1,931	4,791	5,054	10,160	6,367	1,524	3,095	3,085	1,459
Texas	228,001	79,295	4,677	14,555	18,356	40,519	24,190	3,012	7,765	9,368	3,648
Utah	38,800	19,013	812	1,777	2,350	4,529	2,135	801	1,350	1,628	944
Vermont	12,783	4,339	341	1,105	1,114	657	674	477	651	834	478
Virginia	114,134	41,165	3,093	11,104	2,370	19,213	9,220	2,373	3,356	4,762	2,695
Washington	96,077	38,959	1,597	6,218	7,463	7,413	5,873	1,833	5,416	3,537	1,396
West Virginia	33,558	11,241	1,535	5,654	2,266	2,494	771	756	1,739	1,854	1,010
Wisconsin	69,302	35,708	1,332	1,839	1,128	7,716	4,688	835	2,586	4,232	1,458
Wyoming	11,172	3,174	180	1,933	553	1,015	539	252	781	592	382

Source: U.S. Department of Commerce, Bureau of the Census, *Public Employment 1991*.
(a) Includes instructional and other personnel.
(b) Includes instructional and other personnel in elementary and secondary schools.

Table 7.21
STATE GOVERNMENT EMPLOYMENT (FULL-TIME EQUIVALENT), FOR SELECTED FUNCTIONS, BY STATE: OCTOBER 1992

| State | All functions | Education | | Selected functions | | | | | | | |
		Higher education (a)	Other education (b)	Highways	Public welfare	Hospitals	Corrections	Police protection	Natural resources	Financial and other governmental administration	Judicial and legal administration
United States	3,856,222	1,285,659	98,186	256,830	211,548	525,441	344,793	86,027	147,294	193,697	110,664
Alabama	81,101	30,109	3,964	4,269	4,510	12,784	3,911	1,073	3,186	3,091	2,629
Alaska	24,246	5,874	477	2,978	1,698	382	1,216	431	2,658	1,369	1,100
Arizona	54,064	18,826	2,649	3,190	4,963	988	6,232	1,670	2,285	3,422	1,032
Arkansas	46,596	14,873	2,650	4,028	3,602	5,008	2,812	870	2,579	2,390	327
California	321,860	106,617	4,494	19,304	3,098	35,803	34,870	11,085	13,252	16,817	2,429
Colorado	53,004	27,328	1,423	3,055	1,254	4,740	3,448	1,017	1,662	2,474	2,670
Connecticut	54,154	12,444	2,676	3,691	4,239	10,550	5,418	1,509	626	3,611	3,115
Delaware	20,179	6,439	231	1,390	1,577	2,179	1,675	735	464	878	1,185
Florida	164,501	36,746	2,557	10,882	9,692	15,757	29,080	3,791	6,874	9,694	8,976
Georgia	114,464	32,774	4,694	6,188	7,525	15,172	14,040	2,051	4,429	3,464	1,163
Hawaii	50,657	7,064	137	859	1,208	2,804	2,026	0	1,534	1,639	2,159
Idaho	20,250	7,138	685	1,767	1,562	1,013	1,139	433	1,660	1,412	363
Illinois	136,623	46,518	2,926	8,873	12,605	20,885	11,806	3,750	3,327	8,778	2,496
Indiana	95,157	45,153	4,970	4,842	5,372	11,690	6,470	1,800	2,700	4,837	925
Iowa	47,354	18,485	1,165	2,764	3,289	8,508	2,092	807	2,866	1,898	2,104
Kansas	47,882	19,906	665	3,671	1,699	7,558	3,558	988	1,983	2,010	1,846
Kentucky	76,254	28,113	4,189	5,752	4,945	5,989	5,093	1,701	3,739	3,990	3,638
Louisiana	88,767	27,355	3,687	5,622	5,865	18,666	6,617	1,077	4,772	3,639	1,334
Maine	22,006	5,652	1,220	2,794	1,868	1,875	1,251	587	1,405	1,523	533
Maryland	82,072	20,164	1,970	5,052	7,105	7,443	8,812	2,276	2,310	5,111	3,685
Massachusetts	84,983	20,694	803	4,651	7,338	17,398	5,311	1,991	2,057	5,956	5,326
Michigan	137,853	65,263	1,970	3,875	12,796	13,037	14,965	3,105	3,757	3,677	2,683
Minnesota	67,332	33,190	1,634	5,110	1,651	7,435	2,455	835	3,496	3,180	1,262
Mississippi	47,433	14,496	1,363	3,481	3,233	7,932	2,965	913	3,979	1,477	469
Missouri	74,049	20,518	2,021	6,329	6,797	13,076	6,280	1,925	2,532	3,548	2,701
Montana	17,095	5,573	731	1,890	1,171	1,310	943	370	1,460	1,297	154
Nebraska	28,746	9,919	742	2,391	2,584	4,184	1,751	673	1,834	959	636
Nevada	19,142	5,985	266	1,449	1,017	939	2,252	499	1,104	1,272	405
New Hampshire	16,296	5,169	308	1,948	1,114	982	900	435	475	725	755
New Jersey	115,770	27,343	2,948	8,272	5,893	19,155	9,791	3,651	2,086	7,691	4,751
New Mexico	42,159	16,735	857	2,725	1,950	5,363	2,628	570	1,641	2,709	1,670
New York	267,429	42,684	5,661	14,897	7396	62,749	33,083	5,481	3,484	17,045	16,414
North Carolina	109,046	38,758	3,041	12,084	1,,156	15,534	12,367	3,107	4,066	3,434	4,945
North Dakota	16,468	6,790	339	1,074	198	1,922	487	224	1,410	611	328
Ohio	140,305	65,959	2,296	8,903	2,137	18,701	10,794	2,289	3,810	5,841	2,112
Oklahoma	67,071	23,633	1,926	3,542	7,944	8,309	4,823	1,730	2,050	2,770	1,726
Oregon	49,704	14,137	1,148	3,851	4,439	6,163	2,709	1,092	2,976	3,912	2,225
Pennsylvania	143,438	48,157	2,658	12,682	9,797	23,246	8,688	5,288	5,346	9,716	2,319
Rhode Island	19,890	5,762	927	977	1,593	1,447	1,821	258	665	1,374	924
South Carolina	77,754	26,103	2,925	5,218	4,966	10,031	7,321	1,773	2,809	3,504	545
South Dakota	13,517	4,280	436	1,257	1,114	1,533	582	282	880	718	555
Tennessee	75,930	28,594	2,009	4,793	4,699	10,061	6,409	1,544	3,576	3,101	1,542
Texas	239,702	81,947	4,763	14,339	15,535	41,208	29,397	3,037	11,232	9,940	3,639
Utah	39,618	19,190	836	1,792	2,556	4,434	2,194	648	1,404	1,620	994
Vermont	12,923	4,454	336	1,096	1,144	554	697	475	652	815	491
Virginia	115,817	42,527	3,123	11,281	2,411	19,210	8,836	2,372	3,350	4,772	2,768
Washington	98,016	39,319	1,667	6,212	7,490	7,203	6,095	1,898	5,532	3,587	1,414
West Virginia	33,597	11,477	1,527	5,764	2,264	2,388	786	811	1,815	1,295	975
Wisconsin	72,674	36,251	1,344	2,114	1,189	8,514	5,422	852	2,690	4,525	1,865
Wyoming	11,274	3,174	152	1,862	300	1,629	475	248	815	579	362

Source: U.S. Department of Commerce, Bureau of the Census, *Public Employment 1992.*
(a) Includes instructional and other personnel.

(b) Includes instructional and other personnel in elementary and secondary schools.

Table 7.22
STATE GOVERNMENT PAYROLLS FOR SELECTED FUNCTIONS,
BY STATE: OCTOBER 1991
(In thousands of dollars)

| State | All functions | Education | | Selected functions | | | | | | | | |
		Higher education (a)	Other education (b)	Highways	Public welfare	Hospitals	Corrections	Police protection	Natural resources	Financial and other governmental administration	Judicial and legal administration
United States	$9,437,078	$3,241,477	$236,383	$612,841	$463,590	$1,208,095	$788,044	$249,534	$348,613	$468,753	$338,111
Alabama............	173,640	68,418	9,544	8,560	9,041	23,689	9,067	2,759	6,761	6,943	6,921
Alaska.............	73,983	13,141	1,551	10,836	4,661	1,275	4,479	1,741	8,451	4,549	3,970
Arizona............	111,043	46,250	4,595	7,220	4,413	1,763	11,085	4,866	4,611	6,797	3,029
Arkansas	84,243	28,047	5,093	8,192	5,808	6,508	4,438	1,881	4,479	4,168	1,174
California..........	1,047,687	362,735	13,655	64,465	9,441	110,497	109,180	36,187	47,069	49,176	10,569
Colorado	157,987	89,101	2,970	8,348	3,879	11,732	9,034	2,954	4,634	6,697	7,941
Connecticut	178,287	41,921	8,311	11,645	12,706	36,025	17,081	5,046	2,956	10,982	9,990
Delaware	45,173	16,106	693	2,587	2,577	4,298	2,213	1,008	1,964	2,782
Florida............	358,559	90,164	5,811	21,223	13,806	30,832	64,259	9,212	15,397	18,353	25,552
Georgia............	226,160	74,688	11,180	12,311	15,389	26,407	18,104	4,929	10,089	7,524	3,433
Hawaii	122,319	23,411	358	1,968	2,370	6,257	4,104	0	3,932	3,964	5,488
Idaho	39,103	13,908	1,202	3,865	2,556	746	2,179	1,096	3,333	2,785	1,270
Illinois............	350,468	118,334	7,675	25,932	30,544	45,039	28,783	12,336	9,843	21,423	10,497
Indiana............	210,306	118,663	7,149	9,003	8,497	22,847	11,378	4,962	5,412	7,813	3,997
Iowa	128,135	57,465	2,829	6,374	8,564	19,830	5,028	3,112	6,466	4,389	5,319
Kansas	101,325	37,854	2,268	8,021	7,036	15,261	7,300	2,272	4,617	4,226	4,279
Kentucky	163,120	65,982	9,738	12,214	9,134	11,381	9,668	4,493	7,566	8,120	7,358
Louisiana..........	181,329	59,232	7,577	10,601	12,747	33,280	14,277	2,436	9,381	7,220	3,950
Maine	52,974	13,308	2,790	6,229	4,834	4,592	3,067	1,600	3,480	3,416	1,600
Maryland	224,036	71,420	5,469	12,058	14,698	17,360	22,554	6,809	5,920	13,073	9,442
Massachusetts	221,572	52,969	2,544	14,169	19,069	41,441	13,583	7,083	5,161	16,591	14,861
Michigan	385,351	161,323	6,487	13,028	36,789	43,603	44,553	10,435	10,859	11,831	9,111
Minnesota	182,832	88,841	4,737	14,570	4,598	19,142	6,324	2,777	9,116	9,217	4,347
Mississippi	86,620	28,334	3,640	5,150	5,129	13,438	4,691	1,916	7,065	3,413	1,320
Missouri	144,132	46,070	4,055	13,396	10,007	21,924	10,627	4,596	4,637	5,587	7,070
Montana...........	36,129	12,243	1,597	4,135	2,310	2,262	1,668	830	3,554	2,664	512
Nebraska	60,364	22,236	1,580	4,978	5,254	7,784	3,332	1,563	3,241	2,132	1,690
Nevada	47,243	14,213	775	3,863	1,822	2,160	5,814	1,497	2,597	3,097	1,349
New Hampshire	36,662	12,812	759	4,036	2,195	2,031	1,949	1,012	966	1,650	1,937
New Jersey..........	349,453	83,671	10,139	26,217	16,565	46,174	29,651	12,849	6,282	21,739	17,781
New Mexico.........	85,024	33,871	1,780	5,396	4,091	10,752	4,961	1,244	3,698	5,427	3,867
New York	802,023	140,918	16,129	37,565	21,248	172,642	92,082	18,568	10,334	46,446	61,606
North Carolina	247,698	95,706	7,327	23,430	3,355	32,597	25,054	7,641	8,924	8,271	12,075
North Dakota	31,263	14,466	781	2,276	271	2,705	681	479	2,533	995	807
Ohio	337,070	153,757	6,933	22,666	5,598	41,675	25,816	6,256	9,639	14,605	5,944
Oklahoma	126,986	44,674	4,038	6,461	14,448	14,179	8,541	3,650	3,872	5,827	4,475
Oregon	123,691	37,585	2,119	7,952	8,698	17,736	6,705	3,558	7,950	9,528	5,594
Pennsylvania	323,904	81,524	5,950	33,324	24,640	55,478	18,843	16,582	14,460	25,323	9,332
Rhode Island	49,445	14,730	2,287	2,131	3,463	2,652	4,631	980	1,560	3,812	2,421
South Carolina	153,620	56,144	6,461	7,390	9,235	16,600	12,950	3,683	4,967	6,950	1,637
South Dakota	26,354	9,782	810	2,535	1,786	1,892	1,016	593	1,669	1,472	1,132
Tennessee	156,928	63,421	4,090	9,128	9,878	19,597	11,874	3,470	5,910	6,474	4,384
Texas..............	525,277	196,926	10,212	31,734	33,631	98,992	43,855	7,996	17,209	22,824	11,670
Utah	81,845	38,007	1,715	4,170	4,805	10,396	4,191	1,973	2,997	3,229	2,455
Vermont	29,851	10,482	833	2,534	2,382	1,236	1,717	1,456	1,571	1,663	1,316
Virginia............	250,564	96,309	8,029	20,832	4,895	35,985	17,282	6,315	7,701	11,170	7,632
Washington	231,047	87,594	3,997	18,656	17,814	16,007	13,947	5,248	13,690	8,430	4,968
West Virginia	63,862	25,939	3,027	9,905	3,346	3,378	1,126	1,716	3,547	3,179	2,100
Wisconsin	188,084	100,499	2,691	5,477	2,596	22,445	11,044	2,121	5,796	10,285	5,222
Wyoming	22,304	6,281	404	4,080	969	1,576	931	540	1,703	1,341	936

Source: U.S. Department of Commerce, Bureau of the Census, *Public Employment 1991.*
(a) Includes instructional and other personnel.

(b) Includes instructional and other personnel in elementary and secondary schools.

Table 7.23
STATE GOVERNMENT PAYROLLS FOR SELECTED FUNCTIONS, BY STATE: OCTOBER 1992
(In thousands of dollars)

State	All functions	Education Higher education (a)	Education Other education (b)	Highways	Public welfare	Hospitals	Corrections	Police protection	Natural resources	Financial and other governmental administration	Judicial and legal administration
United States	$9,828,247	$3,456,791	$241,819	$625,915	$471,050	$1,224,262	$843,513	$246,947	$354,739	$475,727	$349,876
Alabama	176,929	70,607	9,158	8,795	9,246	23,537	8,513	3,325	6,982	7,125	6,990
Alaska	76,792	13,592	1,569	11,481	5,054	1,186	4,524	1,741	8,763	4,692	4,109
Arizona	121,955	45,213	5,836	7,220	11,113	1,728	11,855	4,826	4,964	6,744	3,295
Arkansas	99,385	36,638	5,629	8,737	5,960	9,705	4,883	2,105	5,150	4,544	1,265
California	1,062,204	367,157	13,364	65,484	9,230	107,782	125,368	32,370	40,456	47,414	10,181
Colorado	165,021	93,297	3,233	8,877	3,654	11,754	9,449	2,954	4,949	6,928	8,232
Connecticut	174,518	41,971	7,749	11,146	13,015	33,955	18,123	5,326	1,983	10,712	10,094
Delaware	49,451	18,803	709	2,822	3,315	4,187	3,685	2,289	1,039	1,901	3,125
Florida	354,591	90,574	5,534	23,565	13,763	29,980	55,225	9,913	14,838	21,439	26,065
Georgia	233,831	78,618	11,459	12,536	15,274	27,456	19,635	4,971	9,663	7,742	3,611
Hawaii	130,808	25,480	360	2,127	2,703	6,543	4,581	0	4,230	4,635	6,061
Idaho	43,387	14,650	1,436	3,977	3,244	2,058	2,366	1,142	3,550	3,079	1,293
Illinois	346,998	117,762	7,628	24,836	30,518	45,039	30,101	11,973	9,115	21,014	10,462
Indiana	227,829	128,320	8,257	9,003	8,916	26,362	11,982	4,117	6,196	8,415	3,438
Iowa	136,016	61,367	3,134	6,975	7,778	20,940	5,472	2,906	7,274	4,788	5,885
Kansas	100,811	38,982	1,448	8,277	3,949	14,729	8,263	2,396	4,652	4,250	4,390
Kentucky	166,307	68,274	9,724	11,959	9,589	11,932	9,608	4,076	7,653	7,928	7,450
Louisiana	190,313	66,139	8,485	11,460	12,681	33,527	12,988	2,487	9,789	7,547	4,229
Maine	51,870	13,588	3,049	6,060	4,019	4,004	2,957	1,585	3,243	3,550	1,551
Maryland	223,037	68,489	5,276	12,050	15,140	16,900	22,117	6,943	5,990	12,419	11,422
Massachusetts	223,416	57,012	2,109	13,945	18,733	39,062	14,284	7,091	5,369	16,334	14,966
Michigan	401,837	179,588	6,407	12,514	36,414	41,671	46,433	10,435	10,628	11,424	9,323
Minnesota	190,889	93,619	4,967	15,253	4,538	19,280	7,019	2,650	9,317	9,082	4,890
Mississippi	93,589	34,634	2,764	5,522	5,097	14,531	4,485	1,865	7,066	3,107	1,694
Missouri	153,212	52,096	4,076	13,747	10,644	23,171	10,538	4,729	5,067	6,446	6,254
Montana	37,577	12,853	1,649	4,554	2,345	2,198	1,922	856	3,306	2,664	542
Nebraska	59,849	20,928	1,814	5,243	4,763	7,784	3,395	1,606	3,277	2,284	1,812
Nevada	49,783	14,213	778	4,001	2,528	2,301	6,153	1,546	2,853	3,308	1,497
New Hampshire	38,410	12,812	726	4,127	2,785	2,265	2,334	1,158	975	1,675	1,895
New Jersey	351,750	89,437	9,945	26,392	16,692	45,324	30,537	12,849	6,647	21,951	18,330
New Mexico	88,128	34,934	1,857	5,509	3,991	10,598	5,289	1,355	3,475	5,632	4,121
New York	832,608	141,165	17,179	41,466	22,321	167,560	106,705	18,687	10,603	46,847	62,851
North Carolina	257,507	100,845	7,349	24,729	2,950	33,554	24,984	7,953	9,356	8,467	12,514
North Dakota	33,979	15,129	642	2,074	336	3,434	926	550	2,767	1,165	866
Ohio	352,935	158,997	6,575	23,595	5,808	46,298	28,106	6,730	9,018	15,213	6,682
Oklahoma	133,413	49,790	4,095	6,359	14,489	15,058	8,470	3,633	3,650	5,724	4,681
Oregon	130,410	42,780	2,890	8,075	10,744	14,714	7,055	3,648	6,913	9,777	5,959
Pennsylvania	400,895	142,989	6,505	28,379	23,555	80,314	20,093	15,338	13,654	23,698	8,781
Rhode Island	54,871	15,378	2,546	2,382	4,912	2,990	5,973	988	1,602	3,479	2,869
South Carolina	157,742	59,094	6,487	7,835	9,229	15,350	12,895	3,667	6,258	7,204	1,618
South Dakota	28,512	10,253	844	2,658	1,960	2,538	1,056	617	1,771	1,577	1,318
Tennessee	160,337	65,199	4,220	9,029	9,560	9,560	19,936	3,537	6,928	6,535	4,647
Texas	552,537	209,704	10,651	31,913	28,411	88,447	57,895	8,341	25,581	24,177	11,712
Utah	80,955	36,450	1,863	4,327	5,372	8,179	4,588	1,664	3,337	3,324	2,662
Vermont	31,270	11,029	868	2,699	2,449	1,143	1,643	1,473	1,679	1,777	1,365
Virginia	252,987	100,640	7,360	21,768	5,068	35,207	16,637	6,156	7,304	10,818	7,647
Washington	249,095	92,913	4,343	19,666	20,481	16,436	15,439	5,653	13,947	10,097	5,284
West Virginia	64,883	26,217	3,184	10,395	3,343	3,380	1,153	1,844	3,756	2,267	2,041
Wisconsin	210,669	110,291	3,749	6,549	2,786	25,628	13,039	2,358	6,454	11,526	7,007
Wyoming	22,149	6,281	339	3,819	584	2,605	810	524	1,698	1,320	900

Source: U.S. Department of Commerce, Bureau of the Census, *Public Employment 1992.*

(a) Includes instructional and other personnel.

(b) Includes instructional and other personnel in elementary and secondary schools.

Finances of State-Administered Public Employee-Retirement Systems

Many public retirement systems are the 800-pound gorillas of the country's financial markets.

by Henry S. Wulf

State government public employee-retirement systems serve a significant social welfare function by ensuring an adequate source of retirement income to a large number of state and local government employees. They also are important as financial organizations, whether viewed from the perspective of the public or private sector.

This discussion will elaborate on these two broad activities of state government retirement systems. It will provide, first, a description of membership and organization. That is followed by an examination of the financial activity of the systems — where they obtain funds, how they disburse monies to beneficiaries and the relationship between their revenues and expenditures. The last part of the finance topic describes the enormous investments and assets of these systems, making them individually and collectively one of the most significant forces in the nation's financial markets. The final section examines some of the important issues facing these systems.

The existence of state retirement systems as both government agencies and influential players in the capital markets means that often they are buffeted by significant economic and political currents simultaneously. The recent recession, for example, had an impact on their ability to earn acceptable returns in investment vehicles such as stocks and real estate, as did the extended period of low interest rates. For state governments, on the other hand, there are political considerations. The recession, rapidly rising costs of state-funded programs such as education, welfare and corrections, and need for capital to stimulate growth has created political pressure to change retirement system funding formulas and make use of the vast resources of the systems to boost regional economies.[1]

Overview

At the end of fiscal year 1991-92 there were 210 state-administered public employee-retirement systems, a total that has remained fairly constant for at least the past decade.[2] When states have changed the composition of the systems, it was usually to create a new class of employees for retirement purposes such as judges or police, consolidate existing systems for administrative or financial reasons, or assume responsibility for local government employee-retirement systems.

The 210 state systems provide retirement coverage not only for their own employees but also to a large number of employees in the political subdivisions of the states. There were 13 million public employees who were members of the approximately 2,400 state and local government employee-retirement systems in fiscal 1992. However, the 210 state systems provided coverage for more than 11.3 million of these employees, or 87 percent.

The total assets of state systems amounted to $720 billion in 1992. The state-administered systems controlled nearly 82 percent of the more than $880 billion in total assets held by all public employee retirement systems. Approximately three-fourths of the state retirement system assets was composed of three

Henry Wulf is special assistant for Programs, Governments Division, Bureau of the Census, U.S. Department of Commerce.

types of investments: federal government securities worth $209 billion (29 percent), corporate stocks worth $199 billion (27.6 percent), and corporate bonds worth $130 billion (18.1 percent). The remaining 25 percent of the portfolio consisted of a variety of other investments such as mortgages, savings deposits and real estate holdings.

Membership

State-administered systems provide retirement coverage to 11.3 million members, both active and inactive. Active members — consisting of current employees of state and local governments — are by far the largest portion with 9.9 million members. Inactive members totaled nearly 1.4 million members, or 14 percent of the total. This latter group is mostly former employees who had acquired a vested right to receive retirement benefits or employees on military or extended leave without pay who still retained retirement credits in the system.

System Coverage

Coverage describes the types of employees eligible for membership in retirement systems. This divides broadly into two categories, general coverage and limited coverage. General-coverage systems include employees in varied and assorted occupations and activities. Limited coverage systems are those that are restricted to specific job categories (teachers, police officers or firefighters) or functions (education, highways or hospitals).

More than 60 of the state-administered systems are general in their coverage. They provide retirement protection for about 60 percent of all state retirement system members. The remaining 40 percent of the membership is covered by nearly 40 limited-coverage systems for education, 50 for public safety activities, and the remainder in a variety of other specific occupations such as judges, assessors and legislators. The number of these limited-coverage systems, however, does not indicate the magnitude of membership or financial importance. For example, the education systems account for about one-third of the membership, the miscellaneous systems 6 percent and the pub-

lic safety systems — the largest number (51) of limited coverage systems — just 2 percent.

System Size

Among administrative organizations — both public and private — state-administered retirement systems are large and, therefore, important. This can be illustrated in a number of ways. Of the 210 systems, for example, 82 had memberships exceeding 25,000 and only 33 had fewer than 100 members. By contrast, although there are about 2,200 locally-administered public employee-retirement systems, there were only eight with memberships greater than 25,000. More than 1,400 of the local systems had 100 or fewer members.

There is a heavy concentration of membership and financial activity in the 82 largest state systems. For example, they provided retirement coverage for 10.9 million members, or about 84 out of every 100 members. The concentration is even greater than that, however. The 10 largest systems alone cover nearly four out of every 10 members and also control about 36 percent of the state system assets. The largest systems were, in order of membership size (membership in parentheses): New York State Employees (614,000), California Public Employees (614,000), Florida Retirement System (546,000), Texas Teachers Retirement Fund (473,000), Ohio Public Employees (329,000), California State Teachers (313,000), Michigan Public School Retirement (297,000), Virginia Retirement System (251,000), New Jersey Public Employees (249,000) and North Carolina Public Employees (228,000).

To demonstrate how significant these large state systems are, it is useful to compare them with similar organizations in the private sector. An annual compilation by *Pensions and Investments* magazine shows assets for the top public and private pension systems. The ranking revealed that state-administered retirement systems held 15 of the first 25 positions and 26 of the top 50. The large state systems control assets comparable to some of the immense private pension funds such as AT&T, General Motors Corp., General Electric, IBM, Ford Motor Co., DuPont, NYNEX, Bell South, GTE, Ameritech and Boeing.[3]

Receipts

State retirement systems obtain revenues from three sources: contributions from employees, contributions from governments and earnings on investments. Of the $101 billion total in state-administered retirement system revenue, nearly 62 of every 100 dollars ($63 billion) is derived from investment earnings, followed by state government contributions ($13.6 billion), employee contributions ($13.5 billion) and local government contributions ($11.5 billion).

The importance of investment earnings to state retirement systems is noteworthy. There has been a definite trend of investment earnings contributing a greater percentage of the total revenues over the past few decades. In 1972, for example, investment earnings were just 28 percent of total receipts, a figure that rose slightly to 32 percent by 1977. The average from 1980 to 1986 jumped to 44 percent. There was another jump from 1987 to 1989 when the average rose to 56 percent and in 1990 it was at 58 percent.

This trend ended in 1991 with the investment earnings contribution dropping to 55 percent, perhaps not surprising in view of the economic downturn that began in late 1990. However, in 1992 the contribution rose to a new historic high of 62 percent. The investment contributions in locally administered public employee retirement systems followed the same trend, dropping from 58 percent in 1990 to 52 percent in 1991, but rising again in 1992 to 58 percent. Overall, investment earnings jumped 34 percent over 1991, more than making up the decrease of almost 10 percent from 1990 to 1991.

If the state retirement systems are able to maintain their investment-earnings pace, the implications for general state finances will be significant. The general financial pressure that state governments find themselves under because of rising social service costs, infrastructure needs and the like, increases pressure on the state retirement systems to provide greater investment revenues. The quid pro quo for the retirement systems may well be permission to diversify investments into more profitable — but potentially more risky — financial ventures.

Employee and government contributions to state systems show muddled trends also. Perhaps buttressing the point about the financial pressure on state governments, the state government contributions in 1992 to their own retirement systems decreased nearly 6 percent from 1991. The average annual change from 1987 to 1992 was only +0.6 percent. Local government contributions to state retirement systems were almost the same from 1991 to 1992 and showed slightly less than a 3 percent average annual increase since 1987. Employee contributions, by contrast, have been steady. They were up just over 7 percent from 1991 to 1992 and for the period from 1987 to 1992 increased 7.4 percent on average each year.

Benefit Payments and Other Outlays

Total state retirement system outlays rose 12 percent from 1991, to a total of $37 billion in 1992. These retirement system expenditures fall into three categories: benefits paid, withdrawals and a miscellaneous category covering direct administrative costs and related incidental payments. The single largest outlay, periodic benefit payments, amounted to more than $34 billion.

Benefit payments have sustained continuously high rates of annual growth from 1987 to 1992, averaging more than 10 percent. Thus, the increase of 12 percent in benefit payments from 1991 to 1992 is certainly within range of recent changes. In the early 1980s the average annual increase was even greater, about 14 percent annually. Interpreting the influences on these changes is difficult because there are many factors involved such as inflation, the composition and number of beneficiaries and the consolidation of smaller local government retirement systems into state systems. The most significant fact about these consistent annual increases in state retirement system outlays is the continual pressure they generate on governments and the system trustees to fund the systems properly.

Benefit Payments in Relation to Other Retirement Programs

State retirement system benefits can be supplemented by a variety of different retirement programs. Chief among these additional programs is federal Social Security. Some states also offer deferred compensation and investment programs. The existence of these supplementary programs can influence the amount of benefits paid directly by the state.

The precise number of state retirement system members who are covered under Social Security is not known. Where information is available, however, Social Security appears to be an important element in the overall provision of retirement benefits. Nearly 97 percent of Florida state retirement system membership is covered by Social Security, 89 percent in South Dakota and 73 percent in Mississippi.

Important changes have occurred, especially in the last decade, in the eligibility for Social Security among state government employees. Before 1951, no public employees were eligible to participate. New federal legislation at that time allowed state governments the option of participating. A number of states chose to participate, but retained the right to withdraw. In 1984, new federal amendments required states who still were covered by Social Security to remain in the system. A further legal change that became effective in 1986 was mandatory coverage for the health insurance portion of Social Security (Medicare) for all newly hired state employees. State governments were given the option with this last change of extending Medicare coverage to all employees.

Beneficiaries and Monthly Benefit Payments

There were more than 3.4 million beneficiaries receiving periodic benefit payments from state retirement systems in 1992. These beneficiaries fall into three groups: the largest — almost 88 percent of the total or 3.4 million beneficiaries — were retired on account of age or length of service; the next largest group is survivors of deceased former members (244,000); and the smallest group is employees retired on account of disabilities (178,000).

The number of beneficiaries has increased over the past decade at a steady rate. From 1982 to 1992, the average annual rise was about 4 percent, which when compounded trans-

lates into more than a 50 percent increase in the number of beneficiaries over that period. However, there was some slowing in this trend from 1991 to 1992 when the number rose less than 2 percent. Beneficiaries translate directly into system payments, so a change in trend is extremely important. State and local government decisions about employment levels, privatization and provision of services all have long-term consequences for retirement systems. There also are short-term effects as state governments shift funding from provision of services through salaries to the government contributions for retirement system beneficiaries.

The average monthly payment for beneficiaries was $738. This was less than a 2 percent increase over 12 months earlier when the average received was $726. As there was a slowing in the number of beneficiaries, there was also a trend change between 1991 and 1992 in the average monthly payments to beneficiaries. Since 1982 the average increase in monthly benefit payments has been about 6 percent — 5.8 percent from 1982 to 1987 and 6.3 percent from 1987 to 1992. In the next few years it will be important to see what occurs with this trend as the state retirement systems balance their responsibilities to the beneficiaries against the unpredictable financial markets and the increased fiscal pressure on state governments.

Reflecting both living and economic conditions, the states show a considerable range in their average monthly benefit payments. The highest ranking states are Alaska ($1,287), Rhode Island ($1,260), Connecticut ($1,166), Maryland ($989), Colorado ($988) and Arizona ($981). Four states had average payments of less than $415: Louisiana ($413), Texas ($395), Kansas ($361) and Iowa ($327). The interpretation of these state averages requires considerable caution because there are so many determinants influencing them. Among these are wage levels in the state, the number and type of employees receiving benefits, and the availability of alternative or supplemental retirement programs, especially Social Security. If there are tiered benefit programs, the analysis becomes even further convoluted. Tiered benefit programs are a development of the past few decades to differentiate among newer and older employees in terms of service qualifications, age criteria and access to benefits.

Receipts Compared with Payments

Receipts for state retirement systems exceeded benefit payments by $64 billion in 1992. Retirement systems must increase their assets each year to meet obligations to future beneficiaries. Conventional wisdom holds that measuring this excess funding against the total of all cash and securities provides a relative measure of the ability to cover these future liabilities.

In 1992, the ratio amounted to 8.9 percent. Although this was higher than the 1991 figure of 8.3, it was still well below the next lowest level of the past decade (10.2 percent in 1990). In 1986, the ratio reached 14 percent but has fallen steadily since.

What does this mean for the state retirement systems? The major issue is whether, as a group, they are taking in sufficient revenues to cover their future financial commitments. Whether the systems were previously overfunded or are now properly funded or underfunded, has important financial, governmental and societal implications. If the ratio continues in this direction, at some point the financial viability of the state systems will come into question and, therefore, this ratio bears close watching.

Investments and Assets

As described in the *Pension and Investments* analysis cited previously, state retirement systems are very important institutional investors by any measure. The composition of their investment portfolio is, therefore, very important to analysts of financial markets.

State retirement systems controlled $720 billion in cash and investment holdings at the end of fiscal 1992. Corporate stocks remained the largest portion of the holdings with 27.6 percent of the total, followed by U. S. Treasury securities (22.7 percent), corporate bonds (18.1 percent), federal agency securities (6.3 percent) and cash and short-term investments (5.5 percent). The remainder — 20 percent of the total — was invested in varied financial vehicles such as repurchase agreements, guaranteed investment accounts, mutual fund shares, international securities, partnerships, real estate holdings, venture capital, leveraged buyouts and junk bonds.

The three major categories — corporate stocks, corporate bonds and U.S. Treasury securities — amounted to slightly more than 68 percent of all assets in 1992. This total has been declining irregularly from the recent peak of almost 76 percent in 1988. It is currently the lowest since 1984, when it was 67 percent.

Where have the state systems invested this money? More and more they are moving into new, non-traditional or less frequently used investments. In 1992, 20 percent of the assets were in a miscellaneous category that used a potpourri of investment vehicles. These totaled less than 12 percent in 1988. This appears now to be a trend in the state system's investment strategy. There has been continuing discussion about expanding investments in options such as private placements, international investments and variations of real estate ventures such as construction loans for single-family developments.[4]

Current Issues

Analysts are focusing on three issues of current importance to the state retirement systems: pension system activism, investment targeting, and potential funding problems and their aftermath. Each of these has been debated at length over the past decade. However, they are worth reviewing to see how current conditions affect them.

Pension System Activism

It is not unusual to see a headline in the pension literature such as, "CalPERS gunning for poor performers."[5] In the past decade, public employee-retirement systems have become active investors, demanding a say in the management of their investments. The undisputed leader in this movement is the California Public Employees' Retirement System, but other state systems have also become extremely active. This activity has taken two broad tacks. Some systems have used their financial clout to demand access to companies to discuss financial performance. Others use their influence in open proxy contests to force the management of companies to take certain directions. The Wisconsin Investment Board has been the leader of this latter tactic.[6] This particular issue seems to ebb and flow based on the personalities of the pension system executives, but, having acquired influence that appears to have benefitted their investments, the retirement systems are unlikely to move away from this position.

Investment Targeting

There are two aspects to this issue. First is the matter always uppermost in the thoughts of pension funds: Where can they get the best return on their investment dollar? Second is the social impact of investments. Relative to where state retirement systems will invest, it appears they are becoming more involved, like other major investors, in the growing stock market.[7] Recent articles point to two other directions, realty and foreign investment.[8] The second issue, investment for social purposes, is a growing phenomenon that generates some controversy because of the potential conflict with the fiduciary responsibility toward retirees. A report on a study done at the Wharton School of the University of Pennsylvania said social investment projects achieved returns slightly below what could be expected.[9] Yet, an article about economically targeted investments (ETIs) cited studies arguing that not only were these investments good social policy, but were sound investments.[10]

Funding Issue

One of the perennial questions about any pension system, public or private, is whether it is adequately funded. Two different studies in the past two years agree that, by and large, state retirement systems are adequately funded. The rule of thumb concerning funding is that an 80 percent level is safe. An official for the Government Finance Officers Association indicated that their figures show state retirement funds are 85 percent funded on average. Yet, there are some stated concerns. Five major states (California, Illinois, Louisiana, Massachusetts and Michigan) have been cited as being significantly underfunded. Also, state pensions plans have been noted as being on average 15 percent less funded than corporate pension funds.[11] As long as there are pension funds, there will be debate on this issue.

State pension systems are an integral part of the social, financial and governmental structures. Forces influencing society at large affect the systems and they, in turn, because of their very significant size, can affect the direction of those social institutions. The trends of the finances are mixed, due to changes in the underlying economic base. If the economy moves strongly, then it likely will pull the state retirement systems in its wake. If not, we are likely to continue seeing mixed signals.

Footnotes

[1] The data in this article derive primarily from U.S. Bureau of the Census annual surveys of state and local government employee retirement systems.

[2] The 1982 Census of Governments conducted by the U.S. Bureau of the Census counted 190 state-administered systems in 1981-82.

[3] "Top 200 Pension Funds/Sponsors," *Pensions and Investments*, January 20, 1992.

[4] For some current examples see: "Alabama Pension Chief Achieves a Rare Feat: He Stirs Controversy," *Wall Street Journal*, February 4, 1994, "Pension Funds Venture Abroad in Search of Big Returns," *Wall Street Journal*, January 9, 1994; and "Virginia Fund Boosts Managed Futures to 4%." *Pensions and Investments*, December 27, 1993, p. 8.

[5] *Pensions and Investments*, January 24, 1994, page 4.

[6] "Wisconsin Pension Fund is Activist Hawk," *Wall Street Journal*, March 18, 1984.

[7] "Institutional Share of U.S. Equities Slips," *Wall Street Journal*, December 8, 1993.

[8] See, for example: "New York police finance exporters," *Pensions and Investments*, November 15, 1993, p. 29; "It's a whole new ball game," *Pensions and Investments*, November 29, 1993, p. 10; "Pension funds venture abroad in search of big returns," *Wall Street Journal*, January 19, 1994; and "Pension funds again turn to real estate," February 4, 1994.

[9] "In-state investments don't boost returns," *Pensions and Investment*, January 24, 1994, p. 7.

[10] "Putting a sharp pencil to ETIs: Economic buoyancy or hopes about to pop?," *Pension World*, December 1993, pp. 9-12.

[11] See: *Report on State Pension Systems, 11th Edition*, Pension Commission Clearinghouse, A. Foster Higgins and Company, Inc. 1992; *1993 Report of Funding Levels for State Retirement Systems*, Wilshire Associates Incorporated, May 21, 1993; "Municipal Pensions Face Funding Crisis," *Pension World*, December 1993, p. 6; and "Albany's way of financing pensions is ruled illegal," *New York Times*, November 17, 1993.

Table 7.24
NUMBER, MEMBERSHIP AND MONTHLY BENEFIT PAYMENTS OF STATE-ADMINISTERED EMPLOYEE RETIREMENT SYSTEMS: 1988-89 THROUGH 1991-92

Item	1991-92	1990-91	1989-90	1988-89
Number of systems	209	203	204	204
Membership, last month of fiscal year:				
Total members	11,884,340	11,653,035	10,641,661	11,022,437
Active members	10,454,302	10,102,942	9,242,854	9,689,662
Other	1,430,038	1,560,093	1,398,807	1,332,775
Percent distribution	100	100	100	100
Active members	88	87	87	88
Other	12	13	13	12
Beneficiaries receiving periodic benefits:				
Total number	3,414,299	3,357,002	3,232,168	3,119,605
Persons retired on account of age or length of service	2,992,401	2,886,903	2,871,047	2,751,691
Persons retired on account of disability	178,074	220,052	148,238	145,945
Survivors of deceased former members	243,824	250,047	212,833	221,969
Percent distribution	100.0	100.0	100.0	100.0
Persons retired on account of age or length of service	87.6	86.0	88.8	88.2
Persons retired on account of disability	5.2	6.6	4.6	4.7
Survivors of deceased former members	7.1	7.4	6.6	7.1
Recurrent benefit payments for last month of fiscal year:				
Total amount (in thousands)	$2,566,152	$2,436,907	$2,188,900	$1,945,999
To persons retired on account of age or length of service	$2,312,671	$2,157,306	$1,990,460	$1,767,199
To persons retired on account of disability	$140,260	$170,723	$105,461	$95,843
To survivors of deceased former members	$112,491	$108,878	$92,979	$82,956
Percent distribution	100.0	100.0	100.0	100.0
For persons retired on account of age or length of service	90.1	88.5	90.9	90.8
For persons retired on account of disability	5.5	7.0	4.8	4.9
For survivors of deceased former members	4.4	4.5	4.2	4.3
Average monthly payment for beneficiaries:				
Average for all beneficiaries (in dollars)	$752	$726	$677	$624
For persons retired on account of age or length of service	$773	$747	$693	$642
For persons retired on account of disability	$788	$776	$711	$657
For survivors of deceased former members	$461	$435	$437	$374

Source: U.S. Department of Commerce, Bureau of the Census, *Finances of Employee Retirement Systems of State and Local Governments.*
Note: Detail may not add to totals due to rounding.

Table 7.25
NATIONAL SUMMARY OF FINANCES OF STATE-ADMINISTERED EMPLOYEE RETIREMENT SYSTEMS: SELECTED YEARS, 1986-1992

	Amount (in millions of dollars)						Percentage distribution			
	1991-92	1990-91	1989-90	1988-89	1987-88	1986-87	1991-92	1990-91	1989-90	1988-89
Receipts	$101,632	$ 85,576	$ 89,165	$ 81,090	$ 76,444	$ 77,706	100.0	100.0	100.0	100.0
Employee contributions............	13,453	12,563	11,648	10,813	9,942	9,428	13.2	14.7	13.1	13.3
Government contributions	25,132	26,007	25,505	24,357	23,394	23,258	24.7	30.4	28.6	30.0
From State Government	13,611	14,455	13,968	13,155	12,978	13,199	13.4	16.9	15.7	16.2
From Local Government.........	11,521	11,553	11,537	11,202	10,596	10,059	11.3	13.5	12.9	13.8
Earnings on investments	63,047	47,006	52,012	45,919	43,108	45,021	62.0	54.9	58.3	56.6
Payments	37,333	33,297	30,512	25,277	30,512	22,734	100.0	100.0	100.0	100.0
Benefits........................	34,169	30,157	27,538	24,861	22,445	20,537	91.5	90.6	90.3	98.4
Withdrawals....................	1,997	2,156	20,041	1,702	1,765	1,652	5.3	6.5	65.7	6.7
Other..........................	1,168	974	933	725	652	545	3.1	2.9	3.1	2.9
Amount of Cash FY	720,200	630,551	575,466	503,074	446,658	407,953	100.0	100.0	100.0	100.0
Cash and Deposits	39,454	36,806	39,323	39,927	28,747	26,961	5.5	5.8	6.8	7.9
Cash and Demand Deposits	3,039	2,589	2,744	1,527	3,096	2,048	0.4	0.4	0.5	0.3
Time or Savings Desposits	36,415	34,217	36,579	38,445	25,650	11,913	5.1	5.4	6.4	7.6
Securities	626,813	548,585	494,469	438,246	400,482	377,750	87.0	87.0	85.9	87.1
Governmental	208,714	155,469	140,062	128,438	118,394	112,660	29.0	24.7	24.3	25.5
Federal Government.............	208,512	155,360	139,956	128,294	118,273	112,570	29.0	24.6	24.3	25.5
U.S. Treasury	163,296	121,290	109,029	97,295	91,114	88,944	22.7	19.2	18.9	19.3
Federal Agency	45,216	34,071	30,927	31,000	27,159	23,626	6.3	5.4	5.4	6.2
State and Local Governments	201	109	106	143	122	90	. . .	. . .	. . .	0.0
Nongovernmental	418,100	393,116	354,407	309,809	282,088	265,090	58.1	62.3	61.6	61.6
Corporate Bonds	130,370	131,050	119,799	109,706	96,359	76,741	18.1	20.8	20.8	21.8
Corporate Stocks	198,723	190,830	170,536	153,476	151,943	133,288	27.6	30.3	29.6	30.5
Mortgages	31,770	22,459	26,699	16,739	19,597	27,117	4.4	3.6	4.6	3.3
Funds held in trust..............	18,079	19,614	14,095	12,303	6,194	7,335	2.5	3.1	2.4	2.4
Other securities	39,157	29,164	23,307	17,585	7,995	7,609	5.4	4.6	4.1	3.5
Other investments................	53,932	45,160	41,657	24,856	17,429	16,243	7.5	7.2	7.2	4.9
Real Property	20,227	16,081	14,083	8,869	6,239	5,523	2.8	2.6	2.4	1.8
Miscellaneous Investments	33,706	29,079	26,689	15,961	11,189	10,720	4.7	4.6	4.6	3.2

Source: U.S. Department of Commerce, Bureau of the Census, *Finances of Employee Retirement Systems of State and Local Governments.*
Key:
. . . — Not available

Table 7.26

MEMBERSHIP AND BENEFIT OPERATIONS OF STATE-ADMINISTERED EMPLOYEE RETIREMENT SYSTEMS: LAST MONTH OF FISCAL YEAR 1990-91

State	Membership, last month of fiscal year	Beneficiaries receiving periodic benefit payments				Periodic benefit payment for the month (in thousands of dollars)			
		Total (a)	Persons retired on account of age or length of service	Persons retired on account of disability	Survivors of deceased former members (no. of payees)	Total (a)	Persons retired on account of age or length of service	Persons retired on account of disability	To survivors of deceased former members
United States	11,653,036	3,357,002	2,886,903	220,052	250,047	2,436,908	2,157,307	170,723	108,878
Alabama	181,091	47,272	46,960	292	20	37,008	36,807	192	8
Alaska	47,555	12,172	11,162	309	701	17,131	16,147	544	440
Arizona	164,321	40,382	28,199	1,062	11,121	39,301	25,247	4,757	9,297
Arkansas	103,835	24,211	20,879	1,929	1,403	13,403	12,122	798	483
California	1,140,898	400,751	318,249	38,265	44,237	342,905	297,494	35,164	10,247
Colorado	119,814	37,564	31,083	4,727	1,754	35,850	28,230	4,110	3,509
Connecticut	112,419	41,842	36,424	2,115	3,303	44,620	40,831	1,674	2,116
Delaware	31,788	12,634	9,382	1,388	1,864	8,319	7,314	553	452
Florida	562,628	112,978	94,227	6,716	12,035	68,993	60,971	2,752	5,270
Georgia	294,254	55,727	46,761	3,346	5,620	49,142	43,234	2,782	3,126
Hawaii	55,604	23,941	22,373	1,294	274	19,406	18,752	579	75
Idaho	50,500	18,563	18,550	1	12	9,293	9,287	1	5
Illinois	43,868	151,732	121,677	4,932	25,123	100,205	89,441	3,430	7,334
Indiana	232,247	68,909	60,249	2,474	6,186	34,812	29,863	592	4,358
Iowa	163,549	50,452	50,288	59	105	15,938	15,770	97	70
Kansas	122,186	39,691	35,755	1,682	2,254	16,795	15,904	892	0
Kentucky	181,326	49,498	47,585	1,033	880	34,349	32,920	919	510
Louisiana	220,475	71,304	58,598	5,779	6,927	72,577	62,792	4,104	5,681
Maine	85,470	23,720	22,699	994	27	15,513	14,845	650	18
Maryland	173,907	47,270	46,923		347	49,540	48,525	0	1,016
Massachusetts	197,967	64,299	21,771	40,483	2,045	57,116	22,073	33,037	2,005
Michigan	418,498	124,627	105,631	5,884	13,112	105,036	89,545	4,789	10,702
Minnesota	275,434	66,787	57,542	1,895	7,350	44,716	41,162	1,103	2,451
Mississippi	189,989	34,615	29,025	2,081	3,509	18,594	15,560	121	1,914
Missouri	157,741	44,455	38,524	1,689	4,242	28,661	26,484	767	1,409
Montana	56,034	18,349	16,314	1,334	701	10,319	9,206	753	361
Nebraska	38,610	6,914	6,470	146	298	2,459	2,280	59	121
Nevada	56,992	12,542	11,081	673	788	12,273	11,249	582	442
New Hampshire	39,838	9,415	9,415			4,971	4,971	0	0
New Jersey	418,150	118,251	115,011	1,897	1,343	93,648	90,677	1,947	1,024
New Mexico	109,089	24,142	21,531	1,132	1,479	18,831	17,460	564	807
New York	836,474	306,791	273,900	16,837	16,054	215,690	198,182	13,027	4,482
North Carolina	390,905	92,640	75,171	8,792	8,677	61,610	52,207	5,492	3,911
North Dakota	27,548	7,272	6,590	134	548	2,902	2,688	42	172
Ohio	742,083	241,351	201,739	18,465	21,147	173,443	145,817	17,804	9,822
Oklahoma	146,671	46,676	39,542	2,068	5,066	38,581	33,449	1,788	3,344
Oregon	156,787	57,026	53,591	3,435		34,619	32,480	2,138	0
Pennsylvania	361,792	207,940	197,683	4,210	6,047	118,065	114,097	2,076	1,912
Rhode Island	36,687	15,750	14,307	748	695	16,361	15,528	399	434
South Carolina	301,412	45,249	36,430	4,964	3,855	32,860	27,793	3,054	2,013

MEMBERSHIP AND BENEFIT OPERATIONS, FISCAL YEAR 1990-91—Continued

		Benefit Operations, last month of fiscal year							
		Beneficiaries receiving periodic benefit payments				Periodic benefit payment for the month (in thousands of dollars)			
State	Membership, last month of the fiscal year	Total (a)	Persons retired on account of age or length of service	Persons retired on account of disability	Survivors of deceased former members (no. of payees)	Total (a)	Persons retired on account of age or length of service	Persons retired on account of disability	To survivors of deceased former members
South Dakota	34,256	10,881	9,165	261	1,455	4,062	3,623	117	341
Tennessee	198,820	54,789	49,113	2,355	3,321	26,449	24,384	714	1,351
Texas	812,353	167,805	138,259	8,605	20,941	118,566	108,789	5,032	4,745
Utah	97,036	19,613	18,963	650		12,244	11,871	373	0
Vermont	23,393	5,680	4,915	344	421	3,023	2,672	166	185
Virginia	380,480	61,467	52,261	8,209	997	37,097	31,870	4,876	351
Washington	232,617	73,467	73,434	11	22	53,516	53,488	9	19
West Virginia	100,814	408	241	57	110	608	423	90	95
Wisconsin	282,355	77,346	71,413	4,299	1,634	60,546	55,880	4,215	451
Wyoming	50,289	9,868	9,868			4,917	4,917	0	0

Source: U.S. Department of Commerce, Bureau of the Census, Finances of Employee-Retirement Systems of State and Local Governments 1990-91.

(a) Detail may not add to totals due to rounding.

Table 7.27
MEMBERSHIP AND BENEFIT OPERATIONS OF STATE-ADMINISTERED EMPLOYEE RETIREMENT SYSTEMS: LAST MONTH OF FISCAL YEAR 1991-92

State	Membership, last month of the fiscal year	Benefit Operations, last month of fiscal year							
		Beneficiaries receiving periodic benefit payments				Periodic benefit payment for the month (in thousands of dollars)			
		Total (a)	Persons retired on account of age or length of service	Persons retired on account of disability	Survivors of deceased former members (no. of payees)	Total (a)	Persons retired on account of age or length of service	Persons retired on account of disability	To survivors of deceased former members
United States	11,844,340	3,414,299	2,992,401	178,074	243,824	2,566,152	2,312,671	140,260	112,491
Alabama	183,663	49,692	49,393	279	20	38,914	38,715	191	8
Alaska	49,288	12,627	11,512	342	773	16,254	15,147	614	493
Arizona	164,388	40,607	28,387	1,074	11,146	39,848	25,745	4,774	9,329
Arkansas	121,653	24,370	21,173	2,062	1,135	14,560	13,021	1,059	480
California	1,173,027	424,214	336,948	40,058	47,208	402,573	356,190	39,436	6,947
Colorado	151,479	39,183	32,438	4,998	1,747	38,713	30,291	4,649	3,773
Connecticut	112,062	45,024	40,153	2,348	2,523	52,509	48,811	2,040	1,658
Delaware	31,694	14,266	10,868	1,449	1,949	9,638	8,561	582	495
Florida	566,144	119,741	100,618	6,796	12,327	77,323	68,647	2,956	5,720
Georgia	292,589	57,912	47,651	3,981	6,280	53,767	47,121	3,127	3,519
Hawaii	57,401	21,779	20,244	952	583	20,802	19,985	733	84
Idaho	59,541	18,563	18,550	1	12	8,539	8,402	1	5
Illinois	460,414	160,561	129,423	4,864	26,274	112,681	101,022	3,767	7,892
Indiana	230,553	71,967	63,037	2,633	6,297	35,884	30,807	620	4,456
Iowa	157,455	51,827	51,655	62	110	16,924	16,736	110	78
Kansas	120,570	38,300	36,016	0	2,284	13,832	13,318	0	515
Kentucky	190,874	51,770	49,795	1,068	907	37,076	35,471	1,025	579
Louisiana	271,860	72,550	63,536	3,060	5,954	29,960	24,759	1,812	3,390
Maine	49,899	24,613	19,827	1,258	3,528	17,321	14,501	1,251	1,570
Maryland	166,539	53,784	53,780	0	4	53,187	53,180	0	7
Massachusetts	177,708	70,322	59,256	3,832	7,234	57,959	49,127	3,059	5,773
Michigan	449,464	140,087	125,220	6,940	7,927	114,679	102,763	5,731	6,185
Minnesota	277,212	70,404	60,646	1,988	7,770	49,828	45,976	1,199	2,653
Mississippi	189,981	34,616	29,016	2,080	3,520	18,592	15,638	1,107	1,847
Missouri	164,341	45,344	40,033	1,652	3,659	30,678	28,770	844	1,063
Montana	57,780	18,499	16,540	1,306	653	11,259	10,191	701	367
Nebraska	38,610	6,914	6,470	146	298	2,459	2,280	59	121
Nevada	56,992	13,518	11,947	715	856	11,651	10,059	478	514
New Hampshire	39,838	9,415	9,415	0	0	4,971	4,971	0	0
New Jersey	434,130	130,229	115,952	2,086	12,191	125,774	112,837	2,397	10,539
New Mexico	116,542	25,434	22,740	1,137	1,557	21,071	19,603	601	867
New York	877,958	327,003	322,277	1,565	3,161	258,813	256,120	1,187	1,506
North Carolina	399,942	97,103	79,321	8,682	9,100	65,863	56,105	5,589	4,170
North Dakota	26,872	7,527	6,795	149	583	3,611	3,316	51	244
Ohio	806,164	243,168	199,318	20,978	22,872	202,682	168,864	23,088	10,730
Oklahoma	139,772	49,777	41,309	2,164	6,304	43,634	36,845	1,941	4,848
Oregon	161,617	58,751	55,212	3,539	0	33,520	31,479	2,041	0
Pennsylvania	364,483	183,689	164,482	8,285	10,922	114,381	106,519	4,270	3,591
Rhode Island	32,046	13,616	13,391	0	225	17,154	17,022	0	132
South Carolina	311,312	47,519	38,106	5,238	4,175	36,384	30,736	3,303	2,346

MEMBERSHIP AND BENEFIT OPERATIONS, FISCAL YEAR 1991-92—Continued

		Benefit Operations, last month of fiscal year							
		Beneficiaries receiving periodic benefit payments				Periodic benefit payment for the month (in thousands of dollars)			
State	Membership, last month of the fiscal year	Total (a)	Persons retired on account of age or length of service	Persons retired on account of disability	Survivors of deceased former members (no. of payees)	Total (a)	Persons retired on account of age or length of service	Persons retired on account of disability	To survivors of deceased former members
South Dakota	35,474	10,885	9,173	263	1,449	4,797	4,263	123	411
Tennessee	166,121	54,789	49,113	2,355	3,321	27,000	24,200	1,200	1,600
Texas	817,272	59,490	48,257	10,744	489	23,492	22,749	730	13
Utah	104,093	20,047	19,387	660	0	14,076	13,662	413	0
Vermont	24,080	5,850	5,041	377	432	3,282	2,890	192	200
Virginia	306,383	69,609	59,858	8,688	1,063	51,798	45,755	5,671	372
Washington	260,555	79,621	79,588	11	22	28,373	28,344	9	19
West Virginia	72,418	38,476	36,355	735	1,386	20,917	19,521	512	884
Wisconsin	290,347	79,091	73,023	4,474	1,594	71,627	66,111	5,018	498
Wyoming	33,740	10,156	10,156	0	0	5,525	5,525	0	0

Source: U.S. Department of Commerce, Bureau of the Census, *Finances of Employee-Retirement Systems of State and Local Governments 1991-92*.

(a) Detail may not add to totals due to rounding.

Table 7.28
FINANCES OF STATE-ADMINISTERED EMPLOYEE RETIREMENT SYSTEMS, BY STATE: FISCAL 1991-92
(In thousands of dollars)

| | | Receipts during fiscal year | | | | Payments during fiscal year | | | |
| | | Government contributions | | | | | | | |
State	Total	Employee contributions	From states	From local governments	Earnings on investments	Total	Benefits	Withdrawals	Other
United States	$101,632,057	$13,453,403	$13,611,322	$11,520,759	$63,046,573	$37,332,994	$34,168,536	$1,996,592	$1,167,866
Alabama	1,562,772	1,562,772	310,584	56,128	978,086	465,518	428,806	29,264	7,448
Alaska	927,347	927,347	114,560	99,288	591,764	258,438	230,239	14,542	13,657
Arizona	1,043,523	1,043,523	23,280	83,702	836,682	460,307	371,483	38,356	50,468
Arkansas	641,046	641,046	158,236	23,009	421,725	198,325	182,520	4,862	10,943
California	13,894,063	13,894,063	811,509	1,125,728	9,545,570	5,376,693	4,927,049	266,986	182,658
Colorado	1,646,647	1,646,647	179,192	269,679	941,688	536,243	487,288	31,810	17,145
Connecticut	1,102,116	1,102,116	393,359	22,641	519,919	628,207	615,458	11,912	837
Delaware	281,668	281,668	67,063	867	195,631	135,822	123,739	1,444	10,639
Florida	4,331,179	4,331,179	584,087	1,752,024	1,974,090	919,692	909,970	2,668	7,054
Georgia	2,466,088	2,466,088	595,412	145,230	1,430,681	736,268	648,408	60,194	27,666
Hawaii	727,239	727,239	77,194	43,233	540,865	305,259	249,240	34,954	21,065
Idaho	268,062	268,062	112,826	0	89,812	118,649	105,153	11,010	2,486
Illinois	3,821,407	3,821,407	474,284	328,331	2,249,146	1,559,880	1,395,479	78,836	85,565
Indiana	1,271,959	1,271,959	304,885	123,386	681,819	467,212	433,015	26,505	7,692
Iowa	720,259	720,259	42,601	132,224	431,094	249,902	206,920	24,223	18,759
Kansas	599,398	599,398	78,284	13,263	392,443	187,827	150,809	19,266	17,752
Kentucky	1,381,967	1,381,967	370,103	88,841	635,096	513,796	482,189	18,845	12,762
Louisiana	1,690,387	1,690,387	631,993	51,482	665,166	856,404	781,390	51,406	23,608
Maine	388,339	388,339	172,090	0	137,770	214,340	201,825	12,515	0
Maryland	2,073,334	2,073,334	622,477	24,605	1,317,211	688,019	638,240	49,779	0
Massachusetts	1,324,105	1,324,105	694,358	14,400	264,253	819,200	695,369	122,072	1,759
Michigan	2,574,407	2,574,407	636,470	397,579	1,310,051	1,409,734	1,375,905	6,347	27,482
Minnesota	2,302,670	2,302,670	92,232	297,217	1,632,197	646,691	590,820	31,744	24,127
Mississippi	877,981	877,981	252,314	127,475	331,983	308,907	243,869	35,948	29,090
Missouri	1,560,850	1,560,850	181,139	211,456	980,554	431,395	381,698	25,710	23,987
Montana	331,283	331,283	25,870	58,662	172,293	148,920	134,508	12,068	2,344
Nebraska	157,751	157,751	59,931	45,318	5,678	49,584	39,167	6,684	3,733
Nevada	750,071	750,071	90,855	238,633	402,392	177,730	164,304	5,876	7,550
New Hampshire	166,198	166,198	29,151	14,168	68,367	74,646	59,650	12,638	2,358
New Jersey	3,420,635	3,420,635	473,507	292,956	2,008,982	1,631,492	1,509,285	60,371	61,836
New Mexico	806,940	806,940	68,007	135,757	439,205	293,552	252,178	33,846	7,528
New York	8,064,437	8,064,437	21,396	767,396	6,928,943	3,405,880	3,235,050	104,954	65,876
North Carolina	2,678,139	2,678,139	421,198	110,501	1,672,170	844,334	771,679	68,545	4,110
North Dakota	148,225	148,225	9,336	20,964	89,653	51,799	40,927	6,056	4,816
Ohio	8,847,235	8,847,235	609,151	1,644,044	5,271,538	3,122,547	2,935,248	119,027	68,272
Oklahoma	1,125,065	1,125,065	271,026	64,028	601,930	568,964	525,281	24,378	19,305
Oregon	2,119,517	2,119,517	142,886	284,065	1,458,744	567,864	465,488	29,406	72,970
Pennsylvania	4,989,688	4,989,688	866,948	492,171	3,078,709	1,775,230	1,660,931	26,897	87,402
Rhode Island	455,013	455,013	20,791	54,236	302,852	218,884	205,369	5,498	8,017
South Carolina	1,442,017	1,442,017	270,054	66,578	829,020	484,484	437,382	40,455	6,647
South Dakota	238,349	238,349	15,032	22,230	161,962	62,337	54,688	5,662	1,987
Tennessee	1,372,449	1,372,449	254,494	32,495	986,220	355,473	331,777	23,696	0
Texas	5,074,381	5,074,381	1,132,862	251,790	2,466,365	2,145,099	1,850,976	258,898	35,225
Utah	596,826	596,826	66,577	134,264	363,850	188,925	168,281	14,466	6,178
Vermont	135,725	135,725	32,159	2,685	87,437	46,699	38,878	670	7,151
Virginia	1,889,777	1,889,777	239,262	455,944	1,135,967	688,075	597,148	35,345	55,582
Washington	1,987,061	1,987,061	91,982	291,154	1,198,868	791,236	749,596	40,429	1,211
West Virginia	420,381	420,381	162,721	18,837	155,153	266,841	252,296	12,599	1,946
Wisconsin	4,677,499	4,677,499	221,591	542,593	3,898,405	799,689	764,600	27,536	7,553
Wyoming	258,582	258,582	34,003	47,502	166,574	79,982	66,968	9,394	3,620

FINANCES OF STATE-ADMINISTERED EMPLOYEE RETIREMENT SYSTEMS, BY STATE: FISCAL 1991-92—Continued
(In thousands of dollars)

State	Total	Cash and deposits	Cash and security holdings at end of fiscal year				
			Governmental securities				
			Federal securities			State and local	Nongovernmental securities
			Total	U.S. Treasury	Federal agency		
United States	$720,199,996	$39,454,353	$208,512,049	$163,296,219	$45,215,830	$201,451	$418,099,702
Alabama............	9,904,826	1,126,514	160,565	160,565	0	0	8,557,997
Alaska.............	5,057,663	22,746	1,315,238	1,228,778	86,460	0	3,531,152
Arizona............	11,216,823	922,381	4,256,544	3,820,035	436,509	0	6,035,074
Arkansas	4,716,171	394,218	1,164,879	1,058,775	106,104	13,125	3,141,641
California	103,592,764	4,669,335	19,756,356	16,551,500	3,204,856	0	70,898,994
Colorado	11,266,471	340,925	928,865	883,820	45,045	30,000	9,067,175
Connecticut	8,275,981	549,307	760,053	727,808	32,245	13,214	6,733,928
Delaware	1,906,017	154,569	191,688	191,688	0	0	647,226
Florida	21,920,312	731,578	5,783,014	2,485,124	3,297,890	0	15,405,720
Georgia............	15,864,955	398,610	5,607,326	5,586,388	20,938	0	9,832,144
Hawaii	4,567,517	389,275	663,862	265,545	398,317	0	3,057,223
Idaho	1,908,688	98,053	756,891	0	756,891	0	875,765
Illinois	21,940,416	1,436,842	1,968,335	1,340,598	627,737	354	15,456,149
Indiana	6,990,985	758,369	3,672,612	2,228,980	1,443,632	1,234	2,558,510
Iowa	5,866,767	90,703	18,630	12,002	6,628	500	4,789,854
Kansas	3,741,427	51,768	547,774	96,757	451,017	0	2,695,655
Kentucky	8,397,216	1,121,877	1,819,114	1,727,043	92,071	0	5,145,126
Louisiana	9,560,282	832,952	4,208,202	2,567,609	1,640,593	0	4,409,345
Maine	2,088,021	152,350	124,434	124,434	0	0	1,759,601
Maryland	12,492,147	164,280	0	0	0	0	103,448
Massachusetts	7,891,474	86,736	55,825	44,570	11,255	1,226	4,069,971
Michigan	20,975,481	4,004,326	3,480,571	3,480,571	0	0	11,516,984
Minnesota	14,369,421	115,307	264,950	262,196	2,754	0	11,313,388
Mississippi	5,182,662	789,060	2,220,723	1,581,822	638,901	0	2,172,879
Missouri	11,176,440	1,113,278	3,479,784	750,539	2,729,245	6,933	6,355,088
Montana...........	1,915,752	50,087	37,930	37,930	0	0	1,757,836
Nebraska	1,298,531	15,906	0	0	0	0	109,451
Nevada	4,230,896	250,637	1,434,783	1,313,429	121,354	0	2,164,097
New Hampshire	1,303,637	119,903	156,887	156,887	0	0	1,016,482
New Jersey.........	26,243,516	31	861,824	0	861,824	0	25,381,661
New Mexico........	4,839,088	247,653	1,590,061	1,400,368	189,693	0	3,001,374
New York	69,214,213	1,537,935	17,169,183	16,582,072	587,111	0	47,093,193
North Carolina	19,277,649	5,453,109	5,523,715	5,523,715	0	0	8,046,111
North Dakota	989,388	12,647	322	0	322	0	963,039
Ohio	58,278,670	1,829,930	30,279,284	21,736,614	8,542,670	2,150	22,562,520
Oklahoma	5,473,204	456,383	1,560,926	605,009	955,917	109,080	3,230,648
Oregon	8,094,470	824,820	1,291,703	1,220,088	71,615	0	4,380,878
Pennsylvania	28,813,653	1,230,386	8,545,341	5,763,002	2,782,339	0	16,995,367
Rhode Island	2,448,905	36,283	1,502,514	1,502,514	0	0	910,108
South Carolina	12,681,888	1,539,906	8,629,122	4,815,820	3,813,302	0	2,512,860
South Dakota	1,662,367	249,824	366,860	266,108	100,752	0	1,024,466
Tennessee	9,708,682	620,053	2,707,898	64,429	2,643,469	0	6,380,731
Texas..............	73,927,021	783,690	51,326,161	44,662,653	6,663,508	0	21,363,854
Utah	4,303,068	274,143	1,102,232	742,529	359,703	0	2,408,434
Vermont	740,717	89,035	79,528	74,658	4,870	0	523,539
Virginia............	12,610,664	1,207,626	1,359,184	1,359,184	0	0	9,332,159
Washington	15,159,862	1,928,251	3,871,191	3,847,504	23,687	0	7,098,701
West Virginia	1,817,538	45,435	1,591,559	835,993	755,566	0	153,009
Wisconsin..........	22,526,373	118,173	4,017,893	3,308,853	709,040	23,635	18,106,691
Wyoming	1,769,317	17,148	299,713	299,713	0	0	1,452,456

Source: U.S. Department of Commerce, Bureau of the Census, *Finances of Employee-Retirement Systems of State and Local Governments.*

Note: Detail may not add to totals due to rounding.

Table 7.29
COMPARATIVE STATISTICS FOR STATE-ADMINISTERED PUBLIC EMPLOYEE RETIREMENT SYSTEMS: FISCAL 1990-91

State	Percent of receipts paid by			Annual benefit payments as a percentage of		Average benefit payments (a)	Investment earnings as a percentage of cash and security holdings	Percentage distribution of cash and security holdings			
									Governmental securities		
	Employee contribution	State government	Local government	Annual receipts	Cash and security holdings			Cash and deposits	Federal	State and local	Nongovernmental securities
United States	14.7	16.9	13.5	38.9	5.3	$ 726	7.5	5.8	24.6	0.0	62.3
Alabama	13.9	19.9	3.6	29.8	4.7	783	9.9	11.4	1.6	0.0	86.4
Alaska	19.0	15.2		39.5	5.4	1,407	7.1	1.0	26.6	0.0	67.7
Arizona	9.9	2.0	13.3	44.9	4.1	973	7.4	7.6	38.9	0.0	53.5
Arkansas	6.7	30.2	7.7	35.0	4.3	554	7.2	16.8	26.3	0.3	56.5
California	17.2	9.6	4.0	34.8	4.8	856	8.4	5.1	18.2	0.0	69.5
Colorado	18.9	11.1	12.5	38.4	4.5	954	5.7	2.6	13.9	0.3	76.2
Connecticut	14.5	40.2	21.0	51.5	7.1	1,066	6.0	6.4	9.2	0.1	82.0
Delaware	9.1	35.1	2.0	42.4	5.2	658	6.8	7.9	14.2	0.0	63.6
Florida	0.7	21.6	64.8	33.4	4.0	611	1.5	8.6	25.5	0.0	65.6
Georgia	13.0	27.4	6.6	26.9	4.3	882	8.4	4.9	47.0	0.0	47.9
Hawaii	12.7	11.6	6.5	57.4	7.2	811	8.6	6.5	18.1	0.0	66.5
Idaho	22.3	13.7	25.6	44.9	7.1	501	6.0	3.9	36.4	0.0	49.8
Illinois	25.7	18.7	10.2	499.8	6.9	660	6.3	5.5	9.4	0.0	71.9
Indiana	13.4	29.9	10.3	35.9	6.8	505	8.7	2.8	59.8	0.0	37.4
Iowa	15.9	5.7	17.7	33.1	4.4	316	8.0	1.5	0.3	0.0	77.7
Kansas	34.3	19.8	7.7	65.4	6.2	423	3.6	3.3	20.0	0.0	74.7
Kentucky	20.6	26.4	6.1	36.5	5.8	694	7.5	20.5	20.7	0.0	55.8
Louisiana	20.3	30.9	4.5	53.2	10.1	1,018	8.4	9.9	36.8	0.0	52.0
Maine	22.3	52.5	0.0	60.3	10.0	654	4.2	4.1	11.9	0.0	81.6
Maryland	6.2	33.1	1.1	40.4	6.5	1,048	9.6	0.0	0	0.0	5.6
Massachusetts	30.5	54.2	1.8	65.1	10.7	888	2.2	1.2	0.7	0.0	51.2
Michigan	7.7	24.9	12.4	50.6	6.5	843	7.0	20.3	17.0	0.0	53.3
Minnesota	16.2	5.9	17.0	35.0	0.0	670	0.1	1.3	1.8	0.0	78.3
Mississippi	18.9	28.7	14.5	35.2	6.0	537	6.4	15.2	42.8	0.0	41.9
Missouri	13.5	14.7	15.1	30.6	4.2	645	7.7	7.4	19.3	0.1	71.8
Montana	22.4	7.2	17.8	45.5	7.6	562	8.8	3.3	3.7	0.0	87.8
Nebraska	25.5	6.4	24.9	220.5	3.5	356	6.9	6.1	28.2	0.0	65.6
Nevada	1.5	11.3	39.2	27.3	4.5	979	7.9	1.6	35.5	0.0	53.1
New Hampshire	32.8	17.5	8.5	44.9	5.7	528	5.2	9.2	12.0	0.0	78.0
New Jersey	15.4	23.7	11.7	35.0	5.5	792	7.7	0.3	5.6	0.1	94.0
New Mexico	27.3	11.8	23.0	47.2	6.2	780	5.0	5.2	33.4	0.0	61.0
New York	5.2	0.2	8.6	91.9	8.7	703	8.2	2.2	22.9	0.0	70.5
North Carolina	18.0	21.2	4.1	31.2	4.5	665	8.2	27.8	28.8	0.0	41.5
North Dakota	22.7	7.3	15.4	38.7	5.3	399	7.5	1.1	0.0	0.0	96.8
Ohio	17.1	7.3	21.1	38.3	5.5	719	7.9	2.5	52.3	0.0	38.0
Oklahoma	19.4	29.1	5.5	58.8	10.8	827	8.5	7.1	35.1	0.0	54.9
Oregon	16.4	10.3	20.7	41.1	4.8	607	6.1	5.4	7.9	0.0	72.8
Pennsylvania	13.6	25.8	15.3	42.1	5.5	568	5.9	2.1	28.1	0.0	63.9
Rhode Island	26.6	0.0	17.0	77.8	10.0	1,039	5.2	16.8	35.1	0.0	47.6
South Carolina	19.7	19.6	4.7	33.1	4.0	726	6.7	4.8	73.7	0.0	21.4

COMPARATIVE STATISTICS: FISCAL 1990-91—Continued

State	Percent of receipts paid by			Annual benefit payments as a percentage of		Average benefit payments (a)	Investment earnings as a percentage of cash and security holdings	Percentage distribution of cash and security holdings			
									Governmental securities		
	Employee contribution	State government	Local government	Annual receipts	Cash and security holdings			Cash and deposits	Federal	State and local	Nongovernmental securities
South Dakota	18.1	7.3	10.9	26.5	3.5	375	8.4	15.5	24.8	0.0	57.9
Tennessee	8.8	22.5	2.6	28.9	3.8	483	8.8	7.9	29.5	0.0	62.6
Texas	19.8	19.2	4.7	32.6	5.3	707	9.1	1.4	38.4	0.0	59.8
Utah	9.2	8.9	29.2	42.4	4.7	624	5.9	6.0	27.9	0.0	53.2
Vermont	11.7	33.0	2.5	42.1	5.7	532	7.2	4.5	11.3	0.0	77.5
Virginia	3.3	13.2	23.8	27.3	4.4	604	9.7	11.7	12.3	0.0	74.9
Washington	18.0	22.9	8.3	36.4	5.0	728	7.0	13.8	18.7	0.0	55.0
West Virginia	14.4	39.0	26.0	44.7	16.4	1,490	7.6	0.2	74.9	0.0	24.9
Wisconsin	0.6	10.3	24.7	36.1	3.7	783	6.6	0.5	17.0	0.1	81.3
Wyoming	4.5	17.0	22.6	38.1	4.6	498	6.7	0.3	12.8	0.0	86.8

Source: U.S. Department of Commerce, Bureau of the Census, Finances of Employee-Retirement Systems of State and Local Governments 1990-91.

(a) Average benefit payment for the last month of fiscal year.

Table 7.30
COMPARATIVE STATISTICS FOR STATE-ADMINISTERED PUBLIC EMPLOYEE RETIREMENT SYSTEMS: FISCAL 1991-92

State	Percent of receipts paid by			Annual benefit payments as a percentage of		Average benefit payments (a)	Investment earnings as a percentage of cash and security holdings	Percentage distribution of cash and security holdings			
									Governmental securities		
	Employee contribution	State government	Local government	Annual receipts	Cash and security holdings			Cash and deposits	Federal	State and local	Nongovernmental securities
United States	13.2	24.7	13.4	36.7	5.2	$ 729	8.8	5.5	29.0	0.0	58.1
Alabama	13.9	23.5	19.9	29.8	4.7	783	9.9	11.4	1.6	0.0	86.4
Alaska	13.1	23.1	12.4	27.9	5.1	1,287	11.7	0.4	.26	0.0	69.8
Arizona	9.6	10.3	2.2	44.1	4.1	981	7.5	8.2	37.9	0.0	53.8
Arkansas	5.9	28.3	24.7	30.9	4.2	597	8.9	8.4	24.7	0.3	66.6
California	17.4	13.9	5.8	38.7	5.2	949	9.2	4.5	19.1	0.0	68.4
Colorado	15.6	27.3	10.9	32.6	4.8	988	8.4	3.0	8.2	0.3	80.5
Connecticut	15.1	37.1	35.7	57.0	7.6	1,166	6.3	6.6	9.2	0.2	81.4
Delaware	6.4	24.1	23.8	48.2	7.1	676	10.3	8.1	10.1	0.0	34.0
Florida	0.5	53.9	13.5	21.2	4.2	646	9.0	3.3	26.4	0.0	70.3
Georgia	12.0	30.0	24.1	29.9	4.6	928	9.0	2.5	35.3	0.0	62.0
Hawaii	9.1	16.6	10.6	42.0	6.7	955	11.8	8.5	14.5	0.0	66.9
Idaho	24.4	42.1	42.1	44.3	6.2	460	4.7	5.1	39.7	0.0	45.9
Illinois	20.1	21.0	12.4	40.8	7.1	702	10.3	6.5	9	0.0	70.4
Indiana	12.7	33.7	24.0	36.7	6.7	499	9.8	10.8	52.5	0.0	36.6
Iowa	15.9	24.3	5.9	34.7	4.3	327	7.3	1.5	0.3	0.0	81.6
Kansas	19.3	15.3	13.1	31.3	5.0	361	10.5	1.4	14.6	0.0	72.0
Kentucky	20.8	33.2	26.8	37.2	6.1	716	7.6	13.4	21.7	0.0	61.3
Louisiana	20.2	40.4	37.4	50.7	9.0	413	7.0	8.7	44.0	0.0	46.1
Maine	20.2	44.3	44.3	55.2	10.3	704	6.6	7.3	6.0	0.0	84.3
Maryland	5.3	31.2	30.0	33.2	5.5	989	10.5	1.3	0.0	0.0	0.8
Massachusetts	26.5	53.5	52.4	61.9	10.4	824	3.3	1.1	0.7	0.0	51.6
Michigan	8.9	40.2	24.7	54.8	6.7	819	6.2	19.1	16.6	0.0	54.9
Minnesota	12.2	16.9	4.0	28.1	4.5	708	11.4	0.8	1.8	0.0	78.7
Mississippi	18.9	43.3	28.7	35.2	6.0	537	6.4	15.2	42.8	0.0	41.9
Missouri	12.0	25.2	11.6	27.6	3.9	677	8.8	10.0	31.1	0.1	56.9
Montana	22.5	25.5	7.8	45.0	7.8	609	9.0	2.6	2.0	0.0	91.8
Nebraska	29.7	66.7	38.0	31.4	3.8	356	0.4	1.2	0.0	0.0	8.4
Nevada	2.4	43.9	12.1	23.7	4.2	862	9.5	5.9	33.9	0.0	51.1
New Hampshire	32.8	26.1	17.5	44.9	5.7	528	5.2	9.2	12.0	0.0	78.0
New Jersey	18.9	22.4	13.8	47.7	6.2	966	7.7	0.0	3.3	0.1	96.7
New Mexico	20.3	25.3	8.4	36.4	6.1	828	9.1	5.1	32.9	0.0	62.0
New York	4.3	9.8	0.3	42.2	4.9	791	10.0	2.2	24.8	0.0	68.0
North Carolina	17.7	19.9	15.7	31.5	4.4	678	8.7	28.3	28.7	0.0	41.7
North Dakota	19.1	20.4	6.3	34.9	5.2	480	9.1	1.3	0.0	0.0	97.3
Ohio	14.9	25.5	6.9	35.3	5.4	834	9.0	3.1	52.0	0.0	38.7
Oklahoma	16.7	29.8	24.1	50.6	10.4	877	11.0	8.3	28.5	2.0	59.0
Oregon	11.0	20.1	6.7	26.8	7.0	571	18.0	10.2	16.0	0.0	54.1
Pennsylvania	11.1	27.2	17.4	35.6	6.2	623	10.7	4.3	29.7	0.0	59.0
Rhode Island	17.0	16.5	4.6	48.1	8.9	1,260	12.4	1.5	61.4	0.0	37.2
South Carolina	19.2	23.3	18.7	33.6	3.8	766	6.5	12.1	68.0	0.0	19.8

COMPARATIVE STATISTICS: FISCAL 1991-92—Continued

| State | Percent of receipts paid by | | | Annual benefit payments as a percentage of | | Average benefit payments (a) | Investment earnings as a percentage of cash and security holdings | Percentage distribution of cash and security holdings | | | |
	Employee contribution	State government	Local government	Annual receipts	Cash and security holdings			Cash and deposits	Federal	Governmental securities State and local	Nongovernmental securities
South Dakota	16.4	15.6	6.3	26.2	3.7	441	9.7	15.0	22.1	0.0	61.6
Tennessee	7.2	20.9	18.5	25.9	3.7	493	10.2	6.4	27.9	0.0	65.7
Texas	24.1	27.3	22.3	42.3	2.9	395	3.3	1.1	69.4	0.0	28.9
Utah	5.4	33.7	11.2	31.7	4.4	702	8.5	6.4	25.6	0.0	56.0
Vermont	9.9	25.7	23.7	34.4	6.3	561	11.8	12.0	10.7	0.0	70.7
Virginia	3.1	36.8	12.7	36.4	5.5	744	9.0	9.6	10.8	0.0	74.0
Washington	20.4	19.3	4.6	39.8	5.2	356	7.9	12.7	25.5	0.0	46.8
West Virginia	19.9	43.2	38.7	63.5	14.7	544	8.5	2.5	87.6	0.0	8.4
Wisconsin	0.3	16.3	4.7	17.1	3.6	906	17.3	0.5	17.8	0.1	80.4
Wyoming	4.1	31.5	13.1	30.9	4.5	544	9.4	1.0	16.9	0.0	82.1

Source: U.S. Department of Commerce, Bureau of the Census, *Finances of Employee-Retirement Systems of State and Local Governments 1991-92.*

(a) Average benefit payment for the last month of fiscal year.

The Council of State Governments **467**

TABLE 7.31
STATE REGULATION OF SELECTED NON-HEALTH OCCUPATIONS AND PROFESSIONS: 1993

State or other jurisdiction	Accountant, Certified Public	Architect	Auctioneer	Barber	Cosmetologist	Embalmer (a)	Engineer, Professional (b)	Funeral Director	Insurance Agent	Insurance Broker	Landscape Architect	Polygraph Examiner	Real Estate Agent	Real Estate Broker	Surveyor, Land
Alabama	L	L	L	...	L	L	L	L	L	L	L	L	L	L	L
Alaska	L	L	...	L	L	L	L	L	L	...	...	...	L	L	L
Arizona	L	L	...	L	L	L	L	L	L	L	L	L	L	L	L
Arkansas	L	L	L	L	L	L	L	L	L	...	L	L	L	L	L
California	L	L	...	L	L	L	L	L	L	...	L	...	L	L	L
Colorado	L	L	...	L	L	...	L	...	L	L	...	...	L	L	L
Connecticut	L	L	...	L	L	L	L	L	L	L	C	...	L	L	L
Delaware	L	L	...	L	L	...	L	L	L	L	L	...	L	L	L
Florida	L	L	L	L	L	L	L	L	L	...	L	...	L	L	L
Georgia	L	L	L	L	L	L	L	L	L	...	L	L	L	L	L
Hawaii	L	L	...	L	L	L	L	L	L	...	L	...	L	L	L
Idaho	L	L	...	L	L	L	L	L	L	L	L	...	L	L	L
Illinois	L	L	...	L	L	L	L	L	L	...	L	L	L	L	L
Indiana	L	L	L	L	L	...	L	L	L	L	...	L	L	L	L
Iowa	L	L	...	L	L	...	L	L	L	...	C	L	L	L	L
Kansas	L	L	...	L	L	L	L	L	L	L	...	L	L	L	L
Kentucky	L	L	L	L	L	L	L	L	L	...	L	L	L	L	L
Louisiana	L	L	L	L	L	L	L	L	L	L	L	L	L	L	C
Maine	L	L	L	L	L	L	L	L	L	L	L	L	L	L	C
Maryland	L	L	...	L	L	...	L	L	L	L	L	...	L	L	L
Massachusetts	L	L	...	L	L	L	L	L	L	L	...	L	L	L	L
Michigan	L	L	...	L	L	...	L	L	L	...	C	L	L	L	L
Minnesota	L	L	...	L	L	...	L	L	L	...	L	...	L	L	L
Mississippi	L	L	...	L	L	L	L	L	L	...	L	...	L	L	L
Missouri	L	L	...	L	L	L	L	L	L	L	C	...	L	L	L
Montana	L	L	...	L	L	...	L	L	L	...	L	L	L	L	L
Nebraska	L	L	...	L	L	L	L	L	L	L	L	L	L	L	L
Nevada	L	L	...	L	L	L	L	L	L	L	L	L	L	L	L
New Hampshire	L	L	L	L	L	L	L	L	L	L	...	...	L	L	L
New Jersey	L	L	...	L	L	...	L	L	L	...	C	...	L	L	L
New Mexico	L	L	...	L	L	...	L	L	L	L	L	L	L	L	L
New York	L	L	...	L	L	L	L	L	L	L	L	...	L	L	L
North Carolina	L	L	L	L	L	L	L	L	L	L	C	L	L	L	L
North Dakota	L	L	L	L	L	L	L	L	L	L	...	L	L	L	L
Ohio	L	L	L	L	L	L	L	L	L	L	L	...	L	L	L
Oklahoma	L	L	...	L	L	L	L	L	L	...	L	L	L	L	L
Oregon	L	L	...	L	L	L	L	L	L	...	L	L	L	L	L
Pennsylvania	L	L	L	L	L	...	L	L	L	L	L	...	L	L	L
Rhode Island	L	L	L	L	L	L	L	L	L	L	L	...	L	L	L
South Carolina	L	L	L	L	L	L	L	L	L	L	L	L	L	L	L
South Dakota	L	L	...	L	L	L	L	L	L	L	L	L	L	L	L
Tennessee	L	L	L	L	L	L	L	L	L	...	L	L	L	L	L
Texas	L	L	L	L	L	L	L	L	L	L	L	L	L	L	L
Utah	L	L	...	L	L	...	L	L	L	L	L	L	L	L	L
Vermont	L	L	L	L	L	L	L	L	L	L	...	L	L	L	L
Virginia	L	L	L	L	L	...	L	L	L	...	C	L	L	L	L
Washington	L	L	R	L	L	L	L	L	L	L	C	...	L	L	L
West Virginia	L	L	L	L	L	L	L	L	L	L	L	L	L	L	L
Wisconsin	L	L	...	L	L	...	L	L	L	L	...	...	L	L	L
Wyoming	L	L	...	L	L	L	L	L	L	L	L	...	L	L	L
Dist. of Columbia	L	L	...	L	L	...	L	L	L	L	...	...	L	L	...

Sources: Council on Licensure, Enforcement and Regulation, *Issues in Professional Regulation,* 1993, and various national associations of state boards.

Key:
C — Certification
L — Licensure
R — Registration

(a) In some states, embalmers are not licensed separately from funeral directors; embalming is part of the funeral director's job.

(b) In addition to licensing professional engineers, some states regulate engineers by specific areas of expertise, such as civil engineers.

Table 7.32
STATE REGULATION OF HEALTH OCCUPATIONS AND PROFESSIONS: 1993

State or other jurisdiction	Acupuncturist	Chiropractor	Counselor, Professional	Counselor, Alcoholism	Counselor, Drug	Counselor, Pastoral	Counselor, Substance Abuse	Dentist	Dental Assistant	Dental Hygenist	Denturist	Dietitian	Emergency Medical Technician (a)	Hearing Aid Dealer & Fitter	Homeopath
Alabama	...	L	L	...	...	...	...	L	...	L	...	L	L	L	...
Alaska	L	L	...	...	...	...	...	L	...	L	...	...	L	L	L
Arizona	...	L	C	...	...	...	C	L	C	L	L	L	L	L	L
Arkansas	...	L	L	...	...	...	...	L	R	L	...	...	L	L	...
California	L	L	...	...	...	...	...	L	L	L	...	C	L	L	...
Colorado	R	L	L	C	C	...	L	L	...	L	...	...	L	L	...
Connecticut	...	L	...	...	C	...	...	L	...	L	...	...	L	L	L
Delaware	...	L	...	C	...	...	...	L	...	L	...	...	L	L	...
Florida	L	L	L	...	...	...	...	L	...	L	...	C	L	L	...
Georgia	L	L	L	...	...	...	...	L	...	L	...	...	L	L	...
Hawaii	L	L	...	...	...	...	C	L	...	L	...	...	L	L	...
Idaho	...	L	L	...	...	...	...	L	...	L	L	L	L	L	...
Illinois	...	L	L	...	...	...	...	L	...	L	...	...	L	L	...
Indiana	...	L	...	...	...	...	...	L	...	L	...	...	L	L	L
Iowa	...	L	...	...	...	...	...	L	...	L	...	...	L	L	...
Kansas	...	L	C	...	...	...	C	L	...	L	...	L	L	L	...
Kentucky	L	L	...	...	R	...	...	L	...	L	...	C	L	L	...
Louisiana	L	L	L	...	L	L	L	L	...	L	...	L	L	L	...
Maine	L	L	C	...	...	...	...	L	R	L	...	L	L	L	L
Maryland	L	L	C	...	...	...	...	L	R	L	...	...	L	L	...
Massachusetts	L	L	...	...	...	...	...	L	...	L	...	L	L	...	...
Michigan	...	L	...	...	...	...	...	L	L	L	...	...	L	L	...
Minnesota	...	L	...	...	C	...	...	L	C	L	...	L	L	L	...
Mississippi	...	L	L	...	...	...	...	L	...	L	...	...	L	L	...
Missouri	...	L	C	...	...	...	...	L	...	L	...	...	L	L	...
Montana	L	L	C	...	...	...	C	L	...	L	L	L	L	L	...
Nebraska	L	L	...	...	...	...	...	L	...	L	...	...	L	L	...
Nevada	...	L	...	...	...	...	C	L	...	L	...	...	L	L	L
New Hampshire	L	L	...	...	...	C	C	L	...	L	...	...	L	L	...
New Jersey	...	L	...	...	...	...	...	L	R	L	...	...	L	L	...
New Mexico	L	L	L	L	L	...	...	L	...	L	...	L	L	L	...
New York	L	L	...	...	...	...	...	L	...	L	...	...	L	L	...
North Carolina	...	L	C	...	...	...	...	L	...	L	...	...	L	L	L
North Dakota	...	L	...	...	L	...	...	L	...	L	...	...	L	L	...
Ohio	...	L	L	...	L	...	L	L	...	L	...	L	L	L	...

See footnotes at end of table.

Key:
C — Certification
L — Licensure
R — Registration
* — Enabling legislation
... — Not regulated

STATE REGULATION OF HEALTH OCCUPATIONS AND PROFESSIONS: 1993—Continued

State or other jurisdiction	Acupuncturist	Chiropractor	Counselor, Professional	Counselor, Alcoholism	Counselor, Drug	Counselor, Pastoral	Counselor, Substance Abuse	Dentist	Dental Assistant	Dental Hygienist	Denturist	Dietitian	Emergency Medical Technician (a)	Hearing Aid Dealer & Fitter	Homeopath
Oklahoma	. . .	L	L	. . .	. . .	. . .	. . .	L	C	L	. . .	L	L	L	. . .
Oregon	L	L	L	. . .	. . .	. . .	. . .	L	. . .	L	. . .	L	L	L	. . .
Pennsylvania	R	L	. . .	. . .	. . .	. . .	C	L	. . .	L	. . .	. . .	L	L	. . .
Rhode Island	L	L	. . .	. . .	. . .	. . .	. . .	L	. . .	L	L	L	L	L	. . .
South Carolina	. . .	L	L	. . .	. . .	. . .	. . .	L	. . .	L	. . .	. . .	L	. . .	. . .
South Dakota	. . .	L	. . .	. . .	. . .	. . .	. . .	L	R	L	. . .	. . .	L	L	. . .
Tennessee	L	L	L	. . .	. . .	. . .	. . .	L	L	L	. . .	C	L	L	. . .
Texas	L	L	L	. . .	L	. . .	. . .	L	. . .	L	. . .	L	L	L	. . .
Utah	L	L	. . .	. . .	. . .	. . .	. . .	L	L	L	. . .	. . .	L	. . .	. . .
Vermont	L	L	. . .	. . .	. . .	. . .	. . .	L	. . .	L	. . .	. . .	L	L	. . .
Virginia	L	L	L	C	C	. . .	C	L	. . .	L	. . .	. . .	L	L	. . .
Washington	L	L	. . .	. . .	C	. . .	. . .	L	. . .	L	. . .	L	L	L	. . .
West Virginia	. . .	L	C	. . .	. . .	. . .	. . .	L	. . .	L	. . .	. . .	L	L	. . .
Wisconsin	L	L	L	. . .	. . .	. . .	. . .	L	. . .	L	. . .	. . .	L	L	. . .
Wyoming	. . .	L	L	. . .	. . .	. . .	L	L	L	L	. . .	. . .	L	L	. . .
Dist. of Columbia	L	L	L	. . .	. . .	. . .	. . .	L	. . .	L	. . .	L	L	. . .	. . .
Puerto Rico	. . .	L	. . .	. . .	. . .	. . .	. . .	L	. . .	L	. . .	L	L	. . .	. . .

Key:
C — Certification
L — Licensure
R — Registration
* — Enabling legislation
. . . — Not regulated

STATE REGULATION OF HEALTH OCCUPATIONS AND PROFESSIONS: 1993—Continued

State or other jurisdiction	Massage Therapist	Nurse, Licensed Practical	Nurse Midwife	Nurse Practitioner	Nurse, Registered	Nursing Home Administrator	Occupational Therapist	Occupational Therapy Assistant	Optician	Optometrist	Osteopath	Pharmacist
Alabama	. . .	L	L	L	L	L	L	L	. . .	L	L	L
Alaska	. . .	L	L	L	L	L	L	L	L	L	L	L
Arizona	L	L	. . .	C	L	L	L	L	L	L	L	L
Arkansas	. . .	L	L	L	L	L	L	L	L	L	L	L
California	. . .	. . .	L	L	L	L	L	L	C	L	L	L
Colorado	. . .	L	L	. . .	L	L	. . .	. . .	. . .	L	L	L
Connecticut	. . .	L	L	. . .	L	L	L	L	L	L	L	L
Delaware	L	L	. . .	. . .	L	L	L	L	. . .	L	L	L
Florida	. . .	L	L	L	L	L	L	L	L	L	L	L
Georgia	. . .	L	L	L	L	L	L	L	. . .	L	L	L
Hawaii	L	L	L	. . .	L	L	L	L	L	L	L	L
Idaho	. . .	L	. . .	. . .	L	L	. . .	. . .	. . .	L	L	L
Illinois	. . .	L	. . .	. . .	L	L	L	L	. . .	L	L	L
Indiana	. . .	L	C	C	L	. . . (b)	L	L	. . .	L	L	L
Iowa	L	L	. . .	L	L	L	L	L	. . .	L	L	L
Kansas	. . .	L	L	L	L	L	C	C	. . .	L	L	L
Kentucky	. . .	L	. . .	. . .	L	L	L	L	. . .	L	L	L
Louisiana	. . .	L	. . .	C	L	L	L	L	. . .	L	L	L
Maine	R	L	. . .	L	L	L	L	L	. . .	L	L	L
Maryland	. . .	L	L	. . .	L	L	L	L	. . .	L	L	L
Massachusetts	. . .	L	. . .	. . .	L	L	L	L	L	L	L	L
Michigan	. . .	L	. . .	C	L	L	. . .	. . .	. . .	L	L	L
Minnesota	. . .	L	. . .	L	L	L	C	C	. . .	L	L	L
Mississippi	. . .	L	L	. . .	L	L	L	L	. . .	L	L	L
Missouri	. . .	L	. . .	. . .	L	L	L	L	. . .	L	L	L
Montana	. . .	L	L	L	L	L	L	L	. . .	L	L	L
Nebraska	L	L	L	L	L	L	L	L	. . .	L	L	L
Nevada	L	L	. . .	. . .	L	L	L	L	. . .	L	L	L
New Hampshire	L	L	L	L	L	L	L	L	R	L	L	L
New Jersey	. . .	L	. . .	L	L	L	. . .	. . .	. . .	L	L	L
New Mexico	L	L	. . .	. . .	L	L	L	L	. . .	L	L	L
New York	L	L	C	L	L	L	L	L	L	L	L	L
North Carolina	. . .	L	C	. . .	L	L	L	L	. . .	L	L	L
North Dakota	L	L	. . .	. . .	L	L	L	L	L	L	L	L
Ohio	L	L	L	L	L	L	L	L	L	L	L	L

See footnotes at end of table.

Key:
C — Certification
L — Licensure
R — Registration
* — Enabling legislation
. . . — Not regulated

STATE REGULATION OF HEALTH OCCUPATIONS AND PROFESSIONS: 1993—Continued

State or other jurisdiction	Massage Therapist	Nurse, Licensed Practical	Nurse Midwife	Nurse Practitioner	Nurse, Registered	Nursing Home Administrator	Occupational Therapist	Occupational Therapy Assistant	Optician	Optometrist	Osteopath	Pharmacist
Oklahoma	...	L	C	C	L	L	L	L	...	L	L	L
Oregon	L	L	C	...	L	L	L	L	...	L	L	L
Pennsylvania	...	L	L	L	L	L	L	L	...	L	L	L
Rhode Island	L	L	L	L	L	L	L	...	L	L	L	L
South Carolina	...	L	L	L	L	L	L	L	L	L	L	L
South Dakota	...	L	L	L	L	L	L	L	...	L	L	L
Tennessee	L	L	...	...	L	L	L	L	...	L	L	L
Texas	L	L	...	L	L	(b)	L	L	L	L	L	L
Utah	L	L	...	L	L	...	L	L	L	L	L	L
Vermont	...	L	...	...	L	L	...	...	L	L	L	L
Virginia	...	L	L	L	L	L	C	...	L	L	L	L
Washington	L	L	L	...	L	L	L	C	L	L	L	L
West Virginia	...	L	L	...	L	L	C	C	...	L	L	L
Wisconsin	...	L	L	...	L	L	L	L	...	L	L	L
Wyoming	...	L	...	L	L	L	L	L	...	L	L	L
Dist. of Columbia	...	L	L	...	L	L	L	L	L	L	L	L
Puerto Rico	...	L	L	L	L	(b)	L	L	L	L	L	L

Key:
C — Certification
L — Licensure
R — Registration
* — Enabling legislation
... — Not regulated

STATE REGULATION OF HEALTH OCCUPATIONS AND PROFESSIONS: 1993—Continued

State or jurisdiction	Physical Therapist	Physical Therapy Assistant	Physician	Physician Assistant	Podiatrist	Psychologist	Radiologic Technologist	Radiation Therapist	Respiratory Therapist	Sanitarian	Social Worker	Speech-Language Pathologist & Aud.	Therapist, Marriage & Family	Veterinarian	Veterinary Technician
Alabama	L	L	L	L	L	L					L	L		L	L
Alaska	L	L	L	L	L	L					C		L	L	L
Arizona	L		L	C	L	L	C	C	L	R	L		R	L	L
Arkansas	L	L	L	C	L	L	C	L	L			L	L	L	L
California	L		L	L	L	L			L			L	L	L	R
Colorado	L		L	C	L	L						L	L	L	
Connecticut	L	R	L	L	L	L	L	L	L	L	L	L	L	L	
Delaware	L	L	L	L	L	L	L	L	L	L	L	L	L	L	L
Florida	L	L	L	L	L	L	L	L	L	L	L	L	L	L	L
Georgia	L		L	C	L	C					L			L	L
Hawaii	L		L	C	L	L		L	R	L	L	L	C	L	L
Idaho	L		L	O	L	L		L		L	L	L		L	L
Illinois	L	L	L	C	L	L	L	*	R	R	L	C		L	L
Indiana	L	L	L	O	L	C	L	L	C		L	L	L	L	L
Iowa	L		L	L	L	L		L	L		L	L	L	L	L
Kansas	C	R	L	C	L	L		L	C	L	L	L	L	L	L
Kentucky	L	L	L	L	L	L	L	*	L	C	C	L		L	L
Louisiana	L	L	L	L	L	L	L	L	L	C	C	L		L	L
Maine	L	L	L	L	L	L		L	L	L	L	L		L	L
Maryland	L	L	L	L	L	O		L	C	O	L	L		L	L
Massachusetts	L	R	L	L	L	L	*		L	L	L	L	L	L	L
Michigan	C	L	L	L	L	L			O	C	O	C		L	
Minnesota	O	L	L	O	L	L		L	L	O	L	L		L	L
Mississippi	L	L	L		L	L			O	L	C	L	L	L	L
Missouri	L	L	L	L	L	L			L	O	L	L		L	L
Montana	L	L	L	O	L	L			L	L	O	L		L	L
Nebraska	L	L	L	C	L	L			O	R	C	C		L	L
Nevada	L	L	L	L	L	L			L		L		L	L	L
New Hampshire	L	C	L	L	L	O		L	L	L	L	L	O	L	L
New Jersey	L	L	L	L	L	L			L		L	L	L	L	L
New Mexico	L	L	L	L	L	L	C	L	L		L	L	L	L	L
New York	L	L	L	L	L	L	L		L		O	L	C	L	L
North Carolina	L	L	L	R	L	L			L		O	L		L	L
North Dakota	L	L	L	R	L	L			L	L	L	L		L	L
Ohio	L	L	L	L	L	L		L	L	L	L	L		L	L

See footnotes at end of table.

Key:
C — Certification
L — Licensure
R — Registration
* — Enabling legislation
. . . . — Not regulated

STATE REGULATION OF HEALTH OCCUPATIONS AND PROFESSIONS: 1993—Continued

State or other jurisdiction	Physical Therapist	Physical Therapy Assistant	Physician	Physician Assistant	Podiatrist	Psychologist	Radiologic Technologist	Radiation Therapist	Respiratory Therapist	Sanitarian	Social Worker	Speech-Language Pathologist & Aud.	Therapist, Marriage & Family	Veterinarian	Veterinary Technician
Oklahoma	L	L	L	L	L	L	L	...	...	L	L	L	L	L	L
Oregon	L	L	L	C	L	L	...	...	...	L	...	L	L	L	L
Pennsylvania	L	R	L	L	L	L	...	...	...	...	...	L	...	L	R
Rhode Island	L	L	L	L	L	L	...	...	L	...	...	L	L	L	...
South Carolina	L	L	L	L	L	L	L	...	L	...	...	L	L	L	L
South Dakota	L	L	L	L	L	L	...	...	...	L	L	...	...	L	L
Tennessee	L	L	L	L	L	L	...	...	L	L	L	L	L	L	...
Texas	L	L	L	L	L	L	L*	L	...	...	L	L	L	L	...
Utah	...	...	L	L	L	L	L	...	...	C	L	...	...	L	...
Vermont	L	L	L	L	L	L	L	...	L	L	L	L	L	L	L
Virginia	L	L	L	L	L	L	C	...	C	...	L	L	...	L	L
Washington	L	L	L	L	L	L	C	...	L	...	L	L	L	L	...
West Virginia	L	L	L	L	L	L	L	...	L	L	L	L	C	L	L
Wisconsin	L	...	L	...	L	L	...	L	...	L	C	L	L	L	L
Wyoming	L	...	L	L	L	L	L	L	...	...	...	...	...	L	...
Dist. of Columbia	L	L	L	L	L	L	...	...	...	...	L	L	...	L	...
Puerto Rico	L	L	L	L	L	L	...	...	...	...	L	L	L	L	...

Source: Council on Licensure, Enforcement and Regulation, *Issues in Professional Regulation,* 1993 and various national associations of state boards.

Key:
C — Certification
L — Licensure
R — Registration
* — Enabling legislation
. . . — Not regulated

(a) There are eight categories of emergency medical technicians, from basic to paramedic to task-specific certifications. No state regulates all categories, but every state regulates at least one category.

(b) In Indiana, Utah and Puerto Rico, nursing home administrators are not licensed as such, but they are licensed more broadly as health facility administrators.

TABLE 7.33
STATUS OF MANDATORY CONTINUING EDUCATION
FOR SELECTED PROFESSIONS: 1993

State or other jurisdiction	Architects	Certified Public Accountants	Dentists	Engineer, Professional	Lawyers	Nurses	Nursing Home Administrator	Optometry	Psychology	Pharmacy	Physical Therapist	Physicians	Real Estate	Social Work	Veterinary Medicine
Alabama	★	★	★	★	★	★	★	★	★	★	★	★	★	★	★
Alaska	...	★	★	...	...	★	...	★	★	★	★	★	★	★	★
Arizona	...	★	...	...	★	★	★	★	★	★	...	★	★	★	★
Arkansas	...	★	...	...	★	...	★	★	E	★	...	E	★	★	★
California	...	★	★	...	★	★	★	★	...	★	...	★	★	...	★
Colorado	...	★	...	...	★	★	...	★	...	...	...	...	★	...	★
Connecticut	...	★	...	...	...	...	...	★	...	★	...	...	★	...	...
Delaware	...	★	★	...	★	★	★	★	★	★	★	★	★	★	★
Florida	E	★	★	...	★	★	★	★	★	★	★	★	★	★	★
Georgia	...	★	★	...	★	...	★	★	★	★	★	★	★	★	★
Hawaii	...	★	...	...	...	...	★	★	...	...	...	...	★	★	...
Idaho	...	★	...	...	★	...	★	★	★	★	...	...	...	E	★
Illinois	...	★	★	...	...	...	★	★	...	★	...	...	E	E	★
Indiana	...	★	★	...	★	...	★	★	...	★	...	...	E	E	E
Iowa	★	★	★	★	★	★	★	★	★	★	★	★	★	★	★
Kansas	...	★	★	...	★	★	★	★	★	★	★	★	★	★	★
Kentucky	...	★	★	...	★	★	★	★	...	★	★	E	★	...	★
Louisiana	...	★	...	...	★	★	★	★	★	★	★	...	★	★	★
Maine	...	★	★	...	...	...	★	★	★	★	...	★	★	★	★
Maryland	...	★	E	...	...	...	★	★	★	★	E	★	★	...	★
Massachusetts	...	★	★	...	★	★	★	★	★	★	...	★	...	★	...
Michigan	E	★	★	E	S	E	★	★	E	★	...	★	★	...	...
Minnesota	...	★	★	E	★	★	★	★	E	★	★	★	★	★	...
Mississippi	...	★	...	...	★	★	★	★	...	★	...	...	★	★	★
Missouri	...	★	...	...	★	...	★	★	...	★	...	...	★	E	...
Montana	E	★	★	...	★	...	★	★	...	★	E	...	★	★	★
Nebraska	...	★	★	...	...	★	★	★	...	★	...	E	★	★	★
Nevada	...	★	★	...	★	★	★	★	★	★	★	★	★	★	★
New Hampshire	...	★	★	...	★	★	★	★	★	★	S	★	★	...	★
New Jersey	...	★	★	...	S	...	★	★	...	★	...	...	★	E	...
New Mexico	...	★	★	...	★	★	★	★	★	★	★	★	★	★	★
New York	...	★	...	...	...	...	★	...	...	...	...	...	★	...	...
North Carolina	E	★	★	...	★	...	★	★	E	★	...	...	...	★	★
North Dakota	...	★	★	...	★	...	★	★	...	★	...	...	★	★	★
Ohio	E	★	★	...	★	★	★	★	...	★	...	★	★	★	★
Oklahoma	...	★	★	E	★	...	★	★	★	★	...	...	★	S	★
Oregon	...	★	★	...	★	★	★	★	★	★	...	...	★	★	★
Pennsylvania	...	★	...	...	★	...	★	★	★	★	...	...	★	E	★
Rhode Island	...	★	★	...	★	...	★	★	★	★	...	★	★	...	...
South Carolina	...	★	...	...	★	...	★	★	★	★	...	...	E	★	★
South Dakota	E	★	★	E	...	...	★	★	...	★	...	...	★	★	★
Tennessee	...	★	★	...	★	...	★	★	...	★	...	...	★	...	★
Texas	E	★	...	...	★	★	★	★	E	★	★	...	★	★	...
Utah	...	★	...	E	★	...	★	★	★	★	...	...	★	...	...
Vermont	...	★	E	E	★	...	...	★	★	★	...	...	★	...	...
Virginia	...	★	...	...	★	...	★	★	...	★	...	...	★	...	...
Washington	...	★	E	E	★	...	★	★	★	★	★	★	★	E	★
West Virginia	...	★	E	E	★	...	★	★	★	★	...	...	★	★	★
Wisconsin	...	...	...	...	★	...	★	★	S	★	...	...	★	E	...
Wyoming	...	★	...	E	★	...	★	★	E	★	...	...	★	★	...
Dist. of Columbia	E	★	★	...	...	★	★	★	★	★	★	★	E	★	E	★

Source: Louis Phillips & Associates, Athens, Ga.
Key:
★ — Required
E — Enabling legislation
S — Under certain circumstances
... — No requirements

Table 7.34
MINIMUM AGE FOR SPECIFIED ACTIVITIES

State or other jurisdiction	Age of majority (a)	Minimum age for marriage with consent (b)		Minimum age for making a will	Minimum age for buying alcohol	Minimum age for serving on a jury	Minimum age for leaving school (c)
		Male	Female				
Alabama	19	14 (d)	14 (d)	19	21	19	16
Alaska	18	16 (e)	16 (e)	18	21	18	16
Arizona	18	16 (e)	16 (e)	18	21	18	16
Arkansas	18	17 (f)	16 (f)	18	21	18	17
California	18	(g)	(g)	18 (h)	21	18	18
Colorado	18	16 (e)	16 (e)	18	21	18	16
Connecticut	18	16 (e)	16 (e)	18	21	18	16
Delaware	18	18 (f)	16 (f)	18	21	18	16
Florida	18	16 (d,f)	16 (d,f)	18	21	18	16
Georgia	18	(g)	(g)	18	21	18	16
Hawaii	18	16 (i)	16 (i)	18	21	18	18
Idaho	18	16 (e)	16 (e)	18 (h)	21	18	16
Illinois	18	16	16	18	21	18	16
Indiana	18	17 (f)	17 (f)	18	21	18	16 (j)
Iowa	18	18 (e)	18 (e)	18	21	18	16
Kansas	18	18 (e)	18 (e)	18	21	18	16
Kentucky	18	18 (e,f)	18 (e,f)	18	21	18	16 (j)
Louisiana	18	18 (e)	18 (e)	18 (h)	21	18	17
Maine	18	16 (e)	16 (e)	18	21	18	17
Maryland	18	16 (f,k)	16 (f,k)	18	21	18	16
Massachusetts	18	14 (n)	12 (n)	18	21	18	16
Michigan	18	16 (f,i)	16 (f)	18	21	18	16
Minnesota	18	16 (e)	16 (e)	18	21	18	16 (l)
Mississippi	18	17	15	18	21	21	16
Missouri	18	15 (i), 18 (e)	15 (i), 18 (e)	18	21	21	16
Montana	18	16	16	18	21	18	16 (m)
Nebraska	19	17	17	18	21	19	16
Nevada	18	16 (e)	16 (e)	18	21	18	17
New Hampshire	18	14 (n)	13 (n)	18	21	18	16
New Jersey	18	16 (e,f)	16 (e,f)	18	21	18	16
New Mexico	18	16 (i)	16 (i)	18	21	18	16
New York	18	14 (n)	14 (n)	18	21	18	16 (o)
North Carolina	18	16 (f,p)	16 (f,p)	18	21	18	16
North Dakota	18	16	16	18	21	18	16
Ohio	18	18 (e,f)	16 (e,f)	18	21	18	18
Oklahoma	18	16 (f)	16 (f)	18	21	18	18
Oregon	18	17	17	18	21	18	18
Pennsylvania	21	16 (i)	16 (i)	18	21	18	17
Rhode Island	18	18 (i)	16 (i)	18	21	18	16
South Carolina	18	16 (f)	14 (f)	18	21	18	17
South Dakota	18	16 (f)	16 (f)	18	21	18	16 (m)
Tennessee	18	16 (i)	16 (i)	18	21	18	17
Texas	18	14 (n)	14 (n)	18 (h)	21	18	17
Utah	18	14	14	18	21	18	18
Vermont	18	16 (e)	16 (e)	18	21	18	16
Virginia	18	16 (d,f)	16 (d,f)	18	21	18	18
Washington	18	17 (i)	17 (i)	18	21	18	18
West Virginia	18	18 (f)	18 (f)	18	21	18	16
Wisconsin	18	16 (i)	16 (i)	18	21	18	18
Wyoming	19	16 (i)	16 (i)	19	21	18	16
Dist. of Columbia	18	16 (d)	16 (d)	18	21	18	17

Sources: Distilled Spirits Council of the United States, Inc.; Education Commission of the States; National Center for State Courts; National Center for Youth Law; Gary Skoloff, Skoloff & Wolfe.

(a) Generally, the age at which an individual has legal control over own actions and business (e.g., ability to contract) except as otherwise provided by statute. In many states, age of majority is arrived at upon marriage if minimum legal marrying age is lower than prescribed age of majority.

(b) With parental consent. Minimum age for marrying without consent is 18 years in all states, except in Mississippi where the minimum age is 21.

(c) Without graduating.

(d) Parental consent not required if minor was previously married.

(e) Younger persons may marry with parental consent and/or permission of judge. In Connecticut, judicial approval.

(f) Younger persons may obtain license in case of pregnancy or birth of child.

(g) No age limits.

(h) Age may be lower for a minor who is living apart from parents or

legal guardians and managing own financial affairs, or who has contracted a lawful marriage.

(i) Younger persons may obtain license in special circumstances.

(j) In Indiana, students between 16 and 18 must submit to an exit interview and have written parental approval before leaving school. In Kentucky, must have parental signature for leaving school between 16 and 18.

(k) If under 16, proof of age and the consent of parents in person is required. If a parent is ill, an affidavit by the incapacitated parent and a physician's affidavit to that effect required.

(l) Age 18, beginning in year 2000.

(m) Or completion of eighth grade, whichever is earlier.

(n) Parental consent and/or permission of judge required. In Texas, below age of consent, need parental consent and permission of judge.

(o) Age 17 in New York City and Buffalo.

(p) Unless parties are 18 or over, female is pregnant, or applicants are the parents of a living child born out of wedlock.

Table 7.35
STATE MOTOR VEHICLE REGISTRATIONS: 1992

State or other jurisdiction	Automobiles (a)	Motorcycles (a)	Buses (a,b)	Trucks (a)	Total registrations 1991	Total registrations 1992	Percentage change
United States	144,213,429	4,065,118	644,732	45,504,067	188,136,469	190,362,228	1.2
Alabama	2,196,269	41,358	8,270	1,099,525	3,483,797	3,304,064	− 5.2
Alaska	307,722	11,191	1,918	176,455	470,903	486,095	3.2
Arizona	1,993,810	71,163	4,394	802,697	2,848,537	2,800,901	− 1.7
Arkansas	974,023	13,905	5,585	521,872	1,479,637	1,501,480	1.5
California	17,219,177	623,046	40,835	4,942,288	22,252,741	22,202,300	− 0.2
Colorado	2,164,815	88,872	5,517	744,953	3,045,247	2,915,285	− 4.3
Connecticut	2,429,120	49,667	8,346	131,698 (c)	2,588,777	2,569,164	− 0.8
Delaware	418,780	9,759	2,155	124,047	533,567	544,982	2.1
Florida	8,131,392	193,739	38,135	2,062,809	9,980,076	10,232,336	2.5
Georgia	4,121,018	80,035	15,399	1,763,020	5,714,189	5,899,437	3.2
Hawaii	668,305	22,846	4,253	101,536	785,004	774,094	− 1.4
Idaho	610,411	33,475	3,717	420,162	1,055,369	1,034,290	− 2.0
Illinois	6,622,277	200,904	16,307	1,343,141	8,192,744	7,981,725	− 2.6
Indiana	3,300,636	95,195	22,451	1,192,763	4,413,624	4,515,850	2.3
Iowa	1,930,784	157,383	9,191	765,779	2,668,436	2,705,754	1.4
Kansas	1,257,929	55,749	3,761	658,878	1,879,442	1,920,568	2.2
Kentucky	1,938,605	35,133	10,325	1,034,290	2,942,102	2,983,220	1.4
Louisiana	2,005,710	35,193	19,681	1,068,120	3,045,788	3,093,511	1.6
Maine	754,331	30,484	2,837	220,966	978,849	978,134	− 0.1
Maryland	3,075,207	52,162	10,990	602,702	3,630,236	3,688,899	1.6
Massachusetts	3,156,214	62,991	10,625	496,561	3,663,843	3,663,400	0.0
Michigan	5,679,842	153,886	23,325	1,607,385	7,244,938	7,310,552	0.9
Minnesota	2,735,867	105,916	15,384	732,579	3,273,153	3,483,830	6.4
Mississippi	1,496,099	27,147	8,911	448,963	1,887,441	1,953,973	3.5
Missouri	2,821,027	60,045	11,713	1,171,322	3,950,125	4,004,062	1.4
Montana	540,739	22,630	2,799	363,251	765,754	906,789	18.4
Nebraska	893,071	19,421	5,261	456,718	1,404,444	1,355,050	− 3.5
Nevada	620,547	19,779	1,784	298,605	881,274	920,936	4.5
New Hampshire	693,573	34,276	1,698	198,376 (c)	906,464	893,647	− 1.4
New Jersey	5,135,703	100,274	18,185	437,466 (c)	5,518,957	5,591,354	1.3
New Mexico	837,707	31,167	3,444	510,544	1,320,488	1,351,695	2.4
New York	8,467,220	193,715	39,667	1,272,667 (c)	9,771,437	9,779,554	0.1
North Carolina	3,778,448	58,635	33,592	1,494,871	5,216,177	5,306,911	1.7
North Dakota	393,518	18,464	2,272	259,545	628,672	655,335	4.2
Ohio	7,304,197	230,291	31,254	1,694,378	8,684,599	9,029,829	4.0
Oklahoma	1,757,742	56,937	13,729	965,484	2,669,312	2,736,955	2.5
Oregon	1,955,443	62,069	11,295	616,667	2,506,950	2,583,405	3.0
Pennsylvania	6,534,865	167,010	31,708	1,612,658 (c)	8,037,808	8,179,231	1.8
Rhode Island	516,895	21,137	1,605	103,525 (c)	628,407	622,025	− 1.0
South Carolina	1,948,340	32,595	14,360	638,229	2,471,245	2,600,929	5.2
South Dakota	426,818	23,408	2,532	290,340	701,987	719,690	2.5
Tennessee	3,726,216	75,059	15,001	903,866	4,541,676	4,645,083	2.3
Texas	8,688,680	164,147	63,742	4,015,016	12,696,540	12,767,438	0.6
Utah	809,676	24,174	1,179	441,413	1,229,730	1,252,268	1.8
Vermont	345,693	16,588	1,796	117,321	446,819	464,810	4.0
Virginia	3,960,758	59,209	16,315	1,261,633	5,022,222	5,238,706	4.3
Washington	3,140,036	111,587	6,569	1,319,238	4,403,604	4,465,843	1.4
West Virginia	778,169	18,251	3,628	491,110	1,273,444	1,272,907	0.0
Wisconsin	2,463,488	175,683	12,161	1,259,062	3,684,938	3,734,711	1.4
Wyoming	248,898	15,537	2,362	231,555	468,566	482,815	3.0
Dist. of Columbia	237,619	1,831	2,769	16,018	246,390	256,406	4.1

Source: Federal Highway Administration, U.S. Department of Transportation (1993). Compiled for the calendar year ending December 31, 1992 from reports of state authorities.

Note: Where the registration year is not more than one month removed from the calendar year, registration-year data are given. Where the registration year is more than one month removed, registrations are given for the calendar year.

(a) Includes federal, state, county and municipal vehicles. Vehicles owned by the military services are not included.

(b) The numbers of private and commercial buses given here are estimates by the Federal Highway Administration of the numbers in operation, rather than the registration counts of the states.

(c) The following farm trucks, registered at a nominal fee and restricted to use in the vicinity of the owner's farm, are not included in this table: Connecticut, 8,548; New Hampshire, 3,315; New Jersey, 5,956; New York, 27,855; Pennsylvania, 22,135; and Rhode Island, 1,027.

Table 7.36
MOTOR VEHICLE OPERATORS LICENSES: 1992

State or other jurisdiction	Years for which issued	Renewal date	Amount of fee	Estimated total licensed drivers during 1992 (in thousands)
Alabama	4	Issuance	$15.00 (a)	2,977
Alaska	5	Birthday	10.00	405
Arizona	4	Birthday	7.00	2,506
Arkansas	4	Birthday	14.25	1,712
California	4	Birthday	12.00	20,111
Colorado	5	Birthday	15.00	2,392
Connecticut	2 and 4	Birthday	35.50 (a,b)	2,358
Delaware	5	Birthday	12.50	501
Florida	4 or 6 (c)	Birthday	15.00 (b)	10,538
Georgia	4	Birthday	4.50	4,600
Hawaii	2 and 4 (d)	Birthday	(d)	717
Idaho	4	Birthday	19.50	721
Illinois	4 and 5 (e)	Issuance	10.00 (e)	7,411
Indiana	3 and 4 (f)	Birth month	6.00 (f)	3,800
Iowa	2 and 4 (f)	Birthday	16.00 (f)	1,859
Kansas	4	Birthday	8.00 - 14.00 (a)	1,692
Kentucky	4	Birth month	8.00	2,457
Louisiana	2 and 4 (f)	Birthday	18.00 (f)	2,617
Maine	4	Birthday	20.00	918
Maryland	5	Birthday	20.00 (b)	3,234
Massachusetts	5	Birthday	35.00 (a,b)	4,170
Michigan	2 and 4 (g)	Birthday	12.00 (g)	6,481
Minnesota	4	Birthday	15.00	2,625
Mississippi	4	Birthday	20.00	1,628
Missouri	3	Issuance	7.50	3,454
Montana	4	Birthday	16.00 - 24.00	597
Nebraska	4 (h)	Birthday	10.00 (h)	1,129
Nevada	4	Birthday	20.50 (f)	957
New Hampshire	4	Birthday	32.00	850
New Jersey	4	Issuance	16.00 - 17.50	5,285
New Mexico	4 (f)	30 days after Birthday	10.00	1,126
New York	4	Birthday	22.25	10,360
North Carolina	4	Birthday	10.00	4,655
North Dakota	4	Birthday	10.00	433
Ohio	4	Birthday	5.00 (i)	9,169
Oklahoma	2 and 4	Issuance	7.00 and 14.00 (b)	2,287
Oregon	4	Birthday	16.25 (b)	2,426
Pennsylvania	2 and 4 (f)	Birth month	22.00 (f)	8,019
Rhode Island	5 (j)	Birthday	30.00 (a,j)	685
South Carolina	4	Birthday	10.00 (a)	2,400
South Dakota	4	Birthday	6.00	498
Tennessee	4	Bithday	14.00 - 16.00	3,486
Texas	4	Birthday	16.00	11,438
Utah	4	Birthday	15.00 (b)	1,143
Vermont	2 and 4	Birthday	12.00 and 20.00 (a)	423
Virginia	5	Birth month	12.00	4,697
Washington	4	Birthday	14.00 (a)	3,627
West Virginia	4	Issuance	10.50	1,314
Wisconsin	4	Birthday	10.00 (a,b)	3,543
Wyoming	4	Birthday	5.00 (b)	343
Dist. of Columbia	4	Issuance	20.00	352

Sources: American Automobile Association, *Digest of Motor Laws* (1993); U.S. Department of Transportation, Federal Highway Administration, *Highway Statistics, 1992.* Status of requirements as of December 31, 1992.

(a) The following examination fees are in addition to the fee shown for a license: Alabama and Rhode Island—$5; Connecticut—$29; Kansas—$3; Massachusetts—$20; South Carolina—$2; Vermont—written examination fee for first examination-$15, $10 for each additional examination; Washington—$7; Wisconsin—$10.

(b) Fee for original license: Connecticut—$28.50 to $43.50; Florida—$20; Maryland—$30; Massachusetts—$43.75; Oklahoma—$18; Oregon—$31.25; Utah—$20 for persons under 21; Wisconsin—$15; Wyoming—$10.

(c) Original license is $19. Renewal fee is $15 for six years if no moving violation convictions within past three years.

(d) Licenses issued for two years to persons 15-24 years and 65 years and over. Fee for two-year licenses: $4.25 to $6; four-year licenses: $8.50 to $12.

(e) $5 for persons 65-80 years; $2 for two-year license for persons 81-86; no cost for one-year license for persons 87 and older.

(f) Indiana—$3 for three-year renewal license for persons 75 years and older; Iowa—$8 for two-year license for persons under 18 or over 70; Louisiana—$9.50 for two-year license for persons over 70 years; Nevada—$15.50 for original or renewal license for persons 65 and over; New Mexico—persons 75 and over renew annually at no charge; Pennsylvania—$12 for two-year license for persons 65 years and over.

(g) Persons with unsatisfactory driving records renew for two-year term at $6.

(h) Original license expires on licensee's birthday in the first year after issuance that licensee's age is divisible by four. Fees: $3.50 for one year; $5.50 for two years; $8 for three years.

(i) A $1.50 issuance fee and $1.00 eye exam fee are charged for licenses and permits.

(j) First license is for two years at $12.

Table 7.37
MOTOR VEHICLE LAWS
(As of 1993)

State or other jurisdiction	Minimum age for driver's license (a)			Liability laws (b)	Vehicle inspection (c)	Transfer of plates to new owner	Child restraints mandatory for passengers up to ___ years (d)	Mandatory seat belt law (e)
	Regular	Learner's	Restrictive					
Alabama	16	15 (f)	14 (g)	S	(h)	★	6	★
Alaska	16	14 (i)	14 (g,i)	S	spot	★	16	★
Arizona	18	15 + 7 mo. (f,i)	16 (i)	C	(j)	★	5	★
Arkansas	16	14-16 (f)	14 (i,k)	S,NF	★	. . .	5	★
California	18	15 (k,l)	16 (l)	(m)	(j)	★	4 (n)	★ (o)
Colorado	21	15 + 9 mo. (f,p)	15 + 6 mo. (l)	S,NF	(j)	. . .	4 (n)	★
Connecticut	16 (l)	16 (l,q)	16 (l)	S,NF	★	. . .	4	★
Delaware	18	15 + 10 mo. (f,i)	16 (i,l)	S,NF	★	★	4 (n)	★
Florida	16	15 (f)	15 (i)	(r)	(j)	. . .	6	★
Georgia	21	15	16 (i)	C,NF	(j)	★	5	★
Hawaii	18	(f)	15 (i)	S,NF	★	★	4	★
Idaho	16 (l)	16 (f,l)	15 (l)	S,C	. . .	. . .	4 (n)	★
Illinois	18	(f)	16 (i,l)	S	(j,s)	. . .	6	★
Indiana	18	16 (k,l,p)	16 + 1 mo. (i,l)	S,C	(j)	. . .	5	★
Iowa	18	14 (l)	14 (i,l)	S	spot	. . .	6	★
Kansas	16	(f)	14 (k)	NF,UM	spot	. . .	14	★
Kentucky	18	(f)	16 (i)	C,NF	. . .	★	(n)	. . .
Louisiana	16	16 (i)	17 (t)	C	★	★	5	★
Maine	17	(f,k)	16 (l)	S,C	★	. . .	4 (o)	. . .
Maryland	18	15 + 9 mo. (f,k)	16 (i,l,t)	C,NF	(u)	. . .	10	★
Massachusetts	18	16 (f)	16 + 6 mo. (i,l,t)	C,NF	★	. . .	12	. . .
Michigan	18	(f)	16 (i,l,v)	C,NF	spot	. . .	4	★
Minnesota	18	(f)	16 (l)	C,NF	spot (h)	★	4	★ (o)
Mississippi	15	(f)		S,F	★	. . .	2	★
Missouri	16	15 (k)	15 + 6 mo. (p)	C	★	. . .	4	★
Montana	18	(f)	15 (i,l)	C	. . .	. . .	4 (n)	★
Nebraska	16	15 (f,k)	(v)	F	. . .	. . .	5 (n)	★
Nevada	18	15 + 6 mo. (f)		F,C	(u)	. . .	5 (n)	★ (o)
New Hampshire	18	(q)	16 (l)	S,F	★	. . .	12	. . .
New Jersey	17	(k)	(v)	S,NF,UJ	★	. . .	5	★ (o)
New Mexico	16	15 (l)	14 (k)	S,C	(j)	. . .	11	★
New York	17 (l)	16 (k)	16 (i,t)	S,C,NF	★	. . .	16 (o)	★ (o)
North Carolina	18	15 (i,k,l)	16	S,C	★	. . .	6	★
North Dakota	16	(f)	14 (i,l)	S,NF,UM,UJ	spot	★	11	. . .
Ohio	18 (w)	16 (i,k)	(v)	S,C	(j)	. . .	4 (n)	★
Oklahoma	16	(p)	15 + 6 mo. (l)	|S,C|	★	★	6	★
Oregon	16	15 (f)	(v)	F,C,NF	spot (j)	★	16	★ (o)
Pennsylvania	16	16 (i,k)	16 (i,t)	C	★ (j)	. . .	4	★
Rhode Island	16	(f)	16 (l)	S	★	. . .	13	★
South Carolina	16	15 (k)	15	C,NF,UM	★	. . .	6	★ (o)
South Dakota	16		14 (t)	F,UM	. . .	★	5	. . .
Tennessee	18	15 (k)	15	S,F	(h)	. . .	4	★
Texas	16 (l)	15 (k,p)	15 (l,v)	S,F,C,UM	★	★	4	★
Utah	16(i,l)	16	15 + 9 mo. (k,p)	S,NF,UM	★	. . .	8	★
Vermont	18	15 (f,k)	16 (k)	S	★	. . .	13	★
Virginia	18	15 + 8 mo. (f,i,k)	16 (i,l)	S,UM	★	. . .	4	★
Washington	18	15 (f,p)	16 (l)	S,F	(j)	★	5	★ (o)
West Virginia	18	15 (f)	15 (i)	S,C	★	. . .	9	. . .
Wisconsin	18 (l)	15 + 6 mo. (f)	16 (i,l)	S	spot	. . .	4	★ (o)
Wyoming	18	15 (i,k)	15 (i,k)	S,C	. . .	. . .	3 (n)	★
Dist. of Columbia	18	(f,k)	16 (i)	C	★	. . .	16	★ (o)
American Samoa	18	16 (f,k)	16 (i,l)	C	★	★	. . .	. . .
Guam	18	15 (i,k)	16 (i)	S	★	. . .	11	★
Puerto Rico	18	(f)	16 (i)	(x)	★	★	. . .	★
U.S. Virgin Islands	18		16 (l)	C	★	★	5 (n)	. . .

See footnotes at end of table.

MOTOR VEHICLE LAWS—Continued

Source: American Automobile Association, *Digest of Motor Laws,* (1993).

Note: All jurisdictions except Guam have chemical test laws for intoxication. All except the District of Columbia have an implied consent provision. (Colorado has expressed consent law).

Key:

★ —Provision.

. . . — No provision.

(a) See Table 7.36, "Motor Vehicle Operators Licenses: 1992" for additional information on driver licenses.

(b) All jurisdictions except Colorado, Hawaii, American Samoa, Guam, Puerto Rico and the U.S. Virgin Islands have a non-resident service of process law. Alabama, Arkansas, California, Georgia, Illinois (applicable to hitchhikers only), Oregon, Texas, Virginia, West Virginia, Wyoming and the U.S. Virgin Islands each have a guest suit law.

In this column only: S—"Security-type" financial responsibility law (following accident report, each driver/owner of the vehicles involved must show ability to pay damages which may be charged in subsequent legal actions arising from accident); F—"Future-proof type" financial responsibility law (persons who have been convicted of certain serious traffic offenses or who have failed to pay a judgment against them for damages arising from an accident must make a similar showing of financial responsibility); C—"Compulsory insurance" law (motorists must show proof of financial responsibility—liability insurance—usually as a condition of vehicle registration); NF—"No-fault insurance" law (vehicle owner looks to own insurance company for reimbursement for accident damages, rather than having to prove in court that the other party was responsible); UJ—"Unsatisfied judgment funds" law (state-operated funds financed with fees from motorists unable to provide evidence of insurance or from assessments levied on auto insurance companies to cover pedestrians and others who do not have no-fault insurance); UM—"Uninsured motorist" law (insurance companies must offer coverage against potential damage by uninsured motorists).

(c) "Spot" indicates spot check, usually for reasonable cause, or random roadside inspection for defective or missing equipment.

(d) The type of child restraint (safety seat or seat belt) required depends on the age of the child. The majority of states allow for substituting adult safety belts by age 5.

(e) These states have enacted mandatory seat belt legislation. Unless otherwise specified, legislation covers driver and front-seat passengers.

(f) Permit required. In Arkansas, for 30 days prior to taking driving test. In Delaware, for up to two months prior to 16th birthday. In Michigan, for 30 days prior to application for first license. In Minnesota, not required if driver can pass road test. In Oregon, not required if applicant can already drive.

(g) Restricted to mopeds.

(h) Cities have authority to maintain inspection stations. In Alabama, state troopers also authorized to inspect at their discretion.

(i) Guardian or parental consent required.

(j) Emission inspections. In Arizona, Colorado, Florida, Georgia, Illinois, Indiana, New Mexico, Ohio, Pennsylvania and Washington, mandatory annual emission inspections in certain counties. In California, biennial inspections are required in portions of counties which do not meet federal clean air standards. In Oregon, biennial inspections in Portland metro area and Jackson County. In Washington, also other checks (e.g., out-of-state vehicles, salvaged).

(k) Driver must be accompanied by licensed operator. In California and Vermont (learner's permit), a licensed operator 25 years or older. In Kansas,

may drive to school or work without licensed operator. In Maine, New York, Texas, Vermont (restrictive license), Virginia and Wyoming, a licensed operator 18 years or older. In Maryland, individual, 21 years or older, licensed to drive vehicle of that class, and licensed for 3 or more years. In Nebraska, a licensed operator 19 years or older. In New Jersey, an individual licensed for same classification as the learner's permit. In Pennsylvania, a licensed operator 18 years or older, licensed in same or equivalent class as learner. In South Carolina, a licensed operator 21 years or older. In American Samoa, must be accompanied by parent, legal guardian, or safety instructor. In Guam, must be accompanied by parent or legal guardian.

(l) Must have successfully completed approved driver education course.

(m) Financial responsibility required of every driver/owner of motor vehicle at all times.

(n) Other restrictions. In California, Colorado, Idaho, Montana, Nebraska, Nevada, Ohio and U.S. Virgin Islands, age restriction or child under 40 pounds. In Delaware, age restriction and under 40 pounds. In Kentucky and Wyoming, 40 inches in height or under.

(o) Covers other passengers in vehicle. California, Nevada, Oregon, South Carolina, Washington, Wisconsin and District of Columbia, all passengers. Maine, passengers between 4-15 years. In Minnesota, driver, front seat passengers, and anyone under 11. New Jersey, driver responsible for all passengers between 5 and 18 years. New York, all back seat occupants under 10 years and over 4 years, as well as all front-seat occupants.

(p) Must be enrolled in driver education course. In Colorado, if not in such course, wait until 15 + 9 mo.; in Washington, 15 + 6 mo.

(q) Required for motorcyclists only. In New Hampshire, otherwise, unlicensed persons who are being taught to drive must be accompanied by licensed operator 25 years or older.

(r) Proof of personal injury protection is required. In event of an accident in which operator is charged with a moving violation, the operator must prove liability insurance in force on date of accident.

(s) Trucks, buses and trailers only. Required for vehicle owners in certain counties.

(t) Driving hours restricted. In Louisiana, drivers under 17 not permitted to operate vehicles between hours of 11 p.m. and 5 a.m. Monday through Thursday; between midnight and 5 a.m. Friday through Sunday. In Maryland, drivers prohibited from driving between midnight and 5 a.m. unless accompanied by licensed driver 21 years or older. In Massachusetts, drivers prohibited from driving between 1 a.m. and 4 a.m., unless accompanied by parent or legal guardian. In New York, drivers 16-17 years old are restricted from driving between 8 p.m. and 5 a.m. (may not drive in New York City at any time). In Pennsylvania, drivers prohibited from driving between midnight and 5 a.m., unless accompanied by parent or spouse 18 years or older or in possession of employer's affidavit. In South Dakota, driver not permitted to operate vehicle between 8 p.m. and 6 a.m., unless accompanied by licensed driver in front seat.

(u) Mandatory inspection only under certain circumstances. In Maryland, all used cars upon resale or transfer. In Nevada, used cars registered to new owner and emissions test for first-time registration in Clark and Washoe counties.

(v) License will be granted at lower age under special conditions. In Michigan (extenuating circumstances), 14. In Nebraska (school permit), 14. In New Jersey (agriculture pursuit), 16. In Ohio (proof of hardship), 14. In Oregon, (special conditions), 14. In Texas (proof of hardship), 15.

(w) Probationary license issued to persons 16-18 upon completion of approved driver education course.

(x) Has financial responsibility law; details not available.

Table 7.38
STATE NO-FAULT MOTOR VEHICLE INSURANCE LAWS

State or other jurisdiction	Purchase of first-party benefits	Minimum tort liability threshold (a)	Maximum first-party (no-fault) benefits			
			Medical	Income loss	Replacement services	Survivors/funeral benefits
Arkansas	O	None	$5,000 if incurred within 2 yrs. of accident	70% of lost income up to $140/wk. beginning 8 days after accident, for for up to 52 wks.	Up to $70/wk. beginning 8 days after accident, for up to 52 wks.	$5,000 (if death occurs within one yr. of accident)
Colorado	M	$2,500 (b)	$50,000 if incurred within 5 yrs. (additional $50,000 for rehabilitation expenses incurred within 5 yrs. of accident)	100% of first $125/wk., 70% of next $125/wk., 60% of remainder up to $400/wk., for up to 52 wks.	Up to $25/day for up to 52 wks.	$1,000
Connecticut	-- (c) --					
Delaware	M	None, but amt. of no-fault benefits received cannot be used as evidence in suits for general damage	------ $15,000 per person, $30,000 per accident overall max. on first-party benefits ------			
			Limited only by total benefits limit, but must be incurred within 2 yrs. of accident	Limited only by total benefits limit, but must be incurred within 2 yrs. of accident	Limited only by total benefits limit, but must be incurred within 2 yrs. of accident	Funeral benefit: $3,000 (must be incurred within 2 yrs. of accident)
Florida	M	No dollar threshold (d)	------------------------- $10,000 overall max. on first-party benefits -------------------------			
			80% of all costs	60% of lost income	Limited only by total benefits limit	Funeral benefit: $5,000
Hawaii	M	Amount set annually by state insurance commissioner (b)	------------------------- $20,000 overall max. on first-party benefits -------------------------			
			Limited only by total benefits limit	Up to $1,200/mo.	Up to $800/mo.	Funeral benefit: $15,00
Kansas	M	$2,000 (b)	$4,500 (additional $4,500 for rehabilitation)	Up to $900/mo. for one yr. (if benefits not subject to taxes, max. 85% of lost income)	$25/day for 365 days	Up to $900/mo. for lost income and replacement services for up to one yr., less disability payments received before death. Funeral benefit: $2,000
Kentucky	(e)	$1,000	------------------------- $10,000 overall max. on first-party benefits -------------------------			
			Limited only by total benefits limit	Up to $200/wk. (If not subject to taxes, benefits can be reduced max. 15%)	Up to $200/wk.	Up to $200/wk. each for survivors' economic loss and survivors' replacement services loss. Funeral benefit: $1,000
Maryland	M	None	------------------------- $2,500 overall max. on first-party benefits -------------------------			
			------------------------- for expenses incurred within 3 yrs. of accident -------------------------			
			Limited only by total benefits limit	Limited only by total benefits limit	Limited only by total benefits limit; payable only to non-wage earners	Funeral benefit: limited only by total benefits limit
Massachusetts	M	$2,000 (b)	------------------------- $8,000 overall max. on first-party benefits -------------------------			
			Limited only by total benefits limit, if incurred within 2 yrs.	Up to 75% of lost income	Up to 75% of actual loss	Funeral benefit: limited only by total benefits limit
Michigan (f)	M	No dollar threshold (d)	$1 million minimum	85% of lost income up to 3 yrs.	$20/day for up to 3 yrs.	Up to $1,475/30-day period for lost income for up to 3 yrs. and $20/day for replacement services. Funeral benefits: not less than $1,750 nor more than $5,000
Minnesota	M	$4,000 (b)	-------------------- $20,000 max. for first-party benefits other than medical --------------------			
			$20,000	85% of lost income up to $250/wk.	$200/wk., beginning 8 days after accident	Up to $200/wk. ea. for survivors' economic loss and survivors' replacement services loss. Funeral benefit: $2,000
New Jersey	M	(g)	Max $250,000 Subject to $250 deductible and 20% co-payment between $250 and $5,000	Up to $100/wk. for one yr.	Up to $12/day for a max. of $4,380/ person	Max. amount of benefits victim would have received. Funeral benefit: $1,000

See footnotes at end of table.

STATE NO-FAULT MOTOR VEHICLE INSURANCE LAWS—Continued

State or other jurisdiction	Purchase of first-party benefits	Minimum tort liability threshold (a)	Maximum first-party (no-fault) benefits			
			Medical	Income loss	Replacement services	Survivors/funeral benefits
New York	M	No dollar threshold (d)	----------------------------$50,000 overall max. on first-party benefits----------------------------			
			Limited only by total benefits limit	80% of lost income up to $2,000/mo. for up to 3 yrs.	$25/day for up to one yr.	$2,000 in addition to other benefits
North Dakota	M	$2,500 (d)	----------------------------$30,000 overall max. on first-party benefits----------------------------			
			Limited only by total benefits limit	85% of lost income up to $150/wk.	Up to $15/day	Up to $150/wk. for survivors' income loss and $15/day for survivors' replacement services. Funeral benefit: $3,500
Oregon	M	None	$10,000	If victim is disabled at least 14 days, 70% of lost income up to $1,250/mo. for up to one year.	If victim is disabled at least 14 days up to $30/day for up to one yr. $15/day for child care, up to $450.	Funeral benefit: $2,500
Pennsylvania	M	(h)	$5,000	(i)	(i)	(i)
South Dakota	O	None	$2,000 if incurred within 2 yrs. of accident	$60/wk. for up to 52 wks. for disability extending beyond 14 days of date of accident	None	$10,000 if death occurs within 90 days of accident
Texas	O	None	----------------------------- $2,500 overall max. on first-party benefits -----------------------------			
			Limited only by total benefits limit if incurred within 3 yrs. of accident	Limited only by total benefits limit if incurred within 3 yrs. of accident	Limited only by total benefits limit if incurred within 3 yrs. of accident. Payable only to non-wage earners	Limited only by total benefits limit if incurred within 3 yrs. of accident
Utah	M	$3,000 (b)	$3,000	85% of lost income up to $250/wk. for up to 52 wks., subject to 3-day waiting period which does not apply if disability lasts longer than 2 wks.	$20/day for up to 365 days subject to 3-day waiting period which does not apply if disability lasts longer than 2 wks.	$3,000 survivors benefit. Funeral benefit: $1,500
Virginia	O	None	$2,000 if incurred within one yr. of accident	Up to $100/wk. for max. 52 wks.	None	Funeral benefit: included in medical benefit
Washington	O	None	Up to $35,000	Up to $35,000	Up to $5,000	Funeral benefit: $5,000
Dist. of Columbia	O	(j)	$50,000 or $100,000 (medical and rehabilitation)	$12,000 or $24,000	Max. of $24,000	Funeral benefit: $4,000

Source: State Farm Insurance Companies, *No Fault Press Reference Manual.*

Key:

O — Optional

M — Mandatory

(a) Refers to minimum amount of medical expenses necessary before victim can sue for general damages ("pain and suffering"). Lawsuits allowed in all states for injuries resulting in death and permanent disability. Some states allow lawsuits for one or more of the following: serious and permanent disfigurement, certain temporary disabilities, loss of body member, loss of certain bodily functions, certain fractures, or economic losses (other than medical) which exceed stated limits.

(b) Victim cannot recover unless economic loss exceeds amount *or* injury results in condition(s) cited in legislation (e.g., permanent disfigurement, disability, dismemberment, fractures, etc.).

(c) Connecticut's no-fault insurance law was repealed, effective January 1994.

(d) Victim cannot recover *unless* injury results in condition(s) cited in legislation (e.g., permanent disfigurement, disability, dismemberment, fractures, etc.). In North Dakota, specified dollar amount *and* conditions cited.

(e) Accident victim is not bound by tort restriction if (1) he has rejected the tort limitation in writing or (2) he is injured by a driver who has rejected the tort limitation in writing. Rejection bars recovery of first-party benefits.

(f) Liability for property damage for all states with no-fault insurance under the state tort system. Michigan has no tort liability for vehicle damage, except in cases where damage does not exceed $500.

(g) Motorist chooses one of two optional limitations.

(h) Motorist chooses between full-tort option, with no limit on general damages, and a limited-tort option.

(i) Optional coverages are available to $177,500 maximum, including income loss benefits, accidental death benefits, and funeral benefits, in addition to medical benefits. An extraordinary medical benefits coverage to maximum $1.1 million is available.

(j) If person chooses "personal injury protection" option, victims who are covered by no-fault benefits have up to 60 days after accident to decide whether to receive no-fault benefits. Victims who choose to get no-fault benefits cannot recover damages unless injury resulted in substantial permanent scarring or disfigurement; substantial and medically demonstrable permanent impairment which has significantly affected the victim's ability to perform professional activities or usual and customary daily activities; a medically demonstrable impairment that prevents victim from performing substantially all of his usual customary daily activities for more than 180 continuous days; or medical and rehabilitation expenses or work loss exceeding the amount of no-fault benefits available.

Table 7.39
STATE PUBLIC UTILITY COMMISSIONS

State or other jurisdiction	Regulatory authority	Members		Selection of chair	Length of commissioners' terms (in years)	Number of full-time employees
		Number	Selection			
Alabama............	Public Service Commission	3	E	E	4	152
Alaska.............	Public Utilities Commission	5	GS	G	6	40
Arizona............	Corporation Commission	3	E	C	6	241
Arkansas	Public Service Commission	3	GS	G	6	114
California...........	Public Utilities Commission	5	GS	C	6	1,029
Colorado	Public Utilities Commission	3	GS	G	4	98.5
Connecticut	Department of Public Utility Control	5	GL	C	4	111
Delaware	Public Service Commission	5	GS	G	5	23
Florida	Public Service Commission	5	GS	C	4	391
Georgia............	Public Service Commission	5	E	(a)	6	139
Hawaii	Public Utilities Commission	3	GS	G	6	24
Idaho	Public Utilities Commission	3	GS	C	6	57
Illinois.............	Commerce Commission	7	GS	G	5	401
Indiana	Utility Regulatory Commission	5	GS	G	4	86
Iowa	Utilities Board	3	GS	G	6	74
Kansas	State Corporation Commission	3	GS	C	4	229.5
Kentucky	Public Service Commission	3	GS	G	4	126
Louisiana	Public Service Commission	5	E	C	6	85
Maine	Public Utilities Commission	3	GL	G	6	69
Maryland	Public Service Commission	5	GS	G	5	135
Massachusetts	Department of Public Utilities	3	G	G	4 (b)	123
Michigan	Public Service Commission	3	GS	G	6	206
Minnesota	Public Utilities Commission	5	GS	G	6	40
Mississippi	Public Service Commission	3	E	C	4	139
Missouri	Public Service Commission	5	GS	G	6	197
Montana............	Public Service Commission	5	E	C	4	47
Nebraska	Public Service Commission	5	E	C	6	59
Nevada	Public Service Commission	5	G	G	4	118
New Hampshire	Public Utilities Commission	3	GC	GC	6	55
New Jersey..........	Board of Regulatory Commissioners	3	GS	G	6	388
New Mexico.........	Public Utility Commission	3	GS	G	6	50
New York	Public Service Commission	5	GS	G	6	685
North Carolina	Utilities Commission	7	GL	G	8	134
North Dakota	Public Service Commission	3	E	C	6	51
Ohio	Public Utilities Commission	5	GS (c)	G	5	490
Oklahoma	Corporation Commission	3	E	C	6	428
Oregon	Public Utility Commission	3	GS	C	4	459
Pennsylvania	Public Utility Commission	5	GS	G	5	581
Rhode Island	Public Utilities Commission	3	GS	G	6	38
South Carolina	Public Service Commission	7	L (d)	(a)	4 (e)	144
South Dakota	Public Utilities Commission	3	E	C	6	24
Tennessee	Public Service Commission	3	E	C	6	281
Texas..............	Public Utility Commission	3	GS	C	6	227
Utah	Public Service Commission	3	GS	G	6	17
Vermont	Public Service Board	3	GS	G	6	14
Virginia............	State Corporation Commission	3	L	(a)	6	592
Washington	Utilities & Transportation Commission	3	GS	G	6	238
West Virginia	Public Service Commission	3	GS	G	6	230
Wisconsin..........	Public Service Commission	3	GS	G	6	184.5
Wyoming	Public Service Commission	3	GS	C	6	30
Dist. of Columbia	Public Service Commission	3	MC	MC	4	82
Guam	Public Utilities Commission	6	GL	N.A.	6	N.A.
Puerto Rico	Public Service Commission	5	GS	GS	4	264
U.S. Virgin Islands	Public Service Commission	9 (f)	GS (f)	C	3	4

Source: National Association of Regulatory Utility Commissioners, *Profiles of Regulatory Agencies of the United States and Canada, Yearbook 1992-1993.* (Washington, D.C.: 1993).

Note: See Table 7.40, "Selected Regulatory Functions of State Public Utility Commissions," for information on commissions' authority.

Key:
G — Appointed by Governor.
GC — Appointed by Governor, with consent of the Governor's Council.
C — Elected by the Commission.
GS — Elected by Governor, with consent of Senate.
L — Appointed by the Legislature.
GL — Appointed by Governor, with consent of entire Legislature.
MC — Appointed by the Mayor, with consent of City Council.
E — Elected by the public.
N.A. — Information not available.

(a) Chairmanship rotates annually.
(b) Co-terminous with governor's.
(c) After nomination by PUC Nominating Council.
(d) Upon recommendation of State Merit Selection Panel.
(e) Concurrent terms.
(f) 7 voting, 2 non-voting. Voting members appointed by governor and confirmed by Senate; nonvoting appointed by Senate president.

Table 7.40
SELECTED REGULATORY FUNCTIONS OF STATE PUBLIC UTILITY COMMISSIONS

State or other jurisdiction	Controls rates of privately owned utilities on sales to ultimate consumers of			Prescribe temporary rates, pending investigation			Require prior authorization of the changes			Suspend proposed rate changes			Initiate rate investigation on its own motion		
	Electric	Gas	Telephone	Electric	Gas	Telephone	Electric	Gas	Telephone	Electric	Gas	Telephone	Electric	Gas	Telephone
Alabama	★	★	★	★	★	...	★	★	★	★	★	★	★	★	★
Alaska	★	★	★	★	★	★	★	★	★	(a)	(a)	(a)	★	★	★
Arizona	★	★	★	★	★	★	★	★	★	★	★	★	★	★	★
Arkansas	★	★	★	★	★	★	★	★	★	★	★	★	★	★	★
California	★	★	★	★	★ (b)	★ (b)	★	★		★	★	★	★	★	★
Colorado	★	★	★	★ (c)	★ (c)	★ (c)	★	★	★	★	★	★	★	★	★
Connecticut	★	★	★	★	★	★	★	★	★	★	★	★	★	★	★
Delaware	★	★	★	★	★	★	★	★	★	★	★	★	★	★	★
Florida	★	★	★	★	★	★	★	★	★	★	★	★	★	★	★
Georgia	★	★	★	★	★	★	★	★	★	★	★	★	★	★	★
Hawaii	★	★	★	★	★	★	★	★	★	(a)	(a)	(a)	★	★	★
Idaho	★	★	★ (d)	★	★	★	★ (e)	★ (e)	★ (e)	★	★	★	★	★	★
Illinois	★	★	★	★	★	★	★	★	★	★	★	★	★	★	★
Indiana	★	★	★	★	★	★ (f)	★	★	★	★	★	★	★	★	★
Iowa	★	★	★ (f)	★	★	★ (f)	★	★	★ (f)	★	★	★ (f)	★	★	★ (f)
Kansas	★	★	★	★	★	★	★	★	★	★	★	★	★	★	★
Kentucky	★	★	★	★	★	★	★	★	★	★	★	★	★	★	★
Louisiana	★	★ (g)	★	★	★	★	★	★	★	★	★	★	★	★	★
Maine	★	★	★	★	★	★	★	★	★	★	★	★	★	★	★
Maryland	★	★	★	★	★	★	★	★	★	★	★	★	★	★	★
Massachusetts	★	★	★ (h)	★	★	★	★	★	★	(a)	(a)	(a)	★	★	★
Michigan	★	★	★ (h)	★ (i)	★ (i)	★ (i)	★	★	★	★	★	★	★	★	★
Minnesota	★	★ (j)	★ (k)	★	★	★	★	★	★ (k)	★	★	★	★	★	★
Mississippi	★	★	★	★	★	★	★	★	★	★	★	★	★	★	★
Missouri	★	★	★	★	★	★	★	★	★	★	★	★	★	★	★
Montana	★	★	★	★	★	★	★	★	★	★	★	★	...	★	★
Nebraska (l)	...	...	★	...	...	...	...	...	...	...	...	★	...	...	★
Nevada	★	★	★	★	★	...	★	★	★	★	★	★	★	★	★
New Hampshire	★	★	★	★	★	★	★	★	★	★	★	★	★	★	★
New Jersey	★	★	★	★	★	★	★	★	★	★	★	★	★	★	★
New Mexico Public Service Comm.	★	★	...	★	★		★	★	...	★	★	...	★	★	...
State Corporation Comm.	...	...	★	...	...	★	...	...	★	...	...	★	...	...	★
New York	★	★	★	★	★	★	★	★	★	★	★	★	★	★	★
North Carolina	★	★	★	★	★	★	★	★	★	★	★	★	★	★	★ (n)
North Dakota	★	★	★ (m)	★	★	...	★	★	...	★	★	...	★	★	★
Ohio	★	★	★	★	★	★	★	★	★	★	★	★	★	★	★
Oklahoma	★	★	★	★	★	★	★	★	★	★	★	★	★	★	★
Oregon	★	★	★	★	★	★	★	★	★	★	★	★	★	★	★
Pennsylvania	★	★	★	★	★	★	★	★	★	★	★	★	★	★	★
Rhode Island	★	★	★	★	★	...	★	★	★	★	...	★	★	★	★
South Carolina	★	★	★	★	★	★	★	★	★	★	★	★	★	★	★
South Dakota	★	★	★ (o)	★	★	★	★	★	★	★	★	★	★	★	★
Tennessee	★	★	★	★ (p)	★ (p)	★	★	★	★	★	★	★	★	★	★
Texas Public Utilities Comm.	★	...	★	★	...	...	★	...	...	★	...	★	★	...	★
Railroad Comm.	...	★ (q)	...	...	★	...	...	★	...	...	★	...	...	★	...
Utah	★	★	★	★	★	★	★	★	★	★	★	★	★	★	★
Vermont	★	★	★	★	★	★	★	★	★	★	★	★	★	★	★
Virginia	★	★	★	★	★	★ (r)	★	★	★ (r)	★	★	★	★	★	★
Washington	★	★	★	★	★	★	★	★	★	★	★	★	★	★	★
West Virginia	★	★	★	★	★	★	★	★	★	(a)	(a)	(a)	★	★	★
Wisconsin	★	★	★ (s)	★	★	★	★	★	★	★	★	★	★	★	★
Wyoming	★	★	★	★	★	★	★	★	★	★	★	★	★	★	★
Dist. of Columbia	★	★	★	★	★	★	★	★	★	★	★	★	★	★	★
Puerto Rico	...	★	★ (t)	...	...	★ (t)	...	...	★ (t)	...	...	★ (t)	...	...	★ (t)
U.S. Virgin Islands	...	...	★	★	...	★	★	...	★	...	...	★	...	...	★

SELECTED REGULATORY FUNCTIONS—Continued

Source: National Association of Regulatory Utility Commissioners, *Utility Regulatory Policy in the United States and Canada*, 1992-1993 (Washington, D.C.: 1993).

Note: Full names of commissions are shown on Table 7.39, "State Public Utility Commissions."

Key:

★ — Yes

. . . — No

(a) Rate changes do not go into effect until approved by Commission.

(b) Authority is not exercised.

(c) No specific statutory authority.

(d) Rates for local exchange companies (LECs) and LECs providing intraLATA toll only.

(e) Rates become effective after expiration of suspension period if Commission does not take action.

(f) Not for companies with less than 15,000 customers and less than 15,000 access lines.

(g) Except no authority over rates charged to industrial customers by any gas company.

(h) Rates for basic local exchange services only.

(i) Interim rates may be prescribed after statutory requirements are met.

(j) Rates not regulated for gas utilities serving fewer than 650 customers.

(k) Five local exchange companies must have prior approval to change rates; other 89 companies must give notice, but do not need PUC approval.

(l) Telephone is the only regulated utility with jurisdiction limited to rate increases for basic exchange service of more than 10 percent during a 12-month period. State has no private power companies. Natural gas is provided by private companies through franchise granted by each local jurisdiction.

(m) PSC does not regulate local rates for 14 telephone cooperatives, six small independents nor rates for resellers.

(n) Upon complaint proceeding only.

(o) PUC does not regulate rates of rural telephone cooperatives, or of 13 independents and three municipals.

(p) Emergency only.

(q) Only over services offered outside corporate limits.

(r) Companies participating in experimental regulatory plan have rate flexibility for services deemed competitive.

(s) Of the 96 LECs operating in the state, only 12 are fully regulated.

(t) The Puerto Rico Telephone Authority, a state public corporation, purchased the Puerto Rico Telephone Company.

State Lobby Laws in the 1990s

States are attempting to place more regulations on lobbying without jeopardizing constitutional rights.

by Joyce Bullock

While the U.S. Constitution guarantees the right for an individual to lobby government, the role of money in the petitioning process has been the focus of lobby law regulations throughout the country. In their ongoing efforts to limit this aspect of access to government officials without jeopardizing constitutional rights, states have developed regulations in the areas of registration, reporting requirements and limitations on lobbying activities such as giving gifts or taking part in fund-raising activities for public officials.

Major New Laws

New major reform laws continue to be linked with the aftermath of scandals. Since 1990, three states have called special legislative sessions and passed new ethics laws containing lobbying provisions due to scandals in their legislatures: Arizona (November 1991), Kentucky (February 1993) and South Carolina (September 1991). Arizona's new law requires lobbyists to itemize expenditures over $20 and prohibits them from giving anything valued at $10 or more to public officials and employees. Lobbyists also are banned from fundraising during legislative sessions. Gone, too, is a loophole that allowed lobbyists to avoid reporting entertainment-related expenditures. Kentucky's new law (S.B. 2) prohibits lobbyists and their employers from giving anything of value to legislators or their immediate family. Meals are exempt under this provision; but lobbyists are limited to $100 per year per legislator, regardless of the number of employers.

South Carolina's comprehensive Ethics Reform Act requires extensive reporting and disclosure by lobbyists and their clients (principals). Lobbyists now must disclose any business dealings among lobbyists, their principals and any public officials or employees. The state now prohibits anyone, not just lobbyists, from giving anything of value to public officials and employees. Lobbyists' principals are limited to gifts of $200 per year per official. The 180 requests for lobby-related advisory opinions the state received during the act's first year indicate that the Ethics Reform Act's impact on how state employees and registered lobbyists do business will be significant.[1]

Banned Lobbyist Activities

Gifts

Does the right to lobby extend to lobbyists the right to give gifts to public officials? California, Connecticut, Michigan, South Carolina and Wisconsin say "no" and restrict the amount a lobbyist may spend per year or per day on each official. (See Table 7.41) Thirty-nine states also prohibit public officials from *accepting* gifts. The gift value and time period for the gift restriction varies. South Carolina now joins Wisconsin in applying the tough "no cup of coffee" provision. Public employees in both states are banned from accepting gifts of value even if it is as inexpensive as a cup of coffee. Almost as stringent is Iowa's 1992 measure (H.F. 2466), which prohibits all gifts to officials except food and drink valued at $3 or less and consumed at one sitting.[2]

Kentucky's new gift restriction is an example of states experimenting with defining a tolerance level for gift restrictions. Lobbyists in Kentucky may not give anything of value to legislators or their immediate family with

Joyce Bullock is a senior policy analyst with the State Policy and Innovations Group of The Council of State Governments.

the exception of meals (limited to $100 per year per legislator) and for informational or promotional items. Similarly, Georgia in April 1992 set a $100 limit on gifts that public officials can accept from lobbyists. By 1992, 15 states set a gift restriction for public employees in the $100 or less range. Disclosure begins at a lower level.[3]

A 1989 national survey conducted by Associated Press/Media General showed that 87 percent of the American public thought it should be illegal for lobbyists to give gifts to legislators.[4] If this sentiment continues, states can be expected to move towards zero tolerance in future gifts restrictions.

Campaign contributions and activities

That same survey showed that 75 percent of the public thought it should be illegal for lobbyists to contribute to legislators' campaigns. Laws passed since 1990 show that the lobbyist's permitted role in such campaign-related activities already is narrowing. Colorado, Kentucky, South Carolina and Vermont completely ban lobbyists from contributing to campaigns at any time. These four, and 18 other states, prohibit lobbyist contributions during a legislative session: Alabama, Alaska, Arizona, Arkansas, Connecticut, Georgia, Iowa, Kansas, Louisiana, Minnesota (also applies to caucuses), Nevada, New Mexico, North Carolina, Oregon, Texas, Utah, Washington and Wisconsin. (See Table 7.41)

New Mexico's new law bans both public officials from soliciting and lobbyists from giving campaign contributions during legislative sessions. Vermont now also prohibits public officials from soliciting any gifts for any purpose while the Legislature is in session. Currently Alabama, Florida, Idaho, Iowa, Maryland, Nebraska, Nevada, Oregon, South Carolina, South Dakota, Utah, Vermont and Wisconsin prohibit officials or employees from soliciting lobbyists for contributions of gifts. Louisiana requires lobbyists to provide written notice of fund-raisers during a session not less than 30 days before the function (1993). Minnesota has placed stricter reporting requirements on lobbyists who directly solicit or cause others to make political contributions in excess of $5,000.[5]

Post-employment Restrictions

Post-employment restrictions are directed at former public officials and employees, however, the desirable effect is to lessen public-employees-turned-professional-lobbyists' impact on the political system. These new lobbyists can use their past professional contacts with present lawmakers and public employees to their clients' advantage. Since companies and interest groups are willing to pay top dollar for former lawmakers and political appointees to lobby their interests, states are experimenting with measures to curb this "revolving door" phenomenon.

In Iowa (H.F. 2466, 1993) former legislators and former state decision-makers now are prohibited for two years after state service from representing someone before their former state agency and from lobbying. Administration of this provision rests with the state's attorney general. Kentucky (S.B. 7, 1993) restricts public employees from lobbying the government for one year and former legislators (S.B. 2, 1993) for two years. (The Kentucky General Assembly's regular session is every two years.) South Carolina now bans legislators from serving on state boards and commissions (with some exceptions). In 1992, Florida extended its two-year revolving door policy for state officers and employees when it mandated county, municipal or special district levels of government to adopt revolving door policies for its officers elected after October 1, 1992.[6]

Currently, 35 states have post-government employment restrictions, many of which were passed since 1988. Seventeen states have set one or two years as the required waiting period following employment.[7]

Registration and Reporting Requirements

Any individual has the right to lobby government. States focus their registration and reporting requirements on professional lobbyists, and to a lesser extent their employers (also referred to as their principals). A common assumption in regulatory policy is that registration and disclosure control the financial aspects of lobbying, and states set policy in these areas to complement outright prohibited activities.

The litmus test used for identifying a lobbyist varies from state to state. Some states use the amount of time, money spent or money earned in lobbying as a determinant, while others are more concerned with who (legislators or administrative agencies' employees) the lobbyists are lobbying. Still other states use a combination of these to define a lobbyist.

All 50 states require lobbyists to register if they lobby the legislature. Newer provisions extend that requirement to lobbyists of the executive branch or require agencies that lobby the legislature to register and report expenditures. South Carolina includes agency lobbying under its 1991 Ethics Reform Act; and Arizona, also in 1991, expanded its lobby law requirements to include universities, towns and cities. Illinois, New Mexico and Vermont all passed measures in 1993 that require lobbyists of the executive branch to register. New Jersey passed a similar measure in 1991. Utah's 1992 lobby law narrows the scope of executive branch lobbying to include only individuals seeking a position regarding rules and regulations and not other citizen contact with the executive branch. Table 7.41 breaks down each state's definition of lobbyists in detail.

In 1992, Georgia became the 49th state (the exception is Wyoming) to establish disclosure requirements for lobbyists. The 49 states require lobbyists to file periodic financial reports of expenditures made in their efforts to access and communicate with government officials. Eleven states have more frequent reporting requirements during legislative sessions to track this activity. (See Table 7.42)

In recent years, states have sought to flesh out more information in these periodic reports. Itemization of expenditures, including the amount per public official and the occasion for the expense is one aspect of new itemization language. Just what must be itemized and the related thresholds for such detailed disclosure vary from state to state. However, 10 states require lobbyists' expenditures to contain some sort of itemization. (See Table 7.42)

Illinois strengthened its lobby requirements by passing a tough new lobby law in August 1993. Now Illinois lobbyists must provide itemized reporting for all expenditures by categories (i.e., travel, gifts, honoraria and entertainment).

In addition, lobbyists' employers, which were previously exempted, must also register and report. A new Louisiana law (H.B.2037, 1993) requires lobbyists to disclose all expenditures, including food or drink. Nevada lobbyists now must report the name and agenda of their employers as well as every expenditure of more than $50 made to a legislator. The latter must specify the amount and the recipient (1993). As of January 1993, lobbyists in Iowa must now disclose the names of their clients and any campaign contributions they make. A 1993 Vermont law requires lobbyists to report on expenditures that include research, consulting, travel, meals and lodging. They must also identify their employers and the agenda for which they lobby.[8]

Technology and Disclosure

Computer technology provides new possibilities for tracking lobbyist activity. With increased technology and auditory authority (such as subpoena of records or people), agencies will be able to track what lobbyists say they gave to what public officials report they received (personal financial disclosure reports). The capability also will be available for lobbyists' reports of campaign contributions to be compared with the actual campaign committees' filed financial reports. The Ohio secretary of state's office has been experimenting with this cross-checking capability.

The Washington Public Disclosure Commission's (PDC's) Micro-computer Access to Grassroots Information on Campaigns (MAGIC) is being copied by other states. The PDC has considered developing a data base on registered lobbyists with possible plans for expansion to include financial information from reports submitted by lobbyists and their employers. Such activity is now pending the outcome of a major revision by the Washington Legislature of the state's ethics laws and their administration.

Georgia's new law provides for the expenditure reports to be kept on disk and made available to the public. The Texas Ethics Disclosure Database (TEDD) went on-line in January 1993, providing electronic access to all information required to be filed by lobbyists, candidates, officeholders, political action committees and state officers. The Texas Ethics Commission plans to provide for electronic filing of reports within the next few years.[9]

Ethics Education for Lobbyists

In 1990, the California Legislature amended its Political Reform Act to require both lobbyists and legislators to attend an ethics orientation course. Lobbyists must take the training class in order to register to lobby. Wisconsin has amended its statutes to permit and encourage the Wisconsin Ethics Board to prepare and present programs and materials for lobbyists, local officials, municipal attorneys and state officials on lobbying practices and standards for state and local officials. The Board will receive credit for copy, postage and location-related expenses.

Looking Ahead

Registration fees

In an atmosphere of budget cuts, a growing number of registered lobbyists and the demand for expanded services, states will continue to experiment with alternatives to subsidizing required services. One such area being tapped is lobbyist registration fees. As of 1992, 29 states had registration fees.[10] Expect to see higher fees passed by states in the future even though opponents say it is like putting a price tag on a constitutional privilege.

Code of conduct for lobbyists

Can a state impose a code of conduct on lobbyists describing how they must carry out their constitutional right to lobby? States are considering the possibility. The Maryland General Assembly considered a code of ethics for lobbyists in 1993. The bill passed the Senate but not the House. In 1992, Florida also considered a code of conduct for lobbyists, but with similar results. Expect to see other states consider measures to test this issue.

Changing definition of lobbyists

States will continue to expand the definition of lobbyists to include agency lobbying, as was discussed earlier. There also will be measures to regulate local/municipal lobbyists at either the state or local level.

Investigatory authority and enforcement

According to Alan Rosenthal, professor with the Eagleton Institute of Politics at Rutgers University, most state governments spend little to monitor lobbying, and half the states have only one or a part-time staffer to oversee the task.[11] Such authority and the manpower to undertake it are the measuring sticks of a lobby agency's ability to enforce the regulations it sets. Many agencies will seek to increase their authority and funding to audit lobbyists' financial reports and to enforce regulations.

Conclusion

Widely publicized scandals at the federal and state level continue to bring ethics and lobbying back as front-burner issues in the states. In light of current public sentiment, lobby-related reform will continue as an active issue. Expect to see state legislatures, which set up lobby laws in the late 1970s, re-examine their programs in light of a movement towards zero tolerance and greater emphasis on agencies' investigatory authority and public access.

Notes

[1] James P. Fields Jr., and Deborah A. Davis, "View From the Regulated: Lawyers in Private Practice Review the Year-old South Carolina Ethics Act," *COGEL Guardian*, Vol. 14, No. 2 (April 1993), p. 5, 9.

[2] "Lobby Disclosure Reform," *Common Cause State Issue Brief*, (Washington, D.C.: Common Cause) January 1994, p. 17.

[3] Joyce Bullock, ed., *COGEL Blue Book*, Ninth Edition, (Lexington, Ky: The Council of State Governments, 1993), pp. 158-162.

[4] Alan Rosenthal, *The Third House: Lobbyists and Lobbying in the States*, (Washington, D.C.: Congressional Quarterly Inc.) 1993, p. 108.

[5] *Lobby Law 1993*. (Los Angeles: Council on Governmental Ethics Laws) January 1994, p. 11.

[6] R. Roth Judd, "Ethics Codes and Commissions: Legislation, 1991-1992," *Ethics and Lobbying 1992: Legislation and Litigation*, (Lexington, Ky: The Council of State Governments) 1992, 1.21.

[7] Bullock.

[8] "Lobby Disclosure Reform," p. 25.

[9] *Lobby Law 1993*, pp. 29-32.

[10] Bullock, pp. 176-179.

[11] Rosenthal, p. 108.

Table 7.41
LOBBYISTS: DEFINITIONS AND PROHIBITED ACTIVITIES

State or other jurisdiction	Definition of a lobbyist includes							Prohibited activities involving lobbyists					
	Legislative lobbying	Administrative agency lobbying	Elective officials as lobbyists	Public employees as lobbyists	Compensation standard	Expenditure standard	Time standard	Making campaign contributions at any time	Making campaign contributions during legislative sessions	Making expenditures in excess of $ per official per year	Solicitation by officials or employees for contributions or gifts	Contingent compensation	Other
Alabama	★	...	...	...	...	...	★	...	★	...	★	★	...
Alaska	★	★	...	...	...	...	★	...	★	...	...	★	...
Arizona*	★	★	...	...	...	...	...	...	★	...	...	...	...
Arkansas	★	★	★	...	...	★	...	...	★	...	...	...	...
California	★	★	...	★	★	...	★	...	...	...	(a)	★	(b)
Colorado	★	...	★	...	★	★	...	★	★	...	...	★	...
Connecticut	★	★	...	...	★	★	★	...	★	...	...	★	(b,c)
Delaware	★	...	...	...	...	...	...	...	...	...	...	...	...
Florida	★	★	...	★	...	...	...	...	★	...	★	★	...
Georgia	★	...	...	★	★	★	...	...	★	...	...	...	(d)
Hawaii	★	★	...	...	★	★	★	...	...	...	★	★	...
Idaho	★	...	★	★	★	...	...	...	...	...	★	★	(e)
Illinois	★	★	...	...	...	...	...	...	...	...	...	★	(f)
Indiana	★	...	...	...	★	★	...	...	...	...	...	★	...
Iowa	★	★	...	...	...	...	...	...	★	(g)	★	★	...
Kansas	★	★	...	...	...	★	...	...	★	$40 (h)	★	★	...
Kentucky	★	...	...	...	★	...	...	★	★	$100	...	...	(i)
Louisiana	★	...	★	...	★	★	...	...	★	...	...	...	...
Maine	★	...	...	...	★	★	★	...	...	...	...	...	(j)
Maryland	★	★	...	...	★	★	★	...	...	...	★	★	...
Massachusetts*	★	★	...	...	★	...	...	...	...	...	...	★	(b)
Michigan	★	★	...	★	★	★	★	...	...	...	★	★	(k)
Minnesota	★	★	★	★	★	★	★	...	...	...	...	★	...
Mississippi	★	★	...	...	★	...	...	...	...	...	...	...	(l)
Missouri	★	★	★	★	★	★	★	...	...	...	...	...	(l)
Montana	★	...	...	★	...	★	...	...	...	...	★ (m)	★	...
Nebraska*	★	...	...	...	...	...	...	...	...	...	★	...	(n)
Nevada	★	...	★	★	...	...	...	...	★	$100	★	★	...
New Hampshire	★	...	...	...	★	...	...	...	...	...	...	...	...
New Jersey	★	★	...	...	★	...	★	...	...	...	...	...	...
New Mexico	★	★	...	★	...	...	...	...	★	...	...	★	...
New York	★	★	...	...	★	★	★	...	★	...	...	★	...
North Carolina	★	...	...	(o)	...	...	...	...	...	...	...	★	...
North Dakota	★	...	...	...	★	★	★	...	...	...	...	★	...
Ohio	★	★	...	★	★	★	...	...	...	...	...	★	...
Oklahoma	★	★	...	...	★	★	...	...	...	...	...	★	(p)
Oregon	★	...	★	★	★	★	★	...	...	...	(q)	★	...
Pennsylvania	★	★	...	...	★	★	...	...	...	...	...	★	...
Rhode Island	★	...	...	...	...	...	...	...	...	...	...	...	...
South Carolina	★	★	...	★	...	...	...	★	★	(r)	★	★	(b,r)
South Dakota	★	...	...	★	...	...	★	...	...	...	★	★	...
Tennessee	★	★	...	★	★	★	...	...	★	...	...	...	...
Texas	★	★	★	★	★	★	★	...	★	(s)	...	★	(t)
Utah	★	★	★	★	★	★	★	...	★	...	★	★	...
Vermont	★	★	...	★	★	★	...	★	★	...	★	★	...
Virginia	----------(u)----------												
Washington	★	★	★	★	★	★	★	...	★	...	...	★	...
West Virginia	★	★	...	...	★	★	...	...	...	...	...	...	...
Wisconsin	★	★	...	★	★	...	★	...	★	...	★	★	...
Wyoming	★	...	...	★	...	...	...	...	...	...	...	...	(v)
Dist. of Columbia	★	★	...	...	★	★	★	...	...	$100	...	...	...

LOBBYISTS: DEFINITION AND PROHIBITED AREAS—Continued

Source: The Council of State Governments' survey, March 1994, except as noted by * where data are from *The Book of the States 1992-93.*
Key:
★ — Application exists
. . . — Not applicable

(a) No prohibition on officials soliciting but officials may only accept gifts from a single source in any calendar year with a total value of $250.

(b) Lobbyists making gifts in excess of the following thresholds to state officials: California, $10 per month per official; Connecticut, $50 for gifts per year, $150 for food and drink per year; Michigan, $37 per month per official; South Carolina, anything of value.

(c) Giving of fees and honoraria banned; "necessary expenses" allowed.

(d) Offering or proposing anything which may be reasonably construed to improperly influence a legislator's official acts, decisions or votes. Lobbying without registering.

(e) Expenditures without full disclosure; lobbying without registering.

(f) Legislative officials, full-time public officials or employees may not receive compensation for lobbying. Lobbying without registering, if compensated.

(g) Expenditures in excess of $3 per official in any one calendar day.

(h) Limit applies only to state officials and employees who license, inspect and regulate the lobbyist.

(i) State employees prohibited from lobbying.

(j) Lobbyist cannot solicit, serve on committees or transmit funds relating to legislative elections. By order of the speaker of the House and president of the Senate, legislators cannot hold fund-raisers during the legislative session.

(k) Commercial use of information on all disclosure programs filed with the Ethical Practices Board.

(l) Employment of non-registered lobbyists.

(m) If over $50 per month.

(n) Instigating the introduction of legislation for the purpose of obtaining employment to lobby in opposition thereto. Making false statements or misrepresentation to legislators or in a registration report concerning lobbying activities. Except during specified periods, acting as a lobbyist without being registered.

(o) State government agency liaisons lobbying on issues concerning their agency (no fee).

(p) May not knowingly make a false statement or representation of fact to legislative, judicial or executive branches; nor knowingly provide, to same, a copy of a document which contains a false statement without written notification of such; nor appear, during session, on the floor of the House or Senate in the absence of an express invitation.

(q) During regular session.

(r) Lobbyists or their principals cannot offer to pay for lodging, transportation, meals, entertainment, beverages, etc., unless all members of the General Assembly, the House or the Senate, or one of the committees, subcommittees, legislative caucuses or county legislative delegations are also invited.

(s) Expenditures in excess of $500 per year for entertainment or gifts.

(t) Lobbying without registering; giving loans or gifts of cash to legislators; pleasure trips; appearing, during session, on the floor of the House or Senate without an invitation.

(u) In early 1994, the Ethics Committee met to consider significant changes to Virginia's laws on lobbyists. No information available as of April 1994.

(v) Lobbying without registering.

Table 7.42
LOBBYISTS: REGISTRATION AND REPORTING

State or other jurisdiction	Agency which administers registration and reporting requirements for lobbyists	Frequency	Legislation/administrative action seeking to influence	Expenditures benefiting public officials or employees	Compensation received [broken down by employer(s)]	Total compensation received	Categories of expenditures	Total expenditures	Contributions received from other for lobbying purposes	Other
Alabama	Ethics Comm.	Monthly (a)	★	...	...	...	★	...	...	...
Alaska	Public Offices Comm.	Monthly (b)	★	★	★	★	★	★	...	...
Arizona*	Secretary of State	Annually (c)	...	(d)	...	...	...	...	...	...
Arkansas	Ethics Comm. (e)	Monthly and quarterly	...	...	...	★	★	...	...	...
California	Fair Political Practices Comm.	Quarterly	★	★	★	★	...	★	★	(f)
Colorado	Secretary of State	Monthly	★	★	★	★	★	★	...	...
Connecticut	State Ethics Comm.	Monthly (a,g)	★	(h)	★	★	★	★	...	(i)
Delaware	Legislative Council	Quarterly	...	★	...	...	★	★	...	...
Florida	Jt. Legislative Mgt. Cmte.	Quarterly	...	★	...	...	★	★	★	...
Georgia	Ethics Comm.	Monthly (b)	★	★	...	...	...	...	...	...
Hawaii	State Ethics Comm.	Jan., March	★	★	...	★	★	★	★	...
Idaho	Secretary of State	Monthly (a) and annually	★	★	...	...	★	★	...	...
Illinois	Secretary of State	Semi-annually and annually	...	★	...	...	★	★	...	(d,j,k)
Indiana	Lobby Registration Comm.	Semi-annually	★	★	...	...	...	★	...	(l)
Iowa	Secretary of Senate, Clerk of House	Monthly (m)	★	★	...	...	...	★	...	...
Kansas	Comm. on Gov't'l. Standards & Conduct	(n)	...	...	...	...	★	...	...	...
Kentucky	Legislative Ethics Comm.	(o)	...	...	★	...	★	★	...	(p)
Louisiana	Secretary of Senate, Clerk of House	Annually	★	★	...	...	...	★	...	...
Maine	Comm. on Gov't'l. Ethics	Monthly (a) and after session	★	★	★	★	★	★	...	...
Maryland	Ethics Comm.	Semi-annually	★	★	★	★	★	★	(q)	...
Massachusetts*	Secretary of State	Semi-annually	★	★	★	★	★	★	...	...
Michigan	Dept. of State	Semi-annually	★	★ (r)	...	...	★	★	...	(s)
Minnesota	Ethical Practices Bd.	Three times a year	★	...	...	...	★	★	★	(t)
Mississippi (u)	Secretary of State	Annually and after session	...	★	★	★	★	★	★	...
Missouri	Ethics Comm.	Monthly (a)	★	★	...	...	★	★	...	(v)
Montana	Commr. of Political Practices		★	★	★	★	★	★	(w)	...
Nebraska*	Accountability & Disclosure Comm.	Monthly (a,x)	★	★	...	★	★	★	(y)	(j)
Nevada	Legislative Counsel Bureau	Monthly (a) and after session	...	★	...	...	★	★	...	...
New Hampshire	Secretary of State	April, Aug., Dec.	★	★	★	...	★	★	...	...
New Jersey	Election Law Enforcement Comm.	Annually and quarterly	★	★	★	★	★	★	★	...
New Mexico	Secretary of State	After session	★	★	...	...	★	★	★	...
New York	State Comm. on Lobbying	Quarterly	★	★	★	★	★	...	...	...
North Carolina	Secretary of State	After session	...	...	(z)	...	★	...	...	...
North Dakota	Secretary of State	Annually	...	...	...	...	...	...	...	(aa)
Ohio	(bb)	Every four months	★	★	...	...	...	★	...	(k)
Oklahoma	Ethics Comm.	Biennially	...	★	...	...	...	...	...	(cc)
Oregon	Gov't. Ethics Comm.	(dd)	★	...	★	...	★	★	...	...
Pennsylvania	Secretary of Senate, Clerk of House	Semi-annually	...	★	...	...	★	...	...	...
Rhode Island	Secretary of State	(ee)	★	...	★	★	★	★	...	...
South Carolina	Ethics Comm.	Semi-annually	★	★	★	★	★	★	★	...
South Dakota	Secretary of State	After session	★	...	...	...	★	★	...	...
Tennessee	Registry of Election Finance	Semi-annually	...	★	...	...	★	★	...	...
Texas	Ethics Comm.	Monthly and annually	★	★	(ff) ★	★	★	★	...	...
Utah	Lieutenant Governor	(gg)	★	★	...	...	...	★	...	...
Vermont	Secretary of State	Semi-annually (hh)	★	★	★	★	...	...	...	(ii)
Virginia	------------------------------ (jj) ------------------------------									
Washington	Public Disclosure Comm.	Monthly	★	★	★	★	★	★	...	...
West Virginia	Ethics Comm.	After session and annually	★	★	...	...	★	★	...	...
Wisconsin	Ethics Board	Biennially	★	(kk)	★	★	★	★	...	(ll)
Wyoming	Legislative Service Office	...	...	...	...	...	...	...	...	(mm)
Dist. of Columbia	Bd. of Elections & Ethics	Biennially	★	★	★	★	★	★	★	...

Source: The Council of State Governments' survey, March 1994, except as noted by * where data are from *The Book of the States 1992-93.*

Key:

★ — Application exists

. . . — Not applicable

(a) During legislative session. In Missouri, filed with the secretary of Senate and clerk of the House.

(b) During legislative session, quarterly thereafter.

(c) Also monthly during those months in which any single expenditure exceeds $25.

(d) Entertainment expense.

(e) Reporting forms are filed with the secretary of state.

(f) Campaign contributions made; lump sum reporting of overhead and other payments in connection with lobbying activities.

(g) Also, first, second and fourth quarters.

(h) In detail, if over $10 per person.

(i) Fundamental terms of lobbying contracts.

(j) Disclosure of honoraria or other money loaned, promised or paid to official or staff of legislative or executive branches of state government.

(k) Categories of expenditures exceeding thresholds.

(l) Compensation and reimbursement to others, receptions, and entertainment. Compensated lobbyists must report on behalf of each client by filing an activity report naming the client.

(m) In the Senate, reports are required only if $15 or more is provided to senators or their staff on any one day.

(n) February, March, April, May, September, and December.

(o) Initial registration begins seven days after engagement to lobby. Updated registration forms are due not later than the 15th day of January, February, March, April, May and September of even-numbered years; the 15th day of January, May and September of odd-numbered years.

(p) Expenditures for individual legislators which exceed $100 on an occasion or $1,000 in a year and expenditures for recognized groups of legislators.

(q) To a limited extent.

(r) Food and beverage expenditures for public officials are disclosed. Expenditures for persons who are not public officials are not disclosed.

(s) Financial transactions of $775 or more are disclosed. Gifts in excess of $37 to a single public official are prohibited.

(t) Metropolitan governmental unit action seeking to influence.

(u) Effective January 1, 1995, Mississippi will require lobbyists to disclose the name of the government official whenever anything of value is given by a lobbyist.

(v) Business relationships with public officials, if over $50.

(w) If over $250.

(x) Also, at end of legislative session and after end of interim between sessions.

(y) Must report names and addresses of persons giving more than $100.

(z) Only if lobbyist is not a full-time employee for employer nor on annual retainer.

(aa) Any expenditure over $25 per occasion.

(bb) Effective May 11, 1994, lobbyist registration function transfers from the Joint Committee on Agency Rule Review to a newly created Joint Committee on Legislative Ethics. Other reporting requirements will also go into effect.

(cc) By whom the lobbyist is reimbursed, retained or employed to lobby, and on whose behalf the lobbying is done.

(dd) Even-numbered years: January 31, July 31; odd-numbered years: January 31, April 30, July 31.

(ee) At specified times during legislative session and at end of legislative session.

(ff) In detail, if over $50 per person.

(gg) After the session, annually, seven days before a general election, and seven days after the end of a special session or veto override session.

(hh) January 20 for preceding year; March 10 for January and February.

(ii) A lobbyist who is compensated, in whole or in part, by an employer for the purpose of lobbying on behalf of another person, group or coalition is required to provide the name of the employer, the name of the person, group or coalition on whose behalf he/she lobbies and a description of the matters for which lobbying has been engaged by the employer.

(jj) During early 1994, the Ethics Committee met to consider significant changes to Virginia's laws on lobbyists. No information available as of April 1994.

(kk) Prohibited.

(ll) Daily record of time spent on specific area; daily record of payments made by organization for lobbying. Reports filed by lobbyist's employer.

(mm) Name and firm only.

Chapter Eight

STATE PROGRAMS & ISSUES

*A review of several state program and issue
areas — including education, corrections and
criminal justice, environmental management,
labor, health care, and highways — with current
information and statistics. Includes a special
feature on innovators in state government.*

Innovators in State Government

Just who are the scientists in this country's "laboratories of democracy"?

by Dennis O. Grady and Keon S. Chi

The devolvement of most domestic policy in state governments during the past decade in conjunction with the often-noted "resurgence" of state governing capacity (Bowman and Kearney, 1990) has made state governments the primary centers of policy activism and creativity in our nation today. The ability, therefore, of our nation to address its problems is largely in the hands of the 4.2 million public servants employed across the 50 states. While national political leaders extol the virtues of "reinventing" government, the mechanics of reinvention have been toiling away in virtual obscurity across state governments for quite some time. Who are these mechanics of reinvention (otherwise known as innovators, although most are too self-effacing to call themselves that)? Where do they get their ideas? How do they get their innovations enacted through the policy process? And how are they connected to others across the country who share similar concerns and responsibilities? These are some of the questions addressed in this essay.

The Sample — Defining an Innovation and Determining the Innovator

The Innovations Transfer Program (ITP) of The Council of State Governments, since 1975, has annually solicited information on innovative state activities. Each year, the ITP receives between 300 and 500 applications which are first reviewed by CSG staff and then by regional panels of experts to determine which of the nominations will be selected for national recognition. To be eligible for consideration, the following standards are applied:

• Is it a state policy or program?

• Does it represent a new and creative approach to a significant problem affecting the state?

• Has the program or policy been implemented and operational for at least one year?

• Is the program or policy relatively unknown across the states?

• Has the program or policy been effective in achieving its goals and purposes?

• Does the program or policy address an issue or problem area that is regional or national in scope?

• Is it applicable and could it be easily transferred to the other states?

Approximately half of each year's nominations are eliminated after the first review process. Those remaining are sent to one of four CSG regional screening committees that select two national winners for each region. The eight ITP winners then are promoted nationally through CSG's *Innovations* publications.

As part of the nomination process for the 1992 Innovations Transfer Program, individuals submitting a nomination were asked to identify the individual(s) responsible for developing the original idea that led to the successful innovation. Those individuals identified by the nominators are defined in this analysis as the innovators. In the 1992 competition, 294 programs were submitted. Of those, 250 of the nominees provided the names and addresses of 272 program originators. These 272 individuals constitute the population for the analysis. An extensive survey was sent to each of the 272 innovators covering their educational and pro-

Dennis O. Grady is professor at Appalachian State University, Department of Political Science/Criminal Justice and Keon S. Chi is senior fellow with the State Policy and Innovations Group of The Council of State Governments.

fessional experiences, organizational environments, communication networks and political environments. One hundred seventy-five members of the population responded to the survey (67 percent response rate). The responses of these 175 innovators form the basis of the analysis.

Profile of the Innovators

The 175 individuals in the sample work in 36 different states and 22 different types of state agencies. Table A displays the sample organized by region and policy area.

Table A demonstrates a significant number of respondents from each of the four regions, with the Eastern and Midwestern regions supplying 58 percent of the innovators, and the Southern and Western regions providing 43 percent. Since Eastern and Midwestern states have relatively higher numbers of state government employees than the other two regions, this distribution is approximately proportional to the distribution of state workers among the regions. The allocation of the sample across policy areas shows that social services and state administration have the highest followed by health, education, environmental protection, infrastructure and other. The "other" category includes agriculture, civil rights, labor, and science and technology departments that did not logically fit into the other more recognizable policy areas.

Table B summarizes the innovators' education, age and gender.

It is evident from the table that the sample is composed of highly educated and mature professionals. Almost two-thirds of the sample have education beyond their undergraduate degrees and nearly one in five has professional degrees. The average age of the sample is 47, and more than one in three are female.

Table C presents the employment characteristics of the sample of innovators.

Almost 60 percent of the sample are permanent civil servants. Interestingly, a large portion of these are a new type of civil servant who is permanent, but not subject to traditional civil service regulations. In essence, they are the state equivalent of the federal Senior Executive Service that emerged from the 1978

Table A
DISTRIBUTION OF INNOVATORS' SAMPLE BY REGION AND POLICY AREA

Region	N	%
East	53	30.3
South	38	21.7
Midwest	48	27.4
West	36	20.6
	175	100.0

Policy Area	N	%
Criminal Justice	28	16.0
Social Services	37	21.1
Education	17	9.7
Environment	17	9.7
Health	20	11.4
Infrastructure	15	8.6
Administration	33	18.9
Other	8	4.6
	175	100.0

Table B
PERSONAL CHARACTERISTICS OF INNOVATORS

Education	N	%
Less than College	12	6.9
College Degree	40	22.9
Graduate School/MA,MS	83	47.4
Professional Degree (MD,LLD,Ph.D.)	33	18.9
Missing	7	4.0

Age Categories	N	%
27 - 35	11	6.3
36 - 45	59	33.7
46 - 55	72	41.1
56 - 67	33	18.9

Gender	N	%
Male	113	64.6
Female	62	35.3

Civil Service Reform Act. About a quarter of the sample are appointed administrators serving at the pleasure of the appointing authority. The remainder serve in a variety of capacities — the largest portion of this group working in nonprofit organizations tied closely to state government programs.

A large proportion of the sample has been working in state government for a significant number of years (the mean for the sample is 15 years). However, in looking at the average number of years in the current agency (8.8 years), and the average number of years in the policy area (6.7 years), it is evident that these innovators have been quite mobile within their state governments. Also, more than a significant majority (56.6 percent) have had experience in a private sector situation in addition to their governmental careers. Only about one in 10 had worked in another state government.

While one should always be hesitant in discussing the "typical" innovator, certain patterns do emerge in reviewing the sample's personal, educational and experiential backgrounds. Some of these patterns conform to conventional wisdom, while others are at odds with it. The notion that new ideas generally spring from highly educated individuals with diverse experience (Rogers, 1983) is surely borne out by this sample. However, contrary to conven-

tional wisdom (Downs, 167; Hummel, 1987), long service in state bureaucracies does not seem to dampen creative impulses nor willingness to experiment with new ideas. Essentially, the innovators in this sample are well seasoned, highly educated professionals with diverse experience within their state bureaucracies and some experience in the private sector.

Before presenting the information obtained from the innovators, it is important to explain why particular information was requested from them. Virtually all previous research on public sector innovation identifies three necessary conditions for an individual in the public sector to successfully alter existing policies and/or procedures (Rogers, 1983; Wilson, 1966; Mohr, 1969; Grady and Chi, 1994). First, innovators must be in information-rich environments where they are continually scanning new ideas that might have relevance to problems within their areas of responsibilities. They then take an idea from this information network and make it suit their particular problem. Frequently, this requires collaboration with others or, at least, concurrence from superiors. Finally, they push their approach through the policy process, relying at this stage on relevant political actors to authorize and legitimize the new departure.

The information to follow is built around this process. First, a description of the innovators' information environment is presented. We then examine the actors involved in the development of the new approach. Finally, we look at the role of internal and external political actors in the successful implementation of the innovation.

The Innovators' Information Environment

The innovators were asked to rate on a seven-point scale (7 being "Very Essential," 1 being "Not Essential") the importance of nine different information sources to stay abreast of developments within their professions. Table D ranks these sources based on the sample means.

It is evident from the ranking that the most important source of information is informal

Table C
EMPLOYMENT CHARACTERISTICS OF INNOVATORS

Employment Status	N	%
Permanent/merit system	68	38.9
Permanent/exempt	36	20.6
Appointed	42	24.0
Private sector	10	5.7
Elected official	6	3.4
Federal/Local employee	3	1.7
Other	7	4.0
Years of State Government Service		
Less than 5	25	14.3
6 - 15	70	40.0
16 - 25	42	24.0
26 or more	34	19.4
Missing	4	2.3
Years in Current Agency		
Less than 5	84	48.0
6 - 15	50	28.6
16 - 25	28	16.0
26 or more	13	7.4
Years in Policy Area		
Less than 5	102	58.3
6 - 15	44	25.1
16 - 25	20	11.4
26 or more	9	5.1

communication with colleagues within the innovators' work environments. The relatively low standard deviation for this source indicates how consistent this perception is across the sample. The second tier of information sources includes peers in other agencies, other states and professional affiliations. It appears that innovators rely extensively on lateral information networks. Next, we find more public sources of information from interest groups and the news media. Finally, the innovators rated information coming from academic sources and federal information as the least significant in maintaining professional currency. But even these are rated "somewhat essential" to the innovators. In general, innovators receive most of their information from immediate peers and professional colleagues sharing similar professional responsibilities across the country. While information in the public domain is considered important, as is more technical information coming from academic and federal sources, the primary spark of a new idea is generated by personal interaction with knowledgeable peers.

A basic tenet of the policy studies literature is that information channels and the policy development process vary among different policy domains. That is, how one goes about altering policy in social services is different from the process in the transportation area. Given this, we can assess differences in the information environments of the innovators controlling for their policy area. Table E rank orders the nine different information sources by the policy areas of the innovators.

When the innovator's policy area is controlled, a few interesting patterns emerge. Regardless of policy area, the innovator's immediate colleagues remain the most important sources of information. Also, the importance of attending professional conferences remains relatively stable across areas. However, significant differences are apparent for the role of other states, professional association information and academic information. Innovators in the environmental and health areas rate cross-state information much higher than innovators in other areas. This could be attributed to the relatively technical but widespread nature of

Table D
RATING OF INFORMATION SOURCES BY SAMPLE

Source	Group Mean	Std. Dev.
Informal Communication Agency Coworkers	6.14	1.23
Informal Communication State Coworkers	5.44	1.43
Professional Conferences and Workshops	5.36	1.43
Informal Communication Other States	5.20	1.59
Professional Association Publications	5.12	1.42
News Media	4.72	1.53
Interest Group Information	4.67	1.62
Academic Journals/ Research Reports	4.30	1.65
Federal Government Publications/Contacts	4.28	1.81

the problems faced by professionals in these two policy domains. Professional association publications are very important to innovators in the social services area but are only moderately important to innovators in the other policy areas. Academic research is moderately important to innovators in the education and health areas but generally rated among the lowest in the other areas.

In looking at experiential and personal factors that influence the innovators' information environments, a few statistically stable (using analysis of variance procedures) and predictable patterns were found. The longer the tenure of the innovator in his/her organization, the more reliance placed on coworker information. Conversely, the shorter the tenure, the higher the value placed on media as a source of information. Also, newer employees regarded academic information as much more instrumental than the sample's more experienced individuals. The more educated the innovator, the greater reliance placed on academic and other state information. Basically, older and less educated innovators place greater reliance on proximate, interpersonal information in searching for new ideas, while younger and more educated innovators rely on non-proximate, more sophisticated information outlets.

Formulating Innovations: The Role of Groups and Individuals

A prevailing model in the study of organizations is that public agencies operate in an open environment receiving demands and support from various elements external to the agency. Given that the innovator is an organizational member, we may also assume that he/she also is influenced by forces external to the particular agency. While we would expect the greatest influences on the innovator to be individuals in closest proximity, we would also anticipate that the innovator is receiving cues from non-agency actors in working on the new idea. To that end, we asked the respondents to rate on a seven point scale (7 being "Very Influential" and 1 being "Not Influential") the role of two internal agency actors and nine external agency actors in the initial formulation of the innovation. Table F presents the groups ranked (by group mean) from highest to lowest.

It is apparent from the ranking that innovators look primarily to immediate coworkers and clients at the earliest stages of innovation development. Interest groups and professional association contacts are in a second tier of

Table E
RANKING OF INFORMATION SOURCES BY POLICY AREA

Sources	Crim Just	Soc Serv	Educ	Env	Health	Infra	Admin
Agency Coworkers	1	1	1	1	1	1	1
State Coworkers	2	3	4	4	5	2	2
Other States	3	4	7	2	2	4	6
News Media	7	6	8	7	9	7	4
Prof. Conferences	3	2	2	3	4	2	3
Prof. Publications	5	5	2	5	3	5	5
Federal Info	6	8	9	8	7	8	9
Interest Group Information	9	7	6	6	7	6	7
Academic Research	8	9	5	9	6	9	8

Table F
RANKING OF GROUPS INVOLVED IN INNOVATIONS' DEVELOPMENT
(All Innovations)

Groups	Mean	Std. Dev.	Median
Supervisor	4.80	2.06	5
Agency Clients	4.01	2.43	4
Agency Coworkers	3.56	1.85	5
Interest Groups	3.54	2.38	3
Professional Associations	3.16	2.06	3
Governor's Office	2.83	2.13	2
Local Governments	2.82	2.18	2
Legislators	2.56	1.89	1
Colleagues in Other States	2.44	1.74	1
Legislative Staff	2.35	1.79	1
Federal Officials	2.21	1.76	1

Table G
COMPARISON OF GROUP INVOLVEMENT IN INNOVATION DEVELOPMENT
CONTROLLING FOR IMPACT OF INNOVATION ON AGENCY OPERATIONS

Groups	Policy Change	Administrative Change	F	Sig.
Supervisor	4.66	4.84	.21	.64
Coworkers	4.47	5.19	4.46	.03
Clients	4.00	4.01	.00	.97
State Coworkers	3.78	3.49	.52	.46
Interest Groups	3.59	3.51	.02	.87
Governor	3.50	2.63	4.73	.03
Legislators	3.33	2.33	8.13	.00
Legislative Staff	3.27	2.08	13.47	.00
Local Officials	2.81	2.83	.00	.98
Prof. Associations	2.69	3.29	2.35	.12
Federal Officials	1.91	2.29	1.30	.25
Other States	1.89	2.60	4.73	.03

influential groups but their involvement is more sporadic across the sample as evidenced by the high standard deviations relative to the group means. The formal institutional actors in the governor's office or in the legislature do not seem instrumental at this stage of the process. Finally, the respondents did not perceive other state or federal officials as influential in sparking the new idea.

However, not all innovations are of the same magnitude. As Chi (1988) has pointed out, some innovations require fundamental alteration of the agency's policy domain while others may be accomplished through less drastic administrative changes. In previous work (Grady and Chi, 1993), significant differences have been found among the groups' involvement at the development stage based upon this distinction. Table G presents the group means for each actor, controlling for whether or not the innovation required a fundamental change in agency operations (defined as a statutory alteration of agency responsibilities). Also displayed is the ANOVA F-statistic and significance level as a way of demonstrating the stability of the differences across the subsamples.

Table G indicates a statistically significant difference in group involvement for five of the 12 actors. As one might expect, governors, legislators and their staffs are much more instrumental in innovation development when a change in the agency's statutory basis is required. Alternatively, agency coworkers and colleagues in other states have more impact when the innovation requires only a modification of administrative rules and procedures. Of note is the consistency of client and interest group involvement across the two types of innovations. This implies that those most affected by the innovation (clients and interest groups) are as involved in the less publicized administrative alterations as they are in the more political domain of statutory change.

In summarizing the process of how the innovator takes an idea and develops it into an operational program, the data indicate a clear pattern. The primary collaborator is the innovator's direct supervisor. As we might expect, there is little reason to pursue the new idea if the agency leadership is opposed to its development. Next, the innovator works with those most affected (agency clients) and agency coworkers in molding the idea to suit both client and organizational needs. If the program requires a statutory change, the innovator then receives input from the state's political leadership. While we observed the important role of other states in the innovators' information environment, when it comes to actually developing the idea, other states have very little impact and federal officials are virtually nonexistent.

Implementing Innovations — The Role of Groups and Individuals

Because of the command and control structure of the public sector, individual public servants rarely have the independent authority to implement changes without the assistance, or at least the concurrence, of others with a stake in the policy area. To assess the involvement of other actors in the innovation implementation process, we asked the respondents to rate on a seven-point scale the support of the same individuals and groups listed in the previous section. The scaling on this survey item differed from the previous one to account for the fact that the innovator might not know the role of a specific actor, a group could be split in support or a particular individual or a group could be totally uninvolved in the innovation's implementation. Therefore, the number 7 through 5 indicated levels of positive support, 4 indicated neutrality or group division, and 3 through 1 levels of nonsupport. Lack of involvement or lack of knowledge of involvement were excluded from the calculations to follow.

At the implementation stage of the innovation process, the respondents generally perceived four groups supportive, three groups neutral or divided, and four groups unsupportive in taking the idea and putting it into practice. Supervisor, agency coworkers, clients and interest groups were all considered important to the successful implementation of the new approach. These rankings speak well to the responsiveness of the innovators to client and interest group concerns, as well as to the willingness of agency leadership and colleagues to experiment with new approaches. State actors not specifically part of the organization (state coworkers, legislators and governors) were generally perceived as neutral at this stage. While lack of support does not necessarily imply outright opposition, local officials, legislative staff, professional associations and federal officials were generally not perceived as facilitators during the implementation stage.

In looking at the sample as a whole, it is evident that most implementation assistance comes from within the agency and from the groups most affected by the new approach. While other non-agency actors were not perceived as opponents, they were not generally perceived as strong supporters either. Table I examines the same data controlling for innovations requiring statutory change in the agencies' enabling legislation.

As expected, when an innovation requires a major alteration in the agency's enabling

Table H
RANKING OF GROUPS INVOLVED IN INNOVATIONS' IMPLEMENTATION
(All Innovations)

Groups	Mean	Std. Dev.	Median
Supervisor	5.91	1.86	7
Agency Coworkers	5.44	1.67	6
Agency Clients	4.09	2.66	5
Interest Groups	3.99	2.71	5
State Coworkers	3.86	2.50	4
Legislators	3.28	2.72	4
Governor's Office	3.16	2.84	4
Local Governments	2.98	2.75	3
Legislative Staff	2.80	2.65	3
Professional Associations	2.54	2.73	1
Federal Officials	2.48	2.63	1

Table I
COMPARISON OF GROUP INVOLVEMENT IN INNOVATION IMPLEMENTATION
CONTROLLING FOR INNOVATIONS REQUIRING CHANGE
IN AGENCY'S ENABLING LEGISLATION

Groups	Policy Change	Administrative Change	F	Sig.
Supervisors	5.63	5.98	.91	.34
Coworkers	5.60	5.40	.40	.52
Legislators	4.69	2.88	12.96	.00
Clients	4.63	3.96	1.56	.21
Governor	4.40	2.81	8.92	.00
Interest Groups	4.35	3.91	.68	.41
State Coworkers	4.18	3.77	.70	.40
Legislative Staff	3.97	2.47	9.19	.00
Local Officials	3.56	2.83	1.73	.19
Professional Associations	2.69	2.50	.11	.74
Federal Officials	2.34	2.52	.12	.73

legislation, the political leadership of the state is perceived as much more instrumental in its implementation. The role of the legislature, its staff and the governor's office increases dramatically both in absolute and relative terms; and this change is statistically stable between the two types of innovation.

Comparing the role of individuals and groups in the innovation development and implementation stages indicates a few noteworthy results. At both stages, regardless of type of innovation, the respondents perceived their supervisors and coworkers as the most instrumental actors in the process. This indicates a healthy agency culture prone to collaborative experimentation. A full exploration of the forces creating this type of organizational environment goes beyond the scope of this investigation.

A second pattern worthy of note is the role of political leadership. While the majority of the innovations did not require statutory alteration for implementation, those that did required the collaboration of political leadership at both stages of the innovation process. It appears that the innovators were cognizant early on that any fundamental change in what the organization did would require the involvement of the states' elected officials. The high involvement of client and interest groups at

both stages is also striking. It is evident that these innovators are very much concerned with the response of those most directly affected by new approaches. And finally, when comparing the role of internal and external actors at the two different stages, they appear more important at the implementation stage than at the development stage. This implies that, while numerous creative ideas may be floating around the halls of public agencies, only those capable of generating internal consensus and external political support will actually bear fruit.

The Professional Environment of Innovators

Recalling the earlier discussion of the information environment of the innovators, the role of professional association information and contacts was noted as a significant factor in the generation of the new ideas. To get a better understanding of how professionally involved the respondents are, we asked a series of questions concerning professional association memberships and conferences attended annually.

In an open-ended question, we requested the respondents to list all professional association memberships held. As expected, the innovators supplied a wide variety of state, regional and national groups representing the professional interests of their members. Seventy-five percent of the sample reported membership in at least one association with the average number of memberships reported as two. Regarding professional conferences, the respondents average 4.5 state conferences, 1.5 regional conferences and 2.3 national conferences annually. Together, the typical respondent attended more than eight professional conferences a year. However, there was considerable variation among the respondents on their reported professional association involvement, which invites more detailed analysis.

While membership in associations and attendance at conferences is not a perfect measure of professional involvement given vagaries among requirements for particular occupations and agency travel budgets, they do represent opportunities for individuals to become aware of developments within their professions and to learn about new ideas. Because our specific interest concerns how innovators learn about new approaches from other states, we constructed an index summing each respondent's number of reported memberships, multistate regional conferences attended and national conference attendance. The resulting index had a mean of 5.75 with a standard deviation of 4.94. Table J examines this index by controlling for relevant differences among the sample of innovators.

The policy area variation in professional involvement shows little stability across policy areas. While innovators in the environment, criminal justice (this area includes a number of lawyers and psychologists) and health areas are relatively the most active within their professional associations, the substantial variation within each policy group precludes any con-

Table J
PROFESSIONAL INVOLVEMENT OF INNOVATORS
BY CHARACTERISTICS OF INNOVATORS

Policy Area	Mean	Std. Dev.	F	Sig.
Environment	7.06	6.55		
Criminal Justice	6.56	4.88		
Health	6.45	5.09		
Education	6.06	3.47		
Social Services	5.91	5.67		
Administration	4.53	4.51		
Infrastructure	4.08	3.47		
			.85	.54
Education				
Less than College	3.67	2.96		
College Degree	4.55	4.41		
Graduate Work or MA	5.63	4.69		
Professional Degree	8.61	5.76		
			5.31	.00
Employment Type				
Permanent/Merit system	4.68	4.27		
Permanent/Exempt	4.85	3.49		
Appointed	7.97	6.36		
Non-state Employee	6.54	4.98		
			4.40	.00
Gender				
Male	5.85	5.41		
Female	5.56	3.94		
			.14	.71

clusion that some policy areas are significantly more professionally active than others. Gender also appears to have little effect on the professional involvement of the respondents. Any notion that either men or women are more involved in professional networking is not borne out by the index. However, the innovators' levels of education and their employment status are clearly associated with professional activism. Not surprisingly, the more educated innovators are also the most professionally active. The 31 respondents with law, medical or Ph.D. degrees are more than twice as active professionally as the 12 respondents with less than a college degree. In terms of employment status, the least active professionally are the permanent civil servants protected by merit systems, while the most active are appointed administrators. While the data are insufficient to state definitively why the innovators' job status should affect his/her professional activism, we might conjecture that the innovators with the least job security are the most aggressive in seeking out new ideas and networking professionally. Alternatively, this activism of appointees could simply be a result of access to the resources necessary to defray the costs of conferences and professional memberships.

Other States as Innovation Models

Along with professional association information as a source of creative inspiration, the respondents also considered other states as primary to their information environments. The idea of some states being pioneers in policy development has long been studied by researchers interested in the diffusion of innovations among the states (Walker, 1969; Gray, 1973).

To determine who this sample of innovators considered leaders within their respective policy spheres, they were asked, "What states (other than your own) do you consider to be particularly creative and/or effective in addressing the problems associated with your area of responsibility?" One hundred three respondents listed at least one other state, and seven innovators listed as many as six. By simply counting the number of times a particular state was iden-

Table K
INNOVATIVE STATES BY REPUTATION

Frequency of Mention	States (# Mentions)
20 or More	CA (32)
19 - 15	FL (18), NY (17)
14 - 10	MN (14), MA (13), MD (12), MI (12), IL (10)
9 - 5	AL (4), KY (4), UT (4), AZ (3), DE (3), CO (3), ID (3), IN (3), MO (3), NM (3), NC (3), OK (3), VT (3), AR (2), HI (2), IA (2), ME (2), MT (2), ND (2), RI (2), TN (2), AK (1), GA (1), MS (1), SD (1), WV (1)

tified in response to this question, we attain a general picture of which states have the reputation as innovation leaders. Table K lists the states by frequency of mention.

The table indicates that while 44 states were considered innovative in at least some policy areas, the reputational concentration centers on eight states constituting almost half of the total mentions. California has, by far, the greatest reputation for creativity and effectiveness, followed by Florida and New York. The next tier comprises states in the industrial Midwest (Minnesota, Michigan, Illinois) and the Atlantic seaboard (Massachusetts and Maryland).

While the reputation for innovation is subject to many reliability problems, what is striking about the ranking of states is their stability over time. From Walker's (1969) earliest work on the attributes of innovative states to the more recent examination of states by Bowman and Kearney (1988), these highly reputed states have maintained their status for creativity and effectiveness. Each of the top eight has professionalized legislative branches, comparatively strong governors as measured by formal powers, high per capita state administrative staffing and spending ratios, and strong, pluralistic interest group systems. These attributes, most typically related to the ability of a state to be responsive and effective, also translate into recognition for creativity by peers across the country.

Particular Circumstances

Finally, state innovators were asked to answer an open-ended question, "Can you recall any particular event or circumstance that sparked your interest in creating the new approach or innovation?" Although several innovators could not recall any particular causes that led them to initiate an innovative program, most respondents offered one or two specific reasons or motivations. These responses can be grouped in five categories: (1) some innovations occurred as a routine management improvement effort; (2) other innovations were initiated as an approach to cut back management; (3) new data and information available to innovators contributed to many of those innovations; (4) top-down directives motivated some innovators; and (5) several innovators were motivated by "outsiders," including federal agencies, consultants and customers.

References

Bowman, Ann O'M. and Richard C. Kearney (1990). *State and Local Government*. Boston: Houghton Mifflin Co.

Brudney, Jeffrey L. and F. Ted Hebert (1987). "State Agencies and Their Environments: Examining the Influence of Important External Actors." *The Journal of Politics*, 49: 186-206.

Chi, Keon S. (1988). "Innovations Transfer In State Governments." Presented at the annual meeting of the American Political Science Association, Washington, D.C.

Downs, Anthony (1967). *Inside Bureaucracy.* Boston: Little, Brown.

Downs, George W. Jr. and Lawrence B. Mohr (1976). "Conceptual Issues in the Study of Innovation." *Administrative Science Quarterly*, 21: 700-714.

Grady, Dennis and Keon S. Chi (1994), "Formulating and Implementing Public Sector Innovations: The Environment of State Government Innovators." *Public Administration Quarterly*, Vol. 14, No. 4: 468-484.

Gray, Virginia (1973). "Innovation in the States: A Diffusion Study." *American Political Science Review*, 67: 1174-1185.

Mohr, Lawrence B. (1969). "Determinants of Innovation in Organizations." *American Political Science Review*, 63: 111-126.

Rogers, Everett M. (1983). *Diffusion of Innovations*. 3ed. New York: The Free Press.

Walker, Jack L. (1969). "The Diffusion of Innovations among the American States." *American Political Science Review*, 63: 880-899.

Wilson, James Q. (1966). "Innovation in Organization: Notes Toward a Theory." In James D. Thompson, ed. *Approaches to Organizational Design*. Pittsburgh: University of Pittsburgh Press. 193-218.

The National Education Goals Panel: State and National Partnerships in Education Reform

Officials from the state and federal level are working together to ensure America's education system is ready for the Twenty-First Century.

by Leslie A. Lawrence and Cynthia D. Prince

Education is chiefly a responsibility of state, rather than federal, government. Among the education policies established by individual states are teacher certification standards, high school graduation course requirements, school attendance and public school finance. In recent years, however, increasing concern over U.S. economic competitiveness and the skills and training of America's workforce has elevated education from a state to a national concern. Proponents of education reform have called for higher education standards and stronger national and state accountability to reverse declining scores on college entrance examinations, weak U.S. performance on international assessments of mathematics and science achievement, increasing school violence and low adult literacy skills.[1,2]

In 1989, President George Bush and the nation's governors (led by former Governor Bill Clinton) met at an education summit in Charlottesville, Va. to address these concerns. Recognizing the need for a sustained commitment to educational improvement and the need for a state and national partnership to achieve the necessary reforms, the president and the governors established six national education goals that all states and the nation would work collectively to achieve by the year 2000.

In 1994, Congress added two new goals on teacher training and parent involvement to the original six, when it enacted the *Goals 2000: Educate America Act*. The National Education Goals cover birth through adulthood and state that by the year 2000:

1. All children in America will start school ready to learn.

2. The high school graduation rate will increase to at least 90 percent.

3. All students will leave grades 4, 8 and 12 having demonstrated competency over challenging subject matter including English, mathematics, science, foreign languages, civics and government, economics, arts, history and geography, and every school in America will ensure that all students learn to use their minds well, so they may be prepared for responsible citizenship, further learning, and productive employment in our Nation's modern economy.

4. The Nation's teaching force will have access to programs for the continued improvement of their professional skills and the opportunity to acquire the knowledge and skills needed to instruct and prepare all American students for the next century.

5. U.S. students will be first in the world in mathematics and science achievement.

6. Every adult American will be literate and will possess the knowledge and skills necessary to compete in a global economy and exercise the rights and responsibilities of citizenship.

7. Every school in the United States will be free of drugs, violence, and the unauthorized presence of firearms and alcohol and will

Leslie A. Lawrence is a research associate, and Cynthia D. Prince is a senior education associate for the National Education Goals Panel in Washington, D.C. Any opinions, findings, conclusions or recommendations presented in this essay are those of the authors and do not necessarily reflect the views of members of the National Education Goals Panel.

offer a disciplined environment conducive to learning.

8. Every school will promote partnerships that will increase parental involvement and participation in promoting the social, emotional, and academic growth of children.

The National Education Goals Panel

In order to determine whether the nation and the states were making progress toward the goals, an independent panel of state and federal policy-makers — the National Education Goals Panel — was formed through a joint agreement between the White House and the National Governors' Association in July 1990. The National Education Goals Panel is a bipartisan panel of state and federal policy-makers composed of eight governors, four state legislators, four members of Congress and two senior-level representatives of the administration.

Participating governors are appointed by the chair and the vice-chair of the National Governors' Association. State legislators are appointed by the president of the National Conference of State Legislatures. Congressional representatives are appointed by the majority and minority leaders of the House and Senate, and representatives of the administration are appointed by the president.

The chair of the National Education Goals Panel serves for a one-year term and is selected by the panel members. The chairmanship alternates political parties each year. Governors who have served as chair are Colorado Governor Roy Romer (D, 1990-91), South Carolina Governor Carroll A. Campbell, Jr. (R, 1991-92), Nebraska Governor E. Benjamin Nelson (D, 1992-93), and Maine Governor John R. McKernan, Jr. (R, 1993-94). Fourteen governors, six representatives of the Bush and Clinton administrations, seven members of Congress and four state legislators have served on the panel thus far (see Table A).

Roles and Responsibilities

Since its inception, the primary responsibility of the National Education Goals Panel has been to monitor and report progress to ward the National Education Goals. When the panel was first formed, members decided to issue a report on state and national progress for policy-makers and for the American public each September, through the year 2000. The panel has published three such reports to date.[3,4,5]

Before the panel could issue its first annual report, however, clear baselines were required in order to establish how far the nation and the states were from the targets set for 2000. In 1991, the panel assembled advisory groups of nationally known experts in each of the goal areas to offer technical advice and counsel on the best available measures to gauge progress, as well as to recommend new measures where necessary data did not yet exist.[6]

Four criteria were applied to the baseline data selected for inclusion in the goals panel reports. First, the data had to be representative of national and state populations. Second, the data had to be comparable across states. Third, the data had to be updated periodically between 1990 and 2000 so that change over time could be assessed. Finally, the indicator had to be directional; that is, it had to be clear whether educational conditions were getting better or worse if the indicator increased or decreased over time.

The panel decided that its annual reports should be distinct from most previous educational reports in four important ways. First, the reports should focus on educational results such as increased student achievement and reduced student dropout rates, rather than educational inputs, such as student-teacher ratios and pupil enrollments. Second, to the extent possible, the reports should employ direct measures of the goals, such as actual student performance in science, rather than indirect measures or proxies, such as the proportion of students who merely enrolled in science courses. Third, since the goals cover birth through adulthood, the reports should include measures such as children's preschool experiences and the post-secondary educational attainment of adults. Most importantly, the panel decided that the reports should focus on state progress over time as measured against each state's own baseline, and should not compare or rank states against each other.

Table A
NATIONAL EDUCATION GOALS PANEL

1990-91

GOVERNORS
Roy Romer, Colorado (D), *Chair*
John Ashcroft, Missouri (R)
Evan Bayh, Indiana (D)
Terry E. Branstad, Iowa (R)
Carroll A. Campbell Jr., South Carolina (R)
Booth Gardner, Washington (D)

MEMBERS OF THE ADMINISTRATION
Lamar Alexander, secretary of education
Richard G. Darman, director, Office of
   Management and Budget
Roger B. Porter, assistant to the president
   for economic and domestic policy
John H. Sununu, White House chief of staff

MEMBERS OF CONGRESS (ex officio)
U.S. Senate Minority Leader Bob Dole, Kansas (R)
U.S. House Majority Leader Richard Gephardt,
   Missouri (D)
U.S. House Minority Leader Robert Michel,
   Illinois (R)

1991-92

GOVERNORS
Carroll A. Campbell Jr., South Carolina (R), *Chair*
John Ashcroft, Missouri (R)
Evan Bayh, Indiana (D)
Terry E. Branstad, Iowa (R)
Howard Dean, Vermont (D)
E. Benjamin Nelson, Nebraska (D)
Barbara Roberts, Oregon (D)
Roy Romer, Colorado (D)

MEMBERS OF THE ADMINISTRATION
Lamar Alexander, secretary of education
Roger B. Porter, assistant to the president
   for economic and domestic policy

MEMBERS OF CONGRESS
U.S. Sen. Jeff Bingaman, New Mexico (D)
U.S. Sen. Thad Cochran, Mississippi (R)
U.S. Rep. William Goodling, Pennsylvania (R)
U.S. Rep. Dale Kildee, Michigan (D)

1992-93

GOVERNORS
E. Benjamin Nelson, Nebraska (D), *Chair*
Evan Bayh, Indiana (D)
Terry E. Branstad, Iowa (R)
Carroll A. Campbell Jr., South Carolina (R)
Arne H. Carlson, Minnesota, (R)
John Engler, Michigan (R)
John R. McKernan Jr., Maine (R)
Roy Romer, Colorado (D)

MEMBERS OF THE ADMINISTRATION
Carol H. Rasco, assistant to the president
   for domestic policy
Richard W. Riley, secretary of education

MEMBERS OF CONGRESS
U.S. Sen. Jeff Bingaman, New Mexico (D)
U.S. Sen. Thad Cochran, Mississippi (R)
U.S. Rep. William Goodling, Pennsylvania (R)
U.S. Rep. Dale Kildee, Michigan (D)

1993-94

GOVERNORS
John R. McKernan Jr., Maine (R), *Chair*
Evan Bayh, Indiana (D)
Arne H. Carlson, Minnesota (R)
Jim Edgar, Illinois (R)
John Engler, Michigan (R)
Michael Leavitt, Utah (R)
E. Benjamin Nelson, Nebraska (D)
Roy Romer, Colorado (D)

MEMBERS OF THE ADMINISTRATION
Carol H. Rasco, assistant to the president
   for domestic policy
Richard W. Riley, secretary of education

MEMBERS OF CONGRESS
U.S. Sen. Jeff Bingaman, New Mexico (D)
U.S. Sen. Thad Cochran, Mississippi (R)
U.S. Rep. William Goodling, Pennsylvania (R)
U.S. Rep. Dale Kildee, Michigan (D)

STATE LEGISLATORS
State Rep. Anne Barnes, North Carolina (D)
State Rep. Spencer Coggs, Wisconsin (D)
State Sen. Robert T. Connor, Delaware (R)
State Rep. Doug Jones, Idaho (R)

State Goals Reports

At the same time that the first National Education Goals report was being developed, the National Governors' Association encouraged states to develop their own State Progress Reports for three reasons. First, State Progress Reports provide the opportunity for states to choose additional indicators to measure progress that may not be included in the national report. Some states have adopted additional education goals that could be monitored.

Second, the national reports thus far have focused solely on education results, and have not addressed programs and policies that have proven effective in achieving the Goals. State Progress Reports provide the opportunity to describe state programs and policies that have been instituted in response to the goals and to present evidence of their success.

Finally, the national goals reports are limited in the amount of state data that can be reported, since only comparable state data from national data collections such as the National Assessment of Educational Progress (NAEP) are used. State Progress Reports, however, can include state-specific data such as the results of the state's own student performance assessments in reading, writing and mathematics that may be collected on a more regular basis than some of the state data reported in the national goals reports.

Local Goals Reports

While the national goals reports do include data on national and state progress, they do not include data on local progress which may also be of great interest to parents, local businesses and industries, local higher education institutions, and communities. Some State Progress Reports do include school district data and school building data to measure local progress in achieving the goals, but others do not.

To assist local communities with this task, the National Education Goals Panel has published a *Handbook for Local Goals Reports.*[7] The handbook gives guidance on types of questions to ask about local progress and suggests possible data sources to answer those questions, so that a community can establish baselines and measure its progress toward the National Education Goals, as well as local goals. In the near future, the handbook will become part of a Goals Panel "community tool-kit" that will provide materials and suggest strategies to help local communities measure their progress and achieve the goals.

Expanding Role of the National Education Goals Panel

The role and responsibilities of the National Education Goals Panel have expanded considerably as a result of Congressional enactment of the *Goals 2000: Educate America Act* in March, 1994. Some of the immediate effects of the bill are to:

1. codify the National Education Goals and establish the National Education Goals Panel in law;

2. create a National Skill Standards Board to motivate the development of a voluntary national system of skill standards and assessments to ensure a highly trained workforce; and

3. create a National Education Standards and Improvement Council (NESIC) to certify voluntary national and state standards that define:

    a. what all students should know in different subject areas (content standards);

    b. the levels of competence students are expected to attain (performance standards); and

    c. the educational conditions necessary for all students to have opportunities to achieve at high levels (opportunity-to-learn standards).

In addition to reporting state and national progress toward the National Education Goals, the *Goals 2000: Educate America Act* has broadened the panel's charge to include building a nationwide, bipartisan consensus on necessary reforms and strategies to achieve the goals; reporting on promising or effective educational policies and practices; and encouraging the development of voluntary national and state content, performance and opportunity-to-learn standards to ensure economic competitiveness and a well-educated citizenry for the 21st century.

Continuous improvement toward goal attainment through the end of the century will depend largely on the continued partnership of schools, communities, states and the nation. The National Education Goals Panel's mission is to catalyze the fundamental changes necessary for that to happen.

Notes

[1] National Commission on Excellence in Education, *A nation at risk: The imperative for educational reform.* (Washington, D.C.: U.S. Department of Education, 1983).

[2] National Council on Education Standards and Testing, *Raising standards for American education: A report to Congress, the Secretary of Education, the National Education Goals Panel, and the American people.* (Washington, D.C.: U.S. Government Printing Office, 1992).

[3] National Education Goals Panel, *The 1991 National Education Goals report: Building a nation of learners.* (Washington, D.C.: U.S. Government Printing Office, 1991).

[4] National Education Goals Panel, *The 1992 National Education Goals report: Building a nation of learners.* (Washington, D.C.: U.S. Government Printing Office, 1992).

[5] National Education Goals Panel, *The 1993 National Education Goals report: Building a nation of learners.* (Washington, D.C.: U.S. Government Printing Office, 1993).

[6] National Education Goals Panel, *Measuring progress toward the National Education Goals, potential indicators and measurement strategies: Compendium of interim Resource Group reports.* (Washington, D.C.: author, March 1991).

[7] National Education Goals Panel, *Handbook for local Goals Reports: Building a community of learners.* (Washington, D.C.: U.S. Government Printing Office, 1992).

Table 8.1
MEMBERSHIP AND ATTENDANCE IN PUBLIC ELEMENTARY AND SECONDARY SCHOOLS, BY STATE: 1991-92 AND 1992-93

State or other jurisdiction	1991-92 (rev. est.)			1992-93 (est.)		
	Estimated average daily membership (ADM)	Estimated average daily attendance (ADA)	ADA as a percent of ADM	Estimated average daily membership (ADM)	Estimated average daily attendance (ADA)	ADA as a percent of ADM
United States......	. . .	38,891,055	. . .	. . .	39,641,924	. . .
Alabama...........	719,629	682,303	94.8	720,409	683,041	94.8
Alaska.............	115,640	100,672	87.1	113,276	103,540	91.4
Arizona...........	653,525	616,928	94.4	667,114	629,981	94.4
Arkansas	436,531	412,107	94.4	429,103	407,190	94.9
California..........	. . .	5,063,809 (a)	. . .	. . .	5,144,342 (a)	. . .
Colorado	. . .	549,976	. . .	. . .	568,158	. . .
Connecticut	482,400	457,934	94.9	482,241	460,377	95.5
Delaware	100,755	93,909	93.2	102,840	95,861	93.2
Florida	1,914,521	1,778,973	92.9	1,956,213	1,817,713	92.9
Georgia...........	1,168,269	1,099,020	94.1	1,197,691	1,126,218	94.0
Hawaii	174,535	163,265	93.5	174,386	163,389	93.7
Idaho	. . .	213,843	. . .	. . .	213,000	. . .
Illinois............	1,759,236	1,630,534	92.7	1,770,537	1,645,930	93.0
Indiana	923,919	880,230	95.3	929,386	885,705	95.3
Iowa	482,992	460,068	95.3	490,899	467,781	95.3
Kansas	424,261	401,474	94.6	434,254	411,887	94.8
Kentucky	603,813	574,226	95.1	609,464	578,991	95.0
Louisiana	783,254	732,518	93.5	763,434	710,413	93.1
Maine	209,225	198,405	94.8	209,929	197,982	94.3
Maryland	734,277	683,649	93.1	749,845	698,146	93.1
Massachusetts	840,588	781,887	93.0	838,096	797,208	95.1
Michigan	. . .	1,455,861	. . .	. . .	1,448,218	. . .
Minnesota	768,183	725,933	94.5	785,547	742,342	94.5
Mississippi	499,719	473,398	94.7	502,361	475,901	94.7
Missouri	. . .	745,276	. . .	. . .	755,503	. . .
Montana...........	147,745	138,880	94.0	151,760	144,172	95.0
Nebraska	274,684	262,012	95.4	275,278	262,474	95.3
Nevada	209,778	195,285	93.1	218,390	205,018	93.9
New Hampshire	171,347	162,726	95.0	174,273	165,559	95.0
New Jersey.........	1,098,698	1,021,789	93.0	1,063,654	983,935	92.5
New Mexico.........	289,481	260,533	90.0	294,699	265,229	90.0
New York	2,565,000	2,350,000	91.6	2,592,000	2,374,000	91.6
North Carolina	1,080,223	1,023,186	94.7	1,094,490	1,036,700	94.7
North Dakota	118,181	113,782	96.3	118,290	113,989	96.4
Ohio	1,691,000	1,581,000	93.5	1,692,000	1,582,000	93.5
Oklahoma	587,100	556,600	94.8	596,000	566,000	95.0
Oregon	493,000	461,640	93.6	504,000	471,940	93.6
Pennsylvania	1,677,500	1,560,100	93.0	1,706,600	1,773,100	103.9
Rhode Island	139,000	128,436	92.4	140,897	131,599	93.4
South Carolina	603,053	578,236	95.9	610,753	591,808	96.9
South Dakota	129,910	124,119	95.5	127,245	121,310	95.3
Tennessee	827,525	774,596	93.6	841,610	785,285	93.3
Texas..............	. . .	3,147,593	. . .	. . .	3,242,508	. . .
Utah	450,758	426,507	94.6	459,854	435,383	94.7
Vermont	94,000	89,300	95.0	94,850	89,214	94.1
Virginia...........	1,008,244	951,208	94.3	1,023,492	965,243	94.3
Washington	866,018	811,459	93.7	895,053	838,665	93.7
West Virginia	317,748	296,191	93.2	314,542	295,479	93.9
Wisconsin..........	780,750	734,814	94.1	791,901	741,616	93.7
Wyoming	98,951	93,926	94.9	99,310	94,294	94.9
Dist. of Columbia.....	78,826	70,939	90.0	79,318	71,544	90.2

Source: Adapted from National Education Association, *Estimates of School Statistics 1992-93* (Copyright 1993. All rights reserved).

Note: Average Daily Membership (ADM) for the school year is an average obtained by dividing the aggregate days of membership by the number of days in which school is in session. Pupils are "members" of a school from the date they are placed on the current roll until they leave permanently. Membership is the total number of pupils belonging — the sum of those present and those absent. Average Daily Attendance (ADA) for the school year is the aggregate days pupils were actually present in school divided by the number of days school was actually in session.

Key:
. . . — Not available

(a) Count includes excused absences.

Table 8.2
ENROLLMENT, AVERAGE DAILY ATTENDANCE AND CLASSROOM TEACHERS IN PUBLIC ELEMENTARY AND SECONDARY SCHOOLS, BY STATE: 1992-93

State or other jurisdiction	Total enrollment (a)	Estimated average daily attendance (a)	Classroom teachers (a)	Pupils per teacher based on enrollment	Pupils per teacher based on average daily attendance
United States	42,550,658	39,641,924	2,466,725	17.2	16.1
Alabama	726,900	683,041	40,900	17.8	16.7
Alaska	121,922	103,540	7,052	17.3	14.7
Arizona	672,477	629,981	34,717	19.4	18.1
Arkansas	440,682	407,190	25,886	17.0	15.7
California	5,184,000	5,144,342 (b)	225,700	23.0	22.8
Colorado	612,635	568,158	33,149	18.5	17.1
Connecticut	481,717	460,377	35,107	13.7	13.1
Delaware	104,321	95,861	6,253	16.7	15.3
Florida	1,979,933	1,817,713	106,965	18.5	17.0
Georgia	1,206,317	1,126,218	72,116	16.7	15.6
Hawaii	176,923	163,389	10,303	17.2	15.9
Idaho	231,668	213,000	11,820	19.6	18.0
Illinois	1,859,808	1,645,930	110,588	16.8	14.9
Indiana	957,902	885,705	55,358	17.3	16.0
Iowa	494,222	467,781	31,490	15.7	14.9
Kansas	451,520	411,887	29,730	15.2	13.9
Kentucky	640,470	578,991	37,698	17.0	15.4
Louisiana	795,690	710,413	45,516	17.5	15.6
Maine	211,825	197,982	15,137	14.0	13.1
Maryland	751,850	698,146	43,416	17.3	16.1
Massachusetts	846,648	797,208	55,645	15.2	14.3
Michigan	1,574,150	1,448,218	81,609	19.3	17.7
Minnesota	838,758	742,342	45,837	18.3	16.2
Mississippi	504,229	475,901	28,010	18.0	17.0
Missouri	838,758	755,503	52,593	15.9	14.4
Montana	159,749	144,172	9,935	16.1	14.5
Nebraska	281,363	262,474	19,031	14.8	13.8
Nevada	222,846	205,018	11,969	18.6	17.1
New Hampshire	181,197	165,559	11,658	15.5	14.2
New Jersey	1,130,560	983,935	80,869	14.0	12.2
New Mexico	294,699	265,229	17,325	17.0	15.3
New York	2,670,800	2,374,000	183,000	14.6	13.0
North Carolina	1,106,876	1,036,700	65,986	16.8	15.7
North Dakota	118,094	113,989	7,793	15.2	14.6
Ohio	1,772,500	1,582,000	102,800	17.2	15.4
Oklahoma	597,100	566,000	38,540	15.5	14.7
Oregon	509,350	471,940	27,200	18.7	17.4
Pennsylvania	1,716,670	1,773,100	101,196	17.0	17.5
Rhode Island	143,043	131,599	9,680	14.8	13.6
South Carolina	632,988	591,808	36,330	17.4	16.3
South Dakota	133,870	121,310	8,631	15.5	14.1
Tennessee	845,411	785,285	45,438	18.6	17.3
Texas	3,564,725	3,242,508	218,988	16.3	14.8
Utah	461,259	435,383	19,387	23.8	22.5
Vermont	98,100	89,214	7,232	13.6	12.3
Virginia	1,032,058	965,243	67,378	15.3	14.3
Washington	898,112	838,665	44,156	20.3	19.0
West Virginia	317,719	295,479	20,833	15.3	14.2
Wisconsin	820,698	741,616	55,110	14.9	13.5
Wyoming	100,313	94,294	6,605	15.2	14.3
Dist. of Columbia	80,937	71,544	6,790	11.9	10.5

Source: Adapted from National Education Association, *Estimates of School Statistics 1992-93* (Copyright 1993. All rights reserved).

(a) Estimated.
(b) State's average daily attendance count includes unexcused absences.

Table 8.3
AVERAGE ANNUAL SALARY OF INSTRUCTIONAL STAFF IN PUBLIC
ELEMENTARY AND SECONDARY SCHOOLS: 1939-40 to 1992-93

State or other jurisdiction	Average annual salary for: (in unadjusted dollars)						
	1939-40	1949-50	1959-60	1969-70	1979-80	1989-90	1992-93
Alabama.............	$ 744	$2,111	$4,002	$ 6,954	$13,338	$26,200	$28,737
Alaska..............	. . .	. . .	6,859	10,993	27,697	43,161	46,400
Arizona.............	1,544	3,556	5,590	8,975	16,180	33,529	38,221
Arkansas	584	1,801	3,295	6,445	12,704	23,296	28,645
California..........	2,351	. . .	6,600	9,980	18,626	39,309	42,800
Colorado	1,393	2,821	4,997	7,900	16,840	31,832	35,212
Connecticut	1,861	3,558	6,008	9,400	16,989	41,888	50,820
Delaware	1,684	3,273	5,800	9,300	16,845	34,620	37,691
Florida	1,012	2,958	5,080	8,600	14,875	30,275	32,453
Georgia............	770	1,963	3,904	7,372	14,547	29,541	32,609
Hawaii	. . .	. . .	5,390	9,829	20,436	32,956	37,856
Idaho	1,057	2,481	4,216	7,257	14,110	24,758	28,334
Illinois.............	1,700	3,458	5,814	9,950	18,271	33,912	39,925
Indiana	1,433	3,401	5,542	9,574	16,256	31,905	27,264
Iowa	1,017	2,420	4,030	8,200	15,776	27,619	31,180
Kansas	1,014	2,628	4,450	7,811	14,513	30,154	34,269
Kentucky	826	1,936	3,327	7,624	15,350	27,482	32,733
Louisiana	1,006	2,983	4,978	7,220	14,020	25,036	29,783
Maine	894	2,115	3,694	8,059	13,743	27,831	31,293
Maryland	1,642	3,594	5,557	9,885	18,308	37,520	40,524
Massachusetts	2,037	3,338	5,545	9,175	18,900	40,175	47,510
Michigan	1,576	3,420	5,654	10,125	20,682	37,286	43,231
Minnesota	1,276	3,013	5,275	9,957	16,654	33,340	38,303
Mississippi	559	1,416	3,314	6,012	12,274	25,079	25,178
Missouri	1,159	2,581	4,536	8,091	14,543	28,166	30,630
Montana............	1,184	2,962	4,425	8,100	15,080	29,526	28,344
Nebraska	829	2,292	3,876	7,855	14,236	27,024	30,463
Nevada	1,557	3,209	5,693	9,689	17,290	31,970	35,764
New Hampshire	1,258	2,712	4,455	8,018	13,508	29,798	36,456
New Jersey..........	2,093	3,511	5,871	9,500	18,851	37,485	46,055
New Mexico.........	1,144	3,215	5,382	8,125	15,406	25,790	27,356
New York	2,604	3,706	6,537	10,200	20,400	40,000	46,300
North Carolina	946	2,688	4,178	7,744	14,445	28,952	30,678
North Dakota	745	2,324	3,695	6,900	13,684	23,788	26,058
Ohio	1,587	3,088	5,124	8,594	16,100	32,467	35,700
Oklahoma	1,014	2,736	4,659	7,139	13,500	23,944	26,977
Oregon	1,333	3,323	5,535	9,200	16,996	32,100	36,882
Pennsylvania	1,640	3,006	5,308	9,000	17,060	34,110	42,736
Rhode Island	1,809	3,294	5,499	8,900	18,425	36,704	38,282
South Carolina	743	1,891	3,450	7,000	13,670	28,453	30,477
South Dakota	807	2,064	3,725	6,700	13,010	22,120	24,470
Tennessee	862	2,302	3,929	7,290	14,193	27,949	30,451
Texas..............	1,079	3,122	4,708	7,503	14,729	28,549	30,452
Utah	1,394	3,103	5,096	8,049	17,403	24,591	27,869
Vermont	981	2,348	4,466	8,225	13,300	29,012	36,217
Virginia............	899	2,328	4,312	8,200	14,655	31,656	35,093
Washington	1,706	3,487	5,643	9,500	19,735	31,828	37,495
West Virginia	1,170	2,425	3,952	7,850	14,395	23,842	31,428
Wisconsin...........	1,379	3,007	4,870	9,150	16,335	32,445	36,668
Wyoming	1,169	2,798	4,937	8,532	16,830	29,047	30,094
Dist. of Columbia ...	2,350	3,920	6,287	11,075	23,027	32,638	39,382

Sources: U.S. Department of Education, National Center for Education Statistics, *Statistics of State School Systems*; National Education Association, *Estimates of School Statistics 1992-93* (Copyright 1993. All rights reserved).

Note: Includes supervisors, principals, classroom teachers, librarians and other related instructional staff.

Key:
. . . — Not available

Table 8.4
STATE COURSE REQUIREMENTS FOR HIGH SCHOOL GRADUATION

State or other jurisdiction	All courses	English/ language arts	Social studies	Mathe-matics	Science	Physical education /health	Electives	Other courses	First graduating class to which requirements apply
Alabama (a)									
Standard diploma . . .	22	4	3	2	2	1½	9½	. . .	1989
Advanced diploma . .	22	4	4	3	3	1½	4	2 foreign languages, ½ home/ personal management	1989
Alaska	21	4	3	2	2	1	9	. . .	. . .
Arizona (b)	20	4	2½	2	2	. . .	9	½ free enterprise	1991
Arkansas (c)	20	4	3	3	2	1	6½	½ fine arts	1988
California (d)									
Standard diploma . . .	13	3	3	2	2	2	. . .	1 fine arts or foreign language	. . .
Advanced diploma . .	16	3	3	3	2	2	. . .	2 in same foreign language, 1 fine arts	. . .
Colorado (e)	. . .	. . .	. . .	. . .	. . .	. . .	. . .	. . .	. . .
Connecticut	20	4	3	3	2	1	6	1 arts or vocational education	1988
Delaware (f)	19	4	3	2	2	1½	6½	. . .	1987
Florida (g)									
Standard diploma . . .	24	4	3	3	3	½	9	½ practical/exploratory vocational education, ½ performing arts or speech & debate, ½ life management skills	1989
Academic scholars . .	26	4	3	4	4	1	7	2 of same foreign language, 1 from a spectrum of fine arts subjects	1989
Georgia (h)									
Standard diploma . . .	21	4	3	3	3	1	6	1 computer technology and/or fine arts and/or education, and/or junior ROTC	1997
Advanced diploma . .	21	4	3	3	3	1	4	2 foreign languages, 1 fine arts, vocational education, computer technology or ROTC	1997
Hawaii	22	4	4	3	3	1½	6	½ guidance	1997
Idaho (i)	21	4	2	2	2	1½	6	3½	1989
Illinois (j)	16	3	2	2	1	4½	2¼	1¼	1988
Indiana (k)									
Standard diploma . . .	19½	4	2	2	2	1½	8	. . .	1989
Academic honors . . .	24	4	3	4	4	1	4 or 5	3 in 1 foreign language or 2 each in 2 foreign languages	1990
Iowa (l)	. . .	. . .	. . .	. . .	. . .	1	. . .	. . .	1989
Kansas	21	4	3	2	2	1	9	. . .	1989
Kentucky (m)									
Standard diploma . . .	20	4	2	3	2	1	7	1	1987
Commonwealth diploma	22	5	2	6	6	. . .	1	1 foreign language in advanced placement	1986
Louisiana (n)									
Standard diploma . . .	23	4	3	3	3	2	7½	½ computer literacy	1989
Scholar program (q)	23	4	3	3	3	2	7½	½ computer literacy	1987
Regents' scholar	24	4	3½	3	3	2	4½	3 foreign languages, 1 fine arts	1983
Maine (o)	16	4	2	2	2	1½	3½	1 fine arts	1989
Maryland (p)	21	4	3	3	2	1	5	1 fine arts, 1 industrial arts/ technology education, home economics, vocational education or computer studies, 1 community service	1997
Massachusetts (q)	. . .	. . .	1	. . .	. . .	4	. . .	. . .	. . .
Michigan (r)									
Standard diploma . . .	. . .	4	3	3	2	1	. . .	2 foreign languages/fine or performing arts or vocational education, ½ computer education	. . .
College preparatory . .	. . .	4	3	3	2	1	. . .	At least 2 years foreign languages	. . .
Minnesota (s)	20	4	3	1	1	1½	9½	. . .	1982
Mississippi (t)	18	4	2	2	2	. . .	8	. . .	1989
Missouri (u)									
Standard diploma	22	3	2	2	2	1	10	1 fine, 1 practical arts	1988
College preparatory . .	24	4	3	3	3	1	8	1 fine, 1 practical arts	1988
Montana (v)	20	4	1½	2	1	1	10½	. . .	1989
Nebraska (w)	. . .	. . .	. . .	. . .	. . .	. . .	. . .	. . .	1991
Nevada (x)	22½	4	2	2	2	2½	8½	1 arts/humanities, ½ computer literacy	1992
New Hampshire (y) . .	19¾	4	2½	2	2	1¼	4	4	1989
New Jersey (z)	21½	4	3	3	2	1	4	1½	1990

See footnotes at end of table.

STATE COURSE REQUIREMENTS—Continued

State or other jurisdiction	All courses	English/ language arts	Social studies	Mathe- matics	Science	Physical education /health	Electives	Other courses	First graduating class to which requirements apply
					Years of instruction in . . .				
New Mexico (aa)	23	4	3	3	2	1	9	1 communication skills	1990
New York (bb)									
Local diploma	18½	4	4	2	2	½	0 to 2	1 art and/or music, ½ health, 2 noncredit units of physical education beyond total	1989
Regents' diploma ...	18½	4	4	2	2	½	0 to 2	3 to 5 in sequence of specific courses (varying on type of diploma) chosen by the student	1989
North Carolina (cc) ..									
Standard diploma ...	20	4	2	2	2	1	9		1987
Scholars program ...	22	4	3	3	3	1	4	2 foreign languages, 2 additional from English, math, science, social science, or foreign language	1994
North Dakota (dd) ...	17	4	3	2	2	1	5	. . .	1994
Ohio (ee)	18	3	2	2	1	1	9		1988
Oklahoma (ff)									
Standard diploma ..	20	4	2	2	2	. . .	10	. . .	1987
College preparatory ..	15	4	2	3	2	. . .	. . .	4 from choice	1988
Oregon (gg)	22	3	3½	2	2	2	8	1½	1988
Pennsylvania (hh)	21	4	3	3	3	1	5	2 arts/humanities	1989
Rhode Island (ii).....									
Standard diploma ..	16	4	2	2	2	. . .	6	. . .	1989
College preparatory ..	18	4	2	3	2	. . .	4	2 foreign languages, ½ computer, ½ arts	. . .
South Carolina (jj)...									
Standard diploma ...	20	4	3	3	2	1	7	. . .	1987
Academic achievement honors............	22	4	3	3	2	1	7	2 foreign languages	1986
South Dakota (kk) ...	20	4	3	2	3	. . .	7	½ computer, ½ fine arts	1989
Tennessee (ll)									
Standard diploma ...	20	4	1	2	2	½	9	½ economics	1989
Honors	20½	4	3	3	3	1½	2	2 in same foreign languages, 2 fine/visual or performing arts	1989
Texas (mm)									
Standard diploma ...	21	4	2½	3	2	1½	7	½ economics/free enterprise	1988
College preparatory ..	22	4	2½	3	3	1½	3	½ economics/free enterprise, 2 foreign languages, 1 computer science, 1 fine arts	1988
Utah (nn)	24	3	3	2	2	2	9½	2½	1988
Vermont (oo)........	14½	4	3	5	5	. . .	1½	1 arts	1989
Virginia (pp)									
Standard diploma ...	21	4	3	2	2	2	6	1 additional math or science, 1 fine or practical arts	1989
Advanced studies diploma	23	4	3	3	3	2	4	3 foreign languages, 1 fine or practical arts	1989
Washington (qq).....	19	3	2½	2	2	2	5½	1 occupational education, 1 fine/visual or performing arts	1991
West Virginia (rr)....	21	4	3	2	2	2	7	1	1989
Wisconsin (ss)	13	4	3	2	2	2	. . .	. . .	1989
Wyoming (tt)........	18	. . .	1	. . .	. . .	. . .	. . .		. . .
Dist. of Columbia (uu).	23½	4	3½	3	3	1½	3½	2 foreign languages, 1 life skills, 1 career/vocational, ½ fine arts, ½ music	1996

Source: Education Commission of the States, *Clearinghouse Notes* (October 1992).

Key:

. . . — No requirement

(a) Students must become computer literate through related coursework. A minimum competency test is required for graduation.

(b) Passage of a minimum competency test is required for graduation.

(c) Social studies options-3 units or 2 units social studies and 1 practical arts.

(d) State board has published Model Graduation Requirements to be used as a guide by local districts. These include specifics in core subjects plus computer studies and foreign language. Dept. of Education has test and cut-off standards for early exit, with parental approval. Passage of a minimum competency test is required for graduation. State has a suggested model of curriculum to guide local districts advising students on requirements for college entry.

(e) Local boards determine requirements. State has constitutional prohibition against state requirements. School accreditation requirements are a total of 30 units, appropriately covering language arts, social studies, science, math, foreign language, fine/vocational/practical arts, health/safety and physical education.

(f) Passing the minimum competency test is required for graduation.

(g) Two of the science units must be in a lab. Students must have a 1.5 grade point average to graduate. Vocational students may substitute certain sequences of vocational courses to satisfy up to 2 of the required credits in each of the areas of English, math and science. For the Academic Scholars Certificate, in addition to the increased requirements, students face a set of specific requirements to qualify for the program as well as the accompanying scholarship program. The state's junior and senior class students may receive dual credits for college courses. The state does require passage of a minimum competency test for graduation.

(h) Other column: 1 fine arts, vocational education or computer technology, ROTC. Students who successfully complete 4 units in vocational education courses in addition to requirements receive a formal seal of endorsement by the SBE. Algebra is required. Passage of a minimum competency test is required for graduation.

(i) Other column: ½ each, reading, speech and consumer education and 2 humanities. Practical arts may substitute for 1 of the 2 units of humanities; total requirement remains the same with electives decreasing. SBE requires either a C average, demonstrated competency in core curriculum on a junior class competency test, or adherence to local district's achievement plan for graduation. State has available a competency test for optional usage by districts. If students pass the test they receive a special proficiency endorsement on their diploma.

STATE COURSE REQUIREMENTS—Continued

(j) Other column: 1/4 consumer education, 1 art, foreign language, music or vocational education. One year of math may be computer technology; 1 year of social studies must be U.S. History or half U.S. History and half American Government. Beginning in 1985-86 the school boards were allowed to excuse pupils in 11-12th grades from physical education to 1) participation in interscholastic athletics or 2) enroll in academic class required for admission to college or in order to graduate from high school. Pupils in 9-12th grades may elect to take a SBE developed consumer education proficiency test; if passed, they will be excused from requirement.

(k) The state board regulations were approved and signed by the governor in September 1983. The state does not use standard Carnegie units.

(l) Legislative requirements in effect for many years. Local districts determine remaining requirements. State allows students in junior and senior classes to receive dual credits for college coursework.

(m) Other column: 1 additional math, science, social studies or vocational education. Additional core subject credit is a legislative requirement passed in 1984 and approved by the state board to be effective for graduates in 1985. Graduates in 1985 and 1986 needed 18 units to graduate.

(n) With an ACT score of 29 or above, 3.5 GPA with no semester grade lower than a B, no unexcused absences and no suspensions students receive a Scholar Program seal on diploma. Algebra is required. Minimum competency test passage is required for graduation.

(o) Enacted by legislature and approved by state board. American History is required. All students must pass computer proficiency standards. One of the science units must include lab study.

(p) Four credits must be earned after Grade 11. Students can now earn statewide certificate of merit with fulfillment of additional requirements. Special education certificates are available for students unable to meet requirements but who complete a special education program. Minimum competency test is required for graduation, as is a writing test and passage of a quiz on citizenship.

(q) Legislative requirements in effect for many years. American History is required. Local boards determine additional requirements.

(r) Legislative requirements in effect for many years. Local boards determine additional requirements. The state board, in January 1984, published graduation requirement guidelines which local districts are urged to incorporate. Included in the recommendations are a minimum of 15 1/2 units, which includes an option of 2 units picked from foreign language/fine or performing arts/vocational education and 1/2 computer education. Recommendations include modified academic coursework for students who are college-bound.

(s) Students in junior and senior classes may receive dual credits for college coursework.

(t) At least one of the science units must include lab. Minimum competency test passage is required for graduation.

(u) The college preparation diploma became available to qualifying graduates in 1985. For college preparation, specific core subjects must be taken.

(v) Core requirements in effect for several years. State board raised the total-1985 graduates needed 19 units; 1986 graduates needed 20. Social studies requirement has 2 alternatives. Effective 7/92 requirements changed to 2 units of social studies, 2 units of science, 1 unit of fine arts and 1 unit of vocational/practical arts.

(w) For graduation, 200 credit hours are required, with at least 80% in core curriculum courses.

(x) Computer literacy may be waived by demonstration of competency. Minimum competency test passage is required for graduation.

(y) Other column: 1/2 arts; 1/2 computer science; 3 from 2 of the following-arts, foreign language, practical arts, vocational education. The usage of minimum competency test passage for high school graduation is an option of the local districts.

(z) Other column: 1 fine, practical or performing arts; 1/2 career exploration. 92 credit hours are required for graduation. The state does not use standard Carnegie units. State does not use graduating class as the base for changes but uses the terminology of the students entering ninth grade class. Minimum competency test passage is required for graduation.

(aa) In 6/84 the state board approved requiring all students achieve computer literacy prior to graduation. In 1989 the legislature approved a bill allowing languages other than English to satisfy the communication skills requirement which emphasizes the areas of writing and speaking. Students preparing for college have an advanced curriculum. A state level minimum competency test is available and the districts have the option of usage. If a student passes the test, a special proficiency endorsement is included on their diploma.

(bb) Electives vary for the local (regular) and the Regents' (college-bound) diploma. Other column: 1 art and/or music for local; 3 to 5 from a sequence of specific courses must be chosen by Regents' diploma students and is an additional requirement for local. The local diploma notes 1/2 for health only, 2 noncredit units of physical education beyond the total are required. For all students, comprehensive tests are required. By 1991, areas covered needed to include reading, writing, math, American History and government, and science/global studies. For a Regents' diploma compre-

hensive exams are required in most subjects. Minimum competency test passage is a graduation requirement for all students.

(cc) One science class must include lab. Minimum competency test passage is required for graduation.

(dd) One unit of higher level foreign language may be substituted for the 4th unit of English; 1 unit of math may be business math. Although 17 units are required, the local education agencies are urged to establish requirements at a minimum of 20 units. As of 7/1/94 social studies must include 1 unit of world history, 1 of U.S. history each with a strong geography component.

(ee) Passage of a minimum competency test is a graduation requirement.

(ff) Other column: For college preparation diploma-choice of foreign language, computer science, economics, English, geography, government, math, history, sociology, science, speech and psychology. There are slight variations between 2- and 4-year and junior colleges. If foreign language is elected, student must take 2 years of same language. Although total hour requirement is less for college prep. path, curriculum is more rigorous and restrictive.

(gg) Other column: 1/2 career development, 1 applied arts, fine arts or foreign language. Minimum competency test passage required for graduation. Honors Degree diplomas are available for students who maintain at least a 3.5 GPA. Recipients have an honors seal on the diploma

(hh) Computer science can be option instead of arts and humanities. State has prescribed learning objectives and curriculum guidelines for 12 goals of quality education. As of 1993, state discontinued use of the Carnegie Unit.

(ii) College-bound students are required to complete 2 units of foreign language, 1/2 arts and 1/2 computer literacy and have a total unit requirement of 18.

(jj) If approved by the state department of education, students may count one unit of computer science for a math requirement. Students who earn 1 unit in science and 6 or more in a specific occupational service area will fulfill the science requirements. State allows students in the junior and senior classes to receive dual credits for college coursework. Students must pass an exit exam of minimum competency.

(kk) Beginning in 1990 the requirements were raised to 3 in science and the electives dropped to 7.

(ll) Minimum competency test passage is a requirement for graduation. Students may meet the economics requirement by: 1 semester in economics, out-of-school experiences through Junior Achievement, or marketing education.

(mm) Other column: For college preparation—1/2 free enterprise, 2 foreign language, 1 computer science, 1 fine arts. 1 1/2 units of physical education and 1/2 of health are required for either regular or college prep. program. Junior and senior students are allowed to receive dual credit for college courses. Minimum competency test passage is a requirement for graduation.

(nn) Other column: 1 1/2 arts, 1 vocational education. The state board makes specific course recommendations for college entry, vocational, etc. If computer literacy isn't obtained in related coursework, 1/2 of the electives may be devoted to computer science.

(oo) To allow more flexibility to both vocational education students and smaller or more rural districts, the previous math and science requirement of 3 units in each was modified to a combination of 5 units which may be 2 of one and 3 of the other.

(pp) Additional math or science requirement included in the Other column may be fulfilled by an appropriate vocational education class or ROTC. Grade average of B or better earns a SBE seal on the diploma. Students in junior and senior classes are allowed to receive dual credits for college coursework. Minimum competency test passage is required for graduation.

(qq) 1985 legislature passed addition of a credit for students graduating in 1991. This may be in fine, visual or performing arts or any of the subject areas currently required.

(rr) Other column: 1 of student's electives must be for choice of applied arts, fine or performing arts or a foreign language. State has approved, and policies reflect, an advanced studies certificate, Certificate of Academic Excellence, which has not yet been implemented.

(ss) Electives are the option of the local school district. The state recommends that districts require a total of 22 units. State recommendations emphasize vocational education, foreign language and fine arts to make up the difference between the 13 mandated and 22 recommended units. State requires that all students in Grades 7-12 be participating in class or a board approved activity each period of the day. Local districts have the option of using minimum competency test passage as a requirement for graduation.

(tt) Requirements in effect a number of years. Accreditation standards indicate 4 units of English/language arts, 3 of social studies and 2 each of math and science.

(uu) Electives must include life skills seminar or students may pass a test in lieu of the seminar. District of Columbia requires 100 hours of community service without credit.

Table 8.5
NUMBER OF INSTITUTIONS OF HIGHER EDUCATION AND BRANCHES, BY TYPE, CONTROL OF INSTITUTION AND STATE: 1992-93

State or other jurisdiction	All institutions			Universities		All other 4-year institutions		2-year institutions	
	Total	Public	Private	Public	Private	Public	Private	Public	Private
United States	3,638	1,624	2,014	94	62	508	1,507	1,024	445
Alabama............	86	55	31	2	0	16	18	37	13
Alaska.............	8	4	4	1	0	2	3	1	1
Arizona............	40	21	19	2	0	1	15	18	4
Arkansas	34	20	14	1	0	9	10	10	4
California..........	322	139	183	2	4	29	143	108	36
Colorado	59	28	31	2	1	11	21	15	9
Connecticut	47	24	23	1	1	6	18	17	4
Delaware	10	5	5	1	0	1	5	3	0
Florida	105	39	66	2	1	7	50	30	15
Georgia............	115	69	46	1	1	18	30	50	15
Hawaii	17	10	7	1	0	2	7	7	0
Idaho	11	6	5	1	0	3	3	2	2
Illinois.............	189	62	107	3	4	9	87	50	16
Indiana	78	28	50	4	1	10	39	14	10
Iowa	61	20	41	2	1	1	34	17	8
Kansas	49	28	21	3	0	5	19	20	2
Kentucky	62	22	40	2	0	6	27	14	13
Louisiana	33	20	13	1	2	13	9	6	2
Maine	31	14	17	1	0	7	12	6	5
Maryland	56	32	24	1	1	12	20	19	3
Massachusetts	117	31	88	1	7	13	65	17	14
Michigan	102	45	57	3	1	12	49	30	7
Minnesota	99	55	44	1	0	9	35	45	9
Mississippi	46	29	17	2	0	7	12	20	5
Missouri	96	29	67	1	2	12	52	16	13
Montana............	19	13	6	2	0	4	3	7	3
Nebraska	37	20	17	1	1	6	14	13	2
Nevada	9	6	3	1	0	1	2	4	1
New Hampshire	29	12	17	1	0	4	13	7	4
New Jersey.........	62	33	29	1	2	13	21	19	6
New Mexico........	31	23	8	2	0	4	6	17	2
New York	320	88	232	2	12	40	171	46	49
North Carolina	122	75	47	2	2	15	36	58	9
North Dakota	20	15	5	2	0	4	4	9	1
Ohio	165	61	104	8	1	17	67	36	36
Oklahoma	46	29	17	2	1	12	10	15	6
Oregon	45	21	24	2	0	6	23	13	1
Pennsylvania	220	84	156	3	4	42	99	19	53
Rhode Island	12	3	9	1	0	1	9	1	0
South Carolina	60	33	27	2	0	10	22	21	5
South Dakota	19	8	11	2	0	5	10	1	1
Tennessee	78	24	54	1	1	9	41	14	42
Texas..............	176	105	71	6	4	34	53	65	14
Utah	16	9	7	2	1	2	3	5	3
Vermont	22	6	16	1	0	3	14	2	2
Virginia............	86	39	47	3	0	12	33	24	14
Washington	62	36	26	2	0	6	21	28	5
West Virginia	28	16	12	1	0	12	10	3	2
Wisconsin..........	64	30	34	1	1	12	28	17	5
Wyoming	9	8	1	1	0	0	0	7	1
U.S. Service Schools ...	10	10	0	0	0	9	0	1	0
Dist. of Columbia	18	2	16	0	5	2	11	0	0
American Samoa	1	1	0	0	0	0	0	1	0
Guam	2	2	0	0	0	1	0	1	0
No. Mariana Islands ...	1	1	0	0	0	0	0	1	0
Republic of Palau	1	1	0	0	0	0	0	1	0
Puerto Rico	58	15	43	1	0	10	32	4	11
U.S. Virgin Islands	2	2	0	0	0	2	0	0	0

Source: U.S. Department of Education, National Center for Education Statistics, Integrated Postsecondary Education Data System (IPEDS).
Note: Because of revised survey procedures, data are not entirely comparable with figures for earlier years. The number of branch campuses reporting separately has increased.

Table 8.6
AVERAGE SALARY OF FULL-TIME INSTRUCTIONAL FACULTY IN INSTITUTES OF HIGHER EDUCATION, BY TYPE AND CONTROL OF INSTITUTION AND STATE: 1991-92

State or other jurisdiction	Public institutions				Private institutions			
		4-year institutions		2-year institutions		4-year institutions		2-year institutions
	Total	University	Other 4-year institutions	2-year institutions	Total	University	Other 4-year institutions	2-year institutions
United States	$43,641	$48,771	$43,518	$38,959	$44,376	$58,794	$39,231	$25,673
Alabama............	37,219	42,472	38,309	32,626	31,813	. . .	31,728	28,716
Alaska..............	45,257	43,094	46,770	. . .	37,237	. . .	37,237	. . .
Arizona.............	44,876	48,037	40,182	42,317	35,234	. . .	35,234	. . .
Arkansas	35,671	41,325	35,686	28,146	32,057	. . .	32,541	13,729
California...........	52,886	64,707	55,514	48,374	51,923	64,144	45,133	29,452
Colorado	41,973	50,219	40,956	30,025	44,751	46,282	42,700	. . .
Connecticut	52,809	58,417	50,938	45,851	52,050	65,517	46,585	31,887
Delaware	46,608	49,905	36,009	37,262	43,380	. . .	43,380	. . .
Florida	39,462	48,085	42,485	33,183	40,329	46,534	38,493	23,461
Georgia............	38,754	43,832	39,509	30,754	38,135	55,501	33,781	28,467
Hawaii	47,882	52,788	43,906	40,898	37,059	. . .	37,059	. . .
Idaho	37,438	42,139	36,449	31,847	26,999	. . .	30,012	28,312
Illinois.............	42,937	46,449	39,904	42,680	47,125	80,861	37,875	26,774
Indiana	42,343	45,390	38,587	30,517	42,531	59,720	37,470	28,137
Iowa	43,575	50,636	41,108	32,098	35,898	44,418	34,547	29,107
Kansas	38,178	42,282	36,486	31,822	25,900	. . .	26,303	20,913
Kentucky	39,419	48,066	38,469	30,330	31,183	. . .	3,145	19,553
Louisiana	37,868	45,955	38,476	30,330	43,756	50,498	32,142	. . .
Maine	39,388	43,321	39,428	32,141	41,535	. . .	41,535	. . .
Maryland	44,701	61,879	44,075	41,245	44,881	61,776	37,872	23,385
Massachusetts	42,875	53,320	43,236	36,182	53,128	60,403	45,506	27,862
Michigan	47,814	54,132	43,965	45,366	38,134	39,297	36,290	24,561
Minnesota	44,184	54,178	41,312	40,186	39,111	. . .	39,354	29,203
Mississippi	31,911	37,647	33,250	27,861	30,024	. . .	30,843	20,549
Missouri	38,594	43,205	38,636	35,707	38,989	51,604	31,440	28,103
Montana............	35,567	37,748	32,481	28,006	28,884	. . .	27,914	23,389
Nebraska	40,745	49,943	38,898	27,749	34,805	40,930	31,382	. . .
Nevada	44,176	48,702	44,685	3,765	39,284	. . .	39,284	. . .
New Hampshire	40,733	46,329	37,929	31,485	43,881	. . .	44,153	20,370
New Jersey.........	52,548	62,985	54,151	43,778	51,321	52,671	43,103	. . .
New Mexico.........	38,029	42,335	34,746	28,879	36,328	. . .	36,328	. . .
New York	48,865	56,904	50,548	44,425	49,053	58,051	43,676	23,262
North Carolina	40,887	48,868	40,507	25,863	38,728	54,997	32,515	27,888
North Dakota	34,706	36,885	33,008	30,607	25,963	. . .	27,174	19,819
Ohio	45,928	49,828	43,811	36,774	39,916	55,372	38,326	30,978
Oklahoma	37,711	43,036	36,674	31,938	33,526	46,322	28,046	21,167
Oregon	27,917	41,925	38,148	35,204	38,382	. . .	38,382	. . .
Pennsylvania	46,226	52,858	44,373	40,888	45,873	59,273	41,785	27,112
Rhode Island	46,054	51,151	43,530	38,958	49,089	. . .	49,089	. . .
South Carolina	36,713	44,980	38,480	27,455	33,140	. . .	33,653	21,656
South Dakota	34,298	34,486	34,004	36,033	29,173	. . .	29,173	. . .
Tennessee	39,001	45,369	39,793	30,741	37,852	57,987	30,876	21,779
Texas..............	39,133	46,955	37,600	34,164	42,444	50,738	35,826	21,320
Utah	37,207	43,568	32,505	29,274	43,202	43,991	31,617	31,381
Vermont............	42,532	45,995	34,616	32,194	37,308	. . .	38,180	18,784
Virginia............	44,493	51,252	44,731	35,446	38,747	. . .	38,878	27,220
Washington	41,636	49,107	41,344	35,049	35,204	3,896	38,926	. . .
West Virginia	35,063	41,074	32,925	37,422	30,261	. . .	30,584	24,329
Wisconsin..........	42,498	53,029	40,769	3,957	38,187	. . .	34,490	. . .
Wyoming	37,502	44,227	. . .	30,413	. . .	. . .	48,463	. . .
U.S. Service Schools ...	50,243	. . .	50,243	. . .	. . .	. . .	. . .	. . .
Dist. of Columbia.....	45,808	. . .	45,608	. . .	50,254	51,806	39,284	. . .
American Samoa	21,411	. . .	. . .	21,411	. . .	. . .	. . .	. . .
Guam	48,459	. . .	60,574	41,842	. . .	. . .	. . .	. . .
No. Mariana Islands...	30,520	. . .	. . .	30,520	. . .	. . .	. . .	. . .
Republic of Palau	30,898	. . .	. . .	30,898	. . .	. . .	. . .	. . .
Puerto Rico	29,435	27,042	31,959	30,289	7,638	. . .	7,749	7,219
U.S. Virgin Islands	43,609	. . .	43,609	. . .	. . .	. . .	. . .	. . .

Source: U.S. Department of Education, National Center for Education Statistics, Integrated Postsecondary Education Data System (IPEDS).
Note: Data include imputations for nonrespondent institution.
Key:
. . . — Data not reported or not applicable

Table 8.7
ESTIMATED UNDERGRADUATE TUITION AND FEES AND ROOM AND BOARD RATES IN INSTITUTIONS OF HIGHER EDUCATION, BY CONTROL OF INSTITUTION AND STATE: 1992-93

State or other jurisdiction	Public 4-year institutions				Private 4-year institutions			
	Total	Tuition (in state)	Room	Board	Total	Tuition	Room	Board
United States	$6,029	$2,352	$1,820	$1,857	$15,128	$10,383	$2,372	$2,363
Alabama............	5,013	1,877	1,503	1,633	10,342	6,744	1,522	2,076
Alaska..............	5,423	1,684	1,950	1,789	10,980	6,678	1,807	2,495
Arizona............	5,695	1,554	1,935	2,206	9,389	5,831	1,567	1,991
Arkansas	4,955	1,660	1,659	1,636	8,410	5,424	1,269	1,717
California..........	8,737	1,975	4,319	2,443	17,455	11,833	2,828	2,794
Colorado	5,940	2,216	1,588	2,136	15,473	10,893	2,420	2,160
Connecticut	7,594	3,253	2,303	2,038	19,765	14,082	3,266	2,417
Delaware	7,276	3,471	2,049	1,756	10,209	6,556	2,417	1,236
Florida	5,940	1,703	1,931	2,306	13,759	9,176	2,188	2,395
Georgia............	5,057	1,842	1,422	1,793	13,198	8,606	2,343	2,249
Hawaii	5,905	1,399	1,625	2,991	9,588	4,986	3,020	1,562
Idaho	4,724	1,416	1,327	1,981	12,858	9,021	1,055	2,782
Illinois............	6,509	2,829	1,738	1,942	14,412	9,938	2,444	2,030
Indiana	6,283	2,452	1,639	2,192	14,238	10,495	1,723	2,020
Iowa	5,213	2,228	1,468	1,517	13,601	10,127	1,613	1,861
Kansas	4,934	1,803	1,461	1,870	10,391	7,037	1,386	1,968
Kentucky	4,766	1,708	1,291	1,767	9,594	6,274	1,580	1,740
Louisiana	4,810	1,840	1,366	1,804	15,938	11,156	2,423	2,359
Maine	7,055	2,896	2,088	2,071	18,923	13,652	2,444	2,827
Maryland	7,575	2,770	2,532	2,273	18,147	12,200	3,092	2,855
Massachusetts	7,898	3,845	2,195	1,858	20,198	13,973	3,241	2,984
Michigan	7,211	3,189	1,801	2,221	11,714	8,008	1,719	1,987
Minnesota	5,686	2,660	1,552	1,474	14,677	10,929	1,790	1,958
Mississippi	5,115	2,366	1,299	1,450	8,284	5,693	1,269	1,322
Missouri	5,646	2,243	1,887	1,516	12,555	8,573	1,885	2,097
Montana...........	6,004	1,834	1,675	2,495	10,033	6,623	894	2,516
Nebraska	4,745	1,859	1,228	1,658	11,254	7,904	1,614	1,735
Nevada	6,425	1,536	2,863	2,026	. . .	7,500	2,400	. . .
New Hampshire	7,274	3,453	2,259	1,562	17,395	12,351	2,599	2,445
New Jersey..........	7,984	3,353	2,768	1,863	17,900	11,692	2,858	3,352
New Mexico........	4,744	1,608	1,470	1,666	13,731	9,826	1,747	2,158
New York	7,326	2,894	2,479	1,953	17,829	11,851	3,144	2,834
North Carolina	4,537	1,266	1,535	1,736	12,891	9,094	1,738	2,059
North Dakota	5,061	2,007	872	2,172	8,756	6,035	1,154	1,567
Ohio	7,286	3,108	2,223	1,955	14,369	10,166	1,993	2,210
Oklahoma	3,831	1,549	818	1,464	10,095	6,733	1,519	1,843
Oregon	6,631	2,658	2,030	1,943	15,530	11,488	1,840	2,222
Pennsylvania	7,836	4,022	1,969	1,845	16,779	11,896	25,835	2,348
Rhode Island	8,097	3,159	2,578	2,360	18,314	12,567	3,098	2,649
South Carolina	6,153	2,643	1,733	1,777	11,767	8,212	1,745	1,810
South Dakota	4,616	2,072	1,046	1,498	10,926	7,366	1,371	2,189
Tennessee	4,806	1,713	1,444	1,649	11,230	8,032	1,462	1,736
Texas	4,720	1,354	1,655	1,711	11,370	7,467	1,785	2,118
Utah	4,879	1,837	1,227	1,815	5,612	2,411	1,244	1,957
Vermont	9,673	5,321	2,675	1,677	18,367	13,490	2,583	2,294
Virginia............	7,231	3,338	2,080	1,813	12,844	8,864	1,881	2,099
Washington	5,973	2,069	1,896	2,008	15,324	10,938	2,309	2,077
West Virginia	5,422	1,759	1,778	1,885	13,462	9,728	1,662	2,072
Wisconsin...........	5,277	2,173	1,582	1,542	13,031	9,542	1,441	2,048
Wyoming	4,652	1,430	1,392	1,830	. . .	. . .	. . .	. . .
Dist. of Columbia ...	. . .	830	. . .	. . .	18,594	12,416	3,509	2,669

Source: U.S. Department of Education, National Center for Education Statistics.
Note: Data are for the entire academic year and are average charges for 4-year institutions. Tuition and fees were weighted by the number of full-time-equivalent undergraduates but are not adjusted to reflect student residency. Room and board are based on full-time students.
Key:
. . . — Data not reported or not applicable

Table 8.8
GENERAL REVENUE OF PUBLIC SCHOOL SYSTEMS, BY SOURCE: 1990-91
(In thousands of dollars)

State or other jurisdiction	Total (a)	Intergovernmental: Total	Directly from federal government	From state: Federal aid distributed by state	From state: Other	From other local governments	From own sources: Total	Taxes	Parent government contributions	Current charges: School lunch	Current charges: Other	Other
United States	$224,225,680	$116,341,568	$6,073,519	$1,351,992	$11,983,328	$99,993,378	$3,012,870	$101,810,593	$69,146,614	$19,135,012	$6,352,990	$7,175,977
Alabama	2,529,262	1,868,340	239,710	13,132	259,642	1,385,806	209,760	421,212	270,199	0	89,292	61,721
Alaska	1,007,282	792,919	0	69,248	37,835	685,836	0	214,363	0	176,533	17,940	19,890
Arizona	3,089,515	1,635,845	546	70,115	177,173	1,280,895	107,662	1,453,124	1,098,390	88	82,650	271,996
Arkansas	1,622,527	966,992	130,052	3,037	144,211	817,089	2,655	525,483	412,068	278,514	74,450	38,965
California	25,547,408	17,816,021	136,049	147,669	1,564,262	16,039,451	64,639	7,595,338	4,928,935		1,003,644	1,384,245
Colorado	2,896,601	1,255,633	0	12,012	123,145	1,119,399	1,077	1,640,968	1,334,779	2,015,271	48,585	206,905
Connecticut	3,753,926	1,527,193	158,351	6,156	119,139	1,260,153	141,745	2,068,382	0	0	10,188	4,526
Delaware	567,574	416,813	1,615	5,663	34,285	376,865	0	149,146	125,499	0	466,405	13,459
Florida	10,843,381	6,146,047	0	42,173	638,961	5,464,913	0	4,697,334	3,884,985	0	126,402	345,944
Georgia	5,428,786	3,299,284	63,139	24,061	319,074	2,924,168	31,981	2,066,363	1,705,833	0		234,128
Hawaii	960,578	926,105	0	59,414	16,674	850,017	0	34,473	206,709	0	16,570	4,410
Idaho	793,239	511,406	39,523	6,669	53,267	451,468	2	242,310		0	217,645	19,031
Illinois	9,368,544	3,709,064	275,971	50,791	485,167	3,165,673		5,383,509	4,777,570	0	181,067	388,294
Indiana	5,277,109	2,925,416	198,218	11,720	212,711	2,658,195	7,433	2,153,475	1,821,541	0	61,603	150,867
Iowa	2,159,431	1,136,115		5,153	78,849	1,052,113	42,790	1,023,316	906,076	0		55,637
Kansas	2,161,657	1,132,663	46,812	14,129	50,124	914,826	153,584	982,182	798,124	0	50,087	122,109
Kentucky	2,653,659	1,732,828	301,525	15,084	234,648	1,483,096	11,373	619,306	533,315	0	50,566	35,904
Louisiana	3,186,528	2,038,267	47,530	19,401	295,346	1,712,147	0	1,100,731	919,359	306,077	24,192	130,806
Maine	1,203,024	586,872	62,605	6,087	52,444	528,341	0	553,547	199,207	0	145,809	24,071
Maryland	4,622,226	1,420,299	488,603	20,965	183,307	1,215,818	209	2,713,324	0	2,537,173		30,342
Massachusetts	5,743,340	2,129,352	292,654	7,900	228,830	1,507,442	385,180	3,321,334	5,495,515	3,090,185	209,496	39,607
Michigan	9,940,530	3,126,842	722,694	33,523	447,492	2,423,791	222,036	6,090,994	1,306,150	0	154,556	385,983
Minnesota	4,292,573	2,672,045	0	15,417	156,369	2,379,149	121,110	1,620,528	342,267	0	67,210	159,822
Mississippi	1,631,569	1,165,999	8,286	16,048	255,301	894,047	603	457,284	660,584	1,645	167,842	46,162
Missouri	3,926,637	2,360,346	0	9,407	208,830	1,521,946	620,163	1,566,291	1,231,134	0		167,315
Montana	765,763	482,246	0	36,325	36,477	346,007	63,437	283,517	219,894	0	111,457	54,021
Nebraska	1,482,189	592,801	0	19,389	61,859	440,325	71,228	889,388	724,067	0	14,538	53,864
Nevada	981,523	678,836	0	5,712	31,541	641,566	17	302,687	245,662	0	23,827	42,487
New Hampshire	974,607	103,665	0	3,095	23,620	76,382	568	870,942	660,584	173,176	111,623	13,355
New Jersey	9,910,893	3,109,535	913,293	12,453	357,539	2,739,543	0	5,888,065	4,773,326	769,936		233,180
New Mexico	1,339,164	1,124,777	9,358	68,621	96,883	959,273	0	205,029	123,339	3,694,437	274,400	49,039
New York	21,389,551	10,212,021	0	21,703	1,001,787	9,087,026	101,505	11,177,530	6,816,985	1,409,675	142,644	391,708
North Carolina	5,377,323	3,644,734	0	38,557	318,941	3,287,236	0	1,732,589		0	29,934	180,270
North Dakota	508,720	281,388	0	10,584	30,846	231,390	8,568	227,332	171,609	0	394,245	25,789
Ohio	8,811,183	4,192,472	15,033	16,425	425,491	3,746,524	4,032	4,603,678	3,930,303	0		279,130
Oklahoma	2,438,766	1,699,821	91,180	48,870	178,031	1,427,126	45,794	647,765	528,985	0	78,280	53,312
Oregon	2,686,963	901,465		42,473	119,646	686,285	53,061	1,785,498	1,587,847	0	229,300	119,371
Pennsylvania	10,367,100	4,184,181	500,732	20,683	550,348	3,599,467	13,683	5,682,187	5,164,206	0	652	288,681
Rhode Island	853,164	410,147	476	5,525	30,284	342,710	31,628	442,541	859,713	437,221	121,086	4,668
South Carolina	2,843,758	1,729,413	44,615	9,129	219,885	1,378,996	121,403	1,069,730		0		88,931

See footnotes at end of table.

GENERAL REVENUE OF PUBLIC SCHOOL SYSTEMS, BY SOURCE: 1990-1991—Continued

State or other jurisdiction	Total (a)	Intergovernmental		From state		From other local governments	From own sources			Current charges		Other
		Total	Directly from federal government	Federal aid distributed by state	Other		Total	Taxes	Parent government contributions	School lunch	Other	
South Dakota	519,888	0	212,413	21,683	34,160	148,556	8,014	307,475	268,893	0	15,467	23,115
Tennessee	2,992,007	159,736	1,741,058	11,822	272,691	1,209,084	247,461	1,091,213	0	874,650	102,138	114,425
Texas	15,196,817	885,557	6,857,701	74,988	964,480	5,803,321	14,912	7,453,559	6,619,226	0	428,527	405,806
Utah	1,356,823	0	899,226	12,166	79,782	807,260	18	457,597	359,372	0	43,317	54,908
Vermont	631,685	15,000	228,215	1,846	28,290	197,069	1,010	388,470	356,774	0	15,328	16,368
Virginia	5,535,374	0	2,551,648	43,213	250,612	2,257,823	0	2,983,726	0	2,767,450	177,677	38,599
Washington	4,578,531	0	3,585,176	60,994	184,236	3,325,261	14,685	993,355	748,252	0	138,832	106,271
West Virginia	1,598,967	224,656	966,457	2,686	122,177	839,408	2,186	407,854	334,617	0	25,696	47,541
Wisconsin	4,624,721	0	2,240,105	14,108	163,835	2,021,636	40,526	2,384,616	2,163,865	0	94,769	125,982
Wyoming	588,854	0	357,659	8,266	22,801	281,460	45,132	231,195	191,440	0	18,352	21,403
Dist. of Columbia	664,440	0	55,702	55,702	0	0	0	608,738	0	602,981	4,143	1,614

Source: U.S. Department of Commerce, Bureau of the Census, *Public Education Finances 1990-91*.
Note: Revenue from state sources for state dependent school systems is included as intergovernmental revenue from state rather than as parent government contributions. Detail may not add to totals due to rounding.

(a) To avoid duplication, interschool system transactions are excluded.

Table 8.9
SUMMARY OF STATE GOVERNMENT DIRECT EXPENDITURES FOR EDUCATION, BY STATE: 1992
(In thousands of dollars)

State	Total (a)	Elementary and secondary — Total	Current operation	Capital outlay — Total	Construction	Other capital outlay	Higher education — Total	Current operation	Capital outlay — Total	Construction	Other capital outlay
United States	$86,650,112	$2,221,660	$1,810,740	$410,920	$70,904,354	$62,696,136	$8,208,218	$13,524,098	$7,178,227	$345,689	$6,000,182
Alabama	1,871,394	24,693	24,693	0	1,437,777	1,310,732	127,045	408,924	338,106	6,115	64,703
Alaska	575,109	216,541	200,717	15,824	296,194	263,376	32,818	62,374	58,092	1,043	3,239
Arizona	1,265,910	0	0	0	1,119,930	1,027,377	92,553	145,980	69,625	1,527	74,828
Arkansas	962,351	0	0	0	766,433	667,471	98,962	195,918	154,952	4,650	36,316
California	9,242,251	136,161	136,161	0	7,630,889	6,894,745	736,144	1,475,201	712,940	3,267	758,994
Colorado	1,489,249	0	0	0	1,395,521	1,257,611	137,910	93,728	35,176	1,695	56,857
Connecticut	939,282	0	0	0	765,691	749,814	15,877	173,591	118,008	7,271	48,312
Delaware	467,576	0	0	0	389,319	361,776	27,543	78,257	54,650	620	22,987
Florida	2,637,569	0	0	0	2,055,294	1,651,473	403,821	582,275	353,587	7,840	220,848
Georgia	1,864,529	0	0	0	1,555,837	1,375,954	179,883	308,692	252,077	15,895	40,720
Hawaii	1,344,015	814,149	703,447	110,702	511,473	456,172	55,301	18,393	10,275	3,939	4,179
Idaho	380,714	0	0	0	325,665	291,143	34,522	55,049	42,697	1,991	10,361
Illinois	3,045,399	118	118	0	2,372,035	2,044,568	327,467	673,246	297,298	14,157	361,791
Indiana	2,462,080	0	0	0	2,186,764	1,937,618	249,146	275,316	108,078	6,639	160,599
Iowa	1,105,383	0	0	0	945,978	864,550	81,428	159,405	57,366	286	101,753
Kansas	1,094,167	0	0	0	978,073	717,110	260,963	116,094	70,520	919	44,655
Kentucky	1,554,117	0	0	0	1,191,749	1,073,702	118,047	362,368	263,649	25,944	72,775
Louisiana	1,511,386	21,256	21,256	0	1,230,884	1,134,768	96,116	259,246	187,382	2,045	69,819
Maine	421,697	8,634	8,402	232	356,489	317,591	38,898	56,574	36,187	333	20,054
Maryland	1,705,008	130,128	130,128	0	1,328,315	1,177,693	150,622	246,565	131,036	3,107	112,422
Massachusetts	1,532,085	0	0	0	1,283,498	1,173,183	110,315	248,587	158,308	799	89,480
Michigan	3,559,987	0	0	0	3,197,078	2,944,889	252,189	362,909	99,253	927	262,729
Minnesota	1,816,561	0	0	0	1,534,564	1,424,252	110,312	281,997	105,391	25,304	151,302
Mississippi	749,078	0	0	0	607,811	556,487	51,324	141,267	97,748	2,755	40,764
Missouri	1,235,778	0	0	0	1,053,559	971,089	82,470	182,219	105,775	3,963	72,481
Montana	312,795	0	0	0	242,138	230,454	11,684	70,657	53,569	2,671	14,417
Nebraska	636,050	0	0	0	561,673	503,748	57,925	74,377	45,380	3,272	25,725
Nevada	410,459	0	0	0	377,052	316,783	60,269	33,407	25,087	177	8,143
New Hampshire	317,992	0	0	0	274,113	273,092	1,021	43,879	12,922	10,264	20,693
New Jersey	2,468,810	421,964	404,107	17,857	1,728,364	1,524,993	203,371	318,482	105,831	2,511	210,140
New Mexico	763,268	0	0	0	685,066	626,557	58,509	78,202	49,945	2,050	26,207
New York	5,078,736	0	0	0	3,901,558	3,387,578	513,980	1,177,178	383,475	19,394	774,309
North Carolina	2,283,928	33,234	24,696	8,538	1,991,335	1,803,976	187,359	259,359	177,525	4,981	76,853
North Dakota	413,522	0	0	0	370,252	328,410	41,842	43,270	27,772	571	14,927
Ohio	3,855,198	0	0	0	3,333,961	2,796,077	537,884	521,237	152,953	52,741	315,543
Oklahoma	1,244,988	14,571	14,571	0	1,085,060	1,010,587	74,473	145,357	84,281	3,274	57,802
Oregon	952,392	0	0	0	833,182	715,729	117,453	119,210	63,854	2,047	53,309
Pennsylvania	4,932,078	69,728	1,167	68,561	3,615,934	2,708,939	906,995	1,246,416	592,718	25,981	627,717
Rhode Island	392,370	0	0	0	288,397	270,095	18,302	103,973	75,971	1,436	26,566
South Carolina	1,482,688	50,268	49,400	868	1,257,832	1,081,020	176,812	174,588	115,467	12,975	46,146

See footnotes at end of table.

STATE GOVERNMENT DIRECT EXPENDITURES FOR EDUCATION: 1992—Continued

State	Elementary and secondary					Higher education				
	Total (a)	Current operation	Capital outlay			Total	Current operation	Capital outlay		
			Total	Construction	Other capital outlay			Total	Construction	Other capital outlay
South Dakota	220,135	0	0	183,681	168,664	15,017	36,454	30,114	1,128	5,212
Tennessee	1,788,541	0	0	1,507,955	1,194,697	313,258	280,586	219,561	7,382	53,643
Texas	5,109,226	91,995	91,995	4,515,000	4,172,790	342,210	502,231	284,491	8,702	209,038
Utah	964,307	0	0	880,025	794,366	85,659	84,282	58,192	183	25,907
Vermont	326,651	0	0	268,608	251,800	16,808	58,043	27,416	341	30,286
Virginia	2,464,157	0	0	2,086,107	1,906,323	179,784	378,050	237,619	5,149	135,282
Washington	2,581,447	188,220	188,220	2,023,231	1,822,659	200,572	369,996	202,246	15,566	152,184
West Virginia	667,217	0	0	551,272	519,208	32,064	115,945	76,484	13,545	25,916
Wisconsin	1,956,125	0	0	1,664,210	1,497,162	167,048	291,915	142,407	5,872	143,636
Wyoming	194,357	0	0	161,528	145,285	16,243	32,829	14,771	445	17,613

Source: U.S. Department of Commerce, Bureau of the Census, *Public Education Finances 1992.*
Note: Detail may not add to totals due to rounding.

(a) To avoid duplication, interschool system transactions are excluded.

The Federalization of Crime and Justice in the United States

Crimes that were once punishable under state laws are now becoming federal offenses.

by Rhonda Reeves

Introduction

The presidential campaign of 1992 was unique, not for the issues that were debated (such as U.S. intervention in Somalia or health care), but for an issue that was excluded from election rhetoric: crime and crime control. President Clinton's strategy to keep the nation's attention focused on "the economy, stupid," diverted the spotlight from criminal justice issues, such as those that dominated the 1988 election.

With the furor the Willie Horton case created in 1988, the Democrats had learned an important political lesson from the failed Dukakis campaign: Never be perceived as soft on crime. Such highly publicized tragedies as the Polly Klaas kidnapping and murder in California; the Pamela Basu carjacking in Maryland; and the murder of German tourist Uwe-Wilhelm Rakebrand in Florida, were devastating episodes that ultimately came to drive public policy — resulting in new (and sometimes redundant) legislation and enforcement provisions. In the aftermath of cases such as these, Clinton's 1993 recommendations to Congress were strong on law enforcement (calling for 100,000 new police) and also focused on options, such as an increase in prison expansion and boot camps.

Congress got the message. In 1994, frustrated with mounting public disgust and fear about governmental inadequacy on the crime issue, Congress debated a sweeping omnibus Crime Bill (H.R. 3355) that essentially eviscerated the state's role in responding to the problems of crime and violence. The bill represented the culmination of 20 years of "get tough" rhetoric

and encompassed such issues as mandatory sentencing, increased prison construction, boot camps, guns and violence. It is part of a comprehensive approach to "federalize" crime and remove the response to such crime from the province of the states. The fiscal and political ramifications of such policies for states are enormous.

This essay will attempt to explore the politics, the rhetoric and the implications surrounding these pivotal issues, while also providing data about what the actual research on these issues has indicated.

Mandatory Sentencing

A February 1994 article in *Time* (Smolowe) recounts the following episode related to mandatory sentencing: A young welfare mother, struggling to make ends meet, accepted a $100 bill from a stranger in return for mailing a package for him. She was allowed to keep the change ($47.70) for mailing the package, which (unknown to her) turned out to contain 232 grams of crack. For her role in this crime, despite her lack of a criminal record or history of drug use, she was sentenced to a 10-year prison term. District Judge Richard Gadbois Jr. was forced to impose this sentence under federal mandatory sentencing guidelines, although he termed the situation "crazy."

Although mandatory minimum sentences were initially conceived as a means of ensuring stiffer (and more uniform) punishments for offenders, many critics are now questioning-

Rhonda Reeves is communications coordinator for the Center for Law and Justice at The Council of State Governments.

ing whether or not these laws are doing that. Policy-makers also have serious questions about mandatory sentencing as a cost-effective means of crime control.

Mandatory minimum sentences have now been in place long enough for significant research to be available on their effectiveness. Although much of the rhetoric surrounding the 1994 crime bill focuses on combating violent crime, according to a recent report by the Campaign for Effective Crime Policy (*Evaluating Mandatory Minimum Sentences*, 1993), "mandatory sentencing has resulted in an increased proportion of non-violent drug offenders in prison and a decrease in incarcerated violent offenders."

The report cites New York as an example of a state that extensively uses mandatory minimums for drug offenses: In that state the percentage of violent offenders in prison declined from 63 percent in 1982 to 34 percent in 1992. In Florida, former Governor Bob Martinez authorized the release of 130,000 inmates over four years (many of them violent offenders) to create prison space for drug offenders sentenced under mandatory laws; one in three went on to commit new crimes (Isikoff 1990).

The implications of mandatory minimum sentences on fiscal policy also is significant. The U.S. Sentencing Commission reported to Congress in 1991 that mandatory minimums resulted in offenders receiving a total of between 4,400 and 7,000 additional years of prison time during fiscal year 1990 at a cost of between $79 million and $125 million (1991).

Questions also have been raised regarding the racial disparity in applying mandatory minimum sentences. Research indicates that such sentences are disproportionately applied to minorities. The Federal Judicial Center reported that in cases where a mandatory minimum could apply, black offenders were 21 percent more likely and Hispanic offenders 28 percent more likely than whites to receive at least the mandatory minimum prison term (Meierhofer, 1992).

There is little evidence to suggest mandatory minimum sentencing has deterred offenders from committing crimes — the theory being that if a potential offender knows he will spend significant time in prison, he or she will decide against committing the crime. This goal ignores the important likelihood that most offenders do not believe they will be caught, and therefore, do not adequately evaluate the penalties for their crime (Ellis & Ellis, 1989). It also does not take into account the common influence of alcohol or drugs on many offenders at the time of the crime, or the poor socioeconomic status of many offenders who would be subject to mandatory minimums — a group unlikely to "engage in cost-benefit analysis" prior to committing a crime (Irwin and Austin, 1987). And as U.S. Attorney General Reno has said, "certainty, not severity, of punishment" has been shown to be a more consistent motivator with respect to deterrence.

The imposition of mandatory minimum sentences have not, however, resulted in a certainty of punishment. Scott Wallace, former counsel to the U.S. Senate Judiciary Committee (and special counsel with the National Legal Aid and Defender Association) describes the "increasing randomization of punishment in America . . . Though sentences may be 10 times as long in the federal system as in the states, the fact that there's a mere 2 percent chance of being hauled into that system — and no clue about how that 2 percent is selected — gives these tough punishments all the predictability of an earthquake. People are not readily deterred, either from crime or from living in Los Angeles, by horrific consequences that always seem to happen to someone else" (Wallace, 1994).

Do mandatory sentences imprison the "right" offenders — thereby making our streets safer? Many experts think not. Oliver J. Keller, past president of the American Correctional Association was quoted in the *Los Angeles Times* as saying, "Many of the people who wind up with mandatory sentences are small-time drug dealers who are taking up valuable prison space. This country has been on a prison-building binge for over 20 years, and if that were the answer [to crime] we'd be crime-free by now" (Eaton, 1994).

United States Attorney General Janet Reno addressed the problems inherent in mandatory minimums when she told the American Bar

Association (1994), "It is so frustrating to me to find people in federal prisons serving 10- and 15-year mandatory minimum sentences as first-time offenders, when three- and four-time offenders in the state systems who have committed terrible violent crimes are getting vastly reduced sentences because we do not have enough state prison cells."

More Prisons/Boot Camps

With 1.2 million people incarcerated in this country, the United States locks up more of its citizens per capita than the former Soviet Union, South Africa or any other industrialized nation. Prison populations have consistently been on the rise in this country for the past 20 years.

The question is: Has this solved the crime problem? Are options the most appropriate solution? Or, as the average citizen has a right to ask, are we any safer? Research indicates that the answer is "no." From 1983 to 1992, the nation's prison population has increased 102 percent, while rates of violent crime rose 40 percent during that period.

In looking at specific states, there is little proportionate relationship between high incarceration rates and reductions in violent crime. For example, Florida ranks first in violent crime, but has the 12th highest incarceration rate in the country. Minnesota, on the other hand, is ranked 37th in violent crime, but has this country's second lowest incarceration rate (Smolowe, 1994).

Andrew L. Sonner, state's attorney for Montgomery County, in Maryland, is a 23-year veteran of elective office who understands the politics of certain incarcerative options within the 1994 crime bill, but he says, "It hasn't been shown in the last 12 years that imprisoning more people is solving our problem. There's a huge price tag on it, and you can't build these prisons overnight . . . We'll be getting a lot of punishment out of it, but not much crime prevention" (Eaton, 1994).

The "three strikes and you're out" clause of the Omnibus Crime Bill has enormous implications for states that are already struggling with increasing prison populations. The provision would mandate that, after a third

felony conviction, offenders go to prison for life. Wallace, special counsel to the National Legal Aid and Defender Association, warns that "three-time loser laws" will eventually turn prisons into nursing homes. He says, "We're going to have a nation with geriatric prisoners — comatose guys in oxygen tents — and nobody will be able to turn those guys loose until they die" (Eaton, 1994).

In his testimony before the House Judiciary Committee, Marc Mauer, assistant director of the Sentencing Project, proposed the following analogy: No one has suggested that the solution to the health-care crisis is to build more hospitals. Prevention is the key to good health care, and hospitals should be used as a last resort. Prisons should be used in the same manner. Mauer further suggested that had the nation embarked on an experiment with prevention in the criminal justice system for 20 years, rather than an experiment with incarceration, our society might be safer and we might have a less expensive criminal justice system.

A frightening societal aspect of increased rates of incarceration is that, far from rehabilitating offenders, prison may actually teach inmates criminal behavior. University of Miami criminologist Paul Cromwell (who served on the Texas Board of Pardons and Paroles) says, "Prison systems are criminogenic, they create criminals" (Smolowe, 1994). Michael Sheahan, the sheriff of Cook County, Ill., says of inmates, "They start as drug offenders they eventually become property-crime offenders, and then they commit crimes against people. They learn this trade as they go through the prison system" (Smolowe, 1994).

Boot camps are another incarcerative option, often intended to scare offenders "straight." They have received wide support from both the president and Congress in 1994 and are an important linchpin in the Omnibus Crime Bill. Doris MacKenzie is a University of Maryland researcher who has studied eight such programs and found little impact on recidivism rates. "We're not finding any significant difference from similar offenders who are put on probation or who serve their time" (Lacayo, 1994).

Guns and Violence

Articles in sources from *USA Today* to *Rolling Stone* debate the Second Amendment issue — does it or does it not guarantee an American citizen's right to own guns? The trend in popular research seems to be to either treat the question as a non-issue, or to interpret the amendment as not intending to affirm such rights. The phraseology in question reads, "a well-regulated militia, being necessary to the security of a free state, the right of the people to keep and bear arms, shall not be infringed." According to the Violence Policy Center (1993), "no gun-control measure has ever been struck down as unconstitutional under the Second Amendment . . . The lower federal courts, in accordance with Supreme Court precedents, have consistently held that there is no individual right to own a gun." Precedent setting cases include: *United States v. Miller* (1939); *United States v. Warin* (1976); and *Lewis v. United States* (1980).

Despite the apparent lack of constitutional opposition to gun control, state legislatures and Congress have been historically unwilling to regulate gun trade and ownership. One likely reason for this is pressure from powerful lobbies that oppose all gun control proposals. For example, the National Rifle Association spends $80 million a year to defeat gun control legislation (Coalition, 1993).

One thing is clear: Gun violence in the United States, where handguns remained essentially unregulated until the 1993 passage of the Brady Bill, is virtually without parallel. According to Franklin Zimring, director of the Earl Warren Legal Institute, "The United States has a violence problem like no other industrialized nation."

Does the ability of a nation to regulate, legislate and control guns have an impact on that country's rate of gun violence? Britain, for example, requires that guns be kept at clubs (as they are intended for sport/hunting purposes) — handguns killed 22 people in Great Britain in 1990. Japan prohibits the ownership of guns except as antiques — handguns killed 87 people in Japan in 1990. Seattle residents, on the other hand, are six times more likely to be homicide victims than residents of Vancouver (which has strict gun regulations), even though the cities are demographically similar and are only 160 miles apart (*USA Today*, 1993).

In their bid to offer hope for reducing firearms violence in America, the Violence Policy Center offers several proposals. The nonpartisan organization promotes a two-pronged approach: 1) "The first step toward reducing firearms violence is to recognize firearms for what they are — inherently dangerous consumer products"; 2) "The second is to design a comprehensive, workable regulatory framework that can be applied to firearms and firearms products" (Sugarman and Rand, 1993). The aim of their comprehensive report on handgun violence is not to prohibit gun ownership, however. Their position is, rather, that "before progress toward a safer, less violent country can be made, there must be a recognition that regulation of firearms is not inconsistent with continued availability . . . It is possible to create a regulatory system that treats firearms just as we currently control other potentially dangerous consumer products." In other words, the regulation of pesticides has not resulted in the elimination of pesticides; it has simply resulted in safer use of what could be a dangerous product.

Conclusion

One thing that most criminal justice experts will agree on is the fact that there are no simple solutions to the problems of crime and violence in this country. This is not a fact easily absorbed or responded to by the political infrastructure. Politicians are elected in short-term increments; solutions can only be achieved through long-term visionary policy development.

As if crime is not a complicated enough phenomenon, the societal factors that contribute to it are even more intricate. Educating the public is not an easy task for any elected official. "When people want action now, it doesn't help much to tell them the root causes are even more intractable problems like joblessness, family disintegration or drugs. But the solution they are most inclined to reach for, more prisons, has a dismal record when it comes to reducing crime" (Lacayo, 1994).

It is ironic that the "easy answers" the public seems to clamor for is part of the same impulse that heavily contributes to criminal activity in this country. "Americans' impatience for quick-fix remedies resembles the frustration that drives inner-city youths to seize on illegal get-rich schemes: They want to cut corners, produce high yields and not pay a price" (Smolowe, 1994).

To effectively deal with the complex issues surrounding crime and violence, long-term policy examination is called for — much in the manner that has led to extensive research in the area of health-care reform. Experts from every level of the system need to be consulted, including the solicitation of perspectives from law enforcement, institutions, community-based corrections, public health agencies, social service providers and all three branches of government. State officials need to become better educated so that they can, in turn, educate their constituencies. Federalization is a trend that is not likely to go away without careful, systematic reform.

References

Campaign for An Effective Crime Policy, *Evaluating Mandatory Minimum Sentences*, October 1993.

Coalition to Stop Gun Violence, Washington, D.C., 1993.

Eaton, William J. "Despite Support, Critics of Crime Bill Abound." *Los Angeles Times*. 25 January 1994.

Ellis, Ralph D. and Ellis, Carol S. *Theories of Criminal Justice: A Critical Reappraisal*. Wolfeboro: Longwood Academic, 1989.

Irwin, John and Austin, James. *It's About Time: Solving America's Prison Crowding Crisis*. San Francisco: National Council on Crime and Delinquency, 1987.

Isikoff, Michael, "Florida's Crime Crackdown is Freeing Felons Early," *Washington Post*. 28 December 1990.

Lacayo, Richard. "Lock 'em Up," *Time*. 7 February 1994.

Mauer, Marc. Testimony before the House Judiciary Committee, Subcommittee on Crime and Criminal Justice on H.R. 3355: an Alternative Approach to Fighting Crime, February 22, 1994.

Meierhofer, Barbara S. *The General Effect of Mandatory Minimum Prison Terms: A Longitudinal Study of Federal Sentences Imposed*, Washington, DC, Federal Judicial Center, 1992.

Smolowe, Jill. "And Throw Away the Key," *Time*. 7 February 1994.

Sugarman, Josh and Rand, Kristen. *Cease Fire: A Comprehensive Strategy to Reduce Firearms Violence*. 1993.

"USA in Its Own League When it Comes to Firearms," in *USA Today*. 29 December 1993.

United States Sentencing Commission, *Mandatory Minimum Penalties in the Federal Criminal Justice System*, August 1991.

Wallace, H. Scott. "When Congress Runs for Sheriff." *State Government News*. March 1994.

Table 8.10
TRENDS IN STATE PRISON POPULATION, 1991-92

State or other jurisdiction	Total population			Population by maximum length of sentence						
				More than a year				Year or less and unsentenced		
	1992 (a)	1991	Percentage change	1992 (a)	1991	Percentage change	Incarceration rate 1992 (b)	1992 (a)	1991	Percentage change
United States	883,593	824,133	7.2	846,695	789,349	7.3	329	36,898	34,784	6.1
Alabama	17,453	16,760	4.1	16,938	16,400	3.3	404	515	360	43.1
Alaska	2,865	2,706	5.9	1,944	1,840	5.7	363	921	866	6.4
Arizona	16,477	15,415	6.9	15,850	14,843	6.8	415	627	572	9.6
Arkansas	8,433	7,766	8.6	8,129	7,722	5.3	332	304	44	590.9
California	109,496	101,808	7.6	105,467	98,515	7.1	332	4,029	3,293	22.4
Colorado	8,997	8,392	7.2	8,997	8,392	7.2	266	0	0	N.D.
Connecticut	11,403	10,977	3.9	8,794	8,585	2.4	269	2,609	2,392	9.1
Delaware	3,977	3,717	7.0	2,665	2,430	9.7	371	1,312	1,287	1.9
Florida	48,302	46,533	3.8	48,302	46,533	3.8	348	0	0	N.D.
Georgia	25,290	23,644	7.0	24,848	22,910	8.5	366	442	734	−39.8
Hawaii	2,926	2,700	8.4	1,922	1,766	8.8	164	1,004	934	7.5
Idaho	2,475	2,143	15.5	2,475	2,143	15.5	234	0	0	N.D.
Illinois	31,640	29,115	8.7	31,640	29,115	8.7	267	0	0	N.D.
Indiana	13,166	13,008	1.2	13,012	12,865	1.1	227	154	143	7.7
Iowa	4,518	4,145	9.0	4,518	4,145	9.0	157	0	0	N.D.
Kansas	6,028	5,903	2.1	6,028	5,903	2.1	234	0	0	N.D.
Kentucky	10,364	9,799	5.8	10,364	9,799	5.8	277	0	0	N.D.
Louisiana	20,810	20,003	4.0	20,603	20,003	3.0	478	207	0	N.D.
Maine	1,515	1,579	−4.1	1,488	1,558	−4.5	116	27	21	28.6
Maryland	19,977	19,291	3.6	18,808	17,824	5.5	380	1,169	1,467	−20.3
Massachusetts	10,056	9,155	9.8	9,382	8,561	9.6	156	674	594	13.5
Michigan	39,019	36,423	7.1	39,019	36,423	7.1	414	0	0	N.D.
Minnesota	3,822	3,472	10.1	3,822	3,472	10.1	84	0	0	N.D.
Mississippi	9,083	8,904	2.0	8,877	8,682	2.3	337	206	222	−7.2
Missouri	16,198	15,897	1.9	16,198	15,897	1.9	309	0	0	N.D.
Montana	1,553	1,478	5.1	1,553	1,478	5.1	192	0	0	N.D.
Nebraska	2,565	2,495	2.8	2,492	2,375	4.9	152	73	120	−39.2
Nevada	6,049	5,503	9.9	6,049	5,503	9.9	461	0	0	N.D.
New Hampshire	1,777	1,533	15.9	1,777	1,533	15.9	150	0	0	N.D.
New Jersey	22,653	23,483	−3.5	22,653	23,483	−3.5	289	0	0	N.D.
New Mexico	3,271	3,119	4.9	3,154	3,016	4.6	197	117	103	13.6
New York	61,736	57,862	6.7	61,736	57,862	6.7	340	0	0	N.D.
North Carolina	20,455	18,903	8.2	20,024	18,272	9.6	291	431	631	−31.7
North Dakota	464	492	−5.7	415	441	−5.9	65	49	51	−3.9
Ohio	38,378	35,744	7.4	38,378	35,744	7.4	346	0	0	N.D.
Oklahoma	14,821	13,340	11.1	14,821	13,340	11.1	463	0	0	N.D.
Oregon (c)	6,596	6,732	−2.0	5,216	6,732	...	173	1,380	0	N.D.
Pennsylvania	24,974	23,388	6.8	24,966	23,386	6.8	204	8	2	300.0
Rhode Island	2,775	2,771	0.1	1,709	1,749	−2.3	168	1,066	1,022	4.3
South Carolina	18,643	18,269	2.0	17,612	17,208	2.4	477	1,031	1,061	−2.8
South Dakota	1,487	1,374	8.2	1,487	1,374	8.2	206	0	0	N.D.
Tennessee	11,849	11,474	3.3	11,849	11,474	3.3	232	0	0	N.D.
Texas	61,178	51,677	18.4	61,178	51,677	18.4	348	0	0	N.D.
Utah	2,699	2,625	2.8	2,687	2,605	3.2	152	12	20	−40.0
Vermont	1,267	1,118	13.3	867	733	18.3	144	400	385	3.9
Virginia	21,199	19,829	6.9	20,989	19,660	6.8	327	210	169	24.3
Washington	9,959	9,156	8.8	9,959	9,156	8.8	193	0	0	N.D.
West Virginia	1,745	1,502	16.2	1,745	1,502	16.2	97	0	0	N.D.
Wisconsin	9,054	7,849	15.4	9,033	7,819	15.5	180	21	30	−30.0
Wyoming	1,022	1,099	−7.0	1,022	1,099	−7.0	223	0	0	N.D.
Dist. of Columbia ..	10,875	10,455	4.0	7,528	7,106	5.9	1,312	3,347	3,349	−0.1

Source: U.S. Department of Justice, Bureau of Justice Statistics, *Prisoners in 1992* (May 1993).
Key:
N.D. — Not defined
(a) Advance count of prisoners is conducted immediately after calendar year ends.

(b) The number of prisoners with sentences of more than one year per 100,000 resident populations.
(c) Before 1992, because of their sentencing guidelines, Oregon reported all prisoners as having a sentence of more than one year. Comparing the number of prisoners sentenced to more than one year in 1992 with the counts from previous years would be inappropriate.

Table 8.11
ADULTS ADMITTED TO STATE PRISONS, 1991

State or other jurisdiction	Prisoner population (1/1/91)	Total	New court commitments	Parole or other conditional release violators returned	Escapees and AWOLs returned	Returns from appeal or bond	Transfers from other jurisdictions	Other admissions
United States	689,596	480,046	317,237	142,100	9,586	922	4,175	6,026
Alabama	15,365	7,908	5,721	1,734	174	181	51	47
Alaska (a,b)	1,851	1,341	1,021	316	0	4	0	0
Arizona	13,781	7,790	6,144	1,283	321	0	42	0
Arkansas	7,274	4,574	3,181	1,218	15	154	6	0
California	94,122	96,865	38,253	57,737	494	. . .	381	0
Colorado (c)	7,671	4,037	2,887	699	361	6	3	81
Connecticut (a,b) . . .	7,771	11,832	6,401	4,711	713	7	0	0
Delaware (a,c)	2,241	1,206	794	34	84	0	. . .	294
Florida	44,380	37,440	33,094	2,981	352	. . .	78	935
Georgia (b)	21,671	15,812	12,189	3,531	92	. . .	0	0
Hawaii (a,d)	1,708	1,750	846	901	3	0	0	0
Idaho	1,961	1,402	1,101	280	9	0	11	1
Illinois (c)	27,516	18,880	14,650	3,995	180	55	. . .	0
Indiana	12,615	5,927	5,503	409	7	. . .	8	0
Iowa	3,967	2,985	1,818	796	208	29	69	65
Kansas (b)	5,775	3,477	2,118	1,305	48	. . .	0	6
Kentucky	9,023	5,116	3,720	1,289	90	. . .	0	17
Louisiana (c)	18,599	8,381	4,200	3,174	100	72	0	835
Maine	1,499	909	672	215	6	6	0	10
Maryland (b,d)	16,734	8,561	7,008	1,422	128	. . .	3	0
Massachusetts (b,d) .	8,014	5,485	2,705	1,536	131	. . .	1,113	0
Michigan	34,267	13,453	9,054	3,381	748	175	95	0
Minnesota	3,176	2,568	1,905	646	17	0	0	0
Mississippi (b)	8,084	3,910	3,294	474	56	. . .	0	86
Missouri	14,943	8,756	6,164	2,278	. . .	. . .	3	311
Montana (b)	1,425	643	489	120	33	0	1	0
Nebraska	2,286	1,404	1,064	328	12	. . .	0	0
Nevada	5,322	3,163	2,421	699	43	. . .	0	0
New Hampshire (b) .	1,342	828	677	136	15	. . .	0	0
New Jersey (b)	21,128	12,134	8,665	2,410	307	. . .	. . .	752
New Mexico	3,067	1,632	1,152	444	23	. . .	13	0
New York (b)	54,895	29,743	24,119	3,284	1,276	108	853	103
North Carolina (c) . .	17,764	21,696	18,056	3,320	280	0	0	40
North Dakota (b) . . .	435	340	293	43	4	0	0	0
Ohio (b,c)	31,822	22,138	18,377	3,476	8	20	257	0
Oklahoma (b,c)	12,285	6,243	5,718	229	294	0	2	0
Oregon (c)	6,492	6,247	3,308	2,694	156	0	. . .	89
Pennsylvania	22,281	9,611	6,435	1,690	54	26	258	1,148
Rhode Island (a,c) . .	1,586	840	589	187	45	7	12	0
South Carolina (b) . .	16,208	7,009	5,342	1,518	126	23	. . .	0
South Dakota	1,341	764	583	166	9	2	4	0
Tennessee (c)	10,388	6,350	4,026	2,209	88	27	0	0
Texas	50,042	37,820	21,417	16,378	25	. . .	0	0
Utah	2,474	1,623	720	875	25	3	0	0
Vermont (a)	681	470	310	77	55	. . .	28	0
Virginia	17,418	12,513	9,716	1,649	19	. . .	. . .	1,129
Washington	7,995	4,905	4,070	606	147	17	0	65
West Virginia	1,565	690	584	101	5	0	0	0
Wisconsin	7,438	3,968	3,208	748	. . .	. . .	0	12
Wyoming (b)	1,110	432	394	31	3	0	4	0
Dist. of Columbia (a,c)	6,798	6,475	1,061	2,337	2,197	. . .	880	0

Source: U.S. Department of Justice, Bureau of Justice Statistics, *Correctional Populations in the United States, 1991* (August 1993).

Key:

. . . — Not available

(a) Figures include both jail and prison inmates; jails and prisons are combined in one system.

(b) New court commitments may include a small number of other admissions.

(c) Counts of inmates by sentence length may be slightly incorrect.

(d) Hawaii, Maryland and Massachusetts estimated the numbers in the admissions categories.

Table 8.12
STATE PRISON CAPACITIES, 1992

State or other jurisdiction	Rated capacity	Operational capacity	Design capacity	Population as a percent of: (a) Highest capacity	Lowest capacity
Alabama	14,788	14,788	14,788	111	111
Alaska	2,472	. . .	. . .	116	116
Arizona	. . .	15,520	. . .	106	106
Arkansas	. . .	7,614	. . .	104	104
California	. . .	. . .	57,367	191	191
Colorado	. . .	7,496	6,136	113	138
Connecticut	10,093	11,102	. . .	103	113
Delaware	4,009	3,987	2,928	99	136
Florida	49,939	55,100	37,887	88	127
Georgia	. . .	25,252	. . .	100	100
Hawaii	. . .	2,382	1,566	123	187
Idaho	2,015	2,158	. . .	106	113
Illinois	24,562	24,562	20,818	129	152
Indiana	11,983	13,817	. . .	95	110
Iowa	3,265	3,265	3,265	138	138
Kansas	6,621	. . .	. . .	91	91
Kentucky	9,119	8,923	. . .	107	110
Louisiana	17,131	17,131	17,131	95	95
Maine	1,353	1,353	1,353	112	112
Maryland	. . .	19,804	12,856	101	155
Massachusetts	. . .	. . .	6,999	144	144
Michigan	27,086	. . .	. . .	144	144
Minnesota	3,678	3,678	3,678	104	104
Mississippi	8,557	9,083	9,007	89	95
Missouri	15,630	16,187	. . .	100	104
Montana	1,160	1,465	1,160	106	134
Nebraska	. . .	. . .	1,706	150	150
Nevada	5,743	5,743	4,770	105	127
New Hampshire	1,358	1,576	1,162	113	153
New Jersey	. . .	. . .	14,980	131	131
New Mexico	3,427	3,290	3,443	95	99
New York	60,054	57,005	49,543	103	125
North Carolina	17,913	20,900	. . .	98	114
North Dakota	. . .	576	576	81	81
Ohio	. . .	. . .	21,738	177	177
Oklahoma	9,130	12,451	. . .	119	162
Oregon	. . .	6,557	. . .	101	101
Pennsylvania	. . .	. . .	16,713	149	149
Rhode Island	3,292	3,292	3,292	84	84
South Carolina	16,216	16,216	12,527	112	145
South Dakota	1,189	1,130	1,189	125	132
Tennessee	11,119	10,837	11,463	94	99
Texas (b)	57,455	54,459	. . .	106	112
Utah	3,184	2,897	. . .	81	89
Vermont	647	852	647	147	193
Virginia	13,852	13,852	13,852	139	139
Washington	6,190	7,779	7,779	128	161
West Virginia	1,680	1,745	1,730	100	104
Wisconsin	6,342	6,342	6,342	139	139
Wyoming	977	977	977	105	105
Dist. of Columbia	11,087	11,087	8,746	95	121

Source: U.S. Department of Justice, Bureau of Justice Statistics, *Prisoners in 1992* (May 1993).
Key:
. . . — Not available

(a) Excludes inmates who had been sentenced to state prison but were held in local jails because of crowding and who were included in the total prisoner count.
(b) Excludes prisoners housed in contract or other non-federal facilities.

Table 8.13
ADULTS ON PROBATION, 1990

State or other jurisdiction	Probation population 1/1/90	1990 Entries	Exits	Probation population 12/31/90	Percent change in probation population during 1990	Probation population (a) Under intensive supervision	Under electronic monitoring
Alabama............	25,519	14,251	12,084	27,686	8.5	705	91
Alaska.............	3,335	1,993	1,729	3,599	7.9	0	0
Arizona............	27,340	11,978	8,921	30,397	11.2	2,232	127
Arkansas (b)	15,552	3,531	3,100	15,983	2.8	0	0
California (c).......	284,437	173,883	152,620 (d)	305,700	7.5	DK	DK
Colorado (c)	28,037	22,310	19,236	31,111	11.0	1,015	248
Connecticut	42,842	28,738	24,940	46,640	8.9	160	6
Delaware (b)	9,701	6,393	3,871	12,223	26.0	951	93
Florida (c)	192,731	266,244	248,194	210,781	9.4	11,215	1,312
Georgia............	125,147	76,042 (e)	66,349 (e)	134,840	7.7	2,820	0
Hawaii	10,960	6,442	5,735	11,667	6.5	22	6
Idaho	4,025	2,024	1,672	4,337	8.7	141	0
Illinois.............	93,944	58,870	57,115	95,699	1.9	660	DK
Indiana (c)	61,177	65,388	58,482 (f)	68,683	12.3	111	983
Iowa (b)	13,722	346	173	13,895	1.3	DK	DK
Kansas	21,675	12,683	12,175	22,183	2.3	(g)	(g)
Kentucky	8,062	3,030	3,610 (h)	7,482	−7.2	506	0
Lousiana...........	32,295	13,310	15,414	30,191	−6.5	50	6
Maine	6,851	4,698	4,000	7,549	10.2	95	10
Maryland	84,456	44,435	45,993 (i)	82,898	−1.8	151	0
Massachusetts (c) ...	88,529	44,486	60,556	72,459	−18.2	0	0
Michigan (b)	122,459	100,151	89,171	133,439	9.0	1,128	1,801
Minnesota	58,648	31,394	30,719	59,323	1.2	(g)	(g)
Mississippi (c)	7,333	3,138	2,250	8,221	12.1	244	0
Missouri (b,c)	44,158	25,000 (j)	26,836	42,322	−4.2	460	96
Montana...........	3,459	1,873	1,280	4,052	17.1	35	19
Nebraska	12,627	17,767	15,740	14,654	16.1	45	45
Nevada (b)	7,065	3,518	2,883	7,700	9.0	718	25
New Hampshire	2,991	1,775	1,620	3,146	5.2	25	10
New Jersey	64,398	33,540	25,597	72,341	12.3	572	263
New Mexico (c)......	5,660	9,650	9,016 (k)	6,294	11.2	270	135
New York	136,686	47,656	39,076	145,266	6.3	3,400	DK
North Carolina	72,325	41,981	36,477	77,829	7.6	1,452	704
North Dakota	1,644	523	436	1,731	5.3	(g)	(g)
Ohio	78,299	59,049 (l)	53,968 (l)	83,380	6.5	2,341	358
Oklahoma (m).......	24,240	12,565	12,394	24,411	0.7	(g)	(g)
Oregon (n).........	31,878	15,742	9,989	37,631	18.0	1,033	380
Pennsylvania	89,491	46,111	38,275	97,327	8.8	10,400	200
Rhode Island	12,231	9,294	6,159	15,366	25.6	0	0
South Carolina	31,623	14,405	13,741	32,287	2.1	1,824	0
South Dakota (o)	2,757	3,995	3,592	3,160	14.6	50	0
Tennessee	30,906	21,925	20,112	32,719	5.9	735	280
Texas (p)	291,156	151,767	134,566	308,357	5.9	7,124	463
Utah	5,524	3,596	3,290 (q)	5,830	5.5	140	0
Vermont	5,399	3,144	2,631	5,912	9.5	230	0
Virginia (c).........	19,085	11,951	9,733 (r)	21,303	11.6	327	0
Washington	74,918	54,791	44,892	84,817	13.2	1,996	50
West Virginia (b)	4,646	2,360 (s)	1,947	5,059	8.9	(g)	(g)
Wisconsin (c)........	27,284	17,806	15,720	29,370	7.6	222	55
Wyoming	3,060	1,557	1,637 (t)	2,980	−2.6	17	17
Dist. of Columbia ...	10,132	8,070	8,460	9,742	−3.8	100	0

Source: U.S. Department of Justice, Bureau of Justice Statistics, *Probation and Parole 1990* (November 1991). Information presented in this table will be updated by the Bureau of Justice Statistics in the forthcoming *Probation and Parole 1992*, BJS Bulletin (1994).

Key:

DK — Number not known

(a) Estimated number. Counts of persons under intensive supervision reported by some states include persons under electronic monitoring. Some states were unable to provide separate counts of probation and parole populations under intensive supervision (see also Table 8.14, "Adults on Parole").

(b) State estimated all or portion of data. Michigan and Nevada estimated entries and exits.

(c) State omitted absconders from their Jan. 1 and Dec. 31, 1990 counts.

(d) Exits include 13,496 transfers of jurisdiction, deaths or loss of jurisdiction.

(e) Entries include 1,945 abandonment and bastardy cases, and interstate compact cases. Exits include 3,621 abandonment and bastardy cases, special termination, and transferred out-of-state cases. All data exclude probationers who have been sent to another state for supervision and include probationers that state supervises for other states.

(f) Exits include 1,435 intrastate transfers and 575 interstate transfers.

(g) State reported either not having persons under intensive supervision and electronic monitoring or not knowing their numbers.

(h) Exits include 13 dismissed cases.

(i) Exits include 4,875 unsatisfactory closings.

(j) Entries include 118 diversion cases without sentence.

(k) Exits include 1,108 closed semi-active cases and interarea transfers.

(l) Include persons transferred between state and county probation agencies.

(m) Data do not include probationers with weekend incarceration.

(n) Data do not include 6,209 probationers supervised by county agencies.

(o) All data are midyear 1990 counts.

(p) All data are for August 1990.

(q) Include 207 revocations and discharges and six reversals of court orders.

(r) Exits include revocations, out-of-state cases terminated and cases closed administratively.

(s) Entries include 50 reinstatements.

(t) Exits include 221 bench warrants, relief of responsibility and interstate transfers.

Table 8.14
ADULTS ON PAROLE, 1990

State or other jurisdiction	Parole population 1/1/90	1990 Entries	1990 Exits	Parole population 12/31/90	Percent change in probation population during 1990	Parole population (a) Under intensive supervision	Parole population (a) Under electronic monitoring
Alabama	5,724	2,225	1,979	5,970	4.3	5	144
Alaska (b)	533	542	507	568	6.6	15	. . .
Arizona	2,048	4,087 (c)	3,424 (c)	2,711	32.4	. . .	116
Arkansas (d)	3,657	2,402	2,088	3,971	8.6	66	. . .
California (d,e)	57,515	91,379	81,332	67,562	17.5	7,207	40
Colorado (d)	1,974	2,149	1,727	2,396	21.4	. . .	45
Connecticut	322	49	80	291	−9.6	10	2
Delaware (b)	1,013	676	406	1,283	26.7	100	10
Florida (d,f)	2,318	645	899	2,064	−11.0	. . .	. . .
Georgia	17,437	16,611	11,402	22,646	29.9	422	. . .
Hawaii	1,287	527	389 (g)	1,425	10.7	70	11
Idaho	238	275	270	243	2.1	DK	DK
Illinois (f)	14,550	16,349 (h)	13,228	17,671	21.5	49	41
Indiana	3,456	2,965	2,643	3,778	9.3	. . .	. . .
Iowa (d,f)	1,900	1,572	1,361	2,111	11.1	269	60
Kansas (d)	5,089	3,107	2,445 (i)	5,751	13.0	(j)	(j)
Kentucky	3,133	2,210 (k)	2,160	3,183	1.6	883	. . .
Louisiana	9,177	6,220	6,520	8,877	−3.3	DK	DK
Maine				(l)			
Maryland	9,862	7,715	6,385	11,192	13.5	541	. . .
Massachusetts (b)	4,688	5,774	5,742	4,720	0.7	34	. . .
Michigan	9,890	8,994	6,983	11,901	20.3	. . .	DK
Minnesota	1,699	2,249 (m)	2,075	1,873	10.2	(j)	(j)
Mississippi (d)	3,349	1,657 (n)	1,528	3,478	3.9	112	. .
Missouri (b,o)	7,545	4,746	3,095	9,196	21.9	. . .	38
Montana	752	406	347	811	7.8	8	. . .
Nebraska	490	840	698	632	29.0	37	1
Nevada	2,417	1,620	1,187	2,850	17.9	912	8
New Hampshire (d,f) .	477	408 (p)	363	522	9.4	41	1
New Jersey	20,062	13,019	9,783 (q)	23,298	16.1	373	49
New Mexico (b,d)	1,151	1,277	1,204	1,224	6.3	54	27
New York	36,885	23,273	17,321	42,837	16.1	. . .	16
North Carolina	7,559	9,148	6,824	9,883	30.7	437	124
North Dakota	138	136	158	116	−15.9	(j)	(j)
Ohio (d)	6,464	5,788 (r)	4,307 (r)	7,945	22.9	. . .	. . .
Oklahoma	1,993	1,990	747	3,236	62.4	(j)	(j)
Oregon	5,794	5,805	3,576	8,023	38.5	65	. . .
Pennsylvania (s)	47,702	28,225 (t)	19,270	56,657	18.8	1,397	223
Rhode Island (u)	393	276	348	321	−18.3	. . .	23
South Carolina (v) . . .	3,386	1,129	972 (w)	3,543	4.6	426	. . .
South Dakota	510	571	461	620	21.6	64	. . .
Tennessee	10,511	5,914	5,098 (x)	11,327	7.8	. . .	. . .
Texas (y)	91,294	46,476 (z)	28,044	109,726	20.2	2,110	306
Utah	1,277	1,244	960	1,561	22.2	199	38
Vermont (d)	220	190	110	300	36.4	34	. . .
Virginia (d)	7,444	8,790 (aa)	7,186 (aa)	9,048	21.5	426	6
Washington	9,832	741	958	9,615	−2.2	. . .	. . .
West Virginia	943	480 (bb)	423	1,000	6.0	(j)	(j)
Wisconsin (d,cc)	4,042	2,736	2,679 (dd)	4,099	1.4	222	55
Wyoming	326	155	168 (ee)	313	−4.0	1	1
Dist. of Columbia . . .	4,915	3,268	2,837	5,346	8.8	198	. . .

ADULTS ON PAROLE, 1990—Continued

Source: U.S. Department of Justice, Bureau of Justice Statistics, *Probation and Parole 1990* (November 1991). Information presented in this table will be updated by the Bureau of Justice Statistics in the forthcoming *Probation and Parole 1992*, BJS Bulletin (1994).

Key:

. . . — No program

DK — Number not known

(a) Estimated number. Counts of persons under intensive supervision reported by some states include persons under electronic monitoring. Some states were unable to provide separate counts of parole and probation populations under intensive supervision (see also Table 8.13, "Adults on Probation").

(b) State estimated all or portion of data. Massachusetts and New Mexico estimated entries and exits.

(c) Entries include 491 interstate compact cases. Exits include 10 early discharges.

(d) State omitted absconders from their Jan. 1 and Dec. 31, 1990 counts.

(e) Data include California Youth Authority cases.

(f) State supervised only persons sentenced to year or more.

(g) Exits include 89 parolees whose maximum sentences had expired.

(h) Entries include 533 out-of-state parolees and 2,060 interstate compact and apprehension cases.

(i) Exits exclude an unknown number of persons returned to prison or jail, parole revocation pending; returned to prison or jail, new charges pending; or transferred to another parole jurisdiction. Exits include 275 absconded, 290 expiration of sentence, 62 pre-revocation confinements and 229 state offenders supervised out-of-state.

(j) State reported either not having persons under intensive supervision and electronic monitoring or not knowing their numbers.

(k) Entries include 489 transfers from out-of-state districts.

(l) State eliminated parole in 1976. Thirty pre-1976 parolees remain under supervision and 25 in prison will become eligible for parole.

(m) Entries include 402 parolees on work release.

(n) Entries include intrastate transfers and two work release cases.

(o) Data exclude 283 parolees from local jails.

(p) Entries include 92 administrative parolees.

(q) Exits include 151 persons recalled by court and discharged by parole authority decree.

(r) Entries include 139 parolees supervised out-of-state. Exits include 31 inactive cases and 67 interstate compact cases.

(s) State supervised 610 parolees from local jails.

(t) Entries include 21,271 parolees released by county courts.

(u) Absconders are removed from parole only if a revocation warrant has been issued.

(v) State excluded youthful offenders from its counts.

(w) Exits include 12 pardoned parolees.

(x) Exits include 436 inactive parolees whose supervision was terminated.

(y) All data are for August 1990.

(z) Entries include about 12,000 parole releases direct from county jail.

(aa) Entries include 367 transfers from other states. Exists include 379 terminated out-of-state cases.

(bb) Entries include 95 interstate compact cases.

(cc) Data do not include parolees supervised out-of-state.

(dd) Exits include 15 administrative closings.

(ee) Exits include 29 administrative closings and pardons.

Table 8.15
STATE DEATH PENALTY
(As of December 1992)

State or other jurisdiction	Capital offenses	Minimum age	Persons on death row	Method of execution
Alabama	Murder during kidnapping, robbery, rape, sodomy, burglary, sexual assault, or arson; murder of peace officer, correctional officer, or public official; murder while under a life sentence; murder for pecuniary gain or contract; aircraft piracy; murder by a defendant with a previous murder conviction; murder of a witness to a crime; murder when a victim is subpoenaed in a criminal proceeding, when the murder is related to the role of the victim as a witness; murder when a victim is less than 14 years old; murder in which a victim is killed while in a dwelling; murder in which a victim is killed while in a motor vehicle by a deadly weapon fired from outside that vehicle; murder in which a victim is killed by a deadly weapon fired from a motor vehicle.	16	124	Electrocution
Alaska	. . .			
Arizona	First-degree murder	None	103	Lethal gas
Arkansas	Felony murder; arson causing death; intentional murder of a law enforcement officer; murder of prison, jail, court or other correctional personnel, or military personnel acting in line of duty; multiple murders; intentional murder of public officeholder or candidate; intentional murder while under life sentence; contract murder	14	32	Lethal injection or electrocution (a)
California	Treason; homicide by a prisoner serving a life term; first-degree murder with special circumstances; train wrecking; perjury causing execution	18	332	Lethal gas
Colorado	First-degree murder; kidnapping with death of victim; felony murder	18	3	Lethal injection or lethal gas (b)
Connecticut	Murder of a public safety or correctional officer; murder for pecuniary gain; murder in the course of a felony; murder by a defendant with a previous conviction for intentional murder; murder while under a life sentence; murder during a kidnapping; illegal sale of cocaine, methadone, or heroin to a person who dies from using these drugs; murder during first-degree sexual assault; multiple murders	18	4	Electrocution
Delaware	First-degree murder with aggravating circumstances	None	11	Lethal injection
Florida	First-degree murder; capital felonies, capital drug trafficking felonies	None	312	Electrocution
Georgia	Murder; kidnapping with bodily injury when the victim dies; aircraft hijacking; treason; kidnapping for ransom when the victim dies	17	101	Electrocution
Hawaii	. . .			
Idaho	First-degree murder; aggravated kidnapping	None	23	Lethal injection or firing squad
Illinois	Murder accompanied by at least one of 11 aggravating factors	18	145	Lethal injection
Indiana	Murder with 12 aggravating circumstances	16	50	Electrocution
Iowa	. . .			
Kansas	. . .			
Kentucky	Aggravated murder; kidnapping when victim is killed	16	29	Electrocution
Louisiana	First-degree murder; treason	16	50	Electrocution
Maine	. . .			
Maryland	First-degree murder, either premeditated or during the commission of a felony	18	15	Lethal gas
Massachusetts	. . .			
Michigan	. . .			
Minnesota	. . .			
Mississippi	Murder of a peace officer or correctional officer; murder while under a life sentence; murder by bomb or explosive; contract murder; murder committed during specific felonies (rape, burglary, kidnapping, arson, robbery, sexual battery, unnatural intercourse with a child, nonconsensual unnatural intercourse); murder of an elected official; forcible rape of a child under 14 years by a person 18 years or older; aircraft piracy	16 (c)	42	Lethal injection (d)

STATE DEATH PENALTY—Continued

State or other jurisdiction	Capital offenses	Minimum age	Persons on death row	Method of execution
Missouri	First-degree murder	16	82	Lethal injection or lethal gas
Montana	Deliberate homicide; aggravated kidnapping when victim or rescuer dies; attempted deliberate homicide, aggravated assault, or aggravated kidnapping by a state prison inmate with a prior conviction for deliberate homicide or who has been previously declared a persistent felony offender	None	8	Lethal injection or hanging
Nebraska	First-degree murder	18	12	Electrocution
Nevada	First-degree murder	16	62	Lethal injection
New Hampshire	Contract murder; murder of a law enforcement officer; murder of a kidnap victim; killing another after being sentenced to life imprisonment without parole	17	0	Lethal injection or hanging (e)
New Jersey	Purposeful or knowing murder; contract murder	18	3	Lethal injection
New Mexico	First-degree murder; felony murder with aggravating circumstances	18	1	Lethal injection
New York	. . .			
North Carolina	First-degree murder	(f)	76	Lethal injection or lethal gas
North Dakota	. . .			
Ohio	Assassination; contract murder; murder during escape; murder while in a correctional facility; murder after conviction for a prior purposeful killing or prior attempted murder; murder of a peace officer; murder arising from specified felonies (rape, kidnapping, arson, robbery, burglary); murder of a witness to prevent testimony in a criminal proceeding or in retaliation	18	121	Electrocution
Oklahoma	Murder with malice aforethought; murder arising from specified felonies (forcible rape, robbery with a dangerous weapon, kidnapping, escape from lawful custody, first-degree burglary, arson); murder when the victim is a child who has been injured, tortured or maimed	16	120	Lethal injection
Oregon	Aggravated murder	18	11	Lethal injection
Pennsylvania	First-degree murder	None	153	Lethal injection
Rhode Island	. . .			
South Carolina	Murder with statutory aggravating circumstances	None	41	Electrocution
South Dakota	First-degree murder; kidnapping with gross permanent physical injury inflicted on the victim; felony murder	(g)	1	Lethal injection
Tennessee	First-degree murder	18	99	Electrocution
Texas	Murder of a public safety officer, fireman, or correctional employee; murder during the commission of specified felonies (kidnapping, burglary, robbery, aggravated rape, arson); murder for remuneration; multiple murders; murder during prison escape; murder by a state prison inmate	17	344	Lethal injection
Utah	Aggravated murder	14	10	Lethal injection or firing squad
Vermont	. . .			
Virginia	Murder during the commission or attempts to commit specified felonies (abduction, armed robbery, rape, sodomy); contract murder; murder by a prisoner while in custody; murder of a law enforcement officer; multiple murders; murder of a child under 12 years during an abduction; murder arising from drug violations	15	49	Electrocution
Washington	Aggravated first-degree premeditated murder	None	11	Lethal injection or hanging
West Virginia	. . .			
Wisconsin	. . .			
Wyoming	First-degree murder including felony murder	16	0	Lethal injection
Dist. of Columbia	. . .			

See footnotes at end of table.

STATE DEATH PENALTY—Continued

Source: U.S. Department of Justice, Bureau of Justice Statistics, *Capital Punishment 1992* (December 1992).

Key:

. . . — No capital punishment statute

(a) State authorizes lethal injection for those whose capital offense occurred after 7/4/83; for those whose offense occurred before that date, the condemned prisoner may select lethal injection or electrocution.

(b) State authorizes lethal gas for those whose crimes occurred before 7/1/88 and lethal injection for those whose crimes occurred on or after 7/1/88.

(c) Minimum age defined by statute is 13, but effective age is 16, based on state attorney general's interpretation of U.S. Supreme Court decisions.

(d) State authorizes lethal injection for those convicted after 7/1/84; execution of those convicted prior to that date is to be carried out with lethal gas.

(e) State authorizes hanging only if lethal injection cannot be given.

(f) Age required is 17 unless the murderer was incarcerated for murder when a subsequent murder occurred; then the age may be 14.

(g) Age 10, but only after a transfer hearing to try a juvenile as an adult.

Emerging Models for Environmental Management

States seek to change the basic model of environmental management by experimenting with alternatives to the command-and-control method.

by R. Steven Brown

Over the past 25 years the states' role and expertise in, and commitment to, environmental management has grown considerably. Research conducted by The Council of State Governments shows that the federal contribution to state environment and natural resource budgets is less than 15 percent per fiscal year.[1] About 70 percent of the key environmental legislation passed by state legislatures has little or nothing to do with federal environmental legislation.[2] State environmental agency directors have noted the states' increasing importance in environmental management. Kathy Prosser, head of Indiana's agency, summed up many state opinions when she said, "I believe we must renegotiate our relationship, and move from paternalism to partnership."[3]

While the states seek to change the basic model of environmental management in the nation, we observe the emergence of alternative models to the tradition of command and control. "Command and control" was a phrase coined to describe the relationship that the U.S. Environmental Protection Agency had with virtually everyone it came into contact with during the first 20 years of its existence. Industries were instructed to meet national standards, states were instructed to conform with implementation policies set at the federal level, local governments were more or less treated like industrial polluters, and so on. This model remained unchallenged until the late 1980s, when the pollution prevention model began to receive attention within the EPA. Now we find the emergence of several environmental management models that do not rely on the traditional command and control techniques. The purpose of this essay is to review some of these models and to predict the likelihood of their implementation.

Sustainable Development

There are probably more than 100 definitions in the literature for sustainable development.[4] A common characteristic of all of them is the acknowledgement that there is an important relationship between the environment and the economy. The incorporation of sustainable policies into state governments is still in its infancy. According to two recent, major CSG surveys, only six states (Wisconsin, New Mexico, California, Maine, Missouri and Washington) list sustainable development as a strategic priority for environmental planning or implementation.[5] This is due in part, no doubt, to the necessity of bringing both state environmental agencies and state development agencies together. Relationships between these two agencies are generally characterized by antagonism at worst, or indifference at best.

Lack of consensus about what defines a sustainable project is likely to thwart states from adopting policies to promote them. For example, one agency may wish to promote forestry projects as inherently sustainable, while another agency may cite the problems with clear-cutting, non-point source pollution and reductions in species diversity due to monocultural practices as non-sustainable indicators.

On the other hand, states able to overcome these obstacles are likely to benefit economically and environmentally. The U.S. market

---

R. Steven Brown is director of the Center for Environment at The Council of State Governments.

for environmental products and services (even under a fairly narrow definition) is about $75 billion annually, with the worldwide market at $200 billion.[6] Several states have begun to promote their environmental industries, most notably Massachusetts and California.

Environmental Indicators

Demands for accountability and performance-based measures of environmental quality have promoted the concept of environmental indicators during the past few years. Traditionally, state-EPA agreements use non-environmental criteria for determining a state's success in implementing federal environmental programs. For example, a state may be required to inspect each major air pollution source once per year or may be judged by how many "notices of violations" it issued during a year.

This sort of reporting is, of course, not a measure of environmental quality, but rather is a measure of bureaucratic accomplishments. A growing number of persons, both in and out of government, is calling for the use of true measures of environmental quality to determine which regions are most successfully protecting the environment. Part of the difficulty is reaching agreement on what constitutes a fair environmental quality measure. Should indicators be technically sophisticated measures, or should measures be used that are easy for the public to understand? Can indicators be agreed upon that all regions of the nation could use, or should they be more locally specific?

Clearly, many states are eager to address these questions. Recent national meetings (1992 and 1994) sponsored by the EPA and others (including CSG), were well-attended by the states. CSG surveys (cited previously) found nine states where use of environmental indicators was a priority item for planning or implementation.[7] The outlook for widespread adoption of environmental indicators is not assured, but the prospect for its usage in an increasing number of states seems likely.

Environmental Mandates

The environmental mandates movement is comprised primarily of local and state govern-

ment officials who believe that the number of federal environmental mandates — particularly unfunded mandates — has increased to the point where the cost exceeds the ability to pay. According to one local government official, the number of federal environmental mandates has increased at the rate of 22 per year between 1987 and 1991.[8] At the same time, federal funding for these mandates has declined, or at least shifted to non-federal sources. Changes in the Clean Water Act in the late 1980s created State Revolving Loan Funds, a pot of federal money that shifted funding from grants to loans. Local governments have to pay these loans. A similar change is likely for the Safe Drinking Water Act when it is reauthorized.

State and local government concern about mandates was focused in October 1993, when several national organizations representing these levels of government held a day of protest against unfunded federal mandates in Washington, D.C. Opposition to mandates often centers on issues of cost-benefit, risk analysis and risk in decline of other services (such as police and parks) if limited local funds are diverted to environmental projects. Cost-benefit and risk analysis arguments often center on the failure of national environmental standards to consider local conditions. The most notorious example was the requirement that Columbus, Ohio, test its drinking water for the presence of a pesticide only known to be used on pineapple crops.

However, state officials are not united in opposition to mandates in general. State environmental agency directors and some legislators have noted privately that the presence of a federal mandate is the only way some environmental legislation can get passed in a few states. Federal mandates create a floor of environmental acceptability that even is occasionally used to spur movement on a state environmental bill, or to defeat bills that forbid the state from exceeding federal rules (using the argument "The federal government is not going to set the rules for our state!").

Controversy over unfunded mandates is likely to continue until sufficient flexibility (that is, opportunity for waivers) is given to state and local governments, or until federal funding is provided.

Pollution Prevention

Pollution prevention was the first alternative management technique to achieve widespread acceptance. Every state now has adopted pollution prevention strategies as part of its environmental management techniques. Pollution prevention is popular because it simultaneously reduces the amounts of pollutants emitted and the amount of environmental paperwork required of both an industry and the state (As pollutants are reduced, it becomes more likely that less environmental permits will be required.) Taken to its ultimate conclusion (zero discharge), an industry ceases to emit any pollutants at all, possibly no longer requiring any environmental permits. Ironically, some environmentalists have argued that a permit still should be required of such a facility in order to make sure that it does not resume its polluting behavior.

Pollution prevention techniques have been adopted in all media — air, water and wastes. Methods to implement this management technique vary from non-regulatory technical assistance to voluntary or mandatory requirements for permitted industries to reduce pollutants. States are very likely to continue not only to use pollution prevention methodologies but to seek ways to increase their use.

Comparative Risk

Comparative risk is a planning process that combines science and judgment to produce strategies and alternatives for environmental managers and the public to select from. Comparative risk has been called a grass-roots effort, because of the perceived failure of federal environmental policy to identify issues of local concern, as well as federal inability to create programs capable of simultaneously dealing with diverse local conditions. In this respect, there is a link between comparative risk and the unfunded environmental mandates movement.

The appeal of comparative risk is its use of risk analysis techniques to identify and prioritize environmental risks in a community or state. This identification procedure then is to be coupled with a management plan that allocates resources to those problems of greatest risk.

The EPA has been very supportive of comparative risk efforts by states and somewhat less of those efforts by cities. As of early 1994, 24 states and eight cities/regions have started or completed comparative risk projects funded in part by the EPA.[9]

Potential difficulties in comparative risk center around the lack of flexibility to move resources from areas of low risk to areas of high risk. This flexibility is lacking because of federal requirements to continue some mandated programs, even if these programs address areas of low concern. State and local resources pay for the bulk of these low priority programs, which means that their resources may be tied up in areas of low concern. Comparative risk projects may produce frustrating results, because if a state finds that its risks are in areas not currently covered by federal law, the state may not be able to shift resources to deal with these areas and may not be able to ask for new resources either.

A second complaint about comparative risk projects centers around the emphasis on the science-based process, which may not take public opinion into consideration. For example, a risk process may find that solid waste management is a low-risk area, but the public may demand municipally subsidized recycling programs anyway. Most comparative risk projects have a public opinion component intended to help alleviate this situation.

Finally, environmentalists worry that comparative risk projects may be a thinly veiled attempt to weaken existing environmental law. Furthermore, risk analyses might show that environmental risk is much less than the public realizes, and thus funding might be diverted from the environment to other areas.

In spite of these problems, comparative risk still has a great deal of appeal, and it is likely that states will continue to explore its possibilities, at least as long as the federal government encourages and subsidizes pilot projects. Whether comparative risk will find its way into routine policy-making will depend, in part, on whether flexibility from federal environmental law, which may be needed to implement the results of these studies, is forthcoming.

Ecosystem Management

Ecosystem management (also called ecosystem protection) is a management technique that emphasizes a holistic, integrated approach to environmental management over traditional media-specific approaches. In ecosystem management, traditional environmental concerns (air, water and waste management) become a part of a larger management of natural resources, in which human health concerns and ecological health concerns (for example, biodiversity) are considered.

Ecosystem management is in its infancy as national policy. The EPA launched its program only in December 1993, and it is still in the design phase. This effort will look at large area applications of ecosystem management, however EPA and others have used the technique on smaller areas for much longer, as noted in Carol Browner's initial memorandum on the subject.[10] These efforts include the national estuary program, the Great Lakes protection effort and several watershed management programs being implemented by the states.

The appeal of ecosystem management is that it recognizes the limitations of managing by specific media (air, water, waste) and substitutes a broader view of protection of an ecosystem. An ecosystem is a place, which can be as small as a rotting log to a much larger area like the Great Lakes. From a regulatory point of view, the smallest area likely to be addressed is a watershed. Watersheds themselves are ambiguous terms: The Mississippi River is a watershed; so is your neighborhood stream. Ecosystem protection recognizes the limitations of traditional environmental protection techniques and recognizes that environmental agencies seldom own or manage the land being affected. Thus, ecosystem protection is by its nature a process that requires collaboration and alliance-building.

Because ecosystem protection is likely to cause major changes in the way the environment is managed, it is potentially threatening to some groups. The challenge rests with the EPA and the states,[11] who want to use it is to address these concerns. States most likely to implement ecosystem protection will be those concerned with failure of traditional techniques to address environmental issues, those with united environmental protection and natural resources agencies, and those accustomed to land-use regulations.

Wise-Use Movement

The wise-use movement is a property rights movement that believes environmental protection efforts have exceeded their authority and that constitutional rights to protection of property have been jeopardized as a result. Advocates believe that environmental rules restricting use of private land must come with compensation and that the compensation generally has been lacking.

"Takings" legislation is one of the results of this movement. A "takings" bill usually requires government to compensate for any loss in property values attributable to land-use or environmental regulation, or alternatively requires governments to conduct fiscal-impact analyses before issuing any regulation. One source cited 24 states with "takings" bills introduced as of February 1994, with activity noted, for example, in Alabama, Virginia and Oregon.[12] Other states have also considered this issue, including Iowa, Florida, Georgia, Rhode Island and Wyoming.

While "takings" legislation appeals to those who believe environmental rules have exceeded property rights, other state officials are concerned about the potential bankrupting costs associated with calculating lost property values, much less paying compensation.

While environmentalists organize to fight this movement, its popularity with property rights advocates cannot be underestimated. This issue is likely to remain at the forefront of environmental discussions for the foreseeable future.

Summary

These management alternatives — sustainable development, environmental mandates, ecosystem protection, property rights movement, pollution prevention, environmental indicators and comparative risk — are not all designed to promote environmental protection. Some clearly place environmental protection below other concerns. Some may result in either weaker or stronger environmental protection, depending on how they are implemented.

These alternatives are not the only ones being discussed. Cross-media (the combination of air, water and waste management — and a typical component of ecosystem management) is gaining attention in some states. Environmental justice issues have emerged as a major concern in some areas. Reliance on technological advances for environmental solutions, a favorite for many years, also continues to have its advocates. The framework of state environmental policies is likely to be built around these issues during the years remaining in this century.

Notes

[1] R. Steven Brown, et al. *Resource Guide to State Environmental Management, Third Edition*. 1993, p. 134.

[2] Ibid., pp. 4-102.

[3] Kathy Prosser, "From Paternalism to Partnership: Changing the State-Federal Relationship," *ecos*, 1:2, November/December 1993, p. 1.

[4] See Michael A. Toman, "The Difficulty in Defining Sustainability," *Resources*. Winter, 1993, pp. 3-6.

[5] "State Reports," *ecos*, 1:4, March/April 1994, pp. 4-7; and Brown, et al., *Resource Guide to State Environmental Management, Third Edition*, (ETC).

[6] See R. Steven Brown, "Environmental Development: Merging Environmental Protection and Economic Development Priorities," *The Book of the States, 1992-93*.

[7] These states are: Florida, Kansas, Minnesota, Missouri, New Mexico, Oklahoma, Rhode Island and Vermont. Vermont and Florida often are cited as two states having particularly emphasized the use of environmental indicators over traditional bureaucratic performance measures.

[8] Michael Pompili, "Case Study," in *State Strategies for Sustainable Development*. (Commonwealth of Kentucky: Louisville) 1994, p. 93.

[9] Personal communication with the Northeast Center for Comparative Risk, April 22, 1994.

[10] Carol Browner, "EPA's Role in Ecosystem Protection," *ecos*, 1:3 January/February 1994, p. 1.

[11] Pennsylvania, among others, has stated that the adoption of ecosystem protection techniques is a major environmental priority.

[12] Constance E. Beaumont, "The Statehouse," *Historic Preservation News*, April/May 1994, p. 12.

Table 8.16
SUMMARY OF STATE ENVIRONMENTAL AND NATURAL RESOURCE EXPENDITURES, FISCAL YEAR 1991

State	Total expenditures in dollars (a)	Per capita expenditures in dollars (b)	As a percentage of state budget (c)	Per manufacturer in dollars (d)
Alabama	$ 41,739,597	$ 22.43	1.02	$ 9,756
Alaska	285,905,900	519.83	5.79	234,349
Arizona	57,280,400	15.63	.73	8,039
Arkansas	60,315,462	25.66	1.29	12,943
California	2,036,746,000	68.44	2.38	27,538
Colorado	225,361,490	68.41	3.22	24,803
Connecticut	68,976,785	20.98	.62	7,237
Delaware	42,434,700	63.70	1.83	41,238
Florida	379,017,945	29.29	1.51	13,536
Georgia	140,500,163	21.69	1.06	10,346
Hawaii	37,728,153	34.00	.84	15,872
Idaho	81,766,425	81.22	3.55	32,028
Illinois	402,028,400	35.17	1.63	13,568
Indiana	77,510,221	13.98	.67	5,699
Iowa	65,922,102	23.74	.97	9,359
Kansas	57,377,912	23.16	1.12	9,486
Kentucky	104,581,645	28.38	1.16	15,563
Louisiana	207,441,837	49.16	1.97	28,972
Maine	58,146,615	47.35	1.66	20,525
Maryland	152,899,913	31.98	1.22	24,347
Massachusetts	235,107,387	39.08	1.16	16,741
Michigan	218,969,211	23.56	.91	8,959
Minnesota	220,934,000	50.50	1.74	16,982
Mississippi	78,262,049	30.41	1.51	15,888
Missouri	257,441,257	50.31	2.78	20,998
Montana	57,791,485	72.32	2.42	33,194
Nebraska	44,023,454	27.89	1.35	13,300
Nevada	55,489,118	46.17	1.61	25,040
New Hampshire	43,815,388	39.50	2.05	12,959
New Jersey	400,796,000	51.85	1.70	21,039
New Mexico	53,968,900	35.62	1.19	18,344
New York	577,049,188	32.08	.90	16,731
North Carolina	112,401,514	16.96	.75	7,449
North Dakota	50,772,534	79.48	2.83	40,456
Ohio	176,375,495	16.26	.64	6,184
Oklahoma	60,147,514	19.00	.83	8,140
Oregon	165,012,301	60.79	2.28	16,685
Pennsylvania	286,679,000	24.13	1.07	11,945
Rhode Island	40,521,693	40.38	1.17	11,306
South Carolina	114,790,267	32.63	1.27	18,163
South Dakota	31,336,587	45.02	2.21	22,272
Tennessee	107,481,321	22.04	.88	10,092
Texas	311,849,015	18.36	1.06	8,130
Utah	75,726,396	43.95	1.84	18,964
Vermont	50,422,699	89.60	2.90	32,014
Virginia	174,901,911	29.27	1.31	18,911
Washington	381,769,409	78.45	1.58	36,358
West Virginia	37,689,843	21.01	.79	17,085
Wisconsin	179,745,860	36.75	1.44	12,866
Wyoming	100,332,716	221.10	5.53	95,554

Source: The Council of State Governments, *Resource Guide to State Environmental Management, Third Edition,* 1993.

Note: See above referenced source for more detailed information.

(a) Amount represents the total dollars spent by each state for environmental and natural resource matters.

(b) Amount represents the environmental/natural resource dollars spent by the state, per state resident.

(c) Percentage of the total state budget spent on environmental/natural resource matters.

(d) Total environmental/natural resource money spent divided by the number of manufacturers in the state.

Table 8.17
STATE ENVIRONMENTAL AND NATURAL RESOURCE SPENDING BY CATEGORY, FISCAL YEAR 1991
(In thousands of dollars)

State	Air quality	Drinking water	Forestry	Fish & wildlife	Geological survey	Hazardous waste	Land management	Marine & coastal programs	Nuclear waste	Pesticides control	Soil conservation	Mining reclamation	Solid waste	Water quality	Water resource management
Alabama	$ 3,875	(a)	$ 24,942	$ 16,384	$ 3,676	(b)	$ 707	$ 1,865	$1,160	$ 1,521	$ 3,986	$ 2,680	$ 8,333	$ 19,491	$ 1,996
Alaska	2,074	5,023	64,405	95,990	10,526	42,707	16,634	4,107	N.A.	266	8,172	25,658	3,073	2,713	4,558
Arizona	6,589	601		14,441	736	983	7,893	N.A.		207	(i)	0	4,577	9,785	11,470
Arkansas	1,432	331	12,396	22,985	1,285	3,156	(d)	N.A.	787	1,383	(d)	2,675	1,062	8,203	4,640
California	88,101	26,159	325,920	112,207	3,159	78,716	34,753	20,289		40,872	2,273	2,065	355,783	219,486	726,963
Colorado	7,792	2,088	5,993	64,845	1,253	1,253	1,865	N.A.	1,344	1,005	750	3,075	920	6,174	11,096
Connecticut	14,132	(a)	5,907	11,389	(a)	(a)	(a)	(a)	(c)	(c)	(a)	N.A.	(c)	15,099	(a)
Delaware	2,110	(d)	1,540	10,843	1,136	1,136	(g)	5,577	(f)	374	(h)	N.A.	(c)	(d)	13,830
Florida	13,144	(a)	44,506	88,744	1,411	1,411	3,927	32,560	(d)	2,692	1,156	1,952	104,305	57,394	27,228
Georgia	5,108	(a)	38,880	32,653	2,755	2,755	3,254	2,354		1,106	2,707	N.A.		44,189	4,889
Hawaii	5,468	(f)	4,308	1,503		1,962	8,769	533	N.A.	804	(i)	N.A.	(f)	(f)	14,381
Idaho	1,769	(a)	11,514	32,952	502	3,769	1,913	N.A.	N.A.		1,630	(i)		16,154	11,565
Illinois	29,817	7,738	5,123	25,276	12,707	42,379	37,254	N.A.	8,603	3,873	3,261	15,755	18,647	179,065	12,531
Indiana	9,599	1,278	7,211	10,040	2,285	11,923		N.A.	876		4,528	3,532	3,139	8,911	15,060
Iowa	1,231	1,735	3,225	24,990	3,782	2,634	8,500	N.A.	(d)	1,258	14,705	939	1,914	8,981	520
Kansas	1,851	(a)	N.A.	9,320	4,825	9,164	466	N.A.	N.A.	(d)	(d)	2,017	(c)	11,751	18,450
Kentucky	4,948	(a)	8,593	17,248	3,097	1,555		N.A.	838	4,120	1,181	43,377	5,980	17,298	84,153
Louisiana	12,867	500	13,438	35,428	1,240	15,916	5,521	20,466	(f)		2,392	999	2,664	13,258	
Maine	1,987	(a)	9,220	15,711	1,272	13,015		2,997		185	185	N.A.	4,914	3,283	43
Maryland	5,540	5,195	10,728	16,929	859	8,960	23,123	10,217	1,234	579	6,076	2,103	19,723	37,895	4,971
Massachusetts	9,158	56,370	8,865	13,140	6,076	29,294	(g)	6,958	500	1,900	2,000	N.A.	3,970	99,480	12,630
Michigan	6,102	204	23,768	51,048		31,618	8,941	12,460	N.A.	2,272	2,945	N.A.	10,210	59,468	802
Minnesota	(a)	7,676	58,404	57,922		28,202	(g)	(d)	N.A.	5,590	(d)		22,888	12,829	21,321
Mississippi		(a)	24,008	18,810	190	2,652		3,238			592	1,567	431	26,644	130
Missouri	3,073	1,062	22,712	37,450	1,949	30,366	1,342	N.A.	N.A.	2,382	24,212	11,365	(c)	120,204	1,325
Montana	1,367	(a)	9,352	22,569	26,444	3,126	641	N.A.	N.A.	1,085	543	7,889	1,292	2,923	5,746
Nebraska	817	820	949	12,499	2,775	4,615	1,981	N.A.	2,695	108	3,520	N.A.	1,052	8,422	3,771
Nevada	2,054	581	13,032	12,134	400	4,591	10,786	N.A.	N.A.	403	156		0	6,437	4,914
New Hampshire	497	931	2,358	11,426		15,749	(g)	1,056		592		N.A.	571	8,636	1,999
New Jersey	19,129	(d)	5,678	24,515	2,795	51,748		18,646	6,764	3,342	3,129	N.A.	25,025	210,827	29,198
New Mexico	1,562	2,088	2,444	15,626	1,115	5,669	5,687	N.A.	1,091			1,981	2,426	5,502	9,893
New York	20,109	(a)	75,577	39,730	893	(b)	(g)	5,028		(b)	11,176	615	96,840	338,034	(a)
North Carolina	5,113		32,331	10,283	556	3,900	5,143	2,635	1,848	2,458	948	N.A.	8,529	26,261	1,831
North Dakota	1,264	596	1,152	10,935	1,867	364	5,905	N.A.	N.A.	948		779	105	1,000	27,168
Ohio	13,434	5,634	9,386	28,601		23,422	13,709	1,030		621	11,362	17,549	11,213	22,877	15,671
Oklahoma	1,934	(a)	7,140	20,358	1,583	13,842	350	N.A.	N.A.	2,587	4,931	2,073	(f)	2,736	2,614
Oregon	8,557	1,603	45,659	65,682	1,052	10,883	8,432	(i)		913	2,492	353	3,210	10,919	7,750
Pennsylvania	10,005	3,607	32,292	56,064	56	42,387	(g)	7,119	11,897	1,371	74	40,781	32,280	44,280	2,102
Rhode Island	773	(a)	2,038	6,896	27	6,394		1,920	63	1,235		N.A.	3,336	9,360	8,406
South Carolina	6,857	9,388	27,701	33,954	1,568	12,083	3,439	4,326	1,468			(i)	(c)	7,803	6,202
South Dakota	4,643	(a)	4,271	15,892	1,594	(f)	362	N.A.	(f)		535	1,582	(f)	2,871	1,169
Tennessee	3,212	(a)	16,619	23,260	1,318	7,575	(i)	N.A.	1,548	2,299	2,162	3,576	4,368	30,931	12,608
Texas	16,990	4,393	12,727	66,197	14,210	776	2,114	1,580	1,430	4,399	3,822	4,378	5,663	159,007	14,962
Utah	3,370	1,517	(i)	22,597	2,373	11,815	6,437	N.A.	944		186		187	12,580	9,340
Vermont	1,128	(a)	6,679	8,122	112	4,845		N.A.	2,279	397		N.A.	6,943	19,943	373

See footnotes at end of table.

STATE ENVIRONMENTAL AND NATURAL RESOURCE SPENDING, FISCAL YEAR 1991—Continued

State	Air quality	Drinking water	Forestry	Fish & wildlife	Geological survey	Hazardous waste	Land management	Marine & coastal programs	Nuclear waste	Pesticides control	Soil conservation	Mining reclamation	Solid waste	Water quality	Water resource management
Virginia	8,252	2,990	22,604	21,936	2,308	51,620	9,334	20,752	665	1,106	779	10,246	6,728	60,345	6,856
Washington	8,775	(c)	23,722	83,393	708	2,119	154,652	10,354	4,673	3,610	750	349	10,751	18,791	9,622
West Virginia	913		3,681	15,215	2,018	(b)	601	N.A.	N.A.	N.A.	2,797	5,299	4,307	234	507
Wisconsin	8,908	10,024	32,174	47,455	N.A.	(b)	N.A.	N.A.	N.A.	N.A.	N.A.	N.A.	48,243	29,214	3,727
Wyoming	1,095	(a)	2,097	27,211	877		2,003	N.A.		(a)	23	29,131	467	4,837	32,582

Source: The Council of State Governments, Resource Guide to State Environmental Management, Third Edition, 1993.

Note: The period covered fiscal year 1991, which ended June 30, 1991, for most states. The figures represented in this table were taken from executive and/or legislative budget documents which listed the actual FY 1991 expenditures. In cases where the budgetary figures could not be obtained from such documents, actual expenditures were requested from the appropriated federal agency officials.

The expenditures totals provided here are combinations of state, federal and other (fees, fines, licenses, etc.) monies which have passed through the state budgetary process. While local government commitments to environmental protection are very substantial in many states, the totals presented herein will reflect only that portion of the local effort that has been passed through the state budget.

Categories may include monies expended on an environmental topic from several agencies, even though there may be designated only one lead agency. The objective was to combine all related expenditures throughout the state within a function-specific category in order to present a more accurate measure of the state's total effort on each particular category of expenditures. In most instances, any discrepancy from a particular agency's record of its expenditures may plausibly be explained by the definitions assigned to the 15 environmental and natural resource categories in the review. In other instances, several agencies' expenditures are combined. In those agencies where administrative overhead was listed as a separate agency-wide item, the overhead has been prorated to each of 'the agencies' subunits. The total state environmental expenditures should reflect, as far as funding is concerned, the individual state's commitment to environmental and natural resource programming.

The following definitions were used during the compilation of the environmental and natural resources expenditures: Air Quality—funds used to administer the states' clean air laws and the Clean Air Act; Drinking Water—funds used to administer the Safe Drinking Water Act, as well as state public drinking water laws, including laboratory testing, and monitoring systems constructions and maintenance; Forestry—funds used to manage and protect the state's forest resources; Fish & Wildlife—funds used to protect, manage and enhance fish and wildlife resources and enforce the state's fish and game laws; Geological Survey—funds used to conduct research on the state's terrain, mineral resources, and possible geological hazards such as earthquakes, faults, volcanoes, etc.; Hazardous Waste—funds used to develop and maintain a comprehensive hazardous waste management program (which could also include remediation of Superfund sites and incidence of leaking underground storage tanks); Land Management—funds used to manage state-owned or state-administered land resources (including rangelands and wetlands not identified as state parks or recreation areas; Marine & Coastal Programs—funds used to plan and implement programs for the orderly development and research of coastal zones (including Federal Sea Grants and related spending); Nuclear Waste—funds used to develop and maintain comprehensive low level and high level nuclear waste management program; Pesticides Control—funds used to regulate the sale, use content and disposal of agricultural and/or commercial pesticides; Soil Conservation—funds used to coordinate and operate programs to conserve and protect the state's soil resources (which may include erosion and sediment control); Mining Reclamation—funds used to enforce mining reclamation standards, clean-up of abandoned mined lands and/or administer state reclamation programs; Solid Waste—funds used to develop and maintain solid waste management programs (including litter control and sustained and pilot recycling programs); Water Quality—funds used to develop and maintain water quality protection programs and water pollution abatement programs (including requisite criteria of the Clean Water Act); Water Resource Management—funds used to administer the state's water conservation, development, use and planning programs. See above referenced source for more detailed information.

(a) Amount included in Water Quality.
(b) Amount included in Solid Waste.
(c) Amount included in Hazardous Waste.
(d) Amount included in Water Resources.
(e) Amount included in Geological Survey.
(f) Amount included in Air Quality.
(g) Amount included in Forestry.
(h) Amount included in Marine/Coastal.
(i) Amount included in Land Management.
(j) Amount included in Mining Reclamation.

Key:
. . . — Data not available
N.A. — Not applicable

Labor Legislation, 1992-93

States have continued to strengthen child labor laws, raise minimum wages and address job discrimination.

by Richard R. Nelson

State labor legislation in 1992 and 1993 covered a wide array of employment standards and included several noteworthy laws.[1]

Trends of the last few years continued as legislation was adopted to address recent issues of restrictions on employee leasing; regulation of drug, alcohol and genetic testing; sexual harassment in the workplace; and bans on employment discrimination because of the lawful use of products outside the workplace, or because of an individual's sexual orientation.

Considerable legislative attention also was given to increasing state minimum wages, restricting child labor, prohibiting discrimination because of disability, containing workers' compensation costs and providing for parental leave.

Wages and Hours

Minimum wages

In 1992, Wisconsin was the only state to raise its minimum hourly wage, and this was by administrative rather than legislative action. 1993 saw a resurgence of activity with rates increased by new legislation in Arkansas, the District of Columbia (for most workers), New Mexico and Washington.[2] The District of Columbia established a single wage rate replacing nine separate occupational wage orders.

Ten jurisdictions had rates higher than the $4.25 federal standard on January 1, 1994[3] (see Table 8.20). The highest was $5.25 in the District of Columbia and Hawaii.

Maine law was amended to change the tip credit against the minimum wage from a dollar amount to a percentage, and to repeal the provision for a subminimum student rate. Utah will no longer permit the payment of a lower rate to adult learners. Legislation in Colorado, Louisiana, North Dakota, Texas, and Utah conformed overtime pay policies for various public sector employees to overtime requirements in the federal Fair Labor Standards Act.

Prevailing wage

Significant changes were made during this biennium in the public construction prevailing wage laws of Alaska, Connecticut, Hawaii, Missouri, Montana, Nevada and Texas.[4] Amendments primarily revised rate determination procedures, increased penalties for violation or strengthened enforcement. Hawaii now permits periodic increases in the prevailing wage rate during the life of a public works contract. Under Connecticut revisions, making a false statement on a certified payroll will now be a felony, and failure to pay the required prevailing wage rates will be larceny. In Nevada, certain unsuccessful bidders may bring civil action against a contractor for damages suffered as a result of not being awarded the contract if the contractor fails to make required payments.

These provisions, and a few enacted in 1990 and 1991, contrast to the past several years when most prevailing wage activity involved attempts to repeal or reduce coverage of the state laws.

The Pennsylvania prevailing wage law was held to be invalid and unenforceable in a 1993 U.S. District Court decision. The court ruled

Richard R. Nelson is a state standards adviser in the Division of State Standards Programs, Wage and Hour Division, Employment Standards Administration, U.S. Department of Labor. The Workers' Compensation section was prepared by Ruth A. Brown, state standards adviser, Division of Planning, Policy and Standards, Office of Workers' Compensation Programs, Employment Standards Administration, U.S. Department of Labor.

that the portion of the law calling for inclusion of benefits in the prevailing wage determination is preempted by the federal Employee Retirement Income Security Act (ERISA) and is not severable from the rest of the act.

Wage Payment and Collection

The labor departments in Colorado, Connecticut, Maine, Tennessee and Texas were authorized to enter into reciprocal agreements with the labor department or corresponding agency in other states to help collect wage claims and judgments from employers who move across state lines. Twenty-six states now have this authority.[5] Colorado and Maine also will permit reciprocal agreements in other labor standards, including minimum wage and overtime, child labor and job safety.

Family Issues

The federal Family and Medical Leave Act of 1993 was enacted on February 5, and took effect for most employers on August 5, 1993. The law entitles eligible private- and public-sector employees to take up to 12 weeks of unpaid, job-protected leave in a 12-month period for the birth or placement of a child for adoption or foster care; to care for a spouse, child or parent with a serious health condition; or for the employee's serous health condition. A covered employer is required to maintain group health insurance coverage for an employee who uses this leave and must restore the employee to his or her original job, or to an equivalent job with equivalent pay, benefits and other employment terms and conditions.

Prior to passage of the federal law, family leave continued as an emerging issue in the states. In 1992 Vermont enacted a law, applicable to both the private and public sector, permitting an unpaid leave of absence for either parent for the birth or adoption of a child, for the employee's own serious illness, or to care for a seriously ill child, parent or spouse. Also, Alaska and Georgia enacted similar legislation for various public-sector employees, and studies of family leave or related issues were requested in other states.

After the federal law was passed, several state family leave bills that had been introduced were withdrawn or failed to move through the legislatures. Of the new measures enacted in 1993, most related to enactment of the federal law. Examples include the California law that was amended to conform most provisions to the federal law; repeal of a provision that would have terminated administration and enforcement of the Washington family leave law upon the effective date of any federal law; a delay in implementation of the Hawaii law in the private sector until July 1, 1994; and amendments to the Maryland law applicable to state employees making certain provisions conform with the federal law. Conversely, Nevada adopted a law applicable to state employees.

Other family issues were addressed by legislation in Illinois and North Carolina, requiring employers to grant employees leave for participation in their children's school activities, and in Utah where employers must now grant time off for parents to accompany their children to juvenile court appearances.

Child Labor

Child labor was one of the most active areas of labor legislation in 1992 and 1993 with laws enacted in several states. Most followed recent trends to strengthen enforcement authority and penalty provisions, to restrict hours of employment, to bring additional minors under coverage or to prohibit work in additional occupations determined to be hazardous.

A comprehensive law in Montana replaced a limited statute. The new law generally conforms to federal standards with respect to working hours for 14- and 15-year-olds, prohibited hazardous occupations for those between 14 and 17 years old, and permitted occupations for 14- and 15-year-olds. Daily, weekly or nightwork hours for minors under 16 also were made to conform to federal standards in California, Indiana, Louisiana and North Dakota (see Table 8.19). Indiana also adopted the federal Fair Labor Standards Act, prohibited occupations for minors under 18, adopted civil penalties for violations, and provided for revocation of a minor's employment certificate if school attendance drops. Labor departments in Louisiana, Tennessee and Texas also were authorized to assess violators civil penalties.

The Louisiana and Maine labor departments will now have rule-making authority.

Children under 16 in Illinois and North Dakota may no longer work in occupations requiring use or carrying of a firearm or any other weapon, or in occupations that involve handling or storing blood, blood products, body fluids and body tissues. North Dakota also prohibits youths under 16 from working in occupations in connection with medical or other dangerous wastes, and door-to-door sales. Work involving door-to-door sales is now prohibited or regulated for some or all minors in 14 states.[6]

Washington revised regulations to limit the work of 16- and 17-year-olds during the school year, reduce the permissible weekly hours for 14- and 15-year-olds, and declare additional occupations hazardous for minors under age 18. Minnesota and North Carolina also acted to restrict the working hours of 16- and 17-year-olds during the school year.

Changes in the Wisconsin regulations eased nightwork restrictions for minors under 16 while making school week work hours and nightwork hours more restrictive for 16- and 17-year-olds.

Restrictions also were eased in California and Maine for certain minors who will now be permitted to work longer hours, and in Louisiana, New Hampshire, North Carolina and Oregon where restrictions were modified for work around alcoholic beverages.

Among other provisions, Alaska and Tennessee now require work breaks for minors; Alaska made provisions for the employment of minors of any age in the entertainment industry; employment certificates in North Dakota will now be issued, and may be revoked, by a minor's parent; and parents in Illinois are to receive copies of employment certificates and may request revocation if they feel it is in the best interest of the child.

Equal Employment Opportunity

Once again, barring various forms of employment discrimination was a major focus of legislative attention this biennium with measures enacted by a majority of the states. Among the more noteworthy was a first-time Civil Rights Act adopted in Arkansas, which includes a ban on employment discrimination because of race, religion, ancestry or national origin, gender or disability; new laws in California, Minnesota, New Jersey and Vermont banning discrimination in employment on the basis of sexual orientation[7] (an anti-gay rights ballot measure was approved in Colorado[8] and another was defeated in Oregon); a ban in California on discrimination against people testing positive for HIV; elimination of the upper age limit in age discrimination provisions in Oklahoma, Pennsylvania and Washington; and provisions in several states to help eliminate sexual harassment in the workplace.

The single most active area of anti-discrimination legislation was discrimination because of disability. Among these measures, a law prohibiting disability discrimination was enacted in Louisiana, and several states adopted provisions similar to those in the federal Americans with Disabilities Act. Most of these laws, as well as new provisions in Minnesota, Mississippi, Nevada and Texas, require employers to make reasonable accommodation to an individual's disability. The New Jersey prohibition against discrimination because of disability was amended to specifically include people with AIDS or HIV.

New York barred discrimination because of various legal activities outside the workplace during nonworking hours such as political activities, use of legal consumable products, legal recreational activities and union membership.

Recent trends continued with Illinois, Minnesota, Montana, North Carolina, and Wisconsin prohibiting discrimination because of the lawful use of any product outside the workplace during nonworking hours; Missouri barring discrimination because of the use of lawful alcohol or tobacco products; and the District of Columbia, West Virginia and Wyoming adopting similar prohibitions because of the use of tobacco products.

Illinois and Kansas broadened the list of unlawful forms of discrimination to include bias on the basis of military status; the District of Columbia made it unlawful for an employer to refuse to make a reasonable accommodation for an employee's religious observance by permitting the employee to make up work; and Texas prohibited the discriminatory use of test scores for employment purposes.

Employee Testing

Genetic testing emerged as an issue during the biennium, with Iowa and Wisconsin barring such testing as a condition of employment, union membership or licensure. Existing law adopted in Oregon in 1989 was amended in 1993 to further restrict the use of genetic testing in employment decisions.

Although fewer drug and alcohol testing laws were enacted than in recent years, measures adopted in Illinois and Oklahoma will permit testing of applicants or employees if certain conditions are met, and more limited laws in North Dakota and Virginia allow school boards to require testing of school bus drivers.

Employee Leasing

Employee leasing continued as an emerging issue with Nevada, New Mexico, Oregon, South Carolina, Texas, and Utah enacting laws requiring licensing or otherwise regulating employee leasing firms. These firms place employees of a client business on their payroll and lease the workers back to the client on an on-going basis for a fee. Laws of this kind were enacted previously in Arkansas, Florida, Maine, Tennessee and Utah.

Workers' Compensation

During 1992-93, Connecticut again changed its method of computing workers' compensation benefits payable for disability or death by reducing the percent of employees' spendable earnings from 80 percent to 75 percent, and by reducing the maximum weekly compensation benefits from 150 percent of the state's average weekly wage to 100 percent.

Cost containment efforts continued as a priority with Arizona, Arkansas, Idaho, Kentucky, Minnesota, Mississippi, Missouri, Montana, Ohio, Oklahoma and Pennsylvania passing legislation allowing, or in some instances requiring, workers' compensation policies to include deductibles. Among those jurisdictions previously authorizing deductibles,[9] Colorado

increased the amount of the maximum deductible under its statute from $1,500 to $5,000.

The issue of fraud received considerable attention as it was addressed in varying degrees in 17 states.[10] A managed health-care plan was introduced into the workers' compensation program of 12 states.[11] Legislation was passed to establish, or to improve existing workplace safety program in 15 states.[12]

Four states provided workers' compensation coverage through alternate sources other than through workers' compensation insurance. Alabama employers may insure for workers' compensation liability by any combination of life, disability, accident, health or other insurance if coverage does not limit or exclude workers' compensation benefits. California implemented a pilot project under which a participating employer may contract with a qualified health care service plan to be the exclusive provider of medical care for work and nonwork injuries and illnesses. Georgia's insurance commissioner was authorized to approve pilot projects that allow employers and employees to enter into agreements to provide employees with workers' compensation medical benefits through comprehensive health insurance that covers workplace injuries and illnesses. Maine passed legislation requiring the superintendent of insurance to adopt rules permitting employers and employees to enter into agreements to provide the employees with health-care benefits covering both workplace and nonworkplace injury and illness.

As a result of reform in Maine's workers' compensation system, legislation was enacted to create an employer's mutual workers' compensation fund to provide a competitive market for workers' compensation coverage. Missouri established the State Mutual Insurance Company, to be funded by the sale of bonds and by a $5 million loan from the Workers' Compensation Administrative Fund, that will focus on employers with premiums of $10,000 or less. The competitive fund is expected to be operational by March 1995. Tennessee established a competitive state workers' compensation insurance fund that will be subject to the same legal and regulatory requirements as any other insurer offering workers' compensation coverage.

Maximum weekly benefit payments were increased in nearly every jurisdiction (see Table 8.18).

Private Employment Agencies

While there were only a few laws enacted concerning regulation of the private employment agency industry, some of these were noteworthy. The Louisiana law was amended to provide for the refund of fees to job applicants under certain conditions, as was the North Carolina law. Virginia adopted several changes, including a requirement that employment counselors be registered with the Department of Commerce.

In a related development, Georgia placed restrictions on labor pools furnishing temporary employees for short-time assignments of casual, unskilled labor.

Whistleblowers

North Dakota and Rhode Island adopted whistleblower laws of general application protecting the jobs of employees who report law violations. Also enacted were laws in Georgia, Nebraska, and South Dakota protecting state employees, and a law in Washington protecting local government workers. Laws of limited application were enacted in three states: Louisiana for insurance companies; Pennsylvania for public utility employers; and Rhode Island for health-care facilities. A number of other state laws were amended, including those in North Carolina, where separate provisions were consolidated into a new Retaliatory Employment Discrimination provision.

Preference

Hawaii, Indiana and Missouri adopted laws granting resident bidders a preference over nonresidents on bids for public contracts. Several other states modified their laws, and the preference law in Arkansas was repealed.

Other Legislation

Among other significant measures adopted during the biennium, employees in Delaware and Tennessee are to receive a meal break if they work the required number of consecutive hours; workers on specified Florida state agency contracts must have access to hospitalization and medical insurance benefits; employers in Kansas may not discharge a permanent employee because of required jury duty; and a polygraph examiners law was reenacted in Mississippi. Kansas, Nebraska, North Carolina and Tennessee will provide paid leave for state employees who are American Red Cross certified disaster service volunteers, and measures in Nebraska and South Carolina encourage employers to grant leave for bone marrow donors. Hawaii banned employers from granting permanent employment to individuals who perform bargaining unit work during a strike or lockout, while a U.S. District Court ruled unconstitutional a similar law enacted in Minnesota in 1991.

Notes

[1] This article does not cover the subjects of unemployment insurance, employment and training, labor relations, employee background clearance, economic development, or occupational safety and health legislation.

[2] In 1992, basic rates also increased in Arkansas, Hawaii, Iowa, New Jersey, North Carolina, Virginia and West Virginia as provided for in previous legislation. Prior actions also resulted in a rate increase for farmworkers in New York, and a rate increase for employees in the watching and protective service industry in Puerto Rico. In 1993, rates rose in Hawaii and North Carolina as the result of prior laws.

[3] Alaska, Connecticut, the District of Columbia, Hawaii, Iowa, New Jersey, Oregon, Rhode Island, the U.S. Virgin Islands and Washington.

[4] Thirty-two states have prevailing wage laws. These are: Alaska, Arkansas, California, Connecticut, Delaware, Hawaii, Illinois, Indiana, Kentucky, Maine, Maryland, Massachusetts, Michigan, Minnesota, Missouri, Montana, Nebraska, Nevada, New Jersey, New Mexico, New York, Ohio, Oklahoma, Oregon, Pennsylvania, Rhode Island, Tennessee, Texas, Washington, West Virginia, Wisconsin and Wyoming. Guam and the U.S. Virgin Islands also have such laws.

[5] Alaska, Arkansas, California, Colorado, Connecticut, Hawaii, Idaho, Illinois, Iowa, Kansas, Maine, Maryland, Montana, Nevada, New York, North Carolina, North Dakota, Oklahoma, Oregon, South Dakota, Tennessee, Texas, Utah, Washington, Wisconsin and Wyoming.

[6] Alaska, Arizona, California, Florida, Massachusetts, Missouri, North Dakota, Ohio, Oklahoma, Oregon, Utah, Virginia, Washington and Wisconsin.

[7] Laws prohibiting discrimination on the basis of sexual orientation were enacted previously in Connecticut, the District of Columbia, Hawaii, Massachusetts and Wisconsin.

[8] On December 14, 1993, a District Court in Colorado struck down the 1992 Constitutional Amendment, approved by the voters, barring state and local laws prohibiting discrimination because of sexual orientation.

[9] Alabama, Colorado, Florida, Georgia, Indiana, Kansas, Maine, Maryland, Montana, Nebraska, New Hampshire, North Dakota, Rhode Island and South Carolina.

[10] Alabama, Arkansas, California, Connecticut, Kansas, Louisiana, Minnesota, Missouri, Montana, Nevada, New Hampshire, Ohio, Oklahoma, Rhode Island, South Dakota, Utah and Virginia.

[11] Arkansas, California, Louisiana, Missouri, Montana, Nebraska, Nevada, New Hampshire, Ohio, Oklahoma, South Dakota and West Virginia.

[12] Arkansas, California, Connecticut, Kansas, Minnesota, Mississippi, Missouri, Montana, Nebraska, North Carolina, Ohio, Oklahoma, Tennessee, Utah and West Virginia.

Occupational Safety and Health

New state legislation is creating safety and health committees to help prevent injury and illness in the workplace.

by Arlene Perkins

Nine states currently have requirements, through regulation or legislation, for employers to establish safety and health programs and/or committees.

Nevada recently passed legislation requiring all employers to establish written safety programs, including training and requiring employers with more than 25 employees to establish safety committees. The legislation also authorizes three additional training and consultation positions so the state can help employers establish such programs.

Under Oregon's new legislation, an employer meets state requirements if it is a member of a multi-employer group operating under a collective bargaining agreement with safety committee requirements equivalent to the state's workplace safety committee rules.

California recently passed legislation that establishes an Injury and Illness Prevention Program (IIPP) for employers and employees in the state. Through the IIPP, employers must establish, implement and maintain in writing, an effective Injury and Illness Prevention Program. The program must include the following criteria: identifying the person with authority and responsibility for implementing the program; ensuring that employees comply with safe and healthful work practices; and convening meetings and training programs, and posting and notifying employees about hazards. Employers may elect to include a labor/management safety and health committee in their IIPP.

California's Target Inspection Program legislation provides for the inspection of employers in the highest hazardous industries on a "worst-first" priority basis. A letter is sent to each high hazard employer indicating that they are in the Target Inspection Program and have been placed on a Targeted Inspection list. The employer is required to establish, implement and maintain an effective Injury and Illness Prevention Program or, if one has already been established, the employer may be required to provide a more effective IIPP. The employer must inform Cal/OSHA, in writing, what they have done to implement an effective program.

North Carolina recently passed legislation to require certain employers to establish safety and health programs and/or committees in the workplace. All employers with an "experience rate modifier" of 1.5 or greater must have a safety program. Experience rate modifiers are ratings the insurance industry uses to determine workers' compensation premiums. Additionally, all employers with 11 or more employees and an experience rate modifier of 1.5 or more must have a safety and health committee.

Tennessee enacted legislation under its Workers' Compensation Act requiring safety and health committees for employers with an experience modification rate applied to the premium in the top 25 percent of all covered employers and self-insured employers. All employers with safety and health committees must also have safety and health programs.

Alaska, Hawaii, Minnesota and Washington have similar requirements.

Standards Adoption

Michigan recently amended its Administrative Procedures Act to eliminate certain promulgation requirements, giving the state the

Arlene Perkins is a project officer in the Office of State Programs, Directorate of Federal-State Operations, Occupational Safety and Health Administration, U.S. Department of Labor.

ability to make known the terms of the rules substantially similar to federal rules within the federally mandated six-month timeframe.

The California Legislature has adopted new legislation that allows Cal/OSHA to temporarily adopt (for six months) and enforce federal standards until an equivalent state standard is adopted, should the state be unable to promulgate its standard within the six-month timeframe.

OSHA's New Seven-Fold Penalty Increase

A congressional amendment to section 17 of the Occupational Safety and Health Act implemented on March 1, 1991, increases penalty levels for violations of the act. As a result of this amendment, states are required to make statutory changes to their occupational safety and health legislation to reflect the new federal penalty maximums of $7,000 for serious, other-than-serious, failure to abate and posting violations; and $70,000 for willful and repeat violations; as well as the $5,000 floor for willful violations.

All 21 states and two territories covering both public- and private-sector employment (Alaska, Arizona, California, Hawaii, Indiana, Iowa, Kentucky, Maryland, Michigan, Minnesota, Nevada, New Mexico, North Carolina, Oregon, South Carolina, Tennessee, Utah, Vermont, Virginia, Washington, Wyoming, Puerto Rico and U.S. Virgin Islands) have enacted

legislation paralleling OSHA's penalty increase. (The New York and Connecticut plans, which cover only state and local government employees, were not required to enact penalty increases.)

Public Sector Penalties

North Carolina recently enacted legislation empowering the Commissioner of Labor to impose penalties against public agencies for OSHA violations and to require local government units to report OSHA citations to its governing boards. (Sixteen of the 25 state plans now impose penalties in the public sector.)

Discrimination

Recent North Carolina legislation created The Workplace Retaliatory Discrimination (WORD) Division to administer complaints of discrimination. The occupational safety and health discrimination function was transferred from the Occupational Safety and Health Division and placed in WORD.

Targeting

North Carolina also created a Special Emphasis Program to target OSHA inspections. These inspections are scheduled because of an employer's high frequency of safety and health standards or because of an employer's high risk or high rate of work-related fatalities or work-related serious injuries or illnesses.

Table 8.18
MAXIMUM BENEFITS FOR TEMPORARY TOTAL DISABILITY
PROVIDED BY WORKERS' COMPENSATION STATUTES
(As of January 1994)

State or other jurisdiction	Maximum percentage of wages	Maximum payment per week		Maximum period		Total maximum stated in law
		Amount	Based on	Duration of disability	Number of weeks	
United States						
FECA (a)	66-2/3 (b)	$1,248.88	(b)	★	. . .	. . .
LS/HWCA (a) . .	66-2/3	738.30	200% of NAWW	★	. . .	. . .
Alabama	66-2/3	419.00	100% of SAWW	★	. . .	. . .
Alaska	80 of worker's spendable earnings	700.00 (c)	. . .	★ (d)	. . .	. . .
Arizona	66-2/3	323.10 (e)	. . .	★	. . .	. . .
Arkansas	66-2/3	267.00	70% of SAWW	. . .	450	. . .
California	66-2/3	336.00	66-2/3% of SAWW	★	. . .	. . .
Colorado	66-2/3	432.25	91% of SAWW	★	. . .	. . .
Connecticut	75 of worker's spendable earnings	638.00	100% of SAWW	★	. . .	. . .
Delaware	66-2/3	339.29	66-2/3% of SAWW	★	. . .	. . .
Florida	66-2/3	444.00 (g)	100% of SAWW	. . .	104	. . .
Georgia	66-2/3	250.00	. . .	. . .	400	. . .
Hawaii	66-2/3	481.00	100% of SAWW	★	. . .	. . .
Idaho	67	351.00	90% of SAWW	. . .	52 (h)	. . .
Illinois	66-2/3	712.92	133-1/3% of SAWW	★	. . .	. . .
Indiana	66-2/3	394.00	. . .	. . .	500	$214,000 (i)
Iowa	80 of worker's spendable earnings	797.00	200% of SAWW	★	. . .	. . .
Kansas	66-2/3	313.00	75% of SAWW	★	. . .	100,000
Kentucky	66-2/3	415.94	100% of SAWW	★	. . .	. . .
Louisiana	66-2/3	319.00 (j)	75% of SAWW	★	. . .	. . .
Maine	80 of worker's after tax earnings	441.00 (j)	90% of SAWW	★	. . .	. . .
Maryland	66-2/3	510.00	100% of SAWW	★	. . .	. . .
Massachusetts	60	565.94 (k)	100% of SAWW	. . .	156	(l)
Michigan	80 of worker's spendable earnings	475.00 (m)	90% of SAWW	★	. . .	. . .
Minnesota	66-2/3	508.20	105% of SAWW	★ (n)	. . .	. . .
Mississippi	66-2/3	243.75	66-2/3% of SAWW	. . .	450	109,687
Missouri	66-2/3	470.06	105% of SAWW	. . .	400	. . .
Montana	66-2/3	362.00 (c)	100% of SAWW	★	. . .	. . .
Nebraska	66-2/3	265.00 (o)	. . .	★	. . .	. . .
Nevada	66-2/3	432.39	100% of SAWW	★	. . .	. . .
New Hampshire	66-2/3	709.50	150% of SAWW	★	. . .	. . .
New Jersey	70	460.00	75% of SAWW	. . .	400	. . .
New Mexico	66-2/3	333.02	85% of SAWW	. . .	700 (p)	(q)
New York	66-2/3	400.00	. . .	★	. . .	. . .
North Carolina	66-2/3	466.00	110% of SAWW	★	. . .	. . .
North Dakota	66-2/3	358.00 (r)	100% of SAWW	★	. . .	. . .
Ohio	72 for first 12 weeks; 66-2/3 thereafter	482.00 (s)	100% of SAWW	★	. . .	. . .
Oklahoma	70	307.00	75% of SAWW	. . .	300	. . .
Oregon	66-2/3	478.95	100% of SAWW	★	. . .	. . .
Pennsylvania	66-2/3	493.00	100% of SAWW	★	. . .	. . .
Rhode Island	75 of worker's spendable earnings	463.00 (t)	100% of SAWW	. . .	500	. . .
South Carolina	66-2/3	410.26	100% of SAWW	. . .	. . .	. . .
South Dakota	66-2/3	338.00	100% of SAWW	★	. . .	. . .
Tennessee	66-2/3	355.97	. . .	. . .	400	142,388
Texas	70 of worker's earnings over $8.50 per hour; 75 for all others	464.00 (u)	100% of SAWW	. . .	104 (v)	. . .
Utah	66-2/3	413.00 (w)	100% of SAWW	. . .	312	. . .
Vermont	66-2/3	644.00 (x)	150% of SAWW	★	. . .	. . .
Virginia	66-2/3	451.00	100% of SAWW	. . .	500	. . .
Washington	60-75	517.16 (c)	105% of SAMW	★	. . .	. . .
West Virginia	70	420.33	100% of SAWW	. . .	208	. . .
Wisconsin	66-2/3	466.00 (c)	100% of SAWW	★	. . .	. . .
Wyoming	66-2/3 of actual monthly earnings	413.00	100% of SAMW	★	. . .	. . .
Dist. of Columbia	66-2/3 or 80 of worker's spendable earnings; whichever is less	679.17	100% of SAWW	★	. . .	. . .
Puerto Rico	66-2/3	65.00	. . .	. . .	312	. . .
U.S. Virgin Islands	66-2/3	287.00	66-2/3% of SAWW	★	. . .	. . .

See footnotes at end of table.

MAXIMUM BENEFITS—Continued

Source: U.S. Department of Labor, Branch of Planning, Policy and Review, Division of Planning, Policy and Standards, Office of Workers' Compensation Programs, Employment Standards Administration.

Key:

SAWW — State's average weekly wage

SAMW — State's average monthly wage

NAWW — National average weekly wage

(a) Federal Employees Compensation Act (FECA) and the Longshore and Harbor Workers' Compensation Act (LS/HWCA). LS/HWCA benefits are for private-sector maritime employees (not seamen) who work on navigable waters of the U.S., including dry docks.

(b) Benefits under FECA are computed at a maximum of 75 percent of the pay of a specific grade level in the federal civil service.

(c) Benefits are subject to Social Security benefit offsets.

(d) Benefits payable for duration of disability or until date of medical stability is reached.

(e) Additional $25 monthly added to benefits of dependents residing in the U.S.

(f) Benefits are subject to Social Security benefit offsets and by benefits from an employer pension or disability plan.

(g) Benefits are subject to Social Security and Unemployment Insurance benefit offsets.

(h) After 52 weeks, benefits are; 67 percent of SAWW for duration of disability.

(i) Effective 7/1/94.

(j) Payments are subject to Unemployment Insurance benefit offsets.

(k) Additional $6 will be added per dependent if weekly benefits are below $150.

(l) Total maximum payable not to exceed 250 times the SAWW in effect at time of injury.

(m) Benefits subject to reduction by Unemployment Insurance and Social Security benefits, and those under an employer disability, retirement or pension plan.

(n) Payments made for duration of disability until 90 days after maximum medical improvement or end of retraining.

(o) Effective 1/1/96, maximum weekly benefit will be 100 percent of the SAWW.

(p) 100 weeks (primary and secondary mental impairment).

(q) Total maximum payable equals the sum of 700 multiplied by the maximum weekly benefit payable at the time of injury.

(r) Additional $10 per week payable for each dependent child, not to exceed worker's net wage. Benefits are reduced by 50 percent of Social Security benefits.

(s) Benefits are subject to offset and if concurrent and/or duplicate with those under employer non-occupational benefits plan.

(t) An additional $9 for each dependent; including a non-working spouse, aggregate not to exceed 80 percent of the worker's average weekly wage.

(u) Each cumulative $10 increase in the average weekly wage for manufacturing production workers will increase the maximum weekly benefit by $7 per week.

(v) Maximum is 104 weeks, or upon reaching maximum medical improvement, whichever is sooner.

(w) Additional $5 for dependent spouse and each dependent child up to 4, but not to exceed 100 percent of the state average weekly wage.

(x) Additional $10 is paid for each dependent under 21 years of age.

Table 8.19
SELECTED STATE CHILD LABOR STANDARDS AFFECTING MINORS UNDER 18 IN NON-FARM EMPLOYMENT
(As of January 1994)
(Occupational coverage, exemptions and deviations usually omitted)

State or other jurisdiction	Maximum daily and weekly hours and days per week for minors (a)		Nightwork prohibited for minors (a)	
	Under 16 years of age	*16 and 17 years of age*	*Under 16 years of age*	*16 and 17 years of age*
Federal (FLSA)	8-40, non-schoolday period Schoolday/week: 3-18 (b)		7 p.m. (9 p.m. June 1 through Labor Day) to 7 a.m.	
Alabama	8-40-6 Schoolday/week: 3-18		7 p.m. (9 p.m. during summer vacation) to 7 a.m.	10 p.m. before schoolday to 5 a.m., if enrolled in school
Alaska	6-day week Schoolday/week: 9 (c)-23	6-day week	9 p.m. to 5 a.m.	
Arizona	8-40 Schoolday/week: 3-18		9:30 p.m. (11 p.m. before non-schoolday) to 6 a.m. 7 p.m. to 6 a.m. in door-to-door sales or deliveries	
Arkansas	8-48-6	10-54-6	7 p.m. (9 p.m. before non-schoolday) to 6 a.m.	11 p.m. before schoolday to 6 a.m.
California	8-40-6 Schoolday/week: 3-28	8-48-6 Schoolday/week: 4-28 (d) except 8 before non-schoolday	7 p.m. (9 p.m. June 1 through Labor Day) to 7 a.m.	10 p.m. (12:30 a.m. before non-schoolday) to 5 a.m.
Colorado	8-40 Schoolday: 6	8-40	9:30 p.m. to 5 a.m. before schoolday	
Connecticut	9-48 8-48-6 in stores and in agriculture (overtime permitted in certain industries)	9-48 8-48-6 in stores (overtime permitted in certain industries)	10 p.m. (midnight before non-schoolday in supermarkets) to 6 a.m.	10 p.m. (midnight before non-schoolday in supermarkets) to 6 a.m. 11 p.m. (midnight before non-schoolday or if not attending school) to 6 a.m. in restaurants or as ushers in non-profit theater
Delaware	8-40-6 Schoolday/week: 4-18 (d)	12 (c)	7 p.m. (9 p.m. June 1 through Labor Day) to 7 a.m.	8 hours of non-work, non-school time required in each 24-hour day
Florida	8-40-6 Schoolday: 3 when followed by schoolday, except if enrolled in vocational program Schoolweek: 15	8-30-6 during schoolyear	7 p.m. before schoolday to 7 a.m. on schoolday (9 p.m. during holidays and summer vacations to 7 a.m.)	11 p.m. to 6:30 a.m., before schoolday
Georgia	8-40 Schoolday: 4		9 p.m. to 6 a.m.	
Hawaii	8-40-6 Schoolday: 10 (c)		7 p.m. to 7 a.m. (9 p.m. to 6 a.m. June 1 through day before Labor Day)	
Idaho	9-54		9 p.m. to 6 a.m.	
Illinois	8-48-6 Schoolday/week: 3|8 (c)|-23 (d)		7 p.m. (9 p.m. June 1 through Labor Day) to 7 a.m.	

See footnotes at end of table.

SELECTED STATE CHILD LABOR STANDARDS—Continued

State or other jurisdiction	Maximum daily and weekly hours and days per week for minors (a)		Nightwork prohibited for minors (a)	
	Under 16 years of age	16 and 17 years of age	Under 16 years of age	16 and 17 years of age
Indiana	8-40 Schoolday/week: 3-18	8-40-6, except if not enrolled in school; 9-48 during summer vacation with written parental permission, minors enrolled in school	7 p.m. (9 p.m. June 1 through Labor Day) to 7 a.m.	10 p.m. (midnight before non-schoolday with written parental permission) to 6 a.m., minors of 16 enrolled in school. 11:30 p.m. to 6 a.m. before schoolday, minors of 17 enrolled in grades 9 through 12 (later with permission up to 2 non-consecutive nights per week)
Iowa	8-40 Schoolday/week: 4-28		7 p.m. (9 p.m. June 1 through Labor Day) to 7 a.m.	
Kansas	8-40		10 p.m. before schoolday to 7 a.m.	
Kentucky	8-40 Schoolday/week: 3-18	6 (8 Saturday and Sunday)-40, if attending school	7 p.m. (9 p.m. June 1 through Labor Day) to 7 a.m.	11:30 p.m. (1 a.m. Friday and Saturday) to 6 a.m. when school in session
Louisiana	8-40-6 Schoolday: 3-18		7 p.m. (9 p.m. June 1 through Labor Day) to 7 a.m.	
Maine	8-40-6 Schoolday/week: 3-18	10-50-6 if enrolled in school; schoolday/week: 4-20, except 8 before non-schoolday, if enrolled in school. (28 hours in a week with multiple days of school closure)	7 p.m. (9 p.m. during summer school vacation) to 7 a.m.	10 p.m. (12 a.m. before non-schoolday) to 7 a.m., if enrolled in school 5 a.m. before non-schoolday
Maryland	8-40 Schoolday/week: 4-23 (d)	12 (c)	8 p.m. (9 p.m. Memorial Day through Labor Day) to 7 a.m.	8 hours of non-work, non-school time required in each 24-hour day
Massachusetts	8-48-6 4-24 in farm work, under 14	9-48-6	7 p.m. (9 p.m. July 1 through Labor Day) to 6:30 a.m.	10 p.m. (midnight in restaurants on Friday, Saturday and vacation) to 6 a.m.
Michigan	10-48-6 Schoolweek: 48 (c)	10-48-6 Schoolweek: 48 (c)	9 p.m. to 7 a.m.	10:30 p.m. to 6 a.m., if attending school 11:30 p.m. to 6 a.m. if not attending school
Minnesota	8-40		9 p.m. to 7 a.m.	11 p.m. to 5 a.m. before schoolday (11:30 p.m. to 4:30 a.m. with written parental permission)
Mississippi	8-44 in factory, mill, cannery or workshop		7 p.m. to 6 a.m. in factory, mill, cannery or workshop	
Missouri	8-40-6		7 p.m. (10 p.m. before non-schoolday and for minors not enrolled in school) to 7 a.m.	
Montana	8-40 Schoolday/week: 3-18 (b)		7 p.m. (9 p.m. during periods outside the school year June 1 through Labor Day, depending on local standards) to 7 a.m.	
Nebraska	8-48		8 p.m. to 6 a.m., under 14 10 p.m. (beyond 10 p.m. before non-schoolday with special permit) to 6 a.m., 14 and 15	

SELECTED STATE CHILD LABOR STANDARDS—Continued

State or other jurisdiction	Maximum daily and weekly hours and days per week for minors (a)		Nightwork prohibited for minors (a)	
	Under 16 years of age	16 and 17 years of age	Under 16 years of age	16 and 17 years of age
Nevada	8-48		...	
New Hampshire	8 on non-schoolday, 48-hour week during vacation, if enrolled in school Schoolday/week: 3-23 if enrolled in school	48-hour week, 6-day week, during vacation if enrolled in school 30-hour week, 6-day week, if enrolled in school	9 p.m. to 7 a.m.	
New Jersey	8-40-6 10-hour day, 6-day week in agriculture Schoolday/week: 3-18	8-40-6	7 p.m. (9 p.m. during summer vacation with parental permission) to 7 a.m.	11 p.m. to 6 a.m. during school term, with specified variations
New Mexico	8-44 (48 in special cases), under 14		9 p.m. to 7 a.m., under 14	
New York	8-40-6 Schoolday/week: 3-18 (b)	8-48-6 Schoolday/week: 4 before schoolday, 8 Friday, Saturday, Sunday or holiday-28, if enrolled in school	7 p.m. (9 p.m. June 21 through Labor Day) to 7 a.m.	10 p.m. (midnight before schooldays with written permission from both parent and school and before non-schoolday with written parental consent) to 6 a.m., while school is in session; midnight to 6 a.m. while school is not in session
North Carolina	8-40 Schoolday/week: 3-18 (b)		7 p.m. (9 p.m. during summer vacation) to 7 a.m.	11 p.m. to 5 a.m. before schoolday while school is in session. Not applicable with written permission from both parent and school
North Dakota	8-40-6 Schoolday/week: 3-18 if not exempted from school attendance	8-48-6	7 p.m. (9 p.m. June 1 through Labor Day) to 7 a.m.	
Ohio	8-40 Schoolday/week: 3-18		7 p.m. (9 p.m. June 1 to Sept. 1 and during school holidays of 5 schooldays or more) to 7 a.m. 7 p.m. to 7 a.m. in door-to-door sales	11 p.m. before schoolday to 7 a.m. on schoolday (6 a.m. if not employed after 8 p.m. previous night) if required to attend school. 8 p.m. to 7 a.m. in door-to-door sales
Oklahoma	8-40 Schoolday/week: 3-18 8 hours on school days before non-schooldays if employer not covered by FLSA		7 p.m. (9 p.m. June 1 through Labor Day) to 7 a.m. 9 p.m. before non-schooldays if employer not covered by FLSA	
Oregon	8-40 Schoolday/week: 3-18 (b)	44-hour week (emergency overtime with permit)	7 p.m. (9 p.m. June 1 through Labor Day) to 7 a.m.	
Pennsylvania	8-44-6 Schoolday/week: 4-26 (d)	8-44-6 28 in schoolweek, if enrolled in regular day school	7 p.m. (10 p.m. during vacation from June to Labor Day) to 7 a.m.	11 p.m. (midnight before non-schoolday) to 6 a.m., if enrolled in regular day school
Rhode Island	8-40	9-48, during school year	7 p.m. (9 p.m. during school vacation) to 6 a.m.	11:30 p.m. (1:30 a.m. before non-schoolday) to 6 a.m., if regularly attending school
South Carolina	8-40 Schoolday/week: 3-18		7 p.m. (9 p.m. June 1 through Labor day) to 7 a.m.	

See footnotes at end of table.

SELECTED STATE CHILD LABOR STANDARDS—Continued

State or other jurisdiction	Maximum daily and weekly hours and days per week for minors (a)		Nightwork prohibited for minors (a)	
	Under 16 years of age	16 and 17 years of age	Under 16 years of age	16 and 17 years of age
South Dakota	8-40 Schoolday/week: 4-20			After 10 p.m. before schoolday
Tennessee	8-40 Schoolday/week: 3-18		7 p.m. to 7 a.m. (9 p.m. to 6 a.m. before non-schooldays)	10 p.m. to 6 a.m. (Sunday-Thursday before schooldays) (midnight, with parental permission, up to 3 nights a week)
Texas	8-48		10 p.m. (midnight before non-schoolday or in summer if not enrolled in summer school) to 5 a.m.	
Utah	8-40 Schoolday: 4		9:30 p.m. to 5 a.m. before schoolday	
Vermont	8-48-6	9-50	7 p.m. to 6 a.m.	
Virginia	8-40, non-school period Schoolday/week: 3-18		7 p.m. (9 p.m. June 1 through Labor Day) to 7 a.m.	
Washington	8-40-6 Schoolday/week: 3 (8 Saturday and Sunday) -16	8-48-6 Schoolday/week: 4 (8 Friday, Saturday and Sunday) -20. 6-28 with special variance agreed to by parent, employer, student and school	7 p.m. (9 p.m. Friday and Saturday when school is not in session) to 7 a.m.	10 p.m. Sunday-Thursday (midnight Friday and Saturday and when school is not in session) to 7 a.m. (5 a.m. when school is not in session). 9 p.m. to 7 a.m. in door-to-door sales
West Virginia	8-40-6		8 p.m. to 5 a.m.	
Wisconsin	8-40-6 Schoolday/week: 4 (8 Friday and non-schoolday)-18 (d)	(f)-50-6 Schoolday/week: 4 (8 Friday and non-schoolday)-26 (d)	8 p.m. (11 p.m. before non-schoolday) to 7 a.m.	11 p.m. (12:30 a.m. before non-schoolday) to 7 a.m. (5 a.m. on non-schoolday) during school week (f)
Wyoming	8-56		10 p.m. (midnight before non-schoolday and for minors not enrolled in school) to 5 a.m.	Midnight to 5 a.m., females
Dist. of Columbia	8-48-6	8-48-6	7 p.m. (9 p.m. June 1 through Labor Day) to 7 a.m.	10 p.m. to 6 a.m.
Guam	8-40-6 Schoolday: 9 (c)	8-40-6 Schoolday: 9 (c)	After 10 p.m. on schoolday	After 10 p.m. on schoolday
Puerto Rico	8-40-6 Schoolday: 8 (c)	8-40-6	6 p.m. to 8 a.m.	10 p.m. to 6 a.m.

Source: U.S. Department of Labor, Division of State Standards Programs, Wage and Hour Division, Employment Standards Administration.

(a) State hours limitations on a schoolday and in a schoolweek usually apply only to those enrolled in school. Several states exempt high school graduates from the hours and/or nightwork or other provisions, or have less restrictive provisions for minors participating in various school-work programs. Separate nightwork standards in messenger service and street trades are common, but are not displayed in table.
(b) Students of 14 and 15 enrolled in approved Work Experience and Career Exploration programs may work during school hours up to 3 hours on a schoolday and 23 hours in a schoolweek.

(c) Combined hours of work and school.
(d) More hours are permitted when school is in session less than 5 days.
(e) Eight hours are permitted on both Saturday and Sunday if minor does not work outside school hours more than 6 consecutive days in a week and total hours worked outside school does not exceed 24.
(f) Wisconsin has no limit during non-schoolweek on daily hours or nightwork for 16-and 17-year-olds. However, they must be paid time and one-half for work in excess of 10 hours per day or 40 hours per week, whichever is greater. Also, 8 hours rest is required between end of work and start of work the next day, and any work between 12:30 a.m. and 5 a.m. must be directly supervised by an adult.

Table 8.20
CHANGES IN BASIC MINIMUM WAGES IN NON-FARM EMPLOYMENT UNDER STATE LAW: SELECTED YEARS 1968 TO 1994

State or other jurisdiction	1968 (a)	1970 (a)	1972	1976 (a)	1979	1980	1981	1988	1991	1992	1993	1994
Federal (FLSA)	$1.15 & $1.60	$1.30 & $1.60	$1.60	$2.20 & $2.30	$2.90	$3.10	$3.35	$3.35	$3.80	$4.25	$4.25	$4.25
Alabama	. . .	. . .	. . .	. . .	. . .	. . .	. . .	. . .	. . .	. . .	. . .	. . .
Alaska	2.10	2.10	2.10	2.80	3.40	3.60	3.85	3.85	4.30	4.75	4.75	4.75
Arizona	18.72-26.40/ wk. (b)	18.72-26.40/ wk. (b)	18.72-26.40/ wk. (b)	. . .	. . .	. . .	. . .	. . .	. . .	. . .	. . .	. . .
Arkansas	1.25/day (b)	1.10	1.20 (b)	1.90	2.30	2.55	2.70	3.25	3.35	3.65	4.00	4.15 (c)
California	1.65 (b)	1.65 (b)	1.65 (b)	2.00	2.90	2.90	3.35	3.35	4.25	4.25	4.25	4.25
Colorado	1.00-1.25 (b)	1.00-1.25 (b)	1.00-1.25 (b)	1.00-1.25 (b)	1.90	1.90	1.90	3.00	3.00	3.00	3.00	3.00
Connecticut	1.40	1.60	1.85	2.21 & 2.31	2.91	3.12	3.37	3.75	4.25	4.27	4.27	4.27
Delaware	1.25	1.25	1.60	2.00	2.00	2.00	2.00	3.35	3.80	4.25	4.25	4.25
Florida	. . .	. . .	. . .	. . .	. . .	. . .	. . .	. . .	. . .	. . .	. . .	. . .
Georgia	. . .	. . .	1.25	1.25	1.25	1.25	1.25	3.25	3.25	3.25	3.25	3.25
Hawaii	1.25	1.60	1.60	2.40	2.65	2.90	3.10	3.85	3.85	3.85	5.25	5.25
Idaho	1.15	1.25	1.40	1.60	2.30	2.30	2.30	2.30	3.80	4.25	4.25	4.25
Illinois	. . .	. . .	1.40	2.10	2.30	2.30	2.30	3.35	3.80	4.25	4.25	4.25
Indiana	1.15	1.25	1.25	1.25	2.00	2.00	2.00	2.00	3.35	3.35	3.35	3.35
Iowa	. . .	. . .	. . .	. . .	. . .	. . .	. . .	. . .	4.25	4.65	4.65	4.65
Kansas	.65-.75 (b)	.65-.75 (b)	.65-.75 (b)	1.60	1.60	1.60	1.60	1.60	2.65	2.65	2.65	2.65
Kentucky	. . .	. . .	. . .	. . .	2.00	2.15	2.15	3.35	3.80	4.25	4.25	4.25
Louisiana	. . .	. . .	. . .	. . .	. . .	. . .	. . .	. . .	. . .	. . .	. . .	. . .
Maine	1.40	1.60	1.40-1.80	2.30	2.90	3.10	3.35	3.65	3.85	4.25	4.25	4.25
Maryland	1.00 & 1.15	1.30	1.60	2.20 & 2.30	2.90	3.10	3.35	3.35	3.80	4.25	4.25	4.25
Massachusetts	1.60	1.60	1.75	2.10	2.90	3.10	3.35	3.65	3.75	4.25	4.25	4.25
Michigan	1.25	1.25	1.60	2.20	2.90	3.10	3.35	3.35	3.35	3.35	3.35	3.35
Minnesota	.70-1.15 (b)	.70-1.15 (b)	.75-1.60	1.80	2.30	2.90	3.10	3.55 & 3.50 (d)	4.25 (e)	4.25 (e)	4.25 (e)	4.25 (e)
Mississippi	. . .	. . .	. . .	. . .	. . .	. . .	. . .	. . .	. . .	. . .	. . .	. . .
Missouri	. . .	. . .	. . .	. . .	. . .	. . .	. . .	. . .	3.80	4.25	4.25	4.25
Montana	1.00	1.00	1.60	1.80	2.00	2.00	2.00	3.35	3.80	4.25 (e)	4.25 (e)	4.25 (e)
Nebraska	1.25	1.30	1.00	1.60	1.60	1.60	1.60	3.35	3.35	4.25	4.25	4.25
Nevada	1.40	1.45-1.60	1.60	2.20 & 2.30	2.75	2.75	2.75	3.55	3.80	4.25	4.25	4.25
New Hampshire	1.40	1.60	1.60	2.20-2.30	2.90	3.10	3.35	3.55	3.85	4.25	4.25	4.25
New Jersey	. . .	1.50	1.50	2.20	2.50	3.10	3.35	3.35	3.80	5.05	5.05	5.05
New Mexico	1.15-1.40	1.30-1.60	1.30-1.60	2.00	2.30	2.65	2.90	3.35	3.35	3.35	3.35	4.25
New York	1.60	1.60	1.85	2.30	2.90	3.10	3.35	3.35	3.80	4.25	4.25	4.25
North Carolina	1.00	1.25	1.45	2.00	2.50	2.75	2.90	3.35	3.35	3.80	4.25	4.25
North Dakota	1.00-1.25	1.00-1.45	1.00-1.45	2.00-2.20	2.10-2.30	2.60-3.10	2.80-3.10	2.80-3.10	3.40	4.25	4.25	4.25
Ohio	.75-1.25 (b)	.75-1.25 (b)	.75-1.25 (b)	1.60	2.30	2.30	2.30	2.30	3.80 (e)	4.25 (e)	4.25 (e)	4.25 (e)
Oklahoma	1.00	1.00	1.40	1.80	2.00	2.00	3.10	3.35	3.80 (e)	4.25 (e)	4.25 (e)	4.25 (e)
Oregon	1.25	1.25	1.25	2.30	2.30	2.90	3.10	3.35	4.75	4.75	4.75	4.75
Pennsylvania	1.15	1.30	1.60	2.20	2.90	3.10	3.35	3.35	3.80	4.25	4.25	4.25
Rhode Island	1.40	1.60	1.60	2.30	2.30	2.65	2.90	3.65	4.25	4.45	4.45	4.45
South Carolina	. . .	. . .	. . .	. . .	. . .	. . .	. . .	. . .	. . .	. . .	. . .	. . .

See footnotes at end of table.

CHANGES IN BASIC MINIMUM WAGE—Continued

State or other jurisdiction	1968 (a)	1970 (a)	1972	1976 (a)	1979	1980	1981	1988	1991	1992	1993	1994
South Dakota	17.00-20.00/wk.	1.00	1.00	2.00	2.30	2.30	2.30	2.80	3.80	4.25	4.25	4.25
Tennessee	...	...	...	...	...	...	...	...	...	...	...	...
Texas	...	...	...	...	...	...	...	3.35	3.35	3.35	3.35	3.35
Utah	1.00-1.15 (b)	1.00-1.15 (b)	1.20-1.35 (b)	1.55-1.70 (b)	2.20-2.45 (b)	2.35-2.60 (b)	2.50-2.75 (b)	2.50-2.75 (b)	3.80	4.25	4.25	4.25
Vermont	1.40	1.60	1.60	2.30	2.90	3.10	3.35	3.55	3.85	4.25	4.25	4.25
Virginia	1.60	1.60	1.60	2.00	2.35	2.35	2.65	2.65	2.65	3.65	4.25	4.25
Washington	1.00	1.00	1.20	2.20-2.30	2.30	2.30	2.30	2.30	4.25	4.25	4.25	4.90
West Virginia	1.25 (b)	1.30 (b)	1.45 (b)	2.00	2.20	2.20	2.75	3.35	3.35	3.80	4.25	4.25
Wisconsin	1.20	1.30	1.50	2.10	2.80	3.00	3.25	3.35	3.80	3.80	4.25	4.25
Wyoming	...	...	...	1.60	1.60	1.60	1.60	1.60	1.60	1.60	1.60	1.60
Dist. of Columbia	1.25-1.40	1.60-2.00	1.60-2.25	2.25-2.75	2.46-3.00	2.50-3.50	2.50-3.75	3.50-4.85	3.70-4.85	3.90-5.45	3.90-5.45	4.25
Guam	1.25	1.60	1.90	2.30	2.90	3.10	3.35	3.35	3.80	4.25	4.25	5.25 (f)
Puerto Rico	.43-1.60	.43-1.60	.65-1.60	.76-2.50	1.20-2.50	1.20-2.50	1.20-3.10	1.20-3.35	1.20-4.25 (f)	1.20-4.25 (f)	1.20-4.25 (g)	1.20-4.25 (g)
U.S. Virgin Islands	NA	NA	NA	NA	2.90	3.10	3.35	3.35	4.65 (c,e)	4.65 (c,e)	4.65 (c,e)	4.65 (c,e)

Source: U.S. Department of Labor, Division of State Standards Programs, Wage and Hour Division, Employment Standards Administration.

Note: Rates are for January 1 of each year, except 1968 and 1972, which show rates as of February. A range of rates, as in Puerto Rico, reflects rates which differ by industry, occupation or other factor, as established under a wage-board type law.

Key:
... — Not applicable
N.A. — Not available

(a) Under the Federal Fair Labor Standards Act (FLSA), the two rates shown in 1968, 1970 and 1976 reflect the former multiple-track minimum wage system in effect from 1961 to 1978. The lower rate applied to newly covered persons brought under the act by amendments, whose rates were gradually phased in. A similar dual-track minimum wage system was also in effect in certain years under the laws in Connecticut, Maryland and Nevada.

(b) For the years indicated, the laws in Arizona, Arkansas, California, Colorado, Kentucky, Minnesota, Ohio, Utah and Wisconsin applied only to women and minors.

(c) A scheduled future increase will raise the minimum rate in Arkansas to $4.25 on July 1, 1994. In the U.S. Virgin Islands, implementation of an indexed rate, which was to have started January 1, 1991, has been delayed.

(d) For the years 1988-1990, Minnesota had a two-tier wage schedule with the higher rate applicable to employers covered by the FLSA and the lower rate to employers not covered by the FLSA.

(e) Minnesota sets a lower rate for enterprises with annual receipts of less than $362,500 ($4.00, January 1, 1991 - January 1, 1994); Montana sets a lower rate for businesses with gross annual sales of $110,000 or less ($4.00 January 1, 1992 - January 1, 1994); Ohio sets a lower rate for employers with gross annual sales from $150,000 to $500,000 ($3.35, January 1, 1991 - January 1, 1994) and for employers with gross annual sales under $150,000 ($2.50, January 1,1991 and $2.80 January 1, 1992 - January 1, 1994); Oklahoma sets a lower rate for employers of less than 10 full-time employees at any one location and for those with annual gross sales of less than $100,000 ($2.00, January 1, 1991 - January 1, 1994); and the U.S. Virgin Islands sets a lower rate for businesses with gross annual receipts of less than $150,000 ($4.30, January 1, 1991 - January 1, 1994).

(f) In the District of Columbia wage orders were replaced by a statutory minimum wage on October 1, 1993. A $5.45 minimum rate remained in effect for the laundry and dry cleaning industry as the result of a grandfather clause.

(g) In Puerto Rico, separate minimum rates are in effect for almost 350 non-farm occupations by industry Mandatory Decrees. Rates higher than those in the range listed are in effect in a few specific occupations.

Table 8.21
STATUS OF APPROVED STATE PLANS DEVELOPED IN ACCORDANCE WITH THE FEDERAL OCCUPATIONAL SAFETY AND HEALTH ACT
(As of February 1994)

State or other jurisdiction	Status of state plan						
	Operational status agreement (a)	Different standards (b)	7(c)(l) On-site consultation agreement (c)	On-shore maritime coverage	Date of initial approval	Date certified (d)	Date of 18(e) final approval (e)
Alaska...............	...	★	★	...	07/31/73	09/09/77	09/28/84
Arizona.............	...	...	...	...	10/29/74	09/18/81	06/20/85
California..........	★	★	★	★	04/24/73	08/12/77	...
Connecticut (f)	...	...	★	...	10/02/73	08/19/86	...
Hawaii.............	...	★	★	...	12/28/73	04/26/78	04/30/84
Indiana	...	...	...	...	02/25/74	09/24/81	09/26/86
Iowa	...	...	★	...	07/12/73	09/14/76	07/02/85
Kentucky	...	...	...	...	07/23/73	02/08/80	06/13/85
Maryland	...	...	★	...	06/28/73	02/15/80	07/18/85
Michigan	★	★	★	...	09/24/73	01/16/81	...
Minnesota	...	...	★	★	05/29/73	09/28/76	07/30/85
Nevada	★	...	...	...	12/04/73	08/13/81	...
New Mexico.........	★	...	...	...	12/04/75	12/04/84	...
New York (f)........	...	...	★	...	06/01/84	...	...
North Carolina	★	...	★	...	01/26/73	09/29/76	...
Oregon	★	★	★	★	12/22/72	09/15/82	...
South Carolina	...	...	★	...	11/30/72	07/28/76	12/15/87
Tennessee...........	...	...	★	...	06/28/73	05/03/78	07/22/85
Utah	...	...	★	...	01/04/73	11/11/76	07/16/85
Vermont	★	...	★	★	10/01/73	03/04/77	...
Virginia.............	...	...	★	...	09/23/76	08/15/84	11/30/88
Washington	★	★	...	★	01/19/73	01/26/82	...
Wyoming	...	...	★	...	04/25/74	12/18/80	06/27/85
Puerto Rico	★	...	...	...	08/15/77	09/07/82	...
U.S. Virgin Islands	...	...	...	...	08/31/73	09/22/81	04/17/84

Source: U.S. Department of Labor, Directorate of Federal-State Operations, Office of State Programs, Occupational Safety and Health Administration.

Key:
★ — Yes
... — No
(a) Concurrent federal jurisdiction suspended.

(b) Standards frequently not identical to the federal.
(c) On-site consultation is available in all states either through a 7(c)(1) Agreement or under a State Plan.
(d) Developmental steps satisfactorily completed.
(e) Concurrent federal jurisdiction relinquished (supersedes Operational Status Agreement).
(f) Plan covers only state and local government employees.

State Health-Care Reform Initiatives

States have developed or implemented various health-care reforms in an effort to ease the crisis and be prepared for national reform plans.

by Elizabeth Buerger

In the past few years, several plans have been introduced on the federal level to deal with the ever-worsening health-care crisis in the United States. However, little has been done to slow the rising costs of health care that leave millions of people uninsured. As debate heats up between President Clinton's proposal for national reform and a number of other plans on the table, states continue to explore different options and experiment with new ideas for state-based reforms. These states are unwilling to wait for what likely will be a lengthy process toward national reform, but recognize the importance of flexibility for the forthcoming national plan.

These state-based plans have taken a variety of forms. Some states have looked first to employers to offer health-care coverage to workers either by mandate or by encouraging them to do so voluntarily. Options for those lacking access to employer-based insurance include expanding Medicaid or other programs for low-income residents. Some states, reluctant to commit to the goal of universal access, have looked to insurance reform to expand access and control costs. Other cost containment measures in state reform plans include provision of services in managed-care settings, group purchasing, community rating requirements, global budgeting, regulation of insurance rates and provider fees, utilization review, and development of uniform claim forms.

States are also in various stages of development with their plans. Some are still in the planning stages while others have implemented or are beginning to implement their plans. Taken together, the state-based reform efforts throughout the nation clearly reflect the importance and priority states place on reforming the health-care delivery system.

Hawaii began to reform its health-care system through the Prepaid Health Care Act of 1974, which requires all employers to provide insurance for their employees. In 1989, the state created the State Health Insurance Program (SHIP) to insure those not covered by Medicaid or the Prepaid Health Care Act. As a result, Hawaii has the lowest percentage of uninsured citizens in the country. The federal government has granted the state's waiver request to begin a new program that involves consolidating three public health assistance programs Medicaid AFDC, SHIP and General Assistance into one comprehensive health-care program. Through the creation of this single purchasing pool, with services delivered in a managed-care setting, the state hopes to ensure that all citizens will continue to have access to quality care at an affordable price. Governor John D. Waihee views this plan as a "second generation health-care initiative" that, in combination with the Prepaid Health Care Act, will reinforce Hawaii's place as a leader in health-care reform.

Oregon spent four years developing its health-care reform package beginning with the passage of the Basic Health Services Act in 1989. The central piece of this package was a Medicaid expansion proposal that involved a controversial plan to ration health-care services. The Health Services Commission developed a prioritized list of conditions and treatments, and the Legislature then determined the number of services it could afford to cover. Medicaid would not pay for services below that level. After a lengthy battle to gain federal

---

Elizabeth Buerger is a research assistant with the States Information Center of The Council of State Governments.

Table A
HEALTH CARE REFORM IN SELECTED STATES: SUMMARIES OF LEGISLATION

FLORIDA

Legal references: Health Care Reform Act of 1992, Ch. 92-33; Health Care and Insurance Reform Act of 1993, Ch. 93-129, Laws of Florida.

Year(s) of enactment: 1992, 1993

Highlights of legislation: Legislation enacted in 1992 created the Agency for Health Care Administration to consolidate state health functions into a single agency and write the Florida Health Plan to ensure voluntary universal access to health care by December 1994.

The 1993 enactment focused on reaching universal access — not through uniform benefit packages for everyone or required employer participation, but by filling in the gaps for the underserved or uninsured (e.g., persons in rural areas, employees of small businesses, and low-income persons ineligible for Medicaid.

Key features of the 1992 and 1993 health care reform enactments include: creation of a rural health network program; creation of MedAccess, a state health insurance program for the uninsured; a requirement that all insurers and health maintenance organizations offer a basic health benefit plan to small employers; creation of voluntary community health alliances to provide health purchasing pools for small employers; and various cost containment and quality assurance provisions.

HAWAII

Legal references: Prepaid Health Care Act, Ch. 393, Hawaii Revised Statutes; State Health Insurance Program, Ch. 421N, Hawaii Revised Statutes.

Year(s) of enactment: 1974, 1989

Highlights of legislation: Since 1974, the Prepaid Health Care Act has been the foundation for providing near-universal health care coverage for Hawaii residents. The legislation requires all employers to provide full-time employees (20 hours per week or more) with health coverage through regular insurance, self-insurance, or health maintenance plans. The act exempts state and local governments, the self-employed, workers on commission, employers of seasonal workers, and those covered under plans negotiated under collective bargaining agreements.

The 1989 legislation created the State Health Insurance Program (SHIP) to offer limited and subsidized health care benefits focusing on preventive and primary care to those not covered by employers.

[In 1993, Hawaii received a federal waiver for QUEST, a project to combine Medicaid, the State Health Insurance Program, and the state's general assistance program into a single managed care program.]

MINNESOTA

Legal references: HealthRight Law (MinnesotaCare), Ch. 549, 1992 Legislative Session Laws; Ch. 345, 1993 Legislative Session Laws.

Year(s) of enactment: 1992, 1993

Highlights of legislation: The 1992 MinnesotaCare legislation expanded an existing state-funded insurance program for children into a new state health insurance program for low-income, uninsured families not covered by Medicaid or general assistance medical care. The act also made individual and small employer health insurance reforms, created a large health insurance purchasing pool for small employers, established an office of rural health to recruit rural providers and improve rural health care, authorized the self-employed to deduct 100 percent of their health care premiums from state income taxes, and created a structure for cost containment and health planning.

The 1993 legislation called for a comprehensive plan leading to universal health coverage by 1997, and authorized the replacement of the existing health care delivery system with Integrated Service Networks (provider networks formed by health maintenance organizations, insurers, hospital providers, local governments, purchasers, or a combination of these groups) and a regulated all-payer system. It also set short-term limits on health care spending, and statutory revenue and spending limits for the Networks and for providers and insurers outside that system.

OREGON

Legal references: Oregon Health Plan, SB 27 of 1989 session, SB 935 of 1989 session, SB 534 of 1989 session, SB 1076 of 1991 session, SB 1077 of 1991 session, SB 44 of 1991 session, SB 5530 of 1993 session [all incorporated into Oregon Revised Statutes, 316.096-317.113, 414.025-414.750, 442.580-442.586, 653.705-653.791, 735.600-735.650, and 743.730-743.745].

Additional enactments: SB 47, SB 757, SB 989 (1993)

Year(s) of enactment: 1989, 1991, 1993

continued on page 566

OREGON (continued)

Highlights of legislation: The legislation adopted from 1989 to 1993 constitutes the Oregon Health Plan. The overall plan is designed to achieve universal access to health care by an expanded Medicaid program (whereby the state assumes health care responsibility for all residents below the federal poverty line); a "play or pay" mandate for employers to either provide health benefits to their employees or pay into a special state insurance fund; and a requirement that small business insurance carriers must offer small businesses a benefit package similar to the state's Medicaid program.

The most publicized portion of Oregon's plan pertained to the "rationing" or cost containment of Medicaid benefits. The act calls for the Oregon Health Services to create and update a prioritized list of health services. The state legislature, which cannot change the order of the items on the list, must, through the appropriations process, determine how far down the priority list money will be available to fund Medicaid services.

Implementation was pending approval of a Medicaid waiver by the Health Care Financing Administration, the U.S. Office of Management and Budget, and the U.S. Secretary of Health and Human Services. In March 1993, the Clinton administration approved the waiver, thus permitting the state to proceed. In doing so, however, it required the state to revise its priority ranking of services to eliminate the possibility of bias against disabled persons, in accordance with the Americans with Disabilities Act.

VERMONT

Legal references: Vermont Health Care Reform Act of 1992, H. 733, Act No. 160.

Year(s) of enactment: 1992

Highlights of legislation: The 1992 legislation created the Vermont Health Care Authority, requiring it to submit both a single-payer and multi-payer plan for universal health care access. The enactment also required the Health Care Board to adopt a targeted budget for all sectors of health care in the state and to design a unified health care data base.

Other key features include: expansion of a state health program for low-income children, establishment of malpractice reforms, establishment of a health insurance purchasing pool for state and municipal governments, and various reforms for coverage of individuals previously covered by insurers who have left the market.

WASHINGTON

Legal references: Washington Health Services Act of 1993 (E2SSB 5304 and related provisions of ESB 5076, ESHB 1855, SHB 1784 and SHB 1721).

Year(s) of enactment: 1993

Highlights of legislation: The 1993 legislation calls for a phase-in of universal access to health care over a six-year period, beginning in 1993. By 1999, every Washington state resident must purchase a Uniform Benefit Package. Employers must offer employees and dependents a choice of three certified health plans and pay 50 percent of the premiums of the lowest cost package for full-time employees and a pro-rated share for part-time employees. The Washington Health Services Commission is required to determine a new set of government regulations for the state's private health insurance and delivery systems.

Other provisions of the enactment include: a requirement that the courts set up a voluntary review of malpractice claims by medical experts before lawsuits are filed; a requirement that the University of Washington prepare a primary care shortage plan to increase residencies to 50 percent by the year 2000; and a directive to the Health Services Commission to study employer-funded medical savings accounts and to submit a plan to integrate long-term health care into the new health reform system by 1999.

Sources: Pioneers in State Health Care Reform: Summaries of Innovative State Legislation, Western Legislative Conference Health Committee, The Council of State Governments, April 1994. Oregon information also taken from "Prioritization of Health Care Act," entry (pp. 12-23) in *Suggested State Legislation 1994,* vol. 53, produced by The Council of State Governments.

Note: Additional information on recent state activity in health care reform may be found in *Health Care Reform Initiatives in the States: A Survey of The Council of State Governments'* States Information Center (3560 Iron Works Pike, P.O. Box 11910, Lexington, Ky. 40578-1910, 606-244-8000).

Suggested State Legislation volumes 51-53 also include summaries of recent state legislative activity in the health care arena: *Access to Health Care (Note),* vol. 51, pp. 1-5; *Health Care Legislation (Note),* vol. 52, pp. 1-5; and *Health Insurance Reform Legislation (Note),* vol. 53, pp. 1-11.

approval, the necessary waivers were granted in March 1993. With the approval of the financing plan in August 1993, Oregon has moved forward with implementation. Still being challenged is the employer mandate included in the 1989 legislation. Debate on this mandate, which would expand health-care coverage to all Oregonians by 1998, rages on.

In the fall of 1992, Minnesota began implementing the MinnesotaCare program. This program extends the eligibility of the existing Children's Health Plan and increases the benefits available. The plan provides for phased-in eligibility for more children and adults. By 1994 all Minnesotans who meet the income requirements will be eligible. Those with incomes exceeding 275 percent of the federal poverty level will be covered through their employers' plans. In 1993, the Legislature enhanced the MinnesotaCare benefits package and introduced the creation of Integrated Services Networks, similar to health maintenance organizations, that would provide services for a fixed price per person.

Florida's road toward comprehensive health-care reform began with the passage of the Health Care Reform Act of 1992. The state is relying on employers to voluntarily offer insurance to their employees to achieve the goal of universal access by December 1994. The Health Care and Insurance Reform Act of 1993 put in place a managed-competition system of Community Health Care Purchasing Alliances (CHPA). The 11 regional CHPAs will provide purchasing services and information on prices, usage and quality to members. Membership will be open to, but optional for, small businesses, the state on behalf of state employees and their dependents, participants in the new MedAccess program, and Medicaid recipients. A Medicaid expansion plan also has been proposed that would require a waiver from the federal government. The Florida Agency for Health Care Administration and the alliance boards expect alliance coverage to begin May 1, 1994.

In April 1993, Tennessee Governor Ned McWherter proposed that the state withdraw from Medicaid and replace it with a state program to be called TennCare. This new program would bring the state's Medicaid recipients together with approximately 500,000 eligible uninsured residents into one health insurance program. The plan is based on the state employees' managed-care health plan and includes many cost containment measures. Participants with incomes under 200 percent of the federal poverty level will be charged on a sliding fee scale based on their ability to pay. Those with incomes below the federal poverty level will receive care free of charge. Delivery of services in a managed-care setting is aimed at achieving the proposal's cost containment goals. The Clinton administration approved the waivers to implement the program on November 18, 1993, and program enrollment began in January 1994.

In May 1993, Governor Mike Lowry signed the Washington Health Services Act. This plan has been cited as a model for national reform as it contains many elements considered by the national task force, including universal coverage, managed care and financing through sin taxes such as taxes on alcohol and tobacco. Washington's plan relies on employers to provide insurance for their employees and requires them to pay at least 50 percent of the premium for full-time workers. The legislation also establishes regional Health Insurance Purchasing Cooperatives that will offer certified health plans to members, establish a rating system and collect members' premiums. The act also includes an expansion of the state's programs for low-income residents, the Basic Health Plan and Medicaid, to cover an additional 195,000 individuals.

In Vermont and Colorado, legislation set in motion extensive studies of health-care plans. In Vermont, the Health Care Authority created by the 1992 reform legislation developed two plans, a single-payer plan and a regulated multi-payer plan, to be considered by the Legislature. The report outlining these plans and other details of reform was released November 1, 1993. Both plans include provisions for universal coverage, portability of coverage, uniform benefits, control of capital expenditures and a binding cap on overall spending. In Colorado, a lengthy study yielded the ColoradoCare feasibility report in September 1993.

This report recommended the creation of regional health purchasing pools to negotiate with insurance companies for the best rates. Employers no longer would select plans for employees who would have a number of choices of health-care plans. Many alternatives for implementation were to be considered, however, Governor Roy Romer has delayed further debate in order to structure state reform according to whatever plan is adopted at the federal level. Efforts continue toward cost containment.

New Jersey's reform was brought on by a court ruling that found that the state's financing of uncompensated hospital care violated federal law. The result was a legislative package of health insurance reforms that included a new funding source for uncompensated care and restructured individual and small group insurance. The legislation established community rating and open enrollment requirements and established five standard benefit packages that all carriers must offer.

Maryland's reform effort does not attempt to provide universal coverage. The focus is on providing health-care coverage for the many uninsured residents employed by small businesses. In the future, the reforms will be extended to the general market. The reform legislation also regulates practitioner fees and a new formula for practitioner reimbursement.

Both New York and California have had many health-reform proposals developed for consideration, but neither has enacted a comprehensive plan. In New York, a proposed plan for a single, publicly financed health-care delivery system failed to pass both houses of the Legislature in 1992, and it is unlikely that it will be considered further. In California, two proposals for health-care reform received national attention. Proposition 166, developed by the California Medical Association, went to the voters in November 1992 and was defeated. "California Health Care in the 21st Century," the plan sponsored by state Insurance Commissioner John Garamendi was defeated as S.B. 6 in the Legislature. While smaller scale programs have been successful in both states, budget concerns and a lack of consensus on the direction reform should take have precluded extensive change of the states' health-care systems.

While these are just some of the states that have developed or are developing health-care reform plans across the country, they do provide insight into the stages of the reform process. Virtually every state has looked at some type of reform in the early 1990s. The involvement of many stakeholders contributes to the development of a comprehensive plan, from the initial period of studying reform and analyzing options to the ongoing implementation. States continue to work toward reform to contain out-of-control costs that strain state budgets and in an effort to be prepared for whatever form the national reform plan takes.

Table 8.22
1991 EXPENDITURES AND AVERAGE ANNUAL GROWTH IN EXPENDITURES, 1980-91, FOR HOSPITAL CARE, PHYSICIAN SERVICES AND PRESCRIPTION DRUG PURCHASES IN RETAIL OUTLETS BY STATE

State	1991 Expenditures (millions of dollars)				Percent of Average Annual Growth: 1980-91			
	Total (a)	Hospital care	Physician services	Prescription drugs	Total (b)	Hospital care	Physician services	Prescription drugs
Alabama	$ 7,494	$ 4,521	$ 2,296	$ 677	10.7	10.0	12.4	10.1
Alaska	1,027	659	312	56	11.4	11.4	11.3	12.0
Arizona	6,420	3,615	2,321	483	11.9	11.5	12.3	13.3
Arkansas	3,968	2,359	1,241	368	10.9	11.1	11.5	8.3
California	58,141	31,128	23,108	3,904	10.3	9.4	11.6	10.5
Colorado	6,100	3,614	2,122	364	10.9	10.4	12.1	10.0
Connecticut	6,844	4,089	2,236	520	11.1	10.3	12.9	10.5
Delaware	1,379	800	488	91	12.0	10.8	14.2	12.4
Florida	27,047	15,210	9,881	1,956	12.5	12.0	13.3	12.5
Georgia	12,476	7,603	3,902	971	12.5	12.2	13.3	11.5
Hawaii	2,144	1,287	719	137	11.4	12.3	10.0	10.9
Idaho	1,282	762	397	123	10.5	11.0	9.9	9.8
Illinois	21,234	13,792	5,731	1,711	8.2	7.5	9.4	10.7
Indiana	9,749	6,024	2,890	835	10.3	9.9	11.1	9.6
Iowa	4,631	2,933	1,294	404	8.9	8.7	9.3	9.0
Kansas	4,307	2,545	1,404	358	9.0	8.1	10.6	9.8
Kentucky	6,362	3,908	1,814	639	11.0	11.1	11.3	10.0
Louisiana	8,335	5,277	2,400	658	10.7	10.6	11.3	9.0
Maine	1,966	1,257	547	162	10.6	9.6	13.1	11.0
Maryland	9,323	5,210	3,284	829	10.6	8.9	13.3	12.6
Massachusetts	14,402	9,097	4,244	1,061	10.3	8.7	14.3	12.5
Michigan	17,383	10,663	5,141	1,578	8.6	8.2	8.7	10.5
Minnesota	8,726	4,607	3,571	548	10.5	9.3	12.6	10.0
Mississippi	3,732	2,425	923	384	9.8	9.9	9.9	9.5
Missouri	10,226	6,660	2,815	751	9.7	9.2	11.1	9.6
Montana	1,164	763	314	87	9.4	10.1	7.8	9.8
Nebraska	2,794	1,789	779	227	9.5	9.2	9.9	9.9
Nevada	2,274	1,195	945	135	12.4	10.8	14.7	12.6
New Hampshire	1,917	1,129	641	146	13.4	12.4	15.7	12.8
New Jersey	14,647	8,829	4,569	1,249	11.3	11.2	11.6	11.4
New Mexico	2,448	1,570	699	179	12.3	12.1	12.9	12.0
New York	38,533	25,345	10,611	2,577	10.1	9.3	12.0	11.0
North Carolina	10,987	6,795	3,200	992	12.0	12.0	12.6	10.2
North Dakota	1,322	796	442	84	9.6	8.8	11.0	10.5
Ohio	20,335	12,628	6,094	1,613	9.4	9.2	9.9	9.3
Oklahoma	4,929	3,016	1,471	442	9.1	9.0	9.5	8.8
Oregon	4,597	2,562	1,738	297	9.8	9.7	10.2	8.2
Pennsylvania	25,178	16,622	6,680	1,876	10.3	9.7	11.8	10.7
Rhode Island	1,924	1,215	543	166	9.7	8.8	11.4	11.8
South Carolina	5,547	3,614	1,455	479	12.4	12.7	12.4	10.9
South Dakota	1,221	799	342	80	10.6	10.3	11.5	9.3
Tennessee	9,948	6,239	2,865	844	11.0	10.8	11.7	10.3
Texas	30,222	18,086	9,754	2,382	11.2	11.4	11.3	9.8
Utah	2,539	1,510	822	207	11.7	11.6	11.6	13.0
Vermont	824	502	243	79	11.2	10.2	13.4	12.4
Virginia	10,825	6,407	3,464	955	11.6	10.8	13.1	12.0
Washington	8,486	4,581	3,336	568	11.7	11.4	12.6	9.4
West Virginia	3,299	2,000	900	329	8.9	8.4	9.6	10.0
Wisconsin	8,733	4,981	3,077	675	9.8	8.9	11.3	10.8
Wyoming	598	394	155	49	8.9	9.4	8.2	7.2
Dist. of Columbia	3,400	2,641	666	93	9.5	9.4	9.8	10.3

Source: Health Care Financing Administration, Office of the Actuary, estimates prepared by the Office of National Health Statistics.
(a) Sum of expenditures for hospital care, physician services, and retail purchases of prescription drugs approximately 70 percent of U.S. personal health care expenditures.

(b) Growth in total equals growth in the sum of expenditures for hospital care, physician services, and retail purchases of prescription drugs.

Table 8.23
TOTAL ROAD AND STREET MILEAGE: 1992
(Classified by jurisdiction)

State or other jurisdiction	Rural mileage				Urban mileage			Total rural and urban mileage
	Under state control	Under local control (a)	Under federal control (b)	Total rural roads	Under state control	Under local control (a)	Total urban mileage	
United States	696,589	2,238,941	181,025	3,116,555	103,648	680,125	785,160	3,901,715
Alabama	9,137	62,765	933	72,835	1,883	17,475	19,366	92,201
Alaska	5,401	3,997	2,588	11,986	448	1,200	1,648	13,634
Arizona	5,663	20,751	14,432	40,846	467	14,627	15,123	55,969
Arkansas	14,967	52,876	1,628	69,471	1,241	6,450	7,691	77,162
California	14,721	55,154	18,517	88,392	3,729	76,250	79,986	168,378
Colorado	8,222	49,921	7,123	65,266	1,022	11,755	12,777	78,043
Connecticut	2,137	6,643	4	8,784	1,835	9,661	11,496	20,280
Delaware	3,434	232	3	3,669	1,453	402	1,855	5,524
Florida	7,592	54,305	106	62,003	4,278	44,359	48,637	110,640
Georgia	14,889	68,693	1,061	84,643	2,949	23,162	26,147	110,790
Hawaii	767	1,469	71	2,307	260	1,505	1,799	4,106
Idaho	4,854	27,311	23,109	55,274	268	3,034	3,314	58,588
Illinois	13,041	90,938	157	104,136	4,328	27,923	32,266	136,402
Indiana (c)	9,623	63,322	. . .	72,945	1,671	17,438	19,109	92,054
Iowa	9,125	94,249	116	103,490	980	8,111	9,096	112,586
Kansas	10,007	114,140	. . .	124,147	665	8,843	9,508	133,655
Kentucky	25,291	36,161	305	61,757	2,293	7,529	10,008	71,765
Louisiana	14,868	30,816	626	46,310	1,779	10,540	12,319	58,629
Maine	7,777	12,059	166	20,002	768	1,707	2,479	22,481
Maryland	3,764	11,795	39	15,598	1,659	11,519	13,574	29,172
Massachusetts	1,729	11,490	87	13,306	1,834	19,153	21,017	34,323
Michigan	7,660	81,848	. . .	89,508	1,972	26,040	28,012	117,520
Minnesota	12,155	101,317	1,627	115,099	1,199	13,324	14,523	129,622
Mississippi	9,639	54,511	757	64,907	829	7,037	7,888	72,795
Missouri	30,737	74,726	563	106,026	1,620	13,778	15,398	121,424
Montana	8,038	45,723	14,248	68,009	162	2,186	2,348	70,357
Nebraska (c)	9,927	77,592	137	87,656	329	4,701	5,030	92,686
Nevada	4,796	22,516	13,832	41,144	502	4,011	4,513	45,657
New Hampshire	3,734	8,603	136	12,473	293	2,147	2,440	14,913
New Jersey	1,592	10,168	23	11,783	1,655	20,830	22,503	34,286
New Mexico	11,050	39,867	4,450	55,367	586	5,242	5,828	61,195
New York	11,724	60,899	. . .	72,623	4,680	34,383	39,063	111,686
North Carolina	68,643	3,712	1,776	74,131	9,231	11,970	21,451	95,582
North Dakota	7,193	76,799	831	84,823	206	1,619	1,825	86,648
Ohio	16,593	65,633	29	82,255	3,934	27,631	31,568	113,823
Oklahoma	12,092	87,973	86	100,151	957	11,322	12,281	112,432
Oregon	10,490	33,418	41,835	85,743	783	8,676	9,494	95,237
Pennsylvania	36,324	48,649	992	85,965	8,097	22,726	30,823	116,788
Rhode Island	365	1,158	. . .	1,523	771	3,826	4,597	6,120
South Carolina	34,736	18,274	602	53,612	6,902	3,615	10,517	64,129
South Dakota	7,738	71,735	1,968	81,441	166	1,691	1,858	83,299
Tennessee	12,117	56,141	572	68,830	2,399	13,915	16,314	85,144
Texas	68,861	147,360	953	217,174	7,982	68,161	76,143	293,317
Utah	5,043	22,421	9,722	37,186	756	5,321	6,084	43,270
Vermont	2,664	10,096	71	12,831	171	1,134	1,314	14,145
Virginia	50,084	949	1,815	52,848	6,357	9,013	15,581	68,429
Washington	17,767	37,417	7,204	62,388	1,113	15,912	17,025	79,413
West Virginia	30,537	642	650	31,829	1,321	1,769	3,090	34,919
Wisconsin	11,025	83,543	962	95,530	1,420	13,421	14,841	110,371
Wyoming	6,256	26,164	4,113	36,533	405	2,081	2,489	39,022
Dist. of Columbia . . .	. . .	. . .	. . .	. . .	1,040	. . .	1,104	1,104

Source: U.S. Department of Transportation, Federal Highway Administration. Compiled for calendar year ending December 31, 1992, from reports of state authorities.

Key:

. . . — Not applicable

(a) Includes mileage not identified by administrative authority.
(b) Mileage in federal parks, forests, and reservations that are not a part of the state and local highway systems.
(c) 1991 base data factored to 1992 levels (1992 base data not available).

Table 8.24
STATE RECEIPTS FOR HIGHWAYS: 1992
(In thousands of dollars)

State or other jurisdiction	State highway user tax revenues	Road and crossing tolls (a)	Other state imposts, general fund revenues	Miscellaneous income	Federal funds Federal highway administration	Federal funds Other agencies	Transfers from local governments	Bond proceeds (b)	Total receipts
United States	30,809,268	2,970,050	2,989,856	2,583,068	15,194,795	392,082	685,040	5,973,529	61,597,688
Alabama	561,066	. . .	3,777	21,612	275,246	2,571	. . .	. . .	864,272
Alaska	42,708	17,700	103,787	25,100	208,110	764	. . .	. . .	398,169
Arizona	541,697	. . .	99,087	46,491	173,265	9,004	134,434	264,860	1,268,838
Arkansas	425,910	. . .	2,255	14,305	174,590	2,738	5,239	. . .	625,037
California	3,268,992	108,595	179,575	310,485	1,574,646	35,971	104,839	. . .	5,583,103
Colorado	489,334	. . .	16	6,976	242,537	3,415	. . .	. . .	742,278
Connecticut	400,487	206	111,874	89,908	373,990	1,778	1,294	273,258	1,252,795
Delaware	102,256	66,820	92,503	14,649	57,495	11,717	. . .	173,360	518,800
Florida	1,284,409	251,691	148,854	123,980	482,116	14,738	21,480	143,226	2,470,494
Georgia	389,300	1,319	422,344	44,414	342,162	2,983	14,636	169,256	1,386,414
Hawaii	121,817	. . .	52,600	20,985	188,422	665	. . .	. . .	384,489
Idaho	205,691	. . .	. . .	. . .	98,279	8,867	2,749	. . .	315,586
Illinois	1,391,171	253,844	33,562	30,276	515,389	5,169	19,336	601,361	2,850,108
Indiana	724,503	57,091	3,705	105,386	409,587	2,177	17,616	74,252	1,394,317
Iowa	550,688	. . .	129,923	28,628	265,223	1,799	2,063	. . .	978,324
Kansas	354,379	42,257	171,368	39,384	149,992	4,013	14,529	376,801	1,152,723
Kentucky	756,978	13,796	35,519	86,764	193,604	2,454	3,235	. . .	1,092,350
Louisiana	570,336	22,683	. . .	32,024	313,050	3,870	. . .	94,445	1,036,408
Maine	182,927	36,053	2,714	4,035	81,226	519	. . .	61,328	368,802
Maryland	718,184	74,415	45,147	43,631	306,003	2,695	4,375	27,720	1,222,170
Massachusetts	660,900	148,546	. . .	59,029	680,287	3,632	495	275,006	1,827,895
Michigan	1,041,054	14,356	97,357	76,931	432,868	4,455	52,610	236,695	1,956,326
Minnesota	843,509	. . .	8,801	61,666	284,535	3,446	32,552	8,008	1,242,517
Mississippi	354,374	. . .	51,946	18,679	176,033	7,476	1,924	. . .	610,432
Missouri	582,675	. . .	113,722	3,521	346,072	2,532	8,101	. . .	1,056,623
Montana	148,531	. . .	1,397	2,975	138,617	6,996	. . .	. . .	298,516
Nebraska	261,762	. . .	99,118	7,466	133,123	1,343	13,812	. . .	516,624
Nevada	233,377	. . .	16,628	10,278	74,196	1,137	. . .	33,729	369,345
New Hampshire	162,514	45,224	4,046	18,091	70,336	742	3,274	2,790	307,017
New Jersey	513,189	524,642	. . .	435,268	442,982	4,891	3,504	1,045,753	2,970,229
New Mexico	262,267	. . .	. . .	10,130	153,435	1,985	. . .	. . .	427,817
New York	682,397	559,658	. . .	178,835	723,729	6,155	. . .	1,526,147	3,676,921
North Carolina	1,083,311	1,346	63,639	90,746	316,473	3,551	14,686	. . .	1,573,752
North Dakota	107,507	. . .	4,163	835	98,548	1,052	9,459	. . .	221,564
Ohio	1,602,789	85,766	. . .	34,415	464,922	5,434	10,875	100,000	2,304,201
Oklahoma	400,052	73,793	21,719	19,954	184,519	2,762	4,195	42,520	749,514
Oregon	498,415	2,483	26,124	29,980	205,212	71,549	7,999	. . .	841,762
Pennsylvania	1,753,983	325,043	. . .	93,108	679,245	7,748	17,128	35,643	2,911,898
Rhode Island	66,170	8,831	. . .	1,125	118,053	1,031	. . .	30,295	225,505
South Carolina	392,990	. . .	. . .	7,982	209,598	5,062	508	. . .	616,140
South Dakota	98,030	. . .	27,135	5,826	103,443	2,387	5,332	. . .	242,153
Tennessee	652,229	54	383,289	7,339	299,260	2,790	16,437	. . .	1,361,398
Texas	2,066,484	43,424	18,909	73,519	887,628	7,985	38,317	. . .	3,136,266
Utah	213,457	220	31,834	2,290	115,462	22,739	1,810	. . .	387,812
Vermont	108,284	. . .	. . .	8,139	74,415	2,320	4,235	12,700	210,093
Virginia	850,076	86,171	326,778	43,162	258,201	2,995	50,192	104,229	1,721,804
Washington	850,020	66,769	106	65,556	401,241	24,261	6,971	30,651	1,445,575
West Virginia	364,782	37,254	10,187	21,888	213,503	3,289	11	. . .	650,914
Wisconsin	720,480	. . .	. . .	33,440	316,055	4,713	32,149	194,503	1,301,340
Wyoming	76,816	. . .	26,531	5,797	92,806	57,193	2,639	. . .	261,782
Dist. of Columbia	74,011	. . .	17,817	66,065	75,066	524	. . .	34,993	268,476

Source: U.S. Department of Transportation, Federal Highway Administration, *Highway Statistics 1992.* Compiled for calendar year 1992 from reports of state authorities.
Note: Detail may not add to totals due to rounding.
Key:
. . . — Not applicable

(a) Toll receipts allocated for non-highway purposes are excluded.
(b) Bonds issued for and redeemed by refunding are excluded.

Table 8.25
STATE DISBURSEMENTS FOR HIGHWAYS: 1992
(In thousands of dollars)

State or other jurisdiction	Capital outlay				Maintenance & traffic services	Administration & highway police	Bond interest	Grants-in-aid to local governments	Bond retirement (a)	Total disbursements
	Federal-aid highways									
	Interstate	Other federal aid systems	Other roads & streets	Total						
United States	19,476,378	6,079,557	2,443,031	28,656,525	8,787,516	8,586,043	2,157,001	2,596,834	8,674,049	59,457,968
Alabama.........	245,382	81,865	46,394	373,641	134,450	112,665	4,382	11,165	183,401	819,704
Alaska..........	107,217	89,325	16,458	213,000	121,900	40,778	2,255	12,996	7,241	398,170
Arizona..........	374,711	66,598	72,595	513,904	68,907	96,615	109,328	59,839	323,733	1,172,326
Arkansas	194,760	121,286	21,572	337,618	113,232	43,296	. . .	. . .	121,499	615,645
California........	1,694,647	177,146	249,188	2,120,981	512,088	1,255,883	5,638	4,194	1,103,567	5,002,351
Colorado	213,069	50,006	141,328	404,403	128,060	54,405	. . .	. . .	157,932	744,800
Connecticut	451,202	81,750	158,328	691,280	60,753	64,071	164,116	191,665	29,887	1,201,772
Delaware	151,987	16,241	25,731	193,959	55,562	80,315	45,565	22,383	3,000	400,784
Florida	1,101,353	304,693	41,107	1,447,153	282,812	369,421	171,533	92,031	264,358	2,627,308
Georgia..........	532,344	158,540	8,265	699,149	185,909	144,113	35,654	266,628	2,183	1,333,636
Hawaii	274,175	42,475	2,919	319,569	19,897	27,463	12,586	16,052	30,805	426,372
Idaho	86,062	25,316	11,039	122,417	49,296	41,197	. . .	. . .	79,098	292,008
Illinois..........	896,728	598,021	78,906	1,573,655	300,307	305,417	116,329	108,599	415,945	2,820,252
Indiana..........	449,351	191,742	28,057	669,150	201,342	98,407	47,901	5,775	295,528	1,318,103
Iowa	304,524	96,167	. . .	400,691	100,801	139,074	. . .	. . .	369,157	1,009,723
Kansas	282,299	89,860	28,724	400,883	81,227	128,753	25,994	107,125	113,567	857,549
Kentucky	277,766	162,743	323,176	763,685	152,056	144,948	101,564	141,472	107,126	1,410,851
Louisiana	437,699	161,860	51,207	650,766	59,191	145,201	79,578	77,555	1,760	1,014,051
Maine	76,269	52,668	16,133	145,070	115,541	40,419	9,033	11,235	19,459	340,757
Maryland	425,695	69,059	18,227	512,981	149,131	196,041	32,571	16,492	304,956	1,212,172
Massachusetts	812,157	87,902	42,468	942,527	146,150	252,454	163,770	232,526	94,628	1,832,055
Michigan	526,662	19,618	90,654	636,934	138,763	310,537	19,188	19,759	592,882	1,718,063
Minnesota	. . .	. . .	. . .	657,559 (b)	144,894	137,272	8,170	10,696	408,145	1,366,736
Mississippi	252,368	111,794	57,025	421,187	54,704	64,663	13,155	34,325	61,833	649,867
Missouri	327,080	130,086	7,484	464,650	210,439	199,520	. . .	. . .	181,191	1,055,800
Montana.........	94,554	76,477	25,088	196,119	43,199	32,924	12,162	. . .	27,575	311,979
Nebraska	151,259	79,847	81,680	312,786	52,011	38,594	. . .	14,760	140,477	543,868
Nevada	54,395	104,167	9,925	168,487	58,785	34,286	2,812	14,760	41,567	320,697
New Hampshire ...	71,204	14,697	6,690	92,591	98,469	112,764	19,981	3,600	611	328,016
New Jersey.......	1,174,203	71,546	65,837	1,311,586	358,862	496,987	223,409	207,172	58,562	2,656,578
New Mexico.......	172,780	70,589	14,749	258,118	63,812	74,278	. . .	. . .	31,608	427,816
New York	1,003,047	225,959	42,154	1,271,160	606,776	557,303	190,658	243,418	399,098	3,268,413
North Carolina	493,896	216,617	63,911	774,424	362,139	229,921	8,287	. . .	82,080	1,456,851
North Dakota	67,051	39,832	2,891	109,774	34,742	25,469	. . .	. . .	42,308	212,293
Ohio	569,407	163,061	21,539	754,007	460,687	464,622	23,969	86,956	633,645	2,423,886
Oklahoma	208,919	78,136	87,629	374,684	88,492	139,124	50,090	34,191	171,796	858,377
Oregon	249,957	109,071	4,703	363,731	120,773	62,251	5,163	6,407	271,280	829,605
Pennsylvania	894,097	307,121	22,053	1,223,271	764,351	344,623	183,035	207,529	264,848	2,987,657
Rhode Island	54,753	26,188	55,382	136,323	23,710	19,495	13,278	18,174	90	211,070
South Carolina	206,672	78,545	60,009	345,226	156,266	101,046	. . .	. . .	19,224	621,762
South Dakota	92,471	77,881	9,915	180,267	33,371	29,236	. . .	. . .	16,614	259,488
Tennessee	378,031	232,374	21,859	632,264	192,392	116,696	878	4,950	229,448	1,176,628
Texas............	1,322,767	316,826	61,422	1,701,015	564,131	491,117	31,920	2,855	135,110	2,926,148
Utah	144,108	53,700	420	198,228	59,893	50,876	. . .	. . .	59,107	368,104
Vermont	36,170	61,216	4,601	101,987	36,077	31,836	1,632	1,397	21,275	194,204
Virginia..........	343,932	220,992	85,048	649,972	468,402	200,538	41,119	157,930	169,597	1,687,558
Washington	404,199	110,410	1	514,610	194,067	241,069	54,092	53,281	319,476	1,376,595
West Virginia	218,878	99,402	38,490	356,770	161,301	40,804	28,106	40,114	. . .	627,095
Wisconsin........	438,418	185,060	80,390	703,868	116,788	102,004	24,965	25,527	254,355	1,227,507
Wyoming	73,840	59,080	14,483	147,403	52,084	35,537	. . .	. . .	11,417	246,441
Dist. of Columbia...	61,863	14,002	25,177	101,042	28,524	19,715	73,135	46,061	. . .	268,477

Source: U.S. Department of Transportation, Federal Highway Administration, *Highway Statistics 1992.* Compiled for calendar year 1992 from reports of state authorities.
Note: Detail may not add to totals due to rounding.
Key:
. . . — Not applicable

(a) Bonds issued for and redeemed by refunding are excluded.
(b) Segregation by federal-aid systems not identified by state.

Table 8.26
APPORTIONMENT OF FEDERAL-AID HIGHWAY FUNDS: FISCAL 1993
(In thousands of dollars)

State or other jurisdiction	Interstate construction, (Fiscal 1994)	National highway system	Surface transportation program	Interstate maintenance	Bridge program	Highway safety (a)	Total (b)
United States (c)....	1,218,685	3,389,937	3,925,486	2,795,955	2,569,765	156,859	17,681,090
Alabama...........	10,251	64,477	84,757	52,242	39,664	2,719	297,732
Alaska.............	...	53,060	117,685	21,563	6,396	788	214,218
Arizona............	...	45,000	56,110	61,005	6,396	2,205	255,040
Arkansas..........	...	38,619	42,270	29,742	34,041	1,819	203,889
California..........	142,554	292,835	355,162	288,956	158,444	15,153	1,655,625
Colorado	5,432	52,724	69,438	50,823	24,279	2,259	211,867
Connecticut	11,968	57,089	79,246	35,786	73,660	1,691	340,102
Delaware	...	17,127	26,585	13,987	6,461	788	70,973
Florida	16,125	132,313	214,141	102,390	46,349	6,962	725,816
Georgia............	27,549	97,052	124,600	98,330	43,587	4,020	510,765
Hawaii	...	17,463	70,079	13,987	14,640	788	122,591
Idaho	...	26,194	40,323	24,718	6,821	1,062	113,698
Illinois.............	...	130,298	176,876	96,463	84,476	6,523	610,521
Indiana	...	73,209	102,760	63,216	35,064	3,416	378,504
Iowa	...	52,724	67,307	38,766	38,325	2,356	215,002
Kansas	...	48,022	51,101	39,842	40,524	2,423	196,672
Kentucky	5,869	55,410	71,000	47,170	33,995	2,354	261,002
Louisiana	7,820	55,746	53,327	49,783	49,476	2,488	267,031
Maine	...	21,157	30,481	13,987	13,495	788	85,848
Maryland	...	52,724	56,963	46,310	41,513	2,457	298,354
Massachusetts	776,000	63,806	5,091	47,834	121,071	3,071	1,065,866
Michigan	14,790	94,030	97,121	89,894	70,490	5,371	489,492
Minnesota	10,489	58,433	80,303	52,565	27,320	3,247	241,795
Mississippi	...	41,977	39,460	32,919	42,467	1,875	197,472
Missouri	...	81,940	66,009	76,359	82,650	3,503	383,723
Montana...........	...	36,940	47,564	43,779	9,998	1,050	166,140
Nebraska	...	35,933	49,711	22,594	26,107	1,618	141,597
Nevada	...	25,858	39,881	24,668	6,396	989	106,233
New Hampshire	...	20,485	29,696	13,987	12,572	788	83,162
New Jersey.........	82,076	87,649	72,494	32,049	136,152	3,850	495,758
New Mexico........	...	35,933	46,655	45,035	6,915	1,234	181,087
New York	...	183,358	141,680	103,408	255,851	9,268	929,701
North Carolina	21,216	84,962	115,064	55,402	62,223	3,940	449,643
North Dakota	...	25,186	41,296	21,408	6,396	1,131	106,904
Ohio	...	121,567	120,456	108,106	105,276	6,038	643,722
Oklahoma	...	51,380	58,819	38,509	43,332	2,521	244,305
Oregon	17,629	41,306	40,540	42,007	30,575	2,228	202,642
Pennsylvania........	...	138,022	48,931	71,660	258,435	6,539	747,040
Rhode Island	...	17,463	23,542	13,987	14,914	788	108,382
South Carolina	9,248	49,701	64,076	47,933	24,476	2,209	218,514
South Dakota	...	27,873	40,151	26,123	10,165	1,125	114,664
Tennessee	2,159	73,880	73,401	69,184	60,300	3,043	357,399
Texas..............	30,600	229,029	317,501	210,326	100,105	10,578	1,136,132
Utah	...	31,903	32,317	46,049	9,150	1,203	128,797
Vermont	...	18,470	23,467	13,987	13,268	788	76,060
Virginia............	...	73,545	75,002	77,632	49,329	3,476	393,376
Washington	4,430	59,104	46,703	58,997	56,042	2,990	402,998
West Virginia	...	41,306	32,588	22,307	58,536	1,154	161,525
Wisconsin	...	56,418	83,378	37,169	34,039	3,297	341,256
Wyoming	...	27,873	35,650	34,432	6,396	788	115,036
Dist. of Columbia.....	22,483	17,798	20,604	13,987	14,286	788	96,174
American Samoa	...	3,392	...	...	...	394	3,786
Guam	...	13,568	...	...	...	394	13,962
No. Mariana Islands...	...	3,392	...	...	...	394	3,786
Puerto Rico	...	19,645	26,126	12,588	16,928	1,734	83,723
U.S. Virgin Islands	...	13,568	...	...	...	394	13,962

Source: U.S. Department of Transportation, Federal Highway Administration, *Highway Statistics 1992.*

Note: Apportioned pursuant to the Intermodal Surface Transportation Efficiency Act of 1991 (ISTEA). Does not include funds from the Mass Transit or the National Recreational Trails accounts of the Highway Trust Fund. ISTEA eliminated the earlier federal-aid highway systems and created a new National Highway System (NHS). Therefore, column headings in this table differ in some cases from previous versions in *The Book of the States.* When the new system is completely designated, it will include the existing interstate routes, a large percentage of urban and rural principal arterials, the defense strategic highway network, and strategic highway connectors. ISTEA also created a new flexible funding program, the Surface Transportation Program (STP), that can be used for roads and streets not functionally classified as local or rural minor collectors, for bridges on any public road, and for transit capital projects. ISTEA continues the interstate construction program through Fiscal Year 1995 and provides the final authorizations for completion of the interstate system.

(a) Includes $19.7 million administered by the Federal Highway Administration and $137.2 million administered by the National Highway Traffic Safety Administration.

(b) Does not include funds from the following programs: Emergency Relief, Federal Lands Highway Programs, mandated projects, National Magnetic Levitation Development, High-Speed Ground Transportation Development, and Intelligent Vehicle-Highway System, among others. These funds are allocated from the Highway Trust Fund.

(c) Detail may not add to totals due to rounding.

Chapter Nine

INTER-GOVERNMENTAL AFFAIRS

A recap of recent developments in the relations between the federal government and the states, the states and local governments, and the impact of free trade agreements on the states. Includes statistics on federal aid and state intergovernmental revenues and expenditures for 1991 and 1992.

Developments in Federal-State Relations, 1992-93

The pattern of the past 25 years is likely to continue, but state and local governments should see more flexibility and some mandate relief.

by John Kincaid

Federal-state relations in 1992-93 remained on a course characteristic of intergovernmental relations during the past 25 years — namely, continual expansion of federal power and involvement in state and local government affairs. Although the 1992 election ended 12 years of Reagan-Bush New Federalism, it did not fundamentally alter the course of federal-state relations, in part because former Governor Bill Clinton of Arkansas won only a plurality of the vote in his race against President George Bush and Texas billionaire Ross Perot. The voters gave Clinton a mandate for change, but not a clearcut mandate for the direction of change.

The president, moreover, is only one actor in intergovernmental affairs. Often more important are the actions of Congress, the federal courts and the interest groups that influence federal policy-making. As with former President Ronald Reagan's New Federalism, which met with minimal success after 1981, the election of a new president frequently produces more rhetoric than real change in federal-state relations.

Furthermore, the course of intergovernmental relations is being driven by two overriding forces: federal deficits and federal policy-making for persons rather than places (i.e., state and local governments).

Annual deficits, which have been incurred by the federal government every year since 1969, virtually require Congress to make policy by enacting mandates that must be carried out by state and local governments with little or no federal funding. The political viability of Congress in today's budget climate rests heavily on its ability to meet interest-group demands through unfunded mandates. In addition, given the U.S. Supreme Court's abandonment of the 10th Amendment in *Garcia v. San Antonio Metropolitan Transit Authority* (1985), the states cannot expect judicial protection against federal policy-making. Although President Clinton expressed strong commitment to deficit reduction, the size of federal deficits and the total federal debt will not relieve the federal government of its fiscal problems for the foreseeable future. Hence, unfunded mandates emerged in 1993 as the leading intergovernmental concern for state and local governments.

Federal policy-making also has been shifting from places to persons during the past 25 years, a trend captured by Clinton's campaign slogan, "Putting People First." This shift from places to persons is reflected in the rising costs of federal entitlement programs and in the changing pattern of federal aid. The proportion of federal aid to state and local governments that is dedicated for payments to individuals increased from 31.8 percent of all aid in 1978 to about 62 percent by 1993. In the past, federal policy-making was highly sensitive to the interests of places because state and local governments were seen as having primary responsibility for the health and well-being of citizens. Today, federal policies, including most unfunded mandates, are increasingly aimed directly at the interests of persons regardless of the interests of places.

John Kincaid is Robert B. and Helen S. Meyner professor of Government and Public Service at Lafayette College, Easton, Pa., and former executive director of the U.S. Advisory Commission on Intergovernmental Relations.

This shift in federal policy-making from places to persons will be difficult to reverse so long as Congress and the Supreme Court regard state and local governments as simply another set of interest groups. Compared to the past, state and local officials also have lost considerable political leverage over members of Congress and presidential candidates. Candidates for Congress and the presidency win election or re-election not so much by gaining the support of state and local officials but by gaining the financial support of political action committees and the political support of interest groups, and by campaigning directly with voters through the media and delivering benefits directly to constituency groups within their states and districts. Federal officials have few incentives to treat state and local officials as partners in governance and many incentives to reward voters with benefits without being held accountable for the costs of those benefits.

A New Federal-State Partnership?

Nevertheless, the election of President Clinton produced enthusiasm among many state and local officials for the possibility of forging a new, more cooperative federal-state partnership. At the invitation of Colorado Governor Roy Romer, chairman of the National Governors' Association, representatives of the "Big 7" state and local government associations and others gathered in Colorado Springs on November 12, 1992 to develop a strategy for working with the new administration on federalism and economic issues. The state and local leaders agreed on several priorities: (1) reducing the federal budget deficit, (2) containing the costs of health care, (3) enhancing strategic investment, (4) improving accountability and efficiency in government, and (5) developing specific proposals to consolidate and simplify government programs.

The U.S. Advisory Commission on Intergovernmental Relations also appealed to the president to focus on eight intergovernmental issues:

1. Federal mandates on state and local governments;

2. Federal pre-emption of state and local powers;

3. Federal regulation of state and local governments;

4. Structural and policy fragmentation within Congress and executive branch;

5. Grant-in-aid fragmentation and multiple conditions of aid;

6. Shifts in federal aid from future investment to current consumption;

7. The decline of historically cooperative federal-state programs; and

8. Federal intrusions upon state and local tax bases.

The president met frequently with the governors and other state and local officials and pledged his support for a revitalized federal-state partnership. The first major statement of the Administration's vision of intergovernmental reform came with the September 1993 report of Vice President Al Gore's National Performance Review, which contained more than 100 recommendations relevant to federal-state-local relations. The six principal intergovernmental recommendations were:

• Create flexibility and encourage innovation by designing a bottom-up solution to the problem of grant proliferation and its accompanying red tape. Also, support the pending proposal for Federal-State Flexibility grants that has been developed by the National Governors' Association and by the National Conference of State Legislatures. Establish a Cabinet-level Enterprise Board to oversee initiatives in community improvement.

• Issue an Executive Order addressing the problems of unfunded federal mandates and regulatory relief and authorize Cabinet Secretaries and agency heads to obtain selective relief from regulation or mandates in programs they oversee.

• Modify OMB Circular A-87, "Cost Principles for State and Local Governments," to provide a fixed fee-for-service option in lieu of costly reimbursement procedures covering actual administrative costs of grant disbursement.

• Simplify OMB's requirements to prepare multiple grant compliance certification by allowing state and local governments to submit a single certification to a single point of contact in the federal government.

• Modify OMB circular A-102, "Grants and Cooperative Agreements to State and Local Governments," to increase the dollar threshold for small purchases by local governments from $25,000 to $100,000.

• Reinvent the Advisory Commission on Intergovernmental Affairs (ACIR) and charge it with responsibility for continuous improvement in federal, state and local partnership and intergovernmental service delivery. Direct the ACIR to identify opportunities to improve intergovernmental service delivery and develop a set of benchmarks.

Clinton's Federalism Initiatives

Initially, the administration got off to a rough start in intergovernmental relations, as was the case in many policy fields. For example, the president's $16.3 billion economic stimulus package, which was strongly supported by many state and local officials, suffered defeat in Congress in April 1993. The president's first assistant for intergovernmental affairs, Regina Montoya, left the office in August 1993 and was succeeded by Marcia L. Hale, who brought a high level of energy and effectiveness to the White House Office of Intergovernmental Affairs.

In the meantime, however, the lack of presidential appointments to fill 10 vacancies on ACIR and appoint a new chairperson for the Commission made ACIR vulnerable in the congressional appropriations process. In June 1993, the House zeroed ACIR out of its fiscal year 1994 appropriations bill by a voice vote on the floor. Funding was restored through the Senate, but only at a level of $1 million, representing a 44 percent cut for ACIR from fiscal year 1993. As a result, ACIR was compelled to downsize from 18 to 12 staff members, reduce office facilities by 43 percent and cut current services.

This attempt to abolish ACIR came on the heels of the elimination of the intergovernmental division that had existed in the U.S. General Accounting Office. These actions reflect another trend in federal-state relations: the dismantling of federal intergovernmental institutions. During the 1980s, Reagan abolished the federal regional councils and OMB's

intergovernmental unit; the Senate reorganized its Subcommittee on Intergovernmental Relations into a Subcommittee on Government Efficiency, Federalism, and the District of Columbia; and the House renamed its intergovernmental subcommittee as Human Resources and Intergovernmental Relations. These actions left the long-term future of intergovernmental relations as an explicit institutional component of the federal government's approach to federal-state relations in doubt.

By the second half of 1993, however, Clinton began to make progress on his intergovernmental agenda. Implementation of elements of the National Performance Review were under way, and on October 20, the president appointed William F. Winter, former governor of Mississippi, as the new chairman of ACIR, along with 10 other new members. The president also met with the Commission on December 1 and pledged his support for forging a new intergovernmental partnership. By the end of 1993, Clinton also had issued six executive orders relevant to his intergovernmental agenda:

1. Creating a community enterprise board to help distressed communities with integrating federal and state efforts to implement the new legislation providing for empowerment and enterprise zones;

2. Ordering executive agencies to eliminate 50 percent of their regulations in order to improve customer service within three years;

3. Streamlining the federal bureaucracy by reducing the executive civilian work force by 252,000 (12 percent) by fiscal year 1999;

4. Ordering all executive agencies to set customer service standards to provide services that match or exceed the best service available in the private sector;

5. Establishing a regulatory review and planning process to ease regulatory burdens by requiring regular consultation between OMB's Office of Information and Regulatory Affairs and state, local and tribal governments; and

6. Ordering executive agencies to reduce unfunded mandates created by administrative rule promulgation, provide state, local, and tribal governments "meaningful and timely input in the development of regulatory pro-

posals containing significant unfunded mandates," and streamline and make more flexible agency processes for waivers of federal rules for state, local and tribal governments.

Public Opinion

Many of these presidential initiatives were responses to "the mandate for change" expressed in the 1992 elections. Public trust and confidence in government, especially in the federal government, continued to slide downward in 1992-93. This slide was reflected in the results of ACIR's 1992 and 1993 national public opinion polls. The proportion of Americans expressing a "great deal" or a "fair amount" of trust and confidence in the federal government tumbled from 68 percent in 1987 to 42 percent in 1992. Citizen concerns about the federal government also spilled over onto state governments, which dropped public trust from 73 percent to 51 percent.

Similarly, when asked, "From which level of government do you feel you get the least for your money?" 49 percent cited the federal government, 18 percent said local government and 16 percent picked state government. The 49 percent saying that the federal government gave them the least for their money was up from 36 and 41 percent in 1989 and 1990, respectively. States fared the best on this 1992 ACIR question. Those choosing state government as giving them the least for their money (16 percent) dropped from 26 percent in 1990 and 25 percent in 1989.

When asked in 1993 which government gives them the most for their money, however, 38 percent of Americans picked local government, 23 percent cited the federal government and 20 percent said state government. These results represented the most positive response for local government and the most negative response for the federal government ever recorded in 20 annual ACIR polls. State governments have averaged around 22 percent. In addition, local government was picked by 43 percent of Americans as spending its tax dollars most wisely, compared to 19 percent citing state government and 11 percent selecting the federal government.

In 1993, 36 percent of Americans also rated the federal income tax as "the worst, that is,

the least fair" among the nation's four major general taxes, compared to 26 percent citing the local property tax as the worst, 16 percent for the state sales tax and 10 percent for the state income tax. The unfavorable 1993 rating of the federal income tax was 10 percentage points more than in 1991, when only 26 percent of the respondents rated the federal income tax as the worst. In contrast, the state income tax has been viewed the most favorably in all ACIR polls conducted since 1972.

Another sign of public discontent was voter approval of ballot initiatives in 14 states in 1992 limiting the terms of members of Congress and, in some cases, state legislators. Term limits garnered 77 percent voter support in Wyoming; more than 70 percent in Arizona, Florida and Missouri; 60 percent or more in Arkansas, California, Michigan, Montana, Nebraska, Ohio, Oregon and South Dakota; 55 percent in North Dakota; and 52 percent in Washington. Whether state-imposed term limits on members of Congress can withstand judicial scrutiny under the U.S. Constitution remains to be seen, but public support for term limits reflects widespread citizen concern about the performance of government. (For a more complete discussion of this issue, see "Term Limits in the States," by Thad Beyle and Rich Jones on pages 28-33 of this volume.)

Federal Mandates

These expressions of public opinion and voter sentiment added fuel to state and local governments' greatest intergovernmental concern in 1992-93: unfunded federal mandates. ACIR issued a report showing Congress had enacted 27 major statutes during the 1980s that imposed new regulations on states and local governments or significantly expanded existing mandates. There were 22 such statutes enacted during the 1970s, 12 in the 1960s, none in the 1950s, one in 1940, and one in 1935. Feeling the political heat to raise taxes and/or reduce services to comply with unfunded federal mandates, state and local government leaders staged a well-publicized protest, National Unfunded Mandates Day, on October 27, 1993.

Two surveys, one of 314 cities conducted by the U.S. Conference of Mayors (USCM) and one of 128 counties conducted by the National Association of Counties (NACo), attempted to estimate the costs of selected mandates. The USCM survey, which focused on 10 specific mandates affecting cities, found current year costs of $6.5 billion and estimated that the costs of those programs will total $54 billion between 1994 and 1998. On average, the 10 mandates were consuming 11.4 percent of locally-raised city revenues. The NACo survey found that counties were spending an estimated $4.8 billion annually to comply with 12 specific mandates, and that the costs of those programs will total $33.7 billion between 1994 and 1998. On average, the 12 mandates consumed 12.3 percent of locally-raised county revenues. The mandates examined by the cities and counties were:

- Underground storage tanks;
- Clean Water Act coverage of wetlands;
- Clean Air Act;
- Subtitle D of the Resource Conservation and Recovery Act (solid waste);
- Safe Drinking Water Act;
- Endangered Species Act;
- Superfund (NACo only);
- Americans with Disabilities Act;
- Fair Labor Standards Act;
- Davis-Bacon Act;
- Arbitrage rules for local government bonds (NACo only);
- Immigration Act (NACo only);
- Asbestos Abatement (USCM only); and
- Lead Paint Abatement (USCM only).

Another survey, conducted by the National Conference of State Legislatures (NCSL), compiled cost estimates from 21 states for compliance with five specific mandates. The survey found total costs of $1.5 billion over several years. The mandates examined by NCSL were (1) transportation requirements under the Americans with Disabilities Act, (2) Medicaid coverage of qualified Medicare beneficiaries, (3) automatic wage withholding for new child support orders, (4) fleet conversion requirements under the Energy Act, and (5) capital improvement requirements under the Safe Drinking Water Act.

In response to the protest, President Clinton issued an executive order on unfunded mandates (E.O. 12875, Enhancing the Intergovernmental Partnership), and by the end of 1993, some 32 mandate-relief bills had been introduced in Congress. The two principal mandate-relief measures presented in these bills were a prohibition on unfunded federal mandates (Kempthorne-Condit) and an improved fiscal notes process, including a point-of-order rule on the House and Senate floors (Moran-Dorgan). At the time, NCSL also reported 132 bills containing mandates being considered by Congress.

The Federal-State Fiscal Partnership

Other factors affecting state and local concerns about federal mandates were tight fiscal conditions for state and local budgets. David Broder, columnist with *The Washington Post*, described the opening of 1992 as one of "economic devastation" for state governments. Although states spent $596 billion in 1992 from all funding sources, the general fund increase between 1991 and 1992 was about 5 percent, compared to an average annual general fund increase of 8 percent during the 1980s. By 1993, however, economic growth had eased the states' fiscal plight, even though budgets remained tight. States limited the growth of their general fund budgets to only 3.3 percent in fiscal 1993.

Of particular concern to state officials was the growth of Medicaid, which had surpassed higher education as the second largest category of state spending. After the 1992 elections, therefore, state officials joined Clinton in pressing for major reforms to contain the costs of health care.

Federal aid to state and local governments increased by 88 percent during the last six Reagan-Bush years, rising from a post-1978 low of 17.3 percent of total state and local government outlays in 1989 to 22 percent by 1992. By 1993, federal aid was growing at a faster rate (about 19 percent) than state and local own-source revenues (about 5 percent).

Although states received about 89 percent of all direct federal aid, the increase in aid was of little solace to the states because it occurred mostly in matching grant entitlement programs, mainly Medicaid and Aid to Families with Dependent Children (AFDC), which drive up state spending as well. About 90 percent of all federal domestic spending increases enacted in 1992 were for Medicaid, food stamps, child nutrition and foster care. Medicaid alone, which accounted for about 35 percent of all federal aid, had grown from 2.5 percent of the federal budget in 1981 to 5.5 percent in 1993, while other federal grants declined from 11.5 percent to 8.5 percent of the federal budget. Furthermore, if there is no major health-care cost containment, federal spending on Medicaid and AFDC is expected to increase by about 66 percent from 1995 to 1999, while federal domestic discretionary spending is expected to decrease by 0.3 percent. In turn, states will spend about $68 billion more on Medicaid and AFDC in 1999 than in 1995.

In addition, the final regulations implementing the Provider-Specific Tax Amendments of 1991 went into effect in December 1992. The legislation limits to 25 percent the allowable share of state Medicaid funds from provider taxes, requires taxes to be broad-based and applied uniformly to classes of providers, places new limits on provider-related donations, and limits payments to hospitals that serve a disproportionate share of indigent patients to 12 percent of total Medicaid expenditures.

Given that states have primary administrative responsibility for the major federal-aid programs, particularly the aid to persons programs, direct federal aid to local governments maintained its post-1978 downward plunge, though at a slower rate in 1992-93. According to a survey of 688 cities by the National League of Cities, federal aid amounted to $63.60 per capita in 1980, but only $29.40 per capita in 1993 — a decline of 53.8 percent. During this same period, state aid increased from $72.40 per capita to $80.20 — a 10.8 percent increase.

As a result, local governments, especially large central cities and urban counties, pressed for state as well as federal mandate relief and for more state and federal aid. In 1992, cities mounted a major effort for more federal aid by announcing 7,252 ready-to-go public works projects kept on hold in 506 cities as a result of federal aid cuts in the 1980s. Local govern-

ments also pressed for renewed revenue sharing through a proposed Local Partnership Act. After the not-guilty verdict in the Rodney King police-brutality case sparked riots in Los Angeles and several other cities in April 1992, congressional and presidential approval of a major urban aid package seemed assured, but while cities received some additional aid for the summer months, they received no major increase in urban aid. Bush vetoed an urban aid tax bill, although he did sign the Housing and Community Development Act of 1992. The prospects for urban aid were further reduced by federal needs to respond to Hurricane Andrew, which struck Florida, Alabama and Louisiana, and Hurricane Iniki, which struck Hawaii in 1992.

Given that the shift in federal aid from places to persons also emphasizes spending for current consumption over capital investment, state and local officials began to express greater interest in federal capital budgeting along with entitlement reform. Capital budgeting is a normal facet of state and local budgeting but not of the federal budget process. Federal infrastructure investment especially captured state and local attention, in part because economic development and growth will be the most lucrative and least politically painful sources of state and local revenues for the foreseeable future and, in part, because development and growth are needed to create more jobs and reduce reliance on public assistance programs.

States, moreover, will share in the pain of federal deficit reduction, although by the end of 1993, states had avoided many major cost shifts from the federal government, especially in financing entitlement programs. An energy tax proposal, which would have cost states some $10 to $12 billion, was defeated along with the Penny-Kasich deficit-reduction proposal, which would have cost states about $5 billion for Medicaid co-payments for home health care.

Major Policy Issues

The major policy issues of concern to the states in 1992-93 were health care, education, economic growth and welfare. However, no significant federal action was taken on these issues because the Bush Administration was unable to advance a credible domestic agenda, the 1992 elections interrupted policy action, the new Clinton Administration needed to organize itself for action and the great floods in the Midwest and riots in Los Angeles diverted public resources.

In the field of health care, states advocated greater flexibility for state innovation and a major role for state governments in any reformed health-care system. In education, states continued to coalesce around and act on the objectives of Goals 2000 and to press for corresponding federal action. On economic growth, however, state officials generally agreed on the end but not the means, especially as the 1992 elections produced great debate on how best to stimulate economic growth and create jobs. State officials did begin to reach consensus positions on welfare reform, particularly a two-year limit on welfare for most recipients, after which they would be required to work in the private sector or in a public service position. The principal concern of state officials, however, is how to pay for a welfare-to-work program.

Other issues of concern for the states were dislocations created by reductions in defense spending, increases in state and local government costs stemming from federal refugee and immigration policies, Indian gaming, and crime control, which was propelled onto the intergovernmental agenda by public opinion in 1993. Many state and local officials, however, also expressed concern about the costs of the get-tough-on-criminals attitudes reflected in such popular ideas as "three strikes and you're out."

Congressional actions favorable to the states in 1992 included increased federal spending on transportation, community development, and Head Start plus $150 million more for state revolving loan funds for clean water. Congress also gave states the right to force environmental cleanups at federal facilities, established a new $1.5 billion defense conversion program, maintained National Guard strength for 1993, re-authorized housing and airport improvement programs, preserved states' rights to tax

non-resident pension income and extended unemployment benefits. Local governments scored a major victory when Congress overrode Bush's veto of the Cable Television Consumer Protection and Competition Act of 1992, thus restoring to local governments some regulatory authority for basic cable rates. However, when the 102nd Congress adjourned in 1992, NCSL counted 15 new mandates enacted into law.

The pace of mandating picked up in 1993, however, with the first session of the 103rd Congress enacting 13 mandates on state and local governments. Many of the mandates were carried over from 1992. Most publicized was the National Voter Registration Act of 1993 (Motor Voter), which Bush vetoed in 1992. This act requires states to provide for federal elections voter registration along with applications for a driver's license, by mail application, and through agency offices that provide services under the Food Stamp, Medicaid, WIC and AFDC programs. States also may provide for voter registration at unemployment compensation offices.

The Family and Medical Leave Act of 1993 requires employers, including state and local governments, having more than 50 employees to provide up to 12 weeks of unpaid job-protected leave annually — with health insurance — for the birth or adoption of a child or a serious illness of the employee or an immediate family member. Other major legislation incorporating mandates included the Brady Bill requiring a waiting period before purchasing a handgun, the Nation Child Protection Act, and the Religious Freedom Restoration Act. Congress also reduced the enhanced federal matching rate for all AFDC and food stamp administrative costs to 50 percent effective April 1, 1994. Through the South African Democratic Transition Support Act of 1993, Congress approved reductions in federal transportation funds for states and localities that do not repeal their economic sanctions against South Africa by the end of fiscal year 1995.

The States in Court

Despite its reduced caseload, the U.S. Supreme Court decided a sizable number of cases affecting federal-state relations in 1992-93, a number of which were favorable to the states.

Most significant was the Court's 6-3 ruling in *New York v. United States* (1992), in which The Council of State Governments played an important role by filing an *amicus brief* on behalf of the states. The majority held that the take-title provision of the Low-Level Radioactive Waste Policy Amendments Act of 1985 was unconstitutional under the 10th Amendment and the Constitution's republican guarantee clause. The take-title provision required that any state not meeting a 1993 deadline for joining interstate compacts or making other arrangements to dispose of low-level radioactive waste would have to take title to all such waste generated within its borders or else forfeit to waste generators the incentive payments it had received from the federal government. In enacting this provision, said the Court, the Congress "crossed the line distinguishing encouragement from coercion." In the aftermath of the Court's 1985 *Garcia* decision, the invocation of the 10th Amendment to help shield the states in this case was a significant development, though still narrow in its application.

The court also issued two rulings affecting cross-boundary solid-waste disposal in 1992. In the *Chemical Waste Management v. Hunt*, the justices struck down, 8-1, an Alabama statute imposing a differential fee on out-of-state hazardous waste. In a 7-2 decision, *Fort Gratiot Sanitary Landfill v. Michigan*, the Court ruled against a state law barring landfill operators from accepting waste generated in other counties.

In a setback for state and local regulatory powers, especially in environmental protection, the Supreme Court ruled in *Lucas v. South Carolina Coastal Council* (1992) that regulations that deny a property owner of all economically viable use of his or her land require compensation without the usual case-specific inquiry into the public interest. In another decision more favorable to the states, though, the Court dismissed a case in which a developer in Puerto Rico sued on the ground that his due process rights had been violated by officials who delayed giving approval for a hotel and residential complex (*PFZ Properties, Inc. v. Rodriquez*, 1992).

In three 1993 civil liberties cases, the Supreme Court (1) struck down several ordinances of Hialeah, Fla., which prohibited animal sacrifice in religious ceremonies, (2) affirmed that a municipality cannot ban the distribution of commercial handbills through free-standing newsracks (*City of Cincinnati v. Discovery Network*), and (3) upheld the authority of states to impose stiffer penalties on people convicted of committing hate crimes (*Wisconsin v. Mitchell*).

In a challenge to state redistricting powers, the Supreme Court ruled unanimously that federal courts must defer to state courts when both are devising voting districts. Justice Antonin Scalia, writing for the court in *Grove v. Emison* (1993), opined that "the Constitution leaves with the states primary responsibility for apportionment. Absent evidence that [states] will fail timely to perform that duty, a federal court must neither affirmatively obstruct state reapportionment nor permit federal litigation to be used to impede it." In a widely publicized 5-4 decision, *Shaw v. Reno* (1993), the Supreme Court ruled, in response to a suit brought by white voters, that the 12th Congressional District in North Carolina, with a 53 percent black majority, was gerrymandered for race reasons in violation of the U.S. Voting Rights Act. The majority opined that purely racial gerrymandering even to ensure "majority-minority" districts violates the equal protection clause of the 14th Amendment.

In *Moreau v. Klevenhagen* (1993), the court gave state and local governments more latitude to provide their employees time off in lieu of overtime pay. The justices held that a 1985 amendment to the Fair Labor Standards Act requires public employers to bargain over compensatory time only when the employees' representative has the authority to negotiate a collective bargaining agreement authorizing the use of compensatory time.

In the field of business regulation, the Court, in *General Motors Corp. v. Romein* (1992), upheld Michigan's authority to require corporations to make back payments of workers' compensation benefits. States and local government also won an important case, *Hartford Insurance Co. v. California* (1993), which cleared the way for attorneys general in 19 states to prosecute four U.S. insurance companies accused of conspiring with British insurance companies to restrict the coverage of commercial general liability insurance policies commonly purchased by city governments, corporations and nonprofit organizations. In another 1993 ruling, however, the Court expanded opportunities for contracting firms to challenge the legality of laws that set aside a certain amount of public contracts for minorities.

In *Rufo v. Inmates of Suffolk County Jail* (1992), the Supreme Court made it easier for state and local governments to challenge court settlements requiring them to improve conditions in prisons and other public institutions. The Court ruled that a federal judge had applied too strict a standard in refusing to change a prohibition against putting two convicts in each cell at the Suffolk County jail. Later, in *Brecht v. Abrahamson* (1993), the Court also made it more difficult for state prisoners to challenge their convictions in federal court. Chief Justice William H. Rehnquist, writing for the Court, held that federal courts should not disturb a state ruling unless the violation "had a substantial and injurious effect or influence in determining the jury's verdict." In *Withrow v. Williams* (1993), however, the Court declined to limit protection under the "Miranda warning," and in *Austin v. United States* (1993), the Court ruled that the excessive fines clause applies to the forfeiture of vehicles and property used, or intended to be used, to carry out certain drug-related crimes. The ruling, therefore, may constrain the value of assets received by the federal, state and local governments from asset forfeitures. In 1992, the federal government confiscated nearly $2 billion in property from people arrested for drug offenses.

In *Franklin v. Gwinnett County Public Schools* (1992), the Supreme Court gave students who experience sexual harassment and other forms of sexual discrimination an expansive right to win money damages from schools that receive federal funds. In a 1993

decision that may prove more costly for state and local governments, however, the Court ruled unanimously in *Florence County School District Four v. Carter*, that parents who withdraw children with special needs from public schools and place them in private schools not approved by local school districts may be eligible for tuition reimbursement. On the other hand, in *Suter v. Artist M.* (1992), the justices ruled that children do not have the right to sue states in federal court to enforce a provision of the Adoption Assistance and Child Welfare Act that requires "reasonable efforts" to prevent out-of-home placement and return of foster children to their families. The Court opined that Congress intended for states to have "a great deal of discretion" to develop plans to comply with federal guidelines. In 1993, however, the justices held, in *Wieder v. Skala*, that Massachusetts could not halt payments for child care for AFDC recipients engaged in job-training programs because Congress in the 1988 Family Support Act told states that participated in the AFDC program that they must put participants with school children into job-training programs and also open those courses to mothers of younger children who wish to participate. The 1988 law also said that states "must guarantee child care" for those getting the vocational education.

The Court also decided a number of important tax cases in 1992-93. In *Quill Corporation v. North Dakota* (1992), the justices opened the door to state taxation of out-of-state mail-order sales by removing any due process impediment to the ability of Congress to enact legislation to allow states to require mail-order companies to collect use taxes. Congress began considering such legislation in 1992, though no action had been taken by the end of 1993. Subsequently, in *Nordlinger v. Hahn* (1992), the Court upheld California's 1978 voter-initiated property tax limitation, Proposition 13. In *County of Yakima v. Confederated Tribes and Bands of Yakima Indian Nation* (1992), the Court upheld state and local authority to tax certain land owned by Indian tribes and their members within reservations.

In *Allied Signal, Inc. v. Director, Division of Taxation* (1992), however, the Court struck down as unconstitutional New Jersey's effort to include nonunitary income in the tax base by endeavoring to tax nonbusiness gains generated by an out-of-state corporation. In *Kraft General Foods, Inc. v. Iowa Department of Revenue and Finance* (1992), the justices voided Iowa's attempt to tax dividends from foreign subsidiaries while exempting dividends from domestic subsidiaries. In *Wisconsin Department of Revenue v. William Wrigley, Jr., Co.* (1992), though, the Supreme Court held that Wisconsin could tax the world's largest chewing gum company because its activities in the state exceeded the scope of the federal statutory definition of "solicitation." This definition holds that a state may not tax the income of a corporation whose only business activities in a state consist of "solicitation of orders" for tangible goods, provided that the orders are sent outside the state for approval and the goods are delivered from an out-of-state location.

In another case divisive for the states, *Delaware v. New York* (1993), the Supreme Court ruled that Delaware could demand hundreds of millions of dollars in unclaimed dividend and interest payments on securities held mostly in New York brokerage houses. In another decision, *Harper v. Virginia* (1993), the Court ruled 7-2 that 16 states owed back taxes to federal government pensioners. This case stemmed from *Davis v. Michigan* (1989), which held that it was unconstitutional for states to tax federal pensioners if they did not tax their own employee's pension benefits.

Overall, the states did not fare too poorly before the U.S. Supreme Court in 1992-93, and may even have breathed a sliver of judicial life back into the 10th Amendment.

International Developments

Continuing another trend of recent decades, states maintained 40 offices in Tokyo, 36 offices in Europe and scattered offices elsewhere in the world, primarily for state export promotion and secondarily for investment attraction and tourist promotion. The National Governors' Association also opened an office in Moscow in 1993. Many state and local officials strengthened other ties abroad as well, not only for purposes of state competition in the global economy but also to share information and provide technical assistance, especially to Eastern Europe and the countries of the former Soviet Union. Receiving foreign visitors and hosting foreign interns also are increasingly commonplace activities for state and local officials and their national organizations.

The most significant development further integrating state and local governments in the world economy in 1992-93 was congressional approval of the North American Free Trade Agreement (NAFTA) in late 1993. Although NAFTA was a highly divisive political issue in Congress and many parts of the country, most governors supported NAFTA in the belief that it would, in the long run, benefit state economies. During the next 15 years, NAFTA will eliminate most tariffs, quotas and investment restrictions among Canada, Mexico, and the United States.

Although NAFTA does not automatically pre-empt state laws, it will pose challenges to state laws in a number of areas, such as labor, economic development and environmental protection. If a state law is found to be inconsistent with NAFTA, the federal government may consult with the state to determine how it can comply with NAFTA. Furthermore, the law implementing NAFTA does not provide for any private right of action against a state for non-compliance. The federal government will also consult with states about any Canadian or Mexican complaints and will involve states in resolving such complaints.

The Office of the U.S. Trade Representative is obligated to help states identify financial and investment laws that conflict with NAFTA. States must identify by January 1, 1995, laws in the financial services area that restrict foreign enterprises. These laws may be placed in an "annex" and can be grandfathered for a further period. State laws that restrict investments (e.g., foreign ownership of land) were excepted from NAFTA's market-opening provisions for two years. These laws must also be identified by states and placed in an "annex" in order to be grandfathered for a longer period. States are asked to open their procurement systems voluntarily to foreign competition by 1998 and to eliminate "buy local" laws.

NAFTA created a Land Transportation Standards Subcommittee, which will attempt to make safety rules and other standards for trucks and buses as compatible as possible across the three countries. States are authorized to send observers to the subcommittee's meetings.

NAFTA's implementing legislation also permits states to establish self-employment assistance programs as part of their unemployment compensation program, and to pay a self-employment allowance in lieu of unemployment compensation to those who establish businesses and seek self-employment.

Conclusion

Federal-state relations showed no sharp departures from patterns that have developed over the past 25 years. The trends evident in 1992-93 are likely to prevail for the foreseeable future, even though state and local governments are likely to win more flexibility and waivers in the administration of federal programs, some mandate relief from Congress, and more favorable rulings from the Supreme Court.

Table 9.1
TOTAL FEDERAL GRANTS TO STATE AND LOCAL GOVERNMENTS
BY STATE: 1984-1993
(In thousands of dollars)

State or other jurisdiction	1993	1992	1991	1990	1989	1988	1987	1986	1985	1984
Total	$195,201	$153,350	$134,457	$121,079	$114,610	$107,962	$112,596	$105,478	$97,209	$92,693
Alabama	3,081	2,347	2,101	1,802	1,721	1,559	1,759	1,719	1,532	1,469
Alaska	948	738	717	663	593	624	664	640	616	541
Arizona	2,640	1,810	1,620	1,305	1,177	1,188	1,206	1,122	990	845
Arkansas	1,855	1,439	1,250	1,106	1,011	1,009	1,123	1,014	946	901
California	21,635	16,885	13,932	11,936	11,676	11,006	11,291	10,589	9,799	9,207
Colorado	2,109	1,707	1,429	1,359	1,241	1,152	1,220	1,166	1,176	1,057
Connecticut	2,691	2,393	1,973	1,771	1,542	1,489	1,501	1,377	1,221	1,189
Delaware	455	386	313	313	319	301	314	318	299	307
Florida	7,579	5,209	4,576	4,095	3,419	3,155	3,244	3,122	2,784	2,817
Georgia	4,408	3,553	3,136	3,089	2,964	2,512	2,732	2,371	2,214	2,110
Hawaii	984	739	598	528	477	460	473	436	459	457
Idaho	712	590	569	501	477	392	435	445	413	380
Illinois	7,845	5,954	5,280	4,989	4,670	4,468	5,010	4,688	4,304	4,189
Indiana	3,732	2,767	2,423	2,115	1,960	1,982	2,000	1,825	1,760	1,611
Iowa	1,737	1,475	1,289	1,183	1,199	1,090	1,158	1,164	1,091	981
Kansas	1,608	1,165	1,021	912	880	848	884	856	805	763
Kentucky	3,041	2,493	2,044	1,853	1,766	1,702	1,784	1,764	1,590	1,488
Louisiana	4,817	3,249	2,658	2,304	2,135	1,919	2,039	1,785	1,776	1,710
Maine	1,166	926	762	688	665	689	672	659	590	575
Maryland	3,310	2,557	2,350	2,156	2,004	2,002	1,959	1,812	1,697	1,790
Massachusetts	5,520	4,709	3,857	3,688	3,328	2,983	3,082	2,842	2,634	2,898
Michigan	6,654	5,426	4,751	4,553	4,243	4,199	4,353	3,961	3,776	3,612
Minnesota	3,297	2,559	2,366	2,269	2,120	2,037	2,110	1,983	1,865	1,765
Mississippi	2,285	1,822	1,595	1,366	1,324	1,274	1,344	1,188	1,176	1,100
Missouri	3,566	2,827	2,177	2,031	1,942	1,926	1,982	1,935	1,775	1,675
Montana	831	687	591	559	546	540	592	584	532	477
Nebraska	1,108	868	779	709	712	607	661	675	637	575
Nevada	767	544	442	389	336	394	418	387	340	356
New Hampshire	652	540	427	411	398	389	404	420	368	352
New Jersey	6,189	4,517	3,977	3,570	3,328	3,327	3,354	2,945	2,798	2,811
New Mexico	1,534	1,118	959	907	831	779	857	891	863	676
New York	21,166	17,226	15,761	13,700	12,494	11,932	12,380	11,093	10,363	10,032
North Carolina	4,498	3,447	2,942	2,498	2,299	2,171	2,281	2,134	1,929	1,878
North Dakota	640	533	471	431	462	419	433	452	454	372
Ohio	7,716	6,220	5,388	4,965	4,693	4,382	4,764	4,158	4,044	3,642
Oklahoma	2,111	1,788	1,568	1,508	1,406	1,317	1,400	1,236	1,167	1,075
Oregon	2,099	1,694	1,708	1,426	1,322	1,243	1,340	1,449	1,246	1,161
Pennsylvania	8,517	6,870	6,125	6,390	5,793	5,271	5,718	4,964	4,667	4,817
Rhode Island	1,107	908	773	684	644	550	570	573	548	486
South Carolina	2,521	2,078	1,892	1,455	1,354	1,280	1,322	1,324	1,169	1,113
South Dakota	654	539	511	464	443	440	457	480	436	361
Tennessee	3,925	3,129	2,717	2,353	2,225	2,018	2,128	2,049	1,885	1,687
Texas	11,035	7,837	6,889	5,974	5,168	4,853	5,225	4,477	4,136	3,805
Utah	1,173	839	838	822	725	784	807	759	708	622
Vermont	557	409	377	356	324	314	334	336	331	312
Virginia	2,945	2,432	2,237	2,119	1,961	1,905	1,995	1,817	1,628	1,665
Washington	3,722	2,832	2,568	2,294	2,170	1,978	1,905	1,826	1,698	1,537
West Virginia	1,884	1,284	1,009	952	1,056	1,028	1,063	904	819	840
Wisconsin	3,397	2,799	2,538	2,312	2,228	2,155	2,310	2,112	2,064	1,904
Wyoming	645	597	568	484	448	449	471	503	556	426
Dist. of Columbia	1,961	1,847	1,718	1,523	1,615	1,515	1,423	1,498	1,382	1,355
American Samoa . . .	59	51	79	75	48	51	46	43	47	37
Guam	161	116	100	116	106	103	127	95	89	63
No. Mariana Islands . .	47	75	62	60	52	46	49	47	44	43
Puerto Rico	3,130	2,916	3,082	2,515	2,390	2,307	2,296	2,348	2,248	2,111
Trust Territory	. . .	. . .	. . .	. . .	. . .	. . .	124	129	143	170
U.S. Virgin Islands . . .	183	175	273	116	121	119	141	132	117	91
Adjustments or undistributed to states	592	711	302	366	2,058	1,331	859	1,856	465	407

Source: U.S. Department of Commerce, Bureau of the Census, *Federal Expenditures by State for Fiscal Year 1993*; and previous annual reports.
Key:
. . . — Not available

The Political Dynamics of State-Local Relations, 1991-93

State mandates on local governments have been the hot topic, with seven states passing laws to ease the fiscal burden on localities.

by Joseph F. Zimmerman and Julie M. Clark

Much activity has taken place within the states over the past two years in the area of unfunded mandates. The most notable development in state-local relations during 1991-93 was that relatively few major new mandates were imposed by state governments upon general-purpose local governments. The state legislatures of seven states enacted statutes reducing permanently or temporarily the burden of state mandates.

Local discretionary authority was broadened by the state legislature for some or all general purpose local governments in 11 states. Federal and state court decisions, on the other hand, generally limited the discretionary authority of these units.

Reports were issued by study groups in 10 states; nine of which were devoted to state mandates. This essay will examine activity in these states, and update state-local relations for each.

New and Expanded State Mandates

The 1992 Arizona Legislature mandated that municipal providers, prior to increasing rates or fees, must prepare and make available a written explanation of the proposed rate increase 30 days prior to holding a public hearing. A council, at a regular meeting, must give notice of its intent to increase charges and to hold a publicly advertised hearing on the question within 30 days.

The 1993 Connecticut General Assembly mandated municipal compliance with state established minimum standards for probate court facilities. However, a specific requirement

may be waived or modified by the probate court administrator after conferring with the probate judge and the responsible municipal officer. The 1993 General Assembly also enacted a law requiring employers, including cities and towns, to submit plans to increase the average passenger occupancy of motor vehicles commuting to and from work sites.

The Georgia Department of Natural Resources in 1992 promulgated regulations implementing the 1991 Mountain and River Corridor Protection Act. The act stipulates that any county containing a river with a water flow of 400 or more cubic feet per second must meet minimum planning standards for river protection, including a 100 foot buffer zone on each side of the river bank. Also, counties with mountains 2,200 feet or more above mean sea level must assess the impact certain activities have on mountain areas and enact specific zoning requirements for proposed structures. Failure to comply will result in lost eligibility for specified grants and loans.

The 1993 Maine Legislature imposed 16 new mandates on local governments. One mandate partially preempts local authority relative to granting permits to motor vehicle recycling businesses. Cities and towns are authorized to apply existing ordinances to an application, but the new state standards must be applied concurrently.

Joseph F. Zimmerman is professor of Political Science, Graduate School of Public Affairs, State University of New York of Albany, and Julie M. Clark is a graduate student in Political Science, Graduate School of Public Affairs, State University of New York at Albany.

The Maryland General Assembly enacted the Economic Growth, Resource Protection, and Planning Act of 1992, which requires municipalities to develop comprehensive plans that meet specified state goals, including protection of sensitive areas and resource conservation, economic growth encouragement and re-routing growth from rural areas to existing population centers. Municipalities possess the authority to adopt the necessary implementing regulations via zoning and land-use ordinances. Failure of a municipality to comply will result in state establishment of sensitive areas standard for that government.

The 1993 North Dakota Legislative Assembly enacted House Bill 1057 requiring the board of county commissioners in each county to establish zoning requirements for solid waste disposal and incineration facilities by July 1, 1994. In addition, a solid waste disposal or incineration facility must meet the zoning requirements of both the county and the township where the facility is located unless the township has relinquished its zoning authority to the county.

Mandate Relief

Connecticut Public Act 93-434 of 1993 stipulates that cities and towns may delay for one year implementation of new statutory mandates if the statutes do not provide for mandate cost reimbursement. A pending 1993 constitutional amendment in Georgia would require state funding for 90 percent of mandated costs unless a mandate is approved by a two-thirds vote of the members of each house of the General Assembly. The 1992 Iowa General Assembly enacted a fiscal note requirement for bills mandating a local government expenditure exceeding specific dollar amounts.

Maine voters in 1992 approved a constitutional amendment requiring the state to provide funds equal to 90 percent of the cost of a mandate.

Chapter 351 of 1993, which implements the constitutional provision, stipulates that the state may not fund mandates by authorizing new tax sources for local governments, or requiring expenditure of previously appropriated funds. The state is not bound to fund mandates arising from federal law, or legislation and judicial decisions arising from certain provisions of the Maine constitution, such as reapportionment requirements and constitutional referenda provisions.

The 1992 Maryland General Assembly squashed two anti-mandate proposals. Article 15 of Chapter 375 of the Minnesota Laws of 1993 created the board of Government Innovation and Cooperation and authorized local governments to request that the board grant a waiver from one or more state administrative rules or a temporary limited exemption from enforcement of state procedural laws relative to service delivery. The board reviews each request to determine if it meets the conditions of the law and that the granting of a waiver or temporary exemption will not "result in due process violations, violations of federal law or the state or federal constitution, or the loss of services to people who are entitled to them."

In 1993, the Nevada Legislature enacted Chapter 419 requiring the Legislature to authorize additional revenue sources if local governments are directed to increase services or programs that require additional funding.

In 1992, the New Hampshire General Court enacted Chapter 161 forbidding state agencies to promulgate rules requiring additional expenditures by cities and towns unless funded by the state. Furthermore, the state may not enhance federal mandates without providing funding.

New York Governor Mario M. Cuomo in 1993 directed the Office of Regulatory and Management Assistance to select certain counties for participation in a mandate relief experiment. Regulatory mandates either will be modified or waived for one year. The counties, in conjunction with state agencies, will analyze the effects of mandate relief on public policy and issue a report offering recommendations.

Although 20 cities and towns requested reimbursement for costs incurred under 23 mandates, Rhode Island did not make payments under its mandate reimbursement program in fiscal year 1993. No reimbursement in 1994 is expected as funds were not included in the 1994 budget.

The 1993 South Carolina General Assembly added section 4-9-55 to the *Code of Laws* stipulating that a county is not bound by any general law requiring the county to spend funds unless the mandate "fulfills a state interest" and is approved by a two-thirds vote of the members of the Assembly. With some exemptions, a simply majority vote is required if the mandate is funded or if a county is authorized a new revenue source sufficient to cover the cost of the mandate.

The Utah Legislature in 1992 enacted a law requiring the potential financial impact on local governments to be included in each bill's fiscal note. The Utah Advisory Council on Intergovernmental Relations (ACIR) has initiated a sunset review process for all state mandates and has achieved a degree of success in promoting the repeal of obsolete mandates.

A 1991 statute enacted by the Virginia General Assembly added section 2.1-51.5:1 to the *Code of Virginia* authorizing the governor on fiscal hardship grounds to suspend temporarily a mandate upon the request of a local government. Education mandates were exempted from the section that contained a sunset provision of July 1, 1993. However, HB1726 of 1993 extended the provision for one year. In a related action, the 1993 General Assembly enacted HB2332, requiring state agencies to review state mandates every four years and determine whether individual mandates should be eliminated or modified.

On May 1, 1992, Wisconsin Governor Tommy G. Thompson established a Governor's Advisory Council on Mandates, which will advise the governor on public policy relating to proposed legislative unfunded mandates.

Mandate Studies

In 1992, California's Commission on State Mandates reviewed eight mandates for potential state reimbursement of incurred costs. Of the two claims accepted by the commission for reimbursement, one involved interviews of potentially dependent children. The 1990 Legislature amended the mandate and the commission could not determine a reimbursement cost. The other accepted mandate, requiring school districts to report crime data, was found to have a statewide cost of approximately $5 million from 1988 to 1994.

The Connecticut General Assembly in 1993 required the State Commission on Intergovernmental Relations (ACIR) to prepare a catalog of all state mandates and a fiscal analysis of each mandate's impact on cities and towns. The report will be presented to the 1994 session of the General Assembly.

The Connecticut ACIR released a report on state mandates enacted by the 1993 General Assembly. Twenty-eight new mandates were enacted, including 10 educational mandates.

The Florida Advisory Council on Intergovernmental Relations released in 1993 an *Intergovernmental Impact Report*, which described the effects of mandates on local governments. Forty-six laws containing mandates were enacted in 1993. Ten laws pre-empted city and county discretionary authority, and 21 laws provided new or expanded revenue sources for local governments.

The Kansas Association of Counties issued a 1993 report containing an analysis of the financial impact of two federal mandates and 10 state mandates on counties in 1992. Revenue restriction mandates imposed the greatest cost on counties and accounted for 71.9 percent of the total cost of the mandates. Counties with high per capita assessed valuation had a lower proportion of total expenditures devoted to mandated costs, suggesting that counties with greater revenue sources are best able to finance mandates.

In 1992, the Maryland Department of Fiscal Services released a *Catalog of State Mandates on Local Governments*, detailing 758 mandates imposed on local governments through the 1991 legislative session. The department also issued a *Report on State Mandates on Local Governments*, based upon the catalog, which concluded that the largest numbers of mandates were educational and environmental. More than one-fourth of the mandates had a significant ($100,000 and above) fiscal impact.

The South Carolina Advisory Commission on Intergovernmental Relations issued in 1993 a *Catalog of State Mandates to South Carolina Local Governments* noting that 20 new mandates were adopted during the 1991-92 legislative session, bringing the total number of state mandates to 1,206.

The Virginia Joint Legislative Audit and Review Commission in 1992 released *Intergovernmental Mandates and Financial Aid to Local Governments* and a 1993 update entitled *Catalog of State and Federal Mandates on Local Governments*. These reports identified concerns of local government officials: inadequate mandate cost reimbursement, inflexible implementation requirements, unequal taxing authority for cities and counties, lack of adequate taxing authority for all local governments, and fiscal pressures due to the 1990-91 recession and reduced federal government aid.

Local Discretionary Authority

The amount of discretionary authority afforded to localities has been both augmented and decreased during the past few years. For example, Alabama, Arkansas and Tennessee preempted the authority of local governments to regulate pesticides in 1992-93.

In 1992, Arizona voters ratified a constitutional amendment — Art. XII, § 20 — authorizing Maricopa and Pima counties to adopt home rule charters. Charter counties are required to perform the same state mandates services and functions as non-charter counties.

Cities and towns in Arizona are authorized until March 31, 1995, to annex territory if owners of at least one-half of the property value subject to taxation sign approval petitions. The territory must be surrounded by the city or town, and have a border at least 75 percent in common with the city or town. Additionally, the 1993 Arizona Legislature enacted Chapter 222, allowing two or more cities, towns, or counties to establish an airport authority that may issue bonds, prescribe user fees and operate and maintain property and facilities related to aviation.

The 1993 Arkansas General Assembly proposed a constitutional amendment that would impose term limits on all elected officials and forbid the General Assembly from increasing the retirement benefits of state officers without voter approval.

Recognizing the need for increasing efficiency in local service delivery, the Georgia General Assembly enacted two laws in 1993 concerning municipal consolidations and terminations. The Local Government Efficiency 2000 Act establishes a grant program for efficiency assessment, consolidation planning and consolidation implementation. The act mandates that every local government unit must complete a specialized performance audit by 1998, and once every 10 years after the year 2000, to determine if cost benefits and efficiency gains could be achieved by consolidation. The second law provides for minimum service standards for active municipalities. Cities that do not provide at least three of 11 specified services, hold at least six monthly or bi-monthly council meetings, or have municipal elections will be terminated on July 1, 1995.

The 1992 Kentucky General Assembly authorized each first-class city to enact a nuisance code and penalties for violations of the code. During that same year, Kentucky education officials dismissed three of five Harlan School Board members on such charges as awarding school contracts to relatives and accepting kickbacks from businesses. A state appointed trustee for the school district will perform board duties until a new school board is selected.

The 1993 Maine Legislature enacted Chapter 369, authorizing non-charter municipalities to establish recall provisions for municipal elected officers. In addition, the Legislature enacted Chapter 279, granting authority to municipalities to enter into interlocal service agreements that span state lines.

The 1993 Nevada Legislature enacted an Interlocal Cooperation Act — authorizing the governing body of a county of a city to consolidate certain services. The affected governments may establish a permanent administrative entity to perform related service delivery functions.

In 1993, the New Mexico Legislature enacted the Solid Waste Authority Act (SB784), which allows counties and municipalities to form a quasi-municipal Solid Waste Authority. Its powers include acquiring, equipping and operating a solid waste system; borrowing money; levying a limited property tax; and setting user fees to gain necessary revenue. The Tobacco Sales Act of 1993 (SBO58) grants New Mexico local governments power to enact ordinances more stringent than state regulations pertaining to tobacco sales to minors.

Similarly, the 1992 New York Legislature enacted Chapter 391 authorizing the City of Troy and four towns in Rensselaer County to form the Greater Troy Area Solid Waste Management Authority.

The 1992 Agricultural Protection Act (Chapter 797 of 1992), enacted by the New York Legislature, places agricultural land and buildings in the lower-taxed homestead bracket. This law requires land buyers in agricultural districts to be notified of local farming practices, assists counties in establishing farm land protection initiatives, and requires complaints against farming practices to be brought to the state Agricultural Commissioner to determine if the practice is a nuisance.

The 1993 New York Legislature enacted Chapter 512 authorizing two or more towns or cities assessing units to consolidate and/or contract with the county for appraisal, exemption and/or assessment services. Chapter 242 of 1993 authorizes counties to establish inter-municipal planning and zoning agreements with cities, towns and villages. In addition, these latter units are authorized to contract with a county to carry out ministerial functions relative to land use.

Most New York municipalities are opting not to regulate cable companies. Apparently daunted by the complexity and cost of the regulatory responsibility, only 5 percent of local governments have chosen to regulate, 84 percent have delegated the responsibility to the state, and 12 percent are allowing the state to regulate while reserving their future right to regulate. The state provides its regulating service to municipalities without cost.

The 1993 North Carolina General Assembly granted local governments authority to require separation of recyclable materials prior to disposal.

Home rule charters drafted by charter commissions appeared on the referendum ballots in Bismarck City and Burleigh County, N.D., in 1992. City voters, by a small margin, approved the proposed charter, but county voters,

by a similar small margin, rejected the proposed county charter.

In a related development, the Bureau of Governmental Affairs of the University of North Dakota released a 1993 report — *Grand Forks City and County Cooperation Study* — that recommended improving city-county communications, possibly locating city and county law enforcement agencies in a single facility, developing a city-county data processing department and appointing a coordinating council for strategic planning purposes.

The 1992 Oklahoma Legislature enacted the County Home Rule Charter Act (HB2257), which authorizes Tulsa County to establish a charter government.

In Pennsylvania, Jacksonville Borough and Black Lick Township in Indiana County merged in 1992. St. Mary's City and Lebanon City adopted home rule charters in 1992, and Johnstown adopted one in 1993.

Meanwhile, the 1993 Rhode Island General Assembly ratified the Town of Smithfield home rule charter that was approved by the town voters in 1992. The General Assembly also ratified home rule charter amendments for North Kingstown and South Kingstown.

The 1993 Tennessee General Assembly enacted three laws relating to municipalities. One stipulates that municipal elections are to be nonpartisan unless a municipal charter provides otherwise. The second statute requires that charter amendments placed on the ballot for voter approval in a home rule city must be accompanied by fiscal estimates prepared by the city's chief financial officer. The third law authorizes the governing bodies of agencies of political subdivisions to enter into interlocal agreements for joint or cooperative action with similar agencies.

The 1993 Vermont General Assembly enacted H. 159, empowering cities and towns to enact anti-smoking ordinances, applicable to the common areas of publicly-owned buildings, that are as protective of the rights of non-smokers as the state law. The Assembly also enacted H. 535, restoring state responsibility for striping local highways and directing the State Agency of Transportation to assume responsibility for scheduled surface maintenance of class 1 highways, which are continuations of state highways through cities, villages and the populous areas of towns.

Legal Decisions

In a 1992 solid waste decision — *B.G. Goodrich Company v. Murtha* (958 F.2d 1192, 2nd Cir.) — the U.S. Court of Appeals held that municipalities are not exempt from the Comprehensive Environmental Response, Compensation, and Liability Act (CERCLA). Municipalities may be liable for cleanup costs if disposal sites for municipal solid waste contain hazardous substances. The case was remanded to U.S. District Court Judge Peter Dorsey in New Haven, Conn., who on December 20, 1993, dismissed the municipalities as defendants because Goodrich and other corporations had not shown that the municipalities placed hazardous substances in the landfills.

The U.S. District Court for the Middle District of Georgia, in *Diamond Waste Incorporated v. Monroe County* [91-379-2-MAC (WDO)], held in 1993 that a county ordinance regulating solid waste imported for disposal violated the interstate commerce clause. To be valid, the county would have to show that a substantial reason existed that necessitated that out-of-state solid waste be treated differently from in-state solid waste.

In *Tetra Technologies, Incorporated v. Harter* (823 F.S. 1116), the U.S. District Court for the Southern District of New York on June 15, 1993, held that New York state law does not require an out-of-state engineering contractor to be licensed; since a locally licensed engineer supervised the work, requiring the contractor to obtain a New York license would violate the interstate commerce clause. The Village of Florida had refused to pay the plaintiff for work done because the contractor was not a licensed New York state engineer.

The Appellate Division of the New York Supreme Court ruled in *C & A Carbone, Incorporated v. Clarkstown* in 1992 that a local ordinance requiring disposal of all solid waste at a specified local facility and forbidding export of solid waste out-of-state is valid and does not impede interstate commerce. In 1992, the New York Supreme Court opined that the

Town of North Hempstead's ordinance requiring all solid waste within the town be deposited at a designated site illegally interferes with village authority to adopt local laws and ordinance regulating solid waste disposal.

The Alabama Supreme Court, in *Evans v. Sunshine Jr. Stores, Incorporated* (25 ABR 6158), found that municipal ordinances that incorporate in general terms all state misdemeanors cannot conflict with state law since the ordinances automatically change as state law is amended by the Legislature.

The Appellate Division of the New York State Supreme Court, in *ILC Data Service Corporation v. County of Suffolk*, invalidated a county ordinance requiring employers with 20 or more video display terminals to meet specific light, noise and seating comfort standards. The court opined that workplace safety can be regulated only by the State Labor Law if it is not pre-empted by federal law.

The Town of York's home rule charter was ruled valid in 1993 by the Supreme Judicial Court of Maine in *School Committee of Town of York v. Town of York and York Charter Commission* (626 A.2d 935). The court opined that the state has not pre-empted local regulation of education. Thus, the charter's establishment of a Budget Committee with the power to determine the school budget to be presented to the voters is legal.

The Minnesota Court of Appeals in 1992, in *Medical Services, Incorporated v. City of Savage* (487 N.W.2d 263), opined the city acted arbitrarily in enacting a moratorium ordinance to stop the issuance of building and special use permits in industrial zones only after an infectious waste processing company was denied a permit and filed a suit against the city.

In 1993, the Minnesota Court of Appeals in *Crooks Township v. ValAdCo* (504 N.W. 2d 267) ruled a township ordinance, requiring a permit for a hog confinement facility, to be preempted by state law.

The New Hampshire Superior Court for Cheshire County decided in 1993 that voters in the Town of Swanzey lacked the authority to repeal zoning laws establishing the height of buildings and trees near the Keene Municipal Airport, which is located in the town.

The Judge found that towns must have airport zoning ordinances which conform to state regulations.

The New Jersey Supreme Court ruled on April 1, 1993, that the state Fair Housing Act prohibits municipalities from reserving one-half of their low-cost public housing for their own residents or municipal employees.

The New York Court of Appeals, in a 4 - 2 decision on July 6, 1993, held that a special school district created for handicapped Satmarer Hasidic students violated a 1971 precedent established in *Lemon v. Kurtzman*, which formulated a three-part test to determine the constitutionality of government involvement in religion. The Court of Appeals opined that as handicapped services are available in a nearby public school, the state is yielding to religious demands.

Generally countering the flexibility given to local governments by state legislatures, legal decisions limited the discretion allotted to localities. The U.S. Supreme Court case of *Presley v. Etowah County Commission* (112 S.Ct. 820) ruled that changes in the decision-making authority of elected officials that have no effect on citizens' voting power are not subject to clearance by the U.S. Department of Justice under the Voting Rights Act of 1965 as amended.

In *Fort Gratiot Sanitary Landfill, Incorporated v. Michigan Department of Natural Resources* (112 S.Ct. 2019), the U.S. Supreme Court in 1992 invalidated a Michigan statute prohibiting the disposal within any county of solid waste generated in another county, state or country unless authorized in the county's solid waste management plan.

On October 9, 1992, the California Court of Appeals unanimously ruled that La Palma lacks authority to impose term limits on local officers since state law governs elections.

On February 13, 1992, the California Superior Court for San Francisco County invalidated a San Francisco ordinance requiring municipal and private employers to provide adjustable chairs and screens, detachable keyboards, and adequate lighting to workers using computer or video display terminals.

The Georgia Supreme Court, in *City v. Shank* (S93A1563) on December 2, 1993, held

that a municipality is liable for creating or maintaining a nuisance constituting the taking of property or a danger to health and life. The plaintiff brought a suit against the city of Thomasville because her home was flooded with raw sewage. The city maintained that a 1990 amendment to the state constitution established a tort claims act waiver to municipal liability for a nuisance and hence the city was entitled to sovereign immunity.

In *Allied Vending Incorporated v. City*, the 1992 Maryland Court of Appeals found that the state has preempted municipal ordinances restricting the placement of state-licensed cigarette vending machines to areas not generally accessible to minors.

In *King v. Cuomo* (81 N.Y.2d 247), the New York Court of Appeals in 1993 invalidated the procedure used by the state Legislature to recall enacted bills from the governor. The case involved a bill forbidding the establishment of a county landfill on agricultural land in Saratoga County. After being recalled from the governor, the bill never was returned to the governor by the Legislature. The Court stipulated that its ruling was prescriptive because of the large number of bills recalled by the Legislature since the mid-19th century and not returned to the governor.

The Texas Supreme Court for the third time held that the system for financing public schools is unconstitutional. The 1992 decision — *Carrollton-Farmers Branch Independent School District v. Edgewood Independent School District* (no. 1469) — invalidated the financing mechanism embodied in Senate Bill 351 which had created County Education Districts (CEDs). The CEDs, composed of several school districts with a per pupil property wealth no greater than $280,000, were responsible for levying and redistributing taxes for school districts. Texas voters in 1993 rejected a proposed constitutional amendment relative to school financing.

State Aid and Finance

Some state funding has become available to localities, but not without a loss in discretionary power. The City of West Haven, Conn., with a deficit of $10.2 million in fiscal year 1993 and a $12.7 million bond debt, requested state financial assistance. The General Assembly approved $35 million in bond guarantees and imposed stricter financial controls on the city. West Haven was denied permission by the General Assembly to file for bankruptcy protection, but was made subject to a state financial review panel with taxing power and approval authority over collective bargaining agreements. The Borough of Jewett City, Conn., also was placed in state receivership.

The 1992 Iowa General Assembly created an investment recovery program for municipalities that invested funds in the Iowa Trust Program. Municipalities are allowed to borrow money for operational purposes at low interest rates until money lost in the investment programs is recovered. The General Assembly also froze the amount cities and counties can collect in property tax revenue for fiscal years 1993 and 1994 at 1992 levels and authorized certain exceptions such as debt service.

The 1992 Kentucky General Assembly established the Local Government Economic Fund, which will receive one-half of severance and processing taxes collected on coal. This fund, administered by the Kentucky Economic Development Finance Authority, will make grants to attract new industry to the coal producing counties, effective July 1, 1995.

Chelsea, Mass. is no longer insolvent, yet remains in state-imposed receivership. The city reduced costs by trimming payroll, renegotiating union contracts, receiving $5 million in restitution for the Tobin Bridge from the Massachusetts Port Authority and attracting a state computer center.

The Michigan Legislature in 1993 eliminated the property tax as a source of financing K-12 public education. Previously, the local government's share of education costs was 60 percent. The Legislature presumably will fund the total costs via increases in business, personal income and sales taxes.

The 1992 Minnesota Legislature enacted Chapter 511 applying the sales tax to local government purchases and repealing the city levy limit. The chapter was enacted instead of the governor's proposed $66 million annual reduction in state aid for cities and the Senate's proposed income tax increase, which was faced with a gubernatorial veto.

The 1993 Minnesota Legislature enacted Chapter 141 expanding protection for agriculture lands in the seven county Twin Cities metropolitan area by stipulating that new public infrastructure improvements on or adjacent to lands or buildings enrolled in agricultural preserves to be of no benefit and hence unassessible.

The 1993 Nevada Legislature expanded a debt-management special law, enacted for Clark County in 1992, to every local government. This law is expected to improve the credit ratings of local governments and coordinate overlapping debt-issuing agencies. Local governments are required to submit debt-management plans to the state in January 1994, including three-year capital improvement forecasts.

In 1993, the New Hampshire General Court enacted the Safe Drinking Water Act (Chapter 341) which provides state funds to cities and towns equal to 20 percent of the annual amortization costs incurred to meet standards established by the federal Safe Drinking Water Act. Similarly, the 1993 Rhode Island General Assembly enacted Chapters 313 and 396 establishing the State Drinking Water Revolving Loan Fund to finance drinking water projects.

The New Hampshire-Vermont Solid Waste Authority filed for Chapter 9 bankruptcy protection on September 16, 1993, in lieu of raising the tipping fee which, at $96 dollars per ton, is the highest in either state. The Authority, involving 29 towns, is engaged in a dispute with Wheelabrator Environmental Systems Inc. over $1.2 million in unpaid bills.

Federal Bankruptcy Court Judge James Yacos informed members of the authority that it must tax or assess member towns in order to gain bankruptcy protection and cited the authority's operating agreement, which stipulates that towns will be assessed for the cost of burning trash. Vermont members of the Authority rejected the judge's advice and the senior New Hampshire assistant attorney general urged the judge to dismiss the filing because only the New Hampshire General Court could authorize New Hampshire members of the authority to file for bankruptcy, and court protection of the authority would make investors wary of purchasing municipal bonds for fear the towns might file for bankruptcy protection in the future.

Citing poor student performance and financial mismanagement, the New Jersey state Education Commissioner appointed an auditor for the Newark school system in 1993. The auditor will review its business and financial operations, and has veto power over school board spending greater than $20,000.

The Appellate Division of the New York Supreme Court in *McDermott v. Regan* in 1993 (191 A.D. 2d 47) invalidated a 1990 state law (Chapter 210) designed to reduce the state deficit and financial burdens of counties by decreasing annual payments to pension funds. Counties in 1995 must commence payments to replenish an approximately $2.1 billion short fall in their pension funds and the state must replenish $1.9 billion not paid to its pension fund.

The North Dakota Legislative Assembly in 1993 enacted Senate Bill 2472 authorizing a city council to carry over the year-end unencumbered cash balance in the general fund, and designate the balance for use in subsequent years.

In addition, the 1993 North Dakota Legislative Assembly enacted Senate Bill 2006 appropriating $480,000 to continue the operation of eight solid waste districts established in 1991. The Assembly also enacted Senate Bill 2214, which established a municipal waste landfill release compensation fund to assist open landfills to initiate corrective action to meet federal government requirements. In addition, House Bill 1391 was enacted, which established the Local Government Computer Grant Programs to assist cities and counties to develop "a uniform communications, accounting, and records maintenance system."

The 1992 Oklahoma Legislature enacted SB853, authorizing counties with a population exceeding 300,000 to levy a sales tax up to 1 percent, subject to voter approval, with the proceeds dedicated to development of facilities for lease or conveyance to the federal government and any necessary infrastructure changes or improvements directly related to the facilities.

The Rhode Island General Assembly in 1993 enacted Chapter 242 authorizing the state di-

rector of administration to appoint a Budget and Review Commission to oversee municipalities in danger of defaulting on their debt obligations.

Study Groups

The California Legislative Analyst's Office in 1993 released a report — *Making Government Make Sense* — identifying seven major state-local relationship problems: counterproductive fiscal incentives, inappropriate assignment of responsibilities, failure to avoid duplication and realize scale economies, inappropriate exercise of administrative oversight, unproductive competition for resources, lack of accountability for program outcomes and erosion of local control. The report offers a model of a more rational governmental system.

In a related development, Governor Pete Wilson of California in 1993 issued Executive Order W-60-93 creating the Governor's Local Government Policy Council, composed of the Director of the Department of Finance, Secretary of State and Consumer Affairs, Secretary of Health and Welfare, and Governor's Director of Intergovernmental Affairs. The council in turn appointed a Realignment Advisory Panel composed of 50 local government officers. The panel organized five task forces that submitted their reports in November 1993. Wilson also devoted a section of his 1994-95 Executive Budget to "Restructuring the State-Local Relationship."

In 1992, the Georgia state Commission on Mental Health, Mental Retardation and Substance Abuse Service Delivery released a report calling for improved service delivery and responsiveness to consumers. The resulting statute removes authority from county boards of health to regulate mental health, mental retardation, and substance abuse, while creating regional community service boards responsible for coordination and planning of services in their respective regions. One-half of the members of the boards must be appointed by the county commissioners.

The final report of the Georgia Governor's Local Governance Commission contains several recommendations to improve financing, service delivery and local government efficiency. Recommendations include state funding of mandated costs, structural and revenue home rule, required minimum levels of services and prohibition of service duplication within counties.

The Maryland Department of Fiscal Services released three reports on local finances and taxation in 1992-93. The latter reported that 11 counties granted tax rebates to their municipal corporations in 1992. The Joint Committee on Federal Relations issued a report in 1992 recommending continued membership in six interstate compacts the committee reviewed. The committee also indicated it would review and cosponsor legislative proposals to limit unfunded state mandates.

The New York State Association of Counties, in conjunction with the New York State County Executive Association, released in 1993 a report entitled *Medicaid Takeover: Relief for County Taxpayers*. Currently, counties must contribute 25 percent of Medicaid costs and 10 percent of the costs of long-term care programs. With Medicaid costs increasing 83 percent since 1989, the report stresses the need for cost containment and state assumption of responsibility for Medicaid.

In 1992, the Legislative Commission of the Legislative Counsel Bureau of Nevada issued a report entitled *Feasibility of Privatizing Provision of Governmental Services*. Recommendations include utilizing a numerical scoring system to determine the feasibility of privatization with emphasis on factors such as cost efficiency, quality of service, employee impact, political resistance and government control.

The Pennsylvania Department of Community Affairs in 1992 released five reports designed to assist local government officers and study groups — *Boundary Change Procedures, Intergovernmental Cooperation Handbook, Municipalities Financial Recovery Act, Home Rule Law* and *Home Rule in Pennsylvania*. The latter two reports detail the powers of home rule charters and procedures for adopting a home rule charter.

The South Carolina Advisory Commission on Intergovernmental Relations (ACIR) issued three reports in 1992-93. Due to increased organization and the corresponding need for efficient service delivery, ACIR recommends that

each urbanized area be authorized to form a charter commission to create a metropolitan council form of government to meet expectations for urban services and the need for centralized county governing authority.

Virginia's Joint Legislative Audit and Review Commission in 1993 released *State/Local Relations and Service Responsibilities: A Framework for Change*. Unfunded federal and state mandates, as well as a need for improved intergovernmental communication, were identified as concerns of local government officers.

The League of Minnesota Cities in 1992 released a *Cooperation and Consolidation Report* containing sections on cooperative and joint agreements, limitations and barriers to agreements, and consolidation of governments. The report concludes that consolidation of general purpose local governments is apt to continue to be rare.

Summary

The 1992-93 biennium was dominated by local governments' protests against unfunded state mandates, enactment of mandate relief statutes and voter ratification of a Maine constitutional mandate reimbursement amendment, and publication of studies of state mandates. The fiscal burdens of state mandates on general purpose local governments were reduced permanently or temporarily by statutes enacted by seven state legislatures.

The state legislatures in 11 states enacted laws broadening the discretionary authority of general purpose local governments, but the expansions of authority generally were limited ones. No state legislature during the biennium devolved broad powers upon its political subdivisions. New and expanded mandates generally offset the grant of additional discretionary authority.

Responding to pressures from local government officers and citizens, many state legislatures established study groups which, together with other organizations, published reports. Nine of the reports were devoted to state mandates.

Developments during 1992 and 1993 suggest that voters, by ratifying constitutional amendments, and state legislatures will continue to provide general purpose local governments relief from unfunded state mandates as the burdens of unfunded federal mandates mount.

References

Local Discretionary Authority

Berman, David R., et al., "County Home Rule: Does Where You Stand Depend on Where You Sit?" *State and Local Government Review*, Spring 1985, pp. 232-34.

Clark, Gordon L., *Judges and Cities: Interpreting Local Automony* (Chicago: University of Chicago Press, 1985).

Fordham, Jefferson B., *Model Constitutional Provisions for Municipal Home Rule* (Chicago: American Municipal Association, 1953).

Libonati, Michael E., "Local Governments in State Courts: A New Chapter in Constitutional Law," *Intergovernmental Perspective*, Summer/Fall 1987, pp. 15-17.

Local Government Autonomy: Needs for State Constitutional, Statutory, and Judicial Clarification (Washington, D.C.: U.S. Advisory Commission on Intergovernmental Relations, 1993).

Martin, Lawrence L., "Assessing Actual Versus Potential County Discretionary Authority," *Southeastern Political Review*, Fall 1991, pp. 214-27.

Model City Charter, 7th ed. (Denver: National Civic League, 1989).

Mott, Rodney L., *Home Rule for America's Cities* (Chicago: American Municipal Association, 1949).

Pagano, Michael A., "State-Local Relations in the 1990s," *The Annals of the American Academy of Political and Social Science*, May 1990, pp. 94-105.

State-Local Relations (Chicago: The Council of State Governments, 1946).

Substate Regional Governance: Evolution and Manifestations Throughout the United States and Florida (Tallahassee: Florida Advisory Council on Intergovernmental Relations, 1991).

Zimmerman, Joseph F., "Issues in State-Local Relations," a paper presented at the Maxwell Graduate School, Syracuse University, Syracuse, N.Y., October 14, 1992.

Zimmerman, Joseph F., *Measuring Local Discretionary Authority* (Washington D.C.: U.S. Advisory Commission on Intergovernmental Relations, 1981).

Zimmerman, Joseph F., *State-Local Relations: A Partnership Approach* (New York: Praeger Publishers, 1983).

State-Local Relations Bodies

State-Local Relations Bodies, State ACIRs, and Other Approaches (Washington D.C.: United States Advisory Commission on Intergovernmental Relations, 1981).

Intergovernmental Fiscal Relations

Aronson, Richard J. and John Hilley, *Financing State and Local Governments*, 4th ed. (Washington, D.C.: The Brookings Institution, 1986).

Clark, Terry N. et al., *Financial Handbook for Mayors and City Managers* (Florence, Ky.: Van Nostrand Reinhold, 1986).

Hale, Dennis, "Proposition 2 1/2 a Decade Later: The Ambiguous Legacy of Tax Reform in Massachusetts," *State and Local Government Review*, Spring 1993, pp. 117-29.

MacManus, Susan A., "Mad About Mandates: The Issue of Who Should Pay for What Resurfaces," *Publius*, Summer, 1991, pp. 59-75.

Proposition 2½: The Fiscal Facts (Boston: Massachusetts Department of Revenue, 1985).

Proposition 13 — How California Governments Coped with a $6 Billion Revenue Loss (Washington, D.C.: U.S. Government Printing Office, 1979).

United States Department of the Treasury, *Federal-State-Local Fiscal Relations: Report to the Congress* (Washington, D.C.: U.S. Government Printing Office, 1985).

State Mandates

Fiscal Effects of State School Mandates (Albany: New York State Legislative Commission on Expenditure Review, 1978).

Local Government Guide to the Mandate Process (Sacramento: California Commission on State Mandates, 1991).

Intergovernmental Mandates and Financial Aid to Local Governments (Richmond: Joint Legislative Audit and Review Commission, Virginia General Assembly, 1992).

1993 Intergovernmental Impact Report (Mandates and Measures Affecting Local Government Capacity) (Tallahassee: Florida Advisory Council on Intergovernmental Relations, 1993).

Mandate Costs: A Kansas Case Study (Topeka: Kansas Association of Counties, 1993).

1993 State Mandates (Hartford: Connecticut Advisory Commission on Intergovernmental Relations, 1993).

Report of State Mandates on Local Governments (Annapolis: Department of Fiscal Services, 1992).

State Mandates to Counties (Albany: New York State Legislative Commission on Expenditure Review, 1981).

State Mandates Study (Salt Lake City: Utah Advisory Council on Intergovernmental Relations, 1991).

Zimmerman, Joseph F., "Relieving the Fiscal Burdens of State and Federal Mandates and Restraints," *Current Municipal Problems*, vol. XIX, no. 2, 1991, pp. 216-24.

Zimmerman, Joseph F., "State Mandated Expenditures Distortions: Is There a Remedy?" a paper presented at the Annual Legislative Conference, Association of County Commissioner of Georgia, Atlanta, Ga., January 13, 1994.

Zimmerman, Joseph F., "The State Mandate Problem," *State and Local Government Review*, Spring 1987, pp. 78-84.

Zimmerman, Joseph F., "State Mandates and Restraints on Local Discretionary Authority," *Comparative State Politics*, December 1990, pp. 49-56.

Zimmerman, Joseph F., *State Mandating of Local Expenditures* (Washington, D.C.: U.S. Advisory Commission on Intergovernmental Relations, 1978).

State Aid to Local Governments, Fiscal 1992

The money local governments get from states is vital because it funds many of the schools and welfare programs in this country.

by Henry S. Wulf

State aid to local governments is one of the most significant activities in which states engage. If we viewed state aid as one program, it would be the single largest individual state program. It is, of course, funneled into a variety of programs — for highways, education, health and the like. The very size of the aid program, relative to other outlays of the states, attests to the considerable responsibility states have assumed for their subordinate governments. If the federal government were to share revenue with the state governments in a proportionate manner, it would total approximately one-half the current total state outlays.[1]

State aid in fiscal year 1992 amounted to $198 billion, or 28 percent of all state expenditures. The increase from fiscal year 1991 was 8 percent. This corresponded with the increases since 1985 which rose an annual average of 7.4 percent. The relatively narrow range of change over this time ran from 9 percent from 1988 to 1989 to 5.7 percent from 1989 to 1990.

The 8 percent increase was well below the increase in total state expenditures of 11.5 percent. Relative to other major types of expenditures, the growth in state aid was considerably behind insurance benefits and repayments, which was up nearly 24 percent, and current operations other than salaries and wages, up almost 18 percent. It was, however, more than 3 percentage points above salaries and wages and capital outlay at 4.7 percent and 4.6 percent respectively. Comparing these aggregated data requires caution, however, because the extremely high increases in insurance benefits and repayments and current operations other than salaries and wages were driven by special circumstances. The former resulted largely from recession-related unemployment com-

pensation expenditures and the latter from the Medicaid program.

State aid, when viewed broadly, would include both direct financial assistance to local governments as well as myriad programs that provide indirect financial assistance. The tables adjoining this analysis (Tables 9.2-9.11) describe, for the most part, only the direct financial assistance. A complete analysis of aid needs to take cognizance of the wide-ranging and often substantial indirect programs. A partial list of the latter might include: subsidization of municipal debt by exempting bond interest from state income taxes; state loan programs; bond banks; local government investment pools; and on-behalf payments for local employees in state retirement systems.[2]

State Aid Historically

In the past two decades, the aid portion of total state expenditures has remained relatively stable in relation to the total. Though generally consistent since 1971, the percentages fall into three distinct periods, 1971 to 1982, 1983 to 1990, and after 1991. In the earliest period, aid averaged 33 percent of the budget and the range was 3 percent, from 31.8 to 34.8. In the second period starting in 1983, the average dropped to 30.9 percent of the budget and ranged from 30.2 percent to 31.5 percent. The likely reason for the drop in 1983 was that a change in legislation for the federal General Revenue Sharing program eliminated states after federal fiscal year 1982. States had passed

---

Henry S. Wulf is special assistant for Programs, Governments Division, Bureau of the Census, U.S. Department of Commerce.

Table A
PERCENT DISTRIBUTION OF STATE AID, SELECTED YEARS 1976-1992

Fiscal year	Total	Distributed by Level of Government		% Distributed by Function				
		To local governments	To federal government	General local government support	Education	Public welfare	Highways	Other
1976	100.0	98.0	2.0	9.8	58.9	16.4	5.6	9.3
1978	100.0	97.8	2.2	10.1	59.6	14.9	5.7	9.6
1980	100.0	97.9	2.1	10.2	62.3	13.0	5.2	9.2
1982	100.0	98.2	1.8	10.2	61.5	13.9	5.1	9.4
1984	100.0	98.4	1.6	9.9	62.3	12.6	5.2	10.0
1986	100.0	98.4	1.6	10.1	62.1	12.4	4.9	10.5
1988	100.0	98.3	1.7	9.8	62.9	11.6	4.6	11.1
1990	100.0	98.1	1.9	9.5	62.4	12.4	4.4	11.3
1992	100.0	98.2	1.8	8.1	62.1	14.6	4.2	

Source: U. S. Bureau of the Census

through a portion of that federal money to local governments.

The data show another change in 1991 when the state aid total dropped to 29.7 percent of total outlays, nearly a full percentage point below the prior year, and in 1992, when it dropped another point to 28.7. The 1992 percentage was the lowest in the past 40 years.

It is unclear where this trend is going. It appears that it is primarily the result of two factors. They are the impact of the recession on state finances generally and the rapid growth of public welfare expenditures. From an aggregate view, it appears that the states might be putting their obligations to local governments below the direct delivery of social services. We must be cautious about drawing that conclusion, however, until we have data from additional years.

Functional Distribution of State Aid

Aid for education takes the single largest piece of the state intergovernmental aid pie. More than $3 out of every $5, or 62.4 percent is for education. The second largest function, public welfare, accounts for only 14.6 percent, followed by general local government support at 8.1 percent, and highways at 4.2 percent. The ratio of education aid to all state aid was very stable through the 1980s and up to 1992 as seen in Table A. The 1992 state aid total for education amounted to $125 billion. The state

leaders in this were California ($19 billion), New York ($12.9 billion), Texas ($8.2 billion), Florida ($6.2 billion) and Pennsylvania ($5 billion). There were 29 additional states that each provided $1 billion or more in this type of aid.

The individual states exhibited wide-ranging variations in their patterns of education aid in 1991 and 1992. Nine states — some large, some small — showed an absolute decrease in their aid amounts. Others had noteworthy increases — among them New York (31.8 percent), Pennsylvania (26.2 percent) and New Jersey (23.4 percent).

The major issue concerning the future of education aid is the outcome of equalization legislation and lawsuits. Equalization is an effort to obtain balance in fiscal resources by redistribution among school systems within a state. The goal is to bring education spending among all districts more in balance on the assumption that additional spending improves educational outcomes. State aid has always been the primary method for achieving some balance, but in many instances it has been inadequate for a variety of reasons.

Two particular cases are noteworthy. Texas, which has been seeking an answer to a thorny equalization problem for a number of years, has seen many potential solutions die in its Legislature or its courts. One of the major obstacles often cited about resolving this matter in Texas is that it relies on two major revenue sources, sales taxes and severance taxes. Income taxes are barred by its constitution and, without access to another broad-based revenue source, Texas is having difficulty devising a satisfactory financial solution. Michigan took a different tack in the spring of 1994. Looking for a way to reduce school system reliance on property taxes, the state voted to substitute a general sales tax at a higher rate. The state will redistribute this additional portion of the sales tax for education aid. A number of other states are looking at Michigan's actions to see whether they might be suitable for them.

Public welfare programs received the next most aid from the states in 1992, $25.9 billion.[3] Unlike education, where state aid programs exist in every state except Hawaii,[4] there are 12 states that provide no welfare aid or less than $5 million each. The reason is that some states have chosen to administer public welfare programs directly instead of through their subordinate governments. California predominates in this type of aid, accounting for about 45 percent of the total. New York comprises another 25 percent. Like nearly all public welfare finances in 1992, state aid increased dramatically over the prior year, rising more than 24 percent.

General local government support, the next largest aid total, amounted to $16.4 billion in 1992. This was a drop of 3.6 percent from the prior year, the first time this has occurred since 1955. Massachusetts had the biggest absolute dollar decrease and percentage decrease (down 23 percent or $244 million). Four states have no general support program — Delaware, Georgia, Kentucky and Utah. The source for most of this money is from the dedication by states of shares in major taxes, very often the general sales tax.

Highway aid, $8.5 billion in 1992, had an annual growth rate of 4.4 percent over 1991, far below the 8 percent overall increase in state aid. Low percentage increases have been a continuing pattern for highway aid since at least the mid-1980s, usually hovering about 5 percent. The long-term decline in the importance of highway aid can be seen by looking at these outlays in relation to the total state aid. In 1972 they were 7.2 percent, a figure that dropped to 5.1 percent in 1982 and stood in 1992 at 4.2 percent.

An additional $22 billion in state aid is scattered in a variety of functional categories. These include, in order of magnitude: health ($6.4 billion); transit subsidies ($3.6 billion); correction ($1.7 billion); housing and community development ($1.1 billion); and sewerage ($706 million). Miscellaneous programs add another $8.6 billion.

Variations Among the States in Aid Programs

Since states organize themselves as they wish, significant variations exist in administration, content and level of state aid programs. Add to this the effect of history and geography and it is not surprising that state aid programs show so much variability from state to state.

It is obvious that patterns exist, mostly on a regional basis. For example, the New England states tend to have similar aid programs, as do the states carved out of the Northwest Territories. Though they manifest similarities, however, there are also distinct peculiarities.

The most obvious differences are seen in the level of aid. The per capita national average for state aid was $791 and the median $636. Both these measures of central tendency, and even Table B, obscure the tremendous range of the per capita expenditures, which extend from $110 in Hawaii and $264 in New Hampshire to $1,396 in Wyoming and $1,787 in Alaska.

Just as there are geographic commonalities, these four outliers demonstrate still other types of commonalities. For example, Hawaii and New Hampshire share a programmatic commonality. In Hawaii, the state has elected to run the elementary and school system and, as was noted before, therefore has no need to provide a flow of funds to local governments for that service. New Hampshire has made a choice in elementary and secondary education that is at the other end of the administrative spectrum, but with practically the same result. New Hampshire makes the funding and administration of elementary and secondary education almost entirely a local government function. About $9 out of every $10 for that service comes from local sources, the highest in the nation. Alaska and Wyoming share both a demographic and geographic commonality.

Table B
PER CAPITA STATE AID DISTRIBUTION, 1992

Per Capita Amount	Number of States
Over $1,100	4
$1,000 - $1,100	3
$900 - $999	1
$800 - $899	3
$700 - $799	7
$600 - $699	13
$500 - $599	14
Less than $500	5

Source: U.S. Bureau of the Census

The demographic aspect is their widely dispersed populations and the geographic facet the natural resource bases they use to support aid programs.

One program that deserves mention because of the variety it introduces into state aid programs is property tax relief. There are two major variations in the way states handle property tax relief payments, only one of which is considered direct state aid. If a state were to target a group for property tax relief — the age group over 65, for example — under the first variation, the local government would reduce its tax bill and charge the state for the amount of the reduction. This is a direct state aid program. Some states, however, do it indirectly by providing payments straight to individuals in the targeted group — often through the vehicle of an income tax. The local government receives the same amount under either scenario, but plays no role in the latter. This would be an indirect subsidy of the local government.

Financing State Aid Programs

There is sometimes a fairly direct connection between a state aid program and its revenue source. The relationship can be programmatic as it is with motor fuel taxes supporting highway or mass transit aid programs; sometimes it is geographic. For example, states sometimes share sales tax revenues with local governments by returning a portion of the taxes that derive from that jurisdiction.

For the majority of state aid programs, however, the financing comes from general revenue sources that may be a mix of different taxes and charges. Further, the state usually distributes the funds based on various measures of need. This is especially true in school aid programs which more and more are designed to distribute resources as evenly as possible.

Issues

There are three interrelated issues that are especially relevant to the future of state aid programs. One is the continuing reliance local governments have on property taxes for providing services. A second is the very delicate matter of unfunded mandates. The very same complaints that states have about the federal government are often voiced by local governments about the states. The third is the issue raised by state officials in which they ask where they are going to find additional funding sources for all the needed programs. It is likely that whatever solutions evolve, they'll be well grounded in the local situation. The solutions, thus, will benefit from one of the real strengths of American federalism, its adaptability.

Footnotes

[1] This calculation is intended only to demonstrate the magnitude of the states' financial commitment. The comparison is probably invalid because of the unique responsibilities borne by the federal government.

[2] For a good discussion of state aid generally and a listing of other state programs that might be included in a total analysis, see the annual report to the National Association of State Budget Officers, *State Aid to Local Government (Year)*.

[3] There is an intergovernmental public welfare payment made by the states to the federal government for repayments to support the Supplemental Security Income (SSI) program. The federal government allows states to combine their supplement to the SSI payments with the federal amount. These intergovernmental flows exist merely as an administrative convenience to allow the states to add in their funds. In 1992 the SSI repayments totaled $3.6 billion. These and a small amount ($39 million) for miscellaneous transactions are excluded from the calculations used in this analysis.

[4] The Hawaii state government runs the elementary and secondary education system.

Table 9.2
SUMMARY OF STATE INTERGOVERNMENTAL PAYMENTS: 1940 to 1992
(In thousands, except per capita)

| | Total | | | | To local governments | | | | |
| | | | | | | For specified purposes | | | |
Fiscal year	Amount	Per capita	To federal governments (a)	For general local government support	Total	Education	Public welfare	Highways	All other
1940	$ 1,654,000	$ 12.63	. . .	$ 1,654,000	$ 181,000	$ 700,000	$ 420,000	$ 332,000	$ 21,000
1942	1,780,000	13.38	. . .	1,780,000	224,000	790,000	390,000	344,000	32,000
1944	1,842,000	13.95	. . .	1,842,000	274,000	861,000	368,000	298,000	41,000
1946	2,092,000	15.03	. . .	2,092,000	357,000	953,000	376,000	339,000	67,000
1948	3,283,000	22.60	. . .	3,283,000	428,000	1,554,000	648,000	507,000	146,000
1950	4,217,000	28.13	. . .	4,217,000	482,000	2,054,000	792,000	610,000	279,000
1952	5,044,000	32.57	. . .	5,044,000	549,000	2,523,000	976,000	728,000	268,000
1953	5,384,000	34.20	. . .	5,384,000	592,000	2,737,000	981,000	803,000	271,000
1954	5,679,000	35.41	. . .	5,679,000	600,000	2,930,000	1,004,000	871,000	274,000
1955	5,986,000	36.61	. . .	5,986,000	591,000	3,150,000	1,046,000	911,000	288,000
1956	6,538,000	39.26	. . .	6,538,000	631,000	3,541,000	1,069,000	984,000	313,000
1957	7,440,000	43.87	. . .	7,440,000	668,000	4,212,000	1,136,000	1,082,000	342,000
1958	8,089,000	46.65	. . .	8,089,000	687,000	4,598,000	1,247,000	1,167,000	390,000
1959	8,689,000	49.26	. . .	8,689,000	725,000	4,957,000	1,409,000	1,207,000	391,000
1960	9,443,000	52.88	. . .	9,443,000	806,000	5,461,000	1,483,000	1,247,000	446,000
1962	10,906,000	58.97	. . .	10,906,000	839,000	6,474,000	1,777,000	1,327,000	489,000
1963	11,885,000	63.34	. . .	11,885,000	1,012,000	6,993,000	1,919,000	1,416,000	545,000
1964	12,968,000	68.15	. . .	12,968,000	1,053,000	7,664,000	2,108,000	1,524,000	619,000
1965	14,174,000	73.57	. . .	14,174,000	1,102,000	8,351,000	2,436,000	1,630,000	655,000
1966	16,928,000	86.94	. . .	16,928,000	1,361,000	10,177,000	2,882,000	1,725,000	783,000
1967	19,056,000	96.94	. . .	19,056,000	1,585,000	11,845,000	2,897,000	1,861,000	868,000
1968	21,950,000	110.56	. . .	21,950,000	1,993,000	13,321,000	3,527,000	2,029,000	1,080,000
1969	24,779,000	123.56	. . .	24,779,000	2,135,000	14,858,000	4,402,000	2,109,000	1,275,000
1970	28,892,000	142.64	. . .	28,892,000	2,958,000	17,085,000	5,003,000	2,439,000	1,407,000
1971	32,640,000	158.39	. . .	32,640,000	3,258,000	19,292,000	5,760,000	2,507,000	1,823,000
1972	36,759,246	176.27	. . .	36,759,246	3,752,327	21,195,345	6,943,634	2,633,417	2,234,523
1973	40,822,135	193.81	. . .	40,822,135	4,279,646	23,315,651	7,531,738	2,953,424	2,741,676
1974	45,941,111	216.07	$ 341,194	45,599,917	4,803,875	27,106,812	7,028,750	3,211,455	3,449,025
1975	51,978,324	242.03	974,780	51,003,544	5,129,333	31,110,237	7,136,104	3,224,861	4,403,009
1976	57,858,242	266.79	1,179,580	56,678,662	5,673,843	34,083,711	8,307,411	3,240,806	5,372,891
1977	62,459,903	285.10	1,386,237	61,073,666	6,372,543	36,964,306	8,756,717	3,631,108	5,348,992
1978	67,287,260	303.88	1,472,378	65,814,882	6,819,438	40,125,488	8,585,558	3,821,135	6,463,263
1979	75,962,980	339.25	1,493,215	74,469,765	8,224,338	46,195,698	8,675,473	4,148,573	7,225,683
1980	84,504,451	374.07	1,746,301	82,758,150	8,643,789	52,688,101	9,241,551	4,382,716	7,801,993
1981	93,179,549	406.89	1,872,980	91,306,569	9,570,248	57,257,373	11,025,445	4,751,449	8,702,054
1982	98,742,976	426.78	1,793,284	96,949,692	10,044,372	60,683,583	11,965,123	5,028,072	9,228,542
1983	100,886,902	431.77	1,764,821	99,122,081	10,364,144	63,118,351	10,919,847	5,277,447	9,442,292
1984	108,373,188	459.49	1,722,115	106,651,073	10,744,740	67,484,926	11,923,430	5,686,834	10,811,143
1985	121,571,151	510.56	1,963,468	119,607,683	12,319,623	74,936,970	12,673,123	6,019,069	13,658,898
1986	131,966,258	548.76	2,105,831	129,860,427	13,383,912	81,929,467	14,214,613	6,470,049	13,862,386
1987	141,278,672	581.88	2,455,362	138,823,310	14,245,089	88,253,298	14,753,727	6,784,699	14,786,497
1988	151,661,866	618.55	2,652,981	149,008,885	14,896,991	95,390,536	15,032,315	6,949,190	16,739,853
1989	165,415,415	667.98	2,929,622	162,485,793	15,749,681	104,601,291	16,697,915	7,376,173	18,060,733
1990	175,027,632	705.46	3,243,634	171,783,998	16,565,106	109,438,131	18,403,149	7,784,316	19,593,296
1991	186,398,234	740.91	3,464,364	182,933,870	16,977,032	116,179,860	20,903,400	8,126,477	20,747,101
1992	201,313,434	791.04	3,608,911	197,704,523	16,368,139	124,919,686	25,942,234	8,480,871	21,993,593

Sources: U.S. Department of Commerce, Bureau of the Census, *State Payments to Local Governments (Census of Governments: 1982,* vol. 6, no. 3) and *State Government Finances.*

Key:
. . . — Not available

(a) Represents primarily state reimbursements for the supplemental security income program. This column also duplicates some funds listed under "Public welfare" and "All other" columns.

Table 9.3
STATE INTERGOVERNMENTAL EXPENDITURE, BY STATE: 1986 to 1992
(Amounts are in thousands of dollars and per capitas are in whole dollars)

State	Amount (in thousands)				Per capita amounts				Percentage change in per capita amounts		
	1992	1990	1988	1986	1992	1990	1988	1986	1990 to 1992	1988 to 1990	1986 to 1988
United States	$201,313,434	$175,027,632	$151,661,866	$131,966,258	$791	$705	$619	$549	12.1	14.1	12.7
Alabama	2,143,312	2,015,484	1,772,140	1,563,108	518	499	432	386	3.9	15.4	12.0
Alaska	1,048,860	909,183	794,294	863,981	1,787	1,653	1,516	1,627	8.1	9.1	−6.8
Arizona	2,996,879	2,432,564	2,014,460	1,913,685	782	664	577	583	17.8	15.0	−1.0
Arkansas	1,465,060	1,176,535	1,053,029	988,755	611	500	440	417	22.0	13.8	5.4
California	39,402,316	35,173,773	29,754,786	24,929,013	1,277	1,182	1,051	923	8.0	12.5	13.8
Colorado	1,969,365	1,816,163	1,601,393	1,459,018	568	551	485	447	2.9	13.7	8.6
Connecticut	2,090,932	1,857,595	1,477,198	1,147,052	637	565	457	359	12.8	23.7	27.2
Delaware	390,542	358,518	317,800	254,127	567	538	482	399	5.3	11.8	20.7
Florida	8,405,800	7,204,813	6,500,752	5,198,824	623	557	527	445	11.9	5.7	18.5
Georgia	3,723,502	3,667,040	2,928,597	2,604,968	552	566	462	427	−2.6	22.6	8.2
Hawaii	127,640	113,673	49,776	30,034	110	103	45	28	7.3	126.3	60.6
Idaho	780,742	584,926	489,765	399,356	732	581	488	398	26.0	19.0	22.6
Illinois	6,706,663	5,856,022	5,274,272	4,797,568	577	512	454	415	12.6	12.8	9.4
Indiana	3,677,893	3,385,370	2,995,457	2,591,875	650	611	539	471	6.4	13.3	14.5
Iowa	2,160,539	1,946,027	1,802,094	1,457,094	768	701	636	513	9.6	10.2	23.9
Kansas	1,440,836	1,311,740	1,073,214	994,956	571	529	430	405	7.9	23.1	6.3
Kentucky	2,392,289	1,913,433	1,741,531	1,415,742	637	519	467	380	22.7	11.1	22.8
Louisiana	2,634,974	2,330,717	1,865,441	1,867,466	615	552	423	415	11.3	30.5	1.9
Maine	711,798	663,588	544,712	427,857	576	540	452	365	6.7	19.5	23.7
Maryland	2,558,591	2,288,000	2,233,494	1,854,629	521	479	483	416	8.9	−1.0	16.2
Massachusetts	4,047,945	4,649,241	4,127,655	3,325,747	675	773	701	570	−12.7	10.3	23.0
Michigan	6,970,998	6,313,931	5,813,874	4,842,870	739	679	629	530	8.7	8.0	18.8
Minnesota	4,733,385	4,277,456	3,621,482	3,124,133	1,057	978	841	742	8.1	16.3	13.4
Mississippi	1,765,089	1,691,111	1,391,664	1,237,181	675	657	531	471	2.7	23.7	12.7
Missouri	2,773,013	2,561,392	2,303,781	1,915,955	534	501	448	378	6.7	11.7	18.5
Montana	610,277	419,878	308,044	319,790	741	526	383	391	40.9	37.3	−2.2
Nebraska	1,047,544	771,891	552,488	537,476	652	489	345	336	33.3	41.8	2.5
Nevada	1,107,607	949,281	725,283	590,225	835	790	688	611	5.7	14.8	12.6
New Hampshire	293,668	220,209	204,898	174,711	264	199	189	170	33.1	5.1	11.0
New Jersey	7,859,234	6,005,632	5,462,250	4,803,345	1,009	777	707	630	29.9	9.8	12.3
New Mexico	1,619,075	1,463,158	1,244,887	1,119,486	1,024	966	826	758	6.0	16.9	9.0
New York	24,711,442	19,443,872	16,767,678	15,182,153	1,364	1,081	936	853	26.2	15.4	9.8
North Carolina	5,523,219	5,084,636	4,066,203	3,402,507	807	767	627	538	5.2	22.4	16.5
North Dakota	402,727	369,588	365,329	399,352	633	578	548	589	9.5	5.6	−7.0
Ohio	7,999,399	7,386,283	6,315,346	5,536,665	726	681	582	514	6.6	17.0	13.3
Oklahoma	2,166,336	1,636,573	1,447,844	1,478,351	674	520	447	448	29.7	16.5	−0.3
Oregon	1,613,334	1,479,025	1,201,765	1,105,928	542	520	434	409	4.1	19.8	6.2
Pennsylvania	8,616,122	6,921,300	6,119,723	5,364,037	717	583	510	451	23.2	14.2	13.1
Rhode Island	500,667	488,214	374,249	347,862	498	487	377	357	2.3	29.1	5.6
South Carolina	2,031,830	1,885,288	1,574,229	1,429,440	564	541	454	423	4.3	19.2	7.3
South Dakota	280,445	241,962	221,219	194,507	394	348	310	275	13.5	12.0	12.9
Tennessee	2,288,949	2,210,631	1,685,450	1,430,475	456	453	344	298	0.5	31.6	15.5
Texas	9,365,415	7,342,620	6,625,955	6,147,106	530	432	393	368	22.7	9.9	6.8
Utah	1,140,214	980,782	842,039	782,272	629	569	498	470	10.5	14.2	6.0
Vermont	303,258	265,368	213,223	158,962	532	471	383	294	12.9	23.1	30.0
Virginia	3,489,912	3,471,957	3,038,790	2,513,086	547	561	505	433	−2.5	11.1	16.6
Washington	4,578,587	3,632,019	3,485,095	3,011,346	891	746	750	675	19.5	−0.5	11.1
West Virginia	1,149,496	959,756	870,197	855,734	634	535	464	446	18.5	15.4	3.9
Wisconsin	4,845,330	4,315,552	3,855,521	3,286,305	968	882	794	687	9.7	11.1	15.6
Wyoming	650,384	583,862	551,480	590,143	1,396	1,286	1,151	1,164	8.5	11.7	−1.1

Source: U.S. Department of Commerce, Bureau of the Census, *State Government Finances in 1992*; and previous annual reports.
Note: Includes payments to the federal government, primarily state reimbursements for the supplemental security income program.

Table 9.4
PER CAPITA STATE INTERGOVERNMENTAL EXPENDITURE, BY FUNCTION AND BY STATE: 1991
(In thousands of dollars)

State	Total	General local government support	Specified functions				
			Education	Public welfare	Highways	Health	Miscellaneous and combined
United States	$ 741.48	$ 67.48	$461.80	$ 96.75	$32.30	$28.99	$ 54.15
Alabama............	499.40	24.55	399.46	1.84	34.35	2.55	36.64
Alaska.............	1,632.15	106.62	993.90	139.72	57.05	95.58	239.28
Arizona............	686.75	154.91	409.66	0.00	89.83	6.13	26.21
Arkansas	530.89	19.38	417.06	0.24	36.86	20.04	37.31
California..........	1,197.76	78.77	607.43	345.34	33.33	82.02	50.86
Colorado	579.31	6.99	377.46	95.58	54.93	6.86	37.48
Connecticut	605.81	67.47	441.22	41.99	9.27	4.51	41.35
Delaware	565.75	0.00	469.84	1.21	4.41	1.20	89.09
Florida	624.59	102.50	481.02	0.02	10.90	6.39	23.75
Georgia............	567.40	1.22	502.98	0.00	2.13	42.72	18.35
Hawaii	91.82	57.20	0.00	9.03	0.00	6.09	19.50
Idaho	640.75	60.58	487.76	0.00	63.39	5.01	24.01
Illinois.............	563.85	66.69	365.61	15.27	39.52	5.19	71.56
Indiana............	673.63	141.60	398.39	46.60	58.53	7.49	21.02
Iowa	757.30	56.54	526.93	12.62	97.36	15.73	48.13
Kansas	563.91	32.87	444.34	0.39	43.28	22.41	20.62
Kentucky	598.22	0.00	502.01	1.84	24.41	21.99	47.98
Louisiana	580.25	38.62	477.09	8.79	10.16	0.32	45.26
Maine	568.20	57.30	453.36	17.70	16.46	4.27	19.13
Maryland	551.90	40.34	338.92	0.01	59.29	49.07	64.27
Massachusetts	750.02	177.91	299.14	77.03	3.93	0.12	191.89
Michigan	703.10	110.04	377.49	36.16	74.18	54.40	50.82
Minnesota	1,101.70	193.82	595.78	140.06	73.32	28.11	70.61
Mississippi	627.77	103.41	457.02	2.16	30.79	10.62	23.77
Missouri	517.88	1.27	442.03	1.85	31.82	1.74	39.17
Montana...........	729.09	54.30	558.22	11.66	17.60	7.26	80.06
Nebraska	559.71	53.72	352.53	3.43	68.57	47.14	34.33
Nevada	807.67	262.93	501.72	6.95	28.18	1.65	6.24
New Hampshire	232.66	28.43	117.53	44.07	14.81	0.28	27.54
New Jersey	791.93	118.59	474.76	113.41	0.71	12.07	72.39
New Mexico........	1,002.72	247.78	702.62	0.00	20.02	1.62	30.68
New York	1,138.60	57.22	541.51	386.64	11.54	33.83	107.87
North Carolina	808.61	70.74	598.39	49.05	17.53	42.82	30.07
North Dakota	611.70	87.53	414.29	2.20	64.86	12.32	30.50
Ohio	710.22	94.44	416.99	82.20	61.09	29.48	26.02
Oklahoma	608.38	7.15	485.12	18.04	52.40	22.08	23.59
Oregon	547.67	27.94	327.04	0.00	113.28	50.19	29.22
Pennsylvania	576.61	8.77	333.91	83.12	24.35	44.69	81.78
Rhode Island	446.03	30.52	355.67	40.69	0.00	0.00	19.15
South Carolina	563.79	62.20	452.04	2.39	3.97	6.27	36.92
South Dakota	384.07	34.32	294.42	0.80	19.59	0.64	34.30
Tennessee..........	496.70	45.79	274.06	88.92	50.87	0.32	36.75
Texas..............	477.76	2.79	426.42	0.11	0.39	20.11	27.94
Utah	599.20	0.00	519.15	1.84	28.73	23.67	25.81
Vermont............	524.19	22.32	408.49	17.93	37.67	0.00	37.79
Virginia............	555.67	3.73	396.64	40.75	24.19	2.11	88.24
Washington	849.62	19.18	665.42	7.36	-48.62	29.80	79.25
West Virginia	654.76	10.13	613.68	0.00	0.00	5.01	25.94
Wisconsin..........	928.14	233.07	424.14	59.27	70.28	55.26	86.10
Wyoming	1,322.59	260.74	776.75	8.49	83.30	53.77	139.54

Source: U.S. Department of Commerce, Bureau of the Census, *State Government Finances 1991.*

Note: Includes payments to the federal government, primarily state reimbursements for the supplemental security income program (under "public welfare" column).

Table 9.5
PER CAPITA STATE INTERGOVERNMENTAL EXPENDITURE, BY FUNCTION AND BY STATE: 1992
(In thousands of dollars)

State	Total	General local government support	Specified functions				
			Education	Public welfare	Highways	Health	Miscellaneous and combined
United States	$ 791.04	$ 64.32	$ 490.86	$115.96	$33.32	$ 24.99	$ 61.58
Alabama............	518.21	24.60	410.81	2.44	35.85	2.71	41.79
Alaska.............	1,786.81	124.81	1,066.24	171.44	56.64	119.78	247.91
Arizona............	782.07	158.46	434.23	59.48	84.28	12.80	32.82
Arkansas	610.70	19.35	483.77	0.26	50.85	22.96	33.50
California..........	1,276.52	77.36	616.93	440.53	38.48	34.01	69.22
Colorado	567.54	7.48	351.58	100.85	54.43	7.64	45.56
Connecticut	637.28	38.91	477.62	59.41	9.24	5.01	47.09
Delaware	566.82	0.00	467.22	1.16	6.92	18.55	72.99
Florida	623.21	104.51	457.95	13.75	12.29	6.82	27.89
Georgia............	551.55	0.00	491.74	0.00	1.74	41.14	16.92
Hawaii	110.03	66.72	0.00	9.06	0.00	15.05	19.21
Idaho	731.72	63.13	567.91	0.00	70.19	5.57	24.91
Illinois............	576.62	65.59	365.37	30.49	37.73	5.67	71.78
Indiana............	649.57	116.51	386.91	53.05	60.36	7.73	25.02
Iowa	768.33	52.40	549.01	14.41	94.64	15.34	42.53
Kansas	571.08	35.07	437.45	5.99	44.86	25.72	21.98
Kentucky	637.09	0.00	537.50	1.89	24.16	24.74	48.81
Louisiana	614.64	35.12	507.49	11.60	9.69	0.57	50.16
Maine	576.35	44.83	476.45	19.51	16.00	4.51	15.07
Maryland	521.31	22.36	355.29	0.02	57.26	47.24	39.14
Massachusetts	674.88	137.14	289.97	51.44	17.02	0.01	179.31
Michigan	738.69	99.69	408.57	31.74	77.07	61.82	59.79
Minnesota	1,056.56	152.64	611.55	118.64	72.21	29.05	72.45
Mississippi	675.24	106.77	475.93	24.14	30.83	11.05	26.51
Missouri	533.99	1.55	441.66	2.99	32.80	1.62	53.38
Montana............	740.63	55.44	555.47	5.96	17.02	14.10	92.65
Nebraska	652.27	90.74	387.85	4.45	68.20	61.28	39.74
Nevada	834.67	253.02	529.49	6.01	30.74	1.20	14.21
New Hampshire	264.33	28.37	134.84	48.82	19.17	0.56	32.58
New Jersey..........	1,009.02	123.76	584.04	163.01	0.02	9.27	128.92
New Mexico.........	1,024.08	252.14	731.21	0.00	9.47	1.02	30.24
New York	1,363.84	49.10	711.59	414.90	4.58	36.84	146.83
North Carolina	807.13	68.54	588.77	53.86	20.18	45.89	29.90
North Dakota	633.22	79.83	427.08	1.50	66.47	27.00	31.33
Ohio	726.16	94.95	420.65	84.88	69.10	31.09	25.48
Oklahoma	674.45	6.04	554.51	17.14	54.34	22.04	20.38
Oregon	541.93	32.51	330.19	0.00	97.12	55.13	26.99
Pennsylvania	717.47	12.50	419.78	115.92	25.91	56.88	86.48
Rhode Island	498.18	20.70	418.98	47.24	0.00	0.00	11.25
South Carolina	563.93	73.78	440.72	2.71	0.35	5.37	40.99
South Dakota	394.44	34.52	295.90	0.88	21.37	0.97	40.80
Tennessee	455.60	46.92	261.16	54.01	49.91	0.17	43.42
Texas..............	530.44	2.86	462.96	12.44	0.47	21.59	30.13
Utah	628.91	0.00	543.97	1.80	27.31	26.76	29.07
Vermont	532.03	18.10	414.16	19.45	37.73	0.00	42.59
Virginia............	547.27	4.09	386.80	42.60	24.21	2.58	86.99
Washington	891.47	17.85	709.25	9.20	56.20	21.05	77.93
West Virginia	634.38	7.33	599.32	0.00	0.00	4.94	22.78
Wisconsin..........	967.71	242.53	446.40	64.95	72.96	65.33	75.53
Wyoming...........	1,395.67	298.96	859.78	5.98	82.55	37.93	110.47

Source: U.S. Department of Commerce, Bureau of the Census, *State Government Finances 1992.*
Note: Includes payments to the federal government, primarily state reimbursements for the supplemental security income program (under ''Public welfare'' column).

Table 9.6
STATE INTERGOVERNMENTAL EXPENDITURE, BY FUNCTION AND BY STATE: 1991
(In thousands of dollars)

State	Total	General local government support	Functions Education	Public welfare	Highways	Health	Miscellaneous and combined
United States	$186,540,238	$16,977,032	$116,179,860	$24,341,214	$8,126,477	$7,292,105	$13,623,550
Alabama	2,042,035	100,400	1,633,403	7,516	140,447	10,432	149,837
Alaska	930,327	60,774	566,525	79,640	32,518	54,483	136,387
Arizona	2,575,296	580,924	1,536,241	0	336,862	22,983	98,286
Arkansas	1,259,279	45,972	989,257	577	87,438	47,542	88,493
California	36,387,815	2,393,006	18,453,791	10,491,350	1,012,651	2,491,794	1,545,223
Colorado	1,956,314	23,604	1,274,683	322,770	185,501	23,177	126,579
Connecticut	1,993,721	222,039	1,452,056	138,189	30,514	14,831	136,092
Delaware	384,710	0	319,492	820	3,000	819	60,579
Florida	8,292,704	1,360,958	6,386,539	276	144,746	84,895	315,290
Georgia	3,757,866	8,058	3,331,239	0	14,100	282,922	121,547
Hawaii	104,219	64,923	0	10,249	0	6,913	22,134
Idaho	665,736	62,942	506,779	0	65,860	5,205	24,950
Illinois	6,508,465	769,800	4,220,261	176,243	456,160	59,948	826,053
Indiana	3,779,085	794,394	2,234,966	261,408	328,361	42,027	117,929
Iowa	2,116,655	158,031	1,472,782	35,261	272,109	43,962	134,510
Kansas	1,406,963	82,007	1,108,633	971	107,985	55,909	51,458
Kentucky	2,221,186	0	1,863,952	6,826	90,642	81,634	178,132
Louisiana	2,467,214	164,217	2,028,603	37,375	43,209	1,344	192,466
Maine	701,731	70,760	559,894	21,855	20,324	5,278	23,620
Maryland	2,682,227	196,070	1,647,152	35	288,151	238,465	312,354
Massachusetts	4,497,141	1,066,751	1,793,660	461,883	23,583	720	1,150,544
Michigan	6,586,640	1,030,847	3,536,310	338,789	694,949	509,618	476,127
Minnesota	4,882,754	859,027	2,640,497	620,765	324,963	124,565	312,937
Mississippi	1,627,186	268,039	1,184,607	5,590	79,820	27,527	61,603
Missouri	2,671,247	6,549	2,280,015	9,525	164,134	8,980	202,044
Montana	589,106	43,875	451,041	9,421	14,220	5,863	64,686
Nebraska	891,619	85,573	561,576	5,461	109,235	75,090	54,684
Nevada	1,037,053	337,608	644,207	8,922	36,187	2,116	8,013
New Hampshire	257,088	31,417	129,870	48,694	16,370	305	30,432
New Jersey	6,145,398	920,280	3,684,163	880,086	5,494	93,650	561,725
New Mexico	1,552,216	383,562	1,087,662	0	30,989	2,513	47,490
New York	20,560,925	1,033,255	9,778,590	6,981,865	208,448	610,914	1,947,853
North Carolina	5,447,610	476,583	4,031,386	330,468	118,078	288,498	202,597
North Dakota	388,431	55,581	263,073	1,400	41,183	7,826	19,368
Ohio	7,769,101	1,033,071	4,561,497	899,207	668,211	322,529	284,586
Oklahoma	1,931,607	22,707	1,540,251	57,273	166,360	70,107	74,909
Oregon	1,600,306	81,638	955,614	0	331,017	146,657	85,380
Pennsylvania	6,896,859	104,938	3,993,875	994,194	291,227	534,487	978,138
Rhode Island	447,817	30,643	357,091	40,857	0	0	19,226
South Carolina	2,007,109	221,447	1,609,258	8,521	14,120	22,328	131,435
South Dakota	270,004	24,128	206,979	562	13,775	449	24,111
Tennessee	2,460,175	226,797	1,357,413	440,400	251,955	1,598	182,012
Texas	8,288,581	48,424	7,397,965	1,840	6,737	348,918	484,697
Utah	1,060,590	0	918,887	3,264	50,860	41,898	45,681
Vermont	297,218	12,656	231,612	10,164	21,358	0	21,428
Virginia	3,492,960	23,462	2,493,303	256,149	152,070	13,272	554,704
Washington	4,263,416	96,224	3,339,059	36,951	243,982	149,522	397,678
West Virginia	1,179,220	18,245	1,105,236	0	0	9,023	46,716
Wisconsin	4,598,923	1,154,885	2,101,612	293,695	348,255	273,836	426,640
Wyoming	608,390	119,941	357,303	3,907	38,319	24,733	64,187

Source: U.S. Department of Commerce, Bureau of the Census, *State Government Finances 1991*.
Note: Detail may not add to totals due to rounding.

Table 9.7
STATE INTERGOVERNMENTAL EXPENDITURE, BY FUNCTION AND BY STATE: 1992
(In thousands of dollars)

| State | Total | General local government support | Functions | | | | |
			Education	Public welfare	Highways	Health	Miscellaneous and combined
United States	$201,313,434	$16,368,139	$124,919,686	$29,511,968	$8,480,871	$6,359,903	$15,672,867
Alabama	2,143,312	101,752	1,699,130	10,079	148,290	11,224	172,837
Alaska	1,048,860	73,266	625,881	100,635	33,245	70,310	145,523
Arizona	2,996,879	607,224	1,663,976	227,926	322,964	49,037	125,752
Arkansas	1,465,060	46,427	1,160,554	634	121,983	55,085	80,377
California	39,402,316	2,387,811	19,042,747	13,597,738	1,187,671	1,049,744	2,136,605
Colorado	1,969,365	25,969	1,219,986	349,956	188,869	26,495	158,090
Connecticut	2,090,932	127,669	1,567,068	194,928	30,331	16,434	154,502
Delaware	390,542	0	321,913	796	4,766	12,779	50,288
Florida	8,405,800	1,409,682	6,176,792	185,515	165,716	91,934	376,161
Georgia	3,723,502	0	3,319,732	0	11,774	277,752	114,244
Hawaii	127,640	77,390	0	10,513	0	17,458	22,279
Idaho	780,742	67,364	605,959	0	74,892	5,947	26,580
Illinois	6,706,663	762,891	4,249,610	354,601	438,823	65,910	834,828
Indiana	3,677,893	659,668	2,190,681	300,366	341,751	43,765	141,662
Iowa	2,160,539	147,354	1,543,803	40,521	266,126	43,147	119,588
Kansas	1,440,836	88,485	1,103,697	15,123	113,182	64,888	55,461
Kentucky	2,392,289	0	2,018,298	7,085	90,727	92,905	183,274
Louisiana	2,634,974	150,566	2,175,623	49,736	41,548	2,462	215,039
Maine	711,798	55,366	588,415	24,089	19,754	5,566	18,608
Maryland	2,558,591	109,737	1,743,746	102	281,024	231,869	192,113
Massachusetts	4,047,945	822,569	1,739,212	308,523	102,112	35	1,075,494
Michigan	6,970,998	940,745	3,855,645	299,561	727,331	583,440	564,276
Minnesota	4,733,385	683,833	2,739,762	531,511	323,519	130,164	324,596
Mississippi	1,765,089	279,100	1,244,088	63,103	80,602	28,894	69,302
Missouri	2,773,013	8,073	2,293,534	15,511	170,305	8,409	277,181
Montana	610,277	45,679	457,707	4,915	14,021	11,615	76,340
Nebraska	1,047,544	145,725	622,890	7,147	109,535	98,419	63,828
Nevada	1,107,607	335,751	702,636	7,977	40,786	1,595	18,862
New Hampshire	293,668	31,517	149,802	54,238	21,294	626	36,191
New Jersey	7,859,234	963,929	4,549,082	1,269,653	168	72,219	1,004,183
New Mexico	1,619,075	398,631	1,156,037	0	14,976	1,620	47,811
New York	24,711,442	889,567	12,893,270	7,517,628	83,069	667,568	2,660,340
North Carolina	5,523,219	468,987	4,028,979	368,591	138,085	313,995	204,582
North Dakota	402,727	50,774	271,626	955	42,273	17,175	19,924
Ohio	7,999,399	1,045,997	4,633,832	935,071	761,250	342,527	280,722
Oklahoma	2,166,336	19,407	1,781,073	55,053	174,540	70,802	65,461
Oregon	1,613,334	96,786	982,966	0	289,115	164,108	80,359
Pennsylvania	8,616,122	150,097	5,041,164	1,392,088	311,140	683,122	1,038,511
Rhode Island	500,667	20,805	421,079	47,477	0	0	11,306
South Carolina	2,031,830	265,822	1,587,925	9,779	1,260	19,345	147,699
South Dakota	280,445	24,543	210,382	628	15,192	688	29,012
Tennessee	2,288,949	235,746	1,312,052	271,361	250,769	876	218,145
Texas	9,365,415	50,417	8,173,962	219,593	8,286	381,141	532,016
Utah	1,140,214	0	986,214	3,268	49,509	48,522	52,701
Vermont	303,258	10,316	236,073	11,087	21,505	0	24,277
Virginia	3,489,912	26,093	2,466,610	271,647	154,384	16,435	554,743
Washington	4,578,587	91,669	3,642,690	47,253	288,632	108,104	400,239
West Virginia	1,149,496	13,279	1,085,976	0	0	8,957	41,284
Wisconsin	4,845,330	1,214,344	2,235,148	325,222	365,310	327,115	378,191
Wyoming	650,384	139,317	400,659	2,785	38,467	17,676	51,480

Source: U.S. Department of Commerce, Bureau of the Census, *State Government Finances 1992.*
Note: Detail may not add to totals due to rounding.

Table 9.8
STATE INTERGOVERNMENTAL EXPENDITURE, BY TYPE OF RECEIVING GOVERNMENT AND BY STATE: 1991
(In thousands of dollars)

State	Total intergovernmental expenditure	Type of receiving government				
		Federal	School districts	Counties, municipalities, and townships	Special districts	Combined and unallocable
United States	$186,540,238	$3,464,364	$95,437,359	$79,302,236	$1,744,388	$6,591,891
Alabama	2,042,035	0	1,633,403	406,753	0	1,879
Alaska.............	930,327	79,640	0	772,400	0	78,287
Arizona............	2,575,296	0	1,536,241	1,018,224	0	20,831
Arkansas	1,259,279	1,412	989,257	206,028	5,460	57,122
California..........	36,387,815	2,309,443	17,505,424	16,185,992	161,664	225,292
Colorado	1,956,314	623	1,274,468	656,758	22,688	1,777
Connecticut	1,993,721	0	18,592	1,804,569	0	170,560
Delaware	384,710	671	319,328	64,711	0	0
Florida	8,292,704	0	6,386,539	1,604,455	57,353	244,357
Georgia............	3,757,866	0	3,331,239	376,364	13,702	36,561
Hawaii	104,219	10,249	0	75,880	0	18,090
Idaho	665,736	1,473	506,779	99,746	1,922	55,816
Illinois............	6,508,465	2,354	4,220,261	1,608,765	352,626	324,459
Indiana	3,779,085	15,819	2,234,966	871,812	3,720	652,768
Iowa	2,116,655	19,233	1,472,782	531,739	0	92,901
Kansas	1,406,963	175	1,108,633	257,343	4,682	36,130
Kentucky	2,221,186	0	1,863,653	321,565	0	35,968
Louisiana	2,467,214	0	2,028,006	401,245	0	37,963
Maine	701,731	7,426	0	20,677	0	673,628
Maryland	2,682,227	35	0	2,644,200	0	37,992
Massachusetts	4,497,141	136,439	260,183	3,170,685	580,152	349,682
Michigan	6,586,640	74,193	3,536,310	2,783,545	2,348	190,244
Minnesota	4,882,754	0	2,640,427	2,124,688	22,265	95,374
Mississippi	1,627,186	0	1,180,327	441,523	0	5,336
Missouri	2,671,247	0	2,280,015	218,662	6,501	166,069
Montana...........	589,106	706	450,158	134,905	0	3,337
Nebraska	891,619	3,990	556,598	139,885	16,698	174,448
Nevada	1,037,053	3,487	644,207	387,468	166	1,725
New Hampshire	257,088	0	20,928	121,520	529	114,111
New Jersey..........	6,145,398	69,734	2,767,573	3,217,997	0	90,094
New Mexico........	1,552,216	0	1,087,662	455,115	0	9,439
New York	20,560,925	440,500	5,057,137	14,985,440	12,258	65,590
North Carolina	5,447,610	0	0	5,441,922	0	5,688
North Dakota	388,431	0	262,889	119,254	5,736	552
Ohio	7,769,101	11,869	4,456,990	2,020,951	10,770	1,268,711
Oklahoma	1,931,607	36,880	1,539,731	272,106	4,689	78,201
Oregon	1,600,306	0	955,335	631,388	10,030	3,553
Pennsylvania	6,896,859	83,188	3,992,433	2,390,203	285,392	145,643
Rhode Island	447,817	12,757	37,918	390,907	0	6,235
South Carolina	2,007,109	0	1,609,258	392,116	1,408	4,327
South Dakota	270,004	14	206,979	55,392	464	7,155
Tennessee	2,460,175	0	18,086	2,418,731	13,115	10,243
Texas..............	8,288,581	0	7,397,107	477,606	3,326	410,542
Utah	1,060,590	1,660	918,887	133,560	0	6,483
Vermont	297,218	10,154	231,611	55,453	0	0
Virginia............	3,492,960	0	0	3,481,067	11,893	0
Washington	4,263,416	25,102	3,336,320	731,685	131,479	38,830
West Virginia	1,179,220	0	1,105,236	61,593	1,295	11,096
Wisconsin..........	4,598,923	105,043	2,101,612	1,884,436	57	507,775
Wyoming	608,390	285	355,871	233,207	0	19,027

Source: U.S. Department of Commerce, Bureau of the Census, *State Government Finances 1991.*
Note: Detail may not add to totals due to rounding.

Table 9.9
STATE INTERGOVERNMENTAL EXPENDITURE, BY TYPE OF RECEIVING GOVERNMENT AND BY STATE: 1992
(In thousands of dollars)

State	Total intergovernmental expenditure	Type of receiving government				
		Federal	School districts	Counties, municipalities, and townships	Special districts	Combined and unallocable
United States	$201,313,434	$3,608,911	$102,961,990	$85,661,763	$2,146,081	$6,934,689
Alabama............	2,143,312	0	1,699,130	441,633	0	2,549
Alaska..............	1,048,860	100,635	0	864,262	0	83,963
Arizona.............	2,996,879	0	1,663,976	1,287,326	0	45,577
Arkansas	1,465,060	1,286	1,160,554	249,235	5,220	48,765
California..........	39,402,316	2,385,970	17,841,736	18,466,485	424,700	283,425
Colorado	1,969,365	15,868	1,219,802	709,570	21,641	2,484
Connecticut	2,090,932	0	22,113	1,902,653	0	166,166
Delaware	390,542	788	321,619	68,135	0	0
Florida	8,405,800	2,211	6,176,792	1,896,926	95,589	234,282
Georgia............	3,723,502	0	3,319,732	348,408	13,527	41,835
Hawaii	127,640	10,513	0	98,136	0	18,991
Idaho	780,742	544	605,959	107,555	1,666	65,018
Illinois.............	6,706,663	2,061	4,249,610	1,752,949	357,703	344,340
Indiana	3,677,893	14,312	2,190,681	971,980	2,836	498,084
Iowa	2,160,539	21,146	1,543,803	482,866	0	112,724
Kansas	1,440,836	18	1,103,697	277,373	4,119	55,629
Kentucky	2,392,289	0	2,018,033	341,596	0	32,660
Louisiana	2,634,974	0	2,175,623	405,252	750	53,349
Maine	711,798	7,445	0	23,484	0	680,869
Maryland	2,558,591	102	0	2,520,533	0	37,956
Massachusetts	4,047,945	147,957	245,856	2,855,110	613,762	185,260
Michigan	6,970,998	55,405	3,855,645	2,884,225	2,090	173,633
Minnesota	4,733,385	0	2,728,781	1,855,398	28,629	120,577
Mississippi	1,765,089	0	1,240,259	522,604	0	2,226
Missouri	2,773,013	0	2,293,534	284,782	6,070	188,627
Montana............	610,277	0	457,707	138,496	0	14,074
Nebraska	1,047,544	4,901	618,209	138,543	22,769	263,122
Nevada	1,107,607	3,619	702,636	398,571	1,106	1,675
New Hampshire	293,668	0	20,835	136,144	654	136,035
New Jersey.........	7,859,234	89,964	3,429,028	4,261,268	0	78,974
New Mexico.........	1,619,075	0	1,156,037	448,964	0	14,074
New York	24,711,442	440,500	7,748,696	16,445,962	12,258	64,026
North Carolina	5,523,219	0	0	5,520,717	0	2,502
North Dakota	402,727	0	271,510	126,168	4,692	357
Ohio	7,999,399	2,136	4,501,745	2,168,824	15,849	1,310,845
Oklahoma	2,166,336	38,662	1,780,682	272,927	4,762	69,303
Oregon	1,613,334	0	981,564	619,011	11,889	870
Pennsylvania	8,616,122	93,641	5,025,322	2,950,106	328,971	218,082
Rhode Island	500,667	14,594	38,428	445,819	0	1,826
South Carolina	2,031,830	0	1,587,925	439,506	919	3,480
South Dakota	280,445	12	210,382	59,487	75	10,489
Tennessee	2,288,949	5,351	7,798	2,256,921	9,443	9,436
Texas..............	9,365,415	0	8,173,276	535,724	2,501	653,914
Utah	1,140,214	1,220	986,214	146,409	0	6,371
Vermont	303,258	11,002	236,061	56,195	0	0
Virginia............	3,489,912	0	0	3,480,261	9,651	0
Washington	4,578,587	26,997	3,640,590	722,958	141,881	46,161
West Virginia	1,149,496	0	1,085,976	51,704	359	11,457
Wisconsin..........	4,845,330	109,866	2,225,351	1,981,825	0	528,288
Wyoming	650,384	185	399,083	240,777	0	10,339

Source: U.S. Department of Commerce, Bureau of the Census, *State Government Finances 1992.*
Note: Detail may not add to totals due to rounding.

Table 9.10
STATE INTERGOVERNMENTAL REVENUE FROM FEDERAL AND LOCAL GOVERNMENTS: 1991
(In thousands of dollars)

State	Total intergovernmental revenue	From federal government					From local government				
		Total (a)	Education	Public welfare	Health & hospitals	Highways	Total (a)	Education	Public welfare	Health & hospitals	Highways
United States	$143,533,607	$134,926,318	$23,336,974	$71,961,293	$6,071,112	$14,098,349	$8,607,289	$715,267	$3,763,025	$512,467	$920,366
Alabama	2,362,160	2,316,135	606,047	1,041,602	75,828	261,559	46,025	8,113	399	309	19,040
Alaska	715,392	706,255	135,832	187,253	20,914	139,535	9,137	3,174	0	177	0
Arizona	1,789,506	1,488,711	384,065	663,224	64,793	161,929	300,795	6,826	170,084	97,353	11,327
Arkansas	1,197,842	1,192,692	193,523	629,494	44,583	152,400	5,150	1,486		672	2,199
California	18,150,980	17,568,690	3,183,716	8,829,895	458,332	1,448,561	582,290	53,619	711	32,556	402,946
Colorado	1,611,107	1,576,805	361,894	638,570	106,335	274,993	34,302	21,937	40	188	9,320
Connecticut	2,132,602	2,128,790	206,357	975,013	158,935	546,147	3,812	254	0		0
Delaware	376,238	362,277	51,951	115,142	21,083	65,910	13,961	2,976	0	0	0
Florida	4,826,682	4,581,729	974,263	2,301,967	314,920	405,787	244,953	1,921	109,544	52,268	31,920
Georgia	3,455,792	3,382,896	662,657	1,759,895	177,810	399,956	72,896	11,431		5	45,308
Hawaii	734,349	731,133	146,413	259,995	35,290	150,911	3,216	343	0	0	0
Idaho	553,947	536,587	91,397	194,243	36,130	106,875	17,360	339	2,630	9,809	3,221
Illinois	4,923,880	4,810,405	979,947	2,304,137	292,776	473,431	113,475	20,241	19,569	0	59,894
Indiana	2,684,747	2,583,224	495,770	1,388,353	139,631	323,937	101,523	2,589	73,903	327	12,618
Iowa	1,519,439	1,449,400	316,369	628,730	136,483	192,016	70,039	322	24,694	41,089	2,615
Kansas	1,149,319	1,131,734	239,240	489,159	62,968	165,654	17,585	3,169	0	0	14,416
Kentucky	2,232,815	2,218,587	363,551	1,338,937	81,144	180,640	14,228	7,423	0	5	564
Louisiana	2,856,778	2,841,098	469,284	1,654,927	143,455	287,574	15,680	2,917	0	5,324	0
Maine	757,361	753,419	96,240	483,372	31,185	70,179	3,942	307	0	0	2,834
Maryland	2,284,169	2,223,856	458,515	1,006,896	126,587	311,027	60,313	16,748	7,019	629	0
Massachusetts	4,455,486	4,035,939	463,694	2,748,663	120,756	278,902	419,547	4,244	124,000	3,808	261
Michigan	5,412,629	5,203,940	913,779	3,034,457	215,344	366,215	208,689	9,692	8,350	96,651	41,972
Minnesota	2,602,191	2,484,953	464,591	1,324,733	114,728	227,518	117,238	1,390	89,740	9,764	11,524
Mississippi	1,840,948	1,825,104	379,460	874,956	76,544	174,132	15,844	4,200	579	5,878	816
Missouri	2,243,693	2,233,294	339,572	1,200,950	143,786	308,892	10,399	318	13	72	4,374
Montana	625,026	610,297	72,447	267,068	32,277	107,436	14,729	1,185	12,035	0	979
Nebraska	767,607	748,876	145,302	360,753	38,343	101,282	18,731	3,126	3,856	2,221	8,156
Nevada	440,835	424,798	91,500	142,266	26,559	73,717	16,037	840	6,266	337	3,695
New Hampshire	499,840	441,244	76,864	182,397	10,886	59,419	58,596	1,695	47,805	11	3,010
New Jersey	4,407,155	4,217,957	546,370	2,214,420	189,222	506,485	189,198	103,614	28,826	4,348	16,522
New Mexico	991,481	921,354	251,808	391,652	56,267	117,054	70,127	42,414	356	25,156	1,949
New York	19,205,336	14,735,440	1,306,323	10,762,683	358,092	624,935	4,469,896	111,886	2,722,241	0	0
North Carolina	3,353,941	3,060,650	623,928	1,598,751	137,982	340,118	293,291	6,598	256,175	2,891	5,128
North Dakota	511,672	490,639	93,126	219,392	19,609	68,540	21,033	493	9,087	0	8,931
Ohio	5,755,502	5,548,900	735,820	3,389,515	247,005	529,984	206,602	21,166	0	52,358	36,941
Oklahoma	1,555,232	1,508,944	279,859	815,967	53,940	203,893	46,288	13,153	0	711	5,847
Oregon	1,857,741	1,822,639	299,367	682,352	171,615	149,947	35,102	6,961	13,339	0	13,595
Pennsylvania	5,633,430	5,571,081	845,116	2,994,586	362,025	687,877	62,349	53,117	0	0	6,403
Rhode Island	783,104	740,233	87,755	372,612	31,704	146,382	42,871	164	0	0	63
South Carolina	2,133,314	2,049,324	367,466	1,132,271	109,328	171,240	83,990	19,792	29,296	6,987	1,647

STATE INTERGOVERNMENTAL REVENUE FROM FEDERAL AND LOCAL GOVERNMENTS: 1991—Continued

State	Total intergovernmental revenue	From federal government					From local government				
		Total (a)	Education	Public welfare	Health & hospitals	Highways	Total (a)	Education	Public welfare	Health & hospitals	Highways
South Dakota	505,291	501,905	68,232	205,055	30,972	98,955	3,386	108	0	1,479	1,019
Tennessee	2,772,431	2,731,190	459,571	1,488,292	117,849	257,418	41,241	9,828	78	4,778	12,373
Texas	7,632,301	7,605,216	1,690,102	3,690,232	315,399	1,036,186	27,085	20,438	0	4,412	0
Utah	1,015,897	976,451	287,729	393,174	53,658	94,578	39,446	29,303	2,390	26	0
Vermont	454,298	450,943	71,722	217,342	26,068	58,964	3,355	3,338	0	17	0
Virginia	2,520,128	2,356,812	619,560	1,018,605	103,968	301,578	163,316	16,094	0	47,455	77,197
Washington	2,842,312	2,769,240	599,314	1,227,621	225,156	409,186	73,072	38,416	0	547	5,621
West Virginia	1,083,802	1,075,074	197,405	523,878	44,974	148,503	8,728	1,185	0	0	0
Wisconsin	2,725,371	2,638,726	501,022	1,496,036	85,172	228,516	86,645	5,578	0	244	26,397
Wyoming	590,508	560,732	41,139	99,810	22,702	101,476	29,776	18,796	0	1,605	7,724

Source: U.S. Department of Commerce, Bureau of the Census, State Government Finances 1991.
Note: Detail may not add to totals due to rounding.

(a) Total includes revenue for other activities not shown separately in this table.

Table 9.11
STATE INTERGOVERNMENTAL REVENUE FROM FEDERAL AND LOCAL GOVERNMENTS: 1992
(In thousands of dollars)

State	Total intergovernmental revenue	From federal government					From local government				
		Total (a)	Education	Public welfare	Health & hospitals	Highways	Total (a)	Education	Public welfare	Health & hospitals	Highways
United States......	$169,902,072	$159,041,447	$25,866,723	$91,090,998	$6,825,210	$14,367,184	$10,860,625	$820,184	$5,898,597	$460,428	$928,997
Alabama............	2,737,180	2,707,431	650,440	1,389,303	79,294	236,403	29,749	7,613	713	317	6,923
Alaska.............	773,106	761,779	114,280	225,249	20,608	185,889	11,327	4,015		168	0
Arizona............	2,110,356	1,851,938	437,100	1,000,589	106,275	154,805	258,418	6,001	153,222	58,457	19,720
Arkansas...........	1,635,962	1,629,989	232,713	1,002,354	45,384	174,522	5,973	1,037		693	2,632
California..........	23,429,204	21,562,045	3,457,270	11,953,680	541,647	1,468,509	1,867,159	61,097	1,214,224	239	484,731
Colorado..........	1,918,574	1,843,382	403,833	854,771	121,693	245,274	75,192	18,481	5,027	242	8,637
Connecticut........	2,274,928	2,270,404	218,135	1,196,713	158,735	455,240	4,524	262	0	0	0
Delaware..........	412,211	396,930	60,274	151,752	29,417	68,685	15,281	3,600	0	15	0
Florida............	5,711,452	5,406,514	1,086,840	2,795,277	395,658	488,673	304,938	3,152	186,102	52,390	12,420
Georgia...........	3,770,676	3,723,847	739,790	2,025,079	199,712	354,309	46,829	13,274	0	2	17,281
Hawaii	848,559	845,455	160,820	312,214	51,753	185,995	3,104	394	0	0	0
Idaho	643,738	616,146	103,202	232,561	45,776	110,019	27,592	33	758	24,344	1,724
Illinois	5,740,717	5,559,369	1,106,680	2,921,284	337,150	493,784	181,348	16,773	101,608	0	36,560
Indiana............	3,203,811	3,098,394	508,332	1,761,486	157,727	392,472	105,417	1,797	65,737	5,272	17,406
Iowa	1,651,321	1,578,926	326,249	709,170	153,829	191,894	72,395	198	28,214	41,401	1,907
Kansas	1,359,425	1,341,483	272,158	640,474	74,064	139,017	17,942	3,464	0	0	14,478
Kentucky	2,609,286	2,593,515	395,780	1,649,944	95,683	186,912	15,771	7,137	0	43	1,272
Louisiana	3,695,255	3,676,223	516,512	2,574,078	166,572	125,250	19,032	2,452	0	5,800	46
Maine	931,856	928,391	106,752	625,083	32,555	72,599	3,465	297	0	0	2,637
Maryland	2,662,442	2,588,468	485,601	1,350,351	162,910	239,127	73,974	22,143	7,477	1,425	11,374
Massachusetts	4,626,979	4,226,446	471,634	2,589,019	118,004	479,068	400,533	4,461	53,730	3,616	255
Michigan	6,134,453	5,903,243	1,025,977	3,451,226	251,514	418,535	231,210	10,860	6,835	98,699	44,408
Minnesota	2,909,750	2,686,951	495,988	1,461,224	130,849	242,456	222,799	5,098	183,096	10,821	18,179
Mississippi	2,077,281	2,011,434	408,168	1,106,993	81,820	182,134	65,847	4,621	52,986	1,482	2,218
Missouri	2,956,376	2,945,026	374,151	1,784,114	160,420	319,325	11,350	88	15	230	9,589
Montana	685,573	670,470	85,688	294,493	39,852	130,229	15,103	930	13,124	0	490
Nebraska	897,151	877,464	161,450	444,721	49,109	111,615	19,687	3,490	3,066	1,544	9,978
Nevada	547,402	523,759	93,627	237,795	25,848	61,714	23,643	758	10,881	492	6,203
New Hampshire.....	799,809	732,951	89,762	449,123	9,769	58,674	66,858	3,086	53,867	0	2,867
New Jersey.........	5,337,844	5,130,058	622,143	2,816,970	211,766	649,704	207,786	139,165	7,961	1,165	12,217
New Mexico........	1,202,897	1,116,316	258,658	565,703	65,169	117,601	86,581	57,205	411	28,508	0
New York..........	22,142,003	17,347,330	1,607,355	12,789,907	395,301	731,819	4,794,673	130,084	3,131,843	0	0
North Carolina.....	4,017,596	3,695,376	701,072	1,970,554	168,970	449,450	322,220	4,245	290,164	2,970	3,526
North Dakota......	580,195	557,510	105,464	216,794	20,250	118,699	22,685	662	8,857	0	10,218
Ohio	6,468,864	6,267,841	855,395	3,946,006	256,202	531,948	201,023	23,753	10,263	51,616	17,533
Oklahoma	1,779,458	1,736,419	296,708	1,021,779	68,244	199,127	43,039	14,627	0	555	4,283
Oregon	2,062,649	2,035,792	352,504	785,479	192,643	176,249	26,857	7,211	14,288	0	3,714
Pennsylvania	8,016,454	7,724,509	1,121,958	4,941,337	374,588	590,863	291,945	56,390	221,400	0	7,051
Rhode Island	988,262	943,046	101,985	589,282	27,887	104,675	45,216	123	0	0	151
South Carolina	2,443,841	2,347,127	390,499	1,396,027	111,358	190,021	96,714	21,220	39,999	7,082	671

STATE INTERGOVERNMENTAL REVENUE FROM FEDERAL AND LOCAL GOVERNMENTS: 1992—Continued

State	Total intergovernmental revenue	From federal government					From local government				
		Total (a)	Education	Public welfare	Health & hospitals	Highways	Total (a)	Education	Public welfare	Health & hospitals	Highways
South Dakota	549,243	544,933	75,958	239,828	35,794	90,667	4,310	129	0	2,661	638
Tennessee	3,427,157	3,384,884	473,522	2,022,888	121,582	307,093	42,273	10,869	224	5,062	16,494
Texas	8,577,914	8,505,210	1,778,422	4,653,902	351,361	810,994	72,704	33,230	29,303	4,259	0
Utah	1,150,310	1,105,748	310,844	480,047	46,691	110,217	44,562	35,003	3,202	12	0
Vermont	509,744	504,489	76,780	242,282	35,616	54,184	5,255	837	0	24	4,394
Virginia	2,725,900	2,563,170	681,747	1,166,248	74,250	298,361	162,730	16,129	0	47,680	73,486
Washington	2,994,704	2,929,999	648,812	1,385,268	259,827	331,293	64,705	38,825	0	0	3,671
West Virginia	1,490,087	1,475,928	223,851	839,771	52,676	194,490	14,159	3,173	0	0	0
Wisconsin	3,015,338	2,921,070	536,486	1,696,201	99,528	241,155	94,268	7,063	0	251	32,460
Wyoming	666,779	646,319	57,354	134,605	11,880	95,446	20,460	13,629	0	891	4,538

Source: U.S. Department of Commerce, Bureau of the Census, *State Government Finances 1992*.

Note: Detail may not add to totals due to rounding.

(a) Total includes revenue for other activities not shown separately in this table.

The Effects of Free Trade Agreements on State Sovereignty

States are beginning to look more closely at NAFTA and GATT provisions for their long-term effects on state sovereignty.

by Benjamin J. Jones

The North American Free Trade Agreement (NAFTA) and the General Agreement on Tariffs and Trade (GATT) form a basis for what many hope will be a period of sustained growth and productivity in both developed and developing nations. Although the greatest impact of those agreements will be in the economic arena — where most of the attention has been focused — the state government community is now paying some attention to the potential long-term implications of such agreements for state sovereignty within the federal system of the United States.

Any binding international agreement inherently limits the ability of a nation, and therefore its constituent governments, to make policy choices contrary to the agreement, and therefore limits to some degree the sovereignty of that nation's central government as well as its subdivisions. Given the high degree of compliance with detailed and pervasive standards and agreements which are called for in the case of truly "free trade," however, the states are beginning to realize that a federal commitment to such free trade carries promises to which they will have to conform as well.

State governments have traditionally regulated and legislated in a wide variety of subject areas where international trade commitments under NAFTA and GATT will produce challenges to the fact and manner of that regulation. Challenges typically will involve claims that a state regulation or statute constitutes a trade barrier because it offers a competitive advantage or a de facto subsidy to U.S., versus foreign, business. This type of complaint is typified by the U.S.-Canada "Beer Wars" and will probably be more frequent under NAFTA than under the more carefully defined GATT agreement. Other cases of contention will likely be banking and insurance, trucking regulations, environmental regulations, government procurement, occupational licensing and export promotion programs.

In the case of GATT, the European Union frequently alleges that the very existence of 50 sets of regulations in areas of state regulatory preeminence constitutes an unfair trade barrier justifying retaliatory action. For example, in the United States, pressures on Congress to preempt state regulatory authority in the banking and financial services sector is increased by European Union threats to retaliate. They maintain that U.S. financial sector businesses must comply with essentially only one set of regulatory requirements to do business within the Union, while European banks, insurance companies and others must comply with different requirements in each state when they attempt to enter the U.S. market. State environmental regulations, product labeling requirements, and preferential procurement laws, also have been frequent targets of European complaints.

Legal Overview

Major free trade area agreements entered into by the United States must be approved by Congress and may not go into force until implementing legislation is enacted. For this reason,

Benjamin J. Jones is the former director of international and legal affairs for The Council of State Governments. Rania Samerdjian, CSG research assistant, provided substantial research and writing assistance to this article.

NAFTA is considered a non-self-executing agreement. The NAFTA agreement is also known as a congressional-executive agreement because of the congressional involvement in its approval. The Trade Act of 1974 established a process known as "fast track," which is designed to involve Congress, through consultations, in the drafting and negotiation of international trade agreements in return for a congressional commitment to vote the final agreement "up or down" as a package with no amendments allowed. Upon conclusion of the negotiating process, the president sends the draft to Congress, which must then enact an implementing bill by which means the agreement is ratified and any necessary statutory changes are made. This means that NAFTA will not immediately become part of the domestic law and will not *itself* directly preempt existing state laws. A non-self-executing treaty is binding under international law, but requires legislative implementation to be incorporated into domestic law.

Upon ratification, such agreements become national commitments — including a commitment to make such agreements superior under domestic law to conflicting state laws. Nations alleging violations of NAFTA or GATT do not enforce their claims through U.S. courts. Instead, a challenge process involving international panels is established which will be reviewed in more detail below.

Specific Areas of Contention

Potential challenges to state laws and regulations are somewhat different under NAFTA than under GATT. In addition, questions regarding the magnitude of NAFTA's effect on state laws and exactly which laws will be affected cannot yet be accurately answered. This uncertainty is due not only to complexities in the treaty and uncertainty regarding which laws will be challenged, but also to an inability to predict the vigor with which the United States government will act to preempt state policies determined to be in conflict with NAFTA. However, specific areas of concern under the NAFTA agreements include the following:

Banking and Insurance: States traditionally have imposed requirements upon foreign (non-U.S.) banks and insurance companies who wish to operate in the states that are not imposed on U.S. banks and insurers. Following the conclusion of a phase-in period, these requirements must be eliminated. States may continue to regulate these industries, but may not discriminate in any way against non-U.S. companies.

Trucking: Under NAFTA, states may continue to regulate the trucking industry. Some laws and regulations imposing special safety training standards, however, will be preempted. For example, California's regulations regarding special labeling for dangerous cargo and special testing and training for drivers of dangerous commercial vehicles will now be unenforceable against Mexican trucks and drivers.

Environmental Regulations: The degree to which state environmental laws and regulations will be affected by NAFTA is unclear. It is clear, however, that in a variety of areas of environmental regulation, state policies will be subject to challenge. The rulings of dispute panels and the degree to which the federal government will act against state laws which have been ruled to constitute a barrier is uncertain. Potential areas of challenge include state incentives for alternative fuel use; laws imposing recycled materials use requirements; restrictions on beverage container plastic holding rings; specifications for beverage containers themselves; and any other environmental regulation that arguably was an unreasonable restraint on trade. At least one commentator has noted that if such challenges become common, the "chilling effect" could result in states being discouraged from developing new environmental regulation programs and policies.

Export Promotion Programs: Almost all states have programs of one sort or another to induce business to locate within the state or to encourage exports. Yet cash transfers from governments to private businesses in the form of financial inducements to locate or expand, or in the form of subsidies for firms to export will likely to subject to challenge under NAFTA and could result in countervailing duties imposed by Mexico and/or Canada. In the event of challenge, substantial federal pressure, perhaps in the form of preemption, may be imposed on states.

Occupational Licensing: NAFTA's goal in the area of occupational licensing is that citizens and residents of the member nations will be able to provide professional services in any other member nation, provided they meet necessary and reasonable requirements that are no stricter than those imposed upon citizens of the state involved. This means that states may keep professional standards in licensing but, after a phase-in period, may not require citizenship or residency for licensure in a particular profession in the state.

State concerns regarding challenges by the European Union and the effects of GATT on state laws are somewhat different than those under NAFTA. Those areas of concern include:

Banking and Insurance: In accordance with the dual banking system in the United States, European banks wishing to become established in the U.S. must comply with both state and federal regulations. The European Union sees this dual system as constituting an unfair trade practice in two different ways. First, the European Union argues that some state requirements violate the "national treatment" principle by placing requirements and restrictions on foreign banks which are not placed on domestic institutions. For example, some states prohibit non-U.S. banks from establishing branches within their borders or do not allow them to take deposits. In other states, branches of foreign banks have to comply with extensive registration requirements to engage in broker-dealer activities with which their U.S. counterparts need not comply. In insurance, many states impose various requirements on non-U.S. insurers, such as special capital and deposit requirements. Others do not permit the operation of insurers owned in part or in whole by a foreign party. In addition to these practices, which are alleged to violate national treatment principles, Europeans also argue that the simple existence of 50 sets of state banking and financial services regulations constitutes an unfair trade practice compared with the more uniform regulation in the member nations of the European Union. States can expect these arguments to add impetus to federal efforts to fully or partially preempt state regulation in the financial services sector.

Government Procurement: The European Union has long expressed dissatisfaction about "Buy American" provisions, procurement preferences for in-state businesses, "local content" preferences, and other such provisions at both the state and federal level. Currently, legislation in at least 40 states provides for some or all of these types of preferences. The GATT agreement has pledged the U.S. government to persuade or, if it elects to do so, *require* states to eliminate such preferential requirements in return for access on an equal basis to European Union government procurement. The extent of federal pressure remains to be seen, as does the willingness of states to voluntarily remove such restrictions.

Labeling and Packaging Requirements: The European Union contends that packaging requirements are still an important barrier for import into the United States. A European Union wine exporter must comply with both federal and state regulations regarding the content of wine bottle labels. An average of three months is required to obtain label approval at the federal level, while the approval time at the state level varies, but may take as long as six weeks. Exporters to the U.S. contend that compliance with different rules in each state makes the approval procedure confusing and time-consuming and constitutes an unfair barrier to trade.

State Tax Policy: Under the General Agreement on Trade and Services (GATS), the European Union may challenge any state taxes that are arbitrarily discriminatory or that constitute a restraint to trade. They argue the national treatment principle requires that European taxpayers be treated the same as U.S. taxpayers.

Some state tax experts argue that GATT could conceivably become an instrument for global corporations to escape tax policies based on arguments under the "national treatment" principle. In the case of state corporate income taxes, a multinational corporation headquartered abroad could be placed at an advantage compared with a U.S. domestic non-multinational company. Because states currently tax earnings by multinational companies differently than domestic corporations — to prevent "hiding" corporate income in low-tax nations using paper transactions that obscure real income earned in that state — questions of national treatment will arise under GATT which currently are not a problem.

Subsidies and Supports: Europeans have long argued that U.S. subsidies to support U.S. exports not only exist, but adversely affect the competitive posture of European firms attempting to export to the states. For example, they maintain a Florida statute that taxes citrus processing, with the purpose of using the proceeds for the marketing of Florida citrus, constitutes a state subsidy for the Florida citrus industry. Similarly, state taxes or other incentives for exporters can also be construed as subsidies. It is unclear, at present, the extent to which the U.S. government, and the states, will be pressed by other nations on these issues under the new GATT agreement.

Dispute Settlement Process

In the event of a dispute over unfair trade practices, the settlement process does not allow for state representation before the international panel. As a result, state governments will not be able to directly defend their state laws and will, of necessity, have to rely on federal representation of their interests. Given the recent history of federal mandates, as well as the inherent differences between foreign policy goals and state priorities, states may be understandably skeptical regarding the degree to which such federal representation may be relied on to safeguard their interests.

The "Dispute Settlement Bodies" will consist of panels of experts appointed by the governments involved in a particular dispute. Rulings of such bodies will not be self-enforcing in the courts of the nation which lost before the dispute panel. Instead, the successful party before such a panel will have to request the unsuccessful government to force compliance with the decision. Should the unsuccessful government fail to enforce the decision (as, so far, in the "Beer Wars" case) the successful government is then authorized under the agreements to take retaliatory trade action against the losing nation's exports.

Preservation of Non-Conforming Regulations

Although state laws and regulations in a wide variety of areas are potentially affected by NAFTA and GATT, the NAFTA treaty in particular does contain some protection for state policies that conflict with the basic principles of the agreement. States can file exemptions and reservations to protect state statutes and regulations that conflict with articles of the treaty. Any such laws the states want to exempt must be registered within two years of entry into force of the agreement with no restrictions on the number of measures that may be so registered. Most important to note, however, is that in some areas non-conforming measures may not be enforced, and states may not completely anticipate and register all non-conforming laws and regulations. In addition, for the duration of the NAFTA agreement, states will be precluded from adopting new laws or regulations inconsistent with the treaty.

States have until January 1, 1996, to list any non-conforming measures they wish to maintain. This is very important as a jurisdiction may keep an exemption indefinitely if it is registered by 1996. In the financial services sector, however, states only have until January 1, 1995, to identify laws that are inconsistent with NAFTA. Once identified, those laws will be placed in an "annex" and grandfathered for a future period. In fact, for the states of California, Florida, Illinois, New York, Ohio and Texas, the date to annex laws inconsistent with NAFTA laws was January 1994. Laws that are inconsistent with the NAFTA agreement are those that violate the national treatment and most favored nation principles. For example, a California law allows a state-licensed foreign bank branch or agency to have virtually none of the trust powers of a state-chartered California bank. Although clearly contrary to national treatment principles, California has annexed this law and may continue to legally deny trust powers to foreign bank branches indefinitely.

The federal government now is in the process of notifying the remaining 44 states of the need to file reservations by the end of 1994. The U.S. Trade Representative (USTR) has pledged to work closely with the states to ensure proper listing of all measures and to assist in identifying what type of state measures need to be reserved. In a case where a dispute is brought against a state measure, the USTR also has pledged to notify and work closely with that state in an effort to resolve the dispute in a manner consistent with NAFTA/GATT principles.

Federal/State Consultation

The USTR is establishing a "NAFTA Coordinator for State Matters" to help identify state laws to be registered, to serve as an information exchange channel for NAFTA working committees and states, and to work with state attorneys general in cases where the dispute process is invoked. The USTR, for some time, has had an Intergovernmental Policy Advisory Committee on Trade (IGPAC) to allow state, county and municipal government leaders to voice opinions and provide advice to the USTR. Many state advocates argue that IGPAC has a poor history of consultation with state officials and is ineffective in representing state views within USTR. The effectiveness of the new mechanism for coordination of the federal-state consultative process has yet to be determined.

Uncertainties of the Process

In addition to the uncertainty caused by lack of advance knowledge as to exactly which state laws and requirements will be challenged by our trading partners, is uncertainty created by an inability to project the extent to which the federal government will in fact press states to comply with adverse decisions of international dispute panels. Moreover, the NAFTA and GATT agreements themselves contain the necessity in many disputes to determine scientific facts about which reasonable experts may in fact disagree. For example, NAFTA provides that as long as an environmental regulation is justifiable on the basis of "scientific proof" then it is permissible even if alleged to be an unfair trade barrier. Obviously however, what may seem "scientific evidence" in one nation may merely be seen as an excuse in another. The degree to which state environmental laws and regulations will be affected by NAFTA is therefore unclear. It is clear, however, that in a wide variety of areas of environmental regulation, state policies are potentially subject to challenge.

An example of such a regulation is the requirement in the California Safe Drinking and Water Enforcement Act that a warning label must be placed on all products containing substances that cause birth defects or reproductive harm. One of these substances is the lead often found in ceramic ware. The requirement has forced European exporters of ceramics to finance a $1 million lead safety information campaign for California consumers. European exporters allege that this is a non-tariff barrier to trade that burdens them with labelling requirements and consumer awareness program expenses not required of a similar U.S. business exporting to Europe. If this case were brought to a dispute panel, European and American scientists might legitimately disagree on whether valid scientific proof exists connecting ceramic ware lead exposure to birth defects.

Critics argue that such numerous areas for scientific disagreement may tend to increase the usage of international standards — which could in fact be lower than U.S. standards. Standards and environmental regulation will certainly raise controversial questions of concern to states over the coming years.

Compliance

Pressure may be increasingly applied on local and state governments to comply with commercial treaty provisions. Yet, in the history of GATT, only one ruling of a dispute panel has directly affected state governments. That ruling stemmed from the continuing "Beer Wars" between U.S. and Canadian brewers. The controversy began when two U.S. brewers decided to export beer to Canada. They discovered that Canadian provinces had laws banning the sale of beer unless it was brewed locally. The American brewers took the case to GATT where the dispute panel ruled in their favor. The Canadians then conducted a study and found hundreds of wine and beer regulations in more than 40 states that were arguably in violation of GATT principles. The regulations and statutes consisted of tax preferences to local producers and discriminatory distribution procedures among others. The Canadians, in turn, took their case to the international trade panel which ruled that these state laws were indeed in violation of free trade. Interestingly, however, almost all the rules and statutes are still in effect in both Canada and the U.S. states and, to date, neither national government has required compliance.

Conclusion

Global interdependence increasingly is becoming a fact of life. State governments effectively no longer have the choice to ignore developments in the international arena. Some negative effects of international trade agreements upon state prerogatives is inevitable. However, by being aware of and involved in national negotiations and Congressional ratification of such agreements, states can minimize the negative effects of such pacts, while realizing the economic advantages that the nation as a whole hopes to reap.

References

Britto, Karen, "NAFTA Will Generate Changes in Some States' Laws," *The Fiscal Letter*, December 1993, 7-8.

Brown, Douglas and Earl Fry ed., "States and Provinces in the International Economy," Institute of Intergovernmental Relations, Queen's University, 1993.

Center for Policy Alternatives, "The New Supremacy of Trade: NAFTA Rewrites the Status of States," 1993.

Congressional Research Service, "NAFTA: Some Legal Basics," March 24, 1993.

Conrad, Weiler, "GATT, NAFTA and State and Local Powers," *Intergovernmental Perspective*, Fall 1993, 38-41.

Katter, Andrea, "The North American Free Trade Agreement and the Banking Industry," *The Journal of Commercial Lending*, December 1992, 11-15.

Kentucky Legislative Research Commission, Staff Briefing on NAFTA, October 1993.

"International State Agreements Threaten State and Local Governments," *State Ties*, December 1993, 1-4.

Lemov, Penelope, "Can the States Live Happily After NAFTA?" *Governing*, December 1992, 20-21.

Multistate Tax Commission, "World Trade Talks Affect State Taxation," December 15, 1993.

"NAFTA Implementing Bill," *Congressional Quarterly*, January 1994, 34-35.

National Trade Data Bank, "NAFTA Respects States' Rights," 1993.

U.S. Department of State Dispatch, "NAFTA Supplemental Agreements," August 23, 1993.

White, Jim "With NAFTA up in the Air, States Paying Little Mind to Free Trade," *Stateline Midwest*, June 1993, 3-5.

The Council of State Governments

After 60 years of service, CSG is looking to the future with pride in its past and a clearer sense of its role among state government organizations.

by Deborah A. Gona

A nonprofit, nonpartisan service organization, CSG is the only national association that serves the executive, legislative and judicial branches of state government. Through its national headquarters in Lexington, Ky., and regional offices in Atlanta, Chicago, New York City and San Francisco, the Council works to improve decision-making and promote effective and innovative problem-solving and partnerships across the states.

Re-examining the Founder's Vision

In 1933, Henry Toll, a former state senator from Colorado, set out to fashion a new organization of the states. Despite initial uncertainty over its name, the reality of the founder's vision was the establishment of an agency designed to meet the states' desire and need to cooperate and to check the tendency toward increased centralization at the federal level of policy and functional areas the states themselves were best suited to control.

With the states' adoption, one by one, of this new organization, they formally recognized it as *their* joint agency — *permanent* machinery that would fill a void in the structure and capacity of their governments and facilitate the adoption of laws, procedures and mechanisms that by their consistency would enhance their effectiveness. By promoting interstate cooperation and awareness in areas outside the reach of the federal government and beyond the capabilities of any single state, this new organization would help ensure the states' preparation to assume responsibility for duties that the founder believed were rightfully theirs.

Toll's vision was of a super-structure organization that would bolster the states' cooperative efforts, identify appropriate state and multi-state actions for problem-solving and head off the encroaching federal presence. In 1993, The Council of State Governments — the organization founded by Toll — celebrated its 60th year of service to those states. In many ways during that long tenure, the organization had met or exceeded the founders' plan. But no matter what Toll's intent, the reality was that the CSG organization could not, in and of itself, stabilize the rapidly-shifting roles and responsibilities of the states in the federal system. And today, the debate over those roles and responsibilities is more fierce than before.

The first four years of this decade alone have been marked by fiscal crises for the nation and its individual states, by pressures and criticisms from citizens, and by an increasingly intense re-examination of governments' capacity — at all levels — to solve problems and make legitimate decisions.

And throughout the Council's history, its own internal capacity and ability both to react to and anticipate the states' needs in the changing federal system fluctuated. While CSG continued to provide thousands of state officials and staff around the country with many of the same notable and strong services and products first envisioned by Toll and nurtured by his successors, during its first 60 years, the Council's framework — its governance and operational structures — changed dramatically in much the same fashion as state governments'.

So it was, during the first years of this last decade of the 20th century, that this creature of the very states that so often have found

Deborah A. Gona is the former director of the State Policy and Innovations group at The Council of State Governments.

themselves struggling to meet immediate service needs and to find their most effective long-term fit in the federalism puzzle, found itself grappling with its companionate role. An organizational commitment to a strategic planning process forced CSG to reexamine Toll's vision, scheme and purpose; to determine its evolutionary course; to clarify its past, current-day and future role among the states; to target more closely the clientele it could and should serve; and to begin identifying the services and assistance that would allow state governments to meet current and future challenges.

Choosing the Path to the Future

By early 1992, all CSG components at the national and regional levels had committed to a comprehensive, long-term strategic planning process, an ongoing improvement process that would produce fundamental decisions and actions to shape and guide the CSG organization in what it is, what it does and why it does it.

An extensive outreach campaign in the summer of 1992 involved a series of strategic planning focus group sessions conducted with state legislators, administrators and staff, as well as CSG's private sector partners. Those sessions resulted in assessments of the organization and analyses of the changing environment for state government officials. Later that year, an ad hoc Strategic Planning Task Force, made up of a diverse group of CSG leaders, including state policy-makers, administrators and key staff, was established to oversee the final stages of the process by clarifying the organization's identity and affirming its mission.

Keying in on environmental trends

In its early deliberations, the Strategic Planning Task Force prioritized nine environmental trends for their current and future impact both on state governments and on CSG operations:
• Fiscal conditions/constraints — recognition that states are entering an era of fiscal readjustment, retrenchment and realignment;
• Term limits/turnover/retirement — resulting in a significant turnover in state government, particularly noteworthy within state legislative leadership positions;

• Public cynicism/ethical conduct — a growing awareness of public disenchantment with and disengagement from American politics and public officials;
• Changing demographics — demographic changes in the American population **and** in state government resulting in more representation by women and minorities;
• Federalism restructuring — a blurring of responsibility between levels of government resulting in a need for a "sorting out" of federal, state and local functions;
• Globalization dynamics — the transition from a cold war economy to one of true global competition and the states' vigorous participation in the international arena;
• Technology infusion — the proliferation of technology revolutionizing the process of state governance and service delivery;
• Management restructuring — growing fiscal uncertainties and cutbacks leading to major initiatives to rethink the structure, design and management of state government; and
• State service competition — a noteworthy growth in the number and scope of organizations serving state governments and its officials.

Renewing the organization's purpose

Following months of discussions on the environment, clients, characteristics and priorities of the organization, in April 1993, CSG's Executive Committee approved a new mission statement — one designed to emphasize CSG's unique features and to clarify its role among other organizations that co-exist in the state governmental arena:

CSG, the multi-branch organization of the states and U.S. territories, champions excellence in state government, working with state leaders across the nation and through its regions to put the best ideas and solutions into practice.

To this end, CSG:
• **Builds leadership skills to improve decision-making;**
• **Advocates multistate problem-solving and partnerships;**
• **Interprets changing national and international conditions to prepare states for the future; and,**
• **Promotes the sovereignty of the states and their role in the American federal system.**

Guiding the organization through change

And to guide the crucial decision-making and implementation phases of the strategic planning process, the Task Force and Executive Committee further adopted a set of criteria for CSG's organizational change:

• **mission consistency and depth** — any CSG organizational change must be consistent with and add clarity and depth to CSG's mission statement;

• **customer focus and responsiveness** — CSG changes must respond to the needs of state leaders and translate into quick, personalized products;

• **value-added quality and capacity** — CSG must devise multiple benefits and spin-offs of effort and maximize collective identity with organizational components and products;

• **institutional problem-solving and emerging needs** — CSG should promote its unique multi-state and multi-branch approach to problem-solving to improve the institutional functioning of state government; and

• **financial responsibility and productivity** — CSG changes should be based on best market principles and be fiscally responsible and accountable.

Addressing governance and structural issues

In its remaining days, the Strategic Planning Task Force considered and recommended to the CSG Executive Committee more than 20 proposals to change or clarify various aspects of CSG governance, structure and relationships. Some proposals, intended to alter the CSG Articles of Organization, required action by the CSG Governing Board at its annual meeting in December 1993. The most substantial involved changes in the composition of the Executive Committee to better represent CSG's constituency and active participants and to more clearly reflect the new mission statement and organizational priorities.

Other recommendations that simply required approval by the CSG Executive Committee included: a restructuring of the national standing committees to differentiate between the operations and management tasks of CSG and the issue-oriented, substantive work carried out by these entities; a commitment to analyze and deliberate on the appropriate role of associated organizations within the CSG family, to give strong preference to cabinet-level, policy-oriented groups of state officials, and to extend services to high-level administrators; a commitment to develop systems to better coordinate CSG headquarters and regional relations and operations; and a reformulation of opportunities and channels for private sector participation in the CSG organization.

Toward implementation

The work begun in earnest in 1992 will continue as various facets of the strategic planning and improvement process are implemented throughout the CSG organization. In 1993, for example, all components of CSG undertook a comprehensive inventory of their programs, products and services — just one step toward evaluating and assessing the fit between CSG operations and the clarified mission statement. The assessment of programmatic information is expected to continue through the 1994-95 period.

The CSG Framework — Governance, Structure, Operations and Affiliations

Governance

Each state has an equal voice in directing CSG activities through representation on its Governing Board. The board includes all of the nation's governors and two legislators from each state and other U.S. jurisdictions. Members of the CSG Executive Committee, with representation from all three branches of state government, also serve as members of the larger body. An annual board meeting, typically held in December, provides an opportunity for the diverse members of the CSG family to interact in sessions on current and emerging state issues.

It is the CSG Executive Committee, however, which deals most closely with the organization's day-to-day operations. To advise its membership on various matters, the committee now operates with six national standing committees:

• *Finance Committee*, which monitors the organization's fiscal affairs and recommends an annual budget and schedule of state appropriations to the Executive Committee and Governing Board;

• *Strategic Planning*, a new committee that inherited the work of CSG's former Organizational Planning and Coordinating Committee and its Strategic Planning Task Force, and which will carry forward and coordinate CSG's short- and long-term organizational and technological planning and assessment activities;

• *Intergovernmental Affairs Committee*, which considers major intergovernmental issues and relevant court cases and decisions, and may recommend resolutions and policy statements concerned with intergovernmental relations;

• *Suggested State Legislation Committee*, which reviews and selects exemplary state legislation on topics of major interest to states, for publication in an annual volume;

• *International Committee*, a new committee (formerly a CSG task force) that will coordinate and develop for the CSG membership a variety of activities in the international arena that are of importance to the states; and,

• *CSG Associates Advisory Committee*, also a new committee, made up of public and private sector representatives who will assist CSG in identifying new Associate members, provide advice on marketing techniques, and recommend potential public/private partnership opportunities.

National issue task forces, particularly in the areas of health and environment, also engage CSG's broad constituency in identifying and communicating about emerging policy issues and concerns and developing potential options for their resolution.

Funding

The Council is funded in part through appropriations by the states, U.S. territories and other non-state jurisdictions. In addition, CSG administers federal and private foundation grants and other contributions that support research and information-gathering projects on topics of interest to state officials. Other sources of revenue result from the sale of CSG publications, from the conduct of workshops and conferences, and from contractual service agreements with some of its associated organizations.

A national and regional structure

The national office, located in Lexington,

Ky. since 1969, is responsible for an array of national programs including research and reference publications, inquiry and referral services, an interstate loan library, innovations transfer, suggested state legislation, secretariat services, data processing services and interstate consulting.

A Washington, D.C. office, also part of CSG headquarters, monitors developments at the federal level and evaluates their impact on state legislation and policies. The office facilitates contact and cooperation among officials at the federal, state and local levels.

CSG's regional structure further distinguishes it among state service organizations. Offices in Atlanta, Chicago, New York City and San Francisco serve regional conferences of state officials and provide elected and appointed state officials with opportunities to address issues pertinent to specific areas of the country. Regional task forces and committees actively address their states' interests in fiscal affairs, economic development, environment and natural resources, international trade, agriculture and rural development, and other priority areas.

The issues and activities of each regional office are selected and directed by a regional executive committee of state officials. These CSG offices organize and conduct annual regional conferences, along with seminars and committee and task force meetings, and produce newsletters and substantive issue and trends reports for officials within the regions.

Associated organizations

From its beginnings, CSG has played the role of "umbrella agency," providing secretariat services to organizations of state government officials and serving as a network both for those associations and for others to which CSG does not provide direct staff services. Over time, the number of groups captured under CSG's umbrella has fluctuated, but today, more than 50 organizations still retain some relationship with CSG.

In 1993, CSG provided a range of staffing services to 27 national organizations of state officials — including lieutenant governors, secretaries of state, treasurers and other top-level managers. In 1994, CSG began the process of re-evaluating its relationships with these various associated organizations with the intent of establishing a new framework of affiliations based on mission compatibility and in accordance with the outcomes of the CSG strategic planning process. The resulting affiliations will continue to add a richness and diversity to the CSG family and afford continued opportunities to engage executive officials and legislators in cross-branch problem-solving.

Major CSG Publications and Reference Works

CSG publishes a variety of materials about state government, including policy reports, reference works, directories, periodicals, information briefs and newsletters. Major CSG publications, which are distributed on a complimentary basis to thousands of state officials across the country, include:

• *The Book of the States* — First published in 1935, this biennial reference guide to major aspects of state government contains hundreds of tables with comparative 50-state data and dozens of essays written by experts on state operations.

• *State Government News* — This monthly magazine on state developments, issues and innovations first appeared in 1958, and currently is distributed on a complimentary basis to all state legislators and thousands of state executive branch officials.

• *State Elective Officials and the Legislatures; State Legislative Leadership, Committees and Staff;* and *State Administrative Officials*

Classified by Function — These biennial directories, first produced as supplements to *The Book of the States,* include the names, addresses and telephone numbers of thousands of state officials, and provide information on functional contacts in state government.

• *Suggested State Legislation* — Published annually since 1940 when it began as "suggested war legislation," this volume is one result of the efforts of CSG's Committee on Suggested State Legislation. Entries are selected to aid state policy makers interested in drafting legislation in specific issue areas and are presented as "suggested" legislation, with neither CSG nor the Committee in the position of advocating their enactment.

• *Spectrum: The Journal of State Government* — This periodical, which first appeared in the early 1930s, was renamed *Spectrum* in 1992 and redesigned to provide a forum for the discussion of state issues from political, academic and practitioner viewpoints.

• *Innovations* — First produced in 1975, this series of reports focuses on state programs selected through an annual awards process in which hundreds of entries are evaluated for their contribution to innovation in the administration of state government.

• *State Trends & Forecasts* — A series initiated in late 1992, these new reports are designed to alert state policy makers and administrators to long-term structural and institutional changes in state government and to policy options based on recent trends and expert forecasts.

THE COUNCIL OF STATE GOVERNMENTS
OFFICERS AND EXECUTIVE COMMITTEE 1994

Chairman
  Representative Robert C. Hunter
  North Carolina
Chairman-Elect
  Assemblyman Robert C. Wertz
  New York
Vice Chairman
  Senate President Stanley J. Aronoff
  Ohio

President
  Governor E. Benjamin Nelson
  Nebraska
President-Elect
  Governor Mel Carnahan
  Missouri
Vice President
  (Vacancy)

Gail Albritton, Director, Special Projects, House of Representatives, Florida*
Senator Alfred Alquist, California
Treasurer Edward T. Alter, Utah
Representative Reginald Beamon, Connecticut
Treasurer Marshall Bennett, Mississippi
Martha Bibbs, Director, Department of Civil Service, Michigan
Kevin Blanchette, Director, Legislative Service Bureau, Massachusetts*
Diane E. Bolender, Director, Legislative Service Bureau, Iowa*
Governor Terry Branstad, Iowa**
Senate President Paul "Bud" Burke, Kansas
Senator Anthony K.U. Chang, Hawaii
Senator John Chichester, Virginia
Senate President Arnold Christensen, Utah**
Senator J. Richard Conder, North Carolina
Senator Robert Connor, Delaware
Representative John Connors, Iowa**
Lt. Governor Joanell Dyrstad, Minnesota
Governor Jim Edgar, Illinois**
Senator Rufus Edmisten, North Carolina
Senator Hugh T. Farley, New York**
Representative Toby Fitch, North Carolina
Speaker Bob Griffin, Missouri
Senator Dick Hall, Mississippi
Senator Jeannette Hamby, Oregon**
Representative Art Hamilton, Arizona
Senator Kemp Hannon, New York
Senator Joe Harrison, Indiana
Representative Roy Hausauer, North Dakota**
Senator Douglas Henry, Tennessee
Assemblyman David Humke, Nevada
Representative Barbara M. Ireland, Connecticut
Representative Stephen Karol, Massachusetts
Governor Bruce King, New Mexico
Senator John J. Marchi, New York**
William G. Marcus, Deputy Attorney General, California
Representative Jane Maroney, Delaware
Treasurer Lucille Maurer, Maryland

Phyllis Mayes, Director, Division of Human Resource Management, South Carolina
Governor Stephen Merrill, New Hampshire
Secretary of State Natalie Meyer, Colorado
Representative John E. Miller, Arkansas**
Governor Zell Miller, Georgia**
Secretary of State Brenda Mitchell, Pennsylvania
Senator Roger D. Moe, Minnesota
Speaker Thomas B. Murphy, Georgia**
Representative Joanne O'Rourke, New Hampshire
Larry Primeau, Director, Department of Administrative Services, Nebraska
Senator Fred Risser, Wisconsin
Senate President Pro Tem John "Eck" Rose, Kentucky
Kenneth C. Royall Jr., Senior Budget Advisor, Office of the Governor, North Carolina
John Ruffin, Chairman, CSG Center for Management and Administration Coordinating Council, Mississippi
Representative Tom Ryder, Illinois
Kent Rose, Director, Division of Purchasing, Alabama
Governor Ed Schafer, North Dakota
Alan M. Schuman, President, American Probation and Parole Association, Virginia
Lt. Governor Melinda Schwegmann, Louisiana
Senator Ronald A. Silver, Florida
Representative Dale Shugars, Michigan
Joseph C. Steele, Court Administrator, Nebraska
Pamela A. Stoops, Executive Director, Legislative Affairs Agency, Alaska*
Treasurer Sally Thompson, Kansas
Chief Justice Jean A. Turnage, Montana
Lt. Governor Olene Walker, Utah
Senator Jeffrey Wells, Colorado
Senator W. Paul White, Massachusetts**
Representative Charlie Williams, Mississippi

* State legislative staff, ex officio, non-voting members
** Former CSG Chairmen and Presidents, ex officio, voting members

THE COUNCIL OF STATE GOVERNMENTS
ASSOCIATED ORGANIZATIONS 1993

Affiliated Organizations

Conference of Chief Justices

Conference of State Court Administrators

Council on Licensure, Enforcement and
Regulation*

National Association of Attorneys General

National Association of Secretaries of State*

National Association of State Auditors,
Comptrollers and Treasurers

National Association of State Directors of
Administration and General Services*

National Association of State Personnel
Executives*

National Association of State Purchasing Officials*

National Association of State Treasurers*

National Conference of Lieutenant Governors*

National Conference of State Legislatures

Cooperating Organizations

Adjutants General Association of the United
States

American Probation and Parole Association*

Association of State Correctional Administrators

Association of State Dam Safety Officials

Association of State Floodplain Managers, Inc.

Association of State and Interstate Water
Pollution Control Administrators

Chief Officers of State Library Agencies*

Coastal States Organization, Inc.

Council on Governmental Ethics Laws*

Federation of Tax Administrators

Interstate Conference on Water Policy

National Association of Government
Training and Development Directors*

National Association of Juvenile Correctional
Agencies

National Association of Regulatory Utility
Commissioners

National Association of State Agencies for
Surplus Property

National Association of State Boating Law
Administrators*

National Association of State Controlled
Substances Authorities*

National Association of State Departments
of Agriculture

National Association of State Facilities
Administrators*

National Association of State Foresters

National Association of State Information
Resource Executives*

National Association of State Juvenile
Correctional Agencies

National Association of State Land
Reclamationists

National Association of State Mental Health
Program Directors

National Association of State Telecommunications
Directors*

National Association of State Units on Aging

National Association of Unclaimed Property
Administrators

National Child Support Enforcement Association

National Conference of Commissioners on
Uniform State Laws

National Conference of State Fleet
Administrators*

National Conference of States on Building
Codes and Standards

National Criminal Justice Association

National Emergency Management Association*

National State Printing Association

Ohio River Basin Commission

Parole and Probation Compact Administrators'
Association*

* Staffed by The Council of State Governments

Adjunct Organizations

Association of Paroling Authorities International*

National Association of Government Deferred Compensation Administrators*

National Association of Governmental Labor Officials*

National Association for Public Worksite Health Promotion*

National Association of State Election Directors*

National Association of State Emergency Medical Services Training Coordinators*

THE COUNCIL OF STATE GOVERNMENTS
REGIONAL CONFERENCES, 1993-94

EAST

*Eastern Regional Conference**
Senator John B. Larson, Connecticut
— Co-Chair
Representative Barbara Ireland, Connecticut
— Co-Chair

*Northeast Recycling Council**
Denise Lord, Director, Off. of Planning, Waste Mgmt. Agency, Maine

MIDWEST

*Midwest Governors' Conference**
Governor E. Ben Nelson, Nebraska

*Midwestern Legislative Conference**
Representative John Connors, Iowa

SOUTH

*Southern Governors' Association**
Governor Zell Miller, Georgia

*Southern Legislative Conference**
Senator Ronald A. Silver, Florida

WEST

*Western Legislative Conference**
Senator Jeffrey Wells, Colorado

* Staffed by The Council of State Governments

THE COUNCIL OF STATE GOVERNMENTS
OFFICES AND DIRECTORS

Daniel M. Sprague, Executive Director

Headquarters
3560 Iron Works Pike, P.O. Box 11910
Lexington, KY 40578-1910
(606) 244-8000

Eastern
Alan V. Sokolow, Director
5 World Trade Center, Suite 9241
New York, NY 10048
(212) 912-0128

Midwestern
Virginia Thrall, Director
641 E. Butterfield Road, Suite 401
Lombard, IL 60148
(708) 810-0210

Southern
Colleen Cousineau, Director
The Lenox Building
3399 Peachtree Rd., N.E., Suite 810
Atlanta, GA 30326
(404) 266-1271

Western
Andrew P. Grose, Director
121 Second Street, 4th Floor
San Francisco, CA 94105
(415) 974-6422

Washington
Abe Frank, Director
Hall of the States, 444 N. Capitol St., N.W.
Washington, DC 20001
(202) 624-5460

Chapter Ten

STATE PAGES

A variety of statistics and information about the states — including capitals, population, land areas, historical data, elected executive branch officials, legislative leaders, and judges of the state high courts. State mottos, flowers, songs, birds and other items unique to the states and other U.S. jurisdictions also are presented.

Table 10.1
OFFICIAL NAMES OF STATES AND JURISDICTIONS, CAPITALS, ZIP CODES AND CENTRAL SWITCHBOARDS

State or other jurisdiction	Name of state capitol (a)	Capital	Zip code	Area code	Central switchboard
Alabama, State of	State House	Montgomery	36130	205	242-8000
Alaska, State of	State Capitol	Juneau	99811	907	465-2111
Arizona, State of	State Capitol	Phoenix	85007	602	542-4900
Arkansas, State of	State Capitol	Little Rock	72201	501	682-1010
California, State of	State Capitol	Sacramento	95814	916	322-9900
Colorado, State of	State Capitol	Denver	80203	303	866-5000
Connecticut, State of	State Capitol	Hartford	06106	203	240-0222
Delaware, State of	Legislative Hall	Dover	19901	302	739-4000
Florida, State of	The Capitol	Tallahassee	32399	904	488-1234
Georgia, State of	State Capitol	Atlanta	30334	404	656-2000
Hawaii, State of	State Capitol	Honolulu	96813	808	586-2211
Idaho, State of	State Capitol	Boise	83720	208	334-2411
Illinois, State of	State House	Springfield	62706	217	782-2000
Indiana, State of	State House	Indianapolis	46204	317	232-3140
Iowa, State of	State Capitol	Des Moines	50319	515	281-5011
Kansas, State of	State Capitol	Topeka	66612	913	296-0111
Kentucky, Commonwealth of	State Capitol	Frankfort	40601	502	564-3130
Louisiana, State of	State Capitol	Baton Rouge	70804	504	342-6600
Maine, State of	State House	Augusta	04333	207	582-9500
Maryland, State of	State House	Annapolis	21401	301	841-3000
Massachusetts, Commonwealth of	State House	Boston	02133	617	727-2121
Michigan, State of	State Capitol	Lansing	48909	517	373-1837
Minnesota, State of	State Capitol	St. Paul	55515	612	296-6013
Mississippi, State of	New Capitol	Jackson	39215	601	359-1000
Missouri, State of	State Capitol	Jefferson City	65101	314	751-2151
Montana, State of	State Capitol	Helena	59620	406	444-2511
Nebraska, State of	State Capitol	Lincoln	68509	402	471-2311
Nevada, State of	Legislative Building	Carson City	89710	702	687-5000
New Hampshire, State of	State House	Concord	03301	603	271-1110
New Jersey, State of	State House	Trenton	08625	609	292-2121
New Mexico, State of	State Capitol	Santa Fe	87503	505	986-4300
New York, State of	State Capitol	Albany	12224	518	474-2121
North Carolina, State of	State Legislative Building	Raleigh	27601	919	733-1110
North Dakota, State of	State Capitol	Bismarck	58505	701	224-2000
Ohio, State of	State House	Columbus	43215	614	466-2000
Oklahoma, State of	State Capitol	Oklahoma City	73105	405	521-2011
Oregon, State of	State Capitol	Salem	97310	. . .	NCS
Pennsylvania, Commonwealth of	Main Capitol Building	Harrisburg	17120	717	787-2121
Rhode Island and Providence Plantations, State of	State House	Providence	02903	401	277-2000
South Carolina, State of	State House	Columbia	29211	803	734-1000
South Dakota, State of	State Capitol	Pierre	57501	605	773-3011
Tennessee, State of	State Capitol	Nashville	37243	615	741-3011
Texas, State of	State Capitol	Austin	78711	512	463-4630
Utah, State of	State Capitol	Salt Lake City	84114	801	538-4000
Vermont, State of	State House	Montpelier	05609	802	828-1110
Virginia, Commonwealth of	State Capitol	Richmond	23219	804	786-0000
Washington, State of	Legislative Building	Olympia	98504	. . .	NCS
West Virginia, State of	State Capitol	Charleston	25305	304	348-3456
Wisconsin, State of	State Capitol	Madison	53702	608	266-2211
Wyoming, State of	State Capitol	Cheyenne	82002	307	777-7220
District of Columbia	District Building	. . .	20004	202	727-1000
American Samoa, Territory of	Maota Fono	Pago Pago	96799	684	633-5231
Guam, Territory of	Congress Building	Agana	96910	671	472-3461
No. Mariana Islands, Commonwealth of	Civic Center Building	Saipan	96950	. . .	NCS
Puerto Rico, Commonwealth of	The Capitol	San Juan	00901	809	721-6040
Republic of Palau	. . .	Koror	96940	. . .	NCS
U.S. Virgin Islands, Territory of	Capitol Building	Charlotte Amalie, St. Thomas	00801	809	774-0880

NCS—No central switchboard.   (a) In some instances the name is not official.

Table 10.2
HISTORICAL DATA ON THE STATES

State or other jurisdiction	Source of state lands	Date organized as territory	Date admitted to Union	Chrono-logical order of admission to Union
Alabama	Mississippi Territory, 1798 (a)	March 3, 1817	Dec. 14, 1819	22
Alaska	Purchased from Russia, 1867	Aug. 24, 1912	Jan. 3, 1959	49
Arizona	Ceded by Mexico, 1848 (b)	Feb. 24, 1863	Feb. 14, 1912	48
Arkansas	Louisiana Purchase, 1803	March 2, 1819	June 15, 1836	25
California	Ceded by Mexico, 1848	(c)	Sept. 9, 1850	31
Colorado	Louisiana Purchase, 1803 (d)	Feb. 28, 1861	Aug. 1, 1876	38
Connecticut	Fundamental Orders, Jan. 14, 1638; Royal charter, April 23, 1662 (e)	. . .	Jan. 9, 1788 (f)	5
Delaware	Swedish charter, 1638; English charter, 1683 (e)	. . .	Dec. 7, 1787 (f)	1
Florida	Ceded by Spain, 1819	March 30, 1822	March 3, 1845	27
Georgia	Charter, 1732, from George II to Trustees for Establishing the Colony of Georgia (e)	. . .	Jan. 2, 1788 (f)	4
Hawaii	Annexed, 1898	June 14, 1900	Aug. 21, 1959	50
Idaho	Treaty with Britain, 1846	March 4, 1863	July 3, 1890	43
Illinois	Northwest Territory, 1787	Feb. 3, 1809	Dec. 3, 1818	21
Indiana	Northwest Territory, 1787	May 7, 1800	Dec. 11, 1816	19
Iowa	Louisiana Purchase, 1803	June 12, 1838	Dec. 28, 1846	29
Kansas	Louisiana Purchase, 1803 (d)	May 30, 1854	Jan. 29, 1861	34
Kentucky	Part of Virginia until admitted as state	(c)	June 1, 1792	15
Louisiana	Louisiana Purchase, 1803 (g)	March 26, 1804	April 30, 1812	18
Maine	Part of Massachusetts until admitted as state	(c)	March 15, 1820	23
Maryland	Charter, 1632, from Charles I to Calvert (e)	. . .	April 28, 1788 (f)	7
Massachusetts	Charter to Massachusetts Bay Company, 1629 (e)	. . .	Feb. 6, 1788 (f)	6
Michigan	Northwest Territory, 1787	Jan. 11, 1805	Jan. 26, 1837	26
Minnesota	Northwest Territory, 1787 (h)	March 3, 1849	May 11, 1858	32
Mississippi	Mississippi Territory (i)	April 7, 1798	Dec. 10, 1817	20
Missouri	Louisiana Purchase, 1803	June 4, 1812	Aug. 10, 1821	24
Montana	Louisiana Purchase, 1803 (j)	May 26, 1864	Nov. 8, 1889	41
Nebraska	Louisiana Purchase, 1803	May 30, 1854	March 1, 1867	37
Nevada	Ceded by Mexico, 1848	March 2, 1861	Oct. 31, 1864	36
New Hampshire	Grants from Council for New England, 1622 and 1629; made Royal province, 1679 (e)	. . .	June 21, 1788 (f)	9
New Jersey	Dutch settlement, 1618; English charter, 1664 (e)	. . .	Dec. 18, 1787 (f)	3
New Mexico	Ceded by Mexico, 1848 (b)	Sept. 9, 1850	Jan. 6, 1912	47
New York	Dutch settlement, 1623; English control, 1664 (e)	. . .	July 26, 1788 (f)	11
North Carolina	Charter, 1663, from Charles II (e)	. . .	Nov. 21, 1789 (f)	12
North Dakota	Louisiana Purchase, 1803 (k)	March 2, 1861	Nov. 2, 1889	39
Ohio	Northwest Territory, 1787	May 7, 1800	March 1, 1803	17
Oklahoma	Louisiana Purchase, 1803	May 2, 1890	Nov. 16, 1907	46
Oregon	Settlement and treaty with Britain, 1846	Aug. 14, 1848	Feb. 14, 1859	33
Pennsylvania	Grant from Charles II to William Penn, 1681 (e)	. . .	Dec. 12, 1787 (f)	2
Rhode Island	Charter, 1663, from Charles II (e)	. . .	May 29, 1790 (f)	13
South Carolina	Charter, 1663, from Charles II (e)	. . .	May 23, 1788 (f)	8
South Dakota	Louisiana Purchase, 1803	March 2, 1861	Nov. 2, 1889	40
Tennessee	Part of North Carolina until land ceded to U.S. in 1789	June 8, 1790 (l)	June 1, 1796	16
Texas	Republic of Texas, 1845	(c)	Dec. 29, 1845	28
Utah	Ceded by Mexico, 1848	Sept. 9, 1850	Jan. 4, 1896	45
Vermont	From lands of New Hampshire and New York	(c)	March 4, 1791	14
Virginia	Charter, 1609, from James I to London Company (e)	. . .	June 25, 1788 (f)	10
Washington	Oregon Territory, 1848	March 2, 1853	Nov. 11, 1889	42
West Virginia	Part of Virginia until admitted as state	(c)	June 20, 1863	35
Wisconsin	Northwest Territory, 1787	April 20, 1836	May 29, 1848	30
Wyoming	Louisiana Purchase, 1803 (d,j)	July 25, 1868	July 10, 1890	44
Dist. of Columbia	Maryland (m)	. . .	. . .	. . .
American Samoa	----------------------------------Became a territory, 1900----------------------------------			
Guam	Ceded by Spain, 1898	Aug. 1, 1950	. . .	. . .
No. Mariana Is.	. . .	March 24, 1976	. . .	. . .
Puerto Rico	Ceded by Spain, 1898	. . .	July 25, 1952 (n)	. . .
Republic of Palau	. . .	Jan. 1, 1981	. . .	. . .
U.S. Virgin Islands	------------------------------Purchased from Denmark, March 31, 1917------------------------------			

See footnotes at end of table.

HISTORICAL DATA—Continued

(a) By the Treaty of Paris, 1783, England gave up claim to the 13 original Colonies, and to all land within an area extending along the present Canadian border to the Lake of the Woods, down the Mississippi River to the 31st parallel, east to the Chattahoochee, down that river to the mouth of the Flint, east to the source of the St. Mary's, down that river to the ocean. The major part of Alabama was acquired by the Treaty of Paris, and the lower portion from Spain in 1813.

(b) Portion of land obtained by Gadsden Purchase, 1853.

(c) No territorial status before admission to Union.

(d) Portion of land ceded by Mexico, 1848.

(e) One of the original 13 Colonies.

(f) Date of ratification of U.S. Constitution.

(g) West Feliciana District (Baton Rouge) acquired from Spain, 1810; added to Louisiana, 1812.

(h) Portion of land obtained by Louisiana Purchase, 1803.

(i) See footnote (a). The lower portion of Mississippi also was acquired from Spain in 1813.

(j) Portion of land obtained from Oregon Territory, 1848.

(k) The northern portion of the Red River Valley was acquired by treaty with Great Britain in 1818.

(l) Date Southwest Territory (identical boundary as Tennessee's) was created.

(m) Area was originally 100 square miles, taken from Virginia and Maryland. Virginia's portion south of the Potomac was given back to that state in 1846. Site chosen in 1790, city incorporated 1802.

(n) On this date, Puerto Rico became a self-governing commonwealth by compact approved by the U.S. Congress and the voters of Puerto Rico as provided in U.S. Public Law 600 of 1950.

Table 10.3
STATE STATISTICS

State or other jurisdiction	Land area In square miles	Land area Rank in nation	Population Size	Population Rank in nation	Percentage change 1980 to 1990	Density per square mile	No. of Representatives in Congress	Capital	Population	Rank in state	Largest city	Population
Alabama	50,750	28	4,040,587	22	3.8	79.62	7	Montgomery	187,106	3	Birmingham	265,968
Alaska	570,374	1	550,043	49	36.9	0.96	1	Juneau	26,751	3	Anchorage	226,338
Arizona	113,642	6	3,665,228	24	34.9	32.25	6	Phoenix	983,403	1	Phoenix	983,403
Arkansas	52,075	27	2,350,725	33	2.8	45.14	4	Little Rock	175,795	1	Little Rock	175,795
California	155,973	3	29,760,021	1	25.7	190.80	52	Sacramento	369,365	7	Los Angeles	3,485,398
Colorado	103,729	8	3,294,394	26	14.0	31.76	6	Denver	467,610	1	Denver	467,610
Connecticut	4,845	48	3,287,116	27	5.8	678.40	6	Hartford	139,739	2	Bridgeport	141,686
Delaware	1,955	49	666,168	46	12.1	340.82	1	Dover	27,630	2	Wilmington	71,529
Florida	53,997	26	12,937,926	4	32.7	239.60	23	Tallahassee	124,773	8	Jacksonville	635,230
Georgia	57,919	21	6,478,216	11	18.6	111.85	11	Atlanta	394,017	1	Atlanta	394,017
Hawaii	6,423	47	1,108,229	41	14.9	172.53	2	Honolulu	365,272	1	Honolulu	365,272
Idaho	82,751	11	1,006,749	42	6.6	12.17	2	Boise	125,738	1	Boise	125,738
Illinois	55,593	24	11,430,602	6	0.0	205.61	20	Springfield	105,227	4	Chicago	2,783,726
Indiana	35,870	38	5,544,159	14	1.0	154.56	10	Indianapolis	731,327	1	Indianapolis	731,327
Iowa	55,875	23	2,776,755	30	-4.7	49.70	5	Des Moines	193,187	1	Des Moines	193,187
Kansas	81,823	13	2,477,574	32	4.8	30.28	4	Topeka	119,883	3	Wichita	304,011
Kentucky	39,732	36	3,685,296	23	0.7	92.75	6	Frankfort	25,968	8	Louisville	269,063
Louisiana	43,566	33	4,219,973	21	0.3	96.86	7	Baton Rouge	219,531	2	New Orleans	496,938
Maine	30,865	39	1,227,928	38	9.1	39.78	2	Augusta	21,325	6	Portland	64,358
Maryland	9,775	42	4,781,468	19	13.4	489.17	8	Annapolis	33,187	22	Baltimore	736,014
Massachusetts	7,838	45	6,016,425	13	4.9	767.60	10	Boston	574,283	1	Boston	574,283
Michigan	56,809	22	9,295,297	8	0.4	163.62	16	Lansing	127,321	5	Detroit	1,027,974
Minnesota	79,617	14	4,375,099	20	7.3	54.95	8	St. Paul	272,235	2	Minneapolis	368,383
Mississippi	46,914	31	2,573,216	31	2.1	54.85	5	Jackson	196,637	1	Jackson	196,637
Missouri	68,898	18	5,117,073	15	4.1	74.27	9	Jefferson City	35,481	15	Kansas City	435,146
Montana	145,556	4	799,065	44	1.6	5.49	1	Helena	24,569	5	Billings	81,151
Nebraska	76,878	15	1,578,385	36	0.5	20.53	3	Lincoln	191,972	2	Omaha	335,795
Nevada	109,806	7	1,201,833	39	50.1	10.95	2	Carson City	40,443	9	Las Vegas	258,295
New Hampshire	8,969	44	1,109,252	40	20.5	123.67	2	Concord	36,006	3	Manchester	99,567
New Jersey	7,419	46	7,730,188	9	5.0	1,041.97	13	Trenton	88,675	6	Newark	275,221
New Mexico	121,365	5	1,515,069	37	16.2	12.48	3	Santa Fe	55,859	3	Albuquerque	384,736
New York	47,224	30	17,990,455	2	2.5	380.96	31	Albany	101,082	6	New York City	7,322,564
North Carolina	48,718	29	6,628,637	10	12.7	136.06	12	Raleigh	207,951	2	Charlotte	395,934
North Dakota	68,994	17	638,800	47	-2.1	9.26	1	Bismarck	49,256	3	Fargo	74,111
Ohio	40,953	35	10,847,115	7	0.5	264.87	19	Columbus	632,910	1	Columbus	632,910
Oklahoma	68,679	19	3,145,585	28	4.0	45.80	6	Oklahoma City	444,719	1	Oklahoma City	444,719
Oregon	96,003	10	2,842,321	29	7.9	29.61	5	Salem	107,786	3	Portland	437,319
Pennsylvania	44,820	32	11,881,643	5	0.1	265.10	21	Harrisburg	52,376	10	Philadelphia	1,585,577
Rhode Island	1,045	50	1,003,464	43	5.9	960.27	2	Providence	160,728	1	Providence	160,728
South Carolina	30,111	40	3,486,703	25	11.7	115.79	6	Columbia	98,052	1	Columbia	98,052
South Dakota	75,896	16	696,004	45	0.8	9.17	1	Pierre	12,906	7	Sioux Falls	100,814
Tennessee	41,220	34	4,877,185	17	6.2	118.32	9	Nashville	488,374	2	Memphis	610,337
Texas	261,914	2	16,986,510	3	19.4	64.86	30	Austin	465,622	5	Houston	1,630,553
Utah	82,168	12	1,722,850	35	17.9	20.97	3	Salt Lake City	159,936	1	Salt Lake City	159,936
Vermont	9,249	43	562,758	48	10.0	60.84	1	Montpelier	8,247	8	Burlington	39,127

See footnotes at end of table.

STATE STATISTICS—Continued

State or other jurisdiction	Land area — In square miles	Land area — Rank in nation	Population — Size	Population — Rank in nation	Percentage change 1980 to 1990	Density per square mile	No. of Representatives in Congress	Capital	Population	Rank in state	Largest city	Population
Virginia	39,598	37	6,187,358	12	15.7	156.26	11	Richmond	203,056	3	Virginia Beach	393,069
Washington	66,581	20	4,866,692	18	17.8	73.09	9	Olympia	33,840	18	Seattle	516,259
West Virginia	24,087	41	1,793,477	34	−8.0	74.46	3	Charleston	57,287	1	Charleston	57,287
Wisconsin	54,314	25	4,891,769	16	4.0	90.07	9	Madison	191,262	2	Milwaukee	628,088
Wyoming	97,105	9	453,588	50	−3.4	4.67	1	Cheyenne	50,008	1	Cheyenne	50,008
Dist. of Columbia	61	. . .	606,900	. . .	−4.9	9,884.40	1 (a)	. . .	. . .	. . .	. . .	. . .
American Samoa	77	. . .	46,773	. . .	44.8	607.44	1 (a)	Pago Pago	3,519	3	Tafuna	5,174
Guam	210	. . .	133,152	. . .	25.6	634.06	1 (a)	Agana	1,139	18	Dededo	31,728
No. Mariana Islands	179	. . .	43,345	. . .	158.8	242.15	. . .	Saipan	38,896	1	Saipan	38,896
Puerto Rico	3,427	. . .	3,522,037	. . .	10.2	1,027.90	1 (a)	San Juan	426,832	1	San Juan	426,832
Republic of Palau	177	. . .	15,122	. . .	24.8	85.44	. . .	Koror	9,000	1	Koror	9,000
U.S. Virgin Islands	134	. . .	101,809	. . .	5.4	760.90	1 (a)	Charlotte Amalie, St. Thomas	12,331	1	Charlotte Amalie, St. Thomas	12,331

(a) Delegate with privileges to vote in committees and the Committee of the Whole.

Source: U.S. Department of Commerce, Bureau of the Census.

Key:

. . . — Not applicable

Alabama

Nickname . . . . The Heart of Dixie
Motto . . . . *Aldemus Jura Nostra Defendere*
    (We Dare Defend Our Rights)
Horse . . . . Racking Horse
Flower . . . . Camellia
Bird . . . . Yellowhammer
Tree . . . . Southern (Longleaf) Pine
Song . . . . *Alabama*
Insect . . . . Monarch butterfly
Rock . . . . Marble
Entered the Union . . . . December 14, 1819
Capital . . . . Montgomery

ELECTED EXECUTIVE BRANCH OFFICIALS

Governor . . . . Jim Folsom Jr.
Lieutenant Governor . . . . Vacant
Secretary of State . . . . Jim Bennett
Attorney General . . . . Jimmy Evans
Treasurer . . . . George C. Wallace Jr.
Auditor . . . . Terry Ellis
Commr. of Agriculture
    & Industries . . . . A.W. Todd

SUPREME COURT

Sonny Hornsby, Chief Justice
Hugh Maddox
Reneau P. Almon
Janie L. Shores
Gorman Houston
Henry B. Steagall II
Mark Kennedy
Kenneth F. Ingram
Ralph D. Cook

LEGISLATURE

President of the Senate . . . . Vacant
President Pro Tem
    of the Senate . . . . Ryan deGraffenried Jr.
Secretary of the Senate . . . . McDowell Lee

Speaker of the House . . . . James Clark
Speaker Pro Tem
    of the House . . . . James M. Campbell
Clerk of the House . . . . Gregg Pappas

STATISTICS

Land Area (square miles) 50,750
    Rank in Nation 28th
Population 4,040,587
    Rank in Nation 22nd
    Density per square mile 79.62
Number of Representatives in Congress 7
Capital City . . . . Montgomery
    Population 187,106
    Rank in State 3rd
Largest City . . . . Birmingham
    Population 265,968
Number of Places over 10,000 Population 50

Alaska

Motto . . . . *North to the Future*
Flower . . . . Forget-me-not
Marine Mammal . . . . Bowhead Whale
Bird . . . . Willow Ptarmigan
Tree . . . . Sitka Spruce
Song . . . . *Alaska's Flag*
Fish . . . . King Salmon
Fossil . . . . Woolly Mammoth
Sport . . . . Dog Mushing
Gem . . . . Jade
Mineral . . . . Gold
Purchased from Russia by the
    United States . . . . March 30, 1867
Entered the Union . . . . January 3, 1959
Capital . . . . Juneau

ELECTED EXECUTIVE BRANCH OFFICIALS

Governor . . . . Walter Hickel
Lieutenant Governor . . . . John B. Coghill

SUPREME COURT

Daniel Moore Jr., Chief Justice
Jay A. Rabinowitz
Robert L. Eastaugh
Warren W. Matthews
Allen Compton
Robert L. Eastaugh

LEGISLATURE

President of the Senate . . . . Rick Halford
Secretary of the Senate . . . . Nancy Quinto

Speaker of the House . . . . Ramona Barnes
Chief Clerk of the House . . . . Suzi Lowell

STATISTICS

Land Area (square miles) 570,374
    Rank in Nation 1st
Population 550,043
    Rank in Nation 49th
    Density per square mile 0.96
Number of Representatives in Congress 1
Capital City . . . . Juneau
    Population 26,751
    Rank in State 3rd
Largest City . . . . Anchorage
    Population 226,338
Number of Places over 10,000 Population 4

Arizona

Nickname .... The Grand Canyon State
Motto .... *Ditat Deus* (God Enriches)
Flower .... Blossom of the Saguaro Cactus
Bird .... Cactus Wren
Tree .... Palo Verde
Songs .... *Arizona March Song* and *Arizona*
Gemstone .... Turquoise
Official Neckwear .... Bola Tie
Entered the Union .... February 14, 1912
Capital .... Phoenix

ELECTED EXECUTIVE BRANCH OFFICIALS

Governor .... Fife Symington III
Secretary of State .... Richard D. Mahoney
Attorney General .... Grant Woods
Treasurer .... Tony West
Supt. of Public Instruction .... C. Diane Bishop
Mine Inspector .... Douglas K. Martin

SUPREME COURT

Stanley G. Feldman, Chief Justice
James Moeller, Vice Chief Justice
Robert J. Corcoran
Thomas A. Zlaket
Frederick J. Martone

LEGISLATURE

President of the Senate .... John Greene
President Pro Tem of the Senate ..... Patricia Wright
Secretary of the Senate .... Shirley L. Wheaton

Speaker of the House .... Mark W. Killian
Speaker Pro Tem
of the House .... Lela Steffey
Chief Clerk of the House .... Norman Moore

STATISTICS

Land Area (square miles) 113,642
  Rank in Nation 6th
Population 3,665,228
  Rank in Nation 24th
  Density per square mile 32.25
Number of Representatives in Congress 6
Capital City .... Phoenix
  Population 983,403
  Rank in State 1st
Largest City .... Phoenix
Number of Places over 10,000 Population 28

Arkansas

Nickname .... The Land of Opportunity
Motto .... *Regnat Populus* (The People Rule)
Flower .... Apple Blossom
Bird .... Mockingbird
Tree .... Pine
Song .... *Arkansas*
Gem .... Diamond
Entered the Union .... June 15, 1836
Capital .... Little Rock

ELECTED EXECUTIVE BRANCH OFFICIALS

Governor .... Jim Guy Tucker
Lieutenant Governor .... Mike Huckabee
Secretary of State .... Bill McCuen
Attorney General .... Winston Bryant
Treasurer .... Jimmie Lou Fisher
Auditor .... Julia Hughs Jones
Land Commr. .... Charlie Daniels

SUPREME COURT

Jack Holt, Jr., Chief Justice
Robert H. Dudley
Steele Hays
David Newbern
Tom Glaze
Donald L. Corbin
Robert L. Brown

GENERAL ASSEMBLY

President
of the Senate .... Lt. Gov. Mike Huckabee
President Pro Tem
of the Senate .... Jerry Jewell
Secretary of the Senate .... Hal Moody

Speaker of the House .... L.L. Bryan
Speaker Pro Tem
of the House .... Lloyd R. George
Chief Clerk of the House .... Jo Renshaw

STATISTICS

Land Area (square miles) 52,075
  Rank in Nation 27th
Population 2,350,725
  Rank in Nation 33rd
  Density per square mile 45.14
Number of Representatives in Congress 4
Capital City .... Little Rock
  Population 175,795
  Rank in State 1st
Largest City .... Little Rock
Number of Places over 10,000 Population 27

California

Nickname . . . . The Golden State
Motto . . . . *Eureka* (I Have Found It)
Animal . . . . Grizzly Bear
Flower . . . . Golden Poppy
Bird . . . . California Valley Quail
Tree . . . . California Redwood
Song . . . . *I Love You, California*
Fossil . . . . Saber-Toothed Cat
Marine Mammal . . . . California Gray Whale
Entered the Union . . . . September 9, 1850
Capital . . . . Sacramento

ELECTED EXECUTIVE BRANCH OFFICIALS

Governor . . . . Pete Wilson
Lieutenant Governor . . . . Leo T. McCarthy
Secretary of State . . . . March Fong Eu
Attorney General . . . . Daniel E. Lungren
Treasurer . . . . Kathleen Brown
Controller . . . . Gray Davis
Insurance Commissioner . . . . John Garamendi
Acting Supt. of
    Public Instruction . . . . William D. Dawson

SUPREME COURT

Malcolm M. Lucas, Chief Justice
Stanley Mosk
Joyce Luther Kennard
Armand Arabian
Marvin Baxter
Ronald M. George
Katherine N. Werdegar

LEGISLATURE

President
    of the Senate . . . . Lt. Gov. Leo T. McCarthy
President Pro Tem
    of the Senate . . . . Bill Lockyer
Secretary of the Senate . . . . Rick Rollens

Speaker
    of the Assembly . . . . Willie Lewis Brown Jr.
Speaker Pro Tem
    of the Assembly . . . . Jack O'Connell
Chief Clerk
    of the Assembly . . . . E. Dotson Wilson

STATISTICS

Land Area (square miles) 155,973
    Rank in Nation 3rd
Population 29,760,021
    Rank in Nation 1st
    Density per square mile 190.80
Number of Representatives in Congress 52
Capital City . . . . Sacramento
    Population 369,365
    Rank in State 7th
Largest City . . . . Los Angeles
    Population 3,485,398
Number of Places over 10,000 Population 383

Colorado

Nickname . . . . The Centennial State
Motto . . . . *Nil Sine Numine*
                (Nothing Without Providence)
Flower . . . . Columbine
Bird . . . . Lark Bunting
Tree . . . . Blue Spruce
Song . . . . *Where the Columbines Grow*
Fossil . . . . Stegosaurus
Gemstone . . . . Aquamarine
Animal . . . . Bighorn Sheep
Entered the Union . . . . August 1, 1876
Capital . . . . Denver

ELECTED EXECUTIVE BRANCH OFFICIALS

Governor . . . . Roy Romer
Lieutenant Governor . . . . C. Michael Callihan
Secretary of State . . . . Natalie Meyer
Attorney General . . . . Gale Norton
Treasurer . . . . Gail S. Schoettler

SUPREME COURT

Luis D. Rovira, Chief Justice
William H. Erickson
George E. Lohr
Howard M. Kirshbaum
Anthony Vollack
Mary J. Mullarkey
Gregory K. Scott

GENERAL ASSEMBLY

President of the Senate . . . . Tom Norton
President Pro Tem
    of the Senate . . . . Tilman M. Bishop
Secretary of the Senate . . . . Joan M. Albi

Speaker of the House . . . . Charles Berry
Speaker Pro Tem of the House . . . . . . Tony Grampsas
Chief Clerk of the House . . . . Judith Rodrigue

STATISTICS

Land Area (square miles) 103,729
    Rank in Nation 8th
Population 3,294,394
    Rank in Nation 26th
    Density per square mile 31.76
Number of Representatives in Congress 6
Capital City . . . . Denver
    Population 467,610
    Rank in State 1st
Largest City . . . . Denver
Number of Places over 10,000 Population 39

Connecticut

Nickname..................The Constitution State
Motto.................... *Qui Transtulit Sustinet*
(He Who Transplanted Still Sustains)
Animal............................Sperm Whale
Flower........................Mountain Laurel
Bird........................American Robin
Tree...............................White Oak
Song......................... *Yankee Doodle*
Mineral.............................Garnet
Insect................European "Praying" Mantis
Entered the Union................January 9, 1788
Capital...............................Hartford

ELECTED EXECUTIVE BRANCH OFFICIALS

Governor....................Lowell P. Weicker Jr.
Lieutenant Governor.........Eunice Strong Groark
Secretary of State..................Pauline Kezer
Attorney General.............Richard Blumenthal
Treasurer......................Francisco Borges
Comptroller.................William E. Curry Jr.

SUPREME COURT

Ellen Ash Peters, Chief Justice
Robert J. Callahan
David M. Borden
Robert I. Berdon
Flemming L. Norcott Jr.
Joette Katz
Richard N. Palmer

GENERAL ASSEMBLY

President
of the Senate......Lt. Gov. Eunice Strong Groark
President Pro Tem
of the Senate..................John B. Larson
Clerk of the Senate...........Thomas P. Sheridan

Speaker of the House............Thomas D. Ritter
Deputy Speakers of the House.....Eric D. Coleman,
Moira K. Lyons, David B. Pudlin
Clerk of the House................Penn J. Ritter

STATISTICS

Land Area (square miles)....................4,845
Rank in Nation.........................48th
Population.........................3,287,116
Rank in Nation.........................27th
Density per square mile..................678.40
Number of Representatives in Congress...........6
Capital City..........................Hartford
Population.........................139,739
Rank in State.........................2nd
Largest City.......................Bridgeport
Population..........................141,686
Number of Places over 10,000 Population........37

Delaware

Nickname.......................The First State
Motto................. *Liberty and Independence*
Flower.......................Peach Blossom
Bird........................Blue Hen Chicken
Tree...........................American Holly
Song........................... *Our Delaware*
Fish.................................Sea Trout
Entered the Union..............December 7, 1787
Capital...............................Dover

ELECTED EXECUTIVE BRANCH OFFICIALS

Governor.........................Tom Carper
Lieutenant Governor...........Ruth Ann Minner
Attorney General............Charles M. Oberly III
Treasurer...................Janet C. Rzewnicki
Auditor...................R. Thomas Wagner Jr.
Insurance Commr............Donna Lee Williams

SUPREME COURT

E. Norman Veasey, Chief Justice
Andrew G.T. Moore II
Joseph T. Walsh
Randy J. Holland
Maurice A. Hartnett III

GENERAL ASSEMBLY

President of the Senate...Lt. Gov. Ruth Ann Minner
President Pro Tem
of the Senate...............Richard S. Cordrey
Secretary of the Senate..........Bernard J. Brady

Speaker of the House.............Terry R. Spence
Chief Clerk of the House..........JoAnn Hedrick

STATISTICS

Land Area (square miles)....................1,955
Rank in Nation.........................49th
Population.........................666,168
Rank in Nation.........................46th
Density per square mile..................340.82
Number of Representatives in Congress...........1
Capital City...........................Dover
Population..........................27,630
Rank in State.........................2nd
Largest City.......................Wilmington
Population..........................71,529
Number of Places over 10,000 Population........5

Florida

Nickname	The Sunshine State
Motto	*In God We Trust*
Animal	Florida Panther
Flower	Orange Blossom
Bird	Mockingbird
Tree	Sabal Palmetto Palm
Song	*The Swanee River (Old Folks at Home)*
Marine Mammal	Manatee
Saltwater Mammal	Porpoise
Gem	Moonstone
Shell	Horse Conch
Entered the Union	March 3, 1845
Capital	Tallahassee

ELECTED EXECUTIVE BRANCH OFFICIALS

Governor	Lawton Chiles
Lieutenant Governor	Buddy MacKay
Secretary of State	Jim Smith
Attorney General	Bob Butterworth
Treasurer/Insurance Commr.	Tom Gallagher
Comptroller	Gerald A. Lewis
Commr. of Education	Betty Castor
Commr. of Agriculture	Bob Crawford

SUPREME COURT

Rosemary Barkett, Chief Justice
Ben F. Overton
Parker Lee McDonald
Leander J. Shaw Jr.
Stephen Grimes
Gerald Kogan
Major B. Harding

LEGISLATURE

President of the Senate	Pat Thomas
President Pro Tem of the Senate	Ander Crenshaw
Secretary of the Senate	Joe Brown
Speaker of the House	Bo Johnson
Speaker Pro Tem of the House	Elaine Bloom
Clerk of the House	John B. Phelps

STATISTICS

Land Area (square miles)	53,997
Rank in Nation	26th
Population	12,937,926
Rank in Nation	4th
Density per square mile	239.60
Number of Representatives in Congress	23
Capital City	Tallahassee
Population	124,773
Rank in State	8th
Largest City	Jacksonville
Population	635,230
Number of Places over 10,000 Population	216

Georgia

Nickname*	The Empire State of the South
Motto	*Wisdom, Justice and Moderation*
Flower	Cherokee Rose
Bird	Brown Thrasher
Tree	Live Oak
Song	*Georgia on My Mind*
Butterfly	Tiger Swallowtail
Insect	Honeybee
Fish	Largemouth Bass
Entered the Union	January 2, 1788
Capital	Atlanta

*Unofficial

ELECTED EXECUTIVE BRANCH OFFICIALS

Governor	Zell Miller
Lieutenant Governor	Pierre Howard
Secretary of State	Max Cleland
Attorney General	Michael J. Bowers
Commr. of Insurance	Tim Ryles
Superintendent of Schools	Werner Rogers
Commr. of Agriculture	Thomas T. Irvin
Commr. of Labor	David Poythress

SUPREME COURT

Willis B. Hunt Jr., Chief Justice
Robert Benham, Presiding Justice
Norman Fletcher
Leah J. Sears-Collins
Carol W. Hunstein
George H. Carley
Hugh Thompson

GENERAL ASSEMBLY

President of the Senate	Lt. Gov. Pierre Howard
President Pro Tem of the Senate	Pete Robinson
Secretary of the Senate	Frank Eldridge Jr.
Speaker of the House	Thomas B. Murphy
Speaker Pro Tem of the House	Jack Connell
Clerk of the House	Robert Rivers Jr.

STATISTICS

Land Area (square miles)	57,919
Rank in Nation	21st
Population	6,478,216
Rank in Nation	11th
Density per square mile	111.85
Number of Representatives in Congress	11
Capital City	Atlanta
Population	394,017
Rank in State	1st
Largest City	Atlanta
Number of Places over 10,000 Population	66

Hawaii

Nickname . . . . The Aloha State
Motto . . . . *Ua Mau Ke Ea O Ka Aina I Ka Pono*
(The Life of the Land Is Perpetuated
in Righteousness)
Flower . . . . Hibiscus
Bird . . . . Hawaiian Goose
Tree . . . . Kukui Tree (Candlenut)
Song . . . . *Hawaii Ponoi*
Entered the Union . . . . August 21, 1959
Capital . . . . Honolulu

ELECTED EXECUTIVE BRANCH OFFICIALS

Governor . . . . John D. Waihee III
Lieutenant Governor . . . . Benjamin J. Cayetano

SUPREME COURT

Ronald Moon, Chief Justice
Robert G. Klein
Steven H. Levinson
Paula Nakayama
Mario Ramil

LEGISLATURE

President of the Senate . . . . Norman Mizuguchi
Vice President
of the Senate . . . . Milton Holt
Clerk of the Senate . . . . T. David Woo Jr.

Speaker of the House . . . . Joseph M. Souki
Vice Speaker of the House . . . . Jackie Young
Chief Clerk of the House . . . . . Patricia Mau Shimizu

STATISTICS

Land Area (square miles) 6,423
    Rank in Nation 47th
Population 1,108,229
    Rank in Nation 41st
    Density per square mile 172.53
Number of Representatives in Congress 2
Capital City . . . . Honolulu
    Population 365,272
    Rank in State 1st
Largest City . . . . Honolulu
Number of Places over 10,000 Population 17

Idaho

Nickname . . . . The Gem State
Motto . . . . *Esto Perpetua* (Let It Be Perpetual)
Flower . . . . Syringa
Bird . . . . Mountain Bluebird
Tree . . . . Western White Pine
Song . . . . *Here We Have Idaho*
Horse . . . . Appaloosa
Gemstone . . . . Idaho Star Garnet
Entered the Union . . . . July 3, 1890
Capital . . . . Boise

ELECTED EXECUTIVE BRANCH OFFICIALS

Governor . . . . Cecil D. Andrus
Lieutenant Governor . . . . C.L. Otter
Secretary of State . . . . Pete T. Cenarrusa
Attorney General . . . . Larry EchoHawk
Treasurer . . . . Lydia J. Edwards
Auditor . . . . J.D. Williams
Supt. of Public Instruction . . . . Jerry L. Evans

SUPREME COURT

Chas F. McDevitt, Chief Justice
Stephen Bistline
Byron Johnson
Linda C. Trout
Cathy R. Silak

LEGISLATURE

President
of the Senate . . . . Lt. Gov. C.L. "Butch" Otter
President Pro Tem
of the Senate . . . . Jerry Twiggs
Secretary of the Senate . . . . Jeannine Wood

Speaker of the House . . . . Michael Simpson
Chief Clerk of the House . . . . Phyllis Watson

STATISTICS

Land Area (square miles) 82,751
    Rank in Nation 11th
Population 1,006,749
    Rank in Nation 42nd
    Density per square mile 12.17
Number of Representatives in Congress 2
Capital City . . . . Boise
    Population 125,738
    Rank in State 1st
Largest City . . . . Boise
Number of Places over 10,000 Population 10

Illinois

Nickname	The Prairie State
Great Seal	*State Sovereignty-National Union*
Animal	White-tailed Deer
Flower	Native Violet
Bird	Cardinal
Tree	White Oak
Song	*Illinois*
Mineral	Fluorite
Fish	Bluegill
Entered the Union	December 3, 1818
Capital	Springfield

ELECTED EXECUTIVE BRANCH OFFICIALS

Governor	Jim Edgar
Lieutenant Governor	Bob Kustra
Secretary of State	George Ryan
Attorney General	Roland W. Burris
Treasurer	Patrick Quinn
Comptroller	Dawn Clark Netsch

SUPREME COURT

Michael A. Bilandic, Chief Justice
Ben Miller
James D. Heiple
Charles E. Freeman
Moses W. Harrison II
Mary Ann G. McMorrow
John L. Nickels

GENERAL ASSEMBLY

President of the Senate	James Philip
Secretary of the Senate	Jim Harry
Speaker of the House	Michael J. Madigan
Chief Clerk of the House	Anthony D. Rossi

STATISTICS

Land Area (square miles)	55,593
Rank in Nation	24th
Population	11,430,602
Rank in Nation	6th
Density per square mile	205.61
Number of Representatives in Congress	20
Capital City	Springfield
Population	105,227
Rank in State	4th
Largest City	Chicago
Population	2,783,726
Number of Places over 10,000 Population	180

Indiana

Nickname	The Hoosier State
Motto	*Crossroads of America*
Flower	Peony
Bird	Cardinal
Tree	Tulip Poplar
Song	*On the Banks of the Wabash, Far Away*
Poem	*Indiana* by Franklin Mapes
Stone	Limestone
Entered the Union	December 11, 1816
Capital	Indianapolis

ELECTED EXECUTIVE BRANCH OFFICIALS

Governor	Evan Bayh
Lieutenant Governor	Frank L. O'Bannon
Secretary of State	Joseph H. Hogsett
Attorney General	Pam Carter
Treasurer	Marjorie H. O'Laughlin
Auditor	Ann G. DeVore
Supt. of Public Instruction	Suellen Reed

SUPREME COURT

Randall T. Shepard, Chief Justice
Richard M. Givan
Roger O. DeBruler
Brent E. Dickson
Frank Sullivan

GENERAL ASSEMBLY

President of the Senate	Lt. Gov. Frank L. O'Bannon
President Pro Tem of the Senate	Robert D. Garton
Principal Secretary of the Senate	Carolyn J. Tinkle
Speaker of the House	Michael K. Phillips
Speaker Pro Tem of the House	Chester F. Dobis
Principal Clerk of the House	Carole C. Devitt

STATISTICS

Land Area (square miles)	35,870
Rank in Nation	38th
Population	5,544,159
Rank in Nation	14th
Density per square mile	154.56
Number of Representatives in Congress	10
Capital City	Indianapolis
Population	731,327
Rank in State	1st
Largest City	Indianapolis
Number of Places over 10,000 Population	64

Iowa

Nickname....................The Hawkeye State
Motto................*Our Liberties We Prize and
Our Rights We Will Maintain*
Flower.............................Wild Rose
Bird.........................Eastern Goldfinch
Tree......................................Oak
Song.........................*The Song of Iowa*
Stone...................................Geode
Entered the Union.............December 28, 1846
Capital.............................Des Moines

ELECTED EXECUTIVE BRANCH
OFFICIALS

Governor......................Terry E. Branstad
Lieutenant Governor..............Joy C. Corning
Secretary of State..................Elaine Baxter
Attorney General...............Bonnie Campbell
Treasurer.................Michael L. Fitzgerald
Auditor....................Richard D. Johnson
Secy. of Agriculture................Dale Cochran

SUPREME COURT

Arthur A. McGiverin, Chief Justice
David K. Harris
Jerry L. Larson
James H. Carter
Louis A. Lavorato
Linda K. Neuman
Bruce M. Snell, Jr.
James Andreasen
Marsha Ternus

GENERAL ASSEMBLY

President
of the Senate...............Leonard L. Boswell
President Pro Tem
of the Senate...............William D. Palmer
Secretary of the Senate.............John F. Dwyer

Speaker of the House.........Harold Van Maanen
Speaker Pro Tem of the House.....Mary A. Lundby
Chief Clerk of the House.............Liz Isaacson

STATISTICS

Land Area (square miles)...................55,875
Rank in Nation..........................23rd
Population.........................2,776,755
Rank in Nation..........................30th
Density per square mile...................49.70
Number of Representatives in Congress...........5
Capital City.......................Des Moines
Population...........................193,187
Rank in State.............................1st
Largest City.......................Des Moines
Number of Places over 10,000 Population........30

Kansas

Nickname....................The Sunflower State
Motto......................*Ad Astra per Aspera*
(To the Stars through Difficulties)
Animal.......................American Buffalo
Flower...................Wild Native Sunflower
Bird.......................Western Meadowlark
Tree...............................Cottonwood
Song......................*Home on the Range*
Reptile.......................Ornate Box Turtle
Insect...................................Honeybee
Entered the Union..............January 29, 1861
Capital................................Topeka

ELECTED EXECUTIVE BRANCH
OFFICIALS

Governor.........................Joan Finney
Lieutenant Governor..........James L. Francisco
Secretary of State.....................Bill Graves
Attorney General...............Robert T. Stephan
Treasurer.......................Sally Thompson
Commr. of Insurance.............Ronald L. Todd

SUPREME COURT

Richard W. Holmes, Chief Justice
Kay McFarland
Tyler C. Lockett
Donald L. Allegrucci
Frederick N. Six
Bob Abbott
Robert E. Davis

LEGISLATURE

President
of the Senate.....................Paul Burke
Vice President
of the Senate.....................Jerry Moran
Secretary of the Senate.................Pat Saville

Speaker of the House.............Robert H. Miller
Speaker Pro Tem
of the House................Tim Shallenburger
Chief Clerk of the House...........Janet E. Jones

STATISTICS

Land Area (square miles)...................81,823
Rank in Nation..........................13th
Population.........................2,477,574
Rank in Nation..........................32nd
Density per square mile...................30.28
Number of Representatives in Congress...........4
Capital City...........................Topeka
Population...........................119,883
Rank in State.............................3rd
Largest City...........................Wichita
Population...........................304,011
Number of Places over 10,000 Population........34

Kentucky

Nickname . . . . The Bluegrass State
Motto . . . . *United We Stand, Divided We Fall*
Animal . . . . Gray Squirrel
Flower . . . . Goldenrod
Bird . . . . Cardinal
Tree . . . . Tulip Poplar*
Song . . . . *My Old Kentucky Home*
Fossil . . . . Brachiopod
Fish . . . . Kentucky Bass
Entered the Union . . . . June 1, 1792
Capital . . . . Frankfort
*Changed from Kentucky Coffee Tree to Tulip Poplar, effective July 1994.

ELECTED EXECUTIVE BRANCH OFFICIALS

Governor . . . . Brereton C. Jones
Lieutenant Governor . . . . Paul Patton
Secretary of State . . . . Bob Babbage
Attorney General . . . . Chris Gorman
Treasurer . . . . Frances Jones Mills
Auditor of Public Accounts . . . . Ben Chandler
Supt. of Public Instruction . . . . John Stephenson
Commr. of Agriculture . . . . Ed Logsdon

SUPREME COURT

Robert F. Stephens, Chief Justice
Thomas B. Spain
Charles H. Reynolds
Joseph E. Lambert
Charles M. Leibson
Donald C. Wintersheimer
Janet L. Stumbo

GENERAL ASSEMBLY

President
   of the Senate . . . . John A. Rose
President Pro Tem
   of the Senate . . . . Charles W. Berger
Chief Clerk of the Senate . . . . Julie Haviland

Speaker of the House . . . . Joe Clarke
Speaker Pro Tem
   of the House . . . . Larry Clark
Chief Clerk of the House . . . . Evelyn Marston

STATISTICS

Land Area (square miles) 39,732
   Rank in Nation 36th
Population 3,685,296
   Rank in Nation 23rd
   Density per square mile 92.75
Number of Representatives in Congress 6
Capital City . . . . Frankfort
   Population 25,968
   Rank in State 8th
Largest City . . . . Louisville
   Population 269,063
Number of Places over 10,000 Population 39

Louisiana

Nickname . . . . The Pelican State
Motto . . . . *Union, Justice and Confidence*
Flower . . . . Magnolia
Bird . . . . Eastern Brown Pelican
Tree . . . . Bald Cypress
Songs . *Give Me Louisiana* and *You Are My Sunshine*
Crustacean . . . . Crawfish
Dog . . . . Catahoula Leopard
Entered the Union . . . . April 30, 1812
Capital . . . . Baton Rouge

ELECTED EXECUTIVE BRANCH OFFICIALS

Governor . . . . Edwin Edwards
Lieutenant Governor . . . . Melinda Schwegmann
Secretary of State . . . . W. Fox McKeithen
Attorney General . . . . Richard Ieyoub
Treasurer . . . . Mary L. Landrieu
Commr. of Agriculture . . . . Bob Odom
Commr. of Insurance . . . . Jim Brown
Commr. of Elections . . . . Jerry M. Fowler

SUPREME COURT

Pascal F. Calogero Jr., Chief Justice
Walter F. Marcus Jr.
James L. Dennis
Jack Crozier Watson
Harry T. Lemmon
Pike Hall Jr.
Catherine D. Kimball
Revius O. Ortique Jr.

LEGISLATURE

President of the Senate . . . . Samuel B. Nunez Jr.
President Pro Tem
   of the Senate . . . . Dennis Bagneris
Secretary of the Senate . . . . Michael S. Baer III

Speaker of the House . . . . John Alario Jr.
Speaker Pro Tem
   of the House . . . . Sherman Copelin
Clerk of the House . . . . Alfred W. Speer

STATISTICS

Land Area (square miles) 43,566
   Rank in Nation 33rd
Population 4,219,973
   Rank in Nation 21st
   Density per square mile 96.86
Number of Representatives in Congress 7
Capital City . . . . Baton Rouge
   Population 219,531
   Rank in State 2nd
Largest City . . . . New Orleans
   Population 496,938
Number of Places over 10,000 Population 45

Maine

Nickname . . . . The Pine Tree State
Motto . . . . *Dirigo* (I Direct or I Lead)
Animal . . . . Moose
Flower . . . . White Pine Cone and Tassel
Bird . . . . Chickadee
Tree . . . . White Pine
Song . . . . *State of Maine Song*
Fish . . . . Landlocked Salmon
Mineral . . . . Tourmaline
Entered the Union . . . . March 15, 1820
Capital . . . . Augusta

ELECTED EXECUTIVE BRANCH OFFICIAL

Governor . . . . John R. McKernan Jr.

SUPREME JUDICIAL COURT

Daniel E. Wathen, Chief Justice
David G. Roberts
Caroline D. Glassman
Robert W. Clifford
Samuel W. Collins Jr.
Paul L. Rudman
Howard H. Dana Jr.

LEGISLATURE

President of the Senate . . . . Dennis L. Dutremble
Secretary of the Senate . . . . Joy J. O'Brien

Speaker of the House . . . . Dan Gwadosky
Clerk of the House . . . . Joseph W. Mayo

STATISTICS

Land Area (square miles) 30,865
  Rank in Nation 39th
Population 1,227,928
  Rank in Nation 38th
  Density per square mile 39.78
Number of Representatives in Congress 2
Capital City . . . . Augusta
  Population 21,325
  Rank in State 6th
Largest City . . . . Portland
  Population 64,358
Number of Places over 10,000 Population 13

Maryland

Nicknames . . . . The Old Line State and
                                              Free State
Motto . . . . *Fatti Maschii, Parole Femine*
                        (Manly Deeds, Womanly Words)
Flower . . . . Black-eyed Susan
Bird . . . . Baltimore Oriole
Tree . . . . White Oak
Song . . . . *Maryland, My Maryland*
Dog . . . . Chesapeake Bay Retriever
Boat . . . . The Skipjack
Fish . . . . Striped Bass
Entered the Union . . . . April 28, 1788
Capital . . . . Annapolis

ELECTED EXECUTIVE BRANCH OFFICIALS

Governor . . . . William Donald Schaefer
Lieutenant Governor . . . . Melvin A. Steinberg
Attorney General . . . . J. Joseph Curran Jr.
Comptroller of Treasury . . . . Louis L. Goldstein

COURT OF APPEALS

Robert C. Murphy, Chief Judge
John C. Eldridge
Lawrence F. Rodowsky
Howard S. Chasanow
Robert L. Karwacki
Robert M. Bell
Irma S. Raker

GENERAL ASSEMBLY

President
  of the Senate . . . . Thomas V. Mike Miller Jr.
President Pro Tem
  of the Senate . . . . Frederick C. Malkus Jr.
Secretary of the Senate . . . . Oden Bowie

Speaker of the House . . . . Casper R. Taylor
Speaker Pro Tem
  of the House . . . . Gary R. Alexander
Chief Clerk of the House . . . . Mary Monahan

STATISTICS

Land Area (square miles) 9,775
  Rank in Nation 42nd
Population 4,781,468
  Rank in Nation 19th
  Density per square mile 489.17
Number of Representatives in Congress 8
Capital City . . . . Annapolis
  Population 33,187
  Rank in State 22nd
Largest City . . . . Baltimore
  Population 736,014
Number of Places over 10,000 Population 99

Massachusetts

Nickname . . . . The Bay State
Motto . . . . *Ense Petit Placidam Sub*
Libertate Quietem
(By the Sword We Seek Peace,
but Peace Only under Liberty)
Animal . . . . Morgan Horse
Flower . . . . Mayflower
Bird . . . . Chickadee
Tree . . . . American Elm
Song . . . . *All Hail to Massachusetts*
Fish . . . . Cod
Insect . . . . Ladybug
Dog . . . . Boston Terrier
Beverage . . . . Cranberry Juice
Gem . . . . Rhodenite
Mineral . . . . Babingtonite
Entered the Union . . . . February 6, 1788
Capital . . . . Boston

ELECTED EXECUTIVE BRANCH OFFICIALS

Governor . . . . William F. Weld
Lieutenant Governor . . . . Argeo Paul Cellucci
Secretary of the
Commonwealth . . . . Michael J. Connolly
Attorney General . . . . L. Scott Harshbarger
Treasurer & Receiver General . . . . Joseph Malone
Auditor of the
Commonwealth . . . . A. Joseph DeNucci

SUPREME JUDICIAL COURT

Paul J. Liacos, Chief Justice
Herbert P. Wilkins
Ruth I. Abrams
Joseph R. Nolan
Neil L. Lynch
Francis P. O'Connor
John M. Greaney

GENERAL COURT

President of the Senate . . . . William M. Bulger
Clerk of the Senate . . . . Edward B. O'Neill

Speaker of the House . . . . Charles F. Flaherty
Clerk of the House . . . . Robert E. MacQueen

STATISTICS

Land Area (square miles) 7,838
Rank in Nation 45th
Population 6,016,425
Rank in Nation 13th
Density per square mile 767.60
Number of Representatives in Congress 10
Capital City . . . . Boston
Population 574,283
Rank in State 1st
Largest City . . . . Boston
Number of Places over 10,000 Population 83

Michigan

Nickname . . . . The Wolverine State
Motto . . . . *Si Quaeris Peninsulam Amoenam*
Circumspice (If You Seek a Pleasant
Peninsula, Look About You)
Flower . . . . Apple Blossom
Bird . . . . Robin
Tree . . . . White Pine
Stone . . . . Petoskey Stone
Gem . . . . Chlorastrolite
Fish . . . . Brook Trout
Entered the Union . . . . January 26, 1837
Capital . . . . Lansing

ELECTED EXECUTIVE BRANCH OFFICIALS

Governor . . . . John Engler
Lieutenant Governor . . . . Connie Binsfeld
Secretary of State . . . . Richard H. Austin
Attorney General . . . . Frank J. Kelley

SUPREME COURT

Michael F. Cavanagh, Chief Justice
Charles L. Levin
James H. Brickley
Patricia J. Boyle
Dorothy Comstock Riley
Robert Griffin
Conrad L. Mallett Jr.

LEGISLATURE

President
of the Senate . . . . Lt. Gov. Connie Binsfeld
President Pro Tem
of the Senate . . . . John J.H. Schwarz
Secretary of the Senate . . . . Willis H. Snow

Speakers of the
House . . . . Curtis Hertel, Paul Hillegonds
Speakers Pro Tem of
the House . . . . Frank Fitzgerald, Raymond Murphy
Clerks of
the House . . . . . . Melvin DeStigter, David H. Evans

STATISTICS

Land Area (square miles) 56,809
Rank in Nation 22nd
Population 9,295,297
Rank in Nation 8th
Density per square mile 163.62
Number of Representatives in Congress 16
Capital City . . . . Lansing
Population 127,321
Rank in State 5th
Largest City . . . . Detroit
Population 1,027,974
Number of Places over 10,000 Population 110

Minnesota

Nickname	The North Star State
Motto	*L'Etoile du Nord* (The North Star)
Flower	Pink and White Lady-Slipper
Bird	Common Loon
Tree	Red Pine
Song	*Hail! Minnesota*
Fish	Walleye
Grain	Wild Rice
Mushroom	Morel
Entered the Union	May 11, 1858
Capital	St. Paul

ELECTED EXECUTIVE BRANCH OFFICIALS

Governor	Arne Carlson
Lieutenant Governor	Joanell Dyrstad
Secretary of State	Joan Anderson Growe
Attorney General	Hubert H. Humphrey III
Treasurer	Michael A. McGrath
Auditor	Mark Dayton

SUPREME COURT

Alexander M. Keith, Chief Justice
Rosalie E. Wahl
John E. Simonett
M. Jeanne Coyne
Esther M. Tomljanovich
Sandra S. Gardebring
Alan Page

LEGISLATURE

President of the Senate	Allan H. Spear
Secretary of the Senate	Patrick E. Flahaven
Speaker of the House	Irv Anderson
Speaker Pro Tem of the House	Jerry Bauerly
Chief Clerk of the House	Edward A. Burdick

STATISTICS

Land Area (square miles)	79,617
Rank in Nation	14th
Population	4,375,099
Rank in Nation	20th
Density per square mile	54.95
Number of Representatives in Congress	8
Capital City	St. Paul
Population	272,235
Rank in State	2nd
Largest City	Minneapolis
Population	368,383
Number of Places over 10,000 Population	73

Mississippi

Nickname	The Magnolia State
Motto	*Virtute et Armis* (By Valor and Arms)
Animal	White-tailed deer
Flower	Magnolia
Bird	Mockingbird
Water Mammal	Bottlenosed Dolphin
Tree	Magnolia
Song	*Go, Mississippi*
Fish	Black Bass
Beverage	Milk
Entered the Union	December 10, 1817
Capital	Jackson

ELECTED EXECUTIVE BRANCH OFFICIALS

Governor	Kirk Fordice
Lieutenant Governor	Eddie Briggs
Secretary of State	Dick Molpus
Attorney General	Mike Moore
Treasurer	Marshall Bennett
Auditor of Public Accounts	Steve Patterson
Commr. of Agriculture and Commerce	Jim Buck Ross
Commr. of Insurance	George Dale

SUPREME COURT

Armis E. Hawkins, Chief Justice
Dan M. Lee
Lenore L. Prather
Michael Sullivan
Ed Pittman
Fred Banks Jr.
Chuck McRae
James L. Roberts Jr.
James W. Smith Jr.

LEGISLATURE

President of the Senate	Lt. Gov. Eddie Briggs
President Pro Tem of the Senate	Walter Graham
Secretary of the Senate	E.J. Russell
Speaker of the House	Tim Ford
Speaker Pro Tem of the House	Robert Clark
Clerk of the House	Charles L. Jackson Jr.

STATISTICS

Land Area (square miles)	46,914
Rank in Nation	31st
Population	2,573,216
Rank in Nation	31st
Density per square mile	54.85
Number of Representatives in Congress	5
Capital City	Jackson
Population	196,637
Rank in State	1st
Largest City	Jackson
Number of Places over 10,000 Population	34

Missouri

Nickname .... The Show Me State
Motto .... *Salus Populi Suprema Lex Esto*
(The Welfare of the People Shall Be
the Supreme Law)
Flower......................... White Hawthorn
Bird .... Bluebird
Insect .... Honeybee
Tree .... Flowering Dogwood
Song........................... *Missouri Waltz*
Rock............................... Mozarkite
Mineral .... Galena
Fossil .... Crinoid
Entered the Union .... August 10, 1821
Capital........................... Jefferson City

ELECTED EXECUTIVE BRANCH OFFICIALS

Governor .... Mel Carnahan
Lieutenant Governor .... Roger Wilson
Secretary of State .... Judith Moriarty
Attorney General .... Jeremiah W. Nixon
Treasurer......................... Bob Holden
Auditor .... Margaret B. Kelly

SUPREME COURT

Ann K. Covington, Chief Justice
John C. Holstein
Duane Benton
Elwood L. Thomas
William Ray Price Jr.
Stephen N. Limbaugh Jr.
Edward D. Robertson Jr.

GENERAL ASSEMBLY

President
of the Senate .... Lt. Gov. Roger Wilson
President Pro Tem
of the Senate .... James L. Mathewson
Secretary of the Senate............. Terry L. Spieler

Speaker of the House............. Robert F. Griffin
Speaker Pro Tem
of the House.................... James Barnes
Chief Clerk of the House .... Douglas W. Burnett

STATISTICS

Land Area (square miles).................. 68,898
Rank in Nation.......................... 18th
Population...........................5,117,073
Rank in Nation 15th
Density per square mile 74.27
Number of Representatives in Congress 9
Capital City .... Jefferson City
Population 35,481
Rank in State........................ 15th
Largest City .... Kansas City
Population 435,146
Number of Places over 10,000 Population 64

Montana

Nickname .... The Treasure State
Motto .... *Oro y Plata* (Gold and Silver)
Animal............................. Grizzly Bear
Flower................................ Bitterroot
Bird .... Western Meadowlark
Tree .... Ponderosa Pine
Song.............................. *Montana*
State Ballad.................... *Montana Melody*
Gem stones .... Sapphire and Agate
State Fossil .... Duck-billed Dinosaur
Entered the Union .... November 8, 1889
Capital............................. Helena

ELECTED EXECUTIVE BRANCH OFFICIALS

Governor .... Marc Racicot
Lieutenant Governor .... Dennis Rehberg
Secretary of State .... Mike Cooney
Attorney General .... Joe Mazurek
Auditor........................Andrea Bennett
Supt. of Public Instruction .... Nancy Keenan

SUPREME COURT

Jean Turnage, Chief Justice
Karla M. Gray
William E. Hunt
Terry Trieweiler
John C. Harrison
Fred J. Weber
James C. Nelson

LEGISLATURE

President of the Senate .... Fred Van Valkenburg
President Pro Tem
of the Senate .... John D. Lynch
Secretary of the Senate .... Claudia Clifford

Speaker of the House .... John Mercer
Speaker Pro Tem of the House...... Marian Hanson
Chief Clerk of the House .... Marilyn Miller

STATISTICS

Land Area (square miles)................. 145,556
Rank in Nation........................... 4th
Population........................... 799,065
Rank in Nation 44th
Density per square mile 5.49
Number of Representatives in Congress 1
Capital City .... Helena
Population 24,569
Rank in State........................ 5th
Largest City .... Billings
Population 81,151
Number of Places over 10,000 Population 10

Nebraska

Nickname . . . . The Cornhusker State
Motto . . . . *Equality Before the Law*
Mammal . . . . White-tailed Deer
Flower . . . . Goldenrod
Bird . . . . Western Meadowlark
Tree . . . . Western Cottonwood
Song . . . . *Beautiful Nebraska*
Insect . . . . Honeybee
Gemstone . . . . Blue Agate
Entered the Union . . . . March 1, 1867
Capital . . . . Lincoln

ELECTED EXECUTIVE BRANCH OFFICIALS

Governor . . . . E. Benjamin Nelson
Lieutenant Governor . . . . Kim Robak
Secretary of State . . . . Allen J. Beermann
Attorney General . . . . Don Stenberg
Treasurer . . . . Dawn E. Rockey
Auditor of Public Accounts . . . . John Brewslow

SUPREME COURT

William C. Hastings, Chief Justice
Leslie Boslaugh
C. Thomas White
D. Nick Caporale
Dale E. Fahrnbruch
David J. Lanphier
John F. Wright

UNICAMERAL LEGISLATURE

President of the
   Legislature . . . . Lt. Gov. Maxine Moul
Speaker of the Legislature . . . . Ron Withem
Chairman of Executive Board,
   Legislative Council . . . . Timothy J. Hall
Vice Chairman of Executive Board,
   Legislative Council . . . . Rex Haberman
Clerk of the Legislature . . . . Patrick J. O'Donnell

STATISTICS

Land Area (square miles) 76,878
   Rank in Nation 15th
Population 1,578,385
   Rank in Nation 36th
   Density per square mile 20.53
Number of Representatives in Congress 3
Capital City . . . . Lincoln
   Population 191,972
   Rank in State 2nd
Largest City . . . . Omaha
   Population 335,795
Number of Places over 10,000 Population 14

Nevada

Nickname . . . . The Silver State
Motto . . . . *All for Our Country*
Animal . . . . Desert Bighorn Sheep
Flower . . . . Sagebrush
Bird . . . . Mountain Bluebird
Tree . . . . Bristlecone Pine and Single-leaf Pinon
Song . . . . *Home Means Nevada*
Fish . . . . Lahontan Cutthroat Trout
Fossil . . . . Ichthyosaur
Entered the Union . . . . October 31, 1864
Capital . . . . Carson City

ELECTED EXECUTIVE BRANCH OFFICIALS

Governor . . . . Robert J. Miller
Lieutenant Governor . . . . Sue Wagner
Secretary of State . . . . Cheryl Lau
Attorney General . . . . Frankie Sue Del Papa
Treasurer . . . . Bob Seale
Controller . . . . Darrel R. Daines

SUPREME COURT

Robert E. Rose, Chief Justice
Charles E. Springer
Thomas L. Steffen
Cliff Young
Miriam Shearing

LEGISLATURE

President
   of the Senate . . . . Lt. Gov. Sue Wagner
President Pro Tem
   of the Senate . . . . Lawrence E. Jacobsen
Secretary of the Senate . . . . Janice L. Thomas

Speaker of the Assembly . . . . Joseph E. Dini Jr.
Speaker Pro Tem
   of the Assembly . . . . Myrna T. Williams
Chief Clerk
   of the Assembly . . . . Mouryne B. Landing

STATISTICS

Land Area (square miles) 109,806
   Rank in Nation 7th
Population 1,201,833
   Rank in Nation 39th
   Density per square mile 10.95
Number of Representatives in Congress 2
Capital City . . . . Carson City
   Population 40,443
   Rank in State 9th
Largest City . . . . Las Vegas
   Population 258,295
Number of Places over 10,000 Population 14

New Hampshire

Nickname . . . . The Granite State
Motto . . . . *Live Free or Die*
Animal . . . . White-tailed Deer
Flower . . . . Purple Lilac
Bird . . . . Purple Finch
Tree . . . . White Birch
Song . . . . *Old New Hampshire*
Insect . . . . Ladybug
Gem . . . . Smoky Quartz
Entered the Union . . . . June 21, 1788
Capital . . . . Concord

ELECTED EXECUTIVE BRANCH OFFICIAL

Governor . . . . Steve Merrill

SUPREME COURT

David A. Brock, Chief Justice
William F. Batchelder
William R. Johnson
W. Stephen Thayer III
Sherman D. Horton Jr.

GENERAL COURT

President of the Senate . . . . . . Ralph Degnan Hough
Clerk of the Senate . . . . Gloria M. Randlett

Speaker
   of the House . . . . Harold W. Burns
Deputy Speaker of the House . . . . Michael Hill
Clerk of the House . . . . James A. Chandler

STATISTICS

Land Area (square miles) 8,969
   Rank in Nation 44th
Population 1,109,252
   Rank in Nation 40th
   Density per square mile 123.67
Number of Representatives in Congress 2
Capital City . . . . Concord
   Population 36,006
   Rank in State 3rd
Largest City . . . . Manchester
   Population 99,567
Number of Places over 10,000 Population 14

New Jersey

Nickname . . . . The Garden State
Motto . . . . *Liberty and Prosperity*
Animal . . . . Horse
Flower . . . . Violet
Bird . . . . Eastern Goldfinch
Tree . . . . Red Oak
Insect . . . . Honeybee
Entered the Union . . . . December 18, 1787
Capital . . . . Trenton

ELECTED EXECUTIVE BRANCH OFFICIAL

Governor . . . . Christine Todd Whitman

SUPREME COURT

Robert N. Wilentz, Chief Justice
Robert L. Clifford
Alan B. Handler
Stewart G. Pollock
Daniel J. O'Hern
Marie L. Garibaldi
Gary S. Stein

LEGISLATURE

President of the Senate . . . . . . Donald T. DiFrancesco
President Pro Tem
   of the Senate . . . . Joseph Palaia
Secretary of the Senate . . . . Dolores A. Kirk

Speaker of the
   Assembly . . . . Garabed "Chuck" Haytaian
Speaker Pro Tem
   of the Assembly . . . . Gerald Zecker
Clerk of the Assembly . . . . Donna Frangakis

STATISTICS

Land Area (square miles) 7,419
   Rank in Nation 46th
Population 7,730,188
   Rank in Nation 9th
   Density per square mile 1,041.97
Number of Representatives in Congress 13
Capital City . . . . Trenton
   Population 88,675
   Rank in State 6th
Largest City . . . . Newark
   Population 275,221
Number of Places over 10,000 Population 162

New Mexico

Nickname . . . . The Land of Enchantment
Motto . . . . *Crescit Eundo* (It Grows As It Goes)
Flower . . . . Yucca (Our Lord's Candles)
Bird . . . . Chaparral Bird
Tree . . . . Pinon
Songs . . . . *Asi es Nuevo Mexico* and
O, Fair New Mexico
Gem . . . . Turquoise
Fossil . . . . Coelophysis Dinosaur
Animal . . . . Black Bear
Entered the Union . . . . January 6, 1912
Capital . . . . Santa Fe

ELECTED EXECUTIVE BRANCH OFFICIALS

Governor . . . . Bruce King
Lieutenant Governor . . . . Casey Luna
Secretary of State . . . . Stephanie Gonzales
Attorney General . . . . Tom Udall
Treasurer . . . . David King
Auditor . . . . Robert E. Vigil
Commr. of Public Land . . . . Jim Baca

SUPREME COURT

Seth D. Montgomery, Chief Justice
Richard E. Ransom
Joseph F. Baca
Gene E. Franchini
Stanley F. Frost

LEGISLATURE

President
of the Senate . . . . Lt. Gov. Casey Luna
President Pro Tem
of the Senate . . . . Manny M. Aragon
Chief Clerk of the Senate . . . . . . Margaret Larragoite

Speaker of the House . . . . Raymond G. Sanchez
Chief Clerk of the House . . . . Stephen R. Arias

STATISTICS

Land Area (square miles) 121,365
    Rank in Nation 5th
Population 1,515,069
    Rank in Nation 37th
    Density per square mile 12.48
Number of Representatives in Congress 3
Capital City . . . . Santa Fe
    Population 55,859
    Rank in State 3rd
Largest City . . . . Albuquerque
    Population 384,736
Number of Places over 10,000 Population 19

New York

Nickname . . . . The Empire State
Motto . . . . *Excelsior* (Ever Upward)
Animal . . . . American Beaver
Flower . . . . Rose
Bird . . . . Bluebird
Tree . . . . Sugar Maple
Song* . . . . *I Love New York*
Gem . . . . Garnet
Fossil . . . . Eurypterus remipes
Entered the Union . . . . July 26, 1788
Capital . . . . Albany
*unofficial

ELECTED EXECUTIVE BRANCH OFFICIALS

Governor . . . . Mario M. Cuomo
Lieutenant Governor . . . . Stan Lundine
Attorney General . . . . Robert Abrams
Comptroller . . . . H. Carl McCall

COURT OF APPEALS

Judith S. Kaye, Chief Judge
Richard D. Simons
Vito J. Titone
Joseph W. Bellacosa
George Bundy Smith
Howard A. Levine
Carmen Beaucamp Ciparick

LEGISLATURE

President of the Senate . . . . Lt. Gov. Stan Lundine
President Pro Tem
of the Senate . . . . Ralph J. Marino
Secretary of the Senate . . . . Stephen Sloan

Speaker of the Assembly . . . . Sheldon Silver
Speaker Pro Tem
of the Assembly . . . . Vincent J. Graber
Clerk of the Assembly . . . . Francine M. Misasi

STATISTICS

Land Area (square miles) 47,224
    Rank in Nation 30th
Population 17,990,455
    Rank in Nation 2nd
    Density per square mile 380.96
Number of Representatives in Congress 31
Capital City . . . . Albany
    Population 101,082
    Rank in State 6th
Largest City . . . . New York City
    Population 7,322,564
Number of Places over 10,000 Population 180

North Carolina

Nicknames .... The Tar Heel State and Old North State
Motto .... *Esse Quam Videri* (To Be Rather Than to Seem)
Flower .... Dogwood
Bird .... Cardinal
Tree .... Long Leaf Pine
Song .... *The Old North State*
Mammal .... Grey Squirrel
Dog .... Plott Hound
Beverage .... Milk
Entered the Union .... November 21, 1789
Capital .... Raleigh

ELECTED EXECUTIVE BRANCH OFFICIALS

Governor .... James B. Hunt Jr.
Lieutenant Governor .... Dennis A. Wicker
Secretary of State .... Rufus L. Edmisten
Attorney General .... Mike Easley
Treasurer .... Harlan E. Boyles
Auditor .... Ralph Campbell
Supt. of Public Instruction .... Bob Etheridge
Commr. of Agriculture .... James A. Graham
Commr. of Labor .... Harry E. Payne Jr.
Commr. of Insurance .... James E. Long

SUPREME COURT

James G. Exum Jr., Chief Justice

Louis B. Meyer	John Webb
Burley B. Mitchell Jr.	Willis P. Whichard
Henry E. Frye	Sarah Parker

GENERAL ASSEMBLY

President
    of the Senate .... Lt. Gov. Dennis A. Wicker
President Pro Tem
    of the Senate .... Marc Basnight
Principal Clerk of the Senate .... Sylvia M. Fink

Speaker of the House .... Daniel T. Blue Jr.
Speaker Pro Tem
    of the House .... Marie W. Colton
Principal Clerk of the House ...... Denise G. Weeks

STATISTICS

Land Area (square miles) 48,718
    Rank in Nation 29th
Population 6,628,637
    Rank in Nation 10th
    Density per square mile 136.06
Number of Representatives in Congress 12
Capital City .... Raleigh
    Population 207,951
    Rank in State 2nd
Largest City .... Charlotte
    Population 395,934
Number of Places over 10,000 Population 52

North Dakota

Nickname .... Peace Garden State
Motto .... *Liberty and Union, Now and Forever, One and Inseparable*
Flower .... Wild Prairie Rose
Bird .... Western Meadowlark
Tree .... American Elm
Song .... *North Dakota Hymn*
March .... *Spirit of the Land*
Fossil .... Teredo Petrified Wood
Fish .... Northern Pike
Entered the Union .... November 2, 1889
Capital .... Bismarck

ELECTED EXECUTIVE BRANCH OFFICIALS

Governor .... Edward Schafer
Lieutenant Governor .... Rosemarie Myrdal
Secretary of State .... Alvin A. Jaeger
Attorney General .... Heidi Heitkamp
Treasurer .... Kathi Gilmore
Auditor .... Robert Peterson
Supt. of Public Instruction .... Wayne Sanstead
Commr. of Agriculture .... Sarah Vogel
Commr. of Labor .... Craig Hagen
Commr. of Insurance .... Glenn Pomeroy
Tax Commissioner .... Robert E. Hanson

SUPREME COURT

Gerald W. VandeWalle, Chief Justice
Herbert L. Meschke
Beryl J. Levine
William A. Neumann
Dale V. Sandstrom

LEGISLATIVE ASSEMBLY

President of the Senate .. Lt. Gov. Rosemarie Myrdal
President Pro Tem
    of the Senate .... Corliss Mushik
Secretary of the Senate .... Carol Siegert

Speaker of the House .... Rick Berg
Chief Clerk of the House .... Roy Gilbreath

STATISTICS

Land Area (square miles) 68,994
    Rank in Nation 17th
Population 638,800
    Rank in Nation 47th
    Density per square mile 9.26
Number of Representatives in Congress 1
Capital City .... Bismarck
    Population 49,256
    Rank in State 3rd
Largest City .... Fargo
    Population 74,111
Number of Places over 10,000 Population 9

Ohio

Nickname	The Buckeye State
Motto	*With God, All Things Are Possible*
Animal	White-tailed Deer
Flower	Scarlet Carnation
Bird	Cardinal
Tree	Buckeye
Song	*Beautiful Ohio*
Stone	Ohio Flint
Insect	Ladybug
Entered the Union	March 1, 1803
Capital	Columbus

ELECTED EXECUTIVE BRANCH OFFICIALS

Governor	George Voinovich
Lieutenant Governor	Michael DeWine
Secretary of State	Bob Taft
Attorney General	Lee Fisher
Treasurer	Mary Ellen Withrow
Auditor	Thomas E. Ferguson

SUPREME COURT

Thomas J. Moyer, Chief Justice
A. William Sweeney
Andrew Douglas
Craig Wright
Alice Robie Resnick
Francis E. Sweeney
Paul E. Pfeifer

GENERAL ASSEMBLY

President of the Senate	Stanley J. Aronoff
President Pro Tem of the Senate	Richard H. Finan
Clerk of the Senate	Martha L. Butler
Speaker of the House	Vernal G. Riffe
Speaker Pro Tem of the House	Barney Quilter
Legislative Clerk of the House	William C. Schaeffer

STATISTICS

Land Area (square miles)	40,953
Rank in Nation	35th
Population	10,847,115
Rank in Nation	7th
Density per square mile	264.87
Number of Representatives in Congress	19
Capital City	Columbus
Population	632,910
Rank in State	1st
Largest City	Columbus
Number of Places over 10,000 Population	164

Oklahoma

Nickname	The Sooner State
Motto	*Labor Omnia Vincit* (Labor Conquers All Things)
Animal	American Buffalo
Flower	Mistletoe
Bird	Scissor-tailed Flycatcher
Tree	Redbud
Song	*Oklahoma*
Rock	Barite Rose (Rose Rock)
Grass	Indiangrass
Entered the Union	November 16, 1907
Capital	Oklahoma City

ELECTED EXECUTIVE BRANCH OFFICIALS

Governor	David Walters
Lieutenant Governor	Jack Mildren
Attorney General	Susan Loving
Treasurer	Claudette Henry
Auditor and Inspector	Clifton H. Scott
Supt. of Public Instruction	Sandy Garrett
Commr. of Labor	Dave Renfro
Insurance Commr.	Cathy Weatherford

SUPREME COURT

Ralph B. Hodges, Chief Justice
Robert E. Lavender, Vice Chief Justice

Robert D. Simms	Yvonne Kauger
Rudolph Hargrave	Hardy Summers
Marian Opala	Joseph P. Watt
Alma Wilson	

COURT OF CRIMINAL APPEALS

Gary L. Lumpkin, Presiding Judge
Charles A. Johnson, Vice Presiding Judge

James F. Lane	Reta M. Strubhar
Charles S. Chapel	

LEGISLATURE

President of the Senate	Lt. Gov. Jack Mildren
President Pro Tem of the Senate	Robert V. Cullison
Secretary of the Senate	Lance Ward
Speaker of the House	Glen D. Johnson
Speaker Pro Tem of the House	Jim Glover
Chief Clerk/Administrator of the House	Larry Warden

STATISTICS

Land Area (square miles)	68,679
Rank in Nation	19th
Population	3,145,585
Rank in Nation	28th
Density per square mile	45.80
Number of Representatives in Congress	6
Capital City	Oklahoma City
Population	444,719
Rank in State	1st
Largest City	Oklahoma City
Number of Places over 10,000 Population	39

Oregon

Nickname...................... The Beaver State
Motto.............. *She Flies with Her Own Wings*
Animal........................ American Beaver
Flower.......................... Oregon Grape
Bird..................... Western Meadowlark
Tree.............................. Douglas Fir
Song..................... *Oregon, My Oregon*
Gemstone........................... Sunstone
Insect.............. Oregon Swallowtail Butterfly
Entered the Union.............. February 14, 1859
Capital................................ Salem

ELECTED EXECUTIVE BRANCH OFFICIALS

Governor...................... Barbara Roberts
Secretary of State................... Phil Keisling
Attorney General........... Theodore Kulongoski
Treasurer............................. Jim Hill
Supt. of Public Instruction......... Norma Paulus
Labor Commr.................. Mary W. Roberts

SUPREME COURT

Wallace P. Carson Jr., Chief Justice
W. Michael Gillette
George A. Van Hoomissen
Edward N. Fadeley
Richard L. Unis
Susan Graber
Robert D. Durham

LEGISLATIVE ASSEMBLY

President of the Senate............. Bill Bradbury
President Pro Tem
    of the Senate....................... Mae Yih
Secretary of the Senate.............. Donna Merrill

Speaker of the House............. Larry Campbell
Speaker Pro Tem of the House....... Bill Markham
Chief Clerk of the House......... Ramona Kenady

STATISTICS

Land Area (square miles)................. 96,003
    Rank in Nation.......................... 10th
Population........................... 2,842,321
    Rank in Nation......................... 29th
    Density per square mile................. 29.61
Number of Representatives in Congress.......... 5
Capital City....................... Salem
    Population........................... 107,786
    Rank in State......................... 3rd
Largest City....................... Portland
    Population........................... 437,319
Number of Places over 10,000 Population........ 43

Pennsylvania

Nickname..................... The Keystone State
Motto.......... *Virtue, Liberty and Independence*
Animal...................... White-tailed Deer
Flower......................... Mountain Laurel
Game Bird...................... Ruffed Grouse
Tree................................ Hemlock
Insect................................. Firefly
Fossil........................... Phacops rana
Entered the Union.............. December 12, 1787
Capital........................... Harrisburg

ELECTED EXECUTIVE BRANCH OFFICIALS

Governor....................... Robert P. Casey
Lieutenant Governor.............. Mark S. Singel
Attorney General.............. Ernest D. Preate Jr.
Treasurer................... Catherine Baker Knoll
Auditor........................ Barbara Hafer

SUPREME COURT

Robert N.C. Nix Jr., Chief Justice
John P. Flaherty
Stephen A. Zappala
Nicholas P. Papadakos
Ralph Cappy
Ronald D. Castille
Frank J. Montemuro Jr.

GENERAL ASSEMBLY

President of the
    Senate................. Lt. Gov. Mark S. Singel
President Pro Tem
    of the Senate................. Robert J. Mellow
Secretary of the Senate......... Mark R. Corrigan

Speaker of the House......... H. William DeWeese
Chief Clerk of the House.......... John J. Zubeck

STATISTICS

Land Area (square miles)................. 44,820
    Rank in Nation......................... 32nd
Population........................... 11,881,643
    Rank in Nation.......................... 5th
    Density per square mile................ 265.10
Number of Representatives in Congress......... 21
Capital City....................... Harrisburg
    Population............................ 52,376
    Rank in State........................ 10th
Largest City........................ Philadelphia
    Population........................... 1,585,577
Number of Places over 10,000 Population....... 102

Rhode Island

Nicknames.....................Little Rhody and
Ocean State
Motto..................................*Hope*
Animal...............................Quahaug
Flower..................................Violet
Bird..........................Rhode Island Red
Tree.................................Red Maple
Song.............................*Rhode Island*
Rock.........................Cumberlandite
Mineral............................Bowenite
Entered the Union..................May 29, 1790
Capital...........................Providence

ELECTED EXECUTIVE BRANCH
OFFICIALS

Governor......................Bruce G. Sundlun
Lieutenant Governor...........Robert A. Weygand
Secretary of State.............Barbara M. Leonard
Attorney General..................Jeffrey B. Pine
Treasurer........................Nancy Mayer

SUPREME COURT

Joseph R. Weisberger, Acting Chief Justice
Florence K. Murray
Donald F. Shea
Victoria Lederberg

GENERAL ASSEMBLY

President
of the Senate.......Lt. Gov. Robert A. Weygand
President Pro Tem
of the Senate................John C. Revens Jr.
Secretary of the Senate
.........Secretary of State Barbara M. Leonard

Speaker of the House...........John B. Harwood
Speaker Pro Tem of the House..Mabel M. Anderson
Reading Clerk of the House.......Louis D'Antuono

STATISTICS

Land Area (square miles)...................1,045
Rank in Nation.........................50th
Population...........................1,003,464
Rank in Nation........................43rd
Density per square mile...............960.27
Number of Representatives in Congress...........2
Capital City........................Providence
Population..........................160,728
Rank in State...........................1st
Largest City.......................Providence
Number of Places over 10,000 Population........15

South Carolina

Nickname....................The Palmetto State
Mottos.................*Animis Opibusque Parati*
(Prepared in Mind and Resources) and
Dum Spiro Spero (While I Breathe, I Hope)
Animal.......................White-tailed Deer
Flower.....................Yellow Jessamine
Bird............................Carolina Wren
Tree..................................Palmetto
Songs....*Carolina* and *South Carolina on My Mind*
Stone...........................Blue Granite
Fish.............................Striped Bass
Entered the Union..................May 23, 1788
Capital............................Columbia

ELECTED EXECUTIVE BRANCH
OFFICIALS

Governor.................Carroll A. Campbell Jr.
Lieutenant Governor............Nick A. Theodore
Secretary of State.....................Jim Miles
Attorney General................T. Travis Medlock
Treasurer..................Grady L. Patterson Jr.
Comptroller General...........Earle E. Morris Jr.
Supt. of Education...............Barbara Nielsen
Commr. of Agriculture...........D. Leslie Tindal
Adjutant General..............T. Eston Marchant

SUPREME COURT

David W. Harwell, Chief Justice
A. Lee Chandler
Ernest A. Finney Jr.
Jean Hoeter Toal
James E. Moore

GENERAL ASSEMBLY

President
of the Senate........Lt. Gov. Nick A. Theodore
President Pro Tem
of the Senate..........Marshall Burns Williams
Clerk of the Senate............Frank B. Caggiano

Speaker of the House...........Robert J. Sheheen
Speaker Pro Tem
of the House................David H. Wilkins
Clerk of the House..........Sandra K. McKinney

STATISTICS

Land Area (square miles)..................30,111
Rank in Nation.........................40th
Population..........................3,486,703
Rank in Nation........................25th
Density per square mile.................115.79
Number of Representatives in Congress...........6
Capital City.........................Columbia
Population..........................98,052
Rank in State...........................1st
Largest City.........................Columbia
Number of Places over 10,000 Population........39

South Dakota

Nicknames . . . . The Coyote State and
The Sunshine State
Motto . . . . *Under God the People Rule*
Animal . . . . Coyote
Flower . . . . American Pasque
Bird . . . . Ringnecked Pheasant
Tree . . . . Black Hills Spruce
Song . . . . *Hail, South Dakota*
Mineral . . . . Rose Quartz
Fish . . . . Walleye
Insect . . . . Honeybee
Grass . . . . Western Wheat Grass
Entered the Union . . . . November 2, 1889
Capital . . . . Pierre

ELECTED EXECUTIVE BRANCH OFFICIALS

Governor . . . . Walter Miller
Lieutenant Governor . . . . Steve Kirby
Secretary of State . . . . Joyce Hazeltine
Attorney General . . . . Mark Barnett
Treasurer . . . . Homer Harding
Auditor . . . . Vernon L. Larson
Commr. of School
and Public Lands . . . . Curtis Johnson

SUPREME COURT

Robert A. Miller, Chief Justice
George Wuest
Frank E. Henderson
Richard Sabers
Robert A. Amundson

LEGISLATURE

President of the
Senate . . . . Lt. Gov. Steve Kirby
President Pro Tem
of the Senate . . . . R. Lars Herseth
Secretary of the Senate . . . . Peggy Cruse

Speaker of the House . . . . Steve Cutler
Speaker Pro Tem
of the House . . . . Harvey C. Krautschun
Chief Clerk of the House . . . . Karen Gerdes

STATISTICS

Land Area (square miles) 75,896
Rank in Nation 16th
Population 696,004
Rank in Nation 45th
Density per square mile 9.17
Number of Representatives in Congress 1
Capital City . . . . Pierre
Population 12,906
Rank in State 7th
Largest City . . . . Sioux Falls
Population 100,814
Number of Places over 10,000 Population 10

Tennessee

Nickname . . . . The Volunteer State
Motto . . . . *Agriculture and Commerce*
Animal . . . . Raccoon
Flower . . . . Iris
Bird . . . . Mockingbird
Tree . . . . Tulip Poplar
Wildflower . . . . Passion Flower
Songs . . . . *When It's Iris Time in Tennessee;*
The Tennessee Waltz; My Homeland, Tennessee;
My Tennessee; and *Rocky Top*
Insects . . . . Lady beetle and Firefly
Gem . . . . Freshwater Pearl
Rocks . . . . Limestone and Agate
Entered the Union . . . . June 1, 1796
Capital . . . . Nashville

ELECTED EXECUTIVE BRANCH OFFICIAL

Governor . . . . Ned McWherter

SUPREME COURT

Lyle Reid, Chief Justice
Frank F. Drowota III
Charles H. O'Brien
E. Riley Anderson
A.A. Birch Jr.

GENERAL ASSEMBLY

Speaker
of the Senate . . . . Lt. Gov. John S. Wilder
Speaker Pro Tem
of the Senate . . . . Robert Rochelle
Chief Clerk
of the Senate . . . . Clyde W. McCullough

Speaker of the House . . . . Jimmy Naifeh
Speaker Pro Tem
of the House . . . . Lois M. DeBerry
Chief Clerk of the House . . . . Burney T. Durham

STATISTICS

Land Area (square miles) 41,220
Rank in Nation 34th
Population 4,877,185
Rank in Nation 17th
Density per square mile 118.32
Number of Representatives in Congress 9
Capital City . . . . Nashville
Population 488,374
Rank in State 2nd
Largest City . . . . Memphis
Population 610,337
Number of Places over 10,000 Population 44

Texas

Nickname	The Lone Star State
Motto	*Friendship*
Flower	Bluebonnet (Buffalo Clover, Wolf Flower)
Bird	Mockingbird
Tree	Pecan
Song	*Texas, Our Texas*
Stone	Petrified Palmwood
Gem	Texas Blue Topaz
Grass	Side Oats Grama
Dish	Chili
Seashell	Lightning Whelk
Fish	Guadalape Bass
Entered the Union	December 29, 1845
Capital	Austin

ELECTED EXECUTIVE BRANCH OFFICIALS

Governor	Ann W. Richards
Lieutenant Governor	Bob Bullock
Attorney General	Dan Morales
Treasurer	Martha Whitehead
Comptroller of Public Accounts	John Sharp
Commr. of Agriculture	Rick Perry
Commr. of General Land Office	Garry Mauro

SUPREME COURT

Thomas R. Phillips, Chief Justice

Raul A. Gonzalez	John Cornyn
Jack Hightower	Robert A. Gammage
Nathan L. Hecht	Craig Enoch
Lloyd Doggett	Rose Spector

COURT OF CRIMINAL APPEALS

Michael J. McCormick, Presiding Judge

Sam Houston Clinton	Charles Baird
Charles Miller	Morris Overstreet
Charles F. Campbell	Frank Maloney
Bill White	Lawrence Meyers

LEGISLATURE

President of the Senate	Lt. Gov. Bob Bullock
President Pro Tem of the Senate	John Montford
Secretary of the Senate	Betty King
Speaker of the House	James Laney
Speaker Pro Tem of the House	Wilhelmina R. Delco
Chief Clerk of the House	Betty Murray

STATISTICS

Land Area (square miles)	261,914
Rank in Nation	2nd
Population	16,986,510
Rank in Nation	3rd
Density per square mile	64.86
Number of Representatives in Congress	30
Capital City	Austin
Population	465,622
Rank in State	5th
Largest City	Houston
Population	1,630,553
Number of Places over 10,000 Population	182

Utah

Nickname	The Beehive State
Motto	*Industry*
Flower	Sego Lily
Animal	Rocky Mountain Elk
Bird	California Seagull
Tree	Blue Spruce
Fish	Rainbow Trout
Song	*Utah, We Love Thee*
Gem	Topaz
Insect	Honeybee
Entered the Union	January 4, 1896
Capital	Salt Lake City

ELECTED EXECUTIVE BRANCH OFFICIALS

Governor	Mike Leavitt
Lieutenant Governor	Olene S. Walker
Attorney General	Jan Graham
Treasurer	Edward T. Alter
Auditor	Tom L. Allen

SUPREME COURT

Michael D. Zimmerman, Chief Justice
I. Daniel Stewart
Richard C. Howe
Christine M. Durham
Leonard H. Russon

LEGISLATURE

President of the Senate	Lane Beattie
Secretary of the Senate	M. Eugene Bridges
Speaker of the House	Rob W. Bishop
Chief Clerk of the House	Carole E. Peterson

STATISTICS

Land Area (square miles)	82,168
Rank in Nation	12th
Population	1,722,850
Rank in Nation	35th
Density per square mile	20.97
Number of Representatives in Congress	3
Capital City	Salt Lake City
Population	159,936
Rank in State	1st
Largest City	Salt Lake City
Number of Places over 10,000 Population	39

Vermont

Nickname . . . . The Green Mountain State
Motto . . . . *Freedom and Unity*
Animal . . . . Morgan Horse
Flower . . . . Red Clover
Bird . . . . Hermit Thrush
Tree . . . . Sugar Maple
Song . . . . *Hail, Vermont!*
Insect . . . . Honeybee
Beverage . . . . Milk
Entered the Union . . . . March 4, 1791
Capital . . . . Montpelier

ELECTED EXECUTIVE BRANCH OFFICIALS

Governor . . . . Howard Dean
Lieutenant Governor . . . . Barbara W. Snelling
Secretary of State . . . . Donald M. Hooper
Attorney General . . . . Jeffrey L. Amestoy
Treasurer . . . . Paul W. Ruse Jr.
Auditor of Accounts . . . . Edward S. Flanagan

SUPREME COURT

Frederic W. Allen, Chief Justice
Ernest W. Gibson III
John A. Dooley
James L. Morse
Denise Johnson

GENERAL ASSEMBLY

President of the Senate . . . . Lt. Gov. Barbara Snelling
President Pro Tem
    of the Senate . . . . John H. Bloomer
Secretary of the Senate . . . . Robert H. Gibson

Speaker of the House . . . . Ralph G. Wright
Clerk of the House . . . . Robert L. Picher

STATISTICS

Land Area (square miles) 9,249
    Rank in Nation 43rd
Population 562,758
    Rank in Nation 48th
    Density per square mile 60.84
Number of Representatives in Congress 1
Capital City . . . . Montpelier
    Population 8,247
    Rank in State 8th
Largest City . . . . Burlington
    Population 39,127
Number of Places over 10,000 Population 3

Virginia

Nickname . . . . The Old Dominion
Motto . . . . *Sic Semper Tyrannis*
                                        (Thus Always to Tyrants)
Animal . . . . Foxhound
Flower . . . . Dogwood
Bird . . . . Cardinal
Tree . . . . Dogwood
Song . . . . *Carry Me Back to Old Virginia*
Shell . . . . Oyster
Entered the Union . . . . June 25, 1788
Capital . . . . Richmond

ELECTED EXECUTIVE BRANCH OFFICIALS

Governor . . . . George Allen
Lieutenant Governor . . . . . . Donald Sternoff Beyer Jr.
Attorney General . . . . James S. Gilmore III

SUPREME COURT

Harry Lee Carrico, Chief Justice
A. Christian Compton
Roscoe B. Stephenson Jr.
Henry H. Whiting
Elizabeth B. Lacy
Leroy R. Hassell
Barbara Milano Keenan
Richard H. Poff

GENERAL ASSEMBLY

President
    of the Senate . . . . Lt. Gov. Donald S. Beyer Jr.
President Pro Tem
    of the Senate . . . . Stanley C. Walker
Clerk of the Senate . . . . Susan Clarke Schaar

Speaker of the House . . . . Thomas Moss Jr.
Clerk of the House . . . . Bruce F. Jamerson

STATISTICS

Land Area (square miles) 39,598
    Rank in Nation 37th
Population 6,187,358
    Rank in Nation 12th
    Density per square mile 156.26
Number of Representatives in Congress 11
Capital City . . . . Richmond
    Population 203,056
    Rank in State 3rd
Largest City . . . . Virginia Beach
    Population 393,069
Number of Places over 10,000 Population 76

Washington

Nickname . . . . The Evergreen State
Motto . . . . *Alki* (Chinook Indian word
                    meaning By and By)
Flower . . . . Coast Rhododendron
Bird . . . . Willow Goldfinch
Tree . . . . Western Hemlock
Song . . . . *Washington, My Home*
Dance . . . . Square Dance
Gem . . . . Petrified Wood
Entered the Union . . . . November 11, 1889
Capital . . . . Olympia

ELECTED EXECUTIVE BRANCH OFFICIALS

Governor . . . . Mike Lowry
Lieutenant Governor . . . . Joel Pritchard
Secretary of State . . . . Ralph Munro
Attorney General . . . . Christine Gregoire
Treasurer . . . . Dan Grimm
Auditor . . . . Brian Sonntag
Supt. of Public Instruction . . . . Judith Billings
Insurance Commr. . . . . Deborah Senn
Commr. of Public Lands . . . . Jennifer Belcher

SUPREME COURT

James A. Andersen, Chief Justice

Robert F. Utter	Charles Smith
Robert F. Brachtenbach	Richard Guy
James M. Dolliver	Charles W. Johnson
Barbara Durham,	Barbara A. Madsen
Acting Chief Justice	

LEGISLATURE

President
  of the Senate . . . . Lt. Gov. Joel Pritchard
President Pro Tem
  of the Senate . . . . R. Lorraine Wojahn
Secretary of the Senate . . . . Marty Brown

Speaker of the House . . . . Brian Ebersole
Speaker Pro Tem
  of the House . . . . Ron Meyers
Chief Clerk of the House . . . . Marilyn Showalter

STATISTICS

Land Area (square miles) 66,581
  Rank in Nation 20th
Population 4,866,692
  Rank in Nation 18th
  Density per square mile 73.09
Number of Representatives in Congress 9
Capital City . . . . Olympia
  Population 33,840
  Rank in State 18th
Largest City . . . . Seattle
  Population 516,259
Number of Places over 10,000 Population 82

West Virginia

Nickname . . . . The Mountain State
Motto . . . . *Montani Semper Liberi*
              (Mountaineers Are Always Free)
Animal . . . . Black Bear
Flower . . . . Big Laurel
Bird . . . . Cardinal
Tree . . . . Sugar Maple
Songs . . . . *West Virginia, My Home Sweet Home;*
              The West Virginia Hills; and
              This Is My West Virginia
Fruit . . . . Apple
Fish . . . . Brook Trout
Entered the Union . . . . June 20, 1863
Capital . . . . Charleston

ELECTED EXECUTIVE BRANCH OFFICIALS

Governor . . . . W. Gaston Caperton III
Secretary of State . . . . Ken Hechler
Attorney General . . . . Darrell McGraw
Treasurer . . . . Larrie Bailey
Auditor . . . . Glen B. Gainer Jr.
Commr. of Agriculture . . . . Gus R. Douglass

SUPREME COURT OF APPEALS

W.T. Brotherton Jr., Chief Justice
Richard Neely
Thomas B. Miller
Thomas E. McHugh
Margaret Workman

LEGISLATURE

President of the Senate . . . . Keith Burdette
President Pro Tem
  of the Senate . . . . William R. Sharpe Jr.
Clerk of the Senate . . . . Darrell E. Holmes

Speaker of the House . . . . Robert Chambers
Speaker Pro Tem
  of the House . . . . Phyllis J. Rutledge
Clerk of the House . . . . Donald L. Kopp

STATISTICS

Land Area (square miles) 24,087
  Rank in Nation 41st
Population 1,793,477
  Rank in Nation 34th
  Density per square mile 74.46
Number of Representatives in Congress 3
Capital City . . . . Charleston
  Population 57,287
  Rank in State 1st
Largest City . . . . Charleston
Number of Places over 10,000 Population 16

Wisconsin

Nickname*	The Badger State
Motto	*Forward*
Animal	Badger
Flower	Wood Violet
Bird	Robin
Tree	Sugar Maple
Song	*On, Wisconsin!*
Fish	Muskellunge
Mineral	Galena
Entered the Union	May 29, 1848
Capital	Madison

*unofficial

ELECTED EXECUTIVE BRANCH OFFICIALS

Governor	Tommy G. Thompson
Lieutenant Governor	Scott McCallum
Secretary of State	Douglas J. La Follette
Attorney General	James Doyle
Treasurer	Cathy Zeuske
Supt. of Public Instruction	John Benson

SUPREME COURT

Nathan S. Heffernan, Chief Justice
Ronald B. Day
Shirley S. Abrahamson
Donald W. Steinmetz
William A. Bablitch
Jon P. Wilcox
Janine P. Geske

LEGISLATURE

President of the Senate	Brian D. Rude
Chief Clerk of the Senate	Donald J. Schneider
Speaker of the Assembly	Walter Kunicki
Speaker Pro Tem of the Assembly	Timothy W. Carpenter
Chief Clerk of the Assembly	Thomas Melvin

STATISTICS

Land Area (square miles)	54,314
Rank in Nation	25th
Population	4,891,769
Rank in Nation	16th
Density per square mile	90.07
Number of Representatives in Congress	9
Capital City	Madison
Population	191,262
Rank in State	2nd
Largest City	Milwaukee
Population	628,088
Number of Places over 10,000 Population	61

Wyoming

Nicknames	The Equality State and The Cowboy State
Motto	*Equal Rights*
Animal	Bison
Flower	Indian Paintbrush
Bird	Western Meadowlark
Tree	Cottonwood
Song	*Wyoming*
Gem	Jade
Entered the Union	July 10, 1890
Capital	Cheyenne

ELECTED EXECUTIVE BRANCH OFFICIALS

Governor	Mike Sullivan
Secretary of State	Kathy Karpan
Treasurer	Stan Smith
Auditor	Dave Ferrari
Supt. of Public Instruction	Diana Ohman

SUPREME COURT

Richard J. Macy, Chief Justice
Richard V. Thomas
G. Joseph Cardine
Michael Golden
William A. Taylor

LEGISLATURE

President of the Senate	Jerry B. Dixon
Vice President of the Senate	Charles K. Scott
Chief Clerk of the Senate	Liv Hanes
Speaker of the House	Douglas W. Chamberlain
Speaker Pro Tem of the House	Patti L. MacMillan
Chief Clerk of the House	Paul Galeotos

STATISTICS

Land Area (square miles)	97,105
Rank in Nation	9th
Population	453,588
Rank in Nation	50th
Density per square mile	4.67
Number of Representatives in Congress	1
Capital City	Cheyenne
Population	50,008
Rank in State	1st
Largest City	Cheyenne
Number of Places over 10,000 Population	8

District of Columbia

Motto . . . . *Justitia Omnibus* (Justice to All)
Flower . . . . American Beauty Rose
Bird . . . . Wood Thrush
Tree . . . . Scarlet Oak
Became U.S. Capital . . . . December 1, 1800

ELECTED EXECUTIVE BRANCH OFFICIAL

Mayor . . . . Sharon Pratt Kelly

DISTRICT OF COLUMBIA COURT OF APPEALS

Judith W. Rogers, Chief Judge
John M. Ferren
John A. Terry
John M. Steadman
Frank E. Schwelb
Michael W. Farrell
Annice M. Wagner
Warren R. King
Emmet G. Sullivan

COUNCIL OF THE DISTRICT OF COLUMBIA

Chairman . . . . David A. Clarke
Chairman Pro Tem . . . . John Ray

STATISTICS

Land Area (square miles) 61
Population 606,900
    Density per square mile 9,884.40
Delegate to Congress* 1

*Privileges to vote only in committees and the Committee of the Whole.

American Samoa

Motto . . . . *Samoa-Muamua le Atua*
                                          (Samoa, God Is First)
Flower . . . . Paogo (Ula-fala)
Plant . . . . Ava
Song . . . . *Amerika Samoa*
Became a Territory of the United States 1900
Capital . . . . Pago Pago

ELECTED EXECUTIVE BRANCH OFFICIALS

Governor . . . . A.P. Lutali
Lieutenant Governor . . . . Tauese P. Sunia

HIGH COURT

F. Michael Kruse, Chief Justice
Roy J.D. Hall
Lyle Richmond

LEGISLATURE

President of the Senate . . . . Letuli Toloa
President Pro Tem
    of the Senate . . . . Lutu T.S. Fuimaono
Secretary of the Senate . . . . Leo'o V. Ma'o

Speaker of the House . . . . Talavou S. Ale
Vice Speaker
    of the House . . . . Moananu Va
Clerk of the House . . . . Wally Utu

STATISTICS

Land Area (square miles) 77
Population 46,773
    Density per square mile 607.74
Delegate to Congress* 1
Capital City . . . . Pago Pago
    Population 3,519
    Rank in territory 3rd
Largest City . . . . Tafuna
    Population 5,174

*Privileges to vote only in committees and the Committee of the Whole.

Guam

Nickname . . . . Hub of the Pacific
Flower . . . . *Puti Tai Nobio* (Bougainvilla)
Bird . . . . *Totot* (Fruit Dove)
Tree . . . . *Ifit* (Intsiabijuga)
Song . . . . *Stand Ye Guamanians*
Stone . . . . Latte
Animal . . . . Iguana
Ceded to the United States
    by Spain . . . . December 10, 1898
Became a Territory . . . . August 1, 1950
Request to become a
    Commonwealth Plebiscite . . . . November 1987
Capital . . . . Agana

ELECTED EXECUTIVE BRANCH
OFFICIALS

Governor . . . . Joseph Ada
Lieutenant Governor . . . . Frank F. Blas

SUPERIOR COURT

Alberto C. Lamorena III, Presiding Judge
Joaquin V.E. Manibusan
Janet Healy Weeks
Ramon V. Diaz
Peter B. Siguenza Jr.
Benjamin J.F. Cruz

LEGISLATURE

Speaker . . . . Joe T. San Agustin
Vice Speaker . . . . John P. Aguon
Legislative Secretary . . . . Pilar C. Lujan

STATISTICS

Land Area (square miles) 210
Population 133,152
    Density per square mile 634.06
Delegate to Congress* 1
Capital City . . . . Agana
    Population 1,139
    Rank in territory 18th
Largest City . . . . Dededo
    Population 31,728

---

*Privileges to vote only in committees and the Committee of the Whole.

Northern Mariana Islands

Flower . . . . Plumeria
Bird . . . . Marianas Fruit Dove
Tree . . . . Flame Tree
Song . . . . *Gi Talo Gi Halom Tasi*
Administered by the United States as a trusteeship
    for the United Nations . . . . July 18, 1947
Voters approved a
    proposed constitution . . . . June 1975
U.S. President signed covenant agreeing to
    Commonwealth status for the
    islands . . . . March 24, 1976
Became a self-governing Commonwealth
    . . . . January 9, 1978
Capital . . . . Saipan

ELECTED EXECUTIVE BRANCH
OFFICIALS

Governor . . . . Froilan C. Tenorio
Lieutenant Governor . . . . Jesus Borja

COMMONWEALTH SUPREME COURT

Jose S. Dela Cruz, Chief Justice
Ramon G. Villagomez
Pedro M. Atalig

LEGISLATURE

President
    of the Senate . . . . Jesus R. Sablan
Vice President
    of the Senate . . . . Henry DLG. San Nicolas
Clerk of Senate . . . . Nicky B. Borja

Speaker of the House . . . . Diego T. Benavente
Vice Speaker of the House . . . . Jesus P. Mafnas
Chief Clerk of the House . . . . Evelyn Fleming

STATISTICS

Land Area (square miles) 179
Population 43,345
    Density per square mile 242.15
Capital City . . . . Saipan
    Population 38,896
Largest City . . . . Saipan

Puerto Rico

Nickname . . . . Island of Enchantment
Motto . . . . *Joannes Est Nomen Ejus*
(John Is Thy Name)
Flower . . . . Maga
Bird . . . . Reinita
Tree . . . . Ceiba
Song . . . . *La Borinquena*
Became a Territory of the United States
. . . . December 10, 1898
Became a self-governing Commonwealth
. . . . July 25, 1952
Capital . . . . San Juan

ELECTED EXECUTIVE BRANCH OFFICIAL

Governor . . . . Pedro J. Rossello

SUPREME COURT

Jose Antonio Andreu-Garcia, Chief Justice
Antonio Negron-Garcia
Francisco Rebollo-Lopez
Miriam Naveira de Rodon
Federico Hernandez-Denton
Rafael Alonso-Alonso
Jaime B. Fuster-Berlingeri

LEGISLATIVE ASSEMBLY

President
of the Senate . . . . Robertro Rexach Benitez
Vice President
of the Senate . . . . Nicolas Nogueras Cartagena Jr.
Secretary
of the Senate . . . . Ciorah J. Montes

Speaker of the House . . . . . Zaida Hernandez Torres
Vice Speaker
of the House . . . . Edison Misla-Aldarondo
Chief Clerk
of the House . . . . Angeles Mendoza Tio

STATISTICS

Land Area (square miles) 3,427
Population 3,522,037
Density per square mile 1,027.90
Delegate to Congress* 1
Capital City . . . . San Juan
Population 426,832
Largest City . . . . San Juan
Number of Places over 10,000 Population 30

*Privileges to vote only in committees and the Committee of the Whole.

U.S. Virgin Islands

Nickname . . . . American Paradise
Flower . . . . Yellow Elder or Ginger Thomas
Bird . . . . Yellow Breast or Banana Quit
Song . . . . *Virgin Islands March*
Purchased from Denmark . . . . March 31, 1917
Capital . . . . Charlotte Amalie, St. Thomas

ELECTED EXECUTIVE BRANCH OFFICIALS

Governor . . . . Alexander Farrelly
Lieutenant Governor . . . . Derek M. Hodge

FEDERAL DISTRICT COURT

Thomas K. Moore, Chief Judge
Jeffrey W. Barnard, Magistrate Judge
Jeffrey L. Resnick, Magistrate Judge

LEGISLATURE

President . . . . Bingley G. Richardson Sr.
Vice President . . . . Mary Ann Pickard
Legislative
Secretary . . . . Judy M. Gomez

STATISTICS

Land Area (square miles)* 134
St. Croix (square miles) 83
St. John (square miles) 20
St. Thomas (square miles) 31
Population 101,809
St. Croix 50,139
St. John 3,504
St. Thomas 48,166
Density per square mile 760.90
Delegate to Congress** 1
Capital City . . . . Charlotte Amalie, St. Thomas
Population 12,331
Largest City . . . . Charlotte Amalie, St. Thomas

*The U.S. Virgin Islands is comprised of three large islands (St. Croix,
St. John, St. Thomas) and 50 smaller islands and cays.
**Privileges to vote only in committees and the Committee of the Whole.

Index

(Page numbers in **boldface** indicate tables.)

M

U

V

The States Information Center
Your direct line to state government information.

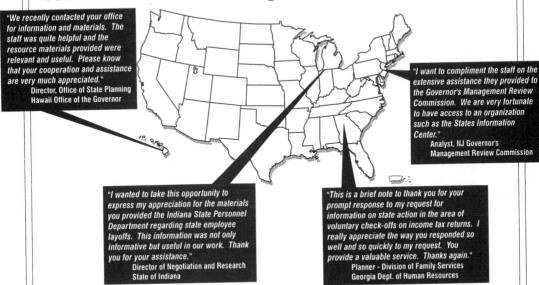

"We recently contacted your office for information and materials. The staff was quite helpful and the resource materials provided were relevant and useful. Please know that your cooperation and assistance are very much appreciated."
Director, Office of State Planning
Hawaii Office of the Governor

"I want to compliment the staff on the extensive assistance they provided to the Governor's Management Review Commission. We are very fortunate to have access to an organization such as the States Information Center."
Analyst, NJ Governor's
Management Review Commission

"I wanted to take this opportunity to express my appreciation for the materials you provided the Indiana State Personnel Department regarding state employee layoffs. This information was not only informative but useful in our work. Thank you for your assistance."
Director of Negotiation and Research
State of Indiana

"This is a brief note to thank you for your prompt response to my request for information on state action in the area of voluntary check-offs on income tax returns. I really appreciate the way you responded so well and so quickly to my request. You provide a valuable service. Thanks again."
Planner - Division of Family Services
Georgia Dept. of Human Resources

CSG's States Information Center (SIC) provides a personalized inquiry and reference service.

The States Information Center staff provides you with. . .

☆ Confidential answers to your questions about any state government issue within 48 hours;

☆ Reports on state issues with comparative data from all 50 states;

☆ *Checklist*, a bimonthly newspaper that keeps you up-to-date on new reference materials on state government issues; and

☆ Access to more than 20,000 documents available on a 30-day loan basis and through ISIS (Integrated State Information System), an on-line information retrieval system to the Council's data base of more than 20,000 titles, abstracts, and full text records.

The services of SIC are *free of charge* to all state government officials and employees. When you need information about state government, call The Council of State Governments' **States Information Center at (606) 244-8253 or send us E-mail via INTERNET: csgmp! mbone @ uunet.uu.net**.